Forensic Psychology

BPS Textbooks in Psychology

BPS Wiley presents a comprehensive and authoritative series covering everything a student needs in order to complete an undergraduate degree in psychology. Refreshingly written to consider more than North American research, this series is the first to give a truly international perspective. Written by the very best names in the field, the series offers an extensive range of titles from introductory level through to final year optional modules, and every text fully complies with the BPS syllabus in the topic. No other series bears the BPS seal of approval!

Many of the books are supported by a companion website, featuring additional resource materials for both instructors and students, designed to encourage critical thinking, and providing for all your course lecturing and testing needs.

For other titles in this series, please go to http://psychsource.bps.org.uk.

Forensic Psychology

Second Edition

EDITED BY

DAVID A. CRIGHTON
GRAHAM J. TOWL

 BPS

WILEY

This second edition first published 2015 by the British Psychological Society and John Wiley & Sons, Ltd.

© 2015 John Wiley & Sons, Ltd.

Edition history: Blackwell Publishing Ltd. (1e, 2010)

Registered Office
John Wiley & Sons, Ltd., The Atrium, Southern Gate, Chichester, West Sussex, PO19 8SQ, UK

Editorial Offices
350 Main Street, Malden, MA 02148-5020, USA
9600 Garsington Road, Oxford, OX4 2DQ, UK
The Atrium, Southern Gate, Chichester, West Sussex, PO19 8SQ, UK

For details of our global editorial offices, for customer services, and for information about how to apply for permission to reuse the copyright material in this book please see our website at www.wiley.com/wiley-blackwell.

The right of David A. Crighton and Graham J. Towl to be identified as the authors of the editorial material in this work has been asserted in accordance with the UK Copyright, Designs and Patents Act 1988.

Library of Congress Cataloging-in-Publication Data

Forensic psychology (Towl)
Forensic psychology / edited by David A. Crighton and Graham J. Towl. – 2nd edition.
    p. ; cm.
  Includes bibliographical references and index.
  ISBN 978-1-118-75778-9 (pbk.)
I. Crighton, David A., 1964– , editor.   II. Towl, Graham J., editor.   III. British Psychological Society, issuing body.   IV. Title.
[DNLM: 1. Forensic Psychiatry–methods–Great Britain.   2. Crime–psychology–Great Britain.   3. Criminals–psychology–Great Britain. W 740]
  RA1148
  614′.15–dc23

                                        2014048411

A catalogue record for this book is available from the British Library.

Cover image: Statue of Lady Justice with retro effect © Rob Wilson / Shutterstock

Set in 11/12.5pt Dante by SPi Publisher Services, Pondicherry, India

1   2015

The British Psychological Society's free Research Digest e-mail service rounds up the latest research and relates it to your syllabus in a user-friendly way. To subscribe go to **www.researchdigest.org.uk** or send a blank e-mail to **subscribe-rd@lists.bps.org.uk**.

Contents

List of Contributors

Editors

David A. Crighton
EBR Associates
Durham University and University of Roehampton

Graham J. Towl
Durham University

Contributors

Joanna R. Adler
Middlesex University

Belinda Brooks-Gordon
Birkbeck University of London

Conor Duggan
University of Nottingham

David P. Farrington
University of Cambridge

David Faulkner
University of Oxford

Yu Gao
University of Southern California

Andrea L. Glenn
University of Southern California

Michael Gossop
Bethlehem Hospital and Institute of Psychiatry,
Kings College London

Lorraine Hope
University of Portsmouth

Richard Howard
University of Nottingham

William Jacks
Middlesex University

Andreas Kapardis
University of Cyprus

Lila Kazemian
John Jay College of Criminal Justice, City University
of New York

Peter Kinderman
University of Liverpool

William R. Lindsay
Danshell Ltd and University of Abertay

Amanda Michie
NHS Lothian, Edinburgh

Melissa Peskin
University of Southern California

David Pilgrim
University of Liverpool

Adrian Raine
University of Pennsylvania

Lawrence W. Sherman
University of Cambridge

Robert A. Schug
University of Southern California

Heather Strang
University of Cambridge

John L. Taylor
Care Principles Ltd and University of Northumbria

Brian A. Thomas-Peter
Douglas College, Canada

Jackie Walton
Durham, United Kingdom

Tammi Walker
Victoria University of Manchester and Bradford University

Jane L. Wood
University of Kent

Yaling Yang
University of California Los Angeles

1 Introduction

GRAHAM J. TOWL AND DAVID A. CRIGHTON

Since the publication of the first edition of this book, there has been a sustained growth in the academic base of forensic practice, which continues to be seen in the availability and popularity of both undergraduate postgraduate courses The popularity of the term 'forensic' has continued to be juxtaposed with a range of areas of academic study, including anthropology, archaeology, computing, engineering, investigation, measurement, psychobiology, psychology and science (UCAS, 2014). This is also evident in much professional practice. In the field of health, this has been seen in the development of forensic psychiatric nursing, psychiatry, occupational therapy and social work. It has also been seen more widely with the development of areas such as forensic accountancy, forensic computing and many others.

There have been a number of significant changes and developments in forensic psychological practice in recent years. The growth in the number of posts in health and criminal justice has slowed internationally. The United Kingdom provides a good illustration of these developments, and the flattening of the total number of psychological staff employed in prisons, probation and secure health settings has continued here. This in part reflects a change in UK government policies, and in particular the cutting back of public services, but it also reflects some of the disappointing evaluation results from interventions aimed at addressing the so called 'dangerous severe personality disorder' and also areas such as sex offender treatment interventions too. There has been a growth of practice in other settings, with an increasing breadth of the areas where forensic psychology is applied. This has included development of work in the courts as well as in areas such as investigation and policing. This has been matched by continued growth in the higher education sector to accommodate new courses and the growth of post-qualification professional training. There has also been a concomitant expansion in the breadth and depth of academic work (Crighton &

Towl, 2008; Towl, Farrington, Crighton, & Hughes, 2008). As noted in the first edition, not all of the developments in forensic psychology have been positive, and at that time we observed an increasingly restricted and narrow focus of practice and the restriction of theoretical perspectives. There has in our view been something of a divergence within forensic psychology since then, with some areas seeing positive developments and others becoming more restricted. In areas such as what might broadly be termed 'community approaches', there has been a marked growth in the quality of practice and the range of perspectives seen. For example, the growth, internationally, in earlier years' interventions were based in large part on the influential work of David Farrington (see Chapters 9 and 10 in this volume). There has also been a notable extension to areas that, in the past, psychologists had little to say about – such as socio-political violence. In this volume, for example, see the work of Brian Thomas-Peter (Chapter 28) and also Joanna Adler (Chapter 27). By contrast, the types of work conducted in correctional settings such as prisons and secure hospitals have continued to largely stagnate, especially perhaps in view of some of the disappointing results from some international evaluation studies. The overinvestment in cognitive behavioural group work, designed with the aim of reducing the risk of re-offending in convicted groups, has continued. Such work has become increasingly standardized, manual-based and also mandated and duly marketed. Examples here would be the development of sexual predator treatment programmes in prisons in the United States (Marques, Wiederanders, Day, Nelson, & Van Ommeren, 2005), but the approach has been replicated to a greater or lesser extent in other correctional contexts.

For the previous edition, we sought to draw together a textbook aimed chiefly but not exclusively at those engaged in forensic practice. That continued to be a major aim of the text here too, but as previously we have been keen to reflect a range of 'voices' and perspectives. Our second aim was to continue to offer a constructively critical analysis of forensic psychology, covering the field in breadth and also depth.

In seeking to do this, we have divided the text into three sections, although any such division is necessarily subject to significant overlaps, and this text is no exception to that. We begin by looking at the legal context and, in particular, go on to elaborate what may be termed 'investigative practice' and cover some of the main ways in which psychology contributes to detection and prosecution. This is followed by a section on working with offending populations, covering adults and children and looking at the various ways in which psychology may be applied to working with offenders. The final section goes on to address a number of the professional, legal and ethical issues that arise in forensic psychology. In covering these areas, we have not sought to simply produce a bland recitation of current practice – there are a number of sources that the reader could seek such an overview from. We have rather engaged with the controversies and challenges seen when psychology is applied to areas that are often socially and politically contentious.

JUSTICE

The justice system in England and Wales is used as an exemplar of such systems internationally and provides a starting point, setting the scene for many of the activities and interests of forensic psychologists. This begins with an initial exploration of what justice means. Such thinking and reflection are perhaps a helpful starting point when considering the ethical underpinning for much of forensic psychology, whether as an area of academic study or professional practice. After outlining some key developments over the past century or so in the criminal justice system, consideration is given to what a crime is. Forensic psychology can potentially derive great benefit from a fuller understanding of such philosophical, social policy and criminological perspectives. It is often in asking the most fundamental questions that some of the most fruitful hypotheses can be developed. Scientifically the methods that are used to collect data on crime will clearly be important in informing our understanding of criminal behaviour, for example, in understanding the prevalence rates for particular crimes. Psychologists who are professionally interested in crime will want to familiarize themselves with the different methodologies commonly used internationally and how these are drawn on in reports of crime or in official figures used for social policy purposes. The social construction of crime, and

indeed the social structures that administer criminal justice processes, is apparent from the chapter. An example of the social construction of crime, which may perhaps be particularly familiar to student readers, is the behaviour of students. In such settings, excessive alcohol consumption and anti-social behaviours are often seen. Sexual violence on campuses is also a common problem (Masoumzadeh, Jin, Joshi, & Constantino, 2013).

Yet, in both cases, if it is detected, such behaviour is unlikely to be recorded as criminal. Individuals may be admonished by their university, but rarely in such circumstances do they find themselves subject to the relevant criminal justice system on charges of criminal damage or for sexual offences. By contrast, similar or identical behaviours by young people in economically deprived areas may be far more readily criminalized. Outside the cosy cloisters of academia, individuals may find themselves charged with criminal offences, although here too there are clear social and environmental biases that operate. The conducts of those working in criminal justice systems also illustrate some questions about the application of laws and issues of justice and criminality. The gratuitous violence of police officers in response to political protestors around the world illustrates very starkly the social construction of crime. Here, the wearing of a uniform or membership of a particular profession may protect one from behavioural labelling (i.e., being designated a criminal). Such protection is, however, not unlimited, and police officers, correctional officers and others are, on occasion, charged with offences; some are found guilty, and some of these go on to become prisoners.

The key structures and institutions of criminal justice processes are addressed throughout the text. It is evident from these discussions that the contributions of psychology and the distribution of psychologists across areas of forensic practice are uneven and irrational. The situation in England and Wales provides a useful illustration. Here, there are only a small (albeit growing) number of psychologists, predominantly in higher-education institutions, concerned with areas such as the prevention and investigation of criminal and anti-social behaviours. By far the largest group of psychologists are located in correctional settings, including prisons and secure hospitals, with a strong concentration in high-security settings. Less visible is the fact that community services concerned with preventing crime such as probation and community mental health services appear to be working beyond what could be seen as reasonable capacity, with few psychologists working in such settings. The distribution of psychology is largely the result of historical precedent, and few would argue that it is optimal in terms of outcomes or the cost-effective use of resources. Equally, it has also generated a range of interests that have little to do with the needs of the criminal justice system or society more generally, but which act as barriers to efforts at positive change.

Internationally, many psychologists will feel grave discomfort at the number of children who are drawn into criminal systems and end up in prisons. It is well known that adolescence is the point at which anti-social and criminal behaviours increase dramatically, and in our view psychology has a major contribution to make in looking for constructive ways of addressing this. Yet, here, forensic psychologists have been comparatively rare. Those working with children have tended to be located in correctional settings and have tended to be the poor relation to adult services. Input into community services with children have not been sufficient when compared with the underwriting of interventions in prisons and secure hospitals, with at best equivocal evidence as to their effectiveness.

Forensic psychologists have been slow to accept the role of economic and social inequality in crime. Indeed, it could be suggested that some have acted to resist such notions by stressing the individual causation of crime, going on to invent and use pseudo-scientific terminology to more firmly locate crime within the individual. Yet, current research suggests that more unequal societies are more unhealthy societies. Relative poverty as well as absolute poverty therefore becomes an important issue for forensic psychologists. Since the first edition of this text, there has still been little real progress in this important area. The investment of resources internationally, in terms of public money, has continued to be considerable. A great deal of money has been invested in various 'assessment tools' and standardized group work, and these may continue to serve the financial and professional interests of some. They continue to fail the public. In some places, this has led to a rowing back from forensic psychology on a large scale, as in the case of Canada. Elsewhere, there has been increased marketization and mutualization of services extending from adults to children and young people. A parallel may be drawn here with the privatization of bus services where the market dictates that only some services are profitable, irrespective of customer needs. The increasing use of manual-based interventions has led some to conclude that there is a real danger of the 'dumbing down' of psychological interventions with a failure to reflect the complexities of human behaviour (Towl, 2004). There have though been continuing signs of more broadly based approaches developing and spreading, for example, the use of more multi-modal interventions such as multi-systemic therapy (MST) approaches with young people.

The issue of sentencing practices has remained central to many areas of forensic practice. The use of more punitive sentences has continued across a number of countries with comparatively little done to address the causes of crime. We see in subsequent chapters how much may be learned from a public-health-based model of crime reduction. Sadly, this appears to be a lesson still to be learnt with an emphasis on assessment and identifying 'risks' overriding investment in preventative interventions.

The so-called 'What works?' literature and the wider debate about such modern political mantras continues to be a live issue (Merrington & Stanley, 2007; Thomas-Peter, 2006). We noted in the previous edition the political resonance in being seen to do 'something' in the domain of criminal justice in general and youth offender work in particular. This is a theme which resonates in areas that have comparatively high levels of public interest. This arguably continues to drive the creation and expansion of interventions characterized more by political expediency than by clinical or empirical rigour.

In setting the context of forensic psychology, the area of expert testimony is central. One feature that distinguishes this as a form of evidence is that opinions are actively sought. A great premium can sometimes be put on such 'expert evidence', and such evidence forms an important as part of the criminal and civil justice process. It is only comparatively recently that psychologists have contributed, and the extent to which this is the case differs markedly across different jurisdictions. The boundaries around the use of psychology in court systems remain contentious, and the conduct of practitioners has at times been controversial. Expert witnesses in most legal systems are present to serve the court or tribunal. They are not there to represent the parties instructing them or to act as an advocate for one party or another. The fact that this has been repeatedly stressed internationally highlights the fact that this fundamental point has been poorly integrated into practice, with psychologists often appearing to testify on behalf of their employers. This has, as noted in the text, often resulted in poor quality and unhelpful testimony that may impair the functioning of court systems. Linked to this, the professional bodies representing psychologists have repeatedly sought to improve guidance (e.g., American Psychological Society, 2010; British Psychological Society, 2014).

EXPERT CONTROVERSIES

One controversy in the area of expert evidence for psychologists, and for psychiatrists too, is that the scientific basis of some of the assertions made about the evidence base may be deeply equivocal. There are major doubts about some aspects of the disciplines of psychology and psychiatry – for example, scientific concerns about the validity of diagnostic categories that may be used in psychology and psychiatry. These tend to be derived from a series of checklists. Although some psychologists have been critical of this approach, many have warmed to it, content to offer their views (and pick up generous salaries or fees for doing so) on whether or not an individual may be deemed fit to be allocated to a particular diagnostic category. In general, scientific research into such diagnostic taxonomies has suggested that they have greater reliability than validity. Many requests for psychological evidence in the forensic domain can hinge upon whether or not an individual is deemed to fit in this or that diagnostic category. In this volume, the challenging and contentious area of psychiatric diagnoses is addressed. This is not merely an empirical issue, but one embedded in professional power and influence. It is every bit as much about us as professionals as it is about patients. Indeed, some legal tribunals have warmed to the use of simplistic categories in 'explaining' behaviour. This is not least perhaps, because these categories appear to provide an explanation for often troubling behaviours and often appear easier to understand than more evidence-informed approaches.

Examples here would include parole or mental health hearings, where the focus may be on whether a prisoner or patient can be 'diagnosed' with 'psychopathy'. The evident circularity of such explanations is rarely considered and is often difficult to convey in such settings. This is also complicated by the recent dramatic growth in the psychometrics industry. The heavily marketed claim is that various psychometric 'tools' may furnish us with much-coveted 'objective' information about psychological aspects of human functioning. Again, the use of psychometrics has a superficial appeal of offering apparently 'objective' information and being relatively easy to convey. Such information needs though to be viewed in the wider context of its use, and this is often missed in practice. Another example of expert testimony has been in relation to memory research. A knowledge and understanding of memory research have perhaps most widely been highlighted in relation to eyewitness testimony as a particular type of expert witness testimony. Indeed this is one application of experimental psychology that is routinely referred to in undergraduate and postgraduate forensic psychology courses. Of course, the scope for applications of our understanding of memory research can potentially go much wider. For example, the application of the understanding of memory to the assessment of offenders subject to indeterminate sentences. Part of the standard assessment methods used for such offenders typically involves the collection of interview-based data or the use of panel interviews in relation to parole hearings. Individuals may be asked to give their recollection of their thoughts, emotions and actions during the commission of their index offence in detail and be judged negatively in relation to any lapses or failures of recall. Some of the findings from memory research though suggests that memory is a constructive process. It is very clear that human beings have very limited recall for distant events and recall is prone to effects from previous accounts and subsequent questioning. This is an area ripe for research, and this is not just in relation to memory research. An understanding of developmental psychology, social psychology and neuropsychology has great potential applications to improving practice in forensic settings.

The area of expert testimony also warrants close scrutiny on ethical and human rights grounds. Laypeople are by definition unlikely to be good at detecting errors in the scientific research presented to them. It is incumbent on the 'expert' to offer not only scientific opinion but to express it in a manner in which a court or tribunal is most likely to understand. They should also clearly explain areas where there is a reasonable range of professional opinion. The ultimate ethical issue for psychologists though continues to revolve around the quality of the science that the 'expert' draws on in giving psychological testimony.

THINKING ABOUT HUMAN RIGHTS AND ETHICS

Human rights and ethical issues are central to much of the psychology practiced in forensic contexts. It has been observed that although the substantive ethical issues are not different to those found elsewhere, they may be brought into sharper focus in the forensic field (Towl, 1994). Ethical issues underpin what we research and how we practise, and it is therefore important to explore some of the philosophical roots to our ethical understanding. Individual rights, generally applicable human rights and a sense of the common good are key considerations that underpin many professional ethical codes of practice. Ethics and ethical thinking and reflection do not occur in a vacuum but rather in the context of power relations in particular cultures during particular times. Power differentials are pervasive across cultures. Professional cultures set the scene for both ethical and unethical behaviour. Some aspects of research and practice may change speedily over time in terms of adjustments to wider societal norms, others more slowly. An underlying concern about professionals in general has been the extent to which they are considered to be self-serving rather than serving the public interest. Professions tend to attract higher levels of pay and related benefits in comparison with the workforce in general. It is perhaps unsurprising, then, that professional ethical guidance can sometimes be seen in the same way, as a means of serving the self-interests of the profession. Psychology and the work of psychologists are not immune to this. Indeed, the numbers of complaints in forensic practice have continued to grow in recent years, particularly in correctional settings. As indicated earlier, forensic practice can bring into sharper focus fundamental ethical issues. If forensic psychologists are criticized, which they frequently are, in service user outlets (see, e.g., Hanson, 2009; Rose, 2009), this can, and all too frequently does, lead to defensive professional practices. These can include the avoidance of some areas of work or an unwillingness to take appropriate and just risks. There is no excuse for such practices. Indeed, such practices themselves may reasonably be deemed unethical. It is important to acknowledge some of the potential dynamics that may come into play. When complained about, individuals may feel hurt or even angry. Complaints may feel as if they are rather personal, whether or not that is the intention of the complainant. There is some good-quality guidance available to forensic psychologists (e.g., the very useful European-wide guidance produced by Lindsay, Koene, Øvreeide, & Lang, 2008). Responses to complaints can be an opportunity for critical reflection on practice and may provide valuable learning. Of course, in forensic practice, there may be more of a tendency for recipients of services to complain in relation to decision-making that may have an impact on their liberty. This is though a perfectly understandable reaction.

We feel it is axiomatic that, in general, the greater the power imbalances the greater the opportunity for abuses, and unethical behaviour. This touches on a tension within the growth of professions. Characteristically, professional groups tend to work towards increasing their power bases rather than decreasing them, and this has certainly applied to psychology in forensic settings. Here there has been, across a number of jurisdictions, a marked growth in the formal and informal power exercised by psychologists. One unintended consequence of such developments is that it becomes ever more likely that some will abuse such powers, and a recipient of such unethical services may well, not unreasonably, complain. More power for a particular profession is not by any means necessarily a good thing, far from it. One important test of professional ethics is the extent to which an individual is willing to 'whistle-blow' about a colleague. Perhaps too often it is easier not to comment, let alone intervene, when a colleague is behaving in a professionally inappropriate manner. Some, of course,

will cover up for the mistakes of colleagues, and this can be a rarely acknowledged ethical problem across professions. However, increased influence or power may, of course, be used positively, and this is the basis of countervailing arguments. Such tensions provide us with a salutary reminder of the need always to treat others with dignity and respect, especially when dealing with differences. Compassion, understanding, justice and kindness are crucial to just, ethical decision-making processes. Another useful 'rule of thumb' test can be not to treat others how we would not wish to be treated ourselves.

Eyewitnesses play an important role in the courtroom. The accuracy, or otherwise, of such testimony may be crucial. For many students of psychology, this will have a real resonance with much of memory research covered during their undergraduate studies. The reconstructive functioning of memory can plausibly lead to biases and inaccuracies in eyewitness testimony. This is an area of forensic psychological research and practice where opportunities to draw from the learning from experimental psychological studies into memory and learning abound. Of course, one feature of the field is the challenge of how results observed in the psychological laboratory may transfer to real-life events. This is largely a question of the ecological validity of such learning.. However, the models and methods developed in laboratories and lecture halls can be convincingly applied to studies in real-world settings. Concepts from memory and learning research can clearly be helpful in assisting our understanding of eyewitness testimony. For example, we may wish to look at errors in encoding information or systematic biases in recall. Memory decay effects may also be an interesting area for further examination. Facial recognition studies also have had an impact, drawing from work in experimental psychology. One practical social policy area of influence drawn from these areas of research in the forensic psychological field has been in relation to the development of procedural guidance relating to the identification of suspects by the police in England and Wales.

DEVELOPMENTAL PERSPECTIVES

A key underpinning theme of the text is the contributions from developmental psychology to forensic contexts, and, in this respect, there is a rich heritage of neuropsychological and biological research into crime and antisocial behaviour. The growth in this area has continued in recent years. Brain research has moved on considerably since the days of clinical lobotomies to control aggressive or disruptive behaviour in psychiatric hospitals. A combination of improved technologies, ethical standards and a more rigorously scientific approach have improved the knowledge and understanding yielded in this complex area of research. Studies have been undertaken with brain-injured patients that have led to links being made between the orbitofrontal cortex and experiences of rage and hostility. Frontal lobe damage or dysfunction has generally been equated with a greater proneness to demonstrate antisocial behaviour. Establishing causal relationships in this area is, however, much more challenging. Our understanding, as a discipline, of causation remains elementary, and there are a range of potential hypotheses as to how the underlying biological mechanisms may impact on behaviour. This is complicated by the interaction of environmental factors and underlying neurobiological mechanisms. The field has moved on dramatically since the intellectually vacuous debates about issues of nature v. nurture. The technology to study the working of the nervous system has also continued to improve at a remarkable rate, and this has been matched by step changes in both research and theory development.

Some forms of psychometric assessment provide us with an avenue to explore e and improve our understanding of specific brain functioning and links to antisocial behaviour. An example here is the reported association between antisocial behaviour and verbal intelligence. From a neurobiological perspective, this may, not unreasonably, be interpreted as linked to left hemispheric damage or, alternatively, dysfunction. The reason for comparatively higher levels of 'performance' intelligence may reflect a lack of educational opportunities. Such explanations are, of course, not mutually exclusive. A lack of specific experiences may lead to areas of the brain failing to develop or function effectively. The causal links or specific mechanisms underpinning the differences that are seen in forensic populations remain poorly understood, and such links are perhaps some of the most challenging to demonstrate.

Forensic neuropsychological research has often been unfairly confused with notions of biological determinism or misused to advance such arguments. The current developing evidence base presents a much more complex and interesting picture that stresses the early plasticity of the brain and also its capacity to recover. This suggests a compelling case for earlier interventions and improved access to such things as educational opportunities, especially for those young children without social and economic advantages. This is a form of intervention that is popular and actively undertaken by many economically and socially advantaged groups to good effect. Educational disadvantage tends to be a feature of

offender populations. It is an encouraging trend that psychologists are increasingly taking an interest in working with children and young people, although this remains limited with a strong bias towards any clinical work being directed towards adults. This bias continues to strike us as odd. To be most effective, it seems probable that such work should be undertaken as early as possible in the trajectory towards crime, and that models of prevention are likely to be more effective than late efforts at 'treatment'. This suggests a need for a major shift of focus in forensic psychology towards work with individual children and young people. The omens here, however, are not good, with, for example, recently developed services in the United Kingdom being cut back before their effects have been assessed.

This is likely to impact on the prevention of the development of criminal behaviour. Effective prevention results in fewer victims and also more individuals living fulfilling and productive lives. One recent trend in some of the research evaluating the efficacy of particular interventions aimed at reducing the risk of (re)offending has been the introduction of measures of 'cost effectiveness' in addition to traditional psychological methods of evaluation. This is a very positive development. It is positive because it allows us not only to focus upon the area of 'treatment impact' but also the financial cost of such impacts. Thus, we have the potential to invest public money more wisely. The idea underlying the developmental prevention of criminality is that 'risk factors' may be identified in advance and addressed early, before the 'risks' manifest themselves behaviourally. Also, 'protective factors' may be identified to further ameliorate the frequency and severity of such 'risks'. Children who have poor parental supervision are exposed to a greater risk of engaging in offending than those who do not. Even in purely financial terms some interventions can be demonstrably effective in saving the public purse. This has been revealed by a number of good-quality cost–benefit-based studies. One comparatively famous 'intensive' intervention involved home visitors giving advice about prenatal and postnatal care to young mothers. There was a focus upon appropriate nutrition and related health advice. In short, it was a general parental education intervention. Postnatal home visits resulted in decreased levels of child neglect and abuse. Children of these mothers had less than half the rate of arrests of a comparison group. These are powerful findings. The quality of the research data here is crucial. It is crucial in making evident the strengths and weaknesses of particular research methods. In public policy terms, the case for the development of a national prevention agency appears to be well made. The arguments are compelling. Such an idea has been implemented elsewhere (e.g., in Sweden and Canada). Such an enterprise would allow for a much more appropriate use of forensic psychologists who could work alongside their educational psychology counterparts.

One of the key problems in the development of forensic psychological services is that there are far fewer of these psychologists engaged in preventative work than are working in correctional settings and, particularly, high-security settings, which we would argue has resulted in severe distortions in forensic psychology services. Even within correctional settings, in terms of the potential impact on crime reduction, there appears to be far too few psychologists working with children and young people. A wiser distribution of resources would target schools, pupil referral units, youth justice services in the community and residential estates and caseloads of 'high-risk' offenders in the probation services.

Psychosocial research has been key in the study of offenders. Offenders tend to be versatile in their criminal activities, sometimes effortlessly switching from one offence type to another, for example, burglary and assaults. The most convicted violent offenders will have convictions for non-violent crimes too.

Early signs of impulsivity can be used to predict an inflated risk of antisocial behaviour. This has perhaps found a recent manifestation in the currently fashionable use of the diagnostic category 'attention deficit hyperactivity disorder' (ADHD). Related perhaps to this is that low school achievement is linked to an increased risk of youth violence. Indeed, there are a host of inter-correlations with subsequent criminal convictions. More recent studies in particular have begun to look, not just at correlations, but also at mediating factors in behavioural outcomes. For example, it has been proposed that the link between low school achievement and delinquency may be mediated by psychological disinhibition. The executive functioning of young brains may well be important in the prediction of future functioning. This is perhaps a good example of future research opportunities, with the need to draw on wider learning within the expanding neuropsychology and cognitive psychology fields to help in our understanding of the developmental trajectories towards crime.

Parenting methods have been looked at in terms of links with future potential crimes. These methods have often been categorized in terms of factors such as parental supervision, discipline and warmth (or coldness). A seminal study in this area provided evidence that poor parental supervision, harsh discipline and a rejecting attitude predicted an inflated chance of subsequent delinquency. Authoritarian parenting styles in particular have been linked to subsequent violence. This is entirely in keeping with social learning theory, which would suggest that brutalization begets brutalization. Attachment theory has also been used to study the psychosocial trajectories towards delinquency. Here, children who lack a secure attachment figure show a variety of adverse outcomes. Subsequent research has built on this initial finding to look at whether specific patterns of attachment are associated with particular types of adverse outcome (Crighton & Towl, 2008; Crittenden, 2008).

The family can be a significant 'protective factor' for some; however, if a child is unfortunate enough to have a father or mother who is involved in crime, then the probability is that they themselves will end up with a criminal record. Although the term 'criminal careers' is widely used in the field, it should perhaps be noted that there is no good evidence that the preceding finding reflects a 'career choice' that the child has moved into the family trade or profession. Far from it. Criminal parents tend to be highly critical of their child's involvement in crime. Family size is also important, with more children being equated with a higher risk of delinquency. This may well be linked to the thinner distribution of emotional, social and financial resources. In the United Kingdom, it has been amply demonstrated that poverty predicts an inflated risk of criminal conviction. Low family income and poor housing tend to characterize those with a higher risk of delinquency. Boys are at a higher risk of conviction while unemployed than when in employment. These findings present some clear moral and related social policy challenges. The potential to inform the design of prevention-based interventions is evident.

Every bit as important as understanding the developmental progression through 'criminal careers' is the need to understand what leads to desistence from crime. One advantage of a developmental perspective is that it lends itself to the notion that at different life stages different factors may come to the fore as the best predictors of desistence. Marriage and stable employment are two factors which have been widely researched in terms of their predictive value in desistence. Others have argued that personal resolve and determination to stop committing crime are also important. Desistence, in one sense, may be likened to 'spontaneous recovery' in medicine. Generally when we are unwell we subsequently recover. This is true of both physical and mental health. This would very often be the case without any medical intervention. A parallel can be drawn with crime. A number of those committing crimes (probably most) will eventually desist from committing crimes. The rate of crime by individual offenders is, in large part, age dependent. Thus, it is clear that one factor that is important in desistence is the ageing process. The field is replete with a lack of agreement about how precisely desistence should be operationalized. Some consider deceleration of the rate or seriousness of the type of crime to be a form of desistence. Others assume that desistence means no longer committing any crime. This remains an under-researched area with great potential and promise for the future.

INVESTIGATION AND PROSECUTION ISSUES

Offender profiling, possibly like no other topic across the forensic psychological field, generates much interest, some of which is prurient, some not. Whatever the motivation, this is an area of the forensic field that has spawned a great deal of interest, including a number of films and television programmes. Some of the increased interest across the field is due to some genuine developments with clear forensic applications (e.g., DNA testing). However, much in this popular area of forensic psychology has amounted in the past to a display of smoke and mirrors, akin to the cold readings practiced by magicians. There has, however, been a recent process of change in this area with a marked growth in scientific and empirical approaches. The field has increasingly concerned itself with higher-frequency crimes and moved away from 'clinical' profiling of rare but high-profile criminal behaviour such as serial homicides. In addition, there has been a greater stress on using psychology to improve the process of investigation. The current evidence base in these areas remains somewhat limited. The move to more scientifically valid methods has though placed this area of practice on a firmer footing.

In terms of a range of criminal and civil justice processes played out in courts and tribunals, one crucial grouping is juries. Jury decision-making has been the subject of much research. References to juries go back a long way in recorded history, but a commonly cited historical reference point is that of the Magna Carta, in 1215. Juries remain prominent in many legal systems in spite of facing frequent challenges and efforts to circum-scribe their freedom of action. This prominence is despite evidence that many members of the jury may struggle to understand particularly complex cases, a finding that has fuelled efforts to limit their role and use. Juries may also struggle to follow the instructions of judges or may disagree with those instructions based on feelings of natural justice. Juries may, when asked, fail to ignore evidence deemed legally inadmissible. Progress in this area has often been limited by the secrecy, in some jurisdictions, that surrounds the jury room.

PSYCHOLOGICAL ASSESSMENT

Power relationships are an important aspect of the context of much forensic work. This is very much the case in the area of the psychological assessment of children and adults. Forensic assessments will generally involve some degree of pressure or coercion. They may also take place in fundamentally coercive environments such as correctional institutions (Towl, 2005a). Psychologists often wield a great deal of influence in forensic contexts and certainly far more than is typically seen in other settings. This has at times been raised as a matter of serious concern among service user groups and by some service users (Leggatt, 2012). This is, or in some cases, perhaps, should be, a key ethical issue in everyday practice. Psychological assessments are, of course, not immune to biases and errors. Each of us, from time to time, will be prone to attributional errors in everyday judgements and decision-making. But at the core of a good psychological assessment is a rigorously scientific approach, applied with appropriate human consideration for the individual or individuals who are the subject of such assessments. A range of theoretical models may be applied but each involves, in some way or another, data collection (ideally from a good range of sources), formulation and judgement (which includes a sense of justice). It is not good enough merely to provide a scientifically accurate report in the forensic domain; there is an ethical responsibility for the psychologist to ensure that their report is also a just report. Whereas the field is replete with examples of discussion and debate over the accuracy of some psychological assessment methods, comparatively rarely is the issue of the justness or fairness of reports covered with such energy and detail. This perhaps reflects poorly on forensic psychology as a profession. One particularly important aspect of assessment is the ability to capture the work within a report form, whether verbal or written. The precise format of reports may vary. However, all should have certain features. They should be evidence based and written in an appropriately respectful and accurate manner. Any recommendations included in such a report should be explicitly linked to the body of data and evidence that characteristically will make up the main body of the report. They need to be both accurate and just.

One area of psychological assessments, which are particularly common in forensic practice, is in the domain of risk assessments. Again, issues of the accuracy and justice of such assessments come into sharp focus (Towl, 2005b). There has been an aggressive marketing of some risk assessment 'tools' in recent years and some hubristic claims made. There are some significant financial gains to be made for psychologists involved in the development and use of such 'tools', often including compulsory training in the application and interpretation of 'the tool'. It is perhaps unsurprising that this has been a key area of development in the 'for profit' (or private) sector in forensic psychology. In assessing the utility of particular structured assessments, it is perhaps worth reflecting on the question of where the benefits from their use lie. This is an area that forensic psychologists have often tended to fight shy of, preferring instead to debate the relative empirical strengths and weaknesses of particular 'tools'. This is clearly very important. However, it is also important that practitioners are aware that businesses, by definition, are on the whole structured to make money, and this will normally be the primary driver for them. It is also notable that, in contrast to some other areas, there have been few 'public domain' assessments developed and adopted within forensic psychology. This reliance on 'for profit' assessments has clear potential to result in conflicts of interest. It is possible for those with financial interests in particular 'tools' to recommend that others use them without being explicit about their conflict of interest. This is, of course, professionally unethical, but challenges to such practices have been comparatively rare. This is perhaps an area of privatization that does not get the same acknowledgement in terms of its impact as, say, the privatization of prisons. It is less salient as a change in the system but no less important.

There is much that can be learnt about the nature of risk assessment across disciplinary boundaries. The contemporary social and political concerns about climate change, international terrorism and transnational banking systems have given rise to a number of interdisciplinary approaches to understanding 'risk'. There are a range of professions and disciplines with an interest in these challenging and fascinating areas. There are a particular set of 'risks' that tend to be focused within forensic psychology. The relevant 'risks' tend to be about the chances of an individual committing crimes, and often violent and sexual crimes. Psychologists have contributed a great deal to improve the accuracy of such 'risk assessments'. Risk assessment reports may be used both to inform judgements about whether or not an individual is released from prison or hospital and also to inform the allocation to particular interventions. White-collar crime is much less commonly a focus of forensic psychological practice. Of course, the impacts of the so-called white-collar crime may well be every bit as serious as those of identified potential violent or sexual offenders. The international 'financial crisis' that appeared to peak in 2008 perhaps provides an illustrative example of this. In the modern world, poverty is a moral crime that

is widespread, including within the 'developed' world. This will result in heightened levels of 'risk' of unnecessary suffering and victimhood for many, and, as has been discussed earlier, an increased chance of ending up on a social and individual trajectory to the perpetration of crime.

Violent and sexual crimes are largely interpersonal. Forensic psychologists though have tended to focus primarily on potential perpetrators rather than potential victims. Not only is this scientifically limited as an approach, it is also questionable in terms of ethical practice. There also perhaps needs to be a wider recognition and acknowledgement that victims and perpetrators, when it comes to violent and sexual crimes, are overlapping groups (see Jackie Walton, Chapter 21 in this volume, in relation to children). This is a real challenge within criminal justice systems as we know many measures that may help to lower crime, are the remit of government departments not concerned with criminal justice. However, forensic psychologists, as a group, are well placed to challenge inappropriate policies and practices. There is something of a history of this among some; for example, forensic psychologists in some jurisdictions have effectively challenged aspects of racism in prisons. Some forensic psychologists have challenged the dubious practices of colleagues who, in the past, have not always obtained fully informed consent before undertaking assessments. It is a healthy sign within a profession if members of that profession are (publicly) prepared to question and, where necessary, challenge the behaviour and conduct of colleagues. This is a sometimes uncomfortable but necessary process. It is essential if, as a discipline, forensic psychologists wish to enjoy the respect of all the public and continue to exercise influence attached to their professional roles.

CRITICAL PSYCHOLOGY

Although some psychologists remain critical or circumspect about the scientific credentials of psychiatric diagnoses, such categorizations continue to be routinely used by many psychologists. Indeed, the use of such categorical approaches has seen a growth within forensic psychology, in marked contrast to other areas of psychology. There can be professional comfort in categorization. Once such an allocation of a diagnostic label has taken place, there is, in effect, purportedly, an 'explanation' of the behaviour that may be of concern or interest. The area of hypothesized links between offending and mental illness is contentious. There can be tensions between psychological and psychiatric knowledge. Unlike in psychology, the focus in psychiatry is with mental disorder rather than 'mental order'. Poverty and social exclusion play a part in informing our understanding of who is and is not diagnosed with mental disorders. Indeed, there is a parallel with recorded crime. Just as there are systematic biases in what crime gets recorded (or is designated as a crime), there are similar such biases in who does or does not get diagnosed with what. Again the issue of power inequalities raises its head.

The issue of power inequalities is arguably more salient in the area of diagnosed mentally disordered offenders with identified intellectual disabilities (Tancred, 2014). This is because it is evident to most of us that intellectual disabilities may well result in a fundamental vulnerability. The term 'learning disabilities' is synonymous with 'intellectual disability' and perhaps reflects particular professional sensibilities in terms of the more or less desirable term to be used. Again, this is an area of practice where the psychometrics industry maintains a firm hold. Screening measures for intellectual disabilities abound and are vigorously marketed. This is a large and financially lucrative market for the psychometrics industry, its proponents and beneficiaries. Much of the territory which may be considered to be 'mental disorder' is subject to the effective ownership of such categories through the auspices of DSM-V and ICD-10, with an array of additional profitable product lines such as psychometric tests for intellectual assessment. The contempt that some of the early test makers had for those with intellectual disabilities was all too evident. This is a field characterized by a history of prejudice, and this is the context in which psychological assessments and interventions take place. Psychologists themselves are also subject to the potential prejudices common in this area, but at least as a professional group should be aware of the effects of such potential prejudices on behaviour and judgements.

One significant area of practice for forensic psychologists is in giving an opinion on fitness to stand trial and enter a plea on behalf of the court. The extent to which the accused party understands the nature of the crime and court process needs to be assessed. Their capacity to 'instruct' their legal representatives needs assessing too. There also needs to be an understanding of the issue of responsibility in criminal law. The level of understanding of the 'wrongness' of the relevant criminal acts by the defendant may well also be a consideration for the courts. Relevant psychological assessments and evidence can lead to a defence of diminished responsibility or not guilty by reason of insanity.

Those with intellectual disabilities may have communication needs different from those of the general population. Effective communication is crucial to psychological assessments. But arguably this need is amplified when working with those with intellectual disabilities whether undertaking assessments or interventions. Arguably this is an aspect of working with offenders that needs more visibility. Such challenges sometimes remain hidden from everyday discourses about offenders.

One increasingly highly visible area of study, policy and practice is in relation to work with those diagnosed as having 'personality disorders'. Historically there has been a discussion and debate about whether or not those diagnosed with personality disorders are simply at the more extreme ends of some key identified dimensions of personality or if they are qualitatively different. In this edition, the coverage of this topic has been expanded to reflect the recent growth in research and practice in this area. Whichever side of that particular debate the reader favours, this is a complex and challenging field and one that has taxed many academics and clinicians. It is an area where both fundamental questions about the putative nature (or existence) of personality disorders may be addressed and also practical clinical questions (e.g., about potentially suitable interventions) may be answered.

In recent years, there has been a great deal of government investment in the 'treatment' of those categorized as having personality disorders. Some 'personality disorders' have been the subject to more study than others within forensic populations. There are some gender differences in such studies, with links between men and 'antisocial personality disorders' and women and 'borderline personality disorders'. This is one of those comparatively few areas of research and practice which has been generously funded by the public. The much-vaunted, but fundamentally flawed, dangerous severe personality disorder (DSPD) units in UK prisons and hospitals were generously funded but have quickly closed or been redesigned and focussed on a broader range of needs. There has also been a massive investment of public money in research in this area, particularly in Europe, with what appears to be very little indeed to show for it in terms of results that will be helpful in policy terms, or in clinical management and practice. This is disappointing, but not remotely surprising. Some of the problems have arisen out of a conceptual confusion regarding what precisely constituted DSPD. From the outset, it was clear that it was not a clinical category, but rather a political one. Another part of the problem was that a range of behavioural disorders appear to have been captured under the muddled rubric. In short, the term was bereft of any intellectual integrity. Of course, this reflects a more general problem when underlying personality traits are attributed to particular behavioural patterns. And it is an argument that could be used to call into question the scientific basis of the construct of personality disorders per se. Many, aware of some of the limitations of such terms, will simply take a pragmatic approach. As we have seen in some other areas of forensic practice, this is an area where financial interests from, for example, the psychometric testing industry are also notable.

SUBSTANCE USE

Drug and alcohol misuse has become an increasingly major problem in relation to both problems of public health and criminal justice. A compulsion to consume such products is an underlying commonality in the often absolutely desperate lives of habitual drug users. Some official estimates have asserted that about half of all recorded crime is drug related. Individuals may commit crimes while under the influence of drugs. Alternatively or additionally they commit crimes to fund their drug habits. Drug addicts may lie and deceive those around them, even their close friends and family, for such is the power of the compulsion to access drugs. The deplorable truth is that drug addicts can often have more chance of receiving treatment if they go to prison than if they do not. This health service inadequacy contributes to the creation of a perverse incentive for addicts who want treatment to commit crime and get caught doing so, with a view to imprisonment. This cannot be right, and it is surely time to move back to a health-care model of managing substance misuse by users rather than the criminal justice models used in many jurisdictions.

Drug crime is also big business, and the relevant markets are vigorously policed and protected by such criminals. Thus, there can be a significant difference between the supplier and the user or consumer of the particular drug. Drug overdose is a relatively common cause of death among regular drug users. It is frequently difficult for individual users to gauge the quality and thereby quantity of the drugs that they are intending to use. Notwithstanding the devastating impacts of drug misuse in both health and crime-related terms, one of the most dangerous drugs routinely used in prisons is nicotine. Stopping smoking in prisons where this has not already been done must surely be the single most significant public health policy that could be implemented. This illustrates the difficulty of departments of state often not being as integrated as they could be in addressing issues that cut across government departmental boundaries. The capacity to function effectively across (and outside) central departmental boundaries is perhaps one of the biggest challenges of public service.

EARLY INTERVENTION

As a general rule, it seems that earlier interventions are potentially more effective. We see from the earlier developmentally orientated chapters that those who go on to commit serious offences as adults can, as a group, be identified comparatively early in their criminal careers. Children and young people who are violent and engage in sexually harmful behaviours particularly warrant our attention. The case for early intervention and support with these children and young people seems unanswerable. This is especially important given the known links between those who have been abused themselves and those who go on to commit acts of abuse. A great deal of such sexually abusive behaviour may go on within the family. For example, teenage children may be trusted to care for younger siblings who then experience abuse. Often such developmental trajectories may well manifest themselves into adulthood from the perspective of both the abuser and abused.

The sex offender assessment and treatment industry boom appears to have levelled off. Again, this is an area where a great deal of public money has been spent internationally. Despite this, however, the evidence of treatment effects in the reduction of risk of reconvictions for a sexual offence is missing. There is some evidence that convicted sex offenders will show clinical improvements on various self-report methods before and after treatment. But it could reasonably be argued that this is simply the result of the demand characteristics present. The elephant in the living room is that the so-called sex offender treatment 'programmes' may not work, or indeed may increase risk. The emerging evidence increasingly suggests that current approaches have not, contrary to some (grandiose) claims, been demonstrated to be effective. In line with this, the use of such 'treatments' outside of the context of experimental trials is at best ethically questionable (Dennis *et al.*, 2012). Researchers in this field have seemed sometimes reluctant to consider such a potentially unpalatable hypothesis. This can lead to a defensiveness which goes beyond the data. Indeed, there is sometimes a sense of desperation and exasperation at the inability of demonstrating improvements on disappointing results. Despite such empirical problems, this has not halted some continued expansion, underpinned by public funding and political imperatives. The industry has also been supported by legislation, with an increased number and range of behaviours being deemed 'sexual offences'. There are also much higher levels of bureaucratic scrutiny that have been implemented. Yet, the disarming truth is that, overwhelmingly, most men who rape will not be brought to trial, and if they are they will have a comparatively strong chance of not being convicted and sent to prison. The same is highly likely to be true with child sexual abuse and other forms of sexual offending. In the unlikely event that a victim of a sexual crime reports it, the chances of a conviction being secured are very slim indeed.

One fundamental caveat to strident assertions about what we 'know about sex offenders' is that much of what is known draws on convicted sex offender populations.

This is clearly the tip of an iceberg. It would also seem highly unlikely that they would be representative of sex offenders as a whole, given the very small sampling involved relative to prevalence and incidence rates. Some sex offenders may be more difficult to detect, let alone convict. Many will enjoy a very high degree of protection. In some occupations, there are increased opportunities to sexually offend – for example, the clergy, medical practitioners in general practice and various specialisms such as gynaecology or paediatrics and many others. 'Trusted' professionals are thus likely to be well protected from detection, prosecution and conviction. The medical profession has typically been fiercely protective of its members and resistant to whistle-blowing about colleagues. As in a number of occupations, it is difficult and, for all intents and purposes, discouraged. Previously, victims of abuse by church leaders have had little voice, but such abuses have increasingly come out into the open. There is no convincing reason to believe that those so motivated will not be distributed across a number of walks of life and some may seek to get themselves into positions where opportunities to abuse abound.

Another problem in the sex offender assessment and treatment industry has been the undue standardization and 'manualization' of the interventions used. It appears implicit in some of the professional literature that we know current interventions work and that there are significant commonalities within and across particular offence types. This understanding is more persuasive in terms of the legal categories that have been assigned to the particular offence type than it is in terms of a psychological understanding of the behaviours involved. This will have implications for interventions.

Imprisoned sex offenders (including alleged sex offenders held on remand) have an inflated risk of suicide. This is a fact that can easily be forgotten in our everyday clinical practice. But by far the most powerful predictor of prisoner suicide is time in the particular prison. There is a compelling case for ensuring that prisoners have access to support early in their time in a given prison. There are some sub-groups that fall out of this general pattern. For example, although life-sentenced prisoners have an inflated risk of suicide they may, on average, complete suicide later in their sentence, possibly linked to particular milestone decisions about their progress (or lack of it) towards parole. Psychologists in prisons have tended to become less involved in this important area of practice, with a shift towards involvement with manualized

interventions to reduce the risk of reoffending. This is unfortunate, because psychologists have contributed much in this important area of public health (e.g., Crighton, 2000; McHugh & Snow, 2000). There are a number of 'suicide myths' in this field, for example, that young people or those held on remand are at a greater risk of suicide than others; the data would suggest otherwise. Yet, such myths still abound and, as late as 2014, the Prison and Probation Ombudsman recommended that 'remand status' be considered a 'risk factor' for suicide in prison. Such an assertion appears to be based upon very limited evidence and, if implemented, may result in misinforming risk assessment processes. However, given that time spent in a prison is the most powerful 'risk factor' for suicide, the 'remand' category may account for disproportionate numbers of those who have only been incarcerated for a short time. Also, interestingly, black prisoners are at a lower risk of suicide; this was first noted in the United Kingdom in the late 1990s (Towl & Crighton, 1998). The precise and sometimes complex links between suicide and intentional self-injury remain unclear. But both remain as significant problems in prisons and healthcare settings. Staff attitudes towards the suicidal can be considerably less than helpful (Crighton, 2000).

JUSTICE RESTORED

There are a range of models of restorative justice, and the research base in this area has recently taken a number of steps forward, with some high-quality evaluations supporting the efficacy of the approach. Lamentably, this is not an area where psychologists have been as active as they might have been. Yet, there is huge potential for psychologists to get more involved in both evaluative research and consultancy advice. Most importantly perhaps, there is the potential to reduce the number of future victims and to help and assist existing victims.

The forensic field is broad, with a growing knowledge base. But it is a knowledge base that could be further developed with more explicit links with the experimental psychology base of much of what is most effective, useful and just in policy and practice.

We remain grateful for the comments we have received on the first edition of *Forensic Psychology*, but hope that readers will agree that the publishing of a second edition is timely.

REFERENCES

American Psychological Society (2010). Guidelines for child custody evaluations in family law proceedings. *American Psychologist, 65*, 863–867.

British Psychological Society (2007). *Psychologists as expert witnesses: Guidelines and procedure for England and Wales*. Leicester: Author.

Crighton, D. A. (2000). Suicide in prisons in England and Wales 1988–1998: An empirical study. Unpublished PhD Dissertation, APU (Cambridge).

Crighton, D. A., & Towl, G. J. (2008). *Psychology in prisons* (2nd edn). Oxford: BPS Blackwell.

Crittenden, P. M. (2008). *Raising parents: Attachment, parenting and child safety*. Cullompton, Devon: Willan.

Dennis, J. A., Khan, O., Ferriter, M., Huband, N., Powney, M. J., & Duggan, C. (2012). Psychological interventions for sex offenders or those who have sexually offended or are at risk of offending. *Cochrane Database of Systematic Reviews 2012, (12)*. Art. No.: CD007507. doi: 10.1002/14651858.CD007507.pub2.

Hanson, C. (2009). Thinking skills? Think again! *Inside Time*, Issue 119, May, p. 20.

Home Office (2000). *Achieving best evidence in criminal proceedings*. London: Author.

Leggatt, T. (2012). Psychology: Off on a tangent again. Insidetime, April 2012. http://www.insidetime.co.uk/articleview.asp?a=1184andc=psychology_off_on_a_tangent_againandcat=Psychology, accessed 14 January 2015.

Lindsay, G., Koene, C., Øvreeide, H., & Lang, F. (2008). *Ethics for European psychologists*. Göttingen, Germany: Hogrefe.

Marques, J. K., Wiederanders, M., Day, D. M., Nelson, C., & Van Ommeren, A. (2005). Effects of a relapse prevention program on sexual recidivism: Final results from California's Sex Offender Treatment and Evaluation Project (SOTEP). *Sexual Abuse: A Journal of Research and Treatment, 17*(1), 79–107.

Masoumzadeh, A., Jin, L., Joshi, J., & Constantino, R. (2013). HELPP zone: Towards protecting college students from dating violence. *iConference 2013 Proceedings*, 925–928. doi:10.9776/13481

McHugh, M. J., & Snow, L. (2000). Suicide prevention: Policy and practice. In G. J. Towl, M. J. McHugh, & L. Snow (Eds.), *Suicide in prisons*. Oxford: BPS Blackwell.

Merrington, S., & Stanley, S. (2007). Effectiveness: Who counts what? In L. Gelsthorpe & R. Morgan (Eds.), *Handbook of probation*. Cullompton, Devon: Willan.

Prison and Probation Ombudsman (2014). *Learning from PPO investigations risk factors in self-inflicted deaths in prisons*. London: Author.

Rose, K. (2009). Has ETS reduced your impulsivity? *Inside Time*, Issue 119, May, p. 21.

Tancred, T. (2014). *Intellectual disabilities – differential treatment within multi agency public protection arrangements*. Unpublished PsychD dissertation, University of Roehampton.

Thomas-Peter, B. (2006). The modern context of psychology in corrections: Influences, limitations and values of 'what works'. In G. J. Towl (Ed.), *Psychological research in prisons*. Oxford: Blackwell.

Towl, G. J. (1994). Ethical issues in forensic psychology. *Forensic Update, 39*, 23–26.

Towl, G. J. (2004). Applied psychological services in HM Prison Service and the National Probation Service. In A. Needs & G. J. Towl (Eds.), *Applying psychology to forensic practice*. Forensic Practice Series. Oxford: BPS Blackwell.

Towl, G. J. (2005a). National offender management services: Implications for applied psychological services in probation and prisons. *Forensic Update, 81*, 22–26.

Towl, G. J. (2005b). Risk assessment. *Evidence Based Mental Health, 8*, 91–93.

Towl, G. J., & Crighton, D. A. (1998). Suicide in prisons in England and Wales from 1988 to 1995. *Criminal Behaviour and Mental Health, 8*(3), 184–192.

Towl, G. J., Farrington, D. P., Crighton, D. A., & Hughes, G. (2008). *Dictionary of forensic psychology*. Cullompton, Devon: Willan.

UCAS (2014). Website. www.ucas.com, accessed 14 January 2015.

Part I
Investigative Practice

2   The Justice System in England and Wales: A Case Study

DAVID FAULKNER

WHAT JUSTICE MEANS

The word 'justice' can be used in several different ways. Social reformers will speak of justice in the sense of the fair distribution of power and wealth among a country's citizens. An organization's workforce may demand justice for themselves in terms of their pay and conditions of service. Minority groups may call for justice in the sense of equal rights and protection from discrimination. Or people may demand justice for an individual who has been unfairly treated, or for the victim of a crime. There will often be contested views about what counts as justice in the situation concerned.

At other times, the word is used – as it is in this chapter – in the context of the courts and issues which have to be resolved through a prosecution in a criminal court, or a civil dispute to be dealt with in the civil or family courts. Even then, the word can be used in two senses. It can refer to an outcome of the process, one which is accepted as fair and legitimate, as one where authority has been properly used and the relevant interests have been suitably represented and taken into account. Or it can refer to the process itself – in criminal matters, the process of arrest, trial and sentence which is centred on the courts but which also involves other agencies of the state. Those agencies include the police, prosecution, prison and probation services, which together make up what has become known as the criminal justice system, sometimes spelt with capital letters and abbreviated to 'CJS'.

Used in the first sense, justice implies a context of moral or social values, and an expectation that they will be shared and respected. Like the rule of law, it stands above the interests of any individual or group, including those of the government. Used in the second sense, the word does not have a normative sense; justice is seen as serving a more instrumental purpose such as protection of the public or satisfaction for the victim, and it is judged by its efficiency and effectiveness in achieving that purpose. It does not have much space for mercy, compassion or forgiveness – a space which supporters of restorative justice try to fill (see the following text).

THE CRIMINAL JUSTICE SYSTEM

The origins of the system of justice as it now exists in England and Wales can be traced back a long way. (There are important differences but similar principles in Scotland and Northern Ireland.[1]) A single framework of law administered consistently throughout the country – the common law – began to be developed in the time of Henry II (1154–1179). Magna Carta (1215) introduced the principles of trial before a jury, proportionate punishment and no imprisonment without trial. Justices of the peace were appointed under the Justices of the Peace Act 1361, although their origins go back another 200 years. The offices of Secretary of State and Lord Chancellor, although of earlier origin, became powerful and prominent at the time of Henry VIII in the persons of Thomas Cromwell and Thomas More.

The Enlightenment, and especially the work of philosophers such as Kant and Locke, of jurists such as Blackstone and Mansfield, and of penal reformers such as John Howard and Elizabeth Fry, brought further influences during the eighteenth century. A 'classical' view of justice emerged which was based on the rule of law, the independence of the judiciary, the presumption of innocence, proportionality of punishment, the adversarial system with 'equality of arms' (an equal contest between the prosecution and the defence), the rule that no one should be tried twice for the same offence

Forensic Psychology, Second Edition. Edited by David A. Crighton and Graham J. Towl.
© 2015 John Wiley & Sons, Ltd. Published 2015 by British Psychological Society and John Wiley & Sons, Ltd.

(no 'double jeopardy'), and the principle that all people are born equal and are entitled to dignity and respect as human beings (although that did not apply to slaves or indigenous people until later). Those principles inspired the constitutions of the United States and the common law countries of the Commonwealth, and they later found expression in the European Convention on Human Rights. The Convention was eventually incorporated into UK domestic law by the Human Rights Act 1998.

The structure of what is now known as the criminal justice system began to take its present shape in the Victorian period, with the formation of regular police forces (1829 in London, later in the provinces), a national prison system (in 1877) and the probation service (in 1907). The pace of change gathered speed from the 1960s, and especially the 1980s, onwards. The changes included the following:

- The reforms of the police under the Police Act 1966, the Police and Magistrates' Courts Act 1994,the Police Reform Act 2002 and the Police Reform and Social Responsibility Act 2011

- The creation of a unified Crown Court under the Courts Act 1971

- The Creation of the Crown Prosecution Service under the Prosecution of Offences Act 1985

- The rapid expansion of the private security industry, performing policing functions alongside the statutory police forces

- Contracting out of some prisons and some prison functions (such as escorts) to the private sector

- Plans to commission the majority of probation functions from the private or voluntary sectors

- Reforms of youth justice, including new powers for youth courts and the formation of the Youth Justice Board and youth offending teams under the Crime and Disorder Act 1998

- New measures for preventing and dealing with terrorism

- The creation of the Ministry of Justice in 2007

Greater attention came to be paid to the treatment of victims of crime, to the position of minority groups, and to antisocial behaviour. The degree of interdependence between different procedures and organizations came to be more widely recognized, and increasing efforts were made to 'manage' the system as a coherent whole.

The assessment, management and avoidance of risk became a major concern, in criminal justice as in national life more generally. Mechanisms for risk assessment include the offender assessment system (OASys) used by probation and prison staff at all stages during an offender's sentence, for example, in deciding the degree of security or supervision that may be required, or a prisoner's readiness for release. They are also used in judging priorities for the police and in preventing crime, including domestic violence and the abuse of children, for example, through the multi-agency public protection arrangements (MAPPA).

Managerial reforms in all public services brought a new emphasis on performance measurement, evidence-based practice, contracting-out and risk assessment and risk management. The National Offender Management Service was created in 2004 with the intention of bringing prisons and probation closer together and of providing for a continuous process of 'offender management' throughout a person's sentence. The two services have a single director-general. Since 2010, measures to reduce public expenditure have led to reductions in the size of police, prison and probation services; in the funds available for legal aid; and in the staff of government departments themselves.

Legislation since 1991 has included between 50 and 60 Criminal Justice or other Acts of Parliament designed to make the system more effective in protecting the public and increasing the public's confidence that offenders are being adequately punished. It increased maximum sentences; restricted judges' discretion to pass sentences which might be considered too lenient; created new indeterminate sentences of imprisonment for public protection (IPP); enabled the police to impose on-the-spot fines for offences of public disorder; made convictions easier to obtain by removing or modifying some of the traditional safeguards; and introduced civil orders such as the antisocial behaviour order (ASBO), or now a criminal behaviour order, for which breach carries a substantial sentence of imprisonment. Special powers were also introduced to deal with terrorism. The number of people in prison doubled between 1992 and 2013, from about 42,000 to about 84,000.

WHAT IS A CRIME?

A 'crime' can be defined for legal purposes simply as an offence against the criminal law (the word may be used more loosely in ordinary language). For nearly all offences the definition is now in statute, although for a few (murder is one example) it is still part of the common law. For some offences such as murder, assault and theft there is widespread agreement through time and across different cultures that the act is wrong, it should be treated as a crime, and the law against it should be effectively enforced. But there are many actions which people consider to be wrong without believing that they should be criminal; or which they may not regard as wrong in themselves but which are made criminal for the sake of good order or public health or safety. Outside the small area of 'obvious' crimes, actions which should and should not be treated as criminal vary over time, and reflect different social attitudes and circumstances, or different economic conditions, and different political priorities on the part of the government of the day. In that sense, crime is what criminologists have called 'socially constructed'.

A recent development has been the growth in 'cyber-crime', essentially crimes involving the use of the Internet, either as a means of committing a 'traditional' crime such as fraud or using a false identity or for new kinds of crime such as hacking or deliberately spreading a computer virus. Some of those offences are difficult to identify or detect, and some people claim that they represent a new area of 'hidden' crime that is not recorded.

No one knows exactly how many criminal offences actually exist. The law reform group JUSTICE calculated that, in 1980, there were about 7,200; an estimate in 2000 suggested that the number had by then grown to about 8,000; and it has been claimed that 3,000 new offences were created between 1997 and 2007. An offence once created is hardly ever abolished, although it may cease to be enforced.

For a fuller discussion of legal and social constructions of crime, see Lacey and Zedner (2012).

MEASUREMENT OF CRIME

Crime is measured in two ways. Statistics have been collected since the mid-nineteenth century to show the number of crimes recorded by the police; the Crime Survey for England and Wales, formerly the British Crime Survey, was first introduced in 1982, and is a survey of households in which people are asked about their experience of crime over the previous 12 months.[2] Neither can give a complete account. Statistics of recorded crime do not include crimes which the police do not record, usually because they are not reported to them or do not otherwise come to their notice; changes in rates of recorded crime may be due to changes in policing priorities or public attitudes to different types of crime or towards the police, as well as changes in the rates themselves. The survey does not cover offences against children or very rare crimes such as murder. Taken together, the two sources do, however, give a reasonable indication of the volume of crime that is committed and especially of changes in the rate at which it is being committed.

The statistics show that recorded crime increased almost continuously during the period from the end of the First World War until 1995. The British Crime Survey uncovered, as had long been suspected, a rate of crime which was about double the rate for recorded crime. Further analysis showed that, for offences in the survey, only about 2% were likely to result in a conviction in court. Other research showed that about 30% of young men were likely to have a conviction for a 'standard list' (roughly speaking, indictable – see the following text) offence by the age of 30; but that about 5% of known offenders were responsible for about 70% of total crime.

Crime rates vary a great deal between different places, both between different parts of the country and different types of neighbourhoods. The highest rates are in the inner city areas of London, Birmingham and Manchester. So do a person's chances of becoming a victim, with young men being most at risk. Many offences are not 'cleared up' – that is to say they are not traced to an offender who admits the offence or is convicted in court. Clear up rates vary from about 20% for burglary and criminal damage, to over 75% for violent and sexual offences and 90% for homicide.

Since 1995, the total volume of crime has fallen sharply, especially for burglary and vehicle offences, which made up about half the total. Crime statistics for the year ended 31 December 2013 show a total of 3.7 million recorded and 7.5 million surveyed offences in that year (http://www.ons.gov.uk/ons/rel/crime-stats/crime-statistics/period-ending-december-2013/index.html, accessed 14 January 2015). Both sources show a fall in the overall crime rate of about 40% since 1995. Violent crime has not fallen so significantly, and for some offences there has been a small increase, so that violent crime now represents a larger proportion of the total (about 20%).

For fuller discussion of crime data and statistics, see Maguire (2012).

THE CRIMINAL JUSTICE PROCESS

The criminal justice process normally begins when an offence is reported to the police or otherwise becomes known to them, for example, if they are already on the scene when the incident takes place. The police investigate the alleged offence, interview witnesses and suspects, and may in due course make an arrest. The person is taken to a police station for further questioning under caution, and may then be detained or released on bail. If detained, the person must as soon as possible be released or charged and brought or bailed to appear before a magistrates' court.

The process up to that point is regulated by the Police and Criminal Evidence Act 1984 (PACE) and codes of practice issued under the Act. There are strict time limits, and rules which cover such matters as the recording of interviews, the suspect's access to legal advice and the granting of bail. A person must normally be charged within 24 hours of being detained by the police, and brought before a court within 36 hours of being charged, with extensions up to 96 hours in certain circumstances on the authority of a senior police officer (for a further 36 hours) or a magistrates' court. A longer period of 28 days applies if the person has been charged with an offence of terrorism.

Alternative procedures allow the police to impose on-the-spot fines in certain cases, or the police or the Crown Prosecution Service (CPS) to administer a caution instead of a charge, provided that the person admits the offence and is prepared to accept the fine or caution. If not, a decision must be taken whether to pursue the case in court in the normal way.

Once a person has been charged, the case goes to the CPS, which decides whether to proceed to prosecution. The decision is taken in accordance with the Code for Crown Prosecutors (http://www.cps.gov.uk/publications/code_for_crown_prosecutors/index.html, accessed 14 January 2015). Prosecution will normally follow unless the CPS decides that there is not enough evidence to obtain a conviction or there are compelling reasons why a prosecution would not be in the public interest. Relevant considerations are set out in the code (e.g., if the person is suffering from a terminal illness). Legal aid is provided for legal advice and representation, but with increasing restrictions on the amount that is available.

The presumption of innocence applies until the person has admitted the offence or been found guilty by a court. The suspect must not be referred to as an offender or a criminal, and the offence must always be described as 'alleged'.

All proceedings begin with a hearing in the magistrates' court, initially to confirm the defendant's identity, to establish that he or she understands the charge and to consider whether bail should be granted or refused. Straightforward cases are then disposed of with (usually) a discharge, a fine or an acquittal; other cases are adjourned and the defendant remanded on bail or in custody. If bail is refused, the defendant is taken to a prison.

The process from then on depends on the nature of the offence. Offences are of three kinds. 'Summary only' cases can only be dealt with in the magistrates' court and include less serious road traffic offences, common assault, and criminal damage where the value is below a certain amount (£5,000 at present). The maximum penalty used is often a fine, although many summary offences carry imprisonment.

'Either way' cases can be dealt with either in the magistrates' court or the Crown Court. They include theft, burglary, assault causing actual bodily harm (ABH) and most offences which involve the possession or supply of drugs. The magistrates' court must decide on mode of trial, normally following representations by the prosecution, and usually with an eye to the sentence which is likely to be appropriate if the person is found guilty and whether it is within the sentencing powers of the magistrates' court (see the following text). The defendant may, however, insist on ('elect') trial at the Crown Court, and therefore before a judge and jury, if he or she chooses.[3]

'Indictable only' offences are the most serious and least numerous and can only be tried in the Crown Court.[4] They include homicide, rape, robbery, assault causing grievous bodily harm with intent (GBH) and conspiracy to commit a crime.

A person convicted and sentenced at a magistrates' court can appeal to the Crown Court, and a person convicted and sentenced at the Crown Court can appeal to the Court of Appeal. An appeal can be against conviction, sentence or both. With Crown Court cases, a further appeal may be made to the Supreme Court when it has been certified that a point of law of general public importance is involved and the Court of Appeal or the Supreme Court grants leave to appeal. A defendant may appeal against his or her conviction as of right on any question of law (e.g., whether the judge properly directed the jury by correctly outlining the ingredients of the offence). In cases which involve questions of fact (e.g., whether the jury should have convicted on the evidence in the case) the offender may only appeal if he or she obtains a certificate from the trial judge that the case is fit for appeal or, more usually, leave from the Court of Appeal.

Appeals to the Court of Appeal against sentence always require the leave of the Court of Appeal. The appeal court may quash a sentence imposed by the Crown Court and in its place substitute any sentence which the lower court could have imposed, but the effect must not be that the applicant is more severely dealt with overall as a result.

The Attorney General may appeal to the Court of Appeal if he or she considers that the Crown Court has passed an unduly lenient sentence. The power is restricted to certain specified (but quite numerous) serious offences. Requests to consider referring a sentence may come from the prosecution, the victim or victim's family, Members of Parliament, pressure groups or members of the public.

Complaints of wrongful conviction sometimes occur when all the normal rights of appeal have been exhausted. Until the mid-1990s, it was a function of the Home

Secretary acting under the Royal Prerogative to consider those complaints and to refer them to the Court of Appeal if he or she considered it appropriate. This was normally done only where there was new evidence or some other substantial consideration which was not before the original trial court. The weakness of that arrangement became evident from a number of notorious miscarriages of justice which took place during the 1980s. The Criminal Cases Review Authority, later the Criminal Cases Review Commission (CCRC), was set up under the Criminal Appeal Act 1995 with authority to review suspected miscarriages of justice and refer them to the Court of Appeal if there is a 'real possibility' that it would not be upheld.

In 2013, a total of 1.76 million individuals were dealt with formally by the criminal justice system in England and Wales, of whom 331,000 were dealt with out of court, and 1.43 million were proceeded against in court. All those figures have been falling during the last 20 years. About 1.2 million were convicted.[5]

For more detailed accounts and fuller discussion of the criminal justice process, see *Handbook of the Criminal Justice Process* (McConville & Wilson, 2002) and *The Criminal Process* (Ashworth & Redmayne, fourth edition 2010).

THE SENTENCING FRAMEWORK

The main sentences or 'disposals' available to the criminal court (some are not strictly sentences) are imprisonment (which may be immediate or suspended) or detention in a young offender institution (YOI); a community sentence; a fine; discharges; compensation orders; and so-called ancillary orders. The maximum sentence for an offence is laid down in legislation, for example, life imprisonment for manslaughter, arson or rape; 14 years for house burglary or blackmail; 10 years for obtaining by deception or indecent assault on a woman; 7 years for theft; 5 years for causing actual bodily harm; 2 years for carrying an offensive weapon (4 years for a knife). For some offences, there are mandatory or minimum sentences – life imprisonment for murder, 5 years for possession of a prohibited firearm, 12 months' disqualification for drunk driving. The Criminal Justice Act 2003 introduced a new and controversial indeterminate sentence for public protection (IPP) for offenders who are considered dangerous. The sentence was modified by the Criminal Justice and Immigration Act 2008 as a result of which courts had more flexibility; it was abolished by the Legal Aid, Sentencing and Punishment

of Offenders Act 2012, but about 6,000 prisoners remained in prison under sentences passed before that date.

The previous range of community-based sentences has been consolidated into a single generic community sentence for which a court may select those requirements that are most suitable for a given offender in a particular case. The possible requirements include unpaid work; taking part in certain activities or programmes; a curfew; residence in a specified place such as an approved hostel; drug rehabilitation; and attendance at an attendance centre (up to age 25). Electronic monitoring (known as 'tagging') can also be added, especially, for example, if a curfew is imposed. The courts can also make a drug treatment and testing order (DTTO), an important feature of which is that it results in offenders being brought back to court so that their progress and the order itself is kept under review. There is now a greater emphasis on enforcement, with more offenders being sent to prison if they do not comply with the conditions of their orders.

For most offences for which the fine is commonly used, the maximum is set at one of five statutory levels – Level 1 (at present £100), Level 2 (£200), Level 3 (£1,000), Level 4 (£2,500) and Level 5 (£5,000). The offender can also be ordered to pay compensation to the victim where appropriate, and courts are encouraged to make compensation orders wherever possible. Both fines and compensation have to take account of the offender's ability to pay. The use of the fine has been falling for many years, partly because of difficulties of enforcement, and partly because many defendants do not have the means to pay fines which the courts consider adequate for the seriousness of the offence. Ancillary orders can cover such matters as disqualification from driving, confiscation or forfeiture of property or assets and a criminal behaviour order. Maximum sentences for 'either way' and 'indictable only' offences are always expressed in terms of sentences of imprisonment. Many of those convicted receive a community rather than a custodial sentence, but community sentences can only be imposed if they are justified by the seriousness of the offence. The Sentencing Council issues guidance on the types and length of sentence to be imposed in particular types of cases – see the following text.

Mention has already been made of the changes in legislation and the new types of offence which they have created. A feature of some of those sentences, especially IPP sentences, is that a person can lose his or her liberty not only for what he or she has done but also for what it is thought they might do in the future. That situation places an expectation of certainty on the assessment of risk and beliefs about 'what works' which the present techniques may not be able to bear (Crighton & Towl, 2008). It also raises questions about the legitimacy of the punishment involved, especially where the judgement is made administratively by the executive and not judicially by a court (Zedner, 2004). Those questions may in due course be tested under the Human Rights Act 1998.

In 2013, of all those persons sentenced, 27% were sentenced to immediate custody, with an average term of 15.5 months. Both figures have been rising during the last 20 years.[5]

The present statutory framework for sentencing is set out in the Criminal Justice Act 2003. For a description of the Act, see Gibson (2004); for a discussion of sentencing more generally, see Ashworth and Redmayne (2010), and Ashworth and Roberts (2012). Statistics on sentencing are included in the *Criminal Statistics*.[2]

THE CRIMINAL COURTS

The courts are at the centre of the justice system, but judges and magistrates are in some ways regarded as separate from it. The constitutional doctrine of the separation of powers requires that the Legislature (Parliament), the Executive (government and statutory services) and the Judiciary should be independent of one another. Neither Parliament nor Ministers can tell the courts what a particular law means or how it should be interpreted or applied in an individual case. Nor should they say what sentence should be imposed on an individual offender.

The criminal courts at present comprise magistrates' courts; youth courts; the Crown Court; and the High Court, Court of Appeal and Supreme Court. The last three are known collectively as the higher courts, but became the new Supreme Court in October 2009 as a result of the Constitutional Reform Act 2005. Courts are serviced by HM Courts and Tribunals Service, an agency of the Ministry of Justice.

Magistrates' courts

The number of *magistrates' courts* has been drastically, and controversially, reduced over the years, and they still vary a great deal in size and the types of case which come before them. There are some 29,000 magistrates, or justices of the peace, who sit part time and are unpaid except for expenses. There are also about 200 district judges who are full-time, salaried professional lawyers.

Magistrates usually sit in threes but a district judge can sit alone. Magistrates' courts are administered by a chief executive and advised by professionally qualified justices' clerks and other legally qualified 'court clerks'. Since 2005, they have formed part of HM Court Service, an executive agency of the Ministry of Justice. The maximum term of imprisonment in the magistrates' court for an individual offence is 6 months; or 12 months in aggregate where consecutive sentences are passed for two or more offences. There is power to double those terms to 12 and 24 months, but it has not so far been brought into effect.

Youth courts

Youth courts were established in 1991 when they took over the work of the former juvenile court. They consist of specially trained magistrates who are members of a statutory youth court panel.

The investigation, processing and outcome of cases involving juveniles follow a similar pattern to that in relation to adults, but with additional safeguards, procedures, and sentencing powers. There are different powers, procedures and considerations in relation to children aged from 10 (the age of criminal responsibility[6]), to 13 years, and for young persons aged from 14 to 17. Investigating police officers have a duty to ensure that someone concerned with the welfare of the juvenile is informed about the person's arrest, and to obtain the involvement of an 'appropriate adult', usually a parent but sometimes a social worker. All first-time offenders are where possible dealt with by the police under a scheme of reprimands and warnings, or where they appear in court by way of a referral order to a youth offending panel composed of two volunteers from the local community and a member of the youth offending team. They meet the young person and their parents or guardians and agree a programme of action for putting things right. The victim is encouraged to be present (for restorative justice more generally, see the following text). Very serious, or 'grave', cases can, and for most serious offences must, be committed to the Crown Court.

The Crown Court

The Crown Court is organized on the basis of six circuits and sits in some 90 locations known as Crown Court Centres, of which the Old Bailey in London is the best known. There about 100 full-time Crown Court judges, and a number of part-time recorders who are also practising lawyers. Cases are heard by a single judge and in a contested trial before a jury. The Crown Court has been administered by HM Court Service since it was formed from the old Assizes and Quarter Sessions in 1972. Crown Court judges are addressed as 'His (or Her) Honour Judge …' or as 'Your Honour' in court.

The High Court

The High Court sits in three divisions – the Queen's Bench Division (QBD), Chancery Division and Family Division – and deals predominantly with the more important civil disputes. But it also has a general supervisory jurisdiction in relation to a wide range of courts, tribunals and public bodies and their officers, including the criminal courts, the police, government departments and their ministers, local authorities, and other public authorities, exercised through the process known as 'judicial review'. There are some 30 High Court judges, who may also sit in the Crown Court to hear especially serious or complicated cases and some of whom may act as the presiding judge for a court centre of circuit. Their judicial form of address is 'His Honour Mr Justice' or 'Her Honour Lady Justice', or 'My Lord' or 'My Lady' in court. High Court judges are automatically appointed to knighthoods and are addressed in the normal way as 'Sir' or 'Dame' (followed by their first name) for non-judicial purposes.

The Court of Appeal (Criminal Division)

The Court of Appeal (Criminal Division) hears appeals from people convicted and sentenced in the Crown Court. Its senior judge is the Lord Chief Justice (LCJ) and its members comprise 30 Lords Justices of Appeal. They may be assisted by High Court judges. As well as giving judgements in particular cases, the LCJ may issue Practice Directions to be followed by other criminal courts, and the Court of Appeal may give guidance on sentencing, although that function has now been largely superseded by the work of the Sentencing Guidelines Council (see the following text). Lords Justices of Appeal become members of the Privy Council on appointment and are addressed formally as 'The Rt. Hon. Lord/Lady Justice ...' and as 'My Lord' or 'My Lady' in court. Non-judicially they are addressed as 'Sir' or 'Dame'.

The Supreme Court

The House of Lords was, until 2009, the final court of appeal in the United Kingdom for both criminal and civil cases. Appeals were heard by an Appellate Committee of the House made up of Law Lords (sometimes called Lords of Appeal in Ordinary), of whom there were usually between 9 and 11. Law Lords were usually judges who became life peers when they were appointed. There was a convention that they did not participate in the general business of the House except where there was a direct legal or judicial context, for example, in debates on Criminal Justice Bills.

For many years, the High Court and Court of Appeal together were loosely called the 'Supreme Court'. A new Supreme Court, in the new sense (for this country) of being the highest court in the land, was created by the Constitutional Reform Act 2005, and began its work in October 2009. It took over the judicial function of the House of Lords and became the final court of appeal for England, Wales and Northern Ireland with regard to criminal cases, and for Scotland with regard to civil cases. Members of the new Supreme Court are known as Justices of the Supreme Court.

POLICE AND POLICING

The police service in England and Wales is organized on the basis of 43 police forces, with a total (in 2013) of about 130,000 police officers (having fallen from about 140,000 in 2008), of whom about 35,000 were women and 6,500 were from minority ethnic groups. There were, in addition, about 14,000 community support officers with more limited powers and duties. Total police strength, including civilian support staff and various technical experts, was about 214,000. Police forces vary a great deal in size, ranging from the Metropolitan Police Service with about 31,000 police officers to several county forces with under 1,500. The highly specialized City of London force has about 750 officers.

Under the Police Act 1964, each force is overseen by a tripartite structure comprising the chief constable who is in operational command, the police authority which has responsibility for administration and the budget, and the Home Secretary who is in charge of overall policy and sets national priorities and targets. Police authorities were originally committees of the local authority, with local councillors and magistrates as members; the Police and Magistrates' Courts Act 1994 made them freestanding bodies, reduced their size and introduced independent members. Under the Police Reform and Social Responsibility Act 2011, they were replaced by directly elected police and crime commissioners who first took office in November 2012.

The operational independence of the chief officer and the discretion of the constable have always been regarded as important principles of British policing, although they have not been seen as having the constitutional importance of the independence of the judiciary. Operational independence requires that the chief officer should not be subject to political direction on the way in which he or she enforces the law in a particular situation or at a particular event; the constable's discretion requires that he or she should be able to use his or her own judgement on when or whether, for example, to make an arrest. Managerial reforms such as the setting of objectives and targets and the publication of 'league tables' have been criticized as undermining that independence, and as distorting police practice by encouraging police to make unnecessary arrests (especially of young people) in order to improve their 'score'.

The numerous municipal police forces which existed before the Police Act 1964 were amalgamated to form the existing structure during the late 1960s and 1970s. But arguments have continued, both for a single national force and for further amalgamations to create a small number of regional forces, and a single national service was formed in Scotland in 2013. Those arguments have for the most part related to the greater efficiency and the economies thought to be achievable through larger units of command and administration, but also the need for specialized resources to deal with terrorism and international crime. They have not so far prevailed against the counterargument that the police need to be locally based and able to identify themselves with their local communities, and the government and the police are themselves developing 'neighbourhood policing' to provide stronger links with local communities.

The police are naturally seen as being concerned primarily with the prevention of crime and the apprehension of offenders. But they have a number of other administrative and regulatory functions, of which the control of road traffic is the most obvious, and 'catching criminals' may be quite a small part of an individual police officer's working life. That fact has led to regular demands for 'more bobbies on the beat' and there is always pressure for police officers to be relieved of bureaucratic responsibilities so that they can spend more time on the 'front line'. A visible police presence on the street undoubtedly helps public confidence, and community support officers perform a valuable role in that respect, but it has always been open to question how having more officers on patrol, in any numbers that could be sustained over time, will have a significant effect on the level of crime, or whether it would only be displaced to other areas or types of crime.

Important central agencies include the *National Crime Agency* and the *College of Policing*, which replaced the former Serious and Organised Crime Agency and National Policing Improvement Agency. The National Crime Agency became operational in 2013 and covers organized crime, border policing (with the UK Border Force), economic crime and child protection. The College of Policing is responsible for setting standards, promoting good practice, accrediting training, supporting partnership working and leading on police ethics and integrity. The *Independent Police Complaints Commission* was established under the Police Reform Act 2002 to provide greater independence, openness and transparency in the investigation of serious complaints against the police. It replaced the former Police Complaints Authority. The Commission has an especially sensitive role in cases where a person dies in police custody or, for example, while being chased by the police.

There is an increasing range of 'policing' functions that are not carried out by police forces as so far described but by other organizations of different kinds – the British Transport Police, local authorities, private security firms, and the Health and Safety Executive are some examples.

Police reform remains a live issue for government and the police themselves, with continuing debate on issues such as structure, accountability, powers and the use of new technology for investigation, surveillance and criminal records.

For a more detailed account of the police and policing, including a discussion of questions such as race, ethnicity and gender; accountability and governance; ethics; leadership; and the use of new technologies, see Newburn (2008) and Newburn and Reiner (2012).

THE CROWN PROSECUTION SERVICE

The CPS is responsible for most public prosecutions in England and Wales, usually taking over from the police at the stage when a suspect has been arrested and charged. The CPS was formed in 1985 as an independent national service – prosecutions had previously been the responsibility of the police or police solicitors – and was one outcome of the Royal Commission on Criminal Procedure set up after irregularities in police procedures had come to light during the 1970s.

The national head of the CPS is the Director of Public Prosecutions (DPP), an office which was first established with more limited functions in the nineteenth century. He or she is appointed by and responsible to the Attorney General. Crown prosecutors are usually solicitors, but may be barristers by training. Prosecutors do not have a role in sentencing as they do in some other countries, but may advise the judge on any relevant guidelines if asked to do so. The Service's role is continuing to develop.

PRISONS AND THE PRISON SERVICE

The prison system in England and Wales in 2014 comprised some 143 establishments, of which 13 were run by private sector companies and the remainder by the national Prison Service (some were due to close). The Prison Service's statement of purpose says:

> Her Majesty's Prison Service serves the public by keeping in custody those committed by the courts. Our duty is to look after them with humanity and help them lead law abiding and useful lives in custody and after release.

The total population of prison establishments in May 2014 was about 84,000, of whom about 80,000 were male and 4,000 were female. The most recent further breakdown of the figures at the time of writing was for March 2013, when, of the same totals, about 11,000 were on remand awaiting trial or sentence; about 1,000 were non-criminal prisoners; and the remainder were serving sentences of various lengths. Of the 80,000 males, about 72,000 were aged 21 or over, 7,000 were aged 18–20 and 1,000 were aged 15–17. Of the 4,000 females, about 3,700 were aged over 21 and 300 under 21, including 23 aged under 18.

Of the British population in prisons, about 10% were black, compared with 2% in the population as a whole, and about 6% were Asian. (On questions of racial discrimination, see the following text.) About 10,000 were foreign nationals.

In 2013, the national Prison Service employed about 43,000 staff, and the total prisons expenditure was about 4.0bn; the average annual cost per prisoner was about £37,000.

Britain has one of the highest rates of imprisonment in Europe – 150 per 100,000 in the population, compared with 93 in Germany and 85 in France. About 65% of prisoners, and 75% of young prisoners, are reconvicted within 2 years of release. The Prison Service has targets for bringing those figures down and claims to have some success, but reoffending is also affected by social and other factors over which the service has no control. (See the following text for the government's plans to commission rehabilitation services from the private and third sectors.)

For fuller accounts of the issues affecting prisons and imprisonment, see Liebling (2005) and Liebling and Crewe (2012). Facts about prisons and imprisonment are conveniently brought together in *Bromley Briefing Factfile*, issued by the Prison Reform Trust and regularly updated. It is available on the Trust's website, www.prisonreformtrust.org.uk (accessed 13 May 2014).

PROBATION

The probation service in England and Wales was formed in 1907 to 'advise, assist and befriend' offenders whom the courts placed under its supervision. Probation orders were made as an alternative to a sentence and were not intended as a punishment. Other duties came to be added over the years, especially the after-care and supervision of prisoners who had been released from custody and the provision and supervision of community service.

In the more punitive climate of the 1990s, probation became a normal sentence of the court and the requirements of probation and community orders began to acquire a 'tougher' and more punitive content. The requirement to 'advise, assist and befriend' was replaced by an emphasis on 'enforcement, rehabilitation and public protection'. The various forms of community order were combined into a single generic 'community sentence' in 2003.

Probation in England and Wales has been reorganized many times. Until 2001, there were 42 separate area services, each with a probation committee composed mainly of local magistrates as the employing authority. In that year, the separate services were combined into a single National Probation Service, with much stronger central direction from the Home Office. Probation committees became probation boards with a different, more business-orientated composition and more limited functions. In 2004, the Service became part of the National Offender Management Service. Further reforms in the Offender Management Act 2007 provided for probation boards to be replaced by 35 probation trusts, with more changes in structure and functions. Then, in 2013, the government announced that the majority of probation work would be commissioned from the private or third sector, with payment 'by results' depending on the contractor's success in reducing reoffending. About 30% of the work, mostly involving reports to court and the supervision of those offenders assessed as presenting the most serious risk, would remain to be undertaken by a single, much smaller, national service. Those changes were in progress at the time of writing.

In 2013, some 225,000 offenders were under the Service's supervision at any one time, 90% of them men and 10% women. Just over a quarter were aged under 21. Just over half were serving community or suspended sentences, and the remainder were on licence after serving the custodial part of a prison sentence. Each year, the Service provides the courts with some 200,000 pre-sentence reports.

The Service also works with victims of crime, for example, in connection with the arrangements for an offender's release from prison and subsequent supervision.

Before the current reorganization, the Service had about 16,000 staff made up of fully qualified probation officers, probation service officers with more limited duties, and support staff of various kinds.

YOUTH JUSTICE

It has been recognized since the nineteenth century that young people should be treated differently from adults in the criminal justice system, with the youngest children being dealt with outside the system altogether and separate arrangements for those who are older. In principle, the person's welfare should be the main concern. Policy and practice have to some extent retreated from that principle since 1997, reflecting a punitive element in public attitudes to children which does not seem to be present in other European countries.

The arrangements for young offenders were substantially reformed in 1998. Responding to a public perception that young people were 'getting away with it' and out of control, the Crime and Disorder Act 1998 established the national Youth Justice Board for England and Wales (YJB) and a network of local youth offending teams (YOTs). The YJB is an executive non-departmental public body. Its 12 board members are appointed by the Secretary of State for Justice; it oversees the youth justice system and works to prevent offending and reoffending by children and young people under the age of 18, 'ensuring that custody for them is safe, secure, and addresses their offending behaviour'. Its functions include advising ministers on the operation of the youth justice system, monitoring its performance, commissioning accommodation for children and young people remanded or sentenced to custody, identifying and promoting effective practice, and publishing information.

Youth offending teams (YOTs) coordinate youth justice services in their area – for example, rehabilitation schemes, activities carried out under community sentences, measures to prevent and reduce crime, and reparation schemes for victims. The team identifies the problems that lead young people to offend, assesses the risk they present to others, and devises suitable programmes which might help to prevent them from reoffending. Each should include people from a wide range of professional backgrounds and different areas of expertise.

HOME OFFICE

Within central government, the main departments concerned with the administration of justice are the Home Office, the Ministry of Justice and the Offices of the Attorney General and Solicitor General (his deputy). Of those, the Home Office is the oldest and has traditionally been the largest and most powerful. The Office of Secretary of State is of medieval origin; it was divided in 1782 between the Home Department and Foreign Affairs and from then on the Home Department or Home Office became the department for all subjects which were not specifically allocated elsewhere. Subjects such as education, health, employment, local government and children were in due course moved to separate departments and by the late twentieth century the Home Office had

become more exclusively identified with maintaining the rule of law and the Queen's Peace, or in modern language crime, criminal justice, the treatment of offenders and immigration. The need to keep the proper balance between public protection and the liberty of the individual became deeply rooted in the department's traditions and culture, although opinions would differ – as they still do – on where the balance should be placed.

Suggestions for dividing the Home Office into a ministry for internal safety and a ministry of justice were made at various times from the 1860s onwards. The arguments were sometimes about efficiency and the volume of the Home Secretary's workload, but a more important issue was whether the balance could be better maintained within a single department or by dividing the relevant functions between two departments, as they are in many other countries. The argument for a single department prevailed for many years, and when responsibility for criminal justice, prisons and probation was transferred to the newly formed Ministry of Justice in 2007, the main reasons given for the change were improved efficiency and effectiveness in the context of the increased threat from terrorism and the internal difficulties which were affecting the Home Office at that time.

The main responsibilities of the Home Office are now security, counter-terrorism, crime reduction and community safety, for which it works through the UK Border Force, UK Visas and Immigration, HM Passport Office, the Criminal Records Bureau and the police services in England and Wales.

MINISTRY OF JUSTICE

The *Ministry of Justice* has its origins in the former Lord Chancellor's Department, which became the Department for Constitutional Affairs for a brief period between 2003 and 2007. The office of Lord Chancellor is also of ancient origin but its supporting department was not formed until the nineteenth century.

For many years, the department's principal concerns were civil law and matters relating to the judiciary; it had few administrative responsibilities. The situation began to change when the structure of the courts was reformed and a national Court Service was formed in 1972. The department grew in size and importance from then onwards and other functions were progressively added – the administration of the magistrates' courts in the 1990s; constitutional affairs in 2003; criminal justice, prisons and probation when it became the Ministry of Justice in 2007.[7] The department's main responsibilities are now constitutional matters; the justice system, including civil justice; criminal law; sentencing policy; and the National Offender Management Service, comprising prisons and probation and now with a single director-general for both prison and probation services.

LAW OFFICERS

The Attorney General and the Solicitor General are together known as the Law Officers of the Crown. The Attorney General is the government's principal legal adviser and certain prosecutions require his or her consent. He or she may also appear as prosecuting counsel in high profile cases or cases where the national interest is involved. The Attorney General is accountable to Parliament for the Crown Prosecution Service, appoints the Director of Public Prosecutions, and is also responsible for certain specialized legal functions within the government. The role is complex and has sometimes been controversial, for example, over the nature of the advice given to the government concerning the legality of the war in Iraq and over investigations and possible prosecutions where political interests may be involved.

OTHER NATIONAL BODIES

The *Parole Board* for England and Wales is an independent body which makes risk assessments to inform decisions on the release and recall of prisoners. It operates in accordance with statutory directions which are issued by the Secretary of State for Justice and cover subjects such as the criteria to be used and the procedures to be followed. The board comprises a chair and some 80 members, of whom a small proportion are full-time. Members include judges, psychologists, psychiatrists, chief probation officers, criminologists and independent members. The work is sensitive, onerous and controversial, and the Board's quasi-judicial functions require an independence from government which is not easy to sustain.

The *Sentencing Guidelines Council* (SGC) was established under the Coroners and Justice Act 2009. It consists of eight judicial members and six non-judicial members. Its purpose is to give authoritative guidance on sentencing to the Crown Court and magistrates' courts; to provide a strong lead on sentencing issues, based on a principled approach which commands general support; and to enable sentencers to make decisions that are supported by information on the effectiveness of sentences and on the most effective use of resources. It also has a remit to raise public awareness and understanding of sentencing issues and seek to match capacity and demand.

Inspectorates have come to play an increasingly prominent role in the oversight of criminal justice services. *HM Inspectorate of Constabulary* has its origins in the nineteenth century; *HM Inspectorate of Probation* dates from before the Second World War. *HM Inspectorate of Prisons* and *HM Inspectorate of the Crown Prosecution Service* are of more recent origin. They now function mainly as part of the system's mechanisms of accountability to central government, with a focus on efficiency, standards and performance. The exception is the prisons inspectorate which is primarily concerned with the treatment and experiences of prisoners, questions of decency and human rights, and the 'health' – in the broadest sense – of the institution as a whole.

The *Prisons and Probation Ombudsman* investigates complaints from those who are or have been in prison or under the supervision of the Probation Service. He or she is not able to issue directions but can make recommendations to the Prison or Probation Service or to the Ministry of Justice.

Each prison establishment has an *Independent Monitoring Board*, composed of unpaid volunteers, which oversees the activities of the prison and the treatment of prisoners. Boards have a long history, going back to visiting committees of magistrates appointed under the Prison Act 1877. They were at one time the main disciplinary authority for the prison. Members have open access to all parts of the prison and may discuss matters with prisoners out of the hearing of prison governors or prison officers. Each board reports annually to the Secretary of State for Justice.

SOME SPECIAL SUBJECTS

Victims of crime

For many years, victims of crime were largely ignored in the criminal justice process unless they were needed as witnesses, and even then they had no special treatment or status. A limited (although by international standards quite generous) scheme of compensation for criminal injuries was introduced in 1964, but otherwise victims' interests were not taken seriously until the rise of the victims' support movement in the 1980s and the publication of the first Victim's Charter in 1990. All criminal justice agencies are now expected to be sensitive and responsive to victims' experience and concerns; help from the national organization Victim Support (www. victimsupport.org.uk, accessed 15 May 2014) is available to any victim who wants it; and the Witness Service provides information, reassurance and practical help for those who have to appear in court.

Issues involving the rights and expectations of victims are not straightforward. Victims deserve proper help, consideration and respect, and there are still instances where the system has let the victim down. It seems natural to argue that anything that could be done for victims ought to be done. But it is not a 'zero sum' where anything that is 'bad' for offenders is 'good' for victims or vice-versa. Victims are able to make statements (known as 'victim impact statements') which can be used in court, but there may be a fine line between a factual statement of the victim's injury or loss, a description of their feelings about what they have experienced, and an emotional account which may unfairly influence the court towards a severe (or occasionally lenient) sentence. There are also special difficulties about cases where intimidation of a victim or witness may be involved, and about the investigation and prosecution of offences of rape, domestic violence and 'honour violence' against a person who has not conformed to the cultural expectations of (usually) her family.

Restorative justice

Restorative justice is a distinctive approach to crime, and to the resolution of conflicts more generally, which concentrates on putting right the harm that has been caused. In criminal justice it may take the form of a conference between the offender and the victim, together with other people who are close to them; it may be instead of or in addition the normal criminal process. The outcome may be an apology and an understanding about future behaviour, sometimes including some form of service or act of reparation. The approach can also be used as part of the management of institutions such as prisons (Edgar & Newell, 2006) or schools, in preventing antisocial behaviour, or in dealing with complaints against public authorities. It has inspired the work of two charities in particular – Circles of Support and Accountability, which works with sex offenders, and Escaping Victimhood, which helps the families of victims of homicide.

After many years in which government and many practitioners and observers were sceptical, restorative procedures are now becoming established at several stages in the criminal process, but much will depend on the detail of the arrangement for commissioning services in the future. See Hoyle (2012), and Chapter 26 in this volume.

Race and racism

Courts and the criminal justice services became increasingly and sometimes painfully aware of the problems of race and racism from the late 1970s onwards. Prison

psychologists were among the first to recognize racist attitudes and behaviour in prisons; the police faced criticism for what was seen as their discriminatory use of their powers of 'stop and search'; and the disproportionate number of black people in prison prompted concern about racial discrimination at the various stages of the criminal justice process and especially in sentencing. Racist behaviour was also found among the staff of the criminal justice services, and the small number of members of minority groups, especially in senior positions, also caused concern.

The Criminal Justice Act 1991 introduced a requirement for the Secretary of State to publish:

> such information as he considers expedient for the purposes of … facilitating the performance by [persons engaged in the administration of criminal justice] of their duty to avoid discriminating against any person on the ground of race, sex or any other improper ground

and reports have been published regularly since that time. The Race Relations (Amendment) Act 2000 went further and placed a duty on all public authorities to be proactive in promoting race equality.

Policies for preventing and dealing with discrimination were in place across the system by the early 1990s, but they were not implemented as consistently or as effectively as might have been hoped. A turning point came with the failure of the investigation into the murder of Stephen Lawrence in 1994 and the subsequent report by Sir William Macpherson and its finding that the Metropolitan Police were 'institutionally racist' (Macpherson, 1999). Instances of racist behaviour were also investigated in prisons, of which one of the most serious was the failure of the Prison Service to prevent the racist murder of Zahid Mubarak in Feltham Young Offenders Institution in 2000. The then Director General of Prisons, Martin Narey, acknowledged that the Prison Service was also institutionally racist, and announced that overt racist behaviour or membership of a racist organization would not be tolerated and would lead to dismissal. A prison officer was later dismissed for wearing the Nazi insignia.

Following those events, efforts to prevent discrimination were redoubled across the criminal justice system, including measures to increase the number and proportion of members of minority groups in all the services. Even so, measures to combat discrimination are still sometimes sneered at as 'political correctness'; racist attitudes are still widespread in the media (Sveinsson, 2008); and racist incidents still occur in the system.

For a general account of race issues in criminal justice, see Phillips and Bowling (2012).

CONCLUSIONS

Crime and criminal justice became the subject of increasing political attention from the late 1970s onwards (Downes & Morgan, 2012). One reason was the increase in crime, so that more people had been victims of crime or knew people who had been victims. Another was a change towards more sensational reporting in the media. A third was the increasingly adversarial style of politics and the sense that governments had to be constantly active, with a solution to every problem.

Until the early 1990s, governments had more or less accepted the conclusion of a Home Office review (Home Office, 1977) that criminal justice measures could have only a marginal effect on the general level of crime. There was then a change of mood,[8] after which successive governments determined to bring forward criminal justice measures that they could claim would have a direct effect in restoring public confidence and reducing crime. The pace accelerated after the change of government in 1997. Ministers not only considered public services to be in desperate need of modernization, but some of them also regarded criminal justice as an outdated system which had grown up haphazardly in a previous age (as the prime minister, Tony Blair, argued in a speech in 2004). It was not capable of dealing with the problems of crime, disorder and antisocial behaviour in a modern, globalized world. Less attention should be paid to traditional principles such as those indicated earlier in this chapter.

A difficulty for criminal justice ministers and administrators is that much of the evidence is counterintuitive. Sentencing does not have much deterrent effect, and sending more people to prison does very little to reduce crime (Halliday, 2001).[9] Having more police officers on the streets reassures the public, but may not have much effect on crime itself. People do not behave better when they are publicly humiliated. A large proportion of the male population has criminal convictions or admits to having committed criminal offences, many victims are or have been offenders, and vice-versa, and it is misleading to talk of 'innocent victims' and the 'law-abiding majority' as if they were separate sections of society. Crime has been falling, but the figures are widely disbelieved. Despite all the reforms of the previous 15 years, there is still in 2014 a sense that the problem of crime is no better than it was and governments still have to do more.

Characteristics of the present approach to crime and criminal justice include economic rather than social ways of thinking; a belief in a 'science' of crime management and evidence-based policy; an instrumental view of justice which sees its purpose as essentially one of public protection, and greater intervention (even 'micromanagement') by government. An alternative or complementary approach would pay more attention to relationships and motivation, drawing on studies of desistance which focus on the factors that influence offenders to stop offending (see McNeill & Weaver 2007, and Chapter 9 in this volume). It could be linked to more locally based and less politicized programmes building on existing initiatives such as neighbourhood policing and community justice.

There have been several accounts, from different perspectives, of the transformation which has taken place over the past 25 years (Garland, 2001; Faulkner, second edition, 2006; Lacey, 2007; Faulkner & Burnett, 2011).

NOTES

1 Some of the most obvious differences in Scotland are the role of the procurator fiscal in prosecutions, the system of sheriff courts, and the arrangements for children's hearings in youth justice.

2 The government regularly publishes statistics on recorded and surveyed crime – http://www.ons.gov.uk/ons/rel/crime-stats/crime-statistics/index.html – and periodical bulletins on particular types of crime. Statistics on more general aspects of crime and criminal justice are available at https://www.gov.uk/government/collections/crime-statistics (accessed 15 January 2015).

3 Various attempts have been made to restrict access to trial before a jury, either to prevent interference with the jury or for cases which were considered too complicated or likely to be too long drawn out (e.g., some types of fraud), and the Criminal Justice Act 2003 made provision for restrictions in those cases. Attempts to prevent 'frivolous' demands for jury trial, for example, by well-to-do defendants charged with minor offences for which a conviction might damage their reputations or careers, have not so far been pursued. No provision has been made in England and Wales for the equivalent of 'Diplock' courts (where judges sat without a jury) which tried terrorist cases in Northern Ireland.

4 'Either way' and 'indictable only' offences are often grouped together and called simply 'indictable offences'. They are almost but not quite the same as 'notifiable offences' which form the basis of statistics of recorded crime: the classification of 'indictable' and summary or non-indictable offences has changed from time to time but the same definition has been kept for statistical purposes so that figures can remain comparable.

5 See *Criminal Justice Statistics, 2013, England and Wales*. Ministry of Justice Statistics Bulletin, May 2014.

6 One of the lowest in Europe and often criticized by children's charities and others. The Crime and Disorder Act 1998 removed the presumption of *doli incapax* under which it had been necessary to prove that a child under 14 knew that what he or she was doing was wrong.

7 The full title of the ministerial head of the Ministry is 'Secretary of State for Justice and Lord Chancellor', the title of Lord Chancellor still being needed for certain special functions which cannot be transferred without legislation or other special authority. The title in normal use is 'Secretary of State for Justice' or 'Justice Secretary', and 'Justice Minister' for less senior ministers appointed to the Ministry or department.

8 The change coincided with the murder of 2-year-old James Bulger by two older children in Liverpool in 1993 – a shocking crime of the kind which arouses an exceptional degree of public feeling and which seems to take place about once in 5 years.

9 It is thought that a 15% increase in the prison population would reduce crime by 1%.

FURTHER READING

Suggestions for further reading on particular aspects of criminal justice have been included at various points in the text.

Bryan Gibson's *Criminal Justice: A Beginner's Guide* (Waterside Press, 2014) is a useful source for more detailed information on most of the aspects covered in this chapter. It gives an authoritative and easy-to-read account of the main features of the system and their latest developments, and includes a useful glossary. Companion volumes on the Home Office and the Ministry of Justice deal similarly with those two departments.

The *Oxford Handbook of Criminology*, edited by Mike Maguire, Rod Morgan and Robert Reiner, fifth edition 2012, is the most comprehensive source of information and discussion on criminology and criminal justice, and its 33 chapters, of over 1,000 pages, its index and the references included in its text provide a good starting point for serious further study of almost any of the subject's various aspects. Many of the references noted earlier are to chapters in the *Handbook*. It also contains material on specialized subjects such as mental health, drugs and alcohol, white-collar crime or organized crime and terrorism which have not been dealt with here – see the chapters by Jill Peay 2012, Fiona Measham and Nigel South 2012, David Nelken, and Martin Innes and Michael Levi 2012, respectively. The *Handbook* also includes a chapter by Clive Hollin 2007, on criminological psychology. References are given the following text.

Criminal Justice by Lucia Zedner (2004) provides a more reflective commentary on criminal justice, its concepts, structures and processes, the central themes and debates, and the historical and cultural contexts in which those debates are now taking place.

REFERENCES

Ashworth, A., & Redmayne, M. (2010). *The criminal process* (4th edn). Oxford: Oxford University Press.

Ashworth, A., & Roberts, J. (2012) Sentencing: Theory, principles and practice. In M. Maguire, R. Morgan, & R. Reiner (Eds.), *Oxford handbook of criminology*, chap. 29. Oxford: Oxford University Press.

Crighton, D., & Towl, G. (2008). *Psychology in prisons* (2nd edn). Oxford: BPS Blackwell.

Downes, D., & Morgan, R. (2012) Overtaking on the left? The politics of law and order in the 'Big Society'. No turning back: The politics of law and order into the millennium. In M. Maguire, R. Morgan, & R. Reiner (Eds.), *Oxford handbook of criminology* (pp. 201–240). Oxford: Oxford University Press.

Edgar, K., & Newell, T. (2006). *Restorative justice in prisons: A guide to making it happen.* Winchester: Waterside Press.

Faulkner, D. (2006). *Crime, state and citizen: A field full of folk* (2nd edn). Winchester: Waterside Press.

Faulkner, D., & Burnett, R. (2011). *Where next for criminal justice?* Bristol: The Policy Press.

Garland, D. (2001). *The culture of control: Crime and social order in contemporary society.* Oxford: Oxford University Press.

Gibson, B. (2004). *The Criminal Justice Act, 2003: A guide to the new procedures and sentencing.* Winchester: Waterside Press.

Gibson, B. (2014). *Criminal justice: A beginner's guide.* Sherfield-on-Loddon: Waterside Press.

Halliday, J. (2001). *Making punishments work: Report of a review of the sentencing framework for England and Wales* (pp. 130–132). London: Home Office.

Hollin, C. (2007). Criminological psychology. In M. Maguire, R. Morgan, & R. Reiner (Eds.), *Oxford handbook of criminology* (pp. 43–77). Oxford: Oxford University Press.

Home Office (1977). *A review of criminal justice policy 1976.* London: HMSO.

Hoyle, C. (2012). Victims, the criminal process and restorative justice. In M. Maguire, R. Morgan, & R. Reiner (Eds.), *Oxford handbook of criminology*, chap. 14. Oxford: Oxford University Press.

Innes, M., & Levi, M. (2012). Terrorism and counter terrorism. In M. Maguire, R. Morgan, & R. Reiner (Eds.), *Oxford handbook of criminology*, chap. 22. Oxford: Oxford University Press.

Lacey, N. (2007). *Criminal Justice*. Oxford: Wiley-Blackwell.

Lacey, N., & Zedner, L. (2012). Legal constructions of crime. In M. Maguire, R. Morgan, & R. Reiner (Eds.), *Oxford handbook of criminology*, chap. 6. Oxford: Oxford University Press.

Liebling, A. (2005). *Prisons and their moral performance: A study of values, quality and prison life*. Oxford: Clarendon Press.

Liebling, A., & Crewe, B. (2012). Prison Life, penal power, and prison effects. In M. Maguire, R. Morgan, & R. Reiner (Eds.), *Oxford handbook of criminology*, chap. 30. Oxford: Oxford University Press.

Macpherson, W. (1999). *The Stephen Lawrence inquiry*. CM4262. London: Stationery Office.

Maguire, M. (2012). Criminal statistics and the construction of crime. In M. Maguire, R. Morgan, & R. Reiner (Eds.), *Oxford handbook of criminology*, chap. 8. Oxford: Oxford University Press.

McConville, M., & Wilson, G. (Eds.) (2002). *Handbook of the criminal justice process*. Oxford: Oxford University Press.

McNeill, F., & Weaver, B. (2007). *Giving up crime: Directions for policy*. Glasgow: Scottish Centre for Crime and Justice Research.

Measham, F., & South, N. (2012). Drugs, alcohol and crime. In M. Maguire, R. Morgan, & R. Reiner (Eds.), *Oxford handbook of criminology*, chap. 23. Oxford: Oxford University Press.

Nelken, D. (2012). White-collar and corporate crime. In M. Maguire, R. Morgan, & R. Reiner (Eds.), *Oxford handbook of criminology*, chap. 21. Oxford: Oxford University Press.

Newburn, T. (Ed.) (2008). *Handbook of policing* (2nd edn). Cullompton, Devon: Willan.

Newburn, T., & Reiner, R. (2012). Policing and the police. In M. Maguire, R. Morgan & R. Reiner (Eds.), *Oxford handbook of criminology*, chap. 27. Oxford: Oxford University Press.

Phillips, C., & Bowling, B. (2012). Ethnicities, racism, crime and criminal justice. In M. Maguire, R. Morgan, & R. Reiner (Eds.), *Oxford handbook of criminology*, chap. 13. Oxford: Oxford University Press.

Sveinsson, K. (2008). *A tale of two Englands – 'race' and violent crime in the press*. London: Runnymede Trust.

Zedner, L. (2004). *Criminal justice* (pp. 39–47). Oxford: Clarendon Press.

3 Offender Profiling

DAVID A. CRIGHTON

Offender profiling involves the use of behavioural data to inform the process of investigating crimes by seeking to predict the likely characteristics of perpetrators of crimes. Doing this has involved efforts to work from available data from crime scenes and other information such as witness accounts. The aim of this is to arrive at useful profiles which aid investigating agencies. Historically, such profiling developed from two main approaches. The first could be characterised as a pragmatic clinical approach and the other as a statistical predictive approach. The practice of offender profiling expanded rapidly from the 1980s onwards to become a regular part of investigations and also popular culture. The early development of offender profiling drew on a limited and weak evidence base and poorly developed practice.

More recently, there has been a growth in the evidence base for practice and clear trends to eliminate ineffective methods. This has brought offender profiling increasingly in line with mainstream forensic psychology practice in terms of its regulation, methodology and research. It is now seen as a developing and largely experimental area of practice, where there is a pressing need to move towards scientifically validated methods.

INTRODUCTION

Offender profiling has been described as the process of observation, reflection and construction using available data to predict the likely characteristics of an offender (Kocsis, 2007). This activity has attracted a number of labels, including Criminal Investigative Analysis (CIA) (Ressler, Burgess, Douglas, Hartman, & D'Agostino, 1986; Tenten, 1989), Investigative Psychology (IP) (Canter, 1989), Profile Analysis (PA) (Jackson & Bekerian, 1997) and Crime Action Profiling (CAP) (Kocsis, 2003;

2007). While each of these labels may reflect differences in emphasis, they are all substantively similar, since they involve common logic and use similar techniques. Offender profiling makes two central assumptions. The first of these is behavioural consistency, meaning that the behaviour exhibited at a crime scene or series of crime scenes is likely to be consistent. The second assumption is one of homology. This is a term derived from developmental biology, and it refers to the notion that similar crime scene behaviour will be associated with similar offender characteristics. Using these assumptions, inferences from the available information are used to produce psychological profiles to assist investigators (Gudjonsson & Copson, 1997).

HISTORICAL DEVELOPMENT

The notion that crime scenes can provide valid and useful information about offenders has a significant history and many of the elements of offender profiling have been reflected in fictional detectives such as Sherlock Holmes (Conan Doyle, 1897/2001) and Hercule Poirot (Christie, 1934) and more recently in books such as *Red Dragon* (Harris, 1981). As early as the 1880s Thomas Bond, a physician, tried to develop a profile of the personality characteristics of the perpetrator of a series of sexual homicides in the East End of London. The perpetrator was never identified in these cases but went on to become notorious as 'Jack the Ripper'. The profiler in this case was a police surgeon and he assisted in the autopsy on one of the victims. He noted the sexual aspects of the murders and made inferences about the apparent rage and hatred of women shown by the offender, as demonstrated by severe pre- and post-mortem injuries. Based on the limited information then available he went on to reconstruct the murder, providing an

Forensic Psychology, Second Edition. Edited by David A. Crighton and Graham J. Towl.
© 2015 John Wiley & Sons, Ltd. Published 2015 by British Psychological Society and John Wiley & Sons, Ltd.

assessment of the behaviour and personality characteristics of the offender. From his analysis of the available evidence he suggested that five out of seven murders committed in that part of London had been perpetrated by a single man acting alone. It was also suggested that the offender was physically strong, composed, and willing to take significant risks, and that the perpetrator was likely to be a relatively quiet and unassuming individual, socially isolated and without regular employment: someone who would generally draw little public attention. Dr Bond went on to suggest a possible diagnosis of satyriasis – what would now probably be termed 'promiscuity'. Contrary to much of the lurid and inaccurate press reporting at the time, and subsequently, he also believed based on post-mortem analysis that the offender had no specialist knowledge as either a surgeon or butcher (Petherick, 2005).

Another key milestone in the history of profiling of criminal offenders followed a series of explosions in New York between 1940 and 1956.[1] A serial offender carried out a campaign of terror by planting explosives in public settings such as cinemas, telephone boxes and railway stations. In 1956, the police commissioned James Brussel, then New York State's assistant commissioner of mental hygiene, to complete a profile. In this profile it was suggested that the offender would be a heavily built middle-aged man. It was also suggested that he would be single, perhaps living with a sibling, have some basic mechanical skills, come from Connecticut, be a Roman Catholic immigrant and harbour an obsessional love for his mother and hatred for his father. Brussel also noted that the offender appeared to have a grudge against the city's power company, on the basis that the first bomb had targeted its headquarters. Curiously, the profile also went on to mention a high probability that the offender would be wearing a 'buttoned' double-breasted suit when arrested. Brussel went on to assist the New York police as an offender profiler until 1972 and published a popular account of his work (Brussel, 1968).

Following completion of this profile, the police began looking at unhappy former employees of the power company and this helped them to identify the offender, George Metesky, who lived in Connecticut. In line with the profile the offender was reported to be heavily built, single, Roman Catholic and foreign-born. It was also reported that when told to get dressed by the police, the offender returned wearing a fully buttoned double-breasted suit as Brussel had predicted. This and other high-profile cases are perhaps responsible for some of the mythical status that has attended offender profiling until recently. In fact, Brussel's work was probably less impressive than the earlier work of Bond in the 1890s. Subsequent reviews have suggested that the profile developed did not, in reality, show much understanding of the offender or his motives. Rather, it involved the generation of a large number of predictions, many of which turned out to be inaccurate or misleading. However, with a high number of predictions, some with high base rates, it was inevitably the case that some would turn out to be accurate. Subsequently these accurate predictions were recalled as positive evidence of accuracy, while inaccurate predictions were forgotten (Gladwell, 2007).

In 1972, the FBI formed a Behavioral Science Unit (BSU) with a remit for developing improved methods for identifying unknown offenders in unsolved cases. The early work of the unit was greatly shaped by the work of Howard Teten, a Californian police officer who had worked for the FBI since the 1960s. With colleagues at the BSU, he went on to develop a methodology called Criminal Investigative Analysis (CIA). The BSU built progressively on these early methods (Tenten, 1989). The unit went on to conduct a series of systematic studies, particularly in relation to serial homicides. These initially involved the intensive study of a group of sexual homicide offenders, using semi-structured interview methods to produce systematic descriptions of these offenders (Ressler et al., 1986). The work was described as involving four stages: data assimilation; crime classification; crime reconstruction; and profile generation. The final stage of profile generation tended to follow a consistent format covering a range of socio-demographic and psychosocial descriptors along with suggestions for interview techniques that might be applicable. Such descriptions were drawn from known offenders, based on the assumption that unknown offenders would show significant similarities. A number of offence types were felt to be particularly suited to such an approach. These included arson and sexual offences, in addition to sexual homicides.

An alternative approach, developed in parallel to the work of the BSU, was undertaken by Keppel and Walter (1999). The methods developed gained wide coverage when they were used to aid in the capture of notorious serial killers Ted Bundy and Gary Ridgway. Walter has worked as a psychologist within the Michigan prison system. Based on his clinical experience, he suggested that all killings and sex crimes could be categorized into four subtypes: power-assertive, power-reassurance, anger-retaliatory, and anger-excitation or sadism.

The development of profiling in Europe occurred somewhat later than in North America and began with attempts to apply a range of techniques to a number of high-profile cases (Britton, 1998; Canter, 1994). Practice in Europe tended to develop along two distinct lines, which have often been misleadingly summarized as 'clinical' and actuarial approaches. This probably relates to the fact that many early profiles were constructed by

NHS-based psychologists and followed a similar pattern to the work of Brussel, with a focus on attempts to identify known patterns of psychopathology. Such approaches were often what was requested by police services and were initially greeted with great enthusiasm. Such efforts, though, have increasingly attracted concern and dissatisfaction from the researchers and the courts (Copson, 1995; *R* v. *Stagg* [1994]). The alternative 'empirical' approach has involved the use of statistical methods such as multidimensional scaling as a means of identifying consistent patterns in offending (Alison, Bennett, Mokros, & Ormrod, D., 2002; Fujita *et al.*, 2013).

APPROACHES TO OFFENDER PROFILING

It has been suggested by some that there is a relatively high level of agreement that, theoretically at least, it ought to be possible to evaluate criminal behaviours on the basis of available data from crime scenes and witnesses and in turn go on to use these to derive some impression of the offender (Kocsis, 2007). A number of differing terms for offender profiling have emerged subsequently, including diagnostic evaluation (DE), criminal investigation analysis (CIA), crime action profiling (CAP), investigative psychology (IP) and a number of others.

Diagnostic evaluation

This approach differs substantively from the three other widely advocated approaches to profiling and is in many respects more akin to the approach to profiling pioneered by Brussel (1968). It essentially involves the use of what might broadly be termed clinical models and methods. These are used to deliver a series of predictions about offenders based on a practitioner's analysis of the crime scene and, often, a mental-health-related diagnosis. The prediction of characteristics is generated in an idiographic manner and appears to be based on prior experience, for example, from work with a series of mental health patients. In many respects, this method is similar to that seen in mental health practice where information from a number of sources may be used to allocate individuals into psychopathological categories which are claimed to have prognostic value, although in the context of offender profiling such methods are being applied in a markedly different context and for different purposes (Copson, Badcock, Boon, & Britton, 2006).

Criminal investigation analysis

The use of criminal investigation analysis (CIA) is the method largely developed by the FBI BSU in North America (Tenten, 1989). The method sought to take a markedly different approach from diagnostic evaluation methods by developing an evidence base on offenders. The method replaced the use of diagnostic terminology with terms commonly in use in forensic science and criminology. These included terms such as 'crime scene analysis' to describe the systematic analysis of the site of the crime, or crimes, and terms such as 'staging' and 'signature' to describe aspects of the scenes. The method was initially directed at crimes which had proved particularly difficult to solve using conventional methods of investigation and detection, such as serial stranger homicides. CIA involves the generation of empirically grounded profiles or typologies of likely offenders based on an analysis primarily of crime scene data. One of the earliest and probably the best known and most influential of these distinctions has been that between 'organized' and 'disorganized' homicide perpetrators. The method has subsequently been expanded to consider other types of offenders, including rapists and arsonists (Kocsis, 2007). The approach has also gone on to be codified into manual form as the *Crime Classification Manual* (Douglas, Burgess, Burgess, & Ressler, 2013), which provides templates of types of offender for use by investigative teams.

Crime action profiling

Crime action profiling (CAP) is largely similar to CIA but has been described as working within the boundaries of forensic psychology and psychiatry (Kocsis, 2007). As with CIA, the focus has tended to be on specific types of offence which have proved difficult to solve using conventional methods. The approach has developed to include the study of other factors surrounding the production of profiles, including such things as logistical factors surrounding profiling, such as data collection and accuracy. CAP has also drawn heavily on the use of a statistical technique called multidimensional scaling (MDS). It is suggested that CAP uses MDS in combination with other statistical tools as a means of developing conceptual models which are, in turn, used to generate predictors contained in profiles (Kocsis, 2003, 2007).

Investigative psychology

The term investigative psychology (IP) is most closely associated with researchers and practitioners at the University of Liverpool in the United Kingdom (Alison & Kebbell, 2006). The approach involves an empirical approach to profiling crimes. IP has been extended to a broad range of crimes beyond the historical focus of profiling, including burglary and domestic violence. It is characterized by the use of ideographic analysis of crime-related behaviours and offender characteristics using empirical methods. In particular, the approach has relied heavily on MDS, leading to the approach often being described, somewhat misleadingly, as an 'empirical' or sometimes a 'statistical' approach. MDS is generally used in this context to analyse both crime-related behaviours and offender characteristics. A concrete example here might be the use of MDS to study domestic violence offenders: separating this group into 'instrumental' and 'expressive' types and defining the characteristics that are more common to each type (Kocsis, 2007).

RECENT DEVELOPMENTS

Since the 1980s, the development of profiling has moved on from initial pioneering techniques towards the development of more evidence-based approaches. This has been generally associated with two major developments in this area of practice. Firstly, in both practice and research it has moved to become a part of mainstream forensic psychology. Secondly, in common with other areas of forensic psychology, there have been clear efforts to develop evidence-based practice. Scientific research and practice in this area has in recent years been primarily concerned with three central questions arising from crime scenes. Firstly, what happened at the crime scene? Secondly, what socio-demographic characteristics is the person who carried out the activities observed at the crime scene likely to have? Thirdly, what are the most likely psychological characteristics of the person concerned (Read & Oldfield, 1995)?

Current scientific practice has also been described as resting on two major assumptions: behavioural consistency and homology. Behavioural consistency refers to the notion that the variance shown by serial offenders will be less than that shown in comparison to a random series of other offenders. Homology in evolutionary biology refers to similarities that reflect shared ancestry. In profiling the term refers to the assumption that the degree of similarity in two offenders, from any given category of crime, will be reflected by similarity in their characteristics (Alison & Kebbell, 2006).

Efforts at evidence-based profiling as a means of identifying and giving investigative priority to offenders has tended, as outlined in the preceding text, to focus on serious violent and sexual crimes. The example used in the following text for illustrative purposes is work on sexual offences, where around half of reported sexual offences are perpetrated by strangers. The use of profiling in such offences has been attractive to police services, since this group of offences is particularly difficult to solve. Investigating officers in such offences are deprived of many of the normal lines of inquiry in what may appear to be random offences, so the appeal of any methods that reduce uncertainty is not difficult to see. The challenge, though, is significant. One of the most widely reported and generally accepted characteristics of sexual offenders is their heterogeneity as a group (Prentky & Burgess, 2000). This has led to numerous attempts to develop valid typologies of sexual offenders, as a means of managing this heterogeneity as an aid to investigation and also to assessment and intervention. Many attempts have been made at such typologies. For example, Cohen, Seghorn, and Calmas (1969) suggested dividing rapists into four subtypes: compensatory; impulsive; sex-aggression diffused; and displaced aggressive. They also suggested dividing child molesters into regressed, aggressive, fixated and exploitative subgroups.

The use of such categories went on to gain wide currency among practitioners and it is still common to see reference to such categories as regressed or fixated paedophiles. It is also easy to see how, if valid, such categories might have significant value within the processes of criminal investigation. While many of the categories have an intuitive appeal, there is little evidence of a firm empirical base. Nor is there much good evidence favouring one model of categorization over another. Such typologies have repeatedly been criticized for the failure to collect data on the reliability and validity of types (Prentky, Knight, & Rosenberg, 1988). It is therefore perhaps not surprising that subsequent research has generally failed to provide support for the utility of such typologies.

There have been subsequent efforts to develop empirically valid categorical systems, such as the Massachusetts Treatment Center (MTC) classification system, currently in its third revision (Prentky, Knight, Rosenberg, & Lee, 1989). While this system has potential clinical utility, it has proved less useful for investigative purposes, since it draws heavily on issues of motivation. In turn these can generally not be discerned from crime scenes (Alison, 2006; Alison et al., 2006).

Recent work in offender profiling has sought to apply scientific approaches to the detection of more mainstream crimes than has historically been the case, with a move away from efforts to identify individual perpetrators of rare high-profile offences such as serial homicide and rape. Increasing efforts have also been made to use profiling methods concerned with behavioural consistency to the risk of terrorist offences Here, statistical approaches such as latent class analysis have been applied to offences that occur with much higher frequency but where the rates of solution have been historically poor. In the United States, for example, only around 12.7% of burglary offences were solved (Federal Bureau of Investigation, 2011). The application of such methods serves primarily to focus the attention of law enforcement agencies on lines of enquiry and reduce the scale of the search necessary to identify potential suspects where there may be limited evidence (Chapman, Smith, & Bond, 2012). In a study of 405 solved burglary offences in Florida, it was reported that offenders could usefully be allocated to one of four types based on different offence characteristics: organized, disorganized, opportunistic and disorganized. In a later study into the utility of these profiles, it was found that agencies using these showed marked increase in arrest rates, and the odds of a burglary being solved tripled (Fox, Farrington, Chitwood, & Janes, in press).

PROFILING DATABASES

Linked to the development of statistical approaches has been the development and use of databases relating to offender characteristics. The increasing relevance of information technology has made such databases increasingly available, and several now exist as tools for police and investigative authorities to draw on. Equally, the increasing ability to capture and store information about individuals has raised legal and ethical concerns as well as concerns about accuracy and data security.

Child Abduction and Serial Murder Investigative Resources Center (CASMIRC)

CASMIRC is a US centre established in order to improve the quality of investigation into violent crimes, by coordinating the work of US federal, state and local authorities. It also acts as a central database for case data on child abductions, disappearances, homicides, and serial homicides. In this manner CASMIRC is described as a means to improve operational support from behavioural services provided by the FBI to investigative authorities.

Violent Criminal Apprehension Program (ViCAP)

ViCAP is a US system introduced by the US Department of Justice in 1985 and run by the FBI. It serves as a database for homicides, sexual assaults, missing persons, and unidentified human remains. The database includes a wide range of case information submitted by investigative authorities. This includes information about the victim, information about offenders and suspects, offence details such as the modus operandi, dates and locations of offences, crime scene details, offence details and what is termed 'holdback' information concerning specific details of offences to be kept confidential. This national database is used to compare incoming cases with the database of past cases to seek out similarities. In addition, incoming cases are reviewed by analysts in an effort to identify any similarities missed by automated searches.

Violent and Sexual Offender Register (ViSOR)

ViSOR is a UK database designed to facilitate the work of Multi Agency Public Protection Arrangements (MAPPA) (National Probation Service, 2007). It contains detailed confidential information on convicted violent and sexual offenders collated by police, probation and prison services. ViSOR is currently used by all police forces in England, Wales, Scotland and Northern Ireland, along with HM Forces and other specialist police units such as the Child Exploitation and Online Protection (CEOP) centre. ViSOR provides a searchable database against which new cases can be compared.

THE EVIDENCE BASE FOR PROFILING

The evidence base in relation to offender profiling is remarkably limited. There is a general lack of good-quality evidence available and that which does exist is often methodologically weak. Early FBI internal research into the effectiveness of criminal investigative analysis methods reported some areas as showing 80% accuracy (Alison, 2006). The reporting of these studies, though, is incomplete and it is unclear how such accuracy ratings were arrived at from the published data. Claims of the accuracy of diagnostic evaluation have also been made. However, such claims often came from the profilers using these methods, often in the absence of empirical data to support these.

A number of criticisms have been made of early approaches to profiling, suggesting that there was a lack of any firm scientific basis to much of the practice in the area, while early efforts drawing on environmental psychology often produced results of limited value (Gladwell, 2007; Towl & Crighton, 1996). Much of the early work of the FBI BSU and its equivalents in Europe and Australasia, it was suggested, lacked credibility.

Gladwell (2007) notes that such profiles have a great deal in common with the 'cold reading' techniques used by many psychics, in that they make a reasonably large number of vague and unspecific predictions, of a kind that people will generally agree to. Similarly, they also make a number of predictions that are not testable and that are therefore not falsifiable. Finally, even where the predictions are demonstrably wide of the mark, some of the vague and general comments will be applicable and may therefore be used to search retrospectively for accurate predictions.

Concerns that practice in this area of forensic psychology has at times run well ahead of the evidence base have been repeatedly raised (Alison, 2006; Copson, 1995; R v. Stagg [1994];[2] West & Alison, 2006). This has also resulted in serious failings within this area of forensic psychology practice, with the potential (sometimes clearly realized) for significant harm. Much of the work in this area of practice has also been popularized through the press and media in a manner that takes little account of scientific weaknesses.

Efforts to look at the accuracy of profilers empirically have yielded mixed results. A study by Pinizzotto and Finkel (1990) sought to compare the accuracy of profilers comparing experienced profilers with a group of non-profilers. A series of closed murder and closed rape cases were used as the basis for the study. Participants were required to construct profiles using a series of multiple choice questions. The authors reported that experienced profilers were significantly better at predicting the characteristics of the group of closed rapist cases but that the groups did not differ for the closed murder cases. A similar method was used by Kocsis (2003) to look at rape and arson cases, where profilers performed better but with two specific limitations. Firstly, the study was based on a small number of profilers, and secondly, there was a high degree of statistical variance among profilers. These findings echo those found in other areas of clinical or expert decision-making where some practitioners appear to perform well, while others perform at chance levels and others perform at markedly below chance levels. Such studies can, though, be criticized on a number of grounds. As already noted, they have tended to be small-sample studies involving only a few practitioners. They also present material in a very artificial manner, quite distinct from what profilers would actually do in practice when seeking to aid an investigation. While this makes for a convenient experimental method and analysis, it does reduce the extent to which such evidence can be generalized to actual practice.

The notion of behavioural consistency that underpins profiling has received some degree of support. It can draw from a considerable evidence base into the development of criminal behaviour where a high level of consistency in behaviour emerges early and persists over long periods of time (Farrington et al., 2006). Such research suggests the development of often quite stable and enduring patterns of criminal behaviour. There has also been some evidence to support notions of behavioural consistency at crime scenes (Grubin, Kelly, & Brunsdon, 2001). A number of studies of sexual offenders have also provided support for the notion that offenders may share characteristics at a group level. For example, among convicted rapists the more violent offenders have been reported to show higher levels of various forms of personality difficulty: showing higher levels on paranoid, narcissistic, histrionic and paranoid sub-scales than less violent rapists (Proulx, Aubut, Perron, & McKibben, 1994). Following on from this work, a study was conducted which divided convicted rapists into three groups: 'sadistic', 'opportunistic' and 'anger' rapists. Allocation to these groups was based on their mode of offending. The authors reported significant differences between the sadistic and opportunistic groups on structured measures of personality disorder (Proulx, St-Yves, Guay, & Ouimet, 1999).

Support for notions of homology though is weak, and a number of studies have failed to support this hypothesis. In one study an attempt was made to integrate crime scene data felt to be predictive, using logistic regression. This failed to show any substantive improvement over base rates for most of the predictors considered (Davies, Wittebrood, & Jackson, 1998). Another study of 50 convicted rapists suggested that they were relatively homogeneous in terms of criminal history, independent of the observed offence characteristics (House, 1997). A larger study of 100 convicted males who raped strangers considered a sample of 28 dichotomous variables. This study found no clear links between crime scene behaviours and background (Mokros & Alison, 2002).

It has been suggested that much of the early work in profiling bears a striking resemblance to naive personality theories (Alison, 2006). These approaches tended to be nomothetic in nature, making group-based predictions. Like naive personality theories, they have also been extensively criticized as being deterministic and failing to adequately consider and address situational effects. Research into personality suggests that these are general trends in our naive efforts to explain personality characteristics (Mischel, Shoda, & Smith, 2004). There is also the possibility of what have been termed 'Barnum' effects in psychology. This is where people routinely accept vague and ambiguous descriptions as accurate descriptions about themselves, even though they are universally applicable (Forer, 1949). This has led to the suspicion that many areas of profiling may bear more than a passing resemblance to the kind of 'cold reading' practised by many psychics (Gladwell, 2007). A clear concrete example of this effect is in newspaper horoscopes. These are widely read and believed by many, but cannot logically be accurate given that each will cover large numbers of people. The way horoscopes get around this is by remaining vague and making multiple predictions: leading individuals to interpret these in the context of their lives and focus on the more accurate assertions while neglecting those that do not apply. Much of what has historically constituted profiling may therefore be legitimately criticized as being a sophisticated example of 'cold reading' based on a series of ambiguous and contradictory statements. The investigator receiving such a 'reading' is then faced with the task of making sense of this material and how it might fit the case. In turn this raises issues of utility in profiling and again there is little good-quality evidence in this area. There have been a number of what might be termed 'consumer' satisfaction surveys. These generally involve asking investigative officers how useful they have found profiles to be (Pinizzotto & Finkel, 1990). In general, the results from such surveys are moderately positive, with investigating officers generally saying they have appreciated and valued such inputs. Yet, it has been noted that this methodology provides little in the way of meaningful utility analysis (Copson, 1995).

A study by Alison et al. (2003) looked at this suggestion empirically. Participants in the study were presented with a questionnaire regarding a sequence of events in a real murder case, an offender profile and the characteristics of either offender, A or B. Offender A was genuine while offender B was a set of fabricated characteristics designed to be quite distinct from profile A. The results suggested that both groups rated the profile as 'generally accurate', with no participant rating the profile as 'generally' or 'very inaccurate'. The findings from this study tend to support the notion that people are seeking to make sense and achieve a fit between profiles and characteristics, largely independent of accuracy.

There is also little good-quality evidence concerned with how profiles and advice from profilers are interpreted and used. There has been some small research into this question which suggests that nearly half the profiles considered included advice that could not be confirmed post conviction, while around a fifth contained information that was vague or open to wide interpretation. In over 80% of profilers' reports, they note that the basis for the advice given was not made clear; although it is perhaps worth noting that this poor practice has been widespread in many areas of psychological reporting (Alison, 2006; Alison et al., 2003). Alison suggests the use of a structured analysis technique developed to systematically consider legal rhetoric (Toulmin, 1958) as a means of assessing offender profiles. This framework

suggests the use of six interrelated components for analysis: the claim; the strength of the claim; the grounds supporting the claim; the warrant that authorizes the grounds for a claim; the backing; and the rebuttal (Alison, 2006; Alison et al., 2006; West & Alison, 2006). It is suggested that there are a number of reasons why such a framework might be useful. These include the fact that there are few formal models available for analysis of offender profiles and, in turn, how, why or indeed if they are effective. There are also increasing pressures on investigating officers to consider the legal basis for their actions and the framework provides a systematic means of considering many of these. The framework is also posited as a useful mechanism for the self-reflective practice that applied psychologists are encouraged to engage in.

It has been astutely observed that many of those most involved in forensic psychology have been the most resistant to developing a critically evaluative approach to profiling (Alison, 2006). The conclusions drawn from profiling approaches and the public and popular claims have also often run well ahead of the very limited evidence base – what Kocsis (2007) evocatively described, with considerable veracity, as 'mountains of conclusions from molehills of evidence'. There has certainly been a tendency to extrapolate from initial research into areas without an evidence base, as in the expansion of methods to new types of crime. There has also been a general failure to consider diversity and cultural issues. An example given here has been the use of profiles developed in North America for serial rapists in other cultures such as Australasia. Such profiles suggest African descent as a marker in such offences but, when used in Australia where the population with African descent is less than 1%, such a 'marker' is not only unhelpful but is misleading (Kocsis, 2007). Surprisingly perhaps, there has been little consideration given to cases where crime scene data are limited or absent. While profiling has been used widely in cases of serial homicide, it has contributed little to cases where offenders retain and hide the body of victims, as in the case of Jeffrey Dahmer.

Some more recent developments in profiling have also faced criticism on the grounds of being irrelevant or obvious. While more scientific in approach, such studies have focused on offences where issues of detection and investigation are generally not significant, for example, studies of offenders perpetrating criminal violence within families (Burgess et al., 1997). Such research appears to overlap with other, perhaps better developed, areas of forensic psychology practice which have approached such characteristics from the direction of clinical assessment and treatment of offenders.

The reliability of profiling data has also been to focus on study as it is, effectively, a form of retrospective classification. Typologies are developed after the event or events have taken place and these are used to provide some understanding of more recent crimes. For this process to be effective requires a number of elements. Most obviously perhaps, it requires that the information used is accurate. In fact, this is somewhat problematic as it often rests on information contained in written records and also the reliability of information elicited from offenders themselves. Both sources are likely to be less than perfect and this, in turn, will impact on the validity of profiling. In addition, there is a lack of uniform definitions within this field, when compared to other areas of practice. Within mental health, for example, there are agreed frameworks for discussing mental health – most notably DSM-IV (American Psychiatric Association, 2000) and ICD-10 (World Health Organization, 1990). While such frameworks are imperfect, it can be suggested that they do at least serve the function of providing a common frame of reference.

Despite the generally poor state of scientific development within profiling, issues of who 'owns' the subject area have been the focus of discussions. A review by the Association of Chief Police Officers (2000) in the United Kingdom concluded that the area should be 'owned' by the police. This perhaps largely reflects justified concerns about the release of sensitive investigative materials and the leakage of such material to offenders and potential offenders. There is here a potential conflict between the needs of science and those of policing services; where the former depends on a high degree of openness and transparency for peer review of material. Such distinctions are, though, easy to overstate and it is not impossible for good science to take place within such sensitive contexts. Certainly discussions of issues of ownership seem premature.

PRACTICE ISSUES

The early development of profiling has been characterized as a largely unregulated free market. This has served to drive up the public profile of the methods and availability from a number of practitioners. This free market approach has also been extensively criticized on a number of grounds. These include the fact that there is little in the way of quality control in terms of what investigative authorities might reasonably expect from such work. It has also proved difficult to gather adequate empirical data on the accuracy and utility of profiles. This is in marked contrast to other areas of forensic practice such as pathology. Here there is a well-established protocol agreement between the central government department overseeing such work (the Home Office) and practitioners

undertaking such work (Home Office, 2005, 2012). It has been widely suggested that a similar process of registration and protocol for practice might usefully be applied within psychology, analogous to that used for forensic pathologists.

It is an open question whether offender profiling as an area of forensic psychology has reached a stage of development where separate accreditation would be appropriate, desirable or achievable in a credible manner. What is largely agreed, though, is the need for more effective professional regulation of such activities and it seems likely that the advent of statutory regulation may effectively drive this process. In addition, there seems to be a broad consensus that future practice in such areas needs to become much more clearly evidence based (Crighton & Towl, 2008).

In moving to more evidence-based practice, it seems clear that the current research base is generally of poor quality. Alison (2006) suggests that the current evidence base available to practitioners can be broken down into research into:

- The type of victim information used
- How this information is used
- What information is of particular value
- Provision of reliable and valid systems of profiling

Historically, it appears that crime scene information and the modus operandi (MO) have been the sources of information most relied upon. Indeed, the MO and what have been termed 'signature' behaviours have been stressed by many engaged in profiling. It has also been suggested that there is a logical distinction here between MO and the 'psychological signature' of an offence (Ressler et al., 1986). The MO is thought to be functionally relevant to the perpetration of the offence but psychologically irrelevant. The psychological signature is felt to be the reverse of this: being psychologically relevant but functionally irrelevant. As such, it has been suggested that the MO will be context dependent and will change with circumstances. The psychological signature by contrast will be context independent. It is, though, unclear how this distinction between MO and psychological signature is drawn in practice (Alison, 2006).

The use of discrete offender behaviours is also potentially problematic given the high degree to which investigators often depend on victim or witness reports. The extent to which these may be unreliable and are subject to systematic biases has been well documented. Additionally, it seems likely that the two areas of MO and psychological signatures will overlap and, in some cases, the latter will be context dependent. An example cited here is sexual behaviours, which may have high base rates, where the meaning may be context dependent (Alison, 2006).

A key aspect of linking offences relates to the consistent use of reliable variables for assigning crimes to a single offender. The decision to link two crimes is a diagnostic question, similar to those addressed in other areas of forensic psychology. It will rest on two key factors:

- Setting a decision threshold for the point at which evidence is sufficient to define two cases as similar
- Identifying information that the decision should be based upon in order to make the most accurate decisions

Setting accurate decision thresholds has been described as requiring:

- Base rates
- Analysis of costs and benefits

Indeed, the use of base rate information for various forms of crime scene behaviours forms an important part of profiling. For example, behaviours with low base rates and high costs to the offender will generally lower the threshold for linking two or more offences. However, the establishment of accurate base rates for such behaviours is far from straightforward and the estimation of costs and benefits is often difficult. There are other means of establishing decision thresholds but these are generally less powerful than the optimal method described.

Swets, Dawes and Monahan (2000) describe diagnostic decision-making as a process of repetitive choices between two competing alternatives. This process may involve the use of a variety of data such as self-report information, behavioural observation and tests of performance. In the case of OP the question facing a psychologist is the probability that two or more offences were committed by a single person. In doing this they need to establish a threshold criterion for linking offences and these will vary, at least in part, depending on the context of the decision-making.

CONCLUSIONS

Profiling of offenders in order to assist investigations has developed rapidly from its early origins in psychiatric and psychological diagnosis. Such growth occurred in light of rising violent crime rates and concerns surrounding serial homicides and other forms of serial offence.

Greater publicity surrounding these comparatively rare offences has been associated with greater public anxiety, although the question of whether such behaviours are new is at best questionable. Early efforts at profiling represented efforts to assist investigators with some of the most difficult crimes to solve, such as stranger homicides. Here investigators were often deprived of the normal means of investigation and left with few avenues to pursue.

It can, though, be convincingly argued that from its inception the development of profiling has tended to quickly outstrip its scientific foundations. It can also be argued that profiling has at times crossed the border between providing scientifically grounded advice towards the realms of pseudo-science. Profiling has also at times crossed the dividing line between scientific advice and criminal investigation. In doing this profiling has strayed into areas that are the legitimate role of police and prosecutors rather than scientific advisers. There is pleasingly now evidence of a rowing back from such practices as profilers are more effectively regulated and as police services develop a clearer understanding of the methodological uses and misuses of profiling.

The field of profiling suffers from a plethora of terminology and acronyms. Yet, these differing terms refer to a common process of seeking to use the information available to investigators, in order to try to predict the likely characteristics of offenders. The use of multiple terms to describe this may well have been as much about marketing (commercial, professional or personal) as it is about the scientific development of this area of forensic practice. Indeed, it can be argued that such marketing has served to limit and sometimes distort the development of both research and practice. As noted in the preceding text, many of the forensic psychologists most involved in profiling have sometimes appeared to be resistant to developing evidence-based practice. The conclusions drawn by forensic psychologists in this area of practice have often run very far ahead of a very limited and tentative evidence base. Consideration of issues such as culture and diversity often received scant or cursory consideration. Early and necessarily tentative research findings were often built on with little consideration for limitations and caveats. More worryingly, research into one type of criminal behaviour was often extrapolated, with limited consideration of the implications, to other types of crime and then applied in practice. Such developments were clearly inappropriate and highlight the dangers of rushing to uncritical application of methods and models that have not been adequately tested.

Profiling has until recently given little consideration to cases where crime scene data are limited or absent. While profiling has been used widely in cases of serial homicide, it has contributed little to cases where offenders retain and hide the body of victims or systematically avoid leaving evidence in other ways. More recent developments in profiling can also be criticized for researching offences where issues of detection and investigation are generally not significant, for example, studies of domestic homicide offenders (Salfati, 2000). It has been suggested that the value of such research in aiding investigators is at best unclear (Alison, 2006; Alison et al., 2006).

The reliability of profiling data has also been the focus of attention as it is, effectively, a form of retrospective classification. Typologies are developed after the event or events have taken place and these are used to provide some understanding of more recent crimes. For this process to be effective a number of elements are required. Information on past crimes needs to be accurate. In fact, this is somewhat problematic and rests on the reliability of information contained in written records and also the reliability of information elicited from offenders themselves. Both sources are notably unreliable and this, in turn, will impact on the validity of profiles. The development of centralized and high-quality relational databases offers the promise of improving this situation, although such datasets raise significant ethical and human rights issues. As yet, in the United Kingdom, these have received little consideration.

Despite the generally poor state of scientific development within profiling, the issue of who 'owns' profiling has quickly become the focus of discussion. Given the 'free market' manner in which profiling has developed this is disappointing but perhaps not a complete surprise. Much of current practice has been developed in haste and for profit. The limited number and expertise of practitioners in the area has meant that investigating authorities may have found impartial information and advice difficult to come by. If profiling becomes more clearly an area of mainstream forensic psychology research and practice, this is something that should improve. Indeed, overall there are grounds for optimism. Profiling is becoming increasingly evidence based, as the scientific foundations improve. It is also seen increasingly (and in common with many other areas of forensic practice) as a largely experimental field. Such developments bode well for the more effective and ethical support of investigative authorities in Europe and beyond.

NOTES

1 During the Second World War, the United States Office of Strategic Services (OSS) commissioned Dr Walter Langer to provide a psychological profile of Adolf Hitler. Langer was psychoanalytically trained and used this as the basis for much of the profile. However, in other respects, the profile was similar to the offender profiles that followed. The profile was, though, far more detailed, arguably because Langer had access to a much richer dataset, including observation of the behaviour of the person being profiled.
2 Unreported, but see Central Criminal Court, 14 September 1994. See F. Gibb, 'Judge attacks police over "murder trap"'. *The Times*, 15 September 1994; M. Doherty, 'Watching the Detectives' (1994) *New Law Journal*, 1525.

FURTHER READING

Alison, L. (Ed.). (2013). *Forensic psychologists casebook: Psychological profiling and criminal investigation*. London: Routledge.
   An update of a previous edited text of 16 chapters covering both offender profiling and aspects of psychological research and practice into criminal investigation. The text adopts a strongly evidence-based approach to policy and practice in the area and provides a good-quality academic review and critique of the evidence base and practice within the field, covering the key areas of application of psychology to investigative processes.
Fox, B. H., & Farrington, D. P. (2012). Creating burglary profiles using latent class analysis a new approach to offender profiling. *Criminal Justice and Behavior*, 39(12), 1582–1611.
   This paper provides a summary of doctoral research undertaken into the area of offender profiling. It illustrates the increasing use of scientific approaches and the effective application of sophisticated statistical techniques to higher-frequency offences such as burglary, which show generally poor clear up rates: in this case, burglary offences in the United States. The work provides a good illustration of recent directions and progress in offender profiling with ongoing moves away from identifying rare high-profile offenders.

REFERENCES

Alison, L. (2006). From trait-based profiling to psychological contributions to apprehension methods. In L. Alison (Ed.), *The forensic psychologists casebook: Psychological profiling and criminal investigation*. Cullompton, Devon: Willan.

Alison, L., Bennett, C., Mokros, A., & Ormrod, D. (2002). The personality paradox in offender profiling. A theoretical review of the processes involved in deriving background characteristics from crime scene actions, *Psychology Public Policy and Law*, 8, 115–135.

Alison, L., Goodwill, A., & Allison, E. (2006). Guidelines for profilers. In L. Alison (Ed.), *The forensic psychologists casebook: Psychological profiling and criminal investigation*. Cullompton, Devon: Willan.

Alison, L., & Kebbell, M. (2006). Offender profiling: Limits and potential. In M. Kebbell & G. Davies (Eds.), *Practical psychology for forensic investigations and prosecutions*. Chichester: John Wiley.

Alison, L. J., Smith, M. D., & Morgan, K. (2003). Interpreting the accuracy of offender profiles. *Psychology, Crime and Law*, 9(2), 185–195.

American Psychiatric Association (2000). *Diagnostic and statistical manual of mental disorders: DSM-IV-TR*. Washington, DC: Author.

Association of Chief Police Officers (2000). *ACPO Crime Committee, Behavioural Science Sub Committee, internal report*. London: Association of Chief Police Officers.

Britton, P. (1998). *The jigsaw man*. London: Corgi Books.

Brussel, J. (1968). *Case book of a crime psychiatrist*. New York: Bernard Geis.

Burgess, A. W., Baker, T., Greening, D., Hartman, Burgess, A. G., Douglas, J. E., & Halloran, R.(1997). Stalking behaviours within domestic violence. *Journal of Family Violence*, 12(4), 389–403.

Canter, D. (1989). Offender profiles. *The Psychologist*, 2(1), 12–16.

Canter, D. (1994). *Criminal shadows*. London: HarperCollins.

Chapman, R., Smith, L. L., & Bond, J. W. (2012). An investigation into the differentiating characteristics between car key burglars and regular burglars. *Journal of Forensic Sciences*, 57(4), 939–945.

Christie, A. (1934). *Murder on the Orient Express*. London: Collins Crime Club.

Cohen, M., Seghorn, T., & Calmas, W. (1969). Sociometric study of the sex offender. *Journal of Abnormal Psychology*, 74(2), 249–255.

Conan Doyle, A. (2001). *A study in scarlet*. Contributor Iain Sinclair (Ed.). London: Penguin Classics. First published 1897.

Copson, G. (1995). *Coals to Newcastle? Part 1: A study of offender profiling*. London: Home Office.

Copson, G., Badcock, R., Boon, J., & Britton, P. (2006). Editorial: Articulating a systematic approach to clinical crime profiling. *Criminal Behaviour and Mental Health*, 7(1), 13–17.

Crighton, D. A., & Towl, G. J. (2008). *Psychology in prisons* (2nd edn). Oxford: BPS Blackwell.

Davies, A., Wittebrood, K., & Jackson, J. L. (1998). *Predicting the criminal record of a stranger rapist*. Special interest series paper 12. London: Home Office Policing and Reducing Crime Unit.

Doherty, M. (1994). Watching the Detectives, *New Law Journal*, 1525–1525.

Douglas, J., Burgess, A. W., Burgess, A. G., & Ressler, R. K. (2013). *Crime classification manual: A standard system for investigating and classifying violent crime*. San Francisco, CA: John Wiley & Sons.

Farrington, D. P., Coid, J. W., Harnett, L. M., Jolliffe, D., Soteriou, N., Turner, R. E., & West, D. J. (2006). Criminal careers up to age 50 and life success up to age 48: New findings from the Cambridge Study in Delinquent Development, 2nd edition. *Home Office Research Study 299*. London: Home Office Research, Development and Statistics Directorate.

Federal Bureau of Investigation (2011). *Uniform Crime Report Crime in the United States 2011*. Washington, DC; US Department of Justice.

Forer, B. (1949). The fallacy of personal validation: A classroom demonstration of gullibility. *Journal of Abnormal and Social Psychology*, 44, 118–123.

Fox, B. H., Farrington, D., Chitwood, M., & Janes, E. (in press). *Developing a profile for burglary*. FBI Law Enforcement Bulletin.

Fujita, G., Watanabe, K., Yokota, K., Kuraishi, H., Suzuki, M., Wachi, T., & Otsuka, Y, (2013). Multivariate models for behavioral offender profiling of Japanese homicide. *Criminal Justice and Behavior*, February, 40(2), 214–227.

Gladwell, M. (2007). *Dangerous minds: Criminal profiling made easy*. New Yorker November 12. Available from www.newyorker.com/reporting/2007/11/12/071112fa_fact_gladwell, retrieved 14 January 2015.

Grubin, D., Kelly, P., & Brunsdon, C. (2001). Linking serious sexual assaults through behaviour. *Home Office Research Study 215*. London: Home Office Research, Development and Statistics Directorate.

Gudjonsson, G. H., & Copson, G. (1997). The role of the expert in criminal investigation. In J. L. Jackson & D. A. Bekerian (Eds.), *Offender profiling: Theory, research and practice* (pp. 61–76). Chichester, UK: Wiley.

Harris, T. (1981). *Red dragon*. New York: Random House.

Home Office (2005). *Register of forensic pathologists disciplinary guidance*. London: Home Office.

Home Office (2012). *Protocol for Home Office registered pathologist* (rev. 2012). Available from: https://www.gov.uk/government/publications/protocol-for-home-office-registered-forensic-pathologists, retrieved 14 January 2015.

House, J. C. (1997). Towards a practical application of offender profiling: The RNC's criminal suspect prioritization system. In J. L. Jackson & D. A. Bekerian (Eds.), *Offender profiling: Theory, research and practice* (pp. 177–190). Chichester: Wiley.

Jackson, L., & Bekerian, D. A. (Eds.) (1997). *Offender profiling theory research and practice*. Chichester: John Wiley.

Keppel, R. D., & Walter, R. (1999). Profiling killers: A revised classification model for understanding sexual murder. *International Journal of Offender Therapy and Comparative Criminology*, 43(4), 417–437.

Kocsis, R. N. (2003). Criminal psychological profiling: An outcome and process study. *Law and Human Behaviour*, 14, 215–233.

Kocsis, R. N. (Ed.) (2007). *Criminal profiling international theory, research, and practice.* Totowa, NJ: Humana Press.

Mischel, W., Shoda, Y., & Smith, R. E. (2004). *Introduction to personality: Toward an integration* (7th edn). New York: Wiley.

Mokros, A., & Alison, L. (2002). Is profiling possible? Testing the predicted homology of crime scene actions and background characteristics in a sample of rapists. *Legal and Criminological Psychology, 7,* 25–43.

National Probation Service (2007). *The Violent and Sex Offender Register (ViSOR).* National Probation Service Briefing Issue 37 (August) . London: Author.

Petherick, W. (2005). *Serial crime: Theoretical and practical issues in behavioral profiling.* Burlington, MA: Academic Press.

Pinizzotto, A. J., & Finkel, N. J. (1990). Criminal personality profiling an outcome and process study. *Law and Human Behavior, 14*(3), 215–233.

Prentky, R. A., & Burgess, A. W. (2000). *Forensic management of sexual offenders.* New York: Kluwer Academic/Plenum.

Prentky, R. A., Knight, R. A., & Rosenberg, R. (1988). Validation analyses on a taxonomic system for rapists: Disconfirmation and reconceptualization. *Annals of the New York Academy of Sciences, 528,* 21–40.

Prentky, R. A., Knight, R. A., Rosenberg, R., & Lee, A. (1989). A path analytic approach to the validation of a taxonomic system for classifying child molesters. *Journal of Quantitative Criminology, 5*(3), 231–257.

Proulx, J., Aubut, J., Perron, L., & McKibben, A. (1994). Troubles de la personalité et viol: Implications théoriques et cliniques [Personality disorders and violence: Theoretical and clinical implications]. *Criminologie, 27,* 33–53.

Proulx, J., St-Yves, M., Guay, J. P., & Ouimet, M. (1999). Les aggresseurs sexuels de femmes: Scénarios délictuels et troubles de la personalitié [Sexual aggressors of women: Offence scenarios and personality disorders]. In J. Proulx, M. Cusson, & M. Ouimet (Eds.), *Les violences criminelles.* Quebec: Les Presses de L'Université Laval.

Read, T., & Oldfield, D. (1995). Local crime analysis. *Police Research Group Paper 65.* London: Home Office.

Ressler, R. K., Burgess, A. W., Douglas, J. E., Hartman, C. R., & D'Agostino, R. B. (1986). (1986). Sexual killers and their victims: Identifying patterns through crime scene analysis. *Journal of Interpersonal Violence, 1,* 288–308.

R v Stagg [1994] 9 Arch News 4.

Salfati, G. (2000). The nature of expressiveness and instrumentality in homicide implications for offender profiling. *Homicide Studies, 4*(3), 265–293.

Swets, J. A., Dawes, R. M., & Monahan, J. (2000). Psychological science can improve diagnostic decisions. *Psychological Science in the Public Interest, 1*(1), 1–26.

Tenten, H. D. (1989). Offender profiling. In W. G. Bailey (Ed.), *The encyclopaedia of police science.* New York: Garland.

Toulmin, S. (1958). *The uses of argument.* Cambridge: Cambridge University Press.

Towl, G. J., & Crighton, D. A. (1996). *The handbook of psychology for forensic practitioners.* London: Routledge.

West, A., & Alison, L. (2006). Conclusions: Personal reflections on the last decade. In L. Alison (Ed.), *The forensic psychologists casebook: Psychological profiling and criminal investigation.* Cullompton, Devon: Willan.

World Health Organization (1990). *International statistical classification of diseases and related health problems, tenth revision.* Available from: www.who.int/classifications/icd/en/index.html, retrieved 1 June 2009.

4   Eyewitness Testimony

LORRAINE HOPE

Eyewitness testimony plays an important role within the criminal justice system and has, over the past four decades, emerged as a significant research area for psychologists and other social scientists. This chapter aims to provide a comprehensive overview of the key findings of an extensive literature on eyewitness identification performance, signposting both classic studies and emergent research strands. Taking the reader through the witnessing experience, from the initial encoding of the perpetrator to the final stage of delivering testimony in court, this chapter identifies the factors likely to lead to mistaken identifications. Theoretical implications and methodological difficulties associated with eyewitness research are also considered. In the second half of the chapter, the difficulties associated with identifications from closed-circuit television (CCTV) are examined and a full overview of the current UK guidelines for the conduct of identifications is provided.

Information obtained from eyewitnesses plays an important role in many forensic investigations. For instance, the positive identification of a suspect can provide major advances in an investigation (Coupe & Griffiths, 1996; Kebbell & Milne, 1998; Wells & Loftus, 2013). Eyewitness testimony is also extremely influential in the courtroom where 'few kinds of evidence are as compelling, or as damning, as eyewitness testimony' (Overbeck, 2005, p. 1895). Yet, identifications are often disputed – and inaccurate. A review of DNA exoneration cases suggests that eyewitness errors have played some part in over 70% of 289 overturned convictions (Innocence Project, 2012; see Scheck, Neufeld, & Dwyer, 2000). That erroneous eyewitness testimony is a leading cause of wrongful convictions suggests that jurors fail to take into account factors which may have influenced or biased the eyewitness and led to a mistaken identification (Boyce, Beaudry, & Lindsay, 2007; Huff, Rattner, & Sagarin, 1996). In this chapter, we examine the performance of eyewitnesses and consider some of the key factors underpinning mistaken identifications.

EYEWITNESS IDENTIFICATION PERFORMANCE

The scientific study of eyewitness identification, which emerged in a programmatic fashion during the 1970s, has mainly been conducted by cognitive or social psychologists and typically adopts a standard scientific experimental model. In the mock witness paradigm, volunteers and/or unsuspecting members of the public are exposed to a selected target (perpetrator) as part of a staged event (or simulated crime) and become eyewitnesses. As the events and target individuals are stipulated by the researcher, the nature of witness errors can be documented and systematic manipulations can be made to establish which recall and recognition errors are most likely under particular, forensically relevant conditions. Thus, the primary purpose of such experiments has been to establish cause-effect relations among variables (Wells & Quinlivan, 2008).

An important question for applied researchers and the legal fraternity concerns the extent to which the findings obtained in laboratory research can be generalized to the experience of actual witnesses. There are, of course, a number of important differences between the experience of (some) witnesses and unsuspecting participants in research. For instance, witnesses to 'real' crimes rarely receive a warning – or may not even be aware they have witnessed something important until after the event. A further concern frequently expressed by those

Forensic Psychology, Second Edition. Edited by David A. Crighton and Graham J. Towl.
© 2015 John Wiley & Sons, Ltd. Published 2015 by British Psychological Society and John Wiley & Sons, Ltd.

in the legal system is that many of the 'witnesses' in such experiments are drawn from rather homogeneous samples of college students. In fact, many studies of eyewitness memory have included community-based samples (e.g., Gabbert, Hope, & Fisher, 2009) while a significant body of research has examined the identification performance of different age groups, including young children (e.g., Pozzulo & Dempsey, 2006) and the elderly (e.g., Badham, Wade, Watts, Woods, & Maylor, 2013; Dodson & Krueger, 2006). Importantly, research consistently demonstrates that college-age students outperform other age populations. Thus, as noted by Wells and Quinlivan (2008), college-age participants may in fact underestimate the magnitude of eyewitness fallibility.

Witnesses to 'real' crime events may experience a higher level of emotional arousal, particularly if the witnessed incident involves weapons or violence and the witnesses feel threatened. For sound ethical reasons, researchers are typically not permitted to induce stress in experimental participants and are, therefore, unable to replicate violent crime scenarios in any meaningful way. Of course, it is also worth noting that the nature of the stress evoked in a controlled experimental setting may differ qualitatively from the stress associated with involvement in an actual criminal event. In brief, the effects of stress and enhanced emotion on memory are complicated, but the results of research conducted in ecologically sound settings suggest that memory is more likely to be impaired than enhanced in a stressful or arousing situation (e.g., Hope, Lewinski, Dixon, Blocksidge, & Gabbert, 2012; Morgan et al., 2004; Morgan, Southwick, Steffian, Hazlett, & Loftus, 2013; Valentine & Mesout, 2008).

Perhaps foremost on the minds of those reluctant to embrace scientific findings on eyewitness performance is the fact that the consequences of an identification decision diverge significantly when that decision is made in a laboratory as opposed to a police identification suite. It is difficult to demonstrate whether or not legal consequences have any actual bearing on witness identification accuracy. However, archival studies of actual witnesses to serious crimes indicate that witnesses taking part in identification parades, where they are presented with a suspect and a number of innocent 'stand-ins', select a foil (i.e., an innocent 'stand-in' or filler) up to 30% on average (Slater, 1994; Wright & McDaid, 1996; Wright & Skagerberg, 2007). These archival data suggest that witnesses can be highly prone to error and do not necessarily become extremely cautious when faced with a high-stake identification decision (see Memon, Vrij, & Bull, 2003b).

Many factors may affect the accuracy of an eyewitness and the research literature examining these factors is extensive (Wells & Olson, 2003). A useful distinction

between these factors was introduced by Wells (1978) who differentiated between *estimator variables* and *system variables*. System variables are factors which are (or could be) under the control of the criminal justice system, specifically identification test factors such as pre-lineup instructions, lineup composition, structure and presentation method. By contrast, estimator variables are not under control of the criminal justice system and, while these are factors which can be manipulated in research (such as exposure duration, age or race of witness, or presence of a weapon), they cannot be controlled in the actual witnessed incident. Therefore, the impact of such factors on witness accuracy has to be estimated, or taken into account, in a *post-hoc* manner.

Working systematically through the witnessing experience, from the encoding of the original incident to eyewitness testimony in court, this chapter examines several important estimator and system factors which have been shown to impair eyewitness identification accuracy. This is not intended to be an exhaustive review of all possible factors but rather a consideration of the more well-researched witness, perpetrator and contextual factors which provide some insight into subsequent witness identification behaviour and accuracy.

THE WITNESSED EVENT

Witness factors

Stable witness characteristics are not, on the whole, useful predictors of identification performance. Research examining factors such as gender, race or intelligence has not revealed any particularly robust effects indicating that members of some groups are better witnesses than others. Nor has research documented any strong relationship between eyewitness accuracy and personality factors. While a small number of studies have examined certain personality characteristics such as self-monitoring (Hosch & Platz, 1984) and trait anxiety (Shapiro & Penrod, 1986), 'no strong theory relating personality to eyewitness identification has emerged' (Wells & Olson, 2003, p. 281).

However, the age of the witness has been consistently associated with identification accuracy, with findings for young children mapping onto the performance of older witnesses under certain test conditions. Specifically, when the originally encoded perpetrator is present in the lineup (a culprit present lineup), both young children and the elderly do not differ significantly from young adults in their ability to correctly identify the perpetrator. However, when the perpetrator is not present in the lineup (a culprit absent lineup), both young children and elderly witnesses are more likely than young adults to make a false identification of an innocent foil (see meta-analysis by Pozzulo & Lindsay, 1998). Research demonstrates that older eyewitnesses (e.g., 60–80 years) tend to make more false identifications than younger adults in both target present and target absent lineups (Memon, Hope, & Bull, 2003a; Memon, Hope, Bartlett, & Bull, 2002). No unifying theory has emerged to fully account for this finding across both age groups. For instance, it appears that young children's identification performance is hampered by a 'choosing problem' (Brewer, Weber, & Semmler, 2005). Keast, Brewer, and Wells (2007) also noted a marked overconfidence in children's judgements relating to their identification decisions, which suggests that children may be poor at monitoring their own memory, a conclusion consistent with the developmental literature (Howie & Roebers, 2007). The mechanisms underlying higher false identification rates for older witnesses are less well explored. Ageing is typically associated with reduced cognitive capacity (such as a decline in attentional resources, see Craik & Byrd, 1982; Salthouse, 1982) and an increased reliance on a more 'automatic' feeling of familiarity rather than a more effortful recollection process (Jacoby, 1999; Mandler, 1980). Thus, it seems unlikely that the explanations for difficulties experienced by younger witnesses will also apply to older witnesses. In a related vein, a recent meta-analytic review by Rhodes and Anastasi (2012) notes a robust own-age bias in face recognition, such that recognition memory for faces in the same age group is superior to memory for faces drawn from other age groups. This own-age bias was found among children, young adults, middle-aged adults and older adults. Although this review focused on face recognition (as opposed to identification) research, a number of identification studies have also noted own-age effects (e.g., Havard, Memon, Laybourn, & Cunningham, 2012; Wright & Stroud, 2002).

A more malleable witness factor at the time of encoding is blood alcohol level. If the witness has been drinking and is intoxicated, both encoding and storage may be impaired (Cutler & Penrod, 1995). In terms of identification performance, Dysart, Lindsay, MacDonald, and Wicke (2002) found that participants with high blood alcohol readings were more likely to make a false identification when faced with a culprit absent identification task. Similarly, Hilliar, Kemp, and Denson (2010) noted that moderate levels of alcohol intoxication was associated with increased false identification rates but did not appear to affect correct identifications. While a number of explanations have been proposed to account for these findings, such as a tendency to focus on salient cues when intoxicated (alcohol myopia hypothesis), research on the performance of intoxicated witnesses is limited due to the associated methodological and ethical difficulties.

Perpetrator factors

Stable factors (such as gender or age of the culprit) have little or no impact on witness ability to correctly identify the perpetrator (excepting the possibility of own-age biases affecting face recognition; see Rhodes & Anastasi, 2012). However, there are a number of well-documented factors that can serve to either impair or enhance recognition ability. For instance, distinctive faces are far more likely to be correctly identified than non-distinctive faces. Similarly, and perhaps due to their distinctiveness, attractive faces are also more easily identified than less attractive or more typical faces. The psychological mechanisms underlying these findings are relatively straightforward. When an encoded face is distinctive or atypical in some way, it will not only attract more attention and greater processing resources but the distinctive feature is also more likely to benefit from an enhanced representation in memory (Ryu & Chaudhuri, 2007; see Brewer et al., 2005, for an interesting examination of the role of distinctiveness).

Unsurprisingly, disguises usually have a negative impact on identification ability (Cutler, Penrod, & Martens, 1987; but see O'Rourke, Penrod, Cutler, & Stuve, 1989). Simple changes, such as covering the head, wearing glasses, growing facial hair or even altering hair style slightly, can significantly impair face recognition (Narby, Cutler, & Penrod, 1996; Shapiro & Penrod, 1986). Most recently, Mansour et al. (2012) manipulated the nature of the disguise used (e.g., stocking mask, sunglasses, knitted hat) and noted that identification accuracy generally decreased with degree of disguise. Furthermore, changes in appearance over time (such as ageing, changes in weight, etc.) also have a negative impact on identification performance. In one study, Read, Vokey, and Hammersley (1990) found that photographs of a target face taken after a 2-year delay were less likely to be recognized than photographs taken nearing the time of original encoding.

An extensive literature has documented the identification impairment that occurs when the perpetrator is from a different race or ethnic group to the witness. Research on own-race (also known as cross-race) bias typically demonstrates that witnesses are less accurate when attempting to identify a target from another race or ethnic group than when tasked with identifying a member of their own race (see meta-analysis by Meissner & Brigham, 2001). Specifically, research documents a higher correct identification rate from target present lineups and a lower false identification rate from target absent lineups when the witness and perpetrator are from the same race. This bias has been demonstrated in both laboratory and field studies (e.g., Wright, Boyd, & Tredoux, 2001), and has been observed across various combinations of ethnic groups (e.g., whites identifying blacks, blacks identifying whites, etc.). Work by Chiroro and Valentine (1995) exploring a basic contact hypothesis suggested that everyday interactions with people of different races may reduce the effect – but not consistently. Other evidence suggests that the quality rather than the quantity of cross-racial interactions may be more important in reducing own-race bias (Lavrakas, Buri, & Mayzner, 1976). Interestingly, a similar pattern of results has been demonstrated for gender and age such that a match between witness and target age and gender can promote recognition accuracy (e.g., Wright & Sladden, 2003; Wright & Stroud, 2002). Taken together, these findings suggest a somewhat preferential processing mechanism for familiar stimuli. In this vein, McClelland and Chappell (1998) have argued that own-race faces may benefit from more accurate and efficient processing due to their familiarity. Recent research by Pezdek, O'Brien, and Wasson (2012) examining recognition memory for both same- and other-race faces suggests that there are systematic and qualitative differences in the social-cognitive processing required for successful cross-race recognition performance.

Situational factors

In any witnessed incident, there may be a number of situational factors which impinge on subsequent eyewitness performance. An important factor which has received surprisingly little attention from researchers is the nature of the exposure duration (i.e., the opportunity, or length of time, the witness had to observe the perpetrator). In their meta-analysis of face recognition studies, Shapiro and Penrod (1986) found the predicted linear relationship between exposure duration and hit rates (i.e., as the amount of time spent viewing the target increases so does the likelihood of a correct recognition decision). A more recent meta-analysis by Bornstein, Deffenbacher, Penrod, and McGorty (2012) replicated this general finding, noting that longer exposure durations lead to better identification performance. However, the authors also noted that the effect of longer exposure was non-linear, in that the greatest effect of increased exposure occurred at short (as opposed to longer) initial durations. Despite these insights, only a handful of studies have actually systematically manipulated exposure duration in an eyewitness context. These studies have typically demonstrated the expected beneficial effect of longer exposure duration on subsequent identification accuracy (e.g., Memon *et al.*, 2003a; Read, 1995). However, inconsistent choosing patterns in target absent conditions require further experimental examination. Similarly, relatively little research attention has been paid to the effect of distance on identification and the ability of eyewitnesses to correctly estimate distances from an incident or perpetrator. Obviously, a correct identification is somewhat unlikely if the witness was unable to *see* the perpetrator so research has tended to focus on identifying a useful 'rule of thumb' with respect to distance. For instance, Wagenaar and van der Schrier (1996) suggested that identification performance was optimal when the viewing distance was less than 15 metres from the target. However, research by Lindsay, R. C. L., Semmler, Weber, Brewer, and Lindsay, M. R. (2008) reveals that the 15-metre rule may not be useful – or accurate – for two reasons. Firstly, if witnesses are unable to estimate distance reliably then they are unlikely to be able to report accurately whether they were less than 15 metres from the target. Secondly, it seems rather unlikely that all identifications made when the viewing distance was less than 15 metres will be correct – or vice versa. In Lindsay *et al.* (2008), over 1,300 participants observed a target person at various distances, estimated the distance to the target, generated a description and attempted an identification of the target from either a target present or target absent lineup. Participants were poor at accurately estimating the distance between themselves and the target (particularly when required to make this estimate from memory). While the reliability of target descriptions was unimpaired up to distances of approximately 50 metres, a decline in identification performance occurred for both target present and target absent lineups as distance between the witness and target at encoding increased. Although this finding is broadly consistent with those of Wagenaar and van der Schrier (1996), Lindsay *et al.* (2008) did not observe any dramatic drop-off in identification accuracy at 15 metres, noting that many participants made correct identifications beyond this distance, suggesting that a 15-metre rule is not a particularly useful diagnostic for the courts.

Another variable aspect of a criminal incident is the amount of stress or fear a witness may experience. Research inducing realistic levels of stress is, for obvious methodological and ethical reasons, difficult to conduct. However, in a field training scenario, Morgan *et al.* (2004) subjected soldiers to either a high- or low-stress interrogation in a mock prisoner of war camp over a 12-hour period. After a 24-hour delay, soldiers who had experienced a high-stress interrogation were significantly less likely to correctly identify their interrogator than those who had experienced the low-stress interrogation. Extending this research, Morgan *et al.* (2013) tested identification accuracy in over 800 military personnel during a stressful prison camp phase of Survival School training. In addition to observing robust misinformation effects, approximately 50% of participants who viewed a target-absent lineup, and were asked to identify the person who had interrogated them, made an incorrect identification. Impaired identification performance has also been observed among police officers placed in challenging physical contexts (e.g., physical exertion; see Hope *et al.,* 2012) Similarly, research on civilian participants in an arousing context (the London Dungeon) demonstrated that high-state anxiety was associated with fewer correct identifications of a target (Valentine & Mesout, 2008).

Other researchers have focused on the forensically relevant problem of witnesses to crimes involving weapons. Although some field research suggests that the emotional arousal associated with violent witnessing conditions may actually serve to benefit memory (e.g., Yuille & Cutshall, 1986; but see Wright, 2006), eyewitness experts have tended to favour the view that incidents involving the presence of a weapon will have a negative impact on eyewitness performance (Kassin, Tubb, Hosch, & Memon, 2001). This phenomenon has become known as the *weapon focus effect* (Loftus, E. F., Loftus, G. R., & Messo, 1987) and occurs when the presence of a weapon adversely affects subsequent eyewitness recall performance such that memory for details such as the perpetrator's facial characteristics and clothing is impaired (e.g., Cutler *et al.,* 1987; Hope & Wright, 2007; Loftus *et al.,* 1987; Maas & Kohnken, 1989; Pickel, French, & Betts, 2003; Steblay, 1992). One explanation is that increased arousal (or stress) due to the presence of a weapon reduces attentional capacity as increased attention is paid to the weapon while peripheral cues are ignored or filtered (Hope & Wright, 2007; Loftus, 1980; Macleod & Mathews, 1991). A meta-analytic review of the effects of stress on eyewitness memory by Deffenbacher, Bornstein, Penrod, and McGorty (2004) concluded that high levels of stress impair the accuracy of eyewitness recall and identification but that the detriment depends on the response mode elicited by the stress manipulation. The authors proposed that some emotion manipulations generate an 'orientating' response while others generate a 'defensive' response (Deffenbacher, 1994; Deffenbacher *et al.,* 2004; see also Klorman, Weissberg, & Wiesenfeld, 1977; Sokolov, 1963). Deffenbacher *et al.* (2004) argued that the orientating response leads to enhanced memory for 'informative aspects' of a scene but that the defensive response can lead to either enhanced memory or significant memory impairment depending on other cognitive and physiological factors. Most recently, a meta-analytic review of the literature on the weapon focus effect by Fawcett, Russell, Peace, and Christie (2013) confirmed a small-to-moderate effect of weapon presence on identification accuracy but noted that this effect was influenced by situational factors (such as exposure duration, retention interview, level of threat, etc.).

BETWEEN THE WITNESSED EVENT AND IDENTIFICATION TASK

Retention interval

In the delay between an individual witnessing a crime and making an identification attempt, the witness's memory is not only prone to decay, but it is also vulnerable to the influence of post-event information from numerous sources. Both delay and post-event information have been shown to compromise recall completeness and accuracy (see Anderson, 1983; Ayers & Reder, 1998; Ellis, Shepherd, & Davies, 1980; Gabbert, Memon, & Allan, 2003; Loftus, Miller, & Burns, 1978; McCloskey & Zaragoza, 1985; Meissner, 2002; Tuckey & Brewer, 2003).

Delay systematically decreases the amount of information that can be recalled (Ebbinghaus, 1885; Kassin *et al.,* 2001; Rubin & Wenzel, 1996; see also Tuckey & Brewer, 2003). Furthermore, a meta-analysis of 128 studies of face recognition suggests that there is a decline in the correct identification of previously seen faces after a delay (Shapiro & Penrod, 1986). Sporer (1992) found a decrease in correct identifications and an increase in false alarms over various intervals up to three weeks. Importantly, the field work by Valentine, Pickering, and Darling (2003b) examining performance of real witnesses suggests that the greatest decline in performance occurs when the delay exceeds one week.

Post-event misinformation

Research conducted by Elizabeth Loftus in the 1970s demonstrated the misinformation effect – a powerful phenomenon resulting in memory distortion (for a review see Loftus, 2005; see also Frenda, Nichols, & Loftus, 2011). In a now classic experiment, Loftus and Palmer (1974) presented participants a short film of a car accident and subsequently tested participant recall for details of the incident. Importantly, they found that simply changing one word in a question pertaining to the speed the car was travelling when the accident occurred resulted in significantly different estimates of speed. Specifically, participants asked to estimate what speed the car was travelling at when it *contacted* the other vehicle provided slower speed estimates (31.8 mph) than those asked to estimate the speed of the car when it *smashed* into the other vehicle (40.5 mph). Including the verb 'smashed' in the question also led to increased false reports of witnessing broken glass at the scene of the accident (no broken glass was ever shown). Several hundred experiments since have demonstrated the misinformation phenomenon, explored boundary conditions of the effect and served the development of theoretical explanations. More pertinent to eyewitness identification accuracy is an emerging body of work on the impact of co-witness influence on memory. In a survey, 86% of real eyewitnesses discussed their memory with a co-witness who was present at the witnessed event (Paterson & Kemp, 2006). Witnesses to an event may share the same experience but their individual recall of the event may differ for many reasons, including naturally occurring differences in attention paid to various details of the event, differences in spatial or temporal location at the scene or perceived differences in ability to recall those details (Gabbert, Memon, & Wright, 2006). Research amply demonstrates that the most likely outcome when two witnesses discuss their memories is that their accounts of the witnessed event become more similar and, hence, seemingly corroborative (Gabbert, Memon, Allan, & Wright, 2004; Wright, Self, & Justice, 2000). A witness is also more likely to be influenced by a co-witness with whom they have a prior acquaintance, such as a friend or partner (Hope, Ost, Gabbert, Healey, & Lenton, 2008). However, very few studies have explored the impact of misleading information on subsequent identifications. Research conducted by Gabbert, Brewer, and Hope (2007) which manipulated co-witness confidence and accuracy across both target present and target absent lineups found that participants were more likely than controls to reject the lineup incorrectly when they were aware that the co-witness had rejected the lineup. However, participants were no more likely than controls to identify the perpetrator correctly after seeing the co-witness make an accurate identification, and the pre-lineup confidence expressed by the confederate did not appear to influence the witness. In a recent examination of the effect of knowing a co-witness's lineup decision on lineup performance, Levett (2013) observed that witnesses who heard that their co-witness had chosen from the lineup were more likely to choose themselves than those who had no information about the co-witness decision or had heard that the co-witness had rejected the lineup. Witnesses who heard co-witness decisions were also influenced by the confidence expressed by their co-witness. In light of these findings (and the wider literature in this field), it is clear that identification decisions should be made independently.

While unbiased lineup procedures should ensure that identification decisions themselves are unlikely to be shared with other witnesses, misinformation concerning descriptive details or pertaining to the general appearance of the target may have a negative impact on eyewitness accuracy, and this hypothesis is worthy of further experimental scrutiny.

INTERMEDIATE RECOGNITION TASKS

Mug shots

In the course of an investigation, witnesses may be asked to search through a set of mug shots (usually photographs of potential suspects). Unsurprisingly, a number of studies have shown that previous exposure to the suspect increases the likelihood that the suspect will be identified in a subsequent lineup. In other words, repeated exposure to a suspect can increase mistaken identifications of an innocent suspect (Brigham & Cairns, 1988; Dysart, Lindsay, Hammond, & DuPuis, 2001; Gorenstein & Ellsworth, 1980; Memon et al., 2002). Research suggests that commitment effects (i.e., commitment to a prior mug shot choice) may be a leading source of identification error when witnesses have been exposed to mug shots (see Goodsell, Neuschatz, & Gronlund, 2009).

Composite production

In an investigation where no suspect has emerged, the police may work with a witness to produce a facial composite of the perpetrator. Previously, this composite might have been produced by a sketch artist but technological advances have led to the use of computerized systems for composite production (such as the E-Fit or Profit identification systems). While research demonstrates that the quality of composites is often rather poor, with little likeness to the appearance of the actual perpetrator (see Wells & Hasel, 2007, for a review), a more important question concerns the extent to which generating a composite might impair identification accuracy. In two studies, Wells, Charman, and Olson (2005) examined whether building a face composite had a negative effect on memory for the target face. Results indicated that building a composite resulted in significantly lower identifications for the original target face (Experiment 1), while a second experiment revealed that the results might be generalized to a standard witness paradigm (Experiment 2). In light of these results, Wells et al. (2005) suggest that where multiple witnesses are available 'it might be possible to use one witness to build a composite and save the other witnesses for any later lineup identification attempts' (p. 155).

The identification task

In this section, we consider several important system variables which can have a significant impact on eyewitness identification performance. These variables are ultimately under the control of the criminal justice system and, to date, research has focused on demonstrating the identification errors resulting from poor practice in the production and administration of identification tests (i.e., lineups) while delivering recommendations for improved procedures.

Pre-lineup instructions

Often witnesses assume that the suspect apprehended by the police and presented to them in the formal setting of a lineup must have a high probability of being the actual perpetrator. In other words, witnesses assume that they would not have been invited to make an identification if there was not a good reason for the police to believe the suspect was the actual perpetrator and their role is to make a positive identification (i.e., choose someone from the array). This bias may be further exacerbated if the witnesses are presented with the task in a misleading manner (i.e., 'Take a good look at the lineup and see if you can identify the offender'). In fact, Memon *et al.* (2003a) found that over 90% of mock witnesses indicated that they expected the perpetrator to be present in a lineup even under unbiased conditions. Therefore, it is extremely important that witnesses are informed that the person they saw 'may or may not be present in the lineup'. Incorrect identifications from target absent lineups are significantly lower when witnesses are given this simple cautionary instruction (see meta-analyses by Steblay, 1997; Clark, 2005). It is also worth noting that the negative effect of biased lineup instructions also holds true for identifications made from video images (Thompson & Johnson, 2008).

Lineup composition

When a suspect disputes his involvement in an incident or claims an identification error, a lineup must be conducted. Here the police face a number of challenges as there are (at least) two important dilemmas with respect to lineup composition, namely, the number of lineup members (or foils) present in addition to the suspect, and how those foils are selected. The requisite number of lineup members is typically specified in law. For instance, in the United Kingdom, a lineup must contain at least eight foils, while in the United States lineups containing five (or more) foils are common. However, researchers have drawn a sharp distinction between the *nominal size* of a lineup (i.e., the number of people appearing in the lineup) and what has been described as the *functional size* of a lineup (Wells, Leippe, & Ostrom, 1979). Functional size refers to the number of plausible lineup members. If an eyewitness describes a perpetrator as a male, in his early twenties with long, dark hair, but then views a lineup in which two of the foils have short dark hair and one other foil is in his 40s, then the functional size of the lineup is reduced by three members, as these foils will be automatically discarded by the witness as they do not match the original description provided. The purpose of the lineup is to provide a fair identification task in which the suspect does not 'stand out' inappropriately from the other foils. Reducing the functional size of the lineup – particularly when the suspect is not the actual perpetrator – significantly increases the chance of a false identification (Lindsay & Wells, 1980; Tredoux, 2002). Thus, the selection of appropriate foils is critical for the production of a fair lineup and has been the focus of a good deal of debate. In the United Kingdom, police are required to select foils that resemble the suspect in what might be described as a 'match to suspect' strategy. In other words, foils are selected on the grounds that they match the appearance of the suspect (rather than the description of the perpetrator). This strategy is problematic as research has documented that foils who do not coincide with a witness's prior verbal description are likely to be disregarded, resulting in a biased lineup and an increased likelihood that an innocent suspect may be mistakenly identified (e.g., Clark & Tunnicliff, 2001). Thus, a 'match to description' strategy (i.e., where foils are selected based on their match to descriptions of the perpetrator provided by the witness) may be preferable (Luus & Wells, 1991). However, research by Darling, Valentine, and Memon (2008) did not identify any differences in either correct or incorrect identifications as a function of these lineup composition strategies. A recent meta-analysis by Fitzgerald, Price, Oriet, and Charman (2013) noted that lineups comprising a suspect and low similarity foils were more likely to elicit suspect identifications – irrespective of whether the suspect was guilty or innocent. Clearly, further research is necessary to identify specifically how alterations to the composition of a lineup affect choosing behaviour.

Investigator bias

Ideally, lineups should take place under double-blind administration where both the witness and lineup administrator are unaware of the identity of the suspect. Where the person conducting the lineup knows which lineup member is the suspect, there is a possibility that they will unintentionally transmit this knowledge to the witness (Harris & Rosenthal, 1985), resulting in increased rates of false identification (Phillips, McAuliff, Kovera, & Cutler, 1999). More recently, Greathouse and Kovera (2009) noted that administrators displayed more biasing behaviours (such as inviting the witness to 'take another look', providing overt cues as to the identity of the suspect, and exerting greater pressure on witnesses to choose) during single-blind administration procedures (i.e., when they knew the identity of the suspect) than under double-blind procedures. Research has also shown that witnesses may be unaware of the influence exerted by a lineup administrator (Clark, Marshall, & Rosenthal, 2009). Similarly, lineup administrators may be unaware of the influence they are exerting (Garrioch & Brimacombe, 2001; Greathouse & Kovera, 2009; see also Dysart, Lawson, & Rainey, 2012).

Lineup procedure: Comparing absolute and relative judgements

The lineup task has probably received greater research attention than any other topic relating to eyewitness testimony. In the traditional lineup (which may involve photographs or live participants, depending on the jurisdiction), the suspect and foils are presented simultaneously. Given witnesses, tendency to assume that the perpetrator will be present in the lineup, the opportunity to examine all lineup members at once can lead witnesses to compare the lineup members with each other and select the lineup member who best matches their original memory. This has been described as a relative judgement strategy (Wells, 1984; Wells & Seelau, 1995). An alternative method of lineup presentation, known as the sequential lineup, was proposed by Lindsay and Wells (1985). Unlike the traditional simultaneous lineup where all lineup members are viewed at once, in the sequential lineup method each lineup member is presented sequentially, one member at a time. The witness is required to make an absolute identification decision for each lineup member (Is this the perpetrator you saw? Yes or No) prior to seeing the next person in the lineup. In the optimal version of the lineup, the witness does not know how many faces will be presented and the lineup terminates when a choice is made, with witnesses not permitted to see any further photos, review previously presented photos or change their identification decision. It has been argued that this lineup method promotes an absolute identification decision as, unlike the simultaneous lineup, witnesses cannot engage in relative comparisons between lineup members but instead have to compare the face presented with their memory for the perpetrator. Many studies have demonstrated that the sequential lineup method significantly reduces false identifications (see Steblay, Dysart, & Wells, 2011 for a recent meta-analysis). However, this reduction in false identifications (from culprit-absent lineups) has been observed in conjunction with a loss of correct identifications (from culprit-present lineups). Steblay et al. (2011) estimated that, in comparison to the simultaneous procedure, the sequential lineup procedure resulted in 22%

fewer false identifications and 8% fewer correct identifications. As the loss of correct identifications is outweighed by the reduction in false identifications, there is an apparent overall gain in accuracy under the sequential procedure (Clark, Howell, & Davey, 2008; Goodsell, Gronlund, & Carlson, 2010; Steblay et al., 2011). The meaning and relevance of these 'lost' identifications has been the topic of robust debate in the field in recent years (e.g., see Clark, 2012b; Laudan, 2012; Newman & Loftus, 2012; Wells, Steblay, & Dysart, 2012; Wixted & Mickes, 2012).

This debate has also focused research attention on the need to determine the mechanisms underpinning witness decision-making in the identification task. One interesting question concerns whether the noteworthy reduction in false identifications under the sequential procedure (in comparison with the simultaneous procedure) is due to a difference in discriminability (i.e., the ability of a witness to discriminate the culprit from other members of the lineup) or, alternatively, a difference in response bias (i.e., decision tendency in respect of the lineup). Taking a signal detection modelling approach to data drawn from 22 studies comparing simultaneous and sequential lineup decisions, Palmer and Brewer (2012) noted that the sequential procedure did not appear to influence discriminability. Instead, witnesses making an identification under the sequential procedure appeared to adopt a more conservative decision criterion that resulted in less biased choosing for sequential lineups. In a similar vein, recent research adopting confidence-based receiver operating characteristic (ROC) analysis suggests that the sequential procedure is actually inferior to the simultaneous procedure with respect to discriminating whether the guilty culprit is present or absent (Mickes, Flowe, & Wixted, 2012). Clearly, further research is necessary to better understand the mechanisms driving choosing behaviour in order to develop accuracy-promoting lineup formats.

Post-identification feedback

Witness confidence is, perhaps, the most influential cue used by juries when evaluating the credibility and reliability of eyewitness testimony (Cutler, Penrod, & Dexter, 1990; Douglass, Neuschatz, Imrich, & Wilkinson, 2010; Lindsay, Wells, & Rumpel, 1981). However, mistaken eyewitnesses can be overconfident (Shaw & McClure, 1996; Wells & Bradfield, 1999), and eyewitness confidence can be highly malleable in the period after making an identification (Luus & Wells, 1994a, 1994b; Wells & Bradfield, 1998). In a classic study of the effect, Wells and Bradfield (1998) found that witnesses who were given positive feedback (e.g., 'Good, you identified the suspect') reported higher confidence and better viewing conditions than those who received no feedback (see meta-analysis by Douglass & Steblay, 2006). Conversely, witnesses given negative feedback were less confident and reported worse witnessing conditions. The effects of feedback have also been shown to occur for both target present and target absent lineups (Bradfield, Wells, & Olson, 2002), when there are long delays between identification and feedback (Wells, Olson, & Charman, 2002), and even extend to witness willingness to testify (Wells & Bradfield, 1998, 1999). Relevant for instances where an eyewitness might be required to view more than one lineup in the course of an investigation, post-identification feedback has also been shown to impair performance on subsequent lineup decisions (Palmer, Brewer, & Weber, 2010). Post-identification effects may be reduced (but not eliminated) by means of warnings (e.g., Lampinen, Scott, Leding, Pratt, & Arnal, 2007), while, more recently, Dysart et al. (2012) noted that blind lineup administration may also protect against the negative effect of post-identification feedback.

The effect of post-identification feedback also extends to the evaluation of the witness by others. Research by Douglass et al (2010) demonstrates that witnesses who received confirming post-identification feedback were evaluated as more accurate and confident by independent evaluators than witnesses who had received no feedback on their identification decision – irrespective of whether explicit statements regarding confidence had been included in their testimony. Clearly, the effects of post-identification feedback are far reaching and have serious implications for the reliability of eyewitness identifications. In light of these findings, identification policy and procedure should prohibit the provision of feedback to witnesses relating to their lineup decisions.

Is confidence related to accuracy?

Police, lawyers, judges and other legal practitioners, in addition to lay jurors, typically consider confidence as a useful indicator of likely eyewitness accuracy (Deffenbacher & Loftus, 1982; Noon & Hollin, 1987; Potter & Brewer, 1999). As we have seen, however, eyewitness confidence is malleable and susceptible to bias which can, in the worst-case scenario, produce highly confident mistaken identifications. But can witness confidence actually tell us anything useful about identification accuracy? Until relatively recently, researchers have tended to take the view that confidence is not reliably associated with accuracy and, in particular, is not a reliable predictor of accuracy given low or non-significant confidence–accuracy correlations (e.g., Bothwell, Brigham, & Deffenbacher, 1987; Sporer, Penrod, Read, & Cutler, 1995; see also Kassin et al., 2001). However, in an extensive programme of research focusing on confidence and adapting alternative analyses,

Brewer and his colleagues have challenged this conclusion (Brewer, 2006; Brewer & Wells, 2006; Sauer, Brewer, & Weber, 2008; Weber & Brewer, 2004). Using a calibration approach, these authors have documented substantial confidence–accuracy relations for lineup choosers (i.e., witnesses who make positive identifications) across various stimuli materials (for extended discussion of this method and the relationship between confidence and accuracy, see Brewer, 2006; Brewer et al., 2005). Research exploiting markers of eyewitness confidence in conjunction with other factors, such as deadline pressure (Brewer, Weber, Wootton, & Lindsay, 2012) or evaluating patterns of confidence judgements (Sauer et al., 2008) are likely to pave the way for the development of fruitful, theoretically informed approaches to eyewitness identification.

IDENTIFICATIONS FROM CCTV

Intuitively, one might expect that identification performance might improve significantly when the 'witness', be that the original witness, a CCTV operator or police officer reviewing the evidence, has access to a video recording of the (alleged) target and, possibly, still photographs of the suspect. With video footage of the incident available, the task would no longer rely so heavily on memory (or prior familiarity with the perpetrator) and would simply require the witness to engage in an apparently simple matching task. However, the identification of individuals from CCTV footage is not necessarily a simple identification task and, like other identification tasks, is prone to error – even under optimal conditions.

There are two quite distinct circumstances where an attempt may be made to identify a face from a video image (Bruce et al., 1999). In the first situation, a spontaneous identification may be made by a member of the public (or perhaps, a CCTV operator or police officer) who claims that the target appearing in the CCTV image is personally known to them. In the second situation, the target appearing in the CCTV footage is compared to an apprehended suspect to establish whether, in fact, the suspect was recorded at the scene of the incident under investigation. Identification accuracy varies under these circumstances with respect to whether the face is previously known or previously unknown to the witness.

In one of the early studies on spontaneous identifications based on prior exposure, Logie, Baddeley, and Woodhead (1987) examined the ability of the general public to identify a live target in a town centre from a previously presented photograph. The photograph had been published in a local newspaper. Despite circulating details of the precise location of the target, the spontaneous detection (i.e., identification) rate for the general public was very low and this was coupled with a high false recognition rate (i.e., false identifications of other 'innocent' passers-by).

These low recognition rates in dynamic interactions where the target face is continually available to the witness have been documented elsewhere. In a field study, Kemp, Towell, and Pike (1997) examined whether credit cards bearing a photograph of the cardholder might serve to reduce credit card fraud. Including a photograph of the legal cardholder on a credit card (or indeed, other identity document) would seem to be a relatively foolproof method of ensuring that the card is used only by the person entitled to use it. In their study, shoppers presented a credit card bearing a photograph of themselves to pay for half the transactions while for other transactions they presented a card bearing the photograph of another individual. Experienced checkout cashiers were required to either accept or decline the card depending on their verification of the cardholder's identity, and rate their confidence that the photograph appearing on the card was, in fact, that of the shopper. More than 50% of the fraudulent cards were accepted by the cashiers – despite the fact that cashiers were aware that a study was under way and indicated that they both spent longer examining cards and had been more cautious than usual.

High error rates in the ability to match a target from CCTV footage have also been documented. Typically, it has been assumed that difficulties in identifying faces from video recordings are largely due to the frequently poor-quality nature of the recording and that were high-quality recordings available such difficulties would be reduced. While it is true that many CCTV images may be of poor quality for a number of technical reasons (such as unsuitable lighting conditions, intermittent image sampling, etc.), the assumption that this alone underpins low accuracy rates in face matching from CCTV has been challenged by research findings.

Bruce and her colleagues (1999) examined how well people were able to match faces extracted from a high-quality video-recording against high-quality photographic images. The results revealed that overall accuracy was relatively poor (averaging only 70% across trials) even under these optimal conditions. Performance was further degraded when the target expression or viewpoint was altered. Furthermore, the use of colour target images (as opposed to black-and-white images) did not appear to lend any particular advantage (or disadvantage) to performance on the matching task. Thus, it would appear that our ability to identify an unfamiliar face – even in the presence of a reference image (such as a CCTV still or a photograph)

is surprisingly error-prone (Davies & Thasen, 2000; Henderson, Bruce, & Burton, 2001).

In contrast, identification accuracy for known or familiar faces can be very accurate – even when the target images are of poor quality. To examine the impact of familiarity on face recognition, Burton, Wilson, Cowan, and Bruce (1999) showed study participants surveillance video footage of a target that was known to some participants but not others. Results indicated a marked advantage for people who were personally familiar with the target – 73% of the poor-quality image targets were recognized *when they were familiar*. In a series of studies exploring the role of familiarity, Bruce, Henderson, Newman, and Burton (2001) found that participants were able to correctly verify (or reject) a familiar target with a high degree of accuracy (over 90%) despite the use of poor-quality video images. When participants were unfamiliar with the targets, the accuracy rate was significantly lower (56%). Subsequent experiments revealed that brief periods of exposure to the target do not necessarily generate sufficient familiarity to improve the recognition or matching of unfamiliar faces – unless some 'deep' or social processing has taken place (i.e., discussing the faces with another person). Simulating the experience of a jury required to determine whether the suspect present in the court is the same individual present in CCTV evidence, Davis and Valentine (2009) examined whether the same high rates of error present when matching a photograph of a stranger to CCTV footage would also occur when matching a physically present stranger to footage. Across three experiments, incorporating both culprit-present and culprit-absent videos, they noted high rates of error, even under conditions of high-quality CCTV footage.

Face recognition is of central importance to investigative police work (Scott-Brown & Cronin, 2007). CCTV has the benefit of providing investigators with a permanent record of an event and, importantly, who may have been involved in it. The availability of CCTV footage – and the speed at which it was analysed – facilitated the rapid identification of the 7/7 and 21/7 bombers from thousands of hours of recordings (Metropolitan Police, 2005). Furthermore, actual CCTV footage is generally considered powerful evidence in court (NACRO, 2002; Scott-Brown & Cronin, 2007; Thomas, 1993). However, relying on CCTV for the recognition and identification of suspects may foster a false sense of security and a potentially dangerous over-reliance on such evidence. We expect to be able to do this task with a high degree of accuracy. However, the research consistently demonstrates that people are poor at this task – even under optimal conditions.

Is eyewitness identification evidence reliable?

Experimental psychological research on eyewitness identification has flourished over the past 40 years, producing hundreds of articles and thousands of identification data-points. Given the size of the literature and the many different designs and research hypotheses deployed, it is often difficult to compare between studies and reach an overall conclusion with respect to our ability to identify correctly a previously seen individual. Correct identification rates often vary widely across experiments, for instance from as high as 80% to as low as 8%. To establish what the results of eyewitness experiments can tell us, Clark *et al.* (2008) conducted a meta-analysis of 94 comparisons between target present and target absent lineups. The most important conclusions to emerge from this analysis were as follows: 1. correct identifications (from target present lineups) and correct non-identifications (target absent lineups) were not correlated; 2. an identification of the suspect is diagnostic of the suspect's guilt but the identification may be less informative if any of the identification procedures are in any way biased (such as lineup composition); and 3. non-identifications were diagnostic of the suspect's innocence while 'don't know' responses were, unsurprisingly, non-diagnostic with respect to guilt or innocence. Based on these, Clark *et al.* (2008) suggest as a basic principle that 'a suspect identification has greater probative value to the extent that it is based on the witness's memory, and less probative value to the extent that it is due to lineup composition or an increase in the witness's conformity, willingness, or desire to make an identification' (p. 211). Thus, when assessing the reliability and likely accuracy of an identification, legal practitioners and juries alike need to consider the extent to which these factors might have played a role in the identification process (see also Brewer & Wells, 2011).

PROCEDURAL GUIDELINES RELATING TO SUSPECT IDENTIFICATION IN THE UNITED KINGDOM

In England and Wales, Code D of the Police and Criminal Evidence Act (PACE) 1984 sets out guidelines, or Codes of Practice, for the conduct of identification procedures by police officers. The main purpose of Code D is to prevent mistaken identifications and the Code sets broad provisions relating to the circumstances and manner in which identification procedures should be conducted and the hierarchy among those procedures. The Code embodies many of the recommendations of the Devlin Report (1976) which was prepared following a number of criminal cases in which biased identification procedures and erroneous witnesses led to the misidentification, and in several instances the wrongful conviction, of the suspect. One such case was that of Laszlo Virag who was convicted of stealing and using a firearm when attempting to escape from police officers in Liverpool in 1969. Despite an alibi and several other evidential contradictions, Virag was identified by eight witnesses as the man who committed the crime. One witness claimed that Virag's face was 'imprinted' on his brain while another had spent some time with him at a hotel bar, yet these identifications were incorrect. Subsequently, another individual confessed to the crime and Virag was pardoned. Cases such as this one led to the conclusion that eyewitness identification evidence could be unreliable and that convictions should not generally rely on such evidence alone.

Under PACE, the Code initially required that a live lineup, otherwise known as an identity parade, must be held when the suspect disputes an identification and holding the lineup is practicable. Unlike in the United States and other international jurisdictions, the presentation of still photographs is not a permitted identification procedure in England and Wales when a suspect has been detained. The Code stipulates the following key requirements for a live identification procedure: the lineup must contain at least eight foils (i.e., volunteers who are known to be innocent) in addition to the suspect and these foils should resemble the suspect in 'age, height, general appearance and position in life'. Unusual or distinctive features (scars, tattoos, etc.) which cannot be replicated across foils may be concealed by means of a plaster or hat so that all members of the lineup resemble each other in general appearance. The suspect may choose their own position in the lineup and their legal representative may also be present during the identification procedure. Importantly, witnesses must be informed that the perpetrator may or may not be present in the lineup, and if they cannot make a positive identification they should say so. Lineup members may be requested to comply with a witness's request to hear them speak, move or adopt a particular pose. Despite these provisions, analyses of archival identification data indicate that witnesses attending a formal police identification parade mistakenly identify a foil over one-fifth of the time. Slater (1994) reported that of 843 witnesses (302 lineups), 36% identified the suspect and 22% identified an innocent foil as the perpetrator while 42% made no positive identification decision. Similarly, Wright and McDaid (1996) reviewed identification decisions for 1,561 witnesses (616 lineups) where 39% of witnesses identified the suspect, 20% identified a foil and the remainder made no identification. A revision to the Code in 2005 made provision for the conduct of a video identification procedure. Specifically, the Code requires that the suspect be initially offered a video identification unless this procedure is not practicable or an identification parade would be 'more suitable'.

Video identification lineups present a video clip of the head and shoulders of each lineup member. Each film clip lasts approximately 15 seconds and follows the following movement sequence: firstly, the lineup member looks at the camera directly for a full-frontal shot of the face and shoulders, then they are required to slowly turn their head to first the left and then the right to present both profile views. Finally, a full-face view is presented once more. Video lineups must comprise at least eight foils who are drawn from over 20,000 foils available from the National Video Identification Database. The database is made up of video clips of volunteers drawn from the general public and, as with the live lineup, suitable foils are selected which resemble the suspect in 'age, height, general appearance and position in life'. In the United Kingdom, two main systems are used for producing video lineups: VIPER (Video Identity Parade Electronic Recording) and PROMAT (Profile Matching). For both systems, a single clip of the suspect performing the movement sequence described is prepared. The witness views at least nine clips presented sequentially on a screen, with each clip identified by a number. As in the earlier code for live lineups, witnesses receive unbiased lineup instructions stating that the perpetrator may not be present. Witnesses are also informed that they may see a particular part of the set of images again, or may have a particular image 'frozen'. There is no limit on the number of times they can view the whole set of images (or any part of the images). The Code also indicates that witnesses should be asked not to make an identification decision until they have viewed the whole set of images at least twice.

Video identification has a number of important advantages over live lineups. Research on actual VIPER video lineups has shown that the lineups produced using this system are fairer to suspects than live lineups (Valentine & Heaton, 1999). Valentine and his colleagues also found that VIPER lineups were fair for both white European and African Caribbean suspects (Valentine, Harris, Colom Piera, & Darling, 2003a). Of course, this is likely due to the availability of a large database of images from which to select foils. The availability of a database of foils has also reduced the delay typically involved in organizing a live identification parade – video lineups can typically be produced within two hours (Valentine et al., 2003b). Lineups are also far less likely to be cancelled (Pike, Kemp, Brace, Allen, & Rowlands, 2000). Finally, the use of video lineups is less threatening for victims, who are not required to be in the physical presence of their attacker at the identification suite. Furthermore, the video lineup can be taken to a victim who may be unable to attend the police station (Valentine, Darling, & Memon, 2006).

While research on photograph arrays suggests that sequential presentation can reduce mistaken identifications when an absolute decision on each lineup member is required (Lindsay & Wells, 1985), the video lineup instructions stipulated under Code D are incompatible with the strict sequential administration procedure discussed earlier in this chapter in that they require the witness to review the entire lineup image set at least twice before making a decision. However, research by Valentine, Darling, and Memon (2007) suggests that strict instructions did not result in a reliably reduced rate of mistaken identification when compared with the existing view-twice procedure used in the United Kingdom. With respect to the benefit of moving lineup images (over still lineup images), combined data from recent research suggests that moving images may yield fewer false identifications in perpetrator absent lineups (Valentine et al., 2007).

The Code also provides for two other forms of identification under certain circumstances: group identification and witness confrontation. Group identification occurs when the witness sees the suspect in an informal group of people and may take place overtly (with the suspect's cooperation) or covertly. In a witness confrontation, under the provision of the Code, the witness is shown the suspect, provided with unbiased instructions and asked 'Is this the person?' Compared with lineup identification procedures, the group identification and witness confrontation procedures may be more susceptible to bias (e.g., due to reduced functional size), thus caution should be exercised when evaluating the reliability of such identifications. The most recent revisions to the Code were made in 2011 (see https://www.gov.uk/government/publications/pace-code-a-2011).

THE EYEWITNESS IN COURT

The final stage of the eyewitness's role within the legal process takes place in court. Courts in many jurisdictions acknowledge that there is a risk that eyewitness evidence may be unreliable and jurors are typically instructed to scrutinize the circumstances under which the witness encountered the suspect (Memon, 2008). For instance, in England and Wales trial judges are required to 'protect against unsafe convictions in cases involving disputed identification' (Roberts & Ormerod, 2008, p. 74). The Turnbull guidelines (*R* v. *Turnbull*) stipulate that if a prosecution case is heavily based on eyewitness identification evidence, where the judge considers that evidence to be weak, of poor or questionable quality, the case must not proceed. When a case involving eyewitness identification evidence does proceed before a jury, the judge is required to provide both a general warning regarding the risks associated with eyewitness evidence and a more specific warning tailored to the nature of the potential weaknesses of the eyewitness evidence in that particular case.

The admissibility of expert testimony concerning eyewitness testimony remains a topic for some debate in legal circles (see Benton, Ross, Bradshaw, Thomas, & Bradshaw, 2006), In most adversarial systems, including North America and the United Kingdom, the judge decides whether expert testimony is admissible against certain criteria (Benton *et al.*, 2006; Kovera, Russano, & McAuliff, 2002; Desmarais & Read, 2011). The one criterion common across most jurisdictions concerns the extent to which issues pertaining to eyewitness memory are considered to be a matter of juror common sense. In the United Kingdom, this means that the jurors are usually expected to make a sound decision about the quality of eyewitness evidence unaided by testimony from an expert. The judicial conclusion that eyewitness memory is indeed a matter of common sense is one of the most frequently cited reasons for the rejection of eyewitness expert testimony (Benton *et al.*, 2006; Leippe, 1995; Yarmey, 2001), and legal experts are often in agreement (e.g., Benton *et al.*, 2006; Stuesser, 2005).

However, jurors are not particularly sensitive to potential eyewitness error – or responsive to judicial instructions on the matter (Kassin & Sommers, 1997). In fact, over a quarter of a century of research has demonstrated that lay understanding of eyewitness psychology is limited – and often mistaken (e.g., Benton *et al.*, 2006; Brigham & WolfsKeil, 1983; Deffenbacher & Loftus, 1982; McConkey & Roche, 1989; Noon & Hollin, 1987; for a meta-analytic review, see Desmarais & Read, 2011). Jurors tend to be unaware of the implications of biased procedures used by law enforcement, such as poorly constructed lineups, misleading feedback or biased instructions (Shaw, Garcia, & McClure, 1999). Potential jurors also find it difficult to distinguish between accurate and inaccurate witnesses (e.g., Lindsay, Wells, & O'Connor, 1989; Lindsay, Wells, & Rumpel, 1981). Legal professionals are also typically rather limited in their understanding of factors affecting eyewitness accuracy (Granhag, Strömwall, & Hartwig, 2005; Wise & Safer, 2004; Wise *et al.*, 2009; Wise & Safer, 2010). Even psychology professionals have limited knowledge of issues pertaining to eyewitness memory (Magnussen & Melinder, 2012). Furthermore, convictions which originally relied heavily on eyewitness testimony, but are now known to have been in error, illustrate quite clearly that jurors are often unable to either generate or apply the common sense expected of them by the courts.

CONCLUSIONS

Eyewitnesses serve an important function in the delivery of justice and can, under the right circumstances, correctly confirm the identity of a criminal. However, caution needs to be exercised with respect to identifications as the leading cause of mistaken convictions is erroneous eyewitness testimony. In particular, consideration must be paid to the conditions under which the witness encoded the perpetrator, the presence of any intervening misleading information, the nature and fairness of the identification procedures and whether the witness received feedback – unwittingly or otherwise.

FURTHER READING

Brewer, N., Weber, N., & Semmler, C. (2005). Eyewitness identification. In N. Brewer & K. D. Williams (Eds.), *Psychology and law: An empirical perspective* (pp. 177–221). New York: Guilford Press.
An excellent and thoughtful overview of key issues in eyewitness research, Specifically, this chapter examines the various stages of the identification process that occur in the real world, from features of the event which may impede the witness to the impact of exposure to inaccurate post-event information and, finally, the identification task. Brewer and his colleagues also critically examine other factors which research suggests may be diagnostic of identification accuracy (e.g., confidence and latency). Throughout the chapter, the authors highlight several important methodological shortcomings which beset the extant research literature, such as underpowered experiments, a limited stimulus set and inadequate lineup conditions. Not only does this chapter provide a comprehensive review of the eyewitness literature and consider some of the problematic methodological issues faced by researchers but, importantly, it also focuses on the need to further develop our theoretical understanding of eyewitness identification behaviour.

Valentine, T., & Heaton, P. (1999). An evaluation of the fairness of police lineups and video identifications. *Applied Cognitive Psychology*, *13*, S59–S72.

Valentine's work evaluating the fairness of VIPER lineups makes an important contribution to our understanding of current UK identification procedures. In this initial study of video identifications, Valentine and Heaton compared the 'fairness' (in terms of non-biased lineup selections) of photo versus video identification stimuli. In a fair lineup the suspect should be chosen, by chance, by 11% of the mock witnesses (i.e., each lineup member should have an equal chance of being selected if the actual perpetrator is not present and correctly identified). However, in this study, 25% of mock witnesses selected the suspect from the photographs of live lineups while only 15% of mock witnesses selected the suspect from video lineups. The authors concluded that the video lineups were fairer than the live lineups. Given that mistaken eyewitness identifications are a significant source of miscarriages of justice, Valentine and Heaton argue that the more widespread use of video identification may actually improve the reliability of identification evidence.

Weber, N., & Brewer, N. (2004). Confidence–accuracy calibration in absolute and relative face recognition judgments. *Journal of Experimental Psychology: Applied*, *10*, 156–172.

This paper introduces an important new conceptual and analytical approach to eyewitness confidence which continues to show promise in determining the likely diagnosticity of eyewitness identification decisions. Confidence–accuracy calibration was analysed for both absolute and relative face recognition judgements. The most interesting finding is that recognition judgements for 'old' (i.e., previously viewed) stimuli demonstrated a strong confidence–accuracy calibration. In other words, there was an association between accuracy and the level of confidence expressed. This finding suggests that there was a meaningful relationship between subjective and objective probabilities of judgement accuracy for previously seen items. However, for 'new' judgements there was little or no association between confidence and accuracy using the calibration approach. See also: Brewer, N. (2006). Uses and abuses of eyewitness identification confidence. *Legal and Criminological Psychology*, 11, 3–23.

Wells, G. L., Memon, A., & Penrod, S. (2006). Eyewitness evidence. Improving its probative value. *Psychological Science in the Public Interest*, *7*, 45–75.

A thorough review of the eyewitness literature and its role within the legal system. In this article, both estimator and system variables are examined and, in particular, the authors focus on how procedures based on scientific research findings can be developed to improve the probative value of eyewitness evidence. Other important questions are addressed, including the frequently occurring tension in applied research between scientific rigour and external validity when moving from the laboratory to real-world contexts. Specifically, the authors consider issues of base rates, multicollinearity, selection effects, subject populations and psychological realism and note how a combination of critical theory and field data can work together to improve the generalizability of eyewitness research.

REFERENCES

Anderson, J. R. (1983). A spreading activation theory of memory. *Journal of Verbal Learning and Verbal Behavior*, *22*, 261–295.

Ayers, M. S., & Reder, L. M. (1998). A theoretical review of the misinformation effect: Predictions from an activation-based memory model. *Psychonomic Bulletin and Review*, *5*, 1–21.

Badham, S. P., Wade, K. A., Watts, H. J. E., Woods, N. G., & Maylor, E. A. (2013). Replicating distinctive facial features in lineups: Identification performance in young versus older adults. *Psychonomic Bulletin and Review*, *20*, 289–295.

Benton, T. R., Ross, D. F., Bradshaw, E., Thomas, W. N., & Bradshaw, G. S. (2006). Eyewitness memory is still not common sense: Comparing jurors, judges and law enforcement to eyewitness experts. *Applied Cognitive Psychology*, *20*, 115–129.

Bornstein, B. H., Deffenbacher, K. A., Penrod, S. D., & McGorty, E. K. (2012). Effects of exposure time and cognitive operations on facial identification accuracy: A meta-analysis of two variables associated with initial memory strength. *Psychology, Crime and Law*, *18*, 473–490.

Bothwell, R. K., Brigham, J. C., & Deffenbacher, K. A. (1987). Correlation of eyewitnesses accuracy and confidence: Optimality hypothesis revisited. *Journal of Applied Psychology*, *72*, 691–695.

Boyce, M., Beaudry, J. L., & Lindsay, R. C. L. (2007). Belief of eyewitness identification evidence. In R. C. L. Lindsay, D. F. Ross, J. D. Read, & M. P. Toglia (Vol. Eds.), *The handbook of eyewitness psychology: Vol. 2. Memory for people* (pp. 501–529). Mahwah, NJ: Lawrence Erlbaum.

Bradfield, A. L., Wells, G. L., & Olson, E. A. (2002). The damaging effect of confirming feedback on the relation between eyewitness certainty and identification accuracy. *Journal of Applied Psychology*, *87*, 112–120.

Brewer, N. (2006). Uses and abuses of eyewitness identification confidence. *Legal and criminological psychology*, *11*, 3–21.

Brewer, N., Weber, N., & Semmler, C. (2005). Eyewitness identification. In N. Brewer & K. D. Williams (Eds.), *Psychology and law: An empirical perspective* (pp. 177–221). New York: Guilford Press.

Brewer, N., Weber, N., Wootton, D., & Lindsay, D. S. (2012). Identifying the bad guy in a lineup using confidence judgments under deadline pressure. *Psychological Science*, *23*, 1208–1214.

Brewer, N., & Wells, G. L. (2006). The confidence–accuracy relationship in eyewitness identification: Effects of lineup instructions, foil similarity and target-absent base rates. *Journal of Experimental Psychology: Applied*, *12*, 11–30.

Brewer, N., & Wells, G. L. (2011). Eyewitness identification. *Current Directions in Psychological Science, 20,* 24–27.

Brigham, J. C., & Cairns, D. L. (1988). The effect of mug shot inspections on eyewitness identification accuracy. *Journal of Applied Social Psychology, 18,* 1394–1410.

Brigham, J. C., & WolfsKeil, M. P. (1983). Opinions of attorney's and law enforcement personnel on the accuracy of eyewitness identifications. *Law and Human Behavior, 7,* 337–349.

Bruce, V., Henderson, Z., Greenwood, K., Hancock, P., Burton, A. M., & Miller, P. (1999). Verification of face identities from images captured on video. *Journal of Experimental Psychology: Applied, 5,* 339–360.

Bruce, V., Henderson, Z., Newman, C., & Burton, A. M. (2001). Matching identities of familiar and unfamiliar faces caught on CCTV images. *Journal of Experimental Psychology: Applied, 7,* 207–218.

Burton, A. M, Wilson, S., Cowan, M., & Bruce, V. (1999). Face recognition in poor quality video: Evidence from security surveillance. *Psychological Science, 10,* 243–248.

Chiroro, P., & Valentine, T. (1995). An investigation of the contact hypothesis of the own race bias in face recognition. *Quarterly Journal of Experimental Psychology A: Human Experimental Psychology, 48A,* 897–894.

Clark, S. E. (2005). A re-examination of the effects of biased lineup instructions in eyewitness identification. *Law and Human Behaviour, 29,* 395–424.

Clark, S. E. (2012a). Costs and benefits of eyewitness identification reform: Psychological science and public policy. *Perspectives on Psychological Science, 7,* 238–259.

Clark, S. E. (2012b). Eyewitness identification reform: Data, theory, and due process, *Perspectives on Psychological Science, 7,* 279–283.

Clark, S. E., Howell, R. T., & Davey, S. L. (2008). Regularities in eyewitness identification. *Law and Human Behavior, 32,* 187–218.

Clark, S. E., Marshall, T. E., & Rosenthal, R. (2009). Lineup administrator influences on eyewitness identification decisions. *Journal of Experimental Psychology: Applied, 15,* 63–75.

Clark, S. E., & Tunnicliff, J. L. (2001). Selecting lineup foils in eyewitness identification: Experimental control and real-world simulation. *Law and Human Behavior, 25,* 199–216.

Coupe, T., & Griffiths, M. (1996). *Solving residential burglary.* Crime Detection and Prevention Series No. 77. London: Home Office.

Craik, F. I. M., & Byrd, M. (1982). Aging and cognitive deficits: The role of attentional resources. In F. I. M. Craik, & S. Trehub (Eds.), *Aging and cognitive processes* (pp. 191–211). New York: Plenum.

Cutler, B. L., & Penrod, S. D. (1995). *Mistaken identifications: The eyewitness, psychology, and the law.* New York: Cambridge University Press.

Cutler, B. L., Penrod, S. D., & Dexter, H. R. (1990). Juror sensitivity to eyewitness identification evidence. *Law and Human Behavior, 14,* 185–192.

Cutler, B. L., Penrod, S. D., & Martens, T. K. (1987). The reliability of eyewitness identification: The role of system and estimator variables. *Law and Human Behavior, 11,* 233–258.

Darling, S., Valentine, T., & Memon, A. (2008). Selection of lineup foils in operational contexts. *Applied Cognitive Psychology, 22,* 159–169.

Davies, G., & Thasen, S. (2000). Closed circuit television: How effective an identification aid? *British Journal of Psychology, 91,* 411–426.

Davis, J. P., & Valentine, T. (2009). CCTV on trial: Matching video images with the defendant in the dock. *Applied Cognitive Psychology, 23,* 482–505.

Deffenbacher, K. A. (1994). Effects of arousal on everyday memory. *Human Performance, 7,* 141–161.

Deffenbacher, K. A., Bornstein, B. H., Penrod, S. D., & McGorty, E. K. (2004). A meta-analytic review of the effects of high stress on eyewitness memory. *Law and Human Behavior, 28,* 687–706.

Deffenbacher, K. A., & Loftus, E. F. (1982). Do jurors share a common understanding concerning eyewitness behavior? *Law and Human Behavior, 6,* 15–30.

Desmarais, S. L., & Read, J. D. (2011). After 30 years, what do we know about what jurors know? A meta-analytic review of lay knowledge regarding eyewitness factors. *Law and Human Behavior, 35,* 200–210.

Devlin Committee Report: *Report of the Committee on Evidence of Identification in Criminal Cases,* 1976. Cmnd 338 134/135, 42.

Dodson, C. S., & Krueger, L. E. (2006). I misremember it well: Why older adults are unreliable eyewitnesses. *Psychonomic Bulletin and Review, 13,* 770–775.

Douglass, A. B., Neuschatz, J. S., Imrich, J., & Wilkinson, M. (2010). Does post-identification feedback affect evaluations of eyewitness testimony and identification procedures? *Law and Human Behavior, 34,* 282–294.

Douglass, A. B., & Steblay, N. (2006). Memory distortion in eyewitnesses: A meta-analysis of the post-identification feedback effect. *Applied Cognitive Psychology, 20,* 859–869.

Dysart, J. E., Lawson, V. Z., & Rainey, A. (2012). Blind lineup administration as a prophylactic against the postidentification feedback effect. *Law and Human Behavior, 36,* 312–319.

Dysart, J. E., Lindsay, R. C. L., Hammond, R., & DuPuis, P. R. (2001). Mug shot exposure prior to lineup identification: Interference, transference, and commitment effects. *Journal of Applied Psychology, 86,* 1280–1284.

Dysart, J. E., Lindsay, R. C. L., MacDonald, T. K., & Wicke, C. (2002). The intoxicated witness: Effects of alcohol on identification accuracy from show-ups. *Journal of Applied Psychology, 87,* 170–175.

Ebbinghaus, H. (1885). *Memory: A contribution to experimental psychology*. Leipzig: Duncker and Humblot.

Ellis, H. D., Shepherd, J. W., & Davies, G. M. (1980). The deterioration of verbal descriptions of faces over different delay intervals. *Journal of Police Science and Administration, 8*, 101–106.

Fawcett, J. M., Russell, E. J., Peace, K. A., & Christie, J. (2013). Of guns and geese: a meta-analytic review of the 'weapon focus' literature. *Psychology, Crime and Law, 19*, 35–66.

Fitzgerald, R. J., Price, H. L., Oriet, C., & Charman, S. D. (2013). The effect of suspect-filler similarity on eyewitness identification decisions: A meta-analysis. *Psychology, Public Policy & Law, 19*, 151–164.

Frenda, S. J., Nichols, R. M., & Loftus, E. F. (2011). Current issues and advances in misinformation research. *Current Directions in Psychological Sciences 20*, 20–23.

Gabbert, F., Brewer, N., & Hope, L. (2007, July). *Effects of co-witness confidence on identification decisions*. Seventh Biennial Conference of the Society for Applied Research in Memory and Cognition, Lewiston.

Gabbert, F., Hope, L., & Fisher, R. (2009). Protecting eyewitness evidence: Examining the efficacy of a self-administered interview tool. *Law and Human Behavior, 33*(4), 298–307.

Gabbert, F., Memon, A., & Allan, K. (2003). Memory conformity: Can eyewitnesses influence each other's memories for an event? *Applied Cognitive Psychology, 17*, 533–543.

Gabbert, F., Memon, A., Allan, K., & Wright, D. B. (2004). Say it to my face: Examining the effects of socially encountered misinformation. *Legal and Criminological Psychology, 9*, 215–227.

Gabbert, F., Memon, A., & Wright, D. B. (2006). Memory conformity: Disentangling the steps towards influence during a discussion. *Psychonomic Bulletin and Review, 13*, 480–485.

Garrioch, L., & Brimacombe, C. A. (2001). Lineup administrators' expectations: Their impact on eyewitness confidence. *Law and Human Behavior, 25*, 299–314

Goodsell, C. A., Gronlund, S. D., & Carlson, C. A. (2010). Exploring the sequential lineup advantage using WITNESS. *Law and Human Behavior, 34*, 445–459.

Goodsell, C. A., Neuschatz, J. S., & Gronlund, S. D. (2009). Effects of mugshot commitment on lineup performance in young and older adults. *Applied Cognitive Psychology, 23*, 788–803.

Gorenstein, G. W., & Ellsworth, P. C. (1980). Effect of choosing an incorrect photograph on a later identification by an eyewitness. *Journal of Applied Psychology, 65*, 616–622.

Granhag, P. A., Strömwall, L. A., & Hartwig, M. (2005). Eyewitness testimony: Tracing the beliefs of Swedish legal professionals. *Behavioral Sciences and the Law, 23*, 709–727.

Greathouse, S. M., & Kovera, M. B. (2009). Instruction bias and lineup presentation moderate the effects of administrator knowledge on eyewitness identification. *Law and Human Behavior, 33*, 70–82.

Harris, M. J., & Rosenthal, R. (1985). Mediation of interpersonal expectancy effects: 31 meta-analyses. *Psychological Bulletin, 97*, 363–386.

Havard, C., Memon, A., Laybourn, P., & Cunningham, C. (2012). Own-age bias in video lineups: a comparison between children and adults. *Psychology, Crime and Law, 18*, 929–944.

Henderson, Z., Bruce, V., & Burton, A. M. (2001). Matching the faces of robbers captured on video. *Applied Cognitive Psychology, 15*, 445–464.

Hilliar, K. F., Kemp R. I., & Denson, T. F. (2010). Now everyone looks the same: Alcohol intoxication reduces the own-race bias in face recognition. *Law and Human Behavior, 34*, 367–378.

Hope, L., Lewinski, W., Dixon, J., Blocksidge, D., & Gabbert, F. (2012). Witnesses in action: The effect of physical exertion on recall and recognition. *Psychological Science, 23*, 386–390.

Hope, L., Ost, J., Gabbert, F., Healey, S., & Lenton, E. (2008). 'With a little help from my friends …': The role of co-witness relationship in susceptibility to misinformation. *Acta Psychologica, 127*, 476–484.

Hope, L., & Wright, D. (2007). Beyond unusual? Examining the role of attention in the weapon focus effect. *Applied Cognitive Psychology, 21*, 951–961.

Hosch, H. M., & Platz, S. J. (1984). Self-monitoring and eyewitness identification. *Personality and Social Psychology Bulletin, 10*, 289–292.

Howie, P., & Roebers, C. M. (2007). Developmental progression in the confidence–accuracy relationship in event recall: Insights provided by a calibration perspective. *Applied Cognitive Psychology, 21*, 871–893.

Huff, C. R., Rattner, A., & Sagarin, E. (1996). *Convicted but innocent: Wrongful conviction and public policy*. Thousand Oaks, CA: Sage.

Innocence Project. (2012). *Innocence blog: Wrongful convictions affect all New Yorkers*. Retrieved from http://www.innocenceproject.org/Content/Wrongful_convictions_affect_all_New_Yorkers.php, retrieved 6 January 2015.

Jacoby, L. L. (1999). Ironic effects of repetition: Measuring age-related differences in memory. *Journal of Experimental Psychology: Learning, Memory, and Cognition, 25*, 3–22.

Kassin, S. M., & Sommers, S. R. (1997). Inadmissible testimony, instructions to disregard, and the jury: Substantive versus procedural considerations. *Personality and Social Psychology Bulletin, 23*, 1046–1054.

Kassin, S. M., Tubb, V. A., Hosch, H. M., & Memon, A. (2001). On the 'general acceptance' of eyewitness memory research. *American Psychologist, 56*, 405–416.

Keast, A., Brewer, N., & Wells, G. L. (2007). Children's metacognitive judgments in an eyewitness identification task. *Journal of Experimental Child Psychology, 97*, 286–314.

Kebbell, M. R., & Milne, R. (1998). Police officers' perceptions of eyewitness performance in forensic investigations. *Journal of Social Psychology, 138*, 323–330.

Kemp, R., Towell, N., & Pike, G. (1997). When seeing should not be believing: Photographs, credit cards and fraud. *Applied Cognitive Psychology, 11*, 211–222.

Klorman, R., Weissberg, R. P., & Wiesenfeld, A. R. (1977). Individual differences in fear and autonomic reactions to affective stimuli. *Psychophysiology, 14*, 45–51.

Kovera, M. B., Russano, M. B., & McAuliff, B. D. (2002). Assessment of the commonsense psychology underlying Daubert – legal decision makers' abilities to evaluate expert evidence in hostile work environment cases. *Psychology Public Policy and Law, 8*, 180–200.

Lampinen, J. M., Scott, J., Leding, J. K., Pratt, D., & Arnal, J. D. (2007). 'Good, you identified the suspect … but please ignore this feedback': Can warnings eliminate the effects of post-identification feedback? *Applied Cognitive Psychology, 21*(8), 1037–1056.

Laudan, L. (2012). Eyewitness identifications: One more lesson on the costs of excluding relevant evidence. *Perspectives on Psychological Science, 7*, 272–274.

Lavrakas, P. J., Buri, J. R., & Mayzner, M. S. (1976). A perspective of the recognition of other race faces. *Perception and Psychophysics, 20*, 475–481.

Leippe, M. R. (1995). The case for expert testimony about eyewitness memory. *Psychology Public Policy and Law, 1*, 909–959.

Levett, L. M. (2013). Co-witness information influences whether a witness is likely to choose from a lineup. *Legal and Criminological Psychology, 18*, 168–180.

Lindsay, R. C. L., Semmler, C., Weber, N., Brewer, N., & Lindsay, M. R. (2008). How variations in distance affect eyewitness reports and identification accuracy. *Law and Human Behavior, 32*, 526–535.

Lindsay, R. C. L., & Wells, G. L. (1980). What price justice? Exploring the relationship between lineup fairness and identification accuracy. *Law and Human Behavior, 4*, 303–314.

Lindsay, R. C. L., & Wells, G. L. (1985). Improving eyewitness identifications from lineups: Simultaneous versus sequential lineup presentation. *Journal of Applied Psychology, 70*(3), 556–564.

Lindsay, R. C. L., Wells, G. L., & O'Connor, F. (1989). Mock juror belief of accurate and inaccurate eyewitnesses: A replication. *Law and Human Behavior, 13*, 333–340.

Lindsay, R. C. L., Wells, G. L., & Rumpel, C. M. (1981). Can people detect eyewitness-identification accuracy within and across situations? *Journal of Applied Psychology, 66*, 79–89.

Loftus, E. F. (1980). *Memory*. Reading, MA: Addison-Wesley.

Loftus, E. F. (2005). Planting misinformation in the human mind: A 30-year investigation of the malleability of memory. *Learning and Memory, 12*, 361–366.

Loftus, E. F., Loftus, G. R., & Messo, J. (1987). Some facts about 'weapon focus'. *Law and Human Behavior, 11*, 55–62.

Loftus, E. F., Miller, D. G., & Burns, H. J. (1978). Semantic integration of verbal information into a visual memory. *Journal of Experimental Psychology: Human Learning and Memory, 4*, 19–31.

Loftus, E. F., & Palmer, J. C. (1974). Reconstruction of auto-mobile destruction: An example of the interaction between language and memory. *Journal of Verbal Learning and Verbal Behaviour, 13*, 585–589.

Logie, R. H., Baddeley, A. D., & Woodhead, M. M. (1987). Face recognition, pose and ecological validity. *Applied Cognitive Psychology, 1*, 53–69.

Luus, C. A. E., & Wells, G. L. (1991). Eyewitness identification and the selection of distracters for lineups. *Law and Human Behavior, 15*(1), 43–57.

Luus, C. A. E., & Wells, G. L. (1994a). The malleability of eyewitness confidence: Co-witness and perseverance effects. *Journal of Applied Psychology, 79*(5), 714–723.

Luus, C. A. E., & Wells, G. L. (1994b). Determinants of eyewitness confidence. In D. F. Ross, J. D. Read, & M. P. Toglia (Eds.), *Adult eyewitness testimony: Current trends and developments* (pp. 348–362). New York: Cambridge University Press.

Maas, A., & Kohnken, G. (1989). Eyewitness identification: Simulating the 'weapon effect'. *Law and Human Behavior, 13*, 397–408.

Macleod, C., & Mathews, A. (1991). Biased cognitive operations in anxiety – accessibility of information or assignment of processing priorities. *Behavior Research and Therapy, 29*, 599–610.

Magnussen, S., & Melinder, A. (2012). What psychologists know and believe about memory: A survey of practitioners. *Applied Cognitive Psychology, 26*, 54–60.

Mandler, G. (1980). Recognizing: The judgment of previous occurrence. *Psychological Review, 87*, 252–271.

Mansour, J. K., Beaudry, J. L., Bertrand, M. I., Kalmet, N., Melsom, E. I., & Lindsay, R. C. L. (2012). Impact of disguise on identification decisions and confidence with simultaneous and sequential lineups. *Law and Human Behavior, 26*, 513–536.

McClelland, J. L., & Chappell, M. (1998). Familiarity breeds differentiation: A subjective-likelihood approach to the effects of experience in recognition memory. *Psychological Review, 105*, 724–760.

McCloskey, M., & Zaragoza, M. (1985). Misleading postevent information and memory for events – Arguments and evidence against memory impairment hypotheses. *Journal of Experimental Psychology – General, 114*, 1–16.

McConkey, K. M., & Roche, S. M. (1989). Knowledge of eyewitness memory. *Australian Psychologist, 24*, 377–384.

Meissner, C. A. (2002). Applied aspects of the instructional bias effect in verbal overshadowing. *Applied Cognitive Psychology, 16*, 911–928.

Meissner, C. A., & Brigham, J. C. (2001). A meta-analysis of the verbal overshadowing effect in face identification. *Applied Cognitive Psychology, 15*, 603–616.

Memon, A. (2008). Eye witness research: Theory and practice. In D. V. Canter & R. Žukauskiene (Eds.), *Psychology and law*. Aldershot: Ashgate.

Memon, A., Hope, L., Bartlett, J., & Bull, R. (2002). Eyewitness recognition errors: The effects of mugshot viewing and choosing in young and old adults. *Memory and Cognition, 30*, 1219–1227.

Memon, A., Hope, L., & Bull, R. H. C. (2003a). Exposure duration: Effects on eyewitness accuracy and confidence. *British Journal of Psychology, 94*, 339–354.

Memon, A., Vrij, A., & Bull, R. (2003b). *Psychology and law: Truthfulness, accuracy and credibility of victims, witnesses and suspects* (2nd edn). Chichester: Wiley.

Metropolitan Police (2005). Police investigation continues into the 7/7 bombings. *Metropolitan Police Bulletin 222*, 18 July 2005.

Mickes, L., Flowe, H. D., & Wixted, J. T. (2012). Receiver operating characteristic analysis of eyewitness memory: Comparing the diagnostic accuracy of simultaneous versus sequential lineups. *Journal of Experimental Psychology: Applied, 18*, 361–376.

Morgan, C. A., Hazlett, G., Doran, A., Garrett, S., Hoyt, G., Thomas, P. et al. (2004). Accuracy of eyewitness memory for persons encountered during exposure to highly intense stress. *International Journal of Law and Psychiatry, 27*, 265–279.

Morgan, C. A., Southwick, S., Steffian, G., Hazlett, G. A., & Loftus, E. F. (2013). Misinformation can influence memory for recently experienced highly stressful events. *International Journal of Law and Psychiatry, 36*, 11–17.

NACRO (2002). *To CCTV or not to CCTV? A review of current research into the effectiveness of CCTV systems in reducing crime.* Publication Number 2002062800. London: Author.

Narby, D. J., Cutler, B. L., & Penrod, S. D. (1996). The effects of witness, target, and situational factors on eyewitness identifications. In S. L. Sporer, R. S. Malpass, & G. Koehnken (Eds.), *Psychological issues in eyewitness identification* (pp. 23–52). Mahwah, NJ: Lawrence Erlbaum.

Newman, E. J., & Loftus, E. F. (2012). Clarkian logic on trial. *Perspectives on Psychological Science, 7*, 260–263.

Noon, E., & Hollin, C. R. (1987). Lay knowledge of eyewitness behaviour: A British survey. *Applied Cognitive Psychology, 1*, 143–153.

O'Rourke, T. E., Penrod, S. D., Cutler, B. L., & Stuve, T. E. (1989). The external validity of eyewitness identification research: Generalizing across subject populations. *Law and Human Behavior, 13*, 385–395.

Overbeck, J. L. (2005). Beyond admissibility: A practical look at the use of eyewitness expert testimony in the Federal courts. *New York University Law Review, 80*(6), 1895–1920.

Palmer, M. A., Brewer, N., & Weber, N. (2010). Postidentification feedback affects subsequent eyewitness identification performance. *Journal of Experimental Psychology: Applied, 16*, 387–398.

Palmer, M. A., & Brewer, N. (2012). Sequential lineup presentation promotes less-biased criterion setting but does not improve discriminability. *Law and Human Behavior, 36*, 247–255.

Paterson, H. M., & Kemp, R. I. (2006). Co-witnesses talk: A survey of eyewitness discussion. *Psychology Crime and Law, 12*, 181–191.

Pezdek, K., O'Brien, M., & Wasson, C. (2012). Cross-Race (but not same-race) face identification is impaired by presenting faces in a group rather than individually. *Law and Human Behavior, 36*, 488–495.

Phillips, M. R., McAuliff, B. D., Kovera, M. B., & Cutler, B. L. (1999). Double-blind photoarray administration as a safeguard against investigator bias. *Journal of Applied Psychology, 84*, 940–951.

Pickel, K. L., French, T. A., & Betts, J. M. (2003). A cross-modal weapon focus effect: The influence of a weapon's presence on memory for auditory information. *Memory, 11*, 277–292.

Pike, G., Kemp, R., Brace, N., Allen, J., & Rowlands, G. (2000). The effectiveness of video identification parades. *Proceedings of the British Psychological Society, 8*, 44.

Potter, R., & Brewer, N. (1999). Perceptions of witness behaviour–accuracy relationships held by police, lawyers and jurors. *Psychiatry, Psychology and Law, 6*, 97–103.

Pozzulo, J. D., & Dempsey, J. (2006). Biased lineup instructions: Examining the effect of pressure on children's and adults' eyewitness identification accuracy. *Journal of Applied Social Psychology, 36*, 1381–1394.

Pozzulo, J. D., & Lindsay, R. C. L. (1998). Identification accuracy of children versus adults: A meta-analysis. *Law and Human Behavior, 22*, 549–570.

Read, J. D. (1995). The availability heuristic in person identification – the sometimes misleading consequences of enhanced contextual information. *Applied Cognitive Psychology, 9*, 91–121.

Read, J. D., Vokey, J. R., & Hammersley, R. (1990). Changing photos of faces: Effects of exposure duration and photo similarity on recognition and the accuracy–confidence relationship. *Journal of Experimental Psychology: Learning, Memory and Cognition, 16*, 870–882.

Rhodes, M. G., & Anastasi, J. S. (2012). The own-age bias in face recognition: A meta-analytic and theoretical review. *Psychological Bulletin, 138*, 146–174.

Roberts, A., & Ormerod, D. (2008). Identification in court. In D. Canter & R. Zukauskien (Eds.) *Bridging the gap between psychology and law: International perspectives*. Aldershot: Ashgate.

Rubin, D. C., & Wenzel, A. E. (1996). One hundred years of forgetting: A quantitative description of retention. *Psychological Review, 103*, 743–760.

Ryu, J. J., & Chaudhuri, A. (2007). Differences in attentional involvement underlying the perception of distinctive and typical faces. *Perception, 36*, 1057–1065.

Salthouse, T. A. (1982). *Adult cognition: An experimental psychology of human aging*. New York: Springer-Verlag.

Sauer, J. D., Brewer, N., & Weber, N. (2008). Multiple confidence estimates as indices of eyewitness memory. *Journal of Experimental Psychology: General, 137*, 528–547.

Scheck, B., Neufeld, P., & Dwyer, J. (2000). *Actual innocence*. New York: Doubleday.

Scott-Brown, K. C., & Cronin, P. D. (2007). An instinct for detection: Psychological perspectives on CCTV surveillance. *The Police Journal, 80*, 287–305.

Shapiro, P. N., & Penrod, S. (1986). Meta-analysis of facial identification studies. *Psychological Bulletin, 100*, 139–156.

Shaw, J. S., III, & McClure K. A. (1996). Repeated postevent questioning can lead to elevated levels of eyewitness confidence. *Law and Human Behavior, 20*, 629–654.

Shaw, J. S., III, Garcia, L. A., & McClure, K. A. (1999). A lay perspective on the accuracy of eyewitness testimony. *Journal of Applied Social Psychology, 29*, 52–71.

Slater, A. (1994). *Identification parades: A scientific evaluation*. London: Police Research Group. Home Office.

Sokolov, E. N. (1963). *Perception and the conditioned reflex*. Oxford: Pergamon Press.

Sporer, S. L. (1992). *Das Wiedererkennen von Gesichtern* [Recognizing faces]. Weinheim: Beltz/Psychologie Verlags Union.

Sporer, S. L., Penrod, S., Read, D., & Cutler, B. (1995). Choosing, confidence, and accuracy: A meta-analysis of the confidence–accuracy relation in eyewitness identification studies. *Psychological Bulletin, 118*, 315–327.

Steblay, N. M. (1992). A meta-analytic review of the weapon focus effect. *Law and Human Behavior, 16*, 413–424.

Steblay, N. (1997). Social influence in eyewitness recall: A meta-analytic review of lineup instruction effects. *Law and Human Behavior, 21*, 283–297.

Steblay, N. K., Dysart, J. E., & Wells, G. L. (2011). Seventy-two tests of the sequential lineup superiority effect: A meta-analysis and policy discussion. *Psychology, Public Policy and Law, 17*, 99–139.

Stuesser, L. (2005). Experts on eyewitness identification: I don't just see it. *International Commentary on Evidence, 3*(1), Article 2.

Thomas, M. (1993). *Every mother's nightmare: The killing of James Bulger*. London: Pan.

Thompson, W. B., & Johnson, J. (2008). Biased lineup instructions and face identification from video images. *Journal of General Psychology, 135*, 23–36.

Tredoux, C. G. (2002). A direct measure of facial similarity and its relation to human similarity perceptions. *Journal of Experimental Psychology: Applied, 8*(3), 180–193.

Tuckey, M. R., & Brewer, N. (2003). The influence of schemas, stimulus ambiguity, and interview schedule on eyewitness memory over time. *Journal of Experimental Psychology: Applied, 9*, 101–118.

Valentine, T., Darling, S., & Memon, A. (2006). How can psychological science enhance the effectiveness of identification procedures? An international comparison. *Public Interest Law Reporter, 11*, 21–39.

Valentine, T, Darling, S., & Memon, A. (2007). Do strict rules and moving images increase the reliability of sequential identification procedures? *Applied Cognitive Psychology, 21*, 933–949.

Valentine, T., Harris, N., Colom Piera, A., & Darling, S. (2003a). Are police video identifications fair to African-Caribbean suspects? *Applied Cognitive Psychology, 17*, 459–476.

Valentine, T., & Heaton, P. (1999). An evaluation of the fairness of police line-ups and video identifications. *Applied Cognitive Psychology, 13*, S59–S72.

Valentine, T., & Mesout, J. (2008). Eyewitness identification under stress in the London Dungeon. *Applied Cognitive Psychology, 23*(2), 151–161.

Valentine, T., Pickering, A., & Darling, S. (2003b). Characteristics of eyewitness identification that predict the outcome of real lineups. *Applied Cognitive Psychology, 17*, 969–993.

Wagenaar, W. A., & van der Schrier, J. H. (1996). Face recognition as a function of distance and illumination: A practical tool for use in the courtroom. *Psychology, Crime and Law, 2*, 321–332.

Weber, N., & Brewer, N. (2004). Confidence–accuracy calibration in absolute and relative face recognition judgments. *Journal of Experimental Psychology: Applied, 10*, 156–172.

Wells, G. L. (1978). Applied eyewitness-testimony research: System variables and estimator variables. *Journal of Personality and Social Psychology, 36,* 1546–1557.

Wells, G. L. (1984). The psychology of lineup identifications. *Journal of Applied Social Psychology, 14,* 89–103.

Wells, G. L., & Bradfield, A. L. (1998). 'Good, you identified the suspect': Feedback to eyewitnesses distorts their reports of the witnessing experience. *Journal of Applied Psychology, 83,* 360–376.

Wells, G. L., & Bradfield, A. L. (1999). Measuring the goodness of lineups: Parameter estimation, question effects, and limits to the mock witness paradigm. *Journal of Applied Psychology, 13,* S27–S39.

Wells, G. L., Charman, S. D., & Olson, E. A. (2005). Building face composites can harm lineup identification performance. *Journal of Experimental Psychology: Applied, 11,* 147–157.

Wells, G. L., & Hasel, L. E. (2007). Facial composite production by eyewitnesses. *Current Directions in Psychological Science, 16,* 6–16.

Wells, G. L., Leippe, M. R., & Ostrom, T. M. (1979). Guidelines for empirically assessing the fairness of a lineup. *Law and Human Behavior, 3,* 285–293.

Wells, G. L., & Loftus, E. F. (2013). Eyewitness Memory for People and Events). In R. K. Otto and & I. B. Weiner (Eds.), *Handbook of Psychology,* Vol. 11 (Forensic Psychology). Hoboken, NJ: John Wiley & Sons.

Wells, G. L., & Olson, E. (2003). Eyewitness identification. *Annual Review of Psychology, 54,* 277–295.

Wells, G. L., Olson, E., & Charman, S. (2002). Eyewitness identification confidence. *Current Directions in Psychological Science, 11,* 151–154.

Wells, G. L., & Quinlivan, D. S. (2008). Suggestive eyewitness identification procedures and the Supreme Court's reliability test in light of eyewitness science: 30 years later. *Law and Human Behavior, 33*(1), 1–24.

Wells, G. L., & Seelau, E. P. (1995). Eyewitness identification: Psychological research and legal policy on lineups. *Psychology, Public Policy, and Law, 1,* 765–791.

Wells, G. L., Steblay, N. K., & Dysart, J. E. (2012). Eyewitness identification reforms: Are suggestiveness-induced hits and guesses true hits? *Perspectives on Psychological Science, 7,* 264–271.

Wise, R. A., Pawlenko, N. B., Safer, M. A., & Meyer, D. (2009). What US prosecutors and defence attorneys know and believe about eyewitness testimony. *Applied Cognitive Psychology, 23,* 1266–1281.

Wise, R. A., & Safer, M. A. (2004). What US judges know and believe about eyewitness testimony. *Applied Cognitive Psychology, 18,* 427–443.

Wise, R. A., & Safer, M. A. (2010). A comparison of what US judges and students know and believe about eyewitness testimony. *Journal of Applied Social Psychology, 40,* 1400–1422.

Wixted, J. T., & Mickes, L. (2012). The field of eyewitness memory should abandon probative value and embrace receiver operating characteristic analysis. *Perspectives on Psychological Science, 7,* 275–278.

Wright, D. B. (2006). Causal and associative hypothesis in psychology: Examples from eyewitness testimony research. *Psychology, Public Policy and Law, 12,* 190–213.

Wright, D. B., Boyd, C. E., & Tredoux, C. G. (2001). A field study of own-race bias in South Africa and England. *Psychology, Public Policy, and Law, 7,* 119–132.

Wright, D. B., & McDaid, A. T. (1996). Comparing system and estimator variables using data from real line-ups. *Applied Cognitive Psychology, 10,* 75–84.

Wright, D. B., Self, G., & Justice, C. (2000). Memory conformity: Exploring misinformation effects when presented by another person. *British Journal of Psychology, 91,* 189–202.

Wright, D. B., & Skagerberg, E. M. (2007). Post-identification feedback affects real eyewitnesses. *Psychological Science, 18,* 172–178.

Wright, D. B., & Sladden, B. (2003). An own gender bias and the importance of hair in face recognition. *Acta Psychologica, 114,* 101–114.

Wright, D. B., & Stroud, J. N. (2002). Age differences in lineup identification accuracy: People are better with their own age. *Law and Human Behavior, 26,* 641–654.

Yarmey, A. D. (2001). Expert testimony: Does eyewitness memory research have probative value for the courts? *Canadian Psychology–Psychologie Canadienne, 42,* 92–100.

Yuille, J. C., & Cutshall, J. L. (1986). A case study of eyewitness memory of a crime. *Journal of Applied Psychology, 71,* 291–301.

5 Jury Decision-Making

ANDREAS KAPARDIS

INTRODUCTION: THE JURY IDEA

The origins of the jury system, of trial by one's peers, are lost in the mist of time. Generally speaking, considering jury systems around the world today (see Kaplan & Martin, 2006), we can distinguish between mixed juries in continental Europe and the jury found in Western, English-speaking, common law countries, namely the United Kingdom, United States, Australia, New Zealand and Canada. The latter can be traced to the following clause in the Magna Carta,[1] which dates back to 1215:

> No freeman shall be seized, or imprisoned, or disposed or outlawed, or in any way destroyed; nor will we condemn him, nor will we commit him to prison, excepting by the lawful judgement of his peers, or by the law of the land. (Clause 39, Magna Carta, 1215)

The idea of a jury of 12 (it is 15 in Scotland) has been an essential feature of English common law and was passed onto the Anglo-Saxons by the Vikings. Unanimous verdicts were introduced in England in 1367 and abolished in 1978. In the United States, the decision in *Johnson v. Louisiana* 32 L.Ed.2d 152 (1972) introduced majority verdicts in non-capital felony cases, and in *Burch v. Louisiana* 441 US 130 (1979) it was stated that 6 person juries must be unanimous. Today, for those living in the European Union, it is comforting to know that Article 6(1) of the European Charter of Human Rights provides for trial by an independent and impartial tribunal. Furthermore, according to the European Court of Human Rights, the fact that the jury give no reasons for their decision to convict is not incompatible with Article 6 of the Charter.[2]

Regarding jury eligibility, since 2003,[3] persons involved in law enforcement and the administration of justice such as police officers and Crown Prosecution Service members as well as Members of Parliament and medical professionals are eligible for jury service, making juries more representative than in the past. In England, the qualification for jury service has ranged from (1) being a freeholder in the early days, to a householder in the nineteenth century; (2) since the Juries Act of 1974, being at least 18 and no more than 70 years of age; (3) on the electoral register for parliamentary or local government elections, one must have been ordinarily resident in Britain for at least 5 years since attaining the age of 13; and, (4) finally, is not a mentally disordered person, and is not otherwise disqualified from jury service. The size of the jury varies between different countries and often depends on whether it is a civil or a criminal trial. Parliament in England has introduced a number of safeguards[4] against corrupt and biased jurors, including[5]: majority verdicts; jury vetting; drawing members of the jury from the panel subject to juror challenges; the sanction of a criminal offence for a disqualified person to serve on the jury; part of the evidence may be heard in camera in cases in which national security is involved and in terrorist cases; and the appropriate court officer and the judge have the responsibility for ensuring that an individual does not serve on the jury if they are not competent to discharge properly the duties of a juror.

Forensic Psychology, Second Edition. Edited by David A. Crighton and Graham J. Towl.
© 2015 John Wiley & Sons, Ltd. Published 2015 by British Psychological Society and John Wiley & Sons, Ltd.

THE NOTION OF AN IMPARTIAL AND FAIR JURY: A CRITICAL APPRAISAL

Those common law and civil law countries that have a jury system differ regarding various aspects of their jury system. Such differences between jurisdictions mean that one should not unquestionably generalize findings about juror decision-making across jurisdictions. Of course, the methods by which people eligible for jury service are summoned, and the criteria used to excuse some of them, affect their representativeness (Airs & Shaw, 1999).

The very concept of the jury itself is problematic (Darbyshire, 1991). The view that it is desirable to be tried by one's 'peers' is based on the argument that: (a) it is good to be tried by a group of individuals who are representative of one's community; and (b) that 'representativeness' makes for impartial, objective, just and fair jury verdicts. Marshall (1975) pointed out that 'the right to trial by an impartial jury' is not an ideal that can be achieved because trial by one's 'peers', 'representativeness' and 'impartiality' do not go together and, even if they did, they would not guarantee that a jury's verdict would be a fair one. The US Supreme Court provided[6] a definition of a constitutionally impartial juror as someone 'who will conscientiously apply the law and find the facts' (Cammack, 1995, p. 458). Finally, the Supreme Court stated[7] clearly that the constitutional requirement of juror impartiality is to be achieved by means of peremptory challenges (p. 447) but these are not to be exercised on the basis of the juror's sex[8] or race[9] because doing so violates the Equal Protection Clause of the Fourteenth Amendment (p. 406).

The well-known English judge Lord Denning (1982, p. 77) argued for a new way of selecting jurors in England on the basis that the ordinary man is no longer suitable to sit on a jury. He also argued that there should be a qualification for service as a juror so that a jury would be 'composed of sensible and responsible members of the community. It should be representative of the best of them of whatever sex or colour and of whatever age or occupation. ... Those on the jury list should be selected in much the same way as magistrates are now'. He also proposed that people could apply or be recommended to go on the jury list, should need to provide references and, finally, be interviewed for suitability. Lord Denning's radical proposal for jury reform seems to have gone largely unheeded.

Before examining empirical studies of juror and jury decision-making, let us first consider some of the arguments put forward against and in favour of the jury (see Kapardis, 2003, pp. 135–176 for more such arguments).

Arguments against jury trials

- In England, Scotland, Australia and New Zealand, the right to trial by jury is not enshrined in their respective constitutions.
- Trial by jury is not the cornerstone of the criminal justice system.
- Juries are not representative of the wider community.
- In some jurisdictions, jury trial has declined drastically.
- A jury does not give reasons and is not accountable for its verdict.
- Jury deliberation is secret.
- No precedent is established by a jury's verdict.
- Juries are unpredictable.
- In a significant number of trials, there is a hung jury. Trials by a judge are speedier and less costly.
- A jury can be interfered with.
- Jury verdicts are influenced by non-legal factors.
- Jurors often lack the ability to understand and judge a legal case adequately.
- Juries acquit too readily.
- Perverse jury verdicts are not uncommon.
- Any form of voir dire is incompatible with both randomness and representativeness.
- In many jurisdictions, there is no longer a need for perverse jury verdicts to counter the death penalty.
- Jury verdicts are not significantly different from a judge deciding alone.
- The jury's function is not for amateurs but for professionals.

Arguments in favour of jury trials

- The jury is an antidote to tyranny.
- Twelve heads are better than one.
- Unlike an experienced judge, a jury brings a fresh perception to each trial.
- Jurors' common sense and experience compensates for their lack of professional knowledge and training.
- Undesirable idiosyncrasies of individual jurors are minimized by jury deliberations.
- Jurors are suitable to decide complex legal cases.

- Unlike a judge, a jury can choose to ignore strict and unfair legal rules and return a verdict that reflects its own social and ethical standards.
- A significant proportion of people who have served on juries have confidence in the jury system and are satisfied with the experience.

The arguments in favour and against the jury listed in the preceding text make it clear that there are two contrasting views of what the function of the jury ought to be, but no amount of juror/jury research will resolve the jury controversy, and, in the end, value judgements remain to be made. What is certain is that the jury trial on both sides of the Atlantic and in the Antipodes will undergo further reforms (see the following text) but its very existence is not seriously threatened.

Since the Chicago Jury Project of the 1950s (Kalven & Zeisel, 1966), the jury has been a very popular research topic for psychologists, especially in the United States. Some mock juror researchers have claimed since the 1970s that they can predict juror verdict preference with such accuracy as to be able to talk about 'scientific jury selection', raising serious ethical issues irrespective of whether their claim is valid or not (Brigham, 2006).

METHODS FOR STUDYING JURIES/JURORS

We need to understand the strengths and weaknesses of different research methodologies in order to be able to interpret the validity and usefulness of psycho-legal research (Kerr & Bray, 2005, p. 328). Let us next take a look at six methods used to study juror/jury decision-making.

Archival research

Two limitations of archival research are that important information of interest to a researcher may well be missing, and it is not possible to draw causal inferences on the basis of such data.

Questionnaire surveys

The best-known jury questionnaire survey is Chicago Law School's Kalven and Zeisel's (1966) pioneering study 'The American Jury'. They sent a questionnaire to 3,500 judges in the United States, of whom 15.8% cooperated, providing data on 3,576 trials. This frequently cited study, which provided the basis for a great deal of the subsequent jury/juror research, however, suffers a number of

very serious limitations (Law Reform Commission of Victoria [LRCV], 1985; Pennington & Hastie, 1990; Stephenson, 1992). To illustrate, the sample of cases surveyed comprised 3% out of the total number of jury trials (60,000) during the 2-year period in question in the 1950s; half of the 3,576 cases were provided by only 15% of the judges; the researchers' changed their questionnaire midway after obtaining data for two-thirds of the cases and lumped the findings from both questionnaires together, thus undermining the reliability and validity of their survey (LRCV, 1985, p. 82). Furthermore, it was judges and not jurors themselves who were asked to assess the jurors' competence in understanding the content of a trial and the quality of the judge–juror communication.

Kalven and Zeisel (1966) found that: (a) the judge agreed with the jury's verdict in 75% of the cases; (b) most jurors decided on their verdict before they retired to deliberate; and, finally, (c) the majority view prevailed. Stephenson (1992, pp. 180–182) analysed the figures on judge–jury agreement provided by the Chicago researchers and showed convincingly that the conclusion that jurors' verdicts are not significantly different from what trial judges themselves would decide is not justified. British researchers have also reported questionnaire surveys (McCabe & Purves, 1972b; Zander, 1974; Baldwin & McConville, 1979; Zander & Henderson, 1994), as have researchers in New Zealand (Young, 2003, 2004; Ogloff, Clough, Goodman-Delahunty, & Young, 2006).

Contrary to what the majority of mock jury researchers have reported (see the following text), Baldwin and McConville (1979, p. 104) found no relationship between the social composition of juries in terms of age, social class, gender and race and their verdicts, indicating that real jury verdicts are perhaps largely unpredictable (see also Dunstan, Paulin & Atkinson, 1995, p. 55).

Mock juries

Mock juror/jury studies have been the most commonly used method (Nietzel, McCarthy, & Kery, 1999), especially in the United States, and have attracted a great deal of criticism. In the literature review by Devine, Clayton, Dunford, and Seying (2001), two-thirds of the 206 studies involved mock juries. Experimental simulation allows one to (a) investigate a number of significant variables while controlling for extraneous influences, and (b) have direct access to the deliberation process. However, the external validity of a great deal of experimental simulation juror research has repeatedly been questioned seriously (see Kerr & Bray, 2005, for a detailed discussion of the issue). As McEwan (2000) points out, since we cannot interview real jurors, 'laboratory experiments and mock trials appear to be the best alternative psychologists can adopt' but 'It would be dangerous to make too much of their findings' (p. 111).

Mock juror/jury studies have reported a significant amount of experimental evidence suggesting that characteristics of both the defendant and the jurors impact on jury decisions about verdict and (in the United States) severity of sentence (see Levett, Danielsen, Kovera, & Cutler, 2005, for a review). Since the early 1980s, the quality of mock jury studies has improved in terms of its sensitivity to the social and legal context of jury decision-making, methodological subtlety and legal sophistication (Hans, 1992, p. 60). On the basis of their in-depth and critical evaluation of the experimental jury research, Kerr and Bray (2005) have argued convincingly that authors of unrealistic jury simulations should qualify their findings and should refrain from putting them forward as the basis for policy changes (p. 358).

Shadow juries

This is the closest one can get to simulating a real jury. McCabe and Purves (1974) studied 30 'shadow juries' (recruited utilizing the electoral roll) sitting in on actual trials. Their deliberations were recorded and transcribed, and shadow jurors were interviewed subsequently. It was found that the verdicts of the real and shadow jury were very similar indeed. While field studies of jury behaviour are more realistic than experimental ones, their findings are difficult to interpret due to possible confounding variables.

Post-trial juror interviews

Post-trial interviews have been used, for example, to ascertain jurors' experience and understanding of judges' instructions (see Bowers, 1995; Costanzo and Costanzo, 1994; Horan, 2004; Ryan, 2003; Tinsley, 2001),[10] and judges' communicating with jurors (Ogloff *et al.*, 2006; Young, 2003, 2004). Despite their limitations, post-trial juror interviews can yield very significant findings. Lengthy face-to-face interviews with capital jurors carried out by university students have been the chief source of data in the national Capital Jury Project (CJP) in the United States,[11] yielding significant findings.

Books by ex-jurors

Some jurors have published their experiences (see Barber & Gordon, 1976; Zerman, 1977; Burnett, 2001). The major limitation of such books is that they are about the experience of one or a few individuals in isolated cases. Nevertheless, such books can still provide an insight into the jury experience.

SELECTING JURORS

As already mentioned, the scope for selecting jurors is very limited in Great Britain, Australia and New Zealand, and there is no voir dire equivalent to that in the United States.[12]

Lawyers and trial consultants in the United States use one or more of three approaches to select jurors (Brigham, 2006, pp. 18–19): (a) focusing on general attitudes or personality characteristics such as legal authoritarianism; (b) case-specific attitudes; and (c) supplemental jurors questionnaires. If the evidence against the defendant is weak, such 'jury packing' can make the difference to the verdict. The whole voir dire process is predicated on the debatable assumption that jurors give honest answers (Seltzer, Venuti, & Lopes, 1991). The question, therefore, arises of whether 'scientific', systematic jury selection is as possible and successful in influencing trial outcome, as some psychologists and jury selection experts claim. As a number of juror/jury decision-making literature reviews testify (Brigham, 2006; Devine *et al.*, 2001; Levett *et al.*, 2005), the use of the term 'scientific jury selection' conveys an impression of accuracy and precision not justified by existing knowledge and methods.

A lot of juror research has concerned itself with how individual jurors in serious criminal cases behave before they retire to deliberate (see Hastie, 1993b, and the following text). This focus stems from a belief that: (a) most jurors have decided on a verdict before they retire to deliberate; and (b) that the pre-deliberation distribution of individual juror's verdict preferences is the best predictor of the final jury verdict (Kalven & Zeisel, 1966; McCabe & Purves, 1974). However, it is the strength of the evidence against the defendant that impacts on the trial result. Mock jurors' personality, physical attractiveness, attitudes and so forth correlate significantly with trial outcome if the evidence against the defendant is weak (Reskin & Visher, 1986). In other words, individual differences among mock jurors are not very good predictors of jury decision-making (Ellsworth, 1993, p. 42; Wrightsman, Greene, Nietzel, & Fortune, 2002). Close examination of jury literature shows that: (a) some enduring characteristics of jurors (e.g., authoritarianism) are useful in understanding the jury verdict (see the following text); and (b) that it is the interaction of juror and case characteristics that should be the focus of the jury researcher since neither set of variables can be said to be operating alone. In the absence of sufficient such research, a certain amount of scepticism is therefore warranted when considering research findings on the relationship between juror characteristics and verdict.

PRE-TRIAL PUBLICITY

Different kinds of prejudice can influence a juror (see Vidmar, 2002, for details). It is the courts' role to ensure a fair trial by, inter alia, enforcing legal restrictions on pre-trial publicity. In the United States, fundamental fairness in prosecuting federal crimes is provided in Article III of the Constitution, the Sixth Amendment, the Due Process Clause of the Fifth Amendment, and the Federal Rules of Civil Procedure (FRCP). In fact, Rule 21 (a) of the FRCP provides for the trial to be held elsewhere to protect an accused from prejudice. Recognizing the real threat posed by prejudicial publicity, restrictions have been imposed on trial publicity by the courts in Britain by the Contempt of Court Act, 1981. This restriction is supported by the weight of the evidence in the empirical literature (see Steblay, Besirevic, Fulero, & Jimenez-Lorente, 1999, meta-analysis of 44 studies), showing that case-specific pre-trial publicity in both civil and criminal cases impacts adversely on prosecution verdicts (i.e., makes a guilty verdict significantly more likely) by potential jurors who are presented with negative pre-trial information about the defendant (Bornstein, Wisehunt, Nemeth, & Dunaway, 2002; Honess, Charman, & Levi, 2003; Hope, Memon, & McGeorge, 2004). As far as the impact of pre-trial publicity on actual jurors is concerned, post-trial interviews of judges, lawyers, and ex-jurors in criminal cases during 1997–2000 by Chesterman, Chan, and Hampton (2001) in New South Wales, Australia, found that 8% of the verdicts were believed to have been influenced more by publicity than by the evidence. Their finding, however, should be treated with caution due to serious methodological flaws of the study (Goodman-Delahunty & Tait, 2006, p. 58). Finally, Vidmar's (2002) research indicates that pre-trial publicity will not impact on jurors with polarized attitudes towards a particular crime or defendant.

Thomas (2010) reported a survey of media reporting and of Internet use with 668 jurors who served on 62 trials in London, Nottingham and Winchester. She found that, in high-profile cases, almost three-quarters of the jurors were aware of media coverage of their cases (p. vii), and, of those, 20% found it difficult to put those reports out of their mind while serving as jurors. Thomas also found that all jurors who looked for information about their cases during the trial looked on the Internet – something they should have been told by the judge not to do (p. viii). In fact, in high-profile cases, 26% said they saw information on the Internet, and twice as many admitted looking for such information on the Internet. Thomas' findings raise questions such as whether jurors realize they are not supposed to use the Internet, whether they also discuss the case on social networking sites and what a judge could do to prevent Internet misuse.

The reported importance of juror characteristics

A number of studies[13] have reported that mock jurors are less likely to find a defendant guilty if he/she is similar to them in terms of beliefs, ethnicity or background. However, if a defendant who is similar to mock jurors is said to have acted in such a way as to bring shame on those similar to him, they are more likely to treat him more harshly (Kerr, Hymes, Anderson, & Weathers, 1995). Concerning the importance of jurors' gender, while women are minimized on juries in England and Wales (Lloyd-Bostock & Thomas, 1999), a follow-up study of jurors in Florida by Moran and Comfort (1982) found no gender differences as far as predeliberation verdict or verdict is concerned. However, the weight of the research evidence shows that female jurors are more likely to convict a defendant charged with rape or child sexual abuse, especially if there had been no eye-contact between the rape victim and the offender during the attack (see Kapardis, 2003). Interestingly, Brekke and Borgida (1988) reported that juror deliberation narrows such gender verdict differences. The large jury simulation study by Thomas (2010) at Crown Courts in England and Wales found that female jurors were more open to persuasion to change their vote during deliberations than male jurors (who rarely changed their mind about the guilt of a defendant). Concerning a juror's *age*, as one might have expected, younger jurors have been found to be more likely to acquit (Hans & Vidmar, 1986). Conflicting findings have been reported concerning the importance of having jurors of a higher educational standard (Hans & Vidmar, 1986; Mills & Bohannon, 1980).

As far as race is concerned, a number of authors (e.g., Zander & Henderson, 1993; Lloyd-Bostock & Thomas, 1999) have drawn attention to the fact that, in England, non-whites/ethnic minorities are under-represented on juries. The US Supreme Court has stated that peremptory challenges (i.e., rejecting a juror during voir dire without giving the court any reason) on the basis of a juror's race are unconstitutional. Baldwin and McConville (1979) found that the racial composition of a jury was not important in explaining the verdict. It was the race of the defendant that emerged as significant – even when a jury was predominantly black, a black defendant was more likely to feature among perverse convictions than acquittals. The meta-analysis of 37 studies by Mazzella and Feingold (1994) found that, perhaps due to jurors' stereotypes, African-Americans were given harsher sentences for negligent homicide, in contrast to whites who were given harsher penalties for economic crimes such as fraud and embezzlement. Evidence for juror prejudice and racial discrimination has also been reported in Canada (Avio, 1988; Bagby, Parker, Rector, & Kalemba, 1994). Devine *et al.*'s literature review (2001) of the racial composition of the jury concluded that 'Jury-defendant bias has thus been observed across a number of studies and contexts and appears to be a robust phenomenon'. Kemmelmeier (2005) maintains that race is a significant factor but primarily in white mock jurors' decision-making. This is supported by a jury simulation study with 68 real 12-member juries at three Crown Courts in England and Wales by Thomas (2010), which found that while all-white juries did not discriminate against black, minority, ethnic (BME) defendants, all-white juries at Nottingham Crown Court had particular difficulty reaching a verdict involving a BME defendant or BME victim, suggesting that local population dynamics may influence jury decision-making. Interestingly, analysis of jury verdicts by Thomas (2010) in all the Crown Courts in England and Wales 2006–2008 showed that there were no significant differences between jury verdicts as a function of a defendant's ethnicity.

According to social psychologists, people scoring high on an authoritarianism scale think in terms of absolutes, are intolerant of others who are different, are hostile towards deviants in society, are pro-death penalty and, finally, accept and do not question the authority of officials (including judges) and institutions. Narby, Cutler, and Moran's (1993) meta-analysis of 20 studies distinguished between 'legal' and 'traditional' authoritarianism and concluded that the latter was a better predictor of verdict preference and that high authoritarians are more likely than low authoritarians to convict and impose harsh sanctions. The same conclusion was reached by Devine *et al.* (2001) on the basis of their literature review. Finally, there is evidence that high-authoritarian mock jurors decide on their verdicts early in the trial (Boehm, 1968). A juror's previous jury experience correlates with a greater likelihood of a guilty verdict (Dillehay & Nietzel, 1985) and severer sentences in both criminal and civil trials (Himelein, Nietzel, & Dillehay, 1991).

According to Brigham (2006), approximately three-quarters of the states and the federal government in the United States authorize the death penalty. Utilizing an in-depth standard protocol to interview ex-jurors in capital cases in 14 states that have the most variation in death penalty sentencing, the Capital Jury Project[14] (CJP) has been an attempt by a consortium of university-based research studies (founded in 1991) to improve on mock jury research with student subjects and to resolve the debate concerning arbitrary or racist death penalties in the United States. By October 2007, a total of 1,198 jurors from 353 capital juries in the 14 states had been interviewed. CJP researchers have found that a defendant's race is a significant factor in understanding jury decisions; more specifically, if the defendant is white, the jury is more likely to assess him as mentally unstable (a mitigating factor) than if he were black. In turn, this mitigating factor influences a jury's penalty decision, resulting in a sentence that is less harsh than the death penalty.

While conflicting views have been expressed about whether death-qualified juries are necessarily conviction prone,[15] the American Psychological Association's (APA's) amicus brief, submitted on behalf of the defendant McCree in *Lockhart v. McCree* 106 S.Ct. 1758 (1986), concluded, on the basis of existing experimental evidence, that such juries are conviction prone. On the basis of data from 916 actual jurors from 257 capital juries in 11 states, Bowers (1995) concluded that a juror's attitude to the death penalty is crucial in understanding how he/she processes trial information and behaves when the jury retires to deliberate. More specifically, jurors with pro-death penalty attitudes were more likely to make up their minds about the defendant's guilt and the appropriateness of the death penalty very early in the trial process and, consequently, were significantly more likely to want to impose the death penalty even when the jury was deliberating whether to find the defendant guilty or innocent.

JUROR COMPETENCE

Comprehending evidence

In support of Heuer and Penrod's (1994b) finding with real jurors, there is overwhelming evidence from mock juror studies (Cutler, Penrod, & Dexter, 1990; Horowitz, ForsterLee, & Brolly, 1996) that as case-complexity increases, juror comprehension of the evidence decreases, and that mock jurors find it difficult to discount a defendant's confession made under pressure (i.e., involuntary) when instructed to do so and proceed to convict (Kassin & Sukel, 1997). Mixed results have been reported by mock jury studies concerning whether jurors are able to ignore inadmissible evidence when instructed to do so by the judge (London & Nunez, 2000). The finding reported by Zander and Henderson (1993) that most of the jurors in their national Crown Court study had been able to understand and remember the evidence is questionable because they did not actually test for jurors' competence. Thomas (2010) analysed data from 797 jurors in her simulated study at three courts and found that 31% actually understood the judge's legal directions to them but such comprehension of directions declined as the age of the juror increased (p. vi). Juror comprehension improved significantly if jurors were given a written summary of the judge's legal directions. Rather alarming in this context is the finding from the Capital Jury Project that, while capital jurors could remember well details about the defendant, they admitted to having hardly understood and could barely recall the legal rules relevant to their decision to impose the death penalty (Luginbuhl & Howe, 1995; Sarat, 1995). The available evidence[16] (Kovera, McAuliff, & Hebert, 1999; McAuliff & Kovera, 2003) shows that some jurors are not able to evaluate scientific evidence proffered by an expert but do so better if judicial instructions to the jury are revised to make them more comprehensible (Grosscup & Penrod, 2002[17]).

Understanding and following the judge's instructions/the jury charge

Inadequacies of the judicial instructions/charges to the jury are grounds for appeal. Drawing on Ogloff and Rose (2005), studies in Canada have reported jury verdict reversal rates by appellate courts ranging from 34% to 74%. In support of Nietzel et al.'s (1999) meta-analysis of 48 published studies, Ogloff and Rose concluded, on the basis of their extensive literature review, that, whatever the method used, 'jurors appear largely incapable of understanding judicial instructions as they are traditionally delivered by the judge' (p. 425).

Suggestions to ameliorate this problem have included rewriting and standardizing judges' instructions to juries (Hans, 1992), allowing jurors to take notes in order to assist their memory of important trial details (see Horowitz & ForsterLee, 2001; Heuer & Penrod, 1994a) and to ask questions during the trial in order to clarify issues (Hollin, 1989) and, finally, to facilitate juror compliance with judicial instruction by presenting that instruction early in the evidence processing task (Goodman-Delahunty & Tait, 2006, p. 64).

The US Supreme Court in Gregg stated a requirement that capital jurors must decide guilt and punishment separately. However, Sandys (1995, p. 1221) found in interviews with 67 capital jurors in Kentucky that they made the decision concurrently, before the penalty stage of the trial, thus rendering irrelevant any subsequent evaluation of information about the defendant's mitigating and aggravating factors in order to decide on the right sentence. Such findings are a cause for concern and call for effective juror guidance by the judge.

The jury foreperson

The juror characteristics that predict foreperson election are: male sex, high socio-economic status, sitting at the end of the jury table and initiating discussion (Baldwin and McConville, 1980, pp. 40–41).[18] The foreperson can, of course, influence the deliberation result by directing discussion, timing poll votes and influencing whether poll votes will be public or secret (see the following text).

The Spanish mock jury study by Arce, Fariña, Novo, and Seijo (1999) reported that in hung juries the foreperson (a) failed to control the deliberation in order to guide it to evaluate the evidence; (b) did not avoid destructive interventions, (c) failed to be persuasive; and (d) did not inspire either authority or respect (p. 269). Similarly, the New Zealand study of post-deliberation interviews of jurors found that if the foreperson was weak in performing his/her role and the deliberation process was unstructured, some jurors would dominate the deliberation and some would feel intimidated by them (Tinsley, 2001). In the light of their findings, Arce et al. (1999) recommended that the foreperson should be trained in order to perform his/her role effectively. A follow-up survey of judicial practices in New Zealand reported that as a result of the juror survey, more judges provided guidance to jurors as far as selection of a foreperson is concerned (Ogloff et al., 2006).

Jury deliberation

What we know today about jury deliberation is from mock and shadow jury studies as well as from a small number of post-trial surveys of real jurors. None of the researchers in this area has observed real juries at their task. Most of the mock research into jury decision-making (see Devine et al., 2001; Levett et al., 2005; Memon, Vrij, & Bull, 2003, for reviews[19]) focuses on juror behaviour at the pre-deliberation stage in the belief (that can be traced back to Kalven and Zeisel's 'liberation hypothesis') that most jurors have already decided on a verdict before they retire to deliberate and that first-ballot majority verdict preferences predict the final verdict reliably. The said prediction has been borne out by some studies[20] but not by others.[21] On the basis of their own work, the well-known American researchers Pennington and Hastie (1990, p. 102) concluded that the relationship between individual jurors' initial verdicts and the final jury verdict is more complex than the simple one proposed by Kalven and Zeisel (1966).

Available empirical evidence (Hastie, Penrod, & Pennington, 1983) indicates that we need to distinguish between: (a) deliberations where jurors announce their verdict preferences before discussion begins in the jury room (known as 'verdict-driven' deliberations); and (b) deliberations in which jurors' verdict preferences are expressed later in the deliberation process (known as 'evidence-driven' deliberations).

If a majority verdict is required, it has been reported by Hastie, Penrod, and Pennington (1983) that minority jurors will participate less and will be paid less attention by the rest of the jury, and that taking a vote very early on speeds up the deliberation process and, also, jury deliberation will take longer if the jury is evidence- rather than verdict-driven, but this will not necessarily result in a different verdict. Real jury studies have found that the longer the retirement, the more likely it will lead to an acquittal (Baldwin & McConville, 1980, p. 42). Multiple charges against the defendant are associated with a greater likelihood of a guilty verdict (Tanford, Penrod, & Collins, 1985) as does knowledge that the defendant has a prior conviction (Greene & Dodge, 1995). Jurors are more likely to acquit if a reasonable doubt standard of proof is emphasized (McCabe & Purves, 1974). Finally, Osborne, Rappaport, and Meyers (1986) found that, following deliberation, jurors shift to a severer decision if the jury is heterogeneous rather than homogeneous. In this sense, the composition of a jury can be said to be related to its verdict.

Thomas' (2010) study of real jury deliberations and impropriety involved 196 jurors at Winchester Crown Court and found that two-thirds of them felt they should be given more information about how to deliberate when they retire to reach a verdict as half of them did not know what to do if something improper happened in the jury deliberation room (p. vi). Thomas also reported that 82% of the jurors believed they should not be allowed to speak about what transpired in the jury deliberation room.

In the 1970s, the US Supreme Court upheld the use of 6 person juries in criminal (*Williams v. Florida*, 399 US 78, 86, 1970) and civil (*Colgrove v. Battin*, 413 US 149, 156, 1973) cases (Cammack, 1995, p. 435). A meta-analysis by Saks and Marti (1997) of studies that investigated 6-member *v.* 12-member juries found that juries of 12: (1) are more representative of the community; (2) contain a range of opinion and experience; and (3) deliberate longer because twice as many people are present, but, on average, each juror contributes the same to the deliberation (Hastie, Penrod, & Pennington, 1983). The finding that each juror on average contributes the same to the deliberation in 6-member and 12-member juries may well be an artefact of the homogeneity of the mock jurors (psychology students) used extensively in US studies. Also, juries of 12 recall more evidence accurately; generate more arguments; and minority views are more likely to be represented. However, while jury size influences deliberation, the evidence indicates it does not make any significant difference to the verdict. Small juries are less likely to recall evidence accurately or to examine the evidence thoroughly or to result in a hung jury (Saks, 1977), and are more likely to hold secret ballots and to convict (Hans & Vidmar, 1986).[22] There are conflicting views on whether jurors in a smaller jury participate less (Saks, 1977) or more (Arce, 1995, p. 567). It becomes clear that the real reason for introducing small-size juries has been economic concerns (Zeisel & Diamond, 1987, p. 204).

Defendant characteristics

A number of studies have reported that a defendant's attractiveness is a good predictor of defendant guilt in mock jury studies (Bagby *et al.*, 1994)[23] and whether mock jurors will apply the reasonable doubt standard (MacCoun, 1990). Interestingly, jurors have been shown to be harsher on an attractive defendant whose good looks enabled them to commit a deception offence (Sigall & Ostrove, 1975). Regarding a defendant's display of remorse in the courtroom, Devine *et al.* (2001) concluded that, on the basis of the review of the relevant studies, no conclusions are possible due to conflicting findings reported.

Victim/plaintiff characteristics

Daudistel, Hosch, Holmes, and Graves, (1999) reported that longer sentences were imposed when the victim and the defendant were of the same race. One of the worrying findings yielded by the Capital Jury Project in the United States is that jurors see the defendant as more dangerous if the victim is white and that the race of the victim plays a significant role in whether they find mitigating factors that would lead them to decide on a lesser sentence than the death penalty. Thus, in the case of a defendant charged with killing a white victim, jurors would be unlikely to find mitigating factors and would decide on the death penalty. Regarding the importance of plaintiff characteristics in civil trials, an interaction effect between a victim's age and race has been reported by Foley and Pigott (1997) who found that when the plaintiff was young jurors considered black plaintiffs as less responsible and awarded them more damages than white plaintiffs in a sexual assault case. However, the reverse was found when the plaintiff was older.

Lawyer and judge characteristics

The importance of lawyer and judge characteristics as far as trial outcome is concerned has been neglected by psycho-legal researchers. Blanck (1985) had observers rate judges' verbal and non-verbal behaviour using videotaped parts of their instruction to the jury and found that the defendant was more likely to be found guilty if the trial judge was rated as less dogmatic, less wise, less dominant and less professional. Regarding the importance of lawyer characteristics, McGuire and Bermant (1977) reported that a higher acquittal rate was associated with the defence lawyer being a male. Lawyers' behaviour in court can sometimes be annoying and even offensive. Kaplan and Miller (1978) found that jury deliberation eliminated any adverse effect (e.g., bias) the annoying or offensive behaviour of lawyers or judges might have for or against the annoying party. Finally, as far as trial tactics are concerned, Spiecker and Worthington (2003) carried out a simulated civil trial and found that using a mixed organizational strategy (i.e., a narrative opening statement and a legal expository closing argument) was more effective for the plaintiff, whereas either a mixed or strict legal expository organizational strategy was more effective for the defence.

HUNG JURIES

Despite the concern by some that, in a number of trials, there is a hung jury, the proportion of hung jury verdicts for real juries has been found to be 1% in the meta-analysis of 17 studies by Saks and Marti (1997) and 8.3%[24] in the New South Wales study of 2,771 jury cases in Australia by Baker, Allan, and Weatherburn (2002). The weight of the empirical evidence[25] indicates that larger juries deliberate for longer (Saks & Marti, 1997), and the number of hung juries increases with jury size when a unanimous verdict is required and when case complexity is high. In order to remedy this weakness in the judicial system, legislators on both sides of the Atlantic have allowed smaller juries (see *Williams v. Florida*, 399, US, 78–145 [1970]) and majority verdicts (10 out of 12) in England and Wales. In Spain, a non-guilty verdict requires a majority verdict of five out of nine and a guilty verdict seven out of nine votes in order to eliminate hung juries (Arce *et al.*, 1999, p. 244). Also, since the case of *Allen v. U.S.*, 164, US, 492 (1896), a judge can ask jurors to reconsider their verdict in order to avoid a hung jury.

MODELS OF JURY DECISION-MAKING[26]

According to Hastie (1993b), there are basically four descriptive models of jury decision-making (see Levett *et al.*, 2005, pp. 370–375 for a discussion): (a) the Bayesian probability theory model (see Hastie, 1993b, pp. 11–17); (b) the algebraic weighted average model (Hastie, 1993b); (c) the stochastic Poisson process model (Kerr, 1993); and (d) the cognitive story model (see Pennington & Hastie, 1993). Thus, we have two broad categories of models of jury decision-making: the mathematical approach ones and the explanation-based/cognitive approach model.

In contrast to mathematical models, the story model (see Hastie, Penrod, & Pennington, 1983; Pennington & Hastie, 1986) assumes that jurors actively construct explanations for the evidence presented to them and decide on a verdict accordingly. In constructing a story,

jurors use three types of knowledge, namely: (a) personal knowledge about the offence; (b) knowledge acquired through the evidence presented during the trial; and (c) jurors' own knowledge or expectation about what constitutes a complete story. Pennington and Hastie (1992) used the story model successfully in three experiments to explain juror decision-making. The story model remains the most influential cognitive model of juror decision-making and has implications for lawyers in court but, also, for suggestions to reform the jury trial.

REFORMING THE JURY TO REMEDY SOME OF ITS PROBLEMS

In support of mock juror research (Penrod & Heuer, 1998; Horowitz & ForsterLee, 2001), the New Zealand juror survey by Young, Cameron, and Tinsley (1999) found that note-taking during the trial helped jurors during their deliberations. Support for allowing jurors to ask questions during the trial has been provided by Penrod and Heuer (1998), who found in their study that jurors felt better informed and in a better position to reach a verdict as a result of having been allowed to ask questions. However, Penrod and Heuer also found that judges and lawyers were not positive about jurors being allowed to ask questions.

The findings reported about New Zealand judges by Ogloff *et al.* (2006) and Young (2004) show that New Zealand is good example of a country where increasingly more judges aid jurors in their difficult task by better introduction to the task at hand, written aids, allowing access to transcripts of testimony, guidance on foreperson selection and on how to avoid impasses in deliberations, requiring juries to reason their verdict and, finally, providing jurors with a special verdict form to help in the process.

ALTERNATIVES TO TRIAL BY JURY

In light of some of the arguments against the jury system mentioned in the preceding text, an obvious alternative to trial by jury is trial by a single judge. A second alternative is a combination of judge and jury (lay persons), as it exists in Germany or as introduced in Japan in 2009 (see Mack, 2012; Ohtsubo, 2006). Lord Denning

(1982, pp. 72–73) was a strong advocate of a mixed jury for fraud trials in England, comprising a High Court judge and two lay assessors. Some commentators have questioned whether, in a mixed jury, the laypersons would outvote the judge often enough (Knittel & Seiler, 1972). Research cited by Antonio and Hans (2001, p. 69) shows that mixed courts limit the impact of lay participation on decision-making because lay judges are often marginalized when they hear and decide cases with professional judges (Kutnjak Ivkovich, 1999; Machura, 2001).[27]

CONCLUSIONS

The concept of the jury in Western, English-speaking, common law countries has been eroded (e.g., with the introduction of majority verdicts, 6 member juries), and the use of juries has declined drastically in some jurisdictions. Despite the problem of both low ecological validity of many mock juror/jury research, as well as conflicting findings reported by experimental simulation and real juror/jury studies, as far as juror competence is concerned, the evidence discussed in this chapter shows that: as trial complexity increases, juror comprehension of the evidence decreases; both mock and real jurors are generally unable to comprehend and apply the law or to evaluate scientific evidence proffered by an expert witness, thus negating the very notion of a fair trial; there is overwhelming evidence that jurors find it difficult to comply with judges' instructions, for example, to discount a defendant's involuntary confession or to ignore inadmissible evidence. 'Scientific jury selection', in itself a controversial practice, is not as possible, nor as successful in influencing trial outcome, as some mock jury researchers and trial consultants have claimed. Inconsistent findings have been reported by experimental studies on the one hand and research into actual jurors on the other.

A certain degree of scepticism is warranted in considering research findings about the relationship between juror characteristics and sentence due to the fact that simulation studies often lack deliberation and conflicting findings have been reported by mock and real juror studies. Juror/jury research should focus more on the interaction between juror and case characteristics. The empirical evidence casts doubt on the wisdom of having 6 member juries, the deliberation process plays a more significant role than was reported by Kalven and Zeisel's (1966) 'liberation hypothesis' in their influential pioneering study and, finally, the 'cognitive story model' of jury decision-making has been shown to be very useful in focusing on juror characteristics. Juridic decision-making is an area where psychologists have contributed and will continue to contribute useful knowledge to a vital debate in society. A number of reforms mentioned earlier will make the jury both more representative of the community and more competent.

It is unlikely that we shall see judges and laypersons deciding criminal cases together in courts in the United States, United Kingdom, Australia or New Zealand in the near future. The notion of the jury has miraculously survived thus far despite its inherent contradictions and an onslaught since the 1960s in Western, English-speaking, common law countries. Psychologists still have a lot to contribute to both improving our understanding of juror and jury decision-making as well as to improving juror competence. Finally, psycho-legal researchers must poise themselves to address the opportunities and challenges that lie ahead as technology, especially the Internet, produces irreversible changes in the world of law (Susskind, 2013).

NOTES

1 See Darbyshire (1991) concerning the controversy surrounding the content and interpretations of this clause in the Magna Carta.

2 *Taxquet v. Belgium* [2010] ECHR (Grand Chamber).

3 Criminal Justice Act (CJA) 2003, s.321, and Schedule 33.

4 This section draws on *Archbold*, 2012.

5 See *Juries Act* 1974 and *Juries Disqualification Act* 1984. The previous disqualification category 'imprisonment for public protection' was abolished by the sentencing provisions of the *Legal Aid, Sentencing and Punishment of Offenders Act* 2012.

6 In *Wainwright v. Witt* 469 US at 423 (1985).

7 In *Holland v. Illinois* 493 US at 482 (1990).

8 *J.E.B. v. Alabama* ex rel.T.B. 114 S.Ct 1419 (1994).

9 *Batson v. Kentucky* 476 US 79 [1986].

10 Horan (2004), Ryan (2003) and Tinsley (2001) are cited in Goodman-Delahunty and Tait (2006).

11 See issues of *Indiana Law Review*, 1995, vol. 70 (3,4).

12 But see *R v. Maxwell* case (*Bishopsgate Investment Management Ltd v. Maxwell* (No 2) [1993] BCLC 814) in which Justice Phillip, over a 2-week period, used a questionnaire to select the jury and reduced 700 potential jurors down to 70 and then selected the jurors by ballot.

13 Amato (1979); Griffitt and Jackson (1973); Kerr *et al.* (1995); Stephan and Stephan (1986).
14 See http://en.wikipedia.org/wiki/Capital_Jury_Project
15 Elliott (1991); Mauro (1991); Nietzel *et al.* (1999); Bowers (1995).
16 Cited by Levett *et al.* (2005).
17 Cited by Levett *et al.* (2005).
18 Similar findings were reported by Saks and Hastie (1978) and Deosoran (1993).
19 See Hastie (1993a), Levine (1992) and Nietzel *et al.* (1999) for earlier reviews.
20 Meyers, Brashers, and Hanner (2001); and Sandys and Dillahay (1995).
21 Ellsworth (1993); Kerr and MacCoun (1985); Hastie, Penrod, and Pennington (1983).
22 Cited in Hollin (1989, 168).
23 See also Izzett and Leginski (1974); Landy and Aronson (1969); Ostrom, Werner, and Saks (1978).
24 9.8% were aborted.
25 Kalven and Zeisel, 1966; Zeisel, 1971; Saks, 1977; Kerr and MacCoun, 1985; Foss, 1981.
26 See Hastie (1993b) and Levett *et al.* (2005) for a discussion.
27 Both studies are cited by Antonio and Hans (2001, 69).

FURTHER READING

Devine, D. J. (2012). *Jury decision making the state of the science.* New York: New York University Press.
This text reviews a broad range of the social and psychological research into juries and their decision-making processes. It provides a wide-ranging but readable overview of the field. Current theoretical accounts of decision-making and studies into jury behaviour, including the effects of contextual and court practices are considered in detail. A good overview and introduction to this area of research is provided.

REFERENCES

Airs, J., & Shaw, A. (1999). *Jury excusal and deferral.* Home Office Research Development and Statistics Directorate Report No.102. London: Home Office.
Amato, P. R. (1979). Juror-defendant similarity and the assessment of guilt in politically-motivated crimes. *Australian Journal of Psychology, 31,* 79–88.
Antonio, M. E., & Hans, V. P. (2001). Race and the civil jury: how does a juror's race shape the jury experience? In R. Roesch *et al.* (Eds.), *Psychology in the courts: International advances in knowledge* (pp. 69–81). Routledge.
Arce, R (1995). Evidence evaluation in jury decision making. In R. Bull & D. Carson (Eds.), *Handbook of psychology in legal contexts* (pp. 565–580). Chichester: Wiley.
Arce, R., Fariña, F., Novo, M., & Seijo, D. (1999). In search of causes of hung juries. *Expert Evidence, 6,* 243–260.
Archbold, J. F. (2012). *Criminal pleading, evidence and practice.* London: Sweet & Maxwell.
Avio, K. L. (1988). Capital punishment in Canada: Statistical evidence and constitutional issues. *Canadian Journal of Criminology, 30,* 331–45.
Bagby, R. M., Parker, J. D., Rector, N. A., & Kalemba, V. (1994). Racial prejudice in the Canadian legal system: Juror decisions in a simulated rape trial. *Law and Human Behavior, 18,* 339–50.
Baker, J., Allan, A., & Weatherburn, D. (2002). Hung juries and aborted trials: An analysis of their prevalence, predictors and effects. *Crime and Justice Bulletin, 66,* 1–19.
Baldwin, J., & McConville, M. (1979). *Jury trials.* Oxford: Clarendon Press.
Baldwin, J., & McConville, M. (1980). Juries, foremen and verdicts. *British Journal of Criminology, 20,* 35–44.
Barber, D., & Gordon, G. (Eds.) (1976). *Members of the jury.* London: Wildwood House.
Blanck, P. D. (1985). The appearance of justice: Judges' and verbal and nonverbal behavior in criminal jury trials. *Stanford Law Review, 38,* 89–164.
Boehm, V. R. (1968). Mr. Prejudice, Miss Sympathy, and the authoritarian personality: An application of psychological measuring techniques to the problem of jury bias. *Wis. L. Rev.,* 734.
Bornstein, B. H., Wisehunt, B., Nemeth, R. J., & Dunaway, D. (2002). Pretrial effects in a civil trial: A two-way street? *Law and Human Behavior, 26,* 3–17.
Bowers, W. (1995). The capital jury project: Rationale, design, and preview of early findings. *Indiana Law Review, 70,* 1043–1068.
Brekke, N. J., & Borgida, E. (1988). Expert psychological testimony in rape trials: A social cognitive analysis. *Journal of Personality and Social Psychology, 55,* 372–86.

Brigham, J. C. (2006). The jury system in the United States of America. In M. F. Kaplan & A. M. Martin (Eds.), *Understanding world systems through social psychological research* (pp. 11–29). New York and Hove: Psychology Press.

Burnett, D. G. (2001). A *trial by jury*. New York: Knopf.

Cammack, M. (1995). In search of the post-positivist jury. *Indiana Law Journal, 70*(2), 405–89.

Chesterman, M., Chan, J., & Hampton, S. (2001). *Managing prejudicial publicity: An empirical study of criminal jury trials in New South Wales*. Sydney, Australia: Justice Research Center, Law and Justice Foundation of New South Wales.

Costanzo, S., & Costanzo, M. (1994). Life or death decisions: An analysis of capital jury decision making under the special issues sentencing framework. *Law and Human Behavior, 18*, 151–170.

Cutler, B. L., Penrod, S. D., & Dexter, H. R. (1990). Juror sensitivity to eyewitness identification evidence. *Law and Human Behavior, 14*, 185–191.

Darbyshire, P. (1991). The lamp that shows that freedom lives – is it worth the candle? *Criminal Law Review*, October, 740–752.

Daudistel, H., Hosch, H., Holmes, M., & Graves, J. B. (1999). Effect of defendant ethnicity on juries' disposition of felony cases. *Journal of Applied Social Psychology, 29*, 317–336.

Denning, Lord. (1982). *What next in the law*. London: Butterworths.

Deosoran, R. (1993). The social psychology of selecting jury forepersons. *British Journal of Psychology, 33*, 70–80.

Devine, D. J., Clayton, L. D., Dunford, B. B., & Seying, R. P. (2001). Jury decision making: 45 years on deliberating groups, *Psychology, Public Police and Law, 7*(3), 622–727.

Dillehay, R. C., & Nietzel, M. T. (1985). Juror experience and jury verdicts. *Law and Human Behavior, 9*, 179–191

Dunstan, S., Paulin, J. & Atkinson, K-a (1995). *Trial by Peers? The Composition of New Zealand Juries*. Department of Justice: Wellington, NZ.

Elliott, R. (1991). On the alleged prosecution-proneness of death-qualified juries and jurors. In, P. J. Suedfeld & P. E. Terlock (Eds.), *Psychology and social policy* (pp. 255–265). New York: Hemisphere Publishing Corporation.

Ellsworth, P. C. (1993). Some steps between attitudes and verdicts. In R. Hastie (Ed.), *Inside the Juror: The Psychology of Juror Decision Making*. Cambridge: Cambridge University Press. .

Foley, L. A., & Pigott, M. A. (1997). Race, age and jury decisions in a civil rape trial. *American Journal of Forensic Psychology, 15*(1), 37–55.

Foss, R. D. (1981). Interactions between jurors as a function of majority vs. unanimity decision rules. *Journal of Applied Psychology, 7*, 38–56.

Goodman-Delahunty, J., & Tait, D. (2006). Lay participation in legal decision-making in Australia and New Zealand: Jury trials and administrative tribunals. In M. F. Kaplan & A. M. Martin (Eds.), *Understanding world systems through social psychological research* (pp. 147–170). New York and Hove: Psychology Press.

Greene, E., & Dodge, M. (1995). The influence of prior record evidence on juror decision making. *Law and Human Behavior, 19*, 67–78.

Griffitt, W., & Jackson, T. (1973). Simulated jury decisions: The influence of jury defendant attitude similarity dissimilarity. *Social Behavior and Personality, 1*, 1–7.

Grosscup, J., & Penrod, S. D. (2002, March). *Limiting instructions' effects on juror assessment of scientific validity and reliability*. Paper session presented at the biennial meeting of the American Psychology-Law Society, Austin, Texas.

Hans, V. P. (1992). Jury decision making. In D. K. Kagehiro & W. S. Laufer (Eds.), *Handbook of psychology and law* (pp. 56–76). New York: Springer.

Hans, V. P., & Vidmar, N. (1986). *Judging the jury*. New York: Plenum

Hastie, R. (Ed.) (1993a). *Inside the jury: The psychology of juror decision making*. New York: Cambridge University Press.

Hastie, R. (1993b). Introduction. In Hastie, R. (Ed) (1993a). *Inside the jury: The psychology of juror decision making* (pp. 3–41). New York: Cambridge University Press.

Hastie, R., Penrod, S. D., & Pennington, N. (1983). *Inside the jury*. Cambridge, MA: Harvard University Press.

Heuer, L., & Penrod, S. (1994a). Juror note taking and question asking during trials: A national field experiment. *Law and Human Behavior, 18*, 121–150.

Heuer, L., & Penrod, S. (1994b). Trial complexity its meaning and effects. *Law and Human Behavior, 18*, 29–51.

Himelein, M., Nietzel, M. T., & Dillehay, R. C. (1991). Effects of prior juror experience on jury sentence. *Behavioral Sciences and the Law, 9*, 97–106

Hollin, C. R. (1989). *Psychology and crime: An introduction to criminological psychology*. London: Routledge.

Honess, T. M., Charman, E. A., & Levi, M. (2003). Factual and affective/evaluative recall of pretrial publicity: Their relative influence on juror reasoning and verdict in a simulated fraud trial. *Journal of Applied Social Psychology, 30*, 1404–1416.

Hope, L., Memon, A., & McGeorge, P. (2004). Understanding pretrial publicity: Predecisional distortion of evidence in mock jurors. *Journal of Experimental Psychology: Applied, 10*, 111–119.

Horan, J. (2004). *The civil jury system: An empirical study*. Unpublished Doctoral Dissertation, University of Melbourne School of Law, Victoria, Australia.

Horowitz, I. A., & ForsterLee, L. (2001). The effects of note-taking and trial transcript access on mock jury decisions in a complex civil trial. *Law and Human Behavior, 25*(4), 373–391.

Horowitz, I. A., Forsterlee, L., & Brolly, I. (1996). Effects of trial complexity on decision making. *Journal of Applied Psychology, 81*, 757–768.

Izzett, R., & Leginski, W. (1974). Group discussion and the influence of defendant characteristics in a simulated jury setting. *Journal of Social Psychology, 93*, 271–279.

Kalven, H., & Zeisel, H. (1966). *The American Jury.* Chicago: University of Chicago Press.

Kapardis, A. (2003). *Psychology and law: A critical introduction.* Melbourne: Cambridge University Press.

Kaplan, M. F., & Martin, A. M. (Eds.) (2006). *Understanding world systems through social psychological research.* New York and Hove: Psychology Press.

Kaplan, M. F., & Miller, L. E. (1978). Reducing the effects of juror bias. *Journal of Personality and Social Psychology, 36*, 1443–1455.

Kassin, S. M., & Sukel, H. (1997). Coerced confessions and the jury: An experimental test of the 'harmless error' rule. *Law and Human Behavior, 21*, 27–46.

Kemmelmeier, M. (2005). The effects of race and social dominance orientation in simulated juror decision making. *Journal of Applied Social Psychology, 35*, 1030–1045.

Kerr, N. L. (1993). Stochastic models of juror decision making. In R. Hastie (Ed.), *Inside the juror: The psychology of juror decision making.* Cambridge: Cambridge University Press.

Kerr, N. L., & Bray, R. M. (2005). Simulation, realism, and the study of the jury. In N. Brewer & K. D. Wilson (Eds.), *Psychology and law: An empirical perspective* (pp. 322–364). New York, London: Guilford Press.

Kerr, N. L., Hymes, R. W., Anderson, A. B., & Weathers, J. E. (1995). Defendant-juror similarity and mock-juror judgments. *Law and Human Behavior, 19*, 545–567.

Kerr, N. L., & MacCoun, R. (1985). The effects of jury size and polling method on the process and product of jury deliberation. *Journal of Personality and Social Psychology, 48*, 349–363.

Knittel, E., & Seiler, D. (1972). The merits of trial by jury. *Cambridge Law Journal, 56*, 223–228.

Kovera, M. B., McAuliff, B. D., & Hebert, K. S. (1999). Reasoning about scientific evidence: Effects of juror gender and evidence quality on juror decisions in a hostile work environment case. *Journal of Applied Psychology, 84*, 362–375.

Kutnjak Ivkovich, S (1999). *Lay Participation in Criminal Trials.* Washington, DC: Austin & Winfield.

Landy, D., & Aronson, E. (1969). The influence of the character of the criminal and his victim on decisions of simulated jurors. *Journal of Experimental Social Psychology, 5*, 141–152.

Law Reform Commission of Victoria (1985). *The jury in a criminal trial.* Melbourne, Australia.

Levett, L. M., Danielsen, E. M., Kovera, M. B., & Cutler, B. L. (2005). The psychology of jury and juror decision making. In Brewer, N. & Wilson, K. D. (Eds.), *Psychology and law: An empirical perspective* (pp. 365–406). New York: The Guilford Press.

Levine, J. P. (1992). *Juries and politics.* Pacific Grove, CA: Brooks/Cole Publishing.

Lloyd-Bostock, S. (1988). *Law in practice: Applications of psychology to legal decisionmaking and legal skills.* London: Routledge/British Psychological Society.

Lloyd-Bostock, S. (1996). Juries and jury research in context. In G. Davies, S. Lloyd-Bostock, M. McMurran, & C. Wilson (Eds.), *Psychology, law, and criminal justice: International developments in research and practice.* New York: Walter de Gruyter.

Lloyd-Bostock, S., & Thomas, C. (1999). Decline of the little parliament: Juries and jury reform in England and Wales. *Law and Contemporary Problems, 7*, 21.

London, K., & Nunez, N. (2000). The effect of jury deliberation on jurors' propensity to disregard inadmissible evidence. *Journal of Applied Psychology, 85*, 932–39.

Luginbuhl, J., & Howe, J. (1995). Discretion in capital sentencing: guided or misguided? *Indiana Law Journal, 70*, 1161–1185.

MacCoun, R. (1990). The emergence of extralegal bias during jury deliberation. *Criminal Justice and Behavior, 17*, 303–314.

Machura, S. (2001). Interaction between lay assessors and professional judges in German mixed courts. *Revue internationale de droit pénal, 72*(1), 451–479.

Mack, R. L (2012). Reestablishing jury trails in Japan: Foundational lessons from the Russian experience. 2 *Creighton International and Comparative Law Journal, 100.*

Marshall, G. (1975). The judgement of one's peers: Some aims and ideals of jury trial. In N. D. Walker & A. Pearson (Eds.), *The British Jury System: Papers presented at the Cropwood Round-Table Conference,* December 1974. Cambridge: Institute of Criminology.

Mauro, R. (1991). Tipping the scales toward death: The biasing effects of death qualification. In P. Suedfeld & P. E. Tetlock (Eds.), *Psychology and social policy* (pp. 243–254). New York: New York Publishing Corporation.

Mazzella, R., & Feingold, A. (1994). The effects of physical attractiveness, race, socioeconomic status, and gender of defendants and victims on judgments of mock jurors: A meta-analysis. *Applied Social Psychology, 24*, 1315–1344.

McAuliff, B. D., & Kovera, M. B. (2003). *Need for cognition and juror sensitivity to methodological flaws in psychological science.* Unpublished manuscript, Florida International University, Miami, FL.

McCabe, S., & Purves, R. (1974). *The jury at work.* Oxford: Blackwell.

McEwan, J. (2000). Decision making in legal settings. In M. Maguire *et al.* (Eds.), *Behaviour, crime and legal processes* (pp. 111–131). Chichester, England: Wiley.

McGuire and Bermant, G. (1977). *Conduct of the voir dire examination: Practices and opinions of federal District Judges.* Washington, DC: Federal Judicial center.

Memon, A., Vrij, A., & Bull, R. (2003). *Psychology and law* (2nd edn). Bognor Regis, UK: Wiley.

Meyers, R. A., Brashers, D. E., & Hanner, J. (2001). Majority/minority influence: Identifying argumentative patterns and predicting argument-outcome links. *Journal of Communication, 50,* 3–30.

Mills, C. J., & Bohannon, W. E. (1980). Juror characteristics: To what extent are they related to jury verdicts? *Judicature, 64,* 23–31.

Moran, G., & Comfort, J. C. (1982). Scientific jury selection: Sex as a moderator of demographic and personality predictors of impaneled felony jury behaviour. *Journal of Personality and Social Psychology, 47,* 1052–1063.

Narby, D. J., Cutler, B. L., & Moran, G. (1993). A meta-analysis of the association between authoritarianism on jurors' perceptions of defendant's culpability. *Journal of Applied Psychology, 78,* 34–42.

Nietzel, M. T., McCarthy, D. M., & Kery, M. (1999). Juries: The current state of the empirical literature. In R. Roesch, S. D. Hart, & J. R. Ogloff (Eds.), *Psychology and law: The state of the discipline* (pp. 23–52). New York: Kluwer Academic/Plenum Publishers.

Ogloff, J. R. P., & Rose, G. (2005). The comprehension of judicial instructions. In N. Brewer & K. D. Wilson (Eds.), *Psychology and law: An empirical perspective* (pp. 407–444). New York: The Guilford Press.

Ogloff, J. R. P., Clough, J., Goodman-Delahunty, J., & Young, W. (2006). *The jury project: stage I – A survey of Australian and New Zealand judges.* Melbourne, Australia: Australian Institute of Judicial Administration Incorporated.

Ohtsubo, Y. (2006). On designing a mixed jury system in Japan. In M. F. Kaplan & A. M. Martin (Eds.), *Understanding world systems through social psychological research* (pp. 199–214). New York and Hove: Psychology Press.

Osborne, Y. H., Rappaport, N. B., & Meyer, R. G. (1986). An investigation of persuasion and sentencing severity with mock juries. *Behavioral Sciences and the Law, 4,* 339–349.

Ostrom, T. M., Werner, C., & Saks, M. (1978). An integration theory analysis of jurors' presumption of guilt or innocence. *Journal of Personality and Social Psychology, 36,* 436–450.

Pennington, N., & Hastie, R. (1986). Evidence evaluation in complex decision making. *Journal of Personality and Social Psychology, 51,* 242–258.

Pennington, N., & Hastie, R. (1990). Practical implications of psychological research on juror and jury decision making. *Personality and Social Psychology Bulletin, 16*(1), 90–105.

Pennington, N., & Hastie, R. (1992). Explaining the evidence: tests of the story model for juror decision making. *Journal of Personality and Social Psychology, 62,* 189–206.

Pennington, N., & Hastie, R. (1993). The story model for juror decision making. In R. Hastie (Ed.), *Inside the juror: The psychology of juror decision making* (pp. 192–221). New York: Cambridge University Press.

Penrod, S. D., & Heuer, L. (1998). Improving group performance; the case of the jury. In R. S. Tindale (Ed.), *Theory and research on small groups* (pp. 127–151). New York: Plenum.

Reskin, B. F., & Visher, C. A. (1986). The impacts of evidence and extralegal factors in jurors' decisions. *Law and Society Review, 20,* 423–38.

Ryan, S. (2003, October). *Jury debriefing and stress.* Paper presented at the Second Annual Jury research Conference, Sydney, Australia. Cited by Goodman-Delahunty and Tait (2006).

Saks, M. (1977). *Jury verdicts: The role of group size and social decision rule.* Lexington, MA: Heath.

Saks, M. J., & Marti, M. W. (1997). A meta-analysis of the effects of jury size. *Law and Human Behavior, 21,* 451–467.

Sandys, M. (1995). Cross overs – capital jurors who change their minds about the punishment: A litmus test for sentencing guidelines. *Indiana Law Journal, 70,* 1183–1221.

Sarat, A. (1995). Violence, representation, and responsibility in capital trials: The view from the jury. *Indiana Law Journal, 70,* 1103–1139.

Seltzer, R., Venuti, M. A., & Lopes, G. M. (1991). Juror honesty during voir dire. *Journal of Criminal Justice, 19*(5), 451–462.

Sigall, H., & Ostrove, N. (1975). Beautiful but dangerous: Effects of offender attractiveness and nature of the crime on juridic judgements. *Journal of Personality and Social Psychology, 31,* 410–414.

Spiecker, S. C., & Worthington, D. L. (2003). The influence of opening statement/closing statement organizational strategy on juror verdict and damage awards. *Law and Human Behavior, 27*(4), 437–456.

Steblay, N. M., Besirevic, J., Fulero, S. M., & Jimenez-Lorente, B. (1999). The effects of pretrial publicity on juror verdicts: A meta-analytic review. *Law and Human Behavior, 23,* 219–235.

Stephan, C. W., & Stephan, W. G. (1986). Habla Ingles? The effects of language translation on simulated juror decisions. *Journal of Applied Social Psychology, 16,* 577–589.

Stephenson, G. M. (1992). The *psychology of criminal justice.* Oxford: Blackwell.

Susskind, R. (2013). *Tomorrow's lawyers: An introduction to your future.* New York: Oxford University Press.

Tanford, S., Penrod, S., & Collins, R. (1985). Decision making in joined criminal trials: The influence of charge similarity, evidence similarity and limiting instructions. *Law and Human Behavior, 9*, 319–337.

Thomas, C. (2010). *Are juries fair?* Research series 1/10. London: Ministry of Justice.

Tinsley, Y. (2001). Juror decision-making: a look inside the jury room. In Tarling, R. (Ed.), *Selected proceedings: Papers from the British Society of Criminology Conference*, Leicester 2000 (Vol.4).

Vidmar, N. (2002). Case studies of pre- and midtrial prejudice in criminal and civil litigation. *Law and Human Behavior, 26*, 73–105.

Wrightsman, L. S., Greene, E., Nietzel, M. T., & Fortune, W. H. (2002). *Psychology and the legal system* (2nd ed.). Belmont, CA: Wadsworth.

Young, W. (2003). Summing up to juries in criminal cases – what jury research says about current rules and practice. *Criminal Law Review*, 665–689.

Young, W. (2004, November). *Judges' assistance to jurors*. Paper presented at the Third Australasian Jury Conference, Victoria, Australia.

Young, W., Cameron, N., & Tinsley, Y. (1999). *Juries in criminal trials*. Law Commission, Preliminary Paper no. 37, New Zealand.

Zander, M. (1974). Why I disagree with Sir Robert Mark. *Police*, April 16.

Zander, M., & Henderson, P. (1993). *Crown court study*. The Royal Commission on Criminal Justice, Research Study No. 19. London: HMSO.

Zander, M., & Henderson, P. (1994). The Crown court study. Royal Commission on Criminal Justice Study No.19. *Research Bulletin, 35*, 46–48. London: Home Office Research and Statistics Department.

Zeisel, H. (1971). '…. And then there were none': the diminution of federal jury. *University of Chicago Law Review, 35*, 35–54.

Zeisel, H., & Diamond, S. S. (1987). Convincing empirical evidence on the six-member jury. In L. S. Wrightsman, S. M. Kassin, & C. E. Willis (Eds.), *In the jury box: Controversies in the courtroom* (pp. 193–208). Newbury Park, CA: Sage.

Zerman, M. (1977). *Call the final witness: The people vs. Mather as seen by the 11th juror*. New York: Harper & Row.

6 Assessment

David A. Crighton

Assessment is a fundamental aspect of forensic practice and serves to underpin a range of activities, including categorization, formulation and treatment. Assessment is characterized by attempts to apply scientific approaches ethically to human functioning, both individually and in social contexts. The use of scientific approaches is in turn characterized by a number of key features. These include the use of theory to derive hypotheses, the use of careful observation and measurement as a means of testing falsifiable hypotheses, in turn leading to possible rejection and reformulation, and the development and refining of more valid theories.

Effective psychological assessment requires a clear understanding of relevant theory, along with the principles that apply to accurate measurement and the appropriate application of measures. Assessment methods can be understood in terms of a range of psychometric qualities, including reliability, validly, specificity, sensitivity and power. Ethical and competent forensic psychological assessments need to be individually tailored in order to produce change most effectively. In order to be ethical, assessment needs to actively address the human rights of those being assessed, as well as issues of potential bias that may apply to all practitioners.

CONCEPTUAL ISSUES IN ASSESSMENT

Forensic psychological assessment can be operationally defined as the use of psychological methods to evaluate a person (or persons) in relation to specific legal purposes. Most of the processes involved in conducting such assessments are common across psychology. Hence, assessments conducted by clinical, counselling, educational and other applied psychologists all share a number of fundamental characteristics. What does distinguish such assessments is the context in which they are undertaken. In forensic psychology, this context is ultimately one which involves legally mandated decisions.

There are several fundamental conceptual and methodological components involved in the assessment and these are interrelated. They include the need to draw on credible theories of human behaviour along with the need to make valid observations and measurements, both quantitative and qualitative, as part of the process of testing and reformulating theory-based explanations. It also involves attempts to systematically evaluate the information and data gathered. The emphasis on scientific approaches in conducting assessments is based on a number of assumptions. These include the notion that using scientific methods to assess people will improve the ability to identify sources of variance relating to psychological characteristics. It forms the basis of the 'scientist-practitioner' model which is currently dominant across applied psychology (Haynes & O'Brien, 2000).

Figure 6.1 provides an idealized and simplified outline of the process of assessment using a 'scientist practitioner' approach.

Within a framework of scientific practice, it is critical to recognize that the beliefs and values of the assessor will strongly influence both the process and what is measured. This is inevitable and is both a technical and an ethical point, in that it is essential to recognize the impacts of such processes on assessment and make appropriate efforts to address them and mitigate any inappropriate effects (Crighton & Towl, 2008). Such efforts are perhaps brought into sharpest relief in forensic practice, where assessments may have a range of legal consequences for those being assessed. This fact also implies that restricted notions of the 'objectivity' of any assessment are misplaced.

A scientific approach to assessment will generally rest, initially, on a basis of careful and detailed observation.

Forensic Psychology, Second Edition. Edited by David A. Crighton and Graham J. Towl.
© 2015 John Wiley & Sons, Ltd. Published 2015 by British Psychological Society and John Wiley & Sons, Ltd.

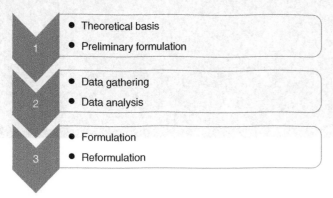

1
- Theoretical basis
- Preliminary formulation

2
- Data gathering
- Data analysis

3
- Formulation
- Reformulation

FIGURE 6.1 *A structure outline of assessment using a 'scientist practitioner' approach.*

This in turn will be associated with processes of hypothesis generation, formulation and reformulation, based on a clear theory base. It will also generally involve an emphasis on careful measurement, the use of multivariate measurements and sometimes efforts to manipulate variables. Measurement in turn can be defined as the process of trying to assign values to specific attributes of a person or variable (Haynes & O'Brien, 2000). Accurate measurement is an essential aid to clinical[1] judgements and more accurate measurement is associated with better ability to estimate covariance and describe causal relationships. An example here might be the suggested association between alcohol use and violence: testing such covariance clearly rests in very large part on the ability to accurately measure 'alcohol use' and 'violence' (Reyes, Foshee, Bauer, & Ennett, 2012).

One of the major functions of assessment often has particular salience in forensic practice and is that of predicting future behaviour. This relates to efforts to establish links between assessment findings and future outcomes (often called 'prognosis' in other applied sciences such as medicine). Efforts at prediction are generally limited by our ability to accurately measure predictor variables (PVs). Hence, any suggested association between, for example, lack of empathy and subsequent violence depends on being able to measure 'lack of empathy' reliably and validly.

Psychological assessment may also be concerned with attempts at categorization or classification (sometimes termed diagnosis). This can be seen as an aspect of accurate measurement, where meaningful categories can be used to aid clinical judgements.

Classification

The use of classification is extensive within science and serves a number of useful functions. Most obvious of these perhaps is that it can support communication about something by ensuring a high degree of consistency between observers. Classification as a concept has made a substantial contribution to a number of sciences in this way, with biological sciences such as botany providing an archetypal example, with the development of detailed taxonomic approaches. Classification, though, may also serve as an aid to thinking about complex problems as in the case of disease categories, or diagnoses, in medicine and surgery.

The virtues of good scientific classification systems include their clarity, with explicit transparent decision rules for inclusion and exclusion. They are comprehensive in that they serve to categorize a population of things, events or behaviours. They have a high degree of acceptability to users, because they are functional and have good utility. Finally they have good levels of fidelity to nature. It is, though, noteworthy that even optimal classification systems yield categories that are concepts and not things, a fact that is often poorly recognized and integrated in practice, where there is often a tendency to reify categories (Rutter & Taylor, 2002).

The best-known and most influential categorical systems within applied sciences are medicine and surgery, which are primarily concerned with the categorization of forms of anatomical or physiological dysfunction termed 'diseases'. In relation to mental health, the best-known and most widely used categorical frameworks in Western practice are DSM-IV (American Psychiatric Association, 2000) and ICD-10 (World Health Organization, 1990). These seek to provide operationally defined categories applicable to psychological dysfunction. This approach has been described by some as the 'medical model', where assessment is concerned with description and categorization (diagnosis), based on an analysis of observable factors (signs) and self-reported factors (symptoms), leading to the estimation of likely outcomes (prognosis) and interventions (treatment). This description is problematic in a number of ways. Whatever the successes of this model within applied biological sciences such as medicine and surgery, it is misleading to suggest that this model is in any way exclusively 'medical'. It might be more accurate to describe this as a 'categorization' model, and it is clearly one that has wide application across science (Crighton & Towl, 2008). It is similarly inaccurate to suggest that the appropriate practice of applied sciences such as medicine and surgery merely involves biological categorization (Clare, 2003; Rutter & Taylor, 2002).

Effective categorization of function and dysfunction may have utility in a number of respects. It potentially creates relatively homogeneous groups which are replicable for research purposes. This has clear advantages in producing testable predictions derived from classification. Practitioners will also need to know how to apply research findings to individuals, and classification systems may be helpful in doing this. However, there are clear areas of difficulty with classification systems which may also serve to mask significant differences within categories and between individuals. This may impact on the relative value of categories across settings. For example, the needs of researchers and practitioners in this respect may be quite different. A classification system that leaves many cases unallocated is not, necessarily, problematic for researchers. Yet, it is likely to have much less utility for practitioners.

Classification approaches have been subject to several critiques. The most fundamental of these, already touched upon, is that classification approaches both exaggerate and reify the power of concepts. This is evident in clinical practice within psychology and psychiatry where 'diagnoses' are normally descriptive rather than explanatory. Antisocial personality disorder (APD) is a description of a person who may be impulsive and aggressive but as a concept it does not explains these behaviours. This can result in entirely circular thinking where a concept such as APD, defined in terms of aggressive and antisocial behaviour, can be misused as an apparent 'explanation' of why an individual behaves in antisocial and aggressive ways. The use of classification approaches in this way serves no useful function.

Diagnostic categories may also serve to obscure assumptions that are being made, such as the dysfunctional nature of behaviours. In the context of an individual's social circumstances the behaviours concerned may in fact be adaptive. For example, high levels of aggression may be functional in environments where others are highly aggressive. Diagnostic categories may also serve to mask considerable heterogeneity within groupings. Those identified within a category such as 'narcissistic personality disorder' show a wide variation in the levels of aggression shown towards others. This variation parallels that seen in many other groups, yet the category may serve to effectively mask this fact.

The implications of such aspects of categorical approaches are the subject of considerable debate and disagreement. It is certainly the case that categories have been misused in the past. Psychological and psychiatric categories have been used to justify a range of abuses, ranging from incarceration in closed institutions through to enforced sterilization and killing of those with mental disorders (Geuter, 1992). The existence of abuses alone though is, of course, not sufficient to justify the absolute rejection of categorical approaches. Categories can have considerable scientific value but their misuse within science underlines the need for a cautious approach to their use, along with a clear appreciation of the strengths and weaknesses of categorization as one form of scientific approach.

Dimensional approaches

The choice between categorical and dimensional approaches has been a significant area of debate within science. There are, though, a number of constraints that have favoured categorical models in clinical practice. Most obvious of these is that there is often a need to make dichotomous decisions during assessment and intervention: either to undertake a particular assessment or not; either to intervene or not; and so on. This becomes a significant difficulty, though, where categories come to be used to dominate assessment and intervention, an approach which is generally inappropriate.

Categorical thinking also appears to be something which is firmly ingrained in human cognition (Macrae & Bodenhausen, 2000) and it is therefore perhaps not entirely surprising that it has tended to result in concepts which develop a life of their own. Dimensional thinking, by contrast, is less natural and has been slower to gain ground. It has, though, become increasingly attractive to researchers and has also had marked impacts in areas of practice such as neuropsychology and behavioural genetics. It is also a poorly recognized fact that, even when using good categorical models, dimensional risk and protective factors will be the norm rather than the exception.

At a more fundamental level it is also easy to exaggerate the differences between dimensional and categorical models and explanations. Generally it is possible to translate between categorical model and dimensions and vice versa. A category can often be described in terms of a set of dimensions or dimensional scores, while dimensions may reciprocally be grouped into categories.

This has a number of significant implications. These include the fact that discrete causes can be associated with problems that are distributed across a continuum. It is, for example, not unusual for genetic disorders to show a range of physical changes across one or more dimensions. It is thus inappropriate to assume that because effects are continuously distributed causal factors must also be, or indeed vice versa. To illustrate this, a child's emotional attachment to its caregivers may be assessed categorically but the effects may be seen and assessed across a number of dimensions.

Overall, the choice between dimensional and categorical approaches within biological sciences (and elsewhere) is not simple, nor is it a straightforward either/or issue. In practice the choice will be complex and challenging and dependent on the assessment context and purpose. Mixed classification patterns are likely to be the norm in psychological assessment, which may involve dimensional data and outcomes but the need to make categorical decisions.

Diagnosis and formulation

The term diagnosis is often used in clinical practice to refer to a specific form of categorization involving the identification of signs and symptoms, and the use of these to allocate to categories which, in turn, are associated with specific outcomes or prognoses and interventions or treatments.

Formulation refers to approaches concerned with analysing specific cases to produce a plausible explanation of one or more specific problems and a prescription of interventions likely to address these. Case formulation includes an analysis of the problems to be addressed and organization of information within a conceptual explanatory schema. This in turn is associated with intervention decisions that lead to specific procedures (Bruch, 1998).

The differences between diagnosis and case formulation are easy to exaggerate. To a large extent they can be seen as differing descriptions of similar analytic processes, with the former being traditionally dominated by medicine and the latter by psychology. Efforts to stress the differences between these could be cynically seen as reflecting demarcation disputes, rather than representing more substantive process differences. In fact, the use of scientific approaches to assessment in this way cannot reasonably be seen as the exclusive province of any professional group (Towl, 2005).

ASSESSMENT

Hypothesis formulation

Clinical case assessment and subsequent formulation (or the integration and interpretation of assessment data) involves the application of scientific method to individual cases (Shapiro, 1985). It is fundamental to the scientist-practitioner approach common across the various specialist areas of applied psychology (Lane & Corrie, 2006).

The first step within this is the adoption of a theoretical orientation as the basis for generating hypotheses. Each theoretical orientation has its own core assumptions and hypotheses. So, for example, cognitive orientations are based on an assumption of the central role of cognitive processes in behaviour. In contrast, radical behaviourist theory would stress the importance of not attempting to address such processes. While every theory will have its core assumptions and hypotheses, it is noteworthy that there may be significant overlap between these. Apparent differences may simply involve different descriptive language or 'packaging' of similar concepts. As an example, cognitive behavioural therapy (CBT) and narrative therapy (NT) both stress the importance of 'faulty cognitions', but describe this concept using quite different language.

There is clearly a wide range of plausible theoretical orientations that might be drawn on explicitly or implicitly to inform assessments, and these will influence the entire process. Ingram (2006), though, suggests seven dominant types within clinical practice:

  i) Biological models
  ii) Crisis and stressful situational transitions
  iii) Behavioural and learning models
  iv) Cognitive models
  v) Existential and spiritual models
  vi) Psychodynamic models
  vii) Social, cultural and environmental models

Psychological assessment requires efforts to generate provisional explanations and hypotheses, followed by processes intended to test and refine these initial explanations. This can be further broken down into a number of activities paralleling those seen in other areas of science (Crighton & Towl, 2008). These would include:

  i) Problem definition
  ii) Theoretical formulation
  iii) Hypothesis generation
  iv) Data gathering
  v) Data analysis
  vi) Specification of outcome goals
  vii) Intervention planning
  viii) Monitoring of intervention effects
  ix) Use of monitoring data to adapt interventions

These processes provide the foundations of psychological assessment. The process of psychological assessment is also one which can be seen as integrative and iterative in nature. In this context the notion of integration refers to the fact that the process can involve gathering and evaluating information at different times or rates, with integration and reformulation taking place at a later time. Iterative refers to the use of incremental strategies, where the assessor will use learning from earlier stages to inform the overall assessment. This can be illustrated with an example from adult forensic neuropsychology as in Figure 6.2. A key aspect of such approaches is that they involve revision and reformulation in the light of information emerging from previous iterations.

The validity and utility of any assessment can be seen to involve a number of generic activities. These include:

  i) Initial theory development
  ii) Consideration of ethical issues

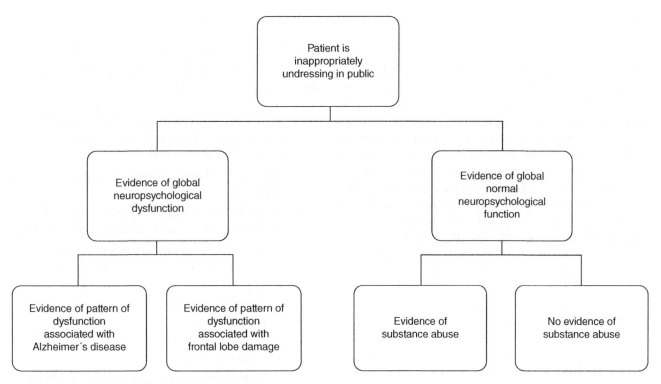

FIGURE 6.2 *Example of an iterative assessment approach.*

iii) Clarification of hypotheses

iv) Development of an overall 'formulation'

v) Priority setting

vi) Planning of intervention strategies

vii) Prediction of responses to interventions

viii) Definition of operational criteria for successful outcomes

ix) Assessment and revisions following failure to respond or blocks to progress

x) Addressing and overcoming individual biases

This outline of assessment leads on sensibly to a discussion of the role of theory, since this can be seen as underpinning the entire process. This is perhaps best illustrated not by an abstract discussion but, rather, by a practical consideration of some major theoretical orientations used in conducting psychological assessments.

Psychodynamic theory

There is no single psychodynamic approach, although all can be traced back to the work of Sigmund Freud (1999). Different schools of thought have, though, developed over the subsequent century. All of these can, however, be seen as sharing a number of common themes:

i) A focus on individual psychological pain and struggle

ii) The existence of an internally constructed world that differs from the external world

iii) The existence of unconscious elements of this internally constructed world which have profound impacts on behaviour

iv) A concern with processes of adaptation to emotional pain and difficulties (Leiper, 2006)

Psychodynamic approaches can be seen as having four main perspectives. They are dynamic in nature, suggesting that all behaviour, however apparently irrational, is purposeful and motivated and explicable as such. The psychological conflicts present in a person will always be unique and are generally too complex for any formulation to fully capture.

They are developmental in nature, suggesting a need to explain the past in order to account for the present and, within psychodynamic approaches, this has often involved stage models of development. The best known of these is perhaps the oral, anal and phallic stages suggested by Freud (1999). However, other psychodynamic theorists have subsequently suggested different stage models of development and often substantive changes to the initial model developed by Freud. Erikson (1966), for example, went on to postulate eight stages of psychosexual development rather than five, suggesting that each person will goes through these in an effort to reach their full developmental potential. He also placed greater stress on the role of the ego as more than a servant of the id. Erikson also placed greater emphasis on the effects of the environment during development in enabling growth, adjustment, self-awareness and the development of a positive 'identity' (Erikson, 1980).

They are structural theories, which suggest the existence of differing conscious and unconscious psychological 'structures' (e.g., the Id, Ego and Super Ego). Importantly, it is generally assumed that the unconscious mind works in a different manner from the conscious. Thus, it has no concept of negation, which allows contradictory propositions to coexist, and it lacks a clear subject–object division, so that one thing might stand for another or many others.

They are also adaptive theories, suggesting that relationships between 'internal' and 'external' worlds are influenced by behaviour and systemic influences. So individual experience will affect the way an individual intersects with the world, through both adaptive and maladaptive processes (Johnstone & Dallos, 2006).

Psychodynamic theories suggest a number of key aspects to assessment that differ from the approaches outlined so far. These would include:

i) The need to go beyond the surface presenting problems however carefully defined and described

ii) The need to focus on the intersection between underlying internal psychodynamic processes and current interpersonal and social situation

iii) The need to focus on early disruption in adjustment and parental relationships in order to address current difficulties in adjustment

iv) That the internal world is the dominant force in structuring perceptions of the world

v) That adjustment to psychological pain and challenges is relative and involves a balance between health and unhealthy approaches

Cognitive behavioural theory (CBT)

CBT represents a fusion of two key theoretical traditions within psychology: behavioural and cognitive psychology. It is perhaps best seen as a broad church of related approaches rather than as being a single unitary approach. In application to specific issues and difficulties it involves a number of fundamental assumptions. It does, though, draw on an extensive, largely empirical, evidence base.

CBT is predicated on a fundamental assumption that any assessment needs to be framed in terms of a 'biopsychosocial' context (Beck, 2005). This involves recognition that simply focusing on psychological factors such as cognitions and behaviours is wholly inadequate. Each individual is part of a much broader and unique matrix of social and biological influences, which are fundamental to effective assessment and subsequent formulation and interventions. This is a notion that, in day-to-day practice, can often be poorly recognized and at times marginalized. In addition, CBT approaches take as their starting point the assumption that the person being assessed is central to the process. More precisely, their perspective and agency are stressed as central.

Johnstone and Dallos (2006) suggest that the approach involves seven key principles:

i) That it draws on cognitive and behavioural psychological theory to inform a better understanding of others

ii) That 'collaborative empiricism' is the basis of the approach

iii) That CBT formulations are provisional and require adapting over the course of interventions

iv) That the approach acts as a framework for assessment, formulation and intervention

v) That a good therapeutic relationship is a necessary but not sufficient condition for a collaborative approach

vi) That the focus should be on current problems and mutually agreed goals

vii) That the approach is complementary to diagnostic categories used in mental health but that such categories are probably only marginal to the course of interventions

There are a range of methods to assist in the process of assessment, which begins with careful identification and description of the presenting issues. This is common to good practice in any assessment, with its stress on the importance of careful observation, clear and agreed definitions and accurate measurement. In CBT approaches, such agreement needs to be between the practitioner and the person they are assessing. Building on such agreement, the process then involves the identification of what may be termed predisposing factors, precipitating factors, perpetuating factors and protective factors (Towl & Crighton, 1996).

CBT approaches provide a variety of methods to assist in this process of assessment, including 'functional analysis', a method which has gone in and out of fashion, but which attempts to systematically establish functional relationships between covariates (Haynes, 1998). While there are multiple ways of completing a functional analysis, all rest on careful observation and data gathering as the basis for interpretation of complex patterns (Daffern, Howells, & Ogloff, 2007; Owens & Ashcroft, 1982).

Systemic theory

Systemic approaches were initially developed in the 1920s, emerging out of the various schools of Gestalt psychology that were then popular. It suggested that individual psychological functioning tended to operate in a holistic and self-organizing fashion. From the 1950s, general systems theory emerged from work within the social and biological sciences and was concerned to offer an explanatory framework for complex 'systems'. Within clinical practice in psychology this often involved the assessment of family 'systems', on the basis that these were the most powerful systems for shaping the development of psychological functioning (Ford & Lerner, 1992; Lerner, Fisher, & Weinberg, 2000). At a theoretical level the approach can still be seen as stressing the role of group social psychological processes to a larger extent than approaches such as CBT which, notwithstanding its own theoretical basis, can often be criticized in practice for often undervaluing these.

Early systemic approaches tended to stress the external analysis of systems interactions but in recent years this has changed. Current systemic approaches stress the need to see therapists themselves as part of the 'system' and at a fundamental level the approach is seen to be based on collaborative interaction between 'helpers' and 'helped' (Dallos & Steadman, 2006).

Systemic assessment can be characterized as involving seven stages:

i) Definition of the problems

ii) Deconstruction of the developmental course of the problems

iii) Establishing links between the problems and 'ordinary difficulties'

iv) Exploration of attempted solutions

v) Beliefs about difficulties and responses to these

vi) Discussion and evaluation of what worked in the past and what did not

vii) Discussion about decisions to persist with some attempted solutions and not to persist with others

A number of clear observations emerge in relation to these stages. The first is perhaps to stress areas of clear overlap with some other theoretical approaches. As noted earlier, while the language differs from that used in CBT, aspects of the logical basis are clearly very similar. What does perhaps differ is the greater influence of constructivist approaches advocated by a number of early (and later) social psychologists (e.g., Kelly, 1955). Because of this influence there is probably a greater tendency within systemic approaches to see case formulations as constructions and propositions than in some other approaches.

Social inequalities theory

Such approaches are, in many respects, similar to systemic theories but differ in drawing more from social psychology and sociological research addressing group differences associated with economic and social inequality. As such they are perhaps especially relevant to forensic practice. Social inequality can be defined as structured differences or hierarchies of power that limit and constrain some and privilege others (Dallos & Steadman, 2006). At a theoretical level the approach is a social constructionist one, with clear links to the work of Max Weber and Karl Marx. It is predicated on the notion that there are clear conflicts of economic interest between groups. The approach can also be seen as a wider challenge to current dominant thinking within Western cultures, with their stress on economic liberalism and individualism (Miller & McClelland, 2006; Rose, 1989).

There is a substantial evidence base which establishes clear links between social and economic inequality and poor health, both physical and mental (Crighton & Towl, 2008; Social Exclusion Unit, 2002). Despite this clear evidence base, issues of social inequality remain largely peripheral in the current practice of applied psychology (Smail, 2004). This is despite the fact that 'low status' groups in society tend to experience the most negative and disempowering contacts with psychologists and psychological therapists (Department of Health, 2003).

The approach differs from many other systemic approaches in stressing the centrality of social, economic and explicit political factors in mental health. The approach sees social agency as inextricably linked to such things as social class, race and gender. The approach also clearly overlaps with systemic approaches in stressing the importance of family systems in mediating the effects of these factors.

Assessment within this model can be characterized as involving five interrelated stages:

i) Definition of difficulties

ii) Analysis of the broad systemic forces that have operated across the person's developmental history

iii) Analysis of the manner in which they have sought to deal with these forces

iv) Analysis of the ways in which the person has gained power and agency in their life

v) Analysis of the ways in which changes to the broader context can contribute to positive changes

This approach to formulation is relatively unusual in often seeing professional psychology (and indeed other professions) as being part of the problem rather than part of the solution. It suggests that there is a need in any society to create ideologies and dialogues that serve to legitimize the status quo, and hence avoid disrupting social and economic inequalities and vested interests. Within this framework mental health professions may be central to legitimizing inequality, by defining excluded groups as 'sick' or 'disordered', setting up a co-dependence between marginalized social groups and professionals (Geuter, 1992; Smail, 2004).

Integrative theories

The term 'integrative theories' refers to systematic efforts to draw from and 'integrate' more than one theoretical approach. These can be in the form of pre-structured approaches or the use of assessment and intervention mixes based on the likelihood of response (Roth, Fonagy, Target, & Woods, 2006).

An example of the former is cognitive analytic therapy (CAT) which, in essence, draws on psychodynamic theory and concepts but integrates this with theory based on cognitive psychology. The posited advantages of this are that it manages to incorporate notions from psychodynamic approaches that are felt to be of value, while also being able to draw on notions and the evidence base from cognitive psychology (Ryle, 1997).

The use of such assessment and intervention 'mixes', based on likely response, is often justified by reference to and analogy with treatment in medicine. Here it is at times appropriate, indeed good practice, to use different drug formulations to address different problems. Such an analogy, though, is open to criticism as something of an intellectual sleight of hand. The use of different drugs in medicine does not necessarily imply the use of different theoretical bases at all. Such approaches also assume an ability to identify evidence on effective treatment components, something which is often, at present, far less applicable to psychological interventions than physiological ones.

DATA GATHERING

The use of theory serves the key function of directing the collection of information, or data. Data gathering, though, presents a range of issues and challenges which need to be addressed. Most obvious of these is perhaps the high degree of dependence within psychology on self-report data. This has a number of implications. Psychological assessment will generally involve the use of at least some self-report data generated via semi-structured and structured interview. It will also frequently involve self-report data derived from psychometric assessments. It may also involve psychometric assessment of behaviours and, more rarely, may involve physical measures associated with psychological functioning.

Another significant challenge is addressing issues of diversity within any assessment. This includes the need to recognize social, economic and political differences as well as issues such as gender, ethnicity, disability, social class and culture. At the most obvious level it is clear that developmental history will differ across individuals based on their social experience. There is also a substantial body of evidence addressing response biases. This refers to the cognitive biases shown when individuals respond to questions in the manner that they believe the person asking them either expects or wants them to answer, as opposed to answering in line with their true behaviour or beliefs. This can result from obvious weaknesses in the approach to assessment, such as the poor use of leading questions. Such biases may also result, though, from the person being assessed seeking to give 'socially acceptable' answers. This is likely to be a factor across many areas of forensic practice where, for example, questions about levels of violence or sexual behaviours are likely to be affected by such considerations. In turn, this will influence the manner in which self-report data may be most usefully gathered. At a more profound level it will open up questions of the need, desirability or ethical basis of assessment. There are, of course, no easy answers. First steps, though, suggest a need for explicit reflection on these issues throughout any assessment and a need to genuinely value the differing experiences of those with problems.[2]

Whatever the theoretical basis used to conduct an assessment, good data gathering will depend on the development of an empathic and trusting relationship. It seems self-evident that few of us would disclose often difficult, generally sensitive, personal information to someone we felt unable to like or trust. This is crucial within psychology, given the extent to which self-report data dominates many assessments. The development of such relationships is also likely to impact markedly on assessment of behaviour and psycho-physiological measures.

Within assessment, it is important to use initial hypotheses as a basis for exploratory work. This needs to be underpinned by a commitment to exploring the individual's problems with them using exploratory questioning. It also requires a fundamental commitment to such hypotheses being provisional and open to revisions or replacement where they do not fit emergent data. This also suggests a need to avoid premature moves to 'fixing' problems and a willingness to use 'trial' approaches as a means of improving the quality of assessment data.

Interviews

The use of interviews is likely to be a key part of any psychological assessment for a number of reasons. These include the fact that this is, generally, a relatively accessible source of self-report information. More fundamentally, for theories such as CBT built on collaborative approaches, it is the main way to establish a positive therapeutic rapport necessary for positive change. Within this model there is no sense that assessment and treatment are mutually exclusive and, in fact, the process of assessment may become a form of treatment. Interviews also have the advantage that they are highly flexible and so can be adapted to address themes and issues as they emerge with individuals. The idiographic nature of interviews, though, also has less positive sides. As an assessment method they tend to have poor reliability. In turn this may be seen to impact on issues of validity and utility. The extent to which interviews are used will also clearly depend on the theoretical basis for the assessment. Assessments based on behavioural theory would, for example, see a very limited role for such self-report information.

Traditional clinical interviews have several well-known weaknesses. Most obviously, the approach has been shown to have relatively low levels of agreement between different interviewers. In terms of categorization, even experienced practitioners have been shown to agree at little better than chance levels (Beck, Ward, Mendelson, Mock, & Erbaugh, 1962). In turn, this has adverse impacts on validity and also the specificity and sensitivity of assessments. Such findings led to efforts to improve the psychometric properties of interviews as an assessment method, generally involving increased use of structuring within interviews. Any interview can be seen as resting on a continuum between low and high levels of structure. At one end of the continuum, such 'interviews' provide an inflexible structure in terms of the questions asked, the order of questions and the ways in which responses are coded. More common has been the development of semi-structured interviews which allow potential for varying degrees of flexibility.

As with all assessments, interviews will have particular psychometric properties, as well as degree of structure, breadth of structure and context of use. The choice of interview approach therefore needs to be tailored to the needs and priorities for any assessment. This means that careful evaluation of the approach adopted is needed. For example, while increasing the structure of an interview may increase reliability, this in turn can also adversely impact on validity and usefulness of the assessment. As an interview becomes more structured and reliable, it may involve questions that are irrelevant to the person being assessed, as well as missing information that is important to inform an accurate and ethical assessment (Towl, 2006).

Choice of assessment here requires consideration of the reliability of the assessment approach used in terms of inter-rater and test–retest reliability, and this is likely to be determined by multiple factors, including:

i) clarity and nature of questions used;
ii) degree of understanding of the questions by the person being assessed and the practitioner conducting the assessment;
iii) training, experience and values of the practitioner;
iv) interview conditions;
v) range of complexity of problems being assessed;
vi) prevalence base rates for what is being assessed;
vii) characteristics of the interviewer.

The validity of an interview will similarly be influenced by such factors, all of which need to be considered in clinical decision-making. The validity of an interview might be seen as its ability to accurately evaluate an operationally defined construct, for example, the capacity of a structured interview to identify an Axis I diagnostic category as defined by DSM-IV (American Psychiatric Association, 2000). An example of an Axis I category here might be a major depressive disorder. A moment's reflection, though, suggests a clear problem with this, in that it can simply become a tautological exercise. It can simply refer to the ability of the interview to accurately identify a collection of factors with varying degrees of association. It does not follow logically that these factors have any theoretical coherence or clinical utility and it is of course possible for an interview to achieve a high degree of reliability and some forms of validity while identifying a clinically meaningless construct (Widiger & Clark, 2000). In the example given in the preceding text of the DSM-IV Axis I category of major depression, the value of allocation to such a diagnostic group depends essentially on the construct validity for this category.

Psychometric assessments

Psychometrics is a specific area within psychological assessment which involves assigning numerical values to one or more properties of an event, using fixed rules. It involves a number of key general considerations and these include the fact that such assessments are seeking to measure psychological attributes which cannot be directly measured. In this respect such assessments are quite different from superficially similar but logically quite different physical measures, concerned with attributes which can be directly measured.

Linked to this point, it is the case that psychological attributes such as 'IQ', 'extraversion' and so on are hypothetical constructs. They cannot be confirmed absolutely. There is also no universal agreement on how to measure such psychological constructs. In reality, the degree or extent to which such constructs can be said to be characteristic of a person can only be inferred from limited samples of the individual's behaviour (McKinnon et al., 2008).

It is also important to note that any measurement of a psychological construct depends on the use of operational definitions. In essence this requires the use of explicit rules of correspondence between the theoretical construct and a sample of observable behaviours. Axiomatically this will always be subject to error. The size of such errors will in turn depend on the accuracy of measurement. Units of measurement in psychological assessments present a range of general problems and are often not well defined. Such measurements need to be based on a clear theoretical basis and may be inter-correlated with other constructs within a theoretical system. Yet, unlike many of the physical and biological sciences, they frequently lack any direct physical measures.

Within psychology a 'test' can be defined as a standard procedure for obtaining a sample of behaviour from a specific domain. It is possible to further subdivide these into:

  i) aptitude, achievement and proficiency tests which comprise a behavioural sample of optimal performance (e.g., IQ tests);

 ii) questionnaires and inventories which comprise a behavioural sample of typical performance (e.g., assessments of personality);

iii) sampling of typical performance in naturalistic settings (e.g., behavioural observation assessments).

Test theory

Most psychological tests have been constructed along the lines of classical test theory (CTT) (Wasserman & Bracken, 2003). This is concerned with the extent to which the specifics of assessment influence the measurements made in a given situation and the methods used to minimize these.

Within classical test theory any observed performance (X) is thought to be composed of the true performance (T) and random error (E). In the population E is assumed to sum to zero and the correlation between T and E is assumed to be zero.

An alternative to classical test theory is item response theory (IRT), which uses more sophisticated forms of data modelling. It is based on the notion that the probability of discrete outcomes on tests is a function of both individual and test item parameters. Within the theory, individual parameters are often termed the 'latent trait', referring essentially to the theoretical construct the test seeks to measure, for example, individual 'intelligence'. IRT provides a logical framework for the estimation of tests. IRT and CTT are sometimes presented as being in opposition to each other but this is potentially misleading. IRT can be seen as a more current and evidence-based theory which serves the functions of allowing greater flexibility in evaluating assessments and achieving higher

levels of reliability by extracting greater detail for individual items (Embretson & Reise, 2000).

DATA ANALYSIS

Reliability

Reliability has a specific statistical meaning within psychological assessment, quite distinct from its day-to-day usage. It is defined as the ratio of the variance in the true score (T) to the variance in the observed score (X) in the population. There are a number of approaches to estimating the reliability of a test. The most frequently used within psychology are:

  i) parallel forms, where parallel versions of a test are used to estimate reliability;

 ii) split-half reliability, where the correlations between item totals for two halves of a test are calculated;

iii) test–retest reliability, where the correlations between repeat administrations of a test are calculated;

iv) standardized item alpha reliability coefficient, where the average correlation of pairs of parallel items is scaled according to test length.

It is important to note that reliability, while it may be a useful measure, is not a goal to be pursued in isolation. It is entirely possible to have high degrees of reliability but little or no validity to an assessment. Clearly low levels of reliability in any assessment are problematic but, in some contexts, increasing reliability may serve to decrease validity (Summerfeldt & Anthony, 2002). It is also important to recognize that reliability is highly context dependent. Assessed levels of reliability will only be applicable across similar conditions. Hence practitioners will always be faced with making clinical judgements of how applicable reliability data (and other psychometric properties) are in the specific context of an assessment.

Validity

Validity can be defined as the potential of the true score (T) to reflect what a test intends to assess (McKinnon, Nixon, & Brewer, 2008). This is the most important and fundamental property of any psychological assessment and it is always a relative property, which needs to be considered in relation to the purpose of any assessment. As such, it is an overall evaluative judgement founded on theoretical rationale and empirical evidence.

As already noted in the preceding text, validity can simply become a tautological exercise where the ability of an assessment to identify a meaningless construct is calculated. Therefore, for validity to be meaningful the core concept being assessed needs to be meaningful. This in turn depends on a mix of a sound theoretical base and inductive and deductive thinking. A number of practical methods have been suggested to improve validity in this respect. For example, in the context of diagnostic categories Spitzer (1983) suggested the Longitudinal observation by Experts using All available Data (LEAD) method, as a means of ensuring that core categories are meaningful. As a method this aims to increase the levels of inter-subjective agreement across a pool of expert observers (Towl, 2005). The method has also been, less charitably, described as the 'best guess' approach (Summerfeldt & Anthony, 2002).

There are three[3] main approaches to estimating the validity of an assessment.

Criterion-related validity

This refers to the extent that one measure correlates with another measure such as a 'gold standard' assessment or subsequent behavioural sample. Criterion-related validity may be further subdivided into concurrent validity, which is concerned with temporally current relationships, and predictive validity, which is concerned with temporally distal relationships. An example here would be the ability of an assessment to predict subsequent violence.

Content validity

This refers to the ability to draw inferences from a test score to a larger item domain similar to those within the test instrument and is often based on expert ratings. An example here would be the extent to which an assessment of depression assessed the relevant dimensions of depression such as the effective aspects and behavioural aspects.

Construct validity

This refers to the extent that an instrument and the theoretical basis of the construct it seeks to measure are mutually verified by way of testable hypotheses. This form of validity generally refers to theoretical constructs that would not be observable directly. An example here might be the extent to which an assessment could measure the hypothetical construct of 'psychopathic personality disorder'.

Specificity, sensitivity and power

Specificity and sensitivity are both statistical concepts with important applications in relation to psychological assessment. Yet, curiously, they are often very poorly integrated into practice and are frequently the focus of confused thinking (Gigerenzer & Selten, 2001).

Specificity refers to the probability that a person who does not have a particular attribute will be correctly identified as not having that attribute, or alternatively the proportion of negative cases correctly identified (true negatives). Sensitivity mirrors this in that it is the probability that a person with a particular attribute will be correctly identified as having it, or alternatively the proportion of positive cases correctly identified (true positives).

The term power here refers to the predictive accuracy of an assessment instrument or the overall proportion of people correctly classified. This is logically related to specificity and sensitivity and can be described in terms of positive or negative predictive power. Negative predictive power is the proportion of those not having a characteristic correctly identified as not having it. Positive predictive power is the proportion having a characteristic correctly identified as having it.

These relationships are often set out algebraically and this perhaps explains the poor application of these concepts to assessment, since there is considerable evidence that people (including those trained in statistics) find such thinking unnatural and difficult to apply. Much easier to understand are examples using natural frequencies, and one example of this in psychological assessment might be efforts to assess the risk of suicide in a forensic setting. Here it is relatively easy to devise a test with good specificity since this involves identifying true negatives. As suicide, even in forensic settings, is a low-frequency event, this can be achieved simply by a decision rule that states that all cases will not complete suicide. The sensitivity of such as assessment, though, would be low as it would miss all the true positives, those who complete suicide. It is therefore critical that as part of any assessment the specificity, sensitivity and power of any assessment is carefully considered (Crighton & Towl, 2008).

Base rates

The term 'base rate' (also sometimes termed 'prior probabilities') refers to the relative frequency of occurrence of an event being studied within the population of interest; one example is the level of violence within a population of men with a diagnosis of major depression. Base rates are a key issue in assessing the psychometric properties of any assessment, since they will markedly impact on the validity of assessments. A key practice implication is that statistical prediction models will not be valid when applied to populations with markedly different base rates from the population for which they were developed.

Normality judgements

Ideas of 'normality' can be approached in a number of ways in relation to psychological tests. These include an approach in terms of mastery, where performance is assessed in relation to a test standard.

Alternatively, it may be approached in terms of statistical normality. This may involve evaluating performance in relation to a specific population or populations. It might alternatively involve evaluation in relation to tolerance limits (e.g., a 95% limit). In turn this might refer to outer tolerance limits (where a score falls outside the limits) and inner tolerance limits (where a score falls within the limits).

Such tolerance limits may be parametric or non-parametric in nature. The former require that the true distribution of original scores be known or can be estimated from a large sample. Non-parametric tolerance limits are those that specify a score as falling at a particular rank in relation to a standardization sample.

Deficit measurement

Deficit measurement presupposes an ideal or normal level of performance which can be used for comparison. For example, within forensic neuropsychological assessments it many involve attempts to compare current and pre-morbid functioning.

Such measurement can involve the use of both normative standards and individual comparison standards using direct and indirect assessment methods. Direct methods involve the use of pre- and post-morbid test scores, such as IQ test scores before and after a specific head injury. Indirect methods involve efforts to estimate this on the basis of estimates based on historical data. Unsurprisingly perhaps, direct measures are rarely available. Indirect measures, though, provide only relatively weak data, leading to efforts to develop tests with good hold properties to facilitate comparisons. An example here has been the efforts to identify tests that are less influenced by neurological damage to provide estimates of pre-morbid functioning (Lezak, 2008).

Single case analysis

Zubin (1967) outlined a number of central issues involved in the analysis of intra-individual observations. Firstly, he suggested that it was essential that individuals should not be prematurely classified into 'patient' groups. Secondly, he noted that individuals will each be characterized by a given level and degree of variability in performance on any given assessment. Thirdly, he stressed that any

assessment result will be the joint product of internal and external causes, which might include such things as spontaneous improvements, impacts of therapeutic interventions and impacts of many other factors. These may also affect the level and scatter of results as well.

In seeking to reach an assessment and formulation for any one person it is important that these issues are addressed. There is often a tendency in practice to reify the results of psychological 'tests' and, regrettably, this is common in both psychologists and non-psychologists alike. In reality, tests in this sense simply contribute to the scientist-practitioner process concerned with theory development, hypothesis generation, testing and reformulation. In this context, tests simply contribute to this by providing data to inform hypothesis formulation or reformulation or both.

CLINICAL JUDGEMENTS AND BIASES

Clinical judgement will generally involve making predictions, inferences or decisions. Good judgements in psychological assessment will need to be informed and influenced by good qualitative and quantitative data. Such judgements in forensic practice will often have important consequences, for example, whether violent offenders can return to the community or be safely managed in less secure settings. The primary purpose of a forensic psychological assessment is therefore to maximize the validity of such judgements. This is likely to be achieved to the extent that they are based on strategies and measurements that are relevant to that specific assessment.

Judgement processes are, however, open to a range of biases (Garb, 1998). These include biases due to such things as the values and beliefs held by the practitioner, their 'intuitions', training and theoretical orientation. This suggests a clear need for practitioners to reflect on these as part of the process of ethical and evidence-based assessment. It also suggests a clear need to develop an on-going willingness to reflect on practice and an openness for reformulating hypotheses and judgements in the light of reflection.

This cuts against idealized but unduly simplistic views of psychological assessment as a process of careful definition, observation, testing using well-validated methods and refining, rejecting and reforming hypotheses to reach a balanced judgement. Faced with complex datasets, practitioners use strategies that oversimplify this, often drawing on a handful of variables. Alternatively, it may result in depending simply on diagnostic categories or single variables thought to have a causal role (Gigerenzer & Selten, 2001; Kahneman, Slovic, & Tversky, 1986). Concrete examples here include efforts to look for the single cause of suicide (e.g., depression) or the single cause of violence (e.g., psychopathic personality disorder).

Another poor approach is to oversimplify complex data by relying simply on standardized assessment 'batteries'. Such approaches may appear superficially attractive to practitioners as providing reliable, valid and cost-effective assessments, but this is almost entirely misplaced. Such standardization may appear to be more cost-effective than more complex and individualized assessments, although this appeal is also misplaced. Mechanistic approaches have tended to increase, not reduce, biases in assessment, and also tend to result in less accurate formulations and decreased efficacy and utility of interventions (Haynes & O'Brien, 2000).

The use of such simplification strategies is also not restricted to new or inexperienced practitioners. Indeed, there is some evidence to suggest that the use of these may explain the finding that, while confidence in judgements increases with experience, validity does not (Garb, 1998).

There is a clear need in conducting psychological assessments to treat it as an iterative scientific process for each assessment. This involves the need to reflect critically on practice and use this to adapt and improve data gathering, formulation and judgement. There are a number of clear practical ways in which the validity of assessments can be increased and biases reduced. These would include:

i)   the use of multiple methods and multiple informants to supply data;

ii) the use of broadly focused and systems-level multivariate assessment strategies;

iii) active consideration of base rates;

iv) the tailoring of assessments to the individual or individual situation;

v)   the collection of data at multiple points over time (time series analysis);

vi) the use of direct and minimally inferential strategies in assessment;

vii) the use of clear and transparent procedures for decision-making;

viii) the use of evidence-based assessment strategies;

ix) avoidance of quick judgements;

x)   treating judgements as both provisional and modifiable in the light of evidence;

xi) avoiding the selection of data that supports preconceptions;

xii) examination of the costs and benefits of judgement errors;

xiii) actively seeking alternative viewpoints from colleagues, supervisors, and other professionals;

xiv) keeping data on the accuracy of clinical judgements;

xv) using transparent procedures to test hypotheses wherever possible (Garb, 1998; Haynes & O'Brien, 2000).

CONCLUSIONS

Assessments within forensic psychology share common logical and scientific underpinnings with those undertaken in other areas of applied psychology. They are, though, often thrown into particularly sharp relief in the context of forensic practice by the legal context of such work. Such contextual factors mean that assessments may have serious consequences and, as a result, are likely to be subject to rigorous and indeed 'forensic' scrutiny.

It is therefore critical that, in conducting assessments and subsequently formulating treatment or intervention approaches, professional practices are followed. This will generally involve the application of scientific method to individual cases in an ethical and evidence-based manner. This presupposes the use of credible theoretical models as the basis for assessment, along with a clear understanding of the models' core assumptions and hypotheses. Assessments also need to actively address issues of diversity, response biases and the biases that any psychologist will bring to their practice and reflect on the process.

Psychological assessment benefits from being seen as a clearly iterative scientific process. This involves the need for earlier steps in an assessment to plausibly inform subsequent steps. It involves a process of critical reflection on practice throughout, and the use of such reflection to adapt and improve the process: including data gathering, formulation, judgements and approaches. In seeking to do this, it is essential that the work is ethically grounded and that the theory base of the work is clear. It is also important that multiple sources of data are drawn on and that these are dealt with in a manner that credibly fits with the available evidence base. In maintaining such standards, critical self-reflection on practice serves as a critical underpinning.

NOTES

1 The term 'clinical' in literal translation means pertaining to the bedside. In practice, its usage is much wider than this, and it is used here, and throughout, to signify structured and systematic approaches to assessment and interventions with an individual or groups of people designed to deliver positive change in relation to their psychosocial functioning. Clearly, clinical activity is a fundamental core competency across applied psychology. Likewise, the term forensic in literal translation is derived from forensic meaning before the forum. In practice, its usage is much wider than simply activities that take place within the context of the judicial and quasi-judicial tribunals which are the modern equivalent of the forum.

2 This is an area where forensic psychology faces significant difficulties and has, arguably, gone backwards from 2005 to date, with the transfer of training costs away from employers and the increase in unpaid internships. This has been associated with a less diverse workforce increasingly made up of young, white, upper-middle-class, privately educated and heterosexual women. It is difficult to think of a social group more different from that seen in forensic practice.

3 Another form of validity sometimes referred to is face validity. This falls outside the definition of validity given in this chapter since it refers to the extent that a test seems relevant to what it seeks to measure. Sometimes seen as a relatively trivial form of validity, it is nonetheless important since it may significantly impact on the acceptability of a test to those completing it.

FURTHER READING

Graham, J. R., & Naglieri, J. A. (Vol. Eds) (2012). *Handbook of psychology. Assessment psychology (2nd edn)*. Irving B. Weiner (Editor in Chief). New York: John Wiley & Sons.

Part of a major updating and revision of the encyclopaedic *Handbook of Psychology*, this volume covers assessment issues over the course of 25 edited chapters. The text is written to exacting academic standards and covers everything likely to be needed for training up to taught doctoral level. The text is generally written in a clear and lucid style, although some chapters involve technical treatments of the subject matter. A critically balanced and evidence-based approach is taken throughout.

Johnstone, L., & Dallos, R. (Eds.) (2013). *Formulation in psychology and psychotherapy (2nd edn)*. London: Routledge.

An expanded and extended version of this introductory text now comprised of 12 chapters. Clearly written and edited, the text covers the interactive nature of assessment and intervention well. It is particularly strong at making clear the essential role of theoretical approaches in delivering ethical and effective psychological approaches. Commendably, the book also covers a broad range of theoretical approaches beyond those that are currently dominant.

Lezak, M. D., Howieson, D. B., Bigler, E. D., & Tranel, D. (2012). *Neuropsychological assessment (5th edn)*. New York: Oxford University Press.

This is an exceptionally detailed and thorough review of the key principles of psychological assessment from a neuropsychological perspective. Written to high academic standards, it has become something of a standard in the field and is essential reading for those engaged in forensic neuropsychology. The text includes a thorough compendium of relevant tests across a broad range of psychological functioning. The current edition has been updated to include colour slides and additional coverage of neuropsychological assessment methods.

REFERENCES

American Psychiatric Association (2000). *Diagnostic and statistical manual of mental disorders: DSM-IV-TR*. Washington, DC: Author.

Beck, A. T. (2005). The current state of cognitive therapy: A 40-year retrospective. Aaron T. Beck. *Archives of General Psychiatry, 62*, 953–959.

Beck, A. T., Ward, C. H., Mendelson, M. D., Mock, J., & Erbaugh, J. K. (1962). Reliability of psychiatric diagnoses: 2. A study of consistency of clinical judgments and ratings. *American Journal of Psychiatry, 119*, 351–357.

Bruch, M. (1998). The development of case formulation approaches. In M. Bruch & F. W. Bond (Eds.), *Beyond diagnosis: Case formulation approaches in CBT*. Chichester: John Wiley.

Clare, A. (2003). *Psychiatry in dissent*. London: Routledge.

Crighton, D. A., & Towl, G. J. (2008). *Psychology in prisons (2nd edn)*. Oxford: BPS Blackwell.

Daffern, M., Howells, K., & Ogloff, J. (2007). What's the point? Towards a methodology for assessing the function of psychiatric inpatient aggression. *Behaviour Research and Therapy, 45*(1), 101–111.

Dallos, R., & Steadman, J. (2006). Systemic formulation. In L. Johnstone & R. Dallos (Eds.), *Formulation in psychology and psychotherapy*. London: Routledge.

Department of Health (2003). *Tackling health inequalities: A programme for action.* London: Author.

Embretson, S. E., & Reise, S. (2000). *Item response theory for psychologists.* Mahwah, NJ: Lawrence Erlbaum.

Erikson, E. H. (1966). Eight ages of man. *International Journal of Psychiatry, 2,* 291–300.

Erikson, E. H. (1980). *Identity and the life cycle.* London: W.W. Norton.

Ford, D. H., & Lerner, R. M. (1992). *Developmental systems theory: An integrative approach.* Newbury Park, CA: Sage.

Freud, S. (1999). *The interpretation of dreams: A new translation by Joyce Crick.* Oxford: Oxford University Press.

Garb, H. N. (1998). *Studying the clinician: Judgment research and psychological assessment.* Washington, DC: American Psychological Association.

Geuter, U. (1992). *The professionalization of psychology in Nazi Germany.* Cambridge: Cambridge University Press. Translation by Richard Holmes.

Gigerenzer, G., & Selten, R. (2001). Rethinking rationality. In G. Gigerenzer & R. Selten (Eds.), *Bounded rationality: The adaptive toolbox.* Cambridge, MA: MIT Press.

Haynes, S. N. (1998). The principles and practice of behavioral assessment with adults. In A. P. Goldstein & M. Hersen (Eds.), *Comprehensive clinical psychology: Assessment volume 4.* Amsterdam: Elsevier Science.

Haynes, S. N., & O'Brien, W. H. (2000). *Principles and practice of behavioral assessment.* New York: Kluwer Academic/ Plenum Publishers.

Ingram, B. L. (2006). *Clinical case formulation matching the integrative treatment plan to the client.* Hoboken, NJ: John Wiley & Sons.

Johnstone, L., & Dallos, R. (2006). Introduction to formulation. In L. Johnstone & R. Dallos (Eds.), *Formulation in psychology and psychotherapy.* London: Routledge.

Kahneman, D., Slovic, P., & Tversky, A. (1986). *Judgement under uncertainty.* New York: Cambridge University Press.

Kelly, G. A. (1955). *The psychology of personal constructs* (vols. 1 and 2). New York: Norton.

Lane, D., & Corrie, S. (2006). *The modern scientist-practitioner.* London: Routledge.

Leiper, R. (2006). Psychodynamic formulation: A prince betrayed and disinherited. In L. Johnstone & R. Dallos (Eds.), *Formulation in psychology and psychotherapy.* London: Routledge.

Lerner, R. M., Fisher, C. B., & Weinberg, R. A. (2000). Toward a science for and of the people: Promoting civil society through the application of developmental science. *Child Development, 71*(1), 11–20.

Lezak, M. D. (2008). *Neuropsychological assessment.* New York: Oxford University Press.

Macrae, C. N., & Bodenhausen, G. V. (2000). Social cognition: Thinking categorically about others. *Annual Review of Psychology, 51,* 93–120.

McKinnon, A. C., Nixon, R. D. V., & Brewer, N. (2008). The influence of data-driven processing on perceptions of memory quality and intrusive symptoms in children following traumatic events. *Behaviour Research and Therapy, 46*(6), 766–775.

Miller, J., & McClelland, L. (2006). Social inequalities formulation – Mad, bad and dangerous to know. In L. Johnstone & R. Dallos (Eds.), *Formulation in psychology and psychotherapy.* London: Routledge.

Owens, R. G., & Ashcroft, J. B. (1982). Functional analysis in applied psychology. *The British Journal of Clinical Psychology, 21*(3), 181–189.

Reyes, H. L. M., Foshee, V. A., Bauer, D. J., & Ennett, S. T. (2012). Heavy alcohol use and dating violence perpetration during adolescence: Family, peer and neighborhood violence as moderators. *Prevention Science, 13*(4), 340–349.

Rose, N. (1989). *Governing the soul: The shaping of the private self.* London: Routledge.

Roth, A., Fonagy, P., Parry, G., Target, M., & Woods, R. (Eds.) (2006). *What works for whom? A critical review of psychotherapy research.* New York: Guilford Press.

Rutter, M. J., & Taylor, E. A. (2002). *Child and adolescent psychiatry* (4th edn). Oxford: Blackwell.

Ryle, A. (1997). *Cognitive analytic therapy for borderline personality disorder: The model and the method.* Chichester: John Wiley.

Shapiro, M. B. (1985). A reassessment of clinical psychology as an applied science. *British Journal of Clinical Psychology, 24,* 1–11.

Smail, D. (2004). Therapeutic psychology and the ideology of privilege. *Clinical Psychology, 38,* 9–14.

Social Exclusion Unit (2002). *Reducing re-offending by ex-prisoners.* London: The Stationery Office.

Spitzer, R. L. (1983). Psychiatric diagnosis: Are clinicians still necessary? *Comprehensive Psychiatry, 24,* 399–411.

Summerfeldt, L. J., & Anthony, M.M. (2002). Structured and semistructured diagnostic interviews. In M. M. Anthony & D. H. Barlow (Eds.), *Handbook of assessment and treatment planning for psychological disorders.* New York: Guilford Press.

Towl, G. (2005). Risk assessment. *Evidence-Based Mental Health, 8,* 91–93.

Towl, G. J. (Ed.) (2006). *Psychological research in prisons.* Oxford: BPS Blackwell.

Towl, G. J., & Crighton, D. A. (1996). *The handbook of psychology for forensic practitioners.* London: Routledge.

Wasserman, J. D., & Bracken, B. A. (2003). Psychometric characteristics of assessment procedures. In J. R. Graham & J. A. Naglieri (Vol. Eds), *Handbook of psychology: Assessment psychology.* Irving B. Weiner (Editor in Chief). New York: John Wiley & Sons.

Widiger, T. A., & Clark, L. A. (2000). Toward DSM-V and the classification of psychopathology. *Psychological Bulletin, 126,* 946–963.

World Health Organization (1990). *International statistical classification of diseases and related health problems: ICD-10.* Geneva: Author.

Zubin, J. (1967). Classification of the behavior disorders. *Annual Review of Psychology, 18,* 373–406.

7 Risk Assessment

David A. Crighton

Risk assessment involves systematic efforts to estimate and evaluate outcomes. It is worth stressing at the outset that risk assessment is a process common to a number of areas including medicine, engineering and the social sciences. Given the breadth of the evidence base the focus of this chapter is on the manner in which psychological risk assessments may be used within legal systems to aid decision-making. The logic behind risk assessment is relatively straightforward and easy to understand, it is neverthelessan area where misunderstandings are commonly seen for a number of reasons. These include issues such as the poor understanding or use of language around the area of risk, the nature of measurement and the meaning and interpretation of risk estimates.

KEY LEGAL ISSUES

There has been a marked growth in the use of risk assessment methods in relation to policy, legal decision-making and the allocation of resources across a number of jurisdictions including the United States (Schwalbe, 2008), Canada (Hanson & Morton-Bourgon, 2009), the United Kingdom (Towl, 2005), Sweden (SBU, 2005), Australia (Mercado & Ogloff, 2007) and New Zealand (Vess, 2008). This has included the use of preventative detention on the basis of risk and the prescription of specific risk assessment instruments, for example, as in the case of Severe Personality Disorder services in the United Kingdom (Towl, 2005) or Sexually Violent Predator statutes in Virginia (Skeem & Monahan, 2011). The use of risk assessment methods in forensic practice has also expanded to include assessments of risk in workplace settings and most recently the risk of violent terrorism (Kebbell & Porter, 2012; Monahan, 2012).

Risk assessment involving psychologists is most commonly seen in three settings: criminal justice, health and social care and child protection. Within criminal justice the traditional focus is generally with a person or group of persons as the source of potential harms to others. In health and social care contexts the individual being assessed is more generally seen as a possible source of harm and of being subject to harm. In child protection settings the emphasis varies across jurisdictions but risk assessment will involve a balance between the risk of harm to a child within difference settings (e.g., within a family or a residential home). The distinction between risk assessment in criminal and civil contexts has been historically dominant within forensic psychology but it is misleading. Offenders often present with a range of mental health problems that make them more likely to be recipients of harm as well as perpetrators of it (Barry, 2007).

Risk can be generally defined as the probability of an adverse event happening. A widely used definition of risk assessment has been that given by Kraemer *et al.* (1997 p. 340) as: 'The process of using risk factors to estimate the likelihood (i.e., probability) of an outcome occurring in a population'. This definition is sufficiently broad to encompass the wide range of risk assessments and can also be applied across disciplines and is the one drawn on here. Risk factors can be defined as some measurable entity which is thought predictive of an outcome and are often sub-divided into historical factors (which are unlikely to change) and clinical factors (which may be amenable to change). Notions of 'dangerousness' are common across a number of legal jurisdictions. These draw on the terms day-to-day use but may also refer to more precise constructions of the word. Legal notions of dangerousness might generally be seen to include two distinct concepts: the risk of an outcome

Forensic Psychology, Second Edition. Edited by David A. Crighton and Graham J. Towl.
© 2015 John Wiley & Sons, Ltd. Published 2015 by British Psychological Society and John Wiley & Sons, Ltd.

and the assessed undesirability of the outcome. To take a concrete example: the probability of violence towards others and the severity of that violence.

As in other areas where scientific method has been usefully applied, risk assessment has progressed through the use of more precisely defined language and systematic analysis of available information. More precisely defined terms have been used to describe the process with the term hazard used to refer to something that might result in an outcome. So, for example, going into a town centre may present the same hazard of being violently assaulted but the probability of occurrence (the risk) may change, depending on whether it is late at night or mid-morning. Risk assessment is therefore concerned with the probability of an outcome associated with exposure to one or more hazards (Reason, 1990). Another convention is that the term 'harm' is used to refer to any adverse outcome, the term hazard therefore refers to anything which has the potential to result in harm.

KEY PRINCIPLES IN RISK ASSESSMENT

It has been suggested that there are currently two dominant models of risk assessment: a risk taking model and a risk minimization model (Davis, 1996). The risk taking model sees exposure to risk as a normal facet of life and places its emphasis on individual rights, abilities, choice and participation. The risk minimization model by contrast sees risk as something requiring control, therefore targeting those most at risk and stressing notions such as health, danger, control and incapacity. These models are perhaps better seen as a continuum than a simple dichotomy and there are marked international differences in which approach to risk is predominant. The risk minimization model is perhaps most clearly seen in the United States, Canada, the United Kingdom and Australia.

A major area of contention within risk assessment has been the question of how harm is determined. It has been convincingly argued that the desirability or otherwise of an outcome is not always self-evident. Harms are in reality social constructs and efforts to minimize harms will also have significant costs in areas such as rights and participation. There will be a range from social constructs that enjoy general agreement, such as the notion that children should be protected from sexual activity with adults to those where agreement is much less universal, for example, in relation to drug use or terrorist activity.[1] Notions of harm are therefore a product of processes of social negotiation (Douglas, 1986). When such ideas were first put forward they were seen as both radical and con-

tentious and were subject to extensive, but ultimately unconvincing criticism. This has led to such a view being increasingly seen as mainstream (Towl, 2005).

There has been an increased focus on risk within criminal and civil justice settings internationally with a number of Government driven reviews and legislation based on notions of risk assessment. Examples here would include the MacLean Committee on Serious & Violent Sex Offenders (1999) in Scotland, the Sex Offenders Act (2003) in England & Wales and the Sexually Violent Predator Act in the United States. There has been an increased and arguably increasing socio-political stress on the measurement and management of risk.

Approaches to risk assessment

Three main approaches to assessing risk that cut across subject boundaries have been evident:

- The expression of all possible outcomes as probabilities
- The expression of particular future outcomes as probabilities on the basis of samples of past events
- The estimation of the likelihood of future events based on the widest range of experience, knowledge and care that can reasonably be applied to the context in question

The first of these approaches is typified by the common statistical paradigm which involves studies of multiple events, such as the results of repeated rolls of dice, or coin tosses, or drawing cards from a deck. Here the *a priori* probability of outcomes is known, such as a 1 in 6 chance of rolling a 5 or a 1 in 52 chance of drawing a the ace of hearts. In the past statistical models drew heavily on such paradigms in developing models of probability. The second approach builds on this and would include such things as actuarial estimates based on populations. Here the *a priori* probabilities are generally not known but, it is argued, may be estimated on the basis of sampling from what are thought to be similar populations. This approach has been of significant commercial value and would include areas such as life insurance and accident insurance. Here the risk ascribed to an individual case is based on historical data drawn from the ostensibly similar population. If these populations are well chosen then they will, on a group basis, predict outcomes at a better than chance level. Actuarial assessments of risk in areas such as child abuse have used a similar approach, where the characteristics of a similar population are used to predict outcomes. The third approach involves using the methods involved in the first two approaches but adding in additional information to produce what might be termed a best estimate. Examples of this would include efforts to merge actuarial measures and clinical judgements in a structured manner, to improve the predictive accuracy of individual assessments.

In its idealized form risk assessment can be seen to involve a number of central methodological principles. These would include:

i) Efforts to precisely specify the hazards being assessed

ii) Efforts to precisely specify possible outcomes

iii) Efforts to assess the probability of specific outcomes

iv) Efforts to assess the severity of specific outcomes

From this, it can be seen that even simple examples of risk assessment can involve complex levels of analysis (Breakwell, 2007). This perhaps explains the oft-reported (and misreported) general finding that people are poor at making unaided assessments of risk (Gigerenzer & Selten, 2001; Kahneman, Slovic, & Tversky, 1982).

This is perhaps not entirely surprising and a number of factors make unaided accurate risk assessment a remarkably difficult task. The first obvious factor is that such assessment will involve the use of imperfect information. Hazards may also be correlated with each other, they may interact and may indeed do so synergistically. Professional and scientific opinion may be genuinely divided and the hazards may be poorly understood. This implies that even relatively simple areas of risk assessment present a complex problem of analysis. A frequently used example here has been the failure of aerospace components. Such hazards are relatively well understood. In addition, the characteristics of such components can be precisely defined and subject to controlled testing and analysis. Yet even here, within well understood and relatively constrained systems, it is evident that components can interact with other components – often in unanticipated ways. In turn, failures may result from such interactions, as well as resulting from the component itself (Reason, 1990; Towl & Crighton, 1996, 1997).

The situation in relation to risk assessment involving what might be broadly termed 'social' settings is much more complicated. There is a generally poor understanding of the determinants of the types of behaviour likely to be of interest, such as violence in families or the association between violence and mental health. The ability to measure and specify in this context is invariably far weaker than in the physical systems referred to earlier. Human behaviour is itself part of relatively unconstrained and unbounded systems. Behaviour is also largely interactional in nature and the nature of these interactions, and the social and cultural context of behaviour, is not well understood. In addition, the role of random events, an issue in any area of risk assessment, is likely to present escalating challenges over time (Towl, 2005). Such difficulties have long been recognized in psychology and may be mathematically formalized as 'random walk' models, which are widely used across both the social and physical sciences, providing a systematized notion of the scale of challenge involved in prediction over a series of events (Pearson, 1905). Interestingly, Pearson appeared to conclude, albeit humorously, that normal cognitive heuristics might indeed serve better than mathematical models in addressing this problem.

In common with other efforts at risk assessment, the aim within forensic psychology has been to improve the accuracy of risk assessment. This can be seen as involving a number of definable and logical steps and it is important that these are well understood. In doing this a variety of structures have been suggested to inform the process of risk assessment. Figure 7.1 outlines an example in the form of the Cambridge Model for Risk Assessment (CAMRA), a public domain structured clinical judgement framework designed primarily for the analysis of risks of violent behaviours.

The methodology involved in completing the risk assessments using this model is similar to other forms of psychological assessment and formulation in that it depends on a high level of skill and an ability to integrate multiple methods of analysis. Effective risk assessment within such models will involve a number of elements fundamental to scientific method. These may include:

- Experimentation, including the use of diagnostic testing, to generate data and/or the use of data from previous experimentation

- The use of simulation based on prior analysis of systems

- Modelling to replicate larger and more complex systems

- The analysis of databases that reflect patterns of previous related incidents

- The use of expert opinion data (itself a form of database)

Such models of risk assessment have experienced a sustained decline in recent years. There are a number of possible reasons for this. They suffer many of the same problems attributed to clinical assessments and judgements more generally. It can be argued that they have relatively weak psychometric properties, or that these properties are not clear or measurable.

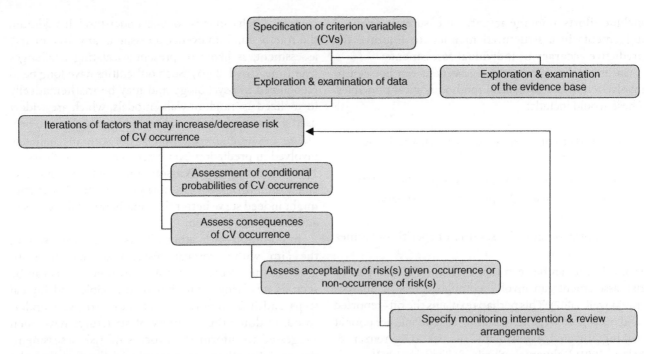

FIGURE 7.1 *Cambridge Model for Risk Assessment. From* Psychology in prisons *(2nd edn) by Crighton, D. A., & Towl, G. J., 2008, Oxford: Blackwell. Reproduced with permission.*

RISK ASSESSMENT INSTRUMENTS

The trend towards developing empirical assessments of behavioural risks can be seen to stem largely from the influential work of Paul Meehl (1954; 1959; 1967; 1973). In these papers Meehl and his collaborators made a distinction between 'actuarial' (statistical) and clinical prediction. It was noted that when cases were pooled, actuarial predictors of risk tended to perform better than clinical judgments commonly used at the time, when seeking to predict future outcomes. A marked growth in the development and application of statistical risk assessments instruments has followed on from this. These instruments generally involved the use of a number of 'risk factors' to estimate an overall probability of a given outcome by means of statistical techniques such as linear regression. In this respect they were similar to the methods used by car insurers, where a series of 'risk factors' such as age, number of years without a claim and so on are used to predict the likelihood of a claim against the policy. Given an adequately large sample of data such instruments are not difficult to devise using fairly straightforward statistical techniques.

There has been, over recent years, an exponential growth in the marketing of such actuarial approaches (sometimes rather curiously termed 'tools') in psychology. Many have been designed to aid in risk assessment in areas of legal interest. An early example of this was the development of instruments for use in the often contentious area of child welfare and these were reviewed in a key paper by Wald and Woolverton (1990). They began by making the central point that efforts to assess risk were only relevant where some balance needed to be struck: in the case of child welfare between the rights of the child and the rights of the parent. If it were simply the case that children should be protected at all costs, then clearly estimates of risk became irrelevant. In reality a balance does need to be struck between the rights of the child and the rights of the family, something which is in fact stressed across jurisdictions and also within human rights frameworks, where a right to family life is stressed as fundamental. As a result Wald and Woolverton (1990) noted the importance of efforts to try to understand the risks to children more effectively. They also raised a number of fundamental concerns about the growth in risk assessment instruments and the application of these in the 1970s and 1980s in the United States.

More recently there has been the development of approaches which fall between the clear distinction between 'actuarial' and 'clinical' assessment. Assessments have generally been developed to address areas of legal concern including violence towards children, violence towards adults, sexual violence and, more recently, areas such as terrorism. These instruments have been variously described as 'second generation', 'third generation', 'new generation' assessments and so on. Critics have suggested that such terms are essentially marketing methods rather than describing any fundamental shifts in paradigm in risk assessment, with the development of new structured clinical assessments not differing fundamentally from earlier approaches (Towl, 2005).

It has been suggested that risk assessment instruments can now be seen as lying on a continuum, with unstructured clinical assessment at one end and structured statistical predictors at the other. In a review of the area, Skeem and Monahan (2011) suggest that risk instruments can be described in terms of the extent to which they provide a structure to four elements:

i)   The identification of risk factors
ii) The measurement of risk factors
iii) The combination of risk factors
iv) The production of a final risk estimate

In a clinical assessment they note that none of these elements are structured in advance and the practitioner would determine which risk factors to measure, how to measure and combine them and how to produce a final estimate. Early advocates of statistical approaches were highly and often unfairly critical of such approaches. For example, it has been noted that when looking at group data:

'clinical judgment has been undervalued in previous research. Not only did clinicians pick out a statistically more violent group, but the violence that the predicted group committed was more serious than the acts of the comparison group. Nonetheless the low sensitivity and specificity of these judgments show that clinicians are relatively inaccurate predictors of violence'.

(Lidz et al., 1993).

There is some evidence to suggest that actuarial and structured clinical approaches may be more accurate than clinical assessment, often due to the low inter-rater reliability and test-retest reliability of clinical assessments (Hanson & Mouton-Borgon, 2009). A number of instruments which use structured clinical judgment approaches have been developed with a view to addressing these weaknesses by using varying degrees of structure to aid clinical assessment. Comparing risk instruments on this basis Skeem and Monahan (2011) looked at five commonly used examples. The use of a standard list of risk factors is the least structured form of judgment in simply identifying a number of risk factors. Assessments such as, for example, the Historical and Clinical Risk 20 (HCR-20), a widely used assessment of risk of violence, go one step further in defining the list of risk factors and how these risk factors are measured. Assessments such as the Classification of Violence Risk (COVR) and Level

of Service Inventory Revised (LSI-R) also determine the way in which risk factors should be combined but allow for clinicians reaching a final risk estimate. The Violence Risk Appraisal Guide (VRAG) and Offender Group Reconviction Scale (OGRS) and similar actuarial assessments provide the rules for determining the final risk estimate without input from the assessor.

Structured clinical judgement has also been developed using techniques commonly seen in the biological sciences and engineering, such as classification and iterative classification tree methods (Appelbaum, Clark Robbins, & Monahan, 2000). Analyses of classification tree approaches have been conducted in relation to a large sample of civil psychiatric patients discharged into the community but yielded disappointing results, with performance slightly poorer than for a more traditional logistic regression approach. In seeking to improve on this level of performance, the curious but then common approach of categorizing risk using a single cut-off point (violent versus non-violent) was looked at afresh (Monahan et al., 2001). An approach using two cut-off points was tested. This created three groups, one where the level of risk appears indistinguishable from the population base rate on the basis of the available risk factors, one where it is lower and one higher (Appelbaum et al., 2000; Monahan et al., 2001).[2] It was hypothesized that by focusing on the two extreme ends of the distribution the accuracy of estimates of risk could be improved.

Drawing on the base rates for violence in their sample, high risk was defined operationally as twice the base rate (>37% over 12 months) and low risk as half the base rate (<9% over 12 months).[3] They found that, using these cut points, 42.9% of the sample were unclassified using the logistic regression main effects approach and 49.2% using the simple classification tree approach (Monahan et al., 2001). In practice, this highlights a major weakness of both models. Even with the addition of a low-risk cut-off point, only slightly over half of those assessed were classified as high or low risk. The remainder were not differentiated from the base rate for violence group, providing little in the way of added utility from the risk assessment.

The researchers went on to look at the use of repeated iterations within a classification tree approach (an iterative classification tree [ICT] model) in an effort to improve on this. This involved conducting repeated iterative analyses on the remaining 'unclassified' group. A second iteration allocated 119 of these individuals to either high- or low-risk groups; a third iteration 63 and a fourth iteration 60, at which point the researchers stopped. Using this form of recursive partitioning the researchers found that 77% of the sample could be allocated to high- or low-risk groups, representing a significant improvement. As a result of the analysis they had identified six low-risk subgroups (49%), four high-risk subgroups (27%) and two average-risk subgroups (23%).[4] The approach was found to be comparable in terms of accuracy to the non-recursive model but was able to classify a significantly greater proportion of cases into high- and low-risk groups.[5] The authors went on to test the model statistically using a technique called 'bootstrapping', which involves mathematically increasing the sample size by randomly duplicating cases. This larger hypothetical 'sample' is then randomly sampled and tested to see how effectively repeated samples fit the new model (Mooney & Duval, 1993). Although open to methodological criticisms, the results from this suggested that the model continued to work effectively.

Of the risk factors included in this analysis, the single factor which performed best was the Psychopathy Checklist – Screening Version (PCL-SV) (Odds Ratio (OR) 2.40), followed by grandiose delusions (OR 2.28), father's drug use (OR 2.18) and drug abuse diagnosis (OR 1.58). The researchers noted that a number of the risk factors included in the initial analysis raised both clinical and economic issues. The use of psychological assessments such as the PCL is labour intensive and expensive, raising the question of whether they have additional utility and, if so, whether this is cost-effective. This was tested by re-conducting the analysis, removing the 28 risk factors that would be most difficult to obtain in a civil mental health context. This included detailed psychological assessments such as the PCL and also details of criminal history. The model was then tested using the remaining 106 risk factors that were relatively easy to obtain. This analysis achieved three iterations allocating 72.6% of individuals to high- or low-risk subgroups and yielding four low-risk subgroups (51%), three high-risk subgroups (22%) and four average-risk subgroups (27%), and performed at a similar level in terms of accuracy (Monahan et al., 2001).

This analysis suggested that the performance of the ICT model was comparable in terms of efficacy using 106 risk factors or using 134.[6] The use of expensive assessments, such as the PCL, appeared to have at best marginal utility. Equally good accuracy in risk assessment could be achieved using relatively straightforwardly obtained clinical risk factors, when analysed appropriately (Appelbaum et al., 2000; Crighton, 2009; Monahan et al., 2001, 2005; Towl, 2005; Towl & Crighton, 1997).

While this model achieved comparable levels of accuracy, it did result in a degree of differential allocation, with 57% of cases being similarly allocated under both approaches (r 0.52, p < 0.001). This is, of course, a general characteristic of any actuarial risk assessments, where approaches will generally be imperfectly correlated with each other. In order to address this issue an analysis was conducted repeating the ICT approach and

combining two models. Interestingly, of those classified as low risk in both models, 3% were violent during the 20-week follow-up period; of those classified as high risk by both models, 64% were violent during the 20-week follow-up period (Monahan et al., 2001).

There have been a number of studies which have looked at the efficacy of such risk assessment instruments. A study by Campbell, French, and Gendreau (2007) suggested that none of the structured risk assessment instruments reviewed were consistently superior in terms of their predictive validity. A later meta-analysis of 28 studies, which controlled well for methodological variation, showed little difference in performance across 9 widely used risk assessment instruments (Yang, Wong, & Coid, 2010). This meta-analysis drew on the Area Under the Curve (AUC) statistic: this plots the false positive rate for an assessment against the true positive rate, across score thresholds. In doing this the statistic describes how well a risk assessment instrument distinguishes between those who are violent and non-violent across all cut offs. The authors concluded that these assessments, which included widely used approaches including the HCR-20, LSI-R and VRAG, were essentially interchangeable, with all estimates falling within a narrow band of accuracy (AUC = .65 to .71).

In another study what were memorably described as 'coffee can instruments' were evaluated (Kroner, Mills, & Reddon, 2005). Here items from a number of widely used structured assessments of violence were printed on strips of paper, which were then placed in a coffee can and drawn out randomly. These randomly drawn items were then used to form new risk assessment instruments. These new assessments went on to predict violence and non-violence with similar accuracy to the original instruments. It has been suggested that all the items used were in reality tapping into four broad and overlapping factors involved in violence: criminal history, an irresponsible lifestyle, psychopathy and criminal attitudes and substance abuse related problems (Skeem & Monahan, 2011).

A meta-analysis of a larger sample of studies was conducted by Singh and Fazel (2010; Singh, Grann, & Fazel, 2011). This systematically reviewed 68 studies involving 25,980 participants. In all nine of the most widely used risk assessments in current use were evaluated: the Level of Service Inventory – Revised (LSI-R), Psychopathy Checklist – Revised (PCL-R), Sex Offender Research Appraisal Guide (SORAG), Static-99, Violence Risk Appraisal Guide (VRAG), the Historical and Clinical Risk-20 (HCR-20), the Sexual Violence Risk 20 (SVR-20), the Spousal Assault Risk Assessment (SARA) and the Structured Assessment of Violence Risk in Youth (SAVRY). Using the median AUC statistic, the findings were similar to those of Yang et al. (2010) with the performance of the assessments being similar. Only modest differences in accuracy from the least to the most accurate (.66 to .78) were noted, suggesting that these assessments were in fact interchangeable.

However, the authors note that while AUC is suggested as the statistic of choice by some experts (Swets, Dawes, & Monahan, 2000) it has a number of weaknesses, when used in the context of conducting meta-analyses. Firstly, it is not sample size dependent and this may be linked in turn to an over optimistic view of structured risk assessments (Sjöstedt & Grann, 2002). It also means that it is not possible to explore heterogeneity by means of meta-regression (Thompson & Higgins, 2002). They therefore went on to use a number of alternative statistical measures of accuracy and a combined estimate of accuracy for each instrument. The Positive Predictive Value (PPV) is the proportion of those predicted to offend who actually did and the Negative Predictive Value (NPV) is the proportion predicted not to offend who did not offend. A difficulty with both these statistics is that they can vary depending on the base rate of the outcome being measured. Singh, Grann, & Fazel (2011) therefore also considered the Diagnostic Odds Ratio (DOR), which is essentially the Odds Ratio of true positives divided by the Odds Ratio of false positives. They noted that this has the advantage of not being dependent on the base rate for the outcome being considered and noted that this statistic is recommended by a number of experts for use in meta-analysis of diagnostic studies (e.g., Deville *et al.* 2002). Use of the DOR also allowed them to use meta-regression to assess sample heterogeneity. When using odds ratio statistics the difference in accuracy between structured assessments of risk appeared more marked than when using the AUC statistic: ranging from 1.2 to 7.9. In addition they went on to calculate a composite index for the assessments, based on a ranking of performance on each of the statistics used to evaluate them and a pooling of these rankings. This suggested a significant degree of variation between the performance of different instruments, with the SAVRY performing best with a score of 60 and the PCL-R and LSI-R worst with 26 and 22, respectively. Based on these findings they suggested that it may in fact be significant which instrument is used to assess risk of violence, with some performing significantly better than others. They concluded that the SAVRY, an assessment focused on young offenders, performed best and the PCL-R and LSI-R performed worst.

A number of risk assessment instruments have been designed to assess risk, as well as direct interventions to reduce and reassess risk. Probably the best known of these is the LSI-R but there has been a recent growth in this approach with, for example, the development of ASSET (designed for use with young offenders in the United Kingdom) (Baker, 2005) and the Violence Risk Scale (VRS) designed for use with adults (Dolan & Fullam, 2007). The approach has also been notably used on a large scale with the Offender Assessment System (OASys). This instrument was developed in England and Wales in the 1990s drawing on the work in Canada from the 1990s (Bonta & Andrews, 2007). Pilot studies were undertaken in 1999 and it was implemented nationally from around 2003, in prisons and probation, for a broad range of those in the criminal justice system. It was designed to assess levels of risk, as well as identifying what were termed 'criminogenic needs'. The assessment was also designed to be used on what was termed a 'multiwave' basis, meaning simply that it could be re-scored. It was argued that this would allow assessment of reductions in risk associated with interventions (Howard & Dixon, 2013).

CRITICAL ISSUES IN RISK ASSESSMENT

There are a number of critical issues involved in the area of risk assessment within forensic psychology. In their paper Wald and Woolverton (1990) expressed serious reservations about the development of risk assessment instruments and the motives for such development. They noted that many instruments were inadequately developed and had poor psychometric properties. Little was known about the inter-rater reliability or the predictive validity of these assessments, yet they were often used or mandated in legal decision-making. They went on to consider why there was such a rush to use inadequate but superficially plausible methods. In the context of child care they noted that structured risk assessment instruments were often adopted as an apparent quick fix. The accurate assessment of child welfare had traditionally depended on highly skilled practitioners and the investment of time and effort in understanding child and family needs. Risk assessment instruments suggested a way that this could be done in a less resource intensive way, without the need to develop and invest in skilled staff. This conversion of risk assessment from complex social care and clinical assessments to checklist based approaches held a clear appeal to managers and service funders. Indeed such approaches may be justified if they were more accurate and improved outcomes. In the case of child welfare Wald and Woolverton (1990) noted that this was not what happened.

In reviewing the adoption of these assessments they firstly noted the haste involved in development and implementation. Assessments were often developed for profit and inadequate efforts to ensure reliability and validation had been made. There was frequently little information on whether these instruments were reliable or valid predictors of any given outcomes across populations and across time. In essence the paper provided an early warning that structured risk assessments in this area may have had the appearance of being scientific, seeming to give precise estimates, but in reality lacking the substance of being properly developed. Such criticisms would seem to remain valid today across a much broader range of applications.

A number of fundamental criticisms of risk assessment have also been raised, particularly where risk minimization models have become dominant. Here it has been suggested that risk assessment has become primarily about the regulation of staff and limiting legal liability when harms occur. The approach has been described as creating 'automated environments' where personal relationships and trust are devalued and the social exclusion of offenders is increased (Hayles, 2006). In this the growth of risk assessment can be seen as a part of a wider growth of a neo-liberal political economy (Rose, 1996). Perhaps one of the most striking example of this has been the large scale implementation of structured assessments in correctional settings and the use of OASys and ASSET in England & Wales provide a clear exemplar. Here traditional approaches of supporting and 'treating' offenders by means of skilled staff have been replaced by a largely automated system of 'offender management'.

In a related critique Brown (2005) has questioned the stress within such risk assessment systems on historical (or 'static') risk factors, suggesting that these are very often seen outside any social context. In turn this leads to such factors being seen as issues for the individual to address, rather than social issues for society to address. Factors such as family breakdown, low family income, single parenthood and low IQ have been shown to be predictive of both poor mental health and criminal justice outcomes (Farrington, 2002). Yet such factors have often become defined as individual 'static' risk factors, when in reality the individual has often had little responsibility for or control over them. In this respect Brown (2005) makes a criticism that is widely directed at forensic psychology: that problem behaviour becomes conveniently individuated and, as such, not matters of social justice or social inclusion.

The use of risk assessment in child protection has been largely driven by a number of tragedies seen internationally and which caught the media spotlight. It is suggested that this led to an increased tension in practice between 'child welfare' and 'family support' approaches. The former have become increasingly dominant in the United States, United Kingdom, New Zealand and Australia; the latter have been more common in Europe and Asia. In Eire a Child Protection Notification System was introduced (Horwarth, 2005) and in New Zealand a national Risk Estimation System (RES) was instituted in the 1990s, using a computer based model of risk. The latter system was unusual in using a model that stressed consensual engagement with families, as well as assessing severity of abuse, vulnerability and likelihood of future abuse. Criticisms of risk assessment have in many respects mirrored those seen in criminal and health and social care contexts and those raised earlier by Wald and Woolverton (1990) in relation to developing US practice. In the United States, where the use of risk assessment instruments has been most widespread, it has been noted that in only half of substantiated child abuse cases is a service offered. This has been in parallel to large scale privatization and deregulation of child welfare services (Jones, 2014). Widely used risk instruments such as the Family Risk Assessment (FRA) show higher than average reliability but only accurately classify two in three cases (Loman & Siegel, 2004), again leading to concerns that the approach is more about control of staff and management of litigation risks, than protecting children from harm.

The issue of the precision of risk assessment instruments as they apply to groups and to individuals has also been the focus of concern. An important paper by Hart, Michie, and Cooke (2007) looked at this via two widely used structured risk assessment instruments: the VRAG which seeks to predict the risk of violence and the Static-99 which seeks to predict the risk of sexual violence. The authors noted that the stakes involved in such assessments are, for the individual concerned, often very high. They may, for example, include indefinite detention in correctional settings. The rationale for choosing the VRAG and Static-99 is not given but perhaps relates to the extent to which such assessments are automated and limit the role of the clinician. Within these actuarial assessments there is no scope to modify or mitigate any risk assessments in light of additional clinical or other information. With these assessments the role of the practitioner is essentially the collection of information and the application of standardized scoring (Harris, Rice, & Quinsey, 1993). As noted earlier, such methods have a clear managerialist appeal. They offer a high degree of control over staff and can be used, among other things, to drive staffing cost savings. They may also be seen as mitigating risks associated with litigation, although such claims are less convincing.

Hart, Michie, and Cooke (2007) looked at the 95% confidence intervals that are involved in making both group and individual predictions of risk using these assessments. Confidence intervals may be defined as an estimated range of values which is likely to include an unknown population parameter, the estimated range being calculated from a given set of sample data. Where independent samples are taken repeatedly from the same population, and a confidence interval calculated for each sample, then a certain percentage (confidence level) of the intervals will include the unknown population parameter (Glasgow University Statistics Laboratory, 2013). It is common practice in a number of research areas to refer to 95% and 99% confidence intervals, although these values are largely arbitrary and in theory an infinite number of confidence intervals could be defined. How wide a confidence interval is gives an indication of the level of uncertainty involved in any estimate. The authors usefully summarize the concept in relation to the instruments being assessed as: 'Given a group of n people with ARAI [Actuarial Risk Assessment Instrument] scores in a particular category, we can state with 95% certainty that the proportion of recidivists will fall between the upper limit and lower limit'.

In calculating confidence intervals (CIs) Hart, Michie, and Cooke (2007) used a method outlined by Wilson (1927) which can be used without access to raw data. Using this method the authors calculated the precision of group estimates for both the instruments. For the VRAG, they reported that the 95% CIs for score categories on the assessment ranged from 13 to 30 percentage points in width, with a mean of around 20 percentage points. For the Static 99 the 95% CIs for score categories ranged from 8 to 19 percentage points in width, with a mean of around 13 percentage points. The VRAG suggests 9 categories of risk and the results suggested that the adjacent score categories on the VRAG overlapped to a large extent: categories 1–4 overlapped and categories 5–7 overlapped. Category 8 also overlapped with category 7 and category 9 overlapped with category 8. Drawing on this the authors suggested that the VRAG was in reality only identifying three reasonably distinct group estimates of risk: 'low', 'moderate' and 'high' risk. For the Static-99 which suggested 7 distinct categories of risk, they likewise found significant overlapping. For this assessment they suggested that it was in fact only distinguishing two groups, a 'low' risk group and a 'high' risk group. Both assessments suggested much less precision than would be suggested by the assessment scores and categorization of risk.

The situation though appeared much worse when they considered the typical case facing forensic psychologists of assessing an individual's level of risk. To do this they looked at the confidence intervals for individual assessments, as opposed to those for data on groups of people. When assessing risk for an individual they found that the 95% confidence interval for the VRAG showed a range from 79 to 89 percentage points, with a mean of around 85 percentage points. The results for the Static-99

showed a range from 82 to 89 percentage points in width, with a mean of around 86 percentage points. This they suggested meant that all of the risk categories overlapped with each other for individual assessments. They went on to conclude that '…any distinctiveness of risk estimates for score categories at the group level did not translate into distinct risk estimates at the individual level' (Hart, Michie, & Cooke, 2007). Such findings have led to the suggestion that the use of a single quantity to characterize a probability distribution should be avoided (Henderson & Keiding, 2005). This raises the concern that such actuarial risk assessment instruments may not meet legal standards for use, in that the margins of error are so wide that individual predictions cannot be meaningfully calculated.

The paper by Hart, Michie, and Cooke (2007) generated significant discussion around the issue. In a response to the criticisms Harris, Rice, and Quinsey (2008) argued that the use of confidence intervals in this manner was inappropriate, as this statistic does not capture the precision of an individual score. They suggested that the standard error of measurement (SEM) is the more appropriate statistic in this case; with the SEM suggesting relatively good levels of performance of actuarial assessments. They also suggest that in their analysis Hart, Michie, and Cooke (2007) used 'precision' and 'accuracy' as synonyms, arguing that the latter is best assessed by specificity, sensitivity and the trade-off between these two measures. They also argued that the notion that it is not appropriate to base individual decisions on post analytic groupings has been effectively refuted (Grove & Meehl, 1996). In defending the VRAG assessment Harris et al. (2008) stated that it is simply an efficient distillation of relevant empirical evidence, which provides a more valid assessment than other available methods and optimizes the balance between public safety and the civil liberties of offenders.

In response Hart, Michie, and Cooke (2008) also drew on the key paper by Grove and Meehl (1996) to question the superiority of actuarial assessments in predicting risk. They note that in their review, Grove and Meehl (1996) had concluded that actuarial assessments were superior to clinical judgement in about 45% of the studies reviewed. In other cases clinical judgment was equally or more accurate. While acknowledging an important trend in the data, they suggest that this is not a sound basis for assessment of individual outcomes. They go on to conclude that '…in forensic mental health, as in many areas of life, good practice does not equate to mindless reliance on simple statistical algorithms' (Hart, Michie, & Cooke, 2008).

The debate outlined in the preceding text has hopefully clarified a number of issues and limitations inherent in efforts to assess risk in the context of forensic practice. Perhaps the most striking limitation though is how little we still know about the types of behaviours of concern. The hazards being assessed are likely to interact in ways that are poorly understood. In addition, any evaluation will only be as good as the data, experiments and simulations used (Ansell, 1992). This presents significant difficulty across the field of risk assessment where, frequently, these sources of information have been very limited. A major concern here is that the development of structured risk assessments may create the impression that our understanding is better than it is and that we are making such assessments drawing on better evidence and knowledge than is in fact the case. Prediction does not of course necessarily equate to scientific understanding. Astrologers were able to make accurate predictions without an accurate understanding of astronomy or the real nature of the universe. The need to make predictions now, to the best of our ability, does not absolve psychologists of the need to improve markedly our scientific understanding of the behaviours of concern (Skeem & Monahan, 2011).

Acceptable risk and rare catastrophic failures

Two issues closely linked to the ascendancy of risk assessment are the acceptability of risks and how to deal with rare but catastrophic failures. These are contentious areas and go to the heart of what risk assessment is about and how it is used. They are also areas that cannot be exclusively addressed in empirical terms in a convincing manner, involving as they do moral and ethical judgements.

Efforts to deal with these have varied across disciplines and contexts. Acceptable risk may be based on standards, such as protecting those most at risk, or alternatively may be framed in terms of some form of cost benefit analysis. Here measures of lifetime risk have been widely used and it has become common to refer to this in terms of hazards which increase deaths or injury per million people. There is some logic to the use of a million, in that this appears to be close to a baseline level of risk which it is not possible to reduce. This does not though address the question of whether an acceptable level of risk is set at 10 times this baseline, or 100 times or 1,000 times. Efforts to address such questions using cost benefit analysis have been extensively advocated and have been increasingly used. Such analyses give the appearance of being empirical and objective but, in reality, are based heavily on often hidden assumptions and value judgements. In reality, levels of acceptable risk seem to be chosen largely for reasons of convenience. For example, setting the acceptable risk of 1 in 100 of harm to a child would result in far higher levels of

children being taken into some form of protective care than an acceptable risk of 1 in 10. Such judgements are made but are often not made transparent.

A related question concerns the cut-off points for decision-making. This may differ between groups within a population. For example, the risk from a given hazard may be very low for 99.9% of the population but very high for the minority group. Response to this in turn is likely to differ on the basis of the characteristics of the sub-population concerned. If the 0.1% refers to premature infants, the response is likely to be quite different from that for criminal drug abusers. Issues of choice also enter into such equations as does the threshold for risks associated with chosen activities (e.g., liver damage following exposure to alcohol). Here they are likely to differ from that for risks associated with hazards in the absence of choice (e.g., exposure to radioactive substances).

Rare catastrophic events present very specific challenges and current approaches to risk assessment are not well suited to these. It has long been recognized that these present a serious difficulty for statistical measures of risk (Meehl, 1959). So while actuarial predictors can deal with regularly occurring events, it is well known that they are poor at dealing with rare events (Crighton & Towl, 2008; Gigerenzer & Selten, 2001). Critics of the risk assessment approach are likely to suggest here that in reality this does not matter. As risk assessment is primarily about controlling staff and managing litigation risk, the prediction of rare and catastrophic events is not necessary or perhaps desirable.

Other cogent criticisms have been raised in relation to these aspects of assessing risk. Perhaps the most persuasive of these is the notion that there is a tendency in risk assessment to overestimate the value of rational explanations. There is a tendency in risk assessment to draw on sets of past data, which are themselves limited and by definition are unlikely to contain rare events. In turn, it is suggested that there is a profound tendency to underestimate the prevalence of random factors (Taleb, 2007). Such analyses suggest that the knowledge of the world available to us is far more incomplete than we imagine and that, because of this, it is inappropriate to naively try to use the past to predict the future. As noted in the preceding text, a poor understating of the phenomena of interest to psychologists has led to a focus on a small number of risk factors as predictors. Often these have relatively weak empirical links and little if any theoretical basis. The role of such uncertainty and randomness particularly in relation to high-impact but low-frequency events have been termed 'black swan' events (Taleb, 2007). Low-probability events, it is argued, are largely discounted, possibly as a result of our desire to see greater structure and predictability in the world than is in fact present.

Taleb (2007) goes on to discuss *the Platonic fallacy*, suggesting that it results in a tendency to distort the world in three key ways relevant to risk assessment:

i) The *narrative fallacy*, which refers to our creating *post hoc* stories that suggest events have an identifiable cause

ii) The *ludic fallacy*, which refers to the assumption that the randomness found in life resembles the randomness found in statistical paradigms such as card and dice games, which underpin much of modern probability theory

iii) The *statistical regress fallacy*, which refers to the belief that the structure of probability can be delivered from a set of data

He also suggests that people are subject to what he terms the *triplet of opacity*. This consists of:

i) An illusion of understanding of current events

ii) A retrospective distortion of historical events

iii) An overestimation of factual information, combined with an overvaluing of the intellectual elite

Gigerenzer and Selten (2001) note that human beings are not designed to understand such things as abstract statistics and that we need context to deal with such information effectively. This is far from an abstract academic critique. Risks assessment has become increasingly based on statistical analyses, used to assure that the analysis is accurate, even where clinical opinion or even 'common sense' may suggest the contrary. Yet, it can be suggested that this has involved a degree of pseudo-science in that it has hidden a generally inadequate understanding.

CONCLUSIONS

The process of risk assessment in forensic psychology serves simply to inform legal decision-making. While current approaches to risk assessment are of assistance in doing this, they remain rather blunt instruments. As outlined in the preceding text, they are often based on very partial understanding of the behaviours of concern.

Risk assessment in forensic psychology has historically been dominated by the distinction between 'actuarial' and 'clinical' approaches. This distinction served to draw attention to the weaknesses evident in unstructured clinical approaches to the area of risk. It was also associated with a growth in the use of actuarial risk assessment and, linked to this, risk management.

Advocates of this approach argue that actuarial risk assessment instruments provide the most accurate and best means of predicting risk by integrating the available evidence in the most effective manner (Harris, Rice, & Quinsey, 2008; Howard & Dixon, 2013). The use of purely actuarial approaches should accordingly lead to the replacement of clinical assessments as inaccurate and lacking in utility.

Advocates of actuarial risk assessment instruments can though be legitimately criticized for overstating their case, dismissing clinical assessment far too quickly on the basis of inadequate research. The evidence base in this area has often pooled results from a range of practitioners to yield disappointing results. Yet, it is well known across a range of areas that the quality and accuracy of expert assessments varies significantly. There is evidence, from a number of areas of risk assessment, to suggest that the inclusion of expert judgement can significantly improve empirical estimations of risk (Gigerenzer, 2008; Skeem & Monahan, 2011; Taleb, 2007). Claims that empirical estimators are the best means of assessing risk do not therefore stand up well to scrutiny and appear hubristic. Considered in terms of characteristics such as the confidence intervals which apply to individual cases, the validity of the use of such methods appears highly questionable, leading some to question the legal admissibility of such assessments (Hart, Michie, & Cooke, 2007).

Perhaps linked to such concerns there has been a marked growth in recent years towards the use of more structured forms of clinical judgement. These approaches have generally sought to disseminate what experienced clinicians do, by developing interview and assessment techniques with varying degrees of structure. Modification of risk estimates in the light of expert judgement is generally part of this type of assessment. Where this is competently done it is suggested this may improve the accuracy of prediction. The flip side of this is of course that where it is not done competently there is the risk of making predictions less accurate. It also needs to be recognized that the frameworks and assessments that are currently available show relatively modest predictive power.

More systemic criticisms have also been raised in relation to recent developments in the area of risk assessment. These have included concerns that the growth in use of structured risk assessments has primarily served the neoliberal agenda that has been dominant since the 1980s. In this it is argued that the purpose of such instruments has been the deskilling and increasing control of staff, reducing costs and managing litigation risks: rather than a concern to meet the needs of, for example, children and families. In this respect, risk assessment instruments can be criticized as part of an increasing culture of automation or 'box ticking' which is often implemented in ways that ignore or minimize contextual factors. Risk assessment instruments are critiqued on the basis that they tend to locate the causes of social problems such as violence and family dysfunction within individuals, rather than setting them within a social and political context. In doing this they are neatly individuated and become a problem with the individual and for them to address. Society more widely is largely absolved of responsibility. The fallacy of this logic is powerfully illustrated in the MacArthur study into violence in North America which showed that individual rates of violence were largely predicted by the affluence of the area that offender were discharged to. Here apparently effective predictors of violence such as ethnicity disappeared when corrected for the affluence of the area (Monahan et al., 2001).

A number of conclusions seem clear from current evidence. The first of these is that the use of purely actuarial risk assessment instruments to individual cases represents poor practice. The use of clinical judgement drawing from the available empirical evidence base appears more useful and, when competently undertaken, may lead to improved accuracy of assessment. This perhaps accounts for the growth of structured clinical assessments as a means of improving the reliability and validity of assessments. The best of these assessments largely replicate what experienced clinicians are felt to do in assessing risk and allow scope to address unusual cases and infrequent characteristics. Where such assessments have been well developed and designed to aid in the assessment of specific groups, such as young offenders, they appear to perform better than more 'generic' assessments. Even here though the results have not been impressive and this brings us back to some of the fundamental issues in risk assessment which remain to be addressed. The most important of these is that we continue to have a poor level of understanding of the behaviours concerned. In the absence of fundamental improvements in understanding risk assessment is likely to involve a recycling of known and moderately predicative risk factors. Linked to this, current risk assessment approaches have undoubtedly contributed to an individuation of risk in child protection, criminal behaviour and violence more generally at the expense of considering broader social and political factors.

NOTES

1 An example here might be the actions of the Norwegian resistance in the Second World War in destroying industrial and transport capacity within Norway associated with the production of materials for the development of nuclear weapons by Germany. This involved the deaths of German combatants and Norwegian civilians. At the time, such actions were clearly illegal and viewed by the German authorities as such, carrying the death penalty for those involved and often for others. The view of the Allied forces at the time and of the vast majority subsequently was that such actions were heroic.

2 The study concerned drew on official records, self-reported violent and aggressive behaviour and collateral reports from family members. The study was designed to maximize willingness to report violence, with no penalties for disclosure. It seems unlikely that such high levels of self-report would be achieved in criminal justice settings, where there are powerful disincentives for honest accounts of such behaviour.

3 Here the definition of 'high'- and 'low'-risk groups is, as with main effects approaches, arbitrary. The inclusion of base rate data does, though, make the basis for the assumptions clear. Unfortunately, in a number of areas of risk assessment such clear base rate data are largely missing and the definition of concepts such as high and low risk becomes less clear as a result.

4 The percentages here have been rounded so do not total to 100.

5 The researchers also conducted this iterative analysis for a logistic regression model. This proved significantly less effective, allocating 62.3% of cases to high- or low-risk groups.

6 This performance is all the more impressive because of the elimination of criminal history factors.

FURTHER READING

Monahan, J., Steadman, H., Silver, E. et al. (2001). *Rethinking risk assessment: The MacArthur study of mental disorder and violence.* New York: Oxford University Press.
This text provides detailed analysis of a major multi-site study into risk funded by the MacArthur Foundation. The study is focused primarily on mental health services in a number of large North American centres but the value of the text goes well beyond this. Detailed coverage is given of major definitional and practice issues in conducting risk assessments and the manner in which these impact on efforts at managing the risk of violence. The book also represents a step change in approaches to risk assessment, moving away from simple models of risk in favour of more sophisticated iterative and clinical approaches.

Breakwell, G. (2007). *The psychology of risk*. Cambridge: Cambridge University Press.

This is a key text and essential reading. It covers the broad area of risk, including the foundations of risk assessment, through to the ways in which risk responses might be changed. The book provides extensive coverage of the experimental evidence base from psychology and also from related disciplines. The text also includes learning aids in the form of a number of text boxes designed to encourage thinking about related questions, or practical examples of risk assessment.

Towl, G. (2005). Risk assessment. *Evidence-Based Mental Health*, 8, 91–93.

This paper provides a thematic review of the current state of play in the area of risk assessment, with particular reference to forensic mental health. The paper adopts a conceptual approach to risk assessment and considers commonalities across areas of research and practice. The main focus is on the social construction of risk in forensic mental health and the ethical implications for the public, policy-makers, and practitioners. The paper critiques the development of simple models and risk assessment tools for profit, going on to consider the appeal of these to both policy-makers and practitioners. The notion of seeking ever better 'tools', in the absence of theoretical understanding, is critically evaluated.

REFERENCES

Ansell, J. (1992). Reliability, industrial risk assessment. In J. Ansell & F. Wharton (Eds.), *Risk analysis, assessment and management*. Chichester: John Wiley & Sons.

Appelbaum, P. S., Clark Robbins, P., & Monahan, J. (2000). Violence and delusions: Data from the MacArthur Violence Risk Assessment Study. *American Journal of Psychiatry*, 157(4), 566–572.

Baker, K. (2005). Is Asset really an asset? Assessment of Young Offenders in Practice. In R. Burnett & C. Roberts (Eds.), *What works in probation and youth justice: Developing evidence based practice*. Cullompton, UK: Willan.

Barry, M. (2007). *Effective approaches to risk assessment in social work: An international literature review*. Edinburgh: Scottish Executive.

Bonta, J., & Andrews, D. A. (2007). *Risk-need-responsivity model for offender assessment and rehabilitation* (User Report 2007–06). Ottawa, Ontario: Public Safety Canada

Breakwell, G. M. (2007). *The psychology of risk*. Cambridge: Cambridge University Press.

Brown, D. (2005). Continuity, rupture, or just more of the 'volatile and contradictory'? Glimpses of New South Wales' penal practice behind and through the discursive. In J. Pratt, D. Brown, M. Brown, & S. Hallsworth (Eds.), *The New Punitiveness*. London: Taylor & Francis.

Campbell, M. A., French, S., & Gendreau, P. (2007). *Assessing the utility of risk assessment tools and personality measures in the prediction of violent recidivism for adult offenders*. Ottawa, ON: Public Safety Canada.

Crighton, D. A. (2005). Risk assessment. In D. A. Crighton & G. J. Towl (Eds.), *Psychology in probation services*. Oxford: Blackwell.

Crighton, D. A. (2006). Methodological issues in psychological research in prisons. In G. J. Towl (Ed.), *Psychological research in prisons*. Oxford: Blackwell.

Crighton, D. A. (2009). Uses and abuses of the Hare Psychopathy Checklist. *Evidence-Based Mental Health*, 12, 33–36.

Crighton, D. A., & Towl, G. J. (2008). *Psychology in prisons* (2nd edn). Oxford: Blackwell.

Davis, A. (1996). Risk work and mental health. *Good Practice in Risk Assessment and Risk Management*, 1, 109–120.

Devillé, W. L., Buntinx, F., Bouter, L. M., Montori, V. M., De Vet, H. C., Van der Windt, D. A., & Bezemer, P. D. (2002). Conducting systematic reviews of diagnostic studies: Didactic guidelines. *BMC medical research methodology*, 2(1), 2–9.

Dolan, M., & Fullam, R. (2007). The validity of the Violence Risk Scale second edition (VRS-2) in a British forensic inpatient sample. *The Journal of Forensic Psychiatry & Psychology*, 18(3), 381–393.

Douglas, M. (1986). *Risk acceptability according to the social sciences*. London: Routledge & Kegan Paul.

Farrington, David P. (2002). Developmental criminology and risk-focused prevention. In M. Maguire, R. Morgan, & R. Reiner (Eds.), *The Oxford handbook of criminology*. Oxford: Oxford University Press.

Gigerenzer, G. (2008). Why heuristics work. *Perspectives on psychological science*, 3(1), 20–29.

Gigerenzer, G., & Selten, R. (2001). Rethinking rationality. In G. Gigerenzer & R. Selten (Eds.), *Bounded rationality: The adaptive toolbox*. Cambridge, MA: MIT Press.

Grove, W. M., & Meehl, P. E. (1996). Comparative efficiency of informal (subjective, impressionistic) and formal (mechanical, algorithmic) prediction procedures: The clinical–statistical controversy. *Psychology, Public Policy, and Law*, 2(2), 293–323.

Hanson, R. K., & Morton-Bourgon, K. (2009). The accuracy of recidivism risk assessments for sexual offenders: A meta-analysis of 118 prediction studies. *Psychological Assessment*, 21, 1–21.

Harris, G., Rice, M., & Quinsey, V. (1993). Violent recidivism of mentally disordered offenders: The development of a statistical prediction instrument. *Criminal Justice and Behaviour*, 20, 315.

Harris, G. T., Rice, M. E., & Quinsey, V. L. (2008). Shall evidence-based risk assessment be abandoned? *British Journal of Psychiatry*, 192, 154.

Hart, S. D., Michie, C., & Cooke, D. J. (2007). Precision of actuarial risk assessment instruments: Evaluating the 'margins of error' of group v. individual predictions of violence. *The British Journal of Psychiatry*, 190(49), s60–s65.

Hart, S. D., Michie, C., & Cooke, D. J. (2008). Authors reply to Harris, G. T., Rice, M. E., & Quinsey, V. L. (2008). Shall evidence-based risk assessment be abandoned? *British Journal of Psychiatry, 192*, 154.

Hayles, M. (2006). Constructing safety: A collaborative approach to managing risk and building responsibility. In K. Gorman, M. Gregory, M. Hayles, & N. Parton (Eds.), *Constructive work with offenders*. London: Jessica Kingsley.

Henderson, R., & Keiding, N. (2005). Individual survival time prediction using statistical models. *Journal of Medical Ethics, 31*(12), 703–706.

Horwath, J. (2005). Assessment and intervention in cases of child neglect: The Irish experience. *Child and Family Social Work, 10*(2), 99–110.

Howard, P. D., & Dixon, L. (2013). Identifying change in the likelihood of violent recidivism: Causal dynamic risk factors in the OASys violence predictor. *Law and human behavior, 37*(3), 163–174.

Jones, R. (2014). Child protection: 40 years of learning but where next? In M. Blythe (Ed.), *Moving on from Munro: Improving children's services*. Bristol, UK: Policy Press.

Kahneman, D., Slovic, P., & Tversky, A. (1982). *Judgment under uncertainty: Heuristics and biases*. Cambridge: Cambridge University Press,

Kebbell, M. R., & Porter, L. (2012). An intelligence assessment framework for identifying individuals at risk of committing acts of violent extremism against the West. *Security Journal, 25*(3), 212–228.

Kraemer, H., Kazdin, A., Offord, D., Kessler, R., Jensen, P., & Kupfer, D. (1997). Coming to terms with the terms of risk. *Archives of General Psychiatry, 54*, 337–343.

Kroner, D. G., Mills, J. F., & Reddon, J. R. (2005). A coffee can, factor analysis, and prediction of antisocial behavior: The structure of criminal risk. *International journal of law and psychiatry, 28*(4), 360–374.

Lidz, C., Mulvey, E., & Gardner, W. (1993). The accuracy of predictions of violence to others. *Journal of the American Medical Association, 269*, 1007–1011.

Loman, A., & Siegel, G. (2004). *Minnesota Alternative Response Evaluation: Final Report*. St. Louis, MO: Institute of Applied Research.

Meehl, P. E. (1954). *Clinical versus statistical prediction: A theoretical analysis and a review of the evidence*. Minneapolis, MN: University of Minnesota.

Meehl, P. E. (1959). Some ruminations on the validation of clinical procedures. *Canadian Journal of Psychology, 13*, 106–128.

Meehl, P. E. (1967). Theory-testing in psychology and physics: A methodological paradox. *Philosophy of Science, 34*, 103–115.

Meehl, P. E. (1973). Why I do not attend case conferences. In P. E. Meehl (Ed.), *Psychodiagnosis: Selected papers*. Minneapolis, MN: University of Minnesota Press.

Mercado, C. C., & Ogloff, J. R. (2007). Risk and the preventive detention of sex offenders in Australia and the United States. *International Journal of Law and Psychiatry, 30*, 49–59.

Monahan, J. (2012). The individual risk assessment of terrorism. *Psychology, Public Policy, and Law, 18*(2), 167.

Monahan, J., Steadman, H., Clark Robbins, P. C., Appelbaum, P., Banks, S., Grisso, T., Heilbrun, K., Mulvey, E. P., Roth, L., & Silver, E. (2005). An actuarial model of violence risk assessment for persons with mental disorders. *Psychiatric Services, 56*, 810–815.

Monahan, J., Steadman, H., Silver, E., Appelbaum, P. S., Robbins, P. C., Mulvey, E. P., Roth, L., Grisso, T., & Banks, S. (2001). *Rethinking risk assessment: The MacArthur study of mental disorder and violence*. New York: Oxford University Press.

Mooney, C., & Duval, R. (1993). *Bootstrapping: A nonparametric approach to statistical inference*. Newbury Park, CA: Sage.

Pearson, K. (1905). The problem of the random walk. *Nature 72*, 294.

Reason, J. (1990). *Human error*. New York: Cambridge University Press.

Rose, N. (1996). The death of the social? Re-figuring the territory of government. *International Journal of Human Resource Management, 25*(3), 327–356.

SBU (2005). *Riskbedömningar inom psykiatrin. Kan våld i samhället förutsägas?* [Risk assessments in psychiatry. Is it possible to predict community violence?]. Stockholm: Swedish Council on Health Technology Assessment (SBU).

Schwalbe, C. S. (2008). A meta-analysis of juvenile justice risk assessment instruments: Predictive validity by gender. *Criminal Justice and Behavior, 35*, 1367–1381.

Singh, J. P., & Fazel, S. (2010). Forensic Risk Assessment A Metareview. *Criminal Justice and Behavior, 37*(9), 965–988.

Singh, J. P., Grann, M., & Fazel, S. (2011). A comparative study of violence risk assessment tools: A systematic review and metaregression analysis of 68 studies involving 25,980 participants. *Clinical Psychology Review, 31*(3), 499–513.

Sjöstedt, G., & Grann, M. (2002). Risk assessment: What is being predicted by actuarial prediction instruments? *International Journal of Forensic Mental Health, 1*, 179–183.

Skeem, J. L., & Monahan, J. (2011). Current directions in violence risk assessment. *Current Directions in Psychological Science, 20*(1), 38–42.

Swets, J., Dawes, R., & Monahan, J. (2000). Psychological science can improve diagnostic decisions. *Psychological Science in the Public Interest, 1*, 1–26.

Taleb, N. N. (2007). *The black swan: The impact of the highly improbable*. London: Allen Lane.

Thompson, S. G., & Higgins, J. (2002). How should meta-regression analyses be undertaken and interpreted? *Statistics in Medicine, 21*(11), 1559–1573.

Towl, G. J. (2005). Risk assessment. *Evidence Based Mental Health, 8*, 91–93.

Towl, G. J., & Crighton, D. A. (1996). *The handbook of psychology for forensic practitioners.* London: Routledge.

Towl, G. J., & Crighton, D. (1997). Risk assessment with offenders. *International Review of Psychiatry, 9*, 187–193.

Vess, J. (2008). Sex offender risk assessment: Consideration of human rights in community protection legislation. *Legal and Criminological Psychology, 13*(2), 245–256.

Wald, M. S., & Woolverton, M. (1990). Risk assessment: The emperor's new clothes? *Child Welfare, 69*(6), 483–511.

Wilson, E. B. (1927). Probable inference, the law of succession, and statistical inference, *Journal of the American Statistical Association, 22*, 209–212.

Yang, M., Wong, S. C. P., & Coid, J. (2010). The efficacy of violence prediction: A meta-analytic comparison of nine risk assessment tools. *Psychological Bulletin, 136*(5), 740–767.

Part II
Working with Offending Populations

8 The Developmental Evidence Base: Neurobiological Research and Forensic Applications

ROBERT A. SCHUG, YU GAO, ANDREA L. GLENN, MELISSA PESKIN, YALING YANG AND ADRIAN RAINE

A significant empirical base for the lifespan development of crime and antisocial behaviour has accumulated through key areas of neurobiological research. Genetic studies indicate significant heritability estimates of antisocial behaviour; and candidate genes for antisociality are becoming identified along with important gene–environment interactions. Neuroimaging research has found structural and functional deficits in frontal, temporal and subcortical regions in antisocial children and adults, and these findings are largely supported by neurological studies of brain trauma in antisocial populations. Neuropsychological studies have reported deficits in verbal, spatial and executive abilities in antisocial adults and children, and risk factors early in childhood appear to predict later forms of antisocial behaviour. Psychophysiological research has focused upon cardiovascular and electrodermal activity, electroencephalogram and event-related potentials, while studies in endocrinology have focused upon hormones such as cortisol and testosterone. Important contributions have also been made from research in areas of moral development and nutrition. This developmental neurobiological evidence base has to date begun to impact various facets of criminal justice systems, including lie detection and judicial process applications; and may enhance forensic psychological assessment and inform policies and procedures regarding the identification, management and treatment of various forms of adult and juvenile offending.

THE DEVELOPMENTAL EVIDENCE BASE: NEUROBIOLOGICAL RESEARCH

Essential to forensic psychology is an empirical understanding of the initiation, maintenance and potential desistance from criminal behaviour. Developmental perspectives of crime – emphasizing lifespan continuities/discontinuities of criminality rather than general causes or correlates – have contributed significantly to this understanding; especially as the neurobiological roots and sociological origins of crime are often present in the earliest years of life. Prominent developmental theories of antisocial behaviour have incorporated both elements. For example, Patterson's (1982) coercion model uses social learning to explain early-onset persistent offending, while Moffitt's (1993) developmental theory of life-course persistent offending emphasizes an additional interactive role of biological factors (i.e., prenatal and perinatal disruptions in neural development which lead to specific neurobiological deficits) in the early-onset trajectory. Both models have received impressive empirical support from studies of childhood antisocial behaviour, aggression and delinquency (Brennan, Hall, Bor, Najman, & Williams, 2003).

Forensic Psychology, Second Edition. Edited by David A. Crighton and Graham J. Towl.
© 2015 John Wiley & Sons, Ltd. Published 2015 by British Psychological Society and John Wiley & Sons, Ltd.

As developmental theories may be ideal for informing future intervention and public policy directions (Brennan *et al.*, 2003), criminal justice systems in general and forensic psychology in particular stand to benefit tremendously from their application. Moreover, neurobiological research – with its extensive contributions to criminological study dating back more than a century (i.e., Lombroso, 1876) – has offered a unique understanding of the aetiological mechanisms underlying antisocial behaviour, and provided a sizeable evidence base for developmental criminological perspectives. This chapter will serve as an integrative review of findings from key areas of neurobiological research on antisocial behaviour, with particular focus upon developmental perspectives and associated theories. Additionally, it will provide an overview of current and potential application of this research within forensic arenas – which may be of value in informing the clinical practitioner.

GENETICS

Genetic predispositions towards antisocial behaviour provide an ideal starting point for a discussion of developmental neurobiological crime research. Twin studies, adoptive studies, studies in twins reared apart and molecular genetic studies have provided substantial evidence for genetic influences on antisocial and aggressive behaviour (Popma & Raine, 2006); and though published estimates of heritability vary widely among studies (Waldman & Rhee, 2006), the genetic contribution is thought overall to be 40–50% (Moffitt, 2005). Variability may be due in part to the use of a variety of semi-overlapping phenotypes (i.e., the detectable expression of an individual's genotype interacting with their environment; Walsh & Ellis, 2007) – including dimensional personality traits (e.g., impulsivity, aggressiveness), psychiatric diagnoses (e.g., antisocial personality disorder [ASPD], conduct disorder [CD]) and behaviour (e.g., crime, delinquency) related to antisociality – which are considered less than ideal (Goldman & Ducci, 2007). Some genetic determinants of antisociality are common to other externalizing disorders (i.e., the aforementioned disorders, along with attention-deficit/hyperactivity disorder [ADHD], alcoholism and other addictions; Goldman & Ducci, 2007), and may be explained by intermediate endophenotypic expressions (Waldman & Rhee, 2006). Additionally, several monoamine neurotransmitter genes have demonstrated a genetic association with antisocial behaviour (Goldman & Ducci, 2007); including those coding for precursor, receptor, transporter, metabolite or conversion elements in the serotonin and catecholamine (i.e., dopamine and norepinephrine)

neurotransmitter systems (e.g., 5-hydroxy-tryptamine receptor 1B [HTR1B], tryptophan hydroxylase [TPH2], 5-hydroxy-tryptamine transporter [HTT], monoamine oxidase A [MAOA], and catchol-O-methyltransferase [COMT]; Goldman & Ducci, 2007; Waldman & Rhee, 2006) – systems thought to modulate aggressive and impulsive behaviour. None of these candidate genes, however, accounts for a large amount of phenotypic variance in antisociality (Goldman & Ducci, 2007). This suggests both that many individual genes are involved in coding the neurobiological risk factors for crime, and also that gene–environment interactions are likely to be important in the developmental progression and expression of antisocial behaviour.

Developmental psychopathology researchers have begun to seek evidence for these interactions. For example, Caspi and colleagues (2002) found maltreated children with a genotype conferring high levels of monoamine oxidase A (a neurotransmitter-metabolizing enzyme) expression to be less likely to become antisocial and violent in adolescence than maltreated children having a genotype conferring low levels of monoamine oxidase A expression. Twin data have also contributed to a developmental neurobiological perspective, demonstrating: (1) most genetic effects upon antisocial behaviour increase with age while shared environmental effects decrease; (2) early-onset persistent antisocial behaviour is more heritable than (later-onset) conduct disorder; (3) family environment is relevant for the initiation and early maintenance of aggression (particularly in men), but its effect fades; and (4) some genes influence antisocial behaviour across the entire lifespan, and others only in adolescence and adulthood (Goldman & Ducci, 2007). The effect of gene–environment interactions is embedded in the social-push theory, which states that biological factors may more likely explain antisocial behaviour in the absence of predispositional social factors (Popma & Raine, 2006). In total, there remains little doubt regarding the role of genetic influences in the developmental progression of antisocial behaviour.

NEUROIMAGING

With the increase in neuroimaging research over the past decade, evidence has accumulated supporting a plausible relationship between brain impairments and antisocial behaviour. The strongest evidence implicates the prefrontal cortex, a result not surprising considering the key multiple functions of this region, which include inhibiting behavioural impulses and regulating emotion generated by subcortical structures such as the amygdala. Structurally, several imaging studies have found significant grey matter volume reduction in the prefrontal cortex in antisocial aggressive individuals (Raine, Lencz, Bihrle, LaCasse, & Colletti, 2000). Functionally, earlier studies found antisocial individuals to show decreased functioning such as glucose metabolism and regional blood flow (rCBF) in this region (Volkow & Tancredi, 1987; Volkow et al., 1995).

The orbitofrontal cortex (OFC) and dorsolateral prefrontal cortex (DLPFC) are the two prefrontal subregions most consistently found to be impaired in antisocial, violent individuals. The orbitofrontal cortex is critical in ethical decision-making and emotion regulation, whereas the dorsolateral prefrontal cortex plays an important role in behavioural control and executive functioning. Structural imaging studies to date have demonstrated reduced volume/thickness in the frontal cortex, particularly the orbitofrontal and dorsolateral prefrontal cortex in antisocial, psychopathic individuals (Laakso et al., 2002; Aoki, Inokuchi, Nakao, & Yamasue, 2013; Bertsch et al., 2013; Howner et al., 2012; Ly et al., 2012; Yang and Raine, 2009; Yang, Raine, Colletti, Toga, & Narr, 2009, 2010), which is consistent with functional imaging studies that revealed abnormal orbitofrontal and dorsolateral prefrontal functioning during cognitive and emotional tasks in antisocials. For example, Raine et al. (1994) found reduced glucose metabolism in the orbitofrontal and dorsolateral prefrontal cortex in murderers during a continuous performance task. Alternatively, antisocial, violent individuals were found more recently to show heightened neural activation in the orbitofrontal and dorsolateral prefrontal areas during emotional processes (e.g., the viewing of affective pictures) compared to controls (Müller et al., 2003; Schneider et al., 2000). Similarly, another study showed reduced activation in the orbitofrontal cortex in psychopathic individuals during empathic processing task (Decety, Skelly, & Kiehl, 2013). Recent studies of frontal networks also found antisocial individuals to show altered structural and functional connectivity compared to normal controls (Tang et al., 2013; Yang et al., 2012). Overall, these findings suggest that impairments in the prefrontal cortex, particularly the orbitofrontal and dorsolateral prefrontal regions, may contribute crucially to the neurobiological pathology in antisocial individuals.

The prefrontal cortex, however, is not the only structure to be linked to violent criminal behaviour. It has long been known that damage to the temporal lobe may result in blunted emotional responses (Klüver & Bucy, 1939), similar to what has been observed in antisocial violent individuals. Indeed, several studies that found prefrontal dysfunction in their antisocial violent subjects also found reduced temporal functioning. For example, Soderstrom, Tullberg, Wikkelsoe, Ekholm, and Forsman (2000) revealed reduced rCBF in the frontal cortex as well as the temporal cortex in violent perpetrators compared to controls. Hirono, Mega, Dinov, Mishkin, and Cummings (2000) also found rCBF reduction in the left anterior temporal cortex in addition to the bilateral dorsofrontal cortex in individuals convicted of impulsive violent offences. Within the temporal region, antisocial and violent behaviour is particularly associated with deficits in the amygdala–hippocampal complex. The amygdala is crucial not only in the reception and production of emotion, but also the processing of fear conditioning, while the hippocampus is involved in emotional memory. Functional abnormalities in the amygdala–hippocampal complex in antisocial, aggressive individuals have been reported in several studies. For example, criminal psychopaths have demonstrated decreased amygdala–hippocampal activations during the viewing of negative affective pictures (Kiehl et al., 2001). Another study (Soderstrom et al., 2000) found reduced hippocampal rCBF in violent perpetrators compared to controls. Together, these findings suggest that deficits in the temporal lobe, particularly the amygdala and hippocampus, may predispose one to a lack of fear of punishment and result in the disruption of normal moral development (see the following text).

Although these studies provide strong evidence for a link between brain impairments and antisocial violent behaviour, the causal effect remains unclear. Studies on children with antisocial personalities have reported brain abnormalities similar to those found in antisocial personality-disordered or aggressive adults (Fairchild et al., 2013; Stevens and Haney-Caron, 2012), suggesting a potential neurodevelopmental pathway to antisocial behaviour. For example, Kruesi, Casanova, Mannheim, and Jonson-Bilder (2004) report significant temporal lobe and non-significant prefrontal lobe volume reductions in early-onset conduct-disordered children, and a trend towards corpus callosum but not prefrontal white matter volume/ratio reductions in youth liars (compared to antisocial controls and healthy volunteers; Kruesi & Casanova, 2006). In aggressive children with epilepsy, Juhasz, Behen, Muzik, Chugani, and Chugani (2001) found a significant correlation between a higher severity of aggression and lower metabolism in the bilateral medial prefrontal and left temporal cortex. Furthermore, Sterzer, Stadler, Krebs, Kleinschmidt, and Poustka (2005) found decreased activation in the right dorsal anterior cingulate cortex in aggressive children with conduct disorders during the viewing of negative affective pictures. Several recent studies showed children with conduct problems or psychopathic traits with decreased activation in similar regions including the anterior cingulate cortex, inferior frontal gyrus, and the amygdala during empathic processing tasks (Lockwood et al., 2013; Marsh et al., 2013) and altered amygdala–prefrontal functional connectivity (Finger *et al.*, 2012). Though prospective imaging studies of antisocial behaviour in children remain largely unreported, these results – along with those in the preceding text – highlight the importance of neuroimaging data in elucidating the developmental neurobiological basis to antisocial behaviour.

NEUROLOGY

Neurological studies of brain trauma in antisocial populations have provided important contributions to the understanding of the pathogenesis of antisocial behaviour. Interestingly, age groups at highest risk for traumatic brain injury (adolescents, young adults, those over age 75, males; Ehrenreich, Krampe, & Sirén, 2007) largely overlap with those associated with increased anti-sociality (see Moffitt, 1993). Some adult antisocial populations are characterized by an unusually high prevalence of adult and childhood brain injury (e.g., Blake, Pincus, & Buckner, 1995; Lewis, Pincus, Feldman, Jackson, & Bard, 1986). More striking evidence comes from case descriptions of frontally damaged patients who subsequently developed marked antisociality (e.g., Phineus Gage [Harlow, 1848] and patient E.V.R. [Saver & Damasio, 1991]; see also Damasio, 1994, and Damasio, Tranel, & Damasio, 1990) – a condition known as 'acquired psychopathy' (Granacher & Fozdar, 2007).

Although damage to different brain areas may result in a variety of emotional and cognitive impairments, studies have shown that individuals are more likely to display aggression when the damage involves the frontal and temporal regions. Grafman *et al.* (1996) found that aggressive and violent attitudes were heightened in Vietnam War veterans who had suffered orbitofrontal lesions when compared to those with lesions in other brain regions. Specifically, patients with temporal injuries reported more feelings of rage and hostility, whereas patients with injuries to the prefrontal cortex, particularly the orbitofrontal cortex, reported a much higher level of violent and aggressive behaviour. These findings are consistent with imaging studies on antisocial violent individuals, and suggests that individuals who suffer brain damage to these two regions may not have sufficient cognitive and emotion-regulation capability to satisfy their desires through socially acceptable channels (e.g., negotiation), thus resorting to aggressive and violent behaviour to achieve their goals (León-Carrión & Ramos, 2003).

Studies examining juvenile criminals and delinquents also report a high prevalence of brain injury history (Andrews, Rose, & Johnson, 1998; Lewis *et al.*, 1988; Pincus & Lewis, 1991), at higher rates than non-delinquents (Lewis, Pincus, Lovely, Spitzer, & Moy, 1987), and with head injuries largely pre-dating violence and law-enforcement contact (Lewis *et al.*, 1986; Sarapata, Hermann, Johnson, & Aycock, 2008); while other studies in children report antisocial and externalizing behavioural sequelae commonly following head injury (Raine, 2002a). Additionally, Anderson, Bechara, Damasio, Tranel, and Damasio (1999) have found that patients who incur damage very early in life (i.e., before age 16 months) develop antisocial tendencies very-similar to those observed in individuals who incur damage as adults, but the tendencies are often more severe and persist throughout development. In aggregate, these findings suggest that the occurrence of brain injury, particularly at an early age, could be a risk factor for developing aggression and other behavioural problems.

It is worth mentioning that head injury, even when resulting in frontal or temporal damage, does not automatically predispose one to delinquency. Criminal behaviour, particularly violent crime, likely results from the complex interaction of risk factors including genetic predisposition, emotional distress, poverty, substance abuse, child abuse and academic underachievement (Filley *et al.*, 2001). For example, for those individuals who suffered from learning disabilities and school behavioural problems, adding a head injury greatly increases the possibility of criminal and violent behaviour later on in life (León-Carrión & Ramos, 2003). In other words, head injuries may act as a trigger that disrupts the neural mechanisms that normally mediate and control behaviour in individuals with socio-biological predispositions to aggression and crime.

These neurological studies support neuroimaging evidence suggesting that impairments in frontal lobe functioning may be involved in the development of antisocial behaviour. However, in some cases, brain damage has not produced behavioural changes, and even reduced aggression in previously aggressive individuals (e.g., Bigler, 2001; Ellenbogen, Hurford, Liebskind, Neimark, & Weiss, 2005; Mataró *et al.*, 2001), though this may be the result of concomitant dorsolateral prefrontal damage (an area spared in the cases of Gage and E.V.R.; Mataró *et al.*, 2001). Alternatively, this may suggest that frontal lobe impairment, particularly in the orbitofrontal cortex, is merely a *risk factor* for antisocial behaviour, but does not *necessarily* result in antisocial behaviour in all cases. Additionally, brain trauma in general and acquired psychopathy in particular may be risk factors for later development of neurodegenerative disorders (Granacher & Fozdar, 2007) which may exacerbate antisocial tendencies. In any event, the literature to date demonstrates that neurological factors can be key contributors to the developmental progression of crime.

NEUROPSYCHOLOGY

Several decades of research have highlighted a growing interest in relating neuropsychological performance to forensic aspects of behaviour (Rasmussen, Almvik, & Levander, 2001). Neuropsychological investigations of violent, aggressive and antisocial behaviour have largely focused on specific domains of cognitive functioning such as verbal and spatial intelligence and executive abilities.

Verbal and spatial intelligence

While general intelligence (e.g., IQ or Full Scale IQ) deficits are the best-replicated cognitive correlate of antisocial, violent and criminal behaviour among non-mentally ill individuals (Wilson & Herrnstein, 1985), identifying component verbal versus spatial/performance intelligence deficits has demonstrated utility in the understanding of the aetiological mechanisms underlying antisociality. Reduced verbal, as opposed to spatial, performance IQ – possibly indicating left-hemispheric dysfunction – is widely reported in adult antisocial populations (Raine, 1993), and appears characteristic of both males and females across studies of antisocial individuals from different age groups (Isen, 2010). However, general intellectual performance or verbal intelligence deficits have not been reported in individuals with antisocial personality disorder and psychopathy (Barkataki, Kumari, Das, Taylor, & Sharma, 2006; Kosson, Miller, Byrnes, & Leveroni, 2007), though some specific psychopathic traits (i.e., criminal versatility and violence) may be related to verbal dysfunction (Rasmussen et al., 2001). Thus, while global and/or verbal IQ deficits may characterize adult antisocials in general, they may not characterize specific subsets of antisocial trait constellations.

Lowered verbal IQ appears largely characteristic of antisocial children and adolescents (Barker et al., 2007; Brennan et al., 2003; Raine, 1993; Teichner & Golden, 2000; Vermeiren, De Clippele, Schwab-Stone, Ruchkin, & Deboutte, 2002). Moffitt, Lynam, & Silva (1994), in a study of children from a New Zealand birth cohort, found that verbal deficits at age 13 predicted delinquency at age 18 for persistent, high-level offending beginning in pre-adolescence – longitudinal neuropsychological evidence which supports Moffitt's (1993) proposed theory. Verbal deficits may affect the development of language-based self-control mechanisms (Luria, 1980), leading ultimately to socialization failure (Eriksson, Hodgins, & Tengström, 2005), although the verbally deficient juvenile offender is thought to have a more positive prognosis, with environmental modifications and therapy (Teichner & Golden, 2000). Additionally,

there is a paucity of literature related to global verbal intelligence in juvenile psychopathy (itself a largely unexplored and controversial topic; Salekin, 2006) – though Loney, Frick, Ellis, and McCoy (1998) found no verbal deficits in children with conduct problems characterized by callous–unemotional traits (CU traits – related to adult psychopathy; Frick et al., 2003); and Salekin, Neumann, Leistico, and Zalot (2004) recently found verbal intelligence to be related positively with the superficial and deceitful interpersonal style traits and inversely with the affective processing-disturbance traits of psychopathy in juvenile prisoners. In all, verbal deficits in antisocial youth populations overall appear relatively consistent, though future investigations of psychopathic youth may help clarify heterogeneity in verbal IQ findings among antisocial juveniles as in adults.

Evidence from longitudinal community-based studies may call into question the classic view (derived primarily from institutionalized samples) of verbal but not performance intelligence impairments in antisocial individuals. Raine et al. (2005) identified both spatial and verbal impairments in a Pittsburgh youth sample including childhood-limited, adolescent-limited and life-course persistent offenders. In a Mauritius sample, Raine, Yaralian, Reynolds, Venables, and Mednick (2002) found spatial but not verbal deficits at age 3 and both spatial and verbal deficits at age 11 in persistently antisocial individuals – suggesting that early spatial deficits contribute to persistent antisocial behaviour, while verbal deficits may be developmentally acquired. These authors proposed an early starter spatial impairment model of antisocial behaviour, in which early visuospatial deficits potentially interfere with mother–infant bonding, and may reflect right hemisphere dysfunction that disrupts the processing and regulation of emotions, in turn contributing to life-course antisociality.

Executive functioning

Executive functioning (EF) refers to the cognitive processes that allow for goal-orientated, contextually appropriate behaviour and effective self-serving conduct (Lezak, Howieson, Loring, Hannay, & Fischer, 2004; Luria, 1980). Executive dysfunction is thought to represent frontal lobe impairment, and is indicated by performance errors on neuropsychological measures of strategy formation, cognitive flexibility or impulsivity (i.e., category, maze-tracing, Stroop interference, card sorting, verbal fluency and tower tests; and go/no-go and gambling tasks). Neuropsychological investigations of EF deficits and antisocial behaviour have traditionally focused on categorical clinical syndromes (i.e., antisocial personality disorder, conduct disorder, psychopathy) and legal/judicial concepts (criminality and delinquency).

Morgan and Lilienfeld's (2000) quantitative review of 39 studies found overall EF deficits in antisocials compared to controls, and strongest effects for the Porteus Mazes test and antisociality defined by judicial status. More recently, EF deficits have been associated with aggressive (e.g., male batterers), violent, and antisocial personality-disordered populations (Dolan, 2012; Dolan & Park, 2002; Hancock, Tapscott, & Hoaken, 2012; Stanford, Conklin, Helfritz, & Kockler, 2007a; Teichner, Golden, Van Hasselt, & Peterson, 2001), property crimes (Barker et al., 2007), paedophilic and non-paedophilic child molesters (Schiffer & Vonlaufen, 2011), suicidal behaviour (Keilp et al., 2013), single as opposed to multiple homicide victims in indigent murder defendants and death row inmates (Hanlon, Rubin, Jensen, & Daoust, 2010), schizophrenic murderers relative to nonviolent men with schizophrenia (Hanlon, Coda, Cobia, & Rubin, 2012), mentally challenged versus nonimpaired forensic hospital patients (Bastert, Schläfke, Pein, Kupke, & Fegert, 2012), and reactive versus instrumental violent offenders (Broomhall, 2005). Executive function has also been shown to be a predictor of responsivity to anti-aggression treatment in schizophrenia patients (Krakowski & Czobor, 2012). Adult psychopathy has not consistently been associated with general EF deficits (Blair & Frith, 2000; Dinn & Harris, 2000; Hiatt & Newman, 2006; Kosson et al., 2007), and recent neuropsychological evidence indicates that psychopathy may be characterized more by orbitofrontal dysfunction (Blair et al., 2006). Additionally, better dorsolateral prefrontal task performance has been demonstrated in successful, uncaught psychopaths relative to unsuccessful psychopaths and controls (Ishikawa, Raine, Lencz, Bihrle, & Lacasse, 2001); and white collar criminals have demonstrated better EF compared to offender controls (Raine et al., 2012). Furthermore, violent ASPD offenders with and without psychopathy have demonstrated similar deficits in terms of 'cool EF' (top-down processes – subsumed by the DLPFC and ventrolateral PFC – that are distinctly cognitive in nature, such as working memory, response inhibition, planning, sustained attention, and attentional set-shifting) and 'hot EF' (processes with an affective, motivational or incentive/reward component – subsumed by ventromedial connections between the mesolimbic reward pathway and the ventromedial PFC – such as appraisal of the motivational significance of a stimulus in emotional decision-making; De Brito, Viding, Kumari, Blackwood, & Hodgins, 2013).

Evidence for executive dysfunction in delinquent children and conduct-disordered adolescents has historically varied depending upon sample characteristics, control groups, assessment measures, executive functioning operationalizations and methodology (Moffitt & Henry, 1989; Teichner & Golden, 2000). Recent findings are mixed, with executive functioning deficits characterizing some antisocial youths (Cauffman, Steinberg, & Piquero, 2005; Kronenberger et al., 2005; Nigg et al., 2004; Raine et al., 2005; White et al., 1994) and not others (Moffitt et al., 1994; Nigg et al., 2004). Important to consider, however, is the development of executive functioning along with the ongoing myelination of the frontal cortex into adolescence and beyond (Nigg et al., 2004; Raine, 2002b), which may explain differential patterns of executive functioning deficits among children and adults. Some findings may reflect this phenomenon. Nestor (1992), for example, found executive functioning impairments in older (i.e., middle-aged) but not younger (i.e., early adulthood) maximum security hospital patients. Blair (2006) found impairments on an orbitofrontal neuropsychological task to be more pronounced in psychopathic adults than psychopathic children. Furthermore, the influences of comorbid hyperactivity and aggression may affect neuropsychological performance (Raine, 2002b; Séguin, Nagin, Assad, & Tremblay, 2004).

Biological versus social influences

Earlier prospective neuropsychological studies have found interactions of neuropsychological/neurobiological dysfunction and adverse social/environmental influences to significantly increase levels of later antisocial behaviour over each factor individually (Raine, 2002b). Recent longitudinal evidence supports these findings, highlights the relative importance of social risk factors and may clarify the nature of these biosocial interactions. For example, *progressive* cognitive dysfunction affected by adverse psychosocial experience may explain early-onset antisociality (Aguilar, Sroufe, Egeland, & Carlson, 2000); and lifetime, cumulative biosocial risk interactions may be stronger predictors of persistent aggression than risks specific to childhood or adolescence (Brennan et al., 2003). More specifically, Brennan and colleagues (2003), in a study of 370 Australian adolescents, identified that an interaction of biological risk factors (i.e., low age 5 vocabulary ability, poor age 15 VIQ and executive functioning, prenatal/birth complications, maternal illness during pregnancy, and infant temperament) and social risk factors predicted life-course persistent aggression in boys and girls, and predicted life-course persistent versus adolescent-onset aggression in boys. Alternatively, an overload of the late-developing prefrontal cortex by the social and executive functioning demands of late adolescence may lead to prefrontal dysfunction, behavioural inhibition failure and significantly increased antisocial behaviour (Raine, 2002b). Clearly, these neuropsychological studies underscore the need for considering biosocial interactions in the lifespan progression of criminality.

In sum, the neuropsychological literature demonstrates how the study of behavioural expressions of brain dysfunction – particularly in verbal, spatial and executive abilities – has informed developmental neurobiological perspectives of crime.

PSYCHOPHYSIOLOGY

Lykken's (1957) seminal work involving psycho-physiological processes in psychopaths largely marks the beginnings of the modern neurobiological investigation of crime. Psychophysiological studies have since focused upon the cardiovascular, electrodermal and electrocortical concomitants of antisocial behaviour.

Heart rate

Heart rate reflects both sympathetic and parasympathetic nervous system activity, and heart rate factors demonstrate an interesting developmental relationship with antisocial behaviour. While heart rate findings in adult antisocials are variable and inconsistent (Herpertz, 2007; Stanford, Houston, & Barratt, 2007b) – with low resting heart rate (an indicator of low autonomic arousal) and heart rate reactivity correlating with aggression but not psychopathy in adults (Lorber, 2004) – low resting heart rate is the best-replicated biological correlate of antisocial behaviour in children and adolescents (Herpertz, 2007; Stanford et al., 2007b). Although greater heart rate reactivity appears characteristic of conduct-disordered children (Lorber, 2004), one recent study found smaller heart rate reactivity in conduct-disordered children with high CU traits (Anastassiou-Hadjicharalambous & Warden, 2008). Low heart rate is diagnostically specific of conduct disorder, and has demonstrated predictive value – being a childhood predictor of adolescent aggression (Raine, 1996), reoffending (de Vries-Bouw et al., 2011), and LCP offending (Moffitt & Caspi, 2001; Jennings, Piquero, & Farrington, 2013). Recently, larger heart rate deceleration when anticipating aversive stimuli has been associated with psychopathic traits in 9–10-year-olds (Wang, Baker, Gao, Raine, & Lozano, 2012), while greater heart rate reactivity to rewards and smaller heart rate reactivity to penalty have been found in children with ODD (Luman, Sergeant, Knol, & Oosterlaan, 2010). Additionally, *high* heart rate appears to protect against the development of criminality, characterizing antisocial boys who later desist from adult criminal offending (Raine, Venables, & Williams, 1995).

Prospective studies indicate that the developmental relationship between heart rate factors and antisocial behaviour may be moderated by social influences. For example, age 3 low resting heart rate was shown to be related to age 11 aggression in high but not low social class individuals (Raine, Reynolds, Venables, & Mednick, 1997). Furthermore, increased heart rate variability has shown a positive relationship with aggression in young adults who have not been violently victimized, but not in those who have (Scarpa, Romero, Fikretoglu, Bowser, & Wilson, 1999). In a recent study, low heart rate was only found to be linked to antisocial behaviour in adolescents who were affiliated with bullies (Sijtsema et al., 2013).

Skin conductance

Skin conductance is controlled exclusively by the sympathetic nervous system, and reflects both arousal (e.g., skin conductance response frequency, level and fluctuations at rest) and responsivity (e.g., skin conductance orientating responses to novel stimuli and task responses to emotionally valenced stimuli). Strongest findings in this area are reduced skin conductance classical conditioning in psychopaths, criminals, delinquents and other antisocials (Raine, 1997). In adults, psychopaths demonstrate fewer skin conductance fluctuations (Raine, 1996), and Lorber's (2004) meta-analysis indicates negative relationships between skin conductance reactivity and both adult aggression and psychopathy. Attenuated task skin conductance responsivity has overall been associated with adult psychopathy, but only for negative stimuli (Lorber, 2004). Finally, antisocial personality-disordered adults have demonstrated reduced skin conductance orientating responses when comorbid for schizophrenia-spectrum personality disorders (Schug, Raine, & Wilcox, 2007), as do antisocial adolescents when additional schizoid features are present (Raine & Venables, 1984).

In children, low skin conductance arousal has been associated with conduct problems (Lorber, 2004; Baker, Shelton, Baibazarova, Hay, & van Goozen, 2013), and reduced skin conductance fluctuations have been reported in conduct-disordered boys (Herpertz et al., 2005) – in fact, together these may be a risk factor for adult criminality (Raine, 2002b). Reduced skin conductance arousal at age 15 has been associated with criminal offending at age 24 years (Raine, Venables, & Williams, 1990b). Orienting deficits and reduced skin conductance fear conditioning have also been reported in conduct-disordered boys (Herpertz et al., 2003) and adolescents (Fairchild, Stobbe, Van Goozen, Calder, & Goodyer, 2010; Fairchild, Van Goozen, Stollerya, & Goodyer, 2008; Herpertz et al., 2005), and the magnitude of conditioned responses were negatively associated with offending rate in juvenile offenders (Syngelaki, Fairchild, Moore, Savage, & Goozen, 2013). In addition, longitudinal studies have shown that low skin conductance fear conditioning responses at age 3 were associated with aggressive behaviour at age 8 and criminal offending at age 23 (Gao *et al.*, 2010a, 2010b), and longer skin conductance half-recovery time (indicating a closed attentional stance to the environment) in response to aversive stimuli at age 3 predisposes to psychopathic personality in adulthood (Glenn, Raine, Venables, & Mednick, 2007). Recent studies have also shown that psychopathic traits or CU traits in youths are associated with reduced skin conductance responses to neutral or aversive stimuli (Isen *et al.*, 2010), during anticipation of aversive stimuli (Fung *et al.*, 2005; Wang *et al.*, 2012) and provocation (Kimonis *et al.*, 2008; Muñoz *et al.*, 2008), similar to that observed in adult psychopaths. Fewer anticipated skin conductance responses may in fact be one of the candidate endophenotypes for psychopathy (Wang *et al.*, submitted).

Cardiovascular and electrodermal underarousal have been interpreted in different ways. Fearlessness theory argues that lack of fear, represented by low heart rate or skin conductance arousal, leads in childhood to poor socialization as low fear of punishment reduces the effectiveness of conditioning. Stimulation-seeking theory argues that underarousal represents an aversive state that is compensated for by stimulation/thrill-seeking and by risk-taking behaviour. In this context, 3-year-old children who show temperamentally high stimulation seeking and reduced fearlessness have been found to show increased aggression at age 11 (Raine, Reynolds, Venables, Mednick, & Farrington, 1998). Finally, prefrontal dysfunction theory argues that reduced skin conductance orienting is a marker for abnormalities in the prefrontal–cortical–subcortical circuitry involved in arousal regulation and stress responsivity – abnormalities associated with attentional and executive deficiencies (Herpertz, 2007). While both fearlessness and stimulation-seeking theories may be complementary in nature (Raine, 2002b), they could also represent independent risk factors as childhood fearlessness and stimulation-seeking have been found to be independent predictors of later aggression (Raine *et al.*, 1998).

Developmental relationships between skin conductance indices and antisociality have been reported, and multiple studies have found that skin conductance deficits show stronger relationships to antisocial behaviour in those from benign childhood social backgrounds that lack classic psychosocial risk factors for crime (Raine, 2002b). For example, reduced age 3 skin conductance orienting is related to age 11 aggression, but only for children from high social class backgrounds (Raine *et al.*, 1997). Additionally, higher heart rate and skin conductance arousal, high orienting and increased conditioning responses distinguished adolescents who desisted from crime by age 29 from those that did not (Raine, Venables, & Williams, 1995, 1996), suggesting a protective role of these mechanisms against antisociality.

Similar psychophysiological protective factors have also been found in the offspring of criminal fathers who desist from adult criminality (Brennan *et al.*, 1997).

Electroencephalogram and event-related potentials

The electroencephalogram (EEG) reflects regional electrical activity of the brain. Extensive reviews indicate that many studies have assessed EEG in antisocial populations such as criminals, delinquents, psychopaths, murderers and violent offenders (Raine, 1993). While a large number of studies have implicated varied EEG abnormalities in violent recidivistic offenders, results from EEG studies of psychopathic individuals are more inconsistent (see Raine, 1993; Herpertz, 2007). Commonly reported are slow-wave (i.e., theta and delta) abnormalities – reflecting underarousal – within frontal and temporal regions (Blake *et al.*, 1995; Evans & Park, 1997; Gatzke-Kopp, Raine, Buchsbaum, & LaCasse, 2001; Green, Leon-Barth, Venus, & Lucey, 2001; Herpertz, 2007; Lindberg *et al.*, 2005), although other regional cortical abnormalities have also been noted (Lindberg *et al.*, 2005).

Key developmental findings have also been reported. For example, alpha wave slowing among children and adolescents has been associated with later delinquency, particularly with thefts (Lindberg *et al.*, 2005). Also, increased age 15 slow-wave EEG activity and decreased autonomic reactivity predicted age 24 criminality in a prospective longitudinal study of 101 male schoolchildren (Raine, Venables, & Williams, 1990a, 1990b). EEG abnormalities may reflect cortical immaturity – a developmental lag in those prone to recidivistic crime (Herpertz, 2007). Additionally, emotion regulation deficits, indexed by abnormal frontal EEG asymmetry, may contribute to antisociality as atypical right > left hemispheric frontal EEG activation has been associated with antisocial/externalizing behaviour problems in children and adults (Baving, Laucht, & Schmidt, 2003; Gatzke-Kopp, Jetha, & Segalowitz, *et al.*, 2012; Harmon-Jones, 2003; Ishikawa & Raine, 2002; Santesso, Reker, Schmidt, & Segalowitz, 2006). Recently, one study has also shown that infants with stable left frontal EEG asymmetry from 10 to 24 months were rated higher in externalizing behaviour by the mother at 30 months (Smith & Bell, 2010).

The event-related potential (ERP) refers to averaged changes in the electrical activity of the brain in response to specific stimuli. Several ERP components appear to be biological markers for antisociality. For example, the P300 (a positive-going waveform occurring approximately 300 milliseconds after a stimulus;

Ishikawa & Raine, 2002) is thought to represent deployment of neural resources to task-relevant information, and P3 amplitude reduction is associated with biological vulnerability to a spectrum of externalizing disorders, such as conduct disorder, antisocial behaviour, and substance use disorders (Bernat, Hall, Steffen, & Patrick, 2007; Gao & Raine, 2009; Gilmore, Malone, & Iacono, 2012; Herpertz, 2007; Patrick, 2008; Yoon *et al.*, 2013), and this association appears to be mediated by genetic factors (Hicks *et al.*, 2007). It is therefore suggested that P300-related measures have potential utility as multivariate endophenotypes for externalizing behaviour (Gilmore, Malone, & Iacono, 2010). In contrast, overall *increased* P300 amplitude was observed in psychopaths on complex tasks, possibly reflecting increased callosal volume (Polich & Hoffman, 1998; Raine *et al.*, 2003a). Additionally, violent but not nonviolent offending has been negatively associated with P300 amplitude (Bernat *et al.*, 2007). Reduced P300 evoked potentials also appear to characterize impulsive but not premeditated aggression (Barratt, Stanford, Felthous, & Kent, 1997).

Developmentally, P300 amplitude decreases from childhood through adolescence, and its sensitivity as a putative marker for antisociality may vary with age (Gao & Raine, 2009). For example, Polich, Pollock, and Bloom, (1994) found reduced P300 amplitudes only in males with a pre-adulthood family history of alcoholism, while Bauer and Hesselbrock (1999) found reduced P300 amplitudes in conduct-disordered adolescents younger than 16.5 years. Prospective studies of P300-antisocial relationships are rare. In one such study, increased N1 amplitudes and faster P300 latencies to warning stimuli at age 15 predicted criminality at age 24 (Raine, Venables, & Williams, 1990c). Iacono, Carlson, Malone, and McGue (2002) similarly observed that reduced P300 amplitude at age 17 predicted the development of substance use disorders at age 20. Though these findings appear somewhat mixed, Gao and Raine's (2009) meta-analysis found a trend for younger antisocials to have twice as large a deficit in P300 amplitudes compared to older antisocials.

Other ERP components have demonstrated relationships with antisociality in adolescents and adults (Racer *et al.*, 2011). Adult psychopaths have shown larger P140 to alternative but not threatening stimuli in a response modulation model (reflect abnormal allocation of attention, Baskin-Sommers, Curtin, Li, & Newman, 2012), reduced frontal N275 amplitudes (thought to reflect response inhibition) during the Go/NoGo task (Kiehl, Smith, Hare, & Liddle, 2000) and reduced N300 amplitudes (thought to be particularly sensitive to affective features of stimuli) while processing positively and negatively valenced emotional faces (Campalla, Vanhoolandt, & Philippot, 2005).

In aggregate, psychophysiological contributions to the understanding of crime have been noteworthy, although much remains to be learned about developmental progressions of antisociality by examining the dynamic interface between psychological and physiological processes.

ENDOCRINOLOGY

Neurobiological research has also explored associations between antisocial behaviour and common hormones such as cortisol (a glucocorticoid stress reactivity hormone) and testosterone (a sex hormone that is part of the hypothalamic–pituitary–gonadal [HPG] axis). In adults, reduced cortisol levels have characterized violent adults (Virkkunen, 1985) and psychopathic offenders (Cima, Smeets, & Jelicic, 2008; Holi, Auvinen-Lintunen, Lindberg, Tani, & Virkkunen, 2006). In children and adolescents, low cortisol levels have been associated with aggression (McBurnett, Lahey, Rathouz, & Loeber, 2000), externalizing behaviour and low anxiety (van Goozen *et al.*, 1998), conduct disorder symptomatology (McBurnett *et al.*, 2000; Oosterlaan, Geurts, & Sergeant, 2005; Pajer, Gardner, Rubin, Perel, & Neal, 2001) and CU traits (Loney, Butler, Lima, Counts, & Eckel, 2006). In one 5-year longitudinal study, Shoal and colleagues (2003) found reduced cortisol in pre-adolescent boys (age 10–12 years) to be associated with low harm-avoidance, low self-control and increased aggression later in adolescence (age 15–17 years). Lower levels of cortisol may suggest reduced responsivity to stressors, which in turn leads to decreased fear of negative consequences such as potential punishment.

Evidence for an association between testosterone and aggressive behaviour has also been reported, a line of inquiry largely based upon the higher male-to-female ratios of antisocial behaviour (e.g., about 4:1 for antisocial personality disorder and as large as 10:1 for violent crimes; van Honk & Schutter, 2007), along with the several-fold increase in testosterone levels in men compared to women. In adults, elevated testosterone levels have been linked to antisocial behaviour and violent crime (Banks & Dabbs, 1996; Dabbs, Frady, & Carr, 1987); however, studies of aggressive children and adolescents have yielded mixed results (Loney *et al.*, 2006; Maras *et al.*, 2003; Pajer *et al.*, 2006). It has been suggested that testosterone may not be linked specifically to aggression, but rather to social dominance (Archer, 2006), which may account for discrepant findings. Either way, antisocial behavioural studies based in endocrinology form an important sector of neurobiological research into crime development.

MORAL DEVELOPMENT

Neurobiological research has increasingly focused upon moral development as a theoretical framework for understanding the initiation and progression of antisocial behaviour over the lifespan. Impaired moral development may result from neurobiological dysfunction, which – when beginning in early childhood – prevents some individuals from successfully passing through critical moral developmental stages. Neurobiological research of moral judgment in children and adults has led to the formulation of three hypothesized pathways to impaired moral development, involving key components to proper moral socialization.

The first is empathy, or the affective response to another's distress (Blair, 1995), which develops as the mental representation of a moral transgression (i.e., causing another harm). Through stimulus–reinforcement learning this generates an aversive emotional response. Children with CU traits have demonstrated reduced recognition of distress cues in others, such as sad and fearful facial expressions (Blair, 1997; Blair, Colledge, Murray, Mitchell, 2001; Blair, Jones, Clark, & Smith, 1997) and fearful vocalizations (Blair et al., 2002), and show autonomic impairments in response to these cues (de Wied, van Boxtel, Matthys, & Meeus, 2012; Blair, 1999). When presented with vignettes describing boys committing antisocial acts, youth with CU traits reported less feelings of guilt than those without CU traits (Feilhauer et al., 2013). Deficits in empathic responding may result from abnormalities in brain regions such as the amygdala and orbitofrontal/ventromedial prefrontal cortex. The amygdala is important in the generation of emotional responses, as well as in stimulus-reinforcement learning – a process which may be important for associating the mental representation of a moral transgression with an aversive emotional response (Blair, 2007). The ventromedial prefrontal region may be important in integrating moral knowledge with emotional cues, understanding the emotional states of others and inhibiting antisocial impulses. Children with CU traits have also demonstrated reduced amygdala activity to fearful facial expressions (Viding et al., 2012) and amygdala/orbitofrontal connectivity reductions associated with CU trait severity (Marsh et al., 2008). These studies suggest that the neurobiological deficits that may underlie reduced empathic responding may be present early in life.

The second deficit involves the ability to calculate risks for harm and utilize this information when making moral judgments. Psychopathic individuals have been found to be insensitive to cues that signal impending punishment. This is shown in laboratory tasks as deficits in fear conditioning (Flor, Birbaumer, Hermann, Ziegler, & Patrick, 2002), indicated by reduced skin conductance responses in anticipation of shock (Lykken, 1957) and reduced fear-potentiated startle (Patrick, Bradley, & Lang, 1993). Birbaumer et al. (2005), using functional magnetic resonance imaging (fMRI), found that criminal psychopaths failed to show normal activations in the amygdala, ventromedial prefrontal cortex, insula and anterior cingulate during fear conditioning, and exhibited no skin conductance responses – suggesting deficits in the fear-conditioning neural circuitry critical to moral development. Thus, moral development may be hindered by this deficit in the inability to use cues to anticipate outcomes of one's actions.

Finally, individuals may have deficits in somatic marker generation. Somatic markers, or bodily signals, are argued to critically guide emotional decision-making (Damasio, 1994). The somatic marker reflects the previous reward/punishment history associated with a behavioural act (e.g., individuals will develop an anticipatory skin conductance response when contemplating a previously risky or disadvantageous action), and is thought to be generated with orbitofrontal cortex involvement. Impaired somatic marker generation is evidenced by individuals with orbitofrontal lesions who choose disadvantageously on the gambling task (a paradigm which simulates real-life decisions in terms of uncertainty, reward and punishment), and fail to develop anticipatory skin conductance responses before selecting disadvantageous responses (Bechara, Damasio, Damasio, & Lee, 1999).

In sum, many of the brain regions that may be critical for moral development have been found to be impaired in antisocial youth, suggesting that these individuals may not have the tools necessary for proper moral development. These deficits may result from genetic or environmental factors. For example, Beauchamp et al. (2013) found that adolescents who had experienced traumatic brain injury demonstrated lower levels of moral reasoning and lower levels of empathy. These studies demonstrate how the theoretical framework of moral development may be particularly useful in understanding antisocial behavioural development.

NUTRITION

There is growing recognition that, along with other neurobiological risk factors, poor nutrition represents a potentially important risk factor for the development of antisocial behaviour in children and adults. Longitudinal studies have shown that increased aggression and attention deficits in childhood are related to malnutrition during infancy (Galler & Ramsey, 1989; Galler, Ramsey, Solimano, Lowell, & Mason, E. 1983a; Galler, Ramsey, Solimano, & Lowell, 1983b). More recent research has found that protein-energy malnutrition in the first year of life is associated with parent reports of externalizing behaviours at ages 9–17 years (Galler *et al.*, 2011) and increased self-reported conduct problems at ages 11–17 years (Galler *et al.*, 2012). Galler and colleagues (2012) found that later susceptibility to increased conduct problems was partially mediated by childhood IQ and home environmental circumstances. A recent meta-analysis also suggested an association between a tendency to develop low blood glucose and aggression (Benton, 2007). Vitamin and mineral deficiencies appear to be related to increased aggression, as evidenced by epidemiological studies (Breakey, 1997; Werbach, 1992) and investigations of individuals with histories of aggressive behaviour. For instance, Rosen *et al.* (1985) reported that one-third of incarcerated juvenile delinquents suffered from iron-deficient anaemia, while others have found violence-prone, assaultive young males to have elevated copper/zinc blood ratios (indicating zinc deficiencies; Cunnane, 1988) compared with individuals with no history of assaultive behaviour (Walsh, Isaacson, Rehman, & Hall, 1997). Furthermore, Neugebauer, Hoek, and Susser (1999) found male offspring of women nutritionally deprived during the first and second trimesters of pregnancy (the period of most rapid fetal brain growth) to have 2.5 times the normal rate of antisocial personality disorder in adulthood.

Studies have also implicated low levels of omega-3 long-chain essential fatty acid in antisocial behaviour. For instance, Corrigan *et al.* (1994) found reduced blood levels of omega-3 essential fatty acids in violent offenders compared to non-criminals. This is consistent with other reports suggesting that violent offenders have abnormalities in essential fatty acid metabolism (Hibbeln *et al.*, 1998; Virkkunen, Horrobin, Jenkins, & Manku, 1987). In addition, a recent study found that omega-3 essential fatty acids were inversely related to CU traits in adolescent boys with attention-deficit hyperactivity disorder (Gow *et al.*, 2013). Other studies have examined whether increased consumption of fish rich in omega-3 essential fatty acids is related to lower levels of violent and aggressive behaviour. For instance, Iribarren *et al.* (2004) reported an association between greater intake of seafood high in omega-3 fatty acids and lower hostility scores in 3,381 male and female adults. In a larger sample of 14,541 pregnant women, mothers who ate more fish during pregnancy had offspring who showed significantly higher levels of prosocial behaviour at age 7 years (Hallahan, Hibbeln, Davis, & Garland, 2007). In addition, a cross-national study of 26 counties observed a correlation of −0.63 between homicide rates and seafood consumption; countries with higher fish consumption had lower homicide rates (Hibbeln, 2001).

Experimental studies have provided more compelling evidence. A recent longitudinal prospective investigation (Liu, Raine, Venables, & Mednick, 2004) demonstrated that children with iron, zinc or protein deficiencies at age 3 had greater externalizing behaviour problems at ages 8, 11 and 17, even after controlling for multiple indicators of psychosocial adversity. In comparison to controls, malnourished children at age 3 were more aggressive or hyperactive at age 8 and had more externalizing behaviour at age 11 and greater conduct disorder and excessive motor activity at age 17. Moreover, a dose–response relationship was found between the extent of malnutrition at age 3 and behaviour problems at ages 8 and 17.

Additionally, research is converging on the idea that malnutrition predisposes to brain dysfunction, and in turn to antisocial behaviour throughout childhood and adolescence (Liu & Raine, 2006; Liu *et al.*, 2004; Liu, Raine, Venables, & Mednick, 2005), an idea which has received support from several studies (Gallagher, Newman, Green, & Hanson, 2005; Liu *et al.*, 2004; Liu, Raine, Venables, & Mednick, 2006; Nakagawasai *et al.*, 2006; Young & Leyton, 2002). For example, in one study, poor nutrition was found to impair cognitive functioning (IQ), which in turn was found to predispose to later antisocial behaviour (Liu *et al.*, 2004). Clearly, nutrition research – along with other key neuro-biological approaches – has a significant role to play in elucidating the important aetiological mechanisms of criminality, and potentially in reducing criminal offending.

FORENSIC APPLICATIONS OF DEVELOPMENTAL NEUROBIOLOGICAL RESEARCH

The potential importance within criminal justice systems of developmental neurobiological crime research is significant. Although technological advances have allowed for new and exciting neurobiological approaches to antisocial behavioural research, forensic applications of biological risk factors for crime are not a novel idea and have their roots in the writings of early positivist criminology (Lombroso, 1876). Thus, of importance to the clinical practitioner is an understanding of how neurobiological research has to date impacted various facets of criminal justice systems, and how future forensic practice may rely more and more heavily upon neurobiological assessment – which can inform policies and procedures regarding the identification, management and treatment of various forms of adult and juvenile offending. More crucial, however, is a thorough understanding of its limitations and of the philosophical, ethical and political dilemmas surrounding its use in the service of justice.

Lie detection

The detection of deception is among the first practical applications of neurobiological measures to the criminal justice system. The polygraph ('lie detector') is the earliest and most well-known physiological measure of lie detection (Trovillo, 1939) and is based upon the assumption that autonomic responses (e.g., increased heart rate, blood pressure, respiration rate and skin conductance response) during questioning indicate anxiety and therefore lying. Polygraph techniques include the control question technique (CQT), directed lie technique (DLT) and guilty knowledge test (GKT). Despite the presumably unfalsifiable nature of psychophysiological indicators of deception, and vehement proponents for its use among law enforcement and national security policymakers, polygraph lie-detection is generally considered by scientists to be fraught with conceptual and methodological weaknesses, and polygraph evidence has generally been excluded from the courts (Iacono, 2007; Iacono & Patrick, 2006).

More recently, an interest in brain-based methods for detecting deception has developed. The most promising line of inquiry has focused on ERP components – particularly the P300 response to significant, infrequent (i.e., 'oddball') stimuli. In a P300-based GKT procedure, crime-relevant information keys constitute the oddball stimuli. Several validation studies of the ERP-GKT appear to indicate its effectiveness, and potential utility within the court system has been noted (Iacono & Patrick, 2006). Neuroimaging approaches to lie detection have also generated recent interest (Langleben & Moriarty, 2013; McCabe, 2011), although the complexities of the structural and functional correlates of deception must be considered. For example, while the first evidence for structural brain abnormalities in pathological liars (i.e., prefrontal grey matter reductions and *increased* inferior, middle and orbitofrontal white matter) has been reported (Yang *et al.*, 2005, 2007), a recent review of 15 functional imaging studies (Sip, Roepstorff, McGregor, & Frith, 2007) indicates multiple areas of cortical and subcortical activation during deception – although dorsolateral prefrontal activation appeared most common across studies (i.e., in 9 out of 15). This, along with the conceptual and methodological issues that

bedevilled the old technology, must still be resolved before neuroimaging may become a viable approach to lie detection (Sip *et al.*, 2007).

Neuropsychological tests have demonstrated utility in the detection of another form of deception – malingering. On intelligence tests, malingering can be detected by an unusual scatter of scores, failing/passing items that legitimate responders would tend to pass/fail, and 'approximately correct' answers. Malingerers appear unable to mimic the performance of brain-injured patients on memory assessments, and often score well below the level of chance on 'forced-choice' tests. Also, malingering may be detected via the evaluation of consistency across measures of common constructs and/or across repetitions of administrations (Ackerman, 1999). Together, these methods demonstrate how neurobiological approaches may soon have much to offer in the way of deception-detection for forensic purposes.

Legal and judicial process

Structural and functional brain imaging have already begun to impact the legal system (Yang, Glenn, & Raine, 2008). Feigenson (2006) reports that approximately 130 court cases have admitted brain imaging data into evidence, a large number considering that the technique has only become more accessible in the past few years – possibly reflecting the belief that brain imaging represents an objective assessment of a defendant's mental functioning. Generally speaking, brain abnormalities as indicated by imaging data have been used to argue for reduced criminal responsibility, and outcomes of homicide cases incorporating this approach have varied, from successful NGRI defences, to sentencing mitigation (i.e., life imprisonment versus death penalty), to failure resulting in guilty verdicts and death sentencing. Though the potential implications of brain imaging within the legal system may seem significant, numerous limitations remain – including the inability of this technique to provide retrospective functional information (i.e., brain functioning at the time of the crime), and the subjectivity of structural interpretations (Yang *et al.*, 2008).

Neuropsychological measures may also have utility in the legal system. For example, a diagnosis of mental retardation (MR) – determined largely by sub-average intellectual functioning (i.e., IQ < 70) can significantly mitigate sentencing outcomes for murder defendants (specifically death penalty candidates), and may now become a key component of pre-trial competency to stand trial evaluations (Dwyer & Frierson, 2006). Additionally, neurotransmitter functioning has been introduced as evidence to support an insanity defence

(Berman & Coccaro, 1998). In sum, the practical application of developmental neurobiological crime research in informing legal and judicial processes is still in its incipient stages and while replication of current findings is needed to allow for more widespread acceptance and implementation, it nonetheless demonstrates significant potential.

Assessment

Initial evidence suggests that neurobiological measures may enhance specificity and effectiveness in key areas of future forensic assessment (Popma & Raine, 2006).

Diagnostic identification

Biological factors may help extend the available range of diagnostic possibilities, assist in identifying difficult-to-assess psychobiological deficits (e.g., using blunted heart rate reactivity rather than self-report measures to identify psychopathic traits, or brain imaging to identify pathological lying or malingering), and increase diagnostic specificity by reducing group heterogeneity within forensic-related psychopathologies. For example, researchers are attempting to identify differential neurobiological profiles of aggression subtypes (e.g., reactive versus proactive; Popma & Raine, 2006). Effective diagnostic identification is crucial within forensic arenas, and developmental neurobiological crime research may soon contribute to increased diagnostic capabilities.

Treatment

Neurobiological assessment approaches which reduce diagnostic heterogeneity may also contribute to improved forensic pharmacological interventions. For example, certain biological types of clinical aggression (i.e., impulsive, as opposed to premeditated) may be more amenable to pharmacological treatment (Moeller & Swann, 2007), whereas a biological subset of disruptive behaviour-disordered children (i.e., with low cortisol stress responsivity) has been associated with poor treatment outcome (Van de Wiel, Van Goozen, Matthys, Snoek, & Van Engeland, 2004). Additionally, certain stimulants (e.g., methylphenidate), which increase arousal and reduce aggressive behaviour (Connor, 2002), may have direct applications within forensic settings.

Furthermore, given the limited financial and staffing resources within correctional settings, clinical decisions must be made regarding the allocation of these resources to those offenders who will most benefit. Developmental neurobiological research may assist in determining the most viable treatment candidates. For example, Moffitt's (1993) theory differentiates life-course persistent from adolescence-limited offending – a normative, late-onset and largely desisting form of antisocial behaviour originating in social mimicry. As such, cognitive-behavioural strategies targeting desistence-related needs (Gendreau, Goggin, French, & Smith, 2006) may be ideal for adolescence-limited but not life-course persistent offenders; and knowledge of characteristic adolescence-limited or life-course persistent developmental histories in juveniles may help forensic practitioners identify those with a potentially better prognosis within criminal justice systems. Alternatively, some offenders with characteristic neurobiological profiles (i.e., psychopaths) may not benefit from non-pharmacological programmes such as therapeutic communities. In fact, these programmes have led to increased violent recidivism in psychopaths (essentially making them worse), although recent views are more optimistic (McGauley, Adshead, & Sarkar, 2007). Nonetheless, knowledge of treatment-resistant psychopathologies may contribute to more efficient use of limited criminal justice system time and monies.

Other non-pharmacological approaches such as nutritional interventions may be more suitable for reducing antisocial behaviour within incarcerated populations. For example, Schoenthaler et al. (1997) found that vitamin and mineral supplementation significantly reduced antisocial behaviour by 28% among incarcerated juvenile delinquents (in 16 of 26 subjects, violent acts were reduced by over 90%), along with improving brain function and reducing electrocortical abnormalities – success which prompted the State of California legislature to amend the Health and Welfare Code to determine if replication was possible among adult male prisoners. In another randomized, double-blind, placebo-controlled trial of 231 English prisoners (Gesch, Hammond, Hampson, Eves, & Crowder, 2002), omega-3 essential fatty acid and multivitamin/mineral treatment for 142 days produced a significant 26.3% reduction in antisocial and aggressive behaviour, and a 37% decrease in serious (including violent) offences. While many interventions for criminal behaviour are time, labour and cost intensive, nutritional interventions may offer a successful, easily implemented, and cost-effective approach for reducing antisocial behaviour in violent populations.

Intervention

Novel non-pharmacological interventions which consider and even alter biological vulnerabilities to juvenile antisocial behaviour also appear promising. For example, biofeedback may be an effective method for increasing physiological arousal in children with attention deficit hyperactivity disorder (Monastra, 2008); and non-pharmacological foster care interventions which normalize abnormally flattened diurnal cortisol-level patterns (Fisher, Stoolmiller, Gunnar, & Burraston, 2007) may reduce aggression associated with these patterns in juveniles (Murray-Close, Han, Cicchetti, Crick, & Rogosch, 2008). Additionally, child studies have shown that daily vitamin, mineral and omega-3 essential fatty acid supplementation can reduce antisocial behaviour as much as 47% in four months (Schoenthaler & Bier, 2000; Stevens et al., 2003), though results have not always been consistent (e.g., Hirayama, Hamazaki, & Terasawa, 2004). Early nutritional guidance (Olds et al. 1998) and enrichment programmes have also successfully reduced crime and antisocial behaviour. One randomized controlled trial (Raine, Mellingen, Liu, Venables, & Mednick, 2003b) demonstrated that environmental enrichment consisting of better nutrition, cognitive stimulation and increased physical exercise from ages 3 to 5 years significantly reduced antisociality at age 17 years and criminality at age 23 years. The fact that the prevention programme was more effective in children with poor nutritional status prior to study entry suggests that better nutrition was an active ingredient in the programme. This environmental enrichment was also shown to produce long-term improvements in arousal and psychophysiological information processing (Raine et al., 2003b; Raine, Liu, Venables, & Mednick, 2006). In fact, biological parameters – useful in devising forensic treatment/intervention approaches – may also be useful in evaluating these approaches (i.e., assessing a certain biological profile that is correlated with behavioural problems before and after treatment/intervention as a measure of outcome; Popma & Raine, 2006). In all, developmental neurobiological research has potentially much to offer in the way of informing the treatment and prevention of crime.

Dangerousness and risk prediction

Biological parameters may also be useful in predicting the risk of future antisocial behaviour (Popma & Raine, 2006). For example, low IQ and high antisociality have been described as components of dangerousness, and these factors have differentiated death-row from life-sentence male murderers (Heilbrun, 1990). Other neuropsychological deficits associated with psychopathy (Hiatt & Newman, 2006) could be used as indices of risk, as elevated psychopathy ratings (i.e., Psychopathy Checklist – Revised; Hare, 2003) are the strongest known actuarial predictors of criminal recidivism (Quinsey, Harris, Rice, & Cormier, 1999). Low levels of cerebrospinal 5-HIAA (a serotonin metabolite) have differentiated recidivistic violent offenders from non-recidivists (Virkkunen, DeJong, Bartko, Goodwin, & Linnoila, 1989), while other neurobiological measures, such as

penile plethysmography, have shown some promise in differentiating child molesters from other sex offenders and non-offenders, non-familial child molesters from incest offenders, and homicidal child molesters from non-homicidal child molesters and non-offenders – though this technique has drawn criticism from the scientific community (Bourget & Bradford, 2008). The prediction of dangerousness and assessment of risk is among the gravest and most imperative roles of the forensic practitioner, and developmental neurobiological research may soon help to increase the capabilities of those called upon to do so.

Though the contributions of neurobiological research to forensic assessment remain largely hypothetical, first evidence appears promising, and further research is both feasible and warranted. Enormous efforts must, however, be undertaken to understand and address the significant philosophical, ethical and political issues – largely centred in arguments of biological determinism versus free will – inherent to neurobiological applications within criminal justice systems (Popma & Raine, 2006; Yang et al., 2008), particularly as forensic psychology may one day be faced with issues such as state-sponsored pre-emptive interventions which deny individual civil liberties, and even implanted behaviour-controlling neurotechnologies. However, underlying these very real and legitimate concerns is perhaps an antiquated notion of the biological nature of crime. For while Lombroso's legacy continues, its foundation has been shaken – we have since learned through developmental neurobiological crime research that biology is not destiny, and that physical properties of mind and body in the criminal can in fact be alterable.

CONCLUSIONS

Key areas of neurobiological research have contributed to a greater empirical understanding of the initiation, maintenance and potential desistance from criminal behaviour. This body of research has also served to inform prominent developmental perspectives of crime. In turn, applications of neurobiological crime research and developmental theories of crime have both become essential to the field of forensic psychology. As such, the three – developmental theories of crime, neurobiological research and forensic applications – are inextricably bound, each serving both to inform and benefit from the other. It is hoped that this interdependence of theory, research and practice will contribute to a growing base of evidence from which the causes and cures of criminality will eventually be revealed.

FURTHER READING

Lorber, M. F. (2004). Psychophysiology of aggression, psychopathy, and conduct problems: A meta-analysis. *Psychological Bulletin*, *130*(4), 531–552.

A meta-analysis of 95 studies was conducted to examine the relationships between three measures of heart rate (HR) and electrodermal activity (EDA) – resting, task and reactivity – and three types of antisocial spectrum behaviour – aggression, psychopathy and conduct problems. Results indicated multiple interactive effects, with an inability in some cases to generalize across antisocial spectrum behaviours. Low resting and task EDA were both associated with psychopathy and conduct problems, though EDA reactivity was positively associated with aggression and negatively associated with psychopathy. Both low resting HR and high HR reactivity were associated with aggression and conduct problems. In some cases, physiology–behaviour relationships varied with age and stimulus valence. Results are considered to have important empirical and clinical implications.

Moffitt, T. E., Lynam, D. R., & Silva, P. A. (1994). Neuropsychological tests predicting persistent male delinquency. *Criminology*, *32*(2), 277–300.

This longitudinal study examined data from a birth cohort of several hundred New Zealand males, ages 13–18, to see if prospective measures of neuropsychological status predict antisocial outcomes. Subjects were administered an extensive neuropsychological battery at age 13 which included verbal, visuospatial and executive function measures. Results indicated that neuropsychological performance at age 13 predicted delinquency at age 18 (measured by official police and court records and self-report inventories) for persistent, high-level offending beginning in pre-adolescence. Findings were strongest for verbal measures, and visuospatial and mental flexibility executive function tasks did not demonstrate these relationships. In contrast, however, age 13 neuropsychological performance appeared unrelated to adolescent-onset offending. Results are considered the first longitudinal neuropsychological evidence for a previously proposed developmental taxon of antisocial behaviour in children and adolescents.

Raine, A., Mellingen, K., Liu, J. H., Venables, P. H., & Mednick, S. A. (2003). Effects of environmental enrichment at 3–5 years on schizotypal personality and antisocial behavior at ages 17 and 23 years. *American Journal of Psychiatry*, *160*, 1627–1635.

In this study, the authors evaluated whether a 2-year nutritional, educational and physical exercise programme for children at ages 3 to 5 reduced rates of schizotypal personality and antisocial behaviour when subjects were 17 and 23 years of age. Children who participated in the enrichment programme were matched on temperament, nutritional, cognitive, autonomic and demographic variables with a control group of children who experienced standard community conditions. Schizotypal personality and antisocial behaviour were assessed through both self-report and objective measures (e.g., court records) when subjects were 17 and 23 years of age. Subjects assigned to the enrichment programme at ages 3 to 5 had significantly lower scores for both schizotypal personality and antisocial behaviour at age 17, and for criminal behaviour at age 23. Children who were malnourished at age 3 benefited more from the enrichment, especially in relation to scores for schizotypal personality and conduct disorder at age 17, and schizotypal personality at age 23. Results add to the growing literature on the beneficial effects of an enriched environment on psychological and behavioural outcomes, and have implications for prevention efforts for schizophrenia and criminal behaviour.

REFERENCES

Ackerman, M. J. (1999). *Essentials of forensic psychological assessment*. New York: John Wiley & Sons.

Aguilar, B., Sroufe, A., Egeland, B., & Carlson, E. (2000). Distinguishing the early-onset/persistent and adolescent-onset antisocial behavior types: From birth to 16 years. *Development and Psychopathology*, *12*, 109–132.

Anastassiou-Hadjicharalambous, X., & Warden, D. (2008). Physiologically-indexed and self-perceived affective empathy in conduct-disordered children high and low on callous-unemotional traits. *Child Psychiatry and Human Development*, *39*(4), 503–517.

Anderson, S. W., Bechara, A., Damasio, H., Tranel, D., & Damasio, A. R. (1999). Impairment of social and moral behavior related to early damage in human prefrontal cortex. *Nature Neuroscience*, *2*, 1031–1037.

Andrews, T. K., Rose, F. D., & Johnson, D. A. (1998). Social and behavioural effects of traumatic brain injury in children. *Brain Injury*, *12*, 133–138.

Aoki, Y., Inokuchi, R., Nakao, T., & Yamasue, H. (2013). Neural bases of antisocial behavior: A voxel-based meta-analysis. *Social Cognitive and Affective Neuroscience. doi: 10.1093/scan/nst104*.

Archer, J. (2006). Testosterone and human aggression: An evaluation of the challenge hypothesis. *Neuroscience and Biobehavioral Reviews*, *30*, 319–345.

Baker, E., Shelton, K. H., Baibazarova, E., Hay, D. F., & van Goozen, S. H. (2013). Low skin conductance activity in infancy predicts aggression in toddlers 2 years later. *Psychological Science*, *24*(6), 1051–1056.

Banks, T., & Dabbs, J. J. M. (1996). Salivary testosterone and cortisol in a delinquent and violent urban subculture. *Journal of Social Psychology*, *136*, 49–56.

Barkataki, I., Kumari, V., Das, M., Taylor, P., & Sharma, T. (2006). Volumetric structural brain abnormalities in men with schizophrenia or antisocial personality disorder. *Behavioural Brain Research, 169*, 239–247.

Barratt, E. S., Stanford, M. S., Felthous, A. R., & Kent, T. A. (1997). The effects of phenytoin on impulsive and premeditated aggression: A controlled study. *Journal of Clinical Psychopharmacology, 17*, 341–349.

Barker, E. D., Séguin, J. R., White, H. R., Bates, M. E., Lacourse, E., Carbonneau, R., & Tremblay, R. E. (2007). Developmental trajectories of male physical violence and theft: Relations to neuro-cognitive performance. *Archives of General Psychiatry, 64*, 592–599.

Baskin-Sommers, A., Curtin, J. J., Li, W., & Newman, J. P. (2012). Psychopathy-related differences in selective attention are captured by an early event-related potential. *Personality Disorders: Theory, Research, and Treatment, 3*(4), 370–378.

Bastert, E., Schläfke, D., Pein, A., Kupke, F., & Fegert, J. (2012). Mentally challenged patients in a forensic hospital: A feasibility study concerning the executive functions of forensic patients with organic brain disorder, learning disability, or mental retardation. *International Journal of Law and Psychiatry, 35*, 207–212.

Bauer, L. O., & Hesselbrock, V. M. (1999). P300 decrements in teenagers with conduct problems: Implications for substance abuse risk and brain development. *Biological Psychiatry, 46*, 263–272.

Baving, L., Laucht, M., & Schmidt, M. H. (2003). Frontal EEG correlates of externalizing spectrum behaviors. *European Child & Adolescent Psychiatry, 12*(1), 36–42.

Beauchamp, M. H., Dooley, J. J., & Anderson, V. (2013). A preliminary investigation of moral reasoning and empathy after traumatic brain injury in adolescents. *Brain Injury, 27*(7–8), 896–902.

Bechara, A., Damasio, H., Damasio, A. R., & Lee, G. P. (1999). Different contributions of the human amygdala and ventromedial prefrontal cortex to decision-making. *Journal of Neuroscience, 19*, 5473–5481.

Benton, D. (2007). The impact of diet on anti-social, violent and criminal behavior. *Neuroscience and Biobehavioral Reviews, 31*, 752–774.

Berman, M. E., & Coccaro, E. F. (1998). Neurobiologic correlates of violence: Relevance to criminal responsibility. *Behavioral Sciences and the Law, 16*, 303–318.

Bernat, E. M., Hall, J. R., Steffen, B. V., & Patrick, C. J. (2007). Violent offending predicts P300 amplitude. *International Journal of Psychophysiology, 66*, 161–167.

Bertsch, K., Grothe, M., Prehn, K., Vohs, K., Berger, C., Hauenstein, K., Keiper, P., Domes, G., Teipel, S., & Herpertz, S. C. (2013). Brain volumes differ between diagnostic groups of violent criminal offenders. *European Archives of Psychiatry and Clinical Neuroscience, 263*(7), 593–606.

Bigler, E. D. (2001). Frontal lobe pathology and antisocial-personality disorder. *Archives of General Psychiatry, 58*, 609–611.

Birbaumer, N., Viet, R., Lotze, M., Erb, M., Hermann, C., & Grodd, W. (2005). Deficient fear conditioning in psychopathy: A functional magnetic resonance imaging study. *Archives of General Psychiatry, 62*, 799–805.

Blair, R. J. (1995). A cognitive developmental approach to morality: Investigating the psychopath. *Cognition, 57*, 1–29.

Blair, R. J. (1997). Moral reasoning in the child with psychopathic tendencies. *Personality and Individual Differences, 22*, 731–739.

Blair, R. J. (1999). Responsiveness to distress cues in children with psychopathic tendencies. *Personality and Individual Differences, 27*, 135–145.

Blair, R. J. (2006). The emergence of psychopathy: Implications for the neuropsychological approach to developmental disorders. *Cognition, 101*, 414–442.

Blair, R. J. (2007). The amygdala and ventromedial prefrontal cortex in morality and psychopathy. *Trends in Cognitive Science, 11*, 387–392.

Blair, R. J., Colledge, E., Murray, L., & Mitchell, D. G. V. (2001). A selective impairment in the processing of sad and fearful facial expressions in children with psychopathic tendencies. *Journal of Abnormal Child Psychology, 29*, 491–498.

Blair, R. J., & Frith, U. (2000). Neurocognitive explanations of the antisocial personality disorders. *Criminal Behaviour and Mental Health, 10*, S66–S81.

Blair, R. J., Jones, L., Clark, F., & Smith, M. (1997). The psychopathic individual: A lack of responsiveness to distress cues. *Psychophysiology, 34*, 192–198.

Blair, R. J., Mitchell, D. G. V., Richell, R. A., Kelly, S., Leonard, A., Newman, C., & Scott, S. K. (2002). Turning a deaf ear to fear: Impaired recognition of vocal affect in psychopathic individuals. *Journal of Abnormal Psychology, 111*, 682–686.

Blair, K. S., Newman, C., Mitchell, D. G. V., Richell, R. A., Leonard, A., Morton, J., & Blair, R. J. (2006). Differentiating among prefrontal substrates in psychopathy: Neuropsychological test findings. *Neuropsychology, 20*, 153–165.

Blake, P. Y., Pincus, J. H., & Buckner, C. (1995). Neurologic abnormalities in murderers. *Neurology, 45*, 1641–1647.

Bourget, D., & Bradford, J. M. W. (2008). Evidential basis for the assessment and treatment of sex offenders. *Brief Treatment and Crisis Intervention, 8*, 130–146.

Breakey, J. (1997). The role of diet and behaviour in childhood. *Journal of Paediatrics and Child Health, 33*, 190–194.

Brennan, P. A., Hall, J., Bor, W., Najman, J. M., & Williams, G. (2003). Integrating biological and social processes in relation to early-onset persistent aggression in boys and girls. *Developmental Psychology, 39*, 309–323.

Brennan, P. A., Raine, A., Schulsinger, F., Kirkegaard-Sorense, L., Knop, J., Hutchings, B., Rosenberg, R., & Mednick, S. A. (1997). Psychophysiological protective factors for male subjects at high risk for criminal behavior. *American Journal of Psychiatry, 154*, 853–855.

Broomhall, L. (2005). Acquired sociopathy: A neuropsychological study of executive dysfunction in violent offenders. *Psychiatry, Psychology, and Law, 12*, 367–387.

Campalla, S., Vanhoolandt, M. E., & Philippot, P. (2005). Emotional deficit in subjects with psychopathic tendencies as assessed by the Minnesota Multiphasic Personality Inventory-2, an event-related potentials study. *Neuroscience Letters, 373*, 26–31.

Caspi, A., McClay, J., Moffitt, T. E., Mill, J., Martin, J., Craig, I. W., Taylor, A., & Poulton, R. (2002). Role of genotype in the cycle of violence in maltreated children. *Science, 297*, 851–854.

Cauffman, E., Steinberg, L., & Piquero, A. R. (2005). Psychological, neuropsychological and physiological correlates of serious antisocial behavior in adolescence: The role of self-control. *Criminology: An Interdisciplinary Journal, 43*(1), 133–176.

Cima, M., Smeets, T., & Jelicic, M. (2008). Self-reported trauma, cortisol levels, and aggression in psychopathic and non-psychopathic prison inmates. *Biological Psychiatry, 78*, 75–86.

Connor, D. F. (2002). *Aggression and antisocial behavior in children and adolescents.* New York: Guilford Press.

Corrigan, F., Gray, R., Strathdee, A., Skinner, R., Van Rhijn, A., & Horrobin, D. (1994). Fatty acid analysis of blood from violent offenders. *Journal of Forensic Psychiatry, 5*, 83–92.

Cunnane, S. C. (1988). *Zinc: Clinical and biochemical significance.* Boca Raton, FL: CRC Press, Inc.

Dabbs, J. M., Frady, R. L., & Carr, T. S. (1987). Saliva testosterone and criminal violence in young adult prison inmates. *Psychosomatic Medicine, 49*, 174–182.

Damasio, A. R. (1994). *Descartes' error: Emotion, reason, and the human brain.* New York: GP Putnam's Sons.

Damasio, A. R., Tranel, D., & Damasio, H. (1990). Individuals with sociopathic behavior caused by frontal damage fail to respond automatically to social stimuli. *Behavioural Brain Research, 41*, 81–94.

De Brito, S. A., Viding, E., Kumari, V., Blackwood, N., & Hodgins, S. (2013). Cool and hot executive function impairments in violent offenders with antisocial personality disorder with and without psychopathy. *PLOS One, 8*(6): e65566. doi:10.1371/journal.pone.0065566

Decety, J., Skelly, L. R., Kiehl, & K. A. (2013). Brain response to empathy-eliciting scenarios involving pain in incarcerated individuals with psychopathy. *JAMA Psychiatry (Chicago, Ill.) 70*, 638–645.

Dinn, W. M., & Harris, C. L. (2000). Neurocognitive function in antisocial personality disorder. *Psychiatry Research, 97*, 173–190.

Dolan, M. (2012). The neuropsychology of prefrontal function in antisocial personality disordered offenders with varying degrees of psychopathy. *Psychological Medicine, 42*(8), 1715–1725.

Dolan, M., & Park, I. (2002). The neuropsychology of antisocial personality disorder. *Psychological Medicine, 32*, 417–427.

Dwyer, R. G., & Frierson, R. L. (2006). The presence of low IQ and mental retardation among murder defendants referred for pretrial evaluation. *Journal of Forensic Sciences, 51*, 678–682.

Ehrenreich, H., Krampe, H., & Sirén, A. L. (2007). Brain trauma. In A. R. Felthous & H. Saβ (Eds.), *International handbook of psychopathic disorders and the law: Vol. 1* (pp.217–236). Chichester: John Wiley & Sons.

Ellenbogen, J. M., Hurford, M. O., Liebskind, D. S., Neimark, G. B., & Weiss, D. (2005). Ventromedial frontal lobe trauma. *Neurology, 64*, 757.

Eriksson, Å, Hodgins, S., & Tengström, A. (2005). Verbal intelligence and criminal offending among men with schizophrenia. *International Journal of Forensic Mental Health, 4*, 191–200.

Evans, J. R., & Park, N. S. (1997). Quantitative EEG findings among men convicted of murder. *Journal of Neurotherapy, 2*, 31–37.

Fairchild, G., Hagan, C. C., Walsh, N. D., Passamonti, L., Calder, A. J., & Goodyer, I. M. (2013). Brain structure abnormalities in adolescent girls with conduct disorder. *Journal of Child Psychology and Psychiatry, and Allied Disciplines 54*, 86–95.

Fairchild, G., Stobbe, Y., Van Goozen, S. H., Calder, A. J., & Goodyer, I. M. (2010). Facial expression recognition, fear conditioning, and startle modulation in female subjects with conduct disorder. *Biological Psychiatry, 68*(3), 272–279.

Fairchild, G., Van Goozen, S. H., Stollerya, S. J., & Goodyer, I. M. (2008). Fear conditioning and affective modulation of the startle reflex in male adolescents with early-onset or adolescence-onset conduct disorder and healthy control subjects. *Biological Psychiatry, 63*(3), 279–285.

Feilhauer, J., Cima, M., Benjamins, C., & Muris, P. (2013). Knowing right from wrong, but just not always feeling it: Relations among callous-unemotional traits, psychopathological symptoms, and cognitive and affective morality judgments in 8- to 12-year-old boys. *Child Psychiatry & Human Development, 44*(6), 709–716.

Feigenson, N. (2006). Brain imaging and courtroom evidence; on the admissibility and persuasiveness of fMRI. *International Journal of Law in Context, 2*, 233–255.

Filley, C. M., Price, B. H., Nell, V., Antoinette, T., Morgan, A. S. Bresnahan, J. F., Pincus, J. H., Gelbort, M. M., Weissberg, M., & Kelly, J. P. (2001). Toward an understanding of violence: Neurobehavioral aspects of unwarranted physical aggression: Aspen Neurobehavioral Conference consensus statement. *Neuropsychiatry, Neuropsychology, and Behavioral Neurology, 14*, 1–14.

Finger, E. C., Marsh, A., Blair, K. S., Majestic, C., Evangelou, I., Gupta, K., Schneider, M. R., Sims, C., Pope, K., Fowler, K., Sinclair, S., Tovar-Moll, F., Pine, D., & Blair, R. J. (2012). Impaired functional but preserved structural connectivity in limbic white matter tracts in youth with conduct disorder or oppositional defiant disorder plus psychopathic traits. *Psychiatry Research, 202*, 239–244.

Fisher, P. A., Stoolmiller, M., Gunnar, M. R., & Burraston, B. O. (2007). Effects of a therapeutic intervention for foster preschoolers on diurnal cortisol activity. *Psychoneuroendocrinology, 32*, 892–905.

Flor, H., Birbaumer, N., Hermann, C., Ziegler, S., & Patrick, C. J. (2002). Aversive Pavlovian conditioning in psychopaths: Peripheral and central correlates. *Psychophysiology, 39*, 505–518.

Frick, P. J., Cornell, A. H., Bodin, S. D., Dane, H. E., Barry, C. T., & Loney, B. R. (2003). Callous-unemotional traits and developmental pathways to severe conduct problems. *Developmental Psychology, 39*, 372–378.

Fung, M. T., Raine, A., Loeber, R., Lynam, D. R., Steinhauer, S. R., Venables, P. H., Stouthamer-Loeber, M. (2005). Reduced electrodermal activity in psychopathy-prone adolescents. *Journal of Abnormal Psychology, 114*(2), 187–196.

Gallagher, E. A., Newman, J. P., Green, L. R., & Hanson, M. A. (2005). The effect of low protein diet in pregnancy on the development of brain metabolism in rat offspring. *Journal of Physiology, 568*, 553–558.

Galler, J. R., Bryce, C. R., Waber, D. P., Hock, R. S., Harrison, R., Eaglesfield, G. D., & Fitzmaurice, G. (2012). Infant malnutrition predicts conduct problems in adolescents. *Nutritional Neuroscience, 15*, 186–192.

Galler, J. R., Bryce, C. R., Waber, D. P., Medford, G., Eaglesfield, G. D., Fitzmaurice, & G. (2011). Early malnutrition predicts parent reports of externalizing behaviors at ages 9–17. *Nutritional Neuroscience, 14*, 138–144.

Galler, J. R., & Ramsey, F. (1989). A follow-up study of the influence of early malnutrition on development. *Journal of the American Academy of Child and Adolescent Psychiatry, 26*, 23–27.

Galler, J. R., Ramsey, F., Solimano, G., & Lowell, W. (1983b). The influence of early malnutrition on subsequent behavioral development. II. Classroom behavior. *Journal of the American Academy of Child and Adolescent Psychiatry, 22*, 16–22.

Galler, J. R., Ramsey, F., Solimano, G., Lowell, W., & Mason, E. (1983a). The influence of early malnutrition on subsequent behavioural development. I. Degree of impairment of intellectual performance. *Journal of the American Academy of Child and Adolescent Psychiatry, 22*, 8–15.

Gao, Y., & Raine, A. (2009). P3 event-related potential impairments in antisocial and psychopathic individuals: A meta-analysis. *Biological Psychology, 82*, 199–210.

Gao, Y., Raine, A., Venables, P. H., Dawson, M. E., & Mednick, S. A. (2010a). The development of skin conductance fear conditioning in children from ages 3 to 8 years. *Developmental science, 13*(1), 201–212.

Gao, Y., Raine, A., Venables, P. H., Dawson, M. E., & Mednick, S. A. (2010b). Reduced electrodermal fear conditioning from ages 3 to 8 years is associated with aggressive behavior at age 8 years. *Journal of Child Psychology and Psychiatry, 51*(5), 550–558.

Gatzke-Kopp, L. M., Jetha, M. K., & Segalowitz, S. J. (2012). The role of resting frontal EEG asymmetry in psychopathology: Afferent or efferent filter? *Developmental Psychobiology, 56*(1), 73–85.

Gatzke-Kopp, L. M., Raine, A., Buchsbaum, M., & LaCasse, L. (2001). Temporal lobe deficits in murderers: EEG findings undetected by PET. *Journal of Neuropsychiatry and Clinical Neuroscience, 13*, 486–491.

Gendreau, P., Goggin, C., French, S., & Smith, P. (2006). Practicing psychology in correctional settings. In I. B. Weiner & A. K. Hess (Eds.), *The handbook of forensic psychology* (3rd edn, pp. 722–750). Hoboken, NJ: John Wiley & Sons.

Gesch, C. B., Hammond, S. M., Hampson, S. E., Eves, A., & Crowder, M. J. (2002). Influence of supplementary vitamins, minerals and essential fatty acids on the antisocial behaviour of young adult prisoners: Randomised, placebo-controlled trial. *British Journal of Psychiatry, 181*, 22–28.

Gilmore, C. S., Malone, S. M., & Iacono, W. G. (2010). Brain electrophysiological endophenotypes for externalizing psychopathology: A multivariate approach. *Behavior Genetics, 40*, 186–200.

Gilmore, C. S., Malone, S. M., & Iacono, W. G. (2012). Is the P3 amplitude reduction seen in externalizing psychopathology attributable to stimulus sequence effects? *Psychophysiology, 49*(2), 248–251.

Glenn, A. L., Raine, R., Venables, P. H., & Mednick, S. A. (2007). Early temperamental and psychophysiological precursors of adult psychopathic personality. *Journal of Abnormal Psychology, 116*, 508–518.

Goldman, D., & Ducci, F. (2007). The genetics of psychopathic disorders. In A. R. Felthous & H. Saß (Eds.), *International handbook on psychopathic disorders and the law: Vol. 1* (pp. 149–169). Chichester: John Wiley & Sons.

Gow, R. V., Vallee-Tourangeau, F., Crawford, M. A., Taylor, E., Ghebremeskel, K., Bueno, A. E., … Rubia, K. (2013). Omega-3 fatty acids are inversely related to callous and unemotional traits in adolescent boys with attention deficit *hyperactivity disorder. Prostoglandins, Leukotrienes, and Essential Fatty Acids, 88*, 411–418.

Grafman, J., Schwab, K., Warden, D., Pridgen, A., Brown, H. R., & Salazar, A. M. (1996). Frontal lobe injuries, violence, and aggression: A report of the Vietnam Head Injury Study. *Neurology, 46*, 1231–1238.

Granacher, R. P., & Fozdar, M. A. (2007). Acquired psychopathy and the assessment of traumatic brain injury. In A. R. Felthous & H. Saß (Eds.), *International handbook of psychopathic disorders and the law: Vol. 1* (pp. 237–250). Chichester: John Wiley & Sons.

Green, J., Leon-Barth, C., Venus, S., & Lucey, T. (2001). Murder and the EEG. *The Forensic Examiner, 10*, 32–34.

Hallahan, B., Hibbeln, J. R., Davis, J. M., & Garland, M. R. (2007). Omega-3 fatty acid supplementation in patients with recurrent self-harm – single-centre double-blind randomised controlled trial. *British Journal of Psychiatry, 190*, 118–122.

Hancock, M., Tapscott, J. L., & Hoaken, P. N. S. (2012). Role of executive dysfunction in predicting frequency and severity of violence. *Aggressive Behavior, 36*, 338–349.

Hanlon, R. E., Coda, J. J., Cobia, D., & Rubin, L. H. (2012). Psychotic domestic murder: Neuropsychological differences between homicidal and nonhomicidal schizophrenic men. *Journal of Family Violence, 27*, 105–113.

Hanlon, R. E., Rubin, L. H., Jensen, M., & Daoust, S. (2010). Neuropsychological features of indigent murder defendants and death row inmates in relation to homicidal aspects of their crimes. *Archives of Clinical Neuropsychology, 25*, 1–13.

Hare, R. D. (2003). *The Hare psychopathy checklist – revised* (2nd edn). Toronto, ON: Multi-Health Systems.

Harlow, J. M. (1848). Passage of an iron bar through the head. *Boston Medical Surgery Journal, 13*, 389–393.

Harmon-Jones, E. (2003). Clarifying the emotive functions of asymmetrical frontal cortical activity. *Psychophysiology, 40*(6), 838–848.

Heilbrun, A. B. (1990). Differentiation of death-row murderers and life-sentence murderers by antisociality and intelligence measures. *Journal of Personality Assessment, 54*, 617–627.

Herpertz, S. C. (2007). Electrophysiology. In A. R. Felthous & H. Saβ (Eds.), *International handbook of psychopathic disorders and the law: Vol. 1* (pp. 187–198). Chichester: John Wiley & Sons.

Herpertz, S. C., Mueller, B., Wenning, B., Qunaibi, M., Lichterfeld, C., & Herpertz-Dahlmann, B. (2003). Autonomic responses in boys with externalizing disorders. *Journal of Neural Transmission, 110*, 1181–1195.

Herpertz, S. C., Mueller, B., Qunaibi, M., Lichterfeld, C., Konrad, K., & Herpertz-Dahlmann, B. (2005). Emotional responses in boys with conduct disorder. *American Journal of Psychiatry, 162*, 1100–1107.

Hiatt, K. D., & Newman, J. P. (2006). Understanding psychopathy: The cognitive side. In C. J. Patrick (Ed.), *Handbook of psychopathy* (pp. 334–352). New York: Guilford Press.

Hibbeln, J. R. (2001). Seafood consumption and homicide mortality: A cross-national ecological analysis. *World Review of Nutrition and Dietetics, 88*, 41–46.

Hibbeln, J. R., Umhau, J. C., Linnoila, M., George, D. T., Ragan, P. W., Shoaf, S. E., Vaughan, M. R., Rawlings, R., & Salem, N. Jr. (1998). A replication study of violent and nonviolent subjects: Cerebrospinal fluid metabolites of serotonin and dopamine are predicted by plasma essential fatty acids. *Biological Psychiatry, 44*, 243–249.

Hicks, B. M., Bernat, E., Malone, S. M., Iacono, W. G., Patrick, C. J., Krueger, R. F., & McGue, M. (2007). Genes mediate the association between P3 amplitude and externalizing disorders. *Psychophysiology, 44*(1), 98–105.

Hirayama, S., Hamazaki, T., & Terasawa, K. (2004). Effect of docosahexaenoic acid-containing food administration on symptoms of attention-deficit/hyperactivity disorder – a placebo-controlled double-blind study. *European Journal of Clinical Nutrition, 58*, 467–473.

Hirono, N., Mega, M. S., Dinov, I. D., Mishkin, F., & Cummings, J. L. (2000). Left frontal temporal hypoperfusion is associated with aggression in patient with dementia. *Archives Neuro-logy, 57*, 861–866.

Holi, M., Auvinen-Lintunen, L., Lindberg, N., Tani, P., & Virkkunen, M. (2006). Inverse correlation between severity of psychopathic traits and serum cortisol levels in young adult violent male offenders. *Psychopathology, 39*, 102–104.

Howner, K., Eskildsen, S. F., Fischer, H., Dierks, T., Wahlund, L. O., Jonsson, T., Wiberg, M. K., & Kristiansson, M. (2012). Thinner cortex in the frontal lobes in mentally disordered offenders. *Psychiatry Research, 203*, 126–131.

Iacono, W. G. (2007). Detection of deception. In J. T. Cacioppo, L. G. Tassinary, & G. G. Berntson (Eds.), *Handbook of psychophysiology* (3rd edn, pp. 688–703), Cambridge: Cambridge University Press.

Iacono, W. G., Carlson, S. R., Malone, S. M., & McGue, M. (2002). P3 event-related potential amplitude and the risk for disinhibitory disorders in adolescent boys. *Archives of General Psychiatry, 59*, 750–757.

Iacono, W. G., & Patrick, C. (2006). Polygraph ('lie detector') testing: Current status and emerging trends. In I. B. Weiner & A. K. Hess (Eds.), *Handbook of forensic psychology* (3rd edn, pp. 552–588). Hoboken, NJ: John Wiley & Sons.

Iribarren, C., Markovitz, J. H., Jacobs, D. R., Schreiner, P. J., Daviglus, M., & Hibbeln, J. R. (2004). Dietary intake of n-3, n-6 fatty acids and fish: Relationship with hostility in young adults – the CARDIA study. *European Journal of Clinical Nutrition, 58*, 24–31.

Isen, J. (2010). A meta-analytic assessment of Wechsler's P>V sign in antisocial populations. *Clinical Psychology Review, 30*, 423–435.

Isen, J., Raine, A., Baker, L., Dawson, M., Bezdjian, S., & Lozano, D. I. (2010). Sex-specific association between psychopathic traits and electrodermal reactivity in children. *Journal of abnormal psychology, 119*(1), 216.

Ishikawa, S. S., & Raine, A. (2002). Psychophysiological correlates of antisocial behavior: A central control hypothesis. In J. Glicksohn (Ed.), *The neurobiology of criminal behavior* (pp. 187–229). Norwell, MA: Kluwer Academic.

Ishikawa, S. S., Raine, A., Lencz, T., Bihrle, S., & Lacasse, L. (2001). Autonomic stress reactivity and executive functions in successful and unsuccessful criminal psychopaths from the community. *Journal of Abnormal Psychology, 110*, 423–432.

Jennings, W. G., Piquero, A. R., & Farrington, D. P. (2013). Does resting heart rate at age 18 distinguish general and violent offending up to age 50? Findings from the Cambridge Study in Delinquent Development. *Journal of Criminal Justice, 41*, 213–219.

Juhasz, C., Behen, M. E., Muzik, O., Chugani, D. C., & Chugani, H. T. (2001). Bilateral medial prefrontal and temporal neocortical hypometabolism in children with epilepsy and aggression. *Epilepsia, 42*, 991–1001.

Keilp, J. G., Gorlyn, M., Russell, M., Oquendo, M. A., Burke, A. K., Harkavy-Friedman, J., & Mann, J. J. (2013). Neuropsychological function and suicidal behaviour: Attention control, memory and executive dysfunction in suicide attempt. *Psychological Medicine, 43*(3), 539–551.

Kiehl, K. A., Smith, A. M., Hare, R. D., & Liddle, P. F. (2000). An event-related potential investigation of response inhibition in schizophrenia and psychopathy. *Biological Psychiatry, 48*, 210–221.

Kiehl, K. A., Smith, A. M., Hare, R. D., Mendrek, A., Forster, B. B., Brink, J., & Liddle, P. F. (2001). Limbic abnormalities in affective processing by criminal psychopaths as revealed by functional magnetic resonance imaging. *Biological Psychiatry, 50*, 677–684.

Kimonis, E. R., Frick, P. J., Skeem, J. L., Marsee, M. A., Cruise, K., Centifanti, L. C., Aucoin, K. J., & Morris, A. S. (2008). Assessing callous-unemotional traits in adolescent offenders: Validation of the inventory of callous-unemotional traits. *International Journal of Law and Psychiatry, 31*(3), 241–252.

Klüver, H., & Bucy, P. C. (1939). Preliminary analysis of functions of the temporal lobes in monkeys. *Archive of Neurological Psychiatry, 42*, 979–100.

Kosson, D. H., Miller, S. K., Byrnes, K. A., & Leveroni, C. L. (2007). Testing neuropsychological hypotheses for cognitive deficits in psychopathic criminals: A study of global-local processing. *Journal of the International Neuropsychological Society, 13*, 267–276.

Krakowski, M. I., & Czobor, P. (2012). Executive function predicts response to antiaggression treatment in schizophrenia: A randomized control trial. *Journal of Clinical Psychiatry, 73*(1), 74–80.

Kronenberger, W. G., Mathews, V. P., Dunn, D. W., Wang, Y., Wood, E. A., Giauque, A. L., &… Li, T. (2005). Media violence exposure and executive functioning in aggressive and control adolescents. *Journal of Clinical Psychology, 61*(6), 725–737.

Kruesi, M. J. P., & Casanova, M. V. (2006). White matter in liars. *British Journal of Psychiatry, 188*, 293–294.

Kruesi, M. J. P., Casanova, M. F., Mannheim, G., & Jonson-Bilder, A. (2004). Reduced temporal lobe volume in early onset conduct disorder. *Psychiatry Research: Neuroimaging, 132*, 1–11.

Laakso, M. P., Gunning-Dixon, F., Vaurio, O., Repo, E., Soininen, H., & Tiihonen, J. (2002). Prefrontal volume in habitually violent subjects with antisocial personality disorder and type 2 alcoholism. *Psychiatry Research Neuroimaging, 114*, 95–102.

Langleben, D. D., & Moriarty, J. C. (2013). Using brain imaging for lie detection: Where science, law, and policy collide. *Psychology, Public Policy, and Law, 19*(2), 222–234.

León-Carrión, J., & Ramos, F. J. (2003). Blows to the head during development can predispose to violent criminal behaviour: Rehabilitation of consequences of head injury is a measure for crime prevention. *Brain Injury, 17*, 207–216.

Lewis, D. O., Pincus, J. H., Bard, B., Richardson, E., Prichep, L. S., Feldman, M. *et al.* (1988). Neuropsychiatric, psychoeducational, and family characteristics of 14 juveniles condemned to death in the United States. *American Journal of Psychiatry, 145*, 584–589.

Lewis, D. O., Pincus, J. H., Feldman, M., Jackson, L., & Bard, B. (1986). Psychiatric, neurological, and psychoeducational characteristics of 15 death row inmates in the United States. *American Journal of Psychiatry, 143*, 838–845.

Lewis, D. O., Pincus, J. H., Lovely, R., Spitzer, E., & Moy, E. (1987). Biopsychosocial characteristics of matched samples of delinquents and nondelinquents. *Journal of the American Academy of Child and Adolescent Psychiatry, 26*, 744–752.

Lezak, M. D., Howieson, D. B., Loring, D. W., Hannay, H. J., & Fischer, J. S. (2004). *Neuropsychological assessment* (4th edn). New York: Oxford University Press.

Lindberg, N., Tani, P., Virkkunen, M., Porkka-Heiskanen, T., Appelberg, B., Naukkarinen, H., & Salmi, T. (2005). Quantitative electro-encephalographic measures in homicidal men with antisocial personality disorder. *Psychiatry Research, 136*, 7–15.

Liu, J., & Raine, A. (2006). The effect of childhood malnutrition on externalizing behavior. *Current Opinion in Pediatrics, 18*, 565–570.

Liu, J., Raine, A., Venables, P., & Mednick, S. A. (2004). Malnutrition at age 3 years predisposes to externalizing behavior problems at ages 8, 11 and 17 years. *American Journal of Psychiatry, 161*, 2005–2013.

Liu, J., Raine, A., Venables, P., & Mednick, S. A. (2005). Behavioral effects of childhood malnutrition. Reply to Galler *et al. American Journal of Psychiatry, 162*, 1629–1761.

Liu, J., Raine, A., Venables, P., & Mednick, S. A. (2006). Malnutrition, brain dysfunction, and antisocial criminal behavior. In A. Raine (Ed.), *Crime and schizophrenia: Causes and cures* (pp.109–128). New York: Nova Science Publishers.

Lockwood, P. L., Sebastian, C. L., McCrory, E. J., Hyde, Z. H., Gu, X., De Brito, S. A., & Viding, E. (2013). Association of callous traits with reduced neural response to others' pain in children with conduct problems. *Current Biology, 23*, 901–905.

Lombroso, C. (1876). *Criminal man.* Milan: Hoepli.

Loney, B. R., Butler, M. A., Lima, E. N., Counts, C. A., & Eckel, L. A. (2006). The relation between salivary cortisol, callous-unemotional traits, and conduct problems in an adolescent non-referred sample. *Journal of Child Psychology and Psychiatry, 47*, 30–36.

Loney, B. R., Frick, P. J., Ellis, M. L., & McCoy, M. G. (1998). Intelligence, psychopathy, and antisocial behavior. *Journal of Psychopathology and Behavioural Assessment, 20*, 231–247.

Lorber, M. F. (2004). Psychophysiology of aggression, psychopathy, and conduct problems: A meta-analysis. *Psychological Bulletin, 130*, 531–552.

Luman, M., Sergeant, J. A., Knol, D. L., & Oosterlaan, J. (2010). Impaired decision making in oppositional defiant disorder related to altered psychophysiological responses to reinforcement. *Biological Psychiatry, 68*(4), 337–344.

Luria, A. (1980). *Higher cortical functions in man* (2nd edn). New York: Basic Books.

Ly, M., Motzkin, J. C., Philippi, C. L., Kirk, G. R., Newman, J. P., Kiehl, K. A., & Koenigs, M. (2012). Cortical thinning in psychopathy. *The American Journal of Psychiatry, 169*, 743–749.

Lykken, D. (1957). A study of anxiety in the sociopathic-personality. *Journal of Abnormal and Social Psychology, 55*, 6–10.

Lykken, D. (1995). *The antisocial personalities.* Hillsdale, NJ: Erlbaum.

Maras, A., Laucht, M., Gerdes, D., Wilhelm, C., Lewicka, S., Haack, D., & Scmidt, M. H. (2003). Association of testosterone and dihydrotestosterone with externalizing behavior in adolescent boys and girls. *Psychoneuroendocrinology, 28*, 932–940.

Marsh, A. A., Finger, E. C., Fowler, K. A., Adalio, C. J., Jurkowitz, I. T., Schechter, J. C., Pine, D. S., Decety, J., & Blair, R. J. (2013). Empathic responsiveness in amygdala and anterior cingulate cortex in youths with psychopathic traits. *Journal of Child Psychology and Psychiatry, and Allied Disciplines, 54*, 900–910.

Marsh, A. A., Finger, E. C., Mitchell, D. G. V., Reid, M. E., Sims, C., Kosson, D. S., Towbin, K. E., Leibenluft, E., Pine, D. S., & Blair, R. J. R. (2008). Reduced amygdala response to fearful expressions in children and adolescents with callous-unemotional traits and disruptive behavior disorders. *American Journal of Psychiatry, 165*, 712–720.

Mataró, M., Jurado, M. A., García-Sánchez, C., Barraquer, L., Costa-Jussá, F. R., & Junqué, C. (2001). Long-term effects of bilateral frontal brain lesion: 60 years after injury with an iron bar. *Archives of Neurology, 58*, 1139–1142.

McBurnett, K., Lahey, B. B., Rathouz, P. J., & Loeber, R. (2000). Low salivary cortisol and persistent aggression in boys referred for disruptive behavior. *Archives of General Psychiatry, 57*, 38–43.

McCabe, D. P. (2011). The influence of fMRI lie detection evidence on juror decision-making. *Behavioral Sciences and the Law, 29*, 566–577.

McGauley, G., Adshead, G., & Sarkar, S. P. (2007). Psycho-therapy of psychopathic disorders. In A. R. Felthous & H. Saβ (Eds.), *International handbook of psychopathic disorders and the law: Vol. 1* (pp. 449–466). Chichester: John Wiley & Sons.

Moeller, F. G., & Swann, A. C. (2007). Pharmacotherapy of clinical aggression in individuals with psychopathic disorders. In A. R. Felthous & H. Saβ (Eds.), *International handbook on psychopathic disorders and the law* (pp. 397–416). Chichester: John Wiley & Sons.

Moffitt, T. E. (1993). Adolescence-limited and life-course-persistent antisocial behavior: A developmental taxonomy. *Psychological Review, 100*, 674–701.

Moffitt, T. E. (2005). The new look of behavioral genetics in developmental psychopathology: Gene–environment interplay in antisocial behavior. *Psychological Bulletin, 131*, 533–554.

Moffitt, T. E., & Caspi, A. (2001). Childhood predictors differentiate life-course persistent and adolescence-limited antisocial pathways among males and females. *Developmental Psychopathology, 13*, 355–375.

Moffitt, T. E., & Henry, B. (1989). Neuropsychological assessment of executive functions in self-reported delinquents. *Development and Psychopathology, 1*, 105–118.

Moffitt, T. E., Lynam, D. R., & Silva, P. A. (1994). Neuropsy-chological tests predicting persistent male delinquency. *Criminology, 32*, 277–300.

Monastra, V. J. (2008). Electroencephalographic feedback in the treatment of ADHD: A model for clinical practice. In V. J. Monastra (Ed.), *Unlocking the potential of patients with ADHD: A model for clinical practice* (pp. 147–159). Washington, DC: American Psychological Association.

Morgan, A. B., & Lilienfeld, S. O. (2000). A meta-analytic review of the relationship between antisocial behavior and neuropsychological measures of executive function. *Clinical Psychology Review, 20*, 113–136.

Müller, J. L., Sommer, M., Wagner, V., Lange, K., Taschler, H., Roder, C. H., Schuierer, G., Klein, H. E., & Hajak, G. (2003). Abnormalities in emotion processing within cortical and subcortical regions in criminal psychopaths: Evidence from a functional magnetic resonance imaging study using pictures with emotional content. *Psychiatry Research Neuroimaging, 54*, 152–162.

Muñoz, L. C., Frick, P. J., Kimonis, E. R., & Aucoin, K. J. (2008). Types of aggression, responsiveness to provocation, and callous-unemotional traits in detained adolescents. *Journal of Abnormal Child Psychology, 36*(1), 15–28.

Murray-Close, D., Han, G., Cicchetti, D., Crick, N. R., & Rogosch, F. A. (2008). Neuroendocrine regulation and physical and relational aggression: The moderating roles of child maltreatment and gender. *Developmental Psychology, 44*, 1160–1176.

Nakagawasai O., Mamadera, F., Sato, S., Taniguchi, R., Hiraga, H., Arai, Y., Murakami, H., Mawatari, K., Niijima, F., Tan-No, K., & Tadano, T. (2006). Alterations in cognitive function in prepubertal mice with protein malnutrition: Relationship to changes in choline acetyltransferase. *Behavioural Brain Research, 167*, 111–117.

Nestor, P. G. (1992). Neuropsychological and clinical correlates of murder and other forms of extreme violence in a forensic psychiatric population. *Journal of Nervous and Mental Disease, 180*, 418–423.

Neugebauer, R., Hoek, H. W., & Susser, E. (1999). Prenatal exposure to wartime famine and development of antisocial personality disorder in early adulthood. *Journal of the American Medical Association, 4*, 479–481.

Nigg, J. T., Glass, J. M., Wong, M. M., Poon, E., Jester, J., Fitzgerald, H. E., Puttler, L. I., Adams, K. M., & Zucker, R. A. (2004). Neuropsychological executive functioning in children at elevated risk for alcoholism: Findings in early adolescence. *Journal of Abnormal Psychology, 113*, 302–314.

Olds, D., Henderson, C. R. J., Cole, R., Eckenrode, J., Kitzman, H., Luckey, D., Pettitt, L., Sidora, K., Morris, P., & Powers, J. (1998). Long-term effects of nurse home visitation on children's criminal and antisocial behavior: 15-year follow-up of a randomized controlled trial. *Journal of the American Medical Association, 280*, 1238–1244.

Oosterlaan, J., Geurts, H. M., & Sergeant, J. A. (2005). Low basal salivary cortisol is associated with teacher-reported symptoms of conduct disorder. *Psychiatry Research, 134*, 1–10.

Pajer, K., Gardner, W., Rubin, R. T., Perel, J., & Neal, S. (2001). Decreased cortisol levels in adolescent girls with conduct disorder. *Archives of General Psychiatry, 58*, 297–302.

Pajer, K., Tabbah, R., Gardner, W., Rubin, R. T., Czambel, R. K., & Wang, Y. (2006). Adrenal androgen and gonadal hor-mone levels in adolescent girls with conduct disorder. *Psychoneuroendocrinology, 31*, 1245–1256.

Patrick, C. J. (1994). Emotion and psychopathy: Startling new insights. *Psychophysiology, 31*, 319–330.

Patrick, C. J. (2008). Psychophysiological correlates of aggression and violence: An integrative review. *Philosophical Transactions of the Royal Society B: Biological Sciences, 363*(1503), 2543–2555.

Patrick, C. J., Bradley, M. M., & Lang, P. J. (1993). Emotion in the criminal psychopath: Startle reflex modulation. *Journal of Abnormal Psychology, 102*, 82–92.

Patterson, G. R. (1982). *A social learning approach: Vol. 3. Coercive family processes.* Eugene, Oregon: Castalia.

Pincus, H. J., & Lewis, O. D. (1991). Episodic violence. *Seminars in Neurology, 11*, 146–154.

Polich, J., & Hoffman, L. D. (1998). P300 and handedness: On the possible contribution of corpus callosal size to ERPs. *Psychophysiology, 35*, 497–507.

Polich, J., Pollock, V. E., & Bloom, F. E. (1994). Meta-analysis of P300 amplitude from males at risk for alcoholism. *Psychological Bulletin, 115*, 55–73.

Popma, A., & Raine, A. (2006). Will future forensic assessment be neurobiologic? *Child and Adolescent Psychiatric Clinics of North America, 15*, 429–444.

Quinsey, V. L., Harris, G. T., Rice, M. E., & Cormier, C. A. (1999). *Violent offenders: Appraising and managing risk.* Washington, DC: American Psychological Association.

Racer, K. H., Gilbert, T. T., Luu, P., Felver-Gant, J., Abdullaev, Y., & Dishion, T. J. (2011). Attention network performance and psychopathic symptoms in early adolescence: An ERP study. *Journal of Abnormal Child Psychology, 39*(7), 1001–1012.

Raine, A. (1993). *The psychopathology of crime: Criminal behavior as a clinical disorder.* San Diego, CA: Academic Press.

Raine, A. (1996). Autonomic nervous system factors underlying disinhibited, antisocial, and violent behavior. *Annals of the New York Academy of Science, 794*, 46–59.

Raine, A. (1997). Classical conditioning, arousal, and crime: A biosocial perspective. In H. Nyborg (Ed.), *The scientific study of human nature: Tribute to Hans J. Eysenck at eighty* (pp. 122–141). New York: Elsevier Science.

Raine, A. (2002a). Annotation: The role of prefrontal deficits, low autonomic arousal, and early health factors in the development of antisocial and aggressive behavior in children. *Journal of Child Psychology and Psychiatry, 43*, 417–434.

Raine, A. (2002b). Biosocial studies of antisocial and violent behavior in children and adults: A review. *Journal of Abnormal Child Psychology, 30*, 311–326.

Raine, A., Buchsbaum, M., Stanley, J., Lottenberg, S., Abel, L., & Stoddard, J. (1994). Selective reductions in prefrontal-glucose metabo-lism in murderers. *Biological Psychiatry, 36*, 365–373.

Raine, A., Laufer, W. S., Yang, Y., Narr, K. L., Thompson, P., & Toga, A. W. (2012). Increased executive functioning, attention, and cortical thickness in white-collar criminals. *Human Brain Mapping, 33*, 2932–2940.

Raine, A., Lencz, T., Bihrle, S., LaCasse, L., & Colletti, P. (2000). Reduced prefrontal gray matter volume and reduced autonomic activity in antisocial personality disorder. *Archives of General Psychiatry, 57*, 119–127.

Raine, A., Lencz, T., Taylor, K., Hellige, J. B., Bihrle, S., LaCasse, L., Lee, M., Ishikawa, S., & Colletti, P. (2003a). Corpus callosum abnormalities in psychopathic antisocial individuals. *Archives of General Psychiatry, 60*, 1134–1142.

Raine, A., Liu, J. H., Venables, P. H., & Mednick, S. A. (2006). Preventing crime and schizophrenia using early environmental enrichment. In A. Raine (Ed.), *Crime and schizophrenia: Causes and cures* (pp. 249–266). New York: Nova Science Publishers.

Raine, A., Mellingen, K., Liu, J. H., Venables, P. H., & Mednick, S. A. (2003b). Effects of environmental enrichment at 3–5 years on schizotypal personality and antisocial behavior at ages 17 and 23 years. *American Journal of Psychiatry, 160*, 1627–1635.

Raine, A., Moffitt, T. E., Caspi, A., Loeber, R., Stouthamer-Loeber, M., & Lynam, D. (2005). Neurocognitive impairments in boys on the life-course persistent antisocial path. *Journal of Abnormal Psychology, 114*, 38–49.

Raine, A., Reynolds, C., Venables, P. H., & Mednick, S. A. (1997). Biosocial bases of aggressive behavior in childhood. In A. Raine, P. A. Brennan, D. P. Farrington, & S. A. Mednick (Eds.), *Biosocial bases of violence* (pp. 107–126). New York: Plenum.

Raine, A., Reynolds, C., Venables, P. H., Mednick, S. A., & Farrington, D. P. (1998). Fearlessness, stimulation-seeking, and large body size at age 3 years as early predispositions to childhood aggression at age 11 years. *Archives of General Psychiatry, 55*, 745–751.

Raine, A., & Venables, P. H. (1984). Electrodermal responding, antisocial behavior, and schizoid tendencies in adolescence. *Psychophysiology, 21*, 424–433.

Raine, A., Venables, P. H., & Williams, M. (1990a). Autonomic orienting responses in 15-year-old male subjects and criminal behavior at age 24. *American Journal of Psychiatry, 147*, 933–937.

Raine, A., Venables, P. H., & Williams, M. (1990b). Relationship between central and autonomic measures of arousal at age 15 and criminality at age 24 years. *Archives of General Psychiatry, 47*, 1003–1007.

Raine, A., Venables, P. H., & Williams, M. (1990c). Relationships between N1, P300, and contingent negative variation recorded at age 15 and criminal behavior at age 24. *Psychophysiology, 27*, 567–574.

Raine, A., Venables, P. H., & Williams, M. (1995). High autonomic arousal and electrodermal orienting at age 15 years as protective factors against criminal behavior at age 29 years. *American Journal of Psychiatry, 152*, 1595–1600.

Raine, A., Venables, P. H., & Williams, M. (1996). Better autonomic conditioning and faster electrodermal half-recovery time at age 15 years as possible protective factors against crime at age 29 years. *Developmental Psychology, 32,* 624–630.

Raine, A., & Yang, Y. (2006). Neural foundations to moral reasoning and antisocial behavior. *Social, Cognitive, and Affective Neuroscience, 1,* 203–213.

Raine, A., Yaralian, P. S., Reynolds, C., Venables, P. H., & Mednick, S. A. (2002). Spatial but not verbal cognitive deficits at age 3 in persistently antisocial individuals. *Development and Psychopathology, 14,* 25–44.

Rasmussen, K., Almvik, R., & Levander, S. (2001). Performance and strategy indices of neuropsychological tests: Relations with personality, criminality and violence. *Journal of Forensic Neuropsychology, 2*(2), 29–43.

Rosen, G. M., Deinard, A. S., Schwartz, S., Smith, C., Stephenson, B., & Grabenstein, B. (1985). Iron deficiency among-incarcerated juvenile delinquents. *Journal of Adolescent Health Care, 6,* 419–423.

Salekin, R. T. (2006). Psychopathy in children and adults: Key issues in conceptualization and assessment. In C. J. Patrick (Ed.), *Handbook of psychopathy* (pp. 389–414). New York: Guilford Press.

Salekin, R. T., Neumann, C. S., Leistico, A. R., & Zalot, A. A. (2004). Psychopathy in youth and intelligence: An investigation of Cleckley's hypothesis. *Journal of Clinical Child and Adolescent Psychology, 33,* 731–742.

Santesso, D. L., Reker, D. L., Schmidt, L. A., & Segalowitz, S. J. (2006). Frontal electroencephalogram activation asymmetry, emotional intelligence, and externalizing behaviors in 10-year-old children. *Child Psychiatry and Human Development, 36*(3), 311–328.

Sarapata, M., Hermann, D., Johnson, T., & Aycock, R. (2008). The role of head injury in cognitive functioning, emotional adjustment and criminal behavior. *Brain Injury, 12,* 821–842.

Saver, J. L., & Damasio, A. R. (1991). Preserved access and processing of social knowledge in a patient with acquired sociopathy due to ventromedial frontal damage. *Neuropsychologia, 29,* 1241–1249.

Scarpa, A., Romero, N., Fikretoglu, D., Bowser, F. M., & Wilson, J. W. (1999). *Community violence exposure and aggression: Biosocial interactions.* Paper presented at the meeting of the American Society of Criminology, Toronto, Canada.

Schiffer, B., & Vonlaufen, C. (2011). Executive dysfunctions in pedophilic and nonpedophilic child molesters. *Journal of Sexual Medicine, 8,* 1975–1984.

Schneider, F., Habel, U., Kessler, C., Posse, S., Grodd, W., & Müller-Gartner, H. (2000). functional imaging of conditioned aversive emotional responses in antisocial personality disorder. *Neuropsychobiology, 42,* 192–201.

Schoenthaler, S. J., Amos, S. P., Doraz, W. E., Kelly M. A., Muedeking G. D., & Wakefield J. A. (1997). The effect of randomised vitamin-mineral supplementation on violent and non-violent antisocial behavior among incarcerated juveniles. *Journal of Nutritional and Environmental Medicine, 7,* 343–352.

Schoenthaler, S. J., & Bier, I. D. (2000). The effect of vitamin-mineral supplementation on juvenile delinquency among American school-children: A randomized, doubleblind-placebo-controlled trial. *The Journal of Alternative and Complementary Medicine, 6,* 19–29.

Schug, R. A., Raine, A., & Wilcox, R. R. (2007). Psychophysio-logical and behavioural characteristics of individuals comorbid for antisocial personality disorder and schizophrenia-spectrum personality disorder. *British Journal of Psychiatry, 190,* 408–414.

Séguin, J. R., Nagin, D., Assad, J. M., & Tremblay, R. (2004). Cognitive-neuropsychological function in chronic physical aggression and hyperactivity. *Journal of Abnormal Psychology, 113,* 603–613.

Shoal, G. D., Giancola, P. R., & Kilrillova, G. P. (2003). Salivary cortisol, personality, and aggressive behavior in adolescent boys: A 5-year longitudinal study. *Child and Adolescent Psychiatry and Mental Health, 42,* 1101–1107.

Sijtsema, J. J., Veenstra, R., Lindenberg, S., van Roon, A. M., Verhulst, F. C., Ormel, J., & Riese, H. (2013). Heart rate and antisocial behavior: Mediation and moderation by affiliation with bullies. The TRAILS study. *Journal of Adolescent Health, 52,* 102–107.

Sip, K. E., Roepstorff, A., McGregor, W., & Frith, C. D. (2007). Detecting deception: The scope and limits. *Trends in Cognitive Sciences, 12,* 48–53.

Smith, C. L., & Bell, M. A. (2010). Stability in infant frontal asymmetry as a predictor of toddlerhood internalizing and externalizing behaviors. *Developmental Psychobiology, 52*(2), 158–167.

Soderstrom, H., Tullberg, M., Wikkelsoe, C., Ekholm, S., & Forsman, A. (2000). Reduced regional cerebral blood flow in non-psychotic violent offenders. *Psychiatry Research: Neuroimaging, 98,* 29–41.

Stanford, M. S., Conklin, S. M., Helfritz, L. E., & Kockler, T. R. (2007a). P3 amplitude reduction and executive function deficits in men convicted of spousal/partner abuse. *Personality and Individual Differences, 43,* 365–375.

Stanford, M. S., Houston, R. J., & Barratt, E. S. (2007b). Psychophysiological correlates of psychopathic disorders. In A. R. Felthous & H. Saβ (Eds.), *International handbook of psychopathic disorders and the law: Vol. 1* (pp. 83–101). Chichester: John Wiley & Sons.

Sterzer, P., Stadler, C., Krebs, A., Kleinschmidt, A., & Poustka, F. (2005). Abnormal neural responses to emotional visual stimuli in adolescents with conduct disorder. *Biological Psychiatry, 57,* 7–15.

Stevens, L., Zhang, W., Peck, L., Kuczek, T., Grevstad, N., Mahon, A., Zentall, S. S., Aronld, L. E., & Burgess, J. R. (2003). EFA supplementation in children with inattention, hyperactivity, and other disruptive behaviors. *Lipids, 38,* 1007–1021.

Stevens, M. C., & Haney-Caron, E. (2012). Comparison of brain volume abnormalities between ADHD and conduct disorder in adolescence. *Journal of Psychiatry & Neuroscience, 37,* 389–398.

Syngelaki, E. M., Fairchild, G., Moore, S. C., Savage, J. C., & Goozen, S. H. (2013). Fearlessness in juvenile offenders is associated with offending rate. *Developmental Science, 16*(1), 84–90.

Tang, Y., Liu, W., Chen, J., Liao, J., Hu, D., & Wang, W. (2013). Altered spontaneous activity in antisocial personality disorder revealed by regional homogeneity. *Neuroreport, 24*, 590–595.

Teichner, G., & Golden, C. J. (2000). The relationship of neuropsychological impairment to conduct disorder in adolescence: A conceptual review. *Aggression and Violent Behavior, 5*, 509–528.

Teichner, G., Golden, C. J., Van Hasselt, V. B., & Peterson, A. (2001). Assessment of cognitive functioning in men who batter. *International Journal of Neuroscience, 111*, 241–253.

Trovillo, P. V. (1939). A history in lie detection. *Journal of Criminal Law and Criminology, 29*, 848–881.

Van de Wiel, N. M. H., Van Goozen, S. M. H., Matthys, W., Snoek, H., & Van Engeland, H. (2004). Cortisol and treatment effect in children with disruptive behavior disorders: A preliminary study. *Journal of the American Academy of Child and Adolescent Psychiatry, 43*, 1011–1018.

van Goozen, S. H. M., Matthys, W., Cohen-Hettenis, P. T., Wied, C. G., Wiegant, V. M., & van Engeland, H. (1998). Salivary cortisol and cardiovascular activity during stress in oppositional defiant disorder boys and normal controls. *Biological Psychiatry, 43*, 531–539.

van Honk, J., & Schutter, D. J. L. G. (2007). Testosterone reduces conscious detection of signals serving social correction: Implications for antisocial behavior. *Psychological Science, 18*, 663–667.

Vermeiren, R., De Clippele, A., Schwab-Stone, M., Ruchkin, V., & Deboutte, D. (2002). Neuropsychological characteristics of three subgroups of Flemish delinquent adolescents. *Neuropsychology, 16*, 49–55.

Viding, E., Sebastian, C. L., Dadds, M. R., Lockwood, P. L., Cecil, C. A., De Brito, S. A., & McCrory, E. J. (2012). Amygdala response to preattentive masked fear in children with conduct problems: The role of callous-unemotional traits. *American Journal of Psychiatry, 169*(10), 1109–1116.

Virkkunen, M. E. (1985). Urinary free cortisol secretion in habitually violent offenders. *Acta Psychiatrica Scandinavica, 72*, 40–44.

Virkkunen, M. E., DeJong, J., Bartko, J., Goodwin, F. K., & Linnoila, M. (1989). Relationship of psychological variables to recidivism in violent offenders and impulsive fire setters. *Archives of General Psychiatry, 46*, 600–603.

Virkkunen, M. E., Horrobin, D. F., Jenkins, D. K., & Manku, M. S. (1987). Plasma phospholipid essential fatty acids and prostaglandins in alcoholic, habitually violent, and impulsive offenders. *Biological Psychiatry, 22*, 1087–1096.

Volkow, N. D., & Tancredi, L. R. (1987). Neural substrates of violent behavior. A preliminary study with positron emission tomography. *British Journal of Psychiatry, 151*, 668–673.

Volkow, N. D., Tancredi, L. R., Grant, C., Gillespie, H., Valentine, A., Mullani, N., Wang, G. J., & Hollister, L. (1995). Brain glucose metabolism in violent psychiatric patients: A preliminary study. *Psychiatry Research, 61*, 243–253.

Vries-Bouw, D., Popma, A., Vermeiren, R., Doreleijers, T. A., Van De Ven, P. M., & Jansen, L. (2011). The predictive value of low heart rate and heart rate variability during stress for reoffending in delinquent male adolescents. *Psychophysiology, 48*(11), 1597–1604.

Waldman, I. D., & Rhee, S. H. (2006). Genetic and environmental influences on psychopathy and antisocial behavior. In C. J. Patrick (Ed.), *Handbook of psychopathy* (pp. 205–228). New York: Guilford Press.

Walsh, A., & Ellis, L. (2007). *Criminology: An interdisciplinary approach.* Thousand Oaks, CA: Sage Publications.

Walsh, W. J., Isaacson, H. R., Rehman, F., & Hall, A. (1997). Elevated blood copper/zinc ratios in assaultive young males. *Physiology and Behavior, 62*, 327–329.

Wang, P., Baker, L. A., Gao, Y., Raine, A., & Lozano, D. I. (2012). Psychopathic traits and physiological responses to aversive stimuli in children aged 9–11 years. *Journal of Abnormal Child Psychology, 40*(5), 759–769.

Wang, P., Gao, Y., Isen, J., Raine, A., Baker, L. A., & Lozano, D. I. (submitted). Genetic covariance between psychopathic traits and anticipatory skin conductance responses to threat: Evidence for a potential endophenotype.

Werbach, M. R. (1992). Nutritional influences on aggressive behavior. *Journal of Orthomolecular Medicine, 7*, 45–51.

White, J. L., Moffitt, T. E., Caspi, A., Jeglum, D., Needles, D. J., & Stouthamer-Loeber, M. (1994). Measuring impulsivity and examining its relationship to delinquency. *Journal of Abnormal Psychology, 103*, 192–205.

de Wied, M., van Boxtel, A., Matthys, W., & Meeus, W. (2012). Verbal, facial and autonomic responses to empathy-eliciting film clips by disruptive male adolescents with high versus low callous-unemotional traits. *Journal of Abnormal Child Psychology, 40*, 211–223.

Wilson, J. Q., & Herrnstein, R. (1985). *Crime and human nature.* New York: Simon & Schuster.

Yang, Y., Glenn, A. L., & Raine, A. (2008). Brain abnormalities in antisocial individuals: Implications for the law. *Behavioral Sciences and the Law, 26*, 65–83.

Yang, Y., & Raine, A. (2009). Prefrontal structural and functional brain imaging findings in antisocial, violent, and psychopathic individuals: A meta-analysis. *Psychiatry Research, 174*, 81–88.

Yang, Y., Raine, A., Colletti, P., Toga, A. W., & Narr, K. L. (2009). Abnormal temporal and prefrontal cortical gray matter thinning in psychopaths. *Molecular Psychiatry 14*, 561–562, 555.

Yang, Y., Raine, A., Colletti, P., Toga, A. W., & Narr, K. L. (2010). Morphological alterations in the prefrontal cortex and the amygdala in unsuccessful psychopaths. *Journal of Abnormal Psychology, 119*, 546–554.

Yang, Y., Raine, A., Joshi, A. A., Joshi, S., Chang, Y. T., Schug, R. A., Wheland, D., Leahy, R., & Narr, K. L. (2012). Frontal information flow and connectivity in psychopathy. *The British Journal of Psychiatry : The Journal of Mental Science, 201*, 408–409.

Yang, Y., Raine, A., Lencz, T., Bihrle, S., Lacasse, L., & Colletti, P. (2005). Prefrontal white matter in pathological liars. *British Journal of Psychiatry, 187*, 320–325.

Yang, Y., Raine, A., Narr, K. L., Lencz, T., LaCasse, L., Colletti, P., & Toga, A. W. (2007). Localisation of increased prefrontal white-matter in pathological liars. *British Journal of Psychiatry, 190*, 174–175.

Yoon, H. H., Malone, S. M., Burwell, S. J., Bernat, E. M., & Iacono, W. G. (2013). Association between P3 event-related potential amplitude and externalizing disorders: A time-domain and time-frequency investigation of 29-year-old adults. *Psychophysiology, 50*(7), 595–609.

Young, S. N., & Leyton, M. (2002). The role of serotonin in human mood and social interaction – Insight from altered tryptophan levels. *Pharmacology, Biochemistry and Behavior, 71*, 857–865.

9 The Developmental Evidence Base: Prevention

DAVID P. FARRINGTON

This chapter aims to review effective prevention programmes that tackle key risk factors for delinquency. It focuses especially on programmes that have been evaluated in randomized experiments that have included a cost–benefit analysis. The chapter reviews family-based programmes, including home visiting by nurses, parent training, functional family therapy, treatment foster care and multi-systematic therapy. It reviews school-based programmes, including preschool intellectual enrichment, teacher training, after-school programmes and anti-bullying projects. It reviews programmes targeted on peer influence, including peer tutoring and mentoring programmes. It reviews cognitive-behavioural skills training programmes targeted on children and adults, and the 'Communities That Care' programme. Recent UK developments are discussed, including the government's action plan for social exclusion and Sure Start. It is concluded that a national agency for early prevention is needed.

INTRODUCTION

The main aim of this chapter is to summarize briefly some of the most effective programmes for preventing delinquency and antisocial behaviour whose effectiveness has been demonstrated in high-quality evaluation research. My focus is especially on programmes evaluated in randomized experiments with reasonably large samples, since the effect of any intervention on delinquency can be demonstrated most convincingly in such experiments (Farrington & Welsh, 2005, 2006). I also focus on randomized experiments with long-term follow-ups, which make it possible to determine if effects persist or wear off (Farrington & Welsh, 2013).

The major methods of reducing crime can be classified as developmental, community, situational and criminal justice prevention (Tonry & Farrington, 1995). Criminal justice prevention refers to traditional deterrent, incapacitative and rehabilitative strategies operated by law enforcement and criminal justice system agencies. Community prevention refers to interventions designed to change the social conditions and institutions (e.g., families, peers, social norms, clubs, organizations) that influence offending in residential communities (Hope, 1995). These interventions target community risk factors and social conditions such as cohesiveness or disorganization. Situational prevention refers to interventions designed to prevent the occurrence of crimes by reducing opportunities and increasing the risk and difficulty of offending (Clarke, 1995). Developmental prevention refers to interventions designed to prevent the development of criminal potential in individuals, especially those targeting risk and protective factors discovered in studies of human development (Tremblay & Craig, 1995). My focus in this chapter is on developmental or risk-focused prevention.

Risk-focused prevention

The basic idea of developmental or risk-focused prevention is very simple: Identify the key risk factors for offending and implement prevention techniques designed to counteract them (Farrington, 2000). There is often a related attempt to identify key protective factors against offending and to implement prevention techniques designed to enhance or strengthen them (Catalano, Hawkins, Berglund, Pollard, & Arthur, 2002). Longitudinal surveys are used to advance knowledge about risk and protective factors, and experimental and quasi-experimental methods are used to evaluate the impact of prevention and intervention programmes.

Risk-focused prevention was imported into criminology from medicine and public health by pioneers such as David Hawkins and Richard Catalano (1992). This

Forensic Psychology, Second Edition. Edited by David A. Crighton and Graham J. Towl.
© 2015 John Wiley & Sons, Ltd. Published 2015 by British Psychological Society and John Wiley & Sons, Ltd.

approach has been used successfully for many years to tackle illnesses such as cancer and heart disease. For example, the identified risk factors for heart disease include smoking, a fatty diet and lack of exercise. These can be tackled by encouraging people to stop smoking, to have a more healthy low-fat diet and to take more exercise.

Risk-focused prevention links explanation and prevention, links fundamental and applied research, and links scholars, policy-makers and practitioners. The book *Saving Children from a Life of Crime: Early Risk Factors and Effective Interventions* (Farrington & Welsh, 2007) contains a detailed exposition of this approach. Importantly, risk-focused prevention is easy to understand and to communicate, and it is readily accepted by policy-makers, practitioners and the general public. Both risk factors and interventions are based on empirical research rather than on theories. This approach avoids difficult theoretical questions about which risk factors have causal effects.

What is a risk factor?

By definition, a risk factor predicts a high probability of later offending (Kazdin, Kraemer, Kessler, Kupfer, & Offord, 1997). For example, children who experience poor parental supervision have an increased risk of committing criminal acts later on. In the Cambridge Study in Delinquent Development, which is a prospective longitudinal survey of 400 London males from age 8 to age 48, 61% of those experiencing poor parental supervision at age 8 were convicted up to age 50, compared with 36% of the remainder, a significant difference (Farrington *et al.*, 2006). Since risk factors are defined by their ability to predict later offending, it follows that longitudinal studies are needed to establish them.

The most important risk factors for delinquency are well known (Farrington, 2007; Murray & Farrington, 2010). They include individual factors such as high impulsiveness and low intelligence; family factors such as poor parental supervision and harsh or erratic parental discipline; peer factors such as hanging around with delinquent friends; school factors such as attending a high-delinquency-rate school; socio-economic factors such as low income and poor housing; and neighbourhood or community factors such as living in a high-crime neighbourhood. My focus is on risk factors that can be changed by interventions. There is also a focus on protective or promotive factors that predict a low probability of offending, but less is known about them (Farrington, Loeber, & Ttofi, 2012; Lösel & Farrington, 2012).

Risk factors tend to be similar for many different outcomes, including delinquency, violence, drug use, school failure and unemployment. This is good news, because a programme that is successful in reducing one of these outcomes is likely to be successful in reducing the others as well. In this chapter, I will review family programmes, then school programmes, then peer-based programmes, and finally, skills training programmes.

Cost–benefit analysis

I will describe some of the most important and best-evaluated programmes, with special reference to programmes that have carried out a cost–benefit analysis. The conclusion from the Perry project (discussed later) that, for every $1 spent on the programme, $7 were saved in the long term (Schweinhart, Barnes, & Weikart, 1993), proved particularly convincing to policy-makers. The monetary costs of crime are enormous. For example, Sam Brand and Richard Price (2000) estimated that they totalled £60 billion in England and Wales in 1999. There are tangible costs to victims, such as replacing stolen goods and repairing damage, and intangible costs that are harder to quantify, such as pain, suffering and a reduced quality of life. There are costs to the government or taxpayer for police, courts, prisons, crime prevention activities and so on. There are also costs to offenders – for example, those associated with being in prison or losing a job.

Mark Cohen (1998) estimated that a high-risk youth in the United States cost society about $2 million at 1997 prices. Mark Cohen and Alex Piquero (2009) updated this analysis using new methods, and concluded that the value of saving a 14-year-old high-risk juvenile from a life of crime ranged from $2.6 million to $5.3 million at 2007 prices. In the Cambridge Study in Delinquent Development, the total cost of offending by the 400 males from age 10 to age 50 was $50 million at 2010 prices, or £123,000 per male, when self-reported as well as official offending was considered (Raffan Gowar & Farrington, 2013).

To the extent that crime prevention programmes are successful in reducing crime, they will have benefits. These benefits can be quantified in monetary terms according to the reduction in the monetary costs of crime. Other benefits may accrue from reducing the costs of associated social problems such as unemployment, divorce, educational failure, drug addiction, welfare dependency and so on. The fact that offending is part of a larger syndrome of antisocial behaviour (West & Farrington, 1977) is good news, because the benefits of a crime prevention programme can be many and varied. The monetary benefits of a programme can be compared with its monetary costs to determine the cost–benefit ratio. Surprisingly, few cost–benefit analyses of crime prevention programmes have ever been carried out (Roman, Dunworth, & Marsh, 2010; Welsh, Farrington, & Sherman, 2001).

FAMILY-BASED PREVENTION

Family programmes are usually targeted on risk factors such as poor parental supervision and inconsistent discipline. The behavioural parent management training developed by Gerald Patterson (1982) in Oregon is one of the most influential approaches. His careful observations of parent–child interaction showed that parents of antisocial children were deficient in their methods of child-rearing. These parents failed to tell their children how they were expected to behave, failed to monitor their behaviour to ensure that it was desirable, and failed to enforce rules promptly and unambiguously with appropriate rewards and penalties. The parents of antisocial children used more punishment (such as scolding, shouting or threatening), but failed to use it consistently or make it contingent on the child's behaviour.

Patterson's method involved linking antecedents, behaviours and consequences. He attempted to train parents in effective child-rearing methods, namely noticing what a child is doing, monitoring the child's behaviour over long periods, clearly stating house rules, making rewards and punishments consistent and contingent on the child's behaviour, and negotiating disagreements so that conflicts and crises did not escalate.

His treatment was shown to be effective in reducing child stealing and antisocial behaviour over short periods in small-scale studies (Dishion, Patterson, & Kavanagh, 1992; Patterson, Reid, & Dishion, 1992). However, the treatment worked best with children aged 3–10 and less well with adolescents. Also, there were problems of achieving cooperation from the families experiencing the worst problems. In particular, single mothers on welfare were experiencing so many different stresses that they found it difficult to use consistent and contingent child-rearing methods. (For a recent review of parent training programmes, see Piquero, Farrington, Welsh, Tremblay, & Jennings, 2009.)

I will now review the most important types of family-based programmes that have been evaluated. These are home visiting programmes (and especially the work of David Olds), parent training programmes (especially those used by Carolyn Webster-Stratton, Stephen Scott, Frances Gardner and Matthew Sanders), home or community programmes with older children (especially those implemented by James Alexander and Patricia Chamberlain) and multi-systemic therapy or MST (used by Scott Henggeler and Alison Cunningham).

Home visiting programmes

In the most famous intensive home visiting programme, David Olds and his colleagues (1986) in Elmira (New York State) randomly allocated 400 mothers either to receive home visits from nurses during pregnancy, or to receive visits both during pregnancy and during the first 2 years of life, or to a control group who received no visits. Each visit lasted about one and a quarter hours, and the mothers were visited on average every two weeks. The home visitors gave advice about prenatal and postnatal care of the child, about infant development, and about the importance of proper nutrition and avoiding smoking and drinking during pregnancy. Hence, this was a general parent education programme.

The results of this experiment showed that the postnatal home visits caused a decrease in recorded child physical abuse and neglect during the first 2 years of life, especially by poor unmarried teenage mothers; 4% of visited versus 19% of non-visited mothers of this type were guilty of child abuse or neglect. This last result is important because children who are physically abused or neglected tend to become violent offenders later in life (Widom, 1989). In a 15-year follow-up, the main focus was on lower-class unmarried mothers. Among these mothers, those who received prenatal and postnatal home visits had fewer arrests than those who received prenatal visits or no visits (Olds et al., 1997). Also, children of these mothers who received prenatal and/or postnatal home visits had less than half as many arrests as children of mothers who received no visits (Olds et al., 1998). Most recently, John Eckenrode and his colleagues (2010) followed up this experiment to age 19, and found that 25% of the treated children were arrested, compared with 37% of the controls; the desirable effects were much greater for girls. Steve Aos and his colleagues at the Washington State Institute for Public Policy (WSIPP) calculated that $2.4 are saved for every $1 expended on this programme (Lee et al., 2012). (For reviews of home visiting programmes, see Bilukha et al., 2005; Olds, Sadler, & Kitzman, 2007.)

Parent management training

One of the most famous parent training programmes was developed by Carolyn Webster-Stratton (1998) in Seattle. She evaluated its success by randomly allocating 426 children aged 4 (most with single mothers on welfare) either to an experimental group which received parent training or to a control group which did not. The experimental mothers met in groups every week for 8 or 9 weeks, watched videotapes demonstrating parenting skills, and then took part in focused group discussions. The topics included how to play with your child, helping your child learn, using praise and encouragement to bring out the best in your child, effective setting of limits, handling misbehaviour, how to teach your child to solve problems, and how to give and get support. Observations in the home showed that the experimental children behaved better than the control children.

Carolyn Webster-Stratton and Mary Hammond (1997) also evaluated the effectiveness of parent training and child skills training with about 100 Seattle children (average age 5) referred to a clinic because of conduct problems. The children and their parents were randomly allocated to receive either (a) parent training, (b) child skills training, (c) both parent and child training, or (d) to a control group. The skills training aimed to foster prosocial behaviour and interpersonal skills using video modelling, while the parent training involved weekly meetings between parents and therapists for 22–24 weeks. Parent reports and home observations showed that children in all three experimental conditions had fewer behaviour problems than control children, in both an immediate and a 1-year follow-up. There was little difference between the three experimental conditions, although the combined parent and child training condition produced the most significant improvements in child behaviour at the 1-year follow-up. It is generally true that combined parent and child interventions are more effective than either one alone.

Stephen Scott and his colleagues (2001) evaluated the Webster-Stratton parent training programme in London and Chichester. About 140 mainly poor, disadvantaged children aged 3-8 who were referred for antisocial behaviour were randomly assigned to receive parent training or to be in a waiting-list control group. The parent training programme, based on videotapes, covered praise and rewards, setting limits, and handling misbehaviour. Follow-up parent interviews and observations showed that the antisocial behaviour of the experimental children decreased significantly compared to that of the controls. Furthermore, after the intervention, experimental parents gave their children more praise to encourage desirable behaviour, and used more effective commands to obtain compliance. This programme was also found to be effective in a later experiment with over 100 children in London (Scott et al., 2010).

Frances Gardner and her colleagues (2006) evaluated the success of the Webster-Stratton programme in Oxfordshire. Over 70 children, aged 2–9, referred for conduct problems, were randomly assigned to receive parent training or to be in a waiting-list control group. Follow-up parent reports and observations again showed that the antisocial behaviour of the experimental children decreased compared with the controls. In a later experiment (Gardner, Hutchings, Bywater, & Whitaker, 2010), over 150 problematic children aged 3–5 from disadvantaged neighbourhoods were randomly assigned to receive parent training or to be in a waiting-list control group. The results showed that the treated children improved in parent-rated conduct problems, and that this was mediated by changes in parenting skills.

Matthew Sanders and his colleagues (2000) in Brisbane, Australia, developed the Triple-P Parenting programme. This programme can either be delivered to the whole community in primary prevention using the mass media or can be used in secondary prevention with high-risk or clinic samples. Sanders evaluated the success of Triple-P with over 300 high-risk children aged 3 by randomly allocating them either to receive Triple-P or to be in a control group. The Triple-P programme involves teaching parents 17 child management strategies, including talking with children, giving physical affection, praising, giving attention, setting a good example, setting rules, giving clear instructions, and using appropriate penalties for misbehaviour ('time-out', or sending the child to his or her room). The evaluation showed that the Triple-P programme was successful in reducing children's antisocial behaviour. The effectiveness of Triple-P was confirmed in a meta-analysis by Thomas and Zimmer-Gembeck (2007). According to WSIPP (Lee et al., 2012), $6.1 are saved for every $1 expended on Triple-P.

Other parenting interventions

Another parenting intervention, termed Functional Family Therapy, was developed by James Alexander in Utah (Alexander & Parsons, 1973). This aimed to modify patterns of family interaction by modelling, prompting and reinforcement, to encourage clear communication between family members of requests and solutions, and to minimize conflict. Essentially, all family members were trained to negotiate effectively, to set clear rules about privileges and responsibilities, and to use techniques of reciprocal reinforcement with each other. The programme was evaluated by randomly allocating 86 delinquents to experimental or control conditions. The results showed that this technique halved the recidivism rate of minor delinquents in comparison with other approaches (client-centred or psychodynamic therapy). Its effectiveness with more serious offenders was confirmed in a replication study using matched groups (Barton, Alexander, Waldron, Turner, & Warburton, 1985; see also Sexton & Alexander, 2000). According to WSIPP (Lee et al., 2012), $10.4 are saved for every $1 expended on FFT.

Patricia Chamberlain and John Reid (1998) in Oregon evaluated treatment foster care (TFC), which was used as an alternative to custody for delinquents. Custodial sentences for delinquents were thought to have undesirable effects especially because of the bad influence of delinquent peers. In treatment foster care, families in the community were recruited and trained to provide a placement for delinquent youths. The TFC youths were closely supervised at home, in the community, and in the school, and their contacts with delinquent peers were minimized. The foster parents provided a structured daily living environment, with clear rules and limits, consistent discipline for rule violations and one-to-one monitoring. The youths were encouraged to develop academic skills and desirable work habits.

In the evaluation, 79 chronic male delinquents were randomly assigned to treatment foster care or to regular group homes where they lived with other delinquents. A 1-year follow-up showed that the TFC boys had fewer criminal referrals and lower self-reported delinquency. Hence, this programme seemed to be an effective treatment for delinquency. Similarly encouraging results were obtained in an evaluation of TFC for delinquent girls (Leve, Chamberlain, & Reid, 2005). The effectiveness of TFC has been confirmed in systematic reviews (Hahn *et al.*, 2005; Macdonald & Turner, 2007). According to WSIPP (Lee *et al.*, 2012), $4.9 are saved for every $1 expended on TFC.

Multi-Systemic Therapy

Multi-Systemic Therapy (MST) is an important multiple-component family preservation programme that was developed by Scott Henggeler and his colleagues (1998) in South Carolina. The particular type of treatment is chosen according to the particular needs of the youth. Therefore, the nature of the treatment is different for each person. MST is delivered in the youth's home, school and community settings. The treatment typically includes family intervention to promote the parent's ability to monitor and discipline the adolescent, peer intervention to encourage the choice of prosocial friends, and school intervention to enhance competence and school achievement.

In an evaluation by Scott Henggeler and his colleagues (1993), 84 serious delinquents (with an average age of 15) were randomly assigned either to receive MST or the usual treatment (which mostly involved placing the juvenile outside home). The results showed that the MST group had fewer arrests and fewer self-reported crimes in a 1-year follow-up. In another evaluation in Missouri, Charles Borduin and his colleagues (1995) randomly assigned 176 juvenile offenders (with an average age of 14) either to MST or to individual therapy focusing on personal, family and academic issues. After 4 years, only 26% of the MST offenders had been rearrested, compared with 71% of the individual therapy group. Later follow-ups to age 29 (Schaeffer & Borduin, 2005) and age 37 (Sawyer & Borduin, 2011) confirmed the cumulative benefits of MST. Other evaluations by Henggeler and his colleagues (1997, 1999, 2002) have also produced impressive results. According to WSIPP (Lee *et al.*, 2012), $4.4 are saved for every $1 expended on MST.

Unfortunately, disappointing results were obtained in a large-scale independent evaluation of MST in Canada by Alan Leschied and Alison Cunningham (2002). Over 400 youths who were either offenders or at risk of offending were randomly assigned to receive either MST or the usual services (typically probation supervision). Six months after treatment, 28% of the MST group had been reconvicted, compared with 31% of the control group, a non-significant difference. Therefore, it is not totally clear how effective MST is when it is implemented independently, although has been successful in Norwegian and Dutch evaluations (Asscher, Dekovic, Manders, Van Der Laan, & Prins, 2013; Ogden & Hagen, 2006). Unfortunately, two meta-analyses of the effectiveness of MST reached contradictory conclusions. Nicola Curtis and her colleagues (2004) found that it was effective, but Julia Littell (2005) found that it was not. Nevertheless, MST is a promising intervention technique, and it is being used quite widely in the United Kingdom (Jefford & Squire, 2004).

Is family-based intervention effective?

Evaluations of the effectiveness of family-based intervention programmes have produced both encouraging and discouraging results. In order to assess effectiveness according to a large number of evaluations, Brandon Welsh and I reviewed 40 evaluations of family-based programmes each involving at least 50 persons in experimental and control groups combined (Farrington & Welsh, 2003). All of these had outcome measures of delinquency or antisocial child behaviour. Of the 19 studies with outcome measures of delinquency, 10 found significantly beneficial effects of the intervention and 9 found no significant effect. Happily, no study found a significantly harmful effect of family-based treatment.

Over all 19 studies, the average effect size (d, the standardized mean difference) was .32. This was significantly greater than zero. When we converted it into the percentage reconvicted, a d value of .32 corresponds to a decrease in the percentage reconvicted from 58% to 42%. Therefore, we concluded that, taking all 19 studies together, they showed that family-based intervention had substantial desirable effects.

SCHOOL-BASED PREVENTION

I now turn to school-based prevention programmes, most of which also had a family-based component. I will first of all review the Perry preschool programme, which is perhaps the most influential early prevention project, because it concluded that \$7 were saved for every \$1 expended (Schweinhart *et al.*, 1993). Then I will review some famous school-based programmes implemented in Seattle by David Hawkins, in Newcastle-upon-Tyne by Israel Kolvin, and in Baltimore by Sheppard Kellam. I will also review anti-bullying programmes by Dan Olweus in Norway and Peter Smith in England.

Preschool programmes

The most famous preschool intellectual enrichment programme is the Perry project carried out in Ypsilanti (Michigan) by Lawrence Schweinhart and David Weikart (1980). This was essentially a 'Head Start' programme targeted on disadvantaged African American children. A small sample of 123 children were allocated (approximately at random) to experimental and control groups. The experimental children attended a daily preschool programme, backed up by weekly home visits, usually lasting 2 years (covering ages 3–4). The aim of the 'plan–do–review' programme was to provide intellectual stimulation, to increase thinking and reasoning abilities and to increase later school achievement.

This programme had long-term benefits. John Berrueta-Clement and his colleagues (1984) showed that, at age 19, the experimental group was more likely to be employed, more likely to have graduated from high school, more likely to have received college or vocational training, and less likely to have been arrested. By age 27, the experimental group had accumulated only half as many arrests on average as the controls (Schweinhart *et al.*, 1993). Also, they had significantly higher earnings and were more likely to be home-owners. More of the experimental women were married, and fewer of their children were born to unmarried mothers.

The most recent follow-up of this programme at age 40 found that it continued to make an important difference in the lives of the participants (Schweinhart *et al.*, 2005). Compared to the control group, those who received the programme had significantly fewer life-time arrests for violent crimes (32% vs. 48%), property crimes (36% vs. 56%), and drug crimes (14% vs. 34%), and they were significantly less likely to be arrested five or more times (36% vs. 55%). Improvements were also recorded in many other important life-course outcomes. For example, significantly higher levels of schooling (77% vs. 60% graduating from high school), better records of employment (76% vs. 62%), and higher annual incomes were reported by the programme group compared to the controls.

Several economic analyses show that the financial benefits of this programme outweighed its costs. The Perry project's own calculation (Barnett, 1993) included crime and non-crime benefits, intangible costs to victims, and even included projected benefits beyond age 27. This generated the famous benefit-to-cost ratio of 7 to 1. Most of the benefits (65%) were derived from savings to crime victims. The most recent cost–benefit analysis at age 40 found that the programme produced \$16 in benefits per \$1 of cost (Schweinhart, 2013). However, according to WSIPP (Lee *et al.*, 2012), \$3 are saved for every \$1 expended on preschool programmes.

Like the Perry project, the Child Parent Center (CPC) in Chicago provided disadvantaged children with a high-quality, active-learning preschool supplemented by family support (Reynolds, Temple, Robertson, & Mann, 2001). However, unlike Perry, CPC continued to provide the children with the educational enrichment component into elementary school, up to age 9. Focusing on the effect of the preschool intervention, it was found that, compared to a control group, those who received the programme were less likely to be arrested for both non-violent and violent offences by the time they were 18. The CPC programme also produced other benefits for those in the experimental compared to the control group, such as a higher rate of high school completion, and had long-term effects (Reynolds, Temple, Ou, Arteaga, & White, 2011).

Desirable results were also obtained in evaluations of other preschool programmes (e.g., Campbell, Ramey, Pungello, Sparling, & Miller-Johnson, 2002). Also, a large-scale study by Eliana Garces and her colleagues (2002) found that children who attended Head Start programmes (at ages 3 to 5) were significantly less likely to report being arrested or referred to court for a crime by ages 18 to 30 compared to their siblings who did not attend these programmes.

School programmes

One of the most important school-based prevention experiments was carried out in Seattle by David Hawkins and his colleagues (1991). They implemented a multiple component programme combining parent training, teacher training and child skills training. About 500 first grade children (aged 6) in 21 classes in 8 schools were randomly assigned to be in experimental or control classes. The children in the experimental classes received special treatment at home and school which was designed to increase their attachment to their parents and their bonding to the school. Also, they were trained in interpersonal cognitive problem-solving. Their parents were trained to notice and reinforce socially desirable behaviour in a programme called 'Catch them being good'. Their teachers were trained in classroom management, for example, to provide clear instructions and expectations to children, to reward children for participation in desired behaviour, and to teach children prosocial (socially desirable) methods of solving problems.

This programme had long-term benefits. By the sixth grade (age 12), experimental boys were less likely to have initiated delinquency, while experimental girls were less likely to have initiated drug use (O'Donnell, Hawkins, Catalano, Abbott, & Day, 1995). In a later follow-up, David Hawkins and his colleagues (1999) found that, at age 18, the full intervention group (those who received the intervention from grades 1 to 6) admitted less violence, less alcohol abuse and fewer sexual partners than the late intervention group (grades 5–6 only) or the control group. However, up to age 27, the beneficial effects on sexual behaviour (e.g., in reducing sexually transmitted diseases) were still apparent, but the beneficial effects on offending had reduced considerably (Hawkins, Kosterman, Catalano, Hill, & Abbott, 2008). The beneficial effects on sexual behaviour continued up to age 30 (Hill *et al.*, 2014). According to WSIPP (Lee *et al.*, 2012), $1.9 are saved for every $1 expended on this programme.

Another important school-based prevention experiment was carried out by Israel Kolvin and his colleagues (1981) in Newcastle-Upon-Tyne. They randomly allocated 270 junior school children (aged 7–8) and 322 secondary school children (aged 11–12) to experimental or control groups. All children had been identified as showing some kind of social or psychiatric disturbance or learning problems (according to teacher and peer ratings). There were three types of experimental programmes: (a) behaviour modification – reinforcement with the seniors, 'nurture work' teaching healthy interactions with the juniors; (b) parent counselling – teacher consultations with both; and (c) group therapy with the seniors, play groups with the juniors.

The programmes were evaluated after 18 months and after 3 years using clinical ratings of conduct disturbance. Generally, the experimental and control groups were not significantly different for the juniors, although there was some tendency for the nurture work and play group conditions to be better behaved than the controls at the three-year follow-up. For the seniors, those who received group therapy showed significantly less conduct disturbance at both follow-ups, and there was some tendency for the other two programmes also to be effective at the three-year follow-up.

In Baltimore, Hanno Petras, Sheppard Kellam, and their colleagues (2008) evaluated the 'Good Behaviour Game' (GBG) which aimed to reduce aggressive and disruptive child conduct through contingent reinforcement of interdependent team behaviour. First grade classrooms and teachers were randomly assigned either to the GBG condition or to a control condition, and the GBG was played repeatedly over 2 years. In trajectory analyses, the researchers found that the GBG decreased aggressive/disruptive behaviour (according to teacher reports) up to grade 7 among the most aggressive boys, and also caused a decrease in antisocial personality disorder at age 19–21. However, effects on girls and on a second cohort of children were less marked (see also Kellam *et al.*, 2014). According to WSIPP (Lee *et al.*, 2012), $31.2 are saved for every $1 expended on the GBG.

There have been a number of comprehensive, evidence-based reviews of the effectiveness of school-based programmes (Gottfredson, Wilson, & Najaka, 2006; Wilson, Gottfredson, & Najaka, 2001; Wilson & Lipsey, 2007). Meta-analyses identified four types of school-based programmes that were effective in preventing delinquency: school and discipline management, classroom or instructional management, reorganization of grades or classes, and increasing self-control or social competency using cognitive-behavioural instruction methods. Reorganization of grades or classes had the largest average effect size ($d = .34$), corresponding to a significant 17% reduction in delinquency.

After-school programmes (e.g., recreation-based, drop-in clubs, dance groups and tutoring services) are based on the belief that providing prosocial opportunities for young people in the after-school hours can reduce their involvement in delinquent behaviour in the community. After-school programmes target a range of risk factors for delinquency, including association with delinquent peers. Brandon Welsh and Akemi Hoshi (2006) identified three high-quality after-school programmes with an evaluated impact on delinquency. Each had desirable effects on delinquency, and one programme also reported lower rates of drug use for participants compared to controls.

Anti-bullying programmes

School bullying, of course, is a risk factor for offending (Farrington, 1993; Ttofi, Farrington, Lösel, & Loeber, 2011; Ttofi, Farrington, & Lösel, 2012). Several school-based programmes have been effective in reducing bullying. The most famous of these was implemented by Dan Olweus (1994) in Norway. The general principles of the programme were: to create an environment characterized by adult warmth, interest in children and involvement with children; to use authoritative child-rearing, including warmth, firm guidance and close supervision, since authoritarian child-rearing is related to child bullying (Baldry & Farrington, 1998); to set firm limits on what is unacceptable bullying; to consistently apply non-physical sanctions for rule violations; to improve monitoring and surveillance of child behaviour, especially in the playground; and to decrease opportunities and rewards for bullying.

The Olweus programme aimed to increase awareness and knowledge of teachers, parents and children about bullying and to dispel myths about it. A 30-page booklet was distributed to all schools in Norway describing what was known about bullying and recommending what steps schools and teachers could take to reduce it. Also, a 25-minute video about bullying was made available to schools. Simultaneously, the schools distributed to all parents a four-page folder containing information and advice about bullying. In addition, anonymous self-report questionnaires about bullying were completed by all children.

Each school received feedback information from the questionnaire, about the prevalence of bullies and victims, in a specially arranged school conference day. Also, teachers were encouraged to develop explicit rules about bullying (e.g., do not bully, tell someone when bullying happens, bullying will not be tolerated, try to help victims, try to include children who are being left out) and to discuss bullying in class, using the video and role-playing exercises. Also, teachers were encouraged to improve monitoring and supervision of children, especially in the playground.

The effects of this anti-bullying programme were evaluated in 42 Bergen schools. Dan Olweus measured the prevalence of bullying before and after the programme using self-report questionnaires completed by the children. Since all schools received the programme, there were no control schools. However, Olweus compared children of a certain age (e.g., 13) before the programme with different children of the same age after the programme. Overall, the programme was very successful, because bullying decreased by half.

A similar programme was implemented in 23 Sheffield schools by Peter Smith and Sonia Sharp (1994). The core programme involved establishing a 'whole-school' anti-bullying policy, raising awareness of bullying and clearly defining roles and responsibilities of teachers and students, so that everyone knew what bullying was and what they should do about it. In addition, there were optional interventions tailored to particular schools: curriculum work (e.g., reading books, watching videos), direct work with students (e.g., assertiveness training for those who were bullied) and playground work (e.g., training lunch-time supervisors). This programme was successful in reducing bullying (by 15%) in primary schools, but had relatively small effects (a 5% reduction) in secondary schools.

Maria Ttofi and I (2011, 2012) completed a systematic review of the effectiveness of anti-bullying programmes in schools. We found 89 high-quality evaluations of 53 different programmes. Overall, anti-bullying programmes were effective. The results showed that bullying and victimization were reduced by about 17–23% in experimental schools compared with control schools.

PEER PROGRAMMES

There are few outstanding examples of effective intervention programmes for antisocial behaviour targeted on peer risk factors. The most hopeful programmes involve using high-status conventional peers to teach children ways of resisting peer pressure; this is effective in reducing drug use (Tobler, Lessard, Marshall, Ochshorn, & Roona, 1999). Also, in a randomized experiment in St. Louis, Ronald Feldman and his colleagues (1983) showed that placing antisocial adolescents in activity groups dominated by prosocial adolescents led to a reduction in their antisocial behaviour (compared with antisocial adolescents placed in antisocial groups). This suggests that the influence of prosocial peers can be harnessed to reduce antisocial behaviour. However, putting anti-social peers together can have harmful effects (Dishion, McCord, & Poulin, 1999).

The most important intervention programme whose success seems to be based mainly on reducing peer risk factors is the Children at Risk programme (Harrell, Cavanagh, Harmon, Koper, & Sridharan, 1997), which targeted high-risk adolescents (average age 12) in poor neighbourhoods of five cities across the United States. Eligible youths were identified in schools, and randomly assigned to experimental or control groups. The programme was a comprehensive community-based prevention strategy targeting risk factors for delinquency, including case management and family counselling, family skills training, tutoring, mentoring, after-school activities and community policing. The programme was different in each neighbourhood.

The initial results of the programme were disappointing, but a 1-year follow-up showed that (according to self-reports) experimental youths were less likely to have committed violent crimes and used or sold drugs (Harrell, Cavanagh, & Sridharan, 1999). The process evaluation showed that the greatest change was in peer risk factors. Experimental youths associated less often with delinquent peers, felt less peer pressure to engage in delinquency, and had more positive peer support. In contrast, there were few changes in individual, family or community risk factors, possibly linked to the low participation of parents in parent training and of youths in mentoring and tutoring. In other words, there were problems of implementation of the programme, linked to the serious and multiple needs and problems of the families.

Peer tutoring was also involved in the Quantum Opportunities Programme, which was implemented in five sites across the United States (Hahn, 1994, 1999). It aimed to improve the life-course opportunities of disadvantaged, at-risk youth during the high school years and included peer tutoring for educational development and adult assistance with life skills, career planning and community service. Participants received cash incentives to stay in the programme, and staff received cash incentives for keeping youth in the programme.

Fifty adolescents aged about 14 were randomly assigned to experimental or control conditions in each site, making an initial sample size of 250. The programme was successful. Experimental adolescents were more likely to graduate from high school (63% versus 42%) and were less likely to be arrested (17% versus 58%). During the 6-month follow-up period, experimental adolescents were more likely to have volunteered as a mentor or tutor themselves (28% versus 8%) and were less likely to have claimed welfare benefits.

A cost–benefit analysis of the Quantum Opportunities Programme (Hahn, 1994) revealed substantial benefits for both the participants and taxpayers. There was a desirable benefit-to-cost ratio of 3.7 to 1. Monetary benefits were limited to gains from education and fewer children, with the benefits from fewer children accruing from reduced costs for health and welfare services for teenage mothers. According to WSIPP (Lee *et al.*, 2012), however, only $1.2 are saved for every $1 expended on this programme.

Community-based mentoring programmes usually involve non-professional adult volunteers spending time with young people at risk of delinquency, dropping out of school, school failure, or other social problems. Mentors behave in a supportive, non-judgmental manner while acting as role models (Howell, 1995, p. 90). Brandon Welsh and Akemi Hoshi (2006) identified seven mentoring programmes (of which six were of high quality) that evaluated the impact on delinquency. Since most programmes found desirable effects, Welsh and Hoshi concluded that community-based mentoring was a promising approach in preventing delinquency.

A systematic review and meta-analysis of 18 mentoring programmes by Darrick Jolliffe and I (2008) found that this was an effective approach to preventing delinquency. The weighted mean effect size was $d = .21$, corresponding to a significant 10% reduction in delinquency. Mentoring was more effective in reducing offending when the average duration of each contact between mentor and mentee was greater, in smaller scale studies and when mentoring was combined with other interventions. According to WSIPP (Lee *et al.*, 2012), $1.7 are saved for every $1 expended on youth mentoring programmes.

SKILLS TRAINING

The most important prevention techniques that target the risk factors of impulsiveness and low empathy are cognitive-behavioural skills training programmes, which

have been recently reviewed by Georgia Zara and myself (2014). For example, Robert and Roslynn Ross (1995) devised a programme that aimed to teach people to stop and think before acting, to consider the consequences of their behaviour, to conceptualize alternative ways of solving interpersonal problems, and to consider the impact of their behaviour on other people, especially victims. It included social skills training, lateral thinking (to teach creative problem solving), critical thinking (to teach logical reasoning), values education (to teach values and concern for others), assertiveness training (to teach non-aggressive, socially appropriate ways to obtain desired outcomes), negotiation skills training, interpersonal cognitive problem-solving (to teach thinking skills for solving interpersonal problems), social perspective training (to teach how to recognize and understand other people's feelings), role-playing and modelling (demonstration and practice of effective and acceptable interpersonal behaviour).

Robert and Bambi Ross (1988) implemented this 'Reasoning and Rehabilitation' programme in Ottawa, and found (in a randomized experiment) that it led to a large decrease in reoffending for a small sample of adult offenders in a short 9-month follow-up period. Their training was carried out by probation officers, but they believed that it could be carried out by parents or teachers. This programme has been implemented widely in several different countries, and forms the basis of many accredited cognitive-behavioural programmes used in the UK prison and probation services, including the Pathfinder projects (McGuire, 2001).

A similar programme, entitled 'Straight Thinking on Probation' was implemented in Glamorgan by Peter Raynor and Maurice Vanstone (2001). Offenders who received skills training were compared with similar offenders who received custodial sentences. After 1 year, offenders who completed the programme had a lower reconviction rate than control offenders (35% as opposed to 49%), although both had the same predicted reconviction rate of 42%. The benefits of the programme had worn off at the 2-year follow-up point, when reconviction rates of experimentals (63%) and controls (65%) were similar to reach other and to predicted rates. However, the reconvicted experimentals committed less serious crimes than the reconvicted controls.

Joy Tong and I (2008) completed a systematic review of the effectiveness of 'Reasoning and Rehabilitation' in reducing offending. We located 32 comparisons of experimental and control groups in four countries. Our meta-analysis showed that, overall, there was a significant decrease in offending for programme participants compared with controls.

Marshall Jones and Dan Offord (1989) implemented a skills training programme in an experimental public housing complex in Ottawa and compared it with a control complex. The programme centred on non-school skills, both athletic (e.g., swimming and hockey) and non-athletic (e.g., guitar and ballet). The aim of developing skills was to increase self-esteem, to encourage children to use time constructively and to provide desirable role models. Participation rates were high; about three-quarters of age-eligible children in the experimental complex took at least one course in the first year. The programme was successful; delinquency rates decreased significantly in the experimental complex compared to the control complex. The benefit–cost ratio, based only on savings to taxpayers, was 2.5 to 1.

The 'Stop Now and Plan' (SNAP) programme is one of the most important skills training programmes for children aged 6–11. It was developed in Toronto by Leena Augimeri and her colleagues (2011). Children referred by the police for problematic behaviour are taught to calm down, take deep breaths, and count to 10 when they are angry. They are also taught coping statements and effective solutions to interpersonal problems. Small-scale experiments by Leena Augimeri and her colleagues (2007) and Christopher Koegl and his colleagues (2008) showed that SNAP was effective in reducing delinquency and aggression. This was confirmed by large-scale independent evaluations in Hamilton, Ontario (Lipman *et al.*, 2008) and Pittsburgh (Burke & Loeber, 2014).

The Montreal longitudinal-experimental study combined child skills training and parent training. Richard Tremblay and his colleagues (1995) identified disruptive (aggressive or hyperactive) boys at age 6, and randomly allocated over 300 of these to experimental or control conditions. Between ages 7 and 9, the experimental group received training designed to foster social skills and self-control. Coaching, peer modelling, role playing and reinforcement contingencies were used in small group sessions on such topics as 'how to help', 'what to do when you are angry' and 'how to react to teasing'. Also, their parents were trained using the parent management training techniques developed by Gerald Patterson (1982).

This prevention programme was successful. By age 12, the experimental boys committed less burglary and theft, were less likely to get drunk, and were less likely to be involved in fights than the controls (according to self-reports). Also, the experimental boys had higher school achievement. At every age from 10 to 15, the experimental boys had lower self-reported delinquency scores than the control boys. Interestingly, the differences in antisocial behaviour between experimental and control boys increased as the follow-up progressed. Later follow-ups showed that fewer experimental boys had a criminal record by age 24 (Boisjoli, Vitaro, Lacourse, Barker, & Tremblay, 2007) and that the experimental boys

self-reported less property crime at age 28 (Vitaro, Brendgen, Giguere, & Tremblay, 2013).

Recent experiments in Germany (Lösel, Stemmler, & Bender, 2013) and Switzerland (Malti, Ribeaud, & Eisner, 2011) also show that child skills training is effective in reducing antisocial behaviour. Friedrich Lösel and Andreas Beelmann (2006) completed a systematic review of the effectiveness of skills training with children and adolescents. They located 89 comparisons of experimental and control groups. Their meta-analysis showed that, overall, there was a significant 10% decrease in delinquency in follow-up studies for children who received skills training compared with controls. The greatest effect was for cognitive-behavioural skills training, where there was an average 25% decrease in delinquency in seven follow-up studies. The most effective programmes targeted children aged 13 or older and high risk groups who were already exhibiting behaviour problems. The latest review by Friedrich Lösel and Doris Bender (2012) also concluded that child skills training was effective.

COMMUNITIES THAT CARE

In the interests of maximizing effectiveness, what is needed is a multiple-component community-based programme including several of the successful interventions listed in the preceding text. Many of the programmes reviewed in this chapter are of this type. However, Communities That Care (CTC) has many attractions (Farrington, 1996). Perhaps more than any other programme, it is evidence-based and systematic: the choice of interventions depends on empirical evidence about what are the important risk and protective factors in a particular community and on empirical evidence about 'What works' (Sherman, Farrington, Welsh, & MacKenzie, 2006). CTC was developed in the United States but has been implemented widely in many other countries, including the United Kingdom.

CTC was developed as a risk-focused prevention strategy by David Hawkins and Richard Catalano (1992), and it soon became a core component of the US Office of Juvenile Justice and Delinquency Prevention's (OJJDP's) Comprehensive Strategy for Serious, Violent and Chronic Juvenile Offenders (Wilson & Howell, 1993). CTC is based on a theory (the social development model) that organizes risk and protective factors. The intervention techniques are tailored to the needs of each particular community. The 'community' could be a city, a county, a small town, or even a neighbourhood or a housing estate. This programme aims to reduce delinquency and drug use by implementing particular prevention strategies that have demonstrated effectiveness in reducing risk factors or enhancing protective factors. It is modelled on large-scale community-wide public health programmes designed to reduce illnesses such as coronary heart disease by tackling key risk factors. There is great emphasis in CTC on enhancing protective factors and building on strengths, partly because this is more attractive to communities than tackling risk factors. However, it is generally true that health promotion is more effective than disease prevention (Kaplan, 2000).

CTC programmes begin with community mobilization. Key community leaders (e.g., elected representatives, education officials, police chiefs, business leaders) are brought together, with the aim of getting them to agree on the goals of the prevention programme and to implement CTC. The key leaders then set up a Community Board that is accountable to them, consisting of neighbourhood residents and representatives from various agencies (e.g., school, police, social services, probation, health, parents, youth groups, business, church, media). The Community Board takes charge of prevention on behalf of the community.

The Community Board then carries out a risk and protective factor assessment, identifying key risk factors in that particular community that need to be tackled and key protective factors that need enhancing. This risk assessment might involve the use of police, school, social or census records or local neighbourhood or school surveys. After identifying key risk and protective factors, the Community Board assesses existing resources and develops a plan of intervention strategies. With specialist technical assistance and guidance, they choose programmes from a menu of strategies that have been shown to be effective in well-designed evaluation research.

The menu of strategies listed by Hawkins and Catalano (1992) includes prenatal and postnatal home visiting programmes, preschool intellectual enrichment programmes, parent training, school organization and curriculum development, teacher training and media campaigns. Other strategies include child skills training, anti-bullying programmes in schools, situational prevention, and policing strategies. The choice of prevention strategies is based on empirical evidence about effective methods of tackling each particular risk factor, but it also depends on what are identified as the biggest problems in the community. While this approach is not without its challenges and complexities (e.g., cost, implementation, establishing partnerships among diverse agencies), an evidence-based approach that brings together the most effective prevention programmes across multiple domains offers the greatest promise for reducing crime and building safer communities.

David Hawkins and his colleagues (2009) have evaluated the effectiveness of CTC in an ambitious large-scale randomized experiment. Twenty-four communities across the United States were placed into 12 matched pairs, and one community in each pair was chosen at random to receive CTC. The effectiveness of CTC was evaluated using annual surveys of over 4,000 students from grade 5 (age 10–11) to grade 8 (age 13–14). The results showed that CTC caused a reduction in delinquency, alcohol use and cigarette use, but not in marijuana use. Nevertheless, these results are extremely encouraging. Furthermore, a cost–benefit analysis of CTC (Kuklinski, Briney, Hawkins, & Catalano, 2012) concluded that between $5.3 and $10.2 were saved for every $1 expended.

RECENT UK DEVELOPMENTS

In September 2006, Prime Minister Tony Blair announced an action plan for 'social exclusion', which is a general concept including antisocial behaviour, teenage pregnancy, educational failure, and mental health problems (Cabinet Office, 2006). This action plan emphasized early intervention, better coordination of agencies, and evidence-based practice (systematically identifying what works and rating evaluations according to methodological quality: see Farrington, 2003). It proposed home visiting programmes targeting at-risk children from birth to age 2, implemented by midwives and health visitors, inspired by the work of David Olds (Olds et al., 1998). It proposed that teenage pregnancy 'hot spots' would be targeted with enhanced social and relationship education and better access to contraceptives. It proposed multi-agency and family-based approaches to tackle behavioural and mental health problems in childhood, including treatment foster care (Chamberlain & Reid, 1998) and multi-systemic therapy (Henggeler et al., 1998). It also proposed interventions for adults with chaotic lives, mental health problems and multiple needs, to try to get more of them into employment. This Action Plan has now been replaced by the Early Intervention Foundation, which was launched by Prime Minister David Cameron in April 2013.

Since the mid-1990s, there has been increasing emphasis on early intervention and evidence-based practice in the United Kingdom (Sutton, Utting, & Farrington, 2004, 2006). In 1995, Child and Adolescent Mental Health (CAMHS) teams were established in every part of the country to provide support for children and young people who were experiencing a range of emotional and behavioural difficulties. The services fall within the remit of the Department of Health and practitioners typically employ a wide range of theoretical approaches.

The major government initiative for preschool children is called Sure Start (www.surestart.gov.uk). The first Sure Start centres were established in 1999 in disadvantaged areas, and there are now over 800 Sure Start programmes in the United Kingdom. These centres provide early education and parenting programmes, integrated with extended childcare, health and family support services. The services are supposed to be evidence-based. Widely used parenting programmes include The Incredible Years (Webster-Stratton, 2000) Triple-P (Sanders *et al.*, 2000), and Strengthening Families, Strengthening Communities (Steele, Marigna, Tello, & Johnson, 1999). A National Academy for Parenting Professionals was established.

It is very difficult to evaluate large-scale national programmes such as Sure Start. The first evaluation compared outcomes for 150 Sure Start areas and 50 non-Sure Start areas (Sure Start-to-be) by assessing a random sample of families with a 9-month-old child or with a 3-year-old child in each locality (Melhuish, Belsky, & Leyland, 2005). The results showed that, for 3-year-old children, with non-teenage mothers (86% of the sample), the children showed greater social competence and had fewer behaviour problems, and there was less negative parenting in the Sure Start areas than in the control group areas. However, among teenage mothers (14% of the sample), in the Sure Start areas the children showed less social competence, had lower verbal ability and had more behaviour problems than in the control areas.

A later evaluation compared outcomes for 93 disadvantaged Sure Start areas with 72 similarly deprived areas in England who took part in the Millennium Cohort Study (Melhuish, Belsky, Leyland, & Barnes, 2008). There were beneficial effects of Sure Start on five outcomes up to age 3: parenting, the child's social development, social behaviour and independence, and the home learning environment. There were no significant effects on the child's vocabulary, the father's involvement with the child or the mother's smoking or life satisfaction.

Sure Start programmes were then developed into Children's Centres, to cover every part of the United Kingdom. Typically, these are service hubs, offering and coordinating information to support children and their parents. One of their implicit objectives is to reduce conduct disorder and aggressiveness among young children through the provision of parenting programmes. The Centres also contribute to the strategic objectives of Every Child Matters, a major government policy document (Chief Secretary to the Treasury, 2003; www.everychildmatters.gov.uk). This applies to all children from birth to age 19 and aims to improve educational achievement and reduce the levels of ill health, teenage pregnancy, abuse and neglect, crime and antisocial behaviour.

CONCLUSIONS

High-quality evaluation research shows that many programmes are effective in reducing delinquency and antisocial behaviour, and that in many cases the financial benefits of these programmes outweigh their financial costs. The best programmes include general parent education, parent management training, preschool intellectual enrichment programmes, child skills training, teacher training, anti-bullying programmes, mentoring and MST. While most is known about programmes for boys, there are also effective interventions designed specifically for girls (Hipwell & Loeber, 2006). Importantly, early intervention programmes have long-lasting benefits (Dekovic *et al.*, 2011; Manning, Homel, & Smith, 2010).

High-quality experimental and quasi-experimental evaluations of the effectiveness of crime reduction programmes are needed in the United Kingdom. Most knowledge about the effectiveness of prevention programmes, such as cognitive-behavioural skills training, parent training and preschool intellectual enrichment programmes, is based on American research. Ideally, prevention programmes should aim not only to tackle risk factors but also to strengthen protective factors, and both risk and protective factors should be measured and targeted. An important development in recent years has been the increasing use of cost–benefit analysis in evaluating prevention programmes. Cost–benefit analyses of the effectiveness of prevention programmes should be given some priority, and a standard how-to-do-it manual should be developed.

Experiments and quasi-experiments should have large samples, long follow-up periods and follow-up interviews. Sample size is particularly important for both individual-and area-based studies. Many interventions have proved effective in small-scale demonstration programmes but less effective in large-scale implementation. More research is needed on the transportability of programmes (Michelson, Davenport, Dretzke, Barlow, & Day, 2013; Welsh, Sullivan, & Olds, 2010). Long-term follow-ups are needed to establish the persistence of effects. This information may indicate the need for booster sessions. Long follow-ups are rare after criminological interventions and should be a top priority of funding agencies. Research is also needed to identify the active ingredients of successful early prevention programmes (Kaminski, Valle, Filene, & Boyle, 2008). Many programmes are multi-modal, which makes it difficult to isolate the independent or interactive effects of the different components. Future experiments are needed that attempt to disentangle the different elements of the most successful programmes.

It is difficult to evaluate large-scale crime reduction strategies, and to answer questions about whether it is better (in terms of crimes saved per £ spent, for example) to invest in risk-focused early prevention, in physical or situational prevention, in more police officers or in more prison cells. Nevertheless, this question is of vital importance to government policy-makers and to the general population. Therefore, research is needed to investigate the cost-effectiveness of risk-focused prevention in comparison with other general crime reduction strategies. Brandon Welsh and I (2011) reviewed the evidence on this and concluded that it was more cost-effective (and saved more crimes) to invest in early prevention than in imprisonment.

Turning to policy implications, consideration should be given to implementing a multiple component risk-focused prevention programme such as CTC more widely throughout the United Kingdom. This programme could be implemented by existing Crime and Disorder Partnerships. However, they would need resources and technical assistance to conduct youth surveys and household surveys to identify key risk and protective factors for both people and places. They would also need resources and technical assistance to measure risk and protective factors, to choose effective intervention methods, and to carry out high quality evaluations of the effectiveness of programmes in reducing crime and disorder.

The focus should be on primary prevention (offering the programme to all families living in specified areas) and not on secondary prevention (targeting the programme on individuals identified as at risk). Ideally, the programme should be presented positively, as fostering safe and healthy communities by strengthening protective factors, rather than as a crime prevention programme targeting risk factors.

Nationally and locally, there is no agency whose main mandate is the primary prevention of crime. A national prevention agency could provide technical assistance, skills and knowledge to local agencies in implementing prevention programmes, could provide funding for such programmes, and could ensure continuity, coordination and monitoring of local programmes. It could provide training in prevention science for people in local agencies, and could maintain high standards for evaluation research. It could also act as a centre for the discussion of how policy initiatives of different government agencies influence crime and associated social problems. It could set a national and local agenda for research and practice in the prevention

of crime, drug and alcohol abuse, mental health problems and associated social problems.

National crime prevention agencies have been established in other countries, such as Sweden (Andersson, 2005) and Canada (Sansfacon & Waller, 2001). These agencies have emphasized three main mechanisms: collaboration with other government departments, development of local problem-solving partnerships and involvement of citizens (Waller & Welsh, 1999). These points specify how evidence-based results can be translated into local practice. Each point specifies concrete actions that a national agency can influence at the local level, but programme success ultimately will depend on local persons. A national agency can influence these implementation issues in a number of ways; for example, by developing guidelines on effective practice and making project funding conditional on the use of evidence-based programmes.

A national agency could also maintain a computerized register of evaluation research and, like the National Institute of Health and Clinical Excellence, advise the government about effective and cost-effective crime prevention programmes. Medical advice is often based on systematic reviews of the effectiveness of health-care interventions organized by the Cochrane Collaboration and funded by the National Health Service. Systematic reviews of the evaluation literature on the effectiveness of criminological interventions, possibly organized by the Campbell Collaboration (Farrington & Petrosino, 2001), should be commissioned and funded by government agencies.

Crime prevention also needs to be organized locally. In each area, a local agency should be established to take the lead in organizing risk-focused crime prevention. In Sweden, 80% of municipalities had local crime prevention councils in 2005 (Andersson, 2005). The local prevention agency could take the lead in measuring risk factors and social problems in local areas, using archival records and local household and school surveys. It could then assess available resources and develop a plan of prevention strategies. With specialist technical assistance, prevention programmes could be chosen from a menu of strategies that have been proved to be effective in reducing crime in well-designed evaluation research. This would be a good example of evidence-based practice.

Recent promising developments in the United Kingdom, such as Sure Start and Every Child Matters (Chief Secretary to the Treasury, 2003), have clearly been influenced by recent research on childhood risk factors and risk-focused intervention strategies. The time is ripe to expand these experimental programmes into a large-scale evidence-based integrated national strategy for the reduction of crime and associated social problems, including rigorous evaluation requirements.

FURTHER READING

Welsh, B. C., & Farrington, D. P. (2012, Eds.) *The Oxford handbook of crime prevention*. Oxford: Oxford University Press.

This handbook comprehensively reviews developmental, community and situational crime prevention. It contains chapters on preventing crime in the preschool years, parent training, child skills training and the prevention of female offending.

Farrington, D. P., & Welsh, B. C. (2007). *Saving children from a life of crime: Early risk factors and effective interventions*. Oxford: Oxford University Press.

This book reviews knowledge about individual, family, socio-economic, peer, school and community risk factors. It then reviews intervention programmes targeted on the individual (e.g., child skills training and preschool intellectual enrichment programmes), family (e.g., home visiting and parent training programmes), peer, school and community. The final chapter sets out the need for a national strategy for early intervention.

Greenwood, P. W. (2006). *Changing lives: Delinquency prevention as crime-control policy*. Chicago: University of Chicago Press.

This book reviews programmes designed to prevent delinquency in children and adolescents, highlighting both effective and ineffective programmes. It is particularly strong in its discussions of cost–benefit analyses, and it includes recommendations about the large-scale national implementation of delinquency prevention programmes.

REFERENCES

Alexander, J. F., & Parsons, B. V. (1973). Short-term behavioral intervention with delinquent families: Impact on family process and recidivism. *Journal of Abnormal Psychology, 81*, 219–225.

Andersson, J. (2005). The Swedish National Council for Crime Prevention: A short presentation. *Journal of Scandinavian Studies in Criminology and Crime Prevention, 6*, 74–88.

Asscher, J. J., Dekovic, M., Manders, W. A., Van Der Laan, P. H., & Prins, P. J. M. (2013). A randomized controlled trial of the effectiveness of multisystemic therapy in the Netherlands: Post-treatment changes and moderator effects. *Journal of Experimental Criminology, 9*, 169–187.

Augimeri, L. K., Farrington, D. P., Koegl, C. J., & Day, D. M. (2007). The SNAP Under 12 Outreach Project: Effects of a community based programme for children with conduct problems. *Journal of Child and Family Studies, 16*, 799–807.

Augimeri, L. K., Walsh, M. M., Liddon, A. D., & Dassinger, C. R. (2011). From risk identification to risk management: A comprehensive strategy for young children engaged in antisocial behaviour. In D. W. Springer & A. Roberts (Eds.), *Juvenile justice and delinquency* (pp. 117–140). Sudbury, MA: Jones & Bartlett.

Baldry, A. C., & Farrington, D. P. (1998). Parenting influences on bullying and victimization. *Legal and Criminological Psychology, 3*, 237–254.

Barnett, W. S. (1993). Cost-benefit analysis. In L. J. Schweinhart, H. V. Barnes, & D. P. Weikart, *Significant benefits: The High/Scope Perry Preschool Study through age 27* (pp. 142–173). Ypsilanti, MI: High/Scope Press.

Barton, C., Alexander, J. F., Waldron, H., Turner, C. W., & Warburton, J. (1985). Generalizing treatment effects of functional family therapy: Three replications. *American Journal of Family Therapy, 13*, 16–26.

Berrueta-Clement, J. R., Schweinhart, L. J., Barnett, W. S., Epstein, A. S., & Weikart, D. P. (1984). *Changed lives: The effects of the Perry Preschool Program on youths through age 19*. Ypsilanti, MI: High/Scope Press.

Bilukha, O., Hahn, R. A., Crosby, A., Fullilove, M. T., Liberman, A., Moscicki, E., Snyder, S., Tuma, F., Corso, P., Schofield, A., & Briss, P. A. (2005). The effectiveness of early childhood home visitation in preventing violence. *American Journal of Preventive Medicine, 28*(2S1), 11–39.

Boisjoli, R., Vitaro, F., Lacourse, E., Barker, E. D., & Tremblay, R. E. (2007). Impact and clinical significance of a preventive intervention for disruptive boys. *British Journal of Psychiatry, 191*, 415–419.

Borduin, C. M., Mann, B. J., Cone, L. T., Henggeler, S. W., Fucci, B. R., Blaske, D. M., & Williams, R. A. (1995). Multisystemic treatment of serious juvenile offenders: Long-term prevention of criminality and violence. *Journal of Consulting and Clinical Psychology, 63*, 569–587.

Brand, S., & Price, R. (2000). *The economic and social costs of crime*. London: Home Office (Research Study No. 217).

Burke, J. D., & Loeber, R. (2014). The effectiveness of the Stop Now and Plan (SNAP) programme for boys at risk for violence and delinquency. *Prevention Science*, in press.

Cabinet Office (2006). *Reaching out: An action plan for social exclusion*. London: Cabinet Office.

Campbell, F. A., Ramey, C. T., Pungello, E., Sparling, J., & Miller-Johnson, S. (2002). Early childhood education: Young adult outcomes from the Abercedarian Project. *Applied Developmental Science, 6*, 42–57.

Catalano, R. F., Hawkins, J. D., Berglund, L., Pollard, J. A., & Arthur, M. W. (2002). Prevention science and positive youth development: Competitive or cooperative frameworks? *Journal of Adolescent Health, 31*, 230–239.

Chamberlain, P., & Reid, J. B. (1998). Comparison of two community alternatives to incarceration for chronic juvenile offenders. *Journal of Consulting and Clinical Psychology*, 66, 624–633.

Chief Secretary to the Treasury (2003). *Every child matters*. London: The Stationery Office.

Clarke, R. V. (1995). Situational crime prevention. In M. Tonry & D. P. Farrington (Eds.), *Building a safer society: Strategic approaches to crime prevention* (pp. 91–150). Chicago: University of Chicago Press.

Cohen, M. A. (1998). The monetary value of saving a high-risk youth. *Journal of Quantitative Criminology*, 14, 5–33.

Cohen, M. A., & Piquero, A. R. (2009). New evidence on the monetary value of saving a high risk youth. *Journal of Quantitative Criminology*, 25, 25–29.

Curtis, N. M., Ronan, K. R., & Borduin, C. M. (2004). Multisystemic Treatment: A meta-analysis of outcome studies. *Journal of Family Psychology*, 18, 411–419.

Dekovic, M., Slagt, M. I., Asscher, J. J., Boendermaker, L., Eichelsteim, V. I., & Prinzie, P. (2011). Effects of early prevention programmes on adult criminal offending: A meta-analysis. *Clinical Psychology Review*, 31, 532–544.

Dishion, T. J., McCord, J., & Poulin, F. (1999). When interventions harm: Peer groups and problem behavior. *American Psychologist*, 54, 755–764.

Dishion, T. J., Patterson, G. R., & Kavanagh, K. A. (1992). An experimental test of the coercion model: Linking theory, measurement and intervention. In J. McCord & R. E. Tremblay (Eds.), *Preventing antisocial behavior: Interventions from birth through adolescence* (pp. 253–282). New York: Guilford.

Eckenrode, J., Campa, M., Luckey, D. W., Henderson, C. R., Cole, R., Kitzman, H., Anson, A., Sidora-Arcoleo, K., Powers, J., & Olds, D. (2010). Long-term effects of prenatal and infancy nurse home visitation on the life course of youths: 19-year follow-up a randomized trial. *Archives of Pediatrics and Adolescent Medicine*, 164, 9–15.

Farrington, D. P. (1993). Understanding and preventing bullying. In M. Tonry & N. Morris (Eds.), *Crime and justice* (vol. 17, pp. 381–458). Chicago: University of Chicago Press.

Farrington, D. P. (1996). *Understanding and preventing youth crime*. York: Joseph Rowntree Foundation.

Farrington, D. P. (2000). Explaining and preventing crime: The globalization of knowledge – The American Society of Criminology 1999 Presidential Address. *Criminology*, 38, 1–24.

Farrington, D. P. (2003). Methodological quality standards for evaluation research. *Annals of the American Academy of Political and Social Science*, 587, 49–68.

Farrington, D. P. (2007). Childhood risk factors and risk-focussed prevention. In M. Maguire, R. Morgan, & R. Reiner (Eds.), *The Oxford handbook of criminology* (4th ed., pp. 602–640). Oxford: Oxford University.

Farrington, D. P., Coid, J. W., Harnett, L., Jolliffe, D., Soteriou, N., Turner, R., & West, D. J. (2006). *Criminal careers up to age 50 and life success up to age 48: New findings from the Cambridge Study in Delinquent Development*. London: Home Office (Research Study No. 299).

Farrington, D. P., Loeber, R., & Ttofi, M. M. (2012). Risk and protective factors for offending. In B. C. Welsh & D. P. Farrington (Eds.), *The Oxford handbook of crime prevention* (pp. 46–69). Oxford: Oxford University Press.

Farrington, D. P., & Petrosino, A. (2001). The Campbell Collaboration crime and justice group. *Annals of the American Academy of Political and Social Science*, 578, 35–49.

Farrington, D. P., & Welsh, B. C. (2003). Family-based prevention of offending: A meta-analysis. *Australian and New Zealand Journal of Criminology*, 36, 127–151.

Farrington, D. P., & Welsh, B. C. (2005). Randomized experiments in criminology: What have we learned in the last two decades? *Journal of Experimental Criminology*, 1, 9–38.

Farrington, D. P., & Welsh, B. C. (2006a). *Saving children from a life of crime: Early risk factors and effective interventions*. Oxford: Oxford University Press.

Farrington, D. P., & Welsh, B. C. (2006b). A half-century of randomized experiments on crime and justice. In M. Tonry (Ed.), *Crime and Justice* (vol. 34, pp. 55–132). Chicago: University of Chicago Press.

Farrington, D. P., & Welsh. B. C. (2007). *Saving children from a life of crime: Early risk factors and effective interventions*. Oxford: Oxford University Press.

Farrington, D. P., & Welsh, B. C. (2013). Randomized experiments in criminology: What has been learned from long-term follow-ups? In B. C. Welsh, A. A. Braga & G. J. N. Bruinsma (Eds.), *Experimental criminology: Prospects for advancing science and public policy* (pp. 111–140). New York: Cambridge University Press.

Feldman, R. A., Caplinger, T. E., & Wodarski, J. S. (1983). *The St. Louis conundrum*. Englewood Cliffs, NJ: Prentice- Hall.

Garces, E., Thomas, D., & Currie, J. (2002). Longer-term effects of Head Start. *American Economic Review*, 92, 999–1012.

Gardner, F., Burton, J., & Klimes, I. (2006). Randomized controlled trial of a parenting intervention in the voluntary sector for reducing child conduct problems: Outcomes and mechanisms of change. *Journal of Child Psychology and Psychiatry*, 47, 1123–1132.

Gardner, F., Hutchings, J., Bywater, T., & Whitaker, C. (2010). Who benefits and how does it work? Moderators and mediators of outcome in an effectiveness trial of a parenting intervention. *Journal of Clinical Child and Adolescent Psychology*, 39, 568–580.

Gottfredson, D. C., Wilson, D. B., & Najaka, S. S. (2006). School-based crime prevention. In L. W. Sherman, D. P. Farrington, B. C. Welsh, & D. L. MacKenzie (Eds.), *Evidence-based crime prevention* (Rev. ed., pp. 56–164). London: Routledge.

Hahn, A. (1994). *Evaluation of the Quantum Opportunities Program (QOP): Did the program work?* Waltham, MA: Brandeis University.

Hahn, A. (1999). Extending the time of learning. In D. J. Besharov (Ed.), *America's disconnected youth: Toward a preventive strategy* (pp. 233–265). Washington, DC: Child Welfare League of America Press.

Hahn, R. A., Bilukha, O., Lowy, J., Crosby, A., Fullilove, M. T., Liberman, A., Moscicki, E., Synder, S., Tuma, F., Corso, P., & Schofield, A. (2005). The effectiveness of therapeutic foster care for the prevention of violence. *American Journal of Preventive Medicine, 28*(2S1), 72–90.

Harrell, A. V., Cavanagh, S. E., Harmon, M. A., Koper, C. S., & Sridharan, S. (1997). *Impact of the Children at Risk program: Comprehensive final report,* vol. 2. Washington, DC: The Urban Institute.

Harrell, A. V., Cavanagh, S. E., & Sridharan, S. (1999). *Evaluation of the Children at Risk program: Results one year after the program.* Washington, DC: US National Institute of Justice.

Hawkins, J. D., & Catalano, R. F. (1992). *Communities that care.* San Francisco: Jossey-Bass.

Hawkins, J. D., Catalano, R. F., Kosterman, R., Abbott, R., & Hill, K. G. (1999). Preventing adolescent health risk behaviors by strengthening protection during childhood. *Archives of Pediatrics and Adolescent Medicine, 153,* 226–234.

Hawkins, J. D., Kosterman, R., Catalano, R. F., Hill, K. G., & Abbott, R. D. (2008). Effects of social development intervention in childhood 15 years later. *Archives of Pediatrics and Adolescent Medicine, 162,* 1133–1141.

Hawkins, J. D., Oesterle, S., Brown, E. C., Arthur, M. W., Abbott, R. D., Fagan, A. A., & Catalano, R. F. (2009). Results of a type 2 translational research trial to prevent adolescent drug use and delinquency: A test of communities that care. *Archives of Pediatrics and Adolescent Medicine, 163,* 789–798.

Hawkins, J. D., Von Cleve, E., & Catalano, R. F. (1991). Reducing early childhood aggression: Results of a primary prevention programme. *Journal of the American Academy of Child and Adolescent Psychiatry, 30,* 208–217.

Henggeler, S. W., Clingempeel, W. G., Brondino, M. J., & Pickrel, S. G. (2002). Four-year follow-up of multisystemic therapy with substance-abusing and substance-dependent juvenile offenders. *Journal of the American Academy of Child and Adolescent Psychiatry, 41,* 868–874.

Henggeler, S. W., Melton, G. B., Brondino, M. J., Scherer, D. G., & Hanley, J. H. (1997). Multisystemic therapy with violent and chronic juvenile offenders and their families: The role of treatment fidelity in successful dissemination. *Journal of Consulting and Clinical Psychology, 65,* 821–833.

Henggeler, S. W., Melton, G. B., Smith, L. A., Schoenwald, S. K., & Hanley, J. H. (1993). Family preservation using multisystematic treatment: Long-term follow-up to a clinical trial with serious juvenile offenders. *Journal of Child and Family Studies, 2,* 283–293.

Henggeler, S. W., Rowland, M. D., Randall, J., Ward, D. M., Pickrel, S. G., Cunningham, P. B., Miller, S. L., Edwards, J., Zealberg, J. J., Hand, L. D., & Santos, A. B. (1999). Home-based multisystemic therapy as an alternative to the hospitalization of youths in psychiatric crisis: Clinical outcomes. *Journal of the American Academy of Child and Adolescent Psychiatry, 38,* 1331–1339.

Henggeler, S. W., Schoenwald, S. K., Borduin, C. M., Rowland, M. D., & Cunningham, P. B. (1998). *Multisystemic treatment of antisocial behavior in children and adolescents.* New York: Guilford.

Hill, K. G., Bailey, J. A., Hawkins, J. D., Catalano, R. F., Kosterman, R., Oesterle, S., & Abbott, R. D. (2014). The onset of STI diagnosis through age 30: Results from the Seattle Social Development Project intervention. *Prevention Science, 15*(S1), S19–S32.

Hipwell, A. E., & Loeber, R. (2006). Do we know which interventions are effective for disruptive and delinquent girls? *Clinical Child and Family Psychology Review, 9,* 221–255.

Hope, T. (1995). Community crime prevention. In M. Tonry & D. P. Farrington (Eds.), *Building a safer society: Strategic approaches to crime prevention* (pp. 21–89). Chicago: University of Chicago Press.

Howell, J. C. (1995). *Guide for implementing the comprehensive strategy for serious, violent, and chronic juvenile offenders.* Washington, DC: Office of Juvenile Justice and Delinquency Prevention.

Jefford, T., & Squire, B. (2004). Multi-systemic therapy: Model practice. *Young Minds, 71,* 20–21.

Jolliffe, D., & Farrington, D. P. (2008). *The influence of mentoring on reoffending.* Stockholm, Sweden: National Council for Crime Prevention.

Jones, M. B., & Offord, D. R. (1989). Reduction of antisocial behaviour in poor children by non-school skill development. *Journal of Child Psychology and Psychiatry, 30,* 737–750.

Kaminski, J. W., Valle, L. A., Filene, J. H., & Boyle, C. L. (2008). A meta-analytic review of components associated with parent training programme effectiveness. *Journal of Abnormal Child Psychology, 36,* 567–589.

Kaplan, R. M. (2000). Two pathways to prevention. *American Psychologist, 55,* 382–396.

Kazdin, A. E., Kraemer, H. C., Kessler, R. C., Kupfer, D. J., & Offord, D. R. (1997). Contributions of risk-factor research to developmental psychopathology. *Clinical Psychology Review, 17,* 375–406.

Kellam, S. G., Wang, W., Mackenzie, A. C. L., Brown, C. H., Ompad, D. C., Or, F., Ialongo, N. S., Poduska, J. M., & Windham, A. (2014). The impact of the Good Behaviour Game, a universal classroom-based preventive intervention in first and second grades, on high-risk sexual behaviours and drug abuse and dependence disorders into young adulthood. *Prevention Science, 15*(S1), S6–S18.

Koegl, C. J., Farrington, D. P., Augimeri, L. K., & Day, D. M. (2008). Evaluation of a targeted cognitive-behavioural programme for children with conduct problems – the SNAP Under 12 Outreach Project: Service intensity, age and gender effects on short and long term outcomes. *Clinical Child Psychology and Psychiatry, 13,* 419–434.

Kolvin, I., Garside, R. F., Nicol, A. R., MacMillan, A., Wolstenholme, F., & Leith, I. M. (1981). *Help starts here: The maladjusted child in the ordinary school*. London: Tavistock.

Kuklinski, M. R., Briney, J. S., Hawkins, J. D., & Catalano, R. F. (2012). Cost-benefit analysis of communities that care outcomes at eighth grade. *Prevention Science, 13*, 150–161.

Lee, S., Aos, S., Drake, E., Pennucci, A., Miller, U., & Anderson, L. (2012). *Return on investment: Evidence-based options to improve statewide outcomes* (Document no. 12-04-1201). Olympia: Washington State Institute for Public Policy.

Leschied, A., & Cunningham, A. (2002). *Seeking effective interventions for serious young offenders: Interim results of a four-year randomized study of multisystemic therapy in Ontario, Canada*. London, Ontario, Canada: London Family Court Clinic.

Leve, L. D., Chamberlain, P., & Reid, J. B. (2005). Intervention outcomes for girls referred from juvenile justice: Effects on delinquency. *Journal of Consulting and Clinical Psychology, 73*, 1181–1185.

Lipman, E. L., Kenny, M., Sniderman, C., O'Grady, S., Augimeri, L., Khayutin, S., & Boyle, M. H. (2008). Evaluation of a community-based programme for young boys at-risk of antisocial behaviour: Results and issues. *Journal of the Canadian Academy of Child and Adolescent Psychiatry, 17*, 12–19.

Littell, J. H. (2005). Lessons from a systematic review of effects of multisystemic therapy. *Children and Youth Services Review, 27*, 445–463.

Lösel, F., & Beelmann, A. (2006). Child social skills training. In B. C. Welsh & D. P. Farrington (Eds.), *Preventing crime: What works for children, offenders, victims, and places* (pp. 33–54). Dordrecht, Netherlands: Springer.

Lösel, F., & Bender, D. (2012). Child social skills training in the prevention of antisocial development and crime. In B. C. Welsh & D. P. Farrington (Eds.), *The Oxford handbook of crime prevention* (pp. 102–129). Oxford: Oxford University Press,

Lösel, F., & Farrington, D. P. (2012). Direct protective and buffering protective factors in the development of youth violence. *American Journal of Preventive Medicine, 43*(2S1), S8–S23.

Lösel, F., Stemmler, M., & Bender, D. (2013). Long-term evaluation of a bimodal universal prevention programme: Effects on antisocial development from kindergarten to adolescence. *Journal of Experimental Criminology, 9*, 429–449.

Macdonald, G. M., & Turner, W. (2007). Treatment Foster Care for improving outcomes in children and young people. *Campbell Systematic Reviews, 9*, 2007.

McGuire, J. (2001). What works in correctional intervention? Evidence and practical implications. In G. A. Bernfeld, D. P. Farrington, & A. W. Leschied (Eds.), *Offender rehabilitation in practice: Implementing and evaluating effective programmes* (pp. 25–43). Chichester: Wiley.

Malti, T., Ribeaud, D., & Eisner, M. P. (2011). The effectiveness of two universal preventive interventions in reducing children's externalizing behaviour: A cluster randomized trial. *Journal of Clinical Child and Adolescent Psychology, 40*, 677–692.

Manning, M., Homel, R., & Smith, C. (2010). A meta-analysis of the effects of early developmental prevention programmes in at-risk populations on non-health outcomes in adolescence. *Children and Youth Services Review, 32*, 506–519.

Melhuish, E., Belsky, J., & Leyland, A. (2005). *Early impacts of Sure Start local programmes on children and families: Report of the cross-sectional study of 9 and 36 months old children and their families*. London: The Stationery Office.

Melhuish, E., Belsky, J., Leyland, A. H., & Barnes, J. (2008). Effects of fully-established Sure Start local programmes on 3-year-old children and their families living in England: A quasi-experimental observational study. *The Lancet, 372*, 1641–1647.

Michelson, D., Davenport, C., Dretzke, J., Barlow, J., & Day, C. (2013). Do evidence-based interventions work when tested in the 'real world'? A systematic review and meta-analysis of parent management training for the treatment of child disruptive behaviour. *Clinical Child and Family Psychology Review, 16*, 18–34.

Murray, J., & Farrington, D. P. (2010). Risk factors for conduct disorder and delinquency: Key findings from longitudinal studies. *Canadian Journal of Psychiatry, 55*, 633–642.

O'Donnell, J., Hawkins, J. D., Catalano, R. F., Abbott, R. D., & Day, L. E. (1995). Preventing school failure, drug use, and delinquency among low-income children: Long-term intervention in elementary schools. *American Journal of Orthopsychiatry, 65*, 87–100.

Ogden, T., & Hagen, K. A. (2006). Multisystemic Treatment of serious behaviour problems in youth: Sustainability of effectiveness two years after intake. *Child and Adolescent Mental Health, 11*, 142–149.

Olds, D. L., Eckenrode, J., Henderson, C. R., Kitzman, H., Powers, J., Cole, R., Sidora, K., Morris, P., Pettitt, L. M., & Luckey, D. (1997). Long-term effects of home visitation on maternal life course and child abuse and neglect: Fifteen-year follow-up of a randomized trial. *Journal of the American Medical Association, 278*, 637–643.

Olds, D. L., Henderson, C. R., Chamberlin, R., & Tatelbaum, R. (1986). Preventing child abuse and neglect: A randomized trial of nurse home visitation. *Pediatrics, 78*, 65–78.

Olds, D. L., Henderson, C. R., Cole, R., Eckenrode, J., Kitzman, H., Luckey, D., Pettitt, L., Sidora, K., Morris, P., & Powers, J. (1998). Long-term effects of nurse home visitation on children's criminal and antisocial behavior: 15-year follow-up of a randomized controlled trial. *Journal of the American Medical Association, 280*, 1238–1244.

Olds, D. L. Sadler, L., & Kitzman, H. (2007). Programs for parents of infants and toddlers: Recent evidence from randomized trials. *Journal of Child Psychology and Psychiatry, 48*, 355–391.

Olweus, D. (1994). Bullying at school: Basic facts and effects of a school based intervention programme. *Journal of Child Psychology and Psychiatry, 35*, 1171–1190.

Patterson, G. R. (1982). *Coercive family process*. Eugene, Oregon: Castalia.

Patterson, G. R., Reid, J. B., & Dishion, T. J. (1992). *Antisocial boys*. Eugene, Oregon: Castalia.

Petras, H., Kellam, S. G., Brown, C. H., Muthen, B. O., Ialongo, N. S., & Poduska, J. M. (2008). Developmental epidemiological courses leading to antisocial personality disorder and violent and criminal behaviour: Effects by young adulthood of a universal preventive intervention in first and second grade classrooms. *Drugs and Alcohol Dependence, 95S*, S45–S59.

Piquero, A., Farrington, D. P., Welsh, B. C., Tremblay, R. E., & Jennings, W. G. (2009). Effects of early family/parent training programmes on antisocial behaviour and delinquency. *Journal of Experimental Criminology, 5*, 83–120.

Raffan Gowar, B., & Farrington, D. P. (2013). The monetary cost of criminal careers. In K. Boers, T. Feltes, J. Kinzig, L. W. Sherman, F. Streng & G. Trueg (Eds.), *Kriminologie, kriminalpolitik, strafrecht (Criminology, crime policy, penal law): Festschrift fur Hans-Jurgen Kerner on the occasion of his 70th birthday* (pp. 441–456). Tubingen, Germany: Mohr Siebeck.

Raynor, P., & Vanstone, M. (2001). 'Straight thinking on Probation': Evidence-based practice and the culture of curiosity. In G. A. Bernfeld, D. P. Farrington, & A. W. Leschied (Eds.), *Offender rehabilitation in practice: Implementing and evaluating effective programmes* (pp. 189–203). Chichester: Wiley.

Reynolds, A. J., Temple, J. A., Ou, S.-R., Arteaga, I. A., & White, B. A. B. (2011). School-based early childhood education and age-28 well-being: Effects by timing dosage and subgroups. *Science, 333*, 360–364.

Reynolds, A. J., Temple, J. A., Robertson, D. L., & Mann, E. A. (2001). Long-term effects of an early childhood intervention on educational achievement and juvenile arrest: A 15-year follow-up of low-income children in public schools. *Journal of the American Medical Association, 285*, 2339–2346.

Roman, J., Dunworth, T., & Marsh, K. (2010). *Cost-benefit analysis and crime control*. Washington, DC: Urban Institute Press.

Ross, R. R., & Ross, B. D. (1988). Delinquency prevention through cognitive training. *New Education, 10*, 70–75.

Ross, R. R., & Ross, R. D. (Eds.) (1995). *Thinking straight: The Reasoning and Rehabilitation programme for delinquency prevention and offender rehabilitation*. Ottawa, Canada: Air Training and Publications.

Sanders, M. R., Markie-Dadds, C., Tully, L. A., & Bor, W. (2000). The Triple P-Positive Parenting Program: A comparison of enhanced, standard and self-directed behavioral family intervention for parents of children with early onset conduct problems. *Journal of Consulting and Clinical Psychology, 68*, 624–640.

Sansfaçon, D., & Waller. I. (2001). Recent evolution of governmental crime prevention strategies and implications for evaluation and economic analysis. In B. C. Welsh, D. P. Farrington, & L. W. Sherman (Eds.), *Costs and benefits of preventing crime* (pp. 225–247). Boulder, CO: Westview Press.

Sawyer, A. M., & Borduin, C. M. (2011). Effects of multisystemic therapy through midlife: A 21.9-year follow-up to a randomized clinical trial with serious and violent juvenile offenders. *Journal of Consulting and Clinical Psychology, 79*, 643–652.

Schaeffer, C. M., & Borduin, C. M. (2005). Long-term follow-up to a randomized clinical trial of multisystemic therapy with serious and violent juvenile offenders. *Journal of Consulting and Clinical Psychology, 73*, 445–453.

Schweinhart, L. J. (2013). Long-term follow-up of a preschool experiment. *Journal of Experimental Criminology, 9*, 389–409.

Schweinhart, L. J., Barnes, H. V., & Weikart, D. P. (1993). *Significant benefits: The High/Scope Perry Preschool Study through age 27*. Ypsilanti, MI: High/Scope Press.

Schweinhart, L. J., Montie, J., Zongping, X., Barnett, W. S., Belfield, C. R., & Nores, M. (2005). *Lifetime effects: The High/Scope Perry Preschool Study through age 40*. Ypsilanti, MI: High/Scope Press.

Schweinhart, L. J., & Weikart, D. P. (1980). *Young children grow up: The effects of the Perry Preschool Program on youths through age 15*. Ypsilanti, MI: High/Scope Press.

Scott, S., Spender, Q., Doolan, M., Jacobs, B., & Aspland, H. (2001). Multicentre controlled trial of parenting groups for child antisocial behaviour in clinical practice. *British Medical Journal, 323*, 194–196.

Scott, S., Sylva, K., Doolan, M., Price, J., Jacobs, B., Crook, C., & Landau, S. (2010). Randomised controlled trial of parent groups for child antisocial behaviour targeting multiple risk factors: The SPOKES project. *Journal of Child Psychology and Psychiatry, 51*, 48–57.

Sexton, T. L., & Alexander, J. F. (2000). *Functional family therapy*. Washington, DC: US Office of Juvenile Justice and Delinquency Prevention.

Sherman, L. W., Farrington, D. P., Welsh, B. C., & MacKenzie, D. L. (Eds.) (2006). *Evidence-based crime prevention* (Rev. ed.). London: Routledge.

Smith, P. K., & Sharp, S. (1994). *School bullying*. London: Routledge.

Steele, M., Marigna, M. K., Tello, J., & Johnson, R. (1999). *Strengthening multi-ethnic families and communities: A violence prevention parent training program*. Los Angeles, CA: Consulting and Clinical Services.

Sutton, C., Utting, D., & Farrington, D. P. (Eds.) (2004). *Support from the start: Working with young children and their families to reduce the risks of crime and antisocial behaviour*. London: Department for Education and Skills (Research Report 524).

Sutton, C., Utting, D., & Farrington, D. P. (2006). Nipping criminality in the bud. *The Psychologist, 19*, 470–475.

Thomas, R., & Zimmer-Gembeck, M. J. (2007). Behavioural outcomes of parent-child interaction therapy and Triple-P positive parenting programme: A review and meta-analysis. *Journal of Abnormal Child Psychology, 35*, 475–495.

Tobler, N. S., Lessard, T., Marshall, D., Ochshorn, P., & Roona, M. (1999). Effectiveness of school-based drug prevention programs for marijuana use. *School Psychology International, 20*, 105–137.

Tong, L. S. J., & Farrington, D. P. (2008). Effectiveness of 'Reasoning and Rehabilitation' in reducing offending. *Psicothema, 20*, 20–28.

Tonry, M., & Farrington, D. P. (1995). Strategic approaches to crime prevention. In M. Tonry & D. P. Farrington (Eds.), *Building a safer society: Strategic approaches to crime prevention* (pp. 1–20). Chicago: University of Chicago Press.

Tremblay, R. E., & Craig, W. M. (1995). Developmental crime prevention. In M. Tonry and D. P. Farrington (Eds.), *Building a safer society: Strategic approaches to crime prevention* (pp. 151–236). Chicago: University of Chicago Press.

Tremblay, R. E., Pagani-Kurtz, L., Masse, L. C., Vitaro, F., & Pihl, R. O. (1995). A bimodal preventive intervention for disruptive kindergarten boys: Its impact through mid-adolescence. *Journal of Consulting and Clinical Psychology, 63*, 560–568.

Ttofi, M. M., & Farrington, D. P. (2011). Effectiveness of school-based programmes to reduce bullying: A systematic and meta-analytic review. *Journal of Experimental Criminology, 7*, 27–56.

Ttofi, M. M., & Farrington, D. P. (2012). Bullying prevention programmes: The importance of peer intervention, disciplinary methods, and age variations. *Journal of Experimental Criminology, 8*, 443–462.

Ttofi, M. M., Farrington, D. P., & Lösel, F. (2012). School bullying as a predictor of violence later in life: A systematic review and meta-analysis of prospective longitudinal studies. *Aggression and Violent Behaviour, 17*, 405–418.

Ttofi, M. M., Farrington, D. P., Lösel, F., & Loeber, R. (2011). The predictive efficiency of school bullying versus later offending: A systematic/meta-analytic review of longitudinal studies. *Criminal Behaviour and Mental Health, 21*, 80–89.

Vitaro, F., Brendgen, M., Giguere, C-E., & Tremblay, R. E. (2013). Early prevention of life-course personal and property violence: A 19-year follow-up of the Montreal Longitudinal-Experimental Study (MLES). *Journal of Experimental Criminology, 9*, 411–427.

Waller, I., & Welsh, B. C. (1999). International trends in crime prevention: Cost-effective ways to reduce victimization. In G. Newman (Ed.), *Global report on crime and justice* (pp. 191–220). New York: Oxford University Press.

Webster-Stratton, C. (1998). Preventing conduct problems in Head Start children: Strengthening parenting competencies. *Journal of Consulting and Clinical Psychology, 66*, 715–730.

Webster-Stratton, C. (2000). *The Incredible Years training series*. Washington, DC: Office of Juvenile Justice and Delinquency Prevention.

Webster-Stratton, C., & Hammond, M. (1997). Treating children with early-onset conduct problems: A comparison of child and parent training interventions. *Journal of Consulting and Clinical Psychology, 65*, 93–109.

Welsh, B. C., & Farrington, D. P. (2011). The benefits and costs of early prevention compared with imprisonment: Toward evidence-based policy. *Prison Journal, 91*(3S1), 120–137.

Welsh, B. C., Farrington, D. P., & Sherman, L. W. (Eds.) (2001). *Costs and benefits of preventing crime*. Boulder, CO: Westview Press.

Welsh, B. C., Sullivan, C. J., & Olds, D. L. (2010). When early crime prevention goes to scale: A new look at the evidence. *Prevention Science, 11*, 115–125.

West, D. J., & Farrington, D. P. (1977). *The delinquent way of life*. London: Heinemann.

Widom, C. S. (1989). The cycle of violence. *Science, 244*, 160–166.

Wilson, D. B., Gottfredson, D. C., & Najaka, S. S. (2001). School-based prevention of problem behaviors: A meta-analysis. *Journal of Quantitative Criminology, 17*, 247–272.

Wilson, J. J., & Howell, J. C. (1993). *A comprehensive strategy for serious, violent, and chronic juvenile offenders*. Washington, DC: US Office of Juvenile Justice and Delinquency Prevention.

Wilson, S. J., & Lipsey, M. W. (2007). School based interventions for aggressive and disruptive behavior: Update of a meta-analysis. *American Journal of Preventive Medicine, 33*(2S), 130–143.

Zara, G., & Farrington, D. P. (2014). Cognitive-behavioural skills training in preventing offending and reducing recidivism. In E. Jiminez & J. L. Alba Robles (Eds.), *Forensic psychology*. Pearson, in press.

10 The Developmental Evidence Base: Psychosocial Research

DAVID P. FARRINGTON

INTRODUCTION

It is plausible to suggest that criminal behaviour results from the interaction between a person (with a certain degree of criminal potential or antisocial tendency) and the environment (which provides criminal opportunities). Given the same environment, some people will be more likely to commit offences than others, and conversely the same person will be more likely to commit offences in some environments than in others (see Farrington, 2005).

Criminological research typically concentrates on either the development of criminal persons or the occurrence of criminal events, but rarely on both. The focus in this chapter is primarily on offenders rather than offences. An advantage of studying offenders is that they are predominantly versatile rather than specialized. The typical offender who commits violence, vandalism or drug abuse also tends to commit theft or burglary. For example, in the Cambridge Study (described later) 86% of violent offenders had convictions for non-violent offences up to age 32 (Farrington, 1991). Also, violent and non-violent but equally frequent offenders were very similar in their childhood and adolescent features in the Cambridge Study, in the Oregon Youth Study (Capaldi & Patterson, 1996) and in the Philadelphia Collaborative Perinatal project (Piquero, 2000). Therefore, in studying offenders, it is unnecessary to develop a different theory for each different type of offence. In contrast, in trying to explain why offences occur, the situations are so diverse and specific to particular crimes that it probably is necessary to have different explanations for different types of offences.

In an attempt to identify possible causes of offending, this chapter reviews risk factors that influence the development of criminal careers. Fortunately or unfortunately, literally hundreds of variables differentiate significantly between official offenders and non-offenders

and correlate significantly with reports of offending behaviour by young people (see Murray & Farrington, 2010). In this chapter, it is only possible to review briefly some of the most important risk factors for the onset and prevalence of offending: individual difference factors such as high impulsivity and low intelligence, family influences such as poor child-rearing and criminal parents, and social influences: socio-economic deprivation, peer, school and community factors. There is not space to review knowledge about protective factors (see Lösel & Farrington, 2012; Farrington, 2003; Farrington, Loeber, & Berg 2012; Farrington & Ttofi, 2012), or risk factors for late onset (see McGee & Farrington, 2010; Murray, Farrington, & Eisner, 2009; Zara & Farrington, 2009).

Within a single chapter, it is obviously impossible to review everything that is known about the psychosocial influences of offending. I will be very selective in focussing on some of the more important and replicable findings obtained in some of the projects with the strongest methodology, namely, prospective longitudinal follow-up studies of large community samples. The better projects are defined here according to their possession of as many as possible of the following criteria:

(a) A large sample size of at least several hundreds

(b) Repeated personal interviews

(c) A large number of different types of variables measured from different data sources (which makes it possible to study the effect of one variable independently of others, or interaction effects)

(d) A longitudinal design spanning at least 5 years (which makes it possible to establish causal order, to study the strength of effects at different ages, and to control extraneous variables better by investigating changes within individuals; see Farrington, 1988)

Forensic Psychology, Second Edition. Edited by David A. Crighton and Graham J. Towl.
© 2015 John Wiley & Sons, Ltd. Published 2015 by British Psychological Society and John Wiley & Sons, Ltd.

(e) A prospectively chosen, community sample (as opposed to retrospective comparisons between prisoners and controls, for example)

(f) Self-reported and official measures of offending (since results replicated with both methods probably provide information about offending rather than about any measurement biases)

Very few projects fulfil all or nearly all of these criteria, and abbreviated details of the most important and long-lasting 20 studies are listed in Table 10.1 (see also Farrington, 2013). This table specifies the principal investigator(s), the sample initially studied, the length of the follow-up period, the most important types of data collected, and a representative publication. I will review results obtained in these projects in this chapter.

TABLE 10.1 *Twenty long-lasting prospective longitudinal surveys of offending*

Elliott, Huizinga (National Youth Survey-Family Study, United States)	Nationally representative US sample of 1,725 adolescents aged 11–17 in 1976. Interviewed in 5 successive years (1977–1981) and subsequently at 3-year intervals up to 1993, and in 2002–2003. Focus on self-reported delinquency, but arrest records collected (Elliott, 1994).
Eron, Huesmann (Columbia County Study, United States)	All 876 third-grade children (aged 8) in Columbia County in New York State first assessed in 1960. Focus on aggressive behaviour. Interviewed at ages 19, 30 and 48. Criminal records searched up to age 48 (Huesmann, Dubow, & Boxer, 2009).
Farrington, West (Cambridge Study in Delinquent Development, United Kingdom)	411 boys aged 8–9 in 1961–1962; all of that age in six London (United Kingdom) schools. Boys interviewed nine times up to age 48, and their children interviewed at age 25. Information also from parents, teachers and peers. Boys and all biological relatives searched in criminal records up to age 56 (Farrington, Piquero, & Jennings, 2013).
Fergusson, Horwood (Christchurch Health and Development Study, New Zealand)	All 1,365 children born in Christchurch in mid-1977. Studied at birth, 4 months, 1 year, annually to age 16, and at ages 18, 21, 25, 30 and 35. Data collected in parental interviews, self-reports, psychometric tests, teacher reports, and official records (Fergusson *et al.*, 2004).
Hawkins, Catalano (Seattle Social Development Project, United States)	808 fifth-grade students (age 10) in 18 elementary schools in Seattle in 1985. Also intervention study. Followed up annually until age 16 and then every 2–3 years up to age 33, with interviews and criminal records (Hawkins *et al.*, 2003).
Huizinga, Esbensen (Denver Youth Survey, United States)	1,528 children aged 7, 9, 11, 13 or 15 in high-risk neighbourhoods of Denver, Colorado, in 1988. Children and parents assessed at yearly intervals up to 1998. Interviews up to age 22–26 in 2003. Focus on self-reported delinquency; arrest data collected up to 2011 (Huizinga, Weiher, Espiritu, & Esbensen, 2003).
Janson, Wikstrom (Project Metropolitan, Sweden)	All 15,117 children born in Stockholm in 1953, and living there in 1963. Tested in schools in 1966. Subsample of mothers interviewed in 1968. Followed up in police records to 1983 (Wikström, 1990).
Kolvin, Miller (Newcastle Thousand Family Study, United Kingdom)	1,142 children born in Newcastle-upon-Tyne in mid-1947. Studied between birth and age 5 and followed up to age 15. Criminal records searched at age 33, and subsamples interviewed (Kolvin *et al.*, 1990).
LeBlanc (Montreal Two-Samples Longitudinal Study, Canada)	Representative sample of 3,070 French-speaking Montreal adolescents. Completed self-report questionnaires in 1974 at age 12–16 and again in 1976. Followed in criminal records to age 50. Males interviewed at ages 30, 40 and 50. Also longitudinal study of 470 male delinquents (LeBlanc & Frechette, 1989).
Loeber, Stouthamer-Loeber, Farrington (Pittsburgh Youth Study, United States)	1,517 boys in first, fourth, or seventh grades of Pittsburgh public schools in 1987–1988 (ages 7, 10, 13). Information from boys, parents, and teachers every 6 months for 3 years, and then every year up to age 19 (youngest) and 25 (oldest). Later follow-ups at ages 28 (youngest) and 34 (oldest). Focus on delinquency, substance use, and mental health problems. Arrests and convictions up to age 35 (Loeber *et al.*, 2003).
Magnusson, Stattin, Bergman, Andershed (Individual Development and Adaptation project, Sweden)	1,027 children aged 10 (all those in third grade) in Orebro in 1965. School follow-up data between ages 13 and 15. Questionnaire and record data up to age 43–45 (Bergman & Andershed, 2009).
McCord (Cambridge-Somerville Youth Study, United States)	650 boys (average age 10) nominated as difficult or average by Cambridge-Somerville (Boston) public schools in 1937–1939. Randomly assigned to treated or control groups. Treated group visited by counsellors for an average of 5 years, and all followed up in 1975–1980 (average age 48) by interviews, mail questionnaires, and criminal records (McCord, 1991).

TABLE 10.1 *(Continued)*

Moffitt, Caspi Dunedin Multidisciplinary Health and Development Study, New Zealand)	1,037 children born in 1972–1973 in Dunedin and first assessed at age 3. Assessed every 2–3 years on health, psychological, education, and family factors up to age 38. Self-reported delinquency measured from age 13. Convictions collected up to age 38 (Moffitt, Caspi, Rutter, & Silva, 2001).
Patterson, Dishion, Capaldi (Oregon Youth Study, United States)	206 fourth-grade boys (age 10) in Eugene/Springfield (Oregon) in 1983–1985. Assessed at yearly intervals, with data from boys, parents, teachers, and peers, to age 37–38. Followed up in criminal records to age 37–38 (Capaldi & Patterson, 1996).
Pulkkinen (Jyvaskyla Longitudinal Study of Personality and Social Development, Finland)	369 children aged 8–9 in Jyvaskyla in 1968. Peer, teacher and self-ratings collected. Followed up five times to age 42 with interviews and questionnaires and in criminal records (Pulkkinen, Lyyra, & Kokko, 2009).
Thornberry, Lizotte, Krohn (Rochester Youth Development Study, United States)	1,000 seventh and eighth graders (age 13–14) in Rochester (New York State) public schools, first assessed in 1988, disproportionally sampled from high-crime neighbourhoods. Followed up initially every 6 months, then every year, then at intervals to age 32. Self-reports and criminal records collected (Thornberry *et al.*, 2003).
Tremblay, Vitaro (Montreal Longitudinal-Experimental Study, Canada)	1,037 French-speaking kindergarten boys (age 6) from poor areas of Montreal assessed by teachers in 1984. Disruptive boys randomly allocated to treatment (parent training plus skills training) or control groups. All boys followed up regularly from age 10 to age 28, including self-reported delinquency and aggression. Criminal records up to age 24 (Tremblay, Vitaro, Nagin, Pagani, & Seguin, 2003).
Wadsworth, Douglas National Survey of Health and Development, United Kingdom)	5,362 children selected from all legitimate single births in England, Scotland and Wales during 1 week of March 1946. Followed in criminal records to age 21. Mainly medical and school data collected, but samples were interviewed at ages 26, 36, 43 and 50 (Wadsworth, 1991).
Werner, Smith (Kauai Longitudinal Study, United States)	698 children born in 1955 in Kauai (Hawaii) assessed at birth and ages 2, 10, 18, 30 and 40. Criminal records up to age 40. Focus on resilience (Werner and Smith, 2001).
Wolfgang, Figlio, Thornberry, Tracy (Philadelphia Birth Cohort Studies, United States)	(1) 9,945 boys born in Philadelphia in 1945 and living there at least from age 10–17. Sample interviewed at age 26 and followed up in police records to age 30 (Wolfgang, Thornberry, & Figlio, 1987). (2) 27,160 children born in Philadelphia in 1958 and living there at least from age 10–17. Followed up in police records to age 26 (Tracy & Kempf-Leonard, 1996).

I will refer especially to knowledge gained in the Cambridge Study in Delinquent Development, which is a prospective longitudinal survey of over 400 London males from age 8 to age 56 (Farrington *et al.*, 2006; Farrington, Coid, & West, 2009; Farrington, Piquero, & Jennings, 2013). Fortunately, results obtained in British longitudinal surveys of delinquency are highly concordant with those obtained in comparable surveys in North America, the Scandinavian countries and New Zealand, and indeed with results obtained in British cross-sectional surveys. For example, a systematic comparison of the Cambridge Study and the Pittsburgh Youth Study showed numerous replicable predictors of offending over time and place, including impulsivity, attention problems, low school attainment, poor parental supervision, parental conflict, an antisocial parent, a young mother, large family size, low family income and coming from a broken family (Farrington & Loeber, 1999).

INDIVIDUAL FACTORS

Temperament and personality

Personality traits such as sociability or impulsiveness describe broad predispositions to respond in certain ways, and temperament is basically the childhood equivalent of personality. The modern study of child temperament began with the New York longitudinal study of Stella Chess and Alexander Thomas (1984). Children in their first 5 years of life were rated on temperamental dimensions by their parents, and these dimensions were combined into three broad categories of easy, difficult and 'slow to warm up' temperament. Having a difficult temperament at age 3–4 (frequent irritability, low amenability and adaptability, irregular habits) predicted poor psychiatric adjustment at age 17–24.

Unfortunately, it was not very clear exactly what a 'difficult' temperament meant in practice, and there was the danger of tautological conclusions (e.g., because the criteria for difficult temperament and 'oppositional defiant disorder' were overlapping). Later researchers have used more specific dimensions of temperament. For example, Jerome Kagan (1989) in Boston classified children as inhibited (shy or fearful) or uninhibited at age 21 months, and found that they remained significantly stable on this classification up to age 7 years. Furthermore, the uninhibited children at age 21 months significantly tended to be identified as aggressive at age 13 years, according to self and parent reports (Schwartz, Snidman, & Kagan, 1996).

Important results on the link between childhood temperament and later offending have been obtained in the Dunedin longitudinal study in New Zealand (Caspi, 2000). Temperament at age 3 years was rated by observing the child's behaviour during a testing session. The most important dimension of temperament was being undercontrolled (restless, impulsive, with poor attention), and this predicted aggression, self-reported delinquency and convictions at age 18–21. In the Pittsburgh Youth Study, Benjamin Lahey and his colleagues (2006) identified three dimensions (low prosociality, negative emotionality and high daring) and showed that all three, measured at age 7, predicted delinquency up to age 17.

Studies using classic personality inventories such as the MMPI and CPI (Wilson & Herrnstein, 1985, pp. 186–198) often seem to produce essentially tautological results, such as that delinquents are low on socialization. The Eysenck personality questionnaire has yielded more promising results (Eysenck, 1996). In the Cambridge Study, those high on both Extraversion and Neuroticism tended to be juvenile self-reported delinquents, adult official offenders and adult self-reported offenders, but not juvenile official delinquents (Farrington, Biron, & LeBlanc, 1982). Furthermore, these relationships held independently of other variables such as low family income, low intelligence, and poor parental child-rearing behaviour. However, when individual items of the personality questionnaire were studied, it was clear that the significant relationships were caused by the items measuring impulsiveness (e.g., doing things quickly without stopping to think). Levine and Jackson (2004) reanalyzed the Eysenck Personality Questionnaire and argued that the most useful scales in relation to self-reported offending were disrespect for rules, need for stimulation, depression and impulsiveness.

Since 1990, the most widely accepted personality system has been the 'Big Five' or five-factor model (McCrae & Costa, 2003). This suggests that there are five key dimensions of personality: Neuroticism (N), Extraversion (E), Openness (O), Agreeableness (A) and Conscientiousness (C). Openness means originality and openness to new ideas, Agreeableness includes nurturance and altruism, and Conscientiousness includes planning and the will to achieve. It is commonly found that low levels of agreeableness and conscientiousness are related to offending (Jones, Miller, & Lynam, 2011; Miller & Lynam, 2001).

Hyperactivity and impulsivity

Impulsiveness is the most crucial personality dimension that predicts antisocial behaviour (Lipsey & Derzon, 1998). Unfortunately, there are a bewildering number of constructs referring to a poor ability to control behaviour. These include impulsiveness, hyperactivity, restlessness, clumsiness, not considering consequences before acting, a poor ability to plan ahead, short time horizons, low self-control, sensation-seeking, risk-taking, and a poor ability to delay gratification. Travis Pratt and his colleagues (2002) carried out a meta-analysis of research on ADHD and delinquency, and concluded that they were strongly associated. Similar conclusions about impulsiveness were drawn by George Higgins and his colleagues (2013) from the US national longitudinal survey of youth.

Many studies show that hyperactivity or 'attention deficit hyperactivity disorder' predicts later offending (e.g., Defoe, Farrington, & Loeber, 2013). In the Copenhagen Perinatal project, hyperactivity (restlessness and poor concentration) at age 11–13 significantly predicted arrests for violence up to age 22, especially among boys whose mothers experienced delivery complications (Brennan, Mednick, & Mednick, 1993). Similarly, in the Orebro longitudinal study in Sweden, hyperactivity at age 13 predicted police-recorded violence up to age 26. The highest rate of violence was among males with both motor restlessness and concentration difficulties (15%), compared to 3% of the remainder (Klinteberg, Andersson, Magnusson, & Stattin, 1993). In the Seattle Social Development Project, hyperactivity and risk taking in adolescence predicted violence in young adulthood (Herrenkohl et al., 2000).

In the Cambridge Study, boys nominated by teachers as lacking in concentration or restless, those nominated by parents, peers, or teachers as the most daring or taking most risks, and those who were the most impulsive on psychomotor tests at age 8–10, all tended to become offenders later in life. Daring, poor concentration and restlessness all predicted both official convictions and self-reported delinquency, and daring was consistently one of the best independent predictors (Farrington, 1992b). Interestingly, hyperactivity predicted juvenile offending independently of conduct problems (Farrington, Loeber, & Van Kammen, 1990). Donald Lynam (1996) proposed that boys with both hyperactivity and conduct disorder were most at risk of chronic offending and psychopathy, and Lynam (1998) presented evidence in favour of this hypothesis from the Pittsburgh Youth Study.

The most extensive research on different measures of impulsiveness was carried out in the Pittsburgh Youth Study by Jennifer White and her colleagues (1994). The measures that were most strongly related to self-reported delinquency at ages 10 and 13 were teacher-rated impulsiveness (e.g., acts without thinking), self-reported impulsiveness, self-reported under-control (e.g., unable to delay gratification), motor restlessness (from video-taped observations), and psychomotor impulsiveness (on the Trail Making Test). Generally, the verbal behaviour rating tests produced stronger relationships with offending than the psychomotor performance tests, suggesting that cognitive impulsiveness (e.g., admitting impulsive behaviour) was more relevant than behavioural impulsiveness (based on test performance). A systematic review (Jolliffe & Farrington, 2009) showed that early measures of impulsiveness (especially daring and risk-taking) predicted later measures of violence.

Low intelligence and attainment

Low IQ and low school achievement also predict delinquency and violence. In the Philadelphia Biosocial project (Denno, 1990), low verbal and performance IQ at ages 4 and 7, and low scores on the California Achievement test at age 13–14 (vocabulary, comprehension, maths, language, spelling) all predicted arrests for violence up to age 22. In Project Metropolitan in Copenhagen, low IQ at age 12 significantly predicted police-recorded violence between ages 15 and 22. The link between low IQ and violence was strongest among lower class boys (Hogh & Wolf, 1983).

Low IQ measured in the first few years of life predicts later delinquency. In a prospective longitudinal survey of about 120 Stockholm males, low IQ measured at age 3 significantly predicted officially recorded offending up to age 30 (Stattin & Klackenberg-Larsson, 1993). Frequent offenders (with four or more offences) had an average IQ of 88 at age 3, whereas non-offenders had an average IQ of 101. All of these results held up after controlling for social class. Similarly, low IQ at age 4 predicted arrests up to age 27 in the Perry preschool project (Schweinhart, Barnes, & Weikart, 1993) and court delinquency up to age 17 in the Collaborative Perinatal Project (Lipsitt, Buka, & Lipsitt 1990).

In the Cambridge Study, twice as many of the boys scoring 90 or less on a nonverbal IQ test (Raven's Progressive Matrices) at age 8–10 were convicted as juveniles as of the remainder (West & Farrington, 1973). However, it was difficult to disentangle low IQ from low school achievement, because they were highly intercorrelated and both predicted delinquency. Low-non-verbal IQ predicted juvenile self-reported delinquency to almost exactly the same degree as juvenile convictions (Farrington, 1992b), suggesting that the link between low IQ and delinquency was not caused by the less intelligent boys having a greater probability of being caught. Also, low IQ and low school achievement predicted offending independently of other variables such as low family income and large family size (Farrington, 1990).

Low IQ may lead to delinquency through the intervening factor of school failure. The association between school failure and delinquency has been demonstrated repeatedly in longitudinal surveys (Maguin & Loeber, 1996). In the Pittsburgh Youth Study, Donald Lynam and his colleagues (1993) concluded that low verbal IQ led to school failure and subsequently to self-reported delinquency, but only for African American boys. An alternative theory is that the link between low IQ and delinquency is mediated by disinhibition (impulsiveness, ADHD, low guilt, low empathy), and this was also tested in the Pittsburgh Youth Study (Koolhof, Loeber, Wei, Pardini, & D'Escury, 2007). In the Christchurch study in New Zealand, low school achievement predicted convictions after controlling for parental criminality, inter-parental violence, single-parent families and deviant peers (Jakobsen, Fergusson, & Horwood, 2012).

A plausible explanatory factor underlying the link between low IQ and delinquency is the ability to manipulate abstract concepts. Children who are poor at this tend to do badly in IQ tests and in school achievement, and they also tend to commit offences, mainly because of their poor ability to foresee the consequences of their offending. Delinquents often do better on non-verbal performance IQ tests, such as object assembly and block design, than on verbal IQ tests (Moffitt, 1993), suggesting that they find it easier to deal with concrete objects than with abstract concepts.

Impulsiveness, attention problems, low IQ and low school achievement could all be linked to deficits in the executive functions of the brain, located in the frontal lobes. These executive functions include sustaining attention and concentration, abstract reasoning, concept formation, goal formulation, anticipation and planning, programming and initiation of purposive sequences of motor behaviour, effective self-monitoring and self-awareness of behaviour and inhibition of inappropriate or impulsive behaviours (Moffitt & Henry, 1991; Morgan & Lilienfeld, 2000). Interestingly, in the Montreal longitudinal-experimental study, a measure of executive functioning based on tests at age 14 was the strongest neuropsychological discriminator between violent and non-violent boys (Seguin, Pihl, Harden, Tremblay, & Boulerice, 1995). This relationship held independently of a measure of family adversity (based on parental age at first birth, parental education level, broken family and low social class). In the Pittsburgh Youth Study, the life-course-persistent offenders had marked neurocognitive impairments (Raine *et al.*, 2005). There is not space here to discuss biological influences on offending (see Raine, 2013).

Low empathy

Numerous other individual factors have been related to delinquency, including depression (Burke, Loeber, Lahey, & Rathouz, 2005), moral judgment (Stams *et al.*, 2006), criminal thinking (Walters, 2002) and social information processing (Lösel *et al.*, 2007). I will focus on empathy, which is related to other concepts such as having callous-unemotional traits (Frick & White, 2008) and being cold, manipulative and Machiavellian (Sutton, Smith, & Swettenham, 1999).

A distinction has often been made between cognitive empathy (understanding or appreciating other people's feelings) and emotional empathy (actually experiencing other people's feelings). Darrick Jolliffe and I (2004) carried out a systematic review of 35 studies comparing questionnaire measures of empathy with official record measures of delinquent or criminal behaviour. We found that low cognitive empathy was strongly related to offending, but low affective empathy was only weakly related. Most importantly, the relationship between low empathy and offending was greatly reduced after controlling for IQ or socio-economic status, suggesting that they might be more important risk factors or that low empathy might mediate the relationship between these risk factors and offending.

Empathy has rarely been investigated in prospective longitudinal studies but there have been important large-scale cross-sectional surveys. In Australia, Anita Mak (1991) found that delinquent females had lower emotional empathy than non-delinquent females, but that there were no significant differences for males. In Finland, Ari Kaukiainen and his colleagues (1999) reported that empathy (cognitive and emotional combined) was negatively correlated with aggression (both measured by peer ratings). In Spain, Maria Luengo and her colleagues (1994) carried out the first project that related cognitive and emotional empathy separately to (self-reported) offending, and found that both were negatively correlated.

Darrick Jolliffe and I (2006) developed a new measure of empathy called the Basic Empathy Scale. An example of a cognitive item is 'It is hard for me to understand when my friends are sad,' and an example of an emotional item is 'I usually feel calm when other people are scared.' In a study of 720 British adolescents aged about 15, we found that low emotional empathy was related to self-reported offending and

violence for both males and females, and to an official record for offending by females (Jolliffe & Farrington, 2007).

FAMILY FACTORS

Child-rearing

Many different types of child-rearing methods predict offending. The most important dimensions of child-rearing are supervision or monitoring of children, discipline or parental reinforcement, warmth or coldness of emotional relationships, and parental involvement with children. Parental supervision refers to the degree of monitoring by parents of the child's activities, and their degree of watchfulness or vigilance. Of all these child-rearing methods, poor parental supervision is usually the strongest and most replicable predictor of offending (Smith & Stern, 1997). In agreement with this, the meta-analysis by Alan Leschied and his colleagues (2008) concluded that parental management that was coercive, inconsistent or lacking in supervision during mid-childhood was a strong predictor of adult criminality.

Many studies show that parents who do not know where their children are when they are out, and parents who let their children roam the streets unsupervised from an early age, tend to have delinquent children. For example, in Joan McCord's (1979) classic Cambridge-Somerville study in Boston, poor parental supervision in childhood was the best predictor of both violent and property crimes up to age 45. In the Cambridge Study, 61% of boys who were poorly supervised at age 8 were convicted up to age 50, compared with 36% of the remainder (Farrington *et al.*, 2009).

Parental discipline refers to how parents react to a child's behaviour. It is clear that harsh or punitive discipline (involving physical punishment) predicts offending (Haapasalo & Pokela, 1999). In their follow-up study of nearly 700 Nottingham children, John and Elizabeth Newson (1989) found that physical punishment at ages 7 and 11 predicted later convictions; 40% of offenders had been smacked or beaten at age 11, compared with 14% of non-offenders. Erratic or inconsistent discipline also predicts delinquency. This can involve either erratic discipline by one parent, sometimes turning a blind eye to bad behaviour and sometimes punishing it severely, or inconsistency between two parents, with one parent being tolerant or indulgent and the other being harshly punitive.

Cold, rejecting parents tend to have delinquent children, as Joan McCord (1979) found in the Cambridge-Somerville study. She also concluded that parental warmth could act as a protective factor against the effects of physical punishment (McCord, 1997). Whereas 51% of boys with cold physically punishing mothers were convicted in her study, only 21% of boys with warm physically punishing mothers were convicted, similar to the 23% of boys with warm non-punitive mothers who were convicted. The father's warmth was also a protective factor against the father's physical punishment. Childhood neglect predicted self-reported and official offending in the Cambridge Study (Kazemian, Widom, & Farrington, 2011).

The classic longitudinal study by Lee Robins (1979) in St. Louis shows that poor parental supervision, harsh discipline and a rejecting attitude all predict delinquency. Also, in the Seattle Social Development Project, poor family management (poor supervision, inconsistent rules and harsh discipline) in adolescence predicted violence in young adulthood (Herrenkohl et al., 2000). Similar results were obtained in the Cambridge Study. Harsh or erratic parental discipline, cruel, passive or neglecting parental attitudes and poor parental supervision, all measured at age 8, all predicted later juvenile convictions and self-reported delinquency (West & Farrington, 1973). Generally, the presence of any of these adverse family background features doubled the risk of a later juvenile conviction.

Laurence Steinberg and his colleagues (1992) distinguished an authoritarian style of parenting (punitively emphasizing obedience) from an authoritative style (granting autonomy with good supervision). In the Cambridge Study (Farrington, 1994), having authoritarian parents was the second most important predictor of convictions for violence (after hyperactivity/poor concentration). Interestingly, having authoritarian parents was the most important childhood risk factor that discriminated between violent offenders and frequently convicted non-violent offenders (Farrington, 1991).

Most explanations of the link between child-rearing methods and delinquency focus on attachment or social learning theories. Attachment theory was inspired by the work of John Bowlby (1951), and suggests that children who are not emotionally attached to warm, loving and law-abiding parents tend to become offenders. Social learning theories suggest that children's behaviour depends on parental rewards and punishments and on the models of behaviour that parents represent (Patterson, 1995). Children will tend to become offenders if parents do not respond consistently and contingently to their antisocial behaviour and if parents themselves behave in an antisocial manner.

James Derzon (2010) carried out a meta-analysis of family factors as predictors of criminal and violent behaviour (as well as aggressive and problem behaviour). This meta-analysis was based on longitudinal studies, but many predictions were over short time periods (less than 4 years in 55% of cases), many outcome variables were measured at relatively young ages (up to age 15 in 40% of cases) and many studies were relatively small (less than 200 participants in 43% of cases). The strongest predictors of criminal or violent behaviour were low parental education ($r = .30$ for criminal behaviour), poor parental supervision ($r = .29$ for violent behaviour), poor child rearing skills ($r = .26$ for criminal behaviour), parental discord ($r = .26$ for criminal behaviour) and large family size ($r = .24$ for violent behaviour). Notably weak predictors were young parents, broken homes and low socio-economic status.

Teenage mothers and child abuse

At least in Western industrialized countries, early childbearing, or teenage pregnancy, predicts many undesirable outcomes for the children, including low school attainment, antisocial school behaviour, substance use and early sexual intercourse. The children of teenage mothers are also more likely to become offenders. For example, Merry Morash and Lila Rucker (1989) analyzed results from four surveys in the United States and United Kingdom (including the Cambridge Study) and found that teenage mothers were associated with low-income families, welfare support and absent biological fathers, that they used poor child-rearing methods and that their children were characterized by low school attainment and delinquency. However, the presence of the biological father mitigated many of these adverse factors and generally seemed to have a protective effect. In the Cambridge Study, teenage mothers who went on to have large numbers of children were especially likely to have convicted children (Nagin, Pogarsky, & Farrington, 1997). In the Newcastle Thousand-Family study mothers who married as teenagers (a factor strongly related to teenage childbearing) were twice as likely as others to have sons who became offenders by age 32 (Kolvin, Miller, Scott, Gatzanis, & Fleeting, 1990).

Several researchers have investigated factors that might mediate the link between young mothers and child delinquency. In the Dunedin study in New Zealand, Sara Jaffee and her colleagues (2001) concluded that the link between teenage mothers and violent children was mediated by maternal characteristics (e.g., intelligence, criminality) and family factors (e.g., harsh discipline, family size, disrupted families). In the Rochester Youth Development Study, Greg Pogarsky and his colleagues (2003) found that the most important mediating factor was the number of parental transitions (frequent changes in caregivers). Much research suggests that frequent changes of parent figures predict offending by children (e.g., Krohn, Hall, & Lizotte, 2009; Thornberry, Smith, Rivera, Huizinga, & Stouthamer-Loeber, 1999).

Children who are physically abused tend to become violent offenders, as Michael Maxfield and Cathy Widom (1996) showed in a retrospective study of over 900 abused children in Indianapolis. In the Cambridge-Somerville study in Boston, Joan McCord (1983) found that about half of the abused or neglected boys were convicted for serious crimes, became alcoholics or mentally ill, or died before age 35. Child maltreatment before age 12 was one of the most consistent predictors of violence and serious theft in the Pittsburgh Youth Study (Loeber, Farrington, Stouthamer-Loeber, & White, 2008). In the Rochester Youth Development Study, child maltreatment under age 12 (physical, sexual or emotional abuse or neglect) predicted later self-reported and official offending (Smith & Thornberry, 1995). Furthermore, these results held up after controlling for gender, race, socio-economic status and family structure. Also, Margaret Keiley and her colleagues (2001) reported that maltreatment under age 5 was more damaging than maltreatment between ages 6 and 9. The extensive review by Robin Malinosky-Rummell and David Hansen (1993) confirms that being physically abused as a child predicts later violent and non-violent offending.

Possible causal mechanisms linking childhood victimization and adolescent offending have been reviewed by Cathy Widom (1994). First, childhood victimization may have immediate but long-lasting consequences (e.g., shaking may cause brain injury). Second, childhood victimization may cause bodily changes (e.g., desensitization to pain) that encourage later aggression. Third, child abuse may lead to impulsive or dissociative coping styles that, in turn, lead to poor problem-solving skills or poor school performance. Fourth, victimization may cause changes in self-esteem or in social information-processing patterns that encourage later aggression. Fifth, child abuse may lead to changed family environments (e.g., being placed in foster care) that have harmful effects. Sixth, juvenile justice practices may label victims, isolate them from prosocial peers and encourage them to associate with delinquent peers.

Parental conflict and disrupted families

There is no doubt that parental conflict and interparental violence predict adolescent antisocial behaviour (Buehler et al., 1997; Ireland & Smith, 2009). In the Christchurch Study in New Zealand, children who witnessed violence between their parents were more likely to commit both violent and property offences according to their self-reports (Fergusson & Horwood, 1998). Witnessing father-initiated violence was still predictive after controlling for other risk factors such as parental criminality, parental substance abuse, parental physical punishment, a young mother and low family income. Parental conflict also predicted delinquency in both the Cambridge and Pittsburgh studies (Farrington & Loeber, 1999).

Many studies show that broken homes or disrupted families predict delinquency. In the Newcastle Thousand-Family Study, Israel Kolvin and his colleagues (1988) reported that marital disruption (divorce or separation) in a boy's first 5 years predicted his later convictions up to age 32. Similarly, in the Dunedin study in New Zealand, Bill Henry and his colleagues (1993) found that children who were exposed to parental discord and many changes of the primary caretaker tended to become antisocial and delinquent. In the US National Longitudinal Survey of Adolescent Health, Stephen Demuth and Susan Brown (2004) concluded that single-parent families predicted delinquency because of their lower levels of parental supervision, closeness and involvement with children.

The importance of the cause of the broken home was demonstrated by Michael Wadsworth (1979) in the UK National Survey of Health and Development. Boys from homes broken by divorce or separation had an increased likelihood of being convicted or officially cautioned up to age 21, in comparison with those from homes broken by death or from unbroken homes. Homes broken while the boy was under age 5 especially predicted offending, while homes broken while the boy was between ages 11 and 15 were not particularly criminogenic. Remarriage (which happened more often after divorce or separation than after death) was also associated with an increased risk of offending, suggesting a possible negative effect of step-parents. The meta-analysis by Edward Wells and Joseph Rankin (1991) also indicates that broken homes are more strongly related to delinquency when they are caused by parental separation or divorce rather than by death.

Most studies of broken homes have focussed on the loss of the father rather than the mother, simply because the loss of a father is much more common. Joan McCord (1982) in Boston carried out an interesting study of the relationship between homes broken by loss of the natural father and later serious offending of the children. She found that the prevalence of offending was high for boys reared in broken homes without affectionate mothers (62%) and for those reared in united homes characterized by parental conflict (52%), irrespective of whether they had affectionate mothers. The prevalence of offending was low for those reared in united homes without conflict (26%) and – importantly – equally low for boys from broken homes with affectionate mothers (22%). These results suggest that it is not so much the broken home which is criminogenic as the parental conflict which often causes it, and that a loving mother might in some sense be able to compensate for the loss of a father.

Few longitudinal studies of offending have begun before age 7 or 8. However, in the British Cohort Study of children born in 1970, Joseph Murray and his colleagues (2010) investigated the extent to which very early risk factors (measured up to age 5) predicted self-reported convictions at ages 30 and 34. Murray and his colleagues found that the strongest early predictors were a single mother, a teenage mother, maternal smoking during pregnancy, loss of a biological parent and family deprivation (low social class, low parental education, poverty and household overcrowding). The likelihood of a conviction increased with the early risk score, from 17% to 44% for boys and from 3% to 11% for girls.

In the Cambridge Study, both permanent and temporary separations from a biological parent before age 10 (usually from the father) predicted convictions and self-reported delinquency, providing that they were not caused by death or hospitalization (Farrington, 1992b). However, homes broken at an early age (under age 5) were not unusually criminogenic (West & Farrington, 1973). Separation before age 10 predicted both juvenile and adult convictions (Farrington, 1992a), and it predicted adult convictions independently of other factors such as low family income or poor school attainment; 60% of boys who had been separated from a parent by their tenth birthday were convicted up to age 50, compared with 36% of the remainder (Farrington et al., 2009). It seems that broken homes caused hyperactivity, which in turn caused offending (Theobald, Farrington, & Piquero, 2013).

Explanations of the relationship between disrupted families and delinquency fall into three major classes. Trauma theories suggest that the loss of a parent has a damaging effect on a child, most commonly because of the effect on attachment to the parent. Life-course theories focus on separation as a sequence of stressful experiences, and on the effects of multiple stressors such as parental conflict, parental loss, reduced economic circumstances, changes in parent figures and poor child-rearing methods. Selection theories argue that disrupted families produce delinquent children because of pre-existing differences from other families in risk factors such as parental conflict, criminal or antisocial parents, low family income or poor child-rearing methods.

Hypotheses derived from the three theories were tested in the Cambridge Study (Juby & Farrington, 2001). While boys from broken homes (permanently disrupted families) were more delinquent than boys from intact homes, they were not more delinquent than boys from intact high conflict families. Overall, the most important factor was the post-disruption trajectory. Boys who remained with their mother after the separation had the same delinquency rate as boys from intact low conflict families. Boys who stayed with their father, with relatives or with others (e.g., foster parents) had high delinquency rates. These living arrangements were more unstable, and other research shows that frequent changes of parent figures predict offending. It was concluded that the results favoured life-course theories rather than trauma or selection theories.

Criminal parents

Lee Robins and her colleagues (1975) showed that criminal, antisocial and alcoholic parents tend to have delinquent sons. Robins followed up over 200 males in St. Louis and found that arrested parents tended to have arrested children, and that the juvenile records of the parents and children had similar rates and types of offences. Joan McCord (1977) also reported that convicted fathers tended to have convicted sons. She found that 29% of fathers convicted for violence had sons convicted for violence, in comparison with 12% of other fathers, but this may reflect the general tendency for convicted fathers to have convicted sons rather than any specific tendency for violent fathers to have violent sons.

In the Cambridge Study, the concentration of offending in a small number of families was remarkable (Farrington et al., 1996). Less than 6% of the families were responsible for half of the criminal convictions of all members (fathers, mothers, sons, and daughters) of all 400 families. Having a convicted mother, father, brother or sister significantly predicted a boy's own convictions. As many as 63% of boys with a convicted parent were themselves convicted up to age 40. Furthermore, convicted parents and delinquent siblings predicted self-reported as well as official offending (Farrington, 1979). Same-sex relationships were stronger than opposite-sex relationships, and older siblings were stronger predictors than younger siblings. Therefore, there is intergenerational continuity in offending.

Similar results were obtained in the Pittsburgh Youth Study. Arrests of fathers, mothers, brothers, sisters, uncles, aunts, grandfathers and grandmothers all predicted the boy's own delinquency (Farrington, Jolliffe, Loeber, Stouthamer-Loeber, & Kalb, 2001). The most important relative was the father; arrests of the father predicted the boy's delinquency independently of all other arrested relatives. Only 8% of families accounted for 43% of arrested family members. Similarly, in the Dunedin study in New Zealand, the antisocial behaviour of grandparents, parents, and siblings predicted the antisocial behaviour of boys (Odgers et al., 2007). Similar results were obtained in a large-scale criminal record study of all families who had a child born in 2006 in a Dutch city (Junger, Greene, Schipper, Hesper, & Estourgie, 2013).

While arrests and convictions of fathers predicted antisocial behaviour of boys, imprisonment of fathers before boys were aged 10 further increased the risk of later antisocial and delinquent outcomes in the Cambridge Study (Murray & Farrington, 2005). Interestingly, the effect of parental imprisonment in Sweden (in Project Metropolitan) disappeared after controlling for parental criminality (Murray, Janson, & Farrington, 2007). This cross-national difference may have been the result of shorter prison sentences in Sweden, more family-friendly prison policies, a welfare-oriented juvenile justice system, an extended social welfare system or more sympathetic public attitudes towards prisoners (see also Murray, Bijleveld, Farrington, & Loeber, 2014).

It is not entirely clear why criminal parents tend to have delinquent children. In the Cambridge Study, there was no evidence that criminal parents directly encouraged their children to commit crimes or taught them criminal techniques. On the contrary, criminal parents were highly critical of their children's offending; for example, 89% of convicted men at age 32 disagreed with the statement that 'I would not mind if my son/daughter committed a criminal offence'. Also, it was extremely rare for a parent and a child to be convicted for an offence committed together. The main link in the chain between criminal parents and delinquent sons seemed to be poor parental supervision (West & Farrington, 1977). In the Rochester Youth Development Study, Terence Thornberry and his colleagues (2009) concluded that the continuity from parental self-reported offending to child antisocial behaviour was primarily mediated by ineffective parenting and parental stress.

There are several possible explanations (which are not mutually exclusive) for why offending tends to be concentrated in certain families and transmitted from one generation to the next. First, there may be intergenerational continuities in exposure to multiple risk factors. For example, each successive generation may be entrapped in poverty, disrupted families, single and/or teenage parenting, and living in the most deprived neighbourhoods. Second, the effect of a criminal parent on a child's offending may be mediated by environmental mechanisms such as poor parental supervision. Third, this effect may be mediated by genetic mechanisms.

Fourth, criminal parents may tend to have delinquent children because of official (police and court) bias against criminal families, who also tend to be known to official agencies because of other social problems (Besemer, Farrington, & Bijleveld, 2013). At all levels of self-reported delinquency in the Cambridge Study, boys with convicted fathers were more likely to be convicted themselves than were boys with unconvicted fathers (West & Farrington, 1977). However, this was not the only explanation for the link between criminal fathers and delinquent sons, because boys with criminal fathers had higher self-reported delinquency scores and higher teacher and peer ratings of bad behaviour.

Large family size

Large family size (a large number of children in the family) is a relatively strong and highly replicable predictor of offending (Ellis, 1988). It was similarly important in the Cambridge and Pittsburgh studies, even though families were on average smaller in Pittsburgh in the 1990s than in London in the 1960s (Farrington & Loeber, 1999). In the Cambridge Study, if a boy had four or more siblings by his tenth birthday, this doubled his risk of being convicted as a juvenile, and large family size predicted self-reported offending as well as convictions (Farrington, 1992b). It was the most important independent predictor of convictions up to age 32 in a logistic regression analysis (Farrington, 1993).

In the National Survey of Health and Development, Michael Wadsworth (1979) found that the percentage of boys who were convicted increased from 9% for families containing one child to 24% for families containing four or more children. John Newson and his colleagues (1993), in their Nottingham study, also concluded that large family size was one of the most important predictors of offending. A similar link between large family size and antisocial behaviour was reported by Israel Kolvin and his colleagues (1990) in their follow-up of Newcastle children from birth to age 33.

There are many possible reasons why a large number of siblings might increase the risk of a child's offending. Generally, as the number of children in a family increases, the amount of parental attention that can be given to each child decreases. Also, as the number of children increases, the household tends to become more overcrowded, possibly leading to increases in frustration, irritation and conflict. In the Cambridge Study, large family size did not predict delinquency for boys living in the least crowded conditions (West & Farrington, 1973). This suggests that household overcrowding might be an important intervening factor between large family size and delinquency.

David Brownfield and Ann Sorenson (1994) reviewed several possible explanations for the link between large families and delinquency, including those focussing on features of the parents (e.g., criminal parents, teenage parents), those focussing on parenting (e.g., poor supervision, disrupted families) and those focussing on economic deprivation or family stress. Another interesting theory suggested that the key factor was birth order: large families include more later-born children, who tend to be more delinquent. Based on an analysis of self-reported delinquency in a Seattle survey, they concluded that the most plausible intervening causal mechanism was exposure to delinquent siblings. In the Cambridge Study, co-offending by brothers was surprisingly common; about 20% of boys who had brothers close to them in age were convicted for a crime committed with their brother (Reiss and Farrington, 1991).

SOCIAL FACTORS

Socio-economic deprivation

The voluminous literature on the relationship between socio-economic status (SES) and offending is characterized by inconsistencies and contradictions, and some reviewers (e.g., Thornberry & Farnworth, 1982) have concluded that there is no relationship between SES and either self-reported or official offending. British studies have reported more consistent links between low social class and offending. In the UK National Survey of Health and Development, Michael Wadsworth (1979) found that the prevalence of official juvenile delinquency in males varied considerably according to the occupational prestige and educational background of their parents, from 3% in the highest category to 19% in the lowest.

Numerous indicators of SES were measured in the Cambridge Study, both for the boy's family of origin and for the boy himself as an adult, including occupational prestige, family income, housing, and employment instability. Most of the measures of occupational prestige (based on the Registrar General's scale) were not significantly related to offending. Low SES of the family when the boy was aged 8–10 significantly predicted his later self-reported but not his official delinquency. More consistently, low family income and poor housing predicted official and self-reported, juvenile and adult, offending (Farrington, 1992a, 1992b).

It was interesting that the peak age of offending, at 17–18, coincided with the peak age of affluence for many convicted males. In the Cambridge Study, convicted males tended to come from low-income families at age 8 and later tended to have low incomes themselves at age 32. However, at age 18, they were relatively well paid in comparison with non-delinquents (West & Farrington, 1977). Whereas convicted delinquents might be working as unskilled labourers on building sites and getting the full adult wage for this job, non-delinquents might be in poorly paid jobs with prospects, such as bank clerks, or might still be students. These results show that the link between income and offending is quite complex.

Socio-economic deprivation of parents is usually compared to offending by children. However, when the children grow up, their own socio-economic deprivation can be related to their own offending. In the Cambridge Study, official and self-reported delinquents tended to have unskilled manual jobs and an unstable job record at age 18. Just as an erratic work record of his father predicted the later offending of the study boy, an unstable job record of the boy at age 18 was one of the best independent predictors of his own convictions between ages 21 and 25 (Farrington, 1986). Between ages 15 and 18, the study boys were convicted at a higher rate when they were unemployed than when they were employed (Farrington, Gallagher, Morley, St. Ledger, & West, 1986), suggesting that unemployment in some way causes crime, and conversely that employment may lead to desistance from offending. Since crimes involving material gain (e.g., theft, burglary, robbery) especially increased during periods of unemployment, it seems likely that financial need is an important link in the causal chain between unemployment and crime.

Several researchers have suggested that the link between a low SES family and antisocial behaviour is mediated by family socialization practices. For example, Richard Larzelere and Gerald Patterson (1990) in the Oregon Youth Study concluded that the effect of SES on delinquency was entirely mediated by parent management skills. In other words, low SES predicted delinquency because low SES families used poor child-rearing practices. In the Christchurch Health and Development Study, David Fergusson and his colleagues (2004) reported that living in a low SES family between birth and age 6 predicted self-reported and official delinquency between ages 15 and 21. However, this association disappeared after controlling for family factors (physical punishment, maternal care, and parental changes), conduct problems, truancy, and deviant peers, suggesting that these may have been mediating factors.

Peer influences

Having delinquent friends is an important predictor of later offending. Sara Battin and her colleagues (1998) showed that peer delinquency predicted self-reported violence in the Seattle Social Development Project. Delinquent acts tend to be committed in small groups (of two or three people, usually) rather than alone. Large gangs are comparatively unusual. In the Cambridge Study, the probability of committing offences with others decreased steadily with age. Before age 17, boys tended to commit their crimes with other boys similar in age and living close by. After age 17, co-offending became less common (Reiss & Farrington, 1991).

The major problem of interpretation is whether young people are more likely to commit offences while they are in groups than while they are alone, or whether the high prevalence of co-offending merely reflects the fact that, whenever young people go out, they tend to go out in groups. Do peers tend to encourage and facilitate offending, or is it just that most kinds of activities out of the home (both delinquent and non-delinquent) tend to be committed in groups? Another possibility is that the commission of offences encourages association with other delinquents, perhaps because 'birds of a feather flock together' or because of the stigmatizing and isolating effects of court appearances and institutionalization. Terence Thornberry and his colleagues (1994) in the Rochester Youth Development Study concluded that there were reciprocal effects, with delinquent peers causing delinquency and delinquency causing association with delinquent peers.

In the Pittsburgh Youth Study, the relationship between peer delinquency and a boy's offending was studied both between individuals (e.g., comparing peer delinquency and offending over all boys at a particular age and then aggregating these correlations over all ages) and within individuals (e.g., comparing peer delinquency and offending of a boy at all his ages and then aggregating these correlations over all boys). Peer delinquency was the strongest correlate of offending in between-individual correlations but did not predict offending within individuals (Farrington, Loeber, Yin, & Anderson, 2002). In contrast, poor parental supervision, low parental reinforcement and low involvement of the boy in family activities predicted offending both between and within individuals. It was concluded that these three family variables were the most likely to be causes, whereas having delinquent peers was most likely to be an indicator of the boy's offending.

It is clear that young people increase their offending after joining a gang. In the Seattle Social Development Project, Sara Battin and her colleagues (1998) found this, and also showed that gang membership predicted delinquency above and beyond having delinquent friends. In the Pittsburgh Youth Study, Rachel Gordon and her colleagues (2004) reported not only a substantial increase in drug selling, drug use, violence and property crime after a boy joined a gang, but also that the frequency of offending decreased to pre-gang levels after a boy left a gang. Terence Thornberry and his colleagues (2003) in the Rochester Youth Development Study and Uberto Gatti and his colleagues (2005) in the Montreal longitudinal-experimental study also found that young people offended more after joining a gang. Several of these studies contrasted the 'selection' and 'facilitation' hypotheses and concluded that future gang members were more delinquent to start with but became even more delinquent after joining a gang. Gang membership in adolescence is a risk factor for later violence (Herrenkohl et al., 2000), but this may be because both are measuring the same underlying construct.

Associating with delinquent friends at age 14 was an important independent predictor of convictions at the young adult ages in the Cambridge Study (Farrington, 1986). Also, the recidivists at age 19 who ceased offending differed from those who persisted, in that the desisters were more likely to have stopped going round in a group of male friends. Furthermore, spontaneous comments by the youths indicated that withdrawal from the delinquent peer group was an important influence on ceasing to offend (West & Farrington, 1977). Therefore, continuing to associate with delinquent friends may be a key factor in determining whether juvenile delinquents persist in offending as young adults or desist.

SCHOOL INFLUENCES

The prevalence of delinquency among students varies dramatically between different secondary schools, as Michael Power and his colleagues (1967) showed many years ago in London. Characteristics of high-delinquency-rate schools are well known (Graham, 1988). For example, such schools have high levels of distrust between teachers and students, low commitment to the school by the students, and unclear and inconsistently enforced rules. However, what is much less clear is how much of the variation between schools should be attributed to differences in school organization, climate and practices, and how much to differences in the composition of the student body.

In the Cambridge Study, attending a high delinquency-rate school at age 11 significantly predicted a boy's later offending (Farrington, 1992b). The effects of secondary schools on delinquency were investigated by following boys from their primary schools to their secondary schools (Farrington, 1972). The best primary school predictor of juvenile delinquency was the rating of the boy's troublesomeness at age 8–10 by peers and teachers, showing the continuity in antisocial behaviour. The secondary schools differed dramatically in their official delinquency rates, from one school with 21 court appearances per 100 boys per year to another where the corresponding figure was only 0.3. Moreover, going to a high-delinquency-rate secondary school was a significant predictor of later convictions.

It was, however, very noticeable that the most troublesome boys tended to go to the high delinquency-rate schools, while the least troublesome boys tended to go to the low delinquency-rate schools. Most of the variation between schools in their delinquency rates could be explained by differences in their intakes of troublesome boys. The secondary schools themselves had only a very small effect on the boys' offending. However, reviews of American research show that schools with clear, fair and consistently enforced rules tend to have low rates of student misbehaviour (Gottfredson, 2001; Herrenkohl, Hawkins, Chung, Hill, & Battin-Pearson, 2001).

The most famous UK study of school effects on delinquency was also carried out in London, by Michael

Rutter and his colleagues (1979). They studied 12 comprehensive schools, and again found big differences in official delinquency rates between them. High-delinquency-rate schools tended to have high truancy rates, low-ability pupils and low-social-class parents. However, the differences between the schools in delinquency rates could not be entirely explained by differences in the social class and verbal reasoning scores of the pupils at intake (age 11). Therefore, they must have been caused by some aspect of the schools themselves or by other unmeasured factors.

In trying to discover which aspects of schools might be encouraging or inhibiting offending, Rutter and his colleagues found that the main school factors that were associated with delinquency were a high amount of punishment and a low amount of praise given by teachers in class. Unfortunately, it is difficult to know whether much punishment and little praise are causes or consequences of antisocial school behaviour, which in turn may be linked to offending outside school. In regard to other outcome measures, they argued that an academic emphasis, good classroom management, the careful use of praise and punishment, and student participation were important features of successful schools. (For a review of research on schools and delinquency, see Payne & Welch, 2013.)

COMMUNITY INFLUENCES

Many studies show that boys living in urban areas are more criminal than those living in rural areas (Derzon, 2010; Foster & Brooks-Gunn, 2013). In the US National Youth Survey, the prevalence of self-reported assault and robbery was considerably higher among urban youth (Elliott, Huizinga, & Menard, 1989). Within urban areas, boys living in high-crime neighbourhoods are more violent than those living in low-crime neighbourhoods. In the Rochester Youth Development Study, living in a high-crime neighbourhood significantly predicted self-reported violence (Thornberry, Huizinga, & Loeber, 1995). Similarly, in the Pittsburgh Youth Study, living in a bad neighbourhood (either as rated by the mother or based on census measures of poverty, unemployment and female-headed households) significantly predicted official and reported violence (Farrington, 1998) and homicide offending (Farrington et al., 2012).

Robert Sampson and his colleagues (1997) studied community influences on violence in the Project on Human Development in Chicago Neighbourhoods. The most important community predictors were concentrated economic disadvantage (as indexed by poverty, the proportion of female-headed families and the proportion of African Americans), immigrant concentration (the proportions of Latinos or foreign-born persons), residential instability, and low levels of informal social control and social cohesion. They suggested that the 'collective efficacy' of a neighbourhood, or the willingness of residents to intervene to prevent antisocial behaviour, might act as a protective factor against crime. In the same project, Sampson and his colleagues (2005) concluded that most of the difference between African Americans and Caucasians in violence could be explained by racial differences in exposure to risk factors, especially living in a bad neighbourhood. Similar conclusions were drawn in the Pittsburgh Youth Study (Farrington, Loeber, & Stouthamer-Loeber, 2003).

It is clear that offenders disproportionately live in inner-city areas characterized by physical deterioration, neighbourhood disorganization and high residential mobility (Shaw and McKay, 1969). However, again, it is difficult to determine to what extent the areas themselves influence antisocial behaviour and to what extent it is merely the case that antisocial people choose to live in deprived areas (e.g., because of their poverty or public housing allocation policies). Interestingly, both neighbourhood researchers such as Denise Gottfredson and her colleagues (1991) and developmental researchers such as Michael Rutter (1981) have argued that neighbourhoods have only indirect effects on antisocial behaviour through their effects on individuals and families. In the Chicago Youth Development Study, Patrick Tolan and his colleagues (2003) concluded that the relationship between community structural characteristics (concentrated poverty, racial heterogeneity, economic resources, violent crime rate) and individual violence was mediated by parenting practices, gang membership and peer violence.

In the Pittsburgh Youth Study, Per-Olof Wikström and Rolf Loeber (2000) found an interesting interaction between types of people and types of areas. Six individual, family, peer and school variables were trichotomized into risk, middle or protective scores and added up. Boys with the highest risk scores tended to be delinquent irrespective of the type of area in which they were living. However, boys with high protective scores or balanced risk and protective scores were more likely to be delinquent if they were living in disadvantaged public housing areas. Hence, the area risk was most important when other risks were not high. In the same study, Donald Lynam and his colleagues (2000) found that the effects of impulsiveness on self-reported offending were greater in low-SES neighbourhoods than in high-SES neighbourhoods, possibly because there were more criminal opportunities in more disorganized neighbourhoods.

Clearly, there is an interaction between individuals and the communities in which they live. Some aspects of an inner-city neighbourhood may be conducive to offending, perhaps because the inner city leads to a breakdown of community ties or neighbourhood patterns of mutual support, or perhaps because the high population density produces tension, frustration, or anonymity. There may be many interrelated factors. As Albert Reiss (1986) argued, high-crime-rate areas often have a high concentration of single-parent female-headed households with low incomes, living in low-cost, poor housing. The weakened parental control in these families – partly caused by the fact that the mother had to work and left her children largely unsupervised – meant that the children tended to congregate on the streets. In consequence, they were influenced by a peer subculture that often encouraged and reinforced offending. This interaction of individual, family, peer and neighbourhood factors may be the rule rather than the exception.

CONCLUSIONS

A great deal has been learned in the last 40 years, particularly from longitudinal surveys, about risk factors for offending and other types of antisocial behaviour. Offenders differ significantly from non-offenders in many respects, including impulsiveness, empathy, low IQ and low school achievement, poor parental supervision, child physical abuse, punitive or erratic parental discipline, cold parental attitude, parental conflict, disrupted families, antisocial parents, large family size, low family income, antisocial peers, high-delinquency-rate schools and high-crime neighbourhoods. These differences are present before, during and after criminal careers. While the precise causal chains that link these factors with antisocial behaviour, and the ways in which these factors have independent, interactive or sequential effects, are not well understood, it is clear that individuals at risk can be identified with reasonable accuracy. More longitudinal studies are needed in different countries, with frequent measurement of risk factors and offending.

The comorbidity and versatility of antisocial behaviour pose a major challenge to scientific understanding. It is important to investigate to what extent research findings are driven by a minority of multiple problem adolescents or chronic delinquents. Often, multiple risk factors lead to multiple problem boys (Farrington, 2002; Loeber, Farrington, Stouthamer-Loeber, & Van Kammen, 1998).

To what extent any given risk factor generally predicts a variety of different outcomes (as opposed to specifically predicting one or two outcomes) and to what extent each outcome is generally predicted by a variety of different risk factors (as opposed to being specifically predicted by only one or two risk factors) is unclear. An increasing number of risk factors leads to an increasing probability of antisocial outcomes, almost irrespective of the particular risk factors included in the prediction measure, but more research is needed on this. There was insufficient space in this chapter to review theories explaining the links between risk factors and antisocial outcomes, but these have to be based on knowledge about the additive, independent, interactive and sequential effects of risk factors (see Farrington, 2005).

While a great deal is known about risk factors for offending, less is known about causes, or about causal pathways or mechanisms. Ideally, intervention programmes should target causes of offending. The best way of establishing causes is to carry out experimental or quasi-experimental analyses. For example, if an intervention experiment succeeded in reducing impulsivity and if there was a consequent reduction in offending, this would indicate that impulsivity might be a cause of offending (Robins, 1992). Similarly, if changes within individuals in parental supervision were reliably followed by changes within individuals in offending, this would indicate that parental supervision might be a cause of offending (Farrington, 1988).

Based on current knowledge, the following factors should be prime targets for intervention efforts: impulsiveness, low school achievement, poor child-rearing methods, young mothers, child abuse, parental conflict and disrupted families, poverty, delinquent peers and deprived neighbourhoods. Efforts should be made to reduce impulsiveness and/or enhance self-control, to increase school achievement, to improve child-rearing, to encourage young people not to have children at an early age, to discourage child abuse, to increase parental harmony, to decrease poverty, to decrease association with antisocial peers and increase association with prosocial peers and to improve bad neighbourhoods. In this way, knowledge from psychosocial research can help to reduce crime and to increase the well-being of individuals and communities.

FURTHER READING

Farrington, D. P., & Welsh, B. C. (2007). *Saving children from a life of crime: Early risk factors and effective interventions.* Oxford: Oxford University Press.
This book discusses the meaning of risk and protective factors, key issues in risk factor research, and major prospective longitudinal surveys of offending. It then reviews individual factors (low intelligence and attainment, personality, temperament, empathy,

impulsiveness and social cognitive skills), family factors (criminal parents, large family size, child-rearing methods, child abuse and neglect, parental conflict and disrupted families, teenage pregnancy) and socio-economic, peer, school and community risk factors for offending.

Thornberry, T. P., & Krohn, M. D. (Eds.) (2003). *Taking stock of delinquency: An overview of findings from contemporary longitudinal studies.* New York: Kluwer/Plenum.

This book contains detailed descriptions of key results obtained in several of the major prospective longitudinal studies of offending summarized in Table 10.1, including the Cambridge Study, the Pittsburgh Youth Study, the Seattle Social Development Project, the Rochester Youth Development Study, the Denver Youth Survey, and the Montreal Longitudinal-Experimental Study. There is a great deal of information about psychosocial factors in the development of offending.

Rutter, M., Giller, H. and Hagell, A. (1998). *Antisocial behaviour by young people.* Cambridge: Cambridge University Press.

This is a very useful textbook on antisocial behaviour and delinquency. It contains chapters on individual factors (including genetic and biological influences, intelligence, temperament, personality and hyperactivity) psychosocial features (including family factors, peer groups, gangs, poverty and social disadvantage), and societal influences (including the mass media, area differences, school effects and ethnic variations). It also reviews gender differences, historical trends, criminal careers and the prevention and treatment of offending.

REFERENCES

Battin, S. R., Hill, K. G., Abbott, R. D., Catalano, R. F., & Hawkins, J. D. (1998). The contribution of gang membership to delinquency beyond delinquent friends. *Criminology, 36*, 93–115.

Bergman, L. R., & Andershed, A-K. (2009). Predictors and outcomes of persistent or age-limited registered criminal behavior: A 30-year longitudinal study of a Swedish urban population. *Aggressive Behavior, 35*, 164–178.

Besemer, S., Farrington, D. P., & Bijleveld, C. C. J. H. (2013). Official bias in intergenerational transmission of criminal behaviour. *British Journal of Criminology, 53*, 438–455.

Bowlby, J. (1951). *Maternal care and mental health.* Geneva, Switzerland: World Health Organization.

Brennan, P. A., Mednick, B. R., & Mednick, S. A. (1993). Parental psychopathology, congenital factors, and violence. In S. Hodgins (Ed.), *Mental disorder and crime* (pp. 244–261). Newbury Park, CA: Sage.

Brownfield, D., & Sorenson, A. M. (1994). Sibship size and sibling delinquency. *Deviant Behavior, 15*, 45–61.

Buehler, C., Anthony, C., Krishnakumar, A., Stone, G., Gerard, J., & Pemberton, S. (1997). Interparental conflict and youth problem behaviors: A meta-analysis. *Journal of Child and Family Studies, 6*, 233–247.

Burke, J. D., Loeber, R., Lahey, B. B., & Rathouz, P. J. (2005). Developmental transitions among affective and behavioural disorders in adolescent boys. *Journal of Child Psychology and Psychiatry, 46*, 1200–1210.

Capaldi, D. M., & Patterson, G. R. (1996). Can violent offenders be distinguished from frequent offenders? Prediction from childhood to adolescence. *Journal of Research in Crime and Delinquency, 33*, 206–231.

Caspi, A. (2000). The child is father of the man: Personality continuities from childhood to adulthood. *Journal of Personality and Social Psychology, 78*, 158–172.

Chess, S., & Thomas, A. (1984). *Origins and evolution of behavior disorders: From infancy to early adult life.* New York: Brunner/Mazel.

Defoe, I. N., Farrington, D. P., & Loeber, R. (2013). Disentangling the relationship between delinquency and hyperactivity, low achievement, depression, and low socio-economic status: Analysis of repeated longitudinal data. *Journal of Criminal Justice, 41*, 100–107.

Demuth, S., & Brown, S. L. (2004). Family structure, family processes, and adolescent delinquency: The significance of parental absence versus parental gender. *Journal of Research in Crime and Delinquency, 41*, 58–81.

Denno, D. W. (1990). *Biology and violence: From birth to adulthood.* Cambridge: Cambridge University Press.

Derzon, J. H. (2010). The correspondence of family features with problem, aggressive, criminal, and violent behaviour: A meta-analysis. *Journal of Experimental Criminology, 6*, 263–292.

Elliott, D. S. (1994). Serious violent offenders: Onset, developmental course, and termination. *Criminology, 32*, 1–21.

Elliott, D. S., Huizinga, D., & Menard, S. (1989). *Multiple problem youth: Delinquency, substance use, and mental health problems.* New York: Springer-Verlag.

Ellis, L. (1988). The victimful-victimless crime distinction, and seven universal demographic correlates of victimful criminal behaviour. *Personality and Individual Differences, 3*, 525–548.

Eysenck, H. J. (1996). Personality and crime: Where do we stand? *Psychology, Crime and Law, 2*, 143–152.

Farrington, D. P. (1972). Delinquency begins at home. *New Society, 21*, 495–497.

Farrington, D. P. (1979). Environmental stress, delinquent behavior, and convictions. In I. G. Sarason & C. D. Spielberger (Eds.), *Stress and anxiety* (vol. 6, pp. 93–107). Washington, DC: Hemisphere.

Farrington, D. P. (1986). Stepping stones to adult criminal careers. In D. Olweus, J. Block & M. R. Yarrow (Eds.), *Development of antisocial and prosocial behavior* (pp. 359–384). New York: Academic Press.

Farrington, D. P. (1988). Studying changes within individuals: The causes of offending. In M. Rutter (Ed.), *Studies of psychosocial risk: The power of longitudinal data* (pp. 158–183). Cambridge: Cambridge University Press.

Farrington, D. P. (1990). Implications of criminal career research for the prevention of offending. *Journal of Adolescence, 13*, 93–113.

Farrington, D. P. (1991). Childhood aggression and adult violence: Early precursors and later life outcomes. In D. J. Pepler & K. H. Rubin (Eds.), *The development and treatment of childhood aggression* (pp. 5–29). Hillsdale, NJ: Lawrence Erlbaum.

Farrington, D. P. (1992a) Explaining the beginning, progress and ending of antisocial behaviour from birth to adulthood. In J. McCord (Ed.), *Facts, frameworks and forecasts: Advances in criminological theory* (vol. 3, pp. 253–286). New Brunswick, NJ: Transaction.

Farrington, D. P. (1992b). Juvenile delinquency. In J. C. Coleman (Ed.), *The school years* (2nd ed., pp. 123–163). London: Routledge.

Farrington, D. P. (1993). Childhood origins of teenage antisocial behaviour and adult social dysfunction. *Journal of the Royal Society of Medicine, 86*, 13–17.

Farrington, D. P. (1994). Childhood, adolescent and adult features of violent males. In L. R. Huesmann (Ed.), *Aggressive behavior: Current perspectives* (pp. 215–240). New York: Plenum.

Farrington, D. P. (1998). Predictors, causes and correlates of male youth violence. In M. Tonry & M. H. Moore (Eds.), *Youth violence* (pp. 421–475). Chicago: University of Chicago Press.

Farrington, D. P. (2002). Multiple risk factors for multiple problem violent boys. In R. R. Corrado, R. Roesch, S. D. Hart & J. K. Gierowski (Eds.), *Multi-problem violent youth: A foundation for comparative research on needs, interventions and outcomes* (pp. 23–34). Amsterdam: IOS Press.

Farrington, D. P. (2003). Key results from the first 40 years of the Cambridge Study in Delinquent Development. In T. P. Thornberry & M. D. Krohn (Eds.), *Taking stock of delinquency: An overview of findings from contemporary longitudinal studies* (pp. 137–183). New York: Kluwer/Plenum.

Farrington, D. P. (2005). The Integrated Cognitive Antisocial Potential (ICAP) theory. In D. P. Farrington (Ed.), *Integrated developmental and life-course theories of offending* (pp. 73–92). New Brunswick, NJ: Transaction.

Farrington, D. P. (2013). Longitudinal and experimental research in criminology. In M. Tonry (Ed.), *Crime and justice 1975–2025* (pp. 453–527). Chicago: University of Chicago Press.

Farrington, D. P., Barnes, G., & Lambert, S. (1996). The concentration of offending in families. *Legal and Criminological Psychology, 1*, 47–63.

Farrington, D. P., Biron, L., & LeBlanc, M. (1982). Personality and delinquency in London and Montreal. In J. Gunn & D. P. Farrington (Eds.), *Abnormal offenders, delinquency, and the criminal justice system* (pp. 153–201). Chichester: Wiley.

Farrington, D. P., Coid, J. W., Harnett, L., Jolliffe, D., Soteriou, N., Turner, R., & West, D. J. (2006). *Criminal careers up to age 50 and life success up to age 48: New findings from the Cambridge Study in Delinquent Development.* London: Home Office (Research Study No. 299).

Farrington, D. P., Coid, J. W., & West, D. J. (2009). The development of offending from age 8 to age 50: Recent results from the Cambridge Study in Delinquent Development. *Monatsschrift für Kriminologie und Strafrechtsreform (Journal of Criminology and Penal Reform), 92*, 160–173.

Farrington, D. P., Gallagher, B., Morley, L., St. Ledger, R. J., & West, D. J. (1986). Unemployment, school leaving, and crime. *British Journal of Criminology, 26*, 335–356.

Farrington, D. P., Jolliffe, D., Loeber, R., Stouthamer-Loeber, M., & Kalb, L. M. (2001). The concentration of offenders in families, and family criminality in the prediction of boys' delinquency. *Journal of Adolescence, 24*, 579–596.

Farrington, D. P., & Loeber, R. (1999). Transatlantic replicability of risk factors in the development of delinquency. In P. Cohen, C. Slomkowski & L. N. Robins (Eds.), *Historical and geographical influences on psychopathology* (pp. 299–329). Mahwah, NJ: Lawrence Erlbaum.

Farrington, D. P., Loeber, R., & Berg, M. T. (2012). Young men who kill: A prospective longitudinal examination from childhood. *Homicide Studies, 16*, 99–128.

Farrington, D. P., Loeber, R., & Stouthamer-Loeber, M. (2003). How can the relationship between race and violence be explained? In D. F. Hawkins (Ed.), *Violent crime: Assessing race and ethnic differences* (pp. 213–237). Cambridge: Cambridge University Press.

Farrington, D. P., Loeber, R., & Ttofi, M. M. (2012). Risk and protective factors for offending. In B. C. Welsh & D. P. Farrington (Eds.), *The Oxford handbook of crime prevention* (pp. 46–69). Oxford: Oxford University Press.

Farrington, D. P., Loeber, R., & Van Kammen, W. B. (1990). Long-term criminal outcomes of hyperactivity-impulsivity-attention deficit and conduct problems in childhood. In L. N. Robins & M. Rutter (Eds.), *Straight and devious pathways from childhood to adulthood* (pp. 62–81). Cambridge: Cambridge University Press.

Farrington, D. P., Loeber, R., Yin, Y., & Anderson, S. (2002). Are within-individual causes of delinquency the same as between-individual causes? *Criminal Behaviour and Mental Health, 12*, 53–68.

Farrington, D. P., Piquero, A. R., & Jennings, W. G. (2013). *Offending from childhood to late middle age: Recent results from the Cambridge Study in Delinquent Development.* New York: Springer.

Farrington, D. P., & Ttofi, M. M. (2012). Protective and promotive factors in the development of offending. In T. Bliesener, A. Beelman & M. Stemmler (Eds.), *Antisocial behaviour and crime: Contributions of developmental and evaluation research to prevention and intervention* (pp. 71–88). Cambridge, MA: Hogrefe.

Farrington, D. P., & Welsh, B. C. (2007). *Saving children from a life of crime: Early risk factors and effective interventions.* Oxford: Oxford University Press.

Fergusson, D. M., & Horwood, L. J. (1998). Exposure to interparental violence in childhood and psychosocial adjustment in young adulthood. *Child Abuse and Neglect, 22,* 339–357.

Fergusson, D., Swain-Campbell, N., & Horwood, J. (2004). How does childhood economic disadvantage lead to crime? *Journal of Child Psychology and Psychiatry, 45,* 956–966.

Foster, H., & Brooks-Gunn, J. (2013). Neighborhood influences on antisocial behavior during childhood and adolescence. In C. L. Gibson & M. D. Krohn (Eds.), *Handbook of life-course criminology* (pp. 69–90). New York: Springer.

Frick, P. J., & White, S. F. (2008). The importance of callous-unemotional traits for developmental models of aggressive and antisocial behaviour. *Journal of Child Psychology and Psychiatry, 49,* 359–375.

Gatti, U., Tremblay, R. E., Vitaro, F., & McDuff, P. (2005). Youth gangs, delinquency and drug use: A test of the selection, facilitation, and enhancement hypotheses. *Journal of Child Psychology and Psychiatry, 46,* 1178–1190.

Gordon, R. A., Lahey, B. B., Kawai, E., Loeber, R., Stouthamer-Loeber, M., & Farrington, D. P. (2004). Antisocial behavior and young gang membership: Selection and socialization. *Criminology, 42,* 55–87.

Gottfredson, D. C. (2001). *Schools and delinquency.* Cambridge: Cambridge University Press.

Gottfredson, D. C., McNeil, R. J., & Gottfredson, G. D. (1991). Social area influences on delinquency: A multilevel analysis. *Journal of Research in Crime and Delinquency, 28,* 197–226.

Graham, J. (1988). *Schools, disruptive behaviour and delinquency.* London: Her Majesty's Stationery Office.

Haapasalo, J., & Pokela, E. (1999). Child-rearing and child abuse antecedents of criminality. *Aggression and Violent Behavior, 1,* 107–127.

Hawkins, J. D., Smith, B. H., Hill, K. G., Kosterman, R., Catalano, R. F., & Abbott, R. D. (2003). Understanding and preventing crime and violence: Findings from the Seattle Social Development Project. In T. P. Thornberry & M. D. Krohn (Eds.), *Taking stock of delinquency: An overview of findings from contemporary longitudinal studies* (pp. 255–312). New York: Kluwer/Plenum.

Henry, B., Moffitt, T., Robins, L., Earls, F., & Silva, P. (1993). Early family predictors of child and adolescent antisocial behaviour: Who are the mothers of delinquents? *Criminal Behaviour and Mental Health, 2,* 97–118.

Herrenkohl, T. I., Hawkins, J. D., Chung, I-J., Hill, K. G., & Battin-Pearson, S. (2001). School and community risk factors and interventions. In R. Loeber & D. P. Farrington (Eds.), *Child delinquents: Development, intervention and service needs* (pp. 211–246). Thousand Oaks, CA: Sage.

Herrenkohl, T. I., Maguin, E., Hill, K. G., Hawkins, J. D., Abbott, R. D., & Catalano, R. F. (2000). Developmental risk factors for youth violence. *Journal of Adolescent Health, 26,* 176–186.

Higgins, G. E., Kirchner, E. E., Ricketts, M. L., & Marcum, C. D. (2013). Impulsivity and offending from childhood to young adulthood in the United States: A developmental trajectory analysis. *International Journal of Criminal Justice Sciences, 8,* 182–187.

Hogh, E., & Wolf, P. (1983). Violent crime in a birth cohort: Copenhagen 1953–1977. In K. T. van Dusen & S. A. Mednick (Eds.), *Prospective studies of crime and delinquency* (pp. 249–267). Boston: Kluwer-Nijhoff.

Huesmann, L. R., Dubow, E. F., & Boxer, P. (2009). Continuity of aggression from childhood to early adulthood as a predictor of life outcomes: Implications for the adolescent-limited and life-course-persistent models. *Aggressive Behavior, 35,* 136–149.

Huizinga, D., Weiher, A. W., Espiritu, R., & Esbensen, F. (2003). Delinquency and crime: Some highlights from the Denver Youth Survey. In T. P. Thornberry & M. D. Krohn (Eds.), *Taking stock of delinquency: An overview of findings from contemporary longitudinal studies* (pp. 47–91). New York: Kluwer/Plenum.

Ireland, T. O., & Smith, C. A. (2009). Living in partner-violent families: Developmental links to antisocial behavior and relationship violence. *Journal of Youth and Adolescence, 38,* 323–339.

Jaffee, S., Caspi, A., Moffitt, T. E., Belsky, J., & Silva, P. A. (2001). Why are children born to teen mothers at risk for adverse outcomes in young adulthood? Results from a 20-year longitudinal study. *Development and Psychopathology, 13,* 377–397.

Jakobsen, I. S., Fergusson, D. M., & Horwood, J. L. (2012). Early conduct problems, school achievement and later crime: Findings from a 30-year longitudinal study. *New Zealand Journal of Educational Studies, 47,* 123–135.

Jolliffe, D., & Farrington, D. P. (2004). Empathy and offending: A systematic review and meta-analysis. *Aggression and Violent Behavior, 9,* 441–476.

Jolliffe, D., & Farrington, D. P. (2006). Development and validation of the Basic Empathy Scale. *Journal of Adolescence, 29,* 589–611.

Jolliffe, D., & Farrington, D. P. (2007). Examining the relationship between low empathy and self-reported offending. *Legal and Criminological Psychology, 12,* 265–286.

Jolliffe, D., & Farrington, D. P. (2009). A systematic review of the relationship between childhood impulsiveness and later violence. In M. McMurran & R. Howard (Eds.), *Personality, personality disorder, and risk of violence* (pp. 41–61). Chichester: Wiley.

Jones, S. E., Miller, J. D., & Lynam, D. R. (2011). Personality, antisocial behavior, and aggression: A meta-analytic review. *Journal of Criminal Justice, 39,* 329–337.

Juby, H., & Farrington, D. P. (2001). Disentangling the link between disrupted families and delinquency. *British Journal of Criminology, 41,* 22–40.

Junger, M., Greene, J., Schipper, R., Hesper, F., & Estourgie, V. (2013). Parental criminality, family violence and intergenerational transmission of crime within a birth cohort. *European Journal on Criminal Policy and Research, 19,* 117–133.

Kagan, J. (1989). Temperamental contributions to social behavior. *American Psychologist, 44*, 668–674.

Kaukiainen, A., Bjorkvist, K., Lagerspetz, K., Osterman, K., Salmivalli, C., Rothberg, S., & Ahlbom, A. (1999). The relationships between social intelligence, empathy, and three types of aggression. *Aggressive Behavior, 25*, 81–89.

Kazemian, L., Widom, C. S., & Farrington, D. P. (2011). A prospective examination of the relationship between childhood neglect and juvenile delinquency in the Cambridge Study in Delinquent Development. *International Journal of Child, Youth and Family Studies, 2*, 65–82.

Keiley, M. K., Howe, T. R., Dodge, K. A., Bates, J. E., & Pettit, G. S. (2001). The timing of child physical maltreatment: A cross-domain growth analysis of impact on adolescent externalizing and internalizing problems. *Development and Psychopathology, 13*, 891–912.

Klinteberg, B. A., Andersson, T., Magnusson, D., & Stattin, H. (1993). Hyperactive behaviour in childhood as related to subsequent alcohol problems and violent offending: A longitudinal study of male subjects. *Personality and Individual Differences, 15*, 381–388.

Kolvin, I., Miller, F. J. W., Fleeting, M., & Kolvin, P. A. (1988). Social and parenting factors affecting criminal-offence rates: Findings from the Newcastle Thousand Family Study (1947–1980). *British Journal of Psychiatry, 152*, 80–90.

Kolvin, I., Miller, F. J. W., Scott, D. M., Gatzanis, S. R. M., & Fleeting, M. (1990). *Continuities of deprivation? The Newcastle 1000 Family Study*. Aldershot: Avebury.

Koolhof, R., Loeber, R., Wei, E. H., Pardini, D., & D'Escury, A. C. (2007). Inhibition deficits of serious delinquent boys of low intelligence. *Criminal Behaviour and Mental Health, 17*, 274–292.

Krohn, M. D., Hall, G. P., & Lizotte, A. J. (2009). Family transitions and later delinquency and drug use. *Journal of Youth and Adolescence, 38*, 466–480.

Lahey, B. B., Loeber, R., Waldman, I. D., & Farrington, D. P. (2006). Child socioemotional dispositions at school entry that predict adolescent delinquency and violence. *Impuls: Tidsskrift for Psykologi, 3*, 40–51.

Larzelere, R. E., & Patterson, G. R. (1990). Parental management: Mediator of the effect of socioeconomic status on early delinquency. *Criminology, 28*, 301–324.

LeBlanc, M., & Frechette, M. (1989). *Male criminal activity from childhood through youth*. New York: Springer-Verlag.

Leschied, A., Chiodo, D., Nowicki, E., & Rodger, S. (2008). Childhood predictors of adult criminality: A meta-analysis drawn from the prospective longitudinal literature. *Canadian Journal of Criminology and Criminal Justice, 50*, 435–467.

Levine, S. Z., & Jackson, C. J. (2004). Eysenck's theory of crime revisited: Factors or primary scales? *Legal and Criminological Psychology, 9*, 135–152.

Lipsey, M. W., & Derzon, J. H. (1998). Predictors of violent or serious delinquency in adolescence and early adulthood: A synthesis of longitudinal research. In R. Loeber & D. P. Farrington (Eds.), *Serious and violent juvenile offenders: Risk factors and successful interventions* (pp. 86–105). Thousand Oaks, CA: Sage.

Lipsitt, P. D., Buka, S. L., & Lipsitt, L. P. (1990). Early intelligence scores and subsequent delinquency: A prospective study. *American Journal of Family Therapy, 18*, 197–208.

Loeber, R., Farrington, D. P., Stouthamer-Loeber, M., Moffitt, T. E., Caspi, A., White, H. R., Wei, E., & Beyers, J. M. (2003). The development of male offending: Key findings from 14 years of the Pittsburgh Youth Study. In T. P. Thornberry & M. D. Krohn (Eds.), *Taking stock of delinquency: An overview of findings from contemporary longitudinal studies* (pp. 93–136). New York: Kluwer/Plenum.

Loeber, R., Farrington, D. P., Stouthamer-Loeber, M., & Van Kammen, W. B. (1998). Multiple risk factors for multi-problem boys: Co-occurrence of delinquency, substance use, attention deficit, conduct problems, physical aggression, covert behavior, depressed mood and shy/withdrawn behavior. In R. Jessor (Ed.), *New perspectives on adolescent risk behavior* (pp. 90–149). New York: Cambridge University Press.

Loeber, R., Farrington, D. P., Stouthamer-Loeber, M., & White, H. R. (2008). *Violence and serious theft: Development and prediction from childhood to adulthood*. New York: Routledge.

Lösel, F., Bliesener, T., & Bender, D. (2007). Social information processing, experiences of aggression in social contexts, and aggressive behaviour in adolescents. *Criminal Justice and Behavior, 34*, 330–347.

Lösel, F., & Farrington, D. P. (2012). Direct protective and buffering protective factors in the development of youth violence. *American Journal of Preventive Medicine, 43*(2S1), S8–S23.

Luengo, M. A., Otero, J. M., Carrillo-de-la-Pena, M. T., & Miron, L. (1994). Dimensions of antisocial behaviour in juvenile delinquency: A study of personality variables. *Psychology, Crime and Law, 1*, 27–37.

Lynam, D. R. (1996). Early identification of chronic offenders: Who is the fledgling psychopath? *Psychological Bulletin, 120*, 209–234.

Lynam, D. R. (1998). Early identification of the fledgling psychopath: Locating the psychopathic child in the current nomenclature. *Journal of Abnormal Psychology, 107*, 566–575.

Lynam, D. R., Caspi, A., Moffitt, T. E., Wikstrom, P-O. H., Loeber, R., & Novak, S. (2000). The interaction between impulsivity and neighborhood context on offending: The effects of impulsivity are stronger in poorer neighborhoods. *Journal of Abnormal Psychology, 109*, 563–574.

Lynam, D. R., Moffitt, T. E., & Stouthamer-Loeber, M. (1993). Explaining the relation between IQ and delinquency: Class, race, test motivation, school failure or self-control? *Journal of Abnormal Psychology, 102*, 187–196.

McCord, J. (1977). A comparative study of two generations of native Americans. In R. F. Meier (Ed.), Theory in criminology (pp. 83–92). Beverly Hills, CA: Sage.

McCord, J. (1979). Some child-rearing antecedents of criminal behavior in adult men. *Journal of Personality and Social Psychology, 37*, 1477–1486.

McCord, J. (1982). A longitudinal view of the relationship between paternal absence and crime. In J. Gunn & D. P. Farrington (Eds.), *Abnormal offenders, delinquency, and the criminal justice system* (pp. 113–128). Chichester: Wiley.

McCord, J. (1983). A forty year perspective on effects of child abuse and neglect. *Child Abuse and Neglect, 7*, 265–270.

McCord, J. (1991). Family relationships, juvenile delinquency, and adult criminality. *Criminology, 29*, 397–417.

McCord, J. (1997). On discipline. *Psychological Inquiry, 8*, 215–217.

McCrae, R. R., & Costa, P. T. (2003). *Personality in adulthood: A five-factor theory perspective.* New York: Guilford.

McGee, T. R., & Farrington, D. P. (2010). Are there any true adult onset offenders? *British Journal of Criminology, 50*, 530–549.

Maguin, E., & Loeber, R. (1996). Academic performance and delinquency. In M. Tonry (Ed.), *Crime and justice*, vol. 20 (pp. 145–264). Chicago: University of Chicago Press.

Mak, A. S. (1991). Psychosocial control characteristics of delinquents and non-delinquents. *Criminal Justice and Behavior, 18*, 287–303.

Malinosky-Rummell, R., & Hansen, D. J. (1993). Long-term consequences of childhood physical abuse. *Psychological Bulletin, 114*, 68–79.

Maxfield, M. G., & Widom, C. S. (1996). The cycle of violence revisited 6 years later. *Archives of Pediatrics and Adolescent Medicine, 150*, 390–395.

Miller, J. D., & Lynam, D. (2001). Structural models of personality and their relation to antisocial behavior: A meta-analytic review. *Criminology, 39*, 765–798.

Moffitt, T. E. (1993). The neuropsychology of conduct disorder. *Development and Psychopathology, 5*, 135–151.

Moffitt, T. E., Caspi, A., Rutter, M., & Silva, P. A. (2001). *Sex differences in antisocial behaviour.* Cambridge: Cambridge University Press.

Moffitt, T. E., & Henry, B. (1991). Neuropsychological studies of juvenile delinquency and juvenile violence. In J. S. Milner (Ed.), *Neuropsychology of aggression* (pp. 131–146). Boston: Kluwer.

Morash, M., & Rucker, L. (1989). An exploratory study of the connection of mother's age at childbearing to her children's delinquency in four data sets. *Crime and Delinquency, 35*, 45–93.

Morgan, A. B., & Lilienfeld, S. O. (2000). A meta-analytic review of the relation between antisocial behavior and neuropsychological measures of executive function. *Clinical Psychology Review, 20*, 113–136.

Murray, J., Bijleveld, C. C. J. H., Farrington, D. P., & Loeber, R. (2014). *Effects of parental incarceration on children: Cross-national comparative studies.* Washington, DC: American Psychological Association.

Murray, J., & Farrington, D. P. (2005). Parental imprisonment: Effects on boys' antisocial behaviour and delinquency through the life-course. *Journal of Child Psychology and Psychiatry, 46*, 1269–1278.

Murray, J., & Farrington, D. P. (2010). Risk factors for conduct disorder and delinquency: Key findings from longitudinal studies. *Canadian Journal of Psychiatry, 55*, 633–642.

Murray, J., Farrington, D. P., & Eisner, M. P. (2009). Drawing conclusions about causes from systematic reviews of risk factors: The Cambridge Quality Checklists. *Journal of Experimental Criminology, 5*, 1–23.

Murray, J., Irving, B., Farrington, D. P., Colman, I., & Bloxsom, C. A. J. (2010). Very early predictors of conduct problems and crime: Results from a national cohort study. *Journal of Child Psychology and Psychiatry, 51*, 1198–1207.

Murray, J., Janson, C-G., & Farrington, D. P. (2007). Crime in adult offspring of prisoners: A cross-national comparison of two longitudinal samples. *Criminal Justice and Behavior, 34*, 133–149.

Nagin, D. S., Pogarsky, G., & Farrington, D. P. (1997). Adolescent mothers and the criminal behavior of their children. *Law and Society Review, 31*, 137–162.

Newson, J., & Newson, E. (1989). *The extent of parental physical punishment in the UK.* London: Approach.

Newson, J., Newson, E., & Adams, M. (1993). The social origins of delinquency. *Criminal Behaviour and Mental Health, 3*, 19–29.

Odgers, C. L., Milne, B. J., Caspi, A., Crump, R., Poulton, R., & Moffitt, T. E. (2007). Predicting prognosis for the conduct-problem boy: Can family history help? *Journal of the American Academy of Child and Adolescent Psychiatry, 46*, 1240–1249.

Patterson, G. R. (1995). Coercion as a basis for early age of onset for arrest. In J. McCord (Ed.), *Coercion and punishment in long-term perspectives* (pp. 81–105). Cambridge: Cambridge University Press.

Payne, A. A., & Welch, K. (2013). The impact of schools and education on antisocial behavior over the life-course. In C. L. Gibson & M. D. Krohn (Eds.), *Handbook of life-course criminology* (pp. 93–109). New York: Springer.

Piquero, A. R. (2000). Frequency, specialization, and violence in offending careers. *Journal of Research in Crime and Delinquency, 37*, 392–418.

Pogarsky, G., Lizotte, A. J., & Thornberry, T. P. (2003). The delinquency of children born to young mothers: Results from the Rochester Youth Development Study. *Criminology, 41*, 1249–1286.

Power, M. J., Alderson, M. R., Phillipson, C. M., Shoenberg, E., & Morris, J. N. (1967). Delinquent schools? *New Society, 10*, 542–543.

Pratt, T. C., Cullen, F. T., Blevins, K. R., Daigle, L., & Unnever, J. D. (2002). The relationship of attention deficit hyperactivity disorder to crime and delinquency: A meta-analysis. *International Journal of Police Science and Management, 4*, 344–360.

Pulkkinen, L., Lyyra, A-L., & Kokko, K. (2009). Life success of males on non-offender, adolescence-limited, persistent, and adult-onset antisocial pathways: Follow-up from age 8 to 42. *Aggressive Behavior, 35*, 117–135.

Raine, A. (2013). *The anatomy of violence: The biological roots of crime.* London: Allen Lane.

Raine, A., Moffitt, T. E., Caspi, A., Loeber, R., Stouthamer-Loeber, M., & Lynam, D. (2005). Neurocognitive impairments in boys on the life-course-persistent antisocial path. *Journal of Abnormal Psychology, 114,* 38–49.

Reiss, A. J. (1986). Why are communities important in understanding crime? In A. J. Reiss & M. Tonry (Eds.), *Communities and crime* (pp. 1–33). Chicago: University of Chicago Press.

Reiss, A. J., & Farrington, D. P. (1991). Advancing knowledge about co-offending: Results from a prospective longitudinal survey of London males. *Journal of Criminal Law and Criminology, 82,* 360–395.

Robins, L. N. (1979). Sturdy childhood predictors of adult outcomes: Replications from longitudinal studies. In J. E. Barrett, R. M. Rose & G. L. Klerman (Eds.), *Stress and mental disorder* (pp. 219–235). New York: Raven Press.

Robins, L. N. (1992). The role of prevention experiments in discovering causes of children's antisocial behavior. In J. McCord & R. E. Tremblay (Eds.), *Preventing antisocial behavior: Interventions from birth through adolescence* (pp. 3–18). New York: Guilford.

Robins, L. N., West, P. J., & Herjanic, B. L. (1975). Arrests and delinquency in two generations: A study of black urban families and their children. *Journal of Child Psychology and Psychiatry, 16,* 125–140.

Rutter, M. (1981). The city and the child. *American Journal of Orthopsychiatry, 51,* 610–625.

Rutter, M., Giller, H., & Hagell, A. (1998). *Antisocial behaviour by young people.* Cambridge: Cambridge University Press.

Rutter, M., Maughan, B., Mortimore, P., Ouston, J., & Smith, A. (1979). *Fifteen thousand hours: Secondary schools and their effects on children.* London: Open Books.

Sampson, R. J., Morenoff, J. D., & Raudenbush, S. (2005). Social anatomy of racial and ethnic disparities in violence. *American Journal of Public Health, 95,* 224–232.

Sampson, R. J., Raudenbush, S. W., & Earls, F. (1997). Neighborhoods and violent crime: A multilevel study of collective efficacy. *Science, 277,* 918–924.

Schwartz, C. E., Snidman, N., & Kagan, J. (1996). Early childhood temperament as a determinant of externalizing behavior in adolescence. *Development and Psychopathology, 8,* 527–537.

Schweinhart, L. J., Barnes, H. V., & Weikart, D. P. (1993). *Significant benefits.* Ypsilanti, MI: High/Scope.

Seguin, J., Pihl, R. O., Harden, P. W., Tremblay, R. E., & Boulerice, B. (1995). Cognitive and neuropsychological characteristics of physically aggressive boys. *Journal of Abnormal Psychology, 104,* 614–624.

Shaw, C. R., & McKay, H. D. (1969). *Juvenile delinquency and urban areas* (rev. ed.). Chicago: University of Chicago Press.

Smith, C. A., & Stern, S. B. (1997). Delinquency and antisocial behavior: A review of family processes and intervention research. *Social Service Review, 71,* 382–420.

Smith, C. A., & Thornberry, T. P. (1995). The relationship between childhood maltreatment and adolescent involvement in delinquency. *Criminology, 33,* 451–481.

Stams, G. J., Brugman, D., Dekovic, M., van Rosmalen, L., Van der Laan, P., & Gibbs, J. C. (2006). The moral judgment of juvenile delinquents: A meta-analysis. *Journal of Abnormal Child Psychology, 34,* 697–713.

Stattin, H., & Klackenberg-Larsson, I. (1993). Early language and intelligence development and their relationship to future criminal behavior. *Journal of Abnormal Psychology, 102,* 369–378.

Steinberg, L., Lamborn, S. D., Dornbusch, S. M., & Darling, N. (1992). Impact of parenting practices on adolescent achievement: Authoritative parenting, school involvement and encouragement to succeed. *Child Development, 63,* 1266–1281.

Sutton, J., Smith, P. K. & Swettenham, J. (1999). Social cognition and bullying: Social inadequacy or skilled manipulation? *British Journal of Developmental Psychology, 17,* 435–450.

Theobald, D., Farrington, D. P., & Piquero, A. R. (2013). Childhood broken homes and adult violence: An analysis of moderators and mediators. *Journal of Criminal Justice, 41,* 44–52.

Thornberry, T. P., & Farnworth, M. (1982). Social correlates of criminal involvement: Further evidence on the relationship between social status and criminal behavior. *American Sociological Review, 47,* 505–518.

Thornberry, T. P., Freeman-Gallant, A., & Lovegrove, P. J. (2009). Intergenerational linkages in antisocial behaviour. *Criminal Behaviour and Mental Health, 19,* 80–93.

Thornberry, T. P., Huizinga, D., & Loeber, R. (1995). The prevention of serious delinquency and violence: Implications from the program of research on the causes and correlates of delinquency. In J. C. Howell, B. Krisberg, J. D. Hawkins and J. J. Wilson (Eds.), *Sourcebook on serious, violent and chronic juvenile offenders* (pp. 213–237). Thousand Oaks, CA: Sage.

Thornberry, T. P., & Krohn, M. (Eds.) (2003). *Taking stock of delinquency: An overview of findings from contemporary longitudinal studies.* New York: Kluwer/Plenum.

Thornberry, T. P., Krohn, M. D., Lizotte, A. J., Smith, C. A., & Tobin, K. (2003). *Gangs and delinquency in developmental perspective.* New York: Cambridge University Press.

Thornberry, T. P., Lizotte, A. J., Krohn, M. D., Farnworth M., & Jang, S. J. (1994). Delinquent peers, beliefs and delinquent behavior: A longitudinal test of interactional theory. *Criminology, 32,* 47–83.

Thornberry, T. P., Lizotte, A. J., Krohn, M. D., Smith, C. A., & Porter, P. K. (2003). Causes and consequences of delinquency: Findings from the Rochester Youth Development Study. In T. P. Thornberry & M. D. Krohn (Eds.), *Taking stock of delinquency: An overview of findings from contemporary longitudinal studies* (pp. 11–46). New York: Kluwer/Plenum.

Thornberry, T. P., Smith, C. A., Rivera, C., Huizinga, D., & Stouthamer-Loeber, M. (1999). *Family disruption and delinquency*. Washington, DC: Office of Juvenile Justice and Delinquency Prevention.

Tolan, P. H., Gorman-Smith, D., & Henry, D. B. (2003). The developmental ecology of urban males' youth violence. *Developmental Psychology, 39*, 274–291.

Tracy, P. E., & Kempf-Leonard, K. (1996). *Continuity and discontinuity in criminal careers*. New York: Plenum.

Tremblay, R. E., Vitaro, F., Nagin, D., Pagani, L., & Seguin, J. R. (2003). The Montreal Longitudinal and Experimental Study: Rediscovering the power of descriptions. In T. P. Thornberry & M. D. Krohn (Eds.), *Taking stock of delinquency: An overview of findings from contemporary longitudinal studies* (pp. 205–254). New York: Kluwer/Plenum.

Wadsworth, M. E. J. (1979). *Roots of delinquency: Infancy, adolescence and crime*. London: Martin Robertson.

Wadsworth, M. E. J. (1991). *The imprint of time*. Oxford: Clarendon Press.

Walters, G. D. (2002). The psychological inventory of criminal thinking styles: A review and meta-analysis. *Assessment, 9*, 278–291.

Wells, L. E., & Rankin, J. H. (1991). Families and delinquency: A meta-analysis of the impact of broken homes. *Social Problems, 38*, 71–93.

Werner, E. E., & Smith, R. S. (2001). *Journeys from childhood to midlife*. Ithaca, NY: Cornell University Press.

West, D. J., & Farrington, D. P. (1973). *Who becomes delinquent?* London: Heinemann.

West, D. J., & Farrington, D. P. (1977). *The delinquent way of life*. London: Heinemann.

White, J. L., Moffitt, T. E., Caspi, A., Bartusch, D. J., Needles, D. J., & Stouthamer-Loeber, M. (1994). Measuring impulsivity and examining its relationship to delinquency. *Journal of Abnormal Psychology, 103*, 192–205.

Widom, C. S. (1994). Childhood victimization and adolescent problem behaviors. In R. D. Ketterlinus & M. E. Lamb (Eds.), *Adolescent problem behaviors* (pp. 127–164). Hillsdale, NJ: Lawrence Erlbaum.

Wikström, P-O. H. (1990). Age and crime in a Stockholm cohort. *Journal of Quantitative Criminology, 6*, 61–84.

Wikström, P-O. H., & Loeber, R. (2000). Do disadvantaged neighborhoods cause well-adjusted children to become adolescent delinquents? A study of male juvenile serious offending, individual risk and protective factors, and neighborhood context. *Criminology, 38*, 1109–1142.

Wilson, J. Q., & Herrnstein, R. J. (1985). *Crime and human nature*. New York: Simon and Schuster.

Wolfgang, M. E., Thornberry, T. P., & Figlio, R. M. (1987). *From boy to man, from delinquency to crime*. Chicago: University of Chicago Press.

Zara, G., & Farrington, D. P. (2009). Childhood and adolescent predictors of late onset criminal careers. *Journal of Youth and Adolescence, 38*, 287–300.

11 The Developmental Evidence Base: Desistance

LILA KAZEMIAN AND DAVID P. FARRINGTON

In recent years, the growing literature on the topic of desistance from crime has generated a large body of knowledge on this dimension of the criminal career. Despite these efforts, it has been suggested that our understanding of the processes underlying desistance remains limited. In particular, very little is known about the causal processes underlying desistance. The objective of this chapter is to offer an overview of the state of knowledge on desistance, and to highlight some unresolved issues in this area of study. It reviews social and cognitive predictors of desistance, as well as the shortcomings of past desistance research. The chapter also offers recommendations for future research.

CURRENT STATE OF KNOWLEDGE ON DESISTANCE

This first section aims to provide a brief summary of some of the key findings from influential studies on desistance research with regard to social and cognitive factors associated with desistance from crime. Desistance may be viewed either as a gradual process or as a sharp termination of offending.

Social predictors of desistance

Although Gottfredson and Hirschi (1990) have argued that associations between life events and desistance from crime are spurious (also see Hirschi & Gottfredson, 1995), a large body of research on desistance has drawn attention to the importance of social bonds in the process of desistance. Desistance from crime is said to be gradual, resulting from an accumulation of social bonds (see

Horney, Osgood, & Marshall, 1995). Irwin (1970) identified three key factors in the explanation of desistance from crime: a good job, a good relationship with a woman and involvement in extracurricular activities. Giordano, Cernkovich, and Rudolph (2002) made reference to the 'respectability package', and argued that marriage and job stability exert a more substantial impact on desistance if they occur jointly. In this respect, turning points (marriage, employment, etc.) are likely to be interdependent.

Horney *et al.* (1995, p. 658) explored the association between crime and local life circumstances, which they defined as '… conditions in an individual's life that can fluctuate relatively frequently'. According to the authors, variables explaining short-term variations in criminal behaviour are similar to variables explaining long-term variations (i.e., strength of bonds to conventional social institutions). Horney *et al.* (1995, p. 669) found that individuals were '… less likely to commit crimes when living with a wife' (see also Farrington & West, 1995; Laub & Sampson, 2003; Rand, 1987; Sampson & Laub, 1993). The authors argued that time invested in conventional social institutions was time away from sources of temptation (bars, delinquent peers, etc.). Horney *et al.* (1995, p. 670) did however admit that local life circumstances may not have been randomly distributed, and that '… local life circumstances can change criminal careers by modifying the likelihood of offending *at particular times*'. Since their analyses were limited to a short period of the life-course, it is difficult to assess whether these changes were permanent, and whether they reflected stable changes in life-course trajectories.

Farrington and Hawkins (1991) argued that predictors of desistance may vary across different periods of the life-course. Similarly, Sampson and Laub's (1993, p. 17; see also Sampson & Laub, 1997) age-graded theory of informal social control emphasizes the idea that '… the

Forensic Psychology, Second Edition. Edited by David A. Crighton and Graham J. Towl.
© 2015 John Wiley & Sons, Ltd. Published 2015 by British Psychological Society and John Wiley & Sons, Ltd.

important institutions of both formal and informal social control vary across the life span'. Sampson and Laub's (1993) argument relies on the premise that changes in social bonds across the life-course can explain offending behaviour, even after accounting for different degrees of self-control. In childhood and adolescence, delinquency is explained by the strength of bonds (or lack thereof) to family and school. In adulthood, variations in offending behaviour are explained by job stability and marital attachment, which are recognized as triggers of the desistance process. How individuals adapt to life-course transitions and turning points may mould the decision to engage in criminal (or non-criminal) behaviour. Thus, life events can either be positive or negative, depending on the 'quality, strength, and interdependence of social ties' (Sampson & Laub, 1993, p. 21). In this respect, adult crime would largely result from weak bonds to social institutions, and desistance from crime would entail some 'social investment' in conventional institutions.

Employment

Using data from the National Supported Work Demonstration Project, Uggen (2000) explored the effect of employment on recidivism. This project recruited participants from underprivileged neighbourhoods and randomly assigned them to control or experimental groups. Offenders, drug users and dropouts were targeted. Individuals in the treatment group were given minimum-wage employment opportunities. The results showed that the programme had a more substantial impact on older individuals (over 26 years of age). Furthermore, 'Offenders who are provided even marginal employment opportunities are less likely to reoffend than those not provided such opportunities' (Uggen, 2000, p. 542). Although the general consensus in the literature is that employment (and employment stability) does exert an impact on desistance, some studies have found that employment did not have an impact on the likelihood of desistance from crime (Giordano et al., 2002; Rhodes, 1989).

The life narratives explored in Laub and Sampson's (2003, p. 129) study suggested that '... stable work may not trigger a change in an antisocial trajectory in the way that marriage or serving in the military does, even though employment may play an important role in sustaining the process of desistance'. Interestingly, analysing data from a random sample of Texas male parolees, Tripodi, Kim, and Bender (2010) found somewhat similar results. Their findings showed that employment is not significantly associated with reductions in the probability of reincarceration, but that it is associated with longer time lags to reincarceration (i.e., more time 'crime-free in the community').

As highlighted by the authors, this interesting finding underlines the importance of studying desistance as a process:

> The explanation for this insignificant finding, however, requires a shift in perspective from a 'black and white' view of ex-prisoners as either recidivists or nonrecidivists. This traditional view of parolees leaves little middle ground for ex-prisoners who are in the process of changing. Instead, a more complex view of offenders is needed to recognize that they may fall on a spectrum of behavior change that consists of various stages (p. 714).

In their explanation of the impact of employment on desistance, Laub and Sampson (2003) continue to emphasize the important role of routine activities. The authors argued that the processes underlying the relationship between work and desistance are similar to those underlying the relationship between marriage and desistance. Employment promotes desistance through four main processes: a reciprocal exchange of social capital between employer and employee, reduced criminal opportunities and the '... probability that criminal propensities will be translated into action', direct informal social control, and the development of a '... sense of identity and meaning' to one's life' (Laub & Sampson, 2003, p. 47). The latter factor leads us to a discussion of the individual factors contributing to the process of desistance from crime (see the following section).

Marriage

Farrington and West (1995, p. 265) found that '... individuals who had married and never separated were the least antisocial at age 32 while those who had married and separated and were now living alone were the most antisocial'. They studied rates of offending before and after marriage, and concluded that getting married led to a decrease in offending compared with staying single. They also discovered that separation from a wife led to an increase in offending compared with staying married. However, they argued that 'It is not clear from these results how far marriage and separation may be causes, consequences, or symptoms' (1995, p. 265). They considered that the effect of marriage may have been dependent on '... the reasons for getting married (e.g., pregnancy), on the happiness of the marriage, and on the extent to which the wife is conventional and prosocial' (1995, p. 278). They concluded that 'Marriage may have a cumulative rather than a sharply-delimited effect' (1995, p. 278). More recent research has also provided support for the positive association between marriage and desistance (Bersani, Laub, & Nieuwbeerta, 2009; Doherty & Ensminger, 2013).

Laub, Nagin, and Sampson (1998) also found that high-rate offenders had weaker marital bonds than other offenders. In agreement with Farrington and West's results, Laub et al. (1998) argued that the timing and quality of marriage were important (see also Rutter, 1996), with stable marriages having an increased preventive effect (see also Sampson & Laub, 1993). In addition to the quality of the relationship, the characteristics of the partner also appear to be important. Van Schellen, Poortman, and Nieuwbeerta (2012) argued that the crime-reduction benefits of marriage may be less among convicted individuals, because they 'have a tendency to marry criminal partners' (p. 567).

Also in agreement with Farrington and West's study, Laub et al. (1998) argued that the inhibiting effect of marriage on crime is gradual rather than abrupt. Laub and Sampson (2003) defined the effect of marriage on crime as an 'investment process'; the more that individuals invest in social bonds (e.g., marriage), the less likely they are to engage in criminal activities because they have more to lose. Laub and Sampson (2003, p. 33) rejected the idea that the effect of marriage on crime is merely a result of self-selection (i.e., people who decide to reform are more likely to get married), and claimed that marital effects remained strong despite selection effects. More recently, Bersani and Doherty (2013) attempted to investigate the processes underlying the marriage-desistance link. The authors found that the dissolution of the marriage is associated with increased offending, prompting them to hypothesize that marriage is likely to exert temporary or situational effects on desistance. Similar results were reported by Theobald and Farrington (2013).

Laub and Sampson (2003) summarized the key processes involved in the effect of marriage on desistance from crime, many of which revolve around shifts in routine activities. Marriage leads to reduced deviant peer associations, new friends and extended family, as well as overall changes in routine activities. Spouses also constitute an extra source of social control, and an effective means of monitoring routine activities. Marriage also often results in residential changes and children, which may also promote changes in routine activities. Laub and Sampson (2003, p. 43) also argued that '... marriage can change one's sense of self'.

In contrast to these results, Knight, Osborn, and West (1977) found that early marriage (under age 21) had little effect on self-reported delinquency, although it was followed by a reduction in drinking and drug use. In a follow-up of the Cambridge Study in Delinquent Development males up to age 48, Theobald and Farrington (2009) found significant declines in the number of convictions after marriage, though this effect was less pronounced for late marriages as opposed to early or mid-range marriages. The authors argue that '... there

may be an interaction effect between marriage and some variable that is correlated with age such as malleability – a willingness to change or be more flexible in behaviour' (p. 512). Also, the later-married men tended to marry older women who had less influence on their offending (Theobald & Farrington, 2011).

Kruttschnitt, Uggen, and Shelton (2000) explored the predictors of desistance among a sample of sex offenders placed on probation in Minnesota in 1992. They found that '... job stability significantly reduces the probability of reoffending among convicted sex offenders, although marital status exerts virtually no effect' (2000, p. 80; see also Giordano et al., 2002). Kruttschnitt et al. (2000) added that their failure to find an association between marriage and reoffending may be a result of the fact that they did not possess any information about the quality of the marital relationship.

Consistent with the hypothesis that turning points are interdependent, Sampson and Laub's (1993) results revealed interaction effects between various social institutions and desistance from crime. For example, they found that the impact of job stability on desistance was not as significant for married men. Whereas their perspective is more consistent with Hirschi's (1969) control theory, others have adopted a social learning or differential association position, which stipulates that the effect of marriage on crime is mediated by peer associations (see Akers, 1990). This perspective attributes desistance to associations with conventional peers, increased noncriminal routine activities, and reduced exposure to definitions favourable to crime.

In desistance research, while marriage is frequently studied as a major turning point, much less attention is given to the effects of cohabitation (for one of the first analyses of cohabitation using longitudinal data, see Farrington & West, 1995). In an analysis based on a sample of Finnish recidivists, Savolainen (2009, p. 300) found that the '... transition to cohabitation is associated with greater reductions in criminal activity than getting married', highlighting once again the relevance of taking into account the stability of the relationship as opposed to uniquely focusing on marital status. Savolainen (2009, p. 301) also noted a cumulative effect of parenthood and union formation on desistance from crime, concluding that 'offenders who formed a union and became fathers enjoyed the greatest reductions in criminal activity'. Drawing on a sample of 500 women living in underprivileged communities in Denver, Kreager, Matsueda, & Erosheva (2010) found that the transition to motherhood was significantly associated with reduced delinquency and substance use, and that this effect was more pronounced than that of marriage. Conjugal relationships often coincide with having children, and further research is needed to better understand the impact of parenthood on desistance.

Peers

Using a sample from the National Youth Survey (NYS), Warr (1993) found that changes in offending behaviour with age were related to changes in peer associations. The author concluded that, when controlling for peer associations, '… the association between age and crime is substantially weakened and, for some offences, disappears entirely' (1993, p. 35). In a later study, Warr (1998) found that married people tend to spend less time with their friends than unmarried people, and that married individuals tend to have fewer delinquent friends than unmarried individuals. According to his argument, the effect of marriage on desistance is mediated by peer influences and more particularly by the reduced involvement with delinquent friends and lower exposure to criminal opportunities.

Wright and Cullen (2004) replicated Warr's (1998) study and also used data from the National Youth Survey (NYS), but focused on work rather than marriage. The authors studied the predictors of changes in rates of offending (using delinquency and drug scales already constructed as part of the NYS). They found that employment increased the interactions with prosocial co-workers, which '… restructure friendship networks by diminishing contact with delinquent peers' (2004, p. 185). Work was said to promote desistance not through the development of increased social capital, but rather through increased associations with prosocial co-workers. In other words, relationships with prosocial co-workers minimized interactions with delinquent peers and promoted desistance from crime. Wright and Cullen (2004, p. 185) did not dismiss Sampson and Laub's position, nor did they deny the important role of adult employment in the process of desistance from crime, but they also suggest that '… the workplace is a social domain in which learning can take place'. Like Sampson and Laub, they also found that adult employment reduces misbehaviour. However, Wright and Cullen (2004, p. 200) argued that the effects of unemployment on desistance were not dependent on the quality of the job (as argued by Sampson and Laub), but rather on the 'quality of peer associations that occur within the context of work'. Wilson and Herrnstein (1985, p. 285) put forth a similar idea regarding the role of school in the development of criminal behaviour, maintaining that '… the school may contribute to criminality because of the peer groups that form there'.

In agreement with these results, Cromwell, Olson, and Avary (1991, p. 83) found that, for some offenders, '… desistance was a gradual process that appeared to be associated with the disintegration of the adolescent peer group, and with employment and the ability to earn money legitimately' (see also Warr, 1998). Rand (1987) also found a positive correlation between gang

membership and offending. Similarly, in his explanation of desistance from family violence offences, Fagan (1989) underlined the importance of replacing old social networks by new prosocial networks that would disapprove of violent behaviour and promote prosocial behaviour. In the debate concerning the relative influences of sibling and peer delinquency on an individual's offending habits, Robins (1966) maintained that associations with delinquent peers were the result of a choice. In this perspective, delinquent peers would exert a more substantial influence on criminal behaviour, since individuals choose their friends but not their siblings.

It is clear that the association with delinquent friends decreases at the same time as a person's own offending decreases. However, it is less clear whether decreasing peer delinquency has a causal effect on a person's offending (in encouraging desistance) or whether it is merely a risk marker (e.g., because many offences are committed in groups, delinquency and delinquent peers could both reflect the same underlying construct). In the Pittsburgh Youth Study, Farrington, Loeber, Yin, and Anderson (2002) found that, while delinquent peers were strongly correlated with delinquency between individuals, delinquent peers did not predict delinquency in within-individual analyses where boys were followed up over time, suggesting that peer delinquency may not have had a causal effect on offending.

Peer networks may be associated with the environment or the neighbourhood. Kirk's (2012) research suggests that residential change may be an important turning point in criminal careers, a dimension that has been largely ignored in life-course research.

Joining the military

Sampson and Laub's (1993; see also 2003) analysis of the Glueck men suggested that joining the military was an important turning point in the life-course of these individuals. In contrast, Bouffard (2005) found that military service was not associated with offending outcomes (see also Craig & Foster, 2013, for similar results). Craig and Foster (2013, p. 219) explain that the divergence in results '… may indicate a change in the military'. There is a need for research with contemporary samples of individuals having completed military service in order to assess the impact of joining the military on desistance from crime.

Cognitive predictors of desistance

The study of subjective changes that promote desistance from crime has generally been addressed in ethnographic studies and qualitative analyses of crime. Maruna (2001, p. 8) argued that 'Subjective aspects of human life (emotions, thoughts, motivations, and goals) have largely been neglected in the study of crime, because the data are presumed to be either unscientific or too unwieldy for empirical analysis'.

According to Gove (1985), desistance from crime is a result of five key internal changes: shifting from self-centredness to consideration for others, developing prosocial values and behaviour, increasing ease in social interactions, greater consideration for other members of the community, and a growing concern for the 'meaning of life'. Through life history narratives, Giordano et al. (2002) discussed the theory of cognitive transformation, which is defined as *cognitive shifts* that promote the process of desistance. The authors described four processes of cognitive transformations. First, the offender must be open to change. Second, through a process of self-selection, the individual exposes himself/herself to prosocial experiences that will further promote desistance (e.g., employment, etc.). Third, the individual adheres to a new prosocial and noncriminal identity. Finally, there is a shift in the perception of the criminal lifestyle, that is, the negative consequences of offending become obvious. As such, desistance is perceived to be a gradual process. Haggard, Gumpert, and Grann (2001, p. 1056) claimed that 'The decision to change one's life seemed only to be the beginning of a long pathway to actual behavioural alterations'.

Shover and Thompson (1992) found that the relationship between age and desistance was mediated by *optimism for achieving success via legitimate pursuits* and *reduced expectations of criminal success*. In this respect, the individual's optimism and genuine desire to adopt a prosocial lifestyle may play an important role in the desistance process. Burnett (2004) also found that pre-release self-assessments of optimism about desistance were positively associated with actual desistance outcomes after release (see Farrall, 2002, for similar results). Maruna (2001, p. 9) concluded that desisting ex-offenders '... displayed an exaggerated sense of control over the future and an inflated, almost missionary, sense of purpose in life'. The individual's motivation and determination to cease offending is also a key component in the desistance process (Burnett, 2004; Moffitt, 1993a; Pezzin, 1995; Shover, 1983; Shover & Thompson, 1992; Sommers, Baskin, & Fagan, 1994).

Through interviews with a sample of incarcerated burglars, Shover (1996) highlighted the importance of *resolve and determination*, which are also essential to the desistance process. He argued that '... men who are most determined to avoid crime are more successful in doing so than their equivocating peers, even allowing for the possible influences of other factors' (1996, p. 130). Some of the interviewees expressed increasing concern about getting caught as they got older, fearing that they might spend the rest of their lives in prison and therefore miss out on the opportunity to make something of their lives (see also Cromwell et al., 1991). Furthermore, with age, some offenders gave less importance to material gain, which reduced the appeal of crime. Overall, crime (and all the pitfalls attached to it) has a cumulative effect on offenders and sooner or later, they get 'worn down' by a life of crime.

These findings suggest that it may not be age in itself that causes a decline in offending (Gottfredson & Hirschi, 1990), but rather the accumulation, over time, of failures, contacts with the criminal justice system, betrayals and other problems associated with crime. Shover (1996, p. 138) suggested that '... aging makes offenders more interested in the rewards of conventional lifestyles and also more rational in decision making'. Individuals will be more willing to shift from crime to non-crime if the perceived benefits of non-crime are greater than those of crime. It is important to highlight here that the perceived benefits may be quite different from the *actual* benefits, and that this assessment is dependent on the offender's perception of reality. These findings suggest that desistance requires both internal and external changes.

The role of identity change in the desistance process

Some authors have highlighted the importance of identity transformation in the process of desistance (Bottoms, Shapland, Costello, Holmes, & Muir, 2004; Burnett, 2004; Gartner & Piliavin, 1988; Giordano et al., 2002; Laub & Sampson, 2003; Maruna, 2001; Meisenhelder, 1977; Shover, 1983). Maruna (2001, p. 7) argued that '... to desist from crime, ex-offenders need to develop a coherent, prosocial identity for themselves' (see also Shover, 1983). In his sample, Maruna identified a need for desisting offenders to separate their past self from their current self (see also Mischkowitz, 1994). *Making good* refers to a process of 'self-reconstruction' (Maruna, 2001). *Making good* entails an understanding of why past offences were committed, and of the reasons supporting the decision to stop offending. Additionally, it also involves an ability to see the link between past mistakes and current accomplishments, to make the best of past experiences and to discover one's 'true self'.

Laub and Sampson (2003) argued that desistance does not necessarily require cognitive transformation. The authors maintained that '... offenders can and do desist without a conscious decision to "make good" ... and offenders can and do desist without a "cognitive transformation"' (p. 279). According to the authors, most offenders desist as a result of changes in adult social bonds. *Desistance by default* refers to the idea that all offenders naturally desist sooner or later (Laub & Sampson, 2003, p. 278). This idea is similar to the notion of 'spontaneous remission' developed by Stall and Biernacki (1986), which suggests that desistance occurs naturally, without the assistance of external forces. Although desistance does eventually occur for all offenders, it occurs earlier for some individuals than others. Evidence from the studies presented in this chapter seems to suggest that, rather than being a process that occurs 'naturally', desistance needs to be prompted and supported by strong social networks and an individual resolve to change.

The role of cognitive deficits in the desistance process

The large body of research that has explored the role of cognitive distortions in the offending process has often been limited to sex offenders (Abel, Becker, & Cunningham-Rathner, 1984; Marshall & Barbaree, 1990; Murphy, 1990; Segal & Stermac, 1990; Ward, Fon, Hudson, & McCormack, 1998; Ward, Hudson, & Marshall, 1995), and these studies have generally found that cognitive deficits promote sex offending (Ward, Hudson, Johnston, & Marshall, 1997; Ward, Keenan, & Hudson, 2000). Cognitive distortions have also been said to promote aggressive behaviour (Abel et al., 1989; Bumby, 1996; Murphy, 1990). It is acknowledged that the term *cognitive deficits* may encompass a wide range of cognitive traits, although there tends to be some redundancy in the literature with regard to some of these traits.

Barriga, Landau, Stinson, Liau, and Gibbs (2000, p. 37) offered a more general definition of cognitive distortions, defining them as '… inaccurate ways of attending to or conferring meaning on experience'. The authors made the distinction between *self-serving* and *self-debasing* cognitive distortions. Self-serving cognitive distortions protect the 'self' from developing a negative self-image, push the blame away from oneself, and promote harmful acts towards others. In contrast, self-debasing cognitive distortions promote self-harm, with individuals being more likely to blame themselves when negative events occur. Self-debasing cognitive distortions include four dimensions: *catastrophizing* (assuming that every situation will turn into a catastrophe), *overgeneralizing* (believing that the same outcome will apply to all future experiences), *personalizing* (blaming oneself when negative events occur and 'interpreting such events as having a personal meaning', Barriga et al., 2000, p. 39) and *selective abstraction* (selectively focusing on the negative elements of a given experience). The four dimensions used to describe self-serving cognitive distortions are drawn from the Gibbs, Potter, and Goldstein (1995) typology. These dimensions include self-centredness (giving central importance to one's own views, needs, rights, etc., and minimal importance to those of others), placing the blame on others (with regard to harmful actions or victimizations), minimizing the harm

caused (see also Bandura, 1991) or labelling others with demeaning titles, and *assuming the worst*.

Barriga et al. (2000, p. 50) found that

> 'Self-serving cognitive distortions were specifically associated with externalizing behaviour problems, whereas self-debasing cognitive distortions were specifically associated with internalizing behaviour problems. However, these cognitive distortions are not necessarily mutually exclusive. In other words, it was possible for these youths to drift from one type of cognitive distortion to another. For instance, they may blame their victims, but also blame themselves if they have been victimized. The authors concluded that the processes linking cognition and behaviour are "reciprocal, interactive, and mutually reinforcing"' (2000, p. 54).

One of the major cognitive-behavioural programmes developed in offending therapy is the Reasoning and Rehabilitation Program (see Ross, 1995; Ross, Antonowicz, & Dhaliwal, 1995), which is a '… multifaceted, cognitive-behavioural program designed to teach offenders social cognitive skills and values which are essential for prosocial competence' (Ross, 1995, p. 195). This programme was designed to develop skills in eight key cognitive areas: impulsivity, concrete thinking, cognitive rigidity, externality, interpersonal problem-solving skills, egocentricity, a self-centred value system and critical reasoning. It is generally effective in reducing reoffending (Tong & Farrington, 2008).

There is still little consensus in the literature as to whether cognitive distortions occur after the act (in which case they would contribute to maintaining offending behaviour and hampering desistance efforts) or whether they occur before the act, which would imply a causal link to the onset and persistence of crime (see Mann & Beech, 2003, for a detailed literature review; see also Ward et al., 1997). Indeed, Ward et al. (1998, p. 147) argued that 'A major problem with most existing research on the cognitions of sex offenders is that it focuses primarily on post-offence cognitions and neglects the possibility that cognitive processes influence all phases of the offending cycle'. *Post-offence cognitive distortions* '… refer to self-statements made by offenders that allow them to deny, minimize, justify, and rationalize their behaviour' (Murphy, 1990, p. 332). This definition is similar to the concept of *techniques of neutralization* developed by Sykes and Matza (1957).

Techniques of neutralization have been regarded as a category of 'thinking errors' that may promote offending behaviour. According to Sykes and Matza (1957), delinquents are bound by law like conventional individuals, but occasionally they engage in illegal behaviours that are justified through *techniques of neutralization*. Sykes and Matza described five techniques used to rationalize criminal acts. The *denial of responsibility* makes reference to the tendency to adopt a victim stance, to attribute one's behaviour to external forces, and to refuse to assume responsibility for one's actions. The *denial of injury* minimizes the harm caused by the act. The *denial of the victim* can occur either when there is the absence of a known and evident victim, or by claiming that some victims deserve to be treated in the way that they were (see Minor, 1981, for an explanation of the limitations associated with this dual definition). The *condemnation of the condemner* involves criticism directed towards those who express disapproval of one's actions. Finally, the *appeal to higher loyalties* refers to the justification of acts through the claim that actions were a response to the '… demands of the smaller social groups to which the delinquent belongs such as the sibling pair, the gang, or the friendship clique' (Sykes & Matza, 1957, p. 669). Attempts to deny, justify or rationalize one's criminal behaviour or lifestyle have been noted in various studies (Abel *et al.*, 1984; Bandura, 1991; Covell & Scalora, 2002; Herman, 1990; Laub & Sampson, 2003; Nugent & Kroner, 1996; Stermac, Segal, & Gillis, 1990; Ward *et al.*, 1995). It should be noted that, although Sykes and Matza have received much recognition for their techniques of neutralization, other researchers had previously explored this question (Festinger, 1957; Redl & Wineman, 1951).

Maruna and Copes (2004) argued that neutralization theory may not be relevant to the onset of offending (i.e., 'primary deviations', see Lemert, 1951), but may contribute to the maintenance of offending behaviour. In other words, neutralization theory is best suited to explain criminal persistence versus desistance from crime. Similarly, Minor (1981, p. 313) argued that '… neutralising excuses may not only *allow* deviance, but also *encourage* it'. Maruna and Copes (2004) further argued that longitudinal data are necessary to determine the sequence of neutralization and offending.

In summary, Laub and Sampson (2001, p. 3) summarized the main elements involved in the process of desistance, '… aging; a good marriage; securing legal, stable work; and deciding to "go straight", including a reorientation of the costs and benefits of crime' (see also Horney, Tolan, & Weisburd, 2012). Shover (1985) found that, with age, offenders developed an increased interest in employment and prosocial relationships. What remains less understood, however, is how the cognitive and social processes interact to cause a shift towards desistance.

The interaction between social and cognitive factors

One of the most interesting dimensions of the desistance process refers to the way individual predispositions and life events converge to promote this process. Piquero

and Pogarsky (2002, pp. 207–208) argued that '… any explanation of crime must address both the person and the person's social situation, and in this sense, the study of crime is intrinsically social-psychological'. Farrington *et al.* (1990, pp. 285–286) suggested that '… criminal behavior results from the interaction between a *person* (with a certain degree of criminal potential or antisocial potential) and the *environment* (which provides criminal opportunities)' (see also Bottoms *et al.*, 2004). Farrington *et al.* (1990) argued that a given environment can promote offending only for certain individuals, whereas others are likely to offend regardless of the environment. Giordano *et al.* (2002, p. 1026) discussed the link between cognitive processes and situational circumstances, and argued that 'Given a relatively "advantaged" set of circumstances, the cognitive transformations and agentic moves we describe are hardly necessary; under conditions of sufficiently extreme disadvantage, they are unlikely to be nearly enough' (see Warr, 2001, for a similar comment on the link between motivation and opportunity). In this perspective, both individual and environmental components should be taken into account in order to better understand the processes underlying desistance.

Giordano *et al.* (2002) supported the idea that permanent desistance from crime may be a result of both cognitive changes and turning points ('hooks for change'). Through a process of self-selection, life events promote shifts in identity and act as *catalysts* for permanent changes in offending. Some of the main hooks for change identified in the narratives were the links to formal institutions (prison and religion) and intimate or informal networks (spouses and/or children), which is consistent with Sampson and Laub's (1993) theory of formal and informal social control. Various other studies have emphasized the important roles of internal and external factors in the explanation of desistance (Fagan, 1989; Farrall & Bowling, 1999; Laub & Sampson, 2003; Sommers *et al.*, 1994; Stall & Biernacki, 1986).

LeBel *et al.* (2008) made the distinction between *social* (i.e., life events, situational factors, 'objective' changes) and *subjective* (i.e., cognitive factors, internal changes) components in the explanation of desistance. The authors explain that these two categories of factors are not necessarily independent of each other. They discussed three models explaining the interaction between social and subjective factors. First, the *strong subjective model* stipulates that it is the individual's motivation and desire to change that increases the likelihood that bonds will be strengthened by conventional social sources (marriage, legitimate employment, etc.). In this respect, turning points that promote desistance would be the result of a process of self-selection and would not cause a change in behaviour. Second, the *strong social model* asserts that life events occur randomly among individuals, and that these turning points are directly responsible for desistance from crime. Thus, from this viewpoint, subjective characteristics are not essential to desistance from crime. Finally, the third model, the *subjective-social model*, supports the idea that life events may contribute to the desistance process, but postulates that the impact of these events will be dependent on the *mindset* of the individuals. As argued in the preceding text, although motivation is a crucial component of change, it still requires support from conventional social networks to maintain desistance efforts. This last model thus integrates both objective and subjective factors (external and internal changes) in its explanation of desistance.

LeBel *et al.*'s (2008) findings suggested that the desistance process is a system in which various internal and external factors interact in different ways. On one hand, the authors suggested that some social problems occur independently of the optimistic views of the offender. On the other, they also concluded that individuals displaying the greatest motivation to change were also the least likely to recidivate. Individuals who had the right mindset and the social networks to support them were better equipped to face problems, resist temptations and avoid setbacks, provided that the problems faced were not tremendous. However, the authors also concluded that the desire to change may be insufficient when social problems are overwhelming and excessive (see also Bottoms *et al.*, 2004; Farrall & Bowling, 1999; Maruna, 2001). Maruna (2001) explained that the decision and desire to desist from crime is often put to the test by situational factors, such as temptations and frustrations, and in such scenarios the desire to desist from crime may not always be sufficient.

Ross and Ross (1995) found that cognitive deficits are related to offending. They also argued, however, that some offenders have highly developed cognitive skills, to the extent that they manage to escape detection and labelling by the criminal justice system. On the other end of the spectrum, some well-adapted individuals may display some of these cognitive deficits. Some environments may provide better opportunities for education, employment, and interactions with prosocial others, and these factors are likely to neutralize the effects of cognitive deficits. Ross and Ross (1995, p. 66) argued that 'Crime is much too complex a phenomenon to allow one to think that a single factor such as faulty thinking could be a useful *explanatory* concept'. Although cognitive deficits may not be the sole cause of offending behaviour, they may contribute to its explanation. By creating academic, employment and social disadvantages, these cognitive deficits put individuals '… at risk of behaving in illegal ways, but they do not cause them to do so' (Ross & Ross, 1995, p. 66).

Genetic factors and desistance

Few studies have explored the role of genetic factors in the desistance process. In a recent study, Barnes & Beaver (2012) investigated the influence of genetic factors in the marriage-desistance link. The authors drew on prior research that examined the genetic foundations of adult social bonds and focused on active rGEs, which '…occur when a person selects into an environment on the basis of his or her genetic propensities' (p. 22). They found significant genetic influences on both marriage and desistance from crime. Marriage remained a significant predictor of desistance even after controlling for genetic influences, but its effect was greatly attenuated. This is a relatively new area of inquiry in the field of desistance, and more research is needed to better understand gene–environment interactions in the explanation of the desistance process.

Summary

Laub and Sampson (2001, p. 38) summarized the key components promoting the desistance process: 'The significant elements to date are the decision or motivation to change, cognitive restructuring, coping skills, continued monitoring, social support, and general lifestyle change, especially new social networks'. This section has shown that a large body of research has suggested the need to integrate both objective and subjective levels of explanation in the analysis of desistance from crime (Bottoms *et al.*, 2004; LeBel *et al.*, 2008; Le Blanc, 2004; Shover, 1983, 1985, 1996). Despite the substantial developments in desistance research in recent years, some important issues remain unresolved. These will be addressed in the following sections.

UNRESOLVED ISSUES IN DESISTANCE RESEARCH

Major unresolved issues have been discussed by Kazemian (2007).

Defining and measuring desistance

In an extensive review of the desistance literature, Laub and Sampson (2001) argued that few studies have offered an operational definition of desistance, and that there is currently no consensus in the literature on this issue (see also Maruna, 2001; Piquero, Farrington, & Blumstein, 2003). For example, 'Can desistance occur after one act of crime?' (Laub & Sampson, 2001, p. 6). Is the desistance process characterized by a reduction in offending frequency or seriousness (Bushway, Piquero, Broidy, Cauffman, & Mazerolle, 2001)? How many years of non-offending are required to be sure that desistance has occurred? (Bushway *et al.*, 2001; Laub & Sampson, 2001, 2003; Maruna, 2001; Piquero *et al.*, 2003). Uggen and Massoglia (2003, pp. 316–317) argued that 'Because conceptual and operational definitions of desistance vary across existing studies, it is difficult to draw empirical generalizations from the growing literature on desistance from crime'. The disparity in definitions inevitably raises the question as to whether it would be useful to reach a consensus on how to define the concept of desistance, in order to achieve some degree of generalizability regarding its predictors.

False desistance

Desistance is often identified at the last officially recorded or self-reported offence. Since most longitudinal studies have followed up individuals over a relatively limited period of the life-course, the issue of false desistance is an important limitation of desistance studies (Blumstein, Cohen, & Hsieh, 1982; Blumstein, Farrington, & Moitra, 1985; Brame, Bushway, & Paternoster, 2003; Bushway, Brame, & Paternoster, 2004; Bushway *et al.*, 2001; Bushway, Thornberry, & Krohn, 2003; Greenberg, 1991; Laub & Sampson, 2001). Many have argued that definite desistance only occurs when individuals have died (Blumstein *et al.*, 1982; Elliott, Huizinga, & Menard, 1989; Farrington & Wikström, 1994). Conversely, individuals may not have desisted if they had not died. Patterns of intermittency may be misinterpreted as 'desistance'. This issue of 'temporary' versus 'permanent' desistance from crime (or 'zig zag', see Laub & Sampson, 2003; Piquero, 2004) has been highlighted by criminal career researchers (Barnett *et al.*, 1989; Bushway *et al.*, 2004, 2001; Laub & Sampson, 2001; Piquero *et al.*, 2003), although very few studies have explored this question in depth (Piquero, 2004; Piquero *et al.*, 2003).

Desistance as a process

Most studies on desistance have adopted a dichotomous measure of desistance (static) rather than a process view of the phenomenon (dynamic). Static studies do not account for *changes* in rates of offending, nor for the progression along the desistance process. In recent years, an increasing number of researchers have acknowledged the relevance of perceiving desistance as a gradual process rather than an event that occurs abruptly (Bottoms *et al.*, 2004; Bushway *et al.*, 2001, 2003; Fagan, 1989; Greenberg, 1975; Haggard *et al.*, 2001; Laub *et al.*, 1998; Laub & Sampson, 2001, 2003; Le Blanc, 1993; Loeber &

Le Blanc, 1990; Maruna, 2001; Shover, 1983). Since complete desistance is difficult to attain (at least in a sudden manner), the definition of desistance as a concrete state (i.e., the absence of offending) may mask the progress made by individuals across various stages of this process (see Bushway *et al.*, 2001 for a similar discussion). Although different individuals may cease offending at the same age, their criminal careers may be distinguished by very different desistance processes (in terms of frequency, seriousness and length). More recent research has made attempts to integrate a process-view of desistance. In their analyses of desistance among parolees, Bahr, Harris, Fisher, and Armstrong (2010, p. 674) did not focus on '…a specific transition or event such as a rearrest or reincarceration but on how well parolees were able to perform across a period of 3 years'. This type of analysis promotes a process-view of desistance.

In summary, in cases where prospective longitudinal data are not available, where observation periods are short and where dichotomous measures of desistance are used, 'desistance' is more likely to refer to a state of 'temporary nonoffending' (Bushway *et al.*, 2001).

Within-individual versus between-individual predictors of desistance

Gottfredson and Hirschi (1990) claimed that, since criminal potential remains stable across time, it is not useful to follow up individuals over long periods. Sampson and Laub (1993, p. 16) responded to this comment by arguing that 'The continuity to which they [Gottfredson and Hirschi, 1990] refer is relative stability, which does not mean that individuals remain constant in their behavior over time'. Relative stability refers to differences observed between individuals rather than within individuals. In a previous study, Huesmann, Eron, Lefkowitz, and Walder (1984) argued a similar point. They found continuity in the levels of aggression displayed in childhood and adulthood, but referred to it as stability in the relative ranking within a group, rather than within-individual stability in the behavioural manifestation.

One interesting paradox in the field of criminology relates to the fact that, although most adult offenders displayed antisocial behaviour as children, most antisocial children do not become adult offenders (Gove, 1985; Robins, 1978); this observation highlights the importance of absolute change in offending behaviour across the life-course. Though studies have shown that the causes of long-term involvement in offending can be traced back to early ages, and that there is a substantial degree of stability in offending behaviour across the life-course (Farrington & Hawkins, 1991; Gottfredson & Hirschi,

1990; Huesmann *et al.*, 1984; Le Blanc & Fréchette, 1989; Loeber & Le Blanc, 1990; Nagin & Farrington, 1992; Sampson & Laub, 1993; Wilson & Herrnstein, 1985), it has also been suggested that adult life events can potentially influence these offending pathways (Farrington & West, 1995; Laub & Sampson, 2003; Sampson & Laub, 1993). An increasing number of researchers seem to agree that there is both stability and change in offending across the life-course (Farrington & West, 1995; Horney *et al.*, 1995; Moffitt, 1993a; Sampson & Laub, 1993). It is important to distinguish between relative stability and absolute change (Farrington, 1990). Sampson and Laub (2003, p. 584) argued that '... life-course-persistent offenders are difficult, if not impossible, to identify prospectively using a wide variety of childhood and adolescent risk factors', and that '... adult trajectories of offending among former delinquents cannot be reduced to the past' (p. 588). The idea that variables measured in childhood cannot always predict desistance from crime in adulthood has been addressed in previous studies (Laub *et al.*, 1998; Nagin, Farrington, & Moffitt, 1995).

Some authors have stressed that little attention has been given to within-individual change in offending patterns across the life-course (Farrington, 1988; Farrington *et al.*, 2002; Horney *et al.*, 1995; Le Blanc & Loeber, 1998; Sampson & Laub, 1992). In their discussion on within-individual change, Le Blanc and Loeber (1998, p. 116) stated that 'An important feature of this approach is that individuals serve as their own controls'. Past research has focused more on differences in offending patterns between offenders, in contrast to changes within individuals. It has been argued that it is more relevant to demonstrate that offending decreases within individuals after getting married, getting a job or moving house than to demonstrate lower offending rates of married compared with unmarried people, employed versus unemployed people, and so on (Farrington, 2007). Unsurprisingly, between-individual analyses tend to show that individuals with higher self and social control are more likely to desist from crime when compared to those with lower self and social control, and this finding has been demonstrated abundantly in the literature. What is lacking in desistance research is not a contrast of desisting versus persisting offenders, but rather a description of the internal and external factors that promote the desistance process for individuals over time. Kazemian, Farrington, and Le Blanc (2009) found that long-term predictions are more accurate when focusing on between-individual differences in offending gravity scores at age 32 than on within-individual change in offending gravity over a 15-year period, suggesting that within-individual variations in patterns of offending may be more dependent on changing life circumstances.

Self-selection and sequencing

The issue of self-selection has been addressed by various researchers (Farrington & West, 1995; Gottfredson & Hirschi, 1990; Horney *et al.*, 1995; Laub & Sampson, 2001, 2003; McCord, 1994; Moffitt, 1993a; Pallone & Hennessy, 1993; Sampson & Laub, 1993, 1997; Uggen, 2000; Uggen & Massoglia, 2003; Warr, 1998). Since turning points and life events are not randomly assigned among individuals, it is difficult to assess whether these events are *causes or correlates* of desistance. Just as children with neuropsychological and other temperamental deficits are not randomly assigned to supportive or non-supportive environments (Moffitt, 1993b), life-course events may not be coincidental; these may occur as the result of a process of self-selection and reflect underlying criminal propensities. The modern method of addressing selection bias is to carry out propensity score matching (see Theobald & Farrington, 2009). Moffitt (1993b) refers to *proactive* interactions, which occur when individuals select environments or situations that support their lifestyle. Laub and Sampson (2001, p. 23) concluded that 'Selection is thus a threat to the interpretation of any desistance study'. This issue highlights the limited state of knowledge regarding the mechanisms underlying desistance from crime.

Many authors have discussed the complexity of establishing temporal or causal order between cognitive processes, situational circumstances and desistance from crime (Bottoms *et al.*, 2004; Laub & Sampson, 2001; Maruna, 2001; Maruna, LeBel, Burnett, Bushway, & Kierkus, 2002; Mischkowitz, 1994; Shover, 1983; Walters, 2002). The unravelling of these sequences is thorny, mainly because external and internal changes are often interdependent and occur simultaneously (Maruna, 2001; Shover, 1983). Le Blanc (1993, p. 56) summarized this idea:

> Some potential variables may occur in such close proximity to desistance that, for all practical purposes, it is impossible to measure which comes first; moreover, they may have reciprocal influences. ... For example, delinquency can be caused by a weak parental attachment and it may also weaken that bond.

Le Blanc (2004) discussed the interactions between self-control, social control and offending, and argued that these two 'general mechanisms of control' interact through various dynamic processes. These cyclical interactions generate criminal behaviour. According to the author, 'chaos' may occur when an individual offends regularly, and displays weak social bonds and self-control. The key postulate in this theory is that dimensions of self and social control are interdependent and interact in complex ways to produce offending behaviour. In short, cognitive and situational processes often occur simultaneously, which makes it difficult to unravel causal sequences.

CONCLUSIONS

Policy relevance of desistance research

It is important to provide information about predicted future criminal careers (e.g., the probability of persistence vs. desistance, predicted residual career length) to sentencers, parole decision-makers and policy-makers. If offenders are about to desist, it is a waste of scarce prison space to lock them up (from the viewpoint of incapacitation). Risk assessment instruments could be developed on the basis of knowledge about the predictors of termination, deceleration and residual career length (Kazemian & Farrington, 2006). It has been suggested that incapacitation could be used more selectively for those offenders who are predicted to be the most frequent and serious (Greenwood & Abrahamse, 1982). It is also important to investigate when (if ever) an ex-offender becomes indistinguishable from a non-offender in the probability of future offending (Kurlychek, Brame, & Bushway, 2006). This probability would obviously depend on criminal career features such as the time since the last offence and the previous frequency of offending. To the extent that ex-offenders are indistinguishable from non-offenders, ex-offenders should not be discriminated against (e.g., in jobs).

Information about protective factors that foster or accelerate desistance would be important in informing interventions after the onset of criminal careers. Information about the desistance process after release from prison or jail could indicate which offenders need particular types of supervision or support. Ideally, implications about effective interventions to foster desistance at different ages or stages of criminal careers should be drawn from knowledge about the predictors and causes of desistance.

The topic of desistance is also particularly relevant to issues relating to the reintegration process among formerly incarcerated individuals. In his interviews with ex-offenders, Maruna (2001) found that individuals who expressed the will to desist from crime were given little support when they tried to reintegrate into the community after their release from prison. Issues relating to prisoner reintegration are now more pressing than ever. Various authors have reported the staggering increase in prison populations in the United States over the past few decades, despite relatively steady crime rates (Maruna, Immarigeon, & LeBel, 2004; Petersilia, 2003; Travis & Petersilia, 2001). This 'mass incarceration' phenomenon

has resulted in critical implications for post-release re-entry efforts (Petersilia, 2003; Travis, 2005). Petersilia (2003, p. 139) reported that 'Recent data tracking inmates released from prison in 1994 show that two-thirds are rearrested, and nearly one-quarter are returned to prison for a new crime within 3 years of their release'; the author also added that these statistics have been relatively stable since the mid-1960s. These figures illustrate the urgent need to facilitate a successful transition from prison to the community among individuals who have been formerly incarcerated.

As such, there is a genuine need to invest more efforts in offender reintegration and to provide individuals with tools that will allow them to maintain desistance efforts and resist temptations to engage in criminal behaviour (Haggard et al., 2001; Laub & Sampson, 2003; Maruna, 2001). Laub and Sampson (2001, p. 58) argued that '... it is critical that individuals are given the opportunity to reconnect to institutions like family, school, and work after a long period of incarceration or any criminal justice contact for that matter'.

Next steps in desistance research

To conclude, although desistance research has greatly contributed to the advancement of knowledge in the past few years, some important shortcomings remain in this area. Considering all the diverse methodologies that can be used in the analysis of desistance from crime, it comes as no surprise that researchers cannot reach a consensus on this question. Farrington (2007) summarized some of the priority questions that need to be addressed in desistance research:

i) How can desistance (defined as either termination or deceleration) be measured?

ii) How do self-report and official measures of offending and desistance compare?

iii) Could there be desistance from one criminal career followed by reinitiation of another?

iv) Do individuals decelerate in offending before they terminate?

v) What factors predict desistance (or residual career length)? Which features of the past criminal career predict the future criminal career?

vi) Are predictors of desistance similar to predictors of late onset and low continuity?

vii) Are there different predictors of early versus later desistance?

viii) What factors cause desistance according to analyses of within-individual changes?

ix) What protective factors encourage or accelerate desistance?

x) What is the relative importance of later life events and earlier risk factors?

xi) Are life events causes or correlates of desistance?

xii) How accurate are predictions about desistance from developmental and life-course theories?

xiii) Is it useful to distinguish types of individuals who differ in their probability of desistance?

xiv) What interventions foster or accelerate desistance?

xv) What are the effects of criminal justice sanctions on desistance?

xvi) Can a risk assessment instrument for desistance be developed, and would it be valuable for criminal justice decisions and reducing crime?

Farrington (2007) further argued that these questions should be addressed for different ages, times and places, ethnic groups and cultures, offence types and types of antisocial behaviour, and for males versus females (for studies comparing the desistance process of men and women, see Bersani et al., 2009, and Craig & Foster, 2013).

Much previous research on desistance has been based on official records. Future research should focus on self-reports of offending as well. Ideally, a new accelerated longitudinal design should be mounted with at least four age cohorts (10, 20, 30 and 40), drawn from the same area to be as comparable as possible, each followed up for 10 years with annual or biannual interviews. At least at ages 20 and 30, offender samples drawn from the same area should be chosen and also followed up for 10 years. All samples should be drawn from the same large city and should consist of at least 500 persons.

There should be repeated measures of offending; individual, family, peer, school and neighbourhood risk factors; life events (e.g., marriage or cohabitation, jobs, joining or leaving gangs, substance use); situational or opportunity factors; cognitive or decision-making processes; and death, disability or emigration. Special efforts should be made to carry out within-individual analyses. The effects of interventions should be investigated, using either experimental designs or quasi-experimental analyses. In summary, despite the substantial progress and advancement of knowledge in desistance research, much remains unknown about this dimension of the criminal career, and a better understanding of the processes underlying desistance is likely to offer valuable insight for post-onset intervention and prevention efforts.

FURTHER READING

Kazemian, L. and Farrington, D. P. (Eds.) (2007). Special issue on desistance from crime. *Journal of Contemporary Criminal Justice, 23*(1). The articles included in this special issue are revised versions of papers presented at a workshop on desistance held in Washington, DC, on 3–4 May, 2006. The workshop was funded by the National Consortium on Violence Research (NCOVR). The workshop was organized by ourselves and attended by the authors of the articles. The special issue includes a variety of papers that address the topic of desistance, from both theoretical and policy viewpoints. The papers emphasize the need to further develop desistance research in order to address essential questions about this key dimension of the criminal career.

Laub, J. H., & Sampson, R. J. (2001). Understanding desistance from crime. In M. Tonry (Ed.), *Crime and justice* (vol. 28, pp. 1–69). Chicago, IL: University of Chicago Press. This chapter offers a comprehensive review of the desistance literature (up to 2001). The authors address issues of measurement and operationalization of desistance, and present an overview of the predictors of desistance. Laub and Sampson also make the parallel between desistance from criminal behaviour and from other forms of antisocial behaviour, discuss relevant theoretical frameworks, and offer insights for future research and policy implications as it relates to desistance from crime.

Maruna, S. (2001). *Making good: How ex-convicts reform and rebuild their lives.* Washington, DC: American Psychological Association. This book offers an in-depth analysis of the desistance process among a sample of desisting ex-inmates. Using concepts deriving from the field of narrative psychology, Maruna uses the narratives of ex-offenders to study the process of change and desistance from crime.

REFERENCES

Abel, G. G., Becker, J. V., & Cunningham-Rathner, J. (1984). Complications, consent and cognitions in sex between children and adults. *International Journal of Law and Psychiatry, 7*, 89–103.

Abel, G. G., Gore, D. K., Holland, C., Camp, N., Becker, J. V., & Rathner, J. (1989). The measurement of the cognitive distortions of child molesters. *Annals of Sex Research, 2*, 135–152.

Akers, R. (1990). Rational choice, deterrence, and social learning theory in criminology: The path not taken. *Journal of Criminal Law and Criminology, 81,* 653–676.

Bahr, S. J., Harris, L., Fisher, J. K., & Armstrong, A. H. (2010). Successful reentry: What differentiates successful and unsuccessful parolees? *International Journal of Offender Therapy and Comparative Criminology, 54*(5), 667–692.

Bandura, A. (1991). Social cognitive theory of moral thought and action. In W. M. Kurtines & J. L. Gewirtz (Eds.), *Handbook of moral behavior and development*: Vol. 1. *Theory* (pp. 45–103). Hillsdale, NJ: Lawrence Erlbaum.

Barnes, J. C., & Beaver, K. M. (2012). Marriage and desistance from crime: A consideration of gene–environment correlation. *Journal of Marriage and Family, 74,* 19–33.

Barnett, A., Blumstein, A., & Farrington, D. P. (1989). A prospective test of a criminal career model. *Criminology, 27*(2), 373–387.

Barriga, A. Q., Landau, J. R., Stinson, B. L., Liau, A. K., & Gibbs, J. C. (2000). Cognitive distortions and problem behaviors in adolescents. *Criminal Justice and Behavior, 27*(1), 36–56.

Bersani, B. E., & Doherty, E. E. (2013). When the ties that bind unwind: Examining the enduring and situational processes of change behind the marriage effect. *Criminology, 51*(2), 399–433.

Bersani, B. E., Laub, J. H., & Nieuwbeerta, P. (2009). Marriage and desistance from crime in the Netherlands: Do gender and socio-historical context matter? *Journal of Quantitative Criminology, 25*(3), 3–24.

Blumstein, A., Cohen, J., & Hsieh, P. (1982). *The duration of adult criminal careers: Final report to the National Institute of Justice.* Pittsburgh, PA: Carnegie-Mellon University.

Blumstein, A., Farrington, D. P., & Moitra, S. D. (1985). Delinquency careers: Innocents, desisters, and persisters. In M. Tonry & N. Morris (Eds.), *Crime and Justice* (vol. 6, pp. 187–219). Chicago, IL: University of Chicago Press.

Bottoms, A., Shapland, J., Costello, A., Holmes, D., & Muir, G. (2004). Towards desistance: Theoretical underpinnings for an empirical study. *The Howard Journal of Criminal Justice, 43*(4), 368–389.

Bouffard, L. A. (2005). The military as a bridging environment in criminal careers: Differential outcomes of the military experience. *Armed Forces & Society, 31*(2), 273–295.

Brame, R., Bushway, S. D., & Paternoster, R. (2003). Examining the prevalence of criminal desistance. *Criminology, 41*(2), 423–448.

Bumby, K. M. (1996). Assessing the cognitive distortions of child molesters and rapists: Development and validation of the MOLEST and RAPE scales. *Sexual Abuse: A Journal of Research and Treatment, 8,* 37–53.

Burnett, R. (2004). To reoffend or not to reoffend? The ambivalence of convicted property offenders. In S. Maruna & R. Immarigeon (Eds.), *After crime and punishment: Pathways to offender reintegration* (pp. 152–180). Cullompton, Devon: Willan.

Bushway, S. D., Brame, R., & Paternoster, R. (2004). Connecting desistance and recidivism: Measuring changes in criminality over the life span. In S. Maruna & R. Immarigeon (Eds.), *After crime and punishment: Pathways to offender reintegration* (pp. 85–101). Cullompton, Devon: Willan.

Bushway, S. D., Piquero, A. R., Broidy, L. M., Cauffman, E., & Mazerolle, P. (2001). An empirical framework for studying desistance as a process. *Criminology, 39*(2), 491–515.

Bushway, S. D., Thornberry, T. P., & Krohn, M. D. (2003). Desistance as a developmental process: A comparison of static and dynamic approaches. *Journal of Quantitative Criminology, 19*(2), 129–153.

Covell, C. N., & Scalora, M. J. (2002). Empathic deficits in sexual offenders: An integration of affective, social, and cognitive constructs. *Aggression and Violent Behavior, 7,* 251–270.

Craig, J., & Foster, H. (2013). Desistance in the transition to adulthood: The roles of marriage, military, and gender. *Deviant Behavior, 34,* 208–233.

Cromwell, P. F., Olson, J. N., & Avary, D. W. (1991). *Breaking and entering: An ethnographic analysis of burglary.* Newbury Park, CA: Sage.

Doherty, E. E., & Ensminger, M. E. (2013). Marriage and offending among a cohort of disadvantaged African Americans. *Journal of Research in Crime and Delinquency, 50,* 104–131.

Elliott, D. S., Huizinga, D., & Menard, S. (1989). *Multiple problem youth: Delinquency, substance use, and mental health problems.* New York: Springer-Verlag.

Fagan, J. (1989). Cessation of family violence: Deterrence and dissuasion. In L. Ohlin & M. Tonry (Eds.), *Family violence* (pp. 377–425). Chicago, IL: University of Chicago Press.

Farrall, S. (2002). *Rethinking what works with offenders: Probation, social context and desistance from crime.* Cullompton, Devon: Willan.

Farrall, S., & Bowling, B. (1999). Structuration, human development and desistance from crime. *British Journal of Criminology, 39*(2), 253–268.

Farrington, D. P. (1988). Studying changes within individuals: The causes of offending. In M. Rutter (Ed.), *Studies of psychosocial risk* (pp. 158–183). Cambridge: Cambridge University Press.

Farrington, D. P. (1990). Age, period, cohort, and offending. In D. M. Gottfredson & R. V. Clarke (Eds.), *Policy and theory in criminal justice: Contributions in honour of Leslie T. Wilkins* (pp. 51–75). Aldershot: Avebury.

Farrington, D. P. (2007). Advancing knowledge about desistance. *Journal of Contemporary Criminal Justice, 23,* 125–134.

Farrington, D. P., & Hawkins, J. D. (1991). Predicting participation, early onset, and later persistence in officially recorded offending. *Criminal Behaviour and Mental Health, 1,* 1–33.

Farrington, D. P., Loeber, R., Elliott, D. S., Hawkins, J. D., Kandel, D. B., Klein, M. W. et al. (1990). Advancing knowledge about the onset of delinquency and crime. In B. B. Lahey & A. E. Kazdin (Eds.), *Advances in clinical and child psychology* (vol. 13, pp. 283–342). New York: Plenum.

Farrington, D. P., Loeber, R., Yin, Y., & Anderson, S. J. (2002). Are within-individual causes of delinquency the same as between-individual causes? *Criminal Behaviour and Mental Health*, 12(1), 53–68.

Farrington, D. P., & West, D. J. (1995). Effects of marriage, separation, and children on offending by adult males. In Z. S. Blau & J. Hagan (Eds.), *Current perspectives on aging and the life cycle* (vol. 4, pp. 249–281). Greenwich, CT: JAI Press.

Farrington, D. P., & Wikström, P.-O. H. (1994). Criminal careers in London and Stockholm: A cross-national comparative study. In E. G. M. Weitekamp & H.-J. Kerner (Eds.), *Cross-national longitudinal research on human development and criminal behaviour* (pp. 65–89). Dordrecht, The Netherlands: Kluwer Academic.

Festinger, L. (1957). *A theory of cognitive dissonance.* Evanston, IL: Row, Peterson and Company.

Gartner, R., & Piliavin, I. (1988). The aging offender and the aged offender. In P. B. Baltes, D. L. Featherman & R. M. Lerner (Eds.), *Life-span development and behaviour* (vol. 9, pp. 287–315). Hillside, NJ: Lawrence Erlbaum.

Gibbs, J. C., Potter, G., & Goldstein, A. P. (1995). *The EQUIP program: Teaching youth to think and act responsibly through a peer-helping approach.* Champaign, IL: Research Press.

Giordano, P. C., Cernkovich, S. A., & Rudolph, J. L. (2002). Gender, crime, and desistance: Toward a theory of cognitive transformation. *American Journal of Sociology*, 107(4), 990–1064.

Gottfredson, M. R., & Hirschi, T. (1990). *A general theory of crime.* Stanford, CA: Stanford University Press.

Gove, W. (1985). The effect of age and gender on deviant behavior: A biopsychological perspective. In A. S. Rossi (Ed.), *Gender and the life course* (pp. 115–144). New York: Aldine.

Greenberg, D. F. (1975). The incapacitative effect of imprisonment: Some estimates. *Law and Society Review*, 9(4), 541–580.

Greenberg, D. F. (1991). Modelling criminal careers. *Criminology*, 29, 17–46.

Greenwood, P. W., & Abrahamse, A. (1982). *Selective incapacitation.* Santa Monica, CA: RAND Corporation.

Haggard, U., Gumpert, C. H., & Grann, M. (2001). Against all odds: A qualitative follow-up study of high-risk violent offenders who were not reconvicted. *Journal of Interpersonal Violence*, 16(10), 1048–1065.

Herman, J. L. (1990). Sex offenders: A feminist perspective. In W. L. Marshall, D. R. Laws & H. E. Barbaree (Eds.), *Handbook of sexual assault: Issues, theories, and treatment of the offender* (pp. 177–193). New York: Plenum.

Hirschi, T. (1969). *Causes of delinquency.* Berkeley, CA: University of California Press.

Hirschi, T., & Gottfredson, M. R. (1995). Control theory and the life-course perspective. *Studies on Crime and Crime Prevention*, 4(2), 131–142.

Horney, J., Osgood, D. W., & Marshall, I. H. (1995). Criminal careers in the short-term: Intra-individual variability in crime and its relation to local life circumstances. *American Sociological Review*, 60, 655–673.

Horney, J., Tolan, P., & Weisburd, D. (2012). Contextual influences. In R. Loeber & D. P. Farrington (Eds.), *From juvenile delinquency to adult crime* (pp. 86–117). Oxford: Oxford University Press.

Huesmann, L. R., Eron, L. D., Lefkowitz, M. M., & Walder, L. O. (1984). Stability of aggression over time and generations. *Developmental Psychology*, 20(6), 1120–1134.

Irwin, J. (1970). *The felon.* Englewood Cliffs, NJ: Prentice Hall.

Kazemian, L. (2007). Desistance from crime: Theoretical, empirical, methodological, and policy considerations. *Journal of Contemporary Criminal Justice*, 23(1), 28–49.

Kazemian, L., & Farrington, D. P. (2006). Exploring residual career length and residual number of offences for two generations of repeat offenders. *Journal of Research in Crime and Delinquency*, 43, 89–113.

Kazemian, L., Farrington, D. P., & Le Blanc, M. (2009). Can we make accurate long-term predictions about patterns of de-escalation in offending behavior? *Journal of Youth and Adolescence*, 38(3), 384–400.

Kirk, D. (2012). Residential change as a turning point in the life course of crime: Desistance or temporary cessation? *Criminology*, 50(2), 329–358.

Knight, B. J., Osborn, S. G., & West, D. J. (1977). Early marriage and criminal tendencies in males. *British Journal of Criminology*, 17, 348–360.

Kreager, D. A., Matsueda, R. L., & Erosheva, E. A. (2010). Motherhood and criminal desistance in disadvantaged neighborhoods. *Criminology*, 48(1), 221–258.

Kruttschnitt, C., Uggen, C., & Shelton, K. (2000). Predictors of desistance among sex offenders: The interaction of formal and informal social controls. *Justice Quarterly*, 17(1), 61–87.

Kurlychek, M. C., Brame, R., & Bushway, S. D. (2006). Scarlet letters and recidivism: Does an old criminal record predict future offending? *Criminology and Public Policy*, 5, 483–503.

Laub, J. H., Nagin, D. S., & Sampson, R. J. (1998). Trajectories of change in criminal offending: Good marriages and the desistance process. *American Sociological Review*, 63, 225–238.

Laub, J. H., & Sampson, R. J. (2001). Understanding desistance from crime. In M. Tonry (Ed.), *Crime and justice* (vol. 28, pp. 1–69). Chicago, IL: University of Chicago Press.

Laub, J. H., & Sampson, R. J. (2003). *Shared beginnings, divergent lives: Delinquent boys to age 70*. Cambridge, MA: Harvard University Press.

LeBel, T. P., Burnett, R., Maruna, S., & Bushway, S. (2008). The 'chicken and egg' of subjective and social factors in desistance from crime. *European Journal of Criminology, 5*(2), 130–158.

Le Blanc, M. (1993). Late adolescence deceleration of criminal activity and development of self- and social control. *Studies on Crime and Crime Prevention, 2*, 51–68.

Le Blanc, M. (2004). *Self-control and social control in the explanation of deviant behavior: Their development and interactions along the life course.* Paper presented at the Conference on the social contexts of pathways in crime: Development, context, and mechanisms, Cambridge, England (December).

Le Blanc, M., & Fréchette, M. (1989). *Male criminal activity from childhood through youth: Multilevel and developmental perspectives.* New York: Springer-Verlag.

Le Blanc, M., & Loeber, R. (1998). Developmental criminology updated. In M. Tonry (Ed.), *Crime and justice* (vol. 23, pp. 115–198). Chicago, IL: University of Chicago Press.

Lemert, E. M. (1951). *Social pathology.* New York: McGraw-Hill.

Loeber, R., & Le Blanc, M. (1990). Toward a developmental criminology. In M. Tonry & N. Morris (Eds.), *Crime and justice* (vol. 12, pp. 375–473). Chicago, IL: University of Chicago Press.

Mann, R. E., & Beech, A. R. (2003). Cognitive distortions, schemas, and implicit theories. In T. Ward, D. R. Laws & S. M. Hudson (Eds.), *Sexual deviance: Issues and controversies* (pp. 135–153). Thousand Oaks, CA: Sage.

Marshall, W. L., & Barbaree, H. E. (1990). An integrated theory of the etiology of sexual offending. In W. L. Marshall, D. R. Laws & H. E. Barbaree (Eds.), *Handbook of sexual assault: Issues, theories, and treatment of the offender* (pp. 257–275). New York: Plenum Press.

Maruna, S. (2001). *Making good: How ex-convicts reform and rebuild their lives.* Washington, DC: American Psychological Association.

Maruna, S., & Copes, H. (2004). Excuses, excuses: What have we learned from five decades of neutralization research? In M. Tonry (Ed.), *Crime and justice* (vol. 32, pp. 221–320). Chicago, IL: University of Chicago Press.

Maruna, S., Immarigeon, R., & LeBel, T. P. (2004). Ex-offender reintegration: Theory and practice. In S. Maruna & R. Immarigeon (Eds.), *After crime and punishment: Pathways to offender reintegration* (pp. 3–26). Cullompton, Devon: Willan.

Maruna, S., LeBel, T. P., Burnett, R., Bushway, S., & Kierkus, C. (2002). *The dynamics of desistance and prisoner reentry: Findings from a 10-year follow-up of the Oxford University 'Dynamics of Recidivism' study.* Paper presented at the American Society of Criminology Annual Meeting, Chicago, Illinois (November).

McCord, J. (1994). Crimes through time. *Contemporary Sociology, 23*(3), 414–415.

Meisenhelder, T. (1977). An explanatory study of exiting from criminal careers. *Criminology, 15*(3), 319–334.

Minor, W. W. (1981). Techniques of neutralization: A reconceptualization and empirical examination. *Journal of Research in Crime and Delinquency, 18*, 295–318.

Mischkowitz, R. (1994). Desistance from a delinquent way of life? In E. G. M. Weitekamp & H.-J. Kerner (Eds.), *Cross-national longitudinal research on human development and criminal behavior* (pp. 303–327). Dordrecht, The Netherlands: Kluwer Academic.

Moffitt, T. E. (1993a). 'Life-course persistent' and 'adolescence-limited' antisocial behavior: A developmental taxonomy. *Psychological Review, 100*, 674–701.

Moffitt, T. E. (1993b). The neuropsychology of conduct disorder. *Development and Psychopathology, 5*, 133–151.

Murphy, W. D. (1990). Assessment and modifications of cognitive distortions in sex offenders. In W. L. Marshall, D. R. Laws & H. E. Barbaree (Eds.), *Handbook of sexual assault: Issues, theories, and treatment of the offender* (pp. 331–342). New York: Plenum Press.

Nagin, D. S., & Farrington, D. P. (1992). The stability of criminal potential from childhood to adulthood. *Criminology, 30*(2), 235–260.

Nagin, D. S., Farrington, D. P., & Moffitt, T. E. (1995). Life-course trajectories of different types of offenders. *Criminology, 33*(1), 111–139.

Nugent, P. M., & Kroner, D. G. (1996). Denial, response styles, and admittance of offenses among child molesters and rapists. *Journal of Interpersonal Violence, 11*, 475–486.

Pallone, N. J., & Hennessy, J. J. (1993). Tinderbox criminal violence: Neurogenic impulsivity, risk-taking, and the phenomenology of rational choice. In R. V. Clarke & M. Felson (Eds.), *Routine activity and rational choice* (Crime Prevention Studies, vol. 5, pp. 127–157). New Brunswick, NJ: Transaction.

Petersilia, J. (2003). *When prisoners come home: Parole and prisoner reentry.* New York: Oxford University Press.

Pezzin, L. E. (1995). Earning prospects, matching effects, and the decision to terminate a criminal career. *Journal of Quantitative Criminology, 11*(1), 29–50.

Piquero, A. (2004). Somewhere between persistence and desistance: The intermittency of criminal careers. In S. Maruna & R. Immarigeon (Eds.), *After crime and punishment: Pathways to offender reintegration* (pp. 102–125): Cullompton, Devon: Willan.

Piquero, A., Farrington, D. P., & Blumstein, A. (2003). The criminal career paradigm. In M. Tonry (Ed.), *Crime and justice* (vol. 30, pp. 359–506). Chicago, IL: University of Chicago Press.

Piquero, A., & Pogarsky, G. (2002). Beyond Stafford and Warr's reconceptualization of deterrence: Personal and vicarious experiences, impulsivity, and offending behavior. *Journal of Research in Crime and Delinquency, 39*, 153–186.

Rand, A. (1987). Transitional life events and desistance from delinquency and crime. In M. E. Wolfgang, T. P. Thornberry & R. M. Figlio (Eds.), *From boy to man, from delinquency to crime* (pp. 134–162). Chicago, IL: University of Chicago Press.

Redl, F., & Wineman, D. (1951). *Children who hate: The disorganization and breakdown of behavior controls*. Glencoe, IL: Free Press.

Rhodes, W. M. (1989). The criminal career: Estimates of the duration and frequency of crime commission. *Journal of Quantitative Criminology, 5*(1), 3–32.

Robins, L. N. (1966). *Deviant children grown up*. Baltimore, MD: Williams and Wilkins.

Robins, L. N. (1978). Sturdy childhood predictors of adult antisocial behavior: Replications from longitudinal studies. *Psychological Medicine, 8*, 611–622.

Ross, R. R. (1995). The Reasoning and Rehabilitation program for high-risk probationers and prisoners. In R. R. Ross, D. H. Antonowicz & G. K. Dhaliwal (Eds.), *Going straight: Effective delinquency prevention and offender rehabilitation* (pp. 195–222). Ottawa: Air Training and Publications.

Ross, R. R., Antonowicz, D. H., & Dhaliwal, G. K. (Eds.) (1995). *Going straight: Effective delinquency prevention and offender rehabilitation*. Ottawa: Air Training and Publications.

Ross, R. R., & Ross, R. D. (1995). *Thinking straight: The Reasoning and Rehabilitation program for delinquency prevention and offender rehabilitation*. Ottawa: Air Training and Publications.

Rutter, M. (1996). Transitions and turning points in developmental psychopathology: As applied to the age span between childhood and mid-adulthood. *Journal of Behavioral Development, 19*, 603–626.

Sampson, R. J., & Laub, J. H. (1992). Crime and deviance in the life course. *Annual Review of Sociology, 18*, 63–84.

Sampson, R. J., & Laub, J. H. (1993). *Crime in the making: Pathways and turning points through life*. Cambridge, MA: Harvard University Press.

Sampson, R. J., & Laub, J. H. (1997). A life-course theory of cumulative disadvantage and the stability of delinquency. In T. P. Thornberry (Ed.), *Developmental theories of crime and delinquency* (Advances in Criminological Theory, vol. 7, pp. 133–161). New Brunswick, NJ: Transaction.

Sampson, R. J., & Laub, J. H. (2003). Life-course desisters: Trajectories of crime among delinquent boys followed to age 70. *Criminology, 41*(3), 555–592.

Savolainen, J. (2009). Work, family and criminal desistance: Adult social bonds in a Nordic welfare state. *British Journal of Criminology, 49*, 285–304.

Segal, Z. V., & Stermac, L. E. (1990). The role of cognition in sexual assault. In W. L. Marshall, D. R. Laws & H. E. Barbaree (Eds.), *Handbook of sexual assault: Issues, theories, and treatment of the offender* (pp. 161–172). New York: Plenum.

Shover, N. (1983). The later stages of ordinary property offender careers. *Social Problems, 31*(2), 208–218.

Shover, N. (1985). *Aging criminals*. Beverly Hills, CA: Sage.

Shover, N. (1996). *Great pretenders*. Boulder, CO: Westview Press.

Shover, N., & Thompson, C. Y. (1992). Age, differential expectations, and crime desistance. *Criminology, 30*(1), 89–104.

Sommers, I., Baskin, D. R., & Fagan, J. (1994). Getting out of the life: Crime desistance by female street offenders. *Deviant Behavior, 15*, 125–149.

Stall, R., & Biernacki, P. (1986). Spontaneous remission from the problematic use of substances. *International Journal of the Addictions, 21*, 1–23.

Stermac, L. E., Segal, Z. V., & Gillis, R. (1990). Social and cultural factors in sexual assault. In W. L. Marshall, D. R. Laws & H. E. Barbaree (Eds.), *Handbook of sexual assault: Issues, theories, and treatment of the offender* (pp. 143–156). New York: Plenum.

Sykes, G., & Matza, D. (1957). Techniques of neutralization: A theory of delinquency. *American Sociological Review, 22*, 664–670.

Theobald, D., & Farrington, D. P. (2009). Effects of getting married on offending: Results from a prospective longitudinal survey of males. *European Journal of Criminology, 6*(6), 496–516.

Theobald D., & Farrington, D. P. (2011). Why do the crime-reducing effects of marriage vary with age? *British Journal of Criminology, 51*, 136–158.

Theobald, D., & Farrington, D. P. (2013). The effects of marital breakdown on offending: Results from a prospective longitudinal survey of males. *Psychology, Crime and Law, 19*, 391–408.

Tong, L. S. J., & Farrington, D. P. (2008). Effectiveness of 'Reasoning and Rehabilitation' in reducing reoffending. *Psicothema, 20*, 20–28.

Travis, J. (2005). *But they all come back: Facing the challenges of prisoner re-entry*. Washington, DC: The Urban Institute Press.

Travis, J., & Petersilia, J. (2001). Reentry reconsidered: A new look at an old question. *Crime and Delinquency, 47*(3), 291–313.

Tripodi, S. J., Kim, J. S., & Bender, K. (2010). Is employment associated with reduced recidivism? The complex relationship between employment and crime. *International Journal of Offender Therapy and Comparative Criminology, 54*(5), 706–720.

Uggen, C. (2000). Work as a turning point in the life course of criminals: A duration model of age, employment, and recidivism. *American Sociological Review, 67*, 529–546.

Uggen, C., & Massoglia, M. (2003). Desistance from crime and deviance as a turning point in the life course. In J. T. Mortimer & M. J. Shanahan (Eds.), *Handbook of the life course* (pp. 311–329). New York: Kluwer Academic/Plenum.

Van Schellen, M., Poortman, A.-R., & Nieuwbeerta, P. (2012). Partners in crime? Criminal offending, marriage formation, and partner selection. *Journal of Research in Crime and Delinquency, 49*(4), 545–571.

Walters, G. D. (2002). Developmental trajectories, transitions, and nonlinear dynamical systems: A model of crime deceleration and desistance. *International Journal of Offender Therapy and Comparative Criminology, 46*(1), 30–44.

Ward, T., Fon, C., Hudson, S. M., & McCormack, J. (1998). A descriptive model of dysfunctional cognitions in child molesters. *Journal of Interpersonal Violence, 13*(1), 129–155.

Ward, T., Hudson, S. M., Johnston, L., & Marshall, W. L. (1997). Cognitive distortions in sex offenders: An integrative review. *Clinical Psychology Review, 17*(5), 479–507.

Ward, T., Hudson, S. M., & Marshall, W. L. (1995). Cognitive distortions and affective deficits in sex offenders: A cognitive deconstruction interpretation. *Sexual Abuse: A Journal of Research and Treatment, 7*, 67–83.

Ward, T., Keenan, T., & Hudson, S. M. (2000). Understanding cognitive, affective, and intimacy deficits in sexual offenders: A developmental perspective. *Aggression and Violent Behavior, 5*(1), 41–62.

Warr, M. (1993). Age, peers, and delinquency. *Criminology, 31*, 17–40.

Warr, M. (1998). Life-course transitions and desistance from crime. *Criminology, 36*(2), 183–216.

Warr, M. (2001). Crime and opportunity: A theoretical essay. In R. F. Meier, L. W. Kennedy & V. F. Sacco (Eds.), *The process and structure of crime: Criminal events and crime analysis* (Advances in Criminological Theory, vol. 9, pp. 65–94). New Brunswick, NJ: Transaction.

Wilson, J. Q., & Herrnstein, R. J. (1985). *Crime and human nature.* New York: Simon & Schuster.

Wright, J. P., & Cullen, F. T. (2004). Employment, peers, and life-course transitions. *Justice Quarterly, 21*(1), 183–205.

12 Crisis Negotiation

David A. Crighton

Crisis negotiation is used here to refer to the application of efforts to reach mutually agreed resolutions to a range of critical incidents, generally involving the holding or threatening individuals, materials or both. It therefore includes incidents of hostage taking, kidnapping and also offences such as piracy, where merchant shipping may be targeted and held for ransom (Bueger, 2013; Forrest, 2012).

Negotiation itself is a common process in much of human interaction. Indeed it is normally a facet of any agreements between people and so would include areas such as politics, social and economic agreements. Given this there is a considerable evidence base on the area of negotiation. This is largely, although not exclusively, concerned with negotiation within organizational contexts. The focus of this chapter is on the manner in which negotiation may be applied to the types of critical incidents outlined in the preceding text. The area of crisis negotiation is one that is often poorly understood, with greater clarity in the area often being held back by an undue focus on some of the more peripheral, and perhaps salacious, aspects of the situations involved. In reality crisis negotiation draws on well understood and researched clinical and counselling skills, common across applied psychology. Such work is also able to draw on extensive research and practice into the use of principled negotiation in other fields, such as industrial relations. The process of crisis negotiation is in reality quite straightforward and easy to understand. It does though present significant challenges in terms of research and practice and throws the skills used into sharp relief, with the costs of poor practice often high.

CONCEPTUAL ISSUES IN CRISIS NEGOTIATION

Crisis negotiation involves the process of trying to resolve a range of situations where a threat of intentional harm is made or implied. Such situations will most commonly involve one or more persons being detained against their will, in order for those detaining them to try to achieve a specific goal. As noted such incidents include cases of kidnapping as well as hostage incidents. It is important to note that the goals involved may or may not be clear, or appear rational, to both parties.

Negotiation involves an effort to come to a mutually agreeable resolution to any given situation by peaceful means and it contrasts with the use of 'tactical' resolutions, where force may be used to release captives or materials, by the overpowering of the perpetrators. Principled negotiation refers to a technique for efficiently obtaining a favourable and fair outcome from any negotiated situation (Zwier, 2013). The approach has been applied to crisis negotiation for some time. It recognizes that for most situations of this type they are not zero sum games[1] (Fisher, 1983; Fisher, Ury, & Patton, 2011). It can be contrasted with approaches such as 'positional' or 'distributional' bargaining approaches, which involve explicit conflict as a gain for one party is seen to represent a loss for the other.[2]

Forensic Psychology, Second Edition. Edited by David A. Crighton and Graham J. Towl.
© 2015 John Wiley & Sons, Ltd. Published 2015 by British Psychological Society and John Wiley & Sons, Ltd.

Types of critical incidents

Firstly it is perhaps worth drawing a distinction between crisis negotiation with 'terrorist' groups and those with 'criminal' or other motives. A universally accepted definition of terrorism is lacking and precise definitions vary markedly. A review of the area in the United Kingdom by Carlile (2007) suggests the definition of terrorism in the Prevention of Terrorism (Temporary Provisions) Act 1989 as a useful starting point:

> … the use of violence for political ends, and includes any use of violence for the purpose of putting the public or any section of the public in fear.

As Carlile (2007) goes on to note this starting definition has a number of significant weaknesses. These include the fact that the definition does not encompass threats of violence, which are clearly relevant. He also notes that there was no requirement for the violence to be serious, meaning that the definition is likely to be over inclusive, capturing non-serious events. A more precise definition is given in the amended *UK Terrorism Act 2000*, and it is this working definition which is used throughout this chapter. This defines terrorism as:

1. Terrorism: interpretation
   (1) In this Act 'terrorism' means the use or threat of action where:
      (a) The action falls within subsection (2).
      (b) The use or threat is designed to influence the government or an international governmental organization or to intimidate the public or a section of the public.
      (c) The use or threat is made for the purpose of advancing a political, religious or ideological cause.
   (2) Action falls within this subsection if it:
      (a) Involves serious violence against a person.
      (b) Involves serious damage to property.
      (c) Endangers a person's life, other than that of the person committing the action.
      (d) Creates a serious risk to the health or safety of the public or a section of the public.
      (e) Is designed seriously to interfere with or seriously to disrupt an electronic system.
   (3) The use or threat of action falling within subsection (2) which involves the use of firearms or explosives is terrorism whether or not subsection (1)(b) is satisfied.
   (4) In this section:
      (a) 'Action' includes action outside the United Kingdom.
      (b) A reference to any person or to property is a reference to any person, or to property, wherever situated.
      (c) A reference to the public includes a reference to the public of a country other than the United Kingdom.
      (d) 'The government' means the government of the United Kingdom, of a Part of the United Kingdom or of a country other than the United Kingdom.
   (5) In this Act, a reference to action taken for the purposes of terrorism includes a reference to action taken for the benefit of a proscribed organization.

The separation of terrorism and criminal violence is generally seen as useful, on the basis that although 'terrorist' incidents may overlap with 'criminal' incidents, they do tend to be qualitatively different in a number of significant ways. Within the definition in the preceding text, the role of motivations is central and includes what might be generally termed social and political motivations. In the past these have ranged from efforts to change the economic and social system in West Germany through to nationalist terrorism in Ireland to religiously motivated groups such as Al Qaeda (Becker, 1977; Post, 2007). Incidents defined as 'terrorism' have an explicit intention of influencing policy, either of governments or international bodies. Such incidents may also involve actions or threats of action including damage conducted at distance, such as damage to electronic infrastructure with the sole aim of engendering fear and anxiety in the general population. Such incidents may also differ in the extent and quality of strategic planning by the perpetrators. Politically motivated groups and states may have the ability to draw on significant external and internal resources including guidance, operational research and materials. Such support may be provided by highly developed states and involve access to sophisticated technologies not otherwise accessible. At a practical level terrorist groups may also have sophisticated command and control structures. As a result negotiations with such groups may present the most significant challenges and complex negotiations.

In relation to crisis negotiation in criminally motivated incidents it has been suggested that it is useful to draw a distinction between those where tangible and 'instrumental' demands are made and those where a person is held for 'non-instrumental', intangible and emotional reasons. It has been suggested that these can be described as 'hostage' and 'non-hostage' incidents, on the basis that the latter type of incidents are fundamentally different (Vecchi, Van Hasselt, & Romano, 2005). This distinction is not used here on the basis that the terminology is potentially confusing and there is little current evidence to support such a clear distinction. However, the notion that incidents in law enforcement and what might be termed 'correctional' settings (including prisons and secure hospitals) will involve a continuum in terms of how 'instrumental' they are is relatively well established. At a practice level such a continuum also appears to have utility in informing crisis negotiation. Such utility would though be easy to overstate. There is evidence to suggest that even in well planned and apparently 'instrumental' crisis incidents, high levels of emotional arousal are typically present regardless of motives (Crighton, 1992). This would appear to be acute during the early stages of most incidents when the level of risk of serious harm may be at its greatest.

It is also possible to usefully divide incidents in terms of the degree of containment. Incidents in correctional settings present crisis incidents that are highly contained. It is generally possible to isolate the scene relatively easily and quickly, to eliminate any outside contact and support and to establish a simple command structure with short lines of communication. This essentially involves two levels of management, one at the scene and often termed 'silver command' and one remote from the incident often termed 'gold command'. Such incidents typically also involve lone or occasionally small numbers of perpetrators and any support that is available to them tends to be limited and of poor quality. Access to means of publicity through the media or Internet is also likely very limited and can generally be controlled by negotiators. The nature of the scene of the incident is also normally well understood, with detailed blueprints of the scene being accessible and the environment is normally designed to facilitate interventions. In turn this means that tactical resolutions are straightforward to plan and implement (Crighton, 1991; 1992; Crighton & Towl, 2008). Highly contained incidents are therefore the most straightforward form of crisis negotiation to manage. There have been exceptions to this pattern in correctional settings and examples here would include the sieges which took place at Attica prison riot in New York State (Wicker, 1994), the Strangeways riot at Manchester prison in the United Kingdom (Boin & Rattray, 2004) and the Carandiru prison riot in Brazil (Willis, 2014). In these incidents the loss of containment by prison authorities overwhelmed their capacity to manage the crisis and resulted in serious human rights violations, injury, loss of life, material and political costs.

Incidents in community settings, typically dealt with by law enforcement agencies (local, regional and national policing services) will generally involve lower levels of containment. Such incidents may more typically involve multiple perpetrators and limiting outside contact is often more difficult and can present serious and ongoing challenges. In such incidents perpetrators will generally not have significant external support and guidance. The use of firearms is also more common than for incidents in correctional settings. In states where access to firearms is relatively easy this can include access to relatively sophisticated equipment which can match, or exceed, that of initial responders. In cases of kidnapping or piracy the location of the perpetrators may be vague and may take significant time to obtain. Tactical resolution in such cases is impossible in the short term and typically will present significant challenges even in the medium or longer term. The level of understanding of the scene is also likely, particularly in the early phases, to be limited and often inadequate to allow a tactical response. Following a history of failed and at times catastrophic tactical interventions, this role is now normally carried out by specialist Police Service units, for example, Special Weapons and Tactics (SWAT) teams used in the United States, Specialist Regional Firearms Units in the United Kingdom or the Special Duties Unit in Hong Kong (Crighton, 1992).[3]

Terrorist incidents will generally show the lowest levels of containment. Incidents may involve negotiations at substantial distances, where at least in the short term intervention is impossible. Incidents may also more typically involve multiple perpetrators. Both of these characteristics are often shared with criminally motivated incidents such as piracy. Terrorist incidents differ though with the likelihood of developed 'cell' and external command structures being present. The ability to isolate and contain the scene, or the perpetrators, may be more limited or indeed nonexistent in such incidents. They may also involve large numbers of hostages or in the cases of kidnappings may involve victims seen as 'high value'. Such incidents clearly present the greatest challenges in terms of crisis negotiation. Tactical resolution in such incidents also tends to particularly difficult and normally rests with state military or paramilitary specialist units such as, for example, GSG 9 in Germany, the Special Air or Boat Services in the United Kingdom, Navy Seal Units in the United States and so on. Tactical resolution in such incidents often presents high potential costs associated with failed interventions. This may include high costs in terms of loss of life, serious injury, economic and political costs. There is also limited opportunity to manage media access. A clear and well understood historical example of the challenges involved would be an operation conducted by the United States to intervene in a hostage incident in Tehran in April 1980. Here a tactical resolution failed, resulting in the deaths of eight and injury of five of the specialist intervention team, the loss of sensitive equipment and materials as well as significant political costs: all with no release of the hostages. The release of the hostages was eventually achieved by means of protracted negotiation and substantial concessions to the hostage takers. Here the failure of tactical intervention served to weaken the negotiating position and served to increase the costs of resolution.

TO NEGOTIATE OR NOT TO NEGOTIATE

There are a number of key issues associated with crisis negotiation and these have been reviewed in detail by Fowler (2007). The first and perhaps most pressing of these is whether the mere fact of negotiating increases the risk of future hostage taking, kidnapping or piracy. It is argued that reaching negotiated settlements gives an incentive to kidnapping and hostage taking. In relation to what might be termed 'criminal' hostage taking this issue seems to have been largely resolved in favour of negotiation. The use of a principled negotiation approach is generally seen as the default response to these incidents. There is a clear possibility here that media coverage may encourage copycat incidents, as a means of trying to resolve similar problems or simply to gain notoriety. This concern needs though to be offset against the high costs of failed tactical responses or indeed non-responding. The situation with terrorist crisis incidents is less clear cut and, as Fowler (2007) notes, most governments have engaged in strong rhetoric against negotiation. An example from 2014 involved the release of a US soldier held by an Islamic group in Afghanistan, in exchange for five prisoners held at the Guantanamo Bay detention facility in Cuba. This exchange was extensively criticized at the time as placing a clear 'premium' on taking US military personnel hostage and also for providing a media opportunity for terror groups in Afghanistan. Perhaps linked to this such exchanges have often been reframed as prisoner of war exchanges (Sherfinski, 2014).

The rhetoric against negotiation appears to be based on notions of deterrence and perhaps also a need to mitigate any political losses. In fact the practical reality is often somewhat different and few governments, whatever their rhetoric, have genuinely refused to engage in negotiation to resolve critical incidents. An example of a government carrying through such rhetoric would be the response of Israel to the Munich Olympics siege, where they refused to negotiate with the Black September

group and after the incident followed up with counter actions (Calahan, 1995; Klein, 2007). Here the hostages were killed following a failed tactical intervention by German police. Subsequently it is clear that Israel has used negotiation resulting in significant prisoner exchanges (Gordon & Lopez, 2000).

GOALS OF CRISIS NEGOTIATION

Crisis negotiation can be seen as involving a number of related processes and for the purposes of exposition these can be set out sequentially. In reality these are likely to interact in a complex and dynamic manner.

Calming the situation

Crisis incidents are by definition those where normal means of resolving difficulties have broken down and the person or group involved see insurmountable obstacles to achieving their goals through normal means (Caplan, 1961; Carkhuff & Berenson, 1977). Such perceptions may or may not be accurate. The primary goal of crisis negotiation though is to seek a mutually agreeable resolution to a critical incident through acceptable means, while avoiding the use of tactical resolution (Crighton, 1991, 1992; Fisher, 2011; Fisher et al., 2011).

The need to reduce the levels of psychological arousal and develop a greater sense of calm is an essential first step to reducing risk and working towards a resolution of difficulties. This is not unique to crisis negotiation and draws on a range of common clinical and counselling skills typically used to address individual crises. A clear example here would be the use of counselling approaches to reduce the risk of intentional self-injury as a means of trying to manage uncontrollable feelings of anger or self-destructive behaviours. This provides striking parallels, where the normal processes of resolving difficulties break down and result in violence, in one case being self-directed and in the other externally directed.

High levels of arousal may be typical in the acute phase of critical incidents where the person or group may appear to be highly emotional and agitated. Examples of incidents here might include the break-up of a relationship and loss of contact with children, resulting in the children or a former partner being held hostage. The combination of emotional arousal and an inability to cope with the challenges being experienced are likely to make it difficult to discuss matters rationally. A primary goal of crisis negotiation in such circumstances is therefore one of calming the situation and progressively reducing arousal. The skills needed to do this are common to those used more generally in counselling (Towl, 2011) and typically would involve the negotiator presenting in calm empathic manner and showing that they are concerned to reach a constructive solution.

Process of crisis negotiation

A variety of models of crisis negotiation have been suggested drawing on the broader clinical and counselling evidence base (Rogan, 2011; Towl, 2011). Such models suggest a process moving from initial calming and the reduction of arousal to the analysis of the situation and a process of constructive problem solving. The acute phase of a crisis tends to be the point where violence is most likely. The model suggested by Fisher *et al.* (2011) has been particularly influential in the development of crisis negotiation in law enforcement settings and this suggests four main themes:

- Separating the person from the problem
- Focusing on interests rather than positions
- Generating options
- Establishing clear criteria for change

These themes have been subject to some criticism and efforts at refinement in a number of respects to meet the needs of critical incident negotiation. These have included concerns that the outline lacks sufficient focus on the calming and rapport building phase of a crisis. Equally it has been argued that the model overemphasizes problem-solving approaches. Concerns have also been raised that the model tends to neglect broader considerations such as intelligence gathering and tactical resolution (Crighton, 1992; Flood, 2003).

Communication and rapport building

Having progressed beyond the initial phase of a critical incident the aim is to develop a process of constructive engagement and communication. This may in the case of correctional settings involve face to face contact or may alternatively involve quite close contact. In community settings it may more typically involve the use of remote communications, for example, by means of telephone contact. Terrorist incidents may involve the least direct communications and may involve remote and delayed communication or the use of electronic means. In this respect such negotiations have been described as being more like playing chess by correspondence (Crighton, 1992). Regardless of the means of communication used though a major aim and challenge is to establish and build rapport.

Rapport can be defined as the development of an empathetic and harmonious relationship. In the absence of this it is less likely that later efforts to engage in negotiation will be effective. Models of rapport building generally stress a number of characteristics of the process. Typically these would stress listening, showing empathy, reflecting back and developing influence.

Listening

The notion of active listening in counselling involves both listening and being seen by others to listen. In doing this counsellors may use a number of key skills This may involve the use of open ended questions and the avoidance of closed questions, where a yes or no answer is possible, to elicit more information. The use of paraphrasing may also be used and this involves summarizing and referring back what is said in a calm and balanced manner. It may also involve a range of other counselling skills and techniques used to defuse tension. These might include the careful use of pauses and silences, to allow the other person to reflect on what has been recently said. It may also involve providing minimal encouragement to allow the person to keep talking. As noted by Vecchi (2003) it might also include the careful use of 'I' statements to develop rapport but it is important not to make presumptions about knowing how the other person feels. It is suggested that statements taking the form 'I can only imagine how that would feel' may help to build rapport, whereas statements taking the form 'I know how you feel' are likely to act as barriers to developing rapport.

There are a number of counselling techniques concerned with the demonstration of active listening. These would include avoiding interruptions. In normal conversation people frequently interrupt and talk over each other but during a crisis this is likely to act as a significant barrier. The use of 'mirroring' and 'reflecting back' in largely unaltered form also demonstrate that the negotiator is listening to what is being said and helps to communicate genuine concern.

Showing empathy

Empathy involves showing the ability to understand and engage with the thoughts and feelings of another person or group. The ability to put themselves in the place of a perpetrator and understand and empathize with them in such a manner is likely to be significant in successful communication by negotiators. An ability to take other perspectives during crisis negotiation is likely to facilitate the development of empathy and, as such, is a core aspect of the process. In addition showing concern for others may often be central. Displays of genuine concern for others are likely to help to develop empathy and also may serve to reduce aggression and violence.

Building rapport

Rapport has been variously described in terms of building a sympathetic and harmonious relationship. Rapport building appears closely linked to the ability to show and build empathy with others and this can involve a variety of skills. Essentially it involves a process of increasing trust and affinity and, in this respect, the ethical conduct of negotiators is critical. Developing trust depends on a high degree of integrity and honesty from negotiators, even where this is uncomfortable or challenging. In addition efforts to reframe issues in a constructive way are likely to build rapport. In contrast efforts to contradict and challenge are likely to reduce rapport. Rapport also appears to be assisted by a process termed Linguistic Style Matching (LSM) (Niederhoffer & Pennebaker, 2002), where parties in successful negotiations appear to converge on similar styles of expression. Higher levels of convergence appear to help the development of rapport and progression towards constructive solutions.

Developing influence

The notion of developing influence builds on the degree of empathy and rapport that can be established and involves processes of developing and elaborating on themes that may help to resolve the situation (Vecchi et al., 2005). This might, for example, involve efforts to reduce the differences in the positions of parties as part of a negotiated resolution. It is likely to be important to stress areas of agreement wherever this is possible and to identify and reinforce any common ground. In turn, this can inform strategies for resolution which can then begin to be discussed jointly.

Gathering intelligence

A fundamental part of negotiation is that the simple passage of time without the occurrence of harm or injury is a positive. There are a number of reasons for this, including the fact that this allows the person or group involved to reduce their levels of arousal and return to normal psychological functioning. As noted this allows efforts at rapport building and negotiation towards an agreed solution to proceed. Reducing levels of arousal is also important in lowering the risk of violence (Spector, 1977) and may allow for the effects of any substances used to dissipate.

Additionally though, the passage of time allows for the gathering of intelligence (Vecchi et al., 2005). This would include efforts to identify those involved in a given incident, the levels of potential lethality and precipitating events. It also allows time to develop better understanding of the location of hostages and the development of better psychological profiles of those involved. Better intelligence may make it more likely that principled negotiation can develop successfully. It also allows for the formulation of better plans for tactical resolution where this is necessary, as well as informing follow-up work with those involved.

CRISIS NEGOTIATION AND TERRORISM

It has been convincingly suggested that crisis negotiation with terrorist groups showed progressive growth through the twentieth and into the twenty-first century (Sherfinski, 2014). This has been the case despite resistance to the idea by governments. Strategies based on not engaging in negotiation however present a number of significant problems which are not easy to dismiss or deal with (Fowler, 2007). These would include the fact that, as noted in the preceding text, negotiation may serve to forestall violence against hostages. Negotiation may also allow for a process of reducing the risks and the costs involved. Examples of this would include the securing of early release of some hostages or groups of hostages, such as children or nationals of other states. This in turn can contribute to working towards a mutually acceptable resolution and reduces the potential costs in terms of loss of life and serious injury. Engaging in negotiation is also important in terms of the longer term morale of staff working in often difficult and dangerous situations. Policies of non-negotiation may serve to markedly increase risk to staff, in turn making it more difficult to engage people to work in what may be volatile and high risk environments. Alternatively blanket injunctions against negotiation may serve to indirectly reduce the effectiveness of those operating in high risk settings, as they increasingly withdraw from some forms of work activity. In turn this may impose significant costs by, for example, reducing the quality of work or the willingness to take constructive risks in dysfunctional and failing states and volatile parts of the world.

The suggestion that negotiation may lead to an increase in hostage taking has often been posited and has an intuitive appeal, based on simple notions of rewarding and reinforcing behaviour. The evidence to support this claim is though remarkably sparse. Such thinking perhaps betrays a poor understanding of the motives that underlie kidnappings and hostage taking in this context. There may often be more than one motive in such incidents and a desire to negotiate with government or other agencies may not be first among these. Aims such as gaining publicity for a cause may be independent of such contact and might indeed be fuelled by an unwillingness to negotiate. It is then perhaps not surprising that there is little credible evidence that non-negotiation or non-engagement approaches serve to deter hostage taking. The use of strong rhetoric in this respect may also serve as a challenge to some individuals and groups, resulting in escalation as a means of publically challenging states and organizations. In the case of some groups it has also been observed that such policies may serve to confirm claims about the opposing state or organization, stressing its intransigent and unwillingness to reach any agreement. It has been suggested that terrorism can often be seen as a form of 'theatre' which thrives on publicity: intransigent governments and policies may simply feed the dramatic value of terrorist actions (Matusitz, 2013).

The use of kidnapping as a means of addressing political and economic grievances has received less attention but its use does not appear to have decreased in recent years. A lowering of political and media attention followed the 9/11 attacks in New York and the growth over time of similar suicidal attacks. This latter form of attack appears designed to maximize the number of deaths as the means of engendering terror in the general population. The use of suicidal tactics has received a lot of recent attention but is far from new, with a lengthy history of use. The recent history of the tactic can probably be traced to an attack on US and French armed forces based at the US Marine Corp Headquarters in the Lebanon in 1983. Here 346 people were killed, either initially or as a result of their injuries (Frykberg, Tepas, & Alexander, 1989; Pape, 2003). It has been suggested that the continuation of such attacks impacted on the United States and Europe and also led Israel to withdraw from Lebanon, giving up gains made during its 1982 invasion (Atran, 2003). Such attacks have suggested a potentially significant objection to the use of principled negotiation, specifically the suggestion that those who engage in such tactics suffer from some form of psychopathology and are therefore unlikely to be amenable or responsive to negotiation which is underpinned by rational exchanges. This is described by Atran (2003) as a clear example of the fundamental attribution error: the tendency to ascribe the behaviour of others to individual characteristics, at the expense of wider situational factors that act on the person. To illustrate this he uses the widely known work of Milgram (1974). In this demonstration members of the public, who showed no evidence of any psychopathology, completed acts which they thought seriously harmed people in the form of serious electric shocks resulting in serious injury. In fact any injury was simulated but participants did not know this and appeared to seriously injure people they did not know on the basis of

a sense of obligation to authority. There are clear parallels here with the harm caused by those acting for terrorist groups. The evidence base would not suggest that psychopathology is a necessary characteristic of terrorists or that such actions can be accounted for in terms of individual characteristics alone (Crenshaw, 2000).

There has been limited recent interest in the use and process of principled negotiation in crisis incidents involving terrorism, with a marked reduction in attention over recent years (Cronin & Ludes, 2004; Garfinkel, 2004; Pillar, 2001). The tradition of psychological studies in this area has though continued, albeit to a limited extent (Donohue & Roberto, 1993; Slatkin, 2010). This decline appears largely to be a result of groups such as Al-Qaeda becoming a primary focus. Such groups have often adopted high profile tactics which did not permit the option of negotiation. This has occurred as part of a rise in what has been termed 'absolutist' terrorism (Hayes, Kaminski, & Beres, 2003). For such groups suicidal attacks have received more attention and generated more fear and anxiety than hostage taking and kidnappings.

APPLYING PRINCIPLED NEGOTIATION DURING TERRORIST INCIDENTS

Some historical examples may serve to illustrate the use and challenges of principled negotiation during terrorist incidents. In 1997, the Tupac Amara group took around 700 hostages at a function hosted by the Japanese ambassador in Peru. A number of early releases were achieved but the group continued to hold a group of 74 hostages and a period of four months of negotiation followed. This proved to be fruitless in terms of an agreed outcome and the incident was resolved by the use of intervention which resulted in 73 hostages being rescued (Faure, 2003). In 2003, an Islamist group seized 31 European tourists in the Algerian Sahara. This was followed by protracted negotiations over 5 months, with the result that 30 hostages were safely released and 1 died as a result of sunstroke (Faure, 2003). In contrast a Chechen group seized 979 theatre goers in Moscow and 2 years later took hundreds of school children and others hostage in Beslan in the Russian Federation. In both cases the authorities opted to intervene early in the process. In Moscow, 128 hostages died and in Beslan there were more than 300 deaths. Both incidents have been described as the result of bungled interventions (Myers, 2004; Finn, 2005). As can be seen any efforts at tactical resolution carry a high risk, particularly where such efforts are rushed, inadequate or poorly thought out.

A notable feature of the more effective negotiations is that they were often very protracted. This is not surprising as perpetrators may be motivated to maximize media and other coverage over time. Taking a principled negotiation approach has faced resistance linked to concerns about this, with the taking of hostages in terrorist incidents being framed in terms of positional bargaining which has often become the default position (Zwier, 2013). Despite this incidents continue to happen and, in addition, the potential seriousness of such incidents has increased with the risk of groups having access to more destructive weapons, including those with the potential for mass destruction of people and property. This possibility raises the stakes involved in negotiation with some groups markedly.

It has been suggested that use of principled negotiation in terrorist incidents has significant potential to improve outcomes. Governments in the past though have tended to reject the approach on at best weak grounds. The use of principled negotiation, it is suggested, provides a sound basis for many forms of conflict resolution and does not depend on both sides embracing the approach (Zwier, 2013).

THE PROCESS OF NEGOTIATION WITH TERRORISTS

Fowler (2007) suggests four overarching principles and seven corollaries involved in the process of principled negotiation during terrorist incidents. These overlap to a large extent with the use of the method in correctional and law enforcement contexts but there are also significant differences in emphasis.

(A) Attempt to establish immediately a working relationship with a forward looking problem-solving rather than a condemnatory approach.
  i) Attempt to understand the hostage takers motives.
  ii) Analyse how culture is influencing extremists' behaviour and avoid cultural misunderstandings in cultivating and maintaining a working relationship.
  iii) Resist growing frustration and antagonism and wherever possible side step inflammatory positions taken by extremists in negotiations.
(B) Use interest based reasoning in an effort to move the negotiations beyond the initial positional exchange characteristic of hostage crises.

  i) Identify objectives and subjective interests held by hostage takers better served by peaceful settlement.
(C) Search for options that would free hostages on acceptable terms to Government and that terrorists see as preferable to violence.
  i) Identify neutral standards based on objective criteria and explore formulaic negotiation in an effort to create options that can overcome lack of trust.
  ii) Consider fractionating the problem.
(D) Weigh any proposed agreement against Governments best current alternatives.
  i) Assess the likelihood of a successful intervention mission.

It is of course the case that in terrorist incidents the negotiation team will face a number of external policy constraints on their actions, which may be more limiting than those typical in other settings. This requires a high level of constructive problem solving and creativity. Whatever the positions taken and initial rhetoric it is rare that governments will not negotiate, either directly, through other states or through other agencies or individuals (Wilkinson, 2014). In practice the process of resolution to such critical incidents does not appear all that different from that seen in law enforcement settings.

THE EXPERIENCE OF HOSTAGES

Those who are taken captive as hostages are a key part of the process of crisis negotiation and will be a focus for any mutually agreeable resolution. Overall the process of crisis negotiation revolves around efforts to ensure the safe release of hostages and the minimization of harm. Ultimately this may take the form of controlled release or the use of tactical resolution to try to secure safe release.

The physical and psychological state of hostages will be an area of concern for negotiators throughout. Being taken hostage is potentially a very traumatic experience and as such is likely to have marked psychological effects during the incident and often following resolution. Much attention has also been focussed on what has become known as the Stockholm syndrome in crisis incidents, not least because of its impacts on the process of negotiation. The term refers to a process of over identification with captors and increasingly negative or confrontational attitudes towards negotiators. The term is named for the reactions seen in a prolonged siege in Stockholm, where some hostages were seen to strongly identify with the perpetrators and to become hostile to the negotiation team. To some degree such responses are perhaps not unexpected in that the hostage is generally made to be heavily dependent on the hostage taker(s) in trying to maintain their safety. In terms of self-preservation the possibility of tactical intervention to resolve the incident also becomes a direct threat. Recent research suggests however that notions of over identification with hostage takers may have been over stated. Empirical research into the effects on hostages following crisis incidents has suggested that while this may occur it is more likely to be seen where hostages are treated poorly (Hillman, 1981; Solomon, 1982). Other research has suggested that over identification may be reduced where negotiators increase their control over time and are effective in minimizing the level of threat to hostages. Where hostages can be protected from a sense of severe threat it appears that over identification can be avoided (Olin & Born, 1983; Fuselier, 1988). A recent systematic review identified 12 papers that met inclusion criteria and found a high degree of inconsistency in the use of the term and a lack of validated criteria. The reviewers also suggested a reporting and publication bias in favour of identifying the presence of such characteristics (Namnyak *et al.*, 2008).

The occurrence of prolonged trauma following such incidents has also been the subject of study (Bisson, Searle, & Srinivasan, 1998). This study involved 71 British servicemen and their families who were held hostage for up to four and a half months, following the 1990 invasion of Kuwait. The mental health of this group was followed up at 6 and 18 months post release using the Impact of Event Scale and the 28-item General Health Questionnaire plus a questionnaire regarding background factors, the trauma and effects of their hostage experience. The authors reported little change on the Impact of Event Scale scores over time but significant reductions in the General Health Questionnaire scores over the 12-month period. They noted a reduction in intrusive and avoidance phenomena and also psychological distress. Witnessing physical violence and a perceived deterioration in physical and mental health were associated with poorer outcomes and poor outcomes at 6 months were strongly correlated with poorer outcomes at 18 months.

CRISIS NEGOTIATION – THE EVIDENCE

The evidence base in relation to the use of principled negotiation is substantial and the level of understanding of the approach is good across a number of domains.

That said there has been relatively little good-quality research into the application in crisis situations and something of a lull in research over recent years. Much of the evidence base is therefore drawn on older research or expert opinion based on practical experience. As a result the field has tended to stagnate in terms of evidence informed policy and practice. The extent to which different organizations have been willing to develop research has also been markedly variable. Correctional organizations, such as HM Prison Service in the United Kingdom, have trended to be resistant to research on the basis that this would have adverse 'security' implications. This is unfortunate since correctional settings provide perhaps the most accessible means of studying the characteristics of crisis negotiations, both effective and failed, in a rigorous manner.

In contrast, those engaged in law enforcement settings and engaging with terrorist negotiations have been more receptive to research. As a result there has been some initial high quality research to improve the understanding of the application of negotiation as it applies to crisis incidents. An example of an early study is that by Donohue and Roberto (1993) who applied negotiated order theory to the study of 10 actual hostage negotiations. The qualitative analysis undertaken into these incidents suggested that successful negotiations depended on building a consensus about the relationship. This seems to have been a key precursor to developing an effective relationship. They also noted that participants in hostage negotiations developed what they termed relational 'rhythms', in the form of fairly stable patterns of either cooperative or competitive behaviour.

Ross and LaCroix (1996) provided a systematic review of the research literature then available on trust in bargaining and mediation. They noted that issues of trust in negotiation had clearly distinct meanings, dependent on the relationship. Trust referred to trait concepts, for example, how trusting or otherwise the negotiator was. Alternatively it referred to state concepts often referring to one of three orientations: (1) cooperative motivational orientation (MO), (2) patterns of predictable behaviour or (3) a problem-solving orientation.

A study by Taylor and Thomas (2008) provides valuable insights into the nature of successful negotiations during crisis incidents. Their study considered the role of Linguistic Style Matching (LSM) in the outcomes of 9 real law enforcement hostage taking incidents. LSM can be described as the degree of coordination of word use between speakers and there is a considerable body of psychological research looking at the role of LSM in negotiated outcomes. LSM tends to emerge whenever two or more people communicate using language. It involves an exchange of cues and responses in an interconnected sequence of events (Auld & White, 1959).

Behaviours here can be verbal or involve various aspects of Non Verbal Communication (NVC), some of which will be more relevant than others. Dependent on the circumstances of any negotiation these could include 'kinesics' (body language) and 'vocalics' (paralanguage) and 'chronemics' (the structuring of time)[4] (Moore, Hickson, & Stacks, 2010).

Accommodation Theory (Giles, Coupland, & Coupland, 1991) suggests that individuals will adopt communication styles that create, maintain or decrease social distance depending on circumstances. Where a reduction in social distance is desirable then we tend to adopt gestures, idioms and behaviour that mirror more closely that of others. There are clear parallels here with other areas of forensic psychology practice such as the provision of expert testimony, where behaviours to alter social distance will vary to accommodate the style of examination in Court settings. The evidence base on non-verbal communication shows consistently that the coordination of communication in a systematic way generally leads to enhanced communication (Ellis & Beattie, 1986).

In looking at negotiation Niederhoffer and Pennebaker (2002) predicted that effective negotiation will be characterized by high levels of LSM and went on to test this via three empirical studies. These studies were concerned with student interactions and also real world interactions. In all cases they found that participants showed significant levels of LSM at both an overall level and in the characteristics of turn-by-turn exchanges. In the real world cases they found that lower levels of LSM were associated with hostile situations where there was often poor coordination of linguistic styles. Such a finding is largely consistent with the evidence base on crisis negotiation (Taylor & Thomas, 2008).

Studies of more effective crisis negotiators suggest a number of characteristics that are present within their negotiations. These would include the ability to increase LSM and reduce social distance in the initial stages of negotiation. Such individuals also appear to use an approach called 'entrainment' more and more effectively. This refers to the ability to adopt and reflect the motivation focus of the other party to a negotiation and, in turn, mirroring this in the dialogue (McGrath & Kelly, 1986). In contrast some studies have suggested that 'hard' verbal tactics can be effective in producing turning points as negotiation progresses but that where the difference between parties is marked, such tactics are likely to produce a crisis (Druckman, 1986, 2001).

All efforts to research crisis negotiations present significant challenges. These would include the methodological challenges associated with research into complex and dynamic negotiations. Recent studies such as those by Taylor and Thomas (2008) and Giebels and Taylor (2009) suggest that such challenges are not insurmountable and that the techniques used to study negotiation in other contexts are applicable to crisis negotiation. Both these studies looked at content and process and involved the systematic analysis of negotiations. In the study by Taylor and Thomas (2008) the negotiations from 9 hostage incidents were analysed across 6 time stages. The authors reported that successful negotiations showed higher levels of LSM. On closer examination, though, this did not appear to be a simple relationship. Both successful and unsuccessful negotiators were using LSM at similar levels but the unsuccessful negotiators showed marked fluctuations in LSM, whereas successful negotiators tended to be consistent over time. They suggest that this showed an inability to maintain rapport and linguistic coordination on the part of the less successful negotiators. Taylor and Thomas (2008) also report an analysis of the turn-by-turn levels of LSM. They suggest that over time the successful negotiators showed greater coordination of turn taking in communication, more reciprocation of positive affect, a stronger focus on the present rather than the past and a focus on alternatives – rather than a stress on competition. Lower levels of some forms of communication were also noted. The use of negatives and negation was seen to be used less by successful negotiators. They also tended not to use communications in the first person singular as much. In addition they tended to show less behaviour which highlighted discrepancies between themselves and the perpetrators.

In a study by Giebels and Taylor (2009) the role of cultural differences in communication was studied in relation to crisis negotiation. This research used audio transcripts of 25 negotiations involving law enforcement agencies that began in the Netherlands or Belgium. These were selected on the basis that the cases had occurred within 10 years of the research study and that a minimum of ten minutes of negotiation transcript was available for analysis. The study included 15 cases of kidnapping and 10 cases of extortion involving telephone negotiations. The results suggested the presence of marked cultural differences which impacted on the process of negotiation. They went on to suggest a need to develop a more sophisticated understanding of how such cross-cultural communication might be improved to achieve resolution of such incidents.

A more recent study of the negotiation process during crisis negotiation (van den Heuvel, Alison, & Power, 2014) also involved the law enforcement context. The study built on long standing research in cognitive psychology to look at the way in which police negotiators analysed and dealt with simulated crisis incidents. This was based on performance during specialist training and focused on the ways in which negotiators managed uncertainty in decision-making. The study was concerned with how trainee negotiators' self-management contributed to their resilience and the effectiveness of their approaches. The method used was analysis of video recordings of a strategic command meeting, held as part of a simulated hostage negotiation. The authors report coding data in relation to three themes: the decision phase, an uncertainty management strategy phase and a decision implementation phase. It was reported that participant trainee negotiators commonly used cognitive reduction strategies to seek additional information and that they also used an iterative approach to update these, drawing on reflection based on previous experience. Negotiators subsequently progressed to a formulation phase, using assumption-based reasoning to mentally simulate intended courses of action. Preferred strategies in turn were subject to an analysis of advantages and disadvantages for each option. Where uncertainty persisted into the execution of plans, it appeared to be managed by relying on standard operating procedures or by intentionally deferring the decision while plans were developed for application in the event of worst-case scenarios.

There also remain significant gaps in the evidence base on crisis negotiation. There is, for example, a wealth of evidence from cognitive psychology as it relates to the way in which people analyse information and the heuristics and biases that are present (Gigerenzer & Selten, 2002; Pachur, Hertwig, & Steinmann, 2012). Such processes undoubtedly have the potential to contribute to improving the quality of crisis negotiation. It is therefore somewhat surprising and concerning that so little research has been undertaken in this area of crisis negotiation, when the stakes involved are potentially so high. Much of the literature in the area has drawn on recent and current practice in a largely atheoretical manner. As a result such work says little about how practice might be refined and developed using this area of cognitive research to improve outcomes.

CONCLUSIONS

A number of themes emerge from the discussion of critical incidents in the preceding text. These include the greater use of principled negotiation approaches to such incidents, to the point where this has become the default response in law enforcement and correctional settings. The use of negotiation in terrorist incidents continued to develop in parallel, despite often strident rhetoric from governments denying this.

After a period of rapid development in the late twentieth century though practice in this area appeared largely stagnant. Isolated examples of psychological research continued in the area but these appeared to have limited impact on policy and practice. The nature of crisis incidents seemed to be understood and the approaches used appeared on the face of it effective. Whether such views were valid is open to question but what is clear is that marked change followed the growth of new forms of crises and the rise of what has been termed 'absolutist' terrorism. This required policy-makers to dramatically rethink existing policy and practice from a state level through law enforcement to the level of correctional settings. This process is still on-going and seems set to continue. Encouragingly there has also been some growth in research directly concerned with the area of crisis negotiation, particularly drawing on developments in areas of cognitive and social psychology. Such research does of course present very significant methodological and ethical challenges for researchers. These have not though proved insuperable and it seems likely that such work will help to move forward the use and efficacy of principled negotiation to crisis incidents.

NOTES

1 The term 'zero sum game' derives from game theory, widely used in psychology and economics. It refers to a mathematical representation of situations where one participant's gain (or loss) of utility is exactly balanced by the losses (or gains) of the utility of the other participant or participants. In such cases where the total gains of all participants are summed and the total losses are subtracted the sum will be zero.

2 A number of models of crisis negotiation have been suggested including the 'Getting Past No' model, the 'SAFE' model, the REACT matrix and others. These are discussed in more detail in Grubb (2010) and McMains and Mullins (2012). Such models appear to be primarily descriptive and tend to be used as both training and practice aids.

3 An exception to this is the offence of piracy where tactical intervention is typically carried out by specialist military units. This may have contributed to some extent to the unhelpful conflation of piracy with maritime terrorism (Singh & Bedi, 2012).

4 Generally of less relevance in crisis incidents would be 'haptics' (touch).

FURTHER READING

Olekalns, M., & Adair, W. L. (2013). *Handbook of research on negotiation.* Cheltenham, UK: Edward Elgar.
A multi-authored text of 19 chapters from a range of international authors providing a review of a wide range of research on negotiation. The text provides an up to date summary of negotiator characteristics, social psychological factors and communication processes. The final section of the book on complex negotiations is the most relevant to forensic psychologists. In particular the chapter by Wells, Taylor & Giebels, entitled 'Crisis negotiation: from suicide to terrorism intervention' provides an excellent review of crisis negotiation. Unusually this provides coverage of the full range of crisis incidents including negotiation in the context of suicidal behaviours.
Fowler, M. R. (2007). The relevance of principled negotiation to hostage crises. *Harvard Negotiation Law Review, 12,* 251–318.
This paper provides a detailed review of the application of principled negotiation to the resolution of hostage crises. The focus is largely on the most complex situations and, in particular the use of such an approach in response to politically motivated incidents. The text is well illustrated with case examples of critical incidents and the author advocates for an increasing use of negotiation.
Ireland, C. A., Fisher, M., & Vecchi, G. M. (Eds.). (2011). *Conflict and crisis communication: Principles and practice.* Oxford: Routledge.
A multi-authored introduction to critical incidents in correctional and policing contexts over ten chapters. The text is unusual in the breadth of coverage including ethical issues, the role of negotiator characteristics and the effects on those held captive.

REFERENCES

Atran, S. (2003). Genesis of suicide terrorism. *Science, 299*(5612), 1534–1539.
Auld, F., & White, A. M. (1959). Sequential dependencies in psychotherapy. *Journal of Abnormal and Social Psychology, S8,* 100–104.
Becker, J. (1977). *Hitler's children: The story of the Baader-Meinhof terrorist gang.* Philadelphia: Lippincott.
Bisson, J. I., Searle, M. M., & Srinivasan, M. (1998), Follow-up study of British military hostages and their families held in Kuwait during the Gulf War. *British Journal of Medical Psychology, 71,* 247–252.
Boin, A., & Rattray, W. A. (2004). Understanding prison riots towards a threshold theory. *Punishment & Society, 6*(1), 47–65.
Bueger, C. (2013). The global fight against piracy. *Global Policy, 4*(1), 63–64.
Calahan, A. B. (1995). *Countering terrorism: The Israeli response to the 1972 Munich Olympic massacre and the development of independent covert action teams* (Dissertation, Marine Corps Command and Staff College).
Caplan, G. (1961). *Prevention of mental disorders in children.* New York: Basic Books.
Carkhuff, R. R., & Berenson, B. G. (1977). *Beyond counseling and therapy.* New York: Holt, Rinehart and Winston.
Carlile, A. (2007). *The definition of terrorism.* A Report by Lord Carlile of Berriew Q.C. Independent Reviewer of Terrorism Legislation (Cm7052). London: HMSO.
Crenshaw, M. (2000). The psychology of terrorism: An agenda for the 21st century. *Political Psychology, 21*(2), 405–420.
Crighton, D. A. (1991). *Psychological contributions to hostage incidents and other serious disturbances: A literature review.* Prison Psychology Conference Proceedings. London: Home Office.
Crighton, D. A. (1992). *Psychological contributions to hostage taking incidents.* Paper presented at the British Psychological Society Annual Conference, Blackpool.
Crighton, D. A., & Towl, G. J. (2008). *Psychology in prisons* (2nd edn). Oxford: BPS Blackwell.
Cronin, A. K., & Ludes, J. M. (Eds.). (2004). *Attacking terrorism: Elements of a grand strategy.* Washington, DC: Georgetown University Press.
Donohue, W. A., & Roberto, A. J. (1993). Relational development as negotiated order in hostage negotiation. *Human Communication Research, 20*(2), 175–198.
Druckman, D. (1986). Stages, turning points, and crises: Negotiating military base rights, Spain and the United States. *Journal of Conflict Resolution, 30,* 327–360.
Druckman, D. (2001). Turning points in international negotiation. *Journal of Conflict Resolution, 45,* 519–544.
Ellis, A., & Beattie, G. (1986). *The psychology of language and communication.* Guildford, UK: Psychology Press.
Faure, G. O. (2003). Negotiating with terrorists: the hostage case. *International Negotiation, 8*(3), 469–494.
Finn, P. (2005). New report puts blame on local officials in Beslan Siege, *Washington Post,* Dec. 29.
Fisher, M. J. (2011). Ethical Considerations in a conflict and crisis situation. In C. A. Ireland, M. J. Fisher, & M. Vecchi (Eds.), *Conflict and crisis communication: Principles and practice.* London: Routledge.
Fisher, R. (1983). What about negotiation as a specialty. *ABAJ, 69,* 1221.
Fisher, R., Ury, W. L., & Patton, B. (2011). *Getting to yes: Negotiating agreement without giving in.* New York: Penguin.
Flood, J. J. (2003). *Hostage barricade database (HOBAS).* Quantico, VA: FBI Academy.
Forest, J. J. (2012). Global trends in kidnapping by terrorist groups. *Global Change, Peace & Security, 24*(3), 311–330.

Fowler, M. R. (2007). The relevance of principled negotiation to hostage crises. *Harvard Negotiation Law Review, 12,* 251–318.

Frykberg, E. R., Tepas, J. J., & Alexander, R. H. (1989). The 1983 Beirut Airport terrorist bombing: Injury patterns and implications for disaster management. *The American Surgeon, 55*(3), 134–141.

Fuselier, G. D. (1988). Hostage negotiation consultant: Emerging role for the clinical psychologist. *Professional Psychology: Research and Practice, 19*(2), 175.

Garfinkel, M. R. (2004). Global threats and the domestic struggle for power. *European Journal of Political Economy, 20*(2), 495–508.

Giebels, E., & Taylor, P. J. (2009). Interaction patterns in crisis negotiations: Persuasive arguments and cultural differences. *Journal of Applied Psychology, 94*(1), 5–19.

Gigerenzer, G., & Selten, R. (Eds.). (2002). *Bounded rationality: The adaptive toolbox.* Cambridge, MA: MIT Press.

Giles, H., Coupland, N., & Coupland, I. (1991). Accommodation theory: Communication, context, and consequence. In H. Giles, J. Coupland, & N. Coupland (Eds.), *Contexts of accommodation. Developments in applied sociolinguistics.* Cambridge: Cambridge University Press.

Gordon, N., & Lopez, G. A. (2000). Terrorism in the Arab-Israeli conflict. In A. Valls (Ed.), *Ethics in International Affairs.* Lanham, MD: Rowman & Littlefield.

Grubb, A. (2010). Modern day hostage (crisis) negotiation: The evolution of an art form within the policing arena. *Aggression and Violent Behavior, 15*(5), 341–348.

Hayes, R. E., Kaminski, S. R., & Beres, S. M. (2003). Negotiating the non-negotiable: Dealing with absolutist terrorists. *International Negotiation, 8*(3), 451–467.

Hillman, G. (1981). *The psychopathology of being held hostage.* Washington, DC: American Psychiatric Association.

Klein, A. J. (2007). *Striking back: The 1972 Munich Olympics Massacre and Israel's deadly response.* New York: Random House LLC.

Lloyd Lord (1996). *Inquiry into legislation against terrorism* (Cm 3420). London: HMSO.

Matusitz, J. A. (2013). *Terrorism & communication: A critical introduction.* Los Angeles: Sage.

McGrath, J. E., & Kelly, J. R. (1986). *Time and human interaction: Towards a social psychology of time.* New York: Guildford Press.

McMains, M. J., & Mullins, W. C. (2010). *Crisis negotiations: Managing critical incidents and hostage situations in law enforcement and corrections.* Providence, NJ: Mathew Bender & Co.

Milgram, S. (1974). *Obedience to authority.* New York: Harper & Row.

Moore, N. J., Hickson, M., & Stacks, D. W. (2010). *Nonverbal communication: Studies and applications.* Oxford: Oxford University Press.

Myers, S. L. (2004). From dismal Chechnya, women turn to bombs. *New York Times, 10.*

Namnyak, M., Tufton, N., Szekely, R., Toal, M., Worboys, S., & Sampson, E. L. (2008). Stockholm syndrome': Psychiatric diagnosis or urban myth? *Acta Psychiatr Scand, 117,* 4–11.

Niederhoffer, K. G., & Pennebaker, J. W. (2002). Linguistic style matching in social interaction. *Journal of Language and Social Psychology, 21,* 337–360.

Olin, W. R., & Born, D. G. (1983). A behavioral approach to hostage situations. *FBI Law Enforcement Bulletin, 52*(1), 18–24.

Pachur, T., Hertwig, R., & Steinmann, F. (2012). How do people judge risks: Availability heuristic, affect heuristic, or both?. *Journal of Experimental Psychology: Applied, 18*(3), 314.

Pape, R. A. (2003). The strategic logic of suicide terrorism. *American Political Science Review, 3,* 343–361.

Pillar, P. R. (2001). Terrorism goes global: Extremist groups extend their reach worldwide. *The Brookings Review, 19,* 34–37.

Post, J. M. (2007). *The mind of the terrorist: The psychology of terrorism from the IRA to al-Qaeda.* London: Palgrave Macmillan.

Rogan, R. G. (2011). Linguistic style matching in crisis negotiations: A comparative analysis of suicidal and surrender outcomes. *Journal of Police Crisis Negotiations, 11*(1), 20–39.

Ross, W., & LaCroix, J. (1996). Multiple meanings of trust in negotiation theory and research: A literature review and integrative model. *International Journal of Conflict Management, 7*(4), 314–360.

Sherfinski, D. (2014). Hagel: US didn't negotiate with terrorists in securing Bergdahl's release. *The Washington Times,* Sunday, June 1.

Singh, C., & Bedi, A. S. (2012). 'War on piracy': The conflation of Somali piracy with terrorism in discourse, tactic and law. *ISS Working Paper Series/General Series, 543,* 1–44.

Slatkin, A. A. (2010). *Communication in crisis and hostage negotiations: Practical communication techniques, stratagems, and strategies for law enforcement, corrections and emergency service personnel in managing critical incidents.* Springfield, IL: Charles C Thomas Publisher.

Solomon, V. M. (1982). *Hostage psychology and the Stockholm syndrome: Captive, captor and captivity* (Doctoral dissertation, Florida Institute of Technology).

Spector, B. I. (1977). Negotiation as a psychological process. *Journal of Conflict Resolution, 21*(4), 607–618.

Taylor, P. J., & Thomas, S. (2008). Linguistic style matching and negotiation outcome. *Negotiation and Conflict Management Research, 1*(3), 263–281.

Towl, G. (2011). Forensic psychotherapy and counselling in prisons. *European Journal of Psychotherapy & Counselling, 13*(4), 403–407.

van den Heuvel, C., Alison, L., & Power, N. (2014). Coping with uncertainty: Police strategies for resilient decision-making and action implementation. *Cognition, Technology & Work, 16*(1), 25–45.

Vecchi, G. M. (2003). Active listening: The key to effective crisis negotiation. *ACR Crisis Negotiation News, 1,* 4–6.

Vecchi, G. M., Van Hasselt, V. B., & Romano, S. J. (2005). Crisis (hostage) negotiation: Current strategies and issues in high-risk conflict resolution. *Aggression and Violent Behaviour, 10,* 533–551.

Wicker, T. (1994). *A time to die: The Attica prison revolt.* Lincoln: University of Nebraska Press.

Wilkinson, P. (2014). *Terrorism versus democracy: The liberal state response.* London: Taylor & Francis.

Willis, G. D. (2014). Antagonistic authorities and the civil police in Sao Paulo, Brazil. *Latin American Research Review, 49*(1), 3–22.

Zwier, P. J. (2013). *Principled negotiation and mediation in the international arena: Talking with evil.* Cambridge: Cambridge University Press.

13 Aspects of Diagnosed Mental Illness and Offending

David Pilgrim

The psychological assessment of people considered to be both criminal and mentally ill brings particular challenges for practitioners. What balance of criminogenic and psychopathological factors should be invoked when attempting a psychological formulation and to what degree are they relevant separately and together? Does a psychological formulation complement or challenge a psychiatric diagnosis? To what extent might the cultural norms of the offender-patient account for what, at first glance, might be seen as individual pathology, if and when we explore their actions in their context of origin? If they are incarcerated when being assessed, which is the commonest scenario, how valid are our assessments and our predictions now that the patient is outside of their normal life setting; they are in a closed system but their offending took place in an open system? To what extent might the symptoms of mental illness be relevant (or irrelevant) to understanding and predicting particular risky action?

These questions apply, by the way, to an extent to *all* criminals, because none of us, including criminals, can ever claim to be perfectly mentally healthy. Psychodynamic psychology in particular emphasizes that we are all, to some degree, mentally ill and so the psychosocial transgressions of all offenders could invite forms of pathologization and psychological expertise. Offenders break the law and few crimes are victimless, so the exploitation of others and the betrayal of mutual trust are ever present. These interpersonal and personal features are the very stuff of psychological interest. Even outside of the psychodynamic tradition, existential, behavioural and cognitive approaches to psychological functioning can be applied to criminal action.

The ambiguities implied by these opening remarks will be explored further in this chapter, via four aims:

1. Mentally disordered offenders and our response to them will be considered in their social context.

2. A summary will be provided of the overlaps and tensions between psychiatric and psychological knowledge.

3. A psychological rather than a psychiatric approach to those with a diagnosis of mental illness in forensic settings will be explored.

4. The evidence about the problematic relationship between diagnosed mental illness and risk will be examined.

THE SOCIAL CONTEXT OF RULE TRANSGRESSIONS: NORMAL AND ABNORMAL OFFENDERS

It is worth noting at the outset that because both criminality and mental health problems are always about rule transgression and frequently about social exclusion, then others, such as criminologists and sociologists, also have had much to say legitimately on this chapter's topic (Prins, 2005 – see Further Reading). Criminality and mental health are social as well as psychological matters. Prison and secure hospital populations are not representative of wider society. Men are overrepresented, as are black people, and of course poverty predicts both law breaking and the 'residual deviance' of mental disorder (Rogers & Pilgrim, 2014). The mentally abnormal offender is thus doubly deviant and more than likely to have origins in deprivation and exclusion.

Those conditions of poverty and social exclusion and their relevance for understanding the uneven social distribution of mental illness were demonstrated around the time of the Second World War by the 'ecological

Forensic Psychology, Second Edition. Edited by David A. Crighton and Graham J. Towl.
© 2015 John Wiley & Sons, Ltd. Published 2015 by British Psychological Society and John Wiley & Sons, Ltd.

wing' of the Chicago School of Sociology (Rogers & Pilgrim, 2003). These poor social conditions are also the likely fate of mentally disordered offenders when, and if, they leave detention. In this context, the chances of risk reduction or minimization cannot be predicted by individual factors alone but rely heavily also on living conditions (neighbourhood and social network characteristics). This point is returned to at the end of the chapter.

Thus, sociology has much to tell us about the social nature of individuals we assess in terms of deviance identification and amplification, in both the lay and professional arenas. This point became apparent during the 1960s from a series of studies from the other wing of the Chicago School of Sociology: symbolic interactionism (Coulter, 1973; Scheff, 1966). A sociological approach also provides us with insights into the organizational apparatus of social regulation used by the State *both* to control offenders being psychologically assessed *and* to employ those, like forensic psychologists, making those assessments (Cohen & Scull, 1985).

It is important, then, that pertinent criticisms of psychiatry, from our disciplinary perspective, do not lead to an overvaluation of psychological accounts of deviance. Replacing medical reductionism with psychological reductionism may not be a great step forward. Psychological formulation certainly has defensible advantages over psychiatric diagnosis but psychologists can learn much from bodies of knowledge outside their discipline.

Penal and psychiatric jurisdiction of mentally abnormal offenders

With these cautions about the social context of criminal action and psychological expertise in forensic settings in mind, let us now return to psychiatry. If 'mental illness' is the discourse of psychiatry, then what features characterize this medical speciality in the shared organizational setting of forensic work? Psychiatrists, because they are medical practitioners, are happy, indeed obliged, to split off 'mental disorder', 'descriptive psychopathology' and 'morbid psychology' from normal psychological functioning. As a consequence, they have a poorly developed lexicon for ordinary thoughts, feelings and actions and have little to say about people who do not fulfil criteria for mental disorder. (Postgraduate students I teach sometimes complain that psychiatrists have a restricted and restrictive medical model. I usually reply that this is not surprising, as they are medical practitioners.)

Psychiatrists are not alone in their ignorance about ordinary experience and behaviour. Most people, medical or otherwise, have little to say about 'mental order'; the strangeness of the term to the ear tells the tale. This is because, outside of contrived psychological research, most of us tend only to become extra-attentive when things go wrong. Life would be tedious and highly disrupted if this were not the case. When things go 'right' (people comply with role–rule expectations) then this is unremarkable and so invites little or no reactive interest.

Thus conformity to role and rule expectations does not demand accountability but, by implication, transgression demands accountability. As Goffman (1971) pointed out, a meta-rule in most societies is that of social intelligibility; we are expected to account for why we break rules if asked by others. The exposed cheat or the detected criminal can disavow or excuse their actions without breaking this meta-rule because they are offering an account of sorts. By contrast, the 'mentally ill' patient breaks rules and is then unable or unwilling to account for their transgressions; they 'lack insight' into their unintelligible actions. Thereby the 'mentally ill' patient, unlike the excuse-making cheat or crook, breaks the social contract about our obligation to account for actions to others when the circumstances require.

To be unable or unwilling to be accountable can be dealt with or reacted to by others as a more serious transgression than other forms of rule breaking. For this reason, those with a diagnosis of mental illness are one of the few social groups of adults who can be detained lawfully without trial; the other obvious group are suspected terrorists. 'Mental health law' (a misnomer, because it is about the coercive social control of one portion of mental disorder, not the promotion of mental health) and terrorist legislation are rare statutes. Moreover, detention without trial is applied to 'civil patients' who have committed no crime; so judgements about prospective risk are not only about offender-patients.

Thus, the confluence of two sorts of deviance – criminal and psychological transgressions – means that two frameworks of sanction might operate together or apart. The first is the normal penal disposal of a defined sentence determined by *past actions*. The other is the organizational peculiarity of secure psychiatric detention, where the patient is detained indefinitely and assessed episodically about their *prospective actions*. It is not unusual for mentally abnormal prisoners to be moved from the first to the second organizational jurisdiction (from a prison to a secure hospital) in order to manage their prospective risk. In the latter setting, mental health professions spend much of their time evaluating risk in conditions of uncertainty and so tend to default to 'false negative' decision-making. These professionals tend not to be sanctioned for detaining a patient unnecessarily, whereas the reoffending discharged patient provokes fierce criticism.

OVERLAPS AND TENSIONS BETWEEN PSYCHIATRIC AND PSYCHOLOGICAL KNOWLEDGE

Outside of medicine, in the human sciences it has been the task of psychologists, anthropologists and sociologists deliberately to pursue the unremarkable and build up pictures of normality – the 'norms and mores', thoughts, feelings and motivations of ordinary people doing ordinary things in their everyday lives. These versions of human science start from this position about ordinary functioning and then might occasionally look to transgressions in order to define normality.

By contrast, psychiatrists start at the other end of the telescope when looking at psychological morbidity – and tend to get stuck there. Consequently, they have little or nothing to say about normal life and so lack a professional capacity to connect their field of interest with wider human functioning. This is an intellectual limitation of the medical model. It also has an important psychosocial consequence of splitting off patients from non-patients, an oppressive process increasingly called 'othering'. If psychologists find themselves too close to that medical model they risk the same problems.

However, the medical model has found some of its most robust critics not within psychology but within psychiatry itself (e.g., Kleinman, 1988; Szasz, 1961). These medical dissenters notwithstanding, most doctors live in a world of digital logic of present or absent ('no abnormality detected', 'no symptoms of mental illness could be elicited', 'the person is not mentally ill', 'the person is fit to plead', etc.). This logic, by the way, is in many ways compatible with a legal context, where questions of insanity and diminished responsibility are deemed to be present or absent by judges and juries.

By contrast, psychologists are socialized differently and so have been encouraged to think in terms of continua rather than categories. In line with their training, psychologists' assessments *ought* to be based on analogue, not digital, reasoning. People are more or less: suspicious; mindful of others; rigid in their thinking; impulsive; moral; egocentric; lacking in insight; prone to idiosyncratic thoughts and perceptions; emotionally labile, etc.

Take the example of 'paranoia'. In psychiatry, this tends to be seen as a morbid condition suffered by individuals are who suspicious, rigid in their thought processes about some matters but not others and express certainty in that rigidity in a way that others do not

understand and fail to challenge successfully. The patient suffers from 'delusions' and these peculiarly morbid ways of thinking are pathognomic of 'paranoid schizophrenia'. All of this suggests that those suffering the latter are, in some sense, *categorically different* from the rest of humanity. But all of us can be suspicious and feel got at (with or without good reason). All of us have beliefs not shared by others. All of us can refuse to accept the reasoning of others. All of us can quickly jump to conclusions, rightly or wrongly. So rather than viewing mentally ill people as categorically different from those who are not, psychologists might be better exploring common psychological processes in all people (Bentall, 2010).

Psychological encounters with 'mental illness' in forensic settings

Psychologists working with offenders will recurrently encounter those who have a pre-existing psychiatric diagnosis. Sometimes they might be involved in assessing the presence and nature of mental health problems in offenders, when a diagnosis is being mooted for the first time. Although both penal and secure mental health settings are places of employment for forensic psychologists, they are more likely to encounter psychiatrists (and clinical psychologists) in the latter. With that engagement come presuppositions about the preferred constructs of these professionals.

The broad points in the following text are relevant to both penal and health settings but the psychiatric discourse is more powerful in the latter because of medical dominance and its traditional enshrinement in law. In the case of Britain there has been a tradition of psychiatrists being central to decision-making as Responsible Medical Officers (RMOs). The admission and discharge of patients (note that name itself is a symbolic marker of jurisdiction rather than 'offender' or 'prisoner') are under their control. Moreover, the viewpoint of the psychiatrist in reports for the Home Office or for Mental Health Review Tribunals tends to have more immediate and automatic authority than views from the members of the multidisciplinary team, such as psychologists.

In Britain, the role of the RMO disappeared under the 2007 Mental Health Act and was replaced by the 'Responsible Clinician', permitting psychologists at 'Consultant' grade to enter the role previously inhabited solely by the RMO. However, the circumstances of psychologists being cast in that role, rather than a psychiatrist, has been largely limited to those with a diagnosis of personality disorder, when considering their fitness for discharge or transfer. Psychiatrists still retain the sole responsibility for admission.

The traditions of psychiatric and psychological knowledge

With the preceding organizational and administrative context in mind, the tradition of diagnosing mental illness can be examined. Here, I focus on mental illness as a subset of mental disorder, but most of the logical and empirical considerations I explore in the following text apply also to 'personality disorder'. A good starting point is the work of Emil Kraepelin, who is attributed with the leading role in developing our current psychiatric theory and practice. Kraepelin (1883) offered his colleagues three axioms about mental illness:

1. They are genetically determined.
2. They are separate, naturally occurring, categories.
3. They are fixed and deteriorating conditions.

Kraepelinian psychiatry elaborated a classification of mental illness, with these emphatic axioms. Kraepelin's focus was on lunacy: 'manic-depressive psychosis' (later 'bipolar disorder') and 'dementia praecox' (later 'schizophrenia'). Since then, the categorization of mental disorder has expanded massively. For example, the current *Diagnostic and Statistical Manual* of the American Psychiatric Association contains nearly 400 categories (when it is revised again in 2010 it is likely to exceed that figure). A century of growth has ensured that the acorn logic of three axioms applied to two main disorders has produced a large tree with many thick branches.

When Kraepelin offered his version of biodeterminism, it was not limited to medicine at the end of the nineteenth century. At that time, eugenics was commonplace and so shaped psychological knowledge as well. In the British, context Francis Galton led the intellectual rationale for a 'tainted gene' pool and its role in undermining the racial stock of the country. A range of relevant disruptive deviance was identified – the prevalence of criminality, lunacy, idiocy, inebriation and prostitution in the underclass of Victorian society was explained by their genetic defectiveness. The eugenic movement sought a range of measures to limit the fecundity of this class and to increase the birth rate in those further up the class pyramid (Pilgrim, 2008).

Thus, while Kraepelin and others were leading forms of psychiatric diagnosis within a eugenic framework, the latter was also the inspiration for the development of an important form of proto-psychology at University College London led by Galton's protégés (Pearson, Spearman and Burt). They developed the early rationale for 'biometrics' – now 'psychometrics' or 'differential psychology' – and the statistical paraphernalia to support the demonstration of the psychological, rather than psychiatric expression of eugenics. The latter, with its diagnostic emphasis, simply assumed the genetic basis for mental illness – with or without empirical evidence to support that view.

By contrast, the psychological expression of eugenics encountered an early logical challenge to genetic explanations, which was that behavioural characteristics very rarely seemed to follow simple Mendelian rules of inheritance. As a consequence, a polygenetic-plus-environmental interaction was postulated to account for the tendency towards the normal distribution of these characteristics in any population (Fisher, 1930). This type of explanation was also to be invoked later by biological psychiatrists to account for the tendency of mental illness to run in families but without following neat genetic rules. However, the mathematical assumption (note that it is an assumption) about the normal distribution of psychological characteristics was stronger and earlier.

Early in the twentieth century, psychological and psychiatric expressions of eugenics encountered some setbacks. The shellshock problem of the First World War was prevalent in 'England's finest blood' (officers and gentlemen and working-class *volunteers*). As a consequence, the eugenic discourse of asylum psychiatry was tantamount to treason. As a result, a space opened up for environmentalist explanations for mental abnormality and formulations about presenting mental health crises (Stone, 1985). Also, Kraepelin's assumption about inevitable degeneration was not evident in practice, with recovery rates in asylum populations being around 25% by the 1920s (Hinsie, 1931). Added to which, the great economic depression of the 1930s was reflected palpably in its individual victims and raised levels of mental distress in civil society during peacetime (Dohrenwend, 1998).

The political and humanitarian catastrophe of the Nazi period confirmed confidence in *environmental* explanations of psychological functioning in the first half of the twentieth century, as well as seriously discrediting the conventional wisdom of eugenics. To complement this period of shame for eugenics, behaviourists showed how to create psychological dysfunction in the laboratory by the simple manipulation of environmental stimuli: the demonstration of 'experimental neurosis' (Watson & Rayner, 1920). Moreover, it is noteworthy, in the context of this chapter, that Pavlov (1941) made his cruelly treated dogs not just miserable but catatonic by manipulating stimuli in the closed system of the psychological laboratory.

Here we begin to see the first pieces of evidence that mammals (not humans alone) can be rendered confused, helpless and crazy by being manipulated, deprived and punished under conditions of no escape. The latter, now called 'entrapment', has been used as a conceptual springboard to explain depression (Brown, Harris, & Hepworth, 1995; Seligman, 1975) and psychosis (Bateson, Jackson, Haley, & Weakland, 1956; Laing & Esterson, 1964). Given that forensic settings permit no escape, this body of knowledge has an additional salience, especially if the institutional regime is not benign and supportive. This point about inherent entrapment applies *much more* to health settings than prisons because there is no estimated date for discharge; a point made earlier about the difference between a penal and a hospital disposal.

A final point to note about doubts from non-medical mental health workers about psychiatric theory and practice is that diagnosis is vulnerable to both pre-empirical and empirical attacks. Diagnoses such as 'schizophrenia' or 'depression' have poor conceptual and predictive validity (Pilgrim, 2007a, 2007b, 2014). Functional mental illnesses *ipso facto* lack aetiological specificity and treatment specificity (usual validating criteria expected for good medical diagnoses). Moreover, although symptom checklists, like those derived from DSM, increase the probability of reliability, a reliable concept is not necessarily a valid one. This has led some psychologists to argue for a complete abandonment of the medical categorization of mental illness in the Kraepelinian tradition, and for new models based in 'normal' psychology to be used instead, when offering formulations for particular patient presentations (Bentall, 2003 – see annotated reference in Further Reading).

The emergence of the biopsychosocial model and neo-Kraepelinian retrenchment

By the middle of the twentieth century, the Nazi stain had discredited but not eliminated a genetic emphasis in the mental health industry. Psychiatric genetics remained strong and was predicated on research in the Nazi period – exemplified by the work of Franz Kallmann in the United States and Eliot Slater in Britain. In psychology, psychometrics remained rooted in eugenic assumptions about genetic determination (Pilgrim, 2008).

At the same time, there was a strong web of environmentalist criticism to contain and even negate this biological enthusiasm. The impact of behaviourism in academic psychology has already been noted. In addition, after the Second World War, concerns about war orphans invited an examination of childhood adversity and its short- and long-term impact on mental health. The conditions of possibility were there to develop attachment theory – a hybrid of psychodynamic and behaviourist ideas (Bowlby, 1951). This theory became a springboard for understanding both mental health problems and delinquency.

Moreover, although the Kraepelinian view remained dominant in peacetime institutional psychiatry, its limits were exposed by the challenges of military psychiatry which, instead, cultivated more environmentalist and psychodynamic ways of understanding mental health. From this tension emerged both social psychiatry and the biopsychosocial model. The first was an interdisciplinary project of socially orientated psychiatrists, clinical psychologists and medical sociologists. The second informed the first and emerged from the work of Adolf Meyer and his 'psychobiology' and the use of General Systems Theory which provides an anti-reductionist and holistic paradigm in the biological and human sciences (Engel, 1980).

Meyer, a Swiss psychiatrist, who spent most of his career in the United States, unlike Kraepelin, did not force patients, Procrustean style, into pre-set, professionally preferred categories. He asked versions of the question 'Why does this patient present with these particular problems at this time in his or her life?' Meyer was proposing the need for formulation to take precedence over diagnosis.

This web of opposition to the Kraepelinian orthodoxy did not displace the latter but it did create a pressure within psychiatry to move towards a compromise in relation to mental illness. That compromise involved a more cautious interactionism about psychological and social, not just biological, causal reasoning, hence the attraction of the biopsychosocial model (Pilgrim, Kinderman, & Tai, 2008). It also softened the eugenic logic in psychology. Thus leaders in clinical psychology such as Hans Eysenck began to ride two horses. One was the eugenic legacy of differential psychology (hence his psychometric devices) and the other was the acceptance of behaviourism to formulate and treat neurotic problems.

However, an outcome of that ambivalence was that Eysenck offered a compromise about jurisdiction for mental illness. He suggested a simple division of labour, between psychologists treating environmentally determined neurotic symptoms with behaviour therapy and psychiatrists treating psychoses using medication, on the grounds that the latter were biologically determined (Eysenck, 1975). For many years up to the present, clinical psychology has been dominated by psychometric routines and the modified legacy of behaviour therapy (cognitive behaviour therapy). That compromise and division of labour was to have a profound effect on the ability of psychologists to think psychologically about psychosis – a point to return to later.

Another compromise across the channel soon emerged in the American Psychiatric Association (APA). The system of classification, the *Diagnostic and Statistical Manual* (DSM), which it had been developing over many years, came into crisis in the run-up to its revision in

1980. Two power blocs in the APA, one of biological psychiatrists and the other of psychoanalysts, were at loggerheads over aetiology.

Psychoanalysts have always been ambivalent about diagnosis. On the one hand, psychoanalysis is a form of biographical psychology and there is the fetish of the illustrative individual case in the 'scientific meetings' of psychoanalytical societies (an idiographic or hermeneutic way of understanding people). On the other hand, analysts have been content to use diagnosis, and even the language of pathology, when describing normal mental processes and development ('the paranoid position', 'schizoid defences', etc). The psychoanalytical insistence on *developmental* aetiology was at odds with biological psychiatry with its own genetic presuppositions.

Another factor in this internal power struggle about DSM-III was that the psychoanalytical position was a threat for the very reason that it was not limited to medical practitioners. This left the door open to the non-medical influence of 'lay analysts' in the APA. Also, at that time, scientific attacks on the tenets of psychoanalysis were beginning to bite and it was suffering a major credibility problem in American culture. As such, it had become a liability to the credibility of psychiatry (Hale, 1995).

The resolution of the political tension within the APA was to drop aetiological claims and emphasize only current and reported *descriptive* criteria for settling on a categorical diagnosis. At first glance the Kraepelinian professional project, with its three medical axioms, looked seriously compromised. As was noted in the preceding text, one of them, about fixed deteriorating prognoses, had been discredited early in the twentieth century (Hinsie, 1931).

And a second axiom was being discounted or at least queried – the assertion about genetic determination. However, and this is why DSM can be quite properly called 'neo-Kraeplinian', there was now the strong reassertion that mental disorders were *naturally occurring categories*. This was crucial to re-establish medical authority about the professional jurisdiction of mental disorder. This had the effect of bringing diagnosis firmly back into the medical model, to the professional relief of psychiatrists (Blacker & Tsuang, 1998). The compromise thus still strongly bolstered a medical view of mental abnormality (Wilson, 1993).

What DSM insisted on and what clinicians then did in practice is worth noting. Biological psychiatrists have not ceased to use diagnoses of mental illness that exclude assumptions of aetiology. For example, since 1980, they have still distinguished between endogenous and reactive depression (McPherson & Armstrong, 2006). Equally though, the stricture about neutrality in relation to aetiology in DSM has been flouted by psychoanalysts in the United States (McWilliams, 1994). The wide-ranging problems associated with psychiatric diagnosis in general, and the DSM system in particular, are reviewed by Horwitz (2002) – see annotated reference in Further Reading.

PSYCHOLOGICAL AND PSYCHIATRIC APPROACHES TO MENTAL ILLNESS IN FORENSIC SETTINGS

In the light of the preceding discussion, psychologists can take three broad positions in relation to people with a diagnosis of mental illness in forensic settings. The first, following Eysenck's offer of the division of labour, can argue that mental illness is a biological condition to be diagnosed and treated medically – which literally means medicinally, with drugs with the grandiose name of 'anti-psychotics'. This leaves no role for the psychologist (except maybe as a psychometrician to offer additional information about the patient's intelligence or personality).

The second position can be found in those psychologists who emphasize that mental illness is a biologically driven condition but that relapse is affected by personal factors. This stance adheres to the 'stress-vulnerability' hypothesis and the emphasis on 'high expressed emotion' and 'communication deviance' in the family of origin or maybe even a ward in a hospital or the wing of a prison. Here the psychologist might offer advice about minimizing the risk of relapse or might offer interventions, such as family therapy or 'psycho-education'. This might be seen as a 'peripheralist' position – the psychologist accepts the primacy of biology and then offers to deal with some of the peripheral fallout of that disease.

The third position is more radical and entails adopting an explicitly psychological approach to assessment and intervention. Recently within the British Psychological Society (BPS), this sharp break with the medical model has been formalized and codified in the approach that should now be adopted by psychologists in relation to both classification and formulation (Division of Clinical Psychology, 2011, 2013). It has also been bolstered by a traumogenic model gaining popularity among research psychologists (Read and Bentall, 2012; Varese *et al.*, 2012).

This now means that all applied psychologists are in a process of reflection about any residual attachment to psychiatric diagnosis.

THE PROBLEMATIC RELATIONSHIP BETWEEN DIAGNOSED MENTAL ILLNESS AND RISK

Historically, the regulation of criminal lunatics preceded the strong biological programme about madness described earlier in the work of Emil Kraepelin, when eugenics was in the political ascendancy (Cohen & Scull, 1985). Accounts of the early Victorian period emphasize two aspects of this regulation. The first is that the co-existence of madness and criminality warranted separate institutional care. The second was that two groups were discernible within this incarcerated population. One seemed to be detached from their original crime and easily managed in the institution but had acute episodes of anger. The other was permanently aggressive and oppositional but less mad. Some conceptual differentiation seemed to be present, then, about those we might now think of as being 'mentally ill' (lunacy) and those that we might now think of as being 'personality disordered' (then, suffering from 'moral insanity').

In more recent times these distinctions have been retained but in practice have shown considerable overlap. Indeed, in forensic settings there are those (considered in Chapter 8) whose main psychological functioning is dominated by egocentric and antisocial action ('antisocial personality disorder' 'dissocial personality disorder' or 'psychopathy') and those whose idiosyncrasies relate more to mood, perceptions and thought processes (what psychiatrists lump together as the functional psychoses of bipolar disorder and the schizophrenias).

'Dual diagnosis' or 'comorbidity'

However, there are problems with these hard-and-fast distinctions between 'mental illness' and 'personality disorder' (PD) as obvious and separate administrative and clinical categories, just as there are problems about neatly separating normal and abnormal behaviour. Habitual criminals often fulfil criteria for ('antisocial' or 'dissocial') personality disorder in a tautological sense, so are they all mentally disordered? And arguably the non-criminal expression of 'personality disorder' can be found in opportunistic politicians, careerists of all types, office bullies, power-obsessed managers in all organizations, shallow light entertainers, boxers and mercenaries. Thus distinctions between normal and abnormal personalities are not easily made. Self-seeking behaviour at the expense of others is sometimes rewarded and even glorified in some social contexts but not others. Thus selfish exploitative action does not always lead to criminal sanctions (Pilgrim, 2001). As for dangerous behaviour, this is sometimes positively socially valued and idolized (in racing-car drivers, mountaineers and astronauts). Thus it is not dangerousness in itself that is the issue, but the way that people are dangerous; the latter may be condemned or glorified depending on the context.

Turning to the merging of personality and psychosis, imagine this scenario (witnessed by the author). In a case review the psychiatrists and nurses present in a medium secure unit argued that the mentally disordered offender being considered must still be detained because they are still showing symptoms of 'schizophrenia'. I argued (to some sceptical looks) something like – 'yes, but why are so many with the very same diagnosis safely in the community or residing in open wards in another part of the NHS down the road from here? Why is *this particular* "sufferer" of "schizophrenia" in a secure setting?' The discussion soon revealed that the answer to this had to be that, like all other offenders, his detention ultimately related to the way he had behaved, been detected and judged by others.

What is obvious, when working with offenders who are diagnosed as being mentally ill, is that they often have much in common with dangerous criminals, whatever their mental state. They are often young, male, poor and poorly educated, with an oppositional attitude, which easily tips into defensive aggression or pre-emptive strikes against others. On the outside they may mix in circles in which reckless behaviour is commonplace and substance misuse is the norm.

Thus, some clear risk factors are not about symptoms of mental illness but are bound up with the *life context* anticipated, if the patient I was recalling were to be discharged. He would go back to a poor environment and reconnect with a social network that drinks excessively and smokes cannabis or crack cocaine regularly. Thus it is not symptoms but the whole behavioural context of open systems that has to be considered for this patient. If this wider context is ignored then the presence of active symptoms of 'mental illness' can too readily become the rationale for detention in conditions of security and become a dubious proxy for dangerousness.

The psychiatric riposte to this observation might be that these patients have a 'dual diagnosis' or suffer from 'comorbidity'. The argument is that this particular patient also 'has' a 'personality disorder' or that they also abuse substances so they have more than one disorder (like having diabetes and arthritis). Indeed, it was common in the nomenclature of the old Mental Health Act for detained patients to be categorized as suffering from *both* 'mental illness' *and* 'psychopathic disorder'. But this social administrative contortion arises because of the reified concepts provided by the Kraepelinian tradition and the questionable assumption that these concepts are valid and separate.

It is only because the neo-Kraepelinian position starts from the unproven assumption that categories are natural and *separately occurring* that it then has to deal with behavioural and experiential complexity by forcing offender-patients onto the Procrustean (double) bed of 'comorbidity'. By contrast, a psychological approach is not obliged to begin with these assumptions about categories. In open systems, with people with particular current and past circumstances, and attributing meanings to these circumstances in particular ways, unique formulations are more likely to be descriptively richer.

A bonus might be that explanatory insights are more robust than those offered by diagnoses. For example, a fragile defensive young man who had been physically and sexually abused in younger days starts to smoke crack and becomes paranoid in his outlook when outdoors. He carries a knife in anticipation of being attacked and believes that street gangs are out to get him. He lives in a very poor area. In streets with gangs on most corners, one day he reacts to a common and apparently inconsequential taunt by using the blade with fatal consequences.

Mental illness and risk to others

The relationship between a diagnosis of mental illness and risk remains controversial. A number of points can be made to summarize this controversy:

Those with a diagnosis of mental illness are predominantly described in the mass media as a risk to others. However, collectively psychiatric patients are at far greater risk from others and to themselves, as victims of crime and exploitation and from self-harm and suicide. Indeed, the selective media attention to mentally disordered offenders ('schizophrenic kills in frenzied knife attack') then distorts the public imagination about the risk posed by psychiatric patients in general (Pilgrim & Rogers, 2003).

Correlational studies, which argue for the raised link between diagnosed mental illness and violence, have to invoke 'dual diagnosis' to justify the relationship persuasively. As a single variable, diagnosed mental illness is a very poor predictor of violence (Monahan, 1992). Some studies suggest raised rates (Laajasalo & Hakkanen, 2005; Shaw *et al.*, 2006; Swanson, 1994) but others note that it is only the co-presence of substance misuse or personality problems that raises the risk of those with a diagnosed mental illness compared to those without (Steadman *et al.*, 1998).

It is important to note that substance misuse is a predictor of violent offending *independent* of mental state.

However, given that substance misuse is relatively common in psychiatric patients living in the community, with prevalence rates recorded of between 20 and 30%, then it is hardly surprising that this is an important matter for both risk assessment and risk management (Hambrecht & Hafner, 1996; Regier *et al.*, 1990). Given that substance misuse is a predictor of violence in both psychiatric and non-psychiatric populations, it is ironic that when the English Mental Health Act was reformed in 2007, substance misuse was *excluded* as a criterion for judging the actions of those with a mental disorder. If we need a clear behavioural criterion to justify preventative social control, then evidence of substance misuse, not mental illness, should be put at the top of the list rather than being excluded from it (Pilgrim, 2007a).

A version of these correlational studies has focused on specific symptoms rather than diagnosis of mental illness *per se* or on treatment compliance as predictors, to some advantage. For example, the risk of violence increases with the presence of positive not negative symptoms (Soyka, 2000). The latter entail social withdrawal, therefore limiting contact with potential victims. Command hallucinations with violent content unsurprisingly predict violence and so need to be taken seriously in any assessment (Junginger, 1995). Similarly, delusions with hostile content, for example, an obsessive grudge about a targeted victim, predict violent action (Taylor, 1985), though the presence of delusions without this focus do not (Appelbaum, Robbins, & Roth, 1999). Treatment compliance in psychotic patients (with medication) reduces but does not eliminate risk (Swartz *et al.*, 1998).

Just as substance misuse is a good predictor of violence in psychiatric and non-psychiatric populations alike, so too with intimacy. Most victims of violent crimes are known to the perpetrator (Estroff & Zimmer, 1994; Lindqvist & Allebeck, 1989). Thus, in risk assessment the anticipated interpersonal field of the patient in the community needs to be mapped out carefully and is more important than the diagnosis given to them. In the light of the previous point, grudges and old scores need particular attention, whether they are delusional or simply bound up with the micro-politics of the patient's social and family network.

The majority of articles in specialist journals, which focus on mentally abnormal offenders (such as the *Journal of Forensic Psychiatry and Psychology*), report studies of factors other than mental illness, such as types of offending (stalking, paedophilia, etc.) and they focus more on other diagnoses of mental disorder, especially personality disorder, rather than mental illness. This balance of articles in dedicated forensic publications is an indication that researchers of offending consider that 'mental illness' *per se* is a poor source of pickings for their inquiries.

Even when correlational studies show raised levels of risk in those with a diagnosis of mental illness, their practical utility for risk assessment and management is undermined by the large presence of non-patients in the relevant offending category. For example, it has been estimated that between 40 and 50% of stalkers are suffering from some form of mental disorder (and note that this includes diagnoses, such as personality disorder, not just mental illness). This means that between 50 and 60% of stalkers *do not* warrant a diagnosis of mental disorder (Zona, Palarea, & Lane, 1998). Take another example, from researchers who argue that mental illness is a worthy focus of prediction. Laajasalo and Hakkanen (2005) point out that 11% of homicides are carried out by those with a diagnosis of mental illness and again, for emphasis, note that these data are dominated by those with a 'dual diagnosis'. Even this relatively high estimate means that nine out of ten homicides are carried out by people who *are not* mentally ill. What predictive use, then, is a diagnosis of mental illness in itself, given these sorts of data?

As with any psychiatric diagnosis (even the circular notion of personality disorder), aggregate data tell practitioners faced with individual risk assessment very little. Certainly a diagnosis such as 'schizophrenia' tells us virtually nothing about risk to others. It is only by using multifactorial formulations specific to the offender that we move towards improved risk assessment and, even then, as I noted at the start of this chapter, those estimates are often being made in the closed system of confinement, not the open system of past or prospective offending. Within that shift from diagnosis to formulation, clinical variables are marginal in two senses. First, aggregate data about other social group membership, such as male gender, membership of violent subculture or low social class, are a better predictor than being in the social group of psychiatric patients. In other words, if we do use actuarial variables for predicting risk (and their practical utility remains in constant doubt), logically we would not start with 'mental illness' but with one or more other variables. Second, for those offenders with a diagnosis of mental illness, just like offenders without, detailed understandings of past-conduct-in-context are more valid ways of predicting risk than focusing on the presence of a diagnosis of mental illness.

Best-practice guidelines about risk assessment for mentally abnormal offenders suggest that unstructured clinical assessments (where the salience of clinical variables tend to get overvalued or narrowly considered) or actuarial assessments (which are evidenced based but tell us little about individuals) need to be superseded by careful professional formulations of offender-patients and their anticipated contexts after discharge. These formulations should utilize research, detailed knowledge of the patient and the patient's own views in combination to assess risk (DH, 2007). Moreover, risk management is not the same as risk assessment. The more the latter shifts to the former, the more it is important to maintain a collaborative relationship with the patient. Thus risk assessment can be 'done to' patients – even then inefficiently if their views are not taken into account – whereas risk management can only be done with any confidence in collaboration with patients.

Finally, and elaborating on the previous point, context is all-important. Offender variables alone are only one aspect of calculating and preventing risk to others. A good formulation should attend to contextual factors. These are what Hiday (1995) calls 'violence inducing social forces' in the life world of the individual. For example, the offender-patient's particular symptoms, personality and personal history need to be understood in the anticipated context of cultural factors, like local base rates of substance misuse and violence, and the family and social networks likely to support, reject or even attack the person. Psychiatric patients and prisoners are often released into localities of 'concentrated poverty', where they are disproportionately exposed to both substance misuse and criminality. Accordingly they are disproportionately at prospective risk, as both victims and perpetrators. Thus a wise emphasis is implied here about an *ecological* approach to risk assessment and management (Silver, Mulvey, & Monahan, 1999).

CONCLUSIONS

This chapter has placed psychiatric diagnosis into a social and historical context in order that forensic psychologists might reflect critically on their work when dealing with people with a diagnosis of mental illness. Psychologists, like psychiatrists, are agents of social control with divided loyalties between their clients, their employers and wider society. Psychologists, unlike psychiatrists, have the educational background to move, if they choose, from digital to analogue reasoning about the mentally abnormal offenders they encounter in their work. This provides an opportunity to challenge common assumptions about diagnosed 'mental illness' on a number of fronts.

'Mental illness' does not have to be seen as a biological condition, which psychologists either avoid cautiously and deferentially or deal with in terms of its peripheral behavioural fallout, when acting as handmaidens to psychiatry. As for risk assessment and management, psychologists, being less invested than medicine in

Kraepelinian assumptions about categories, can ask more straightforward but sophisticated questions about the individual in their life context. They can more readily resist the seduction of diagnosis as a reductionist focus of explanation and prediction. In other words, the experience and behaviour of a mentally abnormal offender might be understood psychologically in the way that the experience and behaviour of any other person might.

FURTHER READING

Prins, H. (2005). *Offenders, deviants or patients?* London: Routledge.

One way of protecting ourselves against the risks of psychological as well as psychiatric reductionism is to read the work of an experienced student of criminality and mental health from outside both disciplines. This book, in its third edition, is an excellent source in this regard. Prins is not particularly critical of psychiatric theory and practice (compared to some sources and arguments used in this chapter). However, the book is a very good transdisciplinary exploration of our topic of interest.

Pilgrim, D. (2014) *Understanding mental health: A critical realist exploration.* London: Routledge.

This is a more comprehensive exploration, by the author of this chapter, of mental health in general, by giving due weight to biological, psychological and social factors. Critical realism is a middle way between positivism, in both psychiatry and psychology, on the one hand, and the popularity of the 'postmodern' or 'linguistic turn' in human science on the other. The book has dedicated chapters on misery, madness and incorrigible egocentricity, all of which may be of interest to forensic psychologists.

Bentall, R. P. (2003). *Madness explained: Psychosis and human nature.* London: Penguin.

This is a very comprehensive and clearly written account of psychosis from a psychological rather than psychiatric viewpoint. The author has spent his whole academic career investigating his topic in this way and this is reflected in the clarity and confidence of the text. Although readers from many backgrounds read this book and find it useful, it speaks most readily to psychologists working with those with a diagnosis of mental illness.

REFERENCES

Appelbaum, P. S., Robbins, P. C., & Roth, L. H. (1999). A dimensional approach to delusions: A comparison across delusional type and diagnosis. *American Journal of Psychiatry, 156,* 1938–1943.

Bateson, G., Jackson, D. D., Haley, J., & Weakland, J. (1956). Toward a theory of schizophrenia. *Behavioral Science, 1,* 251–264.

Bentall, R. P. (2010). *Doctoring the mind.* London: Penguin

Blacker, D., & Tsuang, M. T. (1998). Classification and DSM-IV. In A. M. Nicholi Jr. (Ed.), *The Harvard guide to psychiatry.* London: Harvard University Press.

Bowlby, J. (1951). Maternal care and mental health. *Bulletin of the World Health Organization* (Monograph), *3,* 355–534.

Brown, G. W., Harris, T. O., & Hepworth, C. (1995). Loss, humiliation and entrapment among women developing depression: A patient and non-patient comparison. *Psychological Medicine, 25,* 7–21.

Cohen, S., & Scull, A. (Eds.). (1985). *Social control and the state.* Oxford: Basil Blackwell.

Coulter, J. (1973). *Approaches to insanity.* London: Martin Robertson.

Department of Health (2007). *Best practice in managing risk.* London: Department of Health.

Division of Clinical Psychology (2011). *Good practice guidelines on the use of psychological formulation.* Leicester: British Psychological Society

Division of Clinical Psychology (2013). *Classification of behaviour and experience in relation to functional psychiatric diagnosis: Time for a paradigm shift.* Leicester: British Psychological Society.

Dohrenwend, B. P. (1998). A psychosocial perspective on the past and future of psychiatric epidemiology. *American Journal of Epidemiology, 147*(3), 222–229.

Engel, G. L. (1980). The clinical application of the biopsychosocial model. *American Journal of Psychiatry, 137,* 535–544.

Estroff, A., & Zimmer, C. (1994). Social networks, social support, and violence among persons with severe, persistent mental illness. In J. Monahan & H. E. Steadman (Eds.), *Violence and mental disorder: Developments in risk assessment.* Chicago, IL: University of Chicago Press.

Eysenck, H. J. (1975). *The future of psychiatry.* London: Methuen.

Fisher, R. A. (1930). *The genetical theory of natural selection.* Oxford: Clarendon Press.

Goffman, E. (1971). *Relations in public: Microstudies of the public order.* New York: Harper.

Hale, N. G. (1995). *The rise and crisis of psychoanalysis in the United States: Freud and the Americans, 1917–1985.* New York: Oxford University Press.

Hambrecht, M., & Hafner, H. (1996). Substance abuse and the onset of schizophrenia. *Biological Psychiatry, 40,* 1155–1163.

Hiday, V. (1995). The social context of mental illness and violence. *Journal of Health and Social Behavior, 36,* 911–914.

Hinsie, L. E. (1931). Criticism of treatment and recovery in schizophrenia. *Proceedings of the association for research in nervous and mental disease for 1928. Schizophrenia (dementia praecox).* Baltimore, MD: Williams & Wilkins.

Horwitz, A. V. (2002). *Creating mental illness.* Chicago, IL: University of Chicago Press.

Junginger, J. (1995). Command hallucinations and the prediction of dangerousness. *Psychiatric Services, 46,* 911–914.

Kleinman, A. (1988). *Rethinking psychiatry.* New York: Free Press.

Kraepelin, E. (1883). *Compendium der Psychiatrie.* Leipzig.

Laajasalo, T., & Hakkanen, H. (2005). Offence and offender characteristics among two groups of Finnish homicide offenders with schizophrenia. *Journal of Forensic Psychiatry and Psychology, 16*(1), 41–50.

Laing, R. D., & Esterson, A. (1964). *Sanity, madness and the family.* Harmondsworth: Penguin.

Lindqvist, P., & Allebeck, P. (1989). Criminal homicide in North West Sweden 1970–1981. Alcohol intoxication, alcohol abuse and mental disease. *International Journal of Law and Psychiatry, 8,* 19–37.

McPherson, S., & Armstrong, D. (2006). Social determinants of diagnostic labels in depression. *Social Science and Medicine, 62*(1), 50–58.

McWilliams, N. (1994). *Psychoanalytic diagnosis: Understanding personality structure in the clinical process.* New York: Guilford Press.

Monahan, J. (1992). Mental disorder and violent behavior: Perceptions and evidence. *American Psychologist, 47,* 511–521.

Pavlov, I. P. (1941). *Lectures on conditioned reflexes: Vol. II. Conditioned reflexes and psychiatry* (trans. W. H. Gantt). London: Lawrence & Wishart.

Pilgrim, D. (2001). Disordered personalities and disordered concepts. *Journal of Mental Health, 10*(3), 253–265.

Pilgrim, D. (2007a). The survival of psychiatric diagnosis. *Social Science & Medicine, 65*(3), 536–544.

Pilgrim, D. (2007b). New 'mental health' legislation for England and Wales: Some aspects of consensus and conflict. *Journal of Social Policy, 36*(1), 1–17.

Pilgrim, D. (2008). The legacy of eugenics in modern psychology and psychiatry. *International Journal of Social Psychiatry, 54*(3), 272–284.

Pilgrim, D., Kinderman, P., & Tai, S. (2008). Taking stock of the biopsychosocial model in the field of 'mental health care'. *Journal of Social and Psychological Sciences, 1*(2), 1–39.

Pilgrim, D., & Rogers, D. (2003). Mental disorder and violence: An empirical picture in context. *Journal of Mental Health, 12*(1), 7–18.

Read, J., & Bentall, R. P. (2012). Negative childhood experiences and mental health: Theoretical, clinical and primary prevention implications. *British Journal of Psychiatry, 200,* 88–91.

Regier, D. A., Farmer, M. E., Rae, D. S., Locke, B. J., Keith, S. L., Judd, L. L., & Goodwin, F. K. (1990). Comorbidity of mental disorders with alcohol and other drug abuse: Results from the epidemiologic catchment area (ECA) study. *Journal of the American Medical Association, 264,* 2511–2518.

Rogers, A., & Pilgrim, D. (2003). *Mental health and inequality.* Basingstoke: Palgrave.

Rogers, A., & Pilgrim, D. (2014). *A sociology of mental health and illness (fifth edition).* Buckingham: Open University Press.

Scheff, T. J. (1966). *Being mentally ill: A sociological theory.* Chicago, IL: Chicago University Press.

Seligman, M. E. P. (1975). *Helplessness: On depression, development and death.* San Francisco, CA: Freeman.

Shaw, J., Hunt, I. M., Flynn, S., Meehan, J., Robinson, J., Bickley, H., Parsons, R., McCann, K., Burns, J., Amos, T., Kapur, N. N., & Appleby, L. (2006). Rates of mental disorder in people convicted of homicide: National clinical survey. *British Journal of Psychiatry, 188,* 143–147.

Silver, E., Mulvey, E. P., & Monahan, J. (1999). Assessing violence among discharged psychiatric patients. Towards an ecological approach. *Law and Human Behavior, 23,* 237–255.

Soyka, M. (2000). Substance misuse, psychiatric disorder and violent and disturbed behaviour. *British Journal of Psychiatry, 176,* 345–350.

Steadman, H. J., Mulvey, E. P., Monahan, J., Robbins, P. C., Appelbaum P. S., Grisso, T., Roth, L. H., & Silver, E. (1998). Violence by people discharged from acute psychiatric inpatient facilities and by others in the same neighbourhood. *Archives of General Psychiatry, 55,* 109.

Stone, M. (1985). Shellshock and the psychologists. In W. F. Bynum, R. Porter & M. Shepherd (Eds.), *The anatomy of madness.* London: Tavistock.

Swanson, J. W. (1994). Mental disorder, substance abuse, and community violence: An epidemiological approach. In J. Monahan & H. J. Steadman (Eds.), *Violence and mental disorder: Developments in risk assessment.* Chicago, IL: University of Chicago Press.

Swartz, M. S., Swanson, J. W., Hiday, V. A., Borum, R., Wagner, H. R., & Burns, B. J. (1998). Violence and severe mental illness: The effects of drug abuse and non-adherence to medication. *American Journal of Psychiatry, 155,* 226–231.

Szasz, T. S. (1961). The use of naming and the origin of the myth of mental illness. *American Psychologist, 16,* 59–65.

Taylor, P. J. (1985). Motives for offending among violent psychotic men. *British Journal of Psychiatry, 147,* 491–498.

Varese, F., Smeets, F., Drukker, M., Lieverse, R., Lataster, L., Viechtbauer, W., Read, J., van Os, J., & Bentall, R. P. (2012). Childhood adversities increase the risk of psychosis: A meta-analysis of patient-control, prospective- and cross-sectional cohort studies. *Schizophrenia Bulletin, 38*(4), 661–671.

Watson, J. B., & Rayner, R. (1920). Conditioned emotional reactions. *Journal of Experimental Psychology, 10,* 421–428.

Wilson, M. (1993). DSM-III and the transformation of American psychiatry: A history. *American Journal of Psychiatry, 150*(3), 399–410.

Zona, M. A., Palarea, R. E., & Lane, J. (1998). Psychiatric diagnosis and the offender – victim typology of stalking. In J. Reid Meloy (Ed.), *The psychology of stalking: Clinical and forensic perspectives.* San Diego, CA: Academic Press.

14 Intellectual Disability: Assessment

WILLIAM R. LINDSAY AND JOHN L. TAYLOR

In developing this and the following chapter, we have considered the post-graduate training requirements for forensic psychology published by the British Psychological Society. In stage one, these include four knowledge dimensions of the context of practice in forensic psychology, applications of psychology to processes within the justice system, working with specific client groups and using and communicating information in practice. There are four core roles in which these knowledge dimensions are applied, and a theme stressed through all of the guidelines is the importance of research and the research base to the profession. We shall outline the main aspects of our knowledge in the field of forensic learning disabilities according to these dimensions, and throughout we will emphasize the importance and reliance on research and its crucial underpinning of practice in the field.

We have used the term 'intellectual and developmental disabilities' (IDD) to refer to the population of individuals studied. 'Learning disability' is a term synonymous with IDD but used only in the United Kingdom and Ireland. Until recently, the term 'mental retardation' was used in the United States and widely across English-speaking countries. In order to accommodate for people with intellectual disabilities and those who also have autism spectrum disorder, the American Association for Intellectual and Developmental Disabilities (AAIDD) recently changed its title from the American Association for Mental Retardation, and the International Association is now termed the International Association for the Scientific Study of Intellectual and Developmental Disabilities (IASSIDD), both with an intention to change the terms referring to the population more generally. However, workers and researchers in the field should know that these various terms are synonymous. We have used 'IDD' since it has gained international recognition with reference to the population.

THE CONTEXT OF PRACTICE IN FORENSIC LEARNING DISABILITIES

The British Psychological Society, along with other major international diagnostic classification systems such as ICD-10 (World Health Organisation, 1992), DSM-V (American Psychiatric Association, 2013) and the American Association on Mental Retardation (1992), specifies the following three core criteria for IDD.

i) *Significant impairment of intellectual functioning* – Assessment of intellectual functioning, particularly in forensic contexts, should be obtained using an individually administered, reliable and valid standardized test, such as the third edition of the Wechsler Adult Intelligence Scale (WAIS-IV[UK]: Wechsler, 2010). Using tests such as the WAIS-IV[UK], based on a normal distribution of general intelligence, a significant impairment of intellectual functioning is conventionally understood to be a score more than two standard deviations below the population mean. Therefore, significant impairment of intellectual functioning is generally defined as an IQ less than 70. Importantly, one must take into account the standard error of the test, and psychologists should always consider the range of two standard errors as an appropriately cautious finding. One should be cautious about using shorter, less-time-consuming assessments of cognitive functioning which estimate or screen for intellectual ability. There are a number of screening measures available to services such as

Forensic Psychology, Second Edition. Edited by David A. Crighton and Graham J. Towl.
© 2015 John Wiley & Sons, Ltd. Published 2015 by British Psychological Society and John Wiley & Sons, Ltd.

the Quick Test (Ammons & Ammons, 1958) or the Hayes Ability Screening Index (Hayes, 2000). Screening measures are designed to be over-inclusive in relation to the population, and, although they will generally have a high correlation with a more comprehensive measure of intellectual ability such as the WAIS, where there are errors they should be overwhelmingly in one direction. Therefore, they are more likely to misclassify individuals without ID as falling within the population.

ii) *Significant associated impairment of adaptive or social functioning* – Adaptive functioning is a broad concept that is concerned with an individual's ability to cope with the day-to-day demands of their environment. It will include the skills necessary for independent functioning, domestic tasks, self-care skills in addition to a range of community integration abilities such as the use of public transport, shopping skills and the ability to use services such as banking, social services, leisure services and health services. As with cognitive assessments, there are a range of assessments of adaptive behaviour. The two in most common usage are the Vineland Adaptive Behaviour Scale and the Adaptive Behaviour Scale – Residential and Community (2nd Edition) (ABS-RC:2) developed by the AAIDD (2008). Depending on the classification system, an individual must have at least two or three significant deficits in adaptive behaviour. The VABS has norms which allow the assessor to review an individual's adaptive behaviour in relation to the general population, while the ABS-RC:2 has norms which enable the assessor to gauge an individual's adaptive behaviour in relation to their peers in residential and community settings. An assessment of adaptive behaviour is considered essential in any classification of ID.

iii) *Age of onset within the developmental period before adulthood* – There is general international consensus that the 'age of onset' criterion means the developmental period during childhood and adolescence (e.g., American Psychiatric Association, 2013; British Psychological Society, 2000; ICD10, 1992). The important aspect is that the assessor should partial out intellectual deterioration that may be caused by traumatic injury or disease which has occurred in adulthood. The latter would be classified as acquired impairment rather than developmental impairment. Therefore, an assessment of IDD is not confined to current abilities but is also concerned with developmental experience and developmental skills.

Because IDD is defined by intellectual ability, adaptive skills and age of onset, the population is by definition heterogeneous. This can be seen if one takes, as an analogy, individuals whose cognitive functioning is two standard deviations above the mean rather than below the mean. In individuals who have an IQ of greater than 130 with a corresponding range of adaptive skills, developmental experiences and abilities, it seems fairly obvious that these classifications represent a cross-section of the population at a certain level of ability. Therefore, all of the fields of psychological enquiry are relevant, as they would be to any cross-section of the population. It follows that work on the range of offence categories, the range of witness and victim investigations and, indeed, the range of diagnostic categories are all relevant to people with IDD.

MENTAL HEALTH LEGISLATION

Mental health legislation in the various jurisdictions of the United Kingdom has sections that concern detention for the assessment and treatment of people with ID who have offended or engaged in offending-like behaviour. The Mental Health Act (MHA) 1983 for England and Wales and the MHA 2006 for Scotland, both contain categories of mental disorder termed 'mental impairment' and 'severe mental impairment'. The acts use the terms 'severe impairment' and 'significant impairment'. These legal categories are not synonymous with the clinical definition of ID, and while they contain two of the three core clinical criteria, they also include a criterion for 'abnormally aggressive or seriously irresponsible conduct'. The acts do not operationally define 'significant' and 'severe' mental impairment, stating that the assessment of the degree of impairment is a matter for clinical judgement. However, the level of impairment (significant or severe) is important, as under the acts different legal sanctions apply to respective classifications. For this reason, the British Psychological Society (2000) recommends that this judgement be based on a full assessment using a reliable and valid test such as the WAIS-IV[UK] along with an appropriate assessment of adaptive behaviour. Significant impairment of intellectual function is represented by an IQ score between two and three standard deviations below the population mean, and severe impairment is represented by a score of more than three standard deviations below the population mean.

During 2005–2006, there were a total of 25,740 admissions to NHS facilities (including high-security hospitals) under the England and Wales MHA 1983 (The Information Centre, 2007). Of the 8,435 detentions under civil sections of the act during this period for which the category of mental disorder was recorded, less than 1% were categorized as mental or severe mental impairment. However, of the 1,304 criminal detentions under court and prison disposals during the corresponding period, just over 4% were categorized as mental or severe mental impairment. Assuming a normal distribution, the proportion of people in the general population with IQ scores under 70 is approximately 2.5%. Thus, it appears that around more than double the expected number of people with impaired intellectual functioning are being detained in NHS facilities under sections of the England and Wales MHA 1983. It should be remembered that these are generally secure facilities and, as we pointed out earlier, the evidence that people with ID commit more crime is highly equivocal.

LEARNING DISABILITY AND CRIME

For almost two centuries, crime and learning disability have been linked with devastating effects on the population. Until the mid-to-late nineteenth century, people with ID were generally considered as a burden on society. Living conditions were harsh for people with ID, especially in urban areas, and in rural areas they tended to work long hours in poverty. Perception changed towards the end of the century, and the population began to be viewed as a menace to society. Scheerenberger (1983) notes that 'By the 1980s, mentally retarded persons were no longer viewed as unfortunates or innocents who, with proper training, could fill a positive role in the home and/or community. As a class they had become undesirable, frequently viewed as a great evil of humanity, the social parasite, criminal, prostitute and pauper' (p. 116). Terman (1911), an author of one of the earliest IQ tests, wrote that 'There is no investigator who denies the fearful role of mental deficiency in the production of vice, crime and delinquency … not all criminals are feebleminded but all feebleminded are at least potential criminals' (p. 11). This cultural prejudice, coming from such an authoritative and, presumably for the time, enlightened source (Terman), gives us today a flavour of the extent of these views that ID was a cause of crime.

One of the most persuasive pieces of research on offending rates and people with IDD was the classic study by Hodgins (1992). She used a census cohort of 15,117 people born in Stockholm in 1953 and still living there in 1963. Those still living in Sweden at the 30-year follow-up period in 1983 were included in the analysis. Intellectual disability was defined as 'those who were placed in special classes for intellectually deficient children in high school and were never admitted to a psychiatric ward' (p478). She found that men with IDD were overrepresented threefold for any offence and fivefold for violent offences when compared with non-disabled offenders. Woman offenders with IDD were overrepresented 25-fold for violent offences. Around 50% of the men with IDD had been convicted of an offence, and the average number of convictions was 10. Lindsay and Dernevick (2013) recently reanalysed this data, investigating who was likely to have been in the sample of Swedish schoolchildren with IDD during the 1960s. After a detailed analysis of the Swedish school system at the time and drawing on the writing of both educationalists and those working in the IDD services, they concluded that 'the people with intellectual disability in the Hodgins (1992) study were not the generality of people with such difficulties but rather represented a sample biased towards inclusion of those with conduct disorder or similar behavioural problems as children or adolescents as well as their intellectual problems' (p155).

Despite the long association between delinquency and low intellectual functioning, it is not clear whether people with ID commit more crime than those without ID (Lindsay, Sturmey, & Taylor, 2004), or in fact whether the nature and frequency of offending by people with ID differs from that committed by offenders in the general population (Holland, 2004). In relation to the prevalence of offending, there are several methodological difficulties resulting in disparity across various studies (Lindsay, Hastings, Griffiths & Hayes, 2007). One of the first problems is that studies have been conducted in a variety of settings including prisons (MacEachron, 1979), high-security hospitals (Walker & McCabe, 1973), appearance at court (Messinger & Apfelberg, 1961), probation services (Mason & Murphy, 2002) and appearance at police stations (Lyall, Holland, Collins, & Styles, 1995). In some settings, it has been reported that particular types of offences are overrepresented among offenders with ID. For example, in their classic study of secure hospitals in England, Walker and McCabe (1973) reviewed 331 men with ID who had committed offences and had been detained under hospital orders to secure provision in England and Wales. They found high rates of fire raising (15%) and sexual offences (28%) when compared with other groups in their secure hospital sample. In a more recent study, Hogue et al. (2006) reviewed a number of characteristics of offenders with ID across community, medium/low-security and high-security settings. They found that rates of arson in the index offence depended on the setting with low rates in the community setting (2.9%) and higher rates in the medium/low-security setting (21.4%). This is a clear example of the fact that the setting in which the data is collected is very likely to influence the results and subsequent conclusions about the population.

MacEachron (1979) noted a second source of influence on prevalence rates. She reviewed the literature for prevalence of offenders with ID in prisons and found a range of 2.6–39.6%. She noted that these previous studies had used a variety of methods to identify intellectual disability and concluded that the methodological variation between studies might produce the highly diverse prevalence rates. In her own more carefully controlled study, employing recognized intelligence tests, she investigated 436 adult male offenders in Maine and Massachusetts State Penal Institutions and found prevalence rates of ID of 0.6–2.3%. A third source of variation is inclusion criteria, particularly if those considered to be functioning in the borderline intelligence range are included. Hayes and McIlwain (1988) conducted a review of the prevalence of ID in the prison population of New South Wales, Australia. At the time, they noted that ID is associated with significant deficits in social and adaptive skills which may make these individuals vulnerable to risks and exploitations within the prison setting. Hayes (1991) commented on this study and other studies which revealed that approximately 2% of the prison population in New South Wales had a measured IQ lower than 70. She also noted that approximately 10% of individuals were placed in the borderline range of IQ between 70 and 80. Clearly, the inclusion of individuals with borderline intelligence significantly increases the prevalence rates, and several studies have used an IQ of 80 or even 85 as a cut-off for intellectual disability (Noble & Conley, 1992).

The influence of social policy changes was demonstrated by Lund (1990) in a follow-up study of 91 offenders with ID on Statutory Care Orders in Denmark. He reported a doubling of the incidence of sex offending when comparing sentencing in 1973–1983 and suggested that this rise may have been a result of policies of deinstitutionalization whereby people with ID are no longer detained in hospital for indeterminate lengths of time. He concluded that those with propensities towards offending would be more likely to be living in the community and, as a result, were likely to be subject to normal legal processes should they engage in offending behaviour. Since 1990, there has been an increase in the amount of research related to offenders with ID and especially related to those living in community settings.

This increase in the knowledge base reflects similar changes in social policy with widespread deinstitutionalization policies throughout the developed world.

The methodological differences between studies continue with two recent pieces of research finding markedly different rates of offenders with ID in criminal justice settings. Several recent studies suggest that these differences still produce varying results. In a variety of settings, differences in prevalence have been reported: probation services (Mason & Murphy, 2002; prevalence 4.8%), pre-trial assessment (Vinkers, 2013; prevalence 4.4%), appearances at court (Vanny, Levy, Greenberg, & Hayes, 2009; prevalence 10%) and prison settings (Holland & Persson, 2011, prevalence 1.3%; Murphy, Harrold, Carey, & Mulrooney, 2000, prevalence 28.8%). Two studies conducted in prison settings illustrate some of the problems. Crocker, Côté, Toupin, & St-Onge (2007) attempted to assess 749 offenders in a pre-trial holding centre in Montreal. For a number of reasons including refusal to participate, administrative difficulties and technical problems, they were only able to assess 281 participants with three subscales of a locally standardized mental ability scale. They reported that 18.9% were in the probable ID range with a further 29.9% in the borderline range. On the other hand, in a study of prisoners in Victoria, Australia, Holland and Persson (2010) found a prevalence rate of less than 1.3% using the Wechsler Adult Intelligence Scale. In the latter study, all prisoners were assessed routinely by trained forensic psychologists while, in the former study, only around one-third of potential participants were included in the study. In the former study, three subscales of an intelligence test were used while, in the latter, a full WAIS was used for all participants. It is difficult to reconcile these two pieces of work, but it is likely that the difference in assessment methods, comprehensiveness of the sample and differences in legal systems were all significant contributors to the disparity and results.

Studies of recidivism rates for offenders with ID suffer from the same methodological and social policy influences. However, they do indicate that the contemporary scientific interest in the field extends back to the 1940s. Wildenskov (1962) reported a 20-year follow-up of offenders with ID and found a re-offending rate of around 50%. While the sophistication of studies has improved considerably since this time, it does point out that a 20-year follow-up reported in 1962 requires data going back to at least 1942. Linhorst, McCutchen, and Bennet (2003) followed up 252 convicted offenders with ID who had completed a case management community programme and found that 25% who had completed the programme were rearrested within 6 months while 43% of those who had dropped out were rearrested during the same period. Klimecki, Jenkinson, and Wilson (1994) reported re-offending rates in previous prison inmates with ID, 2 years after their release. They found that over-all, re-offending rates were 41.3%, with higher rates for less serious offences. However, the lower re-offending rates (around 31%) for sex offences, murder and violent offences were artificially reduced because a number of those individuals were still in prison and therefore unable to re-offend.

Due to a lack of controlled studies involving ID and mainstream offenders, it is difficult to make direct comparisons of recidivism rates. However, it would appear that recidivism rates for offenders with ID are consistent with those for populations of mainstream offenders. In one recent study, Gray, Fitzgerald, Taylor, MacCulloch, and Snowden (2007) conducted a 2 year follow-up of 145 offenders with ID and 996 offenders without ID, all discharged from independent-sector hospitals in the United Kingdom. The ID group had a lower rate of reconviction for violent offences after 2 years (4.8%) than the non-ID group (11.2%). This trend also held true for general offences (9.7% for the ID group and 18.7% for the non-ID group).

Pathways into and through offender services

While there is an established relationship between low IQ and offending (Farrington, 1995, 2000, 2004), most of the studies done in this area are investigating the predictive value or differences between groups at one or two standard deviations below the mean (IQ < 85). It is interesting to note the small amount of information which specifically reviews individuals with an IQ less than two standard deviations below the mean. McCord and McCord (1959) evaluated an interesting early intervention study with 650 underprivileged boys in Massachusetts. The Cambridge-Sommerville Youth Study was set up '[t]o prevent delinquency and to develop stable elements in the characters of children' (McCord & McCord, 1959, p. 2). The boys were divided into 325 matched pairs and assigned to treatment and control conditions. There was a relationship between IQ and rates of conviction in that, for the treatment group, 44% of those in the IQ band 81–90 had a conviction while 26% of those with an IQ above 110 had a conviction. However, the 10% of individuals in the lowest IQ group (less than 80) had an intermediate rate of conviction at 35% – that is, lower than that recorded in the IQ band 81–90. Furthermore, of those in the higher IQ band who were convicted of crime, none went to penal institutions, while the highest percentage going to penal institutions, 19%, were in the lowest IQ band. The results were similar in the control group, with 50% in the IQ band 81–90 convicted of crime

and 25% in the IQ band less than 80 convicted. Maughan, Pickles, Hagell, Rutter, and Yule (1996) and Rutter et al. (1997) followed up children who had shown severe reading difficulties at school. It might be considered that a significant proportion of children with severe reading difficulties had developmental and intellectual disabilities. They found that the rate of adult crime among boys who had had significant reading difficulties were slightly lower than the rate of adult crime in the general population comparison group. This finding held true independent of psychopathology or social functioning. Similarly, antisocial behaviour in childhood was less likely to persist into adult life when it was accompanied by reading difficulties. Therefore, while the relationship between IQ and delinquency seems firmly established, there is some evidence that this relationship does not hold when considering individuals 1.5 or more standard deviations below the mean.

One of the main pieces of work to influence views on IDD as a risk factor for offending has been that of Hodgins (1992). She used the census cohort of 15,117 people born in Stockholm in 1953 and still living there in 1983. Only participants living in Sweden at the 30-year follow-up period were included in the analysis. IDD was defined 'as those who are placed in special classes for intellectually deficient children in high school and were never admitted to a psychiatric ward' (p. 478). She reported that crime almost doubled in the group with IDD. Lindsay and Dernevik (2013) questioned this classic study on a number of bases. Hodgins (1992) methodology did not take account of the Swedish education system at the time, which included special schools and special hospitals for people with ID. Therefore, the sample was more likely to be made up of people who had attended special classes in mainstream schools for reasons of intellectual limitations or behaviour disorders. Therefore, while low IQ remained a risk for crime, IDD itself was not included or minimally included in the sample.

When we consider the pathways of people who are referred into forensic IDD services, we can look at a number of studies published in the last few years. The first and most obvious variable to consider is the level of IDD, whether mild, moderate, severe or profound. It is interesting that Brown and Courtless (1971) completed a comprehensive survey of correctional institutions in the United States and found that 1.6% of the population of prisoners had an IQ of < 55 and a few cases even fell below an IQ of 25. An IQ of <25 indicates a profound IDD, and one wonders about the accuracy of the intellectual assessment in these cases, but individuals of this level of ability would not now enter into the criminal justice system. The Northgate, Cambridge, Abertay Pathways (NCAP) project is a fairly large-scale study of 477 individuals with IDD referred to a range of forensic IDD services. The project included generic community services that were comfortable accepting forensic referrals, community forensic IDD services, acute assessment and treatment units for people with IDD who accepted forensic cases, and low-security, medium-security and maximum-security services all for offenders with IDD. Wheeler *et al.* (2009) reported on 237 cases from the NCAP study referred to community services for anti-social or offending behaviour. Those individuals with an IQ of <50 were far less likely to have criminal justice involvement than those with an IQ of 51–75. Those individuals who displayed anti-social behaviour with an IQ of <50 were more likely to remain within generic ID community services and less likely to enter into forensic services. Employing data from all 477 referrals in the NCAP study, Carson *et al.* (2010) constructed a regression model to predict factors influencing whether or not participants were referred to secure or community provision. One of the strongest predictors for referral to secure provision was IQ of >50. Therefore, not only was intellectual ability a major determinant of pathways into criminal justice services (Wheeler *et al.*, 2009), it was also a predictor for pathways into secure services for people with IDD who commit anti-social offending behaviour. The reason for this is fairly obvious, in that those in the lower IQ bands are likely to be assessed as lacking *mens rea* and as such cannot be expected to understand the laws and conventions of society. Because of this, they cannot be considered to have criminal responsibility for their actions.

An important study on the effect of IQ was conducted by Emerson and Halpin (2013) with a secondary analysis of the Longitudinal Study of Young People in England data set that included 15,772 young people, 532 of whom were identified as having mild IDD. For the group as a whole, living with a single parent and four indicators of social, economic and environmental adversity were significant risk factors for contact to the police and anti-social behaviour. Teenagers with IDD were significantly more likely than other children to be exposed to all risk factors including living with a single parent, living in an area of deprivation, living in rented accommodation, living in a workless household and being eligible for free school meals. Although teenagers with mild IDD were significantly more likely to have police contact and to report anti-social behaviour, when these risk factors were controlled, IDD itself was significantly associated with *lower rates* of anti-social behaviour. This study on a very large data set suggests that IDD on its own may not be a risk factor. Rather, it serves as a proxy for other potent risk factors of deprivation and childhood adversity.

Childhood adversity and behaviour problems

The experience of family disruption is a major factor in the histories of those individuals who go on to develop serious and chronic criminality (Farrington, 1995, 2000; Harris, Rice, & Quinsey, 1993; Ward *et al.*, 2010). In the NCAP study, Lindsay, O'Brien *et al.* (2010) and O'Brien *et al.* (2010) found that one-third of the population had experienced deprivation in childhood, and that the most frequent form of deprivation/abuse was socio-economic deprivation. Sexual abuse and non-accidental injury also featured at 10% and 12%, respectively. Lindsay, Carson *et al.* (2010) compared 197 referrals accepted into forensic services with 280 who were not accepted and found that severe deprivation in childhood was recorded at 36% for those accepted into services, compared to 16% for those not accepted. Therefore, severe deprivation in childhood would appear to be a significant variable determining pathway into forensic services for offenders with IDD. In relation to specific offences, several authors in mainstream forensic research have found that the experience of sexual abuse in childhood is more frequent in adult, male sex offenders than in control groups, while the experience of physical abuse in childhood is related to aggression in adulthood (Fago, 2006; Jespersen, Lalumiere, & Seto, 2009). Lindsay, Steptoe, and Haut (2012) compared the physical and sexual abuse histories of 156 sexual and 126 non-sexual offenders with IDD. They found that 33% of the sexual offenders and 18% of the non-sexual offenders had experienced sexual abuse in childhood, while 16% of the sexual offenders and 33% of the non-sexual offenders had experienced physical abuse. The small cohort of female offenders ($n = 27$) reported high levels of both types of abuse in childhood. However, it is important to note that, while those trends were significant, around two-thirds of participants did not report sexual or physical abuse in childhood.

In a study of violent men with IDD, Novaco and Taylor (2008) investigated 105 male forensic patients to determine whether their exposure to parental anger and aggression was related to assault and violence in a hospital setting. Historical records, staff ratings, self-reports and clinical interviews were employed to assess participants' propensity towards anger and aggression and childhood exposure to parental anger and aggression. They found that witnessing parental violence in childhood was significantly related to anger and aggression in adulthood. Therefore, childhood adversity appears as a significant variable in the careers of offenders with IDD not only as a general risk factor but also as a risk factor specific to different types of offending. It should be remembered that Emerson and Halpin (2013) also found that IDD was associated with several indicators of deprivation and childhood adversity.

In mainstream research on criminality, childhood behaviour problems have been shown to be highly predictive of a criminal career (Farrington *et al.* 2006; Livingston, Stewart, Allard, & Ogilvie, 2008; Barratt, 1994; Quinsey *et al.*, 2005). In the NCAP study, O'Brien *et al.* (2010) noted that the most frequent psychiatric disorder in the cohort was attention deficit hyperactivity disorder (ADHD), and that this had continued from childhood. Using the same cohort, Lindsay, O'Brien *et al.* (2010) found that those referred to secure services had significantly higher rates of ADHD/conduct disorder than those referred to community services. Over 25% of those referred to secure services had these childhood disorders, while 8%–15% of those referred to different community services were recorded with these difficulties. Comparing those with and without ADHD/conduct disorder, Lindsay, Carson *et al.* (2013) noted that those with a history of ADHD/conduct disorder had a higher frequency of the most aggressive offences such as physical aggression, damage to property and a high level of previous offending in most categories including sexual and non-sexual offences. In the context of previous literature on ADHD, they concluded that ADHD was not a significant risk factor on its own but that, in combination with conduct disorder, it is a potent risk for criminality.

It should be noted that, with both of the previous variables, childhood adversity and childhood behaviour problems, by no means had all individuals who had committed specific categories of crime experienced associated difficulties in childhood. Neither was it the case that the experience of specific types of adversity in childhood inevitably led to specific types of crime in adulthood. Rather, it should simply be noted that there is a tendency for those variables (physical abuse or sexual abuse in childhood) to be more prevalent in offenders with IDD and to be associated with particular types of crime and therefore considered as risk factors in the trajectory of criminal careers.

Adult psychiatric disorders

We have seen that one of the principal adult psychiatric disorders associated with criminality has been intellectual disability. While this has been the case to a greater or lesser extent over the last 100 years, the available evidence, when analysed in some detail, is not persuasive. Other studies have investigated major mental illness in relation to offending and found that, while it is at least as prevalent in offenders with IDD when compared to the general population of people with IDD, it is not consistently associated with offending or any particular type of

incident. Lunsky *et al.* (2011) compared large cohorts of forensic and non-forensic patients with IDD. The forensic group had lower frequencies of mood disorder with no differences in other mental illnesses. However, the forensic group had significantly higher rates of personality disorder. Lindsay *et al.* (2011) and Lindsay, Steptoe, Wallace, Haut, & Brewster (2013) reported no differences between sexual offenders and violent offenders in their rates of mental illness although rates for both groups were consistent with findings from other populations with IDD at around 35%. Vinkers (2013), in a large study on 12,186 individuals in the Netherlands who had been subject to pre-trial psychiatric reports, found that those with an IQ <70 had lower rates (although not significant) of psychiatric disorder than those with an IQ of >85. In contrast with the studies finding no differences in mental illness in offenders, Raina and Lunsky (2010) reported that a small forensic sample with IDD ($n = 79$) had a significantly higher frequency of psychosis diagnosis than a matched sample of non-forensic patients with IDD.

Personality disorder has been particularly implicated as a risk factor for criminal behaviour in all types of offenders (Monahan *et al.*, 2001; Quinsey, Harris, Rice, & Cormier, 2005). Alexander *et al.* (2010) compared 77 patients with personality disorder against 61 without (all had IDD). They found significantly higher rates of previous violent offending, significantly higher rates of substance abuse and significantly higher previous detention under 'criminal' sections of mental health legislation in the personality disorder group. Hogue *et al.* (2006) constructed a regression model for the prediction of secure or community provision in 212 offenders with IDD. They included a range of offences, and diagnostic and legal detention variables. Personality disorder diagnosis and variables indicating a history of previous anti-sociality emerged as strong predictors of admission to secure provision. However, they noted that clinicians working in maximum-security hospitals were more comfortable in making a personality disorder diagnosis, and this was likely to have influenced the result. Indeed, Lindsay *et al.* (2006) conducted a series of personality disorder evaluations on the same sample and found a much more even distribution of evaluated PD diagnoses between secure and community settings.

In the NCAP study (Lindsay, Carson *et al.*, 2010, Lindsay, O'Brien *et al.*, 2010), adult mental illness diagnosis was not a significant discriminator between referrals to community and secure provision. Apart from personality disorder and ADHD/conduct disorder, already discussed, there were no consistent trends on any specific diagnosis. For personality disorder, the overall rate recorded in the 477 referrals was 8.4%. The differences between groups were significant with maximum-security provision recording 30%, low/medium-security recording 188% and all community services between 2% and 3%. However, the same observation noted by Hogue *et al.* (2006) is relevant in that secure services are much more familiar and comfortable with these diagnoses than community services, giving rise to a possible serious bias in the findings. The variable was not retained in the regression analysis predicting referral pathways for all referrals (Carson *et al.*, 2010), community referrals (Wheeler *et al.*, 2009) or sexual referrals (Carson *et al.*, 2013, in press). Therefore, while mental disorder has a high prevalence in offenders with IDD, it appears not to predict any particular form of pathway or be associated with any particular type of offending.

Specific offence types and pathways into services

In mainstream research, previous violence has been found to be a significant risk factor in pathways to future violence (Webster, Eaves, Douglas, & Wintrup, 1995). A specific test of the predictive value of previous aggression was conducted by MacMillan, Hastings, and Caldwell (2004) when they compared actuarial assessment and clinical judgement for the prediction of physical violence in a forensic IDD sample. They found that previous assaults predicted future violence with a medium-to-large effect size. In terms of pathway into violence, the presence of previous assaults allowed a reasonable prediction of who was at risk for future violence in a forensic population with IDD. In the NCAP study, Carson *et al.* (2010) constructed a regression model to predict community or secure referral participants. If the index behaviour included physical aggression, the referral was significantly more likely to be made to secure services than community services. For the community referrals in this sample, Wheeler *et al.* (2009) found that current physical aggression had a strong relationship with referral to criminal justice services, while, paradoxically, previous physical aggression was associated with no referral to criminal justice. They explained this finding by suggesting that several individuals who were already in care may have shown aggressive behaviour for long periods of time. Their care staff might subsequently be habituated to persistent aggressive outburst and less inclined to call the police. In support of this finding, Raina, Arenovich, Jones, and Lunsky (2013) studied 138 individuals with IDD in crisis and found that police were more likely to arrest someone if the incident involved aggression and if he/she was living independently or with their own family in the community. Once again, the presence of physical aggression led to a more serious criminal justice involvement.

In addition to the predictive value of physical aggression, Carson *et al.* (2010) found that if a referral included a diversity of problem behaviours, it was more likely to be made to secure provision than to community services. With each additional index behaviour, there was 1.6 times added probability of the individual being referred to secure services. Wheeler *et al.* (2009) found that previous criminal justice involvement increased the probability of the person being referred to the criminal justice service for the current index behaviour. Therefore, a diversity of problem behaviours, previous criminal justice service involvement and being currently charged all increase the likelihood of a more serious outcome for the individual.

There has also been a considerable amount of work done on factors influencing sexual offending pathways in men with IDD. This research has included social, psychological and environmental variables extensively. Green, Gray, and Willner (2002) studied court appearances and convictions in sex offenders with IDD. They found that those who had committed offences against children were significantly more likely to be reported to the criminal justice service than men who had committed sexual offences against adults. They felt that any group of offenders with IDD would be likely to have an over-representation of men who had committed sexual offences against children as a result of this ascertainment bias.

Coming to a very different conclusion based on a more biological underpinning, Blanchard *et al.* (2008) also found that sex offenders with lower intellectual functioning were more likely to commit offences against young children and male children although the proportion of variants in their studies was not high. These authors compared referrals from a number of different sources in order to test the hypothesis that the ascertainment bias would increase the number of offenders with IDD who had assaulted children. They found little difference between the referral sources. In a reanalysis of data on 5,647 sexual offenders and 16,222 non-sexual offenders, Cantor, Blanchard, Robichaud, and Christensen (2005) found a similar effect, but again the average IQ for offenders against children, while significantly lower than offenders against adults, remained in the low average range. Rice, Harris, Lang, and Chaplin (2008) compared 69 sex offenders with IDD and 69 control participants without IDD. They found that the offenders with IDD had a higher rate of paedophilic interests than the control group but were not more likely than the comparison offenders to exhibit preferences for coercive sex with children or to exhibit deviant adult activity preferences, nor where they more likely to reoffend. All of these studies drew similar conclusions that sex offenders with IDD may suffer from organic perturbation that predisposes certain individuals to sexual preferences towards children.

On the other hand, a large study of 2,286 male sexual offenders was conducted by Langevin and Curnoe (2008). Over half of the participants had had a full intellectual assessment using a version of the WAIS, and all participants had further assessments with learning disability as well as intellectual disability. Across this population, there was no increase in the level of IDD (2.4% of the whole population) compared to the proportion expected in the general population. In addition, there were no differences in offence type between adults with and without IDD. In relation to those studies that did find an increase in paedophilic interest in sex offenders with IDD, Blanchard *et al.* (2008) noted the small effect sizes and wrote 'the statistical relations of IQ … to paedophilia, although valuable as potential clues to the aetiology of this disorder, are far too small to permit those variables to be used as diagnostic indicators' (p. 308).

In another NCAP study, Carson *et al.* (2013) presented a more detailed analysis of the 131 participants who were referred to community and secure services for sexual offending. There were a number of consistent patterns with those referred to community provision showing less physical aggression in both an index and previous offences. Those referred to secure provision had a higher rate of contact sexual offences although almost half of those referred to community services had contact offences. They were also less likely to be currently living in the community and far more likely to have a history of substance abuse. Despite these various differences, only two variables were retained in a regression model predicting community or secure provision. The diversity of problem behaviour increased the probability of referral to secure services, while currently living in the community increased the probability of being referred to community services.

As a final variable to pathways into services, one should note the changes that have occurred in social policy. As provision for people with IDD has changed dramatically over the years, there is a far greater likelihood of all participants in all studies, including studies on criminal behaviour, living in community settings. We have seen that living in the community is a powerful variable influencing pathway into services (Carson *et al.*, 2010, Wheeler *et al.*, 2009, Raina *et al.* (2013). In a 20-year follow-up of a community forensic IDD service, Lindsay, Haut, and Steptoe (2011) found that one of the most notable aspects was the change in referral source over the 20 years. They split their referrals into three cohorts for approximately 7 years each: 1989–1995; 1996–2002; and 2003–2008. In the earlier time period, 24% of the referrals came from the court, 35% from community services and 40% from other sources such as psychiatrists and psychologists. In the final time period, 83% of referrals came from the court while only 3% came from

community sources and 14% from other sources. Therefore, a far higher percentage of offenders with IDD are passing through criminal justice services rather than being diverted to community services or other NHS routes. It is another indication that offenders with IDD are both living in the community and using community facilities such as police and court services rather than being diverted into social or health services. These individuals may then go onto assessment and treatment services provided by social or health. However, the important point is that they may continue to live in the community while having access to suitably adapted assessment and treatment. This is a significant and major change in the pathway for offenders with IDD, and it has happened over the years 1980–2010. It emphasizes the point beyond doubt that criminal justice services must continue to adapt their procedures to take account of the IDD itself and to make appropriate provision for people with IDD in the process and outcomes if justice is to be fair and reoffending reduced.

APPLICATIONS OF PSYCHOLOGY TO PROCESSES WITHIN THE JUSTICE SYSTEM

People with ID are vulnerable within the criminal justice system at every stage, since the degree of their disability can affect their ability to understand their rights on arrest, to deal with police questioning and interrogation, to provide valid statements or confessions, to enter a plea, to understand court proceedings and to instruct their counsel. Therefore, they are likely to be at considerable disadvantage from stages of apprehension through arrest, indictment and trial to conviction and sentencing. Responsibility and competence are key concepts in criminal justice systems around the world and are particularly pertinent in relation to offenders with ID. In the pre-trial phase, the issue of competence in relation to ID defendants is relevant to the individual's susceptibility to provide self-incriminatory statements or confessions and to enter a plea of guilty or not guilty. In England and Wales, the Police and Criminal Evidence Act (PACE) 1984 provides protection to people detained by the police for questioning. PACE and its accompanying codes of practice have particular provisions for people with ID with regard to police questioning and confessional evidence (Sanders & Young, 2000). It is now the practice across the United Kingdom that, for those individuals with ID, or those who appear to have ID, police interviews require the presence of 'an appropriate adult'. An appropriate adult is different to a solicitor or legal advisor and can be a relative or guardian of the interviewee, someone with experience of working with the population such as a social worker, or, in Scotland, a member of the Appropriate Adult Service. These individuals are not employed by the police service.

The process of police interview

The issue of suggestibility of accused persons with ID during police interviews has received a significant amount of attention. Gudjonsson (1992) wrote that certain categories of people with ID were more susceptible to yielding to leading questions and shifting their answers under interrogation by police and, as such, were more suggestible and liable to give false information and a false confession. Clare and Gudjonsson (1993), in a study of 20 participants with ID compared with 20 participants of average intellectual ability, found that those with ID confabulated more and tended towards greater acquiescence. Everington and Fulero (1999) also found the participants with ID were more likely to alter their answers in response to negative feedback. Both studies concluded that people with mild ID were more suggestible under conditions of interrogative interview. However, Beail (2002) reviewed a number of studies which led him to question the link between the test situation and the real-life situation. He pointed out that the Gudjonsson suggestibility scale (GSS) (Gudjonsson, 1997), which assessed suggestibility through memory of a narrative story, may be limited in its applicability to criminal justice proceedings because 'the results are based on an examination of semantic memory, whereas police interviews are more concerned with episodic or autobiographical event memory. Also, experienced events usually involve multi-modal sensory input, resulting in a more elaborate trace in associative memory' (p. 135).

White and Willner (2004) tested this hypothesis with 20 individuals with ID by comparing their ability to recall information from a standard passage when compared to a further 20 who are asked to recall an actual experienced event. They found that participants recalled greater amounts of information and they were significantly less suggestible, in relation to the experienced situation when compared to the standard verbally presented passage. Willner (2008) also demonstrated a reduction in suggestibility when events were familiar to the individual being questioned. Willner (2009) summarizes some of the research and also reviews the British Psychological Society guidelines on the assessment of mental capacity (BPS, 2006), which includes discussions of both capacity to appear as a witness and fitness to plead. He cleverly uses the illustrations in the BPS guidelines to undermine the assessors' reliance on GSS, pointing out that, although

the individual in the vignette is unable to retain much of the spoken passage, the individual displays an ability not to acquiesce to questions. We would not go so far as Willner in recommending that use of the GSS should be discontinued in people with ID. However, we would advise caution because of the effects reviewed by Willner (2009, 2011) and Beail (2002).

The legal process and offenders with ID

Having made these points with regard to suggestibility, there remain concerns regarding the competency of people with ID in court proceedings, because confessional evidence should be considered to be valid only if it is voluntary, knowing and intelligent (Baroff, Gunn & Hayes, 2004). People with ID can be vulnerable to coercion, threats and promises of leniency, thus raising concerns about the voluntary nature of their confessions. The understanding that one has a right to silence, as well as other rights to protect oneself are rarely tested in ID suspects, and such interviewees may be more likely to answer questions in the manner and direction they believe they are expected to. Baroff (1996) has called this 'sociable desirability bias'. In the stressful and confusing context of arrest and interrogation, it may be difficult for suspects with ID to make a reasoned choice concerning the information they will volunteer or withhold, and such interviewees are perhaps unlikely to grasp fully the implications of their responses to police questions (Baroff et al., 2004). With regard to valid confessions, the suspect with ID may have difficulty understanding that, in waiving rights, such as the right to silence, they are placing themselves in jeopardy.

In assessing competence or fitness to stand trial and enter a plea, a defendant's abilities in the following areas should be considered: (a) understanding of the crime of which they are accused; (b) knowledge of the purpose of the trial and the roles of the principal officers; and (c) ability to instruct one's counsel (Baroff et al., 2004). In England and Wales, if a defendant claims at trial to be unfit to stand trial because, as a result of their ID, they are unable to comprehend the trial or its processes, then a jury will consider the matter by hearing expert medical evidence. If it is decided that the defendant is not fit to stand trial, then a 'trial of the facts' takes place in which the case against the defendant is tested. The outcome of this process cannot result in a conviction; however, one consequence might be that the defendant with ID is considered to have committed the offence without having had the opportunity to raise a defence. In this event, the court can make one of several orders, including an absolute discharge or admission to hospital under mental health legislation.

Research in the United States has indicated that the issue of competence to stand trial is introduced in just 5–7% of cases, with only 16% of those defendants deemed as incompetent to stand trial (Hurley, 2003). There are a number of assessments for testing a defendant's understanding of court proceedings, all based on the criminal justice procedures in the United States. The Competence Assessment to Stand Trial – Mental Retardation (CAST-MR: Everington & Luckasson, 1992) assesses competence in three areas related to court systems – basic legal concepts, skills to assist the defence counsel and understanding of court procedures. The CAST-MR was used by 45% of the psychologists surveyed about practices used when evaluating juvenile competence to stand trial (Ryba, Cooper & Zapf, 2003). However, this and similar assessments have a number of limitations, including the lack of an underlying conceptual structure, no standardized administration procedures, no criterion-based scoring and limited normative data (Otto *et al.*, 1998).

In addition to the issue of competence to stand trial is the issue of responsibility in criminal law. The commission of criminal act (*actus reus*) is distinguished from the intent to commit a crime (*mens rea*), and, historically, people with severe ID were considered incapable of forming such intent and were thus not responsible for their actions (Fitch, 1992). Traditionally, in the English Criminal Justice System, the judgement on responsibility for a person with ID was made in terms of their ability to distinguish right from wrong. However, more recently, the courts have moved away from this dichotomous approach to 'moral understanding' in favour of case-by-case considerations (Baroff *et al.*, 2004).

In the legal system of England and Wales, *mens rea* is only considered in relation to serious crimes of murder, rape and violence. A lack of *mens rea* means that the person's powers of reasoning have been affected by a disease of the mind (including ID). It must be established that the defective reason resulted in either the defendant not knowing what they were doing, or not knowing what they did was legally wrong (as opposed to morally wrong). Usually an attempt to claim a lack of *mens rea* in effect results in a defence of not guilty by reason of insanity (Baroff *et al.*, 2004). A defence of diminished responsibility is pertinent only to the charge of murder and, if accepted, results in a conviction of manslaughter. Diminished responsibility requires impaired mental responsibility for one's acts as a result of an 'abnormality of the mind' (Homicide Act, 1957). Intellectual disability can be considered as an abnormality of the mind causing diminished responsibility that results in a person's involvement in a killing. If, on the balance of probabilities, diminished responsibility is proven, a range of sentencing options are available to the court for manslaughter, as opposed to the mandatory penalty of life imprisonment for murder. In both the defences of insanity and diminished responsibility, the courts will seek expert evidence to assist them in determining if there was, in individual cases, defective reasoning or impaired mental responsibility.

In summary, there have been a number of important developments in relation to the criminal justice system concerning the assessment of responsibility and competency which acknowledge that defendants with ID require accommodation and special consideration in order to participate in legal procedures in a valid and just manner. Psychologists have been involved in the assessment of such competence through the use of cognitive assessments, the use of assessments concerning understanding of criminal justice processes and through assessments of ability to cope with the police investigative system.

WORKING WITH OFFENDERS WITH ID

Assessment issues

We have already dealt with assessment related to the justice system in previous sections on the way that psychology is applied to the legal process. In this section, we will confine ourselves to the assessment of offenders and the way in which assessment has been developed to inform on strengths and deficits and monitor and guide the treatment process. There have been several significant developments in assessment related to people with ID in general and offenders in particular. These fall into two broad categories, both of which have the same aims.

First, it is important that any assessment can be understood by the clients completing it. Since this client group is typified by significant deficits in literary and comprehension skills, all assessments must be suitably adapted to simplify the language and concepts employed. Lindsay and Skene (2007) give an example of the way in which an assessment can be extremely complex in its conceptual structure and requires adaptation. One item on the Beck Depression Inventory (BDI: Beck, Steer, & Brown, 1995) deals with the extent to which the respondent feels guilty. As with all the questions, it is arranged on a four-point Likert Scale indicating increased levels of emotion – in this case, 'guilt'. However, as the response increases from 0 to 3, the concept of guilt and responsibility shift from feeling guilty about one's actions to feeling guilty for everything bad that happens in the world. Lindsay and Skene (2007) found that the concept required simplification to deal in a straightforward fashion with personal feelings of guilt – from feeling no guilt to feeling extremely guilty – without the complicating aspect of feeling responsible for all human disasters and atrocities. A more obvious simplification is that of language. The Bumby Rape and Molest Scales have been shown to be reliable and valid with mainstream sex offenders (Bumby, 1996). However, they are difficult to use with sex offenders with ID because of the linguistic complexity of the items. For example, item 27 in the Rape Scale contains the following: 'Before the police investigate a woman's claim of rape, it is a good idea to find out what she was wearing, if she had been drinking and what kind of person she is'. This item contains the somewhat difficult words 'investigate' and 'claim' (as a noun rather than a verb), and contains a series of concepts including police investigation, an 'idea' that might precede investigation and three linked aspects of the victim. It also conveys an unstated implication that the characteristics of the woman may be used as mitigation by certain sex offenders. All of these are complex cognitive and linguistic characteristics of the statement which require understanding prior to the expression of an opinion. If the individual being assessed has intellectual limitations, then these linked concepts may be harder to understand. Lack of understanding is likely to lead to unreliable responding. Therefore, simplification of language and conceptual structure is crucial, so that the assessment is basically usable in the context of forensic ID.

The second consideration, and an important one in the context of lengthy forensic assessments, is that, because of literacy deficits, all material will have to be read and explained to respondents. Therefore, both the item and the response categories require to be explained. These issues have been dealt with extensively elsewhere (e.g., Taylor & Novaco, 2005; Lindsay, 2008), and it is not our intention to review them in detail here. However, this has two consequences. Assessment will take much longer, and it is impossible to give the respondent a series of questionnaires and receive them back the following week. Secondly, because the assessor has to read the item and explain the responses, all such assessments take the form of a structured interview. The respondents' reactions to questions, their tangential comments and their emotional response will all be available to the assessor as part of the process. This is an enormous strength of conducting assessments with this client group, and it is information that can add to the richness of any assessment process and report.

It is now clear that the adaptations required for assessment of offenders with ID are extensive. Both the assessment instrument and the process require a different approach. Following on from this, it is extremely important that the psychometric properties of the assessment remain intact and that the integrity of the process not be undermined or reduced by these adaptations. One of the first studies in this regard was conducted by Lindsay, Michie, Baty, Smith, and Miller (1994) when they investigated the psychometric properties of several psychological assessments with 73 participants with intellectual disability. All participants were taking part in a study on community living and community integration and, as such, were representative of a heterogeneous population of people with mild ID. They found that adapted versions of the Zung Anxiety Scale, the Zung Depression Inventory and the Goldberg Health Questionnaire could be used reliably by participants. In addition, there was a highly significant degree of convergent validity among the tests. As a further indication of validity, the assessments of emotion had a significant, orderly relationship with the Eysenck-Withers Personality Test, in that they correlated positively with the neuroticism factor but not at all with the extraversion factor. This was an early indication that suitably adapted assessments could be used effectively with this client group.

Finlay and Lyons (2001) reviewed the available literature on the assessment of emotion and other psychotherapeutic issues in people with ID and concluded that there was ample evidence that suitably adapted assessments could be understood and used appropriately by the client group. In addition, there was a lesser amount of emerging evidence that these assessments retained their psychometric properties during these studies.

Since the publication of these studies, there have been a few further pieces of work on generic populations of people with ID, strengthening the conclusions. Kellet, Beail, Newman, and Hawes (2004) conducted a factor analytic study of the Brief Symptom Inventory (BSI). The BSI screens for symptoms related to somatization, interpersonal sensitivity, anxiety, depression, phobia, paranoid ideation, hostility, psychoticism and obsessive compulsive disorders. They had previously established the usability and reliability of the BSI (Kellet, Beail, Newman, & Frankish, 2003), and, in this subsequent study, in addition to further evidence on reliability, they found that the factor structure when used with this client group was essentially similar to the original studies on mainstream populations. Lindsay and Skene (2007), in a study of 108 individuals with ID, reported that the Beck Anxiety Inventory and Beck Depression Inventory both had similar factor structures when used with this client group in comparison to mainstream populations. Therefore, there is a significant amount of emerging evidence that, when assessments are suitably adapted to aid understanding in people with ID, they can be used effectively to reflect emotional states and other issues relevant to therapeutic input, and their psychometric integrity remains broadly intact. In fact, the BSI is an extremely useful assessment to screen for a range of problems in offenders with ID. Any indications of difficulty can be followed up with other, offence-specific assessments discussed later in this chapter.

Assessment of anger and aggression

Aggression and anger in individuals with ID are areas which have attracted a reasonable amount of research when compared with other areas of socio-affective functioning. Studies by Benson and Ivins (1992) and Rose and West (1999) have indicated that a modified self-assessment measure of anger reactivity ('the anger inventory') has some limited reliability and validity with people with ID. Oliver, Crawford, Rao, Reece, and Tyrer (2007) reported that the Modified Overt Aggression Scale (MOAS: Sorgi, Ratey, Knoedler, Markert, & Reichman, 1991), an informant-rated measure of the frequency and severity of aggression, had high levels of inter-rater reliability when administered for a small number of people with ID as part of a treatment outcome research study.

Novaco and Taylor (2004) evaluated the reliability and validity of several specially modified anger assessment measures with detained male offenders with ID. The Novaco Anger Scale (NAS: Novaco, 2003), the Spielberger State-Trait Anger Expression Inventory (STAXI: Spielberger, 1996), both self-report measures of anger disposition, and the Provocation Inventory (PI: Novaco, 2003), a self-report anger reactivity scale, along with the Ward Anger Rating Scale and the informant-related anger attributes measure (WARS: Novaco, 1994), were evaluated. The modified anger self-report measures were found to have high internal consistency and less robust, but reasonable, test–retest reliability. The STAXI and NAS showed substantial intercorrelation providing evidence for the concurrent validity of these instruments. WARS staff ratings of patient anger were found to have high internal consistency and to correlate significantly with patient anger self-reports. Anger, self-reported by the patients, was significantly related to their record of assault behaviour in hospital. The NAS was found to be significantly predictive of whether the patient has physically assaulted others following admission to hospital, and the total number of physical assaults carried out.

In a further development, Taylor, Novaco, Guinan, and Street (2004) developed the Imaginal Provocation Test (IPT) as an additional idiographic anger assessment procedure with people with ID that taps key elements of the experience and expression of anger, is sensitive to change associated with anger treatment and is easily modifiable for idiographic uses. The IPT produces four indices relevant to the individual client's experience of anger: anger reaction, behavioural reaction, a composite of anger and behavioural reaction, and anger regulation. They administered the IPT to 48 patients prior to beginning an anger treatment and showed that the indices had respectable internal reliabilities and reasonable concurrent validity when correlated with the STAXI and NAS. Therefore, it would appear that there are rapid, flexible and sensitive idiographic assessments of anger among people with ID and that these assessments have reasonable psychometric properties.

Alder and Lindsay (2007) also produced a Provocation Inventory (Dundee Provocation Inventory, DPI) which is easily accessible and easy to use. It is based on Novaco's (1975, 1994) analysis and construction of anger as an emotional problem. One of the facets of Novaco's analysis is that the individual may misconstrue internal and external stimuli and respond to a perception of threat rather than a more appropriate, less aggressive response. The DPI was administered to referrals with ID, and Alder and Lindsay (2007) found good reliability and convergent validity. The DPI correlated significantly with the NAS ($r = 0.57$) and highly significantly with the PI ($r = 0.75$), indicating that the DPI and PI have good convergence. They also found a five factor structure consisting of threat to self-esteem, external locus of control, disappointment, frustration and resentment. The strongest factor was threat to self-esteem, and this certainly accords with Novaco's analysis of anger and its relationship with threat. The factors can also be considered as basic self-schemata, and self-esteem has been considered a major dynamic risk factor in sex offenders by several authors (Beech, Friendship, Erikson, & Hanson, 2002; Boer, Tough, & Haaven, 2004). Therefore, the DPI may provide a quick assessment of provocation in relation to a range of relevant factors in offenders with ID.

Willner, Brace, and Phillips (2005) developed the Profile of Anger Coping Skills (PACS) to assess the use by people with ID of specific skills in managing angry situations. Informants are asked to rate the client's use of eight anger management strategies in specific anger-coping situations salient to that individual. The strategies assessed include use of relaxation skills, counting to 10, walking away calmly, requesting help, use of distraction activities, cognitive reframing and being assertive. The PACS was found to have acceptable test, retest and inter-rater reliability coefficients. The PACS was also shown to be sensitive to change associated with an anger intervention. Following involvement in a community-based anger management group, informants reported that the clients' PACS scores were significantly improved compared with scores for clients in a no-treatment control group. The treatment group participant's coping skills had improved significantly in terms of cognitive reframing, assertiveness, walking away and asking for help. These latter two areas of skill improvement were maintained at 6-month follow-up. One of the most important aspects of this study and its method of assessment is that it attests to the importance of anger management treatment and the concepts employed. For many individuals, counting to 10 and relaxing (calming down) are the most common pieces of advice given to clients. It may also be thought that the relaxation component is the most important in anger management treatment. However, by these reports, these two skills were used least frequently in the range of anger-coping skills developed during treatment.

Assessment for sexual offenders

Some work has been completed on knowledge and beliefs in relation to sexual interaction with sex offenders with ID. With this client group, it is important not only to review cognitive distortions but also to consider the level of sexual knowledge that an individual may have. Indeed, one of the first hypotheses put forward to account for inappropriate sexual behaviour in this group was that lack of sexual knowledge may lead the individual to attempt inappropriate sexual contact precisely because they are unaware of the means to establish appropriate interpersonal and sexual relationships. This hypothesis of 'counterfeit deviance' was first mentioned by Hingsburger, Griffiths, and Quinsey (1991), and has been recently reviewed and revised to account for more recent research findings by Lindsay (2008). The term refers to behaviour that is undoubtedly deviant but may be precipitated by factors such as lack of sexual knowledge, poor social and heterosexual skills, limited opportunities to establish sexual relationships and sexual naivety rather than a preference or sexual drive towards inappropriate objects. Following this, remediation should focus on educational issues and developmental maturation rather than inappropriate sexuality. Griffiths, Quinsey, and Hingsburger (1989) gave a number of examples illustrating the concept of counterfeit deviance and developed a treatment programme, part of which was based significantly on sexual and social education.

In a review of variables associated with the perpetration of sexual offences in men with ID, Lindsay (2005) noted that, surprisingly, there were no controlled tests on this hypothesis. Counterfeit deviance would suggest that some men with ID commit sexual offences because they have poorer social and sexual knowledge, do not understand the rules and conventions of society and they are unaware of taboos relating to sexuality. Therefore, men with ID who have committed sexual offences should have poorer social and sexual knowledge than those who do not.

There have now been two tests of this hypothesis. Michie, Lindsay, Martin, and Grieve (2006) completed a test of counterfeit deviance by comparing the sexual knowledge of groups of sex offenders with ID and control participants using the SSKAT (Wish, McCombs, & Edmonson, 1979, Griffiths & Lunsky, 2003). In the first study comparing 17 sex offenders with 20 controls, they found that of 13 subscales in the SSKAT, three comparisons, birth control, masturbation and sexually transmitted diseases, showed significant differences between the groups and, in each case, the sex offenders had higher levels of sexual knowledge. There were no differences between the groups on age or IQ. In a second comparison, 16 sex offenders were compared with 15 controls. There were significant differences between the groups on seven scales and, in each case, the sex offenders showed a higher level of sexual knowledge. These authors then pooled the data for all 33 sex offenders and 35 control participants. They found a significant positive correlation between IQ and SSKAT total score for the control group ($r = 0.71$), but no significant relationship between IQ and SSKAT total score for the sex offender cohort ($r = 0.17$). They presented two possible reasons for this finding. The first was that, by definition, all of the sex offender cohort have some experience of sexual interaction. It is unlikely that these experiences of sexual interaction are random, and one might therefore conclude that these sex offenders have given some thought and attention to sexuality at least in the period prior to the perpetration of the inappropriate sexual behaviour or sexual abuse. Therefore, we can be sure that they have at least some experience of sexual activity, which is not the case for the control participants. The second possible explanation was that these individuals might have a developmental history of increased sexual arousal. This in turn may have led to selective attention and interest in sexual information gained from informal sources. Such persistence of attention would lead to greater retention of information through rehearsal and perhaps to a higher level of associated appropriate sexual activity such as masturbation. These behavioural and informal educational experiences would lead to a higher level of sexual knowledge. This latter hypothesis in combination with sexual arousal and sexual preference, is suggested to have an interactive effect with knowledge acquisition and, perhaps, attitudes and beliefs.

In the second, more sensitive comparison, Lunsky, Frijters, Griffiths, Watson, and Williston (2007) once again compared sexual offenders with controls but divided the sexual offenders into deviant persistent offenders (those who committed contact sexual offences and offences against children) and naïve offenders (public masturbation, indecent exposure). They found that the naïve offenders did indeed have a lower level of sexual knowledge than the deviant offenders, although the naïve offenders did not have poorer knowledge than the control group, as might be expected from the counterfeit deviance hypothesis. However, the fact that they found differences in these subgroups of sexual offenders with ID underlines the importance of assessment of sexual knowledge.

Although a number of assessments have been developed to assess cognitive distortions in sex offenders, as has been pointed out earlier, the language requires to be simplified considerably in order to be understood by individuals with ID. Kolton, Boer, and Boer (2001) employed the Abel and Becker Cognitions Scale and found that the response options of the test needed to be changed from a four-choice system (1 = agree, 4 = strongly disagree) to a dichotomous system (agree/disagree) to reduce extremity bias in the sample. The revised assessment provided 'adequate' total score to item correlations and test–retest reliability; internal consistency was 'acceptable' (values not reported); and the psychometric integrity of the assessment was preserved. As has been pointed out, other tests such as the Bumby Rape and Molest Scales have not been used with this client group, but have the drawbacks of having contained complex concepts, difficult words and complex response choices in their syntax.

There have been a number of more recent developments specific to the assessment of sex offenders with ID. Keeling, Rose, and Beech (2007a) investigated the psychometric properties of adapted versions of a number of assessments relevant to this population. One of the difficulties of their study was that it was a population of convenience and, in the Australian Correctional System, the population of 'special needs offenders' had been identified. This population was more diverse than offenders with ID and included significant literacy deficits, the presence of an acquired brain injury and poor communication skills. Although their population was predominantly individuals with ID, it also included men with borderline intelligence and even low average IQ, and they had access to only a small sample of 16 men with special needs. In order to assess the validity and integrity of their adaptations, they compared these individuals with 53 mainstream sexual offenders. They found that the 'Social Intimacy Scale', 'Criminal Sentiment Scale' and 'Victim Empathy Distortion Scale' broadly retained their psychometric integrity after adaptation and simplification. Their least successful adaptation was in the 'Relationship Scale Questionnaire', which had low internal consistency. Test–retest reliability was high, and there were good correlations between the original and adapted versions, especially for the Social Intimacy Scale and the Victim Empathy Scale.

Williams, Wakeling, and Webster (2007) also assessed the psychometric properties of six self-report measures with sex offenders with ID. Their population was 211 men who had undertaken HM Prison Services' adapted sex offender treatment programme. Average IQ was 71.9, and the accepted participants had an IQ up to 80, well outside the range of ID. However, the literacy skills seem similar, in that they were required to read all the questionnaires to participants and aid them with their answers. Three assessments had good internal consistency, and the other three were reasonable. Factor analyses revealed interesting structures but accounted for a low 30–40% of the common variance. Unfortunately, because of time constraints, test–retest reliability was not conducted.

Lindsay, Whitefield, and Carson (2007) reported on the development of the Questionnaire on Attitudes Consistent with Sexual Offences (QACSO), which is designed to be suitable for offenders with ID. The QACSO contains a series of scales which evaluate attitudes across a range of different types of offences including rape and voyeurism, exhibitionism, dating abuse, homosexual assault, offences against children and stalking. They compared 41 sex offenders with ID, 34 non-sexual offenders with ID, 30 non-offenders with ID and 31 non-ID controls who had not committed sexual offences. They ensured that all items had an appropriate reading ease score, and the response choices were dichotomous. The assessment was revised following tests of reliability, discriminant validity and internal consistency in order to ensure that all three psychometric properties were robust. They found that six of the seven scales in the QACSO were valid and reliable measures of cognitive distortions held by sex offenders with ID (the exception was homosexual assault). Lindsay et al. (2006) also found that the Rape and Offences Against Children Scale in particular discriminated between offenders against adults and offenders against children in the hypothesized direction, with offenders against adults having higher scores on the rape scale and lower scores on the offences against children scale than child molesters. Therefore, it would appear that cognitive distortions in sex offenders with ID can be assessed with some reliability and validity. However, these authors were cautious when considering the relationship of cognitive distortions to risk. They wrote that changes in attitudes may reflect a number of processes such as suppression, influence by social desirability and even lying. They recommended that the results from the QACSO be considered in relation to a range of risk assessment variables including actuarial risk, socio-affective functioning and self-regulation abilities.

Assessment of fire raising

Despite the importance of this issue in societal terms, there are relatively few published studies concerning the assessment and treatment of adult fire setters, and the literature concerning clinical practice with fire setters with ID is even more limited. Murphy and Clare (1996) interviewed 10 fire setters with ID concerning their cognitions and feelings prior to and after setting fires, using a newly developed Fire Setting Assessment Schedule (FSAS). Participants were also asked to rate their feelings in relation to a series of fire-related situations described in a new 14-item Fire Interest Rating Scale (FIRS). The construction of the FSAS was guided by the functional analytical approach to fire setting proposed by Jackson, Glass, and Hope (1987), in which it is proposed that fire setting is associated with a number of psychological functions including the need for peer approval, need for excitement, a need to alleviate or express sadness, mental illness, a wish for retribution and a need to reduce anxiety.

Murphy and Clare (1996) found that the participants in their study identified antecedents to fire setting with more reliability than consequences. The most frequently endorsed antecedents were anger, followed by being ignored and then feelings of depression. This assessment has proven to be clinically useful since its inception, but there has been little further research on its reliability and validity until Taylor, Thorne, Robertson, and Avery (2002) used the FSAS in the assessment and treatment of a group of 14 people with ID to review the effectiveness of a fire setting programme for this client group. Consistent with the results of Murphy and Clare (1996), Taylor, Novaco, Gillmer, and Thorne, (2002) found that anger, being ignored and depression (in rank order) were the most frequently endorsed items on the FSAS in terms of antecedents to and consequences of participants' fire setting behaviour. In a further study on women with ID who had set fires, Taylor, Robertson, Thorne, Belshaw, and Watson, A. (2006) also found that anger and depression were the most frequently endorsed items in participants prior to fire-raising incidents.

Risk assessment

The review of social, psychological, behavioural and biological pathways related to offending (see earlier) is essentially a review of candidate risk factors for the prediction of future offending pathways. Once identified, the task is to develop more effective risk management and treatment systems that can divert and prevent these offending trajectories. Over the last 20 or 30 years, significant progress has been made in the assessment of risk for future offending in criminal and forensic psychiatric populations. Generally, studies have used Receiver Operator Characteristics to evaluate the significance of the risk predictions. The effect size is termed 'area under the curve' (AUC), and an AUC of .5 is no better than chance, an AUC of .56 is a small effect size, .64 a medium and .72 or over is a large effect size (Rice & Harris 2005;

for an explanation of this statistic, see MacMillan, Hasting, & Caldwell, 2004).

Based on the work already described (Harris et al., 1993), Quinsey, Harris, Rice, and Cormier (2005) constructed the Violence Risk Appraisal Guide (VRAG). In an analysis of 42 candidate variables, 11 contributed to a regression model that was significantly successful in predicting who would and who would not commit a further violent offence (Harris et al., 1993). The VRAG has been cross-validated on a variety of forensic psychiatric populations and prisoner samples and, in their original evaluation, Quinsey et al. (2005) found that it was as accurate with offenders who had an ID (IQ less than 80) as with offenders who did not. However, the sample sizes for those with lower intellectual functioning were very small. As research on risk assessment developed, several groups of researchers compared the predictive accuracy of different risk assessment instruments on a range of databases for violent and sexual recidivism (Yang, Wong, & Coid, 2010). The VRAG and Static-99 (Hanson & Thornton, 1999) have become standard static risk assessments for violent and sexual recidivism, respectively, in mainstream offender populations. These assessments depend wholly on historical, unchangeable variables for inclusion.

Contiguous with the development of actuarial risk assessments, risk assessments based on structured clinical judgement related to the same variables as those used in actuarial assessment were also being developed. The first and most important of these was the Historical Clinical Risk-20 items (HCR-20; Webster et al., 1995). The HCR-20 is organized into historical (10 items), clinical (5 items) and risk (5 items) sections, and has been researched in many settings for mainstream offenders in correctional and mental health facilities with AUCs of over .70 (e.g., Dolan & Khawaja 2004; de Vogel & de Ruiter, 2005).

There have now been a number of studies using risk assessments on offenders with ID. Fitzgerald, Gray, Taylor, and Snowdon, (2011) followed up 149 offenders with ID for 2 years and found significant differences on a range of criminogenic variables between those who had and had not reoffended. These results essentially provided validation for the relevance of these variables for this group, as well as for those found for mainstream offenders. In a previous study by the same research group, Gray et al. (2007) assessed the predictive accuracy of the HCR-20, the VRAG and other assessments. They employed 118 men and 27 women with ID who had been discharged from hospital following admission for a criminal offence or exhibiting behaviour that might have led to a conviction in different circumstances. This ID group was compared with a similar control group of 843 men and 153 women who were mentally ill offenders without

ID. Following up these individuals for 5 years, Gray *et al.* (2007) found that all the instruments predicted violent recidivism with medium-to-large effect sizes (AUCs = .64–.81). These predictive values were better than those found with the non-ID group. The corresponding results for the VRAG predictive ability with the offenders with ID was AUC = .74, a result almost identical to that for the offenders without ID. They concluded that these risk assessment instruments were comparable in predicting future violence for offenders with ID and the control population. The same research group (Fitzgerald *et al.* 2013, in press) tested both the VRAG and HCR20 on two samples of 25 offenders with ID and a group of 45 mentally disordered offenders over a period of 6 months. They found that, for the group with ID, the VRAG had an AUC for any aggressive incidents of .87 and, for the HCR20, an AUC of 0.77 (both large effect sizes). Both results were superior to those found with the mentally disordered offenders without ID.

Lindsay *et al.* (2008) tested the predictive abilities of the VRAG and the HCR-20 in a sample of 212 forensic psychiatric patients with ID in high-security, medium/low-security and community forensic services. After follow-up of 1 year, the predictive levels for these tests were AUCs of .71 and .72, respectively.

Quinsey, Book, and Skilling (2004) investigated the predictive validity of the VRAG in 58 men with ID with serious histories of anti-social and aggressive behaviour, followed up for an average of 16 months. They found a significant AUC with a medium effect size of .69. In a further study, Camilleri and Quinsey (2008) reanalysed data from a subsection of participants on the MacArthur Violence Risk Assessment Study (MacArthur.Viriginia.edu/risk.html) to test the application to psychiatric patients with ID. They used the vocabulary scores from the WAIS-R to identify a sample of men and women with borderline intelligence and ID. For all those participants within the ninth percentile cut off, the VRAG predicted just as well as it did for those above the ninth percentile cut off (AUC = .70). Excluding individuals under the second percentile slightly weakened the predictive accuracy among the target group.

For sexual offenders with ID, similar results had been found for risk assessments. Lindsay *et al.* (2008) investigated the accuracy of the Static-99 with the sex offenders in their sample and found it to have an AUC of .71. Wilcox, Beech, Markall, and Blackler (2009) used the Static-99 on a smaller sample of 27 sex offenders with ID and found an AUC of .64, a small-to-medium effect size. Lofthouse *et al.* (2013a, in press) also investigated the predictive value of the Static-99 with 64 adult males with ID and a history of sexual offending behaviour. They found that the Static-99 had an AUC of .75. These results on the

Static-99 converge around an AUC of .70, which is consistent with research from mainstream groups.

One final study (Blacker, Beech, Wilcox, & Boer, 2011) on sexual offenders with ID used the Sexual Violence Risk-20 items (Boer, Hart, Kropp, & Webster, 1997) to predict future sexual incidents over a mean follow-up period of 8.8 years. They assessed a mixed group of 'special needs' offenders that included participants with ID and borderline intelligence. For the full special needs group, the SVR-20 was no better than chance at predicting future sexual incidents, but for the 10 offenders with an IQ less than 75 (those with the diagnostic cut off of IQ of 70 plus two standard errors of the test), the AUC was .75.

It can be seen that risk assessments that have been shown to be predictors, with medium-to-large effect sizes for future incidents with mainstream offenders and other types of mentally disordered offenders, have been shown to perform with similar predictive values on participants with ID. Some of these samples have been fairly large, suggesting that these assessments can provide a risk context for those of us working with offenders with ID. For example, we are likely to know whether we are working with a low-risk individual, a medium-risk or a high-risk offender. It seems therefore that similar variables are applicable to the pathways to offending in populations with ID as have been found with mainstream populations.

One word of caution should be added for the treatment decisions made on offenders with ID in relation to their risk. Lindsay *et al.* (2010) correlated assessed risk and level of security. They graded forensic ID services from generic community services, through community forensic services to low-, medium- and maximum-security services. There were significant correlations between level of security and VRAG score ($r = 0.24$) and Static-99 ($r = 0.32$), representing small effect sizes. This suggests that there were likely to have been a number of individuals in secure settings who were assessed as being a low risk and a number in community settings assessed as being a high risk, and, given the extensive decision-making in relation to these individuals, it seems a somewhat disappointing result. Therefore, a number of factors are likely to account for treatment decisions other than assessed levels of risk.

The role of dynamic risk assessment in the management of offenders with ID

Dynamic risk assessments contrast with static risk assessment in that the variables are able to be changed through treatment and management of the individual. Therefore, these variables are able to be incorporated into effective risk management plans for offenders with ID. Studies investigating the predictive value of dynamic variables have suggested that they are as good as static variables in predicting future offences. Three early studies suggested the importance of clinical and dynamic indicators with this client group. Lindsay, Elliot, and Astell (2004) found that dynamic indicators of risk such as poor treatment compliance and anti-social attitudes correlated with reoffending with a value as high as or higher than static variables such as childhood behavioural and attachment problems. Quinsey *et al.* (2004), in the previously described study, found that, in addition to the static variables on the VRAG, anti-social attitude (a dynamic indicator) also had a significant relationship with reoffending. MacMillan, Hastings, and Caldwell (2004) reported that a clinical rating of risk made by the multi-disciplinary team was as good a predictor of future violence as previous violent incidents.

Lindsay *et al.* (2004) and Steptoe *et al.* (2006) developed the dynamic risk assessment and management system (DRAMS), including ratings of mood, anti-social behaviour, self-regulation, compliance and other clinical items. They found that the total score predicted violence over the next 2 days with an AUC of .73. This was a particularly powerful result since the occurrence or absence of the incident was so proximal. In relation to sexual incidents, Boer, Tough, and Haaven (2004) developed a dynamic assessment and management system (ARMIDILO). The predictive value of this was assessed by Blacker *et al.* (2010) in their study comparing 44 special needs with 44 mainstream offenders. With the special needs offenders, the ARMIDILO predicted incidents with AUCs between .73 and .76, and, with the small sub group of offenders with ID ($n = 10$), it predicted incidents with AUCs between .75 and .86. In the study by Lofthouse *et al.* (2013a, in press) on 64 sex offenders with ID over a period of 6 years, predictive values for different sections of the ARMIDILO ranged between AUC .79 and .90 with an AUC of .92 for total score. These studies certainly suggest that the dynamic risk assessment may be a potent addition to risk management in this client group.

Because there seemed to be an emerging powerful relationship between dynamic risk factors and future incidents for this client group, Lofthouse *et al.* (2013b) reanalysed the risk assessment data published by Lindsay *et al.* (2008) where they had found that both the VRAG and the Short Dynamic Risk Scale (SDRS), an easily and quickly completed dynamic risk assessment, had equivalent risk predictive values of AUC = .71 and .72, respectively. They used the model to investigate the functional relationships between risk factors developed by Kraemer *et al.* (2001) which enables the investigator to determine whether the risk factors are overlapping, independent, mediating, moderating or acting as a proxy. They found that the dynamic variables on the SDRS acted as a proxy for the variables in the VRAG. They concluded that, since these risk factors captured elements of the same underlying risk associated with violence, and since dynamic variables were more accessible and contributed towards risk management regimes, dynamic assessments could provide immediate information more relevant to intervention planning and the reduction of presenting risk.

An alternative understanding of risk has been advanced by Wheeler, Clare, and Holland (2013) in a study on the importance of environmental and contextual variables. In a regression analysis, they found that poor personal relationships were the best predicting variables for recidivism in offenders with ID. In work on mainstream sexual offenders, Willis and Grace (2009) showed that discharge planning including organization (or lack of it) of accommodation, employment and social support predicted recidivism as well as with familiar criminogenic variables (AUC = .71).

These developments may have significant implications for the assessment and management of risk for violent and sexual incidents in people with ID. The extent to which these studies can be replicated is extremely important for the future management of offenders with ID. If we can establish that proximal indicators are not only more accessible but also as predictive as static indicators, this will have a huge impact on procedures and practice in helping offenders with ID to access better services. It is a familiar experience for those of us working in the field to be restricted in our recommendations because static risk assessment (which by definition will never change) places the person in the category of high risk, despite the fact that they may not have perpetrated any incident for several years. With the advent of these new possibilities, this position may gradually become eroded. The crucial aspect is for further studies to be conducted in this area.

CONCLUSIONS ON ASSESSMENT

Broadly, we have attempted to present this review of offenders with intellectual disability within the framework for the diploma in forensic psychology. We have presented information on the context for the practice of forensic psychology, on the applications within the justice system and, of course, on work on the assessment of a specific client group of offenders with ID. The policy of deinstitutionalization on services for people with ID has had an enormous impact on offenders with ID who are now more visible in the wider community than before. Larger numbers of people with ID who engage in offending, or offending-type behaviour, are being dealt with through regular criminal justice system channels, and courts are mandating more people with ID to forensic mental health programmes for access to offence-related interventions. While people with IDD have historically been associated with crime, there is no empirical justification for any link. Some of the principal arguments for an association have recently been undermined (Lindsay & Dernevik, 2013). We now know much more regarding pathways into forensic services for this client group.

We have presented some research concerning the prevalence and nature of offending by people with ID and have noted the lack of consistency between these studies. Some progress has been made in helping offenders with ID to engage with the criminal justice process, and we have noted approaches and assessments which will aid the forensic examiner. More recent studies have investigated the pathways into and through criminal justice services and the offence types related to different pathways. Aggression and violence are always associated with more serious disposals, but diversity of offending is also related to more secure pathways.

A number of assessments have been adapted or developed to aid forensic psychologists in their work with the population of offenders with ID. Assessments include screening measures and general measures of psychological and psychiatric problems in the population as well as offence-specific assessments for fire raising, anger and aggression and cognitive distortions related to sexual offending. From the evidence of published reports, it would seem that these adaptations of relevant assessments began in the early 1990s and have continued with increasing pace until the present day. There have also been significant advances in the identification of risk factors for the client group and investigation into the effectiveness of risk assessments for violence and sexual offending. In general, the data from these predictive studies suggest that risk assessments are generally as effective for this client group as they are for mainstream offenders. Perhaps the major developments in this area are to establish the importance of dynamic risk factors for this client group.

FURTHER READING

Lindsay, W. R., Taylor, J. L., & Sturmey, P. (2004). *Offenders with developmental disabilities*. Chichester: John Wiley.

This multi-authored text provides a wide-ranging review of undertaking psychological assessments and interventions with people who have developmental disabilities. The text is international in approach and provides an up-to-date account of evidence-informed practice in this area.

Morrissey, C., Hogue, T., Mooney, P., Allen, C., Johnston, S., Hollin, C., Lindsay, W. R., & Taylor, J. (2007a). Predictive validity of the PCL-R in offenders with intellectual disabilities in a high secure setting: Institutional aggression. *Journal of Forensic Psychology & Psychiatry, 18*, 1–15.

Morrissey, C., Hogue, T., Mooney, P., Lindsay, W. R., Steptoe, L., Taylor, J., & Johnston, S. (2005). Applicability, reliability and validity of the psychopathy checklist – revised in offenders with intellectual disabilities: Some initial findings. *International Journal of Forensic Mental Health, 4*, 207–220.

Morrissey, C., Mooney, P., Hogue, T., Lindsay, W. R., & Taylor, J. L. (2007b). Predictive validity of psychopathy in offenders with intellectual disabilities in a high security hospital: Treatment progress. *Journal of Intellectual & Developmental Disabilities, 32*, 125–133.

REFERENCES

Alder, L., & Lindsay, W. R. (2007). Exploratory factor analysis and convergent validity of the Dundee Provocation Inventory. *Journal of Intellectual & Developmental Disabilities, 32*, 179–188.

Alexander, R. T., Green, E. N., O'Mahoney, B., Guneratna, I., Gangadharan, S., & Hoare, S. (2010). Personality disorders in offenders with intellectual disability: A comparison of clinical, forensic and outcome variables and implications for service provision. *Journal of Intellectual Disability Research, 54*, 650–658.

American Association on Mental Retardation (1992). *Mental retardation: Definitions, classification and systems of supports* (9th edn). Washington, DC: AAMR.

American Psychiatric Association (2013). *Diagnostic and statistical manual of mental disorders* (5th edn). Washington DC: Author.

Ammons, R. B., & Ammons, C. H. (1958). *The quick test manual*. Southern Universities Press, Psychological Test Specialists.

Baroff, G. S. (1996). The mentally retarded offender. In J. Jacobsen and J. Mulick (Eds.), *Manual of diagnosis and professional practice in mental retardation*. Washington DC: American Psychological Association.

Baroff, G. S., Gunn, M., & Hayes, S. (2004). Legal issues. In W. R. Lindsay, J. L. Taylor, & P. Sturmey (Eds.), *Offenders with developmental disabilities* (pp. 37–66). Chichester: John Wiley.

Barratt, E. (1994). Impulsivity and aggression. In J. Monahan & H. J. Steadman (Eds.), *Violence in mental disorder*. Chicago: University of Chicago Press.

Beail, N. (2002). Interrogative suggestibility, memory and intellectual disability. *Journal of Applied Research in Intellectual Disabilities, 15*, 129–137.

Beck, A. T., Steer, R. A., & Brown, G. K. (1995). *Beck depression inventory –Second edition*. New York: Psychological Corporation.

Beech, A., Friendship, C., Erikson, M., & Hanson, R. K. (2002). The relationship between static and dynamic risk factors and reconviction in a sample of UK child abusers. *Sexual Abuse: A Journal of Research & Treatment, 14*, 155–167.

Benson, D. A., & Ivins, J. (1992). Anger, depression and self-concept in adults with mental retardation. *Journal of Intellectual Disability Research, 36*, 169–175.

Blacker, J., Beech, A. R., Wilcox, D. T., & Boer, D. P. (2011). The assessment of dynamic risk and recidivism in a sample of special needs sexual offenders. *Psychology, Crime & Law, 17*, 75–92.

Blanchard, R., Kella, N. J., Cantor, J. M., Classen, P. E., Dickey, R., Kuban, M. E., & Black, T. (2008). IQ, handedness and paedophilia in adult male patients stratified by referral source. *Sexual Abuse: A Journal of Research & Treatment, 19*, 285–309.

Boer, D. P., Hart, S. D., Kropp, P. R., & Webster, C. D. (1997). *Manual for the sexual violence risk – 20: Professional guidelines for assessing risk of sexual violence*. Vancouver, British Columbia: British Columbia Institute on Family Violence & Mental Health, Law & Policy Institute, Simon Fraser University.

Boer, D. P., Tough, S., & Haaven, J. (2004). Assessment of risk manageability of developmentally disabled sex offenders. *Journal of Applied Research in Intellectual Disabilities, 17*, 275–284.

British Psychological Society (2000). *Learning disability: Definitions and contexts*. Leicester: BPS.

British Psychological Society (2006). Mental capacity. *Assessment of capacity in adults: Interim guidance for psychologists*. Leicester: Author.

Brown, B. S., & Courtless, T. F. (1971). The Mentally Retarded Offender, Department of Health, Education, and Welfare Publication no (HSM) 72-9039. Washington, DC, US Government Printing Office.

Bumby, K. M. (1996). Assessing the cognitive distortions of child molesters and rapists: Development and validation of the MOLEST and RAPE scales. *Sexual Abuse: A Journal of Research & Treatment, 8*, 37–54.

Camilleri, J. A., & Quinsey, V. L. (2008). Appraising the risk of sexual and violent recidivism among intellectually disabled offenders. *Psychology, Crime & Law, 17*, 59–74.

Cantor, J. M., Blanchard, R., Robichaud, L. K., & Christensen, B. K. (2005). Quantitative reanalysis of aggregate data on IQ in sexual offenders. *Psychological Bulletin, 131*, 555–568.

Carson, D., Lindsay, W. R., Holland, A. J., Taylor, J. T., O'Brien, G., Wheeler, J. R., Steptoe, L., & Johnston, S. (2013). Sex offenders with intellectual disability referred to levels of community and secure provision: Comparison and prediction of pathway. *Legal and Criminological Psychology, 19*(2), 373–384.

Carson, D., Lindsay, W. R., O'Brien, G., Holland, A. J., Taylor, J. T., Wheeler, J. R., Middleton, C., Price, K., Steptoe, L., & Johnston, S. (2010). Referrals into services for offenders with intellectual disabilities: Variables predicting community or secure provision. *Criminal Behaviour and Mental Health, 20*, 39–50.

Clare, I. C. H., & Gudjonsson, G. H. (1993). Interrogative suggestibility, confabulation and acquiescence in people with mild learning disabilities (mental handicap): Implications for reliability during police interrogations. *British Journal of Clinical Psychology, 37*, 295–301.

Crocker, A. G., Côté, G., Toupin, J., & St-Onge, B. (2007). Rate and characteristics of men with an intellectual disability in pre-trial detention. *Journal of intellectual and developmental disability, 32*(2), 143–152.

de Vogel, V., & de Ruiter, C. (2005). The HCR-20 in personal disordered female offenders: A comparison with a matched sample of males. *Clinical Psychology and Psychotherapy, 12*, 226–240.

Dolan, M., & Khawaja, A. (2004). The HCR-20 and post discharge outcome in male patients discharged from medium security in the UK. *Aggressive Behaviour, 30*, 469–483.

Emerson, E., & Halpin, S. (2013). Antisocial behaviour and police contact among 13–15 year English adolescents with and without mild/moderate intellectual disability. *Journal of Applied Research in Intellectual Disabilities, 26*, 362–369.

Everington, C., & Fulero, S. (1999). Competence to confess: Measuring understanding and suggestibility in defendants with mental retardation. *Mental Retardation, 37*, 212–220.

Everington, C. T., & Luckasson, R. (1992). *Competence assessment for standing trial for defendants with mental retardation*. Worthington: International diagnostic systems, Inc.

Fago, D. P. (2006). Comorbid psychopathology in child, adolescent and adult sexual offenders. In C. Hilarski & J. Wodarski (Eds.), *Comprehensive mental health practice with sex offenders and their families* (pp. 139–218). Binghamton, NY: Haworth Press, Inc.

Farrington, D. P. (1995). The development of offending and antisocial behaviour from childhood: Key findings from the Cambridge study in delinquent development. *Journal of Child Psychology & Psychiatry, 36*, 929–964.

Farrington, D. P. (2000). Psychosocial causes of offending. In M. G. Gelder, J. J. Lopez-Ibor, & N. Andreasen (Eds.), *New Oxford textbook of psychiatry* (Vol. 2, pp. 2029–2036). Oxford: Oxford University Press.

Farrington, D. P., Coid, J. W. Harnett, L. M., Jolliffe, D., Soteriou, N., Turner, R. E., & West, D. J. (2006). *Criminal careers up to age 50 and life success up to age 48: New findings from the Cambridge Study in Delinquent Development* (2nd edn). London, UK: Home Office Research, Development and Statistics Directorate.

Finlay, W. M., & Lyons, E. (2001). Methodological issues in interviewing and using self-report questionnaires with people with mental retardation. *Psychological Assessment, 13,* 319–335.

Fitch, W. L. (1992). Mental retardation and criminal responsibility. *The George Washington Law Review, 53,* 414–493.

Fitzgerald, S., Gray, N. S., Alexander, R. T., Bagshaw, R., Chesterman, P., Huckle, P., Jones, S. K., Taylor, J., Williams, T., & Snowden, R. J. (2013). Predicting institutional violence in offenders with intellectual disabilities: The predictive efficacy of the VRAG and the HCR-20. *Journal of Applied Research in Intellectual Disabilities, 26,* 384–393.

Fitzgerald, S., Gray, N. S., Taylor, J., & Snowdon, R. J. (2011). Risk factors for recidivism in offenders with intellectual disabilities. *Psychology Crime and Law, 17,* 43–58.

Gray, N. S., Fitzgerald, S., Taylor, J., MacCulloch, M. J., & Snowden, R. J. (2007). Predicting future reconviction in offenders with intellectual disabilities: The predictive efficacy of VRAG, PCL-SV and the HCR-20. *Psychological Assessment, 19,* 474–479.

Green, G., Gray, N. S., & Willner, P. (2002). Factors associated with criminal convictions for sexually inappropriate behaviour in men with learning disabilities. *Journal of Forensic Psychiatry, 13,* 578–607.

Griffiths, D., & Lunsky, Y. (2003). *Sociosexual Knowledge and Attitudes Assessment Tool (SSKAAT-R).* Wood Dale, IL: Stoelting Company.

Griffiths, D. M., Quinsey, V. L., & Hingsburger, D. (1989). *Changing inappropriate sexual behaviour: A community based approach for persons with developmental disabilities.* Baltimore, MD: Paul H. Brookes.

Gudjonsson, G. H. (1992). *The psychology of interrogations, confessions and testimony.* Chichester: Wiley.

Gudjonsson, G. H. (1997). *Gudjonsson suggestibility scales.* Hove, Sussex: Psychology Press.

Hanson, K., & Thornton, D. (1999). Static 99. *Ontario: Public Works and Government Services Canada.*

Harris, G. T., Rice, M. E., & Quinsey, V. L. (1993). Violent recidivism of mentally disordered offenders: The development of a statistical prediction instrument. *Criminal Justice & Behaviour, 20,* 315–335.

Hayes, S. (1991). Sex offenders. *Australia & New Zealand Journal of Developmental Disabilities (Journal of Intellectual & Developmental Disabilities), 17,* 220–227.

Hayes, S. C. (2000). *Hayes ability screening index (HASI) manual.* University of Sydney, Sydney: Behavioural Sciences in Medicine.

Hayes, S., & McIlwain, D. (1988). *The prevalence of intellectual disability in the New South Wales prison population – an empirical study.* Report to the Criminology Research Council, Canberra.

Hingsburger, D., Griffiths, D., & Quinsey, V. (1991). Detecting counterfeit deviance: Differentiating sexual deviance from sexual inappropriateness. *Habilitation Mental Health Care Newsletter, 10,* 51–54.

Hodgins, S. (1992). Mental disorder, intellectual deficiency and crime: Evidence from a birth cohort. *Archives of General Psychiatry, 49,* 476–483.

Hogue, T. E., Steptoe, L., Taylor, J. L., Lindsay, W. R., Mooney, P., Pinkney, L., Johnston, S., Smith, A. H. W., & O'Brien, G. (2006). A comparison of offenders with intellectual disability across three levels of security. *Criminal Behaviour & Mental Health, 16,* 13–28.

Holland, A. J. (2004). Criminal behaviour and developmental disability: An epidemiological perspective. In W. R. Lindsay, J. L. Taylor, & P. Sturmey (Eds.), *Offenders with developmental disabilities* (pp. 23–34). Chichester: John Wiley.

Holland, S., & Persson, P. (2010). Intellectual disability in the Victorian prison system: Characteristics of prisoners with an intellectual disability released from prison in 2003–2006. *Psychology, Crime and Law, 17*(1), 25–41.

Hurley, J. (2003). *Missouri institute of mental health policy brief: Competency to stand trial.* School of Medicine, University of Missouri, Columbia.

Jackson, H. F., Glass, C., & Hope, S. (1987). A functional analysis of recidivistic arson. *British Journal of Clinical Psychology, 26,* 175–185.

Jespersen, A. F., Lalumiere, M. L., & Seto, M. C. (2009). Sexual abuse history among adult sex offenders and non sex offenders: A meta-analysis. *Child Abuse & Neglect, 33,* 179–192.

Keeling, J. A., Rose, J. L., & Beech, A. R. (2007a). A preliminary evaluation of the adaptation of four assessments for offenders with special needs. *Journal of Intellectual & Developmental Disability, 32,* 62–73.

Kellet, S. C., Beail, N., Newman, D. W., & Frankish, P. (2003). Utility of the Brief Symptom Inventory (BSI) in the assessment of psychological distress. *Journal of Applied Research in Intellectual Disabilities, 16,* 127–135.

Kellet, S.C., Beail, N., Newman, D. W., & Hawes, A. (2004). The factor structure of the Brief Symptom Inventory: Intellectual disability evidence. *Clinical Psychology & Psychotherapy. 11,* 275–281.

Klimecki, M. R., Jenkinson, J., & Wilson, L. (1994). A study of recidivism among offenders with an intellectual disability. *Journal of Intellectual and Developmental Disability, 19*(3), 209–219.

Kolton, D. J. C., Boer, A., & Boer, D. P. (2001). A revision of the Abel and Becker Cognition Scale for intellectually disabled sexual offenders. *Sexual Abuse: A Journal of Research & Treatment, 13,* 217–219.

Kraemer, H. C., Stice, E., Kazdin, A. & Kupfer, D. (2001). How do risk factors work together to produce an outcome? Mediators, moderators, independent, overlapping and proxy risk factors. *American Journal of Psychiatry, 258,* 848–856.

Langevan, R., & Curnoe, S. (2008). Are the mentally retarded and learning disordered overrepresented among sex offenders and paraphilics. *International Journal of Offender Therapy and Comparative Criminology, 52*, 401–415.

Lindsay, W. R. (2008). *The treatment of sex offenders with intellectual disability*. Chichester: John Wiley.

Lindsay, W. R., Carson, D. R., O'Brien, G., Holland, A. J., Johnston, S., Taylor, J. L., Wheeler, J. R., Middleton, C., Price, K., Steptoe, L., & Johnston, S.(2010b). The relationship between assessed risk and security level for offenders with intellectual disabilities. *Journal of Forensic Psychiatry and Psychology, 21*, 537–540.

Lindsay, W. R., Carson, D., Holland, A. J., Taylor, J., O'Brien, G., & Wheeler, J. (2013a). The impact of known criminogenic factors on offenders with Intellectual disability: Previous findings and new results on ADHD. *Journal of Applied Research in Intellectual Disabilities, 26*, 71–80.

Lindsay, W. R., & Dernevick, M. (2013). Risk and offenders with intellectual disabilities: Reappraising Hodgins (1992) classic study. *Criminal Behaviour & Mental Health, 23*, 151–157.

Lindsay, W. R., Elliot, S. F., & Astell, A. (2004). Predictors of sexual offence recidivism in offenders with intellectual disabilities. *Journal of Applied Research in Intellectual Disabilities, 17*, 299–305.

Lindsay, W. R., Hastings, R. P., Griffiths, D. M., & Hayes, S. C. (2007). Trends and challenges in forensic research on offenders with intellectual disability. *Journal of Intellectual & Developmental Disability, 32*, 55–61.

Lindsay, W. R., Haut, F., & Steptoe, L. (2011). Changes in referral patterns for offenders with intellectual disability: A 20 year follow up study. *Journal of Forensic Psychiatry and Psychology. 22*, 513–517.

Lindsay, W. R., Hogue, T., Taylor, J. L., Steptoe, L., Mooney, P., Johnston, S., O'Brien, G., & Smith, A. H. W. (2008). Risk assessment in offenders with intellectual disabilities: A comparison across three levels of security. *International Journal of Offender Therapy & Comparative Criminology, 52*, 90–111.

Lindsay, W. R., Michie, A. M., Baty, F. J., Smith, A. H. W., & Miller, S. (1994). The consistency of reports about feelings and emotions from people with intellectual disability. *Journal of Intellectual Disability Research, 38*, 61–66.

Lindsay, W. R., Michie, A. M., Whitefield, E., Martin, V., Grieve, A., & Carson, D. (2006). Response patterns on the questionnaire on attitudes consistent with sexual offending in groups of sex offenders with intellectual disability. *Journal of Applied Research in Intellectual Disabilities, 19*, 47–54.

Lindsay, W. R., Murphy, L., Smith, G., Murphy, D., Edwards, Z., Grieve, A., Chettock, C., & Young, S. J. (2004). The Dynamic Risk Assessment and Management System: An assessment of immediate risk of violence for individuals with intellectual disabilities, and offending and challenging behaviour. *Journal of Applied Research in Intellectual Disabilities, 17*, 267–274.

Lindsay, W. R., O'Brien, G., Carson, D. R., Holland, A. J., Taylor, J. L., Wheeler, J. R., Middleton, C., Price, K., Steptoe, L., & Johnston, S. (2010). Pathways into services for offenders with intellectual disabilities: Childhood experiences, diagnostic information and offence related variables. *Criminal Justice & Behaviour, 37*, 678–694.

Lindsay, W. R., & Skene, D. D. (2007). The Beck Depression Inventory II and The Beck Anxiety Inventory in people with intellectual disabilities: Factor analyses and group data. *Journal of Applied Research in Intellectual Disability, 20*, 401–408.

Lindsay, W. R., Steptoe, L., & Haut, F. (2012). The sexual and physical abuse histories of offenders with intellectual disability. *Journal of Intellectual Disability Research, 56*, 326–331.

Lindsay, W. R., Steptoe, L., Wallace, L., Haut, F., & Brewster, E. (2013). An evaluation and 20-year follow-up of a community forensic intellectual disability service. *Criminal Behaviour and Mental Health, 23*(2), 138–149.

Lindsay, W. R., Sturmey, P., & Taylor, J. L. (2004). Natural history and theories of offending in people with developmental disabilities. In W. R. Lindsay, J. L. Taylor, & P. Sturmey (Eds.), *Offenders with developmental disabilities* (pp. 3–22). Chichester: John Wiley.

Lindsay, W. R., Taylor, J. L., & Sturmey, P. (2004). *Offenders with developmental disabilities*. Chichester: John Wiley.

Lindsay, W. R., Whitefield, E., & Carson, D. (2007). An assessment for attitudes consistent with sexual offending for use with offenders with intellectual disability. *Legal & Criminological Psychology, 12*, 55–68.

Linhorst, D. M., McCutchen, T. A., & Bennett, L. (2003). Recidivism among offenders with developmental disabilities participating in a case management program. *Research in Developmental Disabilities, 24*(3), 210–230.

Livingston, M., Stewart, A., Allard, T., & Ogilvie, J. (2008). Understanding juvenile offending trajectories. *The Australian and New Zealand Journal of Criminology, 41*, 345–363.

Lofthouse, R. E., Lindsay, W., Totsika, V., Hastings, R. P., Boer, D., & Haavan, J. (2013a). Prospective dynamic assessment of risk of sexual reoffending in individuals with an intellectual disability and a history of sexual offending behaviour. *Journal of Applied Research in Intellectual Disabilities. 26*, 394–403.

Lofthouse, R. E., Totsika, V., Hastings, R., Lindsay, W., Hogue, T., & Taylor, J. (2013b). How do static and dynamic risk factors work together to predict violent behaviour amongst offenders with an intellectual disability? *Journal of Intellectual Disability Research*, in press.

Lund, J. (1990). Mentally retarded criminal offenders in Denmark. *British Journal of Psychiatry, 156*, 726–731.

Lunsky, Y., Frijters, J., Griffiths, D. M., Watson, S. L., & Williston, S. (2007). Sexual knowledge and attitudes of men with intellectual disabilities who sexually offend. *Journal of Intellectual & Developmental Disability, 32*, 74–81.

Lunsky, Y., Gracey, C., Koegl, C., Bradley, E., Durbin, J., & Raina, P. (2011). The clinical profile and service needs of psychiatric inpatients with intellectual disabilities and forensic involvement. *Psychology Crime and Law, 17*, 9–25.

Lyall, I., Holland, A. J., Collins, S., & Styles, P. (1995). Incidence of persons with a learning disability detained in police custody. *Medicine, Science & the Law, 35,* 61–71.

MacEachron, A. E. (1979). Mentally retarded offenders prevalence and characteristics. *American Journal of Mental Deficiency, 84,* 165–176.

McCord, W., & McCord, J. (1959). *Origins of crime: A new evaluation of the Cambridge-Somerville.* New York: Columbia Press.

MacMillan, D., Hastings, R., & Caldwell, J. (2004). Clinical and actuarial prediction of physical violence in a forensic intellectual disability hospital: A longitudinal study. *Journal of Applied Research in Intellectual Disabilities, 17,* 255–266.

Mason, J., & Murphy, G. (2002). Intellectual disability amongst people on probation: Prevalence and outcome. *Journal of Intellectual Disability Research, 46,* 230–238.

Maughan, B., Pickles, A., Hagell, A., Rutter, M., & Yule, W. (1996). Reading problems and antisocial behaviour: Developmental trends in comorbidity. *Journal of Child Psychology & Psychiatry, 37,* 405–418.

Messinger, E., & Apfelberg, B. (1961). A quarter century of court psychiatry. *Crime & Delinquency, 7,* 343–362.

Michie, A. M., Lindsay, W. R., Martin, V., & Grieve, A. (2006). A test of counterfeit deviance: A comparison of sexual knowledge in groups of sex offenders with intellectual disability and controls. *Sexual Abuse: A Journal of Research & Treatment, 18,* 271–279.

Monahan, J., Steadman, H., Silver, E., Appelbaum, P., Robbins, T., Mulvey, E., Roth, L., Grisso, T., & Banks, S. (2001). *Re-thinking risk assessment: The MacArthur study of mental disorder and violence.* New York: Oxford University Press.

Murphy, G. H., & Clare, I. C. H. (1996). Analysis of motivation in people with mild learning disabilities (mental handicap) who set fires. *Psychology, Crime and Law, 2,* 153–164.

Murphy, M., Harrold, M., Carey, S., & Mulrooney, M. (2000). *A survey of the level of learning disability among the prison population in Ireland.* Dublin: Department of Justice, Equality and Law Reform.

Noble, J. H., & Conley, R. W. (1992). Toward an epidemiology of relevant attributes. In R. W. Conley, R. Luckasson, & G. Bouthilet (Eds.), *The criminal justice system and mental retardation* (pp. 17–54). Baltimore: Paul Brookes Publishing.

Novaco, R. W. (1975). *Anger control: The development and evaluation of an experimental treatment.* Lexington, MA: Heath.

Novaco, R. W. (1994). Anger as a risk factor for violence among the mentally disordered. In J. Monahan & H. J. Steadman (Eds.), *Violence in mental disorder: Developments in risk assessment.* Chicago, IL: University of Chicago Press.

Novaco, R. W. (2003). *The Novaco Anger Scale and Provocation Inventory Manual (NAS-PI).* Los Angeles: Western Psychological Services.

Novaco, R. W., & Taylor, J. L. (2004). Assessment of anger and aggression in offenders with developmental disabilities. *Psychological Assessment, 16,* 42–50.

Novaco, R. W., & Taylor, J. L. (2008). Anger and assaultiveness of male forensic patients with developmental disabilities: Links to volatile parents. *Aggressive Behaviour, 34*(4), 380–393.

O'Brien, G., Taylor, J. L., Lindsay, W. R., Holland, A. J., Carson, D., Steptoe, L., Middleton. C., Price, K., & Wheeler, J. R. (2010). A multi-centre study of adults with learning disabilities referred to services for antisocial or offending behaviour: Demographic, individual, offending and service characteristics. *Journal of Learning Disabilities and Offending Behaviour, 1,* 5–15.

Oliver, P. C., Crawford, M. J., Rao, B., Reece, B., & Tyrer, P. (2007). Modified Overt Aggression Scale (MOAS) for people with intellectual disability and aggressive challenging behaviour: A reliability study. *Journal of Applied Research in Intellectual Disabilities, 20,* 368–372.

Otto, R. K., Poythress, N. G., Nicholson, R. A., Edens, J. F., Monahan, J., Bonnie, R. J., Hoge, S. K., & Eisenberg, M. (1998). Psychometric properties of the MacArthur Competence Assessment Tool – Criminal adjudication. *Psychological Assessment, 10,* 435–443.

Quinsey, V. L., Book, A., & Skilling, T. A. (2004). A follow-up of deinstitutionalised men with intellectual disabilities and histories of antisocial behaviour. *Journal of Applied Research in Intellectual Disabilities, 17,* 243–254.

Quinsey, V. L., Harris, G. T., Rice, M. E., & Cormier, C. A. (1998). *Violent offenders: Appraising and managing risk.* Washington DC: American Psychological Association.

Quinsey, V. L., Harris, G. T., Rice, M. E., & Cormier, C. A. (2005). *Violent offenders, appraising and managing risk: Second edition.* Washington, DC: American Psychological Association.

Raina, P, Arenovich, T, Jones, J., & Lunsky, Y. (2013). Pathways into the criminal justice system for individuals with intellectual disabilities. *Journal of Applied Research in Intellectual Disabilities, 26,* 404–409.

Raina, P., & Lunsky, Y. (2010). A comparison study of adults with intellectual disability and psychiatric disorder with and without forensic involvement. *Research in Developmental Disabilities, 31*(1): 218–223.

Rice, M. E., & Harris, G. T. (2005). Comparing effect sizes in follow-up studies: ROC area, Cohen's *d,* and *r. Law and Human Behaviour, 29,* 615–620.

Rice, M. E., Harris, G. T., Lang, C., & Chaplin, T. (2008). Sexual preferences and recidivism of sex offenders with mental retardation. *Sexual Abuse: A Journal of Research and Treatment. 20,* 409–425.

Rose, J., & West, C. (1999). Assessment of anger in people with intellectual disabilities. *Journal of Applied Research in Intellectual Disabilities, 12,* 211–224.

Rutter, M., Maughan, B., Meyer, J., Pickles, A., Silberg, J., Simonoff, E., & Taylor, E. (1997). Heterogeneity of antisocial behaviour: Causes, continuities and consequences. In D. W. Osgood (Ed.), *Motivation and delinquency* (pp. 45–118). Lincoln: University of Nebraska Press.

Ryba, N. L., Cooper, V. G., & Zapf, P. A. (2003). Juvenile competence to stand trial evaluations: A survey of current practices and test usage among psychologists. *Professional Psychology: Research in Practice, 34*, 499–507.

Sanders, A., & Young, R. (2000). *Criminal justice* (2nd edn). London: Butterworths.

Scheerenberger, R. C. (1983). *A history of mental retardation.* London: Brooks Publishing Co.

Sorgi, P., Ratey, J., Knoedler, D. W., Markert, R. J., & Reichman, M. (1991). Rating aggression in the clinical setting a retrospective adaptation of the Overt Aggression Scale: Preliminary results. *Journal of Neuropsychiatry, 3*, 552–556.

Spielberger, C. D. (1996). *State-trait anger expression inventory professional manual.* Florida: Psychological Assessment Resources Inc.

Steptoe, L., Lindsay, W. R., Forrest, D., & Power, M. (2006). Quality of life and relationships in sex offenders with intellectual disability. *Journal of Intellectual & Developmental Disabilities, 31*, 13–19.

Steptoe, L., Lindsay, W. R., Murphy, L., & Young, S. J. (2008). Construct validity, reliability and predictive validity of the Dynamic Risk Assessment and Management System (DRAMS) in offenders with intellectual disability. *Legal & Criminological Psychology, 13*, 309–321.

Taylor, J. L., & Novaco, R. W. (2005). *Anger treatment for people with developmental disabilities: A theory, evidence and manual based approach.* Chichester: Wiley.

Taylor, J. L., Novaco, R. W., Gillmer, B., & Thorne, I. (2002). Cognitive behavioural treatment of anger intensity among offenders with intellectual disabilities. *Journal of Applied Research in Intellectual Disabilities, 15*, 151–165.

Taylor, J. L., Novaco, R. W., Guinan, C., & Street, N. (2004). Development of an imaginal provocation test to evaluate treatment for anger problems in people with intellectual disabilities. *Clinical Psychology & Psychotherapy, 11*, 233–246.

Taylor, J. L., Robertson, A., Thorne, I., Belshaw, T., & Watson, A. (2006). Responses of female fire-setters with mild and borderline intellectual disabilities to a group based intervention. *Journal of Applied Research in Intellectual Disabilities, 19*, 179–190.

Taylor, J. L., Thorne, I., Robertson, A., & Avery, G. (2002). Evaluation of a group intervention for convicted arsonists with mild and borderline intellectual disabilities. *Criminal Behaviour and Mental Health, 12*, 282–293.

Terman, L. (1911). *The measurement of intelligence.* Boston: Houghton Mifflin Co.

Vanny, K. A., Levy, M. H., Greenberg, D. M., & Hayes, S. C. (2009). Mental illness and intellectual disability in magistrates courts in New South Wales. *Journal of Intellectual Disability Research, 53*, 289–297.

Vinkers, D. (2013). Pre-trial reported defendants in the Netherlands with intellectual disability, borderline and normal intellectual functioning. *Journal of Applied Research in Intellectual Disabilities, 26*, 357–361.

Walker, N., & McCabe, S. (1973). *Crime and insanity in England.* Edinburgh: Edinburgh University Press.

Ward, A. K., Day, D., Bevc, I., Sun, Y., Rosenthal, J. S., & Duchesne, T. (2010). Criminal trajectories and risk factors in a Canadian sample of offenders. *Criminal Justice and Behavior, 11*, 1278–1300.

Webster, C. D., Eaves, D., Douglas, K. S., & Wintrup, A. (1995). *The HCR-20: The assessment of dangerousness and risk.* Vancouver, Canada: Simon Fraser University and British Colombia Forensic Psychiatric Services Commission.

Wechsler, D. (2010). *Wechsler Adult Intelligence Scale – Fourth UK Edition: Administrative and Scoring Manual.* London: The Psychology Corporation.

Wheeler, J. R., Clare, I. C., & Holland, A. J. (2013). Offending by people with intellectual disabilities in community settings: A preliminary examination of contextual factors. *Journal of Applied Research in Intellectual Disabilities, 26*, 370–383.

Wheeler, J. R., Holland, A. J., Bambrick, M., Lindsay, W. R., Carson, D., Steptoe, L., Johnston, S., Taylor, J. L., Middleton, C., Price, K., & O'Brien, G. (2009). Community services and people with intellectual disabilities who engage in anti-social or offending behaviour: Referral rates, characteristics, and care pathways. *Journal of Forensic Psychiatry & Psychology, 20*, 717–740.

White, R., & Willner, P. (2004). Suggestibility and salience in people with intellectual disabilities: An experimental critique of the Gudjonsson suggestibility scale. *Journal of Forensic Psychiatry & Psychology, 16*, 638–650.

Wilcox, D., Beech, A., Markall, H. F., & Blacker, J. (2009). Actuarial risk assessment and recidivism in a sample of UK intellectually disabled sexual offenders. *Journal of sexual aggression, 15*(1), 97–106.

Wildenskov, H. O. T. (1962). A long term follow-up of subnormals originally exhibiting severe behaviour disorders or criminality. In *Proceedings of the London Conference on the scientific study of mental deficiency.* London: May and Baker.

Williams, F., Wakeling, H., & Webster, S. (2007). A psychometric study of six self-report measures for use with sexual offenders with cognitive and social functioning deficits. *Psychology, Crime and Law, 13*(5), 505–522.

Willis, G. M., & Grace, R. C. (2009). Assessment of community reintegration planning for sex offenders: Poor planning predicts recidivism. *Criminal Justice and Behavior, 36*(5), 494–512.

Willner, P. (2008). Clarification of the memory artefact in the assessment of suggestibility. *Journal of Intellectual Disability Research, 52*, 318–326.

Willner, P. (2009). *Assessment of capacity to participate in court proceedings, with particular reference to the assessment of suggestibility.* Leicester: British Psychological Society.

Willner, P. (2011). To have capacity to participate in court proceedings: A selective critique and some recommendations. *Psychology, Crime and Law, 17*, 117–132.

Willner, P., Brace, N., & Phillips, J. (2005). Assessment of anger coping skills in individuals with intellectual disabilities. *Journal of Intellectual Disability Research, 49,* 329–339.

Wish, J. R., McCombs, K. F., & Edmonson, B. (1979). *The socio-sexual knowledge and attitudes test.* Wood Dale, IL: Stoelting Company.

World Health Organization (1992). *Tenth revision of the international classification of diseases and related health problems (ICD-10).* Geneva: Author.

Yang, M., Wong, S., & Coid, J. (2010). The efficacy of violence prediction: A meta analytic comparison of nine risk assessment tools. *Psychological Bulletin, 136,* 740–767.

15 Intellectual Disability: Treatment and Management

WILLIAM R. LINDSAY, JOHN L. TAYLOR AND AMANDA MICHIE

At the outset of this chapter, we wish to make the important point that most forensic work with offenders with intellectual disability (ID) happens in community settings. As we have seen in the previous chapter, the link between ID and crime has been seriously questioned, but that does not mean that people with ID do not commit crime. Indeed, the available literature would suggest that they commit crime at broadly the same frequency as other groups. The research on pathways indicated that aggression is both a frequently referred problem and a major factor in determining outcome. Therefore, any treatment service should pay attention to the salience of aggression in this client group. These findings are pertinent to all services including community forensic services.

It is often difficult to separate out treatment and management in offenders with ID. To state the obvious, in treatment, individuals attend a course of therapy, and the effects can be evaluated over months and years both in terms of improvement in personal characteristics, such as a propensity towards aggression, and outcomes, such as the number of violent incidents. Management implies that carers and significant others in the person's life monitor and control that individual so that any propensities towards aggression are identified and prevented, irrespective of the person's self-regulation. With offenders with ID, the two are often confounded in a way that would not occur with offenders without mental impairment. The difficulties in evaluation are placed into focus in a treatment study on six sex offenders with ID reported by Craig, Stringer, and Moss (2006). They completed a 7-month programme incorporating sex education, addressing cognitive distortions and promoting relapse prevention in participants but found no significant improvements in proximal measures including the assessment of sexual knowledge. However, they also reported no further incidents of sexual offending during a 12-month follow-up. In the description of individual participants, they wrote that all six received 24-hour supervision and so, presumably, had little or no opportunity to reoffend.

It is impossible to evaluate treatment outcome in the absence of reasonable recordings of behaviour in uncontrolled settings, and few conclusions can be drawn about the treatment that would be relevant for social policy. Social impact is germane to the evaluation of work on offenders and offenders with ID. Many treatments, such as those for anxiety or depression, use self-reports or reports from others as an outcome. In offender work, these can only be considered proximal, while from a social policy point of view, only evidence of whether or not another offence has been committed is of interest. From a societal stance, it is of little value to know that an offender reports low levels of anger or better problem-solving abilities if he or she continues to commit an equivalent number of violent offences following treatment. If an individual continues to be supervised 24 hours a day, we cannot know whether or not treatment has had any effect on the commission of further incidents.

There is a respectable history with regard to long-term evaluation of forensic ID services. Wildenskov (1962) followed up 47 men with borderline IQ (IQ 70–79) who had been convicted of a variety of offences. These individuals had been treated for a period in hospital and were then followed up for 20 years. Wildenskov found that the reoffending rates were 51%, and, although one can criticize this early study for a number of methodological limitations, it does show that interest in evaluating such services goes back over 40 years. Tong and MacKay (1969) followed up 423 male patients with IDD who had been discharged from high-security hospitals. They found 40% reconviction rates with follow-up periods of 1–12 years. In a seminal piece of work in which they followed up all patients from high-security hospitals in England and Wales, Walker and McCabe (1973) identified 370 individuals with IDD. These offenders were reviewed 1 year after discharge, and

Forensic Psychology, Second Edition. Edited by David A. Crighton and Graham J. Towl.
© 2015 John Wiley & Sons, Ltd. Published 2015 by British Psychological Society and John Wiley & Sons, Ltd.

it was found that 39% had reoffended. Gibbens and Robertson (1983) reviewed 250 male offenders with IDD who had been on hospital orders. After a follow-up period of 15 years, they found that 68% of them had been reconvicted and 41% had three or more reconvictions. This higher rate of reoffending was also noted by Lund (1990) when he followed up 83 offenders with IDD.

In a series of evaluations of a comprehensive in-patient forensic service (the MIETS unit), Clare and Murphy (1993) and Xenitidis, Henry, Russell, Ward, and Murphy (1999) followed up six and 64 patients, respectively. Clare and Murphy (1993) noted that all patients were living in less restrictive environments but did not report reoffending. Xenitidis *et al.* (1999) reported that, while only 18% of referrals had been admitted from community facilities, 84% were discharged to the community, and that there was a significant reduction in challenging and offending behaviour. In a 12-year follow-up study from a medium-security unit, Alexander Crouch, Halstead, and Piachaud (2006), when following up 64 patients discharged from medium-security services, found that, while only 11% had been reconvicted, 58% had shown offending-like behaviour that had no legal consequence. The presence of personality disorder, previous theft and young age increased the likelihood of reconviction.

Lindsay and colleagues (Lindsay, Allan *et al.*, 2004; Lindsay, Steele, Smith, Quinn, & Allan, 2006; Lindsay, Steptoe, Wallace, Haut, & Brewster, 2013) have followed up offenders accepted into a community forensic IDD service. In their most recent evaluation (Lindsay *et al.*, 2013), they reported on 309 participants followed up for up to 20 years. They consisted of 156 sex offenders, 126 non-sexual male offenders and 27 women. During the study period, 16% of the male sexual offenders, 43% of the non-sexual male offenders and 23% of the women committed at least one further offence. All but 15 of the 309 participants continued to have restricted access to the community throughout the follow-up period. Analysis of the number of incidents following referral, in comparison to 2 years prior to referral, revealed that there was a 90–95% reduction, representing a significant amount of harm reduction. Survival analysis revealed that, for the non-sexual male offenders, well over half of the reoffending happened within 2 years, and almost all of the reoffending took place up to 4 years after referral. For the sexual offenders, most reoffending occurred within 1 year but for some individuals reoffending occurred up to 9 years after their referral.

Service evaluation for offenders with IDD has been conducted regularly over the last 50 or 60 years. Results suggest that at least half of the offenders are likely to commit another incident throughout the follow-up period. Sex offenders are less likely to reoffend than non-sexual offenders who commit predominantly violent

and acquisitive offences. However, there is also evidence to suggest that those individuals who commit further offences are likely to commit significantly fewer offences than they did prior to treatment. Gray, Fitzgerald, Taylor, MacCulloch, and Snowden (2007) conducted a follow-up study of patients with mental disorder discharged from secure hospital settings. They compared 145 patients with ID against 996 without ID and found that, for violent offences, 4.8% of those with ID and 11.2% of those without ID reoffended, while for general offences, reoffending rates were 9.7% for those with ID and 18.7% for those without.

TREATMENT FOR SPECIFIC NEEDS

Aggression

There is a reasonable research base for intervention in two main areas of offender treatment: violence and sexual offending. The best developed of these are treatments for violent and aggressive behaviour, and the most extensive literature concerning treatment of aggression is in the applied behavioural analysis (ABA) field. Taylor and Novaco (2005) summarized the literature in this area, describing several extensive reviews, and concluding that ABA-type behavioural interventions that are generally applied to low-functioning individuals in institutional settings may not be as effective for anger and aggression problems observed in forensic ID populations. These populations are relatively high functioning in intellectual terms, display low frequency but very serious aggression and violence, and live in relatively uncontrolled environments. The majority of research on interventions for aggression with offenders with ID has evaluated the anger management treatment approach of Novaco (1975, 1994). In contrast to ABA-type treatments, anger management is a 'self-actualizing' treatment that promotes generalized self-regulation of anger and aggression. The approach employs cognitive restructuring, arousal reduction and behavioural skills training. Importantly, anger management treatment incorporates Meichenbaum's (1985) stress inoculation paradigm.

Taylor (2002) and Taylor and Novaco (2005) reviewed a number of case series studies and uncontrolled group anger treatment studies involving individual and group therapy formats, incorporating combinations of cognitive behavioural techniques including relaxation and arousal reduction, skills training and self-monitoring. Generally, they produced good outcomes in reducing anger and aggression, and these were maintained at follow-up. Several case studies have reported successful outcomes in people with histories of aggressive behaviour in hospital and community settings (Murphy & Clare, 1991; Black & Novaco, 1993; Rose & West, 1999). There have also been a small number of studies of cognitive behavioural anger treatment involving offenders with ID that have yielded positive outcomes. Allan, Lindsay, Macleod, and Smith (2001) and Lindsay, Allan, Macleod, Smith, and Smart (2003) reported on group behavioural anger interventions for a series of five women and six men with ID, respectively. The participants in these studies were living in community settings, and they had all been referred following violent assaults resulting in criminal justice system involvement. In both studies, improvements were reported for all participants at the end of treatment that were maintained at 15 months follow-up. Burns, Bird, Leach, and Higgins (2003) reported on the results of a CBT-framed group anger management intervention for three offenders with ID residing in a specialist NHS medium-security unit. Using multiple assessment points to carry out time series analyses, the results for the participants were mixed in terms of self-reported anger and informant-related aggression measures. The authors suggested that the relatively short length of the modified intervention and unstable baseline measures contributed to the limited treatment effects observed.

More recently, there have been a number of treatment trials that have shown the effectiveness of group cognitive behavioural anger treatment over waiting list/no treatment control conditions with clients with ID living in community settings (Rose, West, & Clifford, 2000; Willner, Brace, & Phillips, 2005; Willner, Jones, Tams, & Green, 2002). Lindsay, Smith et al. (2004) reported a controlled study of cognitive behavioural anger treatment for individuals living in the community and referred by the court or criminal justice services. Several outcome measures were used including the DPI, provocation role plays and self-report diaries over a follow-up period of 15 months. Aggressive incidents and re-offences were also recorded for both the treatment group and the waiting list control group. There were significant improvements in anger control on all measures with significant differences between the treatment and control groups. In addition, the treatment group recorded significantly fewer incidents of assault and violence at the post-treatment assessment point (14% vs. 45%). There was evidence that anger management treatment had a significant impact on the number of aggressive incidents recorded in these participants in addition to improvements in the assessed psychological variables.

Taylor, Novaco, Gillmer, and Thorne (2002), Taylor, Novaco, Guinan, and Street (2004), and Taylor, Novaco, Gillmer, Robertson, and Thorne (2005) have evaluated individual cognitive behavioural anger treatment with detained male patients with mild-borderline ID and significant violent, sexual and fire-raising histories in a series of waiting-list-controlled studies. The 18-session treatment package included a six-session broadly psycho-educational and motivational preparatory phase, followed by a 12-session treatment phase based on individual formulation of each participant's anger problems and needs, which follows the classical cognitive behavioural stages of cognitive preparation, skills acquisition, skills rehearsal and then practise in vivo. These studies showed significant improvements on self-reported measures of anger disposition, anger reactivity and behavioural reaction indices following intervention in the treatment groups compared with scores for the control groups, and these differences were maintained for up to 4 months following treatment. Staff ratings of study participants' anger disposition conferred with patients' reports but did not reach statistical significance.

Although these controlled evaluations mean that AMT as a treatment programme is the best evaluated treatment in the field of offenders with ID, there has been little analysis of each treatment component. This is of interest because some of the methods may contribute nothing to the effectiveness of the approach as a whole while others may indeed reduce the effectiveness or work against the effectiveness of the more potent procedures. As an example, one carefully controlled case series (Travis & Sturmey, 2013, in press) focuses on the stress inoculation aspect of AMT and demonstrates considerable effectiveness for this truncated anger treatment in a series of three carefully controlled case studies.

Several of the controlled trials that found significant differences between the treatment group and comparison group were not conducted on forensic cases (Willner et al., 2002; Rose, Loftus, Flint, & Carey, 2005; Rose, Anderson, Hawkins, & Rose, 2012). Studies which have been conducted on forensic cases (Lindsay, Smith et al., 2004; Taylor et al., 2002, 2005) have shown significant improvements following AMT, and one study found a significant reduction in aggressive incidents for the treated group.

In summary, building research evidence suggests that cognitive behavioural interventions can be effective for this population with regard to its self-report and informant anger measures and socially valid indices of the number of incidents carried out by offenders with ID following treatment.

Sexual offending

Until relatively recently, behavioural management approaches dominated the field of intellectual disability and, as with interventions for aggression, the most common psychological treatments for management of sexual offending have been ABA-type approaches (Plaud, Plaud, Colstoe, & Orvedal, 2000). These authors noted that the purpose of a behavioural treatment programme is to improve patients' behavioural competency in daily living skills, general interpersonal and educational skills and specialized behavioural skills related to sexuality and offending. Griffiths, Quinsey, and Hingsburger (1989) developed a comprehensive behavioural management regime for sex offenders with ID. Their programme included addressing deviant sexual behaviour through education, training social competence and improving relationship skills, reviewing relapse prevention through alerting support staff and training on issues of responsibility. In a review of 30 cases, they reported no reoffending and described a number of successful case studies to illustrate their methods. Others have also described similar positive outcomes with behavioural management approaches (Haaven, Little, & Petre-Miller, 1990; Grubb-Blubaugh, Shire, & Baulser, 1994). In their review, Plaud *et al.* (2000) describe aversion therapy techniques and masturbatory retraining techniques in some detail. Although there are few reports on the use of these methods with offenders with ID, Lindsay (2004) has described the successful employment of imagined aversive events to control deviant sexual arousal and routines.

Behavioural treatments continue to be conducted on the assessment and treatment of deviant sexual arousal, often using phallometric measures (Rayes *et al.*, 2006; Rayes, Vollmer, & Hall, 2011). These studies have demonstrated both the utility and limitations of such assessments. The limitations are clear in that phallometric measures continue to be difficult to use on people with IDD. Often, those individuals do not realize the considerable long-term consequences that can be imposed as a result of continued non-compliance with assessment and treatment. The immediate response to the intrusive nature of the assessment that results in non-compliance far outweighs any consideration of possible long-term consequences of non-compliance. There have also been some recent case descriptions of treatment for inappropriate sexual behaviour based on behavioural principles such as role play, reinforcement and extinction. Dozier, Iwata, and Warsdell (2011) treated a man diagnosed with autism who had a 20-year history of inappropriate masturbation. Two interventions were ineffective or impractical but response interruption and time out interventions proved successful after a few sessions and maintained for a further 40 sessions. However, in this case, sessions were conducted three to five times per day; 5 days a week, and 65 sessions could not have lasted much more than a month. Therefore, only short-term follow-up was available. This is a continuing

difficulty with behavioural interventions, in that they often demonstrate effectiveness of treatment over periods of relatively short, intensive, well-controlled treatments (Vollmer, Rayes, & Walker 2012). This presents the clinician with three practical difficulties. The first is that these highly intensive, well-controlled environments are often difficult to replicate in clinical settings. As we have indicated previously, much offender treatment requires self-actualization and self-regulation that does not require any reliance on the external immediate contingencies. In other words, individuals have to carry around the self-regulation contingencies within themselves. The second difficulty is that inappropriate sexual behaviour often does not occur with such high frequency as is seen in these behavioural demonstrations. Indecent exposure or sexual assault may happen once a week at most, and, with these low-frequency acts, it is very difficult to establish and maintain environmental controlling contingencies. The third and possibly most pressing problem with behavioural interventions for inappropriate sexual behaviour is the lack of appropriate follow-up. It is well known that sex offence recidivism should be reviewed for at least a year and, preferably, for up to 10 years. In a recent study, Lindsay *et al.* (2013) demonstrated that while most recidivism, if it happened, was likely to occur within 4 years, there were still occasional instances of reoffending up to 10 years after treatment. Behavioural studies generally show maintenance for weeks, and such short periods of time are clearly highly unsatisfactory for work in forensic settings.

A major recent development in the use of psychological treatment for sex offenders with ID has been the employment of cognitive and problem-solving techniques within therapy. These methods have been developed to a sophisticated degree with mainstream offenders. Hanson *et al.* (2002) reported in a meta-analytic study that those treatments that employed cognitive techniques showed greater reductions in recidivism rates compared to treatments employing other techniques, including behavioural treatments. The essential assumption in cognitive therapy is that sex offenders may hold a number of cognitive distortions regarding sexuality which support the perpetration of sexual offences. These cognitive distortions include mitigation of responsibility, denial of harm to the victim, thoughts of entitlement, mitigation through the claim of an altered state, denial of any intent to offend and complete denial that an offence occurred. Assessments already described represent attempts to review the extent to which each sex offender holds a range of cognitive distortions, and the QACSO is specifically designed for this purpose in offenders with ID.

Support for the centrality of cognitive distortions in the offence process came from a qualitative study of nine male sex offenders with ID by Courtney, Rose, and

Mason (2006), using grounded theory techniques. In the analysis of interviews with participants, they concluded that all aspects of the offence process were linked to offender attitudes and beliefs such as denial of the offence, blaming others and seeing themselves as the victims. Therefore, a crucial aspect of treatment is to explore these issues of denial and other cognitive distortions. Lindsay *et al.* (1998a, b, c) reported on a series of case studies with offenders with ID using a cognitive behavioural intervention in which various forms of denial and mitigation of the offence were challenged over treatment periods of up to 3 years. Strategies for relapse prevention and the promotion of self-regulation were also component parts of the treatment. Across these studies, participants consistently reported positive changes in cognitions during treatment. Each of these reports provides examples of how cognitive distortions are elicited and challenged during treatment. This component of the intervention was evaluated using the QACSO (Lindsay, Whitefield, & Carson, 2007). Reductions in the number of endorsements given to cognitive distortions were found following extended treatment periods, and these improvements maintained for at least 1 year following cessation of treatment. More importantly, lengthy follow-up of these cases (4–7 years) showed that none had reoffended following initial conviction.

Rose *et al.* (2002) reported on a 16-week group treatment for five men with ID who had perpetrated sexual abuse. The group treatment included self-control procedures, consideration of the effects of offences on victims, emotional recognition and strategies for avoiding risky situations. Individuals were assessed using the QACSO attitudes scale, a measure of locus of control, a sexual behaviour and victim empathy scale. Significant differences from pre- to post-treatment were found only on the locus of control scale. The authors noted that the length of treatment was somewhat short in comparison to the majority of sex offender treatment programmes, which usually last from 12 to 18 months. However, they reported that participants had not reoffended at 1-year follow-up.

Although there are a number of treatment comparison studies evaluating the effects of sex offender treatment, they tend to fall well short of adequate experimental standards, and it is important to consider the results in light of their methodological shortcomings. Lindsay and Smith (1998) compared seven individuals who had been in treatment for 2 years or more with another group of seven clients who had been in treatment for less than 1 year. Therefore, the numbers were low, and the comparison was serendipitous in that time, and treatment reflected the length of the probation orders made by the court. There were no significant differences between the

groups in terms of severity or type of offence. The group that had been in treatment for less than 1 year showed significantly poorer progress, and those in this group were more likely to reoffend than those treated for at least 2 years. Therefore, it seemed that shorter treatment periods might be of limited value for this client group. In another comparison of convenience, Keeling, Rose, and Beech (2007) compared 11 'special needs' offenders and 11 mainstream offenders matched on level of risk, victim choice, offence type and age. The authors noted a number of limitations including (1) the fact that 'special needs' was not synonymous with ID, and, as a result, they were unable to verify the intellectual differences between the mainstream and special needs populations, (2) the fact that the treatments were not directly comparable and (3) the fact that assessments for the special needs population were modified. There were few differences between groups post-treatment but follow-up data identified that none of the offenders (neither completers nor non-completers) in either group committed further sexual offences, although completers had a longer average post-release period.

In a further series of comparisons, Lindsay and colleagues have compared individuals with ID who have committed sexual offences with those who have committed other types of offences. Lindsay, Allen *et al.* (2004) compared 106 men who had committed sexual offences or sexually abusive incidents with 78 men who had committed other types of offences or serious incidents. There was a significantly higher rate of reoffending in the non-sexual offender cohort (51%) when compared to the sex offender cohort (19%). In a subsequent, more comprehensive evaluation, Lindsay *et al.* (2006) compared 121 sex offenders with 105 other types of male offenders and 21 female offenders. Reoffending rates were reported for up to 12 years after the index offence. There were no significant differences between the groups on IQ, and the sex offender cohort tended to be older than the other two cohorts. Female offenders had higher rates of mental illness, although rates for male cohorts were generally high at around 31%. These high rates of mental illness in sex offender cohorts have been found by other researchers (Day, 1994). The differences in reoffending rates between the three groups was highly significant, with rates of 23.9% for male sex offenders, 19% for female offenders and 59% for other types of male offenders. The significant differences were evident for every year of follow-up except year 1. These authors also investigated harm reduction by following up the number of offences committed by recidivists and found that, for those who reoffended, the number of offences following treatment, up to 12 years, was a quarter to a third of those recorded before treatment, indicating a considerable amount of harm reduction as a result of intervention. Therefore, although these treatment comparisons have been less than satisfactory in terms of their experimental design, there are some indications that treatment interventions may significantly reduce recidivism rates in sex offenders with ID. Where recidivism does occur, treatment may result in fewer abusive incidents.

A number of large-scale studies have been published reviewing the outcome of sex offender treatment programmes. Unfortunately, the main treatment comparison studies have a number of serious limitations. The first is that they have not used a waiting list control group or no treatment control group. Most of the reports have employed comparisons of convenience, such as other types of offenders or sex offenders without IDD. The second limitation is that, in at least one of the studies (McGrath, Livingstone, & Falk, 2007), most of the participants continued to be supervised and monitored at all times. The third difficulty is that, in some of the studies, the numbers are very small (e.g., Lindsay & Smith 1998). In a more recent small-scale study, Keeling et al. (2007) compared 11 special needs offenders and 11 other mainstream offenders matched on level of risk, sex of victim, offence type and age. All participants were treated in prison, and all were released into the community with an average time from release of 16 months. There were no significant differences between the groups on any assessments on victim empathy, emotional loneliness and social intimacy, but no further sex offences were recorded for any of the special needs disciplines at the follow-up point. This was noteworthy since, following release from prison and discharge from treatment, the participants did not continue to be monitored.

In a large-scale study, McGrath et al. (2007) evaluated the effect on sex offenders of a total deinstitutionalization programme in Vermont, United States. They reviewed the treatment and management regimes of 103 adult sex offenders with IDD, all of who lived in staffed or private homes with paid caregivers. Social and daily living skills were taught to participants, and they were encouraged to interact in the community. There were also treatments to promote skills in managing risk. In an 11-year follow-up period, with an average of 5.8 years follow-up, they reported 10.2% reoffending. The 11 individuals who reoffended committed 20 new sexual offences. As a comparison, they reported on 195 treated and untreated adult male sexual offenders without IDD who had been followed up for an average period of 5.7 years. These individuals had received a prison sentence and from these 21.3% were charged with a new sexual offence at some point within the follow up period. One of the difficulties with the McGrath et al. (2007) evaluation was that 62% of participants received 24-hour supervision, which presumably limited access to potential victims. However, the authors also considered that the level of supervision resulted in a more comprehensive identification of future incidents when compared to the comparison cohort. Importantly, they also reported a considerable amount of harm reduction, in that 83% of the participants were classified as contact sexual offenders while only 45% of the reoffences were contact offences. The rest were typified by exhibitionism and public masturbation.

Murphy et al. (2010) conducted a treatment study on 46 sex offenders with IDD who were living in community settings. Treatment groups ran over a period of 1 year, and assessments included several attitudinal measures including the QACSO. Treatment was manualized and conducted across a number of different settings and services. The manual described methods for dealing with a number of issues and any treatment effect is difficult to ascribe to any particular treatment procedure. They found that sexual knowledge, victim empathy and cognitive distortions had improved significantly following treatment but that only improvements in sexual knowledge and reduced cognitive distortions were maintained at 6-month follow-up. They also reported that 8.7% of their sample reoffended after the treatment programme. Although they had intended to include a control group, this proved impossible because of procedural difficulties. Heaton and Murphy (2013) have demonstrated further effectiveness in a follow-up study over 1 year for these participants.

In a 20-year follow-up of the community forensic IDD service, reported earlier, Lindsay et al. (2013) followed up 156 sexual offenders. All had received at least 4 weeks assessment and appropriate treatment directed at their criminogenic need. Survival analysis found that, although around half of the recidivism for the sex offenders happened within 1 year, some individuals continued to reoffend for up to 9 years. However, following that, there was no further recidivism for up to 20 years. Of the 156 sexual offenders, 16% reoffended in this lengthy follow-up period. These authors also calculated the amount of harm reduction that occurred when comparing the number of offences prior to the referral and up to 20 years after referral. They found that there was over 95% harm reduction in this comparison.

Four additional treatment studies, all of which have been conducted on community referrals, have been published relatively recently. Lindsay, Michie et al. (2011) conducted a comparison between 15 men with IDD who had committed sexual offences with adults and another 15 with IDD who had committed sexual offences against children. All were treated for 36 months using approaches manualized by Lindsay (2009); repeated measures were taken on cognitive distortions supporting or mitigating sexual offences, and records were kept on reoffending for all individuals. By the end of treatment, both groups endorsed cognitive distortions at a low rate consistent with non-offending and non-sexual offending males (with a large effect size). All individuals were followed up for at least 6 years, and, of the 30 participants, seven went on to another incident giving a reoffending rate of 23.3%, a result which was consistent with other reported studies.

Craig, Stringer, and Sanders (2012) reported on 14 sexual offenders treated under probation orders or prison licenses. Participants improved in all measures, and there had been no further incidents at 12-month follow-up. One important note in their report was that all group members were living in the community without daily supervision. Therefore, in contrast to some previous reports (e.g., Craig et al., 2005, McGrath et al., 2007), the participants in this study could have offended at any time. Rose et al. (2012) conducted a treatment study in a community setting with 12 men who had free, unescorted access to the community. Following treatment, there were improvements on measures of sexual attitudes and knowledge, and, at 18 months follow-up, one of the men had a further sexual incident. Again, the essential point about this study is that the men had unescorted access to the community. Unfortunately, in both these previous reports, there were no control conditions. A final study by Michie and Lindsay (2012) was a controlled evaluation of a treatment component within a sex offender programme designed to enhance empathy in participants with IDD. They compared 10 sex offenders and 10 matched controls with IDD and found significant improvements in the treatment group compared to the control group who were receiving sex offender treatment without the empathy component. These improvements continued to the 6-month and 9-month follow-up assessments.

The three reports by Lindsay et al. (2013), McGrath et al. (2007) and Murphy et al. (2010) constitute major evaluations of sex offender IDD treatment services. All have demonstrated significant treatment effectiveness in the one area that is of paramount importance for social policy – that is, reduction in offending incidents over long periods of time. In all three reports, these reductions in reoffending have been shown to be the case both in comparison to other sex offender groups and in comparison to the rate of previous offending. In three reports (Craig et al. 2012; Lindsay et al. 2013; Murphy et al. 2010), therapists have followed detailed, manualized treatment. In addition, the major evaluations have been conducted by different research groups. However, the comparison groups are ones of convenience and are not optimum. There has been no random allocation to treatment conditions and no waiting list control except for the study by Michie and Lindsay (2012), which evaluated only one component of the sex offender treatment programme. While all the studies had at least 12 months follow-up, and up to 20 years follow-up, and some are uncontaminated by constant supervision, they did not have alternative treatment conditions and, because of the nature of treatment and the retention of information, the studies cannot employ a condition whereby participants return to baseline circumstances as would be the case in a planned behaviour analysis. Despite that, there is an undoubted weight of evidence that would support the use of sex offender treatment within a forensic IDD setting.

Based on the limited evidence available, it is possible to conclude tentatively that, in terms of treatment of sex offenders with ID, psychologically informed and structured interventions appear to yield reasonable outcomes. Cognitive behavioural treatment may have a positive effect on offence-related attitudes and cognitions, and longer periods of treatment result in better outcomes that are maintained for longer periods.

Interventions for other offence-related problems

A number of case studies have been reported on the treatment of fire setters with ID. In an early study, Rice and Chaplin (1979) conducted a study that involved the delivery of a social skills training intervention to two groups of five fire setters in a high-security psychiatric facility in North America. One of the groups was reported to be functioning in the mild-borderline ID range. Following treatment, both groups improved significantly on a reliable observation scale of role-played assertive behaviour. At the time of reporting, eight out of the 10 patients treated in the study had been discharged for around 12 months with no reconviction or suspected fire setting. Clare, Murphy, Cox, and Chaplin (1992) reported a case study involving a man with mild ID who had been admitted to a secure hospital following convictions for two offences of arson. He had a prior history of arson and making hoax calls to the fire service. Following his transfer to a specialist in-patient unit, using a comprehensive treatment package, including social skills and assertiveness training, development of coping strategies, covert sensitization and facial surgery (for a significant facial disfigurement), significant clinical improvements were observed in targeted areas. Clearly, it is difficult to parcel out the impact of various components, especially the psychological treatment against facial surgery, but the client was discharged to a community setting and had not engaged in any fire-related offending behaviour at 30 months follow-up.

Taylor, Thorne, and Slavkin (2004) reported a case series of four detained men with ID and convictions for arson offences. They received a cognitive behavioural, 40-session, group-based intervention that involved work on offence cycles, education about the costs associated with setting fires, training skills to enhance future coping with emotional problems associated with previous fire-setting behaviour and work on personalized plans to prevent relapse. The treatment successfully engaged these patients, all of who completed the programme delivered over a period of 4 months. Despite their intellectual and cognitive limitations, all participants showed high levels of motivation and commitment that were reflected in generally improved attitudes with regard to personal responsibility, victim issues and awareness of risk factors associated with their fire-setting behaviour. In a further series of case studies on six women with mild-borderline ID and histories of fire setting, Taylor et al. (2006) also employed a group intervention. The intervention successfully engaged participants in the therapy process, all completed the programme, and scores on measures related to fire treatment targets generally improved following the intervention. All but one of the treatment group participants had been discharged to community placements at 2-year follow-up, and there had been no reports of participants setting any fires or engaging in fire-risk-related behaviour. The results of these small and methodologically weak pilot studies do provide some limited encouragement and guidance to practitioners concerning the utility of group-based, cognitive behavioural interventions for fire-setting behaviour in people with ID.

One of the main developments in offender rehabilitation over the last 15 years has been the introduction of programmes to improve cognitive skills in relation to social and offence-related problem situations such as those involving violence, theft and fire-raising offences. These cognitive skills programmes aim to change beliefs and attitudes that support offending. The purpose of cognitive skills programmes is to equip offenders with thinking skills which will promote alternative, pro-social means of approaching social situations, including high-risk situations in which the person is at risk of offending. In a wider context, these alternative thinking skills will allow the individual to move out of the habits of an offending lifestyle which may have been reinforced by inadequate and criminal thinking styles.

Several criminal thinking programmes have emerged, and the two most dominant approaches have been Moral Reconation Therapy (MRT: Little & Robinson, 1988) and Reasoning and Rehabilitation (R&R: Ross & Fabiano, 1985). A number of reviewers have considered the effectiveness of up to 20 evaluation studies and have concluded that there is reasonable evidence for significant reductions in offending for programme participants (Wilson, Bouffard, & MacKenzie, 2005; Allan, MacKenzie, & Hickman, 2001; Joy Tong & Farrington, 2006). Given the difficulties that offenders with ID are likely to have

with intellectual and moral development, it is surprising that these programmes have not spread to this field, other than some pilot investigations (Doyle & Hamilton, 2006). Recently, Lindsay, Hamilton et al. (2011) have conducted a study reviewing the effectiveness of an adapted cognitive skills programme for offenders with ID. The programme is based on the theoretical work of D'Zurilla and Nezu (1999), drawing heavily on the 'Stop and Think' programme (McMurran, Fyffe, McCarthy, Duggan, & Latham, 2001), which is an offence-related problem-solving programme for offenders with personality disorder. In an evaluation of 10 participants who had completed the programme, they found reductions in measured impulsiveness and increases in positive style and orientation towards social problem-solving. Therefore, there was some limited evidence that assessment and treatment of criminal thinking styles may be a suitable addition to general work on offenders with ID.

CONCLUSIONS

Evaluations for forensic IDD services have been conducted over the last 60 years and are continuing. When one considers that the first evaluation was a 20-year follow-up published in 1962, then researchers have been gathering outcome data since the early 1940s. Studies have shown that, while the reoffending rates are relatively high at around 50%, the number and severity of incidents is considerably lower, indicating significant amounts of harm reduction.

There have been a number of important advances and developments in the treatment of offenders with ID. Treatment methods have been based on cognitive behaviour therapy and have also employed specific methods to adapt procedures for the client group. The most significant treatment innovations have been in the field of anger management, where structured programmes have been published, and these programmes have been evaluated by a number of controlled comparisons. The comparisons have employed waiting list controls and random allocation, and there have been no systematic pre-treatment differences reported between experimental and control groups. As a result, the positive outcomes can be regarded with some confidence, and it may be suggested that anger management treatment programmes should be incorporated into the general management of violence and aggressive offenders with ID. The second main development to treatment has been in cognitive behavioural approaches for sexual offenders. There have been a number of single-case reports producing encouraging results and, more importantly, employing lengthy follow-up periods of up to 7 years. Controlled comparisons have produced positive outcomes, although their methodological integrity has not been particularly sound, and results should be treated with critical caution. For other offence-related programmes, the evidence is more piecemeal. There have been several treatment case studies for fire raisers with ID, all of which have provided promising outcomes. Controlled evaluation of these treatment techniques is certainly required. In relation to social problem-solving and offence-related thinking, one study has been conducted on the development of a suitably adapted programme for offenders with ID. The results were positive, suggesting improvements in cognitive skills for participants.

Major outcome studies for offenders with ID have shown significant impacts that services have had on reduced reoffending and harm reduction.

The upshot of the last 25 years of clinical and research work in the field is that appropriate assessments are now available for a range of criminal justice issues and offence-related difficulties, and many of these assessments have been applied to this population with appropriate reliability, validity and factor analytic studies. We know the effects of risk assessment and risk management and have some initial understanding into criminal justice trajectories. A number of treatments have been adapted and may be employed for a range of relevant difficulties, although some of these have not been subjected to controlled experimental trials.

FURTHER READING

American Psychiatric Association (1994). *Diagnostic and statistical manual of mental disorders* (4th edn). Washington DC: Author.

Hayes, S. (1991). Sex offenders. *Australia & New Zealand Journal of Developmental Disabilities (Journal of Intellectual & Developmental Disabilities)*, 17, 220–227.

Hingsburger, D., Griffiths, D., & Quinsey, V. (1991). Detecting counterfeit deviance: Differentiating sexual deviance from sexual inappropriateness. *Habilitative Mental Healthcare Newsletter*, 10, 51–54.

Jackson, H. F., Glass, C., & Hope, S. (1987). A functional analysis of recidivistic arson. *British Journal of Clinical Psychology*, 26, 175–185.

Lindsay, W. R. (2009). *The treatment of sex offenders with developmental disabilities: A practice workbook*. Chichester, UK: John Wiley & Sons. This text provides a detailed account of working with sex offenders with developmental disabilities. The text covers background research and practice issues in the area and goes on to cover clinical practice issues in detail.

Lindsay, W. R., Smith, A. H. W., Law, J., Quinn, K., Anderson, A., Smith, A., Overend, T., & Allan, R. (2002). A treatment service for sex offenders and abusers with intellectual disability: Characteristics of referrals and evaluation. *Journal of Applied Research in Intellectual Disability*, 15, 166–174.

Lunsky, Y., Frijters, J., Griffiths, D. M., Watson, S. L., & Williston, S. (2007). Sexual knowledge and attitudes of men with intellectual disabilities who sexually offend. *Journal of Intellectual & Developmental Disability*, 32, 74–81.

Novaco, R. W., & Taylor, J. L. (2004). Assessment of anger and aggression in offenders with developmental disabilities. *Psychological Assessment*, 16, 42–50.

Sturmey, P. (2004). Cognitive therapy with people with intellectual disabilities: A selective review and critique. *Clinical Psychology & Psychotherapy*, 11, 222–232.

Wheeler, J. R., Holland, A. J., Bambrick, M., Lindsay, W. R., Carson, D., Steptoe, L., Johnston, S., Taylor, J. L., Middleton, C., Price, K., & O'Brien, G. (2009). Community services and people with intellectual disabilities who engage in anti-social or offending behaviour: referral rates, characteristics, and care pathways. *Journal of Forensic Psychiatry & Psychology*, 20, 717–740.

REFERENCES

Alexander, R. T., Crouch, K., Halstead, S., & Piachaud, J. (2006). Long-term outcome from a medium secure service for people with intellectual disability. *Journal of Intellectual Disability Research*, 50, 305–315.

Allan, L. C., MacKenzie, D. L., & Hickman, L. J. (2001). The effectiveness of cognitive behavioral treatment for adult offenders: A methodological, quality-based review. *International Journal of Offender Therapy and Comparative Criminology*, 45(4), 498–514.

Allan, R., Lindsay, W. R., Macleod, F., & Smith, A. H. W. (2001). Treatment of women with intellectual disabilities who have been involved with the criminal justice system for reasons of aggression. *Journal of Applied Research in Intellectual Disabilities*, 14, 340–347.

Black, L., & Novaco, R. W. (1993). Treatment of anger with a developmentally disabled man. In R. A. Wells & V. J. Giannetti (Eds.), *Casebook of the brief psychotherapies*. New York: Plenum Press.

British Psychological Society (2000). *Learning disability: Definitions and contexts*. Leicester: BPS.

Burns, M., Bird, D., Leach, C., & Higgins, K. (2003). Anger management training: The effects of a structured programme on the self-reported anger experience of forensic inpatients with learning disability. *Journal of Psychiatric and Mental Health Nursing, 10,* 569–577.

Clare, I. C. H., & Murphy, G. H. (1993) MIETS (Mental impairment evaluation and treatment service): A service option for people with mild mental handicaps and challenging behaviour and/or psychiatric problems. *Mental Handicap Research (Journal of Applied Research in Intellectual Disabilities), 6,* 70–91.

Clare, I. C. H., Murphy, G. H., Cox, D., & Chaplin, E. H. (1992). Assessment and treatment of fire setting: A single case investigation using a cognitive behavioural model. *Criminal Behaviour & Mental Health, 2,* 253–268.

Courtney, J., Rose, J., & Mason, O. (2006). The offence process of sex offenders with intellectual disabilities: A qualitative study. *Sexual Abuse: A Journal of Research & Treatment, 18,* 169–191.

Craig, L. A., Stringer, I., & Moss, T. (2006). Treating sexual offenders with learning disabilities in the community. *International Journal of Offender Therapy & Comparative Criminology, 50,* 111–122.

Craig, L. A., Stringer, I., & Sanders, C. E. (2012). Treating sex offenders with intellectual limitations in the community. *The British Journal of Forensic Practice, 14,* 5–20.

Day, K. (1994). Male mentally handicapped sex offenders. *British Journal of Psychiatry, 165,* 630–639.

Doyle, M. C., & Hamilton, C. (2006). An evaluation of a social problem solving group work programme for offenders with ID. *Journal of Applied Research in Intellectual Disabilities, 19,* 257.

Dozier, C., Iwata, B., & Worsdell, A. (2011) Assessment and treatment of foot – shoe fetishism displayed by a man with autism. *Journal of Applied Behaviour Analysis, 44,* 133–137.

D'Zurilla, T. J., & Nezu, A. M. (1999). *Problem solving therapy: A social competence approach to clinical interventions* (2nd edn). New York: Springer.

Gibbens, T. C., & Robertson, G. (1983). A survey of the criminal careers of restriction order patients. *British Journal of Psychiatry, 143,* 370–375.

Gray, N. S., Fitzgerald, S., Taylor, J., MacCulloch, M. J., & Snowden, R. J. (2007). Predicting future reconviction in offenders with intellectual disabilities: The predictive efficacy of VRAG, PCL-SV and the HCR-20. *Psychological Assessment, 19,* 474–479.

Griffiths, D., & Lunsky, Y. (2003). *Sociosexual knowledge and attitudes assessment tool* (SSKAAT-R). Wood Dale, IL: Stoelting Company.

Griffiths, D. M., Quinsey, V. L., & Hingsburger, D. (1989). *Changing inappropriate sexual behaviour: A community based approach for persons with developmental disabilities.* Baltimore: Paul Brooks Publishing.

Grubb-Blubaugh, V., Shire, B. J., & Baulser, M. L. (1994). Behaviour management and offenders with mental retardation: The jury system. *Mental Retardation, 32,* 213–217.

Haaven, J., Little, R., & Petre-Miller, D. (1990). *Treating intellectually disabled sex offenders: A model residential programme.* Safer Society Press: Orwell, V.T.

Hanson, R. K., Gordon, A., Harris, A. J. R., Marques, J. K., Murphy, W., Quinsey, V. L., & Seto, M. C. (2002). First report of the collaborative outcome data project on the effectiveness of psychological treatment for sex offenders. *Sexual Abuse: A Journal of Research & Treatment, 14,* 169–194.

Heaton, K., & Murphy, G. (2013). Men with intellectual disabilities who have attended sex offender treatment groups: A follow up. *Journal of Applied Research in Intellectual Disabilities, 26,* 489–500.

Keeling, J. A., Rose, J. L., & Beech, A. R. (2007). Comparing sexual offender treatment efficacy: Mainstream sexual offenders and sexual offenders with special needs. *Journal of Intellectual & Developmental Disability, 32,* 117–124.

Lindsay, W. R. (2004). Sex offenders: Conceptualisation of the issues, services, treatment and management. In W. R. Lindsay, J. L. Taylor, & P. Sturmey (Eds.), *Offenders with developmental disabilities* (pp. 163–186). Chichester: John Wiley.

Lindsay, W. R. (2009) *The treatment of sex offenders with intellectual disability: A manualised approach.* Chichester: John Wiley.

Lindsay, W. R., Allan, R., Macleod, F., Smart, N., & Smith, A. H. W. (2003). Long term treatment and management of violent tendencies of men with intellectual disabilities convicted of assault. *Mental Retardation, 41,* 47–56.

Lindsay, W. R., Allan, R., Parry, C., Macleod, F., Cottrell, J., Overend, H., & Smith, A. H. W. (2004). Anger and aggression in people with intellectual disabilities: Treatment and follow-up of consecutive referrals and a waiting list comparison. *Clinical Psychology & Psychotherapy, 11,* 255–264.

Lindsay, W. R., Hamilton, C., Moulton, S., Scott, S., Doyle, M., & McMurran, M. (2011). Assessment and treatment of social problem solving in offenders with intellectual disability. *Psychology, Crime & Law, 17,* 181–197.

Lindsay, W. R., Marshall, I., Neilson, C. Q., Quinn, K., & Smith, A. H. W. (1998a). The treatment of men with a learning disability convicted of exhibitionism. *Research on Developmental Disabilities, 19,* 295–316.

Lindsay, W. R., Michie, A. M., Haut, F., Steptoe, L., & Moore, F. (2011). Comparing offenders against women and offenders against children on treatment outcome for offenders with intellectual disability. *Journal of Applied Research in Intellectual Disability, 24,* 361–369.

Lindsay, W. R., Neilson, C. Q., Morrison, F., & Smith, A. H. W. (1998b). The treatment of six men with a learning disability convicted of sex offences with children. *British Journal of Clinical Psychology, 37,* 83–98.

Lindsay, W. R., Olley, S., Jack, C., Morrison, F., & Smith, A. H. W. (1998c). The treatment of two stalkers with intellectual disabilities using a cognitive approach. *Journal of Applied Research in Intellectual Disabilities, 11*, 333–344.

Lindsay, W. R., & Smith, A. H. W. (1998). Responses to treatment for sex offenders with intellectual disability: A comparison of men with 1 and 2 year probation sentences. *Journal of Intellectual Disability Research, 42*, 346–353.

Lindsay, W. R., Smith, A. H. W., Law, J., Quinn, K., Anderson, A., Smith, A., & Allan, R. (2004). Sexual and non-sexual offenders with intellectual and learning disabilities: A comparison of characteristics, referral patterns and outcome. *Journal of Interpersonal Violence, 19*, 875–890.

Lindsay, W. R., Steele, L., Smith, A. H. W., Quinn, K., & Allan, R. (2006). A community forensic intellectual disability service: Twelve year follow-up of referrals, analysis of referral patterns and assessment of harm reduction. *Legal & Criminological Psychology, 11*, 113–130.

Lindsay, W. R., Steptoe, L., Wallace, L., Haut, F., & Brewster, E. (2013). An evaluation and 20 year follow up of recidivism in a community intellectual disability service. *Criminal Behaviour and Mental Health, 23*, 138–149.

Lindsay, W. R., Sturmey, P., & Taylor, J. L. (2004). Natural history and theories of offending in people with developmental disabilities. In W. R. Lindsay, J. L. Taylor, & P. Sturmey (Eds.), *Offenders with developmental disabilities* (pp. 3–22). Chichester: John Wiley.

Lindsay, W. R., Taylor, J. L., & Sturmey, P. (2004). *Offenders with developmental disabilities*. Chichester: John Wiley.

Lindsay, W. R., Whitefield, E., & Carson, D. (2007). An assessment for attitudes consistent with sexual offending for use with offenders with intellectual disability. *Legal and Criminological Psychology, 12*, 55–68.

Little, G. L., Robinson, K. D. (1988). Moral reconation therapy: A systematic step-by-step treatment system for treatment resistant clients. *Psychological Reports, 62*, 135–151.

Lund, J. (1990). Mentally retarded criminal offenders in Denmark. *British Journal of Psychiatry, 156*, 726–731.

McGrath, R. J., Livingston, J. A., & Falk, G. (2007). Community management of sex offenders with intellectual disability: Characteristics, services and outcome of a Statewide programme. *Intellectual and Developmental Disabilities, 45*, 391–98.

McMurran, M., Fyffe, S., McCarthy, L., Duggan, C., & Latham, A. (2001). Stop and think!: Social problem solving therapy with personality disordered offenders. *Criminal Behaviour & Mental Health, 11*, 273–285.

Meichenbaum, D. (1985). *Stress inoculation training*. New York: Pergamon Press.

Michie, A. M., & Lindsay, W. R. (2012) A treatment component designed to enhance empathy in sex offenders with intellectual disability. *The British Journal of Forensic Practice, 14*, 40–48.

Murphy, G. H., Sinclair, N., Hays, S. J., Heaton, K., Powell, S., Langdon, P., Stagg, J., Williams, J., Scott, J., Mercer, K., Lippold, T., Tufnell, J., Langheit, G., Goodman, W., Leggett, J., & Craig, L. (SOTSEC-ID) (2010). Effectiveness of group cognitive-behavioural treatment for men with intellectual disabilities at risk of sexual offending. *Journal of Applied Research in Intellectual Disabilities, 26*, 537–551.

Murphy, G., & Clare, I. (1991). MIETS: A service option for people with mild mental handicaps and challenging behaviour or psychiatric problems. *Mental Handicap Research, 4*, 180–206.

Novaco, R. W. (1975). *Anger control: The development and evaluation of an experimental treatment*. Heath, Lexington, MA.

Novaco, R. W. (1994). Anger as a risk factor for violence among the mentally disordered. In J. Monahan & H. J. Steadman (Eds.), *Violence in mental disorder: Developments in risk assessment*. Chicago: University of Chicago Press.

Plaud, J. J., Plaud, D. M., Colstoe, P. D., & Orvedal, L. (2000). Behavioural treatment of sexually offending behaviour. *Mental Health Aspects of Developmental Disabilities, 3*, 54–61.

Rayes, J. R., Vollmer, T. R., & Hall, A. (2011). The influence of presession factors in the assessment of deviant arousal. *Journal of Applied Behaviour Analysis, 44*, 707–717.

Rayes, J. R., Vollmer, T. R., Sloman, K., Hall, A., Reid, R., & Jensen, G. (2006). Assessment of deviant arousal in adult male sex offenders with developmental disabilities. *Journal of Applied Behaviour Analysis, 39*, 173–188.

Rice, M. E., & Chaplin, T. C. (1979). Social skills training for hospitalised male arsonists. *Journal of Behaviour Therapy & Experimental Psychiatry, 10*, 105–108.

Rose, J., Anderson, C., Hawkins, C., & Rose, D. (2012). A community based sex offender treatment group for adults with intellectual disabilities. *British Journal of Forensic Practice, 14*, 21–28.

Rose, J., Loftus, M., Flint, B., & Carey, L. (2005). Factors associated with the efficacy of a group intervention for anger in people with intellectual disabilities. *British Journal of Clinical Psychology, 44*, 305–317.

Rose, J., Jenkins, R., O'Conner, C., Jones, C., & Felce, D. (2002). A group treatment for men with intellectual disabilities who sexually offend or abuse. *Journal of Applied Research in Intellectual Disabilities, 15*, 138–150.

Rose, J., & West, C. (1999). Assessment of anger in people with intellectual disabilities. *Journal of Applied Research in Intellectual Disabilities, 12*, 211–224.

Rose, J., West, C., & Clifford, D. (2000). Group interventions for anger and people with intellectual disabilities. *Research in Developmental Disabilities, 21*, 171–181.

Rose, J., Willner, P., Shead, J., Jahoda, A., Gillespie, D., Townson, J., Lammie, C., Woodgate, C., Stenfert Kroese, B., Felce, D., MacMahon, P., Rose, N., Stimpson, A., Nuttall, J., & Hood, K. (2013). Different factors influence self-reports and third-party reports of anger by adults with intellectual disabilities. *Journal of Applied Research in Intellectual Disabilities, 26*, 410–419.

Ross, R. R., & Fabiano, E. A. (1985). *Time to think: A cognitive model on delinquency prevention and offender rehabilitation*. Tennessee: Institute of Social Sciences and Arts.

Taylor, J. L. (2002). A review of the assessment and treatment of anger and aggression in offenders with intellectual disability. *Journal of Intellectual Disability Research*, 46(Suppl. 1), 57–73.

Taylor, J. L., & Novaco, R. W. (2005). *Anger treatment for people with developmental disabilities: A theory, evidence and manual based approach*. Chichester: Wiley.

Taylor, J. L., Novaco, R. W., Gillmer, B., & Thorne, I. (2002). Cognitive behavioural treatment of anger intensity among offenders with intellectual disabilities. *Journal of Applied Research in Intellectual Disabilities*, 15, 151–165.

Taylor, J. L., Novaco, R. W., Gillmer, B. T., Robertson, A., & Thorne, I. (2005). Individual cognitive behavioural anger treatment for people with mild-borderline intellectual disabilities and histories of aggression: A controlled trial. *British Journal of Clinical Psychology*, 44, 367–382.

Taylor, J. L., Novaco, R. W., Guinan, C., & Street, N. (2004a). Development of an imaginal provocation test to evaluate treatment for anger problems in people with intellectual disabilities. *Clinical Psychology & Psychotherapy*, 11, 233–246.

Taylor, J. L., Robertson, A., Thorne, I., Belshaw, T., & Watson, A. (2006). Responses of female fire-setters with mild and borderline intellectual disabilities to a group based intervention. *Journal of Applied Research in Intellectual Disabilities*, 19, 179–190.

Taylor, J. L., Thorne, I., & Slavkin, M. L. (2004b). Treatment of fire setting behaviour. In W. R. Lindsay, J. L. Taylor, & P. Sturmey (Eds.), *Offenders with developmental disabilities* (pp. 221–240). Chichester: John Wiley.

Tong, J. E., & MacKay, G. W. (1969). A statistical follow-up of mental defectives with dangerous or violent propensities. *British Journal of Delinquency*, 9, 276–284.

Travis, R., & Sturmey, P. (2013). Using behavioral skills training to teach anger management skills to adults with mild intellectual disability . *Journal of Applied Research in Intellectual Disability*, 26, 481–488.

Vollmer, T. R., Rayes, J. R., & Walker, S. (2012). Behavioral assessment and intervention for sex offenders with intellectual and developmental disabilities. In J. Luiselli (Ed.), *The handbook of high risk challenging behaviors in people with intellectual and developmental disabilities* (pp. 121–144). Baltimore. Paul Brooks Publishing.

Walker, N., & McCabe, S. (1973). *Crime and insanity in England*. Edinburgh: Edinburgh University Press.

Wierzbicki, M., & Pekarik, G. (1993). A meta-analysis of psychotherapy drop out. *Professional Psychology: Research & Practice*, 24, 190–195.

Wildenskov, H. O. T. (1962). A long term follow-up of subnormals originally exhibiting severe behaviour disorders or criminality. *Proceedings of the London conference on the scientific study of mental deficiency* (pp. 217–222). London: May & Baker.

Willner, P., Brace, N., & Phillips, J. (2005). Assessment of anger coping skills in individuals with intellectual disabilities. *Journal of Intellectual Disability Research*, 49, 329–339.

Willner, P., Jones, J., Tams, R., & Green, G. (2002). A randomised controlled trial of the efficacy of a cognitive behavioural anger management group for clients with learning disabilities. *Journal of Applied Research in Intellectual Disabilities*, 15, 224–253.

Willner, P., Rose, J., Jahoda, A., Stenfert Kroese, B., Felce, D., Cohen, D., MacMahon, P., Stimpson, A., Rose, N., Gillespie, D., Shead, J., Lammie, C., Woodgate, C., Townson, J., Nuttall, J., & Hood, K. (2013). Group-based cognitive–behavioural anger management for people with mild to moderate intellectual disabilities: Cluster randomised controlled trial. *British Journal of Psychiatry*, 203(3), 288–296.

Wilson, D. B., Bouffard, L. A., & MacKenzie, D. L. (2005). A quantitative review of structured group orientated cognitive behavioural programmes for offenders. *Criminal Justice & Behaviour*, 32, 172–204.

Xenitidis, K. I., Henry, J., Russell, A. J., Ward, A., & Murphy, D. G. (1999). An in-patient treatment model for adults with mild intellectual disability and challenging behaviour. *Journal of Intellectual Disability Research*, 43, 128–134.

16 Personality Disorders: Assessment and Treatment

CONOR DUGGAN AND RICHARD HOWARD

This chapter divides into two main sections. In the first, we address some broad questions regarding the nature of personality disorder (PD), and argue that PD can only properly be understood with reference to normal personality functioning. In the second section, we turn to more practical issues regarding how PD can be assessed and treated in a forensic context. We conclude by considering some issues in the assessment and treatment of PD that will need to be addressed in the future. In addressing these and other questions, we draw heavily on the work of John Livesley, who has made a major contribution to placing the field on a sound scientific footing (Livesley, 2003, 2007a, 2007b).

ISSUES SURROUNDING THE CONCEPT OF PD

What is 'personality disorder'?

We concur with Livesley (2007a) in believing that the study of PD needs to take normal personality functioning as its starting point. The question, then, is whether PDs are simply extreme variations of normal personality, or whether there is a discontinuity between normal and abnormal personality traits.

Differently stated: Is it possible to derive PDs from scores on conventional measures of normal personality variation such as the 'Big Five' from the Five Factor Model (FFM) of Costa and McCrae (1992)? In short, is there something qualitatively different about PD that distinguishes it from the normal range of personality variation, or is there merely a quantitative difference, with disorder representing an extreme position on some traits or dimensions? Livesley and others (e.g., Blackburn, 2000) have argued that the latter position confuses extreme scores on a trait or dimension with disorder – high or low levels on a given trait such as agreeableness or conscientiousness are neither necessary nor sufficient to indicate disordered functioning (Parker & Barrett, 2000; Wakefield, 1992). Blackburn points out that there is an important difference between the extreme of normal conscientiousness – striving for excellence in everything – and the maladaptive conscientiousness associated with obsessive compulsive PD. The same point is made by Livesley (2007a) when he states: 'With PD, it is difficult to see how an extreme position on dimensions such as agreeableness, sociability, or conscientiousness is necessarily pathological. Some additional factor needs to be present to warrant the diagnosis' (p. 203).

What is this additional factor? Livesley (1998) appeals to evolutionary biology in suggesting that PD can be said to be present when 'the structure of personality prevents the person from achieving adaptive solutions to universal life tasks' (p. 141). More specifically, from this evolutionary perspective, PD can be seen as a failure to solve adaptive life tasks relating to three areas: identity or self, intimacy and attachment and prosocial behaviour. Livesley suggests that PDs can be expressed at three different levels: intrapersonal, interpersonal and societal (see Figure 16.1). At the intrapersonal level, PD involves poorly developed or fragmented representations of the self and others. At the interpersonal level, it involves difficulties resolving attachment problems and developing the capacity for sustained intimacy. At the group level, it involves problems with prosocial behaviour, altruism and maintaining the cooperativeness needed for effective social functioning. Problems with prosocial behaviour are of particular concern to forensic psychologists who are confronted with personality-disordered individuals, of whom it is often said that they are difficult, unpleasant and troublesome, and (sometimes) given to breaking social rules, laws and codes of conduct. As with normal personality theorists, clinical classification systems

Forensic Psychology, Second Edition. Edited by David A. Crighton and Graham J. Towl.
© 2015 John Wiley & Sons, Ltd. Published 2015 by British Psychological Society and John Wiley & Sons, Ltd.

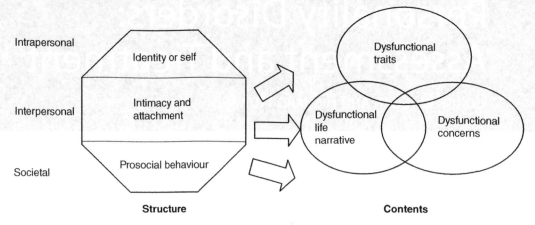

FIGURE 16.1 *A schematic representation of Livesley's conception of personality disorder.*

adopt, either explicitly or implicitly, the trait as the basic taxonomic unit. The International Classification of Diseases-10th revision (ICD-10), for example, defines PD as '… deeply ingrained and enduring behaviour patterns, manifesting themselves as inflexible responses to a broad range of personal and social situations. They represent either extreme or significant deviations from the way the average individual in a given culture perceives, thinks, feels, and particularly relates to others' (ICD-10; World Health Organization, 1992, p.200).

Do the traits of PD overlap with the traits that reflect normal personality variation?

To some extent, the traits of PD are certainly continuous with normal traits. Livesley (2003) points out that it is possible to see a correspondence or continuity between the Big Five factors – Neuroticism, Agreeableness, Extraversion, Conscientiousness and Openness – and major dimensions of PD derived from multivariate analysis of PD traits. Four broad dimensions of PD identified in this way – Emotional Dysregulation, Dissocial Behaviour, Inhibitedness and Compulsivity[1] – correspond broadly to Neuroticism, low Agreeableness, low Extraversion and high Conscientiousness (the 'Big Five') in the Five Factor Model of Costa and McCrae (1992). If one looks, for example, at the primary traits of PD in Table 16.1, derived from phenotypic and behavioural genetic analyses of the Dimensional Assessment of Personality Pathology (DAPP) questionnaire, one sees some examples of overlap. Anxiousness overlaps with Neuroticism, for example, and Stimulus Seeking with Impulsivity. However, most of the primary traits listed in Table 16.1 describe traits that are dysfunctional, in the sense that they are inimical to the attainment of major life tasks, and as such they represent 'the dark side' of a normal personality. Another instrument that was developed to capture the range of dysfunctional traits found in PDs is the MMPI-based PSY-5, which identifies five major domains: Neuroticism, Disconstraint, Introversion/Low Positive Emotionality, Aggressiveness and Psychoticism (Harkness & McNulty, 1994). A comparison of the PSY-5 with the Five Factor Model conducted by Bagby, Sellbom, Costa, and Widiger (2008) found the PSY-5 to be superior in capturing four of the PDs most associated with externalizing and disturbance of thought, namely: paranoid, schizotypal, antisocial and narcissistic PDs. The Neuroticism, Disconstraint, and Introversion/Low Positive Emotionality domains identified in the PSY-5 correspond rather closely to the domains of Emotional Dysregulation, Dissocial Behaviour and Inhibitedness, respectively, in Livesley's schema shown in Table 16.1. We can conclude, in answering the question raised at the beginning of this section, that while there is some continuity between normal and abnormal traits, personality-disordered individuals nonetheless show a range of dysfunctional traits that are not well captured by instruments designed to measure normal personality variation.

This is illustrated by considering a global trait such as impulsivity. It is particular facets of this trait that appear to be dysfunctional in PDs, in particular the sensation-seeking and risk-taking aspects captured by some (e.g., Blackburn's [1971] MMPI-derived measure), but by no means all impulsivity measures. Derivation of the primary traits shown in Table 16.1 was informed by behavioural genetic analyses which indicated that the genetic factor that explained most of the variance in sensation seeking and recklessness did not explain the genetic variance in impulsivity, which was influenced by a genetic factor specific to itself. Therefore, stimulus seeking, originally a primary trait, was split into the separate primary traits of Impulsivity and Sensation Seeking, shown in Table 16.1. A recent review of longitudinal studies linking childhood impulsivity to adult violence (Jolliffe & Farrington, 2009) concluded that the sensation-seeking/risk-taking aspect of impulsivity best predicts violent offending in later life. A neurophysiological correlate of Blackburn's Impulsivity measure, capturing

TABLE 16.1 *Thirty primary traits organized into four secondary domains (Livesley, 2007a; 2007b). The four secondary domains are said to be aetiologically distinct insofar as all traits in a domain are influenced by the same general genetic module which has minimal effect on other domains (Livesley, 2008, p. 46).*

Secondary Domain	Primary Trait
Emotional Dysregulation	Anxiousness
	Emotional reactivity
	Emotional intensity
	Pessimistic anhedonia
	Submissiveness
	Insecure attachment
	Social apprehensiveness
	Need for approval
	Cognitive dysregulation
	Oppositional
	Self-harming acts
	Self-harming ideas
Dissocial Behaviour	Narcissism
	Exploitativeness
	Sadism
	Conduct problems
	Hostile-dominance
	Sensation seeking
	Impulsivity
	Suspiciousness
	Egocentrism
Inhibitedness	Low affiliation
	Avoidant attachment
	Attachment need
	Inhibited sexuality
	Self-containment
	Inhibited emotional expression
	Lack of empathy
Compulsivity	Orderliness
	Conscientiousness

the sensation-seeking aspect of impulsivity, has been found to predict with reasonable accuracy both general and violent reoffending in mentally disordered offenders released into the community (Howard & Lumsden, 1996, 1997). It can be concluded from these findings that it is the sensation-seeking and affective dyscontrol aspects of impulsivity, representing its 'dark side', that predispose to antisocial behaviour.

Is PD no more than a set of dysfunctional traits?

Livesley (2007b) argues cogently that there is much more to PD than simply a set of dysfunctional traits:

The pathology associated with PD includes not only problems with the contents of personality – regulatory problems, maladaptive behaviours and cognitions, and dysfunctional traits – but also severe disturbances in the structure or organization of personality. These disturbances range at the most global level from the failure to forge a cohesive self-structure capable of integrating cognitions and affects and connecting different aspects of self-experience. Such focal problems are illustrated by the failure of many patients to recognize the situational and experiential factors that trigger a variety of problematic behaviours such as deliberate self-harm or interpersonal violence (p. 30).

Thus, Livesley suggests two levels of construct in addition to the trait level: *personal concerns*, including motives, roles, goals and coping strategies; and *the life narrative*, which provides an integrated account of the past, present and future.

A curious feature of trait-based theories of personality, and accounts of PD, is that they assume temporal and situational stability. Yet, as pointed out by some personality theorists (e.g., Apter, 2005), what characterizes normal human behaviour and experience is precisely a *lack* of stability, evidenced by a tendency for people to switch rapidly between opponent modes of experiencing the world and their actions in it – for example, between a playful, hedonistic state and a serious-minded, future-orientated state. According to this view, stability, rather than instability, is dysfunctional and characterizes the experience and behaviour of personality-disordered individuals, who often appear 'stuck' in a particular experiential mode. Someone who is 'stuck' in a playful state, for example, would be constantly striving to avoid boredom by seeking high-arousal situations, and would lack any focus on the future. This accords with Livesley's description of personality-disordered patients, most of whom '… live in the present and have difficulty formulating and working towards long-term goals' (Livesley, 2007b, p. 40). This lack of changeability is acknowledged by Diagnostic and Statistical Manual (DSM) when it refers to the traits of personality-disordered individuals as *rigid and inflexible*.

What is the implication of this for the assessment of PD, to which we turn next? First, it would be as mistaken to classify PDs just in terms of normal personality variation as it would be to classify language disorders simply in terms of normal language. To do so, in either case, would be to ignore the discontinuity that exists between the normal and the abnormal, albeit the boundary between the two is sometimes unclear. Second, while an assessment of dysfunctional traits is a necessary component in an assessment of a PD, particularly for an assessment of what Livesley (2007a) refers to as the *contents* of personality, it is not sufficient. Also required is an assessment of the disturbance in the structure or organization of personality. In particular, one needs to address the question, first, of whether a PD is present. Livesley (2003) points out that a set of criteria needs to be worked out to assess this in terms of global disturbance in the three domains outlined earlier: intrapersonal, interpersonal and societal. Then, in addition to an assessment of dysfunctional traits, one ideally would like an assessment of the individual's motives, roles, goals and coping strategies as he or she experiences them, as well as the experienced life narrative. In the next section, we will review briefly the assessments that are currently available for an evaluation of PDs, particularly in forensic contexts. To a large extent, these are confined to an assessment of dysfunctional traits. The development of assessment tools to tap the other two levels mentioned earlier has largely been neglected, with two notable exceptions, the General Assessment of Personality Disorder (GAPD) and the Personal Concerns Inventory: Offender Adaptation (PCI-OSA). See the Self-Report measures in the following text.

Problems with assessing PD

There are major problems with the current classification of PD, especially as conceived by DSM-1V (for a review, see Tyrer *et al.*, 2007). These difficulties include poor reliability between differing instruments and a problem of overlap between the differing PD diagnoses (Benjamin, 1993), but also of inadequate capture of important aspects of personality pathology for the clinician (Westen & Arkowitz-Westen, 1998). Moreover, in addition to the convergent validity between differing instruments being poor, current classifications are found wanting in two crucial aspects for a clinician as they fail to indicate prognosis and do not provide clear guidance on treatment interventions (Clark, 2007; Clark, Livesley, & Morey, 1997).

While it is tempting therefore to dismiss the current classification in the assessment of PD and start again, this approach is unhelpful for the student who will be faced with personality-disordered individuals to assess and manage. Many of these will be familiar to the practitioner, and it seems pointless to adopt a completely new system, however flawed the old system may be. This section will therefore critically examine some of the approaches to the assessment of PD before indicating an approach that is practical and has a sound theoretical basis. Among the key questions in assessment are the

following: Which is the best method for assessing PD? Who should be the informant? What level of training is required to conduct the assessment?

Methods of assessing PD

Methods of assessment can be conveniently grouped into: (a) unstructured clinical interview; (b) self-report inventories and semi-structured interviews; and (c) observer-rated measures.

Unstructured clinical interviews

The main problem in using unstructured clinical interviews is their poor reliability (Zimmerman, 1994). For instance, Mellsop, Varghese, Joshua, and Hicks (1982) found a kappa coefficient of .41 for the presence of any PD, with the coefficient for specific disorders ranging from .01 to .49, when they assessed the reliability of clinical assessment of PD. Thus, the reliability of unstructured clinical interview is so low that it ought to be discouraged.

Self-report questionnaires

The main advantages of self-report questionnaires are: (a) their ease and low cost of administration; (b) their freedom from systematic interviewer bias; and (c) their results can be compared to normative data. There are a number of self-report instruments available to assess PD, including: the Millon Clinical Multiaxial Inventory, now in its third version (MCMI-III; Millon, T., Millon, C., & Davis, 1994); the Personality Diagnostic Questionnaire – Revised (PDQ-R; Hyler & Rieder, 1987); the Personality Assessment Inventory (PAI; Morey, 1991); and the Antisocial Personality Questionnaire (APQ; Blackburn & Fawcett, 1999). Despite their advantages, the evidence is that questionnaires tend to over-diagnose PDs when compared to semi-structured interviews, and that they do so by a significant order of magnitude (e.g., Hunt & Andrews, 1992; Hyler, Skodol, Kellman, Oldham, & Rosnick, 1990, Hyler, Skodol, Oldham, Kellman, & Doidge, 1992). The MCMI in particular has been criticized for yielding excessive prevalence rates (Zimmerman, 1994). Although questionnaires tend to yield higher prevalence rates of disorder, they tend, as Blackburn (2000) points out, to have high specificity – that is, they detect most patients without disorder. On these grounds, it has been suggested that questionnaires may be more useful as screening tools, with detailed interviews being reserved for those who screen positive (Zimmerman, 1994). Some believe that the MCMI in particular may have only limited utility even as a screening instrument because of its high false positive rate (Cantrell & Dana, 1987).

The APQ (Blackburn & Fawcett, 1999) has the advantage that it focuses on personality deviations relevant to offenders, having been developed originally using data acquired in the UK Special Hospitals (its precursor was the Special Hospitals Assessment of Personality and Socialization [SHAPS; Blackburn, 1982]). It is a short (125 items, answered in a 'yes/no' format), multi-trait, self-report inventory that measures intrapersonal and interpersonal dispositions of relevance to antisocial populations (Blackburn & Fawcett, 1999). Its advantages are first, its brevity; second, its focus on traits associated with social deviance; and third, its validity in discriminating both within offenders and between offenders and non-offenders. There are eight scales (self-control, self-esteem, avoidance, paranoid suspicion, resentment, aggression, deviance and extraversion), all having acceptable reliabilities (Cronbach's alphas between .79 and .88 in patients). Two higher-order factors emerged from principal components analysis: one, labelled 'hostile impulsivity', contrasts aggression, resentment, deviance and paranoid beliefs with self-control; the other, labelled 'social withdrawal', contrasts avoidance and poor self-esteem (neurotic introversion) with stable extraversion. A two-dimensional space defined by these factors has been used to define a useful typology of personality-disordered offenders (reviewed in Blackburn, 2009; see Figure 16.2). The impulsivity factor, incorporating elements of emotional dyscontrol (anger, irritability, loss of temper), loads highly on a higher-order International Personality Disorder Examination (IPDE) 'antisocial' or 'psychopathy' factor (Blackburn, Logan, Renwick, &

Donnelly, 2005) and correlates highly with hostile dominance as measured using the Chart of Interpersonal Reactions in Closed Living Environments (CIRCLE; see the following text) (Blackburn et al., 2005). Blackburn's dimension of hostile impulsivity likely reflects the combination of *meanness* and *disinhibition*, two elements of Patrick, Fowles and Krueger's (2009) reconceptualization of psychopathy (the remaining element is *boldness*) which are moderately highly intercorrelated. While *meanness* relates to low levels of empathy and high levels of narcissism and egocentricity, both *meanness* and *disinhibition* are related to impulsivity, negative affect, aggressiveness and a tendency to blame others (Stanley, Wygant, & Sellbom, 2013). These are cardinal features of Blackburn's hostile impulsivity.

Finally, two self-report measures designed to tap the presence of PD in general, and personal concerns and goals in the personality-disordered offender, merit mention. First, the General Assessment of Personality Disorder (GAPD), which is based on Livesley's psycho-evolutionary (impaired adaptation) approach, comprises two main scales, self and interpersonal pathology, each consisting of several facets. GAPD has been reported to discriminate successfully between mentally disordered patients with and without PD, with a sensitivity (the probability of successfully identifying patients with PD) of 77.3% and a specificity (the probability of successfully

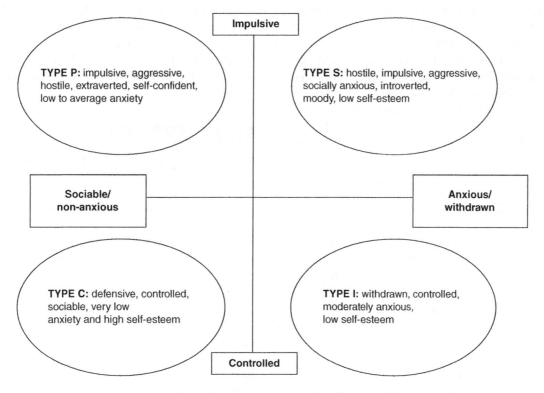

Type P: Primary psychopaths; Type S: Secondary psychopaths; Type I: Inhibited; Type C: Controlled

FIGURE 16.2 *The two-dimensional space defined by impulsivity and social withdrawal. Source: after Blackburn (2009).*

identifying patients without PD) of 86.5% (Hentschel & Livesley, 2012). Second, the Personal Concerns Inventory: Offender Adaptation (PCI-OA) is a semi-structured interview that helps offenders identify what they want to achieve or change in their life, and thereby may improve treatment engagement (Sellen, Gobbett, & Campbell, 2013; Campbell, Sellen, & McMurran, 2010). It asks respondents to describe their current concerns in 14 life areas: self-changes; employment and finance; partner, family and relatives; education and training; home and household matters; substance use; my offending behaviour; friends and acquaintances; health and medical matters; hobbies, pastimes and recreation; current living arrangements; love, intimacy and sexual matters; spiritual matters; other areas. Respondents then rate, on a 0–10 scale, their goals for resolving their current concerns on 12 dimensions related to goal value, goal attainability and perceived control over goals. From these ratings, measures of adaptive and maladaptive motivation are calculated. Compared with no additional interview, use of the PCI interview in a randomized controlled trial with community adults in a PD treatment service as a pre-therapy preparation session led to them having significantly clearer treatment goals, being rated by staff as more engaged in subsequent treatment and attending more sessions in the first 3 months of treatment (McMurran, Cox, Whitham, & Hedges, 2013).

Semi-structured interviews

A number of semi-structured interviews have been developed to address the problem of low reliability of unstructured clinical interviews. Some of these (the International Personality Disorder Examination (IPDE) and Structured Clinical Interview for DSM-IV Axis II Personality Disorders (SCID-II)) also have self-report versions that can be used as a screening instrument to give some guidance to the subsequent interview. Unique to the SCID-II (First, Spitzer, Gibbon, Williams, & Benjamin, 1994) is that the interviewer inquires only about criteria that are endorsed on the questionnaire, thereby reducing the length of the interview.

An advantage of semi-structured interviews is their flexibility. In addition to standard questions, optional probes and unstructured questions are used to elicit relevant information. When using IPDE (Loranger et al., 1994) to assess 99 DSM-defined traits, there are three phases to the assessment of each trait: (a) is it present or absent? (b) if the answer to (a) is 'yes', is the severity of the trait sufficient to have a significant clinical impact on the individual's level of functioning? (c) if the answers to (a) and (b) are in the affirmative, does the motivation behind the behaviour satisfy the relevant DSM criteria? An example is the following question to elicit an avoidant personality trait: 'Q. Do you usually try to avoid jobs or things you have to do at work (school) that bring you into contact with other people?' (This is the structured question and must be asked in this format.) If the answer is 'yes', the individual is then asked to provide examples to provide the interviewer with convincing evidence that the patient's avoidant behaviour satisfies the three 'Ps' of PD (i.e., that it is persistent, pervasive and pathological). Finally, the interviewee is asked: 'Why do you do that?' Here, the interviewer is inquiring about the motivation in the mind of the interviewee for this behaviour, since, according to the DSM manual, the reason for the avoidance must be fear of criticism, disapproval or rejection.

The inter-rater reliability of these semi-structured instruments is moderate to good. In his review, Zimmerman (1994) found that 80% of the 15 joint interview studies reported a kappa of .6 or above, and 60% had a kappa of .70 and above. The temporal stability of the IPDE has been assessed at 6 months by Loranger et al. (1994), who found a low moderate consistency for categorical diagnoses (median $k = .48$) but a superior rating for the dimensional diagnoses (median ICC $= .79$ for DSM-III-R). Of special relevance for the forensic practitioner, the antisocial PD rating has the greatest temporal stability as it is largely based on antisocial, including criminal, behaviour (Grilo, McGlashan, & Oldham, 1998).

Despite their reasonable reliability, the convergent validity between different interview-based instruments, and between these and questionnaire measures, is only poor to fair (Zimmerman, 1994). In the largest study comparing the SCID-II with the PDE, Skodol, Oldham, Rosnick, Kellman, and Hyler (1991) found that the mean kappa for the 11 DSM-III-R PDs was .45, only dependent PD achieving a kappa greater than .6. When similar comparisons are made for Axis I conditions, the agreement is no better (Hasin & Grant, 1987a, 1987b).

MEASURES OF INTERPERSONAL STYLE

As disordered interpersonal functioning is a crucial aspect of PD, another approach to consider in PD assessment stems from interpersonal theory and the interpersonal circle (IPC; Leary, 1957). The latter represents interpersonal styles as a circular array or circumplex, around two dimensions of power or control (dominance versus submission) and affiliation (hostile versus friendly: see Blackburn, 2000, for a fuller description). The IPC is of particular relevance to mentally disordered offenders because, as Blackburn (2000) points out, hostile-dominant styles are associated with interpersonal conflict and aggression. Blackburn and colleagues have developed a nurse-rating measure for use with forensic psychiatric inpatients, the Chart of Interpersonal Reactions in Closed Living Environments (CIRCLE: Blackburn & Renwick,

1996). It contains 49 statements describing discrete social behaviours – for example, 'Joins in group activities', that are independently rated by two members of staff who know the patient well, and the scores are combined and used to calculate the individual's relative position in the eight octants of the IPC (Dominant, Coercive, Hostile, Withdrawn, Submissive, Compliant, Nurturant, Gregarious). A single point that characterizes a particular individual can be plotted within the IPC. There is evidence that the categories of PD in DSM can be mapped on to the IPC; for example, antisocial, narcissistic and histrionic PDs show hostile-dominant styles, and hostile dominance as measured by CIRCLE loads strongly on the higher-order IPDE Antisocial factor described earlier. Hostile dominance correlates significantly (.46) with Psychopathy Checklist Revised (PCL-R) total score (Blackburn et al., 2005) and with APQ scales contributing to the higher-order APQ Impulsivity factor (Blackburn & Fawcett, 1999). Despite the superior theoretical and empirical underpinnings of this approach, this has not as yet become a mainstream evaluation among forensic psychologists.

PRACTICAL CONSIDERATIONS

An important (and unanswered) question is: Who should provide the information when assessing PD – the individual concerned or someone who knows him or her well? Allied to this is if (and how) collateral information (e.g., from files) should be used. It could be argued that since PD patients usually see their disorder as ego-syntonic (i.e., an inevitable or natural part of the person's life), an informant interview would be a more accurate indication of the psychopathology. On the other hand, several of the questions in personality assessment refer to internal mental states (e.g., a feeling of emptiness) or to unusual perceptual and cognitive experiences. It is difficult to see how an informant would be able to provide useful information in these areas. Again, as with the comparison between different instruments, when the two sources are compared, there is often poor agreement between them. For example, Zimmerman, Pfohl, Coryell, Stangl, and Corenthal (1988) compared the views of patients and informants using the Structured Interview for DSM-III PDs (SIDP) in 66 depressed patients and found poor agreement ($k = .13$ for any PD and for all individual PDs $k < .35$). What this tells us is that there is likely to be poor agreement when more than one source of information is provided. What it does not tell us, however, is which of the sources is more valid. While many suggest that two sources of information ought to be collected and then combined, it is unclear how this is to be done if the information is discrepant. This is of particular relevance in a forensic context where there may be a considerable incentive for individuals to downplay their psychopathology in order to minimize the length of a custodial sentence or to avoid admission to a secure hospital. Unfortunately, these instruments were not designed to detect this degree of denial or deception and hence have to be used very cautiously in such a context.

Another practical issue is that of the experience, training and qualifications deemed necessary in order to administer the interviews. The degree of training required and clinical experience expected varies between the various semi-structured interview instruments. For instance, the Personality Interview Questionnaire was designed deliberately to avoid preconceived clinical biases so that it used lay interviewers. Conversely, the Personality Disorder Examination (PDE; Loranger, 1988) and IPDE were designed for use by experienced practitioners, and the manual for the latter explicitly states that it should *not* be used by '… research assistants, nurses, students and other clinicians early in their training …'. Other instruments (e.g., the Structured Interview for Personality Disorders [SIPD; Stangl, Pfohl, Zimmerman, Bowers, & Corenthal, 1985]) recommend a more intermediate level of experience. In the United Kingdom, PCL requires 3 days' expensive basic training, and additional advanced training to receive the PCL manual. Its use is restricted to those with a degree in behavioural or social science. Clearly, a minimum level of training is necessary for administering any instrument, but beyond this, experience in the interpretation of responses is required to arrive at a valid assessment when using and interpreting additional probes to clarify answers.

SUMMARY: ASSESSMENT OF PD

Our review of the evidence on the assessment of PD shows that, while there is agreement in certain areas, there remain significant uncertainties. Nonetheless, we believe that the following conclusions may be drawn:

1. The reliability of unstructured clinical interviews is only poor to fair and hence ought not to be recommended.
2. Judicious and selective use of self-report inventories is required since some over-diagnose, making their interpretation difficult and the planning of interventions near impossible. However, we have pointed to particular merits attaching to one self-report inventory, the Antisocial Personality

Questionnaire (Blackburn & Fawcett, 1999), which has the additional merit of tapping not just dysfunctional traits relevant to mentally disordered offenders, but also traits related to normal personality variation such as Neuroticism, Extraversion and possibly Agreeableness from the Big Five.

3. Semi-structured assessments have reasonable reliability but the convergent validity between the instruments is only poor to fair. Thus, it is unclear as to which (of any of these) ought to be recommended, but research using the IPDE has yielded consistent evidence for a higher-order Antisocial factor (we prefer the label 'Antisocial Dyscontrol') that correlates highly with PCL psychopathy and a coercive interpersonal style on the CIRCLE.

4. Patients and informants do not agree on the patients' personality evaluation, and it is unclear as to which of these is the more valid. One might assume that there would be a reasonable congruence between the PD diagnosis and the problems that the individual PD patient identifies as most salient to them. Relevant to this, Huband, Evans, Duggan, and Khan (2012) asked 141 treatment-seeking patients with PD to describe the five things they most wanted to change about themselves, and these were then compared with the PD diagnosis obtained from the IPDE. Congruence between the target problems identified by patients and their PD traits was weak; doubting the trustworthiness of others was the most commonly reported target problem. The authors concluded that PD diagnosis was a poor indicator of the problems patients cited as the most important, again underscoring deficiencies in the current diagnostic system of PD.

5. The training and experience required by the differing semi-structured instruments varies considerably, and this will have an effect on the cost and accuracy of the assessment.

PROCEDURAL RECOMMENDATIONS IN ASSESSING PD

We endorse Livesley's suggestion that an initial focus should be on assessing whether the general criteria for PD are met, in terms of intrapersonal, interpersonal and societal dysfunction as described earlier in the first section. A set of specific criteria remain to be articulated, but as Livesley (2003, p. 172) points out, 'The definition

of personality disorder could be developed through a conceptual analysis of the functions of normal personality and the way these functions are disturbed in personality disorder'. Only then should one proceed to assessment of individual differences in personality, using a variety of assessment instruments. We would suggest that a basic assessment of dysfunctional traits be carried out using measures from all three domains: self-report, interview-based and observer-rated. Based on the considerations outlined earlier, including economy of time and cost, we would suggest a triad of APQ, IPDE and CIRCLE. If thought appropriate, for example, for delineating specific treatment targets, more specific areas of dysfunction could then be explored using instruments designed for their measurement. If, for example, emotional dysregulation needed to be assessed, the General Emotional Dysregulation Measure (GEDM; Newhill, Mulvey, & Pilkonis, 2004) could be administered.

Given, first, the high proportion of mentally ill offenders who also suffer from a PD (some 60%), and second, the high co-morbidity between DSM Axis I and Axis II disorders (e.g., McGlashan et al., 2000), an assessment of PD should be carried out on all individuals undergoing a routine psychiatric assessment. Indeed, Livesley (2003) suggests that PD should be included together with other psychiatric disorders on a single Axis I in any future reformulation of the DSM nosology. This raises the issue of how to interpret measures of PD that may be inflated by co-morbid Axis I disorders (Zimmerman, 1994). While it has been argued that this reflects over-diagnosis of PD, Blackburn (2000) points out that the reduction in personality pathology following remission of acute symptoms of mental illness may reflect genuine personality change. Nevertheless, he points out that assessing PD in acutely disturbed patients remains an unresolved problem.

TREATMENT OF PD: SOME CAVEATS

There are a number of general issues to discuss before considering some of the specifics in the treatment of PD. First, does PD change, and, if so, *what* changes? Considering that one of the defining features of personality, and hence of PD, is its long-term stability, does it make sense to attempt to treat that which, by definition, is unchanging?

This issue can be addressed at two levels. First, there is recent evidence from naturalistic follow-up studies – and this especially applies to those with borderline PD – that change is indeed possible, with a significant reduction in key symptoms over the medium term (Skodol et al., 2007:

Zanarini, Frankenberg, Hennen, Reich, & Silk, 2005). For example, about 74% failed to meet criteria for the disorder 6 years follow-up, and once remission occurred, recurrences were uncommon (about 6%). While a number of acute symptoms in borderline personality disorder (BPD) such as self-mutilation, help-seeking behaviour and suicidal threats resolve rapidly, regardless of intervention, other symptoms that are not specific to BPD, such as chronic feelings of intense anger, resolve much more slowly, if at all (Zanarini et al., 2005). All studies concur in suggesting that, over time, BPD patients improve psychosocially, that the prognosis for patients with BPD is better than previously recognized, and that, while some aspects of BPD change, others are more resistant to change. Similarly, in the case of men with antisocial PD, while impulsivity, and hence also rates of reoffending, declines over time, major problems in interpersonal relationships persist (Black, Baumgard, & Bell, 1995; Grilo et al., 1998; Weissman, 1993).

Second, an important implication of this is that caution is required when interpreting results of clinical trials purporting to show changes in behaviours such as self-harm which are likely to remit spontaneously over time. Such results beg the question of whether the intervention has achieved a greater reduction in the target behaviour compared with the mere passage of time, and highlight the importance of properly designed trials, a feature that unfortunately does not characterize research in PD. With regard to treatment, relatively brief interventions may augment changes in those more malleable aspects of personality that are likely to change spontaneously with the passage of time, while other, less malleable aspects are more resistant to change and, therefore, require a longer and more sophisticated intervention.

TREATMENT ISSUES

In his review of treatments for personality-disordered offenders, Livesley (2007b) notes that a wide spectrum of treatments, from psychodynamic psychotherapy at one end to antipsychotic medication at the other, has been used to treat PD; while there is evidence of limited success for all, this also suggests that none is especially effective. There have been recent reviews of the efficacy of treatments for PDs in general (Duggan et al., 2007, 2008; Oldham, 2007; Soloff, 1998) as well as more specific reviews of particular PDs, for example, reviews supporting NICE Guidelines for borderline and antisocial PD and Cochrane reviews of borderline (Binks et al., 2006) and antisocial (Gibbon et al., 2009) PDs. The main conclusion from these is that, if one considers only those studies that adopt as standard a high level of evidence, that is,

well-conducted randomized controlled trials (RCTs), then the evidence base is very thin. Duggan et al. (2007, 2008), for example, reviewed RCT evidence for both psychological and pharmacological interventions for any PD. Only 49 trials up to December 2006 could be included that met their inclusion criteria, and, of these, almost half focused on borderline PD and only five involved antisocial PD. The reason why this evidence base is so thin is not difficult to identify, given the difficulties that we have identified in the preceding text. First, since many of the assessment instruments have such poor convergent validity, one cannot be certain that individuals entering the trial with the same diagnosis but assessed with differing instruments are the same. Second, as a result of frequent disagreement between studies concerning relevant outcome measures, there is considerable variability in those chosen, making cross-study comparisons very difficult. Finally, most of the trials are underpowered, with a very brief follow-up period, making findings difficult to interpret. In summary, relying on this evidence base will not take the practitioner very far; as it is unlikely to change in the near future, an alternative approach is necessary.

Livesley (2007b) makes the important point that, contrary to what many of the proponents of specific interventions might claim, there is very good evidence that it is the common factors shared between therapies, rather than their specific aspects, that lead to a successful outcome. Treatment should, therefore, optimize the non-specific effects that are common to all types of treatment. Livesley advocates an eclectic approach, based on what works, requiring an array of interventions selected systematically from different treatment models – psychotherapeutic, cognitive behavioural, pharmacological, etc. – to target specific problems. He goes further in suggesting that such a comprehensive treatment for personality-disordered offenders requires not only interventions aimed at bringing about changes in the *contents* of personality, but at promoting more cohesive personality functioning, for example, to foster integration and to construct a more adaptive and prosocial life script. A systematic treatment approach should progressively target: first, those aspects of PD that are most susceptible to change (e.g., symptoms and states); then those aspects that are less changeable, such as affective impulse control and maladaptive modes of thinking; and finally those aspects that are least susceptible to change, such as core schemata central to self and identity.

An outline of a possible approach is provided in Figure 16.3. This identifies three therapeutic tasks: (a) establishing therapeutic engagement; (b) reducing behavioural dyscontrol; (c) integration of self-states. Establishing therapeutic engagement is best achieved, in our view, by focusing on the individual's difficulties in functioning and relating these to the content of the personality assessment.

Thus the processes of assessment and treatment are connected. We have found that providing information on the individual's personality difficulties through a process of psychoeducation strengthens therapeutic engagement (Banerjee, Duggan, Huband, & Watson, 2006; Huband, McMurran, Evans, & Duggan, 2007). It is the case, however, that specific PD diagnoses have limited value in deciding on specific treatments or indicating prognosis. After conducting one of the semi-structured interviews described earlier, one often finds that the individual assessed meets criteria for more than one, and sometimes several, PDs, so that the practitioner is then faced with making a choice as to which of these ought to be prioritized. In addition, psychological and pharmacological interventions are used to treat specific behaviours (e.g., self-harming behaviour) or dimensions such as cognitive-perceptual symptoms – not specific disorders. This is a limitation of our current assessment process but one that Livesley's approach, as discussed, would overcome.

If this process identifies difficulties in behavioural control, then this becomes the second target of treatment. This can be effected by either psychological interventions (e.g., social problem solving, biofeedback training) or medication to reduce impulsive behaviour so that the individual thinks before he or she acts. In both phases, building up a therapeutic relationship and dealing with behavioural dyscontrol, the therapy is relatively directive so that the level of anxiety experienced by the patient/client is low. In addition, the skill level demanded is relatively modest.

However, as has been pointed out, there is more to PD than improving behaviour: the third stage in Figure 16.3 involves tackling core schemata that are central to the individual's identity and is a major task of treatment. This is a much more challenging task and requires a greater level of sophistication and training. As core issues concerning the patient's identity are confronted, a greater level of anxiety is evoked, so that there is greater resistance to change.

Thus, as in many other areas of therapeutic intervention, a stepped care approach is adopted. This ranges from relatively simple interventions that can be offered to many, to more sophisticated interventions that, because of both the degree of time involved and the level of expertise demanded, are likely to be offered to very few. This is important, as there are significant shortfalls in expertise in programme delivery for those with PD. Hence, it is important to be able to match expectations with available resources.

Dealing with drop-outs from treatment

Prevention of treatment drop-out is an important component of service delivery for the following reasons. First, high drop-out rates are seen in PD patients undergoing treatment, particularly in borderline patients undergoing psychodynamic therapy (Gunderson *et al.*, 1989; Skodol, Buckley, & Charles, 1983; Waldinger & Gunderson, 1984), although lower rates have been reported for other

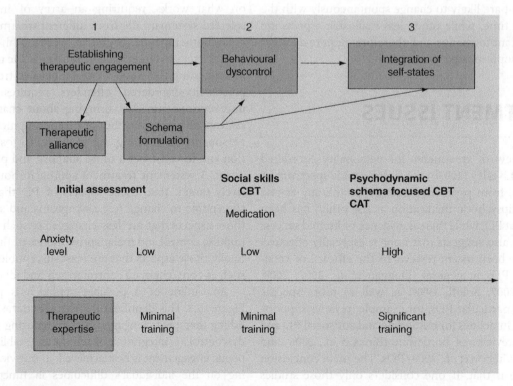

FIGURE 16.3 *A stepped care model of therapeutic intervention.*

approaches (e.g., Bateman & Fonagy, 1999; Linehan, Armstrong, Suarez, Allmon, & Heard, 1991; Stevenson & Meares, 1992).

Second, a high drop-out rate is an uneconomical use of resources that, as already noted, are very limited. Third, drop-outs have a detrimental effect on both patient and therapist. For example, those offered treatment who then drop out are more likely to reoffend compared with those left untreated (McMurran & Theodosi, 2007).

Predicting and preventing drop-out

Factors found to be associated with dropping out of treatment include: low educational attainment and poor social support; young age; more symptoms and a high PCL-R score; high levels of anger; and a low capacity to work collaboratively (Huband *et al.*, 2007). These characteristics are common in those who come to the attention of forensic psychologists.

In the light of these findings, it is not surprising that attention is increasingly being given to reducing the likelihood of dropping out. While improving the motivation for treatment has always been a preoccupation of service providers, this has recently been extended to assessing 'readiness' for treatment. Readiness denotes more than just the individual's motivation to engage in treatment; it involves consideration of the match between the individual's capacity to engage with the treatment and the provider's capacity to meet that individual's needs. The correctional literature indicates that the closer the fit between these, the more likely is the intervention offered to be effective (Andrews & Bonta, 2003). A final aspect of 'readiness' is the organization's commitment and structure to deliver the programme. All too often, the impact of programmes introduced with enthusiasm by practitioners is severely curtailed because they are not supported by the larger organization. An example is the introduction of programmes for individuals in prison who require a stable period of placement. All too often, the authorities ignore this and move inmates around the prison estate due to other pressures. This, more comprehensive, matching of the therapeutic need with the organization's capacity to respond to it is well captured in the 'MORM' concept of Ward, Day, and Howells (2004).

Managing ruptures in the therapeutic relationship

An important consideration in those with PD is the active management of the therapeutic rupture, defined as a breakdown in the emotional relationship between patient and therapist. This is evidenced by the individual arriving late or missing sessions, not complying with homework or medication and so on. When faced with this type of change, instead of ignoring the rupture or confronting the patient, it is suggested that, rather than being seen as a problem stemming from the patient, the rupture should be explored as an exchange between co-equal partners. This kind of dialogue may then model a kind of non-value-laden exploratory activity that the patient might internalize (Safran & Muran, 2000).

CURRENT ISSUES IN THE ASSESSMENT AND TREATMENT OF PD

Currently, the field of PDs is in a state of flux, with DSM-5 having rejected a hybrid categorical/trait-based system, which would have represented a rapprochement with Livesley's proposal outlined earlier. Instead, DSM-5 has retained the categories contained in DSM-IV, with the radical (hybrid) revision included in a separate chapter in Section III to encourage its further study. The revised ICD-II for PDs takes a different tack. It proposes to abolish all individual categories of PD, to be replaced by four severity levels which will be qualified by trait domains. The severity categories range from personality difficulty to mild and moderate PD through to complex and severe PD. Severity will be defined by: (a) overlap of the trait domains, so that the more domains involved, the more severe the disorder; (b) the degree of social dysfunction; and (c) the risk to self and others. The four trait domains comprise: internalizing (neurotic), externalizing (antagonistic), schizoid (detached) and anankastic. As such, they match fairly closely with Livesley's trait domains, described earlier (Table 16.1).

Perhaps the greatest criticism of both the radical DSM and ICD revisions is that neither provides sufficient continuity with what has gone before. Is one supposed, with this tabula rasa, to begin completely afresh? Since their criteria will have changed, will the information about specific PDs gleaned from current and past clinical trials be of no further value and therefore no longer carry any weight? Similarly, will the information from follow-up studies that has been meticulously gathered over many decades no longer be relevant? While no one disputes that the current nomenclature for PDs is deficient, such radical departures as advanced by both the DSM and ICD proposals appear to us to be a step too far. Some continuity with what has gone before, such as is suggested in the following paragraph, is necessary if the field is to advance in an orderly fashion.

The challenge facing those involved with PDs is, as Livesley has pointed out, to derive an evidence-based, aetiologically informed system to describe individual differences in PD. By combining traits across different trait domains (e.g., Livesley's Dissocial and Emotional Dysregulation domains, see Table 16.1) it should be possible to identify significant constellations of traits that reflect the co-morbidity shown to exist across DSM categories of PD. Take, for example, the co-occurrence of DSM-IV antisocial and borderline PDs which, as we shall see in the following chapter, is highly prevalent in forensic samples. The selective co-occurrence of these PDs likely reflects unique risk factors that they share in common, over and above those factors that convey risk for cluster B PDs in general (Torgersen *et al.*, 2008). Antisocial/borderline PD co-morbidity is associated with distinct clinical and criminological correlates: *severe* childhood conduct disorder (more severe than that associated with antisocial PD alone: Freestone, Howard, Coid, & Ullrich, 2012; Howard, Huband, & Duggan, 2012); greater severity of PD, indexed by a higher prevalence of co-occurring PDs (Howard *et al.*, 2012) and greater DSM Axis I co-morbidity (Freestone *et al.*, 2012); greater prevalence of antisocial outcomes in general, including violence (Freestone *et al.*, 2012); and a clear tendency to re-offend early following release from secure care (Howard, McCarthy, Huband, & Duggan, 2013). Antisocial/borderline PD co-morbidity can therefore be considered to be what Livesley refers to as a 'focal disorder', with elevated levels in a subset of

primary traits across the Dyssocial and Emotion Dysregulation domains. From a forensic point of view, it is clearly important to identify this pattern of co-occurring traits which, in terms of the ICD-II revision, would presumably be classed as both highly severe and conveying high risk of harm (the lower risk conveyed by schizoid traits would need to be factored into the risk equation). By requiring the presence of childhood conduct disorder for a diagnosis of antisocial PD, DSM-IV had implied that disordered childhood conduct and adult antisocial personality were functionally linked. While this linkage may still hold (albeit only about 50% of children with conduct disorder progress to adult antisocial PD), the more accurate picture that is emerging is that *severe* childhood conduct disorder, along with its associated callous–unemotional traits, is linked to the particularly severe form of personality pathology represented by co-occurring antisocial and borderline PDs. In principle, the ICD-II revision should be in a position to capture this 'high-severe, high-risk' constellation of personality traits, but it remains to be seen whether it can deliver on this promise.

We conclude by noting that, while great strides have been made in our understanding of PD over the last 25 years, the field is clearly in a state of flux, with many outstanding issues still to be resolved. It will be interesting to see how the field develops over the next 25 years, particularly in the forensic context.

NOTE

1 While studies vary in terms of three versus four higher-order factors and the labels attached to them (see Tyrer *et al.*, 2007), nonetheless there is consensus across studies for a higher-order factor comprising antisocial, narcissistic–histrionic, paranoid and borderline traits, in forensic psychiatric patients (Blackburn *et al.*, 2005), prison inmates (Ullrich & Marneros, 2004, 2007), and in a community sample (Howard, Huband, Duggan, & Mannion, 2008). While Livesley uses the term 'dyssocial' to describe this factor, we prefer to use the term 'Antisocial Dyscontrol' to describe this dimension.

FURTHER READING

Livesley, W. J. (2007). A framework for integrating dimensional and categorical classifications of personality disorder. *Journal of Personality Disorders, 21,* 199–224.

This paper is a good introduction to the views of John Livesley on PD, summarized here in Figure 16.1. Livesley outlines his attempt to combine categorical and dimensional diagnoses of PD in an integrated framework. He adopts a two-component classification that distinguishes between the diagnosis of PD in general (a breakdown in the structure of personality) and individual differences in the form the disorder takes, assessed in terms of a set of empirically derived primary traits. The strength of his approach is that it introduces an aetiological perspective, derived from behavioural genetic studies, to the classification of PDs. It also points to the need to develop instruments for the assessment of areas of content, such as concerns and the life narrative, other than dysfunctional traits. Implicit in Livesley's account is the idea that a breakdown in the structure of personality gives rise to measurable changes in the content of personality, as shown by the arrows in Figure 16.1. However, it is not clear from his account whether the structure of PD has some kind of neurobiological substrate, nor how deformations of the structure give rise to dysfunctional traits, abnormal concerns and a lack of coherence in the life narrative.

REFERENCES

Andrews, D. A., & Bonta, J. (2003). *The psychology of criminal conduct* (3rd edn). Cincinnati, OH: Anderson.

Apter, M. J. (2005). *Personality dynamics: Key concepts in reversal theory*. Loughborough: Apter International.

Bagby, R. M., Sellbom, M., Costa, P. T., & Widiger, T. A. (2008). Predicting diagnostic and statistical manual of mental disorders-IV personality disorders with the five-factor model of personality and the personality psychopathology five. *Personality and Mental Health, 2,* 55–69.

Banerjee, P., Duggan, C. Huband, N., & Watson, N. (2006). Brief psycho-education for people with personality disorder – a pilot study. *Psychology and Psychotherapy; Theory, Research and Practice, 79,* 385–394.

Bateman, A., & Fonagy, P. (1999). Effectiveness of partial hospitalization in the treatment of borderline personality disorder: A randomized controlled trial. *American Journal of Psychiatry, 156*(10), 1563–1569.

Benjamin, L. S. (1993). *Interpersonal diagnosis and treatment of personality disorder*. New York: Guilford Press.

Binks, C., Fenton, M., McCarthy, L., Lee, T., Adams, C. E., & Duggan, C. (2006). Psychological therapies for people with borderline personality disorder. *Cochrane Database of Systematic Reviews*, Issue 1. Art. No.: CD005652. DOI: 10.1002/14651858.CD005652.

Black, D. W., Baumgard, C. H., & Bell, S. E. (1995). A 16- to 45-year follow-up of 71 men with antisocial personality disorder. *Comprehensive Psychiatry, 36*(2), 130–140.

Blackburn, R. (1971). MMPI dimensions of sociability and impulse control. *Journal of Consulting and Clinical Psychology, 37,* 166.

Blackburn, R. (1982). *The special hospitals assessment of personality and socialization*. Unpublished manuscript, Park Lane Hospital, Liverpool.

Blackburn, R. (2000). Classification and assessment of personality disorders in mentally disordered offenders: A psychological perspective. *Criminal Behaviour and Mental Health, 10,* S8–S32.

Blackburn, R. (2009). Subtypes of psychopath. In M. McMurran & R. Howard (Eds.), *Personality, personality disorder and violence*. Chichester: John Wiley & Sons.

Blackburn, R., & Fawcett, D. (1999). The antisocial personality questionnaire: An inventory for assessing personality deviation in offender populations. *European Journal of Psychological Assessment, 15,* 14–24.

Blackburn, R., Logan, C., Renwick, S. J. D., & Donnelly, J. P. (2005). Higher-order dimensions of personality disorder: Hierarchical structure and relationships with the five factor model, the interpersonal circle, and psychopathy. *Journal of Personality Disorders, 19*(6), 597–623.

Blackburn, R., & Renwick, S. J. (1996). Rating scales for measuring the interpersonal circle in forensic psychiatric inpatients. *Psychological Assessment, 8,* 76–84.

Campbell, J., Sellen, J. L., & McMurran, M. (2010). Personal aspirations and concerns inventory for offenders: Developments in the measurement of offenders' motivation. *Criminal Behaviour and Mental Health, 20*(2), 144–157.

Cantrell, J. D., & Dana, R. D. (1987). Use of the Millon Clinical Multiaxial Inventory (MCMI) as a screening instrument at a community mental health center. *Journal of Clinical Psychology, 43,* 366–375.

Clark, L. A. (2007). Assessment and diagnosis of personality disorder: Perennial issues and an emerging reconceptualization. *Annual Review of Psychology, 58,* 227–257.

Clark, L. A., Livesley, J. W., & Morey, L. (1997). Personality disorder assessment: The challenge of construct validity. *Journal of Personality Disorders, 11,* 205–231.

Costa, P. T., & McCrae, R. R. (1992). *Revised NEO personality inventory: Professional manual*. Odessa, FL: Psychological Assessment Resources.

Duggan, C., Huband, N., Smailagic, N., Ferriter, M., & Adams, C. (2007). The use of psychological treatments for people with personality disorder: A systematic review of randomized controlled trials. *Personality and Mental Health, 1,* 95–125.

Duggan, C., Huband, N., Smailagic, N., Ferriter, M., & Adams, C. (2008). The use of pharmacological treatments for people with personality disorder: A systematic review of randomized controlled trials. *Personality and Mental Health, 2,* 119–170.

First, M. B., Spitzer, R. I., Gibbon, M., Williams, J. B. W., & Benjamin, L. (1994). *The Structured clinical interview for DSM-1V Axis II personality disorders (SCID-11) (Version 2.0)*. New York: Biometrics Research, New York State Psychiatric Institute.

Freestone, M., Howard, R. C., Coid, J., & Ullrich, S. (2012). Adult antisocial syndrome co-morbid with borderline personality disorder is associated with severe conduct disorder, substance dependence and violent antisociality. *Personality and Mental Health, 7*(1), 11–21.

Gibbon, S., Duggan, C., Stoffers, J. M., Huband, N., Völlm, B. A., Ferriter, M., & Lieb, K. (2009). Psychological interventions for antisocial personality disorder (Protocol). *Cochrane Database of Systematic Reviews 2009*, Issue 1. Art. No.: CD007668. DOI: 10.1002/14651858.CD007668.

Grilo, C. M., McGlashan, T. H., & Oldham, J. M. (1998). Course and stability of personality disorders. *Journal of Practical Psychiatry and Behavioral Health, 4,* 61–75.

Gunderson, J. G., Frank, A. F., Ronningstam, E. F., Wachter, S., Lynch, V. J., & Wolf, P. J. (1989). Early discontinuance of borderline patients from psychotherapy. *Journal of Nervous and Mental Disease, 177*(1), 38–42.

Harkness, A. R., & McNulty, J. L. (1994). The personality psychopathology five (PSY-5): Issues from the pages of a diagnostic manual instead of a dictionary. In S. Strack & M. Lorr (Eds.), *Differentiating normal and abnormal personality* (pp. 291–315). New York: Springer.

Hasin, D. S., & Grant, B. F. (1987a). Psychiatric diagnosis of patients with substance abuse problems: A comparison of two procedures, the DIS and the SADS-L. *Journal of Psychiatric Research, 21*, 7–22.

Hasin, D. S., & Grant, B. F. (1987b). Diagnosing depressive disorders in patients with alcohol and drug problems: A comparison of the SADS-L and the DIS. *Journal of Psychiatric Research, 21*, 301–311.

Hentschel, A. G., & Livesley, W. J. (2012). Differentiating normal and disordered personality using the General Assessment of Personality Disorder (GAPD). *Personality and Mental Health, 7*(2), 133–142.

Howard, R. C., Huband, N., & Duggan, C. (2012). Adult antisocial syndrome with co-morbid borderline pathology: Association with severe childhood conduct disorder. *Annals of Clinical Psychiatry, 24*, 127–134.

Howard, R. C., Huband, N., Duggan, C., & Mannion, A. (2008). Exploring the link between personality disorder and criminality in a community sample. *Journal of Personality Disorders, 22*(6), 589–603.

Howard, R. C., & Lumsden, J. (1996). A neurophysiological predictor of re-offending in Special Hospital patients. *Criminal Behaviour and Mental Health, 6*, 147–156.

Howard, R. C., & Lumsden, J. (1997). CNV predicts violent outcomes in patients released from special hospital. *Criminal Behaviour and Mental Health, 7*, 237–240.

Howard, R. C., McCarthy, L., Huband, N., & Duggan, C. (2013). Re-offending in forensic patients released from secure care: The role of antisocial/borderline co-morbidity, substance dependence, and severe childhood conduct disorder. *Criminal Behaviour and Mental Health*. Epub ahead of print edition, Jan 31, 2013. doi: 10.1002/cbm.1852.

Huband, N., Evans, C., Duggan, C., & Khan, O. (2012). Personality disorder traits and self-reported target problems in a treatment-seeking sample. *Clinical Psychology and Psychotherapy*. Epub ahead of print edition, doi: 10.1002/cpp.1825.

Huband, N., McMurran, M., Evans, C., & Duggan, C. (2007). Social problem-solving plus psychoeducation for adults with personality disorder: A pragmatic randomised clinical trial. *British Journal of Psychiatry, 190*, 307–313.

Hunt, C., & Andrews, G. (1992). Measuring personality disorder: The use of self-report questionnaires. *Journal of Personality Disorders, 6*, 125–133.

Hyler, S. E., & Rieder, R. O. (1987). *PDQ-R: Personality diagnostic questionnaire – Revised.* New York: New York State Psychiatric Institute.

Hyler, S. E., Skodol, A. E., Kellman, D., Oldham, J. M., & Rosnick, L. (1990). Validity of the Personality Diagnostic Questionnaire – Revised: Comparison with two structured interviews. *American Journal of Psychiatry, 147*, 1043–1048.

Hyler, S. E., Skodol, A. E., Oldham, J. M., Kellman, D., & Doidge, N. (1992). Validity of the Personality Diagnostic Questionnaire – Revised: A replication in an outpatient sample. *Comprehensive Psychiatry, 33*, 73–77.

Jolliffe, D., & Farrington, D. P. (2009). A systematic review of the relationship between childhood impulsiveness and later violence. In M. McMurran & R. Howard (Eds.), *Personality, personality disorder and violence* (pp. 41–61). Chichester: John Wiley & Sons.

Leary, T. (1957). *Interpersonal diagnosis of personality.* New York: Ronald Press.

Linehan, M. M., Armstrong, H. E., Suarez, A., Allmon, D., & Heard, H. L. (1991). Cognitive-behavioral treatment of chronically parasuicidal borderline patients. *Archives of General Psychiatry, 48*, 1060–1064.

Livesley, W. J. (1998). Suggestions for a framework for an empirically based classification of personality disorder. *Canadian Journal of Psychiatry, 43*.

Livesley, W. J. (2003). Diagnostic dilemmas in the classification of personality disorders. In K. A. Phillips, M. B. First, & H. A. Pincus (Eds.), *Advancing DSM: Dilemmas in psychiatric diagnosis.* Washington, DC: American Psychiatric Press.

Livesley, W. J. (2007a). A framework for integrating dimensional and categorical classifications of personality disorder. *Journal of Personality Disorders, 21*, 199–224.

Livesley, W. J. (2007b). The relevance of an integrated approach to the treatment of personality disordered offenders, *Psychology, Crime and Law, 13*, 27–46.

Livesley, W. J. (2008). Toward a genetically-informed model of borderline personality disorder. *Journal of Personality Disorders, 22*, 42–71.

Loranger, A. W. (1988). *Personality Disorder Examination (PDE) manual.* Yonkers, NY: DV Communications.

Loranger, A. W., Sartorius, N., Andreoli, A., Berger, P., Buchheim, P., Channabasavanna, S. M., Coid, B., Dahl, A., Diekstra, R. F., & Ferguson, B. (1994). The International Personality Disorder Examination: The World Health Organization and Alcohol, Drug Abuse and Mental Health Administration international pilot study of personality disorders. *Archives of General Psychiatry, 551*, 215–224.

McGlashan, T. H., Grilo, C. M., Skodol, A. E., Gunderson, J. G., Shea, M. T., Morey, L. C., Zanarini, M. C., & Stout, R. L. (2000). The Collaborative Longitudinal Personality Disorders Study: Baseline Axis I/II and II/II diagnostic co-occurrence. *Acta Psychiatrica Scandinavica, 102*, 256–264.

McMurran, M., & Theodosi, E. (2007). Is treatment non-completion associated with increased reconviction over no treatment? *Psychology, Crime and Law, 13*, 333–343.

McMurran, M., Cox, W. M., Whitham, D., & Hedges, L. (2013). The addition of a goal-based motivational interview to treatment as usual to reduce dropouts in a personality disorder treatment service: Results of a feasibility study for a randomized controlled trial. *Trials, 14*, 50. DOI: 10.1186/1745-6215-14-50.

Mellsop, G., Varghese, F., Joshua, S., & Hicks, A. (1982). The reliability of Axis II of DSM-III. *American Journal of Psychiatry, 139,* 1360–1361.

Millon, T., Millon, C., & Davis, R. D. (1994). *Millon Clinical Multiaxial Inventory – III.* Minneapolis, MN: National Computer Systems.

Morey, L. C. (1991). *Personality assessment inventory.* Lutz, FL: Psychological Assessment Resources.

Newhill, C. E., Mulvey, E. P., & Pilkonis, P. A. (2004). Initial development of a measure of emotional dysregulation for individuals with Cluster B personality disorders. *Research on Social Work Practice, 14,* 443–449.

Oldham, J. M. (2007). Psychodynamic psychotherapy for personality disorders. *American Journal of Psychiatry, 164,* 1465–1467.

Parker, G., & Barrett, E. (2000). Personality and personality disorder: Current issues and directions. *Psychological Medicine, 30,* 1–9.

Patrick, C. J., Fowles, D., & Krueger, R. (2009). Triarchic conceptualization of psychopathy: Developmental origins of disinhibition, boldness and meanness. *Development and Psychopathology, 21,* 913–938.

Safran, J. D., & Muran, J. C. (2000). *Negotiating the therapeutic alliance: A relational treatment guide.* New York: Guilford Press.

Sellen, J. L., Gobbett, M., & Campbell, J. (2013). Enhancing treatment engagement in sexual offenders: a pilot study to explore the utility of the Personal Aspirations and Concerns Inventory for Offenders (PACI-O). *Criminal Behaviour and Mental Health, 23*(3), 203–216.

Skodol, A. E., Buckley, P., & Charles, E. (1983). Is there a characteristic pattern to the treatment history of clinic outpatients with borderline personality? *Journal of Nervous and Mental Disease, 171,* 405–410.

Skodol, A. E., Johnson, J. G., Cohen, P., Sneed, J. R., & Crawford, T. N. (2007). Personality disorder and impaired functioning from adolescent to adulthood. *British Journal of Psychiatry, 190,* 415–420.

Skodol, A. E., Oldham, J. M., Rosnick, L., Kellman, H. D., & Hyler, S. E. (1991). Diagnosis of DSM-III-R personality disorders: A comparison of two structured interviews. *International Journal of Methods in Psychiatric Research, 1,* 13–26.

Soloff, P. (1998). Symptom-orientated psychopharmacology for personality disorders. *Journal of Practical Psychiatry and Behavioral Health, 4*(1), 3–11.

Stangl, D., Pfohl, B., Zimmerman, M., Bowers, W., & Corenthal, C. (1985). A structured interview for the DSM-III personality disorders: A preliminary report. *Archives of General Psychiatry, 42,* 591–596.

Stanley, J. H., Wygant, D. B., & Sellbom, M. (2013). Elaborating on the construct validity of the triarchic psychopathy measure in a criminal offender sample. *Journal of Personality Assessment, 95*(4), 343–350.

Stevenson, J., & Meares, R. (1992). An outcome study of psychotherapy for patients with borderline personality disorder. *American Journal of Psychiatry, 149,* 358–362.

Torgersen, S., Czajkowski, N., Jacobson, K., Reichborn-Kjennerud, T., Røysamb, E., Neale, M. C., & Kendler, K. C. (2008). Dimensional representations of DSM-IV cluster B personality disorders in a population-based sample of Norwegian twins: A multivariate study. *Psychological Medicine, 38*(11), 1617–1625.

Tyrer, P., Coombs, N., Ibrahimi, F., Mathilakath, A., Bajaj, P., Ranger, M., & Din, R. (2007). Critical developments in the assessment of personality disorder. *British Journal of Psychiatry, 190*(Suppl. 49), s51–s59. doi: 10.1192/bjp.190.5.s51.

Ullrich, S., & Marneros, A. (2004). Dimensions of personality disorders in offenders. *Criminal Behaviour and Mental Health, 14,* 202–213.

Ullrich, S., & Marneros, A. (2007). Underlying dimensions of ICD-10 personality disorders: Risk factors, childhood antecedents, and adverse outcomes in adulthood. *Journal of Forensic Psychiatry and Psychology, 18*(1), 44–58.

Wakefield, J. C. (1992). The concept of mental disorder: On the boundary between biological facts and social values. *American Psychologist, 47,* 373–388.

Waldinger, R. J., & Gunderson, J. G. (1984). Completed psychotherapies with borderline patients. *American Journal of Psychotherapy, 38,* 190–202.

Ward, T., Day, A., & Howells, K. (2004). The multifactor offender readiness model. *Aggression and Violent Behaviour, 9,* 645–673.

Weissman, M. M. (1993). The epidemiology of personality disorders: A 1990 update. *Journal of Personality Disorders,* Suppl., 44–62.

Westen, D., & Arkowitz-Westen, L. (1998). Limitations of Axis II in diagnosing personality pathology in clinical practice. *American Journal of Psychiatry, 155,* 1767–1771.

World Health Organization (1992). *10th revision of the International Classification of Diseases (ICD-10).* Geneva: WHO.

Zanarini, M. C., Frankenberg, F. R., Hennen, J., Reich, B., & Silk, K. (2005). The Mclean Study of Adult Development (MSAD): Overview of the first six years of prospective follow-up. *Journal of Personality Disorders, 19,* 505–523.

Zimmerman, M. (1994). Diagnosing personality disorders: A review of issues and research methods. *Archives of General Psychiatry, 51,* 225–245.

Zimmerman, M., Pfohl, B., Coryell, W., Stangl, D., & Corenthal, C. (1988). Diagnosing personality disorder in depressed patients: A comparison of patient and informant interviews. *Archives of General Psychiatry, 45,* 733–737.

17 Personality Disorders: Their Relation to Offending

RICHARD HOWARD AND CONOR DUGGAN

In this chapter, which should be seen as a sequel to the preceding chapter, we raise questions about whether, and how, personality is linked to offending, particularly to violent offending. We start by examining the relationship between personality disorder and offending in general, and proceed to an examination of how this relationship might be mediated, with a focus on different types of violence. We then examine the relationship between 'psychopathy' and violence, with a focus on the subtypes of 'psychopath'. A model is then outlined, with reference to a case example, to illustrate how the link between personality disorder and violence might operate. We conclude with a discussion of some current issues, in particular, recent changes in the general strategy for identifying and intervening with those offenders with personality disorder who are deemed at particularly high risk for harm both to themselves and others.

IS PERSONALITY DISORDER LINKED TO OFFENDING?

There is no doubt that the prevalence of personality disorder, which is around 4% of the general UK population (Coid, Yang, Tyrer, Roberts, & Ullrich, 2006), is markedly raised in criminal populations. In a systematic review of 62 surveys of prisoners in 12 countries, Fazel and Danesh (2002) reported that, of 18,530 men, 65% had a personality disorder and 47% had an antisocial personality disorder (ASPD). The equivalent figures for women were 42 and 21%, respectively. In the five studies that measured it, borderline personality disorder (BPD) showed a moderately high prevalence among women prisoners (25%).

A proportion of offenders transferred from prison, the courts and other psychiatric hospitals to high-security forensic hospitals under the various sections of the UK Mental Health Act (1983, revised 20082) are admitted under the 'Psychopathic Disorder' category.[1] The precise figure has fluctuated over the past 30 years, but it averages about 20–25% of high-security hospital admissions. 'PD' is a catch-all label which comprises patients with a variety of personality disorders, most commonly borderline, antisocial, narcissistic and paranoid types (Coid, 1992). This is not to say that patients admitted under the Mental Illness (MI) category are not personality disordered: roughly 60% of MI patients meet clinical criteria for personality disorder (Blackburn, 2000), and some patients are admitted with a dual (MI + PD) legal classification. The co-occurrence of personality disorders, both with other personality disorders and with Axis I mental disorders, is very high in forensic psychiatric samples, yet systematic study of patterns of co-morbidity found in mentally disordered offenders has been lacking. Coid (1992) noted in passing that a proportion of his forensic sample had both antisocial and borderline PD 'in devastating combination' (p. 89), and this combination was said by Mullen (1992, p. 238) to represent '… a very particular constellation of abnormalities of mental state with a wide range of disorderly conduct' – abnormalities said to be developmental in origin. The co-occurrence of antisocial and borderline personality disorders varies with level of security, being most common in very-high-security samples, and least common in the general community (see Duggan & Howard, 2009, figure 2). The question of the nature of the relationship between personality disorder and violence, and more importantly, of how they are they linked together (see following section), has been systematically explored in a recent volume (McMurran & Howard, 2009). The personality disorder most often found to associate with violence is antisocial PD (e.g., Coid, Kahtan, Gault, & Jarman, 1999). In forensic psychiatric samples, antisocial PD has been found to correlate, albeit very modestly ($r = .23$), with a history of violence

Forensic Psychology, Second Edition. Edited by David A. Crighton and Graham J. Towl.
© 2015 John Wiley & Sons, Ltd. Published 2015 by British Psychological Society and John Wiley & Sons, Ltd.

(Blackburn, 2007). Blackburn pointed out that the correlation between ASPD and violent offending was inflated by criterion contamination, and interpreted his results as suggesting that '… none of the personality disorders is strongly associated with persistent offending' (Blackburn, 2007, p. 155). However, recent results from the UK Prisoner Cohort Study (Coid, Yang, Ullrich, Zhang, & Roberts, 2008) confirm that antisocial PD predicts violent reoffending in prisoners followed up after their release, even in the absence of a high (>/= 30) PCL psychopathy score. The propensity to violence associated with antisocial PD appears particularly high when this co-occurs with borderline PD, both in community samples (Howard, Huband, Duggan, & Mannion, 2008; Freestone, Howard, Coid, & Ullrich, 2012) and in forensic psychiatric samples (Howard, Khalifa, & Duggan, under review). In the latter study, both the antisocial deviance factor of PCL psychopathy and antisocial/borderline PD co-morbidity made independent contributions to the prediction of violence. A triad of severe childhood CD, substance dependence (particularly when this occurs in adolescence) and antisocial/borderline co-morbidity appears to be a particularly toxic combination with regard to the occurrence of violent antisociality in adulthood (Freestone et al., 2012). This toxic triad, associated with antisocial/borderline PD co-morbidity, has been found to be associated with early re-offending in forensic patients following their release from secure care into the community (Howard, McCarthy, Huband, & Duggan, 2013).

HOW IS PERSONALITY DISORDER LINKED TO VIOLENCE?

It is important to note that an association between personality disorder and violence does not necessarily imply a causal link between them, and evidence for such a link in the case of antisocial PD is lacking (Duggan & Howard, 2009). It appears that it is the co-morbidity, both between different personality disorders (e.g., borderline and antisocial) and between personality disorders and DSM Axis I disorders, that is key to understanding this relationship and the mechanisms that mediate it (Freestone et al., 2012). Co-morbid substance (including alcohol) abuse is very high in those personality-disordered individuals who act violently, particularly when it is combined with another Axis I mental disorder. The striking co-occurrence of substance misuse, mental illness and antisocial personality disorder in violent men is well illustrated by results of a study of 90 male mentally ill

homicides by Putkonen, Kotilainen, Joyal, and Tühonen (2004). Men showing this diagnostic triad were responsible for two-thirds of all homicidal acts committed by those who, comprising 50% of the sample, received a double diagnosis of mental illness (mostly schizophrenia) and substance abuse.

The critical question, then, is: What is the mechanism through which mental disorder in general becomes linked to violence? DeBrito and Hodgins (2009) suggested co-morbid childhood conduct disorder as the critical intervening variable, while Howard and McMurran (2013) have outlined a developmental trajectory leading from childhood and adolescence to a heightened risk of alcohol-related violence in adulthood. These authors proposed that the effect on adult antisociality of severe conduct disorder, known to be associated with callous–unemotional traits, is mediated by severe early-onset alcohol abuse (Howard, Finn, Gallagher, & Jose., 2012; Khalifa Duggan, Howard, & Lumsden, 2012). Excessive alcohol use in adolescence is said to subsequently disrupt development of a neural cognitive control system that develops in late adolescence and supports mature self-regulation (Albert and Steinberg, 2011). Incomplete or delayed maturation of this system as a result of excessive alcohol use in adolescence will, it was argued, result in a variety of self-regulatory deficits, including deficiencies in social problem-solving, error monitoring and behavioural inhibition. Important among these deficits is an inability to self-regulate emotionally. Emotional dysregulation has recently been found to mediate effects of both borderline PD and antisocial traits on violence (Newhill, Eack, & Mulvey, 2012). This suggests that the inability to self-regulate emotionally is key to explaining the link between PD (particularly antisocial/borderline PD co-morbidity) and violence.

When addressing this question, it must be borne in mind that different types of violence exist, and that particular personality disorders may be differentially linked to the various types. A typology of violence, suggested by Howard (2009), expands upon the instrumental vs. affective distinction, which is considered too simplistic. The revised typology suggests a distinction between appetitively and aversively motivated violence, the former associated with positive affect, the latter with negative affect. Within each of these, violence may be impulsive or controlled, yielding a 2 × 2 matrix (see table 1 in Howard, 2009), with four distinct types of violence: Appetitive/Impulsive, Appetitive/Controlled, Aversive/Impulsive and Aversive/Controlled. Since this typology was first proposed, it has been validated in a Norwegian sample of antisocial youth using a self-report questionnaire, the Angry Aggression Scale (AAS), developed to tap these four motivationally distinct types of violence (Bjørnebekk & Howard, 2012a;

Bjørnebekk & Howard, 2012b). The latter study confirmed that the quest for excitement was an important motivation for antisocial behaviour in delinquent youth. Scores on the thrill-seeking AAS measure correlated most strongly with the most serious types of offence, in particular violence, carrying hidden weapons, and destroying others' property. It will be a task for future research to attempt to map different types of personality disorders onto this typology. Howard (2009) argued that antisocial PD may be particularly associated with the impulsive type of appetitively motivated violence (i.e., violence that is motivated by a quest for excitement), while borderline PD may be associated with the impulsive type of aversively motivated violence (i.e., violence that is motivated by fear or social threat). This now seems overly simplistic, given the results of a study by Camp, Skeem, Barchard, Lilienfeld, and Poythress (2013), which retrospectively examined the motivations for violence in a sample of 158 American male offenders. Results suggested that individuals with greater disinhibition and a history of past criminal behaviour were more likely to commit violence for material gain or as part of gang involvement, and were less likely to commit violence as an angry response to provocation. In contrast, the violence of those offenders showing core interpersonal-affective traits of psychopathy was less motivated by feelings of fear or threat, raising the question: what did motivate their violence? One might speculate, in terms of Howard's violence typology, that their violence was primarily motivated by the goal of inflicting harm on others to satisfy a desire for excitement (Howard, 2011). However, until violence in personality-disordered offenders is examined through the lens of the quadripartite violence typology, such a conclusion would be premature.

IS 'PSYCHOPATHY' RELATED TO VIOLENCE?

Not all forensic psychiatrists regard psychopathy as a genuine clinical entity (e.g., Mullen, 2007), and it did not feature under personality disorders in earlier editions of the DSM. Nonetheless, it has crept into the nomenclature of the DSM-5 hybrid revision under the title 'antisocial/psychopathic PD' (see Chapter 20), and many working in the field consider that it falls among the personality disorders. The Psychopathy Checklist (PCL), originally developed in the early 1980s as a research scale for the assessment of psychopathy (Hare, 1980), has resulted in a proliferation of research on psychopathy, and its use, and potential misuse, in the criminal justice system has been critiqued by numerous authors

(e.g., Skeem, Polaschek, Patrick, & Lilienfeld, 2011). The PCL is loosely based on Cleckley's psychopathy criteria, although it should be noted that there is not complete overlap between PCL criteria and Cleckley's (1988) checklist. Loss of insight, for example, is not captured by the PCL, and by including items related to criminal behaviour, the PCL goes well beyond Cleckley's criteria (Blackburn, 2007). Development of the PCL in criminal populations resulted in it being strongly biased in favour of disinhibitory psychopathology (Skeem et al., 2011). The most recent revision of the PCL (Hare, 2003) yields, in addition to a total score, scores on two factors – selfish, callous and remorseless use of others (F1), and chronically unstable and antisocial lifestyle (F2). Each factor subsumes two facets, so that F1 subsumes the facets Interpersonal and Affective, while F2 subsumes the facets Lifestyle and Antisocial.

Most relevant to the present context is the PCL's increasing use as a measure of risk within the criminal justice system. Its early promise in this regard led Blackburn (2000) to conclude: 'There is a compelling case for including the PCL-R routinely in the assessment of personality disorder among mentally disordered offenders' (p. S10). This conclusion has been tempered by more recent research that has cast doubt on the PCL's accuracy in predicting both violent and non-violent recidivism. Three large meta-analyses of recidivism data (Leistico, Salekin, DeCosta, & Rogers, 2008; Walters, 2003; Yang, Wong, & Coid, 2010) all reported significantly better predictive accuracy for Factor 2 than for Factor 1. The UK Prisoner Cohort Study (Coid et al., 2008) compared the ability of a range of possible risk measures, including the PCL, to predict violent and nonviolent reoffending in high-risk prisoners. PCL performed relatively poorly as a predictor of reoffending in comparison with a measure – the Offender Group Reconviction Scale – that relied solely on past offending. PCL items that predicted reoffending mainly reflected antisociality and impulsivity. A study that examined PCL's predictive accuracy using a very large database across six separate samples showed that only facet 4 (Antisocial) displayed incremental validity in predicting recidivism relative to facets 1, 2 and 3. In contrast, facets 1, 2 and 3 failed to attain a consistent level of incremental validity relative to facet 4 (Walters, Knight, Grann, & Dahle, 2008). A methodologically rigorous meta-analysis carried out by Yang and colleagues (2010) showed that, in males, only PCL-R Factor 2 predicted violence; the first PCL factor, representing core interpersonal and affective traits of psychopathy, failed to predict above chance level. Furthermore, the core PCL-R interpersonal and affective traits (Factor 1) have been found not to interact with the behavioural/lifestyle traits (Factor 2) in the prediction of violence (Kennealy, Skeem, Walters, & Camp, 2010). A recent prospective study by

Camp *et al.* (2013) assessed the predictive accuracy of psychopathy facets measured using the PCL-R and the Psychopathic Personality Inventory (PPI: Lilienfeld & Andrews, 1996). Total PCL-R score did not significantly predict violence over a 3-month follow-up period. However, Impulsive Antisociality measured with the PPI did significantly predict proximate violence, mostly in the prison environment, and arrests for violence in the community 1 year after release. Results of this and other studies challenge the idea that the interpersonal and affective traits of psychopathy – that is, those traits that distinguish it from general antisocial deviance – predict violence. Rather, it appears to be the combination of criminal behaviour and poor behavioural controls (irritability, aggression and inadequate control of anger) that, among traits tapped by the PCL, accurately predicts future violent and non-violent offending. This combination seems very similar to the traits subsumed under the IPDE Antisocial Dyscontrol factor that appear to be particularly criminogenic (Howard *et al.*, 2008).

Patrick and colleagues' recent triarchic reconceptualization of psychopathy in terms of the three phenotypic domains of *boldness*, *meanness* and *disinhibition* represents an important advance not just in our understanding of psychopathy but also, potentially, in its assessment and treatment (Patrick, Fowles, & Krueger, 2009; Patrick, Drislane, & Strickland, 2012). Patrick (2010) developed a brief self-report inventory, the Triarchic Psychopathy Measure (TriPM), to capture these three domains. Results from a study in which TriPM, along with other relevant measures, was applied to a sample of 141 incarcerated offenders showed that it had good construct validity (Stanley, Wygant, & Sellbom, 2013). However, it is not clear whether, and to what extent, the three elements of boldness, meanness and disinhibition are independent of one another or are causally interrelated. The Stanley *et al.* (2013) study indicated that TriPM meanness and disinhibition were significantly intercorrelated (r ~ 0.4), which implies a possible causal relationship between them. For example, as proposed by Howard and McMurran (2013), meanness may lead to early substance abuse which, in turn, via effects on the brain, may give rise to the panoply of traits included under disinhibition, including poor impulse control, failure to delay gratification, irresponsibility, and poor emotional and behavioural self-regulation.

Subtypes of 'psychopath'

'The psychopath', considered as a homogeneous entity, is almost certainly a chimera, a myth manufactured in the popular media. Insofar as it can be considered as a unitary construct, psychopathy is 'like love, a many-splendoured thing' (Howard, 1986). This is supported by recent research indicating that several sub-types of PCL psychopath exist, who differ in important ways such as their offending histories and DSM Axis I and Axis II correlates (see Figure 17.2 in Blackburn, 2009). Type S, originally labelled 'secondary psychopaths', show a high rate of co-morbid Axis I disorders, a high rate of post-traumatic stress disorder, a high rate of sexual abuse, and the most severe personality pathology measured by IPDE. Type S, importantly, shows antisocial/borderline PD co-morbidity and a high level of both childhood and adult antisociality (see Figure 6.1 in Blackburn, 2009). Type P in Figure 17.2 show high rates of conviction for violence and early onset of antisocial disorder; they appear similar to McCord psychopaths. Borderline, histrionic, narcissistic, and adult/child antisocial traits are prominent in both Type P and Type S. Type C show a high rate of sexual offending, higher IQ and the least severe personality pathology measured using IPDE; of all four types, they approximate most closely to Cleckley psychopaths. The implication of these findings is that, if PCL psychopaths are so heterogeneous, a high score on the PCL may tell us little more about the individual than that he or she is a high PCL scorer – one may just as well call him or her 'a bastard', of which there are equally different sorts. Different permutations of meanness, boldness and disinhibition, as conceptualized in Patrick's triarchic reconceptualization of psychopathy outlined earlier, may be informative in distinguishing between these various subtypes of psychopaths. Type C, for example, might be expected to show a preponderance of boldness with lesser degrees of meanness and disinhibition, while Type S and Type P would be expected to show a predominance of disinhibition with varying degrees of meanness.

A caveat

To conclude this section, it is perhaps appropriate to warn the reader against the naive assumption that all violent people are personality disordered, and that all personality-disordered people are violent. In the Howard, Khalifa, and Duggan (2014, under review) study, for example, schizoid traits were negatively associated with severe violence in personality-disordered offenders. Consistent with this, a recent study found a high (92%) prevalence of personality disorder in incarcerated American adolescents, and that those with schizoid PD were no more aggressive, distressed, angry, delinquent or lacking in restraint than those without PD (Kaszynski *et al.*, 2013). Results of the Camp *et al.* (2013) study warn against the naïve assumption that psychopathic individuals are, as these authors state, driven towards predatory violence for material gain. Rather, their violence, in a proportion of cases at least, appears to be driven by a quest for excitement (Howard,

2009). Both the strength and nature of the relationship between personality disorder and violence are far from clear, and will only become apparent when further longitudinal studies are conducted.

TOWARDS A MODEL OF PERSONALITY DISORDER AND VIOLENCE

We will use a clinical example (Case 4 from Coid, 1998) to illustrate a model of how personality disorder might play a role in instigating an act of violence.[2] The patient, who suffered from narcissistic personality disorder, became increasingly angry and jealous in the course of a telephone conversation with his ex-girlfriend, whom he had telephoned regarding the collection of some of his personal belongings, including a pullover which, he suggested, her new boyfriend might make use of. His girlfriend's mother then interrupted the telephone conversation to suggest that the pullover would be too small for the new boyfriend. This was taken by the narcissistic patient as a demeaning comment about his physique, triggering a rage reaction that resulted in the violent killing of his ex-girlfriend's new partner. Prior to the final murderous act, he had travelled by bus to his ex-girlfriend's house, and had interrupted his journey to buy the weapon, a butcher's knife, used to commit the murder. The trigger factor that precipitated the act of violence (the ex-girlfriend's mother's comment) acted in tandem with his narcissism, a significant predisposing factor. The act of violence can be interpreted as directed at the goal of removing a significant threat to his self-esteem, motivated by revenge. It illustrates the 'aversive/controlled' type of violence in Howard's (2009) typology, which is accompanied by ruminative anger.

In the model, outlined in Figure 17.1, the brain mediates the effects of triggering events and predisposing factors, producing, as outputs, cognitions (e.g., ruminative thoughts of revenge), affective/somatic reactions (e.g., a fight/flight reaction, with sympathetic autonomic arousal) and motor behaviour (including the actions involved in committing the act of murder). Since there was a considerable delay between formation of the

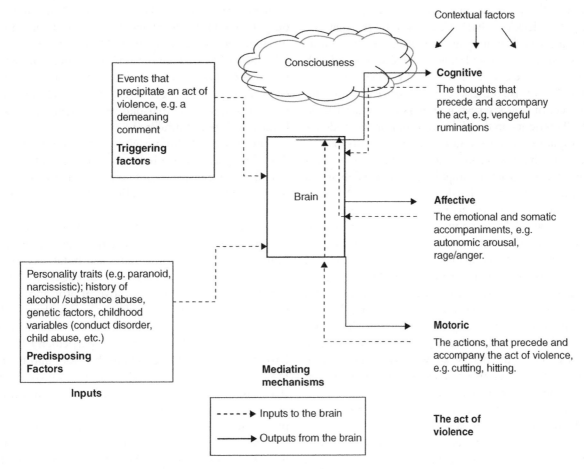

FIGURE 17.1 *A schematic model of how personality disorder may result in violence.*

intention to commit the murder and the consummation of the act, we need to distinguish between a preparatory phase of the act, comprising actions in preparation for its consummation – walking to the bus-stop, buying a bus ticket, getting on the bus, breaking the journey to buy a knife in a hardware store, locating the address of the person to be attacked – and the final consummation of the act. Contextual factors can also influence the final output. For example, if the phone conversation triggering the act had occurred at night, the buses might not have been running, the shops might have been closed, and so on, so that the act of violence might have been delayed or even aborted.

Also shown in Figure 17.1 is the feedback (sometimes called 'reafference') from the cognitive, affective and motor outputs from the brain. Only the cognitive feedback gains direct access to consciousness, but feedback from affective and motor outputs can, by accessing the cognitive processing stream in the brain, gain access to consciousness. In this way, we normally have coherent, conscious representations of our acts, and of ourselves as authors of those acts, allowing us to monitor our own thoughts, affects and behaviours and to consciously reflect on them. This self-monitoring is thought to be defective in people with personality disorder, particularly in psychopaths where it can manifest as a 'specific loss of insight' (Cleckley, 1941). Cleckley remarks that the psychopath 'has absolutely no capacity to see himself as others see him' (p. 350) and shows 'a total absence of self-appraisal as a real and moving experience' (p. 351). Livesley (2007a) also remarks on the absence of the evaluative aspect of self-observation in personality-disordered people. This deficit in the ability to monitor the feedback from cognitive, affective and motor outputs appears to have a neural basis, since individuals ('externalizers') having a propensity to act out impulsively show a deficit in a brain wave, the error-related negativity (ERN) that is evoked when behavioural errors are made (Hall, Bernat, & Patrick, 2007). This brain-wave is thought to be generated in the anterior cingulate cortex (Dehaene, Posner, & Tucker, 1994). Psychopathic personality-disordered offenders (those who scored high on PCL-R psychopathy) have also been reported to show a deficient neural response to a signal conveying negative feedback ('you responded too slowly') in a go/no-go reaction time paradigm (Varlamov, Khalifa, Liddle, Duggan, & Howard, 2010). A similar brain mechanism would putatively evaluate errors in the cognitive and affective outputs, so that these can be corrected. A 'crazy' thought or an inappropriate affective reaction such as jealous rage, for example, could be monitored in this way and corrected.

Dysfunctional personality traits, in conjunction with a variety of other predisposing factors, bias motivational neural circuits such that they respond to particular triggering events, leading to the initiation of an act of violence. This may be impulsive or controlled, appetitive or defensive. Once having initiated an act of violence, which would include actions preparatory to the act as well as its consummation, personality-disordered individuals fail to adequately process the feedback (indicated by dashed arrows) from the motor, cognitive and affective outputs from the brain (indicated by solid arrows). Consequently, their brains fail to register 'errors' which would normally act to inhibit or abort the violent act.

Despite its apparently static appearance, the model shown is in fact a highly dynamic one – the only static elements are the predisposing influences that set the thresholds for detecting and responding to inputs (triggering factors and feedback from outputs, shown as dashed lines in Figure 17.1). Thus, in our example of the narcissistic patient, several successive triggers would have operated subsequent to the initial trigger of the demeaning comment. For example, having arrived at his ex-girlfriend's house and rung the doorbell, the appearance of the new boyfriend triggered the final murderous act. Nonetheless, it is the failure to monitor the feedback from cognitive, affective and motoric outputs that was arguably critical to the fatal outcome. Normally, these outputs would, via feedback, be appraised and an error message registered which would lead to interruption or inhibition of the behaviour. It is, we argue, a characteristic of the personality-disordered individual that these error messages fail to get detected in the relevant neural mechanism, so that maladaptive thoughts, affects and behaviours are not inhibited.

The traits of impulsivity and compulsivity will doubtless play a key role here. To the extent that individuals are impulsive cognitively (their acts lack premeditation and forethought), affectively (their emotional impulses are poorly controlled) and motorically (their actions are rash and precipitate), they will be more liable to failure in detecting an error message. In short, the brains of impulsive individuals will putatively be deficient in the ability to detect error messages contained in the feedback from their cognitive, motor and affective outputs. Those who are affectively impulsive, whose offending is driven by negative affective states such as reactive anger and boredom, are particularly likely to have criminal, including violent, histories and to manifest a combination of borderline and antisocial traits (Howard et al., 2008). Their error-detection deficit is likely to be most salient in situations where an inappropriate affective reaction is manifested in, for example, extreme sensation-seeking or extreme reactive (threat-induced) aggression. At the other extreme are those with obsessive compulsive traits, which correlate inversely with a history of criminal and violent offending (Howard et al., 2008) and are inversely related to a broad PD dimension of antisocial dyscontrol (Fossati et al., 2007). In their case, the error message is likely to be too sensitively detected (the threshold for error detection is set too low), so that any action performed is flagged with an error message. Having detected the error message, the brain 'instructs' that the action be repeated, which again throws up an error message leading to further, compulsive repetition of the action.

An alternative (and perhaps complementary) account of the deficit shown by personality-disordered patients in terms of the model shown in Figure 17.1 would suggest that when motoric or affective errors occur, mismatch signals are generated but are of insufficient strength, so that they fail to connect with the cognitive processing stream. As a consequence, affective and motoric mismatch signals fail to be processed cognitively and hence fail to gain access to consciousness – a type of 'disconnection syndrome'. The result would be a failure of 'cross-talk' between the affective and cognitive systems in the brain such as has been suggested to occur when the brain's cognitive control system fails to develop normally (Albert & Steinberg, 2011). Such a disconnection between cognition and affect recalls the 'failure to forge a cohesive self-structure capable of integrating cognitions and affects and connecting different aspects of self-experience' noted by Livesley in many patients with personality disorder, resulting in their failure '… to recognise the situational and experiential factors that trigger a variety of problematic behaviours such as deliberate self-harm or interpersonal violence' (Livesley, 2007b, p. 30).

Current issues

A major current issue concerns the general strategy for identifying, and intervening with, those individuals with PD who are deemed at particularly high risk for harm both to themselves and others. In the 1990s, the UK government initiated the Dangerous and Severe Personality Disorder (DSPD) programme, to pilot the assessment and treatment of patients with severe personality disorders supposedly linked functionally to their dangerousness (see Duggan & Howard, 2009). Despite its many successes, as well as its failings (see Duggan, 2011), the DSPD programme has now been abandoned in favour of a new initiative focusing on high-harm offenders with PD (see Joseph & Benefield, 2012). A cynic might argue that the old DSPD wine has simply been re-bottled under the label 'high-harm offenders with personality disorder'. Despite the change of focus from patients detained in high-security psychiatric facilities to high-risk offenders detained in the prison estate, Howard and McMurran (2012) point out that many questions remain to be addressed, and among them: is PD a *correlate* of violence, a *risk factor* for violence or a *casual risk factor* for violence? What is it about people with PD that may explain an association with an increased likelihood of violence? It is perhaps the latter question that is most urgently in need of an answer, an approximation to which is suggested by recent evidence pointing to a developmental trajectory from *early psychosocial deprivation*, leading to *disordered childhood conduct* associated, in its severest form, with *callous–unemotional traits* and *early substance abuse*. This, in turn, gives rise, via adverse effects of substance abuse on the developing adolescent brain, to the multitude of traits associated in adulthood with *antisocial dyscontrol* (Howard & McMurran, 2013).

NOTES

1 Note that, following revision of the Mental Health Act by the UK Parliament, the distinction between 'Psychopathic Disorder' and 'Mental Illness' was abolished in favour of the generic term 'mental disorder', defined (in an entirely circular fashion) as 'any disorder or disability of the mind'.
2 Care should be taken to distinguish between an act, defined by an intended goal or outcome (in the case of a violent act, the infliction of harm and suffering), and the actions taken to achieve the outcome.

FURTHER READING

Howard, R. C., & McMurran, M. (2013). Alcohol and violence in developmental perspective. In M. McMurran (Ed.), *Alcohol-related violence: Prevention and treatment* (pp. 81–102). Chichester: Wiley-Blackwell.
This chapter deals in greater detail with many of the arguments and issues addressed in the present chapter. In particular, the quadripartite model of violence referred to here is described in greater detail, as is the developmental trajectory starting from infancy and continuing through adolescence and into adulthood. It describes the developmental risk factors that lead to an increased likelihood of adult alcohol-related violence. Both risk and protective factors, operating over time and at a range of levels, include: individual

characteristics, family functioning, school bonding and academic attainment, peer associations, leisure pursuits and employment. An interactive effect is described between the at-risk individual and his or her social environment, which may exacerbate or mitigate problems. In examining alcohol use in relation to violence, the authors organize their material in three sections: childhood, adolescence and early adulthood. In each section, risk factors are examined in the intrapersonal, interpersonal and social domains.

Coid, J. (1998). Axis II disorders and motivation for serious criminal behaviour. In A. E. Skodol (Ed.), *Psychopathology and violent crime* (pp. 53–97). *Review of psychiatry*, Vol. 17. Washington, DC: American Psychiatric Association.

This was one of the first studies to systematically explore the relationship between personality disorder in criminal offenders and violent crimes. It was unique in also exploring the motivations behind the criminal offending in the personality disordered, and attempted to draw up a taxonomy of motivations. The study samples were male and female psychopaths from three maximum-security hospitals, and male inmates of three special units for dangerous prisoners, a total sample of 243. All underwent detailed psychiatric assessment to ascertain personality-disorder diagnoses and level of psychopathy using the Psychopathy Checklist. The text is illustrated with several interesting case studies, including Case 4 (p. 322), the narcissistic offender referred to in this chapter. A drawback of the study is that it is correlational, so that no causal inferences can be drawn regarding the relationship between personality disorder and violent offending.

REFERENCES

Albert, D., & Steinberg, L. (2011). Peer influences on adolescent risk behaviour. In M. T. Bardo, R. Milich, and D. H. Fishbein (Eds.), *Inhibitory control and drug abuse prevention* (pp. 211–226). New York: Springer.

Bjørnebekk, G., & Howard, R. C. (2012a). Validation of a motivation-based typology of angry aggression antisocial youth in Norway. *Behavioral Sciences and the Law*, 30, 167–180.

Bjørnebekk, G., & Howard, R. C. (2012b). Sub-types of angry aggression, frequency of anti-social acts, and teachers perceptions of social competence, emotional and behavioural problems. *Personality & Individual Differences*, 53(3), 312–316. doi: 10.1016/j.paid.2012.03.033.

Blackburn, R. (2000). Classification and assessment of personality disorders in mentally disordered offenders: A psychological perspective. *Criminal Behaviour and Mental Health*, 10, S8–S32.

Blackburn, R. (2007). Personality disorder and antisocial deviance: Comments on the debate on the structure of the Psychopathy Checklist – Revised. *Journal of Personality Disorders*, 21, 142–159.

Blackburn, R. (2009). Subtypes of psychopath. In M. McMurran & R. Howard (Eds.), *Personality, personality disorder and violence* (pp. 113–132). Chichester: John Wiley & Sons.

Camp, J. P., Skeem, J. L., Barchard, K., Lilienfeld, S. O., & Poythress, N. G. (2013). Psychopathic predators? Getting specific about the relation between psychopathy and violence. *Journal of Consulting and Clinical Psychology*, 81(3), 467–480.

Cleckley, H. (1941). *The mask of sanity*. Oxford: Mosby.

Cleckley, H. (1988). *The mask of sanity* (5th edn). St. Louis, MO: Mosby. Retrieved 14 September 2009 from http://www.cassiopaea.org/cass/sanity_1.PdF

Coid, J. (1992). DSM-III diagnosis in criminal psychopaths: A way forward. *Criminal Behaviour and Mental Health*, 2, 78–94.

Coid, J. (1998). Axis II disorders and motivation for serious criminal behaviour. In A. E. Skodol (Ed.), *Psychopathology and violent crime* (pp. 53–97). *Review of Psychiatry*, Vol. 17. Washington, DC: American Psychiatric Association.

Coid, J., Kahtan, N., Gault, S., & Jarman, B. (1999). Patients with personality disorder admitted to secure forensic psychiatry services. *British Journal of Psychiatry*, 175, 528–536.

Coid, J., Yang, M., Tyrer, P., Roberts, A., & Ullrich, S. (2006). Prevalence and correlates of personality disorder in Great Britain. *British Journal of Psychiatry*, 188, 423–431.

Coid, J., Yang, M., Ullrich, S., Zhang, T., & Roberts, A. (2008). *Predicting and understanding risk of re-offending: The Prisoner Cohort Study*. Final report. London: Home Office/Department of Health.

DeBrito, S. A., & Hodgins, S. (2009). Antisocial personality disorder. In M. McMurran & R. Howard (Eds.), *Personality, personality disorder and violence*. Chichester: John Wiley & Sons.

Dehaene, S., Posner, M. I., & Tucker, D. M. (1994). Localization of a neural system for error detection and compensation. *Psychological Science*, 5, 303–305.

Duggan, C. (2011). Dangerous and severe personality disorder. *British Journal of Psychiatry*, 198(6), 431–433.

Duggan, C., & Howard, R. C. (2009). The 'functional link' between personality disorder and violence: A critical appraisal. In M. McMurran & R. Howard (Eds.), *Personality, personality disorder and violence* (pp. 19–37). Chichester: John Wiley & Sons.

Fazel, S., & Danesh, J. (2002). Serious mental disorder in 23 000 prisoners: A systematic review of 62 surveys. *The Lancet*, 359, 545–550.

Fossati, A., Barratt, E. S., Borroni, S., Villa, D., Grazioli, F., & Maffei, C. (2007). Impulsivity, aggressiveness, and DSM-IV personality disorders. *Psychiatry Research*, 149, 157–167.

Freestone, M., Howard, R. C., Coid, J., & Ullrich, S. (2012). Adult antisocial syndrome co-morbid with borderline personality disorder is associated with severe conduct disorder, substance dependence and violent antisociality. *Personality and Mental Health*, *7*(1), 11–21.

Hall, J. R., Bernat, E. M., & Patrick, C. J. (2007). Externalizing psychopathology and the error-related negativity. *Psychological Science*, *18*, 326–333.

Hare, R. D. (1980). A research scale for the assessment of psychopathy in criminal populations. *Personality and Individual Differences*, *1*, 111–119.

Hare, R. D. (2003). The Hare Psychopathy Checklist – Revised (2nd edn). Toronto: Multi-Health Systems.

Howard, R. C. (1986) Psychopathy: A psychobiological perspective. *Personality and Individual Differences*, *7*(6), 795–806.

Howard, R. C. (2009). The neurobiology of affective dyscontrol: Implications for under-standing 'dangerous and severe personality disorder'. In M. McMurran & R. Howard (Eds.), *Personality, personality disorder and violence*. Chichester: John Wiley & Sons.

Howard, R. C. (2011). The quest for excitement: A missing link between personality disorder and violence? *Journal of Forensic Psychology and Psychiatry*, *22*(5), 692–705.

Howard, R. C., Finn, P. R., Gallagher, J., & Jose, P. E. (2012). Adolescent-onset alcohol abuse exacerbates the influence of childhood conduct disorder on late adolescent and early adult antisocial behaviour. *Journal of Forensic Psychiatry & Psychology*, *23*, 7–22.

Howard, R. C., Huband, N., Duggan, C., & Mannion, A. (2008). Exploring the link between personality disorder and criminality in a community sample. *Journal of Personality Disorders*, *22*(6), 589–603.

Howard, R., Khalifa, N., & Duggan, C. (2014). Antisocial personality disorder comorbid with borderline pathology and psychopathy is associated with severe violence in a forensic sample. *Journal of Forensic Psychiatry and Psychology*, *25*(6), 658–672.

Howard, R., McCarthy, L., Huband, N., & Duggan, C. (2013). Re-offending in forensic patients released from secure care: The role of antisocial/borderline co-morbidity, substance dependence, and severe childhood conduct disorder. *Criminal Behaviour and Mental Health*, Epub ahead of print edition, Jan 31, 2013. doi: 10.1002/cbm.1852.

Howard, R. C., & McMurran, M. (2012). Editorial: Whither research on 'high harm' offenders with personality disorders? *Criminal Behaviour and Mental Health*, *22*, 157–164.

Howard, R. C., & McMurran, M. (2013). Alcohol and violence in developmental perspective. In M. McMurran (Ed.). *Alcohol-related violence: Prevention and treatment* (pp. 81–102). Chichester: Wiley-Blackwell.

Joseph, N., & Benefield, N. (2012). A joint offender personality disorder pathway strategy: An outline summary. *Criminal Behaviour and Mental Health*, *22*(3): 210–217.

Kaszynski, K., Kallis, D. L., Karnik, N., Soller, M., Hunter, S., Haapanen, R., Blair, J., & Steiner, H. (2013). Incarcerated youth with personality disorders: Prevalence, comorbidity and convergent validity. *Personality and Mental Health*, published online in Wiley Online Library (wileyonlinelibrary.com), doi 10.1002/pmh.1241.

Kennealy, P. J., Skeem, J. L., Walters, G. D., & Camp, J. (2010). Do core interpersonal and affective traits of PCL-R psychopathy interact with antisocial behavior and disinhibition to predict violence? *Psychological Assessment*, *22*, 569–580.

Khalifa, N., Duggan, C., Howard, R., & Lumsden, J. (2012). The relationship between child-hood conduct disorder and adult antisocial behavior is partially mediated by early-onset alcohol abuse. *Personality Disorders: Theory, Research, and Treatment*, *3*(4), 423–432.

Leistico, A.-M., Salekin, R. T., DeCosta, J., & Rogers, R. (2008). A large-scale meta-analysis relating the Hare measure of psychopathy to antisocial conduct. *Law and Human Behavior*, *32*, 28–45.

Lilienfeld, S. O., & Andrews, B. P. (1996). Development and preliminary validation of a self-report measure of psychopathic personality traits in noncriminal populations. *Journal of Personality Assessment*, *66*, 488–524.

Livesley, W. J. (2007a). A framework for integrating dimensional and categorical classifications of personality disorder. *Journal of Personality Disorders*, *21*, 199–224.

Livesley, W. J. (2007b). The relevance of an integrated approach to the treatment of personality disordered offenders. *Psychology, Crime and Law*, *13*, 27–46.

McMurran, M., & Howard, R. C. (2009). *Personality, personality disorder and violence*. Chichester: John Wiley & Sons.

Mullen, P. E. (1992). Psychopathy: A developmental disorder of ethical action. *Criminal Behaviour and Mental Health*, *2*, 234–244.

Mullen, P. E. (2007). On building arguments on shifting sands. *Philosophy, Psychiatry and Psychology*, *14*, 143–147.

Newhill, C. E., Eack, S. M., & Mulvey, E. P. (2012). A growth curve analysis of emotion dysregulation as a mediator for violence in individuals with and without borderline personality disorder. *Journal of Personality Disorders*, *26*, 452–467.

Patrick, C. J. (2010). *Triarchic personality measure (TriPM)*. Unpublished manuscript. Down-loadable from: https://www.phenxtoolkit.org/toolkit_content/supplemental_info/psychiatric/measures/Triarchic_Psychopathy_Measure_Manual.pdf (accessed 11 January 2015).

Patrick, C. J., Drislane, L. E., & Strickland, C. (2012). Conceptualizing psychopathy in tricharcic terms: Implications for treatment. *International Journal of Forensic Mental Health*, *11*, 253–266.

Patrick, C. J., Fowles, D., & Krueger, R. (2009). Triarchic conceptualization of psychopathy: Developmental origins of disinhibition, boldness and meanness. *Development and Psychopathology*, *21*, 913–938.

Putkonen, A., Kotilainen, I., Joyal, C. C., & Tühonen, J. (2004). Comorbid personality disorders and substance use disorders of mentally ill homicide offenders: A structured clinical study on dual and triple diagnoses. *Schizophrenia Bulletin, 30,* 59–72.

Skeem, J. L., Polaschek, D. L. L., Patrick, C. J., & Lilienfeld, S. O. (2011). Psychopathic Personality: Bridging the gap between scientific evidence and public policy. *Psychological Science in the Public Interest, 12*(3), 95–162.

Stanley, J. H., Wygant, D. B., & Sellbom, M. (2013). Elaborating on the construct validity of the triarchic psychopathy measure in a criminal offender sample. *Journal of Personality Assessment, 95*(4), 343–350.

Varlamov, A., Khalifa, N., Liddle, P., Duggan, C., & Howard, R. C. (2010). Cortical correlates of impaired self-regulation in personality disordered patients with traits of psychopathy. *Journal of Personality Disorders, 25*(1), 74–87.

Walters, G. D. (2003). Predicting institutional adjustment and recidivism with Psychopathy Checklist factor scores: A meta-analysis. *Law and Human Behavior, 27,* 541–558.

Walters, G. D., Knight, R. A., Grann, M., & Dahle, K.-P. (2008). Incremental validity of the Psychopathy Checklist facet scores: Predicting release outcome in six samples. *Journal of Abnormal Psychology, 117,* 396–405.

Yang, M., Wong, S. C. P., & Coid, J. (2010). The efficacy of violence prediction: A meta-analytic comparison of nine risk assessment tools. *Psychological Bulletin, 136,* 740–767.

18 Beyond 'Disorder': A Psychological Model of Mental Health and Well-Being

PETER KINDERMAN

Much of mental health-care is based on a profoundly flawed ethos. We must move away from the 'disease model', which assumes that emotional distress is merely a symptom of biological illness, and instead embrace a psychological and social approach to mental health and well-being.

Taking a lead from physical health-care, our mental health-care system applies quasi-medical 'diagnoses' to emotional, behavioural and psychological issues. Once illnesses are diagnosed, people's life experiences and their views on the origin of their problems are often unfortunately seen as effectively irrelevant as the 'aetiologies' of those supposed 'illnesses' are investigated. And then, 'treatments' are prescribed. If, on the other hand, an illness is not diagnosed, it is difficult – perhaps impossible – to receive help. As a result, vulnerable people, people in acute emotional distress, frequently suffer.

This 'disease model' threatens our ability to empathize. Because behaviours are seen as irrational, and as the products of 'illnesses', even diseases, we stop trying to understand the human reasons why people might be feeling or acting in the ways they do. When people are experiencing great distress and feel that their sanity, even their life, is threatened, they need empathy and compassion more than ever.

DROP THE LANGUAGE OF DISORDER

One of the main problems with the 'disease model' of mental health and well-being is that it relies heavily on diagnosis in order to 'treat' our anguish. Psychiatric diagnoses are based on the idea that people's emotional difficulties can be understood in the same way as bodily diseases. One consequence is that we fail to look for meaning in people's 'disordered' responses and experiences. It also means that people are assumed to need 'expert' help and that their own skills and resources are not enough. Perhaps worse, diagnoses are used as pseudo-explanations for troubling behaviours – for example, 'this person is hearing voices *because* they have schizophrenia'. Many people, perhaps even most people, who hear voices do not find them distressing. But for others they *are* distressing, and these are the people who might seek help from mental health services and receive a diagnosis. Within the disease-model approach, the voices ('hallucinations') are seen as symptoms of 'schizophrenia'. That is, it is assumed that there is a 'mental illness' called 'schizophrenia', and hallucinations are a common 'symptom' of that illness. But, at the same time, the hallucinations are caused by the schizophrenia – 'why is that person hallucinating?', 'because she has schizophrenia'; 'how do we know she has schizophrenia?', 'because she's experiencing hallucinations'. It is a circular argument. It is conveniently forgotten that many people hear similar voices but are not upset by them, a fact that rather tends to undermine the idea of a simple disease model.

Apart from its circular nature, the diagnostic approach fails to appreciate the person's experiences in a broader context. Diagnoses take little account of whether a person has had significant losses, has been victimized or abused (whether recently or as a child), or has experienced any other environmental stresses. There are two striking exceptions to this – two diagnoses that do include such information. The diagnosis of 'post-traumatic stress disorder' or PTSD is distinctive in that, in order to receive this diagnosis, the person must have experienced a very stressful (traumatic, potentially life-changing) event. There is also a diagnosis of 'adjustment disorder', which

Forensic Psychology, Second Edition. Edited by David A. Crighton and Graham J. Towl.
© 2015 John Wiley & Sons, Ltd. Published 2015 by British Psychological Society and John Wiley & Sons, Ltd.

can be cynically interpreted as the 'something bad has happened and you've been upset by it … disorder'.

Many of my colleagues (both psychologists and psychiatrists) often point out that a diagnostic approach is useful because there are very significant differences between 'real' problems that are 'hugely distressing' and the normal ups and downs of everyday life. That is absolutely true. We all experience emotional distress occasionally; few of us are crippled by this distress. When things go wrong in our lives – when a relationship ends, or we make a mistake at work or someone close to us is seriously unwell – we (all of us) sometimes feel low, unmotivated, have problems sleeping, etc. That is, we experience some of the so-called symptoms of depression. I am not, of course, claiming that this is, in any sense, as serious a problem – or is the same problem – as somebody who has been depressed for years, has harmed themselves, is reliant on medication and is contemplating taking their own life. But I am saying that the experiences and emotions lie on a continuum. Many important things, life-threatening things, lie on continua. Many of us, especially these days, are overweight. Some people could do with losing a few kilos, but some people are in serious and acute danger. These issues lie on continua, and, just because the experience at one end of the continuum is qualitatively different from the experience at the other, it does not follow that the continuum is invalid. Extreme poverty and extreme wealth are very different one from another, but wealth is, obviously, a continuous issue.

Reliability

For scientists, the first test of a diagnostic system is its reliability. A reliable diagnostic system would ensure that two people both agree on which diagnosis to use in a particular situation. Although people do change over time, a reliable diagnostic system would also mean that the same decision – the same diagnosis – would be assigned again if you repeated the assessment. One of the reasons that the diagnostic manuals (DSM and ICD) were developed in the first place, and one of the reasons they have been revised, is to ensure reliability. Several years ago, research suggested that clinicians in different countries (the researchers particularly studied the United States and United Kingdom) tended to make rather different diagnoses when presented with identical sets of problems (World Health Organization, 1973). What would then have led to a diagnosis of, for instance 'schizophrenia' in one country would have led to a diagnosis of 'bipolar disorder' if you were to consult with a clinician in another country. While there are clearly lots of reasons why this might have happened (the people reporting the problems might have behaved differently or said different things, the person making the diagnosis might have interviewed people in a different manner, the environment might have been different, etc.), a central issue was that different countries tended to have different diagnostic systems – different rules for combining symptoms and different systems of naming the 'disorders' that were diagnosed. The DSM and ICD diagnostic systems were drafted specifically to address these kinds of problems; the issue of reliability was addressed by international agreement on criteria, and by rules for which 'symptoms' would count towards which diagnosis.

Another way that people tried to improve reliability was by developing standardized interviews. In these interviews, a person is asked standard questions about his or her experiences, with very little deviation from the prepared script. Although the interviews can sometimes therefore be a little stilted, reliability is improved, and this is the reason why such interviews are often used in research projects. However, it is rather different in routine clinical practice. In practice, clinicians seldom use such standardized interviews. In any event, the subject matter of psychiatric diagnoses is usually subjective reports of behaviours, thoughts and emotions. These can almost never be independently verified (which is why, incidentally, the legal reports of psychiatrists and psychologists tend to use the phrase 'she reported that' very frequently – we cannot claim to know what she *thought*; all we can say is what she *said* she thought). So, when we make these sorts of decisions, we have to ask questions about personal experiences, and it is often a matter of some judgment as to whether (in the words of DSM-5) they 'cause clinically significant distress or impairment in social, occupational, or other important areas of functioning'.

There are three important things to note here. First, although these diagnostic manuals have improved the reliability of psychiatric diagnosis considerably, it is still rather poor. In fact, reliability appears to be getting progressively worse with each new edition of DSM (Carney, 2013). Secondly, as supporters of psychiatric diagnosis sometimes point out, the reliability of some diagnoses in the arena of physical health is also poor. So, for example, pathologists may be mistaken about the cause of death on as much as a third of occasions when their expert judgements are compared with the results of post-mortems, and even diagnoses of illnesses such as tonsillitis can be less reliable than those for 'schizophrenia'. However, there is one important difference: in the arena of physical health, post-mortem examinations and laboratory tests can confirm or refute clinical impressions. There are no such laboratory tests for mental health problems. Indeed, any such laboratory tests might well be largely meaningless even if they existed, because depression and other mental health issues are essentially problems of experience, not biology. If you were to be experiencing major problems, a negative test result would still leave you with problems, and they would need to be addressed. A positive test would tell you nothing more than you already knew, although it might offer spurious scientific confirmation (Noll, 2006). And this raises a third issue. Even if psychiatric diagnoses were reliable, that would not be enough. Diagnoses also need to be 'valid' – that is, to be meaningful and to represent real 'things'.

Validity

It is quite possible for a diagnosis to be completely reliable, but still not be valid. For example, we might imagine a hypothetical disorder called 'Kinderman Syndrome'. Kinderman Syndrome might be diagnosed if someone possesses all of the following 'symptoms': having thinning brown hair, a south-east English accent and protruding ears. This diagnosis would probably be quite reliable. Although some interviewers (especially if not native to the United Kingdom) might be poor at deciding upon the presence of a 'south-east English' accent, and some might be uncertain as to the exact definition of 'thinning' hair, I suspect a rigorous investigation would establish that any panel of suitably selected and trained clinicians would be able to agree at least 75% of the time as to whether these criteria are met. We might have to develop the criteria carefully and perhaps revise them – we might have to define 'protruding ears' carefully, and even define the exact shade of 'brown' we meant. Hence, there might be some work needed to refine the definitions, and we might need to train our diagnosticians. But I suspect we could get high reliability.

However, is it valid? Is there in any real sense a syndrome, a disorder, a mental illness that – validly – exists merely because we can define it? Of course not. I am sure many of the people I have encountered in my professional life would leap at the idea of 'Kinderman Syndrome' (although they probably would not use physical descriptors). But we cannot accept that 'mental illnesses' exist merely because we can name them. We cannot accept that reliability alone makes a 'disorder' a valid concept.

This is not just a theoretical argument. In early versions of psychiatric diagnostic manuals, 'homosexuality' was listed as a mental illness. The World War II code-breaker Alan Turing committed suicide after being prosecuted for an indecency offence – he had been the victim of a theft by his lover, and when he reported it to the police, his sexuality was both criminalized and pathologized. Forced to take female sex hormones to emasculate himself, Turing killed himself with a bite from a cyanide-coated apple. If homosexuality were still categorized as a 'mental illness', no doubt we would be seeing frequent publication of academic articles exploring the genetic basis of the 'disorder', its biochemical and neurotransmitter profile and randomized controlled

trials of medication designed to 'cure' it. We do see occasional attempts by religiously motivated therapists to this end. But largely, we celebrate peoples' rights to live their lives and express their sexuality as they see fit. We can see life beyond the diagnostic paradigm.

'OPPOSITIONAL DEFIANT DISORDER' ... REALLY?

Many people unfamiliar with psychiatric diagnostic practices are surprised to learn that the DSM-5 includes a diagnosis of 'oppositional defiant disorder'. This diagnosis, used with children, is defined by 'a pattern of negativistic, hostile, and defiant behaviour lasting at least 6 months'. The specific diagnostic criteria include: actively defying or refusing to comply with adults' requests or rules, deliberately annoying people, blaming other people for his or her mistakes or misbehaviour and being angry and resentful. In DSM-5, these are grouped into three types: angry/irritable mood, argumentative/defiant behaviour and vindictiveness.

Children can sometimes be painfully unhappy. Children can sometimes be entirely unresponsive to their parents, or, indeed, to other authority figures. I certainly would not want to imply that such problems do not exist or that they are trivial. I just do not think they are 'illnesses'. I am – to be clear – absolutely convinced that children and young people can be negativistic. They can be hostile. They can actively refuse to comply with adults' requests or rules. I have to say, these kinds of problems are often indications that the child has experienced some significant trauma. But, in any case, I do not wish to make light of real, painful problems. These kinds of difficulties can have terrible consequences for children and their parents. But I simply do not think it is sensible, useful, scientifically appropriate or clinically justifiable to suggest that the children have a 'disorder'. Apart from anything else, this kind of labelling makes people think that these problems are not really normal human problems at all, but instead are 'symptoms of mental illness'. We do not like it when our children are defiant or refuse to comply with our requests. But they are not mentally ill.

Another example of the problems with the idea of 'mental illnesses' is the contentious issue of 'personality disorder'. 'Personality disorders' are defined as 'long-standing patterns of maladaptive behaviour that constitute immature and inappropriate ways of coping with stress or solving problems'. It is fascinating and horrible how a person's whole character can be rendered into a 'disorder'. Examples of personality disorder include; 'antisocial personality disorder', 'paranoid personality disorder', 'narcissistic personality disorder', 'schizoid personality disorder', etc. Antisocial personality disorder is particularly interesting in the context of the validity of diagnoses of mental disorder, because it illustrates the weird circularity of these ideas. Do people do bad things because they are suffering from 'antisocial personality disorder' or do they get labelled with 'antisocial personality disorder' because they do bad things?

'Personality disorders' are interesting in part because the authors of diagnostic manuals seem to be entirely undecided as to how many of these 'disorders' there are – DSM-5 and ICD-10 do not agree. Discussions and debates frequently occur as to whether 'personality disorders' could be entirely expunged from the diagnostic manuals (replaced, perhaps, with a description of personality traits). So they appear to have a fleeting, ghost-like reality – written into existence; potentially deleted – as the committees deliberate. But, despite their oddity, their circularity, their tenuous claimed validity, it can be significant if you receive a diagnosis of 'personality disorder'. The UK government linked an entire offender management programme – the Dangerous and Severe Personality Disorder programme, designed to help manage very seriously dangerous offenders – to the concept.

In my professional opinion, we need to question the validity of all mental health diagnoses. As my colleagues and I said in a recent paper – we should 'drop the language of disorder' (Kinderman, Read, Moncrieff, & Bentall, 2013).

MOVING BEYOND THE CONCEPT OF 'ABNORMALITY'

The idea that there is a quintessential distinction between normal emotions and 'mental illness' is widespread. People talk about 'clinical depression' to distinguish it from 'ordinary' depression. One influential journalist in the field of popular science recently decried how people fail to distinguish everyday feelings of depression from (real) 'depressive symptoms'. The disease model of mental health tends to reinforce the idea that the experiences and emotions of people whose problems are placed in diagnostic categories such as 'depression', 'schizophrenia' and 'bipolar disorder' are qualitatively different from 'normal' emotions and experiences. And this faces us with a real contrast. Traditional psychiatry, the 'disease model' of mental health and the diagnostic approach all conceptualize, or at least present a vision of, 'mental illnesses' as qualitatively different to and separable from normality. Research suggests some- thing rather different: that there is no dividing line between 'normal' and 'abnormal' emotions, experiences or behaviours.

Many people, especially clinical psychologists, have suggested that these supposed 'symptoms' of mental illnesses in fact lie on a continuum with normality. Sometimes experiences and emotions become problematical, but this is the same with anything else: any human experience or tendency can become a problem if it is extreme. This idea is neither new nor unusual. In Herman Mellville's novel *Billy Budd*, the narrator discusses the inadequacies of a categorical approach to emotional distress:

> Who in the rainbow can draw the line where the violet tint ends and the orange tint begins? Distinctly we see the difference of the colors, but where exactly does the one first blendingly enter into the other? So with sanity and insanity. In pronounced cases there is no question about them. But in some supposed cases, in various degrees supposedly less pronounced, to draw the exact line of demarcation few will undertake tho' for a fee some professional experts will. There is nothing nameable but that some men will undertake to do it for pay.[1]

An editorial in the *Times* from 1854 expresses it equally eloquently:

> Nothing can be more slightly defined than the line of demarcation between sanity and insanity. Physicians and lawyers have vexed themselves with attempts at definitions in a case where definition is impossible. There has never yet been given to the world anything in the shape of a formula upon this subject which may not be torn to shreds in five minutes by any ordinary logician. Make the definition too narrow, it becomes meaningless; make it too wide, the whole human race are involved in the drag-net. In strictness, we are all mad as often as we give way to passion, to prejudice, to vice to vanity; but if all the passionate, prejudiced, vicious, and vain people in this world are to be locked up as lunatics, who is to keep the keys to the asylum?[2]

I agree. I cannot see how we can draw 'a line of demarcation between sanity and insanity'. I can see why the idea that there is such a dividing line is popular: it reassures us that mental health problems are discrete, diagnosable entities, experienced by people who are different to us. But, in truth, all these experiences lie on continua.

This continuum approach is best understood by thinking about common experiences such as anxiety. All of us will have experienced anxiety at some point in our lives. Some of us have experienced sheer terror, or perhaps become extremely anxious very frequently. Many more of us are often anxious, but to a lesser degree. Only a minority of us will ever experience extremes of anxiety such as a series of panic attacks, crippling obsessions or compulsions to do certain things that would be recognized in the diagnostic textbooks as justifying a diagnosis of an anxiety 'disorder'. Many of us will have had unusual perceptual experiences from time to time, but most of us will have not been disturbed by them and will have dismissed them as transient and trivial events. Others are plagued by continual psychosis. Some people hear disembodied voices, but regard the experience as 'normal'. Other people are terrified by what they hear. We all feel low from time to time, but some people feel so bad that they contemplate suicide. And – and this is important – all shades of experience fall in between.

Madness and sanity are not qualitatively different states of mind, but should instead be seen as lying at the extreme ends of several spectra of experience. In fact, sanity cannot really be seen as occupying the opposite end to madness on any realistic 'normal' spectrum of experience. If we imagine madness at one end of a continuum, the opposite end will be a never-experienced utopia where we are gloriously happy, rational at all times, clear-sighted and with the acute and precise hearing of an owl, and, in the words of the *Times* editor, free from all passion, prejudice, vice and vanity.

The editor of the *Times* also pointed out another fundamental truth that I am attempting to express. The factors that lead to madness are aspects of normal psychology. The *Times* editorial states that we are all mad so long as we give way to passion, prejudice, vice and vanity. These are – in the slightly poetic prose of a Victorian journalist – normal psychological processes. If passion, prejudice, etc., change how we think about the world, then we will blur the lines that separate 'sanity' from 'insanity'.

THERE IS AN ALTERNATIVE TO DIAGNOSIS

We need a wholesale revision of the way we think about psychological distress. We should recognize that distress is an unfortunate but nevertheless normal, not abnormal, part of human life. People experience many difficult circumstances in their lives, and often become distressed as a result. This needs to be reflected in the way we identify, describe and respond to that distress. We also need to acknowledge the overwhelming evidence that severe distress or unusual experiences (which now attract the misleading label of 'psychiatric symptoms') lie at one end of continua with less unusual and distressing mental states. That means there is no easy 'cut-off' between 'normal' experience and 'mental health problems'.

Some people obviously feel that diagnostic labels are helpful. They say that it is important for them to learn that their problems have a name. But, in reality, this sense that a diagnosis is helpful or reassuring cannot come from any greater understanding of the problems, any better knowledge of their causes or aetiology, appropriate treatment or prognosis – because diagnoses simply cannot offer that information. Instead, the sense of helpfulness seems to result from the person knowing that they have been listened to (and heard), that their problems have been recognized (in both senses of the word), understood, validated, that these problems can be explained (and are themselves explicable rather than simply 'mad') and that some help can be offered. In the flawed world of present-day services, however, people often find that they are reassured by (or at least accept) a diagnosis, feel some immediate reassurance, but then find that any real help is illusory. The diagnoses convey very limited useful information, will not explain things, will not guide treatment and will not help predict the future. Instead, a clear description of a person's real problems would be much more useful. A description of an individual's actual problems would provide more information and be of greater communicative value than any diagnostic label.

OPERATIONALLY DEFINED PROBLEM LISTS

A perfectly appropriate alternative to diagnosis would be simply to list a person's problems. A simple list of problems (properly defined) would be more than sufficient as a basis for individual care planning, for communicating between professionals, as the basis for research and for the design and planning of services.

It would be inappropriate to try to list every problem that it is possible to experience. But we can easily see how some of the diagnoses already mentioned could be replaced with more appropriate language. We understand what it means when someone is feeling low, has intrusive anxious thoughts or feels compelled to carry out certain behaviours such as checking things. We understand what attention problems are, what it means to hear voices, and so on. There should be no particular surprise that we can identify and define such specific phenomena. The Oxford English Dictionary defines the scientific method as: 'a method or procedure that has characterized natural science since the 17th century, consisting in systematic observation, measurement, and experiment, and the formulation, testing, and modification of hypotheses'. So scientists use operational (precise) definitions of relevant concepts. We develop hypotheses. And we collect data. We do not need to meet the challenge of a new technological alternative to diagnosis and the 'disease model'. We have had it since the seventeenth century.

THE DRUGS DO NOT WORK

Not surprisingly (since the diagnoses do not match onto any patterns of problems we recognize in the real world, and do not relate to any 'biomarkers' – indicators of underlying biological abnormalities), the drugs offer only minimal benefit. It is not surprising that pharmaceutical chemicals can affect our mood; the vast majority of us regularly buy mind-altering chemicals every day. Coffee, tea, alcohol and nicotine show both that chemicals can affect our thoughts, moods and behaviour, and that these can have effects (both good and bad) without necessarily treating any illnesses.

Although there are over 47 million prescriptions per year for antidepressant medication in the United Kingdom alone, there is plenty of evidence that antidepressants are much less effective than we would like. Careful research comparing the long-term outcomes for people taking antidepressant medication with people taking placebos suggests, at best, only a very marginal benefit.

The same applies to the long-term so-called 'anti-psychotic' medication. These drugs often have serious, life-changing (and occasional very noticeable) adverse effects. Because they affect various physical systems, such as our heart, liver and kidneys, as well as our brains, and because one of the common adverse effects is a significant gain in weight (which is, of course, very harmful), these drugs can significantly affect one's health (Moncrieff, 2013). Outcomes for patients suffering from 'schizophrenia' have not improved since the Victorian age, and an increasing number of people are disabled by mental health problems. This contrasts with what has happened in physical medicine, where genuine advances have led to improved outcomes and reduced disability (Bentall, 2009; Whitaker, 2010). There is evidence that some forms of pharmacological medication may be helpful in the short term (Moncrieff, 2009; 2013). But this is, first of all, unsurprising – drugs that act on the brain are not new in human history, and we are well aware of their effects on mood and behaviour. It is also important to note that these effects are not 'cures' (and are even probably not 'treatments') and can have significant negative effects in the longer term. And all this is without mentioning electroconvulsive therapy (ECT).

Coercion

Mental health-care is unusual within health-care specialities in the use of coercion. While the usual argument goes that coercion is necessary because people 'lack insight', my experience suggests that the main reason is different. While there is a great deal of demand for care, the 'care' and 'treatment' on offer are often not what people want or need. Indeed, it can be aversive to the extent that we need to coerce people into accepting it. At any one time, nearly 20,000 people are being detained in psychiatric hospitals against their will, 'sectioned' under the Mental Health Act. These are not just extreme or rare cases, as people with a wide range of problems can find themselves caught up in coercive practices (Care Quality Commission, 2014). The history of mental health-care is an unfortunate history of coercion, with many mental health treatments clearly rooted in moral judgements and punitive approaches (Porter, 2002; Shorter, 1997). Today, in the context of a general disquiet about a perceived lack of compassion in health-care, the extent and nature of coercion in mental health-care is a clear cause for concern.

Some form of mental health legislation may well be needed, as some people's low mood, risk of suicide, confusion or disturbed behaviour puts them at extreme risk or, in very unusual cases, renders them a risk to others. I contributed to the drafting of both the Mental Health Act and the Mental Capacity Act. It is important to legislate for people whose difficulties put them at significant personal risk, or who pose a risk to others. But this is a social and psychological problem, not a medical one. Diagnosis and even severity of an 'illness' do not relate to risk and dangerousness. Decisions do need to be made about the necessary care of people with serious problems who are at risk. And, after the fact, decisions need to be made about how to deal with people who have committed crimes. In both cases, current practice in a 'disease model'-driven system is flawed. A more coherent and fair approach would be to agree to take decisions on behalf of other people if they are unable to make decisions for themselves, regardless of whether they have a diagnosis, and to make judicial decisions in the criminal justice field on the same basis. This does not mean 'letting them off'; it means making appropriate decisions on rational bases.

Prevention

Advances in the psychological understanding of mental health and well-being allow us to foresee a future beyond the 'disease model'. First, it is important to address the root causes of distress. The ethos of mental health that I would like to see does place the person at the centre of their universe, and emphasizes our individual agency, but it does not imply that people (or their thinking) can be blamed for their distress. The way that people make sense of what happens to them plays an important role and is often a useful focus when we are trying to help someone. However, the most powerful determinants of mental health are the events and circumstances of people's lives. If we are to protect people's mental health, we need wider social or even political change. This is often a neglected topic, but social and political changes are likely to make much more difference overall than anything individuals can do alone.

For example, many people diagnosed with 'psychosis' have experienced poverty. Addressing poverty is rightly the cornerstone of government, and few politicians suggest differently (although many of us fear that right-wing governments pay only lip-service to this aspiration, while presiding over policies that actually increase inequalities). With a very specific focus on mental health, however, measures to reduce or eliminate poverty, especially childhood poverty, would be hugely beneficial. However, absolute income is not the only important issue. Evidence shows that a major contribution to serious emotional distress is income inequality – the growing gap between the richest and poorest people in society. In their book *The Spirit Level*, sociologists Richard Wilkinson and Kate Pickett demonstrate that mental health problems are highest in those countries with the greatest gaps between rich and poor, and lowest in countries with smaller differences (Wilkinson & Pickett, 2009). This suggests that an effective way to reduce rates of mental health problems might be to reduce inequality in society.

Experiences of abuse in childhood are also hugely important. Rates of mental health problems would plummet if we found better ways of protecting children from abuse. This means working with teachers, social workers, community nurses, GPs and the police to identify and then respond to early warning signs that children might be exposed to sexual, physical or emotional abuse or neglect. It also means taking a serious look as a society at what we can do to bring down overall rates of abuse. Bullying – that is, peer-on-peer bullying in school and in leisure settings – is also important, and again here teachers and youth leaders could help, and thereby help prevent later mental health problems.

In that context, we also know that experiences of discrimination are important – people who have been subjected to racism, homophobia and sexual discrimination are put at risk by these experiences. Society – and important agents in society – can help. We can help to make societies less discriminatory. On the other side of this equation, we can perhaps think of ways in which community leaders could help make communities more trusting, more open to help one another – more 'prosocial' in psychological jargon.

And finally, many recreational drugs are associated with mental health problems. Alcohol is unquestionably the most serious substance-related public health issue, but cannabis and other more traditional 'drugs' have been associated with mental health problems in general and psychosis in particular. This certainly does not mean that we need a stronger clamp-down on drugs – the so-called 'war on drugs' does not appear to have been won,

and many people argue that decriminalizing the possession and use of drugs would be an important positive step towards protecting people's health.

The most effective way of reducing rates of mental health problems would be to focus on the social causes of distress. This involves all of us, not just mental health professionals. Politicians in particular have a very important role to play in passing legislation that could protect our health, strengthen our community and prevent mental health problems.

So a new ethos for mental health – moving away from the 'disease model' – would embrace social change. But we must also address the issue of biology. Every thought we have involves a brain-based event. All learning involves changes in associative networks, depolarization thresholds, synaptic biomechanics, even gene expression. My view is a challenge to neuroscience or psychiatry. But our brains are learning engines – biological systems that are the servants of learning. We are not the slaves of our brains, our brains are the organs with which we learn. So, of course, every thought involves brain-based activity. But this is not the same as biomedical reductionism. Our biology provides us with a fantastically elegant learning engine. But we learn as a result of the events that happen to us – it is because of our development and our learning as human beings that we see the world in the way that we do.

This approach contrasts with the approach taken by biological psychiatry. Strong proponents of biological psychiatry argue that all psychological concepts will disappear from the psychiatric lexicon as we understand the neural basis of behaviour (Guze, 1989; Kandel, 1998). Their logic is that any changes in our thinking or behaviour – whether that means learning during childhood, the impact of life experiences or even therapy – reflect physical changes in the neural associative networks. So, they argue, when we understand the physical changes that happen in the brain – the changed 'excitation thresholds', the new synapses, etc. – we will understand human behaviour. On one level, this analysis is obviously true. Any learning must involve biological changes in the brain at the molecular and synaptic levels. But such an argument is intellectually trivial. All learning – all human behaviour – is dependent on the functioning of the brain. But merely invoking 'the brain' does not explain the learning satisfactorily, at least not for me. Of course, a well-functioning brain is necessary for all human activities. But it does not really explain why we do one thing in one situation (whereas somebody else behaves differently) or why we behave differently in other situations. To understand that, we need to ask whether such differences between people are best explained by differences in their biology.

Everybody recognizes that there are changes in our brains that can affect our thinking, moods and behaviour. All over the world, people use a range of chemicals – cannabis, alcohol, even caffeine – that affect our psychological functioning because of the effects they have on our brain. Individual differences between people, including genetic differences, naturally affect our behaviour and thinking. There is nothing un-psychological and certainly nothing unscientific about understanding that biological factors can affect our psychological functioning – and thereby affect our moods, thinking and behaviour. But there is a world of difference between acknowledging these influences and accepting a 'disease model'. In particular, the available literature suggests that the influence of biological variance between people has much less influence on their subsequent emotional life than the variance in their social circumstances.

PATHWAYS TO MENTAL HEALTH

We must also remain clear-sighted as to *how* biological, and, for that matter, social and circumstantial factors affect our mental health and well-being. And, again, the alternative to the 'disease model' is already with us. It is already part of our scientist–practitioner model, and already well-established within psychological science. As just one example, in one piece of research that I have been involved in, we used fMRI technology – functional magnetic resonance imaging – to study regional blood flow during a 'self-referential' task – that is, a task in which the research participants were asked to decide whether particular words were good descriptors of their personality. We found that specific areas of the brain were associated with self-referential thinking, and that these areas were more active in people seeking help for depression. So, when we think – in this example – of ourselves, as opposed to thinking of another person, it is abundantly clear that specific neural pathways are involved. Since thought involves neural signals in the brain, it is hugely unsurprising that thoughts of all kinds involve identifiable brain circuitry.

But identifying a pathway to a particular thought process does not imply that a pathological mechanism has been found. In fact, a much simpler explanation is that, if a particular neural pathway is found to be associated both with emotional and interpersonal difficulties and a key psychological process, then this is an important scientific finding that applies to us all, not just those of us unfortunate enough to have somebody attach an 'illness' label to our emotions. This is not a style of thinking

compatible with the 'disease model'. Because every thought must involve a neurological process, merely finding a neurological correlate of emotional distress or psychological process is not the same as identifying a pathology or an 'illness'.

A PSYCHOLOGICAL MODEL OF MENTAL HEALTH AND WELL-BEING

We need to develop and implement a new approach to understanding mental health problems. Real positive progress may only be possible when we realize that we are discussing a psychological and social phenomenon, not a medical one. Many people have called for radical alternatives to traditional models of care. I agree. But I do not think that we need to develop new alternatives. We already have robust and effective alternatives; we just need to use them.

I have argued for a long time (Kinderman, 2005) that mental health is an essentially psychological phenomenon, and that biological, social and circumstantial factors affect our mental health and well-being by disrupting or disturbing psychological processes. This places psychology at the heart of mental health. The well-established ethos of the clinical psychologist as 'scientist–practitioner' means that we can offer evidence-based scientific models of both mental health problems and well-being. These describe how the social determinants of health and well-being interact with psychological processes. Fundamentally, our thoughts, our emotions, our behaviour and therefore our mental health, are largely dependent on our understanding of the world, our thoughts about ourselves, other people, the future and the world. This understanding, of course, has itself been and continues to be shaped by our experiences. Essentially, things

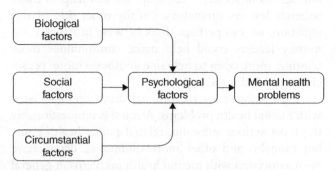

FIGURE 18.1 *A psychological model of mental health © Peter Kinderman (2014).*

happen to us, we make sense of those events and respond to them, and there are consequences. We all differ in the ways we respond to events, and there are many reasons for those differences. There are as many different reasons for these different responses as there are people in the world. Biological factors, social factors, circumstantial factors – our learning as human beings – affect us as those external factors impact on the key psychological processes that help us build up our sense of who we are and the way the world works (see Figure 18.1).

One colleague suggested I was proposing a 'psychobio-social model'. I quite like that.

NOTES

1 Billy Budd is now out of copyright and freely available on the internet, for instance at: http://www2.hn.psu.edu/faculty/jmanis/melville/billy-budd.pdf
2 The *Times* is, remarkably, searchable online from as early as 1785. The Editorial quoted is for Saturday, 22 July 1854, p. 8.

FURTHER READING

Kinderman, P. (2014). *The new laws of psychology: Why nature and nurture alone can't explain human behaviour*. London: Constable & Robinson.

An accessible psychology science book for the intelligent lay reader. It proposes a common-sense, cognitive, account of human behaviour – arguing that our thoughts, emotions, actions and therefore mental health can be largely explained if we understand how people make sense of their world and how that framework of understanding has been learned. This approach challenges notions such as 'mental illness' and 'abnormal psychology' as old-fashioned, demeaning and invalid, argues that diagnoses such as 'depression' and 'schizophrenia' are unhelpful, and proposes that psychological accounts offer a more helpful way to address emotional distress.

Kinderman, P. (2014). *A prescription for psychiatry*. Basingstoke, UK: Palgrave MacMillan.

Takes the psychosocial approach to mental health and well-being outlined in *New Laws of Psychology* and builds upon this to recommend a wholesale revision of our mental health services. Arguing that the origins of distress are largely social, and that therefore we need a change from a 'disease model' to a 'psychosocial model', the book argues that we should reject traditional psychiatric diagnosis, significantly reduce our use of psychiatric medication, tailor help to each person's unique needs, invest in greater psychological and social therapies and place mental health and well-being services within a social rather than a medical framework.

Read, J., Mosher, L., & Bentall, R. (2004). *Models of madness*. Hove and New York: Taylor & Francis.

Develops the theme that serious mental health issues such as hallucinations and delusions are understandable reactions to life events and circumstances rather than symptoms of a supposed genetic predisposition or biological disturbance. Edited by three very well-respected clinical psychologists, it features a range of respected international contributors who critique the 'medical model' of madness, examine the dominance of the 'disease-model' approach from historical and economic perspectives, document the role of drug companies and outline possible alternatives drug-based solutions.

REFERENCES

Bentall, R. P (2009). *Doctoring the Mind: Why psychiatric treatments fail*. London: Allen Lane.
Care Quality Commission (2014). *Monitoring the Mental Health Act in 2012/13*. http://www.cqc.org.uk/sites/default/files/media/documents/cqc_mentalhealthsummary_2012_13_07.pdf URL last accessed 14th June 2014.
Carney, J. (2013, March 26). *The DSM-5 field trials: Inter-rater reliability ratings take a nose dive*. http://www.madinamerica.com/2013/03/the-dsm-5-field-trials-inter-rater-reliability-ratings-take-a-nose-dive/ URL last accessed 14th June 2014.
Guze, S. B. (1989). Biological psychiatry: Is there any other kind? *Psychological Medicine, 19*, 315–323.
Kandel, E. R. (1998). A new intellectual framework for psychiatry. *American Journal of Psychiatry, 155*, 457–468.
Kinderman, P. (2005). A psychological model of mental disorder. *Harvard Review of Psychiatry, 13*, 206–217.
Kinderman, P., Read, J., Moncrieff, J., & Bentall, R. P. (2013). Drop the language of disorder. *Evidence Based Mental Health, 16*, 2–3. doi:10.1136/ eb-2012–100987.
Moncrieff, J. (2009). *The myth of the chemical cure: A critique of psychiatric drug treatment*. London: Palgrave Macmillan. ISBN 9780230574328.
Moncrieff, J. (2013) *The bitterest pills: The troubling story of antipsychotic drugs*. London: Palgrave Macmillan. ISBN 9781137277435.
Noll, R (2006). The blood of the insane. *History of psychiatry, 17*(4), 395–418.

Porter, R. (2002). *Madness: A brief history*. Oxford: Oxford University Press. ISBN 0192802666.

Shorter, E. (1997). *A history of psychiatry: From the era of the asylum to the age of Prozac*. New York: John Wiley & Sons. ISBN 9780471245315.

Whitaker, R. (2010). *Anatomy of an epidemic: Magic bullets, psychiatric drugs, and the astonishing rise of mental illness in America*. New York: Crown (Random House). ISBN 9780307452412.

Wilkinson, R., & Pickett, K. (2009). *The spirit level: Why more equal societies almost always do better*. London: Allen Lane. ISBN 9780241954294.

World Health Organization (1973). *The international pilot study of schizophrenia*. Geneva: World Health Organization.

World Health Organization (1979). *Schizophrenia: An international follow-up study*. New York: Wiley.

19 Substance Use Disorders

MICHAEL GOSSOP

CONSUMPTION BEHAVIOURS, PROBLEMS AND DEPENDENCE

Substance use disorders can be thought of in terms of consumption behaviours, problems and dependence. These dimensions are conceptually distinct and separate: in reality, they tend to be related (sometimes closely) in a number of ways (Gossop, 2003).

The behavioural parameters of drug-taking include such issues as substance type and frequency and quantity of drug use. Certain drugs are regularly identified as leading to dependence and other drug problems. Heroin is most frequently identified as a 'main drug' by drug users in UK treatment services. Other problematic drugs include crack cocaine, amphetamines and benzodiazepines. Alcohol is one of the most widely used psychoactive drugs and it is also associated with many problems. Alcohol use disorders are common in the general population and even more prevalent among offenders in the criminal justice system.

Problematic substance use often involves the concurrent or sequential use of different substances. Reasons for multiple drug use include: *drug enhancement* (through combined psychoactive effects); *modification of effect* (to counteract the adverse or unwanted effects of one or more drugs); *substitution* (if the preferred drug is not available); and *social* (influence of the social setting and the behaviour of other drug users).

Routes of drug administration include: oral (tablets, liquids), intranasal/snorting/sniffing (e.g., cocaine powder, heroin powder), smoking (cannabis, opium), inhalation (chasing the dragon/heroin, volatile substances) and injection (intravenous, intramuscular, subcutaneous/skin popping). Route of administration influences the dependence liability of the drug, risk of overdose and the risk of infections and other health problems.

Initially, drugs are used for many reasons, but the decision to use drugs represents a voluntary choice. With the development of dependence, the relationship between the user and their drug is altered. The person become increasingly preoccupied by the drug and feels some degree of compulsion to use it. The initial reasons for drinking or taking drugs may or may not still be present, but the development of dependence introduces new factors which increase the likelihood, intensity and persistence of drug-taking. Even when the user wants to cut down or to give up using altogether, they experience great difficulty in giving up the habit. They may have withdrawal reactions and become unwell when they stop taking the drug, and they become preoccupied with thoughts about it. Despite their wishes to stop using, they frequently fail in their efforts to do so.

The cognitive, behavioural and physiological components of the dependence syndrome include:

- A feeling of compulsion to take drugs
- A desire to stop taking drugs
- A relatively stereotyped pattern of drug-taking
- Signs of neuroadaption (tolerance and withdrawal symptoms)
- The salience of drug-taking behaviour relative to other priorities and the tendency to return to drug-taking after a period of abstinence

A central characteristic of dependence is the psychological desire for drugs. Of the various elements of dependence, the sense of compulsion is an essential ingredient.

Traditionally, the ICD and DSM classification systems have regarded dependence as a categorical disorder (is this person dependent/addicted?). A contrasting

Forensic Psychology, Second Edition. Edited by David A. Crighton and Graham J. Towl.
© 2015 John Wiley & Sons, Ltd. Published 2015 by British Psychological Society and John Wiley & Sons, Ltd.

approach to assessment regards dependence as being distributed along a dimension (how severely dependent/ addicted is this person?). The dimensional view is more in keeping with current understanding of disorders as learned behaviours.

Progression from occasional to dependent use of drugs is not inevitable. Nonetheless, many users find drug effects rewarding and continue to use, sometimes with increasing frequency and regularity, until they are taking drugs every day and several times a day. When this happens, the amounts usually increase, and often they experience social, psychological and physical problems associated with their drug-taking (increased financial costs, legal and criminal problems, infections and ill-health).

DRUGS AND CRIME

Drug-related crime imposes substantial economic and psychological costs upon society and upon the victims of crime, and it has high priority in public opinion, media and political views of the problem. Many studies have found high levels of criminal activity among drug misusing populations and UK police estimates have suggested that about half of all recorded crime may be drug-related.

A number of factors may be implicated in the association between substance use disorders and crime. No single relationship applies to all cases, and the direction of effect may differ. Many drug misusers have been involved in crime before they started taking drugs, and crime and drug use often share common psychological and social lifestyle factors. High levels of crime and drug use often coexist in economically disadvantaged and socially deprived neighbourhoods.

Different drugs are associated with different problems. Although only about 5% of illicit drug users take heroin, approximately 20% of the total economic costs of illicit drug use have been linked to heroin use (Harwood, Hubbard, Collins, & Rachal, 1988). An important association between illicit drug dependence and crime concerns the need to support the drug habit. The regular use of illicit drugs places an excessive economic burden upon the user which, in most cases, cannot be met by normal means. The main options for supporting a drug habit tend to be crime, drug dealing and prostitution. The onset of addiction is associated with increased levels of criminal behaviour which continue during periods of addiction (Ball, Shaffer, & Nurco, 1983). Acquisitive crimes involving theft are among the most frequent ways of obtaining money for drugs, and one of the most frequent offences is shoplifting (Stewart, Gossop, Marsden, & Rolfe, 2000).

Crime and addiction do not inevitably go together. Half of the patients recruited to NTORS[1] had not committed any acquisitive crimes during the 3 months prior to treatment, and, of those who were involved in crime, the majority were relatively low-rate offenders. The majority of acquisitive crimes were committed by a minority of the drug users, with 10% of them committing 76% of the crimes (Stewart *et al.*, 2000). Those who were more heavily involved in crime were more severely dependent on heroin and/or cocaine. Drug selling offences are common among illicit drug users. However, as with acquisitive crimes, the majority of drug users were not involved in selling drugs. Less than one third reported selling drugs, and for most of those, this was an infrequent activity. Half of the drug sellers reported purchasing drugs for their own use, and dealers tended to use the same drug that they sold, especially with regard to heroin and crack cocaine (Reuter, MacCoun, & Murphy, 1990). Gains are associated both with being able to buy drugs more cheaply if bought in bulk, and through the ability to cream off a percentage of the drug by passing on costs to lower-level buyers.

Unlike heroin or crack cocaine, where drug use is often linked to acquisitive crime, the relationship between alcohol and crime is less clear. One link is that between alcohol and violent crime. This is more often related to binge drinking and intoxication than to alcohol use *per se*, and the association tends to be complex, being mediated by individual propensity for violence and by social and contextual events. Exact figures are difficult to estimate and are disputed, but high estimates suggest that either the offender or victim has consumed alcohol in 65% of homicides, 75% of stabbings, 70% of assaults and half of all domestic assaults (Institute of Alcohol Studies, 2007). The use of stimulant drugs has also been associated with increased risk of violent offences (Darke, Kaye, McKetin, & Duflou, 2008). Drug users with a history of violent crime are more likely to be involved in violent crime both during and after treatment. However, rates of violent offences are reduced when drug users receive treatment (Havnes *et al.*, 2012).

High rates of criminal behaviour among drug users are reflected in high rates of contact with the criminal justice system. Large numbers of drug users are incarcerated in prisons and this leads to its own problems. Drug users tend to have fewer educational qualifications, lower rates of employment, more housing difficulties, poorer physical health, as well as more behavioural, psychological and psychiatric problems than other, non-drug using prisoners. Where drug-dependent offenders are incarcerated, the likelihood of illicit drug use within prisons increases. Among offenders who were using heroin at the time of imprisonment, more than half were found to persist with heroin use while in prison, and the probability of heroin use in prison was greatest among those who were dependent on heroin (Strang *et al.*, 2006). More than a fifth of those who used heroin inside prison used the drug by injection.

The societal costs of drug abuse cannot be calculated precisely but they are known to be massive. Every year the problems associated with drug abuse and its consequences cost billions of pounds. The costs include expenditure on prevention, treatment and rehabilitation programmes. Further human and social costs are associated with impaired health, damaged relationships and lowered productivity, as well as the distress caused to others by drug-related crime.

ASSESSMENT OF SUBSTANCE USE DISORDERS

Clinical assessment should provide information to determine suitability for treatment, to evaluate patient needs and to devise a treatment plan. Assessment is not an impersonal and routine procedure to be completed before the more interesting and important business of treatment: it is an important first stage of the therapeutic process.

Assessment has a pragmatic function. It should identify the presenting problems, and the reasons why the person is making contact. Basic assessment issues are: the types of substances that are being used, the routes of administration and the sorts of associated problems; and if the user wants to give up all drugs, or if they just want to stop taking a particular drug that they believe to be causing them problems.

The assessment of severity of dependence is important and will influence treatment decisions. Interventions for dependent drug-using offenders will differ in important ways from those for non-dependent drug users. Questions need to be asked concerning the obstacles to maintaining change after giving up drugs. Assessment should identify the antecedents (environmental, emotional and cognitive) of episodes of addictive behaviour, and the consequences that maintain the behaviour.

Limitations in treatment resources may tempt staff to select patients who are believed to be more likely to respond well to treatment. It is extremely difficult to predict who will respond well or fail to respond to treatment. 'Clinical judgement' provides a poor basis for such predictions (Gossop & Connell, 1983). It has also proved difficult to identify treatment nonresponders on the basis of pre-treatment patient characteristics, behaviours and problems (Belding, McLellan, Zanis, & Incmikoski, 1998).

In a clinical setting, the interview is the main source of information during assessment. This is heavily reliant upon self-reported problems and behaviours, typically obtained through semi-structured interviews which may or may not also include some use of structured instruments. Commonly used assessment instruments include the AUDIT: this is a short (10-item) questionnaire that provides a composite measure of alcohol consumption, problems and dependence during the previous year (Saunders, Aasland, Babor, de la Fuente, & Grant, 1993). The Severity of Dependence Scale (SDS) is a short (five items) scale that assesses the psychological components of dependence and which can be used to assess dependence upon any drug, including alcohol (Gossop *et al.*, 1995). The Short Opiate Withdrawal Scale (SOWS) is a self-completion questionnaire for the assessment of the opiate withdrawal syndrome (Gossop, 1990). This scale assesses 10 commonly reported symptoms. It is quick and easy to administer, and provides clinically useful information which is relevant to the planning and delivery of treatment programmes.

In a criminal justice setting, the validity of self-reported substance use may be compromised, and greater reliance may be placed upon 'objective' or independent sources of information. Biochemical methods which can be used are analysis of blood, breath, saliva, urine, sweat and hair samples for direct metabolites of abused substances, or for indirect evidence of biological changes related to drug use. The choice of screening method will be influenced by the pharmacokinetics of the drugs which are being investigated, and will depend also on the questions being asked. Biological testing may be useful to monitor and maintain drug-free therapeutic prison wings.

Self-reported drug misuse can have high validity which correlates well with objective measures (Weiss *et al.*, 1998) and self-report remains an essential tool. In many circumstances it is the most practical way to obtain information, and in some circumstances it is the only possible way of obtaining information (as with internal states). Self-report and laboratory tests can also be used interactively. Rates of agreement between self-reported drug use and urinalysis increased when urine was taken for testing prior to interview (Hamid, Deren, Beardsley, & Tortu, 1999).

MANAGEMENT OF DETOXIFICATION

Withdrawal from drugs, or 'detoxification',[2] represents an intermediate treatment goal, and a preliminary phase of abstinence-oriented treatments. Detoxification is not, in itself, a treatment for drug dependence. Detoxification alone leads to little or no improvement compared to no-treatment conditions. Nonetheless, the importance of the treatment and management of withdrawal should not be underestimated. Drug withdrawal can be painful and unpleasant and it should be managed with as little discomfort as possible for the patient.

The main criteria by which the effectiveness of detoxification should be judged are: symptom severity, duration of withdrawal and completion rates (achieving a drug-free state at the end of the detoxification programme). A detoxification treatment may be fully effective in terms of these criteria but still not touch upon the psychosocial and other factors associated with relapse. The majority of the factors which put the ex-user at risk of relapse are different to and separate from withdrawal symptoms and their treatment.

Heroin (and other opiates)

Heroin withdrawal symptoms include: vomiting, diarrhoea, stomach cramps, hot and cold flushes, muscular aches, yawning, sneezing and insomnia. About 8 hours after heroin is discontinued, the addict will start to feel uncomfortable. After about 12–15 hours, withdrawal symptoms increase in severity and are at their most intense between 24 and 72 hours. Thereafter, the symptoms gradually lessen in intensity, though it may be a week or more before the person feels well again.

One of the most widely used opiate detoxification methods involves gradually reducing doses of oral methadone. Methadone is often regarded as the most effective pharmacotherapeutic agent currently used for detoxification (Kreek, 2000). Typically, detoxification takes place with gradually reducing doses of methadone over periods of 10–28 days (Gossop, Griffiths, Bradley, & Strang, 1989).

Centrally acting alpha-2 adrenergic agonists such as clonidine and lofexidine have also been used. Clonidine produces a rapid reduction of withdrawal symptoms (Gossop, 1988), but it may require additional medication to modify residual symptoms. The hypotensive effects of clonidine may restrict the manner in which it can be used since treatment requires relatively close medical supervision. Lofexidine has comparable efficacy to clonidine, but fewer side effects, particularly with regard to postural hypotension (Buntwal, Bearn, Gossop, & Strang, 2000). Detoxification with lofexidine can also be achieved over periods as short as 5 days (Bearn, Gossop, & Strang, 1998).

Stimulants

Some drug users become dependent upon stimulants in the sense that they have impaired capacity to control their use of these drugs. It is unclear whether cocaine and amphetamines have a true withdrawal syndrome, though abstinence after regular use of amphetamines can lead to disrupted sleep patterns with a reduction in sleep time accompanied by daytime drowsiness and night-time wakefulness (Gossop, Bradley, & Brewis, 1982). There are no pharmacotherapies of proven value for the effective treatment of stimulant withdrawal. Non-pharmacological detoxification treatments for stimulants, including auricular (ear) acupuncture, are sometimes used, though with little evidence to support their effectiveness.

Alcohol

Alcohol dependence has a well-defined withdrawal syndrome. Mild or moderate degrees of dependence may lead to only moderate discomfort during withdrawal. This may require low levels of medication and in some cases, no medication may be required. In other cases, alcohol detoxification may require medication with a benzodiazepine for a few days, though detoxification regimes of more than 7–10 days are rarely necessary for uncomplicated alcohol withdrawal.

Trembling is a common alcohol withdrawal symptom with increasing tremor appearing 12–24 hours after the last drink, often accompanied by restlessness, agitation and insomnia. The most severe form of alcohol withdrawal is Delirium Tremens. This may develop 2–5 days after alcohol abstinence. Its onset is often abrupt, but may be preceded by nightmares, restlessness and agitation, then by panic, confusion and hallucinations. Delerium Tremens usually subsides in 2–3 days but has a significant morbidity and mortality due to injuries sustained during periods of confusion, and from dehydration, hypothermia and pneumonia.

Multiple drug detoxification

Drug users may be dependent upon several drugs. Common multiple dependencies which require detoxification involve combinations of opiates, benzodiazepines and alcohol. Where drug users require multiple detoxification, treatment is most appropriately provided in a setting with resources and facilities for intensive clinical supervision and the medically safe treatment of complicated withdrawal states.

The management of withdrawal in custody

The treatment of withdrawal symptoms presents few clinical problems when conducted in a medical setting. Providing detoxification for drug addicts in police custody may be more problematic. The accuracy of self-reported drug use may be compromised in this setting.

Police doctors often stay with the suspect for only a few minutes and the next doctor to attend may be a different one. In most cases, resources or facilities do not allow the medical and physical state of the addict to be observed by trained staff.

When addicts are taken into police custody, some treatment intervention may be required to prevent the onset of acute withdrawal. There is often uncertainty and disagreement among police surgeons about how to respond to drug withdrawal syndromes. Police doctors may have conflicting views about methadone prescribing, coupled with negative attitudes towards drug addicts and a lack of knowledge of current drug-misuse treatment practice.

The management of drug-dependent suspects in police custody presents a dilemma. If untreated, they will develop withdrawal symptoms. If given drugs, they may become intoxicated. Both of these states may impair the suspect's capacity to respond appropriately to a police interview and this may subsequently be relevant to the acceptability of statements and confessions in court.

TREATMENT

(i) Motivation and coercion

Drug users give various reasons for seeking treatment. In addition to drug problems, the person may have physical or psychological problems (a serious infection, depression), or social pressure (from a partner or employer). Facing an imminent court case or having been convicted can be powerful reasons for seeking treatment. Although the person may be aware of the need to change, they are often ambivalent both about drugs and about treatment.

Many drug users in US treatment programmes are directly referred by the criminal justice system (Hubbard *et al.*, 1989). However, direct referral is a relatively insensitive measure of the influence of the criminal justice system, and many more are facing some form of legal pressure such as parole or probation. It has been suggested that legal pressures or mandatory referrals from the criminal justice system can be used productively. However, the results of research studies are inconsistent. Some studies found comparable outcomes among coerced and non-coerced groups (Anglin, 1988; De Leon, 1988). Other studies found that coercion may lead to worse outcomes (Friedman *et al.*, 1982). The heroin users in NTORS who were facing pressure from the criminal justice system had worse heroin use outcomes at follow-up (Gossop, Stewart, Browne, & Marsden, 2002).

Motivation and treatment readiness are complex, and include readiness for personal change, and readiness to engage with the treatment programme and with specific intervention activities. Readiness also includes patient attributes, skills/resources, confidence/self-efficacy, as well as motivation. Many treatments presume a commitment to change. Motivational interviewing (MI) assumes that the drug user is characterized by ambivalence about their drug-taking behaviour, and sees itself as 'an approach designed to help clients build commitment and reach a decision to change' (Miller & Rollnick, 1991). Motivational interventions may be particularly suitable for those drug and alcohol users whose substance use is problematic but not dependent, since these can be delivered as a brief, low-intensity intervention.

MI is seen primarily as a counselling *style* rather than a technique. Motivation is regarded as the product of an interpersonal process in which the therapist has considerable influence on the subsequent attributions and behaviour of the patient. MI is used to help explore and resolve ambivalence about change. Its aim is to increase levels of cognitive dissonance until sufficient motivation is generated for the patient to consider options and interventions for change. Reflective listening is used selectively to elicit self-motivational statements which can orientate the patient towards change. The therapist assists the patient in identification of appropriate goals and in the implementation of strategies to achieve these changes. MI has been found to be a useful tool in many stages of treatment but it has been particularly useful in helping people who are still at an early stage of committing themselves to treatment or to changing their behaviour.

Drug users who received MI were more likely to attend treatment sessions (Carroll, Libby, Sheehan, & Hyland, 2001), to remain in treatment and to show more commitment to treatment goals, more compliance with treatment requirements and to remain abstinent after treatment (Baker, Boggs, & Lewin, 2001). Among drug misusers who received court orders to undergo treatment, those who received MI were more likely to attend treatment sessions and to complete the programme (Lincourt, Kuettel, & Bombardier, 2002).

(ii) Treatment interventions

Cognitive behavioural treatments

Basic assumptions underlying the various cognitive behavioural treatments are that: substance use disorders are mediated by cognitive and behavioural processes; these disorders and their associated cognitive behavioural processes are, to a large extent, learned and can be modified; treatment should facilitate the acquisition of coping skills for resisting drug-taking and for reducing drug-related problems (Liese & Najavits, 1997). Such treatments vary in the precedence given to the development of cognitive or behavioural skills.

One treatment which is based on the principles of social-learning theory is a self-management programme designed to enhance the habit-change process. Relapse prevention (RP) teaches individuals who are trying to change their behaviour how to anticipate and cope with the problem of relapse. It is similar to other cognitive behavioural treatments and combines behavioural skill training, cognitive interventions and lifestyle change procedures (Marlatt, 1985).

The key components of treatment are the identification of high-risk situations which increase the risk of relapse, and the development and strengthening of effective coping responses. High-risk situations may be situations, events, objects, cognitions or mood states associated with drug use. Most lapses are related to negative emotional states, social pressure and interpersonal conflicts (Bradley, Phillips, Green, & Gossop, 1989).

Relapse is often linked to contact with other drug users. The majority of lapses among heroin addicts occur in the company of drug takers or in a social context related to drug-taking (Gossop *et al.*, 1989). More than three-quarters of the opiate addicts in an outpatient treatment programme met other drug users during the previous week: nearly two-thirds had been offered drugs on at least one occasion during the previous week, and 14% had been offered drugs every day (Unnithan, Gossop, & Strang, 1992). Under such circumstances, the likelihood of a lapse to drug-taking is greatly increased for even the most strongly motivated patient.

The provision of treatment within a relapse prevention framework involves an individualized assessment of high-risk situations. Patients are taught to recognize high-risk situations and to avoid or to cope with these risks. RP requires the development of specific coping strategies to deal with risk situations. These may include skills training and the development or strengthening of coping strategies that address issues of lifestyle imbalance and antecedents of relapse.

Positive expectancies and self-efficacy beliefs engender feelings of hope and optimism which facilitate treatment effectiveness. Efficacy expectations reflect the individual's sense of personal control and influence – whether they initiate coping behaviour, what degree of effort is devoted to that behaviour and how long it is maintained in the face of obstacles. Self-efficacy refers to the person's expectations about their capacity to cope with specific high-risk situations. It is concerned with perceived ability to perform a coping response, and not with the general ability to exercise willpower to resist temptation.

Self-efficacy beliefs may apply to the development of addictive behaviour, choice of treatment goals and the maintenance of behaviour change during recovery (Annis & Davis, 1988). Treatment should take account of cognitive appraisals of past successes and failures in relation to drug-taking situations. Where a coping response is successfully performed, self-efficacy beliefs will be strengthened, and repeated experiences of success will reduce the risk of future lapses or relapse in such situations.

Conversely, where an individual fails to cope with a high-risk situation, their beliefs about their own capacity are undermined, and the probability of relapse increases. Loss of confidence may be particularly pronounced among those who rely upon willpower alone to deal with risk situations, since there is nothing they can 'do' to cope. This reinforces the sense of failure, helplessness and lack of control. Addicts who saw relapse episodes as being more amenable to their personal control were more likely to avoid a relapse to opiate use after treatment (Bradley, Gossop, Brewin, Phillips, & Green, 1992).

Relapse prevention procedures may be applied to anticipate and prevent a relapse or to help the individual recover from a 'lapse' before it escalates into a full-blown relapse. In principle, RP procedures can be used regardless of the theoretical orientation of the therapist or the intervention methods used during the initial treatment phase. Once a heroin addict has stopped using drugs, for example, RP can be used to support continued abstinence, regardless of the methods used to initiate abstinence (e.g., attending 12-step meetings, psychotherapy, or voluntary cessation) (Marlatt, 1985).

Although relapse prevention models have often been used to treat offenders, there have been relatively few controlled outcome research studies evaluating their effectiveness. However, a meta-analysis of relapse prevention interventions found moderate mean reductions in recidivism (Dowden *et al.*, 2003). Certain specific elements of relapse prevention (e.g., training significant others to support the programme and identifying the offence chain) were found to be effective, as were the clinically relevant and psychologically informed principles of risk, need and general responsivity.

Twelve-step treatments and therapeutic communities

Twelve-step treatments and therapeutic communities (TCs) differ in several respects but they also share many common features. They share a common focus upon abstinence as the overriding goal of treatment. They see recovery from addiction as requiring a profound restructuring of thinking, personality and lifestyle, and involving more than just giving up drug-taking.

Narcotics Anonymous (NA) is a direct descendant of Alcoholics Anonymous. Both AA and NA have flourished in many countries throughout the world. AA/NA has a philosophy of mutual-help, group affiliation and identification. Reliance upon the fellowship is seen as one of the primary therapeutic agents which sets AA/NA apart from other forms of treatment. Group meetings are one of the best known aspects of AA/NA. Meetings may be 'open' or 'closed'. When individuals join AA/NA, they are usually encouraged to attend more than one meeting a week, and a target of attending 90 meetings in 90 days is often set (DuPont & McGovern, 1994).

AA/NA offers a number of social and psychological support systems for the recovering addict. The peer group can support efforts to achieve and maintain abstinence, and provides a structure for the member's free time (Brown, Kinlock, & Nurco, 2001). Twelve-step programmes provide a form of cognitive restructuring therapy and can help to tackle the faulty beliefs and maladaptive cognitions which need to be changed in recovery.

The 12 steps are the essential principles and ingredients of the recovery process. Progression through the steps is seen as essential for achieving and maintaining abstinence. The steps emphasize two general themes: spirituality/belief in a 'higher power' (which is defined by each individual), and pragmatism (belief in doing 'whatever works' for the individual, meaning doing whatever it takes in order to avoid returning to substance use).

AA/NA sees addiction as an illness that permeates all aspects of the individual's life, and which can only be controlled by lifelong abstinence. The 'disease concept' of addiction has provoked opposition on the grounds that it may serve 'to absolve the alcoholic [or drug addict] from moral responsibility for his actions' (Heather & Robertson 1989). This view is strongly rebutted by AA/NA, which emphasizes the need for addicts to take responsibility for their own behaviour and to participate actively in their own recovery (Wells, 1994).

AA/NA has also been criticized for its 'religious' orientation. Six of the 12 steps make some reference to God, and prayer and meditation are seen as important parts of the recovery process. However, members of the fellowship are encouraged to interpret the 'higher power' based upon their own personal understanding. Examples of this may include the power of the group, the power of nature, love, truth or honesty (Wells, 1994). Attitudes towards the 12 steps vary greatly. Addicts tend to show more willingness to accept 'Personal Responsibility' steps than those related to a 'Higher Power' (Best et al., 2001).

Therapeutic communities are used both within and outside the criminal justice system. As with AA/NA, the basic goal for problem drug users in TCs requires them to undergo a complete change in lifestyle involving abstinence from drugs, avoidance of antisocial behaviour, the development of prosocial skills and personal honesty. The essential element of the TC approach is the community. This provides both the context and method in the change process, and the community element distinguishes the TC from other treatment or rehabilitative approaches to substance abuse and related disorders.

Treatment length varies from short-term with aftercare, to long-term programmes of more than 1 year duration. At one time, treatments were much longer, and some are still provided over extended periods. TCs usually divide their programme into three phases of induction/orientation, treatment and re-entry (Kennard, 1998). Induction/orientation may last for a few weeks or up to 2 months. The core, treatment phase involves the resident living, working and relating to others exclusively in the community, and progressing through the community hierarchy. In the re-entry phase, the resident has passes to go out while still living in the community. Some TCs also operate 'half-way' houses with patients living in semi-independent accommodation after completing the main programme.

Three important psychological principles underlying the processes of change within TCs are social role training, vicarious learning and efficacy training (De Leon, 2000). The resident positions within the TC hierarchy provide experience of work roles, and as individuals learn their various social roles in the community, they undergo a wide range of social and psychological changes. Role training builds new behaviours, skills and attitudes that are socially and psychologically supportive to the individual in their recovery. Peers and staff provide role models for appropriate behaviours and attitudes. Meeting community expectations in performance, responsibility, self-examination and autonomy leads to increased self-efficacy and self-esteem.

Drug maintenance and other pharmacotherapies

Maintenance treatments for opiate dependence are widely used throughout the world. About 600,000 people in Europe are currently receiving maintenance treatment: of these, more than 400,000 are receiving methadone treatment. Methadone maintenance is a long-term treatment for opiate dependence which involves the prescription of daily doses of (usually oral) methadone, and can help shift the orientation and lifestyle away from drug seeking and related crime towards more socially acceptable behaviours.

Methadone maintenance has been extensively studied in different countries, with different treatment groups and over a period of four decades. It is the most thoroughly evaluated form of treatment for drug dependence. A meta-analysis of methadone maintenance studies, reported consistent associations between maintenance treatment and reductions in illicit opiate use, HIV risk behaviours and drug and property crimes (Marsch, 1998).

Opiate-dependent individuals show reduced illicit drug use and criminal behaviour when maintained on methadone compared to no treatment or simple detoxification conditions. Methadone patients who are retained in treatment longer have better outcomes than clients with shorter treatment courses, and better outcomes have been found when patients are maintained on higher (50–100 mg) rather than lower doses (Ward, Mattick, & Hall, 1998). Methadone maintenance treatment has been found to have one of its strongest effects in terms of reducing drug-related criminal behaviours (Marsch, 1998).

Maintenance treatments are used in both specialist (e.g., addiction services) and non-specialist (e.g., GP) settings. Maintenance treatments are also increasingly used in criminal justice settings though its use in such settings continues to be controversial. One reason for the reluctance to provide maintenance treatment in prisons is because of the fear of diversion of an opioid drug within the prison. This risk of diversion can be greatly reduced if not eliminated by means of appropriately supervised consumption of medication. This requires that the treatment be provided with adequate resources and facilities.

In a randomized clinical trial, methadone maintenance treatment in prison was found to be superior to a counselling-only intervention in leading to greater treatment entry in the community after release from prison and to reduced opiate use (confirmed by urine testing) after release (Kinlock et al., 2007). Methadone maintenance treatment in prison has also been found to lead to reduced injecting risk behaviour in prison (Dolan, Wodak, & Hall, 1998). A systematic review of studies of maintenance treatment in prison settings (Hedrich et al., 2012) found that maintenance was associated with reduced heroin use, injecting and syringe-sharing in prison, and also with increased treatment entry and retention after release. Associations with post-release outcomes were weaker, and the evidence regarding crime and re-incarceration was equivocal.

Buprenorphine is a mixed agonist-antagonist unlike full opiate agonists such as heroin or methadone. It is readily absorbed through the mouth and it has been administered both as a solution and as tablets. Although methadone remains the most widely used maintenance medication in the United Kingdom (83% of all prescriptions in 2005), the prescription of buprenorphine is increasing (Strang et al., 2007).

Research studies have demonstrated the efficacy of buprenorphine for maintenance and detoxification treatments. Buprenorphine and methadone have broadly comparable efficacy (Marsch et al., 2005). Buprenorphine can be as effective as methadone in retaining patients in treatment (Mattick, Oliphant, Ward, & Hall, 1998) and in leading to reductions in heroin use and to abstinence from heroin (Johnson et al. 2000).

Buprenorphine and methadone are often used in different treatment settings and this is an issue of potential importance to the provision of maintenance treatment in the prison setting. Whereas the prescription of methadone has often been restricted to specialist clinics buprenorphine has been more widely used in primary care settings.

Buprenorphine's partial agonist effects may be of particular relevance to the use of maintenance treatment in prisons. Buprenorphine produces less severe respiratory depression than full-agonist opioids and the death rate for buprenorphine is lower than for methadone (Auriacombe, 2001).

More recent research has looked at the possible uses of opioid receptor antagonists that block the reinforcing effects of opioids. In a study comparing the effects of in-prison treatment with naltrexone implants (a long-acting formulation of an antagonist) and methadone, reductions were found in the frequency of illicit drug use, as well as criminality, 6 months after prison release (Lobmaier et al., 2010). Other research is exploring the possible uses of naloxone (also an opioid antagonist). A trial (starting in 2012) is currently investigating whether heroin overdose deaths post-prison release can be prevented by prior provision of a take-home emergency supply of naloxone (Strang et al., 2013).

(iii) Effectiveness of treatment

Major national outcome studies have consistently shown improvements in problem behaviours after treatment. US studies showed that treatment leads to reductions in use of heroin and other illicit drugs (Hubbard et al., 1989). Also, predatory crime was reduced during treatment, and remained lower than baseline levels after treatment.

In the United Kingdom, NTORS found improvements in a wide range of problem behaviours after treatment, including reductions in use of heroin and other illicit drugs, improvements in psychological health and reductions in crime. Frequency of heroin use after 1 year, for example, was reduced to about half of the intake levels, and remained at this lower level throughout the 5-year follow-up period (Gossop, Marsden, Stewart, & Kidd, 2003).

There were also substantial reductions in criminal behaviour. Acquisitive crimes were reduced to one-third of intake levels, and the rate of involvement in crime was reduced to about half of intake levels (Gossop, Marsden, Stewart, & Rolfe, 2000). The number of shoplifting offences was reduced to about one-third of intake levels, and burglary offences were reduced to less than one-quarter of intake levels. Changes in offending behaviour were linked to reductions in drug use after treatment, and especially to reduced heroin use. The greatest reductions in criminal activity occurred among the most highly active offenders (Gossop *et al.*, 2000) where crimes were reduced to 13% of intake levels. This represents a huge reduction in criminal behaviour.

The economic costs imposed upon society by drug addicts are largely due to criminality. Treatment has been found to be cost-effective and cost-beneficial with the costs of treatment being recouped during treatment, and further cost-benefits accrued as a result of reduced post-treatment drug use (Harwood *et al.*, 1988). There is a range of economic benefits from treatment for drug dependence, based solely on costs of crime. Even without the numerous other benefits in addition to reductions in crime, the financial resources expended in treating drug-dependent patients provided a return that justified the cost of treatment. The provision of treatment yielded an immediate cost saving in terms of the reduced victim costs of crime, as well as cost savings within the criminal justice system. The true cost savings to society are likely to be even greater than these crime-focussed estimates (Godfrey, Stewart, & Gossop, 2001).

Treatment within prisons can also reduce post-release drug use and reoffending (Wexler, Falkin, & Lipton, 1990; Knight, Simpson, Chatham, & Camacho, 1997). In many respects, the issues involved in providing effective treatment in prison are similar to those for treating addicts in a standard clinical setting. Good results have been found for participation in residential programmes. Studies of therapeutic community programmes within prisons found that programme participation, time spent in treatment, programme completion and the provision of aftercare were all associated with improved outcomes (Martin, Butzin, Saum, & Inciardi, 1999).

Studies of the treatment needs of drug misusers in prison suggest that inmates need a range of treatment modalities, and that the provision of correctional treatment is often inadequate relative to need (Belenko & Peugh, 2005). About one-third of male and more than half of female US prison inmates were estimated to need long-term residential treatment.

One response to the lack of treatments in US correctional services involved the expansion of community-based alternatives such as drug courts or diversion programmes (Hser *et al.*, 2003). Drug Treatment and Testing Orders (DTTOs), based upon the US drug courts, were introduced in the United Kingdom in 1998. These sought to provide treatment in the community for drug-misusing offenders. The drug user is required to attend a treatment programme for between 6 months and 3 years, and to provide urine specimens for testing. An evaluation of DTTOs found that reconviction rates were high (80%), and completion rates were low, with only 30% of the sample completing their programmes (Hough, Clancy, McSweeney, & Turnbull, 2003). Studies from other countries have found poor outcomes among drug users processed through drug courts (Vermeulen & Walburg, 1998; Belenko *et al.*, 1994).

The importance of aftercare is widely accepted, and studies have demonstrated the importance of aftercare support for offenders (Martin *et al.*, 1999). Relapse Prevention can also provide an aftercare programme for substance abusers after completion of an intensive treatment intervention (Brown, Seraganian, Tremblay, & Annis, 2002). The period immediately after leaving a residential setting (hospital or prison) is one of massively high risk of relapse and the best possible support should be provided during this period. Unfortunately, few services have sufficient resources to provide adequate aftercare, and generally, little is done during this critical period.

Because of its self-supporting nature, AA/NA provides a form of aftercare at no cost to existing services and offender programmes can make use of AA/NA as an aftercare resource merely by recommending participation and encouraging attendance at meetings.

FURTHER COMPLICATIONS

Psychiatric comorbidity

The co-occurrence of substance use and psychiatric problems creates particular difficulties for intervention. Anxiety and depression are common among individuals with substance use disorders. Psychiatric disorders and drug misuse can coexist with varying degrees of association or independence. Some disorders may be due to intoxication, or withdrawal states. In some cases, anxiety and depressive symptoms are associated with drug use and will remit with abstinence (Gossop, Marsden, & Stewart, 2006).

Stimulant psychosis may occur after high-dose and/or prolonged use of stimulants. Stimulant psychosis has some similarities with schizophrenia, but unlike schizophrenia, the onset of stimulant psychosis is rapid and is often accompanied by an agitated or manic mood state. When stimulant use is discontinued, a stimulant psychosis would be expected to clear within days. The continuation of psychotic symptoms after the drug has ceased to be excreted (usually within a maximum of 7 days) should be regarded not as stimulant psychoses but as of possible schizophrenic aetiology.

Some individuals use drugs or alcohol to self-medicate psychological problems. Drug use and psychiatric disorders may also coexist by chance since both disorders are relatively common. Even in these circumstances, psychiatric problems are likely to influence the course and outcome of substance use disorders, and may require a specially tailored treatment approach.

The presence of comorbid psychiatric disorders among substance misusers is generally associated with a poorer treatment prognosis, as is the severity of psychiatric disorders (Ward et al., 1998). The provision of appropriate treatment for underlying psychiatric or psychological disorders leads to improved treatment outcomes (Rounsaville & Kleber, 1985).

It has frequently been reported (e.g., Ruiz et al., 2012) that offenders with substance use problems are more likely than others to have increased mental health problems and risk factors for suicide or aggression. Psychiatric comorbidity among female substance-using offenders may be a particular problem. In a study of lifetime psychiatric disorders among offenders newly admitted to a prison substance abuse programme, although men and women did not differ in severity of substance use prior to incarceration, women were more likely to report a lifetime psychiatric disorder and a lifetime severe disorder (Zlotnick et al., 2008). Women reported greater lifetime major depression, post-traumatic stress disorder and eating disorder.

Limited resources often create challenges in providing appropriate screening, assessment and treatment for such problems. Staff in criminal justice settings may need enhanced training to improve their ability to detect, assess and respond to those with comorbid or dual diagnosis disorders. Female offenders with substance use disorders are a population with complex medical and mental health needs and are likely to be high users of services within the correctional system. One of the most difficult challenges is where substance abusing offenders suffer from schizophrenia or other serious mental illnesses. In such cases, the complexities of providing an effective treatment response within the criminal justice system are likely to be beyond all but the most specialized services.

Suicide

Substance use disorders are strongly associated with suicide. Suicidal ideation and suicide attempts are relatively common among substance misusers. Post-mortem studies have consistently reported that at least one-third of those whose death was due to suicide met criteria for alcohol abuse or dependence. Early onset of substance use problems is associated with increased risk of suicide, and in young people the risk of suicidal behaviours is increased among those with substance misuse problems (Hallfors et al., 2004). Substance use disorders are also associated with a greater frequency of suicide attempts, greater seriousness of intention and greater suicidal ideation.

The prison environment may itself increase suicide risk, and the risk is high during the period immediately after incarceration. One-third of suicides within prison occur during the first week after reception (Shaw et al., 2004). Known risk factors include psychiatric disorders and substance use disorders. Suicide risk after intake to prison is particularly high among women prisoners and remand prisoners. Pre-existing risk of suicide may be increased where the treatment of withdrawal symptoms is not done effectively after admission to prison.

In most prisoners who commit suicide, there is evidence of suicide risk at reception screening (Shaw et al., 2004). In this respect, many suicides could be regarded as being, at least in principle, preventable. However, it is extremely difficult to attempt to predict suicidal behaviour in individual cases.

Physical comorbidity

Many substance abusers have poor physical health. Drug abuse can adversely affect a range of organ systems, and damage to health may be both direct and indirect. Alcohol can also cause damage to nearly every tissue and body system with the possibility of consequent disability or disease. Between 20 and 40% of admissions to general hospital wards may be alcohol-related (Lieber, 1995).

The majority of drug- or alcohol-dependent patients tend to have at least one physical health problem at admission to treatment, and many have multiple health problems. Physical health problems are particularly frequent among persons with alcohol dependence. The most common health problems among alcohol-dependent patients are cardiovascular, neurological and gastro-intestinal and liver disorders. Special arrangements may be required in prisons for the clinical management of these health problems.

Drug-dependent patients often suffer from respiratory disorders and from chronic liver disease due to viral hepatitis. Hepatitis C infection is extremely prevalent among drug injectors. A study of London heroin users found a seropositivity rate of 86% for HCV (Best et al., 1999). Although drug users are generally aware of the risk of hepatitis, their beliefs about their own viral status are frequently inaccurate. This may lead to continued injection risk behaviours both within and outside prisons. Physical health problems among opiate addicts are reduced by opioid maintenance treatment. Drug-related hospital treatment episodes were much lower during maintenance treatment compared to before treatment and increased greatly among those who dropped out of treatment (Skeie et al., 2011).

The health risk behaviours of drug users have been the focus for various preventive activities. Dissemination of information about the transmission of blood-borne infections is one of the least controversial prevention responses. This has been widely used and in some circumstances may be effective. Needle and syringe exchange schemes have been more controversial, though these have now been established in many countries throughout the world. Some services provide needles and syringes but make no requirement for the return of used equipment. In other services, needles and syringes are provided on an exchange basis. All services make arrangements for the safe disposal of returned used needles and syringes.

There has often been extreme resistance to providing access to sterile injecting equipment within criminal justice settings. However, it is known that illicit drugs can often be obtained within prisons, and that such drugs may be used by injection (Strang *et al.*, 2006). Where drugs are injected by multiple users who have access only to shared injection equipment this creates a situation of maximum risk for the potential transmission of blood-borne diseases.

Overdose

Despite the greater attention that is generally given to HIV/AIDS, drug overdose is a more frequent cause of death among drug misusers. Although fatal and non-fatal overdoses are commonly attributed to the use of opiates, these are seldom due simply to the use of opiates. The risk of overdose is strongly linked to, and increased by, polydrug use. Both fatal and non-fatal overdoses which are attributed to heroin are more likely to involve the combined use of opiates and alcohol or other sedatives. The mortality rate of the drug users in the NTORS cohort was 1.2% – this is about six times higher than in the general population: deaths were mainly due to overdose (Gossop, Marsden, Stewart, & Treacy, 2002).

The achievement of a drug-free state is not a risk-neutral event. Among patients who have been detoxified in residential programmes, an initial lapse to opiate use often occurs soon after leaving the programme, and the first few weeks after discharge are a critical period (Gossop *et al.*, 1989). The same problem arises when detoxified drug addicts are released from prison. The risk of drug-related death is seven times higher immediately after release (specifically during the first fortnight) than at any subsequent time (Bird & Hutchinson, 2003; Merrall *et al.*, 2010). Prison services need to be aware of the potential overdose risk among previously addicted prisoners who have been withdrawn from opiates and have lost their tolerance to the effects of opiates.

NOTES

1 The National Treatment Outcome Research Study (NTORS) was a 5-year prospective, national study of more than 1,000 drug-dependent patients in addiction treatment services across England.

2 The term 'detoxification' is widely used, and it is retained here to avoid the cumbersome if more accurate phrase 'treatment of the withdrawal syndrome'.

FURTHER READING

Tonry, M., & Wilson, J. Q. (1990). *Drugs and crime*. Chicago: University of Chicago Press.

This edited volume presents a collection of essays which review the various complex interrelationships between drug-taking and crime. It includes chapters which examine these issues from the perspectives of drug-law enforcement, prevention and treatment as the basic components of public policy strategies. Despite its age and its focus upon problems in the United States, it provides a useful overview of many of the key issues within a single volume.

Gossop, M., Trakada, K., Stewart, D., & Witton, J. (2005). Reductions in criminal convictions after addiction treatment: Five year follow-up. *Drug and Alcohol Dependence, 79,* 295–302.

As part of the National Treatment Outcome Research Study (NTORS), changes in criminal convictions were investigated among 1,075 drug-misusing clients admitted to 54 drug-misuse treatment services across England. Convictions data during the year prior to treatment, and at 1 year, 2 years and 5 years after treatment intake, were collected from the Home Office Offenders' Index, a national database of all convictions in adult and youth courts. During the year prior to treatment, 34% of the sample had been convicted of at least one offence. Conviction rates at all follow-up points were significantly lower than at intake. Reductions in convictions were found for acquisitive, drug-selling and violent crimes. These reductions in crime were linked to reductions in regular heroin use and represent substantial changes in behaviour. As well as the personal, social and clinical significance of these behavioural changes, the reduced criminality also provides substantial economic benefits to society.

Merrall, E., Kariminia, A., Binswanger, I., Hobbs, M., Farrell, M., Marsden, J., Hutchinson, S., & Bird, S. (2010). Meta-analysis of drug-related deaths soon after release from prison. *Addiction, 105,* 1545–1554.

In a meta-analysis of the risk of deaths among drug-using offenders in the first 12 weeks after release from prison, this study looked at 612 drug-related deaths. A three- to eightfold increased risk of drug-related death was found when comparing weeks 1 + 2 with weeks 3–12. The findings confirm that there is an increased risk of drug-related death during the first 2 weeks after release from prison and that the risk remains elevated up to at least the fourth week. Such findings point to the need for investment in, and further evaluation of, prison-based interventions for drug abusers to reduce the risk of death during the immediate post-release period.

REFERENCES

Anglin, M. D. (1988). A social policy analysis of compulsory treatment for opiate dependence. *Journal of Drug Issues, 18,* 527–545.

Annis, H., & Davis, C. (1988). Self-efficacy and the prevention of alcoholic relapse. In, T. Baker & D. Cannon (Eds.), *Addictive disorders: Psychological research on assessment and treatment.* New York: Praeger.

Auriacombe, M. (2001). Deaths attributable to methadone vs buprenorphine in France. *Journal of the American Medical Association, 285,* 45.

Baker, A., Boggs, T., & Lewin, T. (2001). Randomized controlled trial of brief cognitive behavioural interventions among regular users of amphetamine. *Addiction, 96,* 1279–1287.

Ball, J., Shaffer, J., & Nurco, D. (1983). The day to day criminality of heroin addicts in Baltimore: A study in the continuity of offence rates. *Drug and Alcohol Dependence, 12,* 119–142.

Bearn, J., Gossop, M., & Strang, J. (1998). Accelerated lofexidine treatment regimen compared with conventional lofexidine and methadone treatment for in-patient opiate detoxification. *Drug and Alcohol Dependence, 50,* 227–232.

Belding, M., McLellan, A. T., Zanis, D., & Incmikoski, R. (1998). Characterising 'nonresponsive' patients. *Journal of Substance Abuse Treatment, 15,* 485–492.

Belenko, S., Fagan, J., & Dumanovsky, T. (1994). The effects of legal sanctions on recidivism in special drugs courts. *Justice System Journal, 17,* 53–81.

Belenko, S., & Peugh, J. (2005). Estimating drug treatment needs among state prison inmates. *Drug and Alcohol Dependence, 77,* 269–281.

Best, D., Harris, J., Gossop, M., Manning, V., Man, L.-H., Marshall, J., Bearn, J., & Strang, J. (2001). Are the Twelve Steps more acceptable to drug users than to drinkers? A comparison of experiences of and attitudes to Alcoholics Anonymous (AA) and Narcotics Anonymous (NA) among 200 substance misusers attending inpatient detoxification. *European Addiction Research, 7,* 69–77

Best, D., Noble, A., Finch, E., Gossop, M., Sidwell, C., & Strang, J. (1999). Accuracy of perceptions of hepatitis B and C status: Cross sectional investigation of opiate addicts in treatment. *British Medical Journal, 319,* 290–291.

Bird, S. M., & Hutchinson, S. J. (2003). Male drugs-related deaths in the fortnight after release from prison: Scotland, 1996–99. *Addiction, 98,* 185–190.

Bradley, B., Gossop, M., Brewin, C., Phillips, G., & Green, L. (1992). Attributions and relapse in opiate addicts. *Journal of Consulting and Clinical Psychology, 60,* 470–472.

Bradley, B., Phillips, G., Green, L., & Gossop, M. (1989). Circumstances surrounding the initial lapse to opiate use following detoxification. *British Journal of Psychiatry, 154,* 354–359.

Brown, B., Kinlock, T., & Nurco, D. (2001). Self-help initiatives to reduce the risk of relapse. In F. Tims, C. Leukefeld, & J. Platt (Eds.), *Relapse and recovery in addictions.* New Haven: Yale University Press.

Brown, T. G., Seraganian, P., Tremblay, J., & Annis, H. (2002). Process and outcome changes with relapse prevention versus 12-step aftercare programs for substance abusers. *Addiction, 97,* 677–689.

Buntwal, N., Bearn, J., Gossop, M., & Strang, J. (2000). Naltrexone and lofexidine combination treatment compared with conventional lofexidine treatment for in-patient opiate detoxification. *Drug and Alcohol Dependence, 59,* 183–188.

Carroll, K. M., Libby, B., Sheehan, J., & Hyland, N. (2001). Motivational interviewing to enhance treatment initiation in substance abusers: An effectiveness study. *American Journal on Addictions, 10,* 335–339.

Darke, S., Kaye, S., McKetin, R., & Duflou, J. (2008). Major physical and psychological harms of methamphetamine use. *Drug and Alcohol Review, 27,* 253–262.

De Leon, G. (1988). Legal pressure in therapeutic communities. *Journal of Drug Issues, 18,* 625–640.

De Leon, G. (2000). *The therapeutic community: Theory, model, and method.* New York: Springer.

Dolan, K. A., Wodak, A. D., & Hall, W. D. (1998). A bleach program for inmates in NSW: An HIV prevention strategy. *Australian and New Zealand Journal of Public Health, 22,* 838–840.

Dowden, C., Antonowicz, D., & Andrews D. A. (2003). The effectiveness of relapse prevention with offenders: a meta-analysis. *International Journal of Offender Therapy and Comparative Criminology, 47,* 516–528.

DuPont, R., & McGovern, J. (1994). *A bridge to recovery: An introduction to 12-step programs.* Washington: American Psychiatric Association.

Friedman, S., Horvat, G., & Levinson, R. (1982). The Narcotic Addict Rehabilitation Act: its impact upon federal prisons. *Contemporary Drug Problems, 82,* 101–111.

Godfrey, C., Stewart, D., & Gossop, M. (2001). *National Treatment Outcome Research Study: Economic analysis of the two year outcome data.* Department of Health, London.

Gossop, M. (1988). Clonidine and the treatment of the opiate withdrawal syndrome. *Drug and Alcohol Dependence, 21,* 253–259.

Gossop, M. (1990). The development of a Short Opiate Withdrawal Scale (SOWS). *Addictive Behaviors, 15,* 487–490.

Gossop, M. (2003). *Drug addiction and its treatment.* Oxford: Oxford University Press.

Gossop, M., Bradley, B., & Brewis, R. (1982). Amphetamine withdrawal and sleep disturbance. *Drug and Alcohol Dependence, 10,* 177–183.

Gossop, M., & Connell, P. (1983). Drug dependence, who gets treated? *International Journal of the Addictions, 18,* 99–109.

Gossop, M., Darke, S., Griffiths, P., Hando, J., Powis, B., Hall, W., & Strang, J. (1995). The Severity of Dependence Scale (SDS): Psychometric properties of the SDS in English and Australian samples of heroin, cocaine and amphetamine users. *Addiction, 90,* 607–614.

Gossop, M., Griffiths, P., Bradley, B., & Strang, J. (1989). Opiate withdrawal symptoms in response to 10-day and 21-day methadone withdrawal programmes. *British Journal of Psychiatry, 154,* 360–363.

Gossop, M., Marsden, J., & Stewart, D. (2006). Remission of psychiatric symptoms among drug misusers after drug dependence treatment. *Journal of Nervous and Mental Disease, 194,* 826–832.

Gossop, M., Marsden, J., Stewart, D., & Kidd, T. (2003). The National Treatment Outcome Research Study (NTORS): 4–5 Year follow-up results. *Addiction, 98,* 291–303.

Gossop, M., Marsden, J., Stewart, D., & Rolfe, A. (2000). Reductions in acquisitive crime and drug use after treatment of addiction problems: One year follow-up outcomes. *Drug and Alcohol Dependence, 58,* 165–172.

Gossop, M., Marsden, J., Stewart, D., & Treacy, S. (2002). A prospective study of mortality among drug misusers during a four year period after seeking treatment. *Addiction, 97,* 39–47.

Gossop, M., Stewart, D., Browne, N., & Marsden, J. (2002). Factors associated with abstinence, lapse or relapse to heroin use after residential treatment: Protective effect of coping responses. *Addiction, 97,* 1259–1267.

Hallfors, D., Waller, M., Ford, C., Halpern, C., Brodish, P., & Iritani, B. (2004). Adolescent depression and suicide risk. *American Journal of Preventive Medicine, 27,* 224–231.

Hamid, R., Deren, S., Beardsley, M., & Tortu, S. (1999). Agreement between urinalysis and self-reported drug use. *Substance Use and Misuse, 34,* 1585–1592.

Harwood, H., Hubbard, R., Collins, J., & Rachal, J. (1988). The costs of crime and the benefits of drug abuse treatment: A cost-benefit analysis using TOPS data. *NIDA Research Monograph No. 86,* 209–235.

Havnes, I., Bukten, A., Gossop, M., Waal, H., Stangeland, P., & Clausen, T. (2012). Reductions in convictions for violent crime during opioid maintenance treatment: A longitudinal national cohort study. *Drug and Alcohol Dependence, 124,* 307–310.

Heather, N., & Robertson, I. (1989). *Problem drinking.* Oxford: Oxford University Press.

Hedrich, D., Alves, P., Farrell, M., Stöver, H., Møller, L., & Mayet, S. (2012). The effectiveness of opioid maintenance treatment in prison settings: A systematic review. *Addiction, 107,* 501–517.

Hough, M., Clancy, A., McSweeney, T., & Turnbull, P. (2003). The impact of drug treatment and testing orders on offending: Two year conviction rates *Findings 184,* Home Office, London.

Hser, Y. I., Teruya, C., Evans, E., Longshore, D., Grella, C., & Farabee, D. (2003). Treating drug-abusing offenders: Initial findings from a five-county study on the impact of California's Proposition 36 on the treatment system and patient outcomes. *Evaluation Review, 27,* 479–505.

Hubbard, R. L., Marsden, M. E., Rachal, J. V., Harwood, H. J., Cavanaugh, E. R., & Ginzberg, H. M. (1989). Drug *abuse treatment: A national study of effectiveness.* London: Chapel Hill.

Institute of Alcohol Studies (2007). *Alcohol and crime.* London: Home Office.

Johnson, R., Chutuape, M., Strain, E., Walsh, S., Stitzer, M., & Bigelow, G. (2000). A comparison of levomethadyl acetate, buprenorphine, and methadone for opioid dependence. *New England Journal of Medicine, 343,* 1290–1297.

Kennard, D. (1998). *An introduction to therapeutic communities.* London: Jessica Kingsley.

Kinlock, T. W., Gordon, M. S., Schwartz, R. P., O'Grady, K., Fitzgerald, T. T., & Wilson, M. (2007). A randomized clinical trial of methadone maintenance for prisoners: Results at 1-month post-release. *Drug and Alcohol Dependence, 91,* 220–227.

Knight, K., Simpson, D., Chatham, L., & Camacho, L. (1997). An assessment of prison-based drug treatment: Texas's in-prison therapeutic community program. *Journal of Offender Rehabilitation, 24,* 75–100.

Kreek, M. J. (2000). Methadone-related opioid agonist pharmacotherapy for heroin addiction. History, recent molecular and neurochemical research and future in mainstream medicine *Annals of the New York Academy of Sciences, 909,* 186–216.

Lieber, C. S. (1995). Medical disorders of alcoholism. *New England Journal of Medicine, 333,* 1058–1065.

Liese, B., & Najavits, L. (1997). Cognitive and behavioral therapies. In J. Lowinson, P. Ruiz, R. Millman, & J. Langrod (Eds.), *Substance abuse: A comprehensive textbook.* Baltimore: Williams and Wilkins.

Lincourt, P., Kuettel, T., & Bombardier, C. (2002). Motivational interviewing in a group setting with mandated clients: A pilot study. *Addictive Behaviors, 27*, 381–391.

Lobmaier, P. P., Kunøe, N., Gossop, M., Katevoll, T., & Waal, H. (2010). Naltrexone implants compared to methadone: Outcomes six months after prison release. *European Addiction Research, 16*, 139–145.

Marlatt, G. A. (1985). Relapse prevention: Theoretical rationale and overview of the model. In G. A., Marlatt & J. R. Gordon (Eds.), *Relapse prevention: Maintenance strategies in the treatment of addictive behavior.* New York: Guildford Press.

Marsch, L. A. (1998). The efficacy of methadone maintenance interventions in reducing illicit opiate use, HIV risk behaviour and criminality: A meta-analysis. *Addiction, 93*, 515–532.

Marsch, L. A., Stephens, M. A., Mudric, T., Strain, E. C., Bigelow, G. E., & Johnson, R. E. (2005). Predictors of outcome in LAAM, buprenorphine, and methadone treatment for opioid dependence. *Experimental and Clinical Psychopharmacology, 13*, 293–302.

Martin, S., Butzin, C., Saum, C., & Inciardi, J. (1999). Three-year outcomes of therapeutic community treatment for drug-involved offenders in Delaware: From prison to work release to aftercare. *The Prison Journal, 79*, 294–320.

Mattick, R., Oliphant, D., Ward, J., & Hall, W. (1998). The effectiveness of other opioid replacement therapies: LAAM, heroin, buprenorphine, naltrexone and injectable maintenance. In J. Ward, R. Mattick, & W. Hall (Eds.), *Methadone maintenance treatment and other replacement therapies.* Amsterdam: Harwood.

Merrall, E., Kariminia, A., Binswanger, I., Hobbs, M., Farrell, M., Marsden, J., Hutchinson, S., & Bird, S. (2010). Meta-analysis of drug-related deaths soon after release from prison. *Addiction, 105*, 1545–1554.

Miller, W. R., & Rollnick, S. (1991). *Motivational interviewing.* New York: Guilford.

Reuter, P., MacCoun, R., & Murphy, P. (1990). *Money from crime: A study of the economics of drug dealing in Washington, DC.* Santa Monica: RAND.

Rounsaville, B. J., & Kleber, H. (1985). Psychotherapy/counseling for opiate addicts: Strategies for use in different treatment settings. *International Journal of the Addictions, 20*, 869–896.

Ruiz, M. A., Douglas, K. S., Edens, J. F., Nikolova, N. L., & Lilienfeld, S. O. (2012). Co-occurring mental health and substance use problems in offenders: Implications for risk assessment. *Psychological Assessment, 24*, 77–87.

Saunders, J. B., Aasland, O. G., Babor, T. F., de la Fuente, J. R., & Grant, M. (1993). Development of the alcohol use disorders identification test (AUDIT): WHO collaborative project on early detection of persons with harmful alcohol consumption. *Addiction, 88*, 791–804.

Shaw, J., Baker, D., Hunt, I. M., Moloney, A., & Appleby, L. (2004). Suicide by prisoners. National clinical survey. *British Journal of Psychiatry, 184*, 263–267.

Skeie, I., Brekke, M., Gossop, M., Lindbaek, M., Reinertsen, E., Thoresen, M., & Waal, H. (2011). Changes in somatic disease incidents during opioid maintenance treatment: results from a Norwegian cohort study *BMJ Open* Aug 6; *1*(1), e000130.

Stewart, D., Gossop, M., Marsden, J., & Rolfe, A. (2000). Drug misuse and acquisitive crime among clients recruited to the National Treatment Outcome Research Study (NTORS). *Criminal Behaviour and Mental Health, 10*, 10–20.

Strang, J., Bird, S. M., & Parmar, M. K. (2013). Take-home emergency naloxone to prevent heroin overdose deaths after prison release: rationale and practicalities for the N-ALIVE randomized trial. *Journal of Urban Health, 90*, 983–996.

Strang, J., Gossop, M., Heuston, J., Green, J., Whiteley, C., & Maden, T. (2006). Persistence of drug use during imprisonment: Relationship of drug type, recency of use, and severity of dependence to use of heroin, cocaine, and amphetamine in prison. *Addiction, 101*, 1125–1132.

Strang, J., Manning, V., Mayet, S., Ridge, G., Best, D., & Sheridan, J. (2007). Does prescribing for opiate addiction change after national guidelines? Methadone and buprenorphine prescribing to opiate addicts by general practitioners and hospital doctors in England, 1995–2005. *Addiction, 102*, 761–770.

Unnithan, S., Gossop, M., & Strang, J. (1992). Factors associated with relapse among opiate addicts in an outpatient detoxification programme. *British Journal of Psychiatry, 161*, 654–657.

Vermeulen, E. C., & Walburg, J. A. (1998). What happens if a criminal can choose between detention and treatment: Results of a 4-year experiment in the Netherlands. *Alcohol and Alcoholism, 33*, 33–36.

Ward, J., Mattick, R., & Hall, W. (1998). *Methadone maintenance treatment and other opioid replacement therapies.* Australia: Harwood.

Weiss, R. D., Najavits, L. M., Greenfield, S. F., Soto, J. A., Shaw, S. R., & Wyner, D. (1998). Validity of substance use self-reports in dually diagnosed outpatients. *American Journal of Psychiatry 155*, 127–128.

Wells, B. (1994). Narcotics Anonymous (NA) in Britain. In J. Strang & M. Gossop (Eds.), *Heroin addiction and drug policy: The British system* (pp. 240–247). Oxford University Press, Oxford.

Wexler, H., Falkin, G., & Lipton, D. (1990). Outcome evaluation of a prison therapeutic community for substance abuse treatment. *Criminal Justice and Behavior, 17*, 71–92.

Zlotnick, C., Clarke, J. G., Friedmann, P. D., Roberts, M. B., Sacks, S., & Melnick G. (2008). Gender differences in comorbid disorders among offenders in prison substance abuse treatment programs. *Behavioral Sciences & the Law, 26*, 403–412.

20 Suicide and Self-Injury in Prisoners

TAMMI WALKER

Suicide and self-injury in offenders are a public health concern due to the increased numbers of episodes in the prison population over recent years. Policy-makers have introduced suicide prevention programmes in prisons following the introduction of a strategy to address the continuing rise in self-inflicted deaths (HM Prison Service, 2001). Suicide and self-injury are rarely the result of a single cause or event, but rather depend on the cumulative and interactive effects of a range of situational and psychosocial factors. This chapter will focus on the individual vulnerable groups of prisoners who are at highest risk for suicide and then move onto a discussion of self-injury in prisoners. It will end with a brief discussion of current interventions and treatments in custody and the prison staff responses to prisoners at risk of harm to self. Attention is also given in the chapter to some of the difficult methodological issues in this area of work.

CONTEXT

The prison population in England and Wales at the end of March 2013 was 83,842 – a decrease of 3% on the previous year – and 79,989 were males and 3,853 were females (Ministry of Justice, 2013a). Prisoners in the United Kingdom tend to come from socially marginalized backgrounds where persistent health inequalities remain (Department of Health, 2004; Social Exclusion Unit, 2002), and they have higher rates of mental health issues, problematic substance misuse, occupational and educational failure, smoking and long-standing illness or disability (Social Exclusion Unit, 2002; Stephenson, 2004). A recent study by Hawton, Linsell, Adeniji, Sariaslan, and Fazel (2014) maintains that suicide rates in

prisoners of both sexes are far higher than in the general population in many countries (Slade & Edelmann, 2013). In the last 20 years, policy-makers have moved to improve and expand the provision of mental health services, court diversion and liaison schemes (Sainsbury Centre for Mental Health, 2009), community forensic mental health teams (Royal College of Psychiatrists, 2013) and resettlement and rehabilitative services (Ministry of Justice, 2013b) as measures of prevention for decreasing the rates of suicide and self-injury in prisoners.

BACKGROUND

Suicide is a complex phenomenon and a serious public health problem in the general population. The World Health Organization (WHO) (2007) estimates that one suicide attempt occurs approximately every 3 seconds, and one completed suicide occurs approximately every minute. The causes of suicide are complex (Task Force on Suicide, 1994), and some individuals appear particularly susceptible to suicide when confronted with problematic life events or a combination of stressors (WHO, 2007). Researchers (WHO, 2007) have identified a variety of factors that interrelate to put an individual at a higher risk of suicide than average rates:

- Young males (ages 15–49)
- Elderly people, especially elderly males
- Indigenous people
- Persons with mental illness
- Persons with alcohol and/or substance abuse
- Persons having made a previous suicide attempt
- Persons in custody

Forensic Psychology, Second Edition. Edited by David A. Crighton and Graham J. Towl.
© 2015 John Wiley & Sons, Ltd. Published 2015 by British Psychological Society and John Wiley & Sons, Ltd.

THE PRISON POPULATION AND SUICIDE

Suicide is often the single most common cause of death in prison settings worldwide, with mortality rates more than three times higher than found in the general population (Hawton, Linsell, Adeniji, Sariaslan, and Fazel, 2014; Slade & Edelmann, 2013; Pratt, Piper, Appleby, Webb, & Shaw, 2006; Shaw, Baker, Hunt, Moloney, & Appleby, 2004). Since 1991, the Prison Service has adopted the term 'Self-Inflicted Death' (SID) to refer to all completed suicides in custody. This all-embracing description covers all deaths arising from non-natural causes that appeared to be directly caused by the actions of the individual concerned. In 2013, the Howard League for Penal Reform produced the *Deaths in Custody Annual Report 2013*, which stated that the number of suicides in prisons in England in Wales was the highest it had been for 6 years. There were 70 SIDs during 2013, 10 more than in 2012, and the largest number of SIDs in prisons since 2007. In 2011, a report by the Independent Advisory Panel (IAP) was published that comprehensively summarized all recorded deaths of individuals detained in state custody between January 2000 and December 2010. This report was the first of its kind as it illustrated a full demographic breakdown of all recorded deaths in a number of custodial sectors – that is, prisons (public and private), police, immigration removal centres, young offender institutes and secure children's homes and training centres. Between January 2000 and December 2010, there were a total of 1,444 SIDs in these custodial sectors. Of these, the most common method of SID was hanging, which accounts for 71% of deaths ($N=1,024$); 6% ($N=89$) of SIDs were as a result of drugs or alcohol overdose, and 68% ($N=985$) of the total SIDs were of white males. Recent trends in the report illustrate that, in 2008, there were 60 SIDs in prisons compared to 58 in 2010. For the 12 months ending September 2012, there were 56 SIDs in prisons in England and Wales, the lowest level in any 12-month period to September in the last 10 years (Prison Reform Trust, 2013).

There are particular individual and environmental factors that may go some way in explaining the higher rates of suicide in prison settings. For example, the social environment in prison and degree of personal control is significantly different from life in the community (Wichmann, Serin, & Motiuk, 2000). Prisoners may receive an unexpected long prison sentence (Huey & McNulty, 2005), the lack of focused and directed activities (Leese *et al.*, 2006), the psychological impact of arrest and incarceration (WHO, 2007) and penal procedures such as adjudications (Cox & Morschauser, 1997). Thus, prisons are repositories for vulnerable groups that are traditionally at the highest risk for suicide, such as young males, persons with mental health issues, people with substance use difficulties and those who have previously engaged in suicidal behaviours (WHO, 2007).

The next part of this chapter will focus on the individual vulnerable groups of prisoners who are at highest risk for suicide, and then move onto a discussion of self-injury in prisoners. The chapter will end with a brief discussion of current interventions and treatments in custody and the prison staff responses to prisoners at risk of harm to self.

SUICIDE IN REMAND PRISONERS

HM Inspectorate of Prisons published a thematic review, *Unjust Deserts*, in 2000 which examined the treatment and conditions for un-sentenced prisoners in England and Wales. The key issues from the review indicated that remand prisoners have a discrete set of needs that differentiate them from the sentenced population and un-convicted and convicted un-sentenced prisoners received notably poorer provision than sentenced offenders. It was concluded by the review that a strategy should be introduced that focused on outcomes for un-sentenced prisoners; however, something is yet to manifest beyond the compilation of *Prison Service Order 4600: Un-convicted, Un-sentenced and Civil Prisoners* (2003). Since *Unjust Deserts* was published, there has been little focus on the remand population until 2012 when HM Inspectorate of Prisons undertook a thematic review which investigated the experience of remand prisoners in adult male and women's prisons and in young offender institutions. This review explored all stages of a prisoner's journey from the point of entry to release, and the treatment, conditions and support they receive throughout. It found that remand prisoners enter custody with multiple and complex needs that are often more commonly seen than in sentenced prisoners (HM Inspectorate, 2012).

Remand prisoners consist of 2,000–13,000 of the prison population, approximately 15% of all prisoners at any one time (Ministry of Justice, 2011). Black and minority ethnic, women and foreign national backgrounds are over-represented within this group (Ministry of Justice, 2011). Remand prisoners are a transient population. For example, the average period spent on remand is 9 weeks, which makes it hard for them to receive purposeful activity.

Further, over three-quarters of remand prisoners reported welfare difficulties on arrival, and a third indicated a drug or mental health problems (HM Inspectorate, 2012). A survey conducted by HM Inspectorate (2012) indicated that remand prisoners are at an increased risk of suicide and self-injury; nearly a quarter (23%) of such prisoners in the survey felt depressed or suicidal when they arrived at prison, and only half of new arrivals had been asked if they needed help and support with these issues. However, some studies have looked more closely at the calculations that produce such statistics and suggest that this is by no means an unequivocal finding. Towl and Crighton (1998) suggest that the remand status of suicidal prisoners has perhaps been overemphasized in previous research, and this may be due to the methodology used to calculate the rates of suicide. They examined all cases of SIDs across all parts of the prison system (i.e., adults, young offenders and women prisoners) recorded by the Prison Service from 5 February 1988 to 5 November 1995. Of the large sample, 369 were men and eight were women. For the men, 181 were sentenced and 188 were on remand: for the women five were sentenced and three were on remand. Towl and Crighton (1998) tabulated separately the rates of SIDs for sentenced prisoners in eight different sentence lengths and examined separately the data for prisoners remanded into prison custody. They found that, when calculating suicide rates among remand prisoners using the average daily populations (ADP), the rate per 100,000 prisoners appear very high (i.e., 238 per 100,000). But, when the rates are calculated using the number of deaths by the number of prisoners received into prison on remand, the rates are markedly lower (i.e., 39 per 100,000). This compares with rates for determinate sentenced prisoners of between 31 and 75 per 100,000 ADP and an overall rate of 31 per 100,000 sentenced receptions per annum. Towl and Crighton's (1998) data suggests that remand prisoners are at a risk of suicide similar to those given short determinate sentences (under 18 months), and are at a lower level of risk than those given longer or indeterminate sentences. Towl (1996) and Towl and Crighton (1998) support the view that remand status, as an individual marker for an increased risk of suicide, has perhaps been overemphasized, and therefore caution needs to be exercised when speculating about the contributing factors for suicide among this population. Furthermore, Crighton (2000) suggests that it can be argued that one would predict a lower rate of suicide among remand prisoners on the grounds that it is likely to be less stressful, since prisoners have not been sentenced and indeed may not be found guilty, and thus they have an element of hope of being released from prison that a sentenced prisoner may have lost.

SUICIDE IN SENTENCED PRISONERS

The number of prisoners sentenced to an indeterminate sentence of imprisonment, where the prisoner must satisfy the authorities she or he is ready for release and does not pose any threat to the community, has increased dramatically over recent years (HMI Probation and HMI Prisons, 2013). Such prisoners now make up 16% of the prison population (as on 31 March 2013), compared with only 9% in 1995. At the end of December 2012, there were 13,577 prisoners serving indeterminate sentences (Ministry of Justice, 2013d). Within the indeterminate sentenced population, 44% were serving an indeterminate sentence for public protection (IPP) (5,920), while 56% were serving life sentences (7,657) (Ministry of Justice, 2013d). Life-sentenced prisoners (for murder and other serious offences) have increased in number, and they are also now serving longer in prison, with judges imposing a longer period of punishment to be served before the prisoner can be considered for release (Prison Reform Trust, 2013).

In 2000, Crighton reported the findings of the largest study of suicide in prisons in England and Wales in which he analysed 525 intentional SIDs that occurred between 1988 and 1998. This represented a sample of 88% of all such deaths in prison custody, and prisoners who completed suicide were analysed in terms of age, gender, ethnicity, index offence, mental health history, legal status, type of establishment, time in custody and history of previous intentional self-injury. Crighton (2000) found that prisoners serving indeterminate sentences were at markedly higher risk of completing a suicide with a rate of 173 per 100,000 ADP, and the risk of suicide also increased for those serving longer sentences and for those sentenced for violent offences (103 per 100,000 ADP). In common with Crighton (2000), Towl and Crighton (1998) noted a general trend towards increased risk of completing a suicide in those serving longer prison sentences. Life-sentenced prisoners appeared to be at an appreciably higher risk of suicide than determinate-sentenced prisoners (Towl & Crighton, 1998). Precipitating factors for their suicide may be due to a conflict within the institution with other prisoners, the prison regime, a family conflict or division, legal frustration due to a negative outcome of an appeal or the rejection of parole (WHO, 2007).

SUICIDE IN YOUNG PRISONERS

Young people are offenders under the age of 18, or in some cases aged 18 but remaining in the under 18 estate, and they can be held in either a Secure Children's Home (SCH), a Secure Training Centre (STC) or a Young Offender Institution (YOI) (Youth Justice Board and Ministry of Justice, 2013). The average population of young people in custody in 2011–2012 (under 18) was 1,963, and this has reduced by 4% in the last year, and by 32% since 2008–2009 (Youth Justice Board / Ministry of Justice, 2013). Between 1990 and 2011, there were 29 suicidal deaths of children and young people in prison aged 14–17, all of which were boys (INQUEST, 2012). The INQUEST report (2012) commissioned by the Prison Reform Trust (PRT) focused on the experiences of 98 children and young people who died between 2003 and 2010, and the report found that young prisoners were placed in prisons with unsafe environments and cells and experienced poor medical treatment. Young prisoners' experience of imprisonment can be particularly difficult due to being separated from their families and friends, and because of some of their group characteristics – for example, relatively high impulsivity levels. Young prisoners who become upset and distressed are particularly dependent on supportive relationships with the staff within the prison regime (Liebling, 2006).

Differing views have been put forward by researchers about the role of prisoners' age in suicide (Crighton, 2000). In four prisons between 1988 and 1990, Liebling (1992) undertook interviews with 50 young prisoners who had attempted suicide and 50 prisoners drawn randomly from the general population within the same establishments. This qualitative study found that younger-age prisoner groups would be at increased risk of suicide relative to older prisoners. In contrast to these findings, Hatty and Walker (1986), in their Australian quantitative study of 155 deaths, which used a questionnaire, found 50–69-year-old prisoners to be over-represented in the completed suicide statistics, and the 15–19-year-old group did not appear to be at increased risk of suicide. Dooley (1990) found that the average age of prison suicides in England and Wales was significantly higher than the average age of the prison population. Further, Towl and Crighton (1998) suggest that young prisoners (i.e., 15–17 years) had higher rates of completed suicide, although this was based on a small number of cases. However, this is the only exception they found, and they argue for the rejection of the hypothesis that younger age groups appear to be over-represented in the suicide figures. This finding was also evident in their earlier study, albeit based on smaller samples, examining suicide data in prisons for the periods 1988–1990 and 1994–1995 (Crighton & Towl, 1997). Overall, although literature reviews have revealed contradictory findings (Livingston, 1997; Lloyd, 1990), there is at least some evidence of an association between age and suicide (Camilleri, McArthur, & Webb, 1999), but caution needs to exercised when interpreting such findings

In 2014, the Youth Justice Board (YJB) published a report of their work that they have undertaken with the government which has explored the learning that has been achieved following the deaths in the under-18 secure estate since 2000. It highlights a summary of some of the key actions taken by them to respond to some of the findings from the deaths of children in custody, such as the introduction of systems to improve the timeliness and quality of information sharing when children enter custody, the development (with the Department of Health) of the Comprehensive Health Assessment Tool (CHAT) to enable the identification and assessment of the health-related needs of children by professionals, commissioning of Health Care Standards for Children and Young People in Secure Settings and Revised National Standards for Youth Justice Services that take account of recommendations from deaths in custody. Furthermore, the Ministry of Justice announced an independent review into the SIDs of young prisoners aged 18–24 years in NOMS (prison) custody. The review, which was ongoing in 2014, conducted by the Independent Advisory Panel (IAP) on Deaths in Custody and will examine cases since the roll out of ACCT was completed in April 2007 to identify whether lessons have been learned from these deaths and, if not, what actions should be taken for reducing the risk of future deaths.

SUICIDE IN RELEASED PRISONERS

Investigations into the suicide rate among released prisoners has highlighted that it was more common than would be estimated in the general population (Graham, 2003; Stewart, Henderson, Hobbs, Ridout, & Knuiman, 2004), particularly in the first 12 months after release from custody (Harding-Pink, 1990; Binswanger et al., 2007). This parallels with the single most robust finding in prisoner suicide research – that is, the time in custody in a given prison is a good predictor at a group level of suicide risk (Crighton, 2000), with, for example, 10% of those who are going to kill themselves doing so within the first 24 hours of such custody and 25% within a week (Crighton, 2000). Pratt *et al.* (2006) undertook a population-based cohort study to investigate suicide rates in individuals within 1 year of release from prison in England and Wales. By comparing the suicide rates per 100,000 person-years in these released prisoners with rates in the general population by using the indirectly age-standardized mortality ratio, they found in England and Wales that released males were eight times and released females 36 times more probable to complete suicide within 1 year of release from custody than would be expected in the general population., In released offenders being supervised by the probation service in England and Wales between 1996 and 1997, Sattar (2001) found that 10% of all suicides had occurred in the first week of release, and 50% by the fourth week. This sample did not include released prisoners who were not under the supervision of probation.

Overall, little is known about the specific risk factors for suicide among released prisoners. A recent piece of research undertaken by Jones and Maynard (2013) attempted to explore this area. They undertook a systematic review to explore the risk of suicide in recently released prisoners, and they argued that the increased risk is likely to be linked to high levels of mental illness documented in prisoners, combined with the stress of the transition from prison to the community.

SUICIDE IN WOMEN PRISONERS

In May 2013, the female prison population in England and Wales was 3,893, which is approximately 5% of the total prison population (Prison Reform Trust, 2013). Men complete suicide at a higher rate than women, on the basis of ADP and receptions into prison (Crighton, 2000). However, Paton and Jenkins (2005) argue that being a woman in custody is also a high risk of suicide factor, and Liebling (1992) has suggested that the rate of suicide among women prisoners is seriously underestimated. Liebling (1994) argued that the completed suicide rate for women and men is similar but by relying on verdicts of suicide, studies tend to find a lower suicide rate for females. Citing the work of Dooley (1990) and drawing comparisons with community studies, Liebling maintains that women prisoner deaths are more likely to be given SIDs other than suicide (e.g., open and death by misadventure). Furthermore, she asserts that the suicide rate for female and male prisoners is similar (Liebling, 1994). Crighton (2000) argues that women prisoners are likely to be even more strongly selected for risk factors in

suicide than the male prison population, in particular because of high levels of prior psychiatric contacts, alcohol and drug abuse, and physical and sexual abuse reported by women in prison. However, in prison, the number of women who complete suicide is small. There were eight in 2000 and three in 2009 (Ministry of Justice, 2009). The small numbers means that it is not possible to reliably analyse for sex differences in completed suicides, and caution is needed. Liebling's work suffers from this common problem of being based on a small sample size, and, although in-depth qualitative analysis was used, the findings are limited to how far they can be generalized in other prisons. Overall, women in prison have lower rates of suicide than men in prison (Towl & Crighton, 1998; Towl, 1999).

LIMITATIONS OF SUICIDE RESEARCH IN PRISON SETTINGS

There are a number of limitations to the studies on suicide. First, there is a focus on identifying risk factors for suicide (Livingston, 1997), and early research studies were based on mental health models (Liebling, 1991) that were mainly concerned with recognizing and describing correlates of suicide. The role of mental health problems and individual characteristics were overstressed in these studies at the expense of other factors, such as the role of the immediate environment. Second, studies were often based on small sample sizes (Dexter & Towl, 1995) or simply one population subgroup, such as young prisoners (Liebling, 1992). Third, suicide rates in prison are criticized as being too high, and completed suicides in custody (and the community) have a statistically low baseline (Towl & Hudson, 1997). Thus, while many individuals enter custody with the recognized risk factors for suicide, relatively few actually undertake these acts. As a result, the screening of prisoners would produce a large number of 'false positives', that is, prisoners identified as having the predispositions linked with a higher risk but who would not then go on to complete suicide. Clearly, 'false positives' can be reduced by categorizing less people as possibly at risk, however, this would raise the possible problem of 'false negatives', that is, prisoners who were not screened as being a high risk but who consequently complete suicide. The possibility for 'false positives' and 'false negatives' during the risk assessment procedure in suicide lends support to the case for exploring situational risk factors for suicide in prisons.

PSYCHOSOCIAL AND SITUATIONAL RISK FACTORS FOR SUICIDE COMMON TO PRISONS

Remanded and sentenced suicidal prisoners share a number of mutual characteristics. With regard to *situational factors*, a report described how prisoners most frequently complete suicide by hanging themselves – this was the case in 51 out of 57 cases in 2011, and the most lethal hangings were carried out using sheets or blankets as ligatures and windows or beds as ligature points (Ministry of Justice, 2011). Further, they tend to occur during periods when staffing is the lowest, such as nights or weekends (Liebling, 2006). A strong link between prisoner suicide and housing accommodation has been found, specifically, a prisoner being placed in and unable to cope with segregation or other housing accommodation such as single-celled may also be at increased risk of suicide (Meltzner & Hayes, 2006). Prisons with low levels of staffing have been found to be at higher risk of prisoner suicide. It is thought that this is because staff in the prison might be unable to carry out effective cell checks or observe prisoner behaviour as frequently as in well-staffed prisons (Prisons & Probation Ombudsman, 2011). It has been suggested by some that overcrowding in prisons may increase vulnerability to suicide as the impact of this leads to prisoners often being 'doubled-up' two to a small cell meant for one, and, in this confined space, they will sleep, eat, wash-up and use the often unscreened lavatory (Howard League, 2005). In 2005, when those prisons which were functioning at more than 125% of their capacity were compared with the number of suicides experienced since January 2004, 90 out of the 159 suicides in prison – over half – had occurred in just a quarter of all prisons (Howard League, 2005). It seems likely that if such a linear effect exists, it will be complicated by a number of factors. First, local and remand prisons tend to be the most overcrowded, but they also tend to have the greatest turnover of prisoner population. There are a number of marked differences between local and remand prisons, and these could well account for differences in suicide rates (Crighton, 2000). Second, the methods of defining and recording of overcrowding can differ by prisons. Third, there is evidence that, when the rates of imprisonment and overcrowding first increase, the rates of suicide decline in United Kingdom prisons.

A range of *psychosocial factors* may contribute to increase the risk of suicide in prisoners, and this can involve reduced social and family support, prior suicidal behaviour (especially within the last 1–2 years), a history of mental health issues and emotional difficulties (WHO, 2007). Additionally, the experience of bullying appears relevant to suicide. In June 2011, the Prisons and Probation Ombudsman released a report revealing evidence of bullying or intimidation in the 3 months prior to their death from other prisoners in 20% of the 47 completed suicide cases in prisons in England and Wales. In one-fifth of these cases, staff reported being unaware of bullying or intimidation from other prisoners until after the suicide had happened (Prisons and Probation Ombudsman, 2011). It should be stressed that, due to the small numbers involved in this study, no statistical significance can be inferred from these findings. A common pathway leading a prisoner to suicide appears to be feelings of hopelessness and loss of routes and opportunities for coping. Suicide comes to be seen as the only way out of a despairing situation. Prisoners voicing such feelings or admitting to suicidal ideation or plans must be considered as at high risk of suicide (WHO, 2007).

SELF-INJURY IN PRISONERS

Self-injury is a challenge for the criminal justice system because it is possibly life threatening, and is a predictor of an inflated risk of suicide. The conceptualization and definition of what has been characterized as 'self-injury' remains problematic. A number of different terms and definitions of 'self-injury' are used in research, policy and practice spheres. Terms such as 'attempted suicide', 'self-injury', 'deliberate self-injury', 'self-mutilation', 'suicidal gesture', 'abortive suicide', 'self-inflicted violence' and 'para-suicide' are used interchangeably. McHugh and Towl (1997) note how terms such as 'self-injury' and 'attempted suicide' pose problems of definition. Individuals may self-injure either with or without any intention to kill themselves. The differing terminology used in the literature demonstrates the ambiguity associated with conceptualizing and analysing self-injurious behaviour (Royal College of Psychiatrists, 2010). Self-injury in prison custody is defined as *any act where a prisoner deliberately harms themselves irrespective of the method, intent or severity of any injury* (Ministry of Justice, 2013c, p. 14).

There are difficulties in gathering accurate statistics on self-injury in the general population. This is because those who self-injure often do so covertly, and many episodes go unreported for many reasons, and individuals may not need hospital treatment. In the United Kingdom, 'Self-injury is one of the top five causes of acute medical admission and those who self-injure have a one in six chance of repeat attendance at A&E within the year' (Department of Health, 2012). In the 12 months to August 2012, hospitals admitted 110,960 self-injury cases, and drug poisoning was the most common reason for self-injury hospital admission in England – almost nine out of 10 admissions were for self-poisoning (89.4%, or 99,200 admissions) (HSCIC, 2012).

Self-injury behaviour, in both prison and community samples, has been criticized due to difficulties in identifying and classifying what behaviours are 'self-injuring and when self-injury is different from a suicide attempt' (Powis, 2002). The motivations for engaging in self-injurious behaviours are very complex, and individuals who have no experience of self-injury may find it an intensely confusing behaviour. Due to the few academic studies looking at the meaning of self-injury for prisoners, the clearest explanations come from the voluntary sector bodies that have attempted to improve public and professional understanding of the self-injury in the community. NICE (2012) states that the methods of self-harm can be divided into two broad groups: self-poisoning and self-injury. However, Sutton (2007) argues that there may be a range of diverse motivations and intentions behind the method chosen by individuals. Further, Lilley, Owens, and Horrocks (2008) found in their study that there was evidence that individuals often change methods of self-injury. Studies indicate that 80% of those who present at accident and emergency departments after self-poisoning have taken an overdose of prescribed or over-the-counter medication (Horrocks, Price, & House, 2003). In the general population, self-injury has been found to possibly be more common than self-poisoning (Hawton, Rodham, & Evans, 2002; Meltzer, Harrington, & Goodman, 2001). Cutting is the most common self-injury method (Hawton et al., 2002; Horrocks et al., 2003), while stabbing, burning, hanging, swallowing or inserting objects, shooting, drowning and jumping from heights or in front of vehicles are less common (NICE, 2012).

Studies of self-injury in prison populations is limited but, in a recent review, Hawton and colleagues (2014) found that cutting and scratching were the most frequent self-injurious methods in both sexes; in female inmates, self-strangulation was common (31% of all episodes), followed by hanging and self-strangulation (Crighton & Towl, 2000; Liebling & Krarup, 1993; Howard League, 2013). Some have argued that the methods of self-injury used by those in prison are more dangerous and harmful than methods they may choose in the community (Towl, 2000); however, Hawton et al. (2014) found that most incidents were of low lethality, particularly in female prisoners. Until 1997, the focus for reporting self-injury incidents in the prison population was on 'attempted suicide', but the problem with this approach was that prisoner intent was frequently unknown (Ministry of Justice, 2013a). Some incidents were more likely to be fatal than others, but the point at which a self-injury incident became an attempted suicide was unclear. From 1997, all self-injury incidents had to be reported, and this led to an increase in reported incidents in the prison population. Further, in 2002, a self-injury monitoring form was introduced based on the F213 'Injuries to Inmate' form (Ministry of Justice, 2013a). As a result, reporting of self-injury incidents improved further throughout 2003. The Ministry of Justice has now omitted self-injury statistics before 2004 from publications because they were considerably under-reported compared with current standards. In 2013, there were 22,977 incidents of self-injury in prison. In the previous 12 months, there were 23,522 incidents, a decrease of 2% (Ministry of Justice, 2013b). The number of reported incidents of self-injuring is therefore lower. However, the number of individuals reported as self-injuring has remained broadly unchanged. This suggests that individuals that do self-injure are doing so fewer times (Ministry of Justice, 2013b).

Reported self-injury continues to decline year-on-year in the prison population, but there are differing trends for male and female reports of self-injury. Hawton et al. (2014) undertook a case-control comparison of prisoners who self-injured and those who did not between January 2006 and December 2009 in all prisons in England and Wales. They found that 139,195 self-injury incidents were recorded in 26,510 individual prisoners between 2004 and 2009; 5–6% of male prisoners and 20–24% of female inmates self-injured every year. The rates were more than 10 times higher in female prisoners than in male prisoners. Repetition of self-harm was common, particularly in women and teenage girls, in whom a subgroup of 102 prisoners accounted for 17,307 episodes. In 2012, for the first time since the current recording system began, the number of male prisoners self-injuring more than 20 times outnumbered female prisoners. In comparison, the self-injury incidents for the female prison population have decreased by 42% over the last 2 years, largely driven by a reduction in the number of repetitive self-injurers within custody. In the 12 months to June 2010, there were 353 females per 1,000 prisoners self-injuring, compared to 266 females per 1,000 prisoners in the 12 months to June 2013. However, even though there have been large reductions in the incidence of female self-injury recently, female offenders still account for a disproportionate amount of self-injury in prison custody.

RISK FACTORS FOR SELF-INJURY IN THE PRISON POPULATION

Associated risk factors with offenders who injure themselves include a history of previous self-injuring (Inch, Rowlands, & Soliman, 1995; Wilkins & Coid, 1991); being a woman (HM Inspectorate of Prisons, 1999;

Singleton, Meltzer, & Gatward, 1998; Social Work Services and Prisons Inspectorates for Scotland, 1998; Wool and Dooley, 1987); substance misuse (Haycock, 1989; Karp, Whitman, & Convit, 1991; Wilkins & Coid, 1991); a dysfunctional childhood (Rieger, 1971); histories of physical (Wilkins & Coid, 1991) and sexual abuse (Wilkins & Coid, 1991); a history of mental disorder (Liebling, 1992; Liebling & Krarup, 1993; Office for National Statistics, 1999; Power & Spencer, 1987), for example, depression (Favazza & Rosenthal, 1993; Haycock, 1989); low self-esteem (Liebling, 1992); high levels of anxiety (Mental Health Foundation, 1997; Wilkins & Coid, 1991); and a reduced capacity to manage stress (deCatanzaro, 1981). Studies have found associations between prison environments and self-injury – that is, being locked up for long periods or being transferred against their wishes affected prisoners' self-injuring rates (Dear, Thomson, Hall, & Howells, 2001; Liebling & Krarup, 1993). Being bullied or intimidated by other prisoners (Dear et al., 2001; Liebling & Krarup, 1993), being alone (Liebling, 1992; 1993), of young age (<20 years), of white ethnic origin, and either a life sentence or being un-sentenced (Hawton et al., 2014) were other contributing risk factors for both male and female prisoners self-injuring. Last, there is evidence that the length of time a prisoner has spent in prison may be a key mediator, with Crighton and Towl (1997) suggesting that just over 10% of suicides occurred within 1 day of arrival at the prison, with 45% of deaths occurring within 1 month. This view is supported by earlier research in Scotland (Bogue & Power, 1995), and is consistent with the finding of Loucks (1998), who reports that rates of self-injury were particularly high during early periods of custody.

CURRENT INTERVENTIONS AND TREATMENTS IN CUSTODY

The Prison Service's strategy used to use a structured administrative process with a guidance document called 'Form 2052 Self-Harm' (F2052SH) to monitor and manage prisoners at inflated risk of suicide or self-injury. Any member of staff could open this form, and the core of this strategy was a case conference approach (The Howard League, 2001). The welfare of the individual prisoners was the focus, and it was an instrument for recording and monitoring prisoners alongside individualized care plans. The Howard League (2001) evaluated the use of the F2052SH tool and found that prison staff

felt it did not provide information about the motives of prisoners engaging in self-injury, and the support offered was often very broad. For example, prisoners would be offered such things as 'health-care' and 'activities', but in practice they often did not receive any extra provision and support (The Howard League, 2001). In April 2006, this was replaced by an amended procedure entitled Assessment, Care in Custody and Teamwork (ACCT), and this offered regular case review meetings, observations and was prisoner-centred, offering a flexible plan which, when used effectively, would reduce risk. The ACCT system has prescriptive timescales, and it is envisaged to improve continuity of staff attending meetings and improve the support offered, so that it is more meaningful for prisoners. The ACCT system remains in current use and was last updated on 1 April 2012.

The role of health-care in the prison system has changed over the last two decades. Prisoners have dramatically higher rates of a whole range of mental health problems including suicide and self-injury compared to the general population (Durcan, 2008). Previously, prisoners identified as being at an inflated risk of harming themselves were often isolated in prison health-care, and it is possible for those who repetitively self-injured that this may worsen their situation (Howard League, 2001). In 2001, the Department of Health introduced the principle of 'equivalence' into prison health-care in England and Wales, which meant that prisoners should receive the same quality of care for their health as they would receive outside prison (Royal College of Nursing, 2010). Some have argued that there is indeed equivalence of care across prisons and the community, in that there remains what is sometimes referred to as a 'postcode lottery' with both such settings (Towl, 2010). Since this time, there has been the creation of new in-reach teams in every prison establishment in England (Royal College of Nursing, 2010). These teams were intended to be the same as community mental health teams that operate outside the prison system, and incorporate within them the outreach and crisis resolution functions of the specialist teams that were developed across the United Kingdom with the publication of the National Service Framework for Mental Health (Department of Health, 1999). Evidence from a review (Royal College of Nursing, 2010) examined what had been achieved in prison mental health by the in-reach teams in England, and it concluded that there had been improved responses to mental ill health among offenders, for example, through better screening on reception to prison, drug treatment and suicide prevention. However, specific reference of the impact of in-reach teams to responding to suicide and self-injuring prisoners was missing from the review.

During the 1980s, the Samaritans became increasingly concerned about escalating levels of suicide and self-injury among prisoners and the need of emotional support which they were unable to access. The Samaritans started to establish links with prisons to inform prisoners and staff of their work and provide support (Samaritans, 1990). They visited prisons to deliver training and awareness sessions to staff and see prisoners, sometimes providing confidential support to them (Samaritans, 1990). After a series of suicides in the early 1990s, a pilot scheme was undertaken in the form of a peer-befriending scheme which formalized prisoners' support of one another (Davies, 1994). Once trialled, the scheme was made available in other prisons at a rapid rate. By 1993, 20 schemes had been established; this grew to 70 schemes in 1995, and by 1996 there were 100 schemes (Samaritans, 2011). Today, the 'Listeners Scheme' in prisons involves Samaritans volunteers visiting prisons to select, train and support prisoners who become known as 'listeners'. They work within the same structure as Samaritans by providing confidential, non-judgemental, emotional support. Any prisoner can volunteer to become a listener to support their peers who are in distress, but they are required to undergo a comprehensive training process. Trained listeners are supported by the local Samaritans branch that regularly visit to support and debrief them, and continue to provide ongoing training (Samaritans, 2011). Currently, there are approximately 120 schemes in England and Wales prisons, and, in some of these institutions, there are particularly high levels of usage by prisoners. For example, one female prison reported almost 500 contacts within a 3-month period during 2001, and 183 of these call-outs were directly related to self-injury (Howard League, 2001); also, a large, busy local male prison reported approximately 8,000 contacts during 2009 (Jaffe, 2012). Some prisoners appear to be afraid of approaching the listeners and hence never use them, as they do not trust them and fear that their problems will be spread around the prison (Howard League, 2001). Some have argued that this is more a perception than reality (Howard League, 2001; Jaffe, 2012). The Listener Scheme is currently the best established and most widespread scheme across the English and Welsh prison system (Jaffe, 2012).

The Prison Service has also adopted other approaches to reduce suicides in prison. For example, training provided for custodial staff has improved their knowledge and understanding of mental health issues, the safer cells programme (Burrows, Brock, Hulley, Smith, & Summers, 2008), changes in reception screening and the development of 'First Night Centres' (HM Inspectorate, 2007).

Different interventions and treatments have been evaluated in community populations of individuals who self-injure, but few have led to clinically significant reductions in such behaviours (Kapur, 2005). With regard to prison populations, these studies are even more challenging. However, in June 2012, the 'Women Offenders Repeated Self Harm Intervention Pilot II' (WORSHIP II) commenced, which the author is currently conducting with Abel and colleagues, at three female prison establishments. This 3-year randomized controlled trial (RCT) is investigating the efficacy of a brief psychological therapy (Guthrie, Kapur, & Mackway-Jones, 2001) aimed at reducing repetitive self-injuring and suicidal ideation in the female prison population. The modified intervention, which is a form of brief talking treatment, was previously piloted in HMP Styal in a sample of female prisoners who had recently self-injured. WORSHIP II aims to establish a women-centred, gender-sensitive and gender-specific approach to women's needs in prisons for those that self-injure.

PRISON STAFF RESPONSES TO PRISONERS AT RISK OF HARM TO SELF

Professionals (in a variety of roles and occupational settings) dealing with prisoners who self-injure experience a variety of anxieties, fears and negative reactions (Taylor, Hawton, Fortune, & Kapur, 2009). It has been suggested that self-injuring clients are engaging in socially unacceptable behaviours which staff may feel responsible for. In fact staff may be relatively powerless to prevent such behaviour (Hayward, Tilley, Derbyshire, Kuipers, & Grey, 2005). These feelings of hopelessness and vulnerability have been described as possibly traumatizing (Deiter & Pearlman, 1998), and may test staff views of autonomy, capability and role (Rayner, Allen, & Johnson, 2005). This, along with the prospective of the individuals actually harming themselves (Fish, 2000) and the pressure of observing and learning about difficult feelings and experiences, may set in motion individual coping mechanisms that cause staff to reject and distance themselves from the client (Huband & Tantam, 2000). There are, of course, variations in staff attitudes from compassion to contempt towards the suicidal.

With regard to prison staff, Marzano, Adler, and Ciclitira (2013) maintain that the pressures they experience are acute and, on the whole, unique. They argue that the environment of the prison is inherently stressful; responding to self-injury might be especially challenging for prison professionals, and not least as reductions in suicide and self-injury rates are repeatedly stated Prison Service targets and priorities (HM Prison Service, 2007). Prison staff often feel unqualified, untrained or unskilled for dealing with repetitive self-injuring prisoners

(Towl & Forbes, 2002), and this is further compounded by the limited support available for staff in prisons (Home Office, 2007). Furthermore, prison officers have to deal with the tension between their custody and care roles when responding to prisoners who self-injure (Home Office, 1991; Towl & Forbes, 2002), which entails them balancing power and authority with empathy and compassion. Conflict and ambiguity may therefore occur within their role (Triplett, Mullings, & Scarborough, 1996), which may cause psychological strain and low job satisfaction (Cox, 1993; Mackay, Cousins, Kelly, Lee, & McCaig, 2004). The perspectives of correctional staff are often overlooked in research that considers self-injuring prisoners. Marzano, Adler, and Ciclitira (2013) considered how those who work in prisons are affected by and respond to repetitive self-injury of male prisoners. Through qualitative interviewing, they explored prison staff experiences, and responses to, and ways of coping with, non-suicidal, repetitive self-injury. The findings from their work indicated high levels of frustration, tensions between health-care and custodial staff, feelings of powerlessness and a low sense of job control. With regard to exploring self-injury among prisoners and prison officers, Kenning et al. (2010) conducted semi-structured interviews at a women's prison and analysed their accounts thematically. The findings suggested that prison staff often attributed motives to self-injury such as 'manipulative' and 'attention-seeking', whereas accounts by female prisoners often proposed explanations that involved issues which affect regulation or self-punishment. They conclude that these differences may in part lie in the lack of training and support that prison officers should receive, and improving this may result in enriched staff–prisoner relationships.

CONCLUSION

Over the past two decades, deaths in custody, suicidal behaviour and self-injury have been the focus of policy-makers in the United Kingdom. The numbers of prisoner self-injury continues to decline year-on-year, but there are differing trends for male and female prisoners. In 2012, for the first time since the current recording system began, the number of male prisoners self-injuring outnumbered female prisoners. However, even though there have been large reductions in the incidence of female self-injury over the last 2 years, which has been largely driven by a reduction in the number of women who repetitively self-injure in custody, female offenders still account for a disproportionate amount of self-injury in prison custody. Studies also continue to demonstrate

that the rates of suicide in the prison population are higher than the general population in England and Wales.

It must be recognized that there are a number of limitations to the methods used to study and investigate this area, and caution needs to be exercised when making comparisons. Research studies are often based on small sample sizes (Dexter & Towl, 1995), no control groups (Bonner, 1992) or one population subgroup, such as young prisoners (Liebling, 1992). Suicide rates in the prison population are also criticized as being too high, and completed suicides in custody (and the community) have a statistically low baseline (Towl & Hudson, 1997). Consequently, while many individuals enter custody with recognized risk factors for suicide, relatively few may actually undertake these acts. As a result, the screening of prisoners would produce a large number of 'false positives' – that is, prisoners identified as having the predispositions linked with a higher risk but who would not then go on to complete suicide. 'False positives' can be reduced by categorizing less people as possibly at risk; however, this would raise the possible problem of 'false negatives' – that is, prisoners who were not screened as being at high risk but who consequently complete suicide. Further, Hawton et al. (2014) argue that the quality of data entry into the prison reporting system is an issue, as it may vary by prison establishment, and the number of unrecorded incidents is unknown. Data for recorded incidents may therefore be accurate, but the numbers of individuals involved are likely to be estimates at the lower limit. Last, there have been few controlled studies of suicide conducted in prison. Caution therefore needs to be exercised when considering the extent to which the current evidence can inform practice.

Future directions in reducing the incidences of suicide and self-injury in prison should be multi-dimensional and incorporate risk factors that individuals have at the time of entry to prison – that is, individual characteristics and experiences – and environmental risk factors, which include the prison-setting influences. Practitioners in the criminal justice system cannot alter the characteristics of individuals who enter the system, but the assessment of suicide or self-injury-inflated risk at the time of reception into prison could include any previous suicidal or self-injuring history in the family, childhood trauma and adequacy of social networks, mental health and levels of self-esteem. A comprehensive plan can then be developed for each prisoner which needs first and foremost to take account of the environment followed by a focus on the individual. This would identify that many prisoners are exceptionally vulnerable to suicide, and that prison can offer them the prospect to break away from their past criminal behaviours.

FURTHER READING

Hawton, K., Linsell, L., Adeniji, T., Sariaslan, A., & Fazel, S. (2014). Self-harm in prisons in England and Wales: An epidemiological study of prevalence, risk factors, clustering, and subsequent suicide. *The Lancet, 383*(9923), 1147–1154.

This paper reports on a case-control study of all prisoners in English and Welsh prisons to ascertain the prevalence of self-harm in this population, associated risk factors, clustering effects and risk of subsequent suicide after self-harm. Records of self-harm incidents in all prisons in England and Wales were gathered routinely between January 2004 and December 2009. A Bayesian approach was also used to look at clustering of people who self-harmed. Prisoners who self-harmed and subsequently died by suicide in prison were compared with other inmates who self-harmed. A total of 139,195 self-harm incidents were recorded in 26,510 individual prisoners between 2004 and 2009; 5–6% of male prisoners and 20–24% of female inmates self-harmed every year. The rates of self-harm were more than 10 times higher in female prisoners than in male inmates. Repetition of self-harm was common, particularly in women and teenage girls, in whom a subgroup of 102 prisoners accounted for 17,307 episodes. The authors highlight that the cost and burden of self-harm in prisoners is considerable, particularly in women. Self-harm in prison is associated with subsequent suicide in this setting. Prevention and treatment of self-harm in prisoners is an essential component of suicide prevention in prisons.

Towl, G., & Crighton, D. (1998). Suicide in prisons in England and Wales from 1988 to 1995. *Criminal Behaviour and Mental Health, 8,* 184–192.

This large-scale study examined 377 case records from the English Prison Service's Suicide Awareness Support Unit of self-inflicted deaths in prisons in England and Wales from 1988 to 1995. The paper also includes a discussion of some of the methodological difficulties in exploring this sensitive area of work. Discussions also include observations on some of the differences between prisoner suicides and others.

REFERENCES

Binswanger, I., Stern, M., Deyo, R., Heagerty, P., Cheadle A., Elmore, J., & Koepsell, T. (2007). Release from prison – a high risk of death for former inmates. *New England Journal of Medicine, 356,* 157–165.

Bogue, J., & Power, K. (1995). Suicide in Scottish prisons, 1976–93. *The Journal of Forensic Psychiatry, 6,* 527–540.

Bonner, R. (1992). Isolation, seclusion and psychological vulnerability as risk factors for suicide behind bars. In R. Maris *et al.* (Eds.), *Assessment and prediction of suicide.* New York: Guilford Press.

Burrows, T., Brock, P., Hulley, S., Smith, C., & Summers, L. (2008). *Safer cell evaluation.* London: University College.

Camilleri, P., McArthur, M., & Webb, H. (1999). *Suicidal behaviour in prisons: A literature review.* School of Social Work, Australian Catholic University: Canberra.

Cox, J., & Morschauser, P. (1997). A solution to the problem of jail suicide. *The Journal of Crisis Intervention and Suicide Prevention, 18,* 178–184.

Cox, T. (1993). *Stress research and stress management: Putting theory to work.* HSE Contract Research Report No 61: Sudbury.

Crighton, D. (2000). *Suicide in prisons in England and Wales 1988–1998: An empirical study.* PhD thesis submitted to Anglia Polytechnic University.

Crighton, D., & Towl, G. (1997). Self-inflicted deaths in England and Wales 1988–1990, and 1994–95, In G. Towl (Ed.), *Suicide and self-injury in prisons.* Leicester: British Psychological Society.

Crighton, D., & Towl, G. (2000). Intentional self-injury. In G. Towl., L. Snow, & M. McHugh (Eds.), *Suicide in prisons.* Leicester: British Psychological Society.

Davies, B. (1994). The Swansea listener scheme: Views from the prison landings. *The Howard Journal, 33*(2), 125–135.

Dear, G., Thomson, D., Hall, G., & Howells, K. (2001). Non-fatal self-injury in western Australian prisons: Who, where, when and why. *Australian and New Zealand Journal of Criminology, 34*(1), 47–66.

DeCatanzaro, D. (1981). *Suicide and self-damaging behaviour: A sociobiological perspective.* New York: Academic Press.

Deiter, P., & Pearlman, L. (1998). Responding to self-injurious behaviour. In P. Kleespies (Ed.), *Emergencies in mental health practice: Evaluation and management.* New York: The Guilford Press.

Department of Health. (1999). *The national service framework for mental health: Modern standards and service models.* London: Department of Health.

Department of Health. (2001). *Changing the outlook – a strategy for developing and modernising mental health services in prisons.* London: Department of Health.

Department of Health. (2004). *Choosing health: Making healthier choices easier.* London: Department of Health.

Department of Health. (2012). *Improving outcomes and supporting transparency.* Part2: *Summary technical specifications of public health indicators.* London: Department of Health.

Dexter, P., & Towl, G. (1995). An investigation into suicide behaviour in prisons. In N. Clark & G. Stephenson (Eds.), *Criminal behaviour: Perceptions, attributions, and rationalities.* Leicester: British Psychological Society.

Dooley, E. (1990). Non-natural deaths in prison. *British Journal of Criminology, 30*(2), 229–234.

Durcan, G. (2008). *From the inside: Experiences of prison mental health care.* London: Centre for Mental Health.

Favazza, A., & Rosenthal, R. (1993). Diagnostic issues in self-mutilation. *Hospital and Community Psychiatry, 44,* 134–140.

Fish, R. (2000). Working with people who harm themselves in a forensic learning disability service: Experiences of direct care staff. *Journal of Learning Disabilities, 4,* 193–207.

Graham, A. (2003). Post-prison mortality: unnatural death among people released from Victorian prisons between January 1990 and December 1999. *Australian and New Zealand Journal of Criminology, 36,* 94–108.

Guthrie, E., Kapur, N., & Mackway-Jones, K. (2001). Randomised controlled trial of brief psychological intervention after deliberate self-poisoning. *British Medical Journal, 323,* 135–138.

Harding-Pink, D. (1990). Mortality following release from prison. *Medicine, Science, and the Law, 30,* 12–16.

Hatty, S. E., & Walker, J. R. (1986). *A national study of deaths in Australian prisons.* Canberra: Australian Centre of Criminology.

Hawton, K., Linsell, L., Adeniji, T., Sariaslan, S., & Fazel, S. (2014). Self-harm in prisons in England and Wales: an epidemiological study of prevalence, risk factors, clustering, and subsequent suicide. *The Lancet, 383*(9923), 1147–1154.

Hawton, K., Rodham, K., & Evans, E. (2002). Deliberate self-harm in adolescents: Self-report survey in schools in England. *British Medical Journal, 325,* 1207–1211.

Haycock, J. (1989). Manipulation and suicide attempts in jails and prisons. *Psychiatric Quarterly, 60,* 85–98.

Hayward, P., Tilley, F., Derbyshire, C., Kuipers, E., & Grey, S. (2005). 'The ailment' revisited: Are 'manipulative' patients really the most difficult? *Journal of Mental Health, 14*(3), 291–303.

HM Prison Service. (2007). *Prison Service Order 2700: Suicide prevention and self-injury management.* London: Home Office.

HMI Probation and HMI Prisons. (2013). *A joint inspection of life sentence prisoners.* London: Home Office.

HM Inspectorate of Prisons. (1999). *Suicide is everyone's concern.* London: Home Office.

HM Inspectorate of Prisons. (2000). *Unjust desserts.* London: Home Office.

HM Inspectorate (2007). *The mental health of prisoners.* London: Home Office.

HM Inspectorate of Prisons. (2012). *Remand prisoners.* London: Home Office.

HM Prison Service. (2001). *Prevention of suicide and self-harm in the prison service: An internal review.* London: HM Prison Service.

Home Office (1991). *Custody, care and justice: The way ahead for the Prison Service England and Wales.* London: Home Office.

Home Office. (2007). *Prison service staff surveys 2002 to 2006.* London: Home Office.

Horrocks, J., Price, S., & House, A. (2003). Self-injury attendances in the accident and emergency department: clinical database study. *British Journal of Psychiatry, 183,* 34–39.

Howard League for Penal Reform. (2001). *Suicide and self-injury prevention 2: Repetitive self-injury among women and girls in prison.* London: The Howard League for Penal Reform.

Howard League for Penal Reform. (2005). *Briefing paper on prison overcrowding and suicide.* London: The Howard League for Penal Reform.

Howard League for Penal Reform. (2013). *Deaths in custody annual report 2013.* London: The Howard League for Penal Reform.

HSCIC. (2012). *Self-harm.* http://www.hscic.gov.uk/article/2430/Self-harm-hospital-admission-rate-per-100000-population-in-North-East-almost-triple-the-rate-in-London (accessed 14 January 2015).

Huband, N., & Tantam, D. (2000). Attitudes to self-injury within a group of mental health staff. *British Journal of Medical Psychology, 73,* 495–504.

Huey, M., & McNulty, T. (2005). Institutional conditions and prison suicide: Conditional effects of deprivation and overcrowding. *The Prison Journal, 85*(4), 477–491.

Inch, H., Rowlands, P., & Soliman, A. (1995). Deliberate self-harm in a young offenders' institution. *Journal of Forensic Psychiatry, 6,* 161–171.

Independent Advisory Panel on Deaths in Custody. (2011). *Statistical Analysis of all recorded deaths of individuals detained in state custody between 1 January 2000 and 31 December 2010.* London: Ministerial Council on Deaths in Custody.

INQUEST. (2012). *Fatally Flawed: Has the state learned lessons from the deaths of children and young people in prison?* London: Prison Reform Trust.

Jaffe, M. (2012). *The Listener Scheme in Prisons: Final report on research findings.* London: The Samaritans.

Jones, D., & Maynard, A. (2013). Suicide in recently released prisoners: a systematic review. *Mental Health Practice, 17*(3), 20–27.

Kapur, N. (2005). Management of self-harm in adults: which way now? *The British Journal of Psychiatry, 187*(6), 497–499.

Karp, J., Whitman, L., & Convit, A. (1991). Intentional ingestion of foreign objects by male prison inmates. *Hospital and Community Psychiatry, 42,* 533–535.

Kenning, C., Cooper, J., Short, V., Shaw, J., Abel, K., & Chew-Graham, C. (2010). Prison staff and women prisoner's views on self-injury; their implications for service delivery and development: A qualitative study. *Criminal Behaviour and Mental Health, 20*(4), 274–284.

Leese, M,. Thomas, S., & Snow, L. (2006). An ecological study of factors associated with rates of self-inflicted death in prisons in England and Wales. *International Journal of Law and Psychiatry, 29*(5), 355–360.

Liebling, A. (1991). *Suicide and self-injury amongst young offenders in custody.* Doctoral dissertation, University of Cambridge.

Liebling, A. (1992). *Suicide in prison.* London: Routledge.

Liebling, A. (1993). Suicides in young prisoners: a summary. *Death Studies, 17,* 381–409.

Liebling, A. (1994). Suicide among women prisoners. *The Howard Journal, 33*(1), 1–9.

Liebling, A., & Krarup, H. (1993). *Suicide attempts in male prisons.* London: Home Office.

Liebling, A. (2006). The role of the prison environment in prison suicide and prisoner distress. In G. Dear (Ed.), *Preventing suicide and other self-injury in prison.* Basingstoke: Palgrave-Macmillan.

Lilley, R., Owens, D., & Horrocks, J. (2008). Methods of self-injury: A multicentre comparison of episodes of poisoning and injury. *British Journal of Psychiatry, 192,* 440–445.

Livingston, M. (1997). A review of the literature on self-injurious behaviour amongst prisoners. In G. Towl (Ed.), *Suicide and self-injury in prisons.* Leicester: British Psychological Society.

Lloyd, C. (1990). *Suicide and self-injury in prison: A literature review.* London: Home Office.

Loucks, N. (1998). HMPI Corton Vale: Research into drugs and alcohol, violence and bullying, suicides and self-injury, and backgrounds of abuse. *Scottish Prison Service Occasional Papers:* 1/98.

Mackay, C., Cousins, R., Kelly, P. J., Lee, S., & McCaig, R. H. (2004). Management standards' and work-related stress in the UK: Policy background and science. *Work and Stress, 18,* 91–112.

Marzano, L., Adler, J., & Ciclitira, K. (2013). Responding to repetitive, non-suicidal self-injury in an English male prison: Staff experiences, reactions, and concerns. *Legal and Criminological Psychology, 12,* 1–14.

Mchugh, M., & Towl, G. (1997). Organizational reactions and reflections on suicide and self-injury. In G. Towl (Ed.), *Suicide and self-injury in prisons.* Leicester: British Psychological Society.

Meltzer, H., Harrington, R., & Goodman, R. (2001). *Children and adolescents who try to harm, hurt or kill themselves: A report of further analysis from the national survey of the mental health of children and adolescents in Great Britain in 1999.* London: Office for National Statistics.

Meltzner, J., & Hayes, L. (2006). Suicide prevention in jails and prisons. In R. Simon & R. Hales (Eds.), *Textbook of suicide assessment and management.* Washington: American Psychiatric Publishing.

Mental Health Foundation. (1997). *Suicide and deliberate self-injury.* London: Mental Health Foundation.

Ministry of Justice. (2009). *Statistics on women and the criminal justice system.* London: Ministry of Justice.

Ministry of Justice. (2011). *Safety in custody.* London: Ministry of Justice Statistics Bulletin.

Ministry of Justice. (2013a). *Guide to safety in custody statistics.* London: Ministry of Justice Statistics Bulletin.

Ministry of Justice. (2013b). *Resettlement prisons.* London: Ministry of Justice.

Ministry of Justice. (2013c). *Safety in custody statistics England and Wales update to June 2013.* London: Ministry of Justice.

Ministry of Justice. (2013d). *Offender management statistics quarterly bulletin July to September 2012.* London: Ministry of Justice.

NICE. (2012). *Self-injury: Longer term management.* London: The British Psychological Society and The Royal College of Psychiatrists.

Office for National Statistics. (1999). *Non-fatal suicidal behaviour among prisoners.* Office for National Statistics, London: The Stationery Office.

Paton, J., & Jenkins, R. (2005). Suicide and suicide attempts in prisons. In K. Hawton (Ed.), *Prevention and treatment of suicidal behaviour: From science to practice.* Oxford: Oxford University Press.

Power, K., & Spencer, A. (1987). Para-suicidal behaviour of detained Scottish young offenders. *International Journal of Offender Therapy and Comparative Criminology, 31,* 227–235.

Powis, B. (2002). *Offenders' risk of serious harm: A literature review.* London: Home Office Research, Development and Statistics Directorate.

Pratt D., Piper, M., Appleby, L., Webb, R., & Shaw, J. (2006). Suicide in recently released prisoners: A population-based cohort study. *Lancet, 368,* 119–123.

Prison Reform Trust. (2013). *Prison: The facts.* London: Prison Reform Trust.

Prisons and Probation Ombudsman. (2011). *Learning from PPO investigations: Violence reduction, bullying and safety.* London: Home Office.

Rayner, G. C., Allen, S. L., & Johnson, M. (2005). Countertransference and self-injury: A cognitive behavioural cycle. *Journal of Advanced Nursing, 50,* 12–19.

Rieger, W. (1971). Suicide attempts in a federal prison. *Archives of General Psychiatry, 24,* 532–535.

Royal College of Nursing. (2010). *Prison mental health: Vision and reality.* London: Royal College of Nursing.

Royal College of Psychiatrists. (2010). *Self-injury, suicide and risk: Helping people who self-injury.* London: Royal College of Psychiatrists.

Royal College of Psychiatrists. (2013). *Standards for community forensic mental health services.* London: Royal College of Psychiatrists.

Sainsbury Centre for Mental Health. (2009). *Diversion: A better way for criminal justice and mental health.* London: Sainsbury Centre for Mental Health.

Samaritans. (1990). *Befriending in prisons.* Slough: The Samaritans.

Samaritans. (2011). *A history of the listener scheme and Samaritans' prison support.* Ewell: Samaritans.

Sattar, G. (2001). *Rates and causes of death among prisoners and offenders under community supervision.* London: Home Office.

Shaw, J., Baker, D., Hunt, I., Moloney, A., & Appleby, L. (2004). Suicide by prisoners: National clinical survey. *British Journal of Psychiatry, 184,* 263–267.

Singleton, N., Meltzer, H., & Gatward, R. (1998). *Psychiatric morbidity among prisoners in England and Wales.* London: The Stationery Office.

Slade, K., & Edelmann, R. (2013). Can theory predict the process of suicide on entry to prison? Predicting dynamic risk factors for suicide ideation in a high-risk prison population. *Crisis, 35*(2), 82–89.

Social Exclusion Unit. (2002). *Reducing re-offending by ex-prisoners.* London: Office of the Deputy Prime Minister.

Social Work Services and Prisons Inspectorates for Scotland. (1998). *Women offenders – A safer way.* Scotland: HMSO.

Stephenson, P. (2004). Mentally ill offenders are being wrongly held in prisons. *British Medical Journal, 328,* 1095.

Stewart, L., Henderson, C., Hobbs, M., Ridout, S., & Knuiman, M. (2004). Risk of death in prisoners after release from jail. *Australian and New Zealand Journal of Public Health, 28,* 32–36.

Sutton, J. (2007). *Healing the hurt within: Understand self-injury and self-injury, and heal the emotional wounds* (revised and updated 3rd edition). Oxford: How To Books.

Task Force on Suicide in Canada. (1994). *Suicide in Canada.* Ottawa: Minister of National Health and Welfare.

Taylor, T., Hawton, K., Fortune, S., & Kapur, N. (2009). Attitudes towards clinical services among people who self-injury: Systematic review. *British Journal of Psychiatry, 194,* 104–110.

Towl, G. (1996). Homicide and suicide, risk assessment in prisons. *The Psychologist,* September, *9,* 398–400.

Towl, G. (1999). Suicide in prisons in England and Wales, 1988–1996. In G. Towl., M. McHugh., & D. Jones (Eds.), *Suicide in prisons: Research, policy and practice.* Brighton, UK: Pavilion Publishing.

Towl, G. (2000). Reflections upon suicide in prisons. *The British Journal of Forensic Practice, 2*(1), 17–22.

Towl, G. (2010). Foreword. In J. Harvey & K. Smedley (Eds.), *Psychological therapy in prisons and other secure settings.* Cullompton, UK: Willan Publishing.

Towl, G., & Crighton, D. (1998). Suicide in prisons in England and Wales from 1988 to 1995. *Criminal Behaviour and Mental Health, 8,* 184–192.

Towl, G., & Hudson, D. (1997). Risk assessment and management. In G. Towl (Ed.), *Suicide and self-injury in prisons.* Leicester: British Psychological Society.

Towl, G., & Forbes, D. (2002). Working with suicidal prisoners. In G. Towl, L. Snow, & M. McHugh (Eds.), *Suicide in prison.* Oxford: BPS Blackwell.

Triplett, R., Mullings, J. L., & Scarborough, K. E. (1996). Work-related stress and coping among correctional officers: Implications from organizational literature. *Journal of Criminal Justice, 24,* 291–308.

WHO. (2007). *Preventing suicide in jails and prisons.* Geneva: World Health Organisation.

Wichmann, C., Serin, R., & Motiuk, L. (2000). *Predicting suicide attempts among male offenders in federal penitentiaries.* Canada: Research Branch, Correctional Service.

Wilkins, J., & Coid, J. (1991). Self-mutilation in female remanded prisoners: I. An indicator of severe psychopathy. *Criminal Behaviour and Mental Health, 1,* 247–267.

Wool, R., & Dooley, E. (1987). A study of attempted suicides in prisons. *Medicine, Science and the Law, 27*(4), 297–301.

Youth Justice Board and Ministry of Justice. (2013). *Youth Justice Statistics 2011/12: England and Wales.* London: Youth Justice Board and Ministry of Justice.

21 Working with Children and Adolescents with Harmful Sexual Behaviour

JACKIE WALTON

In this chapter, I set out to provide an overview of some of the key issues pertinent to working with children and adolescents who have developed harmful sexual behaviour. I begin with an exploration of the definitional issues that have emerged during the development of services to address such behaviours over the past 25 years, specifically in relation to the language used to describe the behaviours, and the children and adolescents who have enacted the behaviours. The historical, legislative and public policy context of the development of these services in the United Kingdom are then outlined – how the problem was first identified by the professionals involved, the search for explanations of causation and assessment and treatment models to address the problems, the public policy and legislative responses, and the extent to which different professionals and public service managers have considered it within their remit to provide services to address the needs of these young people. The key findings from research on prevalence rates and recent developments in assessment and treatment models for children and adolescents will then be critically summarized. The chapter concludes with an overview of the lessons learnt from recent developments in this area of work, which is now beginning to inform work with adult sex offenders. This may be of particular relevance to forensic practitioners working with adult sex offenders, given the recent evidence suggesting that current adult sex offender treatment programmes are not working.

DEFINITIONAL ISSUES AND THE USE OF LANGUAGE

There has been an on-going debate and dialogue among practitioners and researchers about the language used to describe children and young people who have developed sexual behaviour problems – in particular, whether it is the child or the behaviour that is being described. This dialogue has been comprehensively reviewed elsewhere in the literature (Calder, 2001; Hackett, 2004). Terms such as 'Young Abuser', 'Adolescent or Juvenile Sex Offender', 'Children Who Molest', 'Abuse-Reactive Children', 'Children Who Sexually Abuse', 'Sexually Aggressive Children' and 'Children and Young People with Harmful Sexual Behaviour' have been variously used by different authors and in different legislative and policy documents. The terms chosen have often reflected the respective professional and organizational backgrounds of the writers and the age of the cohort of children they have worked with. This debate, however, would also appear to reflect tensions inherent in adopting adult models of treatment to children and young people and the desire to balance a public protection/punishment agenda with a need to engage children and young people in meaningful change that will reduce their need to engage in further harmful sexual behaviour. These tensions appear to have been at the core of the debate and dialogue among professionals that has informed service development since the early 1980s. How do we both acknowledge and address the often significant harm that the child or young person has caused to others, and at the same time acknowledge and address the needs of the young person who has harmed others, most of whom have encountered significant problems throughout their childhood? In this chapter, I have used the term 'harmful sexual behaviour', which acknowledges the harm such behaviour causes to victims while at the same time recognizing the pejorative association of the terms 'abuse' and 'abuser', which imply an established pattern of sexually offending behaviour that is neither relevant or helpful to the children and young people who develop this behaviour.

Forensic Psychology, Second Edition. Edited by David A. Crighton and Graham J. Towl.
© 2015 John Wiley & Sons, Ltd. Published 2015 by British Psychological Society and John Wiley & Sons, Ltd.

HISTORICAL CONTEXT SETTING

In 1990, the Training Advisory Group on Sexually Abused Children (TAGOSAC), the Child Abuse Training Unit at the National Children's Bureau and Childline convened a national conference in the United Kingdom to bring together professionals who were working with children and young people who were considered to have 'sexually abused' others (Hollows & Armstrong, 1991). This conference was shortly followed by the Report of the Committee of Enquiry into Children and Young People Who Sexually Abuse Other Children, published by the National Children's Home (NCH, 1992). Significantly, it was third-sector children's organizations, and the professionals working with or alongside them, that first brought these concerns into the public domain. The report found significant gaps in service provision for these children and young people, and highlighted a lack of consistent and coordinated approaches and inadequate training, supervision and expertise for those who were attempting to respond to the problem. Two sources of information were of particular influence in shaping professional concern about this issue: (1) the number of children who were contacting Childline to talk about either their experience of being sexually abused by another child, or of having sexually abused another child; and (2) the findings from interviews with adult sex offenders who reported that they had developed sexually abusive behaviour in childhood or adolescence (Abel, Mittelman, & Becker, 1985).

In the absence of research data, and tested methods of working with this cohort of children and adolescents, models of working with adult sex offenders, which had largely influenced models of working with adolescent sex offenders imported from the United States, were adopted in the development of assessment and treatment services for children and young people in the United Kingdom at this time. These interventions drew heavily on cognitive behavioural approaches and an addiction model of sexual offending (Ryan, 1986). Children and young people were expected to acknowledge responsibility for their behaviour, to identify the stages of what was construed as their 'offending cycle', to recognize their 'cognitive distortions' and to develop victim empathy and relapse prevention strategies. In keeping with adult intervention models, a confrontational rather than collaborative approach was taken in encouraging the young person to acknowledge responsibility for their behaviour (Calder, 2008). Interventions that were 'sex offence specific', as opposed to interventions that addressed the broader emotional and welfare needs of the young person, were considered to be the most effective means of addressing this behaviour. There was also a preference for group work as opposed to individual interventions (Bentovim, 1991). A central tenet of this approach, therefore, was to separate the welfare needs of the young person from the need to address their harmful sexual behaviour. There was also a view at this time that this work should, where possible, be court mandated, either through criminal proceedings in relation to sexual offences committed by the young person, or through public law proceedings if the young person was considered to be at an unacceptably high risk of harm to themselves. The implication was that, if treatment programmes were to be successful, young people would require a level of coercion to acknowledge and address their harmful sexual behaviour (Bentovim, 1991; Myers, 1998).

Following the implementation of the Sexual Offences Act 2007, children as young as 11 years of age were placed on the Sex Offender Register, following conviction, with all the consequent implications for their long-term life chances in terms of employment opportunities, ability to take part in group sport and leisure activities and indeed the opportunity to have children of their own in adulthood (Longo & Calder, 2005). This again appeared to be based on the un-evidenced assumption that children and young people who committed sexual offences would develop into adult sex offenders. Young people in these circumstances were often deprived of a sense of hope for their future, which understandably negatively impacted on their motivation to engage in treatment services.

Specialist assessment and treatment services for children and young people with sexual abuse problems were few and far between, and were largely locally driven by professionals who had a specific interest in this area of work. There was a lack of clarity as to which public services were responsible for providing these services. Local Authority Social Services Departments, as the lead child protection agency, were responsible for investigating allegations of sexual abuse from one child to another. However, they often lacked the financial and (expensive) specialist resources and staff to undertake risk assessment and treatment work. Very few of these children were convicted of sexual offences, and therefore did not have access to any developing service provision within the Youth Justice System at this time. Child and Adult Mental Health Service (CAMHS) professionals generally did not consider this behaviour a 'mental health issue', and therefore children and young people who were exhibiting harmful sexual behaviour would not be offered a service unless they had other diagnosed mental health disorders. In these circumstances, any focused work on the young person's harmful sexual behaviour would generally not be undertaken by CAHMS teams, with the exception of a few specialist tertiary-level services such as the Child Sexual Abuse Unit at Great Ormond Street Hospital. It was largely third-sector children's services, namely the National Society for the Prevention of Cruelty to Children (NSPCC), Barnardo's and National Children's Home (NCH) Action for Children (now known as Action for Children) that filled this gap in service provision. These services were predominately staffed by social workers and varied in the extent to which they co-opted, consulted or employed other professionals, such as psychologists and psychiatrists, to assist or advise on the services they provided.

The absence of statutory guidance and procedures to ensure a co-ordinated multi-agency response to these children began to be addressed with the publication of Working Together to Safeguard Children (Department of Health, Home Office and Department for Education and Employment, 1999). This guidance emphasized the need for the key public services to develop a coordinated approach to service provision, that the needs of the children and young people who abused others should be considered separately to the needs of their victims, and that an assessment should be carried out in each case, appreciating that these children may have considerable unmet developmental needs, as well as specific needs arising from their sexual behaviour. Under this guidance, children and young people with harmful sexual behaviour, in addition to their child victims, were often the subjects of child protection case conferences. The child considered to have been the 'perpetrator' was not placed on the child protection register unless they were considered to be at an inflated risk of sexual abuse themselves. They were, however, identified as 'young abusers', and a multi-agency protection plan was put in place to reduce their inflated risk of sexually harming other children. Children within the family, considered to have been victims, or potential victims, of this child were placed on the child protection register, and a multi-agency child protection plan put in place to reduce the risk to them of sexual abuse from their 'young abuser' sibling. Children in this context were either victims or perpetrators of sexual abuse, and the child protection system found it very difficult to address their needs as both. Although many child 'perpetrators' were suspected, or known, to have been victims of sexual abuse, their perpetrator status took priority. Professionals working with these children were often erroneously required to ascertain which child was the victim and which child the perpetrator, often in situations when several children within one family were reported to have engaged in inappropriate sexual behaviour with each other. This was particularly problematic when several children in one household were exhibiting inappropriate sexual behaviour within their sibling group in a family context of intergenerational child sexual abuse.

Incidence rates

Ministry of Justice statistics from 2011–2012 indicate that 12.4% of all those cautioned or convicted for a sexual offence were between 10 and 17 years of age. As is the case with most offences, conviction rates are likely to underestimate the actual prevalence of this behaviour. This is particularly the case for sexual offences which rely largely on victim reports in the absence of other witnesses. This effect is likely to be even further amplified by the fact that sexually harmful behaviours may not be classified as 'offences' even if they come to the attention of the relevant authorities. Various retrospective studies suggest that around one-quarter of all alleged sexual abuse involves young, mainly adolescent, male perpetrators (Calder, 2008).

In terms of sexual recidivism, rates for children and young people are much lower than for adults who commit sexual offences and fall between 5% and 14%. Non-sexual recidivism rates, however, are higher at between 16% and 54% (Worling & Curwen, 2001; Nisbet et al., 2004; Waite et al., 2005). Sexual recidivism is associated with a variety of developmental, social and criminological factors, but few studies identify those characteristics that are most strongly associated with an inflated risk of a continuation of sexual offending into adulthood. There is currently no accepted system to determine which children and young people who sexually offend are most likely to pose a subsequently inflated risk of sexual recidivism (HM Inspectorate of Probation, 2013).

ASSESSMENT AND TREATMENT INTERVENTIONS WITH ADOLESCENTS

The development of assessment and treatment services for young people over the past 20 years has paralleled an increasing recognition of the developmental differences between adolescents and adults who sexually offend. Adolescence is characterized developmentally as a period of considerable change in the physical, emotional, cognitive and behavioural functioning of the young person. The developmental challenge of adolescence is primarily one of identity formation (Erikson, 1982). Adolescence can represent a period of increased vulnerability for the young person, specifically in relation to the development of antisocial, criminal and sexually harmful behaviours. Sexual maturation and the development of secondary sexual characteristics, neurological changes affecting the regulation of behaviour and emotions and the perception and evaluation of risk (Steinberg, 2005), and the reliance on peer friendships for identity formation are all considered to be of significance in the development of both sexual and non-sexual offending behaviours. This is particularly the case for young people who have encountered trauma, significant disruption in their family and home circumstances, parental abuse or neglect and social and economic disadvantage. Adolescence can also represent a critical period in the opportunity to intervene to effectively address harmful sexual behaviour that has emerged during or prior to this stage in the young persons' development. Patterns of harmful sexual behaviour have become less established or entrenched, and the young person's drive to develop a positive self-identity and new ways of being can be harnessed if effectively engaged in treatment services. It is important therefore that these developmental differences be taken into consideration when designing treatment services, in terms of both informing the assessment of the young person's needs and the methods and techniques adopted to work with them.

Although there are no validated assessment tools for use with children and young people who commit sexual offences, unsurprisingly, specialist structured assessment tools do appear to show a higher level of accuracy in predicting sexual recidivism than non-specialist, or unstructured, assessments. Tools such as Assessment, Intervention and Moving On 2 (AIM); Juvenile Sex Offender Assessment Protocol-II (J-SOAP-II); Juvenile Sexual Offence Recidivism Risk Assessment Tool-II (J-SORRAT-II); and Estimate of Risk of Adolescent Sexual Offence Recidivism (ERASOR) may therefore be considered for use in addition to core assessment tools such as the ASSET (the YJB structured assessment tool for children and young people who offend). A useful overview of these assessment tools is provided by Calder (2008). Practitioners, however, need to be careful to balance the interests of the public and shareholder return of the testing tools, which sometimes tend to raise service costs considerably. Such tools also are very limited in terms of what they can offer in terms of evaluation (Towl & Crighton, 2008). Their most useful application is, in general, in terms of the structuring of initial assessments. However, a good clinician will outperform a good assessment tool, and therefore experienced practitioners need to have confidence in their own judgements and not be overly reliant upon psychometric testing, whatever its (often spurious) claims of scientific validity. These assessment tools are derived from group-based data, so their application to any individual is always a matter of judgement. It is, however, important that experienced practitioners are aware of the available evidence to strengthen their clinical decision-making.

There would appear to be a broad consensus on the key issues that need to be considered during the assessment process, as described in the following text.

1. Assessments should be systemic and involve significant adults in the young person's life, including parents/carers and professionals who are or have been involved with the young person. Most adolescents remain dependent on their parents, carers and other key adults, both financially and in terms of meeting their basic care needs. They will therefore require the support of these adults to assist them to engage in the assessment process and to facilitate any additional services or support that are identified as part of a programme of intervention. A systemic approach is also considered essential in the acquisition of information about the young person, in terms of their developmental history and the onset and extent of their harmful sexual behaviour, and the monitoring and review of this behaviour during and after treatment.

2. The developmental history of the young person, including any trauma, disruptions in family/care, abusive or neglectful parenting and attachment difficulties that may have impacted on the development of the harmful sexual behaviour.

3. The onset and development of the young person's harmful sexual behaviour, including the nature of the sexual behaviour, the victims involved and the extent to which coercion, threats and violence have been used.

4. The young persons' sexual knowledge and experience and the extent to which they may have been exposed to inappropriate sexual behaviour or sexual images, either by their parents/carers, the influence of their peers or through social media and Internet websites.

5. An assessment of the young persons' educational and cognitive development should inform the materials and techniques used during assessment interviews with the young person and subsequent treatment approaches. This is particularly significant for young people with identified learning difficulties.

6. The capacity of parents/carers to support the young persons in addressing their harmful sexual behaviour, specifically their acknowledgement of the concerns and willingness to engage with the assessment and treatment process.

7. The young person's capacity to engage in the assessment and treatment process, and any identified strengths, interests, ambitions and life goals that may motivate them to change.

In terms of the range of treatment options for young people, there would appear to have been a growing recognition among professionals working in this field that a narrow focus on 'offence-specific' cognitive behavioural approaches in the absence of any attempts to acknowledge and address the young person's broader welfare needs has been at best ineffective and at worst unhelpful. Cognitive behavioural approaches have historically been favoured over and above other more psychotherapeutic/counselling models due to research findings that, some have argued, indicated that they have been more effective in addressing sexual and non-sexual behaviour problems in children and adolescents (see, e.g., Fonagy *et al.*, 2005).

It has been suggested that the development of treatment approaches in the United Kingdom has been marked by 'professional tribalism', with those supporting cognitive behavioural approaches and those supporting psychotherapeutic/psychoanalytical approaches split over questions of theory and practice. Most often, these professionals have worked in isolation from each other, employed by different organizations, with little opportunity for dialogue and enquiry into their respective views, and each group largely dismissing or ignoring the other's contribution.

Gail Ryan and colleagues (Ryan, 1998), working in the United States, began to switch the emphasis from a purely cognitive behavioural approach to incorporate the significance of the young person's developmental stage, attachment relationships and internal working models of self in relation to others, which often impact on the young person's capacity to empathize with others. This was paralleled in the United Kingdom with increasing recognition of the significance of attachment difficulties to the aetiology of harmful sexual behaviour in children (Santry & McCarthy, 1999; Smallbone, 2005). To this extent, it was acknowledged that cognitive behavioural approaches in isolation were insufficient in helping the young person process any earlier traumatic or abusive experiences or to address any developmental deficits resulting from inadequate or inconsistent care they received during their childhood. The previously held view that the victim and perpetrator experiences of the young person needed to be addressed separately was now recognized as unhelpful, and the need to develop an integrated or holistic approach to addressing the needs of the young person became more widely accepted.

It has been argued that the most significant contribution of a psychotherapeutic approach to treatment interventions is the use of the therapeutic relationship to help the young persons to integrate their victim and perpetrator experiences in the development of their maturation and personality. He acknowledges, however, that psychotherapy needs to be offered within the context of a systemic, multi-agency treatment plan that incorporates other approaches and addresses the young person's broader social and welfare needs.

This emphasis on the significance of the relationship between the practitioner and the young person has been increasingly acknowledged and recognized by professionals developing services for young people with harmful sexual behaviour both in the United Kingdom and internationally (Longo, 2002; Hackett, 2004; Rich, 2011). These models advocate a holistic approach that incorporates a range of treatment techniques and methods, but emphasizes the centrality of a relationship of mutual respect and trust between the practitioner and young person in the effectiveness of the interventions adopted. The therapeutic relationship is considered the focal point of treatment and as essential to positive treatment outcomes. Holistic approaches, such as the Good Lives Model developed by Ward (2010, 2011), have been particularly influential in the development of UK treatment services in recent years (McCrory, 2010; Calder, 2008). This model incorporates a strengths-based approach as opposed to a deficits-based approach to working with the young person, largely informed by research on resilience (Hackett, 2006), with an emphasis on the search for skills, strengths and positive life goals rather than an exclusive focus on the reduction of problem behaviours. It is based on the premise that these young persons need to develop empathy for themselves and their own victim experiences before they can develop empathy and compassion for others, including their victims and potential victims. The young person's victim status therefore becomes the starting point for intervention, rather than a secondary consideration once they have acknowledged and addressed the harm they have caused to others. The significance of 'shame' as a potential obstacle to the effective engagement of the young person and therefore their capacity to change their behaviour is also emphasized by these approaches (Worling, Josefowitz, & Maltar, 2011). The adoption of a non-judgemental and non-punitive approach that continues to hold the young person accountable for his or her behaviour, but does so with respect for the young person and a collaborative rather than a coercive working relationship with him or her, is also seen as important.

Political critiques have been developed of statutory and therapeutic intervention programmes that have ignored the politics of disadvantage and the imbalance of power in the relationships between children and adults. Here it is argued that young males from disadvantaged groups are more likely to enter the criminal justice system than their more privileged contemporaries who have access to economic, legal and cultural mechanisms and structures to avoid being held accountable for their actions. It has been maintained that we need to respect the young persons' experiences of disadvantage and deprivation if we expect them to respect their victims' experiences.

There would appear to be a lack of clarity in the literature about the nature of a 'therapeutic relationship'. Recognizing the needs of young people as unique, acknowledging the difficulties they have encountered in their lives and treating them in a respectful and courteous manner amounts to basic professionalism and good ethical practice. This should form the basis of all professional practice with vulnerable clients, whether they are children or adults. A therapeutic relationship, however, in the context of the provision of counselling and psychotherapy to address significant trauma and attachment issues, refers to a relationship that is established between therapist and client through the provision of a safe, consistent and reliable therapeutic space where the young person can be enabled to process earlier traumatic or abusive life experiences and develop insights into the impact of these experiences on how they view themselves in relation to others and on the development of maladaptive coping strategies that have resulted in harm to themselves and others. This requires specific therapeutic skills and training on the part of the therapist, which are often time-intensive and thereby costly services, and not always necessary for all young people who have developed harmful sexual behaviour. Increasing professional awareness of the importance of process over and above technique is a positive step towards providing a holistic service for young people who often present with complex and multiple needs. It is nevertheless important to distinguish between good professional and ethical practice with these vulnerable young people in all aspects of the services provided to them and their specific therapeutic needs in terms of connecting past adverse life experiences to their current problematic behaviours.

The emphasis on the importance of developing a courteous and respectful relationship with the young person is critical to the successful engagement of the young person in the assessment and treatment process, and thereby on the outcomes of these services. Although most young people in the United Kingdom are not mandated by courts to attend treatment services, they rarely attend these services completely of their own volition. They have not chosen to be there but have been persuaded, or at times pressured, to attend by the adults responsible for their care. It requires considerable skill and sensitivity on the part of the professionals who first meet with the young persons to engage them to invest in the service being offered as something that may be of help to them, while at the same time addressing the concerns about their sexually harmful behaviour towards others. It is a testament to the skilled and dedicated work of many of the professionals working in these services that they have been successful in doing so, and perhaps lessons can be learnt for the provision of services to adult sex offenders who are mandated to attend treatment programmes.

ASSESSMENT AND TREATMENT WORK WITH CHILDREN

There is a general consensus within the literature that the needs of pre-pubescent children (aged 11 and under) who develop harmful sexual behaviour differ to those of adolescents. Although very young children can engage other children in the full range of adult sexual behaviours, and their bodies can physiologically respond to sexual stimulation, their motivation to do so is rarely based on attempts to meet their own sexual needs (Sanderson, 2004; Johnson, 2005). Very young children are not aware of the social context of sexual relationships, and their development of age-inappropriate or harmful sexual behaviour towards other children is more likely to result from information they have acquired from adults and older children, either through direct involvement in sexual activity, or exposure to adult sexual activity, or through encouragement to engage in sexualized behaviour by adults responsible for their care. Young children learn behaviour by modelling and imitating the behaviour of adults around them, and this is how they also acquire sexual behaviour. Children who develop harmful sexual behaviour often become very confused about their bodies and their developing sexuality. These children require information about safe and unsafe touching and the difference between private and public body parts. For example, children who become excessively preoccupied with masturbating publicly, often as a means of self-soothing to manage stress and anxiety, need an educative approach that teaches the child that this is a private behaviour, which does not result in the child feeling shamed for the behaviour and which also provides the child with other strategies for self-soothing.

This is not to infer that the harmful sexual behaviour of young children is any less serious in terms of its impact on their child victims, particularly if it involves physical coercion and threats. Indeed, this group of children often raises particularly strong feelings in professionals, with responses ranging on a continuum between a desire to frame the behaviour as normative childhood sexual exploration and thereby not to 'label' the child as an abuser at one end of the spectrum, and a fear that the child represents the same risk as an adult sex offender and should be removed from school, or from other social contact with children on the other end of the spectrum. There is often a considerable lack of information and understanding among professionals about the differences between normative or typical sexual development for young children and atypical and potentially harmful sexual behaviour. This can lead to under- or over-anxiety about these children when their sexual behaviour first comes to the attention of professionals. Children under the age of 10 (the legal age of criminal responsibility in the United Kingdom) cannot be convicted of sexual offences and, therefore, regardless of the seriousness of their behaviour in terms of its victim impact, they are often not referred to costly specialist services until they have been charged with their first offence. Hence, there have often been missed opportunities to work with these children at an earlier age when early intervention may have been helpful to the child and may have prevented further victimization of other children. The corollaries to this are situations when children whose normative sexual behaviour is misconstrued as sexually harmful behaviour by unduly anxious professionals, resulting in unnecessary or inappropriate intervention that may in itself be potentially harmful to the child's sexual development and future life chances.

In terms of causation, children who develop harmful sexual behaviour, similar to adolescents, have not necessarily been victims of sexual abuse themselves; however, they are likely to have encountered other adverse life experiences that may have contributed to this behaviour – such as parental physical abuse and neglect, exposure to domestic violence and adult sexual activity, poor sexual boundaries within the family home and disruptions to their care and home circumstances (Johnson, 2005).

Johnson (2005, 2009) has developed a typology of sexual behaviours for children under the age of 12. She has identified four groups of children, which range on a continuum from children who exhibit normative sexual behaviour to children who develop harmful sexual behaviour. This typology has been conceptualized from clinical experience of children referred to her service since 1987 due to concerns about their sexual behaviour. The first group of children, by far the largest, are children who display 'natural and healthy sexual behaviours'. The next three groups involve children who have developed atypical or 'problematic' sexual behaviour. Johnson identifies these three groups as 'sexually reactive', 'children engaged in extensive mutual sexual behaviours' and 'children who molest'.

'Sexually reactive children', typically, are children who use sexual behaviour to manage anxiety relating to previous abuse or other traumatic or distressing memories. These children often engage in self-stimulating behaviours but can also attempt to involve other children and adults in this behaviour. Significantly, these children do not coerce others into engaging in their sexual behaviour, but act out their confusion on them. Their behaviour is often impulsive and therefore less likely to be hidden or kept secret from adults. 'Children who engage in extensive mutual sexual behaviours' most often have had poor experiences of parental care and consequently feel abandoned and distrustful of adults. In the absence of positive and supportive relationships with adults, they seek emotional connection with other children through sexual behaviour. Significantly, these children do not coerce other children into sexual behaviours but seek out other children with similar attachment difficulties who engage in mutual sexual behaviour with them. These children, typically, have encountered emotional abuse and neglect and have often lived in home environments where there are poor sexual boundaries between children and adults and limited parental supervision and support. Significantly, it is only the last group of children – 'children who molest' – that Johnson considers to have developed sexually harmful, or abusive, behaviour. These children are the smallest in number of all children exhibiting problematic sexual behaviours. They have typically progressed through the other groups. Their sexual behaviour has now developed into the use of coercion to force or intimidate other children to engage in sexual activity, and motivationally their sexual behaviour serves to act out negative emotions towards their intended victims. These children have been unresponsive to previous attempts made by adults to address their problematic sexual behaviour, and they have demonstrated a continued unwillingness to accept the attempts made by others to say 'no' or to avoid or disengage from their sexual behaviour.

Johnson makes the useful distinction between atypical and abusive sexual behaviour: 'A behaviour that is not expected or considered 'normative' in children cannot necessarily be defined as abusive' (Johnson, 2005, p. 37). She cautions that the transformation of developmentally advanced sexual behaviour into abusive behaviour is a common mistake made by professionals. For example, oral–genital contact between pre-school children would not be considered normative, but this does not necessarily imply that one child has coerced the other child into engaging in this behaviour. Both children may have mutually agreed to engage in the behaviour, and this is often very difficult to establish, since, when questioned about this behaviour, children quickly sense that the behaviour is considered unacceptable by adults and often resort to denial or blaming each other.

Although this typology has not been subjected to clinical verification, it provides a very useful assessment tool, particularly in differentiating between children who do and do not require intervention to address their sexual behaviour. This is a critical component of any assessment of children who have been referred to services to address concerns about their sexual behaviour. A child who has merely been engaging in normative sexual behaviour, which has been misconstrued as sexually harmful by the adults who observed the behaviour, may be subjected to unnecessary intervention which is likely to impair their normative sexual development and cause undue stress to both them and their family. The consequences for the child in terms of their future life chances are potentially very damaging indeed.

Key issues to consider in assessments of children

1. Assessments need to be systemic and incorporate the views of the significant adults and professionals who have had involvement with the child and who can provide as much detailed information as possible about the child's concerning behaviour.

2. Information about the details of the child's sexually concerning behaviour needs to be systematically ascertained, including the nature and frequency of the behaviour, the child's responses to previous attempts made by adults to modify this behaviour and, in particular, any attempts made by the child to coerce or manipulate other children into engaging in sexual behaviour. Johnson has developed a child sexual behaviour checklist that can provide a useful template for the collation of this information (http://www.tcavjohn.com/products.php#Assessment).

3. Information about the child's developmental history and their current level of cognitive, behavioural and social functioning is also important in terms of informing how to engage the child in the assessment process and any recommended treatment programme.

4. The extent to which the child has been exposed to or involved in adult sexual activity, domestic violence, abusive and/or neglectful parenting or home environments that lack appropriate sexual boundaries and adequate adult supervision and care, all of which may have contributed to the child's problematic sexual behaviour.

5. The child's capacity to form positive relationships with other children and adults and any indication of attachment difficulties or other non-sexual behaviour problems.

6. The extent to which the child's parents or carers are concerned about the child's sexual behaviour, the steps they have taken to intervene to address the behaviour when appropriate, and their capacity to support the child in modifying their behaviour through the implementation of appropriate sexual boundaries within the home.

7. The child's strengths and other resilience factors that can be utilized to engage the child in working towards an abuse-free life.

Key issues to consider in treatment programmes developed for children

1. The available research on treatment outcomes (reviewed by Johnson, 2005, pp. 53–54) indicates that it is essential to involve parents and carers in parallel treatment work, either individually or in groups. This is particularly important in treatment work with young children, whose home environments, and in particular the behaviour of the adults who are responsible for their care, are often significant factors in precipitating and sustaining their harmful sexual behaviour. Parents and carers are also essential in supporting and reinforcing the child's learning of new behaviours and in monitoring the child's behaviour outside the treatment sessions.

2. It is also important that any treatment programme forms part of a broader, multi-agency plan to consider the safety of other children while the child receives help to modify his or her harmful sexual behaviour. Such plans need to be based in a developmental context and change as the child develops self-control and an improved understanding of appropriate sexual behaviour and boundaries. It is important that the child not remain isolated from other children indefinitely, and that they are given an opportunity to practice new social skills under appropriate adult guidance and supervision. This is essential to providing the child with a more positive sense of self and self-efficacy and can be a strong motivational factor in effectively engaging the child in the treatment process.

3. Cognitive behavioural, or psycho-sexual, educative approaches are considered most effective in helping children to differentiate between normative and sexually harmful behaviours and to learn new ways of meeting their emotional needs. A useful example of this approach is the 'Stop and Think' programme developed by Butler and Elliott (1999). This is a model of working with children aged 10 and under, utilizing an interpersonal problem-solving approach based on cognitive-behavioural theories. It can be used individually or with children in groups and helps the child to identify thoughts, feelings and actions in relation to their harmful sexual behaviour. Johnson has developed a

'Sexuality Curriculum for Abused Children and Young Adolescents, and Their Parents' (http://www.tcavjohn.com/products.php#Assessment), which is a useful educative resource for working with children and their carers.

4. A strengths- and resilience-based approach to treatment programmes is equally important to young children as well as for adolescents. In addition to work that focuses specifically on their concerning behaviour, it is also important that they are provided with opportunities to engage in activities that help them develop pro-social behaviour and to develop positive relationships with other children and adults.

5. Children who are known to have been sexually abused or subjected to other traumatic or abusive experiences may also require individual therapy specifically aimed at helping them to process this trauma.

CONCLUSIONS

We appear to have come full circle from the adoption of adult models of treatment, with an emphasis on a victim/perpetrator dichotomy and the coercion of young people to acknowledge and address their harmful behaviour, to a holistic, strengths-based approach which emphasizes the importance of the development of a therapeutic or professional relationship, based on collaboration and respect, with the young person, and which focuses on strengths, resilience and working towards a more positive abuse-free life. Such approaches, however, are time and resource intensive and do not represent the 'quick fix' that statutory funding bodies often expect when commissioning services for young people, particularly when the primary goal of the intervention is one of public protection. In the absence of a national strategy on the development and provision of these services, and a lack of clarity as to which agencies should fund or provide these services, together with a backdrop of public service budgetary constraints, there will continue to be tension between the development of services that can respond to the individual (and often longer-term) needs of the young people concerned and the need for these services to demonstrate 'evidence' of (often short-term) reductions in recidivism.

It is important, therefore, that assessment and treatment services are evaluated, both in terms of process and outcomes, to demonstrate their efficacy and hopefully increase the chances of these services being available to children and young people who need them. It is likely that, in keeping with research on early interventions work with the development of criminal behaviour in general, that this work may be more effective than later attempts to address this behaviour if it continues into adulthood.

The good practice that has developed in the assessment and treatment of children and adolescents may also helpfully inform such work with adult sex offenders – in particular, the emphasis on addressing the individual needs of the offenders, their developmental pathways into offending and the significance of any childhood trauma and attachment difficulties on the development of their sexual offending, and on their subsequent capacity to change this behaviour. This approach runs counter to the current standardized treatment programmes which assume that all adult sex offenders require the same intervention. Given the recent critique of these programmes, it is perhaps timely to consider the lessons that can be learned from the development of this work with children and adolescents.

FURTHER READING

McCrory, E. (2010). *A treatment manual for adolescents displaying harmful sexual behaviour: Change for good.* London: National Society for the Prevention of Cruelty to Children (NSPCC).

This book provides a useful overview of a strengths-based treatment programme informed by the good lives model, including a detailed outline of treatment sessions accompanied by a CD-ROM.

Johnson, T. C. (2009). *Helping children with sexual behavior problems: A guidebook for professionals and caregivers* (4th edn). www.tcavjohn.com.

This is an invaluable resource for practitioners who work with young children who have developed problematic sexual behaviour. Johnson has also developed a range of resources that can be used in assessment and treatment work with young children and their carers, which are available from her website.

Calder, M. C. (2008). Young people who sexually abuse: Risk refinement and conceptual developments. In M. C. Calder (Ed.), *Contemporary risk assessment in safeguarding children.* Dorset: Russell House Publishing.

This chapter provides a useful summary of the standardized assessment tools developed for working with adolescents with harmful sexual behaviour.

REFERENCES

Abel, G., Mittelman, M. S., & Becker, J. (1985). Sexual offenders: Results of assessment and recommendations for treatment. In H. H. Ben-Aron, S. I. Hucker, & C.D. Webster (Eds.), *Clinical criminology* (pp. 191–205). Toronto, Ontario, Canada: MM Graphics.

Bentovim, A. (1991). Children and young people as abusers. In A. Hollows & H. Armstrong (Eds.), *Children and young people as abusers: An agenda for action*. London. National Children's Bureau.

Butler, L., & Elliott, C. (1999). Stop and think: Changing sexually aggressive behaviour in young children. In M. Erooga & H. Masson (Eds.), *Children and young people who sexually abuse others* (pp. 183–203). London: Routledge.

Calder, M. C. (2001). *Juveniles and children who sexually abuse: Frameworks for assessments*. Dorset: Russell House Publishing.

Calder, M. C. (2008). Young people who sexually abuse: Risk refinement and conceptual developments. In M. C. Calder (Ed.), *Contemporary risk assessment in safeguarding children* (pp. 240–253). Dorset: Russell House Publishing.

Department of Health, Home Office and Department for Education and Employment (1999). *Working together to safeguard children: A guide to inter-agency working to safeguard and protect the welfare of children*. London: The Stationery Office.

Erikson, E. H. (1982). *The life cycle completed*. New York: Norton and Company.

Fonagy, P., Target, M., Cottrell, D., Phillips, J., & Kurtz, Z. (2005). *What works for whom? A critical review of treatments for children and adolescents*. New York: Other Press.

Hackett, S. (2004). *What works for children and young people with harmful sexual behaviours?* London: Barnardo's.

Hackett, S. (2006). Towards a resilience-based intervention model for young people with harmful sexual behaviours. In M. Erooga & H. Masson (Eds.), *Children and young people who sexually abuse others: Current developments and practice responses* (2nd edn). London: Routledge.

HM Inspectorate of Probation (2013). *Responses to children and young people who sexually offend: A joint inspection of the effectiveness of multi-agency work with children and young people in England and Wales who have committed sexual offences and were supervised in the community*. London: Ministry of Justice.

Hollows, A., & Armstrong, H. (Eds.). (1991). *Children and young people as abusers: An Agenda for action*. London: National Children's Bureau.

Johnson, T. C. (2005). Children with sexual behaviour problems: What have we learned in the last two decades? In M. Calder (Ed.), *Children and young people who sexually abuse: New theory, research and practice developments* (pp. 32–58). Dorset: Russell House Publishing.

Johnson, T. C. (2009). *Helping children with sexual behavior problems: A guidebook for professionals and caregivers* (4th edn). www.tcavjohn.com

Longo, R. E. (2002). A holistic approach to treating young people who sexually abuse. In M. Calder (Ed.), *Young people who sexually abuse: Building the evidence base for your practice*. Dorset: Russell House Publishing.

Longo, R. E., & Calder, M. C. (2005). The use of sex offender registration with young people who sexually abuse. In M. Calder (Ed.), *Children and young people who sexually abuse: New theory, research and practice developments* (pp. 334–352). Dorset: Russell House Publishing.

McCrory, E. (2010). *A treatment manual for adolescents displaying harmful sexual behaviour: Change for good*. London: National Society for the Prevention of Cruelty to Children (NSPCC).

Myers, S. (1998). Young people who sexually abuse: Is consensus possible or desirable? *Social Work in Europe, 5*(1), 53–56.

Nisbet, I. A. et al. (June 2004). A prospective longitudinal study of sexual recidivism among adolescent sex offenders. *Sexual Abuse: A Journal of Research and Treatment, 16*(3), 223–234.

NCH. (1992). *Report of the committee of enquiry into children and young people who sexually abuse other children*. London: NCH

Rich, P. (2011). *Understanding, assessing and rehabilitating juvenile sexual offenders*. New Jersey: John Wiley & Sons.

Ryan, G. (1986). An annotated bibliography: Adolescent perpetrators of sexual molestation of children. *Child Abuse and Neglect, 10*, 125–132.

Ryan, G. (1998). The relevance of early life experiences to the behaviour of sexually abusive youth. *Irish Journal of Psychology, 19*(1), 32–48.

Sanderson, C. (2004). *The seduction of children: Empowering parents and teachers to protect children from child sexual abuse*. London: Jessica Kingsley Publishers.

Santry, S., & McCarthy, G. (1999). Attachment and intimacy in young people who sexually abuse. In M. Calder (Ed.), *Working with young people who sexually abuse: New pieces of the jigsaw puzzle* (pp. 71–88). Dorset: Russell House Publishing.

Smallbone, S. W. (2005). Attachment insecurity as a predisposing and precipitating factor for sexually abusive behaviour by young people. In M. Calder (Ed.), *Children and young people who sexually abuse: New theory, research and practice developments* (pp. 6–18). Dorset: Russell House Publishing.

Steinberg, L. (2005). Cognitive and affective development in adolescence. *Trends in Cognitive Sciences, 9*(2), 69–74.

Towl, G. J., & Crighton, D. A. (2008). *Psychology in prisons* (2nd edn.). Oxford: Wiley-Blackwell.

Waite, D., Keller, A., McGarvey, E. L., Wieckowski, E., Pinkerton, R., & Brown, G. L. (July 2005). Juvenile sex offender re-arrest rates for sexual, Violent nonsexual and property crimes: A 10-year follow-up. *Sexual Abuse: A Journal of Research and Treatment, 17*(3), 313–331.

Ward, T. (2010). The good lives model of offender rehabilitation: Basic assumptions, etiological commitments, and practice implications. In F. McNeill, P. Raynor, & C. Trotter (Eds.), *Offender supervision: New directions in theory, research and practice* (pp. 41–64). Devon, UK: Willan Publishing.

Ward, T. (2011). *The good lives model of offender rehabilitation: A strengths based approach.* www.goodlivesmodel.com

Worling, J. R., & Curwen, T. (2001). Estimate of risk of adolescent sexual offense recidivism (Version 2.0: The 'ERASOR'). Reprinted in M. Calder (Ed.), *Juveniles and children who sexually abuse: Frameworks for assessment* (2nd edn, pp. 372–397). Dorset: Russell House Publishing.

Worling, J. R., Josefowitz, N., & Maltar, M. (2011). Reducing shame and increasing guilt and responsibility with adolescents who have offended sexually: A CBT-based treatment approach. In M. Calder (Ed.), *Contemporary practice with young people who sexually abuse: Evidence-based developments.* Dorset: Russell House Publishing.

22 Sexually Harmful Adults

BELINDA BROOKS-GORDON

This chapter provides a critical reflection of sexually harmful adults. First, the notion of sexual harm will be considered, then the theories that have been put forward to explain sexually harmful behaviour will be outlined, along with the tools that have been developed to assess the risk of sexually harmful behaviour. The treatments that are used in interventions to amend the behaviour of, or rehabilitate, sexually harmful adults will be described, and then an exploration will be undertaken of how, in an era of evidence-based treatment, these interventions are tested for their efficacy.

Sexual harm is also an intensely political issue, so the second part of this chapter provides a critical analysis of some of the main controversies surrounding sexually harmful behaviour. These controversies include (a) the increase over the past two decades in the variety and type of behaviours considered sexually harmful in legislation, (b) the disparity in policy between sexual harm and sexual offending, and (c) how public fear, and the political perception of public fear, can result in the overly mechanist application of tools and policies to manage risk. These three issues will be discussed to show how some contemporary measures to reduce risk may be counterproductive and may actually result in greater risk for the vulnerable and others for whose protection the measures were intended.

WHO AND WHAT IS A SEXUALLY HARMFUL ADULT?

A sexually harmful adult is someone over the age of 18 years of age whose behaviour to another person causes harm. Such behaviour may be sexual in and of itself or the behaviour may result in sexual behaviour of another. Sexually harmful behaviours can be divided into contact

and non-contact behaviours (Craig, Browne, & Beech, 2008). Non-contact behaviours include exhibitionism and the viewing of child pornography. Sexually harmful contact behaviours include rape of a male or female, and sexual assault on a minor under 16 years of age (often called 'child molestation' and sometimes associated with paedophilia). A sexually harmful adult may be male or female, but research indicates that sexual harm is predominantly a male activity with 80–95% of contact sex offences being committed by men. They may be highly intelligent, socially skilled, or have a low IQ, be learning disabled and not fully understand the consequences of their actions (Cantor, Blanchard, Robichaud, & Christensen, 2005).[1]

PREVALENCE AND INCIDENCE[2] OF SEXUALLY HARMFUL BEHAVIOURS

While overall police-recorded sexual crimes increased during the last decade from 33,090 to 53,540 incidents, there was a reduction of 7% in police-recorded sexual offences in 2008 on the previous year. So the process was obviously not one of continuous increase; indeed, any rise in the most serious sexual crimes (including rapes, sexual assaults and sexual activity with children) halted with a peak in the middle of the previous decade and figures have fallen every year since. For example, the most serious sexual crimes numbered 31,334 crimes in 1997, peaking in 2003–2004 at 48,732 crimes and falling every year since to the recent figure of 41,460 incidents in the 2007–2008 survey (Kershaw, Nicholas, & Walker, 2008), whereas less serious sexual offences (which include soliciting, prostitution

Forensic Psychology, Second Edition. Edited by David A. Crighton and Graham J. Towl.
© 2015 John Wiley & Sons, Ltd. Published 2015 by British Psychological Society and John Wiley & Sons, Ltd.

offences and unlawful sexual activity between consenting adults) increased from 1756 in 1997 to a peak of 15,320 in 2004–2005 following the creation of many controversial new offences in the Sexual Offences Act 2003 (see Bainham & Brooks-Gordon, 2004). The number of incidents subsequently fell to 12,080 in 2007–2008.

Police-recorded crime, however, is subject to the vagaries of reporting whereas victim surveys such as the British Crime Survey are not affected by changes in reporting, police recording or local police activity, and it has been measured in a consistent way since the survey began in 1981. Such surveys show that that a proportion of violent and sexual crimes are not reported. Non-reporting occurs most commonly because victims feel the police could not do anything, or the victim may consider the issue to be a private matter and wish to deal with it themselves. It can be inconvenient to report, or an incident may be reported to other authorities. There may be fear of reprisal or a dislike or fear of the police, especially if there has been previous bad experience with the police or the courts. All of these issues may affect the reporting of sexually harmful behaviour.

While self-report surveys provide a better estimate of hidden crimes such as intimate violence, victim willingness to disclose incidents may depend on the sensitivity of the information, and this can be difficult to disclose face to face. For this reason British Crime Survey (BCS) interviews since 2004–2005 have included self-completion modules on intimate violence (for those aged 16–59 years of age). Based on the 2006–2007 BCS self-completion module on intimate violence, approximately 3% of women and 1% of men had experienced a sexual assault (including attempts) in the previous 12 months. The majority of these were accounted for by less serious sexual assaults. Less than 1% of both men and women reported having experienced a serious sexual assault (Kershaw et al., 2008).

Despite increased public and legal awareness of sexually harmful behaviour, the measures above show that some behaviour goes unreported and therefore undetected and unconvicted. The raft of historic offences only just being uncovered by Operation Yewtree into behaviour by well-known personalities such as Jimmy Savile and Max Clifford illustrates how victims fear to come forward, and think that even if they do, they will not be believed against a powerful or manipulative abuser. Yet, research has focused on the subset of individuals who are reported, detected, arrested and convicted.[3] The evidence base must therefore be interpreted with this bias to the fore (see Crighton & Towl, 2007).

THEORIES OF SEXUALLY HARMFUL BEHAVIOUR

There are five main theories of why adults sexually harm others. According to Palmer (2008), these are: the preconditions model; quadripartite model; the pathways model; interaction model; and the integrated model.

'Four Preconditions' model (Finkelhor, 1984)

This is a model to explain sexually harmful behaviour towards a child. The model proposes that there are four steps or preconditions that must take place before an adult commits child sexual abuse: (1) motivation – in which there is *sexual arousal* towards a child, *emotional congruence* with a child, and *blockage* whereby the adult's sexual needs are not met by a suitable sexual partner; (2) internal inhibition to cause sexual harm must be overcome – whereby self-regulation against the behaviour is overridden by internal factors such as distorted beliefs about the harm caused, or by the disinhibiting effect of alcohol, drugs or extreme stress; (3) external inhibition must be overcome – such as gaining the trust of the child or their family; (4) resistance of the child must be overcome – through strategies such as force, fear, bribery or other grooming techniques.

Quadripartite model (Hall & Hirschman, 1992)

This is a model to explain sexually harmful behaviour to a child or adult and it also accounts for the differences between adults who sexually harm children. The theory suggests that sexually harmful behaviour requires the following conditions: (1) deviant physiological sexual arousal (or preference) to a child; (2) distorted beliefs of children as competent sexual partners able to make decisions about sexual activity; (3) emotional disturbance or lack of emotional management or control; and (4) problematic personality traits and/or vulnerability from own adverse early experiences.

Integrated theory (Marshall & Barbaree, 1990)

This is a general model to explain all sexually harmful behaviour. It aims to explain the background of such behaviour through early attachment and experiences. It suggests that poor early experiences lead to low self-worth, poor emotional regulation, poor problem-solving and inadequate social coping. Such states can all be reinforced by difficult social interactions with peer groups and prospective sexual partners and reinforced by other cultural influences such as the media or social norms. All of these developmental, sociocultural and situational factors make people vulnerable to being psychologically inadequate as well as being susceptible to inappropriate sexual and antisocial behaviour.

Pathways model (Ward & Siegart, 2002)

This is a theory which combines elements of all the above models into a more complex and comprehensive understanding of sexually harmful behaviour towards children. It is maintained that early life experience, biological factors and cultural influences may lead to vulnerability, which can lead to deviant sexual preferences, intimacy deficits, inappropriate emotions and/or cognitive distortions. These four issues can be dismantled into smaller components which are organized into pathways that lead to the abusive behaviour of a child (see Ward, Polaschek, & Beech, 2006 for further analysis of and a unified theory using these components). It is probably the most influential model of sexually harmful behaviour in research and practice today.

Confluence model of sexual aggression (Malamuth, Heavey, & Linz, 1993)

This peripheral model is a theory, and one of rape only, which suggests that rape occurs when two paths, sexual promiscuity and hostile masculinity, meet and provide the site for rape to take place. It draws on social learning and feminist theory of a certain type of risk-taking, dominant, competitive male who enjoys power to try to explain the role of sexual behaviour in maintaining self-esteem and peer status. However, this theory remains to be validated using a sample known to have committed sexually harmful behaviours, and is less widely adhered to than the above models.

Evolutionary theory of sexual offending (Thornhill & Palmer, 2000)

Even more controversially, this model dismisses the influence of culture and psychological strategies of power and control to suggest that rape is a result of evolutionary mating strategies. It puts forward a notion that males have evolved with profound sexual desire in order to pass on genes, and this manifests itself in the motivation for sexual activity and the need for multiple partners. Its proponents suggest that rape would only be employed when the conditions are favourable; these would include lack of psychological or physical resources,

social alienation, limited sexual access to females, and unsatisfying sexual relationships (Craig et al., 2008).

There are, of course, questions to be asked of all of these theories and in all cases explanatory power is limited when tested against the circumstances and victims of sexually harmful acts. For example, the Thornhill and Palmer (2000) theory does not explain why men would rape non-procreative beings such as men or children. The confluence model does not explain why female adults carry out sexually harmful behaviour.

ASSESSING THE RISK OF SEXUALLY HARMFUL ADULTS

The utility of risk prediction is that it is possible to prevent the circumstances under which a sexually harmful act may occur. These include the ability: (1) to identify high-risk groups from early antecedents of later harmful behaviour, with a view to providing preventative services; (2) to construct aetiological theories in the view that antecedent correlates of behaviour *may* equate to causes, and (3) to derive predictive information for use in criminal justice decision-making, for example, in placement or release decisions (Blackburn, 1995). A number of psychometric instruments have been devised to determine risk and these divide into actuarial and clinical risk prediction instruments. Actuarial or statistical predictive indices objectively indicate an optimal decision, whereas clinical prediction involves a subjective evaluation of risk based on the client as well as clinical experience of the client group.

Although there continues to be opposition to the use of actuarial risk scales, these scales are in general use in the field of risk assessment and prediction of violent and sexually harmful behaviours and recidivism (Harris, Rice, Lalumière, Boer, & Lang, 2003).

There are four main actuarial instruments currently in use for sexually harmful behaviour. These include the Violence Risk Appraisal Guide (VRAG; Harris, Rice, & Quinsey, 1998), the Sex Offender Risk Appraisal Guide (SORAG; Quinsey, Harris, Rice, & Cormier, 1998), the Rapid Risk Assessment for Sexual Offense Recidivism (RRASOR; Hanson, 1997), and the STATIC-99 (Hanson & Thornton, 2000).

The VRAG (Harris et al., 1998) was developed for use with men known to have committed a violent offence (whether sexual or not) and to predict any new sexual or violent contact offences. It contains 12 items and the item weights are based on the empirical relationship between the predictor and violent behaviours. Individuals are assigned to one of nine risk categories on the basis of their scores. The Hare Psychopathy Checklist (PCL-R; Hare, 1993, 2003) is a major part of the VRAG and is the biggest influence on overall score. The PCL-R scores are based on semi-structured interviews and a review of the file information.[4] It aims to measure characteristics such as impulsivity, irresponsibility and callousness. The SORAG is a modification of the VRAG, with 14 items (10 common to the VRAG), and is designed to predict violent recidivism in men who have already committed sexually harmful contact behaviour. Again the PCL-R score is the most influential.

The RRASOR (Hanson, 1997) was developed for men who have been convicted of at least one sexual offence and is designed specifically to predict sexual recidivism. It has four items: number of prior charges or convictions for sexual offences; age upon release from prison or anticipated opportunity to reoffend in the community; any male victims; or any unrelated victims. Items on the scale are weighted to reflect the magnitude of its relationship with sexual recidivism. The STATIC-99 (Hanson & Thornton, 2000) was developed for men who were known to have committed at least one sexual offence. It is designed to predict either violent recidivism or specifically sexually recidivism. It has ten items, of which four are the same as the RRASOR, and it was constructed by combining the RRASOR with a non-actuarial instrument. On the basis of their score, individuals are allocated to one of seven risk categories.

All the preceding are actuarial risk scales which are objectively scored and give probabilistic estimates of risk based on the established empirical relationship between their items and the outcome (i.e., sexual harm). Probabilistic estimates suggest the percentage of people with the same score who would be expected to harm sexually within a specified period of opportunity. These scales have good predictive validity and have been cross-validated in new samples of those who sexually harm. The scales contain similar items because they were all empirically derived and their developers drew upon the same sex offender recidivism literature for items (Seto, 2005).

INTERVENTIONS FOR SEXUALLY HARMFUL ADULTS

Psychological interventions, including behavioural, cognitive-behavioural and psychodynamic therapies, are all used to help change the behaviour of sexually harmful adults. In addition, drug treatment may be given alongside or instead of these therapies. Cognitive-behavioural interventions are the basis of sex offender treatment in prison systems and community programmes in England, Canada, New Zealand and the United States (Ministry of Justice, 2010). In the UK National Health Service, however, psychodynamic approaches are common (Grubin, 2002).

Behavioural interventions are associated with traditional classical and operant learning theory and are generally referred to as behaviour modification or behaviour therapy. The hallmark of these interventions is an explicit focus on changes in behaviour by administering a stimulus and measuring its effect upon overt behaviour. Within sex offender treatment this is often used to address deviant sexual interest alongside penile plethysmography (PPG) for 'objective' measurement. Examples include aversion therapy (exposure to deviant material followed by aversive stimulus), covert sensitization (imagine deviant sexual experience until arousal and then imagine a powerful negative experience), olfactory conditioning (an unpleasant odour is paired with a high-risk sexual situation) and masturbation satiation/orgasmic reconditioning (masturbation to an appropriate sexual fantasy).

A range of interventions falls under the heading of cognitive-behavioural treatment. These interventions have been characterized on a continuum, in the middle of which are interventions seeking to change the individual's internal (cognitive and emotional) functioning as well as their overt behaviour (McGuire, 2000). This best represents cognitive-behavioural treatment as that which has developed from social learning theory. Finally, there are cognitive therapies in which the focus is exclusively on changing some aspect of the individual's cognition. This approach is arguably more likely to have a base in some variant of cognitive theory, such as information processing, than in learning theory. Cognitive-behavioural treatment attempts to change internal processes – thoughts, beliefs, emotions, physiological arousal – alongside changing overt behaviour, such as social skills or coping behaviours. Cognitive behavioural therapy is where the intervention involves: (a) recipients establishing links between their thoughts, feelings and actions with respect to target symptom/s; (b) correction of persons' misperceptions, irrational beliefs and reasoning biases related to target symptom/s; and (c) either or both of the following: (i) recipients monitoring their own thoughts, feelings and behaviours with respect to target symptom/s, and (ii) promotion of alternative ways of coping with target symptom/s.

Psychodynamic psychotherapy involves regular individual therapy sessions with a trained psychotherapist, or a therapist under supervision. Therapy sessions are based on a variety of psychodynamic or psychoanalytic models. Sessions rely on a variety of strategies, including explorative insight-orientated, supportive or directive activity, applied flexibly with therapists working with transference (the unconscious transfer of feelings to a person which do not befit that person and which actually apply to another; Greenson, 1967). Psychoanalytic interventions are many and various but usually include regular individual sessions with a trained psychoanalyst three to five times a week working at the infantile sexual relations level of psychoanalytic theory.

Drug treatments administered specifically for sexually harmful behaviour or impulses are sometimes incorrectly referred to as 'chemical castration' or more correctly 'pharmacological diminution of an abnormal sex drive'. These drugs include leuprorelin (Prostap), which switches off the production of testosterone. High testosterone levels are linked with an abnormally high sex drive in paedophiles. Other drugs, such as cyproterone (Androcur), work in a different way, by opposing the action of testosterone in the body instead of interfering with its production. The effect is the same and results in a lowered or absent sex drive and an inability to have sex. Some sexually harmful men are treated with flouxetine (Prozac), an antidepressant that is also prescribed for obsessive compulsive disorders (OCD) along with psychological therapy.

MEASURING INTERVENTIONS

The rise of evidence-based medicine, the philosophical origins of which extend back to mid-nineteenth-century Paris, has influenced ways of working with those who sexually harm others. Evidence-based practice is the 'conscientious, explicit, and judicious use of current best evidence in making decisions about the care of individual patients' (Sackett, Rosenberg, Gray, Haynes, & Richardson, 1996). The practice of evidence-based medicine means integrating individual clinical expertise with the best available external clinical evidence from systematic research. By clinical expertise, Sackett *et al.* (1996) mean the proficiency and judgement that individual clinicians acquire through clinical experience and clinical practice. They suggest that when asking questions about therapy 'we should try to avoid the non-experimental approaches, since these routinely lead to false positive conclusions about efficacy. Because the randomized trial, and especially the systematic review of several randomized trials, is so much more likely to inform and so much less likely to mislead us' (p. 72). Evidence-based practice is a key feature of psychological interventions and rehabilitative therapies for this group of people within the prison service (Crighton & Towl, 2008).

PAST META-ANALYSES OF INTERVENTIONS WITH SEXUALLY HARMFUL ADULTS

Hall (1995) carried out a meta-analysis of 12 studies that compared sexual offender treatment with a comparison condition (alternative treatment or no treatment) and provided recidivism data for sexual offences. A small overall effect size was found for institutionalized treatment, and a medium effect size for outpatient samples. Both cognitive-behavioural and hormonal treatments appeared to be superior to behavioural treatments, although a possible criticism of Hall (1995) is that it may have overestimated the effectiveness of treatment because of its use of official recidivism data, which may underestimate actual sexually aggressive behaviour. The results suggested that the effect of treatment with sexual offenders was robust, albeit small, and that treatment was most effective with outpatient participants and when it consisted of hormonal or cognitive-behavioural treatments. A subsequent Cochrane review of randomized controlled trials (RCTs) identified only two relevant studies (total $n = 286$) and no clear effects of relapse prevention/group therapy (White, Bradley, Ferriter, & Hatzipetrou, 2000).

In a later meta-analysis, Gallagher, Wilson, Hirschfield, Coggeshall, & MacKenzie (1999) quantitatively synthesized the results of 22 studies (25 treatment comparisons) evaluating the effectiveness of different types of treatment for sexual offenders. Like Hall (1995), cognitive-behavioural therapies were considered promising while less support was found for behavioural, chemical and more general psychosocial therapies. Some of the studies had problematic threats to validity because they involved comparisons between treatment completers and non-completers. This is important, because it is acknowledged amongst practitioners that non-completers are more likely to reoffend.

In Hanson *et al.* (2002), most of the results were based on matching/incident assignment studies. In incidental assignment studies, comparison groups were selected from offenders in which there were no reasons to expect differences in the treatment group. That analysis showed for the first time a significant difference between recidivism rates for sex offenders who were treated and those who were not, suggested Hanson's team. The study revealed, among the research sample, sexual recidivism rates of 17.3% for untreated offenders, compared with 9.9% for treated offenders. Though that is not a large reduction, the large sample size and widely agreed-upon research methods make it statistically reliable and of practical significance.

Hanson, Broom, and Stephenson (2004) found that examination of individual treatment programmes did not yield any difference in recidivism rates. While the study did not allow conclusions about what was effective or ineffective in the CSOP (Community Sex Offender Program) interventions, the findings do suggest that some 'highly plausible interventions may have little overall effect' and the findings of the review certainly contrast with the positive effects of cognitive-behavioural treatment found in previous reviews (e.g., Gallagher et al., 1999, Hanson et al., 2002). Controversy remains as to the merits of treatment, and the relevant evaluative research on the effectiveness of psychological treatments for sexual offenders is not straightforward (Quinsey et al., 1998). Disappointing results from interventions in England and Wales have been discussed by proponents of treatment who suggest that greater effects might be present yet only detectable using more sensitive psychometric measurement instead of reconviction data (Friendship, Falshaw, & Beech, 2003).

Losel and Schmucker (2005) reported a meta-analysis on controlled outcome evaluations of interventions for sexual offenders. Allowing a wide remit for acceptable studies, the 69 studies containing 80 independent comparisons between 'treated' and 'untreated' offenders. Effects for violent and general recidivism were in a similar range. Medical treatments such as surgical castration or pharmaceutical medication showed larger effect sizes than psychosocial interventions. Of the psychological interventions, cognitive-behavioural approaches had the most robust effect. Overall, Losel and Schmucker found a 6 percentage point reduction in sexual recidivism following treatment, compared to untreated controls (see also Schmucker & Losel, 2008).

Langstrom et al. (2013) explored RCTs and prospective observational studies and found eight studies with low to moderate risk of bias and found weak evidence for interventions aimed at reducing reoffending in identified sexual abusers of children.

The largest systematic study was carried out by Brooks-Gordon et al. (2006) and also published as a Cochrane review. This study reports a systematic review of RCTs reporting the effectiveness of sexual offender treatment programmes. Electronic and hand searches were carried out for RCTs published between 1998 and 2003. Searches resulted in nine RCTs and these contained data on interventions for 567 men, 231 of whom were followed up for a decade. Analysis of the nine trials showed that cognitive-behavioural therapy in groups reduced reoffence at one year for child-molesters compared with standard care ($n = 155$). When CBT was compared with a trans-theoretical counselling group

therapy, the former may have increased poor attitudes to treatment. The largest trial compared broadly psychodynamic group therapy with no treatment for 231 men guilty of paedophilia, exhibitionism or sexual assault. Rearrest over 10 years was greater for those allocated to group therapy. These findings and the subsequent use of RCTs in clinical policy and research are important, because while they may not be popular with those who want to believe that current interventions work for all sexually harmful men forever, they raise important conceptual questions about interventions for sexual harm. For example, do interventions need to be longer term, with community-based relapse prevention (such as Alcoholics Anonymous)? In a parallel study, the same authors (Bilby et al., 2006) also analysed quasi-experimental outcome evaluations and process evaluations in qualitative studies.

Harkins and Beech (2006) review the various research methods of examining treatment effectiveness, and random assignment, risk band analysis and matched control groups are discussed. They conclude that different designs confer different advantages and also have methodological shortcomings. While there are those who feel that only the most scientifically rigorous methodology must be employed if one hopes to draw meaningful conclusions, others feel that less stringent criteria in terms of comparison groups can yield meaningful inferential results. As a means of overcoming some of the shortcomings of recidivism outcome studies discussed, they suggest that the examination of more proximate outcomes, such as change within treatment, provide a useful addition to studies of treatment effectiveness (Harkins & Beech, 2006). The last two meta-analytic reviews reported here represent the two sides of this equation. The strictly defined Brooks-Gordon et al. (2006) review conforms to the rigorous Cochrane collaboration methodology to provide a stringent evidence-based measure which meets the so-called 'gold standard'. And the other reviews, by Schmucker and Losel (2008) and Langstrom et al. (2013), take the wider, more pragmatic remit in which treatment usually takes place in England and Wales.[5]

There are enormous difficulties in carrying out RCTs to evaluate interventions with sexually harmful adults. RCTs are often complex and difficult to carry out. It is not ethical to carry out double-blind randomized trials in which neither participant nor clinician knows which group an individual had been allocated to and then wait for the individual to produce sexually harmful behaviour. There is also controversy regarding denial of treatment to this population. Given the belief inherent in policy that treatment works, despite weak evidence, there are human rights and ethical implications should a potentially helpful treatment be withheld within a controlled trial, not to mention implications for future potential victims. It is feasible that such a study could deny a sexually harmful adult an effective treatment, and could also affect the security classification of such a prisoner and decisions regarding parole (Friendship, Beech, & Browne, 2002). Prisoners allocated to non-treatment groups could be denied an intervention package that could affect their chances of early release or re-categorization to a lower security level (Hood, Shute, Feilzer, & Wilcox, 2002). And as Prentky and Schwartz (2006) have pointed out: 'treatment is not likely to be effective for all offenders and that treatment is likely to be effective for some offenders. Essentially, such a conclusion is accurate and, for most of us, obvious. Given the extraordinary variation in sex offenders, it would be only logical that some, but not all, offenders would benefit from treatment. Stated otherwise, treatment undoubtedly will help to restore some offenders to a non-offending lifestyle and will fail to touch other offenders.' It is therefore important to ascertain with as much accuracy as possible whose behaviour is made less harmful by interventions.

IMPROVING THE QUALITY OF TREATMENT OUTCOME

A collaboration formed to ascertain the quality of sexual offender treatment outcome research recommended that interventions use strong research designs, including random assignment to treatment and comparison conditions. It was also recommended that offenders are matched on risk prior to being assigned to treatment. Random assignment studies are politically unpopular and difficult to implement, but the benefits of these studies are such that researchers should advocate for random assignment studies whenever possible. Researchers using random assignment studies, however, should be prepared for breakdown in the randomization procedure. Consequently, it was recommended that all participants (treatment and control) should be assessed pre-treatment on risk-relevant variables, and that researchers are vigilant to problems of treatment integrity, attrition, and crossover (comparison group receiving equivalent services) (Beech *et al.*, 2007).

But many difficulties still hamper researchers wishing to undertake evaluative studies and, as a result, RCTs are seldom undertaken in criminal justice settings. In such a situation, the 'next best' evidence has to be considered. Not surprisingly, there are a number of pragmatic trials carried out in quasi-experimental designs. In addition, more sophisticated randomized research designs, which address some of the difficulties associated with traditional RCTs such as cluster randomization, might profitably be explored for the evaluation of programmes.

CLUSTER RANDOMIZATION

Increasingly, 'cluster randomization' is employed in medical or educational interventions where traditional randomization trials are not possible. It is a method whereby clusters of individuals rather than independent individuals are randomly allocated to intervention groups. In the case of those who have sexually harmful behaviour, this could be in secure communities or secure accommodation unit clusters. This approach has many advantages. The reasons for adopting this method might be: administrative convenience, to obtain cooperation of investigations, ethical considerations, to enhance participant compliance, to avoid treatment group compliance, and/or to apply the intervention naturally at cluster level. An important property of cluster randomization trials is that inferences are frequently intended to apply at the individual level while randomization is at group or cluster level. Thus the unit of randomization may be different from the unit of analysis.

Analysis and pooling of clustered data, however, does pose some problems. The lack of independence among individuals in the same cluster (i.e., between-cluster variation of different offender characteristics such as motivation could be due to differences in characteristics of the therapist) can create methodological challenges in both design and analysis. Authors must account for intra-class correlation in clustered studies, to avoid 'unit of analysis' error (Divine, Brown, & Frazer, 1992) which pushes down p values and could lead to overestimating statistical significance and to Type I errors (Bland & Kerry, 1997; Gulliford, Ukoumunne, & Chinn, 1999). In addition, loss of precision can also occur due to: the intervention being applied on a group basis with little or no attention paid to individual study participants; permitting the entry of new participants to a group (cluster) after baseline; entire clusters, rather than individuals, being lost to follow-up; overoptimistic expectations regarding effect size.

Precision can be improved in cluster randomization trials, argue Donner and Klar (2000), first by establishing a cluster-level eligibility criterion to reduce between-cluster variability, second by increasing the number of clusters randomized, even if only in the control group. Then match or stratify the design by a baseline variable having prognostic importance. Also, obtain baseline measures of other possible prognostic variables, and take repeated assessments over time from the same clusters or from different clusters of subjects. Finally, develop a detailed protocol for ensuring compliance and minimizing loss to follow-up. Interpretational difficulties will be present, and the ratio of the total number of participants required using cluster randomization to the number required using simple randomization is called the 'design effect'. Thus, a cluster randomized trial which has a large design effect will require many more participants than a trial of the same intervention which randomizes individuals (Kerry & Bland, 1998).

So far, this chapter has explored the theories of sexually harmful behaviour by adults, the ways in which risk is assessed in these adults, and if risk is present, what interventions can be used to address and/or change behaviour. In addition, the first section of the chapter explored how the effectiveness of interventions is measured. While none of these issues is without controversy, there are major controversies around what actually constitutes sexual harm and what steps are legitimate to monitor risk. The next section of this chapter proceeds to discuss these two major issues.

WHEN THE 'SEX OFFENDER' IS NOT SEXUALLY HARMFUL

There has been a marked increase over the past two decades in the variety and type of sexual behaviours criminalized in legislation as policy makers have responded to calls for action with unparalleled increases in legislation. This occurred most notably in the Sexual Offences Act 2003 and has continued ever since – in the Criminal Justice and Immigration Act 2008, and the Policing and Crime Act 2009. The review of sexual offences, *Setting the Boundaries*, took the view that what was wrong in sexual relationships depended upon the principle of *harm* and an assessment of harm done to the individual. However, that which is 'sexual' was defined in the Sexual Offences Act 2003 to be what 'a reasonable person' would consider to be 'sexual' (s.70), and this broad statutory definition is highly problematic.

There is a difference between being sexually harmful and being a sexual offender. For example, in a year when there were 25,000 offenders on the sexual offenders register, only 26 had committed a serious sexual or violent offence (*Daily Telegraph*, 2004). One of the reasons for this is that the number of new sexual offences on the statute book has increased, many of which have little to do with sexual harm and more to do with regulating behaviour or appeasing a perceived public understanding of safety. There were 62,081 recorded sexual offences in England and Wales from 2005 to 2006 (Walker, Kershaw, & Nicholas, 2006) but not all sexually harmful behaviours

will necessarily be recorded as offences, and many sexual offences will not be sexually harmful.

Adult women working in prostitution who are good parents and adults may, because of their working lives in the commercial sex industry, end up with a conviction for prostitution. This conviction now constitutes a sexual offence. Those working in the sex industry who, because they wish to keep their working lives separate from their home lives, or for reasons of safety or company wish to work with other sex workers, prefer to rent rooms or work in a sauna or 'parlour'. Yet, those renting out rooms or running parlours (often ex-sex workers or past receptionists, known as 'maids') now fall foul of the laws on brothel-keeping and on conviction are subject to a 2-year sentence according to Sentencing Guidelines Council recommendations under laws of brothel-keeping. This too counts as a sexual offence. These two examples show how misleading the statutory categories are.

The ultimate sanction of the criminal law, however, should be used sparingly and only for those behaviours which are demonstrably harmful. There has a been a highly punitive legislative approach resulting in the criminalization, as opposed to toleration of, sexual diversity (Bainham & Brooks-Gordon, 2004) and this has created a situation whereby what is a sexual offence is not that which is necessarily sexually harmful. And this situation even extends to so-called 'child offences' whereby two young people under the age of 16 years engaged in mutual sexual experimentation are breaking the law.

THE POLITICIZATION OF SEXUAL HARM

The electorate and the media expect policy makers to be accountable for the effects of their responses to sexual offending (Hansard, 2002). The politicization of sexual harm, following a number of high-profile child murders and with politicians aware of global media coverage, added to the statute book new laws in England and Wales and new punitive measures to old laws, in an up-tariffing and redefining of what is sexually harmful. In the United States, such concerns led to Megan's Law in 1996, which allows private and personal information on those registered as sex offenders against children to be made available to the community (Office of the Attorney General, 2004). One of the many examples of political or populist punitiveness in England and Wales came in the Sexual Offences Act which also redefined 'child' as a person under 18 years of age, which would have the effect of criminalizing a same-age couple sending pictures to each other over the Internet.

In the United Kingdom, provisions in the Sexual Offences Act 2003 included substantial increases in sentence length for many sexual offences and increased state control, in terms of notification requirements and supervision, for up to 10 years after a sentence has been spent. Exaggerating the risk of sexual harm is problematic and may increase public fear, and stigmatize and hinder rehabilitation of offenders who have changed their lifestyles, while wasting valuable resources on unnecessary surveillance (Soothill, Francis, Sanderson, & Ackerley, 2000).

SEXUAL HARM AND THE CULTURE OF FEAR

From 2002, anyone who worked with children in any capacity (even as a volunteer) had to be vetted by the Criminal Records Bureau (CRB). This followed the deaths of Holly Wells and Jessica Chapman who were murdered by the school caretaker Ian Huntley, and suspicion of grown-up behaviour towards children has fostered a climate in which it has become normal for some parents to trust only adults who possess official clearance. In some quarters it is argued that the culture of 'vetting' is damaging relationships with adults and children, and the moral panic over paedophilia has arguably become a panic bordering on hysteria.

The 'War on Terror' has polarized ideas of security vs. liberty; this, a political practice, a speech act, is *one* way of framing, naming and constructing problems. It seeks to mobilize forces behind the idea that 'we' face a threat that calls for immediate decisions and special measures, argues Loader (2006). Legislative hyperactivity articulates genuine public insecurities about crime, immigration and social disorder. It generates a climate that inhibits, even actively deters, critical scrutiny of the state's claims and practices, and risks fostering a vicious circle of insecurity (atrocity–fear–tough response–atrocity) that ratchets up state powers in ways that become difficult to temper, dismantle and reverse.

In a report called *Licensed to Hug* for the think-tank, Civitas, Furedi and Bristow (2008) show how adults have become less inclined to volunteer for mundane activities such as school trips, cricket umpiring or football coaching because they are fearful of being thought predatory or sexually harmful adults. The authors state that the whole notion of harm requires re-examination as 'child protection policies are poisoning the relationship between the generations and damaging the voluntary sector' (Furedi & Bristow, 2008). In addition, parents were sceptical about the efficacy of the vetting procedure and felt it was burdensome and confusing.

Institutionalization of the vetting of adults with CRB checks

Since October 2009, adults have had to register with the new Independent Safeguarding Authority (ISA), so it is estimated that one in four (or 11.3 million) people have been affected by the scheme. The alleged protective effects of a system of vetting are considered to be largely illusory by Furedi and Bristow (2008), who conclude that the national vetting scheme represents an exercise in impression management rather than offering effective protection. Aside from the fallibility of record-keeping and technical systems, vetting only takes account of what someone has done in the past; it cannot anticipate what they may do in future. The situation de-skills adults, who then also have a diminished sense of responsibility towards children. Adults feel increasingly nervous around children, unwilling to exercise authority or play a positive role. Such intergenerational unease has not made children safer in the past but rather creates conditions for greater harm, as adults lose the nerve or will to look out for any child that is not their own (see also Furedi, 2005). Perversely, it encourages adults to avoid their responsibility to look out for the well-being of children in their community. Thus, the policy of attempting to prevent paedophiles coming into contact with children will result in the estrangement of all children from all adults – the very people who would otherwise protect them from paedophiles and other dangers.

While fear and risk were explored in the 1990s through 'ontological insecurity' in a risk society (Bauman, 2000; Beck, 1992). Walklate and Mythen (2008) take this further to argue that the view has developed to the extent that if risk constitutes one side of ontological security, then trust and trust relationships comprise the other. They question the extent to which forensic research has fully accounted for the impacts of global structures and processes that shape human agency on the formation of individual anxieties, and state that, notwithstanding the efforts of Gadd and Jefferson (2007), 'fear-of-crime' research 'has not adequately appreciated the full macro climate of this doubt and uncertainty or the way in which it articulates with localized individual experience' (p. 215). Governments become embroiled in the politics of fear, and widespread practices and processes result in the paralysis of the 'culture of fear' where not just individuals but whole communities are being scrutinized and surveyed as subject identities are made up through risk discourses, socially determined according to whether they fit the profile of offenders or innocents. A situation then reigns whereby the risk of sexual harm is greater than before.

CONCLUSIONS

This chapter has explored sexual harm by outlining firstly the theories that have been developed to understand the behaviour. It proceeded to discuss the interventions currently used to rehabilitate sexually harmful behaviours, and how those treatments have been evaluated and measured, before going on to discuss the difficulties in measurement and evaluation in meta-analytic studies, the ethics of such analysis and ways of overcoming such pitfalls.

The second part of the chapter shows how sexual harm has become a major challenge for social policy, and the social and political panic around sexual offending and sexual harm is discussed, showing how more laws were introduced to appease perceived public disquiet. The law is now so encompassing that even consensual adult activity in private has become confused in statute with sexual offending. In this way, the law fails to equate sexual harm with sexual offending, and the result is confusion, conflict and further strain on stretched resources. The consequence has been to foster a climate of concern around children that has resulted in fewer activities for them to do, less freedom and therefore less ability to deal with risk. The resulting culture of fear is, it is argued, a threat to security and safety.

NOTES

1 These authors found that although adult males who commit sexual offences scored lower on IQ tests overall than adult males who commit non-sexual offences, IQ differences did not occur across all sexual offender subtypes – the younger the victim age, the lower the sample group's mean IQ. Non-sexual offenders' IQs equated to general population means.

2 The terms prevalence and incidence are not synonymous. How widespread a practice is at a single point in time (its prevalence) and how often it occurs (its incidence) are different entities. A sexually harmful behaviour may be highly prevalent (i.e., be widespread) but have low incidence (i.e., not occur frequently). An example of this is rape by an adult known to the adult victim or so-called 'date-rape'. Other behaviours may not be so prevalent in the population(s) studied but may have high incidence. An example of this might be abuse by teachers of their pupils, whereby the frequency of the abuse happening may be high to one individual but the prevalence of such abuse in the teacher population (and indeed the pupil population) may be low.

3 The bias is greater in research in England and Wales than in the United States where self-referral and diversion schemes operate for individuals who are at risk, or fear they are at risk, of offending (e.g., see Scheela, 1992).

4 Clinical files usually contain some or all the following information: (a) a summary of institutional files, including police records, court records, previous psychological reports, case management reports; (b) notes from semi-structured interview with the miscreant, including information on family background, education, employment, substance use, relationships, mental health, criminal history and future plans; (c) psychological test results; and (d) treatment reports written by the group therapist and the treatment manager.

5 This review may have been unduly weighted by its inclusion of physical/biological interventions such as physical castration and anti-libidinal pharmaceutical treatment.

FURTHER READING

Ward, T., Polaschek, D. L. L., & Beech, A. R. (2006). *Theories of sexual offending*. Chichester: Wiley.
This text provides a good overview of the theories of sexually harmful behaviours.
Brooks-Gordon, B. M., Bilby, C., & Wells, H. (2006). Sexual offenders: A systematic review on psychological interventions. Part I: Quantitative studies. *Journal of Forensic Psychiatry and Psychology*, 17(3), 442–466.
Bilby, C., Brooks-Gordon, B. M., & Wells, H. (2006). Sexual offenders: A systematic review of psychological interventions. Part II: Qualitative studies. *Journal of Forensic Psychiatry and Psychology*, 17(3), 467–484.
These two studies provide the most comprehensive systematic review of the effectiveness of interventions for sexually harmful adults. The first study is a meta-analysis, followed in the second study by an analysis of lesser data in quasi-experimental studies, and all of the qualitative research on psychological interventions. Between them, these studies provide a comprehensive overview of what is known about the efficacy of treatment at the current time to stringent Cochrane Collaboration standards.
Furedi, F., & Bristow, J. (2008). *Licensed to hug*. London: Civitas.
This study provides a critical look at the culture of fear around sexual harm.

REFERENCES

Bainham, A., & Brooks-Gordon, B. (2004). Reforming the law on sexual offences. In B. M. Brooks-Gordon, L. R. Gelsthorpe, M. H. Johnson, & A. Bainham (Eds.), *Sexuality repositioned: Diversity and the law* (pp. 260–296). Oxford: Hart.

Bauman, Z. (2000). *Liquid modernity*. Cambridge: Polity.

Beck, U. (1992). *Risk society*. Cambridge: Polity.

Beech, A., Bourgon, G., Hanson, R. K., Harris, A. J. R., Langton, C., Marques, J., Miner, M., Murphy, W., Quinsey, V., Seto, M., Thornton, D., & Yates, P. M. (2007). *Sexual offender treatment outcome research: CODC guidelines for evaluation*. Public Safety Canada. Retrieved 14 January 2015 from http://www.publicsafety.gc.ca/cnt/rsrcs/pblctns/sxl-ffndr-trtmnt/index-eng.aspx.

Bilby, C., Brooks-Gordon, B. M., & Wells, H. (2006). Sexual offenders: A systematic review of psychological interventions. Part II: Qualitative studies. *Journal of Forensic Psychiatry and Psychology, 17*(3), 467–484.

Blackburn, R. (1995). *The psychology of criminal conduct: Theory, research and practice*. Chichester: Wiley.

Bland, J. M., & Kerry, S. M. (1997). Trials randomised in clusters. *British Medical Journal, 315,* 600.

Brooks-Gordon, B. M., Bilby, C., & Wells, H. (2006). Sexual offenders: A systematic review on psychological interventions. Part I: Quantitative studies. *Journal of Forensic Psychiatry and Psychology, 17*(3), 442–466.

Cantor, J. M., Blanchard, R., Robichaud, L. K., & Christensen, B. K. (2005). Quantitative reanalysis of aggregate data on IQ in sexual offenders. *Psychological Bulletin, 131*(4), 555–568.

Craig, L. E., Browne, K. D., & Beech, A. R. (2008). *Assessing risk in sex offenders: A practitioners' guide*. Chichester: Wiley.

Crighton, D., & Towl, G. (2007). Experimental interventions with sex offenders: A brief review of their efficacy. *Evidence-Based Mental Health, 10,* 35–37.

Crighton, D., & Towl, G. (2008). *Psychology in prisons*. Oxford: Blackwell.

Daily Telegraph (2004). *Sex offenders register grows by 15 per cent*, 28 July.

Divine, G. W., Brown, J. T., & Frazer, L. M. (1992). The unit of analysis error in studies about physicians' patient care behavior. *Journal of General Internal Medicine, 7*(6), 623–629.

Donner, A., & Klar, N. (2000). *Design and analysis of cluster randomization trials in health research*. London: Arnold.

Finkelhor, D. (1984). *Child sexual abuse: New theory and research*. New York: Free Press.

Friendship, C., Beech, A. R., & Browne, K. D. (2002). Reconviction as an outcome measure in research: A methodological note. *British Journal of Criminology, 42,* 442–444.

Friendship, C., Falshaw, L., & Beech, A. (2003). Measuring the real impact of accredited offending behaviour programmes. *Legal and Criminological Psychology, 8*(1), 115–127.

Furedi, F. (2005). *Culture of fear*. London: Continuum.

Furedi, F., & Bristow, J. (2008). *Licensed to hug*. London: Civitas.

Gadd, D., & Jefferson, T. (2007). *Psychosocial criminology*. London: Sage.

Gallagher, C. A., Wilson, D. B., Hirschfield, P., Coggeshall, M. B., & MacKenzie, D. L. (1999). A quantitative review of the effects of sex offender treatment of sexual offender. *Corrections Management Quarterly, 3,* 19–29.

Gulliford, M. C., Ukoumunne, O. C., & Chinn, S. (1999). Components of variance and intraclass correlations for the design of community-based surveys and intervention studies: Data from the Health Survey for England 1994. *American Journal of Epidemiology, 149,* 876–883.

Greenson, R. R. (1967). *The technique and practice of psychoanalysis*. New York: International Universities Press.

Grubin, D. (2002). *Expert paper: Sex offender research*. Liverpool: NHS Programme on Forensic Mental Health Research and Development. London: Department of Health.

Hall, G. C. N. (1995). Sexual offender recidivism revisited: A meta-analysis of recent treatment studies. *Journal of Consulting and Clinical Psychology, 63*(5), 802–809.

Hall, G. C. N., & Hirschman, J. R. (1992). Sexual aggression against children: A conceptual perspective of etiology. *Criminal Justice and Behavior, 19,* 8–23.

Hansard (2002, 6 February). Columns 980W and 982W.

Hanson, R. K. (1997). *The development of a brief actuarial risk scale for sexual offense recidivism*. User Report 1997-04. Ottawa: Department of the Solicitor General of Canada.

Hanson, R. K., Broom, I., & Stephenson, M. (2004). Evaluating community sex offender treatment programs: A 12-year follow-up of 724 offenders. *Canadian Journal of Behavioral Science, 2,* 87–96.

Hanson, R. K., Gordon, A., Harris, A. J. R., Marques, J. K., Murphy, W., Quinsey, V. L., & Seto, M. C. (2002). First report of the Collaborative Outcome Data Project on the effectiveness of treatment for sex offenders. *Sexual Abuse: A Journal of Research and Treatment, 14,* 169–194.

Hanson, R. K., & Thornton, D. (2000). Improving risk assessments for sex offenders: A comparison of three actuarial scales. *Law and Human Behaviour, 24,* 119–136.

Hare, R. D. (1993) *Without conscience: The disturbing world of psychopaths among us.* New York: Pocket Books.

Hare, R. D. (2003). *Manual for the Revised Psychopathy Checklist* (2nd ed.) Toronto, ON, Canada: Multi-Health Systems.

Harkins, L., & Beech, A. (2006). Measurement of effectiveness of sex offender treatment. *Aggression and Violent Behaviour, 12*(1), 36–44.

Harris, G. T., Rice, M. E., Lalumière, M. L., Boer, D., & Lang, C. (2003). A multisite comparison of actuarial risk instruments for sex offenders. *Psychological Assessment, 15*(3), 413–425.

Harris, G. T., Rice, M. E., & Quinsey, V. L. (1998). Appraisal and management of risk of sexual aggressors. *Psychology, Public Policy, and Law, 4,* 73–115.

Hood, R., Shute, S., Feilzer, M., & Wilcox, A. (2002). Sex offenders emerging from long-term imprisonment: A study of their long-term reconviction rates and of parole board members' judgements of their risk. *British Journal of Criminology, 42*(2), 371–394.

Kershaw, C., Nicholas, S., & Walker, A. (2008). *Crime in England and Wales 2007/08. Findings from the British Crime Survey and police recorded crime.* Home Office Statistical Bulletin. London: Home Office.

Kerry, S. M., & Bland, J. M. (1998). Statistics notes: Sample size in cluster randomization. *British Medical Journal, 316,* 549.

Langstrom, N., Enebrink, P., Lauren, E.-M., Lindblom, J., Werko, S., & Hanson, R. K. (2013) Preventing sexual abusers of children from reoffending: Systematic review of medical and psychological interventions. *BMJ, 347,* f4630.

Loader, I. (2006). *Civilizing security: The 2006 John Barry Memorial Lecture.* University of Melbourne, 23 November.

Losel, F., & Schmucker, D. (2005). The effectiveness of treatment of sexual offenders: A comprehensive meta-analysis. *Journal of Experimental Criminology, I,* 117–146.

Malamuth, N. M., Heavey, C. L., & Linz, D. (1993). Predicting men's antisocial behavior against women: The interaction model of sexual aggression. In G. C. N. Hall, R. Hirschman, J. R. Graham, & M. S. Zaragoza (Eds.), *Sexual aggression: Issues in etiology, assessment and treatment* (pp. 63–97). Washington, DC: Taylor & Francis.

Marshall, W. L., & Barbaree, H. E. (1990). An integrated theory of sexual offending. In W. L Marshall, D. R. Laws, & H. E. Barbaree (Eds.), *Handbook of sexual assault; Issues, theories and treatment of the offender* (pp. 257–275). New York: Plenum.

McGuire, J. (2000). Defining correctional programs. *Forum on Corrections Research, 12,* 5–9.

Ministry of Justice (2010) *What works with sex offenders?* National Offender Management Service May 2010. London: Ministry of Justice.

Office of the Attorney General (2004). *Megan's law.* Sacramento, CA: Author. Retrieved 11 September 2009 from www. meganslaw. ca.gov/pdf/2004LegReportcomplete.pdf.

Palmer, E. J. (2008). Contemporary psychological contributions to understanding crime. In G. Davies, C. Hollin, & R. Bull (Eds.), *Forensic psychology* (pp. 29–56). Chichester: Wiley.

Prentky, R., & Schwartz, B. (2006). *Treatment of adult sex offenders.* Harrisburg, PA: VAWnet, a project of the National Resource Center on Domestic Violence/Pennsylvania Coalition Against Domestic Violence. Retrieved 12 January 2015 from www.vawnet.org.

Quinsey, V. L., Harris, G. T., Rice, M. E., & Cormier, C. (1998). *Violent offenders.* Washington, DC: American Psychological Association.

Sackett, D. L., Rosenberg, W. M. C., Gray, J. A. M., Haynes, R. B., & Richardson, W. S. (1996). Evidence based medicine: What it is and what it isn't. *British Medical Journal. 312,* 13 January, 71–72.

Scheela, R. (1992). The remodeling process: A grounded theory study of perceptions of treatment among adult male incest offenders. *Journal of Offender Rehabilitation, 18*(3/4), 167–189.

Schmucker, M., & Losel, F. (2008). Does sexual offender treatment work? A systematic review of outcome evaluations. *Psicothema, 20*(1), 10–19.

Seto, M. (2005). *Sex offenders in the community.* Cullompton, Devon: Willan.

Soothill, K., Francis, B., Sanderson, B., & Ackerley, E. (2000). Sex offenders: Specialists, generalists or both? A 32-year criminological study. *British Journal of Criminology, 40,* 56–67.

Thornhill, R., & Palmer, C. T. (2000). *A natural history of rape.* Cambridge, MA: MIT Press.

Walker, A., Kershaw, C., & Nicholas, S. (2006). *Crime in England and Wales 2005/06.* Home Office Statistical Bulletin, 12/06. London: Home Office.

Walklate, S., & Mythen, G. (2008). How scared are we? *British Journal of Criminology, 48,* 209–225.

Ward, T., Polaschek, D. L. L., & Beech, A. R. (Eds.). (2006). *Theories of sexual offending.* Chichester: Wiley.

Ward, T., & Siegart, R. J. (2002). Toward a comprehensive theory of child sexual abuse: A theory knitting perspective. *Psychology Crime and the Law, 9,* 319–353.

White, P., Bradley, C., Ferriter, M., & Hatzipetrou, L. (2000). Managements for people with disorders of sexual preference and for convicted sexual offenders. In *The Cochrane Library, 4.* Oxford: Update Software. CD000251.

23 Gang Members: Group Processes and Social Cognitive Explanations

JANE L. WOOD

That gangs facilitate increased levels of deviancy in members is a consistent research finding. However, it is not fully clear why this is so. This chapter seeks to explain this effect by examining, first, the likely impact that group processes have on gang members and, second, the likely social cognitive effects that gang membership is likely to elicit. It concludes by noting the importance of psychology in gang membership and how psychologists need to develop further research to explain the specifics of gang membership as it impacts on youth.

GANG MEMBERSHIP

Gang members generally have higher rates of delinquency than nonmembers ... but they have statistically significantly higher rates only when they are in the gang.

(Thornberry, Krohn, Lizotte, Smith, & Tobin, 2003, p. 121).

Group membership is a fundamental aspect of human social existence. Most people will become members of several groups across their lifespan. Family groups, ethnic groups, friendship networks and work groups provide an infrastructure to our identities and enable us to define who we are – and who we want to be. Most groups provide us with key aspects of life. They help to shape our beliefs, attitudes, feelings and behaviours, and many provide us with support, love and loyalty. However, groups can also provide negative influences – albeit via positive mediums such as support and loyalty. Gangs are examples of such groups. Gangs can provide members with positive elements such as protection, support and loyalty, but they can also

promote and facilitate violence, which results in gang members contributing disproportionately to crime levels, especially crimes of violence (e.g., Chu, Daffern, Thomas, & Lim, 2012). To date, there is a paucity of research examining specifically the psychological processes that underpin gang membership and its associated increase in delinquent behaviour. The purpose of this chapter is to consider the psychological effects that group and social cognitive processes have on individual gang members, and how these fundamental processes contribute to the escalation in delinquency of individual gang members.

GANG MEMBERS: DELINQUENCY LEVELS

It is accepted that street gang membership facilitates violent behaviour over and above association with offender peers, even prolifically offending peers (Klein, Weerman, & Thornberry, 2006). However, other findings note how, once they have left the gang, gang members' involvement in violent events is not worse than non-gang comparison groups (e.g., Melde & Esbensen, 2012). This suggests that there is something specific about gang membership that facilitates delinquency, and particularly violent delinquency. Yet, to date, there are no conclusive explanations as to why delinquency escalates with gang membership.

Criminological theories, such as *social disorganization* (Thrasher, 1927; Shaw & McKay, 1942), *cultural transmission* of criminogenic norms (Shaw & McKay, 1942), *differential association* (Sutherland, 1937), *strain theory* (Cohen, 1955), *differential opportunity* (Cloward & Ohlin, 1960) and *control theory* (Gottfredson & Hirschi, 1990;

Forensic Psychology, Second Edition. Edited by David A. Crighton and Graham J. Towl.
© 2015 John Wiley & Sons, Ltd. Published 2015 by British Psychological Society and John Wiley & Sons, Ltd.

Hirschi, 1969), have provided gang researchers with a century's worth of valuable propositions and empirical findings. However, these theories have each been accused of being limited in what they can tell us about gang membership and its influence at an individual level. For instance, they have been charged with considering youth as motiveless vessels that are simply filled with societal burdens (e.g., Emler & Reicher, 1995). They have been charged with taking a unidirectional rather than a reciprocal view of the causal factors of delinquency (e.g., Thornberry, 1987). And they have been charged with paying scant attention to the social psychological processes involved in gang membership (e.g., Thornberry et al., 2003; Wood & Alleyne, 2010).

With foundations based in Durkheim's tradition of social control, Thornberry (1987) developed the interactional theory to address some of the theoretical gaps in gang research. Interactional theory builds on existing criminological theories by taking a reciprocal perspective of gang membership. It posits that gang membership results from a mutual relationship between the individual and peer groups, social structures (e.g., poor neighbourhood and poor family), weakened social bonds, and a learning environment that fosters and reinforces delinquency (Hall, Thornberry, & Lizotte, 2006).

Interactional theorists, noting the prevalent and persistent finding in existing research (e.g., Short & Strodtbeck, 1965; Hagedorn & Macon, 1998) that gang members have higher levels of delinquency than non-gang youth, identified three theoretical models to explain the relationship between gang membership and delinquency (see Thornberry, 1998; Thornberry, Krohn, Lizotte, & Chard-Wierschem, 1993). The first, selection model, maintains that gangs recruit members based on their existing high levels of delinquency. This 'kind of person' model posits that gangs do not cause their members' delinquency – but rather they enlist already delinquent youth. If this model is accurate, it would logically be expected that gang members would have consistently high levels of delinquency before, during and after their gang membership. In other words, delinquency rates for these youth would not differ with gang membership.

The second model is facilitation. This kind of group model proposes that gang members do not differ from nonmembers in their levels of delinquency. However, when they become gang members, the group processes and normative structures of the gang work to facilitate their delinquency. In short, gang membership causes an increase in delinquent behaviour. If this model is accurate, then we would expect that gang members' delinquency rates would be higher than nonmembers' levels – but only while they are in a gang. Before gang membership and after gang membership, their delinquency levels should not differ from nonmembers' levels.

The third model, enhancement, is a kind of person combined with a kind of group model, and is therefore a hybrid of the previous two models. This model suggests that selection and facilitation effects work in concert to create the high levels of delinquency in gang members. The accuracy of this model would be supported if (1) gang members have higher levels of delinquency than nonmembers when they are not the gang, and (2) their levels of delinquency escalate during the period of gang membership.

In their longitudinal examination of these potential models, Thornberry et al. (2003) found no evidence to support the selection model – that is, gang members were not significantly more delinquent than nonmembers before or after gang membership. They did, however, find consistent evidence to support a facilitation effect – that is, gang members' delinquency increased substantially during their gang membership. Importantly, the research also showed that, when members leave the gang, their delinquency levels decrease. There was also some limited support for an enhancement effect since some gang members had somewhat higher delinquency rates than nonmembers before joining a gang – but these rates spiralled dramatically when they joined a gang.

Research evidence is, however, not conclusive on which of the three models best describes pre- and post-gang delinquency levels (see Lacourse, Nagin, Tremblay, Vitaro, & Claes, 2003, and Hall et al., 2006). This may be due to the individual differences of gang members, which is acknowledged by interactional theory when it notes that not all gang members are alike. For instance, while some youth are stable and enduring (core) members, others are temporary or transient (peripheral) members (e.g., Esbensen, Huizinga, & Weiher, 1993; Thornberry et al., 2003; Alleyne & Wood, 2010), and research suggests that these differences in membership commitment may be influenced by pre-gang delinquency levels – that is, youth who had high levels of delinquency before becoming gang members are more likely to become core members, while youth who were not prior delinquents are more likely to be peripheral members (Gatti, Tremblay, Vitaro, & McDuff, 2005). Nonetheless, during gang membership, both core and peripheral gang members are more deviant than non-gang youth (e.g., Alleyne & Wood, 2010), and this supports the prevailing consensus that, regardless of delinquency levels before or after gang membership, during their time in a gang, members' delinquency levels are likely to escalate significantly. As Thornberry et al., observe: 'Put simply, when gang members are in a gang, their behavior worsens; when they are not in a gang, it improves' (Thornberry et al., 2003, p. 185).

BECOMING A GANG MEMBER: GROUP PROCESSES

Gangs probably form for the same reasons that any other groups form – because they offer members something that they want or need (Goldstein, 2002); yet, so far, research has paid little attention to gangs as groups (Hughes, 2013). Gangs are acknowledged as reflecting universal needs among young people for status, identity and companionship (Klein, 1995). Gangs are perceived as offering a way to gain respect (Anderson, 1999), and they radiate social powers that attract youth (Knox, 1994). They emit a coercive power (threat or use of force and violence) and a power to pay, buy, impress and delegate status to members (Knox, 1994). As a result, young boys look up to gang members, mimic them and aspire to gang membership (Hughes & Short, 2005). Media portraits of gangs, such as gang films depicting characters rewarded for gang-like behaviours, act as a blueprint for young aspiring gang members (Przemieniecki, 2005), and youth living in a culture that strongly identifies success with material wealth are particularly motivated to gang membership (Toy & Stanko, 2008).

Research shows that youth who experience feelings of alienation and stress within legitimate social controls, such as the family, education and community contexts, are motivated to join gangs (e.g., Marshall, Webb, & Tilley, 2005). Gangs offer members friendship, pride, identity development, enhanced self-esteem, excitement and financial resources that may not be available legitimately (Goldstein, 2002). They also offer group protection, alleviation of fears, emotional bonding and a sense of belonging (Vigil, 1988), a strong psychological sense of community, a physical and psychological neighbourhood, a social network and social support (Goldstein, 1991). Consequently, youth may adapt, modify or discard their existing social controls in favour of what they *perceive* as the attractive or even 'glamorous' attributes of gang membership.

GANG IDENTITY AND IDENTIFYING WITH THE GANG

Gangs have a group identity without which we cannot discuss gangs and gang membership, and a central hallmark of that identity is involvement in criminal activity (Weerman *et al.*, 2009). As Klein and Maxson (2006) note,

'Crime and group identity are not merely fellow travelers in the gang world: they are mutual reinforcers' (p. 205). Consequently, deviant behaviour has, for many, but not all (see Wood & Alleyne, 2010, for a fuller discussion), become integral to a gang's group identity and a defining characteristic for many researchers. For example, the Eurogang Network defines a gang as: 'a street gang (or troublesome youth group corresponding to a street gang elsewhere) is any durable, street-oriented youth group whose identity includes involvement in illegal activity' (Weerman *et al.*, 2009, p. 20). In this definition, the group's identity refers specifically to what is normal and accepted behaviour for the group – and, in this definition, criminal activity (rather than nuisance behaviour) is important. However, although individual members, must, by virtue of their membership, contribute to the creation and maintenance of the group's identity, the definition does not refer to their personal self-image (Weerman *et al.*, 2009), which leaves us knowing little about how the group's identity helps shape a youth's personal identity.

Research suggests that a youth's personal identity can be forged within a gang if they focus on how their individual needs can combine with the group's characteristics and function (Vigil, 1988). This conceptualization of how group membership may help shape a youth's social identity is supported by evidence from social psychology. For instance, the social identity approach, which includes *social identity theory* and *self-categorization theory*, maintains that the extent to which an individual identifies with a group helps dictate the view that they have of themselves and also how they behave (Tajfel, 1972). A key tenet of the social identity approach is that part of an individual's self-concept (i.e., how they think about themselves) develops from their membership of groups (e.g., Hogg & Reid, 2006). If gangs offer youth power, status, identity, friendship, etc. (as outlined earlier), then this would suggest that gang membership may help youth develop a more positive self-concept (i.e., people like me, I have a lot of friends, I am worth knowing). Social psychology also shows how group membership can influence the way individuals *feel* about themselves. The self-esteem hypothesis points out that people are motivated to have a positive view of themselves (Hogg & Abrams, 1988), and research shows how group membership can increase members' self-esteem – even if their association with the group is limited to basking in reflected glory (e.g., supporting a successful football team). The positive affect that people experience from their group membership then serves to cement their association with the group (e.g., Cialdini *et al.*, 1976). For instance, research demonstrates how youth who feel good about their abilities as students translate this positive affect into confidence about having a successful career in the future – which, in turn, makes them less interested in becoming gang members (Dukes, Martinez, & Stein, 1997). In contrast, youth who join gangs do not generally feel good about themselves in an academic sense, have comparatively lower confidence in their educational abilities and are less integrated into legitimate social institutions such as school (Dukes *et al.*, 1997). However, their gang membership helps enhance their self-esteem by providing support and affirmation of them as members and, when the gang's esteem increases (mainly due to success in delinquent and antisocial activities), so too does the individual self-esteem of previously low-esteem gang members (Duke *et al.*, 1997).

So, it is possible to see how youth may identify with a gang – especially if available alternatives (e.g., school) are unsuccessful and lack appeal. Once they have identified with a gang whose identity is characterized by its deviant activity, then the chances are that the member will adopt a deviant lifestyle – on behalf of the gang. Research examining social identity in gang members shows how identifying with a gang can dramatically reduce the deterrence effect of potential punishment for delinquency (Hennigan & Spanovic, 2012). This research showed that youth who identified with their gang, compared to non-gang youth, put gang norms of deviancy before any personal concerns they had regarding being caught and punished for criminal activity. As Hennigan and Spanovic (2012) note: 'Since crime and violence are normative among gang-involved youth, personal estimates of getting caught and punished have little or no influence on their criminal and violent behaviors' (p. 143). Consequently, it seems that identifying with a gang can counteract the effects of deterrents such as potential punishment that work to prevent non-gang youth from offending. In short, identifying with a gang is likely to help increase a youth's involvement in deviant behaviour.

CONFORMITY, PLURALISTIC IGNORANCE AND COHESION

When people join a group, they are likely to experience pressure to conform to group norms. The considerable power of normative influences was neatly demonstrated by Asch's (1951) classic research which demonstrated how people will conform to decisions made by others (in this case, confederates of the researcher) on issues as trivial as deciding the length of lines – even when those others are clearly wrong. Findings further show that people want to be accepted, and that they will comply with social norms in order to gain others' approval (Cooper, Kelly, & Weaver, 2004). This is especially true

if they value or admire the group (e.g., David & Turner, 1996) and, as noted above, gangs may be admired by youth – particularly youth who have become alienated from legitimate social controls – such as family or school. Once they have been admitted into the group, members become more willing to accept social influences from the group – especially if they strongly identify with it (Cooper *et al.*, 2004). However, group members are also likely to adhere to and follow in-group norms because they fear the social sanctions that may result following norm violation (e.g., Rimal & Real, 2003), and rejection by friends or by admired others is especially threatening (Baron & Kerr, 2003). So, given the power of in-group influences and individuals' readiness to accept them, it seems likely that youth who join gangs, compared to non-gang youth, will experience greater social pressures to become involved in group norms such as delinquency (Viki & Abrams, 2012). Even if group members accept the group's norms, it does not necessarily follow that they always agree with them. *Pluralistic ignorance* refers to when individuals privately reject a social norm but still go along with it because they believe (often wrongly) that other group members accept it (O'Gorman, 1986). Because each group member believes that they are alone in their private rejection of the norm, no one publicly opposes it, and this, in turn, perpetuates the belief among group members that the norm is accepted by the majority. To illustrate, research with university students has shown that, although most students believed that other students were happy with the drinking habits of other students, they personally were not comfortable with the accepted levels of drinking (Prentice & Miller, 1993).

Pluralistic ignorance has also been noted in gang activity, where gang members privately expressed extreme discomfort with some of their criminal activities (e.g., Matza, 1964). Consequently, gang members may adhere to and publicly support gang norms which they privately reject. The net effect of this is that some gang members may go along with acts of deviance that they might not, on their own, become involved in. However, there is also evidence that the more that a person identifies with their chosen group, the more likely they will be to believe in the group norms (e.g., Reid, Cropley, & Hogg, 2005). This suggests that core gang members may *genuinely* endorse the accepted group norms that more peripheral gang members may privately reject. Either way, regardless of whether gang members' private beliefs are consistent or inconsistent with group norms, gang members are likely to publicly accept group norms and behave in accordance with them. If those norms involve delinquency, then it is feasible that gang members will become more delinquent as they keep up with the prescribed norms of their group.

In turn, involvement in delinquency can contribute to gang cohesiveness (Klein & Maxson, 2006).

Cohesion underpins a gang's social interactions and its behaviours (e.g., Klein, 1995). It is claimed that gang cohesion derives from three processes: (1) the *attraction* that members feel towards the gang and its members; (2) the *motivation* that members have to participate in the gang's activities and to contribute to the overall goals of the gang; and (3) the *coordination* of gang member effort (Goldstein, 2002). Psychological perspectives on cohesion stem from contributions in the 1940s and 1950s by Festinger and his colleagues, who defined cohesion as a 'field of forces' which works on individuals to remain in the group (Festinger, Schachter, & Back, 1950). Social psychologists explain cohesion as a bi-dimensional construct consisting of *vertical* cohesion, derived from the extent that members trust and respect the group's leaders, and *horizontal* cohesion, derived from the feelings, respect and trust that members have for each other. A further bi-dimensional conceptualization of cohesion is *perceived* cohesion, which is, '… an individual's sense of belonging to a particular group and his or her feelings of morale associated with membership in the group' (Bollen & Hoyle, 1990, p. 482). Thus, perceived cohesion reflects the individual's evaluation of his/her relationship with their group, and this is derived from cognitive elements such as their appraisal of their experiences within the group and from affective elements based on their feelings about those experiences.

Cohesion is considered to be a powerful driving force in a group's functioning. It is, in Klein's (1995) words, '… the quintessential group process' (p. 43). A meta-analysis examining group cohesion has shown how highly cohesive groups are more productive than less cohesive groups (Evans & Dion, 1991), and, as Klein (1995) observes, gangs produce crime. Cohesion can generate loyalty, commitment and sacrifice from group members who regard the group with pride and respect (Crocker, Luhtanen, Blaine, & Broadnax, 1994). In turn, this produces a form of group esteem, which replaces individual self-esteem (Vigil, 1988). Hence, cohesiveness in gangs may be expected to lead to high levels of delinquency and violence as members identify strongly with their group, share similar attitudes and are willing to adhere to group norms that endorse criminality (Hughes, 2013). Highly cohesive gangs may also be more efficient in mobilizing their membership and accessing commodities such as drugs and weapons (Hughes, 2013).

However, cohesion has been found to work both ways. Although some research findings suggest that low cohesion results in low levels of delinquency (e.g., Klein, 1971), other findings suggest that gangs do not need to be cohesive to be delinquent (e.g., Jansyn, 1966). Hughes (2013) further notes how low cohesion can contribute to increased levels of delinquency since low cohesion may result in members fighting among themselves. Indeed, evidence suggests that gang member murders occurs more *within* gangs than *between* gangs (Decker & Curry, 2002). Consequently, it seems that cohesiveness – either strong or weak – is a factor that contributes to elevated levels of delinquency among gang members.

INTERGROUP CONFLICT AND STATUS ENHANCEMENT

Social psychologists argue that groups only exist because there are out-groups (e.g., Hogg, 2004), and so people need to sort out where they belong in reference to others (Bruner, 1957). This understanding then forms the basis for action in social contexts. For example, belonging to a gang provides a meaningful understanding of one's relationship with members of one's own gang, with members of other gangs, non-gang members and the police (Viki & Abrams, 2012). To achieve this understanding, people employ the basic cognitive process of categorization. Categorization enables not only an understanding of self and others' social group membership, but also allows the individual to attach an emotional value to those groups (Tajfel, 1978). Social psychological findings have robustly demonstrated how people use the categorization process as a foundation for biases – which may be derived from the barest minimum of information – even about one's own group. For instance, classic research shows how temporary groups founded arbitrarily (e.g., minimal groups – grouped by whether they overestimated or underestimated numbers of dots on a piece of paper), with no history of conflict and no potential for future conflict, resulted in in-group favouritism when members were asked to allocate money to anonymous in-group or out-group others (e.g., Tajfel & Turner, 1979). Various explanations have been offered for this minimal group effect. For instance, some assert that in-group favouritism occurs because people assume that this is what is expected of them (Wilder, 1986), or that people expect in-group members to show reciprocal favouritism (e.g., Jetten, Spears, & Manstead, 1996). Whatever the explanations, and work is still being conducted to establish the reasons for the minimal group effect, the upshot is that people are prone to create 'them and us' categorizations and then use these as a basis to make distinctions.

Gangs are no exception to this categorization approach. Gangs are often formed according to members' region of origin (e.g., Densley, 2013), and their identities defined by their reference to other gangs – in particular, their existing intergroup conflict with such gangs (Papachristos, Hureau, & Braga, 2013). In short, gangs use other groups as a point of reference, by which they assess their own actions and status (e.g., Decker, 1996). Social psychological theories such as Social Dominance Theory (Sidanius & Pratto, 1999) help to explain the processes that underpin group competition for status. Social Dominance Theory explains that group members who have a high social dominance orientation (SDO) may feel compelled to enhance, or reinforce, the place of their group within a social hierarchy. To achieve status, the theory goes on to explain, social hierarchies may be arbitrarily constructed to respond to situational factors such as competition for valued resources, and these arbitrary hierarchies generally involve informal groups such as gangs. So, for example, street gangs may strive to enhance or reinforce their status in comparison to other street gangs in an arbitrary-set system where illegal resources (e.g., narcotics) are the valued resource. Although research examining social dominance theory in the context of gangs is still in its infancy, findings so far indicate that individuals involved in gang activity have high levels of SDO (e.g., Wood, Alleyne, Mozova, & James, in press).

As a result of efforts to enhance the gang's status, or in response to what they perceive as threats to its existing reputation, inter-gang violence is often triggered (Decker & Van Winkle, 1996; Aldridge & Medina, 2008). As Densley (2013) observes, 'Violence is central to gang life…' (p. 118), and gang members consider violence as a necessary response to protect territory and/or gang business. As a result, intergroup conflict is common between rival gangs (Bourdieu & Wacquant, 1996), and it functions on a struggle for power and domination built on reputation, respect and status (Harding, 2012). Transgressions cannot go unpunished, and reciprocation is perhaps the most common reason for gang violence (e.g., Hughes and Short, 2005; Papachristos, 2009) as gangs address a perceived wrong or block a threat. In turn, this helps gangs to save face, protect members and exact revenge on opponents (Papachristos et al., 2013). It also sends the message that the gang is able to look after its interests and its membership – which, accordingly, enhances the gang's existing reputation (Papachristos et al., 2013).

Gangs offer members the chance to enhance their personal social status and, as research shows, this occurs in those involved in prison gang activity (e.g., Wood et al., in press; Wood, Moir, & James, 2009; South & Wood, 2006), and in street gangs where both core and peripheral members value social status more than do non-gang youth (e.g., Alleyne & Wood, 2010). Once they have joined a gang, the acquisition of social status emerges from the reputation that the individual develops as a gang member. Reputation enhancement theory contends that youth will select a self-image that they want to display in front of specific others (Emler & Reicher, 1995). These others then provide feedback that reinforces the image that the individual member wants to develop within the group. For gang members bent on developing their reputation within the gang, delinquency will be key, since delinquency is a valued gang product. Delinquency, particularly violence, also serves as a defence mechanism which protects the member from being victimized (Emler & Reicher, 1995).

Research shows how gang members have normalized violence by using it even when committing 'petty crimes' (Harris et al., 2011). Research also confirms the tenets of reputation enhancement theory by showing how violence is used to achieve status, enhance reputations as well as to express members' commitment to the gang's activities and to avoid being excluded from the group (Harris et al., 2011). In short, violence is gang currency by which members negotiate their positions in the gang. As Densley (2013, p. 85) observes in his ethnographic study of gang youth, 'Interviewees were clear that serious violence was the fastest way to rise to the top'. However, the caveat to this was that violence should be sufficient to enhance both the individual's and the gang's reputation, but not so much that it attracts too much police attention and threatens gang business (Densley, 2013). Gang members also consider violence as necessary for obtaining material possessions and a comfortable high-status lifestyle (Harris et al., 2011). The authors further observed that gang members expected an extremely violent response from any member whose status was being undermined:

> Not reacting with often extreme violence was experienced as tantamount to abject failure. There was a sense of being worse than nothing if a once-held status is lost. This was not only due to loss of respect, but also a sense of inevitable attacks and victimisation from others
>
> (Harris et al., 2011, p. 20).

So, for a youth joining a gang, becoming more deviant than they were – even if they were already deviant – may be essential for developing and maintaining a positive reputation as a gang member. Elevated deviance appears to be a norm for many gangs, and the expectation that gang members will behave violently to achieve and maintain personal and gang status is probably one of the main reasons why gang membership increases delinquency. The value that gang members attach to status and the necessity of delinquency in achieving and maintaining status as a gang member suggest that delinquency levels will always increase with gang membership for as long as gang membership is perceived as providing status and reputation.

BEING A GANG MEMBER: SOCIAL COGNITIVE PROCESSES

While it is useful to understand the group processes that contribute to an escalation in delinquency, particularly violent delinquency, during gang membership, we still know little about the specific psychological influences that joining a gang has on individual members which help to facilitate this escalation. As already noted (see earlier), criminological theories that explain gang membership pay little attention to the social psychological processes involved in gang membership (Thornberry *et al.*, 2003). However, this is changing as individual differences gain conceptual importance in the study of gangs.

The unified theory of gang involvement (see Wood & Alleyne, 2010) draws on both criminological and psychological concepts to explain why youth may or may not join a gang. It illustrates pathways into gang membership as well as pathways into delinquency more generally and pathways that avoid delinquency and/or gang membership. However, importantly, it also highlights the importance of the development and influence of social cognitions and attitudes that may be associated with delinquent behaviour and gang membership. For instance, the theory also explains how gang members' existing social cognitions and attitudes will be shaped as they are exposed to group norms, new informal social controls and new or increased opportunities for criminal learning and involvement in criminal activity. Although still in its infancy this theory posits that greater attention needs to be paid to the psychological processes that influence individuals as they become gang members.

MORAL DISENGAGEMENT

Unified theory maintains that, to become criminally active, youth will need to learn how to set aside their existing moral standards (morally disengage). This strategy is necessary for them to be able to justify their personal involvement in deviant behaviour. Moral disengagement is a social cognitive process that enables individuals to justify harmful acts and avoid the cognitive dissonance and self-condemnation that is associated with violating one's personal moral standards (Bandura, Barbaranelli, Caprara, & Pastorelli, 1996).

Moral disengagement consists of eight socio-cognitive mechanisms which operate at three levels of social processing. The *first level* works by altering the interpretation of an inhumane act. For instance, it may employ *moral justification* (the behaviour is for a worthy cause – e.g., furthering the gang's status), *euphemistic language* (sanitizing the description of harm – e.g., acts of violence may be described as 'gang business') and *advantageous comparisons*, which involves comparing one's own behaviour with that of others considered to be worse (e.g., we only assault – others kill). The *second level* reinterprets inhumane actions by *displacement of responsibility* on to authority figures for personal behaviour (i.e., one's behaviour results from authority figures' diktats – so there is no personal responsibility); *diffusion of responsibility* (responsibility for the harm done is shared by several perpetrators – thus diluting or dispensing with individual blame) and *distorting the consequences* of harm (by ignoring, minimizing or disbelieving the harm done to others). The *third level* involves distorting the way the victim is viewed to deny them their victim status via *dehumanization* tactics (the victim is seen as subhuman and is thus devoid of normal human qualities) or by *blaming* them (they brought it on themselves – they deserved it).

Empirical evidence supports that youth do, indeed, set aside their moral standards if, by doing so, their chosen group will accept them (e.g., Emler & Reicher, 1995). Evidence further shows that street gang members (e.g., Alleyne & Wood, 2010) and those involved in prison gang activity (e.g., Wood *et al.*, 2009; Wood *et al.*, in press) do indeed set aside their moral standards to engage in inhumane behaviour. Research further shows how an ability to morally disengage links to increased levels of violence (e.g., Bandura *et al.*, 1996). Moral disengagement also mediates pathways between impoverished neighbourhoods, which are strongly associated with gang membership (e.g., Hill, Lui, & Hawkins, 2001), and antisocial behaviour and between low levels of empathy and antisocial behaviour (e.g., Hyde, Shaw, & Moilanen, 2010). As Hyde *et al.*, observe:

> In more modern contexts, urban youth living in impoverished homes and neighborhoods that offer them little hope or opportunity for socially acceptable pathways to success may develop a moral code of behavior that is not bound by mainstream prohibitions against committing antisocial actions, particularly when such actions are associated with the means to obtain financial success (e.g., dealing illicit drugs) or ensuring safety (e.g., joining a gang) (p. 198).

If they are already involved in delinquent behaviour, then chances are that youth will have already begun to use moral disengagement strategies to justify their delinquency. However, although their pre-gang delinquency may have brought them some gains (e.g., financial), they are also likely to have encountered external moral condemnation (e.g., from parents, teachers, etc.). In contrast, once they join a gang, their deviant behaviour is likely to be positively reinforced, not only from the acquisition of material profit (e.g., from drug sales), but also from the approval of other gang members. Such positive endorsement will additionally further reinforce their commitment to the group (e.g., Esbensen, Huizinga, & Weiher, 1993), and is likely to negate any reduction in their delinquency that others' moral condemnation may have triggered since now it is condoned. Importantly, it is also likely to exacerbate and intensify the moral disengagement process.

Being a gang member may also provide additional scope for using moral disengagement strategies. Gang members, compared to non-gang youth, are more likely to be violently victimized, sexually assaulted (males or females) and suffer serious injuries from fighting (e.g., Taylor, Freng, Esbensen, & Peterson, 2008). They are also more likely to be victimized by rival gangs (e.g., Sanders, 1994). As such, they may feel justified in being involved in violent retaliations against rival gang members. This idea is supported by research which shows that street gang members, compared to non-gang youth, use more victim blaming disengagement strategies (e.g., Alleyne & Wood, 2010). Research further shows how peripheral gang members, more than non-gang youth, use more displacement of responsibility disengagement tactics to justify their delinquent behaviour (e.g., Alleyne & Wood, 2010). This is understandable. In a group with an established hierarchy of membership such as peripheral and core membership, it is feasible that peripheral members, eager to establish their value to the gang, will follow the lead and/or instructions of more established members. In other words, they follow orders – or at least they believe they are doing so (e.g., Alleyne & Wood, 2010). Either way, it seems that being part of a gang is likely to help foster and broaden members' moral disengagement strategies and, as they learn to sideline their moral standards more and more, gang members are able to become more involved in acts of delinquency.

OFFENCE SUPPORTIVE COGNITIONS

Unified theory maintains that gang membership is likely to generate and/or foster pro-aggression cognitions, beliefs and attitudes that underline delinquent behaviour. Cognitive schemas are essentially cognitive structures which people use to screen, encode and evaluate social stimuli (Beck, 1964). They are parts of memory that hold previous knowledge and contain attitudes, beliefs and assumptions about oneself, other people and the world (e.g., Mann & Beech, 2003). They are, in short, categories of information that people create based on their past experiences. Some theorists prefer to think of schema more as *implicit theories* (ITs), since they maintain that this term more accurately explains the way that people develop theories to explain the world, and develop and test hypotheses on which they base predictions about future events (Ward, 2000). ITs therefore bear some similarity to scientific theories inasmuch as people use them to interpret evidence accumulated regarding other people's behaviours, desires and motives (Ward, 2000). In short, ITs are conceptually *lay* theories that '… enable individuals to explain and understand aspects of their social environment, and, therefore, to make predictions about future events' (Ward, 2000, p. 495). ITs are called implicit because they are seldom explicitly expressed by the holders (Ward, 2000), and they function on two main psychological constructs: beliefs and desires (Polaschek, Calvert, & Gannon, 2009). Accordingly, beliefs about oneself, the world and other people are the driving force behind subsequent actions that are employed to achieve personal desires.

ITs may be revised if new information suggests that existing theoretical constructs held by the individual are wrong (Polaschek *et al.*, 2009). However, people are highly motivated to interpret information in a way that is consistent with their ITs, which can be deeply entrenched and resistant to change (Ward, 2000). This makes it more likely that inconsistent incoming information will be re-interpreted until it is consistent with the individual's existing ITs (Polaschek *et al.*, 2009). To achieve this consistency, people may skew or *cognitively distort* incoming information. For example, research shows how people who hold ITs that others are generally hostile and self-serving are likely to interpret an accidental bump from another person as stemming from malevolent intentions (Epps & Kendall, 1995). Offending populations, in particular, have been found to hold cognitive distortions (i.e., distorted or deviant beliefs).

Consequently, when a youth becomes a gang member and accepts the gang's norms, strives to achieve status via delinquent acts and acquires the in-group/out-group biases associated with their new group membership, then he or she is likely to develop ITs and associated cognitive distortions that support pro-gang, pro-delinquency activities. In addition, the reinforcement that the new gang member receives from peers for acts of aggression on behalf of the gang will probably lead to a positive appraisal of personal aggression. Such personal appraisal will help to foster further cognitive distortions in a pro-aggressive direction, which is then assimilated into the gang member's memory and corresponding ITs to act as a guide for future behaviour.

Research into ITs has mostly been conducted with sexual offenders where the value of this perspective has been amply demonstrated (e.g., Polaschek & Ward, 2002; Ward & Keenan, 1999). However, an IT approach has been used to examine intimate partner violence (e.g., Gilchrist, 2008; Weldon & Gilchrist, 2012; see also Pornari, Dixon, & Humphreys, 2013, for a review), firesetting (e.g., Ó Ciardha & Gannon, 2012) and violent offending (e.g., Polaschek *et al.*, 2009). Although gang affiliation has not been directly examined from an IT perspective, qualitative work highlights that gang members' violence functions on beliefs of traditional male gender values and beliefs associated with aggression (Lopez & Emmer, 2002). Gang violence is also committed in accordance with gang rules, norms and values (Lopez & Emmer, 2002), which suggests that gang members adopt the beliefs and values of the gang as ITs and supports findings that they put what they perceive to be the beliefs and values of the gang before their personal beliefs and values (see also earlier re-commitment). As the authors observed:

> In contrast to the vigilante and self-preservation crimes, the individual self-identity was not mentioned or even alluded to in the commission of the aforementioned violent offenses. Instead, the focus was on the gang as a system with its own beliefs, rules, and norms
> *(Lopez & Emmer, 2002, p. 37).*

Taking a grounded theory approach, Polaschek *et al.* (2009) looked to identify the specific ITs of violent offenders and identified four core ITs that they held. The first and arguably the most important IT as it underpins several of the others, is *normalization of violence*. Violent offenders saw violence as an effective form of communication in terms of resolving conflicts, as persuasive tactics and to make others respect you. Consequences of violence for victims – either physical and/or psychological – were minimized (see also moral disengagement strategies discussed in the preceding text), and so was personal victimization. The second IT is *beat or be beaten* and includes two subtypes (*self-enhancement* and *self-preservation*). The underlying assumption of this IT is the need to strike first in the violence stakes – otherwise, others will gain the advantage in what is perceived by the individual as a violent world. The self-enhancement subtype may be particularly relevant to gang youth inasmuch as it maintains that violence is necessary in order to achieve and/or maintain status and to demonstrate one's dominance over others. The self-preservation subtype relates to their mistrust of others and how they perceive violence as a necessary response to others who will walk all over them

– if they are not violent first. The third IT is *I am the law* and refers to violent offenders' beliefs that they are superior to others and entitled or even obliged to assault or harm others to discipline them. Violence is seen as necessary to protect others or the social order. It is, the authors contend, a hallmark of vigilantism – where violence is delivered as a response to the perceived harm caused by others. Hence, this IT could also be relevant to gang members – particularly core members' disciplining of peripheral members and retaliatory attacks on other gangs. Gangs have also been known to offer social control to their communities and to 'police' neighbourhood events even better than the police (Patillo, 1998). The final IT that violent offenders held was *I get out of control*. This IT refers to problems that violent offenders have with self-control and regulation of their behaviour. They may view their behaviour as stemming from rage or uncontrollable anger. Links between gang membership and a lack of self-control have been well established in theory (e.g., Gottfredson & Hirschi's [1990] general theory of crime), and empirical findings which show how a lack of self-control is a key predictor of gang membership (e.g., Esbensen & Osgood, 1999). Research further shows how gang youth use their gang membership as a coping strategy for negative emotions such as anger, frustration and anxiety (Eitle, Gunkel, & van Gundy, 2004; Klemp-North, 2007). Recent findings also confirm that gang members suffer from high levels of anxiety disorder and psychosis (Coid *et al.*, 2013), which in turn have been linked to a lack of self-control (e.g., Novaco, 1997).

Although ITs have not been examined directly in terms of gang membership, the preceding discussion suggests that becoming a gang member is likely to support and help develop a youth's offence supportive cognitions – or implicit theories. Since research regarding the psychology of gang membership is still in its infancy, we cannot yet say whether gang membership is a causal factor in the development of pro-delinquent ITs. However, the preceding evidence suggests that even if gang membership does not *cause* pro-delinquent ITs, it is likely to strengthen any that already exist as the youth adopts and assimilates the pro-delinquency gang norms and values.

RUMINATION, DISPLACED AGGRESSION AND ENTITATIVITY

Although it is noted in the preceding text that gangs may not be particularly cohesive (Klein & Maxson, 2006), research does show that gangs develop an 'oppositional culture' where they set the group in opposition to legitimate authorities such as the police, schools, etc. (Moore & Vigil, 1989). Research findings show how street gang membership (Alleyne & Wood, 2010) and involvement in prison gang activity (Wood *et al.*, in press) links strongly to anti-authority attitudes. As gangs are targeted in gang prevention programmes leading to persistent contact with authorities, this also helps to reinforce their gang identities (e.g., McAra & McVie, 2005; Ralphs, Medina, & Aldridge, 2009) and amplifies the oppositional culture (e.g., Klein & Maxson, 2006). In turn, gangs may come to view themselves as victims of oppression who are unfairly victimized (Lien, 2005). This then encourages members to consider themselves as defenders of their group which is being victimized by society. Speaking of how gang members in an Oslo sample perceived their membership and victimization by society, Lien (2005) notes:

> He develops ideas of compassion, love, and sacrifice in relation to his friends, and he (sic) explains his acts through a construction of himself as a victim of society. The victimization point is necessary in order to justify the criminal act. He cannot be blamed, the act is heroic rather than evil, and the victims get what they deserve (p. 121).

This is even more likely if the transgressors are members of a rival gang since empirical evidence confirms that a significant amount of gang-related violence stems from retributive inter-gang violence (e.g., Klein & Maxson, 1989). What this shows is that gang members do not have to be personally victimized in order to retaliate with acts of violence – since they are obligated to retaliate on *behalf* of the gang and the victimization of any of its members. In turn, this is likely to add to the reasons why individual gang members' levels of deviance increase when they join a gang. He or she offends as a representative of others as well as for himself/herself.

Rumination

There are of course, psychological processes that underpin the development of this heightened level of deviance. The intensity of a provocation by others is positively associated with the process of rumination (Horowitz, 1986). According to response styles theory (Nolen-Hoeksema, 1991), rumination involves an individual thinking repetitively about something that has caused them distress. It can involve consistent thoughts about one's own thoughts and feelings as well as their causes, in addition to consistent thoughts about the provoking event (e.g., Bushman, Bonacci, Pedersen, Vasquez, & Miller, 2005). Consequently, perceptions

that the gang is being victimized are likely to cause members to ruminate on how this makes them feel and also about the provoking event. In short, the individual gang member is likely to 'dwell' on the harm that they perceive another has to their gang and how this makes them feel.

Ordinarily, when an individual is provoked, the negative affect that emanates from that event will dispel after a short period of time (e.g., Bushman *et al.*, 2005). However, rumination can help maintain the negative affect long after the provocation by producing a focus on one's feelings about the event and its causes (e.g., Lyubomirsky & Nolen-Hoeksema, 1995). Rumination is associated with psychopathologies such as depression, anxiety, binge eating and drinking and self-harm (e.g., Nolen-Hoeksema, Wisco, & Lyubomirsky, 2008). In such cases, the focus of rumination is primarily on the self. However, the focus of rumination can also be externalized via hostile and vengeful ruminative thoughts (e.g., Bandura *et al.*, 1996). As Bandura *et al.* (1996) note, hostile rumination heightens aggressiveness but people can often ruminate hostilely without acting on their feelings. However, if moral disengagement strategies have freed them from their normal moral constraints (see earlier), then they will be more likely to respond aggressively to perceived wrongs (Bandura *et al.*, 1996). As Bandura *et al.* (1996) note:

> Effective moral disengagement creates a sense of social rectitude and self-righteousness that breeds ruminative hostility and retaliatory thoughts for perceived grievances (p. 366).

Research findings confirm that gang members ruminate more than do other populations – even violent populations. For instance, findings show how, compared to non-gang youth, gang youth ruminate more (e.g., Vasquez, Osman, & Wood, 2012). Research comparing gang members' and other violent men's psychiatric morbidity also highlights the importance of rumination in gang members (Coid *et al.*, 2013). This research showed how, even though both violent men and gang members reported holding positive attitudes to violence, gang members reported more frequent violent ruminations and a greater inclination to respond with violence to perceived disrespect than did violent men who were not gang members. Gang members were also more likely to be victims of violence than were violent men. Interestingly, this research further showed how violent ruminations, combined with experiences of being violently victimized and their fear of future victimization, explained the links between gang membership and both anxiety disorders and psychosis (Coid *et al.*, 2013).

Displaced aggression

Although an individual may be motivated to retaliate against their transgressor when provoked, there will be occasions when this is not possible. This may then lead to aggression being directed at another victim. This is known as *displaced aggression* – aggression that targets either an innocent victim (Dollard, Doob, Miller, Mowrer, & Sears, 1939) or a target that has not provided sufficient justification for the levels of aggression meted on them (e.g., Pedersen, Gonzales, & Miller, 2000). Displacement targets are likely to occur in situations where, for instance, the original provocateur has left the scene, or is intangible such as a social construct (e.g., economic hardship), or the provocateur provokes concerns of retaliation that the individual would rather avoid (e.g., the police and prosecution).

Researchers theorize that gang members will be more inclined to engage in displaced aggression (e.g., Vasquez, Lickel, & Hennigan, 2010). Their argument is that gang members are more likely to experience adverse events that prevent them from retaliation against the provocateur. For example, their street orientation may mean that gang members have an antagonistic relationship with authority figures, which in turn may foster a strong sense of being victimized (e.g., Lien, 2005). This is even more likely if the authorities employ gang suppression tactics, which findings suggest can lead to an increase in the number of gangs (e.g., Hagedorn, 2008) as gangs commit more crime to defend their group identity (e.g., Ayling, 2011). As Klein and Maxson (2006) observe, 'The war on gangs justifies the warring gang' (p. 206). Gang members' deviance is also likely to bring them in to conflict with parents and teachers, and lack of parental management (e.g., Thornberry, 2003) or authoritarian parenting styles (e.g., Klein, 1995) may leave a gang member experiencing negative affect from sources against which they are often unable to retaliate (Vasquez *et al.*, 2010). Consequently, another 'scapegoat' may be selected as a target onto which the gang member can vent his/her aggression.

The effects of the initial provocation may also exacerbate and amplify the level of displaced aggression. For example, a meta-analysis shows how the more the negative the setting of the interaction between the individual and the target of displaced aggression and the greater the similarity between the original provocateur and the target of displaced aggression, the more the target will be perceived as deserving of victimization, which in turn serves to increase the magnitude of the displaced aggression (Marcus-Newhall, Pedersen, Carlson, & Miller, 2000). This suggests that if gang members have been provoked by rival gang members, then all members of that rival gang are likely to be perceived as similar to the provocateur – and hence justified displacement targets. Also, the effects of the initial provocation will exacerbate the aggressive response to the displacement target if the provocation occurred in the presence of others (e.g., Vasquez *et al.*, 2013). This may be due to feelings of humiliation and a motivation to 'save face' with others (Vasquez *et al.*, 2013). In essence, provocation, particularly provocation that occurs in front of others, may result in rumination and subsequent retaliation against targets that do little to deserve victimization. As Vasquez *et al.* (2013) note, 'If they stew about a provoking incident and focus on their bad mood, they may in turn lash out against others who provide only the slightest excuse for aggressive retaliation' (p. 28). In a gang context, many of the provocations that members experience are likely to be in a public arena. Gangs are street-oriented groups, and their deviance is likely to be committed with other members (e.g., Weerman *et al.*, 2009). So, the motivation for individual gang members to retaliate against any slight is likely to be heightened by the presence of an audience. In turn, this is likely to exacerbate levels of aggression in gang members.

Entitativity

A further factor that may feed a gang member's disproportionate response to an innocent target is *entitativity*. Entitativity refers to the extent to which a group is perceived of as an entity (i.e., it possesses unity and coherence). Campbell (1958) coined the term to differentiate between real groups and collections of individuals. For example, intimate groups such as a family have entitativity, while a group of people waiting at a bus stop do not (Lickel *et al.*, 2000). Campbell argued that a group of people could be perceived as having entitativity if they moved together, resembled each other, were close to each other and formed a coherent figure. Building on Campbell's ideas, researchers have since proposed that there are five antecedents to entitativity: the importance of the group to its members; the similarity of group members; the extent to which members interact with each other; the extent to which members share common goals; and the extent to which members experience common outcomes (Lickel *et al.*, 2000). The idea that high similarity results in perceptions that the group is high in entitativity has been confirmed in research findings (e.g., Hamilton, Sherman, & Rodgers, 2004).

It is easy to see why gangs might be considered as high in entitativity. They share patterns of age (members are primarily adolescent), they are often exclusively male, and they are often ethnically homogeneous (Klein, Weerman, & Thornberry, 2006) – although, in the United Kingdom, both street (e.g., Mares, 2001) and prison (e.g., Wood, 2006) gangs tend to form along regional lines. In addition, gangs often adopt descriptors that serve as identifiers. For instance, they may adopt colours, clothing, argot, tattoos, hand signals and emblems (Klein *et al.*, 2006), which they use to emphasize their own identity. As a result, such descriptive elements of gang membership may further exacerbate the perceived entitativity of the group, particularly by rival gang members. In turn, their entitativity may be used as justification for selecting *any* member as a target for displaced aggression that emanates from a previous altercation with another member of that gang. Such a situation is potentially even more likely if it is difficult to identify the provocateur (e.g., in a drive-by shooting). In short, any member of the rival gang will do as a target in terms of vengeance – since they are all the same.

CONCLUSIONS

The aim of this chapter was to provide an analysis of the group and individual psychological influences that stem from gang membership. The enduring finding that gang membership increases individuals' levels of deviance, but *only* during gang membership, suggests strongly that gang member youth are not inherently different from other youth. Instead, it suggests that gangs exert a unique impact on those who join them – *while* they are members. The theoretical propositions and empirical evidence outlined in this chapter go some way to explain how this inimitable influence might occur. Social psychologists have robustly demonstrated how group attachment and commitment to a group facilitate an individual's identification with their group and, in turn, influence the way that members think and feel about themselves. By subscribing to the group's norms, members may develop more positive esteem – and so too may the group. As the group continues to exact its implicit authority over members via group process effects, members work to further group goals, and – as noted in the preceding text – gang goals are criminal in nature.

Continuing from the theme of group process effects, the chapter then sought to emphasize the importance of individual effects of gang membership by showing how social cognitive processes may contribute to gang members' elevated deviancy. The theoretical propositions and empirical evidence presented was by no means exhaustive, and the causal relationship between social cognitions and gang membership still need to be fully established. However, the chapter sought to establish the multitude of social cognitive processes that result from gang membership and, in doing so, it demonstrated the powerful influence that gangs have on members at an individual level. Members may set aside their moral constraints, develop pro-offending cognitions and, via rumination processes, aggress against innocent targets. In short, this chapter highlights the powerful effect that gangs can have on the psychology of members.

So far, psychology has given the issue of gang membership little specific attention, and so many of the points made in this chapter are speculative. However, this is beginning to change as psychologists embark on developing empirical and theoretical propositions that emphasize the importance of examining the social cognitive processes that underpin gang membership. In many ways, gangs can be conceptualized as a unique collective of groups since they produce negative outcomes (i.e., acts of deviance) while providing members with positive and necessary life enhancements (e.g., social support, identity, emotional bonding and financial resources). Consequently, it is not difficult to see why youth, particularly youth who feel marginalized from legitimate institutions such as schools, are attracted to gang membership. However, we need to continue to develop research strategies that aim to establish the explicit psychological influence that gangs have on their members – and this is particularly important if we are to develop effective treatment programmes to negate those effects. Therefore, gang research is vital, and a deeper involvement of all relevant disciplines will be critical as we strive to comprehend exactly how gangs influence their members to become particularly deviant.

FURTHER READING

Alleyne, E., & Wood, J. L. (2010). Gang involvement: Psychological and behavioral characteristics of gang members, peripheral youth, and non-gang youth. *Aggressive Behavior, 36*(6), 423–436.
The paper reports the results of an empirical study of young people involved in gang activity in terms of their psychological and behavioural characteristics. The study compared gang members with young people involved at the periphery of gangs and those with no involvement. Significant differences emerged between the groups studied.
Melde, C., & Esbensen, F. A. (2013). Gangs and violence: Disentangling the impact of gang membership on the level and nature of offending. *Journal of Quantitative Criminology, 29*(2), 143–166.
An empirical study which looked at the membership of youth gangs, and the role of these as a social context for violence. The study examined the effects of gang participation on the odds of violent offending independently of involvement in general delinquent and criminal behaviours.

The study looked at seven cities, sampling over 3,700 young people. The results suggested that active gang membership was associated with a 10–21% increase in the odds of involvement in violent incidents. When restricted to young people who reported being gang members, the proportionate increase in the odds of violence associated with gang activity was similar for males and females. Leaving the gang resulted in a return to baseline risk of violence, although general offending remained elevated. The study illustrates the power of social processes on violence.

REFERENCES

Aldridge, J., & Medina, J. (2008). *Youth gangs in an English city: Final report*. ESRC: Swindon.

Alleyne, E., & Wood, J. L. (2010). Gang involvement: Psychological and behavioural characteristics of gang members, peripheral youth and non-gang youth. *Aggressive Behavior, 36*, 423–436.

Anderson, E. (1999). *Code of the street: Decency, violence and the moral life of the inner city*. New York, NY: Norton and Company.

Asch, S. E. (1951). Effects of group pressure upon the modification and distortion of judgment. In H. Guetzkow (Ed.), *Groups, leadership and men*. Pittsburgh, PA: Carnegie Press.

Ayling, J. (2011). Gang change and evolutionary theory. *Crime, Law and Social Change, 56*, 1–26.

Bandura, A., Barbaranelli, C., Caprara, G. V., & Pastorelli, C. (1996). Mechanisms of moral disengagement in the exercise of moral agency. *Journal of Personality and Social Psychology, 71*, 364–374, doi:10.1037/0022-3514.71.2.364

Baron, R. S., & Kerr, N. L. (2003). *Group process, group decisions, group action*. Philadelphia, PA: Open University Press.

Beck, A. T. (1964). Thinking and depression: II. Theory and therapy. *Archives of general psychiatry, 10*(6), 561–571.

Bollen, K., & Hoyle, R. H. (1990). Perceived cohesion: A conceptual and empirical examination. *Social Forces, 69*(2), 479–504.

Bourdieu, P., & Wacquant, L. J. D. (1996). The purpose of reflexive sociology (The Chicago Workshop). In P. Bourdieu & L. J. D. Wacquant (Eds.), *An invitation to reflexive sociology* (pp. 61–215). Chicago, IL: University of Chicago Press.

Bruner, J. S. (1957). On perceptual readiness. *Psychological Review, 64*, 123–152, doi: 10.1037/h0043805

Bushman, B. J., Bonacci, A. M., Pedersen, W. C., Vasquez, E. A., & Miller, N. (2005). Chewing on it can chew you up: Effects of rumination on triggered displaced aggression. *Journal of Personality and Social Psychology, 88*, 969–983.

Campbell, D. T. (1958). Common fate, similarity, and other indices of the status of aggregates of person as social entities. *Behavioural Science, 3*, 14–25.

Chu, C. M., Daffern, M., Thomas, S., & Lim, J. Y. (2012). Violence risk and gang affiliation in youth offenders: A recidivism study. *Psychology, Crime & Law, 18*, 299–315.

Cialdini, R. B., Borden, R. J., Thorne, A., Walker, M. R., Freeman, S., & Sloan, L. R. (1976). Basking in reflected glory: Three (football) field studies. *Journal of Personality and Social Psychology, 34*, 366–375, doi: 10.1037/0022-3514.34.3.366

Cloward, R., & Ohlin, L. (1960). *Delinquency and opportunity*. New York: Free Press.

Cohen, A. K. (1955). *Delinquent boys: The culture of the gang*. Glencoe, IL: Free Press.

Coid, J. W., Ullrich, S., Keers, R., Bebbington, P., DeStavola, B. L., Kallis, C., Yang, M., Reiss, D., Jenkins, R., & Donnelly, P. (2013). Gang membership, violence, and psychiatric morbidity. *American Journal of Psychiatry 2013*. 10.1176/appi.ajp.2013.12091188

Cooper, J., Kelly, K. A., & Weaver, K. (2004). Attitudes, norms, and social groups. In M. B. Brewer & M. Hewstone (Eds.), *Social cognition*. Oxford, UK: Blackwell Publishers.

Crocker, J., Luhtanen, R., Blaine, B, & Broadnax, S. (1994). Collective self-esteem and psychological wellbeing among White, Black, and Asian college students. *Personality and Social Psychology Bulletin, 20*, 503–513.

David, B., & Turner, J. (1996). Studies in self-categorization and minority conversion: Is being a member of the out-group an advantage? *British Journal of Social Psychology, 35*(1), 179–199, doi:10.1111/j.2044-8309.1996.tb01091.x

Decker, S. H. (1996). *Life in the gang: Family, friends, and violence*. Cambridge: Cambridge University Press.

Decker, S. H., & Curry, G. D. (2002). Gangs, gang homicides, and gang loyalty: Organized crimes or disorganized criminals? *Journal of Criminal Justice, 30*, 343–352.

Decker, S. H., & Van Winkle, B. (1996). *Life in the gang: Family, friends, and violence*. New York: Cambridge University Press.

Densley, J. A. (2013). *How gangs work: An ethnography of youth violence*. Oxford: Palgrave Macmillan.

Dollard, J., Doob, L., Miller, N., Mowrer, O., & Sears, R. (1939). *Frustration and aggression*. New Haven, CT: Yale University Press.

Dukes, R. L., Martinez, R. O., & Stein, J. A. (1997). Precursors and consequences of membership in youth gangs. *Youth and Society, 29*, 139–165.

Eitle, D., Gunkel, S., & van Gundy, K. (2004). Cumulative exposure to stressful life events and male gang membership. *Journal of Criminal Justice, 32*, 95–111.

Emler, N., & Reicher, S. (1995). *Adolescence and delinquency*. Oxford, UK: Blackwell Publishers Ltd.

Epps, J., & Kendall, P. C. (1995). Hostile attributional bias in adults. *Cognitive Therapy and Research, 19*, 159–178.

Esbensen, F.-A., Huizinga, D., & Weiher, A. W. (1993). Gang and non-gang youth: Differences in explanatory factors. *Journal of Contemporary Criminal Justice, 9*, 94–116.

Esbensen, F.-A., & Osgood, D. W. (1999). Gang resistance education and training (GREAT): Results from the national evaluation. *Journal of Research in Crime and Delinquency, 36*, 194–225.

Evans, C. R., & Dion, K. L. (1991). Group cohesion and performance: A meta-analysis. *Small Group Research, 22*(2), 175–186.

Festinger, L., Schachter, S., & Back, K. (1950). *Social pressures in informal groups: A study of human factors in housing*. Stanford, CA: Stanford University Press.

Gatti, E., Tremblay, R. E., Vitaro, F., & McDuff, P. (2005). Youth gangs, delinquency and drug use: A test of the selection, facilitation, and enhancement hypotheses. *Journal of Child Psychology and Psychiatry, 46*, 1178–1190.

Gilchrist, E. (2008). Implicit thinking about implicit theories in intimate partner violence. *Psychology, Crime and Law, 15*(2–3), 131–145.

Goldstein, A. P. (1991). *Delinquent gangs: A psychological perspective*. Champaign, IL: Research Press.

Goldstein, A. P. (2002). *The psychology of group aggression*. Chichester, UK: John Wiley & Sons.

Gottfredson, M. R., & Hirschi, T. (1990). *A general theory of crime*. Stanford, CA: Stanford University Press.

Hagedorn, J. M. (2008). *A world of gangs: Armed young men and gangsta culture*. Minneapolis MN: University of Minnesota Press.

Hagedorn, J. M., & Macon, P. (1998). *People and folks: Gangs, crime and the underclass in a rustbelt city*. Chicago, IL: Lake View Press.

Hall, G. P., Thornberry, T. P., & Lizotte, A. J. (2006). The gang facilitation effect and neighbourhood risk: Do gangs have a stronger influence on delinquency in disadvantaged areas? In J. F. Short, & L. A. Hughes (Eds.), *Studying youth gangs* (pp. 47–61). Oxford: Altamira Press.

Hamilton, D. L., Sherman, S. J., & Rodgers, J. S. (2004). Perceiving the groupness of groups: Entitativity, homogeneity, essentialism, and stereotypes. In V. Yzerbyt, C. M. Judd, & O. Corneille (Eds.), *The psychology of group perception: Perceived variability, entitativity, and essentialism*. Philadelphia, PA: Psychology Press.

Harding, S. (2012). *Unleashed: The phenomena of status dogs and weapon dogs*. Bristol: The Policy Press.

Harris, D., Turner, R., Garratt, I., & Atkinson, S. (2011). *Understanding the psychology of gang delinquency: Implications for defining effecting violence interventions*. London: Ministry of Justice.

Hennigan, K., & Spanovic, M. (2012). Gang dynamics through the lens of social identity theory. In F. A. Esbensen & C. L. Maxson (Eds.), *Youth gangs in international perspective*. New York; Springer.

Hill, G. H., Lui, C., & Hawkins, J. D. (2001). *Early precursors of gang membership: A study of Seattle youth*. Juvenile Justice Bulletin, Washington, DC: US Department of Justice, Office of Justice Program, OJJDP.

Hirschi, T. (1969). *Causes of delinquency*. Berkeley and Los Angeles, CA: University of California Press.

Hogg, M. A. (2004) Social categorization, depersonalization, and group behavior: Self and social identity. In M. B. Brewer & M. Hewstone (Eds.), *Self and social identity, Perspectives on social psychology* (pp. 203–231). Oxford: Blackwell Publishing.

Hogg, M. A., & Abrams, D. (1988). *Social identifications: A social psychology of intergroup relations and group processes*. London: Routledge.

Hogg, M. A., & Reid, S. A. (2006). Social identity, self-categorization, and the communication of group norms. *Communication Theory, 16*, 7–30, doi: 10.1111/j.1468-2885.2006.00003.x

Horowitz, M. J. (1986). *Stress response syndromes* (2nd edn). Northvale, NJ: Aronson.

Hughes, L. A. (2013). Group cohesiveness, gang member prestige, and delinquency and violence in Chicago, 1959–1962. *Criminology*, doi: 10.1111/1745-9125.12020

Hughes, L. A., & Short, J. F., Jr. (2005). Disputes involving youth street gang members: Micro-social contexts. *Criminology*, doi:10.1111/j.0011-1348.2005.00002.x

Hyde, L. W., Shaw, D. S., & Moilanen, K. L. (2010). Developmental precursors of moral disengagement and the role of moral disengagement in the development of antisocial behavior. *Journal of Abnormal Child Psychology, 38*(2), 197–209.

Jansyn, L. R., Jr. (1966). Solidarity and delinquency in a street corner group. *American Sociological Review, 31*, 600–614.

Jetten, J., Spears, R., & Manstead, A. S. R. (1996). Intergroup norms and intergroup discrimination: Distinctive self-categorization and social identity effects. *Journal of Personality and Social Psychology, 71*, 1222–1233, doi:10.1002/(SICI)1099-0992(199709/10)27:5<603::AID-EJSP816>3.0.CO;2-B

Klein, M. W. (1971). *Street gangs and street workers*. Englewood Cliffs, NJ: Prentice-Hall.

Klein, M. W. (1995). *The American street gang: Its nature, prevalence, and control*. New York: Oxford University Press.

Klein, M. W., & Maxson, C. K. (1989). Street gang violence. In N. Weiner & M. Wolfgang (Eds.), *Violent crime, violent criminals*. Newbury Park, CA: Sage.

Klein, M. W., & Maxson, C. L. (2006). *Street gang patterns and policies*. New York, NY: Oxford University Press.

Klein, M. W., Weerman, F. M., & Thornberry, T. P. (2006). Street gang violence in Europe. *European Journal of Criminology, 3*, 413–437.

Klemp-North, M. (2007). Theoretical foundations of gang membership. *Journal of Gang Research, 14*, 11–26.

Knox, G. W. (1994). *An introduction to gangs*. Bristol, OM: Wyndham Hall Press.

Lacourse, E., Nagin, D. S., Tremblay, R. E., Vitaro, F., & Claes, M. (2003). Developmental trajectories of boys' delinquent group membership and facilitation of violent behaviors during adolescence. *Developmental Psychopathology, 15*, 183–197.

Lickel, B., Hamilton, D. L., Wieczorkowska, G., Lewis, A., Sherman, S. J., & Uhles, A. N. (2000). Varieties of groups and the perception of group entitativity. *Journal of Personality and Social Psychology, 78*, 223–246.

Lien, I.-L. (2005). The role of crime acts in constituting the gang's mentality. In S. H. Decker & F. M. Weerman (Eds.), *European street gangs and troublesome youth groups: Findings from the Eurogang research program* (pp. 35–62). Walnut Creek, CA: AltaMira Press.

Lopez, V. A., & Emmer, E. T. (2002). Influences of beliefs and values on male adolescents' decisions to commit violent offenses. *Psychology of Men and Masculinity, 3,* 28–40.

Lyubormirsky, S., & Nolen-Hoeksema, S. (1995). Effects of self-focused rumination on negative thinking and interpersonal problem solving. *Journal of Personality and Social Psychology, 69,* 176–190.

McAra, L., & McVie, S. (2005). The usual suspects?: Street-life, young people and the police. *Criminal Justice, 5,* 5–36.

Mann, R., & Beech, A. R. (2003). Cognitive distortions, schemas and implicit theories. In T. Ward, D. R. Laws, & S. M. Hudson (Eds.), *Theoretical issues and controversies in sexual deviance* (pp. 135–153). London: Sage.

Mares, D. (2001). Gangstas or lager louts? Working class street gangs in Manchester. In M. W. Klein, H. J. Kerner, C. L. Maxson, & E. G. M. Weitekamp (Eds.), *The Eurogang paradox* (pp. 153–164). Dordrecht, The Netherlands: Kluwer.

Marcus-Newhall, A., Pedersen, W. C., Carlson, M., & Miller, N. (2000). Displaced aggression is alive and well: A meta-analytic review. *Journal of Personality and Social Psychology, 78,* 670–689.

Marshall, B., Webb, B., & Tilley, N. (2005). *Rationalisation of current research on guns, gangs and other weapons: Phase 1.* London: University College London Jill Dando Institute of Crime Science.

Matza, D. (1964). *Delinquency and drift.* New York: Wiley.

Melde, C., & Esbensen, F.-A. (2012). Gangs and violence: Disentangling the impact of gang membership on the level and nature of offending. *Journal of Quantitative Criminology, 29,* 143–166. doi: 10.1007/s10940-012-9164-z

Moore, J., & Vigil, J. D. (1989). Chicano gangs: Group norms and individual factors related to adult criminality. *Aztlan, 18,* 27–44.

Nolen-Hoeksema, S. (1991). Responses to depression and their effects on the duration of depressive episodes. *Journal of Abnormal Psychology, 100,* 569–582.

Nolen-Hoeksema, S., Wisco, B. E., & Lyubomirsky, S. (2008). Rethinking rumination. *Perspectives on Psychological Science, 3,* 400–424.

Novaco, R. W. (1997). Remediating anger and aggression with violent offenders. *Legal and Criminological Psychology, 2,* 77–88, doi: 10.1111/j.2044-8333.1997.tb00334.x

Ó Ciardha, C., & Gannon, T. A. (2012). The implicit theories of firesetters: A preliminary conceptualization. *Aggression and Violent Behavior, 17*(2), 122–128, doi:10.1016/j.avb.2011.12.001

O'Gorman, H. (1986). The discovery of pluralistic ignorance: An ironic lesson. *Journal of the Historic and Behavioral Sciences, 22,* 333–347, doi: 10.1002/1520-6696(198610)22:4<333::AID-JHBS2300220405>3.0.CO;2-X

Papachristos, A. (2009). Murder by structure: The social structure of gang homicide. *American Journal of Sociology, 115,* 74–128.

Papachristos, A. V., Hureau, D. M., & Braga, A. A. (2013). The corner and the crew: The influence of geography and social networks on gang violence. *American sociological review,* 0003122413486800.

Patillo, M. E. (1998). Sweet mothers and gang-bangers: Managing crime in a black middle-class neighborhood. *Social Forces, 76,* 747–774.

Pedersen, W. C., Gonzales, C., & Miller, N. (2000). The moderating effect of trivial triggering provocation on displaced aggression. *Journal of Personality and Social Psychology, 78,* 913–927.

Polaschek, D. L. L., Calvert, S. W., & Gannon, T. A. (2009). Linking violent thinking: Implicit theory-based research with violent offenders. *Journal of Interpersonal Violence, 24*(1), 75–96, doi:10.1177/0886260508315781

Polaschek, D. L. L., & Ward, T. (2002). The implicit theories of potential rapists: What our questionnaires tell us. *Aggression and Violent Behavior, 7,* 385–406.

Pornari, C. D., Dixon, L., & Humphreys, G. W. (2013). Systematically identifying implicit theories in male and female intimate partner violence perpetrators. *Aggression and Violent Behavior, 18,* 496–505.

Prentice, D. A., & Miller, D. T. (1993). Pluralistic ignorance and alcohol use on campus: Some consequences of misperceiving the social norm. *Journal of Personality and Social Psychology, 64,* 243–256, doi: 10.1037/0022-3514.64.2.243

Przemieniecki, C. J. (2005). Gang behavior and movies: Do Hollywood gang films influence violent gang behavior? *Journal of Gang Research, 12,* 41–71.

Ralphs, R., Medina, J., & Aldridge, J. (2009). Who needs enemies with friends like these? The importance of place for young people living in known gang areas. *Journal of Youth Studies, 12,* 483–500.

Reid, S. A., Cropley, C., & Hogg, M. A. (2005). *A self-categorization explanation of pluralistic ignorance.* Top three paper presented at the International Communication Association, New York.

Rimal, R. N., & Real, K. (2003). Understanding the influence of perceived norms on behaviors. *Communication Theory, 13,* 184–203, doi: 10.1111/j.1468-2885.2003. tb00288.x

Sanders, W. B. (1994). *Gangbangs and Drive-bys: Grounded culture and juvenile gang violence.* New York: Aldine de Gruyter.

Shaw, C. R., & McKay, H. D. (1942). *Juvenile delinquency and urban areas.* Chicago, IL: University of Chicago Press.

Short, J. F., Jr., & Strodtbeck, F. L. (1965). *Group process and gang delinquency.* Chicago, IL: University of Chicago Press.

Sidanius, J., & Pratto, F. (2003). Social dominance theory and the dynamics of inequality: A reply to Schmitt, Branscombe, & Kappen and Wilson & Liu. *British Journal of Social Psychology, 42*(2), 207–213.

South, R., & Wood, J. (2006). Bullying in prisons: The importance of perceived social status, prisonization and moral disengagement. *Aggressive Behavior, 32*, 490–501, doi:10.1002/ab.20149

Sutherland, E. H. (1937). *The professional thief.* Chicago, IL: University of Chicago Press.

Tajfel, H. (1972). Social categorization. In S. Moscovici (Ed.), *Introduction à la psychologie sociale* (Vol. 1, pp. 272–302). Paris: Larousse.

Tajfel, H. (Ed.). (1978). *Differentiation between social groups: Studies in the social psychology of intergroup relations.* London: Academic Press.

Tajfel, H., & Turner, J. C. (1979). An integrative theory of intergroup conflict. In W. G. Austin & S. Worchel (Eds.), *The social psychology of intergroup relations* (pp. 33–47). Monterey, CA: Brooks/Cole.

Taylor, T. J., Freng, A., Esbensen, F.-A., & Peterson, D. (2008). Youth gang membership and serious violent victimization: The importance of lifestyles and routine activities. *Journal of Interpersonal Violence, 23*, 1441–1464, doi: 10.1177/0886260508314306

Thornberry, T. P. (1987). Toward an interactional theory of delinquency. *Criminology, 25*, 863–891.

Thornberry, T. P. (1998). Membership in youth gangs and involvement in serious and violent offending. In Loeber, R. & Farrington, D. P. (Eds.), *Serious and violent offenders: Risk factors and successful interventions* (pp. 147–166). Thousand Oaks, CA: Sage.

Thornberry, T. P. (Ed.). (2003). *Gangs and delinquency in developmental perspective.* Cambridge: Cambridge University Press.

Thornberry, T. P., Krohn, M. D., Lizotte, A. J., & Chard-Wierschem, D. (1993). The role of juvenile gangs in facilitating delinquent behavior. *Journal of Research in Crime and Delinquency, 30*, 55–87.

Thornberry, T. P., Krohn, M. D., Lizotte, A. J., Smith, C., & Tobin, K. (2003). *Gangs and delinquency in developmental perspective.* Cambridge: Cambridge University Press.

Thrasher, F. (1927; 1963). *The gang: A study of 1,313 gangs in Chicago.* Chicago: University of Chicago Press.

Toy, J., & Stanko, B. (2008). *Die another day: A practitioners review with recommendations for preventing gang and weapon violence in London in 2008.* http://www.mac-uk.org/wped/wp-content/uploads/2013/03/Jonathon-Toy-Die-Another-Day-Practitioners-Report-2009.pdf (accessed 12 January 2015).

Vasquez, E. A., Lickel, B., & Hennigan, K. (2010). Gangs, displaced, and group-based aggression. *Aggression & Violent Behavior, 15*, 130–140.

Vasquez, E. A., Osman, S., & Wood, J. L. (2012). Rumination and the displacement of aggression in United Kingdom gang-affiliated youth. *Aggressive Behavior, 38*, 89–97, doi:10.1002/ab.20419

Vasquez, E. A., Pedersen, W. C., Bushman, B. J., Kelley, N. J., Demeestere, P., & Miller, N. (2013). Lashing out after stewing over public insults: The effects of public provocation, provocation intensity, and rumination on triggered displaced aggression. *Aggressive Behavior, 39*, 13–29.

Vigil, J. D. (1988). *Barrio gangs: Street life and identity in Southern California.* Austin: University of Texas Press.

Viki, G. T., & Abrams, D. (2012). The social influence of groups on individuals. In J. L. Wood & T. A. Gannon (Eds.), *Crime and crime reduction: the importance of group processes.* East Sussex; Routledge.

Ward, T. (2000). Sexual offenders' cognitive distortions as implicit theories. *Aggression and Violent Behavior, 5*, 491–507.

Ward, T., & Keenan, T. (1999). Child molesters' implicit theories. *Journal of Interpersonal Violence, 14*(8), 821–838.

Weerman, F. M., Maxson, C. L., Esbensen, F., Aldridge, J., Medina, J., & van Gemert, F. (2009). *Eurogang program manual background, development, and use of the Eurogang instruments in multi-site, multi-method comparative research.* http://www.umsl.edu/ccj/Eurogang/eurogangpublications.html (accessed 14 January 2015).

Weldon, S., & Gilchrist, E. (2012). Implicit theories in intimate partner violence offenders. *Journal of Family Violence, 8*, 761–772.

Wilder, D. A. (1986). Social categorization: Implications for creation and reduction of intergroup bias. In L. Berkowitz (Ed.), *Advances in experimental social psychology* (Vol. 19, pp. 293–355). New York: Academic Press.

Wood, J. L. (2006). Gang activity in English prisons: The prisoners' perspective. *Psychology, Crime & Law, 12*, 605–617, doi:10.1080/10683160500337667.

Wood, J. L., Alleyne, E., Mozova, K., & James, M. (in press). Predicting involvement in prison gang activity: Street gang membership, social and psychological factors. *Law and Human Behavior.*

Wood, J., & Alleyne, E. (2010). Street gang theory and research: Where are we now and where do we go from here? *Aggression and Violent Behavior, 15*, 100–111.

Wood, J., Moir, A., & James, M. (2009). Prisoners' gang-related activity: The importance of bullying and moral disengagement. *Psychology Crime and Law, 15*, 569–581, doi:10.1080/10683160802427786

24 Genocide and Hate Crime

WILLIAM JACKS AND JOANNA R. ADLER

This chapter opens with an outline of historical and definitional issues in genocide and hate crime. Each construct is framed within a legal context, and an example is given. We then move to a discussion of the socio-cognitive and psychological processes that have been drawn on to explain these crimes. These processes will be considered both at the individual and group levels. The chapter then considers how insights from psychological theory have influenced interventions – for both victims and offenders – and responses to hate crime and genocide. We conclude with a summary and a set of recommendations for future research and action.

Hate crime and genocide are separate constructs with distinct legal definitions and bodies of scholarship. They have been included together in this chapter because the aetiology of each crime can be conceptualized in terms of similar psychological processes. Fundamentally, both hate crime and genocide are about patterns of prejudice and hate that result in demonization of the 'other', persecution and violence. In-group/out-group theories derived from Tajfel and Turner (1986), as well as wider debates on stigma, dehumanization, societal competition, discrimination, prejudice and demonization, are pertinent to both constructs.

> Individuals and groups change as a result of their actions. Victims are increasingly devalued, violence intensifies as it continues. Destructive actions can become increasingly normal and probable, a characteristic of a system, a group – or a person
>
> *(Staub, 2011, p. 33).*

WHAT IS GENOCIDE?

Genocide is an atrocious, state-led crime. It sits within international law as a crime against humanity and an act that degrades human dignity. The International Alliance to End Genocide states that 'Genocide is the world's worst intentional human rights problem. But it is different from other problems and requires different solutions. Because genocide is almost always carried out by a country's own military and police forces, the usual national forces of law and order cannot stop it. International intervention is usually required' (IAEG, 2012).

The term 'genocide' was created specifically to distinguish a particularly heinous kind of mass killing, one with the intention of destroying a national group. The word itself was offered by Raphael Lemkin in 1943, but he had already published many of the ideas about it, and first presented his suggestion to create an international convention against 'Acts of Barbarity' to the Legal Council of the League of Nations in 1933, at the Madrid conference (Lemkin, 1933). By 1943, he had come to 'genocide':

> This new word, [...] is made from the ancient Greek word *genos* (race, tribe) and the Latin *cide* (killing) [...] genocide does not necessarily mean the immediate destruction of a nation [...] It is intended rather to signify a coordinated plan of different actions aiming at the destruction of essential foundations of the life of national groups, with the aim of annihilating the groups themselves. Genocide

Forensic Psychology, Second Edition. Edited by David A. Crighton and Graham J. Towl.
© 2015 John Wiley & Sons, Ltd. Published 2015 by British Psychological Society and John Wiley & Sons, Ltd.

is directed against the national group as an entity, and the actions involved are directed against individuals, not in their individual capacity, but as members of the national group

(Lemkin, 1944, p. 79).

Lemkin proposed that genocide should be recognized as the purposeful destruction of a nation or ethnic group, and that it should be treated as a crime against international law and prosecuted accordingly. Genocide was first adopted legally in 1944. In the aftermath of the Holocaust in 1948, the Convention on the Prevention and Punishment of the Crime of Genocide (Article II) refined the definition to: 'any of the following acts committed with intent to destroy, in whole or in part, a national, ethnical, racial or religious group, as such: (a) killing members of the group; (b) causing serious bodily or mental harm to members of the group; (c) deliberately inflicting on the group conditions of life calculated to bring about its physical destruction in whole or in part; (d) imposing measures intended to prevent births within the group; and (e) forcibly transferring children of the group to another group'.

Despite its legal status, there is still no universally accepted definition of genocide (Andreopoulos, 1994; Staub, 2011). Staub offers: 'a government or some group acts to eliminate a whole group of people, whether by directly killing them or creating conditions that lead to their deaths or inability to reproduce' (Staub, 2011, p. 100).

For an accessible summary of the position in international law, see Stanton (2002). Of key importance is 'the intent to destroy in whole or in part a racial, ethnic, religious, or national group as such, by killing members of the group or imposing conditions inimical to survival' (Kuper, 1994). It is important to note that what defines genocide is not solely the causing of death. Genocide can also include grievous mental or bodily harm, imposing measures intended to prevent births within a group, and forcibly transferring children away from a particular group (Fein, 1994). Similarly, mass killings are not genocidal unless there is the intention to destroy a group within that mass killing. This distinction is far from simple and, as Staub (2012) highlights, can result in political inertia:

… mass killing … can be a way station to genocide. Therefore, prevention must focus on preventing increasing violence between groups, not specifically genocide. In actuality, a focus on genocide has become a problem. While the international community usually remains passive even in the face of genocide, it feels even less obligated to act in the face of mass killing or intense, mutual violence. Arguing

about definitions, nations and the UN tend to resist calling a genocide what it is, in order to avoid the obligation to act

(Staub, 2012, p. 55).

International law is notoriously difficult to uphold, and the term 'genocide' is politically loaded and controversial. Problems seem to arise particularly in relation to establishing genocidal intent ('intent to destroy') and in the precise identification of those to charge. Popular outrage about mass killings and 'ethnic cleansing' are not sufficient. The international community may stand by unless, and until, it formally recognizes such actions as genocide. Only if that is possible are the signatories to the Convention obliged to intervene. If this is combined with the reluctance to label genocide as such (e.g., Staub ibid), then it is possible to see why limited intervention or apparent inertia may seem to prevail. When writing this chapter, such matters were highlighted within the cases of Syria, (e.g., Slaughter, 2013), the Central African Republic (e.g., Ki-moon, 2014) and South Sudan.[1]

It was after atrocities of the mid-1990s that we saw tribunals set up to investigate and prosecute crimes against humanity. These tribunals were focused on the former Yugoslavia and on Rwanda.

EXAMPLE: GENOCIDE

Massacres that we would now classify as genocides have been present throughout human history and are recorded in religious and historical texts, both ancient and modern. Looking at recent history, the systematic eradication of the Armenian population by the Turkish State informed Lemkin's definition of genocide, and, 20 years later, those actions were drawn on directly by Adolf Hitler as he outlined his plans for the attack on Poland to the German High Command:

… our war aim does not consist in reaching certain lines, but in the physical destruction of the enemy. Accordingly, I have placed my death-head formations in readiness – for the present only in the East – with orders to them to send to death mercilessly and without compassion, men, women, and children of Polish derivation and language. Only thus shall we gain the living space (lebensraum) which we need. Who, after all, speaks today of the annihilation of the Armenians?

(Berenbaum [2004] or see http://www.teachgenocide.org/background/ hitler.htm, accessed 12 January 2015).

BOX 24.1   THE RWANDAN GENOCIDE

RWANDA: Over the course of 100 days in 1994, the small East African country of Rwanda became the site of one of the most violent episodes of genocide in the twentieth century. A government-led, but largely-civilian-enacted genocide was the culmination of ethnic tensions between the minority Tutsi and majority Hutu population that resulted in an estimated 800,000 people being killed out of the country's total population of 7.5 million (Des Forges, 1999; Gourevitch, 1998). Perpetrators aimed to kill every dissident and every Tutsi and eradicate the Tutsi minority from Rwanda. Over 100,000 of the Hutu majority took part in the killings either voluntarily or under coercion. Most people were killed in their local communities by perpetrators who were well known to them; teachers killed students, doctors killed patients and family members killed other family members. The genocide ceased in July 1994 when the regime fell to an army of Rwandan exiles, but its repercussions are still felt today, both in Rwanda and its neighbouring countries.

WHAT IS HATE CRIME?

The term 'hate crime' is an umbrella concept used to describe crimes motivated by prejudice towards an individual's identity, or towards an individual who is seen to represent a group, and is widely used in political, legal and moral discourse. Hate crimes are aimed towards a particular characteristic of a victim – be it their race, faith, sexual orientation, gender identity, perceived disability or anything else that means they are identified as 'other'. Hate crimes are also recognized as having particular impacts on individuals, groups and their wider communities (Iganski, 2002).

The concept of 'hate crime' originated in the United States, where it dates back to the civil rights campaigns of the 1960s, but there has also been an awareness of the racist element of antisocial behaviour in Britain for some time (for a comprehensive review of hate crime in Britain, see Bowling, 1998). During the 1980s and 1990s, various government initiatives (e.g., Home Affairs Committee, 1994; Home Office, 1981, 1989; House of Commons, 1986), campaigning bodies and victim groups tried to highlight how the racist element of antisocial behaviour and criminal acts was minimized by agencies, perpetrators and the country at large, with limited success. It was not until the racially motivated murder of Stephen Lawrence in 1993 – the third high-profile, racist murder within a year in the London borough of Greenwich – that there was a shift in the public's awareness, and widespread concern was raised. The Lawrence campaign lead by Stephen's family pushed for an inquiry into a police and Crown Prosecution Service investigation that was widely perceived as racist and flawed, and to expose the lack of public concern and awareness about the experiences of racial harassment.

The public inquiry into the death of Stephen Lawrence was published 6 years later (MacPherson, 1999), and was hailed by the then home secretary Jack Straw as a 'watershed' moment in practice and policy. It served to place the issues of hate victimization and policing in England and Wales 'under a spotlight of unprecedented intensity', and found individual, cultural and institutional racism in the policies and practices of the Metropolitan Police Service that resulted in a failure to deliver either quality or equality of service to ethnic minority victims (Bowling, 1998). The inquiry highlighted the need for a holistic overhaul of the justice system, and the ways it deals with racial offending and hate crime in general (Macpherson, 1999).

Over a decade on from the inquiry, it is clear that the MacPherson report has had a significant impact on policing policy, and a wide variety of measures have been implemented to address the highlighted failings. These have included: various legislation governing hate speech and other hate offences (e.g., Criminal Justice Act, 2003), the publication of a national hate crime policies (e.g., Home Office, 2009; HM Government, 2012), guidance documents governing the policing and prosecution of hate crime (e.g., CPS or Home Office and ACPO, 2005) and marked emphasis on community cohesion and interfaith dialogue (Home Office, 2009). An awareness of 'institutional racism' (MacPherson, 1999) and requirements under the Equality Act (2010) have improved many of the ways in which criminal justice agencies work. There have been renewed efforts for an increase in multi-agency intelligence sharing, as well as responses to community demographics, increased awareness of community tensions, and an understanding of the importance of addressing community grievances (Dixon, 2010).

In line with an increased policy focus, the last 15 years have seen an explosion in empirical and theoretical research investigating the prevalence of hate crime, its aetiological causes and the harm it inflicts (Herek & Berrill, 1992; Levin & McDevitt, 1993; Jacobs & Potter, 1998; Perry, 2001; Iganski, 2008). This research has shown hate crime to be a wide-ranging, multi-faceted and complex problem that incorporates a wide variety of offender motivations. This work has also seen European and wider international network forms where practitioners, academics, and governmental and non-governmental representatives work alongside industry and voluntary sector partners to exchange best practice and evaluate effective interventions. One area of concern has been that of trans-border offending and challenges posed both to jurisdictional authority and legislative lag. The EU has begun to tackle this with responses such as Framework Decision 2008/913/JHA, which brings partial harmonization to EU member states' laws on racism and xenophobia.

In the years following the MacPherson Inquiry, there have been some successful prosecutions for high-profile 'hate' murders including those of Anthony Williams, a black teenager from Liverpool, and Jody Dobrowski, a young man targeted for his sexuality and beaten to death on Clapham Common. These cases have demonstrated a growing awareness of preventative policies and procedures alongside improved system capacity and expertise. However, the deaths of Fiona Pilkington[2] and her severely disabled daughter Francecca Hardwick in 2007 followed at least 11 years of harassment and abuse from local youths that persisted despite repeated calls to local police and the council, who each failed to enforce both their own policies and legally imposed injunctions. Serious case reviews of other cases such as the murder of Gemma Hayter also highlight the need for unrelenting vigilance to continue to improve and monitor services (Dixon & Ray 2007; Warwickshire Safeguarding Adults Partnership, 2011).

Definitions

As Jacobs and Potter (1998) suggest, constructing a definition of hate crime is far from straightforward. Choices have to be made about the meaning of prejudice, the nature and strength of the causal link between the prejudice and the offence, as well as the types of crimes to be included. The crucial factor is often who decides whether an offence is motivated by hate; the victim's, perpetrator's and justice agency's interpretations of the same crime may vary significantly.

When considering a definition of hate crime, we start with the definition provided by the Association of Chief Police Officers (ACPO) of England Wales and Northern Ireland that was incorporated into the then government's policy. ACPO defines hate crime as: 'Any offence/incident committed against a person or property which is motivated, in whole or in part, by the offender's bias against a race, colour, religion, gender, disability, sexual orientation or ethnicity. It may also be where a person is targeted or selected because of their status, group characteristics or affiliation' (Home Office, 2009).

This definition is deliberately broad and inclusive, which is important in order to facilitate policing and to cover community needs. The breadth of the definition means that hate crimes can refer to incidents with a wide spectrum of severity – from low-level incidents through to more serious incidents of murder and some forms of terrorism. It is also important that victimized groups can be identified based on common beliefs and practises as well other divisions such as nationality, ethnicity or disability.

The areas of hate mentioned in the preceding text are those that are officially monitored (e.g., see current guidance from the College of Policing, 2014). The monitored strands are those for which data on reported incidents, prosecutions, etc., are routinely gathered, but these strands are not meant to be exhaustive. Similarly, it is recognized that not all incidents will meet the threshold for prosecution, even within the monitored strands, so the preceding definition is not the only one used by police and local authority partnerships. For example, both of the next two extracts originated with ACPO (2005) and can be found routinely incorporated into websites and manuals used by a wide variety of practitioners and police departments.

An incident may be: 'Any hate incident, which may or may not constitute a criminal offence, which is perceived by the victim or by any other person as being motivated by prejudice and hate' (ACPO, 2005).

A crime is: 'Any hate incident which constitutes a criminal offence, perceived by the victim or any other person, as being motivated by prejudice or hate' (ACPO, 2005, 2011).

These definitions emphasize the perspective of the victim or others who are involved, rather than focusing solely on the motivations of the perpetrator. The way in which hate crime is officially defined and conceptualized will influence both the volume and nature of recorded incidents, which in turn has very serious implications for law enforcement in terms of workload, resourcing, investigative practices, occupational health and, of course, the amount and quality of service provision to victims (Hall, 2013).

Prevalence

Relying uncritically on official police data to understand the prevalence of hate crimes and various motivations for hate is somewhat problematic. All the available information suggests that hate crime is underreported (e.g., Guasp, Gammon, & Ellison, 2013 or Sin et al., 2009), and victims of hate crime are less likely to report crimes to the police compared to victims of other crimes (HM Government, 2012). The most recent tranche of statistics on hate crime in England and Wales was compiled by three agencies – the Home Office, Office of National Statistics and Ministry of Justice (2013). This work draws on officially recorded data from the police and court outcome statistics alongside survey data from the Crime Survey in England and Wales. They report

BOX 24.2   VULNERABLE ADULTS

Mate hate is a form of victimization where vulnerable adults are 'groomed' by people whom they believe to be their friends. This can involve the theft of the disabled person's benefits, use of their property and has been associated with other forms of disability hate crime. In some of the most severe cases, it has led to homicide. Gemma Hayter had severe learning difficulties, and, in 2010, at 27 years of age, she was murdered by five ostensible mates, who tortured her with beating, strangulation and stabbing, eventually discarding her on a railway line near where they lived. This was after she had experienced years of sexual exploitation, abuse and was known to social services as a vulnerable adult. To at least one of her killers, she was just 'that thing', a phrase noted in most reports of the trial. Three years earlier, Brent Martin was tortured and punched to death, apparently for a £5 bet, by three people he had believed to be his friends. When reporting that trial, many media outlets had mentioned that one of those perpetrators (Stephen Bonallie) was quoted as subsequently saying 'I'm not going down for a muppet'.

that, within the CSEW data, approximately 278,000 hate crimes were estimated for 2011–2012 and 2012–2013. However, as they go on to point out, the confidence intervals for these data are quite wide, as the reporting rate even within this survey is relatively low. As such, the figures for the CSEW can be seen as being somewhere between 212,000 and 344,000 incidents, of which the overwhelming majority were racially motivated.

When considering hate crime, research and debate has often focused primarily on religious or racially motivated hate. These crimes made up the majority of monitored hate crimes reported in England and Wales, around 154,000 of the crimes considered in CSEW, 2012–2013. If we consider the officially recorded police figures, then overall levels of recorded hate crime drop to 43,927, of which 35,885 (approximately 82%) were racially aggravated offences. Both police and CSEW indicate that hate crime victims are more likely than other victims of crime to be repeat victimized.

Research has shown that hate crimes against LGBT people or people with disabilities are rarely reported by victims – approximately 11% and 4%, respectively, in the police recorded 2012–2013 figures – and, in reality, these occur far more frequently than official figures suggest (Guasp, 2013; MIND, 2007). The low figures for disability-related hate crime seem even less representative when considering the findings from Mencap (2000) or MIND (2007), where only 18% of respondents reported feeling

safe most or all of the time, 71% reported victimization in the preceding 2 years and 41% reported ongoing victimization. The under-representation in recorded crime and prosecution figures of homophobic hate crime was demonstrated by Dick (2008), who reported that 60% of lesbian and gay people have been a victim of some kind of hate incident or crime, with one-sixth of these being physical assaults. However, 75% of those incidents were not reported to the police, and 70% were not reported to any third party until the Gay British Crime Survey (2008) was conducted. This pattern was repeated when Stonewall and YouGov repeated the survey 5 years later (Guasp et al., 2013). The Hate Crime action plan (HM Government, 2012) also highlights under-reporting as a particularly significant issue among new migrant communities, including asylum seekers and refugees as well as the gypsy, Irish traveller and Roma communities.

PSYCHOLOGICAL EXPLANATIONS OF GENOCIDE AND HATE CRIME

In the immediate aftermath of World War II and the Holocaust, in an attempt to identify, predict and even prevent future genocides, scholars started to search for explanations as to why and how people are willing to commit such heinous crimes.

Initially, social scientists considered theories identifying stable, consistent characteristics of individual perpetrators. These attempts promoted the idea of a 'fascist mentality' or 'authoritarian character' (Adorno et al., 1950) that emphasized an individual mindset of obedience with concomitant propensity for harm. However, numerous studies since Milgram's classic work on obedience (1974) have shown that genocides are not committed by intrinsically evil people with extraordinary personal characteristics. Instead, research has shown that genocides are enacted by 'normal' individuals who are placed in extraordinary social circumstances that bear certain similarities (Smith, 2009; Staub, 1989; Zimbardo, 2004). It is not easy for people to kill great numbers systematically; genocides are not spontaneous, sudden, unexpected events. Long processes of societal and psychological change are needed but once in place, genocide and other crimes against humanity can be elicited out of ordinary psychological processes (Staub, 1989).

Hate crime can also be seen as a societal product and the result of an interaction between a wide variety of social forces. Sibbitt's (1997) Home Office-funded review into the perpetrators of hate crime concluded that it was very difficult to find a stereotypical racist offender. Sibbitt writes about perpetrator communities rather than individuals – and while she ties certain types of offending to age, no stereotypical offending type emerged. Iganski, (2008) revives Arendt's idea of the banality of evil when he sets hate crime within 'routine incivilities', where racism is normal.

This still leaves the question of why some groups should be persecuted by members of others. The in-group/out-group theories derived from Tajfel and Turner (1986), and debates surrounding stigma, dehumanization and societal competition, are of direct pertinence when considering the aetiology of both genocide and hate crime offenders. We now turn to these theories, considering them within a wider body of socio-cognitive and societal explanations.

Origins of prejudice: conflict and hardship

Genocide and hate crime can be framed in the context of intractable, intergroup conflicts and long-term (often institutionalized) discrimination (Staub & Bar-Tal, 2003; Coleman, 2003). The source of this intergroup conflict could lie in competition for scarce resources (such as land, material distribution of privilege or goods), or it could be symbolic (e.g., values, beliefs, opinions) (Sherif, 1966). They may also lie in the frustrated basic human needs of one group, or a perceived injustice carried out by the out-group (Staub, 1999). At the most fundamental level, the origins of most intergroup conflict can be traced back to some kind of inequality between groups (Fein, 1993).

Genocides are often perpetrated in times of economic hardship, increased insecurity or social change. Understanding the complex social, historical and economic processes that lead to that suffering is often difficult; people look for simple, rarely accurate explanations of their own worsening circumstances in an attempt to make their world orderly and predictable again. When basic human needs, such as feeling secure or being justly treated, are not satisfied, people may look for alternative explanations in order to understand their situation. These explanations may be negative and include blaming another group for their misfortune (Staub, 1999). Passing blame onto another group is both cognitively and emotionally easier for the individual, and benefits cohesiveness and mobilization within an in-group.

In Nazi Germany, pre-existing anti-Semitism was fanned and inflamed during the economic crisis of the 1920s and 1930s. In Rwanda in 1994, conflict over land possession and tribal delineations resulted in a series of massacres and wars. The 1994 genocide was predictable and was preceded by much racist propaganda and overt preparation for killings.

When basic human needs such as feeling secure, receiving just treatment or being autonomous are not met, individuals and groups turn to destructive ways to seek their satisfaction (Burton, 1987; Staub, 1999). In their research into UK hate attacks, Bowling (1998) and Hewitt (1996) highlighted many racist attacks on people with Asian, Irish or Somali heritage. They proposed that hate offenders were reacting to perceived injustices committed by these groups. The offenders felt the minority groups were responsible for problems such as unemployment and social deprivation that their friends and families, their in-group, were currently experiencing and which had gone unchallenged by the authorities. As such, perpetrators felt that the only way that they could get justice would be to take matters into their own hands. Although these explanations are offered for criminal behaviour, they resonate strongly with commentary provided in the wake of the 2014 European elections. Held at a time of continued uncertainty and austerity, voters mirrored pan-European rises of far right (Front National in France, or the Danish People's Party in Denmark), far left (Syriza in Greece, where Golden Dawn on the far right, also gained its first seat) and other anti-immigration parties such as the United Kingdom Independence Party. Traynor (2014) concluded:

> … after five years of currency and debt crisis, recession, and savage austerity, the results exposed a Europe of division: extremely volatile, fragmented, with voters disenchanted and those choosing to vote cutting their support for the mainstream in favour of fringe parties

NURTURING PREJUDICE: DEMONIZING AND DEGRADING THE OUT-GROUP

As tensions escalate between groups, origins of a conflict or prejudice often cease to be important. What remain important are the established divisions between social groups and increasing inter-group animosity. Perpetrators of genocides or hate crimes are not motivated by an aversion towards victims as individuals, but rather because they are representative of a group perceived as possessing a reviled set of characteristics (Herek, Cogan, & Gillis, 2002).

Frustrations are focused and vented in persecution of the stigmatized group. Members of one group increasingly scapegoat or blame the out-group and develop ideologies and social constructions that promise a better future (Staub, 2012). According to Social Identity Theory (Tajfel & Turner, 1986) and Social Categorization Theory (Turner *et al.*, 1987), people function differently when they think about themselves as members of a social group rather than individuals. As social divisions become intractable, people become more threatened, and their thoughts become emotionally charged. People often think about themselves and others as representatives of 'us' versus 'them' (Sumner, 1906; Tajfel & Turner, 1986). Subsequently, rational thought, along with the understanding of the nuances and complexities of situations, diminishes, giving way to dichotomous reasoning (Castano, 2008; Suedfeld & Tetlock, 1977).

Similarities between members of the in-group and differences they have to the out-group are accentuated. Individual characteristics that are shared with other members of the in-group are emphasized in the self-image (e.g., Biernat, Vescio, & Green, 1996), with the own group clearly favoured (Tajfel & Turner, 1986) and seen as innocent and superior (Gurr, 2000; Sidanius & Pratto, 1999).

In-group favouritism (Brewer & Brown, 1998) is often followed by out-group derogation (Tajfel & Turner, 1986). The out-group is deeply devalued, and generalized, negative judgments are made about the group as a whole. These judgments are not based on actual behaviours of all members of a group, but are reported as being a threat to the in-group's well-being or even continued existence.

The 'other' is ascribed less-human features and emotions (Haslam, 2006; Leyens *et al.*, 2000), as well as other evil characteristics (Castano *et al.*, 2002) – out-group members are perceived as similar to each other in representing these features. Differences between groups are essentialized – that is, treated as being rooted in the very nature of the members of the groups (Castano *et al.* ibid). As this derogation continues, the out-group is seen as a threat to the well-being or continued existence of the in-group, and can be characterized as anything from an obstacle to achieving ideal and desirable social arrangements, to a mortal enemy. As such, prejudice, discrimination, hostility and violence are socially reinforced, becoming normative. This can be reinforced by the benefits of being a member of the in-group, which helps to forge a stronger sense of community and creates a collective identity (Perry, 2000). It can help convince even the most ardent extremist that they are not alone and that their views are not, in fact, extreme at all (Gerstenfeld, Grant, & Chiang, 2003).

BOX 24.3   STAGES OF GENOCIDE

The 10 Stages of Genocide

    Classification→
    Symbolization→
    Discrimination→
    Dehumanization→
    Organization→
    Polarization→
    Preparation→
    Persecution→
    Extermination→
    Denial

Stanton, 2013

As the collective understanding of the inter-group situation loses nuance, escalation begins: actions of one group against the other are reciprocated with ever more ferocity, and it becomes extremely difficult to break this vicious exchange (e.g., Coleman, *et al.*, 2007). In the case of genocide, this has been modelled as part of a 10-stage process (Stanton, 2013). We now turn to such descriptions of processes and explanatory theories, both in genocide and hate crime.[3]

HATE CRIME: BEYOND GROUP EXPLANATIONS

While inter-group conflict has been highlighted as a major motivating factor in genocide and other extremist crimes, it would be somewhat simplistic to suggest that all prejudice and genocidal actions are triggered solely by group motivations.

The term 'hate crime' brings to mind hate-fuelled individuals, consciously acting out their 'hate' for a particular group via the offences they commit (Iganski, 2011). While this may be true for a small number, many offenders are 'ordinary people' who offend during their everyday lives (Iganski, 2008). Hate offences are not always prompted by a particularly strong ideological conviction. Rather, offenders are expressing attitudes that lie beneath the surface of everyday cognitions for many people (Iganski, Kielinger, & Paterson, 2005), and rise to the surface when an opportunity to vent their prejudices presents itself.

Brewer (1999) suggested that the desire to be accepted within one's own group is a stronger motivator to commit hate crime than the hate felt towards at an out-group. Ray, Smith and Wastell (2004) highlighted, for example, shame and envy as possible motivations for committing hate crime against members of an out-group perceived to have a greater social capital. Convicted hate offenders often emphasize feelings of powerlessness and exclusion, and express resentment towards those they see as more successful than themselves (Scheff, 1997). Perceptions that other cultures are stronger and richer than their own can also result in negativity towards these cultures and motivate hate crime.

Looking specifically at the motivations behind hate crime, McDevitt, Levin and Bennett (2002) developed a typology based on police files from Boston, Massachusetts; four distinct motivations for committing hate crime were identified. This typology has been influential in the treatment of hate crime offenders and highlights that offenders' actions are fuelled by a variety of motivations. *Thrill seekers* appear to be led by a desire for excitement or power – the 'buzz' of committing the crime, whereas *defensive offenders* are provoked by a need to protect resources they feel are threatened. *Retaliatory offenders* are apparently motivated to avenge a perceived injustice, and *mission offenders* perceive themselves as champions for their in-group. Mission offenders are premeditated and targeted in the nature of their offending, and, while only accounting for a small minority of offenders, they seem to present the highest level of risk for serious, repeat offending (McDevitt *et al.*, 2002).

ACTING OUT PREJUDICES: PSYCHOLOGICAL PROCESSES THAT FACILITATE VIOLENCE IN GENOCIDE

Alone, the existence of inter-group conflict or prejudice is not enough to result in genocide. The systematic killing of large numbers of people requires co-ordination, commitment and the organization of a great many people. The forces that help unify these actions include a justifying ideology, with organizations that socialize and 'train' individuals to be capable of autonomous, systematic mass-killings and of reproducing killing structures (Darley, 1992). Social organizations and institutions spread the 'ideology of antagonism' (Staub, 1989) to justify stigmatizing (Castano, 2008) and discrimination of designated social groups. Propaganda, 'the cognitive conditioning of hate' (Zimbardo, 2004), is used on many levels, through multifarious social structures including schools, social institutions, families and, increasingly, social media (INACH, 2014).

In Rwanda, the government (composed predominantly of members of the Hutu people) spread negative propaganda against Tutsis, mainly via hate radio (Straus, 2007). Pseudo-scientific information indicating genetic superiority of Hutu over Tutsi people was distributed as fact – a technique also used by Nazi Germany (for an accessible, brief summary of Nazi propaganda techniques, see USHMM, 2013).

In attempting to understand how individuals move from group membership to taking action, Bandura (1999) describes four ways in which people disengage from the moral significance of their actions, and reduce their own cognitive dissonance when committing acts of genocide (Festinger, 1957):

1. The perception of violent actions against members of a stigmatized group is altered and re-interpreted.

2. Minimizing and misconstruction of the negative effects of the actions for the victims.

3. Displacement of individual responsibility to authority figures and dispersal between unidentified others who commit similar acts.

4. Devaluing, de-legitimizing and dehumanizing the victims.

People's attitudes and beliefs are transformed by social processes; individuals socialized to believe and act on an ideology of antagonism learn to commit atrocities against other human beings incrementally. The higher ideology of the cause that the group is serving is used as justification for the evolution of increasing violence and hostility. They come to believe that the other can be hurt, is to be hurt and that they themselves can do the hurting (e.g., Staub, 1989, 1999; Zimbardo, 2004). Ultimately, genocide ceases to be morally wrong and instead becomes the right, justifiable thing to do (Haslam & Reicher, 2008).

PASSIVE BYSTANDERS

Not all of the perpetrators of genocide or hate crime are required to act with equal zeal to achieve a group's goal. There are those who internalize the hostile ideology and believe that harming others is actually moral. Others act on behalf of their group, not necessarily believing in the ideology that devalues the other group but believing that they should act to protect their own in-group. Others still may act through compliance, obedience and conformity. Finally, there are also bystanders who contribute to the possibility of mass harm through their own inaction. Inaction serves to reaffirm the perpetrators' belief in what they are doing, that their acts can go unpunished or are implicitly approved. A new social norm is set: perpetrators, victims and bystanders learn that this is now an acceptable and soon to be normative behaviour for this social group.

There are many processes at work that contribute to bystander passivity: diffusion of responsibility, pluralistic ignorance (Latane & Darley, 1970), belief in the impossibility of one person making a difference and the difficulty in organizing and joining with others of an alternative belief, in societies that are often autocratic (Staub *et al.*, 2010). Inaction can be rationalized as the movement towards violence is taken in such small steps. Just World Theory (Lerner & Simmons, 1966) suggests that those who witness harmful actions against a person are likely to devalue that person if they have reason to believe that the harm and suffering will continue. Observers might also suspend judgment about the meaning of events, attempt to justify the harm that has been done, adopt an observer perspective or avoid information about the harmful actions and others' suffering. Research where participants have been told to take an observer perspective versus imagining themselves in that situation has shown that those with the observer orientation respond with less empathy (Aderman & Berkowitz, 1970). According to the process of informative social influence, in situations that can be seen as ambiguous or unclear (harming an individual or punishing a member of an 'evil' group), the behaviour of others is used as guidance (Sherif, 1954).

Leaders

The role of the charismatic leader, in acts of hate crime and genocide, should not to be underestimated. In difficult circumstances, groups look to leaders for direction and guidance. In all cases, leaders have some leeway in how they deal with intergroup conflict. They can choose to bring groups together in an attempt to unify rather than divide people and improve conditions for all. However, leaders are often motivated to attract followers and enhance their authority, and as such it can be in their interest to offer quick simplistic solutions to ingroup problems. An individual or relatively small leadership group can influence the majority of society, and media coverage can fuel prejudice and divisions and cement stereotypes (Neilsen, 2002). Leaders frequently intensify already existing hostility and often play a key role in propagating an ideology of hate (Kressel, 1996). They enhance devaluation and fear of the other and seek to maintain differences in status between groups. Intense propaganda and the creation of paramilitary groups also facilitate a speedy evolution to intense violence. After the Rwandan genocide, much focus was rightly placed on the role that the Tutsi leadership had at all stages of the genocide (Staub & Pearlman, 2006).

Doubling

In an attempt to explain how people can be loving parents and staunch community members, yet actively participate in killing other men, women and children, the concept of *doubling* has arisen (Lifton, 1986). Based on interviews with Nazi doctors, lawyers, judges and with concentration camp survivors, Lifton's idea of a double self draws on psychoanalytic perspectives. Doubling could be manifested in that it allows perpetrators to live normal lives through the cognitive and emotional separation of social identities in different social roles (e.g., Lifton looked at how doctors could still see themselves as physicians and return to their families, while, at the camps, selecting who should go to the gas chambers). This is an alternative explanation for processes that would result in similar effects to those described earlier when considering cognitive dissonance.

CHARACTERISTICS OF CULTURES DISPOSED TO GENOCIDE AND HATE CRIME

The processes that lead to hostility and violence, and the evolution of hate and genocide, are more likely to occur in groups with certain characteristics (Staub, 2012). Groups that have been victimized in the past (or that harbour the perception that they were victimized) are likely to feel vulnerable to attack. They are more likely to see the world as a dangerous place and respond to perceived danger by engaging in excessive violence under the pretence of self-defence (Staub & Pearlman, 2006). Groups that have a history of dealing with conflicts by engaging in violence are often more willing to engage in violence subsequently.

Triggering event

After the societal and psychological preparations, genocidal actions may well involve symbolic events that are used as an excuse to begin destruction of property, imprisonment and mass killings. Trigger events are usually followed by disproportionate reactions. For example, the assassination of Ernst vom Rath, a junior diplomat of the German Embassy in Paris, was used as a trigger for *Kristallnacht* in November 1938 – the pogrom that predicated more systematic extermination of Jews in Germany. In Rwanda, the assassination of the president Juvenal Habyarimana was used to catalyse the genocide that started hours after his aeroplane was shot down (HRW, 1999).

Some hate crimes may also be triggered by a specific event. Hate offenders that fall into the defensive or retaliatory sections of the McDevitt, Levin, and Bennett (2002) hate offending typology are more likely to be motivated by a perceived injustice and react to a specific event. This can be seen by the increase in reported anti-Muslim hate crime in the aftermath of the 7 July bombings in London (McClintock & LeGendre, 2007). This returns us to how the reporting and incidence of hate crimes are intrinsically part of societal and communal relations. Individual, group and structural explanations need to be considered within this domain. Psychological theories can be evaluated alongside social policy, international relations and wider sociological and criminological literature. This applies both to aetiology and to consideration of how to intervene. Should intervention be at a state level, individual level, early to prevent, or later to challenge? We begin to frame these questions further in the text that follows.

REHABILITATION OF HATE CRIME OFFENDERS

In the 'post-MacPherson era', there has been pressure on the criminal justice system in the United Kingdom to engage with the perpetrators of hate crime and reduce offending. Understanding the impulses and motivations that lead to hate crime has been seen as essential to designing rehabilitation measures/services for offenders. Research into the development and implementation of such interventions has been convincing in its conclusion that hate crime requires a different approach (Iganski, 2002).

To date, interventions have been primarily delivered within the criminal justice system. Interventions based on psychological and social science research are increasingly being used to alter individual offending behaviour, protect victims and meet demands for public protection (Dixon, 2002).

The Diversity, Awareness and Prejudice Pack (DAPP) (Dixon, 2002) was developed by what was then the London Probation Service. While the DAPP toolkit is not the only intervention developed to work with hate offenders (for a full review of all interventions that have been developed to work with hate offenders, see Iganski and Smith, 2011), to date it is widely used in the United Kingdom. It aims to promote an offender's positive racial and cultural identity, reduce disengagement and dissonance, challenge targeted offending, and then reflect on past behaviours through this new lens (Ray, Smith, & Wastell, 2004). By focusing on issues of race, cultural identity and the need to develop skills to manage anger and aggressions in a single

programme, the DAPP aims to manage, contain and ultimately alter offender prejudices.

Practitioners work on a one-to-one basis with offenders. Active engagement within the community is an important part of the programme, and certain modules require offenders to develop victim awareness, learn about the local area and gain a different perspective on their offence. Racist victimization does not occur in a moment, but rather is dynamic and embedded in time, space and place. The DAPP programme is therefore designed to be flexible and to encourage practitioners to adapt to the changing presentations of offending, moving targets and for increasing confidence in the capacity to promote change in offenders (Dixon & Court, 2003). Targeted interventions with offenders who have been convicted of hate crimes may thus be beginning to alter specific beliefs and perceptions at an individual level, but in order to address root causes of prejudice, it seems essential that wide-reaching, group-level interventions are also required to try to address the root causes of such behaviour.

Political will and a culture of social reflection are needed to shift thinking in societies, to challenge normative racism and to challenge institutions, organizations and structures to drive forward long-term, social change (Chakraborti & Garland, 2014; Lemos, 2005). The Cantle Report (2001), which examined community relations in areas of the United Kingdom affected by the riots of 2001, identified how racial tensions can fuel community discord and racial conflict. The report highlighted the increasingly divisive nature of different communities leading 'parallel lives', and the fear and ignorance about 'others' that this generates. More recently, the All Parliamentary Inquiry into Electoral Conduct highlighted the ways in which discriminatory practices can be used during electoral campaigns (APPG, 2013) and suggested ways to challenge them.

Moving back to an individual level briefly, the use of restorative justice practices has also been suggested with hate crime offenders; however, work to date has been limited, and concerns about risk to victim–survivors are high (Gavrielides et al., 2008). Some of the impetus behind such approaches is similar to other initiatives designed simply to bring together members of in-groups with out-groups. If done successfully, this can be a powerful tool to disrupt prejudicial processes, but if mishandled, such encounters can reinforce prejudice and resentment. Contact hypothesis, first put forward by Allport (1954), suggests that, in order to persuade people to reconsider their views about others, they need to have contact with that group, and, ideally, work with one another successfully towards a common purpose. Contact hypothesis, or what is now known as inter-group contact theory (Hodson & Hewstone, 2013), has had notable successes (Brown, 2000) and has been used to break down prejudice and stereotypes in a variety of groups (Ihlanfeldt & Scafidi, 2002).

There was also a feeling that education would enlighten those with prejudiced views of others, something that has been reinforced by the response to Internet-based cyber-crime – where it is believed that greater critical engagement with material by users will be more effective than trying to prevent hate, or other criminal material from being promulgated in the first place (e.g., ICCA, 2013). As Bowling (1998) highlighted, these issues involve relationships and an emotional component that would need addressing alongside possible cognitive distortions and factual inaccuracy. Schools have had some success in the endeavour to promote tolerance – for example, the citizenship curriculum has helped promote community cohesion initiatives (Cowan, et al., 2002). In the last decade, schools, NGOs and Youth Clubs have worked to devise programmes of intervention to develop tolerance and an appreciation of diversity with some success.

PREVENTING GENOCIDE

'Preventing genocide and mass atrocities is not an idealistic addition to our core foreign policy agenda. It is a moral and strategic imperative'
(Allbright & Cohen, 2008).

When examining the social and psychological processes that lead to genocide, it cannot be said that it is unpredictable, and it should therefore be preventable. As such, the focus of those working to prevent genocide must be on early identification and flagging up of areas where genocide might take place. Stanton (1996) summarized much of the material outlined earlier in this chapter and initially put forward 8 *Stages of Genocide*, subsequently revised to 10, as outlined earlier. These stages are used by Genocide Watch to create a list of countries at different levels of risk (or actual incidence) of genocide.

If areas where genocides are likely to occur can be identified, then reactions or interventions can take place while perpetrators' 'commitment to violence' is still limited. The motivation for mass killing or genocide may not yet have fully evolved, and inhibitions against violence may not have disappeared. A plan of action or a system to execute it may not exist. Persistent efforts by external bystanders, nations and the international community are likely to be effective and could prevent action being taken (Staub, 1999), providing that the will and means are there. When cultural preconditions for group violence exist, but there has been no significant increase

in harm-doing, there is still time for preventive action. Economic development, increasing security at the time of post-conflict reconstruction (and thereby preventing new cycles of violence), an effective justice system and other structural elements have been proposed as means of prevention (Carnegie Commission on the Prevention of Deadly Conflict, 1997). These steps are important, but have a long-range horizon, and by themselves are not sufficient.

Outside, third parties have the potential to be either bystanders or to assert influence over a perpetrator nation. These include individuals, community groups, NGOs, governments and federations of states and international organizations. Additionally, there are a number of organizations set up specifically to monitor, report, raise awareness and help to prevent genocide; these include: Genocide Watch (www.genocidewatch.net), Prevent Genocide International (www.preventgenocide.org), the United States Holocaust Memorial Museum (www.ushmm.org/conscience), Survivors' Rights International (www.survivorsrightsinternational.org) and the Aegis Trust (www.aegistrust.org). Finally, countries that have close links to the perpetrator nation have significant potential influence (Fein, 1994) and a responsibility to act. Yet, as we have already noted, governments may vacillate over recognizing genocide as such, and international law is hard to enforce.

Although a number of crimes against humanity have been codified, it is only when genocidal intention has been recognized that the international signatories to the Rome Convention have the legal obligation to intervene. The resulting apparent inertia in the face of crimes against humanity and a reluctance to call any of them 'genocide' has led to a new approach that is led by human rights and known as the 'Responsibility to Protect' (RtoP or R2P) – this is a concept agreed at the World Summit of 2005. It is under the human rights norms of RtoP that UN Security Council (UNSC) resolutions were passed to intervene in conflicts such as Darfur (resolution 1706 established the UN deployment of over 17,000 troops on a peacekeeping mission) and Libya (resolutions 1970 and 1973), and led to the appointment of a special advisor on genocide to the United Nations and RtoP (RtoP, 2013). Under RtoP, any intervention must be sanctioned by the United Nations, which explains the vital importance of UNSC resolutions and the dilemmas posed when allies to a (potentially) genocidal state effectively block such resolutions.

This is partly why, despite being an organization with international backing, the UN has seemed particularly ineffective in intervening in genocides in Rwanda and elsewhere. However, the more recent interventions in Cote d'Ivoire and Libya under RtoP have demonstrated that international response is possible and could be incrementally gaining ground.

SUMMARY

In this chapter, we have provided a historical backdrop for both hate crime and genocide. We have framed these constructs in a legal setting and have tried to elucidate some of the complexity around definition and classification. We have outlined some of the controversies around the law on genocide and the difficulties in reporting on hate crime.

While genocide and hate crime are separate concepts with their own bodies of academic study, we have explained some of the underlying socio-cognitive and psychological processes that sit behind both of these crimes at an individual and group level. We have summarized the patterns of prejudice and hate that result in demonization of the 'other', persecution and violence, while also covering debates on stigma, societal competition, discrimination and prejudice that are pertinent to both concepts.

We have finished with a brief discussion of how insights from psychological theory have influenced interventions (for both victims and offenders), and considered responses to hate crime and genocide – looking at prevention and intervention at the individual and state levels.

NOTES

1 These are only three examples that we have selected of the 14 countries where exterminations were in progress, identified on the Genocide Watch website (Genocide Watch, 2014).
2 In 2007, Fiona Pilkington set her car on fire, while both she and her daughter Frankie were inside. They had been victims of hate abuse for more than 11 years. The abuse is thought to have initially begun when Ms Pilkington's other child, Anthony, was being bullied in relation to dyslexia.
3 Please note that some of this material has been previously considered in Adler and Golec de Zavala (2010).

FURTHER READING

We have suggested here three additional readings, two of which we have already mentioned in the chapter. We have selected these readings as cogent representations of three different areas of endeavour, and start with our suggestion for some in-depth consideration of relevant applied social psychology:

Reading 1: Hodson, G., & Hewstone, M. (Eds.). (2013). *Advances in intergroup contact*. Hove: Psychology Press.

In this chapter, we have mentioned the importance of 'contact hypothesis' as a route to potentially help minimize harm and prevent prejudice. This relatively recent edited collection draws together a substantial body of work concerned with the implementation and refinement of contact hypothesis as it has morphed into the 'Intergroup Contact Theory'. This is a higher-level book, but starts with basic principles, guiding the reader throughout. It is, however, an edited collection, and although this adds both breadth and depth to the book, it may mean that shifts in narrative voice are not to every reader's liking.

Reading 2: Hall, N. (2013). *Hate crime* (2nd ed.). Abingdon: Routledge.

This next text is more criminological in orientation, although it does have a section devoted to prejudice and other ideas that can be considered both sociologically as well as psychologically. Nathan Hall's work has always synthesized approaches that are directly useful to police, while being properly grounded in theory and research. This book starts with basic definitions and moves on to look at the who, what, when, where and why classic questions, applying them to prevalence and consequences of hate crime. This book is relevant widely but retains a useful focus on English and Welsh norms.

Reading 3: Staub, E. (2011). *Overcoming evil: Genocide, violent conflict and terrorism*. Oxford: Oxford University Press.

In selecting all of these readings, we have had to refine down from a plethora of accessible, informative work. By selecting any authors or editors, we have necessarily cut out others. In this case, the problem was worsened by there being so much recent work by the same author. Eventually, we decided that this book was the most relevant to this particular chapter as it is the one where Ervin Staub articulates clearly the inter-connectedness of mass violence, whether it is genocidal or another form of asymmetric violence. One reason for selecting something by Staub is his forthright stance on 'evil' and the arguments he makes not to avoid labelling acts as 'evil'. The stance he takes is that evil acts occur in explainable and avoidable circumstances, and he draws on both individual and group psychology to better understand the processes that are at play. We also selected this book as Professor Staub is someone who has direct experience of drawing on theory to inform policy and practice internationally.

REFERENCES

ACPO (2005). *Hate Crime: Delivering a better service. Good practice and tactical guidance.* London: ACPO.

ACPO (2011). *The national standard for incident recording.* http://www.acpo.police.uk/documents/LPpartnerships/2010/20110831%20LPPBA%20The%20National%20Standard%20for%20Incident%20Recording_April%202011.pdf (accessed 13 January 2015).

Aderman, D., & Berkowitz, L. (1970). Observational set, empathy, and helping. *Journal of Personality and Social Psychology, 14,* 141–148.

Adler, J. R., & Golec de Zavala, A. (2010). Genocide. In J. M. Brown & E. Campbell (Eds.), *Cambridge handbook of forensic psychology.* Cambridge: CU Press.

Adorno, T. W., Frenkel-Brunswik, E., Levinson, D. J., & Sanford, R. N. (1950). *The authoritarian personality.* New York: Harper.

Allbright, M. K., & Cohen, W. S. (2008, 21st December). Never again for real. *New York Times.*

Allport, G. W. (1954). *The nature of prejudice.* Cambridge, MA: Addison-Wesley.

Andreopoulos, G. J. (Ed.). (1994). *Genocide: Conceptual and historical dimensions.* Philadelphia: University of Pennsylvania Press.

APPG (2013). *Report of the all-party parliamentary inquiry into electoral conduct.* http://www.electoralconduct.com/, accessed 14 January 2015.

Bandura, A. (1999). Moral disengagement in the perpetration of inhumanities. *Personality and Social Psychology Review* [Special Issue on Evil and Violence], *3,* 193–209.

Berenbaum, M. (2004). Case Study III: The Holocaust. In S. Totten (Ed.), *Teaching about genocide: Issues, approaches and resources.* Charlotte, NC: Information Age Publishing.

Biernat, M., Vescio, T. K., & Green, M. L. (1996). Selective self-stereotyping. *Journal of Personality and Social Psychology, 71,* 1194–1209.

Bowling, B. (1998). *Violent racism: Victimization, policing and social context.* Oxford: Clarendon Press.

Brewer, M. B. (1999). The Psychology of prejudice: in group love out group hate? *Journal of Social Issues, 55*(3), 429–444.

Brewer, M. B., & Brown, R. J. (1998). Intergroup relations. In D. T. Gilbert, S. T. Fiske, & G. Lindzey (Dir.), *The handbook of social psychology.* New York: McGraw Hill.

Brown, R. J. (2000). *Group processes: Dynamics within and between groups* (2nd ed.). Oxford: Blackwell.

Burton, J. W. (1987), *Resolving deep-rooted conflict: A handbook.* Lanham (Maryland) and London: University Press of America.

Carnegie Commission on the Prevention of Deadly Conflict. (1997). *Preventing deadly violence final report.* New York: Carnegie Foundation.

Castano, E. (2008). On the perils of glorifying the in-group: Intergroup violence, in-group glorification, and moral disengagement. *Social and Personality Psychology Compass, 2*(1), 154–170.

Castano, E., Yzerbyt, V., Paladino, M., & Sacchi, R. (2002). I belong, therefore, I exist: ingroup identification, ingroup entitativity, and ingroup bias. *Personality and Social Psychology Bulletin, 28,* 135–143.

Chakraborti, N., & Garland, J. (Eds.). (2014). *Responding to hate crime: The case for Connecting policy and research.* Bristol: The Policy Press.

Coleman, P. (2003). Characteristics of protracted, intractable conflict: Toward the development of a metaframework–I. Peace and conflict. *Journal of Peace Psychology, 9,* 1–37.

Coleman, P. T., Vallacher, R., Nowak, A., & Bui-Wrzosinska, L. (2007). Intractable conflict as an attractor: Presenting a dynamical-systems approach to conflict, escalation, and intractability. Paper presented at the International Association for Conflict Management Meetings.

College of Policing (2014). Hate crime operational guidance. http://www.college.police.uk/cps/rde/xchg/cop/root.xsl/21807.htm, accessed 14 January 2015.

Cowan, G., Resendez, M., Marshall, E., & Quist, R. (2002). Hate speech and constitutional protection: Priming values of equality and freedom. *Journal of Social Issues, 58*(2), 247–263.

Crown Prosecution Service (CPS) (no date). *Guidance on prosecuting cases of disability hate crime.* http://www.cps.gov.uk/legal/d_to_g/disability_hate_crime/, accessed 13 January 2015.

Darley, J. (1992). Social organization for the production of evil. *Psychological Inquiry, 3,* 199–217.

Des Forges, A. (1999). *Leave none to tell the story: Genocide in Rwanda.* New York: Human Rights Watch.

Dick, S. (2008). *Homophobic hate crime: The Gay British crime survey 2008.* London: Stonewall.

Dixon, L. (2002). Tackling racist offending: A targeted or generalised approach? *Probation Journal, 49*(3), 205–216.

Dixon, L. (2010). Tackling hate by driving diversity: A New Labour success story? *The Journal of Community and Criminal Justice, 57*(3), 314–321.

Dixon, L., & Court, D. (2003). Developing good practice with racially motivated offenders. *Probation Journal, 50*(2), 149–153.

Dixon, L., & Ray, L. (2007). Current issues and developments in race hate crime. *The Journal of Community and Criminal Justice, 54*(2), 109–124.

Fein, H. (1993). Accounting for genocide after 1945: Theories and some findings. *International Journal on Minority and Group Rights, 1*, 79.

Fein, H. (1994). Genocide, terror, life integrity, and war crimes. In G. J. Andreopoulos (Ed.), *Genocide: Conceptual and historical dimensions* (pp. 95–107). Philadelphia: University of Pennsylvania Press.

Festinger, L. (1957). *A theory of cognitive dissonance.* Stanford, CA: Stanford University Press.

Gavrielides, T., Parle, L., Salla, A., Liberatore, G., Mavadia, C., & Arjomand, G. (2008). *Addressing hate crime through restorative justice and cross-sector partnerships: A London study.* London: ROTA.

Genocide Watch (2014). *Recent alerts.* http://genocidewatch.net/alerts-2/new-alerts/, accessed 14 January 2015.

Gerstenfeld, P. B., Grant, Diana R., & Chiang, C. P. (2003). Hate online: A content analysis of extremist Internet sites. *Analyses of Social Issues and Public Policy, 3*(1), 29–44.

Gourevitch, P. (1998). *We wish to inform you that tomorrow we will be killed with our families: Stories from Rwanda.* New York: Farrar, Straus & Giroux.

Guasp, A., Gammon, A., & Ellison, G. (2013). *Homophobic hate crime: The Gay British crime survey, 2013.* London: Stonewall and YouGov.

Gurr, T. R. (2000, May/June). Ethnic warfare on the wane. *Foreign Affairs, 79*(3), 52–64.

Hall, N. (2013). *Hate crime* (2nd edn). Abingdon: Routledge.

Haslam, N. (2006). Dehumanization: An integrative review. *Personality and Social Psychology Review, 10*, 252–264.

Haslam, S. A., & Reicher, S. D. (2008). Questioning the banality of evil. *The Psychologist, 21*(1), 16–19.

Herek, G. M., & Berril, K. (1992). Documenting the victimization of lesbians and gay men: Methodological issues. In G. Herek & K. Berrill (Eds.), *Hate crimes* (pp. 270–286). Thousand Oaks, CA: Sage.

Herek, G. M., Cogan, J. C., & Gillis, J. R. (2002). Victim experiences in hate crimes based on sexual orientation. *Journal of Social Issues, 58*(2), 319–339.

Hewitt, R. (1996). *Routes of Racism: The social basis of racist attack.* Stoke On Trent: Trentham Books.

HM Government (2012). *Challenge it, Report it, Stop it: The Government's plan to tackle hate crime.* London: HM Government.

Hodson, G., & Hewstone, M. (Eds.). (2013). *Advances in intergroup contact.* Hove: Psychology Press.

Home Office (1981). *Racial attacks: Report of a Home Office study.* London: Home Office.

Home Office (1989). *The response to racial attacks and harassment: Guidance for statutory agencies Report of the Inter-Departmental Racial Attacks Group.* London: Home Office.

Home Affairs Committee (1994). *Racial attacks and harassment.* London: HMSO Volumes 1 and 2.

Home Office (2009). *Hate crime: The cross-government action plan.* London: Home Office.

Home Office (2009a). *The cross-government action plan.* London: Home Office.

Home Office Police Standards Unit and ACPO (2005). Hate crime: Delivering a quality service: Good practice and tactical guidance. London: Home Office and ACPO.

Home Office, Office of National Statistics, & Ministry of Justice (2013). An overview of hate crime and England and Wales. London. http://www.report-it.org.uk/files/ons_hate-crime-report_2013.pdf accessed 26.5.14

House of Commons (1986). *Racial attacks and harassment.* Third report from the Home Affairs Committee, Session 1985–86 (London: HMSO).

Human Rights Watch (HRW) (1999). *Leave none to tell the story: Genocide in Rwanda.* http://www.hrw.org/reports/1999/rwanda/ (accessed 13 January 2015).

IAEG (2012). http://www.genocidewatch.org/alliancetoendgenocide/about.html (accessed 13 January 2015).

ICCA (2013). Task force on Internet hate report and recommendations of the co-chairs. London: ICCA.

Iganski, P. (Ed.). (2002). *The hate debate.* London: Profile.

Iganski, P. (2008). *Hate crime and the city.* Bristol: Policy Press.

Iganski, P. (2011). *Racist violence in Europe.* Brussels: Open Society Foundation.

Iganski, P., Kielinger, V., & Paterson, S. (2005). *Hate crimes against London's Jews.* London: Institute for Jewish Policy Research and the Metropolitan Police Service.

Iganski, P., & Smith, D. (2011). Rehabilitation of hate crime offenders. Equality and Human Rights Commission Scotland.

Ihlanfeldt, K, R., & Scafidi, B. (2002). Black Self-regulation as a cause of housing segregation: Evidence from the multi city study of urban inequality. *Journal of Urban Economics, 51*(2), 366–390.

INACH (2014). http://www.inach.net/news.php.

Jacobs, J. B., & Potter, K. A. (1998). *Hate crime, criminal law and identity politics.* New York, NY: Oxford University Press.

Ki-moon, B. (2014). *New York, 20 February 2014 – Secretary-General's remarks to the Security Council on the situation in the Central African Republic.* http://www.un.org/sg/statements/index.asp?nid=7471, accessed 13 January 2015.

Kressel, N. J. (1996). *Mass hate: The global rise of genocide and terror.* Boulder, CO: Westview Press.

Kuper, L. (1994). Theoretical issues relating to genocide: Uses and abuses. In G. J. Andreopoulos (Ed.), *Genocide: Conceptual and historical dimensions* (pp. 31–46). Philadelphia: University of Pennsylvania Press.

Latane, B., & Darley, J. (1970). *The unresponsive bystander: Why doesn't he help?* New York: Appleton-Crofts.

Lemkin, R. (1933) (translated by J. Fussel). *Acts Constituting a General (Transnational) Danger Considered as Offences Against the Law of Nations. Additional explications to the Special Report presented to the 5th Conference for the Unification of Penal Law in Madrid (14–20 October 1933).*

Lemkin, R. (1944, reprinted in 2005). *Axis rule in occupied Europe: Laws of occupation, analysis of government, proposals for redress.* Carnegie Endowment for International Peace–The Lawbook Exchange, Ltd., New Jersey, 2005.

Lemos, G. (2005). *The search for tolerance: Challenging and changing racist attitudes and behaviour among young people.* York: Joseph Rowntree Foundation.

Lerner, M. J., and Simmons, C. H. (1966). The observer's reaction to the 'innocent victim': Compassion or rejection? *Journal of Personality and Social Psychology, 4,* 203–210.

Levin, J., & McDevitt, J. (1993). *Hate crimes: The rising tide of bigotry and bloodshed.* New York: Plenum.

Leyens, J. Ph., Paladino, P. M., Rodriguez, R. T., Vaes, J., Demoulin, S., Rodriguez, A. P., & Gaunt, R. (2000). The emotional side of prejudice: The role of secondary emotions. *Personality and Social Psychology Review, 4,* 186–197.

Lifton, R. J. (1986). *The Nazi doctors: Medical killing and the psychology of genocide.* New York: Basic Books.

Macpherson, W. (1999). *The Stephen Lawrence inquiry report,* Cm. 4262–1. London: HMSO.

McClintock, M., & LeGendre, P. (2007). *Islamophobia, 2007 Hate crime survey.* New York: Human Rights First.

McDevitt, J., Levin, J., & Bennett, S. (2002). Hate crime offenders and extended typology. *Journal of Social Issues, 58*(2), 303–318.

Mencap (2000). *Living in fear.* London: Mencap.

Milgram, S. (1974). *Obedience to authority: An experimental view.* New York: Harper and Row.

MIND (2007). *Another assault.* London: Mind the National Association for Mental Health.

Neilsen, L. B. (2002). Subtle, pervasive, harmful: Racist and sexist remarks in public as hate speech. *Journal of Social Issues, 58*(2), 265–280.

Perry, B. (2001). *In the name of hate.* New York: Routledge.

Ray, L., Smith, D., & Wastell, L. (2004). Shame, rage and racist violence. *British Journal of Criminology, 44,* 350–368.

RtoP (2013). http://responsibilitytoprotect.org/, accessed 14 January 2015.

Scheff, T. J. (1997). *Emotions, the social bond and human reality: Part/whole analysis.* Cambridge: Cambridge University Press.

Sherif, M. (1954). Socio-cultural influences in small group research. *Sociology and Social Research, 39,* 1–10.

Sherif, M. (1966). *In common predicament: Social psychology of intergroup conflict and cooperation.* Boston: Houghton-Mifflin.

Sibbitt, R. (1997). *The perpetrators of racial harassment and violence.* Home Office Research Study 176. London: Home Office.

Sidanius, J., & Pratto, F. (1999). *Social dominance: An intergroup theory of social hierarchy and oppression.* New York: Cambridge University Press.

Sin, C. H., Hedges, A., Cook, C., Mguni, N., & Comber, N. (2009). *Disabled people's experiences of targeted violence and hostility.* Manchester: Equality and Human Rights Commission.

Slaughter, A. M. (2013). *Obama should remember Rwanda as he weighs action in Syria.* The Washington Post , 27 April.

Smith, S. (2009). Massacre at Murambi: The rank and file killers of genocide. In N. Loucks, S. Smith-Holt, & J. R. Adler (Eds.), *Why we kill: Understanding violence across cultures and disciplines.* London: Middlesex University Press.

Stanton, G. H. (1996). *The 8 stages of genocide: A briefing paper for the United States State Department* [Electronic Version]. http://www.genocidewatch.org/aboutgenocide/8stagesofgenocide.html (accessed 13 January 2015).

Stanton, G. H. (2002). *What is genocide?* http://www.genocidewatch.org/genocide/whatisit.html (accessed 13 January 2015).

Stanton, G. H. (2013). *The ten stages of genocide.* http://genocidewatch.net/genocide-2/8-stages-of-genocide/(accessed 13 January 2015).

Staub, E. (1989). *The roots of evil: The origins of genocide and other group violence.* New York: Cambridge University Press.

Staub, E. (1999). The roots of evil: Social conditions, culture, personality, and basic human needs. *Personality and Social Psychology Review, 3,* 179–192.

Staub, E. (2011). *Overcoming evil: Genocide, violent conflict and terrorism.* Oxford: Oxford University Press.

Staub, E. (2012). The roots and prevention of genocide and related mass violence. Chapter 2 in M. Anstey, P. Meerts, & I. W. Zartman (Eds.), *The slippery slope to genocide: Reducing identity conflicts and preventing mass murder.* New York: Oxford University Press.

Staub, E., & Bar-Tal, D. (2003). Genocide, mass killing and intractable conflict: Roots, evolution, prevention and reconciliation. In D. O. Sears, L. Huddy, & R. Jervis (Eds.), *Oxford handbook of political psychology* (pp. 710–751). New York: Oxford University Press.

Staub, E., & Pearlman, L. A. (2006). Advancing healing and reconciliation. In L. Barbanel & R. Sternberg (Eds.), *Psychological interventions in times of crisis* (pp. 213–245). New York: Springer-Verlag.

Staub, E., Pearlman, L. A., Weiss, G., & Hoek, A. (2010). Public education through radio to prevent violence, promote trauma healing and reconciliation, and build peace in Rwanda and the Congo. In E. Staub (Ed.), *The panorama of mass violence: Origins, prevention and reconciliation.* New York: Oxford University Press.

Straus, S. (2007). What Is the relationship between hate radio and violence? Rethinking Rwanda's 'Radio machete'. *Politics & Society, 35*(4), 609–663, doi: 10.1177/0032329207308181.

Suedfeld, P., & Tetlock, P. (1977). Integrative complexity of communications in international crises. *Journal of Conflict Resolution, 21,* 169–184.

Sumner, W. G. (1906), *Folkways*. New York: Ginn.

Tajfel, H., & Turner, J. C. (1986). The social identity theory of intergroup behavior. In S. Worchel & W. G. Austin (Eds.), *Psychology of intergroup relations* (pp. 7–24). Chicago: Nelson-Hall Publishers.

Traynor, I. (2014). Front National wins European parliament elections in France. *Guardian*, 25 May.

Turner, J. C., Hogg, M. A., Oakes, P. J., Reicher, S. D., & Wetherell, M. S. (1987). *Rediscovering the social group: A self-categorization theory*. Oxford: Basil Blackwell.

USHMM (United States Holocaust Memorial Museum, 2013) encyclopedia entry: *Nazi propaganda*. http://www.ushmm.org/wlc/en/article.php?ModuleId=10005202 (accessed 13 January 2015).

Warwickshire Safeguarding Adults Partnership (2011). *Serious case review: The murder of Gemma Hayter 9th August, 2010*. http://www.warwickshire.gov.uk/seriouscasereview, accessed 13 January 2015.

Zimbardo, P. (2004). A situationist perspective on the psychology of evil: Understanding how good people are transformed into perpetrators. In A. Miller (Ed.), *The social psychology of good and evil: Understanding our capacity for kindness and cruelty*. New York: Guilford.

25 Restorative Justice as a Psychological Treatment: Healing Victims, Reintegrating Offenders[1]

LAWRENCE W. SHERMAN AND HEATHER STRANG

A substantial body of scientific evidence now shows that restorative justice conferencing (RJC) is an effective psychological treatment for offenders and their victims. While there are many varieties of programmes described as 'restorative', only RJC, in which offenders and victims meet in person with family or friends, has been subjected to extensive and rigorous testing. The evidence is particularly strong with respect to violent crimes, even though RJ may be most difficult to arrange in such cases. Results from 12 randomized controlled trials (RCTs) in the United Kingdom, Australia and the United States cover adult and youth crime, violent and property crime, offenders in prison as well as in the community, RJC as diversion and as a supplement to ordinary prosecution and sentencing. Outcomes for offenders include reduced frequency of reconviction and cost of crimes committed. Outcomes for victims include reduced post-traumatic stress symptoms, anger, desire for violent revenge, fear and anxiety. Forensic psychologists may be in an ideal position to provide access to RJC for far more victims and offenders than are presently offered opportunities for it in the United Kingdom. They may also be able to enhance the evidence base by conducting and reporting small-scale RCTs in their own practices.

INTRODUCTION

Restorative justice is any response to crime that emphasizes repair of existing harm (restoration) over infliction of additional harm (retribution). Such responses have a long history, a contemporary social movement and an uncertain future. Historically, pre-bureaucratic societies made widespread use of restorative justice (RJ) as a means of preventing long and damaging blood feuds between families or tribes (Braithwaite, 2002; Huxley, 1939). While the rise of nation-states and offences against the Crown (Christie, 1977) greatly restricted RJ in favour of retributive punishments, the late twentieth century saw a resurgence of restorative practices in a global social movement (United Nations, 2002). It also saw the commissioning of a substantial programme of experimental research to compare RJ conferencing (RJC) to strictly retributive responses. While the RJC test results are generally favourable (Shapland et al., 2008; Sherman & Strang, 2007, forthcoming), the findings are not widely known or understood. Until they are, it is not clear that victims and offenders will be provided widespread access to RJC even when they request it.

Forensic psychologists may be in a critical position to translate the research results into action. The evidence suggests that it is appropriate to view RJ as a psychological treatment that benefits both offenders and victims. It is therefore appropriate for psychologists to inform their clients about those benefits and how the treatment operates. The evidence suggests that in order to convey a full and complete understanding of RJ, at least one hour of one-on-one discussion is required. Psychologists in forensic settings may be better placed to provide that kind of intensive explanation than many other professionals. If their offender or victim clients elect to undertake RJ in any volume, forensic psychologists may be better placed than most to conduct their own RCTs of

Forensic Psychology, Second Edition. Edited by David A. Crighton and Graham J. Towl.
© 2015 John Wiley & Sons, Ltd. Published 2015 by British Psychological Society and John Wiley & Sons, Ltd.

the effects of RJC (or other RJ) on a range of outcomes. Adding more RCTs for specific kinds of offenders at specific points of the justice system could bring far greater precision to the evidence base. It could also help to support the expansion of resources needed to make such treatments more widely available to crime victims and offenders. This chapter provides an independent overview of the knowledge forensic psychologists need to provide their clients with more access to restorative justice. This knowledge includes when RJ is *not* recommended, given evidence on when RJ is contraindicated due to offence or offender characteristics. It begins by describing the wide range of restorative practices. It then narrows the focus to the one method that has been subjected to RCTs, and to generally the most extensive field testing: face-to-face RJC meetings of 1–3 hours among victims, their offenders and their respective friends or family members, led by a trained RJ facilitator. After presenting some of the theories of change by which RJC is predicted to affect both victim and offender, the chapter then addresses the practicalities of delivering RJC. These logistical issues set the stage for describing the science and ethics of randomized trials of RJC, followed by summaries of what they show about its effects on offenders and victims. A brief review of other RJ approaches besides conferencing precedes the concluding reflections on the role of forensic psychologists in RJ in general and RJC in particular.

VARIETIES OF RESTORATIVE JUSTICE

Contemporary usage of the term 'restorative justice' embraces a wide range of definitions. These definitions may be classified on several dimensions. One is the method by which the programme operates. A second is the stage of the criminal process at which it operates, if it is associated with criminal justice. A third is the range of other institutions and settings in which restorative responses to harm – criminal or not – may be organized.

All three of these dimensions fall within the broader definition of RJ adopted by the Home Office in 2003: '... a process whereby all the parties with a stake in a particular offence come together to resolve collectively how to deal with the aftermath of the offence and its implications for the future' (Marshall, 1999). This definition is arguably so broad that it would include a lynch mob or a gang fight. Yet, when added to the essential focus on repair rather than revenge (Strang, 2002), the definition is consistent with more philosophical statements such as the one Desmond Tutu (1999) used to guide the Truth and Reconciliation

Commission in South Africa. These ideas about RJ, in fact, have great appeal for the tragic challenges facing post-conflict societies (Strang, 2010). The present chapter limits its focus, however, to everyday crime in stable common law democracies, since virtually all of the evidence reviewed comes from the United Kingdom, Australia, the United States, New Zealand and Canada.

RJ methods

Several methods are commonly advertised as 'restorative' in nature. These may be arranged on a continuum from 'indirect' to 'direct' restoration of one or more individual victims harmed by an offender, where crimes entailed such victims.

Programmes for offenders who directly harmed no personal victim at all (a so-called 'victimless' crime) are sometimes called restorative, as in the RCTs we conducted in Canberra (Australia) with persons caught driving with legally excessive blood alcohol levels and with under-18 shoplifters caught in large department stores (Sherman & Strang, 2007). In both RCTs, the restorative method entailed an RJ conference without a direct victim present, but with frequent participation of a community or store 'representative' in a meeting with the offender, his or her family, friends and a police officer facilitating the discussion. RJ programmes for offenders who had direct victims may be classified by 'directness' as follows, moving from the least to the most direct method of communication among all parties affected by a crime:

- Orders by judges that offenders must pay restitution or reparations to their victims via the Probation Service, without ever meeting their victims.

- Discussions between professionals and offenders in prison or on probation about how the offenders' crimes hurt their victims, sometimes as a motivation for rehabilitation.

- Videotaped presentations to offenders by victims of other criminals, in which the victims discuss the harm they suffered from crime.

- Group discussions of offenders with live crime victims present, but not their own victims, such as the Sycamore Tree Programme (Prison Fellowship, 2008) and some types of cognitive-behavioural therapy (Landenberger & Lipsey, 2005).

- One-way communication from offenders to their own victims, such as sending letters of apology.

- 'Indirect mediation': two-way communication between offenders and their own victims, conveyed by a 'shuttle' mediator who delivers messages face to face.

- 'Direct mediation': two-way mediation between an offender and a victim, face to face, with a mediator present, possibly supervised by a court or prosecutor, focused on a direct payment of cash or in-kind services by offenders to victims, OR
- 'Restorative Justice Conferencing' (RJC): a face-to-face meeting inviting all persons directly affected by a crime, including one or more offenders who participated in the crime and one or more of the personal victims of the crime, with respective friends or family, hosted by a trained RJC facilitator, focused on offender understanding of the harm that was caused and how it might be repaired across all parties affected by it.

To one side of this continuum, we might place the 'family group conference' (FGC): an event, focused on offenders, that victims may attend but sometimes don't (as in New Zealand). The FGC is made up of the young person, his or her youth advocate if one has been arranged, members of the family and whoever they invite, the victim and supporters (or representative of the victim), the police, the youth justice coordinator and sometimes a social worker.

RJC methods are described here in greater detail, given their prevalence in the research literature. Virtually all of the facilitators who led the conferences evaluated in controlled trials have been trained in the same method, often by the same trainers. Two Australian RJ pioneers from New South Wales, Terry O'Connell and John McDonald, developed a conferencing model based in part on traditional Maori practice in New Zealand. One or both of them trained police in Canberra, Indianapolis, London and Northumbria, as well as probation, prison and civilian mediation staff in Thames Valley. They also trained others who became trainers, and who provide training services widely in the United Kingdom and abroad. The main elements of the RJC this training calls for are as follows:

- Facilitators should prepare for the conference by one-on-one discussions with as many participants as possible.
- Facilitators should ask questions but not express personal views.
- They should try to engage all persons present in saying something.
- A conference must be held in a closed room with no distractions.
- All participants must be mutually entrained, with one person speaking at a time.

- The structure of the conference should focus on three questions that all present are invited to answer:
  1. What happened?
  2. Who was affected by it and how?
  3. What should be done to try to repair the harm?
- Facilitators can conclude the conference by summarizing what was said and preparing a written agreement that may be signed by the offender, and perhaps others present.
- Someone should follow up, over months and years, to ensure that agreements are kept.
- Any use of the outcome agreements in court or for other official purposes should be clarified and accepted by all parties in advance.

Both RJC and other methods vary widely in the extent and kind of any agreement offenders make with the professional involved to try to repair the harm to victims, rehabilitate themselves, or prevent any recurrence. The extent to which these agreements are binding on offenders and subject to penalties for non-completion depends, in turn, on the stage of the criminal justice process in which the RJ occurs.

Stages of criminal process

RJ processes can, in principle, be inserted almost anywhere in the criminal process. In practice, RJC has had the broadest application. RCTs on RJC have now been completed both with diversion from prosecution and as a supplement to criminal prosecution and sanctions, as follows:

- An added kind of diversion for offenders under 18 (Northumbria final warnings and Indianapolis).
- A diversion from prosecution in court for both adults and juveniles (Canberra).
- At adjournment for pre-sentence reports in both magistrates' courts (Northumbria) and crown courts (London) in the United Kingdom, with results sometimes taken as mitigation in sentencing.
- After sentencing to probation as a means of deciding the treatment plan, sometimes by court order (Thames Valley).
- After sentencing to prison, in anticipation of resettlement on release (Thames Valley).

Other institutions

In addition to governmental criminal justice, RJ and especially RJC have been used increasingly in schools, businesses, medicine, community organizations and religious courts.

Schools

RJ and RJC are used in primary and secondary schools to deal with matters that might or might not be considered criminal or delinquent, in ways that deflect the cases entirely from the criminal or youth justice process. Fights, bullying, sexual harassment and many other matters have been dealt with in this fashion. Even matters arising from injuries that students cause to teachers or other staff have been dealt with in this way. Unfortunately, no rigorous evaluations or controlled trials are available on the use of RJ in such settings.

Businesses

Conflicts among employees arise in businesses, just as in schools, on matters including race, gender, harassment, religion and bullying. Facilitators trained in RJ methods have been retained to deal with these matters, if only as an attempt to prevent costly civil litigation.

Medicine

Just as some crimes are negligent rather than intentional (as in reckless driving or accidental death), medical injuries give rise to a great sense of injustice and anger. Medical institutions are increasingly attempting to use apologies and restorative practices to resolve these matters in a way that achieves reconciliation of staff with patients and their families.

Community organizations

Conflicts arising in communities over land use, parking, noise, pets, gardens and other matters can sometimes break into violence. Preventive RJ responses to these situations have been used by community organizers, sometimes in conjunction with police.

Religious courts

There is evidence that both Jewish and Muslim (Sharia) religious courts in the United Kingdom, as abroad, have been using restorative practices to resolve a wide range of crimes and lesser matters. Rather than bringing these matters to the police or Crown Prosecutors, the victims have chosen to use an authority system in which they or their offenders may have more trust or confidence. Whatever the complex legality of using these arrangements, it is a contemporary example of RJ that provides some victims with access not presently provided by criminal justice.

THEORIES OF CHANGE FOR VICTIMS AND OFFENDERS

Placing these methods into theories of change is essential for understanding RJ and interpreting the evidence about it. Many people have been sceptical about a single encounter of several hours having any impact on people's lives, let alone affecting their future offending behaviour. Yet, the hypothesis that RJ alone, quite apart from other treatments, can change behaviour is consistent with theories of trauma, reintegration and interaction ritual.

PTSD for victims and offenders

The best-known effect of a critical event of short duration is post-traumatic stress disorder (PTSD). In the space of a few seconds, let alone hours, witnessing a traumatic incident can change (and shorten) people's lives. A roadside bomb in Iraq, a jungle firefight in Vietnam, a fire in one's home at night, a suicide bomber in a restaurant – these and other events can happen in an instant, but then inflict lifelong damage to physical as well as mental health (Kubzansky, Koenen, Spiro, Vokonas, & Sparrow, 2007). Charles Dickens' death on 9 June 1870 occurred on the fifth anniversary of the horrifying Staplehurst train crash that he survived – a fact that is often interpreted as more than coincidence, given the sharp decline in his output after suffering the crash at age 53.

The PTSD theory of an RJC turns the brevity of harm on its head. For a victim, it hypothesizes that an intensive reversal of the power the offender exercised over the victim during the crime can lead to a sudden amelioration of post-traumatic stress symptoms (PTSS). This theory is not unlike the basis for what Edna Foa and her colleagues have developed as a behaviourist treatment for PTSD suffered by rape victims and others. This treatment, called Prolonged Exposure (PE) Therapy, requires the crime victim to relive the crime experience repeatedly as described in her own voice – often by listening to an audio tape of the client telling the story of the crime. By doing this in safe places without the crime happening again, the client can associate the story of the crime with a feeling and reality of safety as the story is repeated. After 12–18 weeks of doing this alone and with a therapist, the evidence suggests substantial drops in PTSS and a high rate of PTSD cure (Rothbaum & Foa, 1999). By extension, through a far more intensive experience, it can be theorized that an RJC in which the offender apologizes will enable the victim to relive the crime in a way that makes the memory 'safe'. And if the victim is able to accept an offender's apology by forgiving the offender, victims may be freed from the burden of vengeful feelings for the rest of their lives (Arendt, 1958). Accepting the apology even without forgiving also appears to have substantial psychological benefits (Strang 2002).

For an offender, the trauma may lie not in the crime, but in the RJC. One offender who experienced an RJC after a self-reported 5,000 crimes describes his reaction in much the same way as PTSD: racing thoughts, nightmares, anxiety and flight reactions. Woolf (2008) reports that he had never been as emotionally distressed by committing a crime, let alone going to prison, as he had been by spending three hours with two of his burglary victims in an RJC. When offenders can no longer deflect the evil of their crimes by techniques of neutralization (Sykes & Matza, 1957), they may find the 120–180 minutes of direct accountability for the harm they cause to be far more painful psychologically than any other experience of criminal sanctions.

Reintegrating offenders

A less punitive theory of offender reform is Braithwaite's (1989) theory of reintegrative shaming, by which social groups can condemn the sin but support the sinner. Using a family model of social control, Braithwaite predicts that RJC experiences will produce more reintegrative shaming than formal justice, while the latter will produce more stigmatic shaming and exclusionary messages than RJC. Evidence from our Canberra experiments suggests that RJC actually produces more of both kinds of shaming than prosecution in court (Ahmed, Harris, Braithwaite, & Braithwaite, 2001). But the evidence of reintegration may be sufficient to confirm the central theoretical premise: that when offenders are invited to rejoin society as fully accepted members once they repair the harm they have caused, it may provide a way to help them stop offending.

Interaction ritual for all participants

Collins (2004) provides a further theory of change for offenders and victims: interaction ritual. This theory predicts that people will become more committed to shared values by experiencing emotionally intense rituals of mutual entrainment, excluding all others from the interaction space who have no moral connection to the ritual. Examples include religious ceremonies, graduations, funerals, weddings and RJC – which Collins explicitly cites as a plausible basis for changing behaviour. The criminal career theory of an offender's 'epiphany' that he should stop committing crime (Sherman, 2003) is consistent with Collins' view that the ritual of an RJC may help to manufacture such an epiphany. Rossner's (2011, forthcoming) analysis of before-and-after differences in rates of offending in Canberra shows that the more often elements of Collins theory were recorded by RJC observers, the greater the decline in the offenders' rate of offending.

Other theoretical perspectives have been suggested for why RJ or RJC might change offender behaviour. What all of them share is the perspective that an RJ experience can be well or badly done. That aspect of the change theories raises the critical importance of delivering the RJ programme, especially an RJC, in a manner consistent with both training and the theories of change.

DELIVERING RJ CONFERENCING

There are many critical questions in the art and logistics of delivering RJC. Few of them can be answered by science, but the following discussion draws on the best evidence available – including our own experience with over 3,000 cases randomly assigned to RJC or control.

Who does RJ best? Police versus others

The question of what kind of person and what kind of professional background is best suited for the actual delivery of RJC has been a controversial one. Debates focus on police versus other service professionals. Empirical evidence is limited by the few opportunities to compare police delivery to other providers. Yet, there has been no shortage of opinion. One opinion, derived in part from observing RJC in several countries, is that police facilitators may be inherently predisposed to be 'on the victim's side' and not impartial, that they will automatically back up their police colleagues' interpretation of the offender's culpability, that offenders will not be inclined to voice complaints about their treatment by arresting police to a police facilitator and that state officials will not be adequately held accountable (Roche, 2003).

These normative criticisms of police delivery are not, however, supported by the empirical evidence available. When we asked juvenile offenders in our RISE experiments in Australia about their experience of that police-run programme they consistently said they rated procedural justice indicators in conferences significantly higher than that experienced in court (www.aic.gov.au/criminal_justice_system/rjustice/rise.aspx). This is despite the fact that juveniles were said to have very bad relations with police in Canberra. They also rated police fairness in their case far higher if they received RJC than if they had not. Nevertheless, it is important to be aware of contraindications of police involvement: for example, the poor response of Aboriginal youth to RJC in Canberra (Sherman & Strang, 2007) may be attributable to historically bad relations between police and Aboriginal communities throughout Australia (Blagg, 1997). We do not have good evidence either about the advantages and disadvantages of other professional backgrounds for facilitators. Social workers, welfare workers, community organizers and volunteers have all been involved in programme delivery but there is little research available on their relative effectiveness. It is likely that every kind of background brings its own strengths and weaknesses and that it remains primarily an issue to be resolved by careful attention to training and to supervision. In our RCTs of RJC in the United Kingdom, five of our seven independently evaluated tests had police-run programmes in which the facilitators were sworn police officers. In the two other tests, where the cases involved offenders sentenced either to terms of imprisonment or to community supervision, the facilitators were probation officers, prison officers and community mediators. Across the seven tests there was higher take-up by victims and offenders and faster conclusion of the RJ process in the police-run programmes. However, these differences may have been a consequence of the different character of post-sentence RJ and of the greater seriousness of the offences. All our facilitators of all Professional backgrounds underwent the same week-long intensive training and all were monitored to ensure they conducted their conferences as they had been trained to do. This was more problematic initially for the mediators whose professional training had been at odds with what was required for conferencing, but they were able to change their style to conform to what was needed under a different theory of practice. As of this writing, we see no reason to exclude any trained facilitator using the same methods as those which have been found effective in RCTs. There is no clear evidence that background makes a difference. Indeed, an RCT comparing different kinds of professionals would be needed to resolve the debate.

Access, referral, recruitment and consent

Access to suitable cases for RJ, absent a satisfactory routine referral arrangement from criminal justice agencies, remains a crucial operational issue in RJ. The dominant justice paradigm assumes a seamless track from police to prosecution to court, with few opportunities for the consideration of alternative or additional stages of the kind RJC represents. Shapland *et al.* (2004) describes the operational difficulties encountered by the Home Office-funded schemes she evaluated, as they began the process of identifying cases eligible for RJ. In addition, all programmes that did not have police facilitators immediately faced problems from the Data Protection Act in obtaining victim contact details, so police inevitably became involved in the process of identifying and approaching victims.

Operational experience with programmes run on restorative justice principles by the youth offending teams provided lessons about how victims could best be approached for RJ. Miers *et al.* (2001) and Newburn *et al.* (2001) revealed the extremely low levels of victim involvement resulting from lack of attention to prioritizing their needs. They also showed that merely writing to victims informing them of the opportunity to meet their offender met with extremely low take-up rates. Our UK RCT's team learned from this and developed a protocol for participant recruitment that proved very successful. When an ostensibly eligible case was identified by our team, the first step was to make contact with offenders to determine whether they accepted full responsibility for the offence and whether they were willing to meet their victim. This was always a face-to-face meeting, almost always arranged by the facilitator who would conduct the conference (early experimenting with different staff interviewing victims and offenders and passing information on to the conference facilitator was soon abandoned as unfeasible).For pre-sentence cases, offenders needed to have pleaded guilty in court to the offence (or to have made full admissions in the case of the youth Final Warning studies). For post-sentence cases, ostensibly eligible offenders were asked whether they accepted responsibility for the offence; if they did so, they were accepted into the programme regardless of whether they had pleaded guilty or not guilty in their court case. Those who were serving prison terms were seen in the prison while those serving community sentences were visited at home. Take-up rates by prisoners were high – in the region of 80% – but much lower for offenders in community supervision cases (Shapland *et al.*, 2006). When offenders had been assessed as eligible and had agreed to participate, facilitators then approached their victims. Initial contact was through a brief letter followed by a phone call asking for a suitable time for a face-to-face visit. It was the open-ended conversation that ensued during this visit that proved the most important element in encouraging victims to attend. Here, victims could voice their anxieties and have their questions answered about what to expect during the meeting.

RJ is essentially a voluntary process. Thus consent by all parties is an essential prerequisite to the deliberative dialogue that is key to the process. In our community supervision RCT, judges sentenced eligible offenders to a process of RJ assessment, which at first glance appeared to be a coercive process; however, the purpose of this order was to allow probation staff to discuss RJ with these offenders, to determine whether they admitted their responsibility for the offence and to ask whether they were willing to meet their victim. If they denied responsibility or were unwilling to meet, RJ did not proceed.

Preparation and delivery – in and out of prison

Careful attention to the preparation of both offenders and victims for the RJ process is absolutely essential. At face-to-face meetings in advance of the RJC, sometimes where the offence is serious and emotions raw, the facilitator needs to describe the RJC process in detail. Since the process is not widely known, it is essential that facilitators take the time to answer all questions frankly if consent is to be truly informed. The roles and responsibilities of all participants must be communicated in straightforward language. The desirability of bringing along to the conference family members or friends as supporters needs to be especially emphasized. Indeed, facilitators should talk to the victim's family and friends as well, given that they can often only envisage the risks rather than the potential benefits associated with such an encounter for their loved one unless they too hear directly from RJC facilitators just what is being proposed.

We found that victims were often more reluctant than offenders to consent to an RJC, saying that they still felt too anxious or frightened. Often, victims said that they did not trust themselves to be in the same room with the offender when they still felt so angry. Facilitators responded that the meeting would give them a chance to explain the full consequences of the crime, that they could tell the offender what they thought of him or her, that they could ask questions about the crime that only the offender could answer – why they had been chosen as the victim, whether there was anything they could have done to avoid the crime – and that they could seek appropriate restitution. Some special preparations are needed for victims whose offenders are in prison, whether on remand awaiting sentence or serving their sentences. Prison procedures need to be explained in detail – where to go upon arrival at the prison, what the security and search arrangements are, who will accompany them to the room set aside for the conference. There must be no surprises for victims, who often are pleased with the opportunity to see the circumstances in which their offender lives.

Aftermath and follow-up

RJ conferences can be emotionally bruising encounters for all participants. Although there have been no reports of physical violence at such meetings anywhere in the world, RJC is sometimes characterized by shouting, tears and powerful feelings. It is the responsibility of the facilitator to allow this level of emotional expression but to ensure that safety is paramount. They should also make sure that by the time the conference finishes all parties have said all they wanted to say. Our conferences were followed by an invitation to all participants to have refreshments together – our facilitators arrived at each prison conference with a suitcase of tea, coffee and biscuits. These often proved to be an extraordinary opportunity for participants to discover what they had in common – worries about their children, shared sporting interests and so on.

A conference can be a cathartic experience for everyone in the room, and participants may leave in a highly emotional state. We were especially conscious of this in the case of imprisoned offenders returning to their cells with little in the way of emotional support available to them. Prison authorities recognized the special vulnerability of these participants and ensured that they were not alone immediately after the conference and that the prison chaplain or Samaritan members were available for them to talk to. The research team also worked to follow up on victims as well as offenders, contacting them within a few days of the conference to ensure that they had not suffered any ill effects from the encounter. There are also practical issues to follow up after the conference in relation to outcomes agreed between the parties. Despite victims being made well aware of the appropriateness of seeking restitution from the offender, these agreements usually focus instead on strategies that would reduce the likelihood of reoffending by the offender – drug and alcohol programmes, literacy and other skills training, letters of apology, reconnection with families and the like. These undertakings often require follow-up action by facilitators who can liaise with prison and other agencies to connect offenders with programmes that meet their needs. Victims often express their desire to be kept informed of their offender's progress and arrangements need to be made to ensure they are told whether they completed what they agreed to do.

RESEARCH ON RESTORATIVE JUSTICE: THE GOLD STANDARD

As in any psychological or medical treatment, the key question is whether high-integrity delivery of the treatment can yield a cost-effective benefit with minimal side effects. Answering that question in forensic settings requires a clear understanding of both the science and the ethics of RCTs. It also requires a clear conception of the outcome measures that will determine whether resources will be provided for widening access to RJC.

The science of randomized trials

The purpose of an RCT is to provide an unbiased estimate of the *average* effects of a treatment, as measured by the difference in outcomes between a treatment group and a comparison group (Cook & Campbell, 1979). An RCT does this by holding constant, or controlling, the percentages of risk factors for any outcome in two different groups. Over large and relatively homogeneous samples, those percentages should be roughly equal, leaving the groups almost identical except for the difference in treatment condition.

RCTs focus on average, rather than individual, effects simply because humans vary in their response to medical treatment, criminal sanctions and psychological treatment. Such variability is the primary reason that random assignment of large samples of cases is necessary in the inexact sciences, from agriculture to psychology to medicine, in contrast to more exact sciences such as physics. Some treatments are found effective (on average) in RCTs even though 75–80% of persons treated experience no change in their condition. The purpose of an RCT is therefore not to find out what works for everyone with a given problem, but what works for groups of relatively similar individuals. The purpose of treatment, however, is to provide the most effective means of helping any one individual. This may seem to create a clash between the product of RCTs and the needs of clients, but it does not. RCTs still offer the best means of finding what works for individuals through a continuous process of identifying non-responsive subgroups within samples in which the average effect of treatment is successful (Doll, 1992). For each non-responsive (or negatively responding) subgroup identified within successful average outcomes, a separate RCT can be devised comparing the success-on-average treatment to some new alternative. At minimum, subgroup analysis can help to identify the groups for whom a treatment does not work, as long as sample sizes are large enough. For these and other reasons, the science of RJC effects can be greatly enhanced by continuing to add RCTs to the evidence base. Since governments may be reluctant to fund further research once an adequate evidence base exists about average effects, it is important for better science – and treatment – that small-scale RCTs continue to be designed, conducted and reported, especially on subgroups with which RJC has yet to be separately tested. Forensic psychologists may be in an ideal position to do this in prison and probation settings, even though it could take several years to accumulate a sample of even 100 cases from the psychologist's own caseload. Yet, for psychologists to undertake such RCTs, they will need to satisfy their colleagues, their supervisors and themselves that such RCTs would be ethical.

The ethics of randomized trials

The ethics of RCTs in general depend upon a state of 'equipoise' (Federal Judicial Center, 1981), in which it is equally likely that a given treatment will help or harm an individual. This condition may seem difficult to satisfy once a substantial body of RCT evidence has been accumulated. Even with such evidence in hand, however, there are two further ethical imperatives that may justify further RCTs. One is the identification of a non-responsive or negatively responding subgroup. The other is the need to ration a scarce treatment within a large population that might benefit from it, on the basis of finding those for whom the greatest benefit may be found for the entire society – for example, future crime victims as well as the offender who is provided with a treatment.

Subgroups of offenders for whom RJC is ineffective or harmful have already been identified within certain samples (see the section titled 'Effects of RJ Conferencing on Offenders'). Even when such subgroups have not been identified, however, there is arguably a state of equipoise for any particular group that has not been directly tested apart from a larger group. With uncertain external validity about the results of a test on men, for example, when applied to women offenders, there is a strong case to be made that separate RCTs should be conducted for women only (since most offenders in RCT samples have been males). Subgroups of offence types may also have equipoise. Homicide offenders about to be released from prison, for example, have never been tested for RJ, since they were excluded from the Home Office–funded RCTs in the United Kingdom. Substantial numbers of homicide offenders leave prison each year, and many may be willing to meet with the surviving family of their victims. If the survivors themselves would consent, there could be substantial benefits – or risks – for both victims and offenders to participate. Many people believe it more ethical to provide treatments without testing than to use random assignment to decide who receives treatment. The Federal Judicial Center (1981) concludes the opposite is true, on two grounds. One is that random assignment eliminates conscious or unconscious biases in selecting some but not all for treatment. The second, more important basis is that it is more unethical to provide an untested treatment (that could cause harm) than to conduct an RCT (where all have an equal chance of being harmed). The common assumption that all treatment is helpful cannot be supported by evidence, especially given the criminogenic effects of RJC on Australian Aboriginals (Sherman et al., 2006). Only an RCT can disturb the state of equipoise, and many cases that forensic psychologists face daily may not fit into a previous RCT. Hence, it may be more ethical to set up even a small RCT than to offer RJ 'off-the-shelf' without a firm evidence base for believing it would be safe and effective to do so.

Outcome measures, costs and benefits

RCTs provide a variety of outcome measures which may not always lead to the same conclusion about the same sample. In RJC tests, for example, the UK results show statistically significant results (in a meta-analysis combining all RCTs) for the *frequency* of reconvictions over a 2-year follow-up period (Shapland *et al.*, 2008, and Figure 25.1). They do not, however, show significant differences for the *prevalence* of the reconvictions between the RJC and control groups. That is, RJC in these RCTs causes significantly fewer offences, but not significantly fewer offenders. Although both prevalence and frequency of reconvictions are lower for RJC than for controls, the magnitude of the effect is much greater for frequency than for prevalence. However, the reduction in prevalence could have been due to chance, by conventional standards, while the reduction in frequency was highly unlikely (1 in 100 odds) to have been due to chance.

Given such a difference, how should outcome measures be interpreted? One answer is to focus on cost. In criminal justice as in medicine, governments must be concerned about cost-effectiveness. Even effective medicines are excluded from the National Health Service, for example, if they exceed a cost–benefit ratio of £30,000 per added year of quality life. Thus if a treatment can pay for itself in relation to a certain cost standard, it may be eligible for widespread implementation. Applying the cost–benefit principle to crime, it will generally be preferable to focus on the frequency of offending across an entire group rather than on the likelihood of a single individual desisting from crime. That is because the total cost of more crimes is generally greater than the total cost of fewer crimes, unless the crimes in question vary substantially in cost (such as a few murders in one group and many shop-thefts in another). The Home Office has made such calculations easier by compiling empirical estimates of the average costs of different kinds of crime, which were in fact used by Shapland and her colleagues in evaluating the UK tests (Shapland *et al.*, 2008). Thus what can be said about RJCs in the largest UK research programme on this treatment is that RJC is effective when judged by the two measures explicitly addressing cost: frequency and cost per crime. It is not effective on the basis of complete desistance from crime, nor on a 10-point ordinal scale of crime severity. For the latter, medical costs and length of prison sentences arguably provide a far more sensitive indicator than a truncated ordinal scale. Conclusions could certainly differ by which criteria one chooses to emphasize and for what reason. Yet, if a forensic psychological treatment is to be evaluated from the standpoint of benefit to society, then the cost-focused criteria would seem to be more appropriate. Once a decision is made to focus on cost, it is important to remember that the UK measurement standards are legalistic and extremely conservative. The convention that only a conviction, and not an arrest or a self-report, can constitute evidence of a crime for *research* purposes creates a bias against detecting treatments as effective. This is especially true for cost measures, where small differences in convictions can indicate large differences in actual offending. In a lifetime self-reported offending study of 411 males born in London in the 1950s, Farrington *et al.* (2006, p. 39) have reported an average of 39 undetected offences for every conviction recorded. The results presented below apply that ratio to differences in convictions in order to estimate the *N* of undetected crimes prevented per year per RJ conference assigned, at least within the window of the follow-up by Shapland *et al.* (2008).[2]

RCT	Odds ratio	Lower limit	Upper limit	*p*-value	Odds ratio and 95% CI
London street crime	0.925	0.433	1.975	0.841	
London burglary	0.825	0.475	1.431	0.493	
Northumbria final warning	0.610	0.372	1.002	0.051	
Northumbria court property	0.694	0.283	1.704	0.425	
Northumbria court assault	0.545	0.185	1.607	0.271	
Thames Valley prison	0.770	0.368	1.612	0.488	
Thames Valley community	0.638	0.261	1.560	0.325	
Fixed	0.715	0.549	0.932	0.013	

	0.01	0.1	1	10	100
	Favours RJ			Favours control	

FIGURE 25.1 *Odds ratio for the frequency of reconviction within the 2 years of the RJ period for JRC trials. From* Does restorative justice affect reconviction? The fourth report from the evaluation of three schemes *by Shapland* et al.*, 2008, London: Ministry of Justice Research Series 10/08, p. 27). © Crown Copyright 2008.*

EFFECTS OF RJ CONFERENCING ON OFFENDERS

RJC has many kinds of effects on offenders. We limit the following discussion to RJC effects on future offending behaviour, as indicated by reconvictions or other official records covering 100% of randomly assigned cases in an 'intention-to-treat' analysis (Piantadosi, 1997).

Overall effects on crime

Using the criterion of frequency of reconviction in 2 years after the random assignment across the population of eligible RCTs, RJC reduces the frequency of reconvictions across 12 tests overall (forest plot $p = .04$), with 10 out of all 12 tests reducing reconvictions, including seven out of all seven tests in the United Kingdom, and nine out of all 10 tests worldwide with crimes involving personal victims. In the seven RCTs of RJ conferencing in the United Kingdom (Shapland et al., 2008: 27), the overall effect was 27% fewer reconvictions in RJC-assigned cases than in control-assigned cases, or 209 fewer convictions per year at risk across 374 offenders assigned to RJC. These results, depicted in Figure 2.6 of Shapland et al. (2008) and reproduced here as our Figure 25.1, are statistically significant at the 0.013 level across all seven tests combined, although not within individual tests.[3]

Using Farrington's undetected offending estimate, RJC may have prevented 8,168 crimes among 374 RJC-assigned offenders per year, or an average of 22 offences per year per RJ conference. These results vary in magnitude across the seven reconviction results that Shapland et al. (2008) report, from five to almost 50 crimes prevented per RJ conference, depending largely on the base rates of the offenders in the control group as well as the effect size. Even without the estimated multiplier for undetected offences, the cost–benefit ratio of the investment in RJC is substantial, at an average of £9 of crime costs prevented to £1 invested in RJC (Shapland et al., 2008). These results were driven heavily by the sample of persistent London burglars, who comprised a large part of the overall cost–benefit sample (23% of RJC cases) and whose crimes were quite costly – but for whom the return on investment was 14 to 1. None of the seven RCTs Shapland et al. analysed using Home Office crime cost values showed a negative ratio; all of them did better than paying for themselves in terms of cost of crime to the victim and the criminal justice system combined (separate estimates not available).

Differences by offence types

While the number of RCTs worldwide is small in relation to the possible subdivisions by offence type, some preliminary insight can be gained from the 12 results to date (which took 15 years to produce). One is that the ten tests of crimes with personal victims did consistently better than the two with only collective, non-personal victims, despite a large decrease in reconvictions of shoplifters in Canberra. A corresponding increase was found in Canberra in convictions for offenders assigned to RJC by diversion from prosecution for driving while intoxicated. This leaves the net effect of collective-victim cases at zero.

More striking is the difference between violent and property crime cases. Taken together in separate meta-analyses (forest plots of standardized mean differences), the five RCTs of violent crime show a statistically significant reduction in reconviction frequency. The RCTs for property crime do not. In the violent crime RCTs, five out of five tests show fewer convictions for RJC than for controls. In the property crime RCTs, one of the four RCTs shows an increase in crime: the Canberra property crime experiment, in which a substantial portion of the offenders were either Aboriginal offenders or chronic offenders or both (see the section titled 'Differences by offender characteristics'). In both UK property crime RCTs, RJC reduced the frequency of reconvictions. Nonetheless, the evidence to date suggests that RJC works better for violent crime than for property crime, even though in most cases it works for both.

Differences by offender characteristics

The highly moral and emotional content of the RJC treatment requires a vigilant examination of possible adverse reactions. So far only one clear adverse effect has emerged by offender characteristics, but some evidence of others has also emerged.

Aboriginals

In a separate analysis, the Aboriginal offenders randomly assigned to RJC had such a large increase in arrest frequency compared to controls that we could only conclude that the idea of attending an RJC, as well as doing it, was in combination highly criminogenic. This was not observed, however, for the white offenders. Adding the handful of Aboriginals in the violent crime RCT to a comparison of white and Aboriginal offenders in the two RCTs shows the same interaction of race and treatment, suggesting that the issue is race and not offence type (Sherman & Strang, 2007).

Females

There is also some evidence that RJC works better for females under 18 than for males the same age, at least in violent crimes. Using the criterion of arrest frequency in Northumbria, Sherman and Strang (2007) found this effect in the first year after random assignment. Insufficient numbers of female offenders have been examined for tests using the lower base rates of reconvictions, so it is unclear how general any gender differences in RJC effects may be.

Crime victims as offenders

Measured by arrest differences between RJC-assigned cases and controls, there is preliminary evidence that offenders who have experienced previous crime victimizations have an adverse reaction to RJC. Bennett (2008, p. 252) reports that London robbery offenders with no previous injury from victimizations against them showed twice as much time to first arrest if they had been assigned to RJC as controls, but the reverse was true for offenders who had been previously injured. It is not clear why this is true, but the difference is statistically significant and the number of crime-free days at stake is large. Among robbery offenders with no previous injury from victimization, RJC had a statistically significant improvement in crime-free days over the control group: 470 days versus 197. But for robbery offenders with previous injury, the direction (though non-significant) was reversed.

Heroin and cocaine addicts

Bennett (2008, p. 212) also found interaction effects between RJC and drug use. Offenders in the London robbery experiment using both heroin and crack cocaine had mean survival to first arrest of 242 days in the RJC group compared to 340 for controls. For those who may have used drugs but not *both* heroin and cocaine, the result was reversed: 447 days mean survival to first arrest for RJC, compared to 355 for controls. Thus RJ may be contraindicated for robbery convicts who use both cocaine and heroin.

Diversion versus supplementation

A very small sample of four diversion-from-prosecution experiments in Canberra and eight RJC in-addition-to-prosecution experiments in the UK shows, on average, that RJC had no effect when used as diversion, with consistently clear effects when used as supplementation. This finding should be treated with great caution, due to the possibly spurious nature of the finding: it is equally well explained by the difference between a part-time facilitator model in the Australian Federal Police versus a full-time facilitator model in UK police, combined with professional mediators in the prison and probation RCTs in the United Kingdom, and a generally more tightly administered process of delivery in the United Kingdom than in Canberra.

Offences brought to justice

One of the most striking benefits of diversion of cases from prosecution, quite apart from reconviction, is the consistently higher rate of offences brought to justice with RJ than without. Sherman and Strang (2007) report that whenever cases are diverted to RJ, whether mediation or RJC, they are more likely to result in offenders being held accountable for their crimes than in the control condition of random assignment to prosecution as normal.

Long-term effects on offenders

In a long-term follow-up of participants in the Canberra diversion experiments, offenders and victims were interviewed again 10 years after the offence that brought them into the study. Both the experimental and control participants were asked about their recollections of the offence, their life experiences in the intervening years and how they now saw their criminal justice experience. Again, all data were analysed on the basis of their randomly assigned treatment rather than treatment as delivered.

About 60% of all the violence and property offenders in the original study were re-interviewed, and about two-thirds of them said that they still remembered their case well. A much higher proportion of those assigned to RJC than to court said they were pleased with the way they were dealt with; this was especially the case for violent offenders.

Substantially more of the RJC-assigned than court-assigned offenders said that, 10 years later, they felt ashamed of themselves for their offending but that they believed the RJC had made up for the crime they had committed. On both these measures, violent offenders were much more positive than property offenders.

When offenders were asked whether they now felt angry about the way they had been treated, there was a substantial difference between court-assigned violent offenders still substantially angrier than those assigned to RJC, though this difference was not apparent with the property offenders. These findings are consistent with those concerning reoffending patterns which show that, in Canberra, RJC was much more effective for violent offenders than for property offenders.

These results indicate that, even for relatively low-level offenders, who made up the bulk of the Canberra cases, long-term effects of the criminal justice experience are evident, and that offenders randomly assigned to RJC tended to be much more positive about that experience than those whose cases were assigned to court.

EFFECTS OF RJ CONFERENCING ON VICTIMS

The effects of RJC on victims are more consistent than for offenders, with larger effect sizes and possibly longer-lasting benefits. Nonetheless, it has proven difficult to attract resources to widen access to RJC based solely on victim benefits. Only evidence on reduced rates of reconvictions seems likely to attract public attention, despite the strong victim preferences for RJC over conventional criminal justice alone.

The evidence base on victim effects comes from two sources. One is the interviews done with victims after the seven RCTs in the United Kingdom reported by Shapland *et al.* (2007) as annotated below, as well as by Strang (2002) with the victims of property and violent crime in Canberra and McGarrell, Olivares, Crawford, and Kroovand (2000) with Indianapolis victims of youth crime. These analyses compare RJC and control groups. In addition, Strang *et al.* (2006) look at before-and-after differences within the RJC group, as they recall how they felt before the conference compared to how they felt after it was over. The latter evidence is less reliable for causal inference than for exploratory analysis of how RJ works, consistent with the theories of change presented in the section titled 'Theories of Change for Victims and Offenders' in the preceding text. Victim effects are clearly limited in external validity to the kinds of victims who consented to participate, and then by the use of an intention-to-treat model. Victims who do not want RJC exclude themselves, thus creating a selection bias. Victims who drop out after beginning the process may be less satisfied than those who complete it, introducing a further selection bias. The present analysis draws entirely on intention-to-treat studies of consenting victims, thereby excluding one (but not both) forms of bias. Of course, RJC can only ever be used with consenting victims, so the consent bias is actually quite useful in generalizing findings to the kinds of victims who are in fact willing to undertake RJC. The problem with generalizing from non-RCT evidence is that programmes vary in the level of effort they put into recruiting cases (see the section titled 'Delivering RJ Conferencing' in the preceding text). Where victims have been more diligently recruited (such as by letting them select the date and time of an RJC), the findings may have stronger external validity. That is the case with most of the RCTs summarized in the following text. The two main effects measured across all of them are satisfaction with justice and desire for violent revenge. A third measure may be even more important: reduction of medically significant post-traumatic stress symptoms.

Satisfaction with justice

Victims are consistently more satisfied with RJC than with conventional justice. Strang's (2002) high interview response rate (approximately 90%) with an intention-to-treat design provided the first clear test. When victims were asked whether they were satisfied with the way their case was dealt with by the justice system, there was a statistically significant difference between the court-assigned and the conference-assigned victims (46 vs. 60%). Significantly more of those who actually *experienced* an RJ conference were satisfied, compared with those who cases were dealt with in court (70 vs. 42%, $p < .001$). There was no difference here between property and violence victims.

Offender apologies appear to play an important role in bringing about emotional restoration of victims. For those Canberra victims assigned to a conference, 72% said their offender had apologized (and 86% of those who actually experienced a conference) compared with 19% of those assigned to court. Furthermore, more conference-assigned victims than court-assigned victims said they felt the apologies they received were sincere (77 vs. 41%).Strang (2002) also found statistically significant improvements for victims between before-conference and after-conference feelings on all the following dimensions: fear of the offender (especially for violence victims); estimated likelihood of revictimization; sense of security; anger towards the offender; sympathy for the offender and the offender's supporters; feelings of trust in others; feelings of self-confidence; and anxiety. The Indianapolis Juvenile Restorative Justice Experiment (McGarrell *et al.*, 2000) was modelled on the Canberra RCTs and produced similar results for crime victims. This study of young (7–14 years) first-time property and minor assault offenders and their victims also found markedly higher levels of satisfaction among victims whose cases were randomly assigned to a conference rather than an array of other court diversions. Furthermore, 97% said they felt involved with the way their case was dealt with, compared with 38% of victims in the control group, and 95% felt they had been able to express their views, compared with 56% of the control group. Our eight trials of RJC in London, Northumbria and Thames Valley contain a number of measures on victims' experience of RJ derived from interviews from over 200 of the approximately 450 victims involved in RJ in the eight trials during the Sheffield evaluation period (Shapland *et al.*, 2007). Overall they found that about 85% of victims (and 80% of offenders) were satisfied with their experience. In particular, only 12% of victims (and 10% of offenders) expressed any doubt about the outcome agreement reached at the end of the conference and almost all thought it was fair. Looking at various dimensions of satisfaction, the evaluation found that more than 70% of victims in all eight experiments said they found the conference useful and fair and that it had given them a sense of closure about the offence.

Revenge

One additional way RJC may prevent crime is by reducing victim desire for violent revenge against their offenders. In a meta-analysis of eight effect sizes across four RCTs (split by victim gender) in London and Canberra, Sherman *et al.* (2005) found a statistically significant pattern of moderately large reductions in victim desire for revenge.

Post-traumatic stress

Given the increased risk of coronary heart disease and mortality from low-level but chronic post-traumatic stress symptoms (Kubzansky *et al.*, 2007), it is very important to note that crime victims treated with RJC experience lower levels of PTSS than controls in early and longer-term follow-ups (Angel, 2005). Based on telephone interviews by a psychiatric nurse using the Impact of Events (Revised) scale, the findings on PTSS show about a 40% reduction in the scale values. Unpublished analysis (Angel, personal communication) shows that this is of major benefit to female victims, with much smaller effect sizes for men. All of this evidence is drawn from the two RCTs we completed in the London crown courts, with robbery and burglary.

Long-term effects on victims

In the follow-up of Canberra victims, around 80% of all those initially interviewed were interviewed again 10 years later. This response rate was similar for both the RJC-assigned and court-assigned victims. Over half of all victims said that, 10 years on, they remembered their case well, but nearly twice as many of the RJC-assigned said that they were pleased with their treatment. Substantial differences between the groups emerged, however, when they were asked about their present emotional states. These differences concerned the court-assigned victims' anxiety about being revictimized, their continuing feelings of anger and bitterness about the offence itself and their higher levels of fear of crime generally. Likewise, many more of the court-assigned victims still said they would harm their offender if they had the chance to do so.

To a remarkable degree, the levels of these emotions and the differences between the two groups, as measured immediately after the disposition of the case, was sustained over the following 10 years. It appears that RJC can work by allowing victims to recover through their own resilience without becoming 'stuck' in a negative emotional state. Even for less serious crimes of the kind in the Canberra study, RJC appears to be an extraordinarily beneficial intervention for victims over the long term.

EVIDENCE ON OTHER RJ OPTIONS

In general, there is far less evidence on the effects of other RJ options, and what evidence we have suggests that RJC is a substantially more effective treatment. The only options with substantial quasi-experimental evidence in the United Kingdom are the direct and indirect mediation projects provided by REMEDI and CONNECT that were evaluated by Shapland *et al.* (2004, 2006, 2007, 2008). Those reports form the evidence base for the following observations assessing the relative benefits of direct and indirect mediation and comparing both of them to RJ conferencing.

Reconviction

Because these programmes did not have a randomized design, the evaluators established a comparison group in which each individual offender in the RJ group was matched on variables that may affect offending, such as the type of offence, offender's age and gender, etc., with individuals who did not experience any kind of mediation. We need to be cautious about findings based on this design, but they do give us some indication of the effects of mediation.

There was no significant difference in the *prevalence*, *frequency* or *severity* of reconviction in the 2 years post-treatment for any of the direct or indirect mediation programmes in respect of adults or youths, compared with the matched offenders who did not experience mediation (Shapland *et al.*, 2008). However, this was also true of the individual RCTs of our RJC methods, whereas the latter achieved significance across a far larger sample combining seven RCTs. The very small number of cases in each of the mediation categories of offenders meant that the effect of mediation on reconviction would have needed to be very great for a significant difference to be detected. The biggest difference from the RJC effects is in the cost–benefit ratios of the respective programmes. Unlike their conclusion for the RJC methods, the evaluators concluded that neither the direct nor the indirect mediation programmes could be justified on grounds of cost savings associated with reduced reconvictions and did not provide positive value for money.

Victim benefits

Both victims and offenders said they had found mediation useful, though offenders were more enthusiastic than victims. This was especially the case for indirect mediation where victims complained about not receiving enough information from the offender and about the offender's response. Their dissatisfaction seemed to derive from the lack of opportunity to convey views directly or to see how these views had been received by the offender. Furthermore, Shapland et al. (2007) concluded that the indirect process makes it difficult to have outcome agreements between the parties because the quantity and quality of interaction needed to achieve a future-orientated agreement cannot practically be achieved by passing information via a third party. Finally, the evaluators state that RJ is more likely to achieve its full potential by direct mediation than indirect mediation, but that RJ conferencing appears to be even more advantageous because the presence of family and friends is particularly important in their role as supporters of each party both during and after the conference.

RJ AND FORENSIC PSYCHOLOGY

To the extent that forensic psychologists may choose which treatments to suggest for offenders, there may be good reason to offer – or at least describe – RJC for many kinds of offenders. This is especially true for violent crimes, where the evidence of reduced reconviction is stronger than for any other crime type.

Opportunities for RJC

Opportunities to suggest RJC – if not other, less evidence-based forms of RJ – may arise in a variety of settings where forensic psychiatry and psychology are found. These include:

- Prisoners completing custodial sentences prior to resettlement
- Prisoners who commit violent crimes against other inmates

- Prisoners on community sentences deciding treatment plans
- Young offenders in YOIs
- Private correctional firms and charities providing services to NOMS

In each of these opportunities, there is likely to be far more work and time involved in delivering RJC than in delivering other 'mass-produced' treatments which may lack RCT-derived evidence. Thus there may be greater confidence that delivering RJC is more likely to be cost-effective in each case than in delivering even a far larger number of cases with an untested treatment.

Arguments against RJC

The difficulties of a forensic psychiatrist or psychologist arranging RJC cannot be underestimated. Coordination with police or probation outside of a prison setting may be difficult to arrange. Victims may live in other parts of the country from a prison or probation setting, and travel costs may need to be provided. Supervisors may object to RJC on these or other grounds.

More often, objections to RJC may be made on the basis of safety or 'revictimization' of the victims. The evidence summarized in this chapter shows that these concerns are generally unfounded. With appropriate preparation for each RJC event, trained facilitators can generally detect any issues of risk and decide not to proceed. If anything, there is a risk of excluding from RJC offenders who are actually good candidates but are not yet remorseful – because they have not yet been treated. Completion of RJC treatment may be exactly what is indicated, even for offenders who may be unrepentant but are at least willing to accept responsibility.

The role of forensic staff

The larger question about RJC concerns the role of forensic staff. It is not clear that such professionals are ideally suited to facilitate RJC. Training in RJC methods is widely available in the United Kingdom, yet it may often be better to broker an RJC delivered by other professionals, people whose only work is to deliver RJC. This may leave forensic staff in the position to deliver hundreds or thousands of RJC events, rather than a mere 20 or 30 per year. By explaining, and perhaps evaluating, RJC on the basis of RCT evidence, they could prevent many crimes and help to heal many lives.

NOTES

1 This chapter is a product of the Australian National University's Regulatory Institutions Network (RegNet) in the Research School of Pacific and Asian Studies, and the Jerry Lee Program of Randomized Trials in Restorative Justice, a collaboration of ANU's RegNet, the University of Pennsylvania, and the Jerry Lee Centre for Experimental Criminology at the University of Cambridge. Points of view or opinions expressed are those of the authors and not of any of the many governmental and private funding agencies that have supported their research.

2 This does not mean that Shapland *et al.* actually conducted a self-report survey. They did not. But Farrington's estimate is based on very high response rates, and is unbiased about any differential in criminal justice response between groups. The application of the estimate from an earlier generation of offenders to Shapland's evaluation of our RCTs must be made with some caution, but if anything there is evidence that convictions represent even more offending in recent UK cohorts (Soothill, Francis, Ackerley, & Humphreys, 2008).

3 While it is not clear how the odds ratios were calculated, our own forest plot using Standardized Mean Difference (SMD) as the effect size statistic shows similar conclusions.

FURTHER READING

Shapland, J., Atkinson, A., Colledge, E., Dignan, J., Howes, M., Johnstone, J. et al. (2004). *Implementing restorative justice schemes (Crime Reduction Programme): A report on the first year.* Home Office online report 32/04. London: Home Office. Retrieved 15 September 2009 from www.homeoffice.gov.uk/rds/pdfs04/rdsolr3204.pdf

In 2001, the Home Office funded the development and testing of three RJ programmes (or 'schemes') to be funded under its Crime Reduction Programme. This decision resulted from political and policy interest provoked by an RJ project operated by the Thames Valley Police, focusing on juvenile offenders, which had been running for some years, together with the results of Australian research indicating the potential of RJ as a crime reduction tool, especially for violent crime. The funded programmes were to target mainly adults, as most research evidence worldwide at that time concerned the effects of RJ on juvenile crime. Professor Joanna Shapland and her team at the University of Sheffield were chosen as the independent evaluator of the selected programmes.

This report, the first of four prepared by the Shapland team, discusses the scope and content of the three RJ programmes and their early efforts to get established. All three subscribed to the Home Office definition (Marshall, 1997) of RJ as 'a process whereby parties with a stake in a specific offence collectively resolve how to deal with the aftermath of an offence and its implications for the future'. However, there were variations in the way the programmes operated, with two of the three using both mediation (including direct and indirect mediation) and RJ conferencing, as defined in the section titled 'Varieties of Restorative Justice' in the preceding text. The CONNECT programme, run by trained mediators, worked with adults who had been convicted in London magistrates' courts of a wide range of offences involving personal victims. Participants were offered direct mediation, indirect mediation and RJ conferencing, all of which took place after conviction but before sentencing. At the end of the first year of operation 59 cases had been referred to the programme, in 12 of which there had been indirect or direct mediation. The REMEDI programme, also run by trained mediators, operated in Yorkshire with both adult and youth offenders who admitted a wide range of property and violent offences. It targeted adults and youths given community sentences, youths given Final Warnings by the police and adults in prison. At the end of the first year 832 cases had been referred, of which 107 had completed direct mediation, most of them involving juvenile offenders. The third programme, directed by the present authors (Sherman and Strang) for the Justice Research Consortium (JRC) of participating agencies and universities, was designed as a series of RCTs of face-to-face RJ conferencing only, in London, Northumbria and the Thames Valley. In London, Metropolitan police officers trained as full-time RJC facilitators implemented two experiments with eligible adult offenders who had pleaded guilty in the Crown Courts to burglary or robbery but had not yet been sentenced. In Northumbria studies, police trained as full-time RJC facilitators implemented four experiments: two RCTs of adults who had pleaded guilty in magistrates' courts (one for property crimes involving a personal victim and one for assaults), and two RCTs for juveniles who admitted personal or violent crimes with personal victims and who were to be given Reprimands or Final Warnings by the police (the two youth RCTs were analysed by Shapland's team as a single RCT but randomly assigned in separate blocks for violent and non-violent crimes). The two Thames Valley studies, where a mix of probation officers, prison officers and mediators all worked together as part-time but fully trained RJ conference facilitators, took adult offenders convicted of violent crimes who were either serving custodial sentences for these offences or had been given community sentences. At the end of the first year, London had 271 referrals, 73 of which had been given an RJ conference; Northumbria had 287 referrals with 73 conferences; Thames Valley had 374 referrals with 41 conferences. It was only towards the end of this year, after the programme was well established, that random assignment to RJ conferencing and control groups commenced. The report discusses difficulties encountered by each of the funded programmes in setting up an RJ programme. The need to operate within the dominant criminal justice paradigm and to negotiate a space within a framework of procedures and values of that culture proved challenging for all of them. As a result, all encountered initial difficulties in obtaining adequate numbers of referrals and considerable effort and ingenuity were entailed in maintaining case flow: in the case of prison, self-referral from prisoners proved an important source. In addition, programmes led by agencies other than the police faced difficulties in obtaining victim contact details, owing to the provisions of the Data Protection Act. Notwithstanding the difficulties of establishing programmes designed to test such a radical idea as RJ in an environment already fully stretched – among other practitioners for whom the concept was alien to their values and procedures – the report judges the first step a success. Within their first year of operation, the three 'schemes' had managed to process a substantial number of cases to completion and demonstrated the feasibility of establishing viable RJ programmes.

Shapland, J. Atkinson, A., Atkinson, H., Colledge, E., Dignan, J., Howes, M. *et al.* (2006) *Restorative justice in practice: The second report from the evaluation of three schemes.* Sheffield: Sheffield Centre for Criminological Research, University of Sheffield.

The second report of the Sheffield evaluation team on the three Home Office-funded RJ programmes focused on the actual RJ meetings conducted by the programmes and the follow-up of outcomes agreed by the victims and offenders in those meetings. It addressed the extent of participation and the content of the meetings.

By the time the Home Office funding ceased in 2004, the London CONNECT programme had completed 50 RJ events: these had been a mixture of indirect mediations ($N = 37$) in which the mediator had 'shuttled' between the victim and the offender, direct mediations ($N = 11$), and two RJ conferences. In the same period, Yorkshire's REMEDI had provided direct mediation in 35 cases and indirect mediation in 97 cases. The JRC had victim and offender consent to all RJC ($N = 723$) cases that reached the point of randomization (where both offender and victim had agreed to take part in a conference) of which about half ($N = 342$) were assigned to an RJ conference. Where there was a choice of forms of RJ, as was the case in REMEDI and CONNECT, most participants (around 75%) opted not to meet the other party. However, when no option of indirect mediation was offered, which was the case in the JRC studies, participation rates were as high as in the other two schemes. There was considerable variation in the percentage of cases where victims agreed to participate, with significantly higher numbers agreeing in cases with juvenile offenders than adults. In both the juvenile and adult programmes offender take-up was generally high, except for post-sentence community sentence offenders whose motivation appeared to be less than that of offenders at other points in the justice system. Shapland *et al.* comment that interviews with participants in direct mediation or RJC showed that even though they had been nervous beforehand, they had been well prepared in terms of their roles and expectations of the RJ meeting. Both offenders and victims tended to emphasize altruistic explanations for taking part, with victims indicating that restitution was not a significant reason for doing so. The JRC conferences were characterized by high levels of perceived procedural justice (Tyler, 1990), with interview results from offenders and victims rating facilitators as non-dominating and impartial. Shapland *et al.* observed a sample of RJCs in which participants contributed more or less equally to the discussion. Participants also rated RJC as safe encounters, despite the high levels of emotion sometimes expressed, with no assaults and almost no threats. Given the total of over 400 RJ conferences completed by JRC without any safety issues, the evidence strongly suggests the safety of victim–offender meetings. While the Sherman–Strang team did abandon two potential conferences on safety grounds, this was in advance of random assignment and part of a more general eligibility screening process. In our JRC conferences, Shapland's team reports that offenders generally admitted a lot of responsibility for the offence. Almost all showed remorse and offered apologies. Victims, who in more than two-thirds of these cases rated themselves as having been considerably affected by the crime, tended in most cases to accept the apologies, though expressed forgiveness was rare. Explicit disapproval of the offence and shaming of the offender occurred in a majority of conferences, but was accompanied by support for the offender in almost all conferences. Each conference concluded with an outcome agreed by all participants. Both parties and their supporters tended to concentrate on the offender's future and how to stop reoffending, rather than on the victim's needs. Outcomes were usually focused on drug or alcohol problems and remedies, literacy, skills training and employment issues for the offender, with reference to financial reparation for the victim rare. Monitoring of our JRC conferences indicated that almost 90% of offenders completed at least some of their undertakings. Of the remainder, many were unable to complete them because of reasons beyond their control. Participation rates in drug and alcohol programmes were particularly high. Shapland *et al.* concluded that all three programmes had been generally well implemented in terms of case flow and in following RJ principles, with good relations maintained with criminal justice officials and with high levels of engagement of both victims and offenders.

Shapland, J. Atkinson, A., Atkinson, H., Chapman, B., Dignan, J., Howes, M. *et al.* (2007). *Restorative justice: The views of victims and offenders. The third report from the evaluation of three schemes.* London: Ministry of Justice Research Series 3/07.

In their third report, the Sheffield team focuses on the views of victims and offenders who had participated in the three programmes. In our JRC RCTs, two attempts were made to interview participants in both the RJ and the control groups on two occasions. The first interview was requested within three weeks of the case finalization to ensure that they had not suffered any ill-effects, and to gain some feedback on their experience. Then, 8–10 months after each case was finalized, Shapland's team approached participants in all three programmes in the evaluation study period and asked them to complete either an interview or a questionnaire. The response rate was variable, ranging from 4% to 80% across all the programmes; most were in the range of 40–60%, with slightly higher figures for victims than offenders. Both victims and offenders in all three programmes said they were pleased with the preparation they had been given and the amount of information they had received about RJ. All were clear that the process was entirely voluntary. Both victims and offenders said they had wanted to take part so as to communicate with each other, to say what they felt about the offence and its effects and to try to solve problems, especially problems behind the offending. Commenting on the content of the RJ conferences, our JRC victims and offenders told Shapland's team that they were very positive about the experience. Over 85% said the conference went well, that they had felt safe, and that the facilitator had been fair and impartial. Victims said that they especially were glad of the opportunity to explain the effects of the offence, to get answers to their questions directly from the offender and to make their own assessment of the offender. Offenders said the best thing was being able to apologize personally and to explain about the offence, even though they had been very apprehensive beforehand about doing so. Very high percentages of both victims and offenders in all JRC RCTS (almost all in excess of 85%) said that they had been able to say what they wanted and that apologies had been expressed and accepted. Victims were as likely to say that they had accepted apologies in the more serious offences as the less serious; for example 100% of the robbery victims and 86% of the prison study victims of serious violent assaults. Overall, 85% of JRC victims and 80% of offenders said that they were satisfied with their conference. Most victims felt that the conference had occurred 'at the right time' after the offence, even though that varied from a matter of a very few weeks to many years, suggesting that there is a broad timeframe in which RJ can be helpful. *RJC in prison.* Many of the JRC conferences were held in the prisons where the offenders were either on remand (the London burglary and robbery cases) or serving their sentence (Thames Valley violence cases). Victims almost never indicated that prison had been a problematic location for their conference; they had been well briefed about what they would encounter arriving at the prison (security routines, etc.) and within the prison. Victims often incurred significant travel and other expenses for the prison conferences, but these were met by the programmes. Future programmes would probably need to make provisions for these costs to yield similar take-up rates. The REMEDI and CONNECT programmes both presented an opportunity to assess the relative benefits of direct and indirect mediation and to compare both of them to RJ conferencing. The evaluators were clear that direct mediation was superior to indirect mediation on important indicators for victims especially, and that RJ conferencing was superior to both of them.

Shapland, J. Atkinson, A., Atkinson, H., Dignan, J., Edwards, L., Hibbert, J. et al. (2008). *Does restorative justice affect reconviction? The fourth report from the evaluation of three schemes.* London: Ministry of Justice Research Series 10/08.

In their fourth report, the focus of the Sheffield team is on the effectiveness of restorative justice in reducing reoffending, using reconviction over the subsequent 2 years as the measure. They also look at the frequency and seriousness of these convictions and the cost of their reoffending, both to victims directly and to the criminal justice process.

Findings from this report on the RCTs conducted by the RJC are summarized in this chapter in section 5C (costs), section 6A (effects on crime) and section 7A (victim effects). Offender and victim effects that emerged from the Remedi and Connect studies also evaluated by the Sheffield team are reported in sections 8A and 8B.

REFERENCES

Ahmed, E., Harris, N., Braithwaite, J., & Braithwaite, V. (2001). *Shame management through reintegration.* Cambridge: Cambridge University Press.

Angel, C. (2005). *Victims meet their offenders: Testing the impact of restorative justice conferences on victims' post-traumatic stress symptoms.* PhD dissertation, University of Pennsylvania.

Arendt, H. (1958). *The human condition.* Chicago, IL: University of Chicago Press.

Bennett, S. (2008). *Criminal careers and restorative justice.* PHD dissertation, University of Cambridge.

Blagg, H. (1997). A just measure of shame? Aboriginal youth and conferencing in Australia. *The British Journal of Criminology, 37,* 481–501.

Braithwaite, J. (1989). *Crime, shame and reintegration.* Cambridge: Cambridge University Press.

Braithwaite, J. (2002). *Restorative justice and responsive regulation.* Oxford: Oxford University Press.

Christie, N. (1977). Conflicts as property. *British Journal of Criminology, 17,* 1–15.

Collins, R. (2004). *Interaction ritual chains.* Princeton, NJ: Princeton University Press.

Cook, T. D., & Campbell, D. T. (1979). *Quasi-experimentation: Design and analysis for field settings.* Boston, MA: Houghton Mifflin.

Doll, R. (1992). Sir Austin Bradford Hill and the progress of science. *British Medical Journal, 305,* 1521–1526.

Farrington, D. P., Coid, J. W., Harnett, L. M., Jolliffe, D., Soteriou, N., & Turner, R. E. (2006). *Criminal careers up to age 50 and life success up to age 48: New findings from the Cambridge Study in Delinquent Development* (2nd edn). London: Home Office.

Federal Judicial Center (1981). Experimentation in the law: Report of the Federal Judicial Center Advisory Committee on Experimentation in the Law. *Journal of Research in Crime and Delinquency, 29*(1), 34–61.

Huxley, E. (1939). *Red strangers.* London: Chatto and Windus.

Kubzansky, L., Koenen, K., Spiro, A., Vokonas, S., & Sparrow, D. (2007). Prospective study of posttraumatic stress disorder symptoms and coronary heart disease in the Normative Aging Study. *Archives of General Psychiatry, 64*(1), 109–116.

Landenberger, N., & Lipsey, M. (2005). The positive effects of cognitive–behavioral programs for offenders: A meta-analysis of factors associated with effective treatment. *Journal of Experimental Criminology, 1,* 451–476.

Marshall, T. (1999). *Restorative justice: An overview*. London: Home Office.

Marshall, T. F. (1997). Criminal justice conferencing calls for caution. *Mediation* (2 parts).

McGarrell, E., Olivares, K., Crawford, K., & Kroovand, N. (2000). *Returning justice to the community: The Indianapolis restorative justice experiment*. Indianapolis, IN: Hudson Institute.

Miers, D., Maguire, M., Goldie, S., Sharpe, K., Hale, C., Netten, A., Uglow, S., Doolin, K., Hallam, A., Enterkin, J., & Newburn, T. (2001). *An exploratory evaluation of restorative justice schemes*. Crime Reduction Series, paper 9. London: Home Office.

Newburn, T., Crawford, A., Earle, R., Goldie, S., Hale, C., Masters, G., & Uglow, S. (2001). *The introduction of referral orders into the youth justice system*. HORS 242. London: Home Office.

Piantadosi, S. (1997). *Clinical trials: A methodologic perspective*. New York: Wiley.

Prison Fellowship (2008). Sycamore tree programme. Retrieved 14 January 2015 from http://www.prisonfellowship.org.uk/what-we-do/sycamore-tree/

Roche, D. (2003). *Accountability in restorative justice*. Oxford: Oxford University Press.

Rossner, M. (2011). Emotions and interaction ritual: A micro analysis of restorative justice. *British Journal of Criminology, 51*(1), 95–119.

Rossner, M. (forthcoming). *Just emotions: Rituals of restorative justice*. Oxford: Oxford University Press.

Rothbaum, B. O., & Foa, E. B. (1999). Exposure therapy for PTSD. *PTSD Research Quarterly*, The National Center for Post-Traumatic Stress Disorder, White River Junction, VT, *10*(2), 1Y8.

Shapland, J. Atkinson, A., Atkinson, H., Chapman, B., Dignan, J., Howes, M., Johnstone, J., Robinson, G., & Sorsby, A. (2007). *Restorative justice: The views of victims and offenders. The third report from the evaluation of Three Schemes*. London: Ministry of Justice Research Series 3/07.

Shapland, J. Atkinson, A., Atkinson, H., Colledge, E., Dignan, J., Howes, M., & Sorsby, A. (2006). Restorative justice in practice: The second report from the evaluation of three schemes. Sheffield Centre for Criminological Research, University of Sheffield.

Shapland, J. Atkinson, A., Atkinson, H., Dignan, J., Edwards, L., Hibbert, J., Howes, M., Johnstone, J., Robinson, G., & Sorsby, A. (2008). *Does restorative justice affect reconviction? The fourth report from the evaluation of three schemes*. London: Ministry of Justice Research Series 10/08.

Shapland, J., Atkinson, A., Colledge, E., Dignan, J., Howes, M., Johnstone, J., Pennant, R., Robinson, G., & Sorsby, A. (2004). *Implementing restorative justice schemes (Crime Reduction Programme): A report on the first year*. Home Office online report 32/04, London, Home Office. Retrieved 14 January 2015 from http://www.restorativejustice.org.uk/resource/ministry_of_justice_evaluation_implementing_restorative_justice_schemes_crime_reduction_programme_the_first_year_report/

Sherman, L. W. (2003). Reason for emotion: Reinventing justice with theories, innovations and research. The 2002 ASC Presidential Address. *Criminology, 41*, 1–38.

Sherman, L., & Strang, H. (2007). *Restorative justice: The evidence*. London: Smith Institute.

Sherman, L., Strang, H., Angel, C., Woods, D., Barnes, G., Bennett, S., & Inkpen, N. (2005). Effects of face-to-face restorative justice on victims of crime in four randomized controlled trials. *Journal of Experimental Criminology, 1*(3), 367–395.

Sherman, L., Strang, H., Barnes, G., & Woods, D. (2006). *Race and restorative justice*. Paper Presented to the American Society of Criminology, November 2006.

Soothill, K., Francis, B., Ackerley, E., & Humphreys, L. (2008). Changing patterns of offending behaviour among young adults. *British Journal of Criminology, 48*, 75–95.

Strang, H (2002). *Repair or revenge: Victims and restorative justice*. Oxford: Oxford University Press.

Strang, H. (2010). Exploring the effects of restorative justice on crime victims for victims of conflict in transitional societies. In *International handbook of victimology*. Thousand Oaks, CA: Sage.

Strang, H., & Sherman, L. (forthcoming). *The effects of restorative justice conferencing on crime victims and offenders: A Campbell Collaboration Crime and Justice Group systematic review*. Cambridge: Jerry Lee Centre for Experimental Criminology, Institute of Criminology, University of Cambridge.

Strang, H., Sherman, L., Angel, C., Woods, D., Bennett, S., Newbury-Birch, D., & Inkpen, N. (2006). Victim evaluations of face-to-face restorative justice experiences: A quasi-experimental analysis. *Journal of Social Issues, 62*(2), 281–306.

Sykes, G. M., & Matza, D. (1957). Techniques of neutralization: A theory of delinquency. *American Sociological Review, 22*, 664–670.

Tutu, D. (1999). *No future without forgiveness*. New York: Rider, Random House.

Tyler, T. (1990). *Why people obey the law*. New Haven, CT: Yale University Press.

United Nations (2002). *Basic principles on the use of restorative justice programmes in criminal matters*. Commission on Crime Prevention and Criminal Justice, April, Vienna.

Woolf, P. (2008). *The damage done*. London: Bantam Press.

Part III
Ethical and Legal Issues

26 Ethical Issues in Forensic Psychological Policy and Practice

GRAHAM J. TOWL

This chapter begins with an outline of some of the philosophical roots which underpin much of what is deemed morally acceptable behaviour in Western societies. In one sense, ethics may be seen as an application of moral philosophic principles which are sometimes explicit but more often implicit.

One distinguishing characteristic of reasonably well-developed professions is that they have sets of ethical guidance. I include a brief review of some germane guidance, drawing upon international and inter-professional sets of guidance.

The focus of the chapter is primarily on psychologists and especially those undertaking work in 'forensic' settings, for example, those working with prisoners. However, the discussion is not intended to be restricted by the work of forensic psychologists, but will be taken to include the work of psychologists from areas where there is work with forensic populations. Indeed, a number of the issues raised could be seen to have some application in a number of professions and not just in a prison or forensic psychiatric service context, but rather in a broader social welfare and health context too. However, although there may very well be relevant learning from other such broader areas, our focus will remain in the forensic domain.

In setting the focus for understanding ethics in forensic practice a key underpinning theme is the contested area of power relationships. A basic conceptual framework is outlined as a heuristic device to aid our understanding and reflection upon the broader context of ethical decision-making in forensic policy and practice.

The chapter will draw to a close with some ideas and reflections upon the development and maintenance of an ethical understanding in forensic policy and practice.

PHILOSOPHICAL ROOTS

Just as with many other areas of study there is a particular language to philosophical ideas in relation to ethics and it is worth briefly outlining some of the relevant terms. Familiarity with such terms will hopefully help in informing some of our thinking, ultimately in relation to decision-making on ethical matters.

Two key types of theory which we need to consider in philosophical thinking are those referred to as teleological and deontological theories (see, e.g., Mendonca & Kanungo, 2007). Teleological or, as they are sometimes described, 'consequentialist' theories are characterized by a focus on outcomes. Thus the notion of 'intent' or motivation may be seen to take a philosophical backseat in such theories. A focus on consequences takes primacy with such theories.

Two major, highly pertinent manifestations of the consequentialist perspective may be seen in what is sometimes termed 'egoistic hedonism' and the much more commonly known 'utilitarianism'.

Egoistic hedonism may broadly be viewed as self-interest, a commonly used implicit philosophical model in much work attempting to understand or predict human behaviour. It is, for example, a popular implicit philosophical model used across a range of professional disciplines, including psychology and economics. Egoistic hedonism has its roots in early Greek philosophical thinking (Mothershead, Jr., 1955) and has been, and remains, a powerful implicit theory in informing our understanding of much human behaviour. Indeed it may often inform much of the behaviour of many individual professionals. However, sometimes professionals may be defensive about such possibilities in *their* practice. But it

Forensic Psychology, Second Edition. Edited by David A. Crighton and Graham J. Towl.

is perhaps worth noting that this was the underpinning philosophical approach adopted by 'New Labour' in the United Kingdom with their health reforms of General Practice – the gatekeepers to more specialist services. And indeed, historically this was a consideration in the setting up of the UK NHS in the post-War period to woo the medical profession to be part of the new organizational structures predicated upon such services being free at the point of service delivery.

Utilitarianism, which is underpinned by the principle of 'utility', has historically had a number of influential proponents such as Hume, Bentham and Mill (Mendonca & Kanungo, 2007). One key difference between egoistic hedonism and utilitarianism is that the latter has as its focus the maximum utility or benefit for the majority. Both theories appear to have at least an implicit disregard for the means, or indeed the motives, to achieve a particular end or consequence. A consideration of 'utility' has underpinned much of the recent deliberations of those engaged in deciding which drugs may or may not be prescribed through the National Health Service in England and Wales. In such cases, the notion of 'utility' is considered in relation to the cost of specified likely benefits. Such 'cost utility' considerations may be compared with other actions or inactions in terms of their cost benefits too. Indeed, it is perhaps worth noting here that inactions are sometimes erroneously conflated with neutrality. In power terms, apparently neutral acts may simply maintain existing power inequalities. An illustrative application of the potential problems which may result from the proposition that inaction means being 'neutral' follows. Many prison staff still struggle to refer to individual prisoners by using the suffix 'Mr'. This is often a term proudly reserved for staff. The (untenable) defence of such an approach by many prison staff is that it is important to distinguish between the status of the prisoner and staff. It is, of course, incumbent upon psychologists working in prisons to challenge such institutionalized abuses of power. I would not wish to suggest that this is a problem exclusive to prisons. Fundamentally, the same sorts of problems arise in hospitals too, but may manifest themselves in different ways, but as institutions dominated by professional power they can be potentially every bit as abusive in terms of the basic dignity and worth (implicitly and explicitly) with which patients are sometimes treated.

In marked contrast with the preceding text, teleological approaches is the deontological perspective. This perspective is about the notion of duties or obligations. In terms of European philosophical thought, one of its leading proponents is Immanuel Kant. Indeed, it is Kant's 'categorical imperative' which is explicitly referred to in the British Psychological Society's most recent set of ethical guidance for practitioner psychologists (British Psychological Society, 2009) as being central to the underpinning moral philosophy of the code. Kant contended that an act was only morally correct if we would be happy to see all (including ourselves) being treated in a particular manner. This does not necessarily sit well with the teleological or consequentialist position that it is the end rather than the means that matters. However, it does sit well with much Eastern and religious thinking. For example, the Far Eastern philosopher Confucius exhorts his students 'Do not impose on others what you yourself do not desire' (The Analects, 15:24 [Confucius, 1979]). There are parallels in Islamic, Christian, Jewish and Buddhist traditions too, among other organized religions. On a practical level, whenever working with a patient, prisoner or client, one useful discipline and 'test' may be when considering particular 'assessments' or 'interventions' to ask ourselves how we would feel about the interaction if the particular recipient of services was someone we loved. The ability to honestly explore and understand one's own motivations in psychological practice is a very challenging area to teach effectively. This change alone may well serve to improve the quality of much forensic practice. This is perhaps especially so given the recent history of forensic psychological practice which has been characterized, some would say unduly, by manualized approaches to group work based interventions often 'delivered' in coercive contexts. Thus the pressures on forensic psychologists to comply rather than question have come more to the professional fore. But such reflection remains an important habit of professional life (Koocher & Keith-Spiegel, 1998).

So, we have noted the respective perspectives of teleological and deontological thinking and we will return to these ideas when looking in more detail at professional policies and practices.

The popular media and political discourse on public service has it that the notion of altruism is important in understanding the motivations and behaviours of a number of professionals, perhaps especially so, purportedly, with health professionals such as nurses and doctors. Prejudices tend to come to the fore in such discourses. Nurses are assumed to be attracted to their work on a vocational basis; in short, they want to help the sick. Similarly, doctors are commonly perceived to have similarly noble motivations to their work, although this reputation has perhaps been somewhat called into question more recently with the substantial pay rises that General Practitioners have received in recent years (Sunday Times, 2008). Professional hospital managers are not afforded the same level of generosity of presumed motivation, nor for that matter are they necessarily assumed to be as competent, unless, of course, they have been previously qualified as doctors or nurses themselves. Often the analysis underlying such arguments is somewhat weak. For example, 'Managers who have been doctors and nurses know how to stop simple conditions becoming expensive illnesses because they have medical training as well as MBAs. Executives from the business schools do not because they only have MBAs' (Cohen, 2008). The key ethical point here is that whatever the background of the individual they need to be competent in the tasks that they are required to undertake whether it is in the domain of management or clinical practice. But the idea that to be an effective manager in the NHS all would have to be previously trained as a doctors or nurses seems to more plausibly reflect the biases of the author in simply parroting the daily discourse of media sound bites alluded to earlier. Many managers lead complex organizations e.g. hospitals, without such specialist backgrounds.

Despite professional self-interests, the notion of altruism remains important to our understanding of the motivations and behaviour associated with much ethical practice. Psychological definitions of altruism have tended to focus upon individual dispositions to help others to meet internal nurturance needs (Krebs, 1982). The selfless helping of others remains widely regarded as a moral virtue, if not always described explicitly in such terms.

Most modern professional ethical guidance appears to draw primarily on deontological perspectives but they by no means ignore the importance of teleological considerations. Such philosophical discussions are, of course, all very well to a point, indeed they are important in informing our understanding.

But what does this mean in terms of how we may improve upon our forensic practice? Our attitudes and beliefs are reflected in our everyday forensic practice. Our behaviour as professionals will be observed closely and will be seen to imply particular attitudes. Working with clients with what is sometimes referred to as a 'positive regard' will convey a sense of respect for the individual. Some professionals are experienced as 'working with' their clients and others may be experienced as being 'dealt with' by the professional. The importance of careful listening, courtesy and kindness in our interactions with our clients should not be underestimated. Such behaviour can be experienced as symbolic of how the professional views the individual client which is part of the basis for any (therapeutic) work.

In the following text, we go on to consider some of the further implications and applications arising from our brief introduction to some of the more relevant philosophical positions underpinning, explicitly or implicitly, many such professional codes of conduct.

ETHICAL GUIDANCE FOR PROFESSIONALS

The widely cited four principles of medical ethics are: respect for autonomy, doing good (or beneficence), doing no harm (non-maleficence) and acting with fairness/equality (Baxter, Brennan, Coldicott, & Moller, 2005). Many other professions would make similar explicit demands on their members. Indeed, as mentioned earlier, one important defining characteristic of an occupation with professional status is that there will be an ethical code. Ethical codes are designed to benefit both recipients of professional services and also the particular professionals themselves. But it is important to remember that although ethical guidance can be very useful in guiding behaviour or expectations about behaviour, it does not provide 'answers' in a categorical and case-specific manner. Nor will it, or should it, ever be so. When drawing on such guidance it is important that professionals possess a range of skills, including critical reasoning skills, as well as drawing upon a clear 'moral compass'. Ethical decision-making needs to be both well-reasoned and fair-minded (Thomson, 2006).

After two World Wars which included some truly appalling and well-documented atrocities (including by health professionals on all 'sides') in and beyond Europe, the General Assembly of the United Nations made a universal declaration of Human Rights (United Nations, 1948). This has provided a useful source document from which professional ethical guidance has drawn. The Declaration is essentially deontological in its approach; it contains both human rights and responsibilities (or duties).

Professional ethical guidance is thus informed by the need to protect human rights while also providing professionals and those in receipt of professional services with guidance about the principles underpinning behavioural expectations. Whereas it is tempting for any professional grouping to concern themselves exclusively with their own professional guidance for ethical practice, it is perhaps fruitful to consider other relevant sets of guidance which might further inform our understanding. The ethical issues of policy and practice are by no means exclusive to the forensic field, although, of course, some matters may come into sharper focus (Towl, 1994). Indeed, similar sorts of critical and often contested considerations have been the subject of a growing literature within social-welfare-based disciplines such as social work (see, e.g., Banks, 2008; Banks & Williams, 2005). In the following text, for illustrative purposes, are some international perspectives within the general discipline of professional psychology and also guidance from the British Association for Counselling and Psychotherapy

(BACP). The BACP guidance is used as an example because, in terms of the processes of interaction with clients and its psychological basis, there is much in common with the professional work of many psychologists. Before going further with this line of reasoning and exploration it is perhaps worth mentioning some caveats. First, a number of modern moral philosophers have called into question whether or not such codes of 'ethical practice' are actually about ethics *per se*. Some have argued that they diminish the level of engagement with ethical issues as a result of the thinking having been pre-prepared for the practitioner (see, e.g., Dawson, 1994). Second, some have noted that a number of moral philosophers question whether or not the codes may confuse ethics with what amounts to 'law or rule making' rather than reflection, argument and understanding (Banks, 2003). There are, of course, other criticisms which may be considered in relation to the development of ethical guidance, but hopefully the reader has a flavour of some of the potential problems from a philosophical and ultimately policy and practice-based perspective. Some of these concerns are perhaps reflected in the development of a European-wide meta-code of ethics. The legal status and organization of professional psychology throughout Europe is somewhat varied. In 1990, the European Federation of Psychologists Associations (EFPA) set up a task force on ethics. The meta-code set out what areas each ethical code should process without being prescriptive about how such areas should be addressed (Lindsay, Koene, Halder & Lang, 2008). This approach reflected recognition of the political, cultural and professional diversity within Europe. But arguably, most importantly it reflected recognition of the importance of reflection, argument and understanding over simple behavioural prescription. The meta-code does, of course, include a significant degree of exhortation in terms of the areas it advocates being covered in individual national codes.

Next we take a brief look at the American Psychological Society ethical guidance. This has been influential in the development of such guidance in the United Kingdom. The first set of ethical guidance prepared for the Division of Criminological and Legal Psychology (DCLP) of the British Psychological Society (BPS) drew heavily upon the work of the APA in its structure and content (DCLP, 1997). In the United Kingdom, specialist ethical guidelines have been dispensed with unlike in the United States (see, e.g., APA, 2013, briefly summarized in the following text). Guidance from Ireland is also considered because of its geographical propinquity and most importantly its practical utility. Such practical utility can help meet some of the criticism and concerns raised by some about the everyday usefulness of such guidance in improving ethical practice.

I also include coverage of the guidance from the Health and Care Professions Council (HCPC).

APA ethical guidance

The APA set of ethical principles and code of conduct has two key sections, one on general ethical principles and the other on ethical standards (APA, 2002). The five general underlying ethical principles are: beneficence and non-maleficence, fidelity and responsibility, integrity, justice, and respect for people's rights and dignity. These are aspirational goals rather than specific rules of behaviour or conduct. However, the ethical standards that follow from these principles are rules which are enforceable through the rules and procedures of the APA. Unsurprisingly, in the event of a complaint, it is not deemed to be a good defence that an individual claims simply not to be aware of specific rules. It is not my intention to go through the details of the code, but rather to give the reader a flavour of the territory covered.

The standards are split into 10 sections which include standards for: Resolving Ethical Issues, Competence, Human Relations, Privacy and Confidentiality, Advertising and Other Public Statements, Record Keeping and Fees, Education and Training, Research and Publication, Assessment, and finally Therapy. The full details of the code are available at http://www.apa.org/ethics for those readers with an interest in examining the American code further.

APA Speciality Guidelines for Forensic Psychology (2013)

The guidance acknowledges the significant growth of forensic psychology in the United States and, hence, it is argued, the pressing need to have some specialist ethical guidelines. The guidance is divided up under eleven sub-headings; responsibilities, competence, diligence, relationships, fees, (informed consent, notification and assent) conflicts in practice, (privacy, confidentiality and privilege) methods and procedures, assessment and finally professional and other public communications. Revision processes for such guidance are included in recognition of the need to periodically make changes as we learn more about ethics and ethical practice and indeed as social and cultural mores change.

The Psychological Society of Ireland (PSI) Code of Professional Ethics

Similar to the APA code, the PSI code is split into two sections, one on four overall ethical principles and the other on specific ethical standards. The PSI principles are:

Respect for the rights and dignity of the person, competence, responsibility and integrity. These principles are used as the headings for all the ethical standards listed. The code also contains two appendices which are informative and worth bringing to the reader's attention.

Appendix A of the code is entitled 'Recommended Procedure for Ethical Decision-Making', which consists of a useful set of seven points to guide the process of an informed ethical decision-making process. It may well be a useful aide-memoire for policy-makers and practitioners alike. The advice is unsurprising but helpful in its focus. It includes the need for defining the relevant issues for parties affected by the decision-making, a scanning of the code for key issues and a careful evaluation of the rights and responsibilities of all concerned. The useful practical suggestion is made that it may be helpful to generate as many alternative decisions as possible while carefully examining likely and possible outcomes. The importance of the effective communication of ethical decision-making is also helpfully addressed. The key and final point in the seven-point structure is that the individual is personally accountable for their decision-making. In other words, although contextual information may be taken into account as possible mitigation, fundamentally psychologists must take personal responsibility for their ethical decision-making. In forensic practice psychologists have a particular responsibility to ensure that the needs of the individual are given due weight. Sometimes it will be most ethical to decline to provide some services. Just because an organizational policy is legal does not mean that it is necessarily morally correct, or ethical. This is why the importance of individual decision-making and personal responsibility and accountability is difficult to overstate. In this respect the statutory regulation of forensic psychologists in the United Kingdom as health professionals under the umbrella regulatory body of the Health Professions Council (HPC) from July 2009 (although now known as the Health and Care Professions Council (HCPC) since social workers were added to the professional register) has provided helpful professional guidance for those concerned with challenging poor policy and practice.

Appendix B of the code usefully lists potential parties who may be affected by ethical decision-making. Again this may well be a useful aide-memoire for policy-makers and practitioners. When the general public are referred to as a party affected by ethical decision-making, it is perhaps culturally interesting that the example given as a potentially controversial issue is that of abortion. This perhaps serves to illustrate the importance of an appreciation of the cultural context of any such code.

On a final point about the PSI code, it is perhaps worth noting that it explicitly, yet disappointingly, excludes a consideration of any wider social concerns.

This has been a point for debate within psychological policy and practice within England and Wales, with some arguing that social concerns and inequalities underpin many ethical issues for psychologists (see, e.g., Gale, 1994; Towl, 1994). Arguably, nowhere is this more so than in forensic psychological practice with a patient/client group characterized by social inequality. This contrasts with the relatively high professional power of practitioner psychologists which serves to amplify the marked power differentials in such relationships.

In the preceding text, ethical guidelines from the United States and Ireland have been drawn on for international comparative purposes. In the following text, I move on to looking at ethical guidance provided for those undertaking counselling and psychotherapeutic work in the United Kingdom. This is done with the aim of considering what we have to learn from practice in a closely related profession to that of professional psychology.

British Association for Counselling and Psychotherapy – Ethical Framework for Good Practice in Counselling & Psychotherapy

One distinctive feature of this guidance is that it is not structured merely with principles and standards, but from the outset contains an explicit set of values (BACP, 2013). Stress is given to the importance of practising with a high degree of cultural sensitivity to the needs of clients. A consideration of the importance of human rights tops the list of values. Again, distinctively, there is an emphasis on a value base which appreciates the value bases of human experiences and culture. Values inform principles.

The principles listed have a resonance elsewhere in the other ethical codes we have touched upon, with the possible exception of the emphasis which is given to the importance of self-respect, defined as fostering the practitioners' self-knowledge and care for the self. Unusually for a code of professional ethics there is a section, albeit aspirational, on personal moral qualities. Moral qualities include: empathy, sincerity, integrity, resilience, respect, humility, competence, fairness, wisdom and courage. Emphasis is given to practitioners continually engaging with the challenge of coming to ethical decisions in practice. I will not list the full range of standards here. Suffice to observe that the standards are derived from the underlying principles mentioned earlier, and also reflect the moral qualities needed to ensure that the counselling and psychotherapeutic values which underpin the guidance are manifest.

What seems clear about the world of counselling and psychotherapy is that there appears to be a greater acknowledgement about the wider context of any psychotherapeutic services when compared with codes for psychologists.

Having briefly considered both some international codes and that of a profession with close theoretical and sometimes practical links with psychology, I will now focus upon the code of ethics and conduct for psychologists in the United Kingdom and then on some of the specific guidance for forensic psychologists. But it is perhaps worth reiterating at this point the need for an emphasis on both underpinning 'values' and the socioeconomic context in understanding the potential application of such ethical codes.

Health and Care Professions Council (HCPC) Standards of conduct, performance and ethics (2012)

The standards as outlined were first published in July 2008 with some amendments when the Health Professions Council (HPC) became the Health and Care Professions Council (HCPC) on 1 August, 2012.

The document begins with a focus upon the duties of the individual practitioner. Fourteen standards follow: (1) 'You must act in the best interests of service users'; (2) 'You must respect the confidentiality of service users'; (3) 'You must keep high standards of personal conduct'; (4) 'You must provide (to us and any other relevant regulators) any important information about your conduct and competence'; (5) 'You must keep your professional knowledge and skills up to date'; (6) 'You must act within the limits of your knowledge, skills and experience and, if necessary, refer the matter to another practitioner'; (7) 'You must communicate properly and effectively with service users and other practitioners'; (8) 'You must effectively supervise tasks you have asked other people to carry out'; (9) 'You must get informed consent to provide care or services (so far as possible)'; (10) 'You must keep accurate records'; (11) 'You must deal fairly and safely with the risks of infection'; (12) 'You must limit your work or stop practising if your performance or judgement is affected by your health'; (13) 'You must behave with honesty and integrity and make sure that your behaviour does not damage the public's confidence in you or your profession'; and (14) 'You must make sure that any advertising you do is accurate'.

What is striking about these exhortations is that the wording is such that the individual is left in no doubt that each of us is responsible for our own conduct. The notion of such personal responsibility is one of the key strengths of this code over the others. The presentation

in the first person serves to reinforce this point. The HCPC is the statutory regulator for 16 health-care professions and most of the guidance readily touched each of the professions. However, standard 11 which refers to dealing fairly and safely with the risk of infection sits as an anomaly for professions such as practitioner psychologists and social workers. Such documentation is periodically reviewed and it will be interesting to see if this is a standard that has longevity.

The British Psychological Society (BPS) Code of Ethics and Conduct (2009)

In 1985, the BPS adopted a code of conduct which has been periodically updated, with some relatively minor revisions over the years. However, the 2006 guidance was, and remains, a marked improvement upon the quality of guidance previously available under the auspices of the BPS. These were subsequently updated with relatively minor amendments in 2009. The single most substantive change is the acknowledgement of the introduction of the statutory regulatory role of the Health Professions Council (HPC).

The introduction to the guidelines explains the rationale and context of the guidance. One fundamental observation which is brought to the reader's attention early on in the document is that ethics are inextricably linked to power relationships. Related to this is the importance of individual responsibility and personal accountability for one's actions. The guidance is there to help inform and not to replace professional decision-making and accountabilities. This may, in part, be seen as having taken account of some of the philosophical criticisms cited in the preceding text about the problems with ethical codes.

On a practical level, practitioners may well find the concise section on decision-making useful for informing the development of local policies and practices. There are similarities with the appendix provided by the Irish code, but there are some additions too. The section concludes with ideas for further reading.

The code is underpinned by four ethical principles: respect, competence, responsibility and integrity. Each of these principles is reflected in a statement of relevant values and a set of specific standards. All this is potentially helpful when trying to make sometimes difficult judgements about ethical decision-making. However, it is lacking in some conceptual clarity. Respect is referred to as a principle rather than a value; some may find this inconsistent, and perhaps somewhat confused. Putting aside this relatively minor beef, essentially the code provides some of the key parameters of professional decision-making while ensuring that individual practitioners are exhorted to retain their accountabilities for their practice.

In sum, the BPS guidance has been improved in recent years and has much in common with not only international codes for psychologists but also those of other related professions.

Specialist BPS forensic guidance

In the late twentieth century and early in the twenty-first century, the Division of Criminological and Legal Psychology (DCLP), which was subsequently renamed the Division of Forensic Psychology (DFP), began to formulate its own specialist guidance (British Psychological Society, 1997, 2002). This guidance was informed by previous APA and BPS guidance and also a number of relevant papers which reflected Divisional activity in this important area (see, e.g., Gale, 1994; Towl, 1994, 1995). More recently, with the advent of the relatively new set of BPS ethical guidance, the specialist guidance has received less attention. This reflects, in part, an acknowledgement that the fundamental concerns associated with ethical guidance are generic to a range of areas of professional practice. In one important sense, then, the forensic domain is no different to anywhere else where issues of power imbalances are to the fore.

In the next section, I will move on to an examination of how we may glean guidance to inform good practice from a consideration of the power imbalances embedded in professional relationships with clients across many professions involved in health or social care. These are the general domains within which forensic policy and practice is situated. All the work of forensic psychologists in courts, police stations, prisons, hospitals and community settings may arguably be construed within this broader health-care and social care context.

POWER RELATIONSHIPS

All professional relationships beget power relationships. Such relationships may be helpfully conceptualized at three levels: socio-political, organizational and individual. The context of these may be viewed through the lenses of 'the state' and 'societal status'.

A similar framework could be used with a range of professional groups in a range of settings. The key point is that to understand what ethical conduct may look like in particular cases and everyday practice, it is important to have an understanding of the power relationships between the professional and the recipient of services. In the forensic context (as is often the case in health more

generally in practice), the recipient of services often has limited 'choices' that they may exercise. A limited choice (if any are tangible) serves to augment the already markedly skewed existing power relationships. Clearly, forensic psychologists need to be mindful of this in their everyday practice, and so do policy-makers.

The framework is not intended to capture every aspect of the layers of the complex power relationships between, in this case, forensic psychologist and offender. However, it does serve as an anchor point in looking at some key characteristics which have a potential impact upon the power relationships with clients.

If we look at the socio-political domain, the state positively supports the work of forensic psychologists. Evidence in support of this can be seen in the large organizational growth in the numbers of posts in the early twenty-first century (Crighton & Towl, 2008). Also, there have been some very significant improvements in pay and conditions for forensic psychologists in England and Wales, Scotland, Northern Ireland and also in other countries. Parole Boards also appear to increasingly and often heavily weight psychological and psychologically based reports when considering whether or not a prisoner may be released.

By marked contrast, prisoners are not allowed to vote in UK state-sponsored elections and are contained within the confines of a prison. At an organizational or institutional level they tend not to have benefited from educational opportunities.

At an organizational level, psychologists benefit from both the strong support of their employers and the support of professional bodies such as the British Psychological Society and Health and Care Professions Council (HCPC). Offenders enjoy no similar such support.

At an individual level, psychologists are state 'successes' with hopefully high levels of verbal intelligence and all the trappings or benefits of professional status. For example, they enjoy the benefits of professional supervision and Continuing Professional Development (CPD) and have access to ethical guidance. By, again, marked contrast, prisoners may be construed, in effect, as 'state failures'. They do not have a ready-made infrastructure for support.

In short, the power inequalities in the relationship start from a position of marked inequality. If we are concerned with the rights of 'another' then we perhaps need to be especially concerned when, as professionals, we hold such power. Many will feel discomfort at the extent of the power differential in such relationships. This may be particularly so among forensic psychologists who will be all too well aware of the potential dangers. As a general rule, the wider the power differential, the higher the risk of power abuses. This is amply illustrated elsewhere in, for example, cases of child abuse and patient abuses by medical practitioners. The child has relatively little power in such circumstances and the same, in practice, can be said for a patient experiencing the potential vulnerabilities associated with illness (whether physical or mental). By marked contrast, the doctor will enjoy the trappings of their professional status and firm power base. Thus the gulf in the power relationship is further amplified. Psychologists need to learn from such problems. This is a very challenging area in need of further research.

Increasingly within psychological practice there has been a growth in awareness about the wider context of the application of ethical guidance. This is illustrated with the more recent BPS guidance cited in the preceding text, the hallmark of which is the importance of our individual responsibility and accountability. The defence of a professional practice on the basis that 'I was only following my organizational (or professional) guidelines' is not in itself good enough in terms of the extent of individual accountability. There is an expectation that a professional will make an informed independent decision, taking account of guidance but retaining *their* accountability for *their* actions and inactions. Sometimes this can be difficult. This may be even more so on occasions when doing the right thing means experiencing a personal or professional disbenefit. However, in terms of statutory regulation for psychologists, the focus on individual practitioners could not be clearer (Health and Care Professions Council, 2012).

CONCLUSIONS

It is important to have some understanding of the philosophical basis of our ethical practice. I have argued that one key underpinning of what is deemed ethical in terms of policy and practice is an understanding of the power relationship between the professional psychologist and offender. These relationships need to be set within their wider social context. Offenders tend to come from socially disadvantaged backgrounds. Psychologists tend to come from socially advantaged backgrounds. A consideration of such factors, in combination with the reading of ethical guidance not just for one's own profession, can clearly be helpful. But arguably most important is the need to engage in discussion and reflection with colleagues about both current and future policy and practices in terms of their potential ethical implications.

A key change since the first edition has been with the statutory regulation of practitioner psychologists. This statutory framework has been a major step forward in encouraging and enabling the individual professional accountability of practitioner psychologists. In view of the 16 health and care professions regulated this may well give the public the added confidence that poly professional regulation more readily lends itself to cross disciplinary learning and questioning which in the ethical domain is a very healthy sign (Towl, 2014).

We have seen how a consideration of one's own values and beliefs is important in the consideration of ethical ideas and practice. On occasion there will be the need to decide what to do next to challenge unethical policies and practices. Active engagement in discussions and actions in relation to ethical practice is sometimes a difficult process. We need to routinely reflect upon who benefits from some areas of our decision-making. There can sometimes be a broad range of potential stakeholders. Self-reflection is an important element of informing ethical decision-making, particularly in relation to a reflection upon one's own values and how they impact upon decision-making. In short, we need to periodically challenge our own ethical practice and its basis.

I hope that there is food for thought within this chapter which will be helpful in such reflections, discussions, deliberations and, most importantly, actions in this intellectually and emotionally challenging field.

FURTHER READING

British Psychological Society (2009). Code of Ethics and Conduct – Guidance published by the Ethics Committee of the British Psychological Society, BPS, Leicester, United Kingdom.
The context, values and principles outlined in the code are essential reading for all practising forensic psychologists. Although forensic settings may beget a sharper focus to some of the ethical tensions and challenges in the field, the fundamental values and principles remain the same. So do many of the required good professional practices. The code provides a highly readable and useful structure (the parameters within which professional judgements may be made) which will be helpful in informing ethical decision-making. There is also an acknowledgement of the statutory regulator role of the HCPC.
Lindsay, G., Koene, C., Overeedide, H., & Lang, F. (2008). *Ethics for European psychologists*. Gottingen, Germany: Hogrefe.
In this recent and stimulating book, the European Federation of Psychologists Associations (EFPA) meta-code of ethics (2nd edition) is detailed, with a number of chapters on key themes in professional practice. Although designed with individual psychological associations primarily in mind, the code can be drawn upon to inform individual practice too. The book contains much material

which may be of practical help to forensic practitioners. For example, appendix 4 covers the potentially uncomfortable professional territory of behavioural expectations of the psychologist when responding to a complaint that has been made. The advice has been taken from a Norwegian source but clearly has a resonance across Europe. The advice is clear, specific and helpful. Complaints about forensic psychologists have increased over the years. In sum, this book will be potentially of much practical help as a resource for the trainee or qualified forensic psychologist.

Standards of conduct, performance and ethics (2012). Health and Care Professions Council, London, UK.

This is essential reading for any registered practitioner psychologist and needs also to be read by those on training routes to qualification in any area of the applied psychology specialisms. The focus of accountability is unambiguously upon the individual practitioner to ensure their appropriate professional standards whatever the organizational context. Failure to adhere to the guidance could result in a Fitness to Practice hearing and one outcome of that can be a loss of registration and inability to practice. This is a must read document for all forensic psychologists especially in view of the coercive nature of the environments within which we practice.

REFERENCES

American Psychological Association (APA) (2002). *Ethical principles of psychologists and code of conduct.* Washington, DC: Author.

American Psychological Association (APA) (2013). *Ethical principles of psychologists and code of conduct.* Including 2010 amendments. Washington, DC: Author.

BACP (2013). *Ethical framework for good practice in counselling and psychotherapy.* London: BACP.

Banks, S. (2003). From oaths to rule books: A critical examination of codes of ethics for the social professions. *European Journal of Social Work, 6*(2), 133–144.

Banks, S. (2008). Critical commentary: Social work ethics. *British Journal of Social Work, 38,* 1238–1249.

Banks, S., & Williams, R. (2005). Accounting for ethical difficulties in social welfare work: Issues, problems and dilemmas. *British Journal of Social Work, 35,* 1005–1022.

Baxter, C., Brennan, M. G., Coldicott, Y., & Moller, M. (Eds.). (2005). *The practical guide to medical ethics and law* (2nd edn). Pastest. Bodmin: MPG Books.

British Psychological Society (2009). *Code of ethics and conduct.* Guidance published by the Ethics Committee of the British Psychological Society, Leicester, UK.

British Psychological Society, Division of Criminological and Legal Psychology (DCLP) (1997). *Ethical guidelines on forensic psychology.* Leicester: Author.

British Psychological Society, Division of Forensic Psychology (DFP) (2002). *Ethical guidelines on forensic psychology.* August. Leicester: Author.

Cohen, N. (2008). Let the PM be the best-paid public servant: Comment. *The Observer,* 23 November.

Confucius (1979). *The analects* (translated with an introduction by D. C. Lau). London: Penguin.

Crighton, D. A., & Towl, G. J. (2008). *Psychology in prisons* (2nd edn). Oxford: BPS Blackwell.

Dawson, A. (1994). Professional codes of practice and ethical conduct. *Journal of Applied Philosophy, 11*(2), 125–133.

Gale, A. (1994). Do we need to think a bit more about ethical issues? *Division of Criminological and Legal Psychology, Newsletter, 37,* 16–22.

Health and Care Professions Council (2012). *Standards of conduct, performance and ethics.* HCPC, London, UK.

Koocher, G. P., & Keith-Spiegel, P. (1998). *Ethics in psychology: Professional standards and cases* (2nd edn). Oxford Textbooks in Clinical Psychology. Oxford: Oxford University Press.

Krebs, D. (1982). Altruism: A rational approach. In H. Eizenberg (Ed.), *The development of prosocial behaviour.* New York: Academic Press.

Lindsay, G., Koene, C., Halder O., & Lang, F. (2008). *Ethics for European psychologists.* Gottinggen, Germany: Hogrefe.

Mendonca, M., & Kanungo, R. N. (2007). Ethical leadership. In C. Brotherton, Series Editor, *Work and organisational psychology.* Maidenhead: Open University Press.

Mothershead, J. R., Jr. (1955). *Ethics: Modern conceptions of the principles of right.* New York: Henry Holt and Company.

Sunday Times (2008). NHS staff earnings, NHS information centre. *Sunday Times,* 30 November, under Freedom of Information Act.

Thomson, A. (2006). *Critical reasoning in ethics: A practical introduction.* London: Routledge.

Towl, G. J. (1994). Ethical issues in forensic psychology. *Forensic Update, 39*(October). Leicester: DCLP, BPS.

Towl, G. J. (1995). Ethics: A framework for forensic psychologists. *Forensic Update, 42*(July). Leicester: DCLP, BPS.

Towl, G. J. (2014). HCPC. *The Psychologist,* April.

United Nations (1948). *Universal Declaration of Human Rights, adopted and proclaimed by General Assembly Resolution 217 A (III) of 10 Dec, 1948.* Geneva: Author.

27   Risk and Resilience

GRAHAM J. TOWL

The field is replete with writings on the forensic risk assessment of individual offenders. In the first edition of this textbook, we touched upon the increasingly aggressive marketing of various risk assessment tool providers with their lucrative structured risk assessment tools for offender assessments. This area of the privatization of a public service gets comparatively little coverage in comparison with, say, the privatization of prisons. But it is every bit as much about a neoliberal political agenda which we have seen played out with the dumbing down of some psychological interventions in prisons in the United Kingdom under a veil of grandiose claims around what is purported to be evidence-based practice. Readers with a broader interest in the work of forensic psychologists in prisons have a number of resources to draw upon (e.g., Towl, 2004, 2010a, 2010b, 2010c; Crighton & Towl, 2007).

Risk assessment and management are core constructs within what has become known under the generic lexicon of 'offender management'. The concepts of risk assessment and management sit well under managerialist models of service organization and implementation. It is perhaps worth noting this language whereby the traditional clinical term of 'treatment' has been largely dispensed with to be replaced by the broader rubicon of 'management' (Towl, 2014a, 2014b). Much of such work is 'evidence light', and this is documented elsewhere in this volume and beyond (e.g., Towl, 2006; Towl & Crighton, 2007; Crighton & Towl, 2008). In short, what is claimed to be evidence-based policy and practice in the general domain of offender management and in particular 'risk assessment' may at best be evidence-informed practice and at worst misinformed with the potential for public harms. Public views on risk play into the political arena, especially perhaps in terms of shaping the risk appetite of politicians. Risk is part of everyday life (Adams, 1998; Breakwell, 2007), and we all make everyday decisions psychologically that amount to what would now be broadly termed 'risk management'. Much of our everyday decision-making may be conscious, preconscious or unconscious, but one advantage of formalized risk management processes is that such approaches tend to be explicit frameworks with policy and practice consequences.

This chapter includes a different approach, looking more widely at what is arguably an undue focus on the individual in our assessments. In view of the power inequalities associated with risk assessment decisions in forensic policy and practice, I consider some key ethical issues. Instead of the forensic focus of risk assessment being restricted to an individual assessment process, a broader more inclusive approach is taken to the concept. Thus, the psycho-politics of risk assessment are considered, as is a conceptual understanding of risk assessment. This is a field of forensic psychology with a particular propensity for what may be termed 'behavioural technologies' to be mistaken for science. In view of such problems, there is a need to inform our understanding in terms of the broader political context – in this case, within the neoliberal area and the development of the resultant narrative on the role of psychologists in relation to the state.

System-based approaches are traditionally given scant recognition in the forensic field, so I seek to contribute to restore an appropriate weighting for such considerations and contributions to our understanding. The relationship between risk and resilience is dynamic, and, as such, to develop our understanding, we need to view our observations through the lens of 'systems' (Meadows, 2009).

For illustrative purposes, I draw conceptual parallels from some recent empirical research with the Port of London Authority (PLA), who are responsible for activities on the Thames, United Kingdom. Complex systems involving the management of a range of risks may be assessed in terms of their overall resilience. I seek to look at some of the learning from an understanding of such

Forensic Psychology, Second Edition. Edited by David A. Crighton and Graham J. Towl.
© 2015 John Wiley & Sons, Ltd. Published 2015 by British Psychological Society and John Wiley & Sons, Ltd.

complex systems to inform our appreciation of links between risk and resilience. Finally, there will be a series of reflections upon the implications of the territory covered for the future of forensic psychology in the United Kingdom and beyond.

THE CONCEPT OF RISK IN FORENSIC PSYCHOLOGICAL POLICY AND PRACTICE

The term 'risk' has been, and is, used in many different ways. Forensic psychologists have characteristically used it to refer to the probability of a specified harm occurring (e.g., Towl & Crighton, 1996); generally, the harm of primary concern is the risk of harm to others. Notions of 'offender' and 'victim' are routinely viewed as dichotomous variables, which is contrary to the evidence. There is much overlap between 'offender' and 'victim' populations; indeed, 'offenders' are, on average, at greater risk of being 'victims' than 'non-offenders' as a group. This serves to bring into focus the importance of the politics of such apparent dichotomies. As we shall see, the policy implications of such distinctions (perpetrator and victim) have consequences.

There are some fundamental problems with the general approach to risk assessment and management in the forensic field. The underlying routine assumption can be that psychological assessments are about making a specific prediction about the behaviour of the assessed offender. This is a common erroneous expectation, sometimes from the practitioner and sometimes from the commissioners of such services, or indeed from both. But such expectations are logically implausible. Indeed, it is this, what may be termed 'predictive fallacy', that continues to permeate much of such work. What the forensic psychologist is characteristically in fact endeavouring to do is to make as accurate an assessment as possible of the probability of a further conviction being recorded. Thus, the test of the efficacy of such risk assessments may most accurately be viewed in terms of such probabilistic outcomes, appropriately informed by the available evidence. Whether or not the individual offender goes on to offend contributes to the group data of furthering our understanding of the overall accuracy of such judgements. An example may serve to further illustrate the point. Of 10 offenders, if the likelihood is that one is deemed to be likely to receive a conviction for a specified offence within 2 years, such an assessment is not about predicting which of the 10 will be convicted. Yet, this is sometimes precisely what is asked for, which

is nonsense. It is nonsense because it represents the antithesis of risk assessment, which is about uncertainty rather than certainty, or indeed the prediction of the behaviour of a specific individual. Yet, there appears to remain, at times, an illusion of certainty (Gigerenzer, 2002). Again, it is perhaps noteworthy that, although a claim is sometimes made that forensic psychological risk assessments are about an estimate of the probability of an offence taking place, the general practice is that data from studies, measured in terms of reconviction rates, are drawn upon to inform such judgements. A more accurate approach would be to consider what we know about the ratios of offence types to conviction rates when making such assessments. This involves greater complexity and another arguably more uncertain data set to be drawn upon, but it does enjoy the advantage of being potentially more accurate if the intention is to assess the probability of actual offending rather than the mere proxy of reconviction rates gleaned from large data sets. Such data sets are most commonly set at the arbitrary cut-off points of 2 years and 5 years, respectively, and there are well-documented limitations to such a subjective approach, albeit sometimes unquestioned in the everyday busy practice of forensic psychologists in the United Kingdom. In the forensic field, long-term-prospective studies are comparatively rare (see, e.g., Joliffe, Farrington, & Howard, 2013). This is an important issue in terms of what some people sometimes claim we 'know' about the effectiveness or otherwise of our interventions, purportedly aimed at reducing the risk of reoffending, measured through the proxy of 'reconviction'.

But the problem of such forensic psychological practice goes deeper than simply being misunderstood. There is a real danger of forensic psychologists failing to acknowledge the humanity of the assessed offender. This is an ethical consequence of the institutionalized political distinction which tends to characterize offenders and victims as independent groups. This tendency may well be greater in some cases than others. For example, in assessing sex offenders, it is comparatively common for the accounts of such offences to be distressing to practitioners. Yet, practitioners in psychological practice are not always encouraged to acknowledge their own personal distress with such cases. But the personal is the professional, which in turn is the political. Psychologically, we do not function as separate beings across these modalities. It could be argued that professional conduct is what mediates between the political and the personal in this context. And the politics of risk assessment are that a disproportionate amount of time and other resource is spent on assessing the risk of reconviction of those with a comparatively low chance of getting reconvicted in highly structured environments (e.g., high-security prisons and high-security hospitals). The numbers of deaths 'saved' by forensic psychological risk assessment is likely to be very modest, even on the most generous take of the data. Arguably, forensic psychologists could, on average, have a much greater impact upon saving lives by having their forensic focus elsewhere much earlier in the trajectory towards criminality. If policy is to be informed by evidence in terms of the risk of reoffending and interventions, then this would result in significant disinvestment from, for example, the high-security prison estate in comparison with, say, young offender institutions, if such investment was restricted within the prison's budget. Thus, in terms of risk management, a disinvestment from the high-security estate would give the potential to reduce the number of crimes committed if that resource was more clearly targeted within the young offender part of the prison estate. There is very little in the way of evidence to suggest that the experimental interventions aimed at reducing the risk of reoffending with prisoners in high-security prisons have any meaningful impact upon their risk of reoffending. Such prisoners live in highly restricted environments, and many are highly unlikely to be released, at least for some considerable time, which leaves us with the genuinely difficult issue of how we may meaningfully measure indicants of a reduced risk of reoffending in such cases. Such self-reported data is necessarily restricted, especially in view of the contingencies involved with such reporting practices in a high-security context. Thus, in terms of the evidence, the movement of rehabilitative resources would potentially be more beneficial, not only in terms of reducing the risk of offending and particularly a more significant impact upon crime rates, but also in terms of reducing prisoner suicides. But the brutal neoliberal politics of imprisonment mean that an escape of a high-security prisoner is invariably viewed as more serious than a suicide. Much earlier interventions would be likely to be more cost and crime control effective, but this broader politically charged debate means that ideology will invariably trump empirical evidence, even at the expense of prospective victims. Other chapters in this volume touch upon this politically challenging area. To put it starkly, if we take, say, sex offender treatment programmes in UK prisons, the balance of evidence is that they do not work in terms of convincingly reducing sexual reoffending rates (Crighton & Towl, 2007). Politically, it may be difficult to appear to have stopped such work. Reinvesting these significant resources in working with children who exhibit harmful sexual behaviours would be a more promising use of such resources if the aim is to reduce the overall number of victims. Other commentators have noted this too (see, e.g., the chapter by Walton in this volume).

DO WE NEED TO THINK MORE ABOUT ETHICAL ISSUES IN RISK ASSESSMENT?

This sub-heading is intended, and hopefully read, as a rhetorical question. The specialist code of ethical conduct for forensic psychologists was first published in 1997 (and subsequently reviewed in 2003), was dispensed with early in the twenty-first century by the Division of Forensic Psychology of the British Psychological Society in the name of the standardization of approaches across the applications of psychological practice.

When the Division of Forensic Psychology (DFP) had been set up originally as the Division of Criminological and Legal Psychology (DCLP), the provision of a code of ethics was highlighted as a key task for the fledgling division to produce. Just over 20 years later, such a code was produced. At the time, this overdue set of guidance was warmly welcomed by the field. Subsequently, this was dispensed with, in recognition that the ethical principles of practice are pervasive to practitioner psychologists. The ideological stances, implicit and explicit, of the range of practitioner psychologists vary. Overall, it is probably a strength to have a broader set of ethical guidance for practitioner psychologists and beyond. One of the benefits of multi-professional regulators in comparison with those regulating just one profession is that there is the opportunity for learning from each other (Towl, 2014a).

Arguably, the importance of the balance and checks of those from other specialisms is especially important with forensic psychology in view of the service user criticisms which seem often to rest upon the argument that such psychologists are effectively 'state psychologists', in that we frequently act as if our 'client' is ultimately the state rather than the individual in front of us for assessment. The, at least, implicit ideology of much of forensic psychological practice for all intents and purposes has a view of the offender as fundamentally 'other'. Thus, such forensic psychologists 'deal with' offenders rather than work together in partnership. This is institutionalized within the discipline, and is amply illustrated in, for example, the official British Psychological Society-endorsed textbook which has a whole section on the characteristically brazenly titled 'Dealing with Offenders'. Again, this is about ideology. Forensic contexts are, by definition, coercive contexts. Coercive contexts beget coercive cultures. We know from social psychological studies that reasonable people will quickly do unreasonable things within particular cultural contexts (e.g., Zimbardo, 2004). This alone should perhaps serve as a salutary reminder of the need to keep ethical issues firmly high on the agenda and salient in the consciousness of the profession. In the early twenty-first century, in prisons, it was all too common a practice for informed consent not to be gained from prisoners when psychometric testing was conducted, and this was especially common with professionally fashionable and (for some) lucrative testing and training procedures. The main reason for this practice changing was that information on how such tests are structured and, crucially, the consequences of high scores for individual prisoners became more widespread. The more transparent and accessible availability of such information has been a very positive outcome of the advent of social media. However irritating it may occasionally be for professionals when the recipients of our services are able to access such information, it is a useful balance and check on our professionalism. Again, there is powerful social psychological evidence around environments that make it harder for (highly educated) individuals to not simply comply with a particular judgement (Asch, 1952) or request, however unethical (Milgram, 1974).

Despite these potential concerns around the withdrawal of a specifically 'forensic' set of ethical guidance, in one sense the forensic context simply amounts to a particular set of power relationships and is thus not qualitatively different from any other area of public policy and practice. Ethical issues may come into sharper focus in forensic environments (Towl, 1993), but fundamentally they are the same issues as elsewhere.

The achievement of the statutory regulation of practitioner psychologists may be viewed in much the same way. The ethical issues across health-care and social-care professions are the same at their core, albeit there may be different manifestations of such issues across professions and agency settings. Indeed, what better checks could psychologists ask for than those of the perspectives of others from different disciplines and with a lay input? This is a much more robust system than any single profession-specific body with the dual role of representation could hope to achieve (Towl, 2014b). Another occasionally unpalatable ethical issue, by no means exclusive to the discipline of psychology, is the spectre of professional self-interests (Towl, 2010a, 2010b, 2012). This underscores the need for effective regulation.

If psychologists are routinely making assessments and judgements around the probability of the risk of reconviction of individual prisoners, which they are, then wielding such professional power needs balances and checks. Historically those undertaking interventions with offenders to reduce their risk of reconviction have oftentimes undertaken risk assessments before and after participation in such interventions. There is clearly a conflict of interest here (e.g., Greenberg & Shuman, 1997), in that a practitioner will have emotional and professional investment in a good result from the intervention. Thus, they are poorly placed to undertake such risk assessments. Fortunately, this practice is increasingly less common, chiefly because it has been challenged effectively in court, again not primarily because of the self-regulation of psychologists. This is important because it perhaps reflects a more general ethical issue which speaks to the importance of professional regulation being predominantly the purview of those not qualified in the profession and therefore more independent in this regard with their judgements. Professional bodies have long argued against such premises, but thankfully this is increasingly becoming the professional norm in, for example, health-care.

Risk assessments undertaken by psychologists employed directly by HM Prison Service have a professional challenge, in that it can be unclear if their reports are written as agents of the prison service, state or as independent practitioners who happen to work for the prison service. Predictably, some adapt to such challenges more effectively than others. Such adaptation can again serve to colour the hue of the evidence for particular risk assessments. Professionally, the assessments should be independent.

But there is another often unspoken but potentially potent issue, which is the delicate and genuinely difficult area of where the individual psychologists' personal experiences may colour their judgements. For illustrative purposes, sex offending may serve as an exemplar for such difficulties. The overwhelming majority of sex offenders in prisons are there for offences against women and girls, resulting in a conviction. The overwhelming majority of forensic psychologists are women, often young women, statistically a number of whom will have been victims of sexual abuses themselves. It would be perfectly understandably unusual for a psychologist to disclose such experiences. It would be unusual statistically for such an offence to have resulted in a public record. Two ethical concerns emerge from this observation. First, what could reasonably be the normative expectation in terms of disclosure? This is chiefly an ethical concern for the practitioner herself (or himself). Second, there may be a conscious, preconscious or unconscious emotional reaction which may colour the report, quite possibly punitively. These are genuinely difficult issues to grapple with, but acting as if they are not potential issues seems to be a response that would be unlikely to contribute to an ethical solution of resolving or at least addressing such matters. Views on sexual offending are unlikely not to tap into some powerful emotions for many of us, and the starting point to addressing such issues must surely be the acknowledgement of such problems, however uncomfortable to tackle. Some generic good practices may help mitigate such possibilities, for example, peer reviews and close supervision. But there may well be more work to do around this difficult area in terms of research so that we can better understand the scale and depth of any such issues, and policy so that we can respond appropriately and in terms of practice to protect the public to include the practitioner and offender in such cases.

Concerns about risk assessment are by no means exclusively the domain of forensic psychologists or, indeed, criminal justice agencies more generally – far from it. Disciplines as far apart as engineering and sociology have rich perspectives on 'risk'. Indeed, in recent years, we have seen the manifestations of the approach to risk in the banking industry and also governmental approaches to risk in terms of the further outsourcing of what social policy theorists would consider to be public goods.

Sociological narratives on risk tend to be characterized by a much broader and more reflective approach to such concepts. Such approaches contrast markedly with the current orthodoxy in criminal justice for risk assessment tools. Such tools can be viewed as about the financial protection of the owner as much they are about public protection. Many sociologists would be quick to observe the importance of such power relations within their cultural context. Some sociologists have used the concept of risk as a lens through which to see modern society. The modern world is awash with the implications of the dominant paradigms of risk. We see this manifest in the growth in regulation, health and safety concerns, auditing, governance and increasing concerns about potential litigation. Such a context can beget defensive professional practices, and we need to be mindful of that.

In the engineering world, safety engineering is concerned with the management of 'risks'. Forensic psychologists have borrowed and built upon some engineering methods for safety such as fault tree analysis. Again, this is so in relation to hazard analysis, which has its parallel with the forensic psychologists looking closely at the full range of offences that the prisoner may be deemed 'at risk (unacceptable or otherwise) of committing'. Arguably, the key commonality with psychologists and engineers in the approach to risk assessments is taken to mean probabilistic risk assessments. Thus, both would specify and try and quantify the 'failure rates' over a set time period. The language of engineering speaks loudly to much forensic psychological practice with the need to contain and/or mitigate risks. Of course, as one set of risks is mitigated, another set is revealed, and sometimes increased. For example, in automotive engineering, there is a trade-off between safety and fuel economy. On average, the heavier the car, the safer the car, but the heavier the car, on average, the less fuel efficient it is. This is an important point because it reflects a

common misconception in much risk management practice, namely that the management of one identified risk may result in other risks increasing or perhaps missed from the analysis totally. With prisoners, the most common example of this would be an undue focus upon the index offence. So, a violent offender would tend to more likely be assessed in terms of his risk of enacting future violence. This is despite evidence which would suggest, for example, that young offenders tend to be multi-skilled in their offence habits and rarely specialize in one offence type. As we shall see, there are parallels to the responses to terrorist attacks. For example, when the twin towers of the World Trade Center collapsed due to hijacked planes crashing into them and dispensing their quickly ignited fuel, there was a marked reduction in air travel within the United States; much more travel was undertaken by car, resulting in significant road traffic deaths, which may otherwise not have occurred. The same may well be true with regard to evacuation policies and procedures around bomb scares. Home Office advice tends to be to err on the side of caution and evacuate in the event of a telephone threat of a bomb. If all such calls were responded to in such a fashion, this would result in economic and social chaos. It may well also arguably increase the probability of such events occurring. The proportion of false threats with such calls hugely outweighs the number of true threats. This brings into question the motivation for the making of such calls. One could hypothesize that the motivation could be linked to the potentially reinforcing impact of seeing the chaos that can result from significant evacuation activity.

Engineering models of risk are mechanistic, based on risk-relevant information for the identified variable. However, there are some curious practices in safety engineering, such as the three-point approach to risk management. The idea is that critical component failure needs to be avoided completely or the risk reduced to a miniscule level. One technique used, for example, in the aviation industry, is the three-point approach to avoiding functional failures. The claim is that three aspects or components of a system would need to fail together for a critical function to catastrophically fail. The assumption is made that each of the three points of potential failure are independent, which they may be prior to one of them failing. But once one such point has failed, the probability of the other two points failing may change. Again, a mechanistic comparison can be made in forensic practice where prisoners have undertaken skills-based interventions and have failed in practice to use at least one of such skills sets appropriately. For example, in anger management work, the offender may have learnt how to relax and is simply more relaxed in throwing a punch at the object of his or her still uncontrolled anger because other crucial aspects of the intervention such as cognitive or behavioural aspects have not worked.

In the United Kingdom, with a relatively temperate climate, it is still the case that there is a greater risk annually of older citizens dying of the weather conditions rather than at the hands of a released life-sentenced prisoner. For citizens, there is a greater risk of death by a car crash rather than at the hands of a released life-sentenced prisoner. The relevance of such observations is to serve to put in perspective the scale of the risk to the public. In practical terms, long-distance lorry drivers, train drivers and pilots have much more everyday responsibility for life and death decisions than do forensic psychologists or medical doctors.

Legal approaches to risk are based on different frameworks to psychological perspectives. Notions of reasonableness are more to the fore, although there is some commonality with language such as 'the balance of probabilities'. But legal processes often tend to reflect the need for decision-making which reflects categorical rather than continuum-based approaches to inform the decision-making.

In sum, in terms of ethical issues for practitioner psychologists, these may be summarized as involving the welcome balances and checks afforded by statutory regulation through the Health and Care Professions Council (HCPC) rather than through a single profession-based regulatory body. The respective roles of the HCPC and the British Psychological Society may be likened to the relationship between the General Medical Council and the British Medical Association (Towl, 2014a, 2014b). Further to these public benefits, the advent of the Internet, with the resultant greater transparency around our professional practices in relation to risk assessment work, is an overwhelmingly positive development, despite the problems. An understanding of the political and social psychology of the context of our risk assessment work on decision-making speaks loudly to the need for us to be ever vigilant to the consequences of the institutionalization of poor practices and, indeed, most difficult, the institutionalization of the research, policy and practitioners.

Moving on from the preceding conceptual and ethical issues, I will now focus upon an understanding of risk in system terms and specifically in relation to resilience.

RISK AND RESILIENCE

The UK cabinet office has a remit for the resilience of national infrastructure. At the time of writing, recent weather events have brought such matters into media and public focus. One of the aims of a recent research project into UK port resilience included an examination of the impact of risk management methods in the port environment to the organizational resilience of the port. Another aim was to explore the extent to which any such conceptual commonalities may be 'imported' into other policy domains – for our purposes, public protection in relation to the risk assessments undertaken by forensic psychologists.

The Port of London is a complex system with a range of stakeholders – in that sense, there is much commonality with the criminal justice system. Such multiple systems are populated by various 'actors'. As we have seen in criminal justice, such environments have their own embedded culture(s). Much of the focus of what has become known as emergency planning and business continuity plans tend to be governed by the management of internal risks, in this case, those captured within the port environment. Rather than focus on specific external 'threats', the focus has been on the mitigation and adaptation to what may emerge as new operating environments. For example, a severe weather event could be disruptive to food supply chains, which has the potential to speedily escalate to widespread disruption and possibly civil disobedience. Other ports may be used as a contingency plan but the extent of the utility of such an approach would be partly based on the extent of the weather events.

But what is the relevance of this in the forensic field? Once the individual under specific assessment is looked beyond, the parallels and potential implications are manifest. The politics of the day can have impacts upon decisions around the sentencing, management and potential release of prisoners. The Port of London Authority (PLA) operates within a mixed economy of actors, some private sector some public sector, not dissimilar to a range of public services, not least prisons, but what both crucially have in common is that both prisons and ports are what social policy theorists would refer to as 'public goods'. Ultimately, this means that, as the public, we experience the consequences directly and indirectly of the hazard in question. The 'risks' for the private sector essentially amount to financial risks – if a particular market no longer provides adequate return on investment, then the investment may well be moved and invested elsewhere. But public services do not enjoy such indulgences of the markets, because they by definition have to provide the service, or, in private sector terms, stay in a potentially hostile market. Thus, the private sector in the port and criminal justice sectors may simply mitigate risk through a resilient financial structure, withdrawing from any markets or pseudo-markets if there is not sufficient return on investment to enhance shareholder value. The values of the public sector are perhaps enshrined in the very notion of a 'public good' – an institution or activity undertaken for the sole purpose of (necessary) public benefit, such as the port-based industry for trade.

Thus, given that we have imprisonment, although some prisons and some supporting services may be under public or private control, the responsibility will ultimately be with government to ensure their effective management. There are direct parallels in the risk management industry discussed earlier. So, this is where the (formal) accountability is held, within government.

But the commonalities are also evident in terms of the complexities of the systems which may influence the outcomes of interest, whether the risk of reoffending by a life-sentenced prisoner or the risk of a bomb being found in a container on a container ship heading for Central London. In terms of the potential numbers of deaths associated with these two examples of decision-making, the individual life-sentenced prisoner would be unlikely to be as prolific in their killing, even if they did go on to reoffend once released. Nonetheless, the trajectory towards the lifer reoffending, or the prospective bomber successfully deploying a bomb on a container ship, are not matters which are solely determined by any one individual. To understand the risk of such potential occurrences, we need to better understand the environments within which both actors would be operating. In the port, this may include the need for the more effective screening and monitoring of individual containers as a preventative measure. In lifer assessment work, this may mean the inclusion of interviews with some of the significant others in the lifer's life.

The problem of a sometimes undue focus on the individual rather than the broader 'systems-based' understanding is important if we are to improve upon our risk assessments. But it is also important to our understanding of resilience and its conceptual links with risk. In forensic psychological parlance, if we were undertaking a risk assessment, we would seek to identify 'protective factors' which may, we would hypothesize, reduce or otherwise mitigate the risk of reoffending. But, for resilience to be manifest, there needs to be some form of stress test (Reich et al., 2010). An individual or organization (system) may be working apparently well yet not be under a state of disruption. It is the collection of responses from the individual offender or institution once under stress that will ultimately test resilience, especially with the benefit of looking through the lens of a significant period of time. Indeed, some researchers (e.g., Harvey & Quinn, 2012) have argued for· an understanding of practitioner resilience which is multi-layered to include individual, proximal and wider systemic factors in contributing to practitioner resilience in demanding roles. Some of the practical applications of the preceding observations are covered in the next section.

So, the political context and system-based approach to understanding risk have been touched upon. The next section acknowledges the importance of biases in human decision-making and, in particular, the biases associated with working in a forensic context, an area not often given sufficient emphasis in forensic risk assessment decision-making.

BIASES IN HUMAN DECISION-MAKING

The literature on decision-making about risks has been detailed elsewhere (e.g., Gigerenzer, Todd, & the ABC Research Group, 1999; Gilovich et al., 2002; Towl, 2014a, 2014b), and the classic exposition on human heuristics and biases in decision-making (Kahneman et al., 1982). What these accounts successfully do is to illustrate systematic biases in human decision-making (e.g., anchoring effects, salience, availability, optimistic bias and so on); such decision-making includes decisions around risk. Competent forensic psychologists will all too well be aware of the impacts of their biases on their decision-making, and will not be persuaded by spurious claims that the so-called 'objective assessment tools' are valuable or bias-free in relation to risk assessment and management – far from it. But what these significant contributions to our understanding of biases in human decision-making do not do is adequately capture the biases in human decision-making associated with the context of the decision-making. In the preceding text, something of the political and systemic context of decision-making has been outlined. Such politics and systems give rise to a series of additional biases in decision-making.

One bias in the forensic context is associated with the professional contingencies in relation to the outcomes. So, to put it starkly, if a recommendation is made for release and the prisoner is released, there is no feedback if no crime is reported to have happened after release. However, if a criminal act is reported, then the psychological assessment (and psychologist) may be viewed as not having made an accurate assessment. This is linked to a lack of understanding about such reports, but nonetheless is politically powerful and will inexorably play a role in shaping what may arguably be the consequentially lower likelihood of a 'positive recommendation' for the lifer. Another bias may well be in relation to a propensity towards action in relation to any such assessment. Sometimes there is nothing to do, or the best choice may be to do nothing. However, if something goes wrong, the leading question for practitioners may well be words to the effect of 'What did you *do*?'. The first of these two potential errors is political and reflects the conflation of *prediction* on the one hand and *risk assessment* on the other. The second may be fundamentally linked to a professional need to have taken an action in response to the presentation of a particular set of problems, here associated with risk assessment. But such decision-making also may be understood in terms of the politics of the risk assessment decision-making.

IMPLICATIONS FOR FUTURE FORENSIC PRACTICE: RISK AND RESILIENCE

The 'predictive fallacy' in criminal justice, whereby 'prediction' is routinely conflated with 'risk assessment', needs to be exposed and dispensed with. Much of what we know about the level of risk of reoffending for particular sub-groups or populations is based upon limited statistical data. It follows that all we can hope to accurately do is ensure that such data is most appropriately used to inform judgements about risk assessment rather than make a prediction about the behaviour of an individual. We need to not go, nor be invited to go, beyond the evidence. We need to resist the illusion of certainty. We cannot sensibly predict the behaviour of an individual in terms of whether or not they will go on to offend, but we can say something of the probability of such an occurrence based largely on group data.

One ethical problem in the domain of what has become termed 'programmes' (experimental group-work-based interventions aimed at reducing the risk of reconviction) has been in relation to the practice of those acting both as 'therapist' and 'forensic assessor', where there is a clear conflict of interest and possibility of bias, either consciously or unconsciously (or both). The therapist in this case would be working towards reducing the risk of reconviction, and the forensic assessor function would be to assess the level of risk subsequent to an experimental intervention.

A second ethical problem, again in the domain of 'programmes', occurred in relation to the issue of whether or not to disclose the nature of a particular psychometric test rather than to describe it merely as a 'personality test'. This was despite consequences dependent upon the scoring for those undertaking such tests. Psychologists eventually withdrew from this practice because information on such tests increasingly became widely available, and there was little point on any grounds in not disclosing the purpose and consequences of such test-taking. Arguments that had been used in support of such an approach tended to be anchored around the need for public protection and the primacy of a notion of 'the public interest' above that of the individual 'offender'. The underpinning ideology of such an approach is captured in the standard British Psychological Society textbook for forensic psychologists, which has a section on 'Dealing with Offenders', which illustrates the ethical point of the offender as routinely seen as 'other', rather than as a member of the public with rights and responsibilities. If we are to work most effectively with offenders, we need to address such ideological approaches.

Ultimately, forensic risk assessments reflect power relationships. Although forensic psychologists do not have executive powers for risk management decision-making, their reports can be very influential. It is thus imperative that they always work to improve upon their practice to include a broader awareness of the complex context and politicized nature of the risk assessments that they make, rather than view them as merely objective accounts.

The notion of resilience can, as we have seen, be linked to risk at a number of levels. Understanding risk in terms of overall individual or organizational resilience brings with it a richer understanding of the bounded and unbounded nature of the risks that are most relevant to us. In forensic practice, the practitioners sometimes proceed as if all risks can be measured and managed, and this is an illusion. It is an unduly bounded view of risk, as if their assessments are made in a vacuum. The same is the case in the UK port industry, which although thorough, can be similarly focussed chiefly upon bounded risks. Many of the 'risks' most relevant to some of our assessments, whether of the individual risk of reoffending or the risk of a terrorist attack on a port, are simply not well understood and are certainly not the focus of such comparatively narrow assessments. The systems based linkages are important to understand. So, with an individual, offender behaviour may be best understood within the community and in a broader cultural context. This is so for staff too (Harvey & Quinn, 2012), and it is the case for ports too, where an understanding of interdependencies is crucial. Too often in the world of risk assessment, presumptions are made which implicitly exclude or minimize historical learning in favour of the fears of the day, be they terrorism or child molestation.

If we are to improve upon our risk assessment processes and the resilience of our systems, whether in criminal justice or ports, we need to capture a much richer understanding of risk, especially as it relates to risk at the level of the individual or, indeed, at a much broader and less bounded and more resilient societal level. Our world is becoming increasingly globalized, marketized and awash with new communications technologies. These changes bring both challenge and opportunity, and we need to embrace these changes as we better understand risk and resilience in the modern world.

FURTHER READING

Breakwell, G. M. (2014). *The psychology of risk* (2nd edn). United Kingdom: Cambridge University Press.

This book includes an informative and wide-ranging overview of the psychological perspectives on risk. It is the leading text in the field. It builds upon the informative and detailed first edition with the recognition of subsequent wider macro-economic and socio-political changes globally. This resonates with the approaches espoused in the forensic field, which represents a welcome shift from narrower, less evidence-informed approaches which took hold in the previous years.

Meadows, D. H. (2009). *Thinking in systems: A primer*. London: Earthscan.

Systems thinking may be viewed as a bridge between our understanding of 'risk' and 'resilience'. The 'bounded rationality' which restricts much risk assessment work may readily be better understood from a systems perspective. This is important if we are to improve upon our risk assessments. I would single out chapters three (on resilience) and four (bounded risks) for special reading attention.

Reich, J. W., Zautra, A. J., & Hall, J. S., (Eds.). (2010). *Handbook of adult resilience*. New York: The Guildford Press.

This is probably one of the more comprehensive texts on human resilience. Genetic, physiological, personal, family, organizational and community processes are covered from the perspective of trying to better elucidate our understanding of human resilience. Resilience is arguably more important in informing our understanding in view of, for example, a move towards more strength-based approaches to working with offenders. But, most importantly, if we are to invest in prevention, which we should, then we need to better understand human resilience, particularly in the early years of development – a core underpinning theme in forensic policy and practice too.

REFERENCES

Adams, J. (1998). *Risk*. London: UCL Press.

Asch, S. E. (1952). Effects of group pressure upon modification and distortion of judgements. In G. E. Swanson, T. M. Newcomb, and E. L. Hartley (Eds.), *Readings in social psychology* (pp. 183–197). New York: Holt, Rinehart & Winston.

Breakwell, G. M. (2014). *The psychology of risk* (2nd edn). Cambridge: Cambridge University Press.

Crighton, D. A., & Towl, G. (2007). Experimental interventions with sex offenders: A brief review of their efficacy. *Evidence Based Mental Health, 10*(2), 35–37.

Crighton, D. A., & Towl, G. J. (2008). *Psychology in prisons* (2nd edn). Oxford: BPS Blackwell.

Gigerenzer, G., Todd, P. M., & the ABC Research Group (1999). *Simple heuristics that make us smart*. Oxford: Oxford University Press.

Gilovich, G., Griffin, D., & Kahneman, D. (Eds.). (2002). *Heuristics and biases: The psychology of intuitive judgement*. Cambridge: Cambridge University Press.

Gigerenzer, G. (2002). *Reckoning with risk; Learning to live with uncertainty*. London: Penguin Books.

Greenberg, S. A., & Shuman, D. W. (1997). Irreconcilable conflict between therapeutic and forensic roles. In *Professional Psychology: Research and Practice, 28*(1), 50–57, February.

Harvey, J., & Quinn, B. (2012). A preliminary model of forensic practitioner resilience within a learning disabilities service. *Journal of Learning Disabilities and Offending Behaviour, 3*(3), 158–169.

Joliffe, D., Farrington, D. P., & Howard, P. (2013). *How long did it last? A 10 year reconviction follow-up study of High Intensity Training for young offenders*. Ministry of Justice, United Kingdom.

Kahneman, D., Slovic, P., & Tversky, A. (Eds.). (1982). *Judgement under uncertainty: Heuristics and biases*. Cambridge: Cambridge University Press.

Meadows, D. H. (2009). *Thinking in systems: A primer*, D. Wright (Ed.). London: Earthscan.

Milgram, S. (1974). *Obedience to authority*. London: Tavistock.

Reich, J. W., Zautra, A. J., & Hall, J. S. (2010). *Handbook of adult resilience*. London: The Guilford Press.

Towl, G. J. (1993). Ethical issues in forensic psychology. *Forensic Update, 39*, 23–26.

Towl, G. J. (2004). Applied psychological services in HM Prison Service and the National Probation Service. In A. Needs & G. J. Towl (Eds.), *Applying psychology to forensic practice*. Oxford: BPS Blackwell.

Towl, G. J. (2006). Introduction. In G. J. Towl (Ed.), *Psychological research in prisons*. Oxford: The British Psychological Society / Blackwell.

Towl, G. J. (2010a). Foreword. In J. Harvey & K. Smedley (Eds.), *Psychological therapy in prions and other secure settings*. Chichester: Willan Publishers.

Towl, G. J. (2010b). Psychology in prisons. In S. Wilson & I. Cumming (Eds.), *Psychiatry in prisons*. London: Jessica Kingsley.

Towl, G. J. (2010c). Psychology in the National Offender Management Service for England and Wales. In J. R. Adler & J. M. Gray (Eds.), *Forensic psychology* (2nd edn), *Concepts, debates and practice*. Oxford: Willan.

Towl, G. J. (2012). Foreword. In P. Jones (Ed.), *Interventions in criminal justice*. Brighton: Pavilion.

Towl, G. J. (2014a). Psychological perspectives on risk and resilience. In J. J. Bissell, C. C. S. Caido, M. Goldstein, & B. Straughtan (Eds.), *Tipping points: Modelling social problems and health.* Chichester: John Wiley & Sons.

Towl, G. J. (2014b). Health and Care Professions Council – perspectives of a new council member. In *The Psychologist*, *27*(4), Leicester: BPS.

Towl, G. J., & Crighton, D. A. (1996). *The handbook of psychology for forensic practitioners.* London: Routledge.

Towl, G. J., & Crighton, D. A. (2007). Psychological services in English and Welsh prisons. In R. K. Ax, & T. J. Fagan (Eds.), *Corrections, mental health and social policy.* Illinois: C.C. Thomas.

Zimbardo, P. (2004). A situationist perspective on the psychology of evil: Understanding how good people are transformed into perpetrators. In Miller, A. G. (Ed.), *The social psychology of good and evil: Understanding our capacity for kindness and cruelty* (pp. 21–50). New York: The Guilford Press.

28 Structural Violence in Forensic Psychiatry

BRIAN A. THOMAS-PETER

Structural violence is a concept borrowed by physician and medical anthropologist Paul Farmer (1999) to focus attention on the political, economic and social organizations of society that result in inequity, disadvantage and suffering of distinct groups of people, usually the poor, in respect of health. The original idea was raised by Johan Galtung (1969), who was concerned about addressing how organizations acted, without intention, to create the circumstances of violence.

There were two kinds of violence he identified: 'We shall refer to the type of violence where there is an actor that commits the violence as personal or direct, and to violence where there is no such actor as structural or indirect. In both cases individuals may be killed or mutilated, hit or hurt in both senses of these words [i.e., physical and psychological], and manipulated by means of stick or carrot strategies. But whereas in the first case these consequences can be traced back to concrete persons as actors, in the second case this is no longer meaningful' (170–171). Later, he introduced a third category of 'cultural' violence, by which he meant 'those aspects of culture … that can be used to justify or legitimize direct or structural violence' (Galtung, 1990, 291).

There have been several contributions to understanding the disadvantages heaped on incarcerated populations with and without mental health challenges. Recent criminological discourses, which collectively have become known as the 'New Punitiveness' (Pratt, Brown, Brown, Hallsworth, & Morrison, 2005), make a convincing argument that the last few decades have been a remarkably unenlightened period. Others have argued that the provision of rehabilitation or therapy in secure services has drawn a 'veil of liberalism' (Moore & Hannah-Moffat, 2005) across narrow-minded if not blatantly anti-therapeutic attitudes, brutal environments and reactionary political trends. The reactionary trend is a 'new intolerance' of deviance (Thomas-Peter, 2007a)

and notes the increasingly risk-averse perspective of criminal justice across the world. Similar arguments describe the 'Death of Liberalism' (Gunn, 2000) in society generally, with a significant impact on caring for mentally disordered offenders. The notion of *caring* for this challenging sector of patients in need has fallen down the list of priorities in favour of *managing* them and the risks they can present. The concept of people in this sector having needs associated with their suffering has been undermined by the preoccupation with *criminogenic need* (Thomas-Peter, 2007b). It is as if people with mental disorder who offend against us may not suffer unless we inflict it upon them, and then we may not identify their experience as suffering or what we do as violent. This would be the end point of the normalizing process that justifies harm to offenders, disguising it behind a veil of liberalism.

The concept of structural violence has been linked to the notions of social injustice and oppression (Farmer, 2004), but the link requires recognizing the everyday machinery of social structures that normalize the injustice through typical experience within stable accepted institutions, rendering it nearly invisible (Gilligan, 1997). It is a chimera of a notion, being neither intended nor obvious, yet profoundly harming victims and notably absent from our reflections on forensic psychiatry.

There have been attempts to apply the concept of structural violence to public health issues, each locating the victims of structural violence as being those who fail to receive the health-care they deserve. These include: neglect of Russian prisoners suffering from a particular form of tuberculosis (Farmer, 1999), treating those with HIV in the United States (Farmer, Nizeye, Stulac, & Keshavjee, 2006), HIV prevention in Haiti (Farmer, 1997), protecting sex workers in Serbia (Simic & Rhodes, 2009) and the treatment of schizophrenia (Kelly, 2005). Health-care provides many examples of how institutionalized

Forensic Psychology, Second Edition. Edited by David A. Crighton and Graham J. Towl.

processes and structures sustain the disadvantage of the vulnerable, who are helpless to remedy their situation.

SUFFERING IN FORENSIC PSYCHIATRY

In a secure mental health unit in North America, a smartly dressed psychologist showed a visitor the facilities. Off a corridor in which administration offices were grouped, a room with a barred door overlaid with Plexiglas appeared misplaced. It was dark in the room, and she led the visitor to it without hesitation. Standing at the bars, she called a name and, after a few moments, a middle-aged man appeared. He was naked, unshaved, his hair was dishevelled and his skin gleamed with perspiration. Warm air extruded from the holes drilled in the Plexiglas, carrying his garbled words and the pungent aroma of sweat and waste. The three were joined by the charge nurse, who introduced himself without taking notice of the man inside the room. The smartly dressed psychologist described the patient's condition and how the unit was caring for him. The charge nurse chimed in proudly. The visitor asked why the bars on the door were covered in Plexiglas and was told that the odour from the room was too much for the staff who had offices nearby. The visitor asked why the patient was totally naked. It was so hot in the room that they allowed him to go without clothing, providing the lights were out, to save the sensibilities of staff that might pass by.

This is a rare occurrence and unusually insensitive, but it does illustrate one important aspect that is not uncommon. Forensic psychiatric staff are vulnerable to losing their moral compass because they stop seeing what is in front of them. Unsurprisingly, the organizations in which they work are resistant to change. It is therefore logical that problems within secure forensic psychiatry hospitals have emerged, on numerous occasions, after long periods of being ignored, avoided or denied. Even so, it is shocking that organizations staffed with health professionals, all endorsing codes of ethics and each claiming high standards of professionalism and good intent, operate in dysfunctional hospitals that perpetrate harm.

Is it possible that the practices of professionals within such organizations have become familiar, regular and normalized to the extent that they are no longer seen with moral disapproval? It is possible, but it would still require some disguise or distraction to prevent it from dawning on someone. There are occasions where abuses have taken years to come to light when nurses, doctors and other health professionals within an institution have

known that there was bad practice and ethical challenges. Moral blindness arising from familiarity is not the only problem leading to the sustained abuse of patients. Other factors are also maintaining it.

In forensic psychiatry, there has long been tension between those who are concerned about staff and public safety on one hand, and patient safety on the other. It has had various guises but it has been an enduring tension that has had an impact on the nature of secure arrangements in secure hospitals (Bowers et al., 2002). Bowers et al. detected different operational security procedures that revealed cultures associated with perspectives of either staff safety or patient safety.

The concern about the harm done to patients, which is the focus of this chapter, is not intended as a rival to those concerns about the risks that patients represent to staff and the community. Concern about assaults on staff working in mental health has increased recently, and rightly so. NHS Protect published figures for the years 2010–2011,[1] indicating that there were more than 39,000 assaults on mental health staff in the United Kingdom, a rate of 195.4 per 1,000 staff. Only some of these occurred in forensic psychiatry, but the point is clear. This is a staggering number of assaults. No one gets paid enough to be injured while working in health-care, and for too long it has been accepted as part of the job (Banerjee et al., 2008). Banerjee et al. (2008) was a self-report-based study, indicating that violence, sexual abuse and racism perpetrated against Canadian residential health-care workers in three provinces is endemic, and it seems likely that other jurisdictions would concur that violence to staff working in mental health services is unacceptable.

In an excellent review of the patient safety literature, Brickell et al. (2009) note opposing views in which patient safety can only be improved through employee safety (Yassi & Hancock, 2005), and staff safety will be improved by ensuring patient safety (Kohn, Corrigan, & Donaldson, 1999). Brickell et al. (2009) suggested that, by pursuing these agendas equally, managers might bring the perspectives together. It may not be as simple as this, since the introduction of security measures as a means of protecting staff may be an important cause of violence in secure environments (Due, Connellan, & Riggs, 2012). However, it invites a consideration of how managers have responded to patient safety issues and the integrity of those efforts.

There is no challenge to these observations of harm done to staff when expressing concern about patient safety, although the representation of these as oppositional concerns reveals something about the interests of the protagonists in addition to their ideological perspectives. Little evidence will be found which contradicts the assertion that work load, staffing levels and working conditions are relevant to understanding conflict in secure environments. However, it is preferable to avoid taking such an ideological divide as a starting point to understanding the issues. A more useful perspective is by simply observing the behaviour of those on either side of the debate, and by recognizing that, as each perspective offers a solution, the nature of the solution reveals their motivation more clearly than the expressed problem. The confusion generated by the polarization of this discussion is such that even the concept of structural violence gets misappropriated.

Bannerjee *et al.* (2008) and, in an extended study, Banerjee *et al.* (2012) drew on the work of Galtung (1969) and Farmer (1997) to identify the heavy workloads, low levels of decision-making autonomy, low status, rigid work routines and insufficient relational care as forms of violence, not to the recipients of care but to the providers. The authors argue that these poor working conditions are experienced as suffering and illustrate organizational structures that result in 'structural' violence. Moreover, as a result, care workers are prevented from providing the kind of care they know they are capable of giving, and are consequently prevented from achieving their potential. This too is an indicator of structural violence.

It must be true that these factors are important, but the problem with this assertion is twofold. First, while the report was sponsored by the Canadian Institute of Health Research and was supported by several universities in Canada and Europe, the larger partners included the Canadian Union of Public Employees (CUPE), the Canadian Auto Workers (CAW), the National Union of Public and General Employees (NUPGE), the Service Employees International Union (SEIU) and the Canadian Federation of Nurses Unions (CFNU), who partnered the research effort and provided 'a range of assistance'. Second, the conflict of interest arising from organized labour involved in a study, purporting to discover structural violence and concluding that this should be remedied by increasing the staffing and authority of care staff, reveals this group, however disadvantaged by their working conditions, to be very different to the HIV victims of Haiti, or any of the other populations identified by Paul Farmer. The fact of there being powerful and sophisticated collective bargaining arrangements renders the concept of structural violence flaccid in this context.

INQUIRIES INTO HARM DONE TO PATIENTS

While the concept of structural violence may not be the appropriate concept to understand how care staff end up in harm's way, it must be acknowledged that everything

that happens within forensic psychiatry is challenging, especially within the secure hospitals that have proliferated since the 1980s. These services are at the difficult end of the spectrum of tasks undertaken by human service and health professionals. It is not always rewarding to work in these environments. There is little sympathy for the work within the communities that they serve: the people they are asked to care for are often distressed, treatment-resistant, grotesquely unwell and typically very troubled even when they are mentally stable. They can act with violence, in ways that are disproportionate to the apparent provocation and, at times, that response cannot be anticipated. It is extremely taxing work, taking a toll on those who work within it.

Paradoxically, the best testimony to this challenge has been the seemingly never-ending number of inquiries into untoward incidents in which the failures of individuals, professionals, managers, hospitals and cross-agency workings are laid bare. It would be reasonable to conclude that this is a difficult job, being done not very well by those charged with the responsibility. Of course, this is self-evidently true where there have been problems, but it is an unfair conclusion for so many dedicated, hardworking, well-meaning professionals who should not be stigmatized by the repetitive and easy criticisms of those who contribute to such reports.[2] Moreover, it is important to recognize that forensic psychiatry services are rarely all bad. It is common for each to have strengths and weaknesses, although where things have gone very bad, it is more difficult to find things that are very good.

Nevertheless, there is a valuable point to be made about the capacity of mental health services to learn effectively from major inquiries into untoward incidents and circumstances leading to patient harm.

MAJOR INQUIRIES: LESSONS LEARNED AND NOT LEARNED

The abuse of forensic patients is not new or even uncommon. Every jurisdiction can find examples, and most have experienced major inquiries that have been established to reform bad practice that has found its way into the light. Those jurisdictions that have not experienced this have, in all probability, not yet looked closely enough. Even with the good intentions and enormously powerful momentum of a shocked public and an embarrassed government, there have been lessons that service providers have failed to learn, going back decades. The Boynton Report (1980) emerged from reports of widespread abuse of patients by nursing staff at Rampton Hospital in England, which turned out to be true. This was a powerful analysis of a high-security forensic psychiatry hospital that should have urged every other forensic hospital to understand the systemic causes of the abuse of patients, and also to recognize that these circumstances could not be attributed to unique events at a single hospital. It appeared to be the inevitable consequence of constructing such service and allowing it to languish in isolation. Whatever lessons were there to be learned, they went unheeded in another high-security hospital.

In 1992, the Blom-Cooper Report lifted the lid on Ashworth Hospital, which had also deteriorated into a situation of widespread abuse of patients by nursing staff. The intention of this report, following a thorough investigation, was to redress the balance of care, placing the patient at the centre of consideration and to reinforce the role of the multi-disciplinary team. It was clear that the wards had been abandoned by other clinicians to the operation of nursing staff. There was little therapy, and punitive attitudes prevailed in a way that was not dissimilar to Rampton Hospital more than a decade earlier.

The response of those responsible for the hospital was to initiate a huge effort to implement the more than 90 recommendations of the Blom-Cooper Report. They formed a Task Force, which possessed great authority, to push through the reforms. Amid a good deal of fanfare, progress was heralded. What happened subsequently has been the subject of many corridor discussions between those who knew the patients, the staff and had some idea of what was happening on the ground. It also became the subject of the Fallon Inquiry[3] (1999).

The Fallon Inquiry was a root and branch investigation of Ashworth Hospital's Personality Disorder Unit (PDU). Despite the thoroughness of the report, discussion about what really happened continued for years following. What is not in dispute is that a patient on a rehabilitation outing from the hospital had absconded, made his way to Amsterdam and, from a bar, telephoned the press in England. He said he would return only if his concerns were addressed. This was followed up with a document entitled 'My Concerns', which claimed that the PDU was replete with pornography, that drugs and alcohol were readily available and that staff were complicit in this and profiting from it. Even more alarming was the allegation that an 8-year-old girl had made regular visits and been allowed to play with a patient who had been convicted of sex offences against children, and without supervision. All of this, and a great deal more, turned out to be true.

The interesting aspect of this example is that, even with the enormous effort of dedicated resources over a prolonged period of time, the organization had not learned the lessons it needed to learn from the Blom-Cooper report. There were significant changes: systems were altered, and staff were changed in accordance with the recommendations. But, in the application of those changes, the wrong lessons seemed to have been learned. Consistent with the spirit of the recommendations, the ward-based staff members were invited to become therapeutic agents with professional attitudes to the care and treatment of patients, in stark contrast to that which had prevailed in the hospital since it started. On the face of it, this was a good thing, but the essential dynamic among clinical teams and ward staff had, arguably, not been dealt with explicitly.

Since the late 1970s and early 1980s, the persistent struggle within the hospital had been played out in clinical decision-making. The battle lines were drawn between nursing staff members, who felt they should have the primary influence on patient care decisions, and other clinicians (psychiatrists, psychologists, social workers, occupational therapists), who believed they should have the influence. Nursing staff members were meant to be part of the clinical teams but, frequently, and in private, they expressed the view that they were outnumbered and overwhelmed by the highly educated clinicians whose written reports and ability to articulate their arguments inhibited the influence of nursing opinion. The nursing perspective was reinforced by the argument that, because they had more numbers and spent more time in the wards, they should have more say in how the patients were managed. Their argument was supported by reasonable complaints that the rest of the clinical team had effectively abandoned nursing staff in the wards to 'get on with it'. The support of other clinicians was neither consistent nor reliable. Even when other clinicians were available and willing, their efforts were unappreciated, being seen as capricious or making unreasonable demands from a lofty and uninvolved position. The prevailing attitudes of nursing staff at that time were less than therapeutic[4] and, faced with the absence of support from their colleagues, it was these attitudes that influenced the culture and patient care.

What the Blom-Cooper report achieved was a very clear direction for the hospital to become more therapeutic. That message was unmistakable, and clinicians of all types were excited by the prospect of working in a genuinely therapeutic environment in forensic psychiatry. Unfortunately, the nursing staff members were yet again left to get on with it and, in the end, did not have the capacity to deliver a genuinely therapeutic environment even with the new opportunity. No single profession has the capacity to achieve this, and there is no reason to believe that nurses are the exception. In any case, the idea of being therapeutic was mistaken for a distorted understanding of being liberal. Some might ask where the harm to patients occurs in these circumstances. The harm is where responsibility for the psychological health, well-being and long-term interests of powerless people has been abandoned by those with power and that responsibility.

The Fallon Inquiry concluded, among other things, that the lack of clinical leadership was key to the failure. The struggle that was played out for decades in clinical decision-making had the impression of being about ideology, but only because clinical decision-making was the battleground. Ideological differences became the means of playing this out. Nurses represented themselves as righteous and concerned about safety and public protection, and were represented by others as reactionary, moralizing and punitive; other clinicians represented themselves as patient-centred and therapeutically minded but by the nursing staff as absent and dangerously liberal. The paradox in this example is that the nurses effectively won the argument by default in the post-Blom-Cooper period, when other clinicians abandoned them, but then themselves became dangerously liberal.

More than 20 years later, in another forensic psychiatry service describing itself as 'world class', the same battle was obvious, but also overlooked. A fraction of inpatients had structured involvement with rehabilitation services, none had integrated multidisciplinary care plans; illicit drugs were ubiquitous; teams failed to meet predictably; nursing staff complained of being abandoned on the wards, had themselves abandoned mandatory training and resented their lack of influence. Practice deteriorated so much that ward staff in some areas took turns sleeping for long periods or departing early. A few patients remained in seclusion for more than a year without plans to get them out. Violence and security issues abounded. Nurses and nursing assistants were represented as reactionary by non-nurses, while other professions were thought of as uncaring of staff or foolishly liberal with patients; each sought the moral high ground with nurses using safety, and clinicians using civil rights and therapeutic liberalism to support their perspective. Clinical decision-making was again the battleground and, just like in Rampton Hospital before the Boynton Report and Ashworth Hospital before Blom-Cooper, subversive authority stifled everything therapeutic. Among senior management, there was a greater motivation to hide the reality than to deal with it. The organization could not make timely decisions and seemed paralyzed in grasping change of any kind. Urgent reforms were being obstructed in order to prevent the calamity of mismanagement coming to light. It was a familiar scenario. It could have been the UK Special Hospitals in 1980.

Interestingly, in a less secure area of the same service, the oppressive practice was not the concern. The regime seemed liberal and without direction. There were numerous exits to the secure area from outside, and the secure perimeter was being used without regulation. No one knew for sure how many staff were in or out of the facility at any time. The whereabouts of patients were not always known. Carving knives were regularly conveyed by patients across an open courtyard used by a variety of patients, staff and visitors. Furtive sexual encounters occurred between male and female patients in the grounds. Occasionally, patients were allowed out into the community – in error and without legal authority to release them. In a general area, some staff watched television while patients mingled unsupervised. Scores were settled in the absence of supervision or purpose. Just as the high-security area failed to understand how to create a therapeutic regime in high-security conditions, the low-security area did not understand how to blend rehabilitation of forensic patients in those circumstances without adding risk to patients, staff and community. There were many well-intentioned staff but they were fearful of expressing concerns about the lack of purpose, as this would transgress their colleagues and not endear them to senior managers. It was clear that rigorously applied therapy and rehabilitation was not the purpose, and this suited some and frustrated others. Meanwhile, the patients failed to make the progress they might have made, and were subject to the slings and arrows of social hierarchies in secure environments.

The underlying issue in these examples has little to do with what has often been portrayed as an ideological battle between conservative and liberal forces, or between professional perspectives. Ultimately, it did not matter to the nursing staff at Ashworth whether they dominated patient care through subversive authority, intimidation and brutality as they did up until the Blom-Cooper report, or by becoming the new 'therapeutic' agent, as they did until the Fallon Inquiry. Equally, in the second example, it did not appear to matter to nurses whether high-security areas were controlled through repressive methods 'in response' to, or in efforts to 'prevent', violence to staff, or to be misguidedly liberal or slack in the low-secure area, provided it was the nursing staff who were in control of that environment. A straightforward conclusion could be offered for both examples. It was never about ideology; it was always about power.[5] None of the inquiries have made much of this, and perhaps this is one reason why lessons have been so difficult to learn, and why they have not been readily transferable.

It is too easy to look just at nursing staff. They are one part of the struggle for power and influence. No less a critique could be levelled at the other professions who also benefit from the circumstances of a dysfunctional institution. This is a key issue in understanding the meaning of structural violence in the context of forensic psychiatry. Who benefits from the structure and the dysfunction? How do the actions of the beneficiaries sustain the disadvantage of those who experience the harm?

In a large, multi-disciplinary group of clinicians, assembled to discuss the changes that needed to take place to improve the quality of a forensic service, an experienced psychiatrist contributed, 'The thing that I have always valued about working here is that I can come and go as I please. If we have to meet regularly as teams, I will have to consider whether I want to work here'. There was a hush in the room as the implications of the contribution were absorbed. Putting aside the admission that regular team meetings were not wanted, it was surprising just how candid and indiscreet the admission was. Colleagues who behaved similarly were taken aback at the sudden exposure of their self-interest. Everyone knew that having flexibility of this kind allowed some psychiatrists to collect a salary, benefit from the affiliation to the local forensic service known to courts and solicitors, and run a thriving private business. Not everyone in the room would connect this conduct with the poor practice that was so evident within the hospital. Psychiatry would, as would other professions in this situation, fight tooth and nail to preserve their benefits, and would never concede any harm done to patients by their profit. That clinical teams rarely met, that care plans were never prepared, that care was left to the least qualified and motivated, that some patients were refused food for being noncompliant, that patients sometimes refused going to rehabilitation programmes because they did not want to miss their psychiatrist should they turn up, would not figure in their calculation. After all, technically and contractually, they were doing nothing wrong; it had always been like that, so how could patients be suffering? Curiously, momentarily, it became immoral when exposed. The discomfort in the room was akin to discovering that your suspicion that the boss has been lying was true. It was only a brief moment until authority and convention was re-established, and it could not again be mentioned. It could not and would not be challenged because of the authority invested in medicine, and many would not have thought to question it because it had become normal. The status quo had the acceptance and tolerance of convention. Precisely because of this acceptance, patients suffered.

It is not just nurses and psychiatrists, although they are often the most powerful by virtue of numbers, statutes and control of processes that define their powers. Psychologists, social workers, occupational therapists and others find autonomy, latitude and flexibility in organizations that are paralyzed and moribund. What critique can be made of a psychologist who does not see many patients, when their reports are never discussed? Does it matter what the occupational therapist does with the patients, providing they are distracted for a while? Who cares if a social worker arrives at 10 o'clock and leaves at 3.30 in the afternoon if the patients in their care

are being warehoused rather than rehabilitated? Without the expectation of high therapeutic standards and accountability to one's inter-professional colleagues, a dull but quiet life can be had. It is attractive to some.

Understanding the benefits of dysfunction is key to understanding the suffering of the vulnerable in forensic psychiatry. It is why circumstances do not change, and why those who suffer are helpless to change their circumstances. The situation needs courageous and morally grounded leadership to be different. Integrity of this quality is not always evident among those with senior management responsibility in forensic psychiatry.

INCIDENTS, COMPLAINTS AND ROOT CAUSE ANALYSIS

Almost two decades ago, I was talking to a consultant psychiatrist and close colleague about an investigation into an untoward incident in another service. We wondered how we would fare if one of our patients was to do something terrible. Independently, we set off to look at our shared case load as if each patient had killed someone. It was a humbling experience. It became clear after looking at just a few cases that, despite being a very experienced, well-oiled and well-functioning multidisciplinary team, we were a long way from being bulletproof on any of our cases. It made us wonder what the value was of these inquiries happening all over the United Kingdom at the time. We concluded that they would always find something to say. There is never an action, course of actions or undertakings that will result in the conclusion, in the event of a homicide, that everything was adequate. How could they conclude that? Consequently, it is unsurprising that many professionals, of all disciplines, and many services appear defensive, and some become preoccupied with risk issues, often at the expense of safety.

Fortunately, the era of major inquiries in the United Kingdom appears now to be over, in favour of less intrusive methods of regulating and responding to individual incidents. While the lessons remain in the history of inquiries in forensic psychiatry services, it is not clear that they have been learned. Neither is it clear that what has replaced the process is more effective. One advantage of a major inquiry is its public element. Not only might the organization learn lessons, but the same lessons are there to be learned by other similar agencies. We have seen that lessons do not always travel, but at least there is a chance of influencing practice elsewhere. What has replaced the large inquiry has been a management process that may be commended for being local, relevant to the immediate circumstances of a single incident and action-orientated, but questions have emerged about its value. Hobbs (2001) writes of the experience of case-specific inquiries in New Zealand, complaining that they are expensive, damaging and ineffective. 'They are liable to over-determine causes and to ignore "near miss" events. There is an excessive reliance on the value of risk assessment and a poor understanding of limitations of prediction, prevention, responsibility and blame' (p. 156).

In the United Kingdom, the Health Care Commission reported of their dealing with a high proportion of cases involving mental health services in 2008: 'The nature of these varies from assaults and rates of suicide among users of services to allegations of abuse by staff and a lack of supervision. These are often accompanied by operational concerns, such as a lack of permanent staff, a lack of training and poor risk management procedures. These issues in turn can lead to intense work pressures and a reduction in the organisation's capacity to report, investigate and take action. A common theme in these referrals is a failure by Trusts[6] to learn from serious untoward incidents' (HCC, *Learning from Investigations*, p. 47).

Not only is there some question about the capacity of mental health organizations to learn lessons from major untoward incidents and dysfunctional hospitals, there is also doubt about the utility of the now ubiquitous process of root cause analysis (RCA) as it is applied to incidents that are serious enough to warrant an investigation without a full inquiry (Neal, Watson, Hicks, Porter, & Hill, 2004). RCA is a process derived from industry and part of total quality management, which has been applied widely in health services Its purpose is to reveal the direct and indirect causes of incidents and what has to be done to prevent a particular incident from occurring again. The accumulated themes that emerge from a series of RCAs are useful to influence whole systems.

Neal *et al.* (2004) expressed doubts about RCA as an answer to the problem of learning lessons in mental health services. Elsewhere, RCA has been described as a 'highly irrational quasi-legal form of local audit' (Salter, 2003). The danger is that RCA has the capacity to appear rigorous and credible, while being less than that. The notion of uncovering a 'root' cause of any single event by this or any other process is unlikely, although it is implied in the description. Neal *et al.* argue that a genuine scientific analysis of human behaviour would not involve inferring causation of a harmful event from a single, uncontrolled case study. Moreover, to assert that a particular action or interaction of events, except in the most obvious of circumstances, is the cause of an adverse outcome is little more than speculation. Perhaps the most challenging notion is where RCA identifies a particular process or methodology that may or may not have been implicated in an adverse event, when that

process has not itself been properly evaluated. The Care Programme Approach might be one such process, as might a range of risk assessment methods.

It is in this realm that subtle and less-than-subtle influences on RCA come into play. At the entirely human and expected level of error would be the likely range of errors in human judgment, including representativeness, availability heuristics and hindsight bias (Schacter, 1999), to name a few. These biases have the effect of leading to conclusions that have face validity. They are satisfying as they allow the pieces of a puzzle to appear to link together in an explanatory way, but they are as likely to be randomly associated as illustrative of what actually happened. Roese and Olson (1995) refer to this effect as 'counterfactual bias'. It describes the tendency to construct alternatives to reality by postulating how things might have turned out in different circumstances. Added to these influences are the range of motives that reveal moral bias, vested interests, professional protectionism and, in a few shameless examples, the desire to obscure the truth in order to prevent the abuse of patients emerging into the light.

The latter might arise from circumstances in which limitations apply to the requirement to disclose information under the freedom of information legislation pertaining to a particular jurisdiction. In one jurisdiction, freedom of information disclosures, or disclosures of any kind, could be avoided by invoking privacy statutes. This could be achieved by designating an incident in which a mistake was made or an injury sustained by staff or patients as a 'patient safety' event. All information would then be subject to restrictions such that it did not have to be disclosed outside the health authority or even circulated within the clinical realm in which it first occurred. The result of this loophole to evade public scrutiny and reflection of clinicians is an unseemly effort to inhibit any expression of concern or opinion in writing or email before the formal designation of 'patient safety' event could be applied. Once the incident is shielded from public scrutiny, it can be managed. In good organizations, RCA might assist lessons being learned. In lesser organizations, the lessons can be obscured with impunity, and sometimes, with the use of the very methods designed to reveal the truth, the truth can be lost. In other words, the legislative framework of civil liberties can be allowed to interact with the management of RCA in such a way as to prevent lessons being learned and patient safety being addressed honestly. The patients would never know, and neither would the clinicians.

The usefulness of RCA really depends on the parameters assigned to it. The advocates of RCA and the new wave of patient safety will protest at the suggestion that RCA is a tool capable of being manipulated, but it is not difficult to illustrate. Take, for example, an incident in which a large patient in a high-security environment became violent one evening, smashing windows and fixtures, and terrifying staff. A great deal of damage was done and at great expense. The RCA considered issues of concern expressed by the staff on duty, as it should have done. These issues included the special circumstances of admitting an unusually large patient with the capacity to overwhelm several staff, the speed of communication in an emergency and the availability of additional staff during the night to cope with such a frightening contingency.

A patient-centred perspective changes the things that are important in this incident. The patient had, in the previous few days, expressed distress at being observed through the glass window in the room door by a female member of staff. Being naked in unfamiliar surroundings, in addition to the patient's mental illness, caused the normal nursing process of making regular observations of patients distressing for this young person. It should have been an easy fix. The patient could have been helped to understand the purpose of observations and that all patients need to be observed to keep them safe. A care plan could have been introduced to remind the patient of how things worked and to ensure each new shift of staff understood what was going on. Perhaps a male member of staff could do the rounds at bedtime. Members of the multidisciplinary team might have been informed to assist in managing the situation, to support the nursing staff. These steps might have prevented the incident from occurring. None of this happened. On the following evening, another female nurse did her duty and looked into the same room at the same individual who happened to be naked at the time, and he exploded in rage. The staff were helpless to stop the rampage that followed.

This fact did not emerge in the RCA because there were issues that would have been exposed if a process with high integrity had occurred. None of the staff on duty that night had completed their mandatory training on managing and de-escalating violent situations. The organization was thousands of hours behind in mandatory training. There was no care plan for that patient prepared before or after the incident. This might have ensured that the information about the patient's concerns was transferred from one shift of nurses to another and prevented the incident from occurring. However, senior clinicians refused to comply with the expectation of preparing and adhering to an integrated multidisciplinary care plan. The significance of this refusal was that the organization had had to satisfy hospital accreditation inspectors that such care plans were integral to patient care in order to achieve national accreditation standards. The RCA could not be allowed to draw attention to the absence of care plans, and so limitations to the remit of the RCA were imposed.

In the immediate aftermath of that incident, the patient was left in seclusion for hours without being seen by a doctor or spoken to by a nurse. He was injured and bleeding, and yet no one knew that the injuries were not serious. Subsequently, when he was seen, his medication was changed so as 'manage' the patient more effectively. There was no longer any justification for medicating the patient – he was no longer angry – but, in the familiar process of medicating the patient, the blame for this incident was being attributed to the patient even before the incident was investigated. This also was not part of the RCA. This would be structural violence of the kind referred to by Farmer.

It is not only the individual RCAs that may be manipulated. Limiting the summary processing of a number of incidents is another well-worn means of inhibiting adverse public scrutiny. For example, everyone accepts that patients may die from time to time under the supervision of any service, and, in each case, there should be an RCA. Where there are a series of deaths, a series of RCAs should be brought together to understand the commonality between the events or any themes that emerge. By preventing a cluster of patient deaths to be examined as a cluster, essential points of learning may not emerge. This may result in the responsible authority evading the eye of adverse public scrutiny, and the agency responsible for the care of patients not changing practice to prevent it occurring again. Such is a desirable outcome for an authority that is morally challenged, but for future patients that die as a result, it reveals a clear organizational process, albeit improper, leading to avoidable death. It is nothing that the patients or relatives would know of or be able to change in anticipation of the possible consequences. As far as they are concerned, the flaw(s) in the defective process appear not as flaws but as normal and would not be seen or questioned.

Also unseen and lost within the RCA process is the recognition that we are not dealing with conventional people of normal capacity or tolerance. Everyone who enters a forensic psychiatry hospital as a patient is unwell and vulnerable. The experience of being incarcerated, for most normal people, would be traumatizing, and acting out of some kind, fear and anger responses, when expected to comply with instruction, are common. But for those with pre-existing vulnerabilities to experiencing interpersonal insult, the impact is compounded.

Compounded vulnerabilities arise when systemic or institutional conditions intersect in a manner that creates additional barriers to the agent's ability to develop or achieve well-being (Guidry-Grimes & Victor, 2012). Guidry-Grimes and Victor make the point that 'disadvantaged populations are susceptible to being kept in disadvantaged positions when an institutional standard or condition plays into, reinforces, and perpetuates the stigma of the population stereotype'. Nothing is more stigmatizing than being designated a 'dangerous offender', psychopath, antisocial, personality-disordered or merely being admitted to a forensic hospital with schizophrenia.

When a label (offender) targets a historically marginalized and disadvantaged population (patient with diagnosis such as schizophrenia), that label compounds the vulnerability to which that population is already subject. People who receive an additional label of this kind are likely to be mistrusted, their agency questioned, their competence maligned, and risk to others is assumed (see Angermeyer & Dietrich, 2006, esp. 170–171), all of which restricts access to opportunity, and renders them easy to blame and additionally vulnerable to harm.

This disadvantage does not arise simply because of how staff members perceive them. Stigma can damage well-being by working from inside the vulnerable (Livingston & Boyd, 2010). Recently, it has been argued that the real effects of internalized stigma for such populations are invisible but profound. 'Hope, self-esteem, empowerment, self-efficacy, overall quality of life, social support, and treatment adherence all suffer considerably for the majority of patients who internalize the stigma of mental illness. The ways in which we perceive the world, navigate our community, perceive evidence, and self-reflect are shaped by social practices. The fact of historical marginalization is enough to make a group or individual vulnerable; when institutional structures bolster that marginalization, vulnerability is compounded by the added difficulties in attaining a sufficient level of well-being' (Livingston & Boyd, 2010). It may be more profound among non-Western immigrant populations (Ghanean, Nojomi, & Jacobsson, 2011).

The point of this discussion is not to suggest that all of the stigma felt by patients can be avoided, or that it is unnecessary to protect the public from the real risks they may represent. It is to ask a question: where, in the application of RCA to a particular incident, does a sensitivity to the impact of stigma in the eyes of the staff, and vulnerability in the disposition of the patient, get recognized? It is obviously relevant to understanding interpersonal incidents within a hospital, but it is generally not admitted to our analysis.

If there is a comfort for forensic psychiatry and mental health services, generally, it is that the limitations of RCA are not confined to them. Writing in the *British Medical Journal* and reporting on the experience of hospital medicine, Taitz *et al.* (2010) conclude, 'given the number of hours per RCA, it seems a shame that the final output of the process may not in fact achieve the desired patient safety improvements' (p. 1).

Higgins (1996) identified a key element of senior management that helps our understanding of why forensic hospitals can be unable to change under their own steam. 'It was all too obvious that the hospitals had been both under-managed and over-managed. They had been under-managed in that no central goals had been set on standards, clinical or managerial, just on security. Decisions had often been driven by knee-jerk responses that were bureaucratic, defensive, and over-conciliatory to reactionary and conservative forces in the hospital, often by concessions and the injection of further wasted resources. The hospitals had been over-managed in that any individuality, innovation, or principled stand at hospital level had been frustrated by central vacillation or obstruction. … It was very difficult to be convinced that the hospitals were being run in the interests of the patients rather than the different and sometimes very self-interested and often adversarial interests of the parties mentioned'. The reform of Special Hospitals in England proceeded with the introduction of general management, setting of standards, requiring multi-disciplinary working among other things, and progress has been obvious. There is a lesson in this for other hospitals and other jurisdictions.

The distance between service delivery in forensic psychiatry and government bodies responsible for the service is critical to understanding the motivation of executives and senior managers, and why over-management can occur. In smaller jurisdictions, the distance tends to be smaller and more difficult to manage. Small incidents make relatively large political ripples, and hence the primary motivation of executives may become containing and controlling information that may be likely to unsettle the political classes. Nothing changes when impression management is more important to a senior executive than the operations and purpose of a service. In the worst examples, there may even be attempts to inhibit or obstruct accountability to statutory bodies established to oversee the service. A more subtle concern is the conflict of interest arising from senior executives with responsibility for a forensic psychiatry service, serving on that body established by legislation for the purpose of overseeing and ensuring accountability to the regional or national government. It is such an obvious source of conflict and corruption, but the nature of small-town politics allows such things to go unseen and unsaid. It means that the strategy of suppression of adverse information goes unacknowledged, and there is never a need to address the structural issues leading to harm.

In larger jurisdictions, there can be more administrative layers between the service and government, which may absorb the ripples and insulate politicians from incidents. This might allow a more rational and honest dealing of the problems encountered, provided the additional layers are effective in focusing on the purpose of the service, the quality of care and service performance.

CONCLUSION

This chapter has attempted to introduce structural violence as a means of conceptualizing the single-most important observation of secure forensic psychiatric hospitals in respect of patient safety. These hospitals have the potential to harm the patients they are responsible for. They do this in ways that have as their source benefits for those who work in or have responsibility for them. The value of using structural violence as a lens with which to see this is that it reveals both the motive and the mechanism of harm done, and how it can be disguised, taking the form of a righteous cause of a staff group or even diligent concern of senior managers. Second, it reveals how convention, routine and familiarity make the process of harm to others nearly invisible. Even those who do see it may be reluctant to identify it. As a consequence, trying to understand how a patient has been injured, or a member of staff has been harmed, is constantly biased by the exclusion of this perspective – excluded by convention in most circumstances, but excluded with clear intent in others.

It is the collective tolerance of this situation that must be most troubling to those of us who seek safe and therapeutic environments to manage this most stigma-ridden population. Failing to acknowledge the process ultimately serves the interests of the powerful and sustains the harm to patients. There cannot be a professional training programme or regulatory body anywhere in the world that would approve of such inaction, even those with the power. Yet, it is only these groups that can make changes. They must be helped to see social justice as a key element of clinical management, and to recognize that, without an understanding of social justice at the heart of clinical care, professional ethics are little more than mechanisms to sustain the vulnerability of the population they manage. Take, as an example, the case of medical ethics, which claims the individual as the focus of concern. All very laudable, but within the complex social organization of a hospital, limiting your perspective to the individual is an easy mechanism to absolve oneself from being concerned about any influence that does the patient harm.

The question here for clinicians of all kinds is about the ethics or the legitimacy for clinicians of ignoring structural violence. To get at this question, we have to ask, is the ubiquitous maxim of 'do no harm', within most ethical frameworks, sufficient to allow a single case of 'this individual only' orientation of clinical decision-making in a hospital where a whole class of disadvantaged and powerless individuals are impacted by a single culture over which they have no influence? Farmer (2003) implies that it is not, and that social and economic rights are at the heart of what must become the new medical ethics, and, further, we need a new ethics of distributive justice in respect of public health. The argument here is not about the need of a new ethics of distributive justice or economic rights, although these would have significant benefits for the mentally unwell who become offenders. The argument here is about being clinically and ethically responsible for the collective well-being of a class of patients while they reside in secure hospitals. Until this responsibility becomes what all our clinicians in forensic psychiatry are charged with delivering, there will be moral blindness, self-interest, suppression of information, distortion of organizational processes and harm to patients.

NOTES

1 http://www.nhsbsa.nhs.uk/Documents/SecurityManagement/2010-11_NHS_Violence_Against_Staff_FINAL_01-11-2011.pdf

2 The author has participated in a number of inquiry teams investigating untoward incidents, given evidence to others, worked on accreditation/inspection teams and acted as consultant to forensic services in the United Kingdom and Australia.

3 The author gave evidence to the Fallon Inquiry in 1998 on behalf of the British Psychological Society. He had been part of a small multidisciplinary group that established a Personality Disorder Unit of Park Lane Hospital (becoming Ashworth Hospital later) and worked there until 1987.

4 Some of the best nursing that the author has ever witnessed occurred at Park Lane/Ashworth Hospital while he worked there between 1982 and 1987. Unfortunately, it was not very common.

5 There has been concern about the strength and influence of the dominant union within the high-security psychiatric facilities in the United Kingdom. The Professional Trades Union for Prison, Correctional and Secure Psychiatric Workers, formally the Prison Officers Association (POA), was the first collective bargaining unit at Broadmoor Hospital (Evans & Cohen, 2009). In 1997, a member of the Blom-Cooper report proposed that the anti-therapeutic aspect of special hospitals would not change until the POA was put out (Murphy, 1997). The same suggestion might be made of any collective bargaining unit where patient care standards are in the hands of the same authority representing only staff interests.

6 A 'Trust' in the United Kingdom is the organizational structure that provides and manages health services.

FURTHER READING

Thomas-Peter B. A. (2007). The modern context of psychology in corrections: Influences, limitations and values of 'what works'. In, G. Towl (Ed.), *Psychology Research in Prisons*. Oxford, UK: Blackwell.

This chapter provides a critique and review of the current practice of psychology within corrections, with a particular emphasis on the 'What Works?' literature.

REFERENCES

Angermeyer, M. C., & Dietrich, S. (2006). Public beliefs about and attitudes towards people with mental illness: A review of population studies. *Acta Psychiatrica Scandinavica, 113*, 163–179.

Banerjee, A., Daly, T., Armstrong, H., Armstrong, P., Lafrance, S., & Szebehely, M. (2008) *'Out of control': Violence against personal support workers in long-term care.* York University and Carlton University.

Banerjee, A., Daly, T., Armstrong, P., Szebehely, M., Armstrong, H., & Lafrance, S. (2012). Structural violence in long-term, residential care for older people: Comparing Canada and Scandinavia. *Social Science & Medicine, 74*, 390–398.

Bowers, L., Crowhurst, N., Alexander, J., Callaghan, P., Eales, S., Guy, S., McCann, E., & Ryan, C. (2002). Safety and security policies on psychiatric acute admission wards: Results from a London-wide survey. *Journal of Psychiatric and Mental Health Nursing, 9*, 427–433.

Brickell, T. A., Nicholls, T. L., Procyshyn, R. M., McLean, C., Dempster, R. J., Lavoie, J. A. A., Sahlstrom, K. J., Tomita, T. M., & Wang, E. (2009). *Patient safety in mental health.* Edmonton, Alberta: Canadian Patient Safety Institute and Ontario Hospital Association.

Due, C., Connellan, K., & Riggs, D. W. (2012). Surveillance, security and violence in a mental health ward: An ethnographic case-study of an Australian purpose-built unit. *Surveillance & Society, 10*(3/4), 292–302.

Evans, D., & Cohen, S. (2009). *The everlasting staircase: A history of the Prison Officers' Association 1939–2009.* London: Pluto Press.

Farmer P. E. (2003). *Pathologies of power: Health, human rights, and the new war on the poor.* Berkeley and Los Angeles: University of California Press.

Farmer, P. (1999). Pathologies of power: Rethinking health and human rights. *American Journal of Public Health, 89*(10), 1486–1496.

Farmer, P. E. (1997). Ethnography, social analysis, and the prevention of sexually transmitted HIV infections among poor women in Haiti. In M.C. Inhorn & P. J. Brown (Eds.), *An anthropology of infectious disease* (pp. 413–438). Amsterdam: Gordon and Breach.

Farmer, P. E. (2004). An anthropology of structural violence. *Current Anthropology, 45*, 305–326.

Farmer. P. E., Nizeye B., Stulac, S., & Keshavjee, S. (2006). Structural violence and clinical medicine. *PLoS Med, 3*(10), 1686–1691.

Galtung, J. (1969). Violence, peace, and peace research. *Journal of Peace Research, 6*(3), 167–191.

Galtung, J. (1990). Cultural violence. *Journal of Peace Research, 27*(3), 291–305.

Ghanean, H., Nojomi, M., & Jacobsson, L. (2011). Internalized stigma of mental illness in Tehran, Iran. *Stigma Research and Action, 1*(1), 11–17.

Gilligan, J. (1997). *Violence: Reflections on a national epidemic.* New York: Vintage Books.

Guidry-Grimes, L., & Victor, E. (2012). Vulnerabilities compounded by social institutions. *International Journal of Feminist Approaches to Bioethics, 5*(2), 126–146.

Gunn, J. (2000). Future directions for treatment in forensic psychiatry. *British Journal of Psychiatry, 176*, 332–338.

Higgins, J. (1996). Future of the special hospitals. *Criminal Behaviour & Mental Health: Supplement, 6*(S1), 65–72.

Hobbs, P. (2001). Inquiries – high costs, unacceptable side effects and low effectiveness: Time for revision. *Australasian Psychiatry, 9*(2), 156–160.

Kelly, J. K. (2005). Structural violence and schizophrenia. *Social Science & Medicine, 61*, 721–730.

Kohn, L. T., Corrigan, J. M., & Donaldson, M. S. (1999). *To err is human: Building a safer health system.* Committee on Quality of Health Care in America, Institute of Medicine.

Livingston, J. D., & Boyd, J. E. (2010). Correlates and consequences of internalized stigma for people living with mental illness: A systematic review and meta-analysis. *Social Science and Medicine, 71*(12): 2150–2161.

Moore, D., & Hannah-Moffat, K. (2005). The liberal veil: Revisiting Canadian penality. In J. Pratt, D. Brown, M. Brown, S. Hallworth, & W. Morrison (Eds.), *The new punitiveness: Trends, theories, perspectives.* Cullhompton: Willan.

Murphy, E. (1997). The future of Britain's high security hospitals. *British Medical Journal, 314*, 1292–1293.

Neal, L. A., Watson, D., Hicks, T., Porter, M., & Hill, D. (2004). Root cause analysis applied to the investigation of serious untoward incidents in mental health services. *Psychiatric Bulletin, 28*, 75–77.

Pratt, J., Brown, D., Hallsworth, S., Brown, M., & Morrison, W. (2005). *The new punitiveness: Trends, theories, perspectives.* Cullompton, UK: Willan.

Report of the review of Rampton Hospital (Chairman Sir John Boynton) (1980). London: HMSO, Cmnd 8073.

Roese, N. J., & Olson, J. M. (1995). *What might have been: The social psychology of counterfactual thinking.* New Jersey: Erlbaum.

Salter, M. (2003). Serious incident inquiries: A survival kit for psychiatrists. *Psychiatric Bulletin, 27,* 245–247.

Schacter, D. L. (1999). The seven sins of memory: Insights from psychology and cognitive neuroscience. *American Psychologist, 54*(3), 182–203.

Simic, M., & Rhodes, T. (2009). Violence, dignity and HIV vulnerability: Street sex work in Serbia. *Sociology of Health & Illness, 31,* 1–16.

Taitz, J., Genn, K., Brooks, V., Ross, D., Ryan, K., Shumack, B., Burrell, T., & Kennedy, P. (2010). System-wide learning from root cause analysis: A report from the New South Wales Root Cause Analysis Review Committee. *Quality Safety in Health Care, 19*(6), e63.

Thomas-Peter B. A. (2007a). The modern context of psychology in corrections: Influences, limitations and values of 'what works'. In G. Towl (Ed.), *Psychology research in prisons.* Oxford, UK: Blackwell.

Thomas-Peter, B. A. (2007b). The needs of offenders and the process of changing them. In G. Towl (Ed.), *Psychology research in prisons.* Oxford, UK: Blackwell.

Yassi, A., & Hancock, T. (2005). Patient safety–worker safety: Building a culture of safety to improve healthcare worker and patient well-being. *Healthc Q, 8,* 32–38.

29 Concluding Themes: Psychological Perspectives and Futures

GRAHAM J. TOWL

INTRODUCTION

As readers may well have noticed in this volume, but also in some of the broader professional developments within the British Psychological Society, the term 'forensic' has come to embrace both criminological and legal psychology in the United Kingdom. It is no longer viewed, as a term, as narrowly, or some would say as technically accurately, as in the past. It would, of course, no longer be accurate, in any meaningful manner in the modern world of forensic psychology. In this volume alone, there is a real breadth of territory covered, which justifies the claim that forensic psychology is becoming a clearly defined branch of applied psychology. The discipline has developed from modest beginnings to emerge as one of the most popular areas of applied psychology with prospective students. The growth is reflected not just in the academic literature but also in the expanding numbers of those in the professional forensic psychological communities. But the field is perhaps at different stages of development in different areas. Some areas are well developed, others much less so. Some areas enjoy the benefits of much empirical evidence, others are considerably less well epistemologically or empirically endowed. Since the first edition, there have been some significant macro-economic and socio-political changes globally. Indeed, the breadth of work in forensic psychology has started to increase markedly, a very positive development, especially in view of a previous narrowness of perspective in much of the field to date.

In the first edition, three pervasive contextual themes emerged from the state of the field. First, there was a large and expanding set of financial interests in the area. The forensic psychological field of courts, probation, prisons, special hospitals, police stations, secure units and related settings is potentially a large market which can accommodate a range of product lines, including psychometric test sales, licensing, administration, interpretation and staff training. Second, the managerialist-based approaches impacted upon much of forensic psychological policy and practice. In particular, there were significant rafts of practice investment driven by managerialist needs rather than evidence-informed practice. Third, and most important, was the need to further develop the professional and ethical basis of much of the forensic field.

The financial interests of those marketing 'treatment programmes' and various psychometric tests remain very much in evidence, although there does appear to be a growing realization that the primary purpose of such businesses is to secure a return on investment to shareholders rather than simply public protection. There is an ethical imperative for practitioners to be mindful of such contingencies when considering the appropriateness or otherwise of any such product. We have seen some product diversification in response to the state market demands. One ethical test for the practitioner is to reflect upon whose need and what need is being met by the use of such products. For example, does it make any sense to simply repeat the administration of programme products against the backdrop of an increasingly poor evidence base and before and after assessments indicating no individual treatment effects? This is intended as a rhetorical question.

Three key psychological perspectives remain evident from much of what is contained within this book, and an additional theme has now come to the fore. First, there are some contested perspectives within (and beyond) the forensic psychological field. We have seen the heavy reliance among many in the field in aping medical perspectives

Forensic Psychology, Second Edition. Edited by David A. Crighton and Graham J. Towl.
© 2015 John Wiley & Sons, Ltd. Published 2015 by British Psychological Society and John Wiley & Sons, Ltd.

with an uncritical reverence of psychiatric taxonomies. This is a topic that has somewhat hit the headlines since the appearance of the first edition. Increasingly, this debate does appear to be eroding the claims of a scientific basis to much of the discipline of psychiatry. The discipline of psychiatry appears to be re-emerging as a manifestation of medical humanities. Second, there appears to be wider agreement on the need to adopt a rigorously scientific approach to forensic work. Third, much may be gleaned from both laboratory and field-based experiments in applying the methods and knowledge base of experimental psychology to the applied forensic psychological knowledge, policy and practice base. Fourth, with the statutory regulation of practitioner psychologists, the discipline is better placed to comment upon and contribute to wider professional debates within and beyond the field of forensic psychology. The scene is set for much learning for us all on this multi-professional regulatory journey.

CONTEXTUAL THEMES

As mentioned earlier, perhaps one of the biggest areas of financial interests in the forensic field is in the domain of psychometric testing. Psychometrics is big business. The forensic field is a substantial market. Since the first issue, there has been more privatization of services, as can be seen perhaps most notably with probation services in England and Wales. Both private companies and some individual psychologists have benefited financially from this. It is an industry that is keen to expand its markets, market share and shareholder value, which is entirely predictable as a business model. Some psychometric tests and 'tools' have been sometimes aggressively marketed in the forensic field. As noted earlier, it is important to consider such matters when looking at the merits and demerits of particular approaches to working with offenders. One fundamental question which is often missed in the everyday business of both research and practice is who benefits from the use of a test or assessment? It is a basic but very important question. It is not unknown for psychologists to recommend particular training or testing from which they may receive a financial benefit. This means that there is a clear conflict of interest in such cases. One useful potential parallel is between the psychometrics industry and the drugs industry. The drugs industry is much more tightly regulated. The quality of the research requirements for the release of new drugs is much more stringent than for psychometric tests. This perhaps reflects, to some degree, the power and influence of such businesses. It is a power and influence that few psychologists appear to question, never mind challenge. This can be due to a lack of aware-

ness, complacency, lack of concern, or can be linked to their individual interests in maintaining the current, sometimes ethically challenging, state of affairs. With the still developing regulatory framework for psychologists, it may be anticipated that such practices will be the subjects of some subsequent scrutiny.

There are some further parallels between big pharmaceuticals industry and the psychometrics industry that may be noted. For example, we may look at the area of the marketing of drugs and also the marketing of psychometric tests. Both present as having a firm scientific basis. Both may attempt to secure favourable quotes for marketing purposes from those in positions of authority. This may be seen to give the particular product some additional 'product authority'. Additionally, there can be an ethically unacceptable use of language in the marketing of the products. For example, the term 'reliability' in terms of test construction has a particular technical usage and meaning. It is a meaning which is fundamentally different from its everyday usage. In everyday parlance the term reliability would refer to that which may be relied upon. In the psychometric testing industry the term is used in the technical sense to refer to consistency. In technical terms a test may have high reliability but low validity. Thus it could be marketed, with apparent legitimacy, as having high reliability. However, this would not mean that it could be relied upon in the everyday sense, very far from it. Such uses of language can be fundamentally misleading. Of course, any literature on individual tests needs to be carefully written to convey technical information but also clear in the way that language is being used so as not to lead to ambiguity and confusion. If psychologists find themselves recommending particular tests then it would seem a bare minimum in terms of ethical expectations that they would declare an interest in the administration of the test should they be gaining any financial benefit directly or indirectly from its usage.

Moving on from markets to managerialism, business is the common denominator between these two influential themes underpinning many of the environments that forensic psychologists populate. Successive governments over recent years have sought to import the methods and language of the private sector into the public sector. One purported purpose of this approach has been to introduce private-sector-based efficiencies into the public sector. The idea is that public sector organizations are inefficient and private sector organizations are efficient. Putting aside whether or not such assertions stand even the most perfunctory scrutiny, the language of business has been imported into much of the public sector. Thus senior managers in probation and prisons will refer to their 'business plans' despite having no business to plan, but rather a probation service or prison to run. There is nothing wrong, and in my view, much right, with being 'business like' in the approach to running some aspects of public services. But prisons, probation, courts and hospitals are not 'businesses' and if such importation is taken too literally, and too far, there can be some rather perverse inefficiencies which result. Some business terms sit uneasily in such an environment; for example, would probation or prison officers be content with serving offenders as customers? Probably not.

Why is this of importance within forensic psychology or to forensic psychologists? It is important because the commitment to managerialism means an unprecedented receptivity to measurement and manualization. What is counted becomes what counts, with scant regard for what may be every bit as important but not as quantifiable. Resources are then allocated accordingly, which is a recipe for the potentially wasteful use of public resources. Probably one of the most powerful and costly illustrations of this has been in relation to the so-called 'offending behaviour programmes'. These are increasingly discredited (e.g. the so-called Dangerous Severe Personality Disorder [DSPD] programmes) discrete interventions with a narrow focus rather than 'programmes', as an integrated set of interventions as more generally understood. 'Success' for such interventions within probation and prisons is measured in terms of the number of people attending the courses. This is, of course, a very limited measure, but nonetheless very easily measurable. And this is part of the problem with managerialist approaches. The 'programmes' themselves have become tainted with some of the fundamental problems of managerialism in public services. Such approaches produce perverse incentives among the staff and offenders. For example, individuals unsuitable for the 'programme' are put on them, or individuals may be sent to repeat a programme to meet institutional targets or 'Key Performance Indicators' (KPIs). Even working within such limited models of measurement, alternative, more accurate and apposite measures have been suggested and not implemented (see Crighton & Towl, 2008). Since the first edition of this book, the much vaunted, but fundamentally flawed, DSPD units and concepts have been acknowledged as a complete failure of policy and practice on any measure. Again, the pervasive and superficially appealing notion of a 'programme' to address individual needs has been shown to be an expensive waste of public money.

There is a popular myth within some of the forensic psychology community that such programmes in probation and prisons thrived simply and chiefly because of the emerging evidence base. This is, at very best, a rather partial truth. Although there was some initially encouraging international evidence, some of which was replicated on a small scale in the United Kingdom, in subsequent years, overwhelmingly there has been a subsequent failure to demonstrate the efficacy of the courses.

In financial terms the courses have provided the public with very poor value for money indeed, yet they continue to be invested in. This is remarkable in times of renewed pressures on the public purse. This is perhaps especially so in view of the purported era of austerity reflected in the reduced overall funding of the public sector under the current government. The largest-scale UK studies have failed to demonstrate a convincing reduction in reconviction treatment effect in cognitive-skills-based courses or in the domain of sex offender treatment. There has never been a successful robust demonstration of the reduction of sexual reconviction rates in the entire, 20-plus-years history of sex offender treatment in prisons in England and Wales. So the argument that such courses are delivered on the grounds of evidence are not even remotely persuasive. They are more plausibly delivered because of political imperatives both in terms of meeting the needs of politicians and those with careers or other investments in such treatment industries.

Interestingly, some of the user community are not fooled by the claims of the efficacy of the courses. Some psychologists may have a professional interest in their continuation, in the short term perhaps. However, in the long term, this cannot be good for the professional reputation of the discipline. In prisons, 'programmes', despite initial promise, have become enmeshed in the broader managerial malaise of running prisons. They are less to do with 'treatment' in any psychologically meaningful sense and more to do with structured activities and institutionalized legitimacy for all concerned. They provide legitimacy for prisoners because the narrative is that they are 'addressing their offending'. They provide legitimacy for psychologists and other staff because they are engaging in the genuinely challenging task of working with offenders to reduce the risk of their reoffending. The Parole Board and its members are likely also to express approval that the offender is undertaking such work in view of their avowed commitment to public protection. This is despite the mainstay of UK evidence. The over-reliance upon some broadly supportive international studies will have a limited shelf life. We are already well past the 'best before' dates of this family of offender 'treatment' industry products. Undoubtedly though, new products will be brought to this lucrative marketplace (as we have seen).

This brings us rather neatly into the domain of professional and ethical issues. It can be extremely challenging in everyday practice to focus on what are the most important professional and ethical issues to address. This is perhaps especially so with 'systems based' problems. Thus an individual may do their level best to act professionally and ethically but in a potentially less than ethical organizational environment. This can be very difficult emotionally and intellectually. There are few easy answers. Difficult choices sometimes need to be made. This can require a great deal of moral, professional and personal courage. Some of the most difficult ethical decisions for professionals can arise when doing the right things means that there will be a personal and professional cost to such assertive behaviour. This is one reason why it is so important for, particularly fully qualified, staff to ensure that all under their supervision and management are enabled to raise concerns and challenge any existing practices. It has been previously observed that psychologists are by no means immune to the processes of institutionalization. Indeed, there are some powerful lessons from history that remind us of this. Starkly put, professional psychology thrived in Nazi Germany (Geuter, 2008). We do need to be ever mindful of the lessons of history rather than give undue focus to the politics or fashions of the moment. Forensic psychology has emerged from being a marginal academic discipline into a profession recognized and sanctioned by the state. With this come some significant responsibilities. In environments characterized by vast differences in power, we need to be especially mindful of our professional responsibilities to protect the vulnerable and, where appropriate, challenge the powerful. This includes raising concerns with colleagues about their professional practices if there are concerns. This is especially the case if the activities are those that are afforded state legitimacy. Ethical issues within the profession tend to focus on the behaviour of individuals or sometimes groups, but comparatively rarely are the broader contextual issues considered. The impact of managerialism and the growing psychometrics and offender courses industry surely warrant closer professional and ethical scrutiny. Such developments have significant impacts on the immediate environments within which many psychologists in the forensic field function.

But the single most significant milestone in the history of the professional regulation of psychologists came into force in July 2009 with the advent of statutory regulation of practitioner psychologists through the Health Professions Council (HPC). This is a very positive development, with an independent regulation system for psychologists. Peer-based regulatory systems tend to lack credibility, with the spectre of professional self-interest looming in the minds of others. It is far more robust and ethical to have a system which draws from a broader and more truly independent set of perspectives in areas such as, for example, misconduct. Many practitioner psychologists will find this reassuring, but more importantly, so will members of the public. The detail of the new arrangements will of course be important. But the principle most surely will be right; it is better to be regulated by a set of independent others than by one's, sometimes close, peers (Towl, 2014). This allows for more robustness and transparency of processes, which is important.

These are exciting times, and statutory regulation is increasingly being viewed as a historical turning point in psychological practice in the United Kingdom.

PSYCHOLOGICAL PERSPECTIVES

There are some contested accounts within the field of mental health, and this is also so for forensic mental health, about the utility and empirical integrity of psychiatric taxonomies. Some of the discussion and debates are reflected in the chapters of this book. Arguably, one problem has been not solely with the taxonomies themselves but with the uses to which they have sometimes been put. It is as if some psychologists assume that there is more scientific rigour to their development than there is. And this is a debate that has come to a head since the first edition of this book. The psychiatric establishment has put its full weight behind the continued but controversial legitimacy of the ever-expanding taxonomies of mental illnesses despite the lack of evidence in support of the approach. This may be taken to mean that such debates are more about the exercising of professional power than they are about informing patient care. The uncritical usage of such imported psychiatric terminology is perhaps all too common. Sometimes the collections of descriptions that make up the taxonomies are taken to be explanations in themselves, rather than simply a constellation of observed signs. Readers can make up their own minds, but such considerations do require critical thinking rather than mere professional compliance with the professionally seductive products of the psychiatric industry standards portfolio.

Much of the forensic field adopts a rigorously scientific approach to the consideration of research methods. And it is important that as the knowledge base develops, such rigour is built upon. Much has been learned about the developmental trajectories towards criminality. There remains a need for further rigorous, independent and scientifically robust randomized controlled trials (RCTs), and also longitudinal research. As illustrated in some of the chapters of this book, there has been a growth of work in the area of witness testimony, including research on children as witnesses. The court decision-making processes have also been the subject of scholarly study. There has also been some excellent work undertaken on risk assessment. Developmental trajectories to criminality are also more widely recognized with a clear evidence base for intervention. If we are to have evidence-informed policy and practice, then there would be a disinvestment from the prison service and high-security hospitals, and increased investment in early interventions.

But one area where there has been rather more of a mix of research quality has been in the domain of the evaluation of interventions aimed at reducing the risk of reoffending. First, there is a dearth of RCTs. Second, there is an overreliance upon self-report and related psychometric measures in the evaluation of courses in prisons and probation aimed at reducing the risk of reoffending.

The quality of some of the 'programme' evaluation research is poor to barely satisfactory in UK prison-based studies. The field has been curiously resistive of the development of RCTs. This perhaps reflects a lack of confidence in the robustness of the interventions themselves. It is unlikely to be fundamentally a financial issue given the very generous amounts of the public purse that have gone into some of these experimental treatments. There have been some ethical concerns raised about the use of RCTs. The primary ethical concern appears to be associated with denying treatment to some who may need it and if they don't get it may go on to harm others. This would perhaps be more persuasive if we knew that the treatments themselves actually worked. We don't know that; that is what we would be seeking to find out. The ethical objection arguably only holds if we have a treatment that works. It could be that some treatments simply teach the participants the appropriate language that they need to learn and use to secure positive reports in support of, e.g. their parole. Some offenders may well take this approach to their courses. But if we think that some of the courses are potentially powerful tools for behavioural change, we need to consider that the change may occur in either direction. That is, for some participants the results may be that they have an increased risk of reoffending as a result of participating in the course. Of course, the hope and expectation is that this will not happen and that change will be positive change. But not all change is positive. In practical terms, one of the implications of this is that we need to be very careful as to how we match prospective participants to courses. This is an ethical issue which, unfortunately, may sometimes be compromised in the name of the managerialist imperative to achieve 'targets' for 'completions' on courses in probation and prisons. As noted earlier, psychologists have a clear ethical responsibility to challenge such practices if and when they occur.

The third psychological perspective to be considered is the exciting potential of the wider application of the knowledge base and methods of experimental psychology to forensic psychological study and practice. There are some areas of forensic research where this is already the routine way of working. For example, in looking at witness testimony an understanding of memory research is routinely drawn upon. It is clear that both psychological laboratory and field-based studies of memory may have utility in improving forensic understanding. Such models and methods need perhaps to be more widely applied within the forensic field. In forensic assessments such as interviews for risk assessments we may be heavily reliant upon the patients' reports of previous events. A fuller understanding of the working of memory could perhaps help inform judgements made in assessment report writing. It would perhaps be helpful to see the more widespread uses and applications of models of human behaviour gleaned from experimental psychology applied to the forensic knowledge base. Encouragingly, the field has moved on in some of these key areas since the first edition. More and more forensic psychologists are drawing upon the wider field of experimental psychology to inform our thinking – for example, in relation to eye witness testimony. What in previous years would have been viewed as 'legal psychology' has also seen a renewed surge of interest. There are numerous opportunities for both laboratory and field-based studies. Opportunities abound in the exciting yet challenging field of forensic psychology.

Since the first edition, the theme of the statutory regulation of practitioner psychologists has very much come to the fore. The chapter on ethical guidance (Chapter 26) notes a theme across the professional codes of psychologists internationally, and indeed across disciplines, which is that it is the individual rather than the organization that the individual happens to be working for who has the personal accountability for their (in) actions. This is useful because it means that, where there is poor organizational practice, the individual has a duty to bring it to the attention of the employer and take appropriate action.

Statutory regulation through a multi-professional register significantly benefits practitioner psychologists, because it allows learning more readily across professional and disciplinary boundaries. I anticipate a growth in such regulation.

FUTURES

With a period of transnational financial recession the pressure on the public purse in the United Kingdom is likely to be greater than was previously the case, especially in the more recent boom years of governmental expenditure on public services, including hospitals, prisons and probation services. Senior managers in these domains have enjoyed the benefits of bigger budgets. A different style of management now may be needed. Although the managerialism referred to earlier is unlikely to disappear, there may well be some refinements of the approach. Large-scale services are likely to have some areas of significant waste, so some large savings could probably be made without a loss of the quality or quantity of service provision.

In terms of the application of the academic discipline of psychology and psychological models there is a need to adopt a more rigorous and empirically consistent approach to the development of some areas of the work. We have seen how, for example, psychologically based courses run with offenders in probation and prisons may well benefit from independent review in terms of the evidence base. Risk assessment is an area that has taken some great strides in recent years, but here again, policy-makers and practitioners need to be better informed by the evidence. And this is a central contribution that psychologists can make to the criminal and civil justice systems – we can bring a level of empirical rigour drawing upon a psychological evidence base and perspective.

However, this is an area which needs more work within the forensic psychology community. That is, the challenge of how we may lever benefits from the broader experimental psychology knowledge base for the benefit of improving forensic psychological understanding and practice. This is a process already well developed in some areas of forensic psychology, as amply illustrated in this volume. In terms of the stage of development of the discipline, forensic psychology has come of age in recent years and we now need to fulfil our initial promise. It is perhaps serendipitous that the advent of statutory regulation has come upon us at this key developmental stage of our discipline. A future that is self-critical and self-reflective and independently regulated, driven by an evidence-informed, ethically underpinned approach, will be a bright future both for psychologists and, most importantly, the public (to include individuals who commit offences).

REFERENCES

Crighton, D. A., & Towl, G. J. (2008). *Psychology in prisons* (2nd edn). Oxford: BPS Blackwell.

Geuter, U. (2008). *The professionalisation of psychology in Nazi Germany, Cambridge Studies in the History of Psychology*. Cambridge: Cambridge University Press.

Towl, G. J. (2014). Reflections of a new HCPC Council member. *The Psychologist*, April.

Index of Names

Abbott, R. D., 147
Abel, G., 330
Abel, K., 241, 323
Ackerman, M. J., 126
Adler, J., 1, 323, 324
Adorno, T. W., 373
Aguilar, B., 120
Ahmed, E., 389
Airs, J., 66
Akers, R., 185
Alder, L., 239
Alexander, J. F., 143, 144
Alexander, R. H., 207
Alexander, R. T., 233, 254
Alison, L., 35, 36, 38, 39, 40–1, 210–11
Allan, A., 73
Allan, R., 257
Allbright, M. K., 379
Alleyne, E., 359
Allport, G. W., 378
Anastasi, J. S., 47
Andershed, A.-K., 162t
Anderson, A. B., 69
Anderson, S., 118, 172, 186
Andersson, J., 153
Andersson, T., 164
Andrews, D. A., 103
Ansell, J., 106
Anthony, M. M., 90, 91
Antonio, M. E., 74
Aos, S., 143
Appelbaum, P. S., 101, 222
Arce, R., 71, 72, 73
Archer, J., 123
Arendt, H., 374, 388
Arenovich, T., 234
Armstrong, A. H., 191
Arteaga, I. A., 146
Asch, S. E., 356, 418
Ashworth, A., 21
Astell, A., 244
Atran, S., 207
Aubut, J., 38
Augimeri, L. K., 150

Auriacombe, M., 308
Avary, D. W., 186

Back, K., 357
Badcock, R., 35
Baddeley, A. D., 53–4
Bagby, R. M., 72, 266
Bahr, S. J., 191
Baker, J., 73
Baker, K., 103
Baldwin, J., 67, 69, 71, 72
Bandura, A., 362, 376
Banerjee, A., 426, 427
Barbaree, H. E., 342–3
Barber, D., 68
Barchard, K., 283
Barnes, H. V., 142, 165
Barnes, J. C., 152, 190
Barnett, W. S., 146
Baroff, G. S., 236, 237
Barriga, A. Q., 188
Barry, M., 97
Bartlett, J., 47
Baskin-Sommers, A., 123
Battin, S. R., 171
Baty, F. J., 238
Bauer, D. J., 82
Beail, N., 236
Beauchamp, M. H., 124
Beaver, K. M., 190
Bechara, A., 118, 124
Beck, A. T., 86, 89
Bedi, A. S., 211n
Beech, A. R., 241, 257, 347
Beelmann, A., 150
Behen, M. E., 117
Bell, M. A., 122
Belsky, J., 152
Bender, D., 150
Bender, K., 184
Bennett, C., 35
Bennett, L., 230
Bennett, S., 376, 378, 395
Bentall, R. P., 217, 220, 294, 296

Benton, D., 125
Berenbaum, M., 370
Bergman, L. R., 162t
Berman, M. E., 127
Bermant, G., 72
Berrueta-Clement, J. R., 146
Bersani, B. E., 185
Besemer, S., 170
Best, D., 307
Biernacki, P., 188
Bihrle, S., 117
Bijleveld, C. C. J. H., 170
Bilby, C., 346
Birbaumer, N., 124
Bisson, J. I., 209
Bjørnebekk, G., 282–3
Blackburn, R., 265, 268–9, 270–1, 272, 282, 283
Blacker, J., 244
Blair, R. J., 124
Blair, Tony, 151
Blanchard, R., 234
Blanck, P. D., 72
Bodenhausen, G. V., 83
Boer, A., 241
Boer, D. P., 241, 244
Boin, A., 203
Bond, Thomas, 33–4
Bonta, J., 103
Book, A., 243
Boon, J., 35
Bor, W., 115
Borduin, C. M., 145
Born, D. G., 209
Bornstein, B. H., 48, 49
Bouffard, L. A., 186
Boulerice, B., 165–6
Bourget, D., 128
Bowers, L., 426
Bowers, W., 70
Bowlby, J., 167, 219
Bowling, B., 28, 374, 379
Boyd, J. E., 433
Brace, N., 239–40

Forensic Psychology, Second Edition. Edited by David A. Crighton and Graham J. Towl.
© 2015 John Wiley & Sons, Ltd. Published 2015 by British Psychological Society and John Wiley & Sons, Ltd.

Index of Subjects

12-step treatments, 306–7

AA (Alcoholics Anonymous), 307,
    309, 346
Abel and Becker Cognitions Scale, 241
abnormality, 294–5
acceptable risk, definition, 106–7
accommodation theory, 210
accountability, 27
active listening, 205
admissible evidence, 57, 126–7
adolescents
    age of criminal responsibility, 22,
        30n, 335
    gang membership, 172, 186,
        353–64
    harmful sexual behaviour,
        329–34, 348
    prisoners, 25, 318
    suicide and self-injury, 318, 321
    see also youth justice
Aegis Trust, 379
aggression, 239–40, 254–5, 363
alcohol, 310
    withdrawal symptoms, 304
Alcoholics Anonymous (AA), 307,
    309, 346
Allen v. U.S. (1896), 73
American Association on Mental
    Retardation, 227
American Psychiatric Association, 40, 82,
    89, 218, 219–20, 227
American Psychological Association
    (APA), 70
American Psychological Society
    (APA), 408
amygdala-hippocampal complex,
    117, 124
anger, 239–40
anti-bullying programmes, 147–8
antisocial behaviour, 115–94, 232–3

and gang membership, 172, 186,
    353–64
neurobiological theories, 115–25
prevention, 124–5, 127, 128,
    141–53
antisocial personality disorder, 281–7
Antisocial Personality Questionnaire
    (APQ), 268–9
appeals, 20–1
archival research, 67
ARMIDILO system, 244
arson (fire raising), 229–30, 241–2,
    259–60
Ashworth Hospital (England),
    428–9, 434n
assessment, 18, 21–2, 81–93, 127,
    215–24
    children and young people, 318,
        331–2, 334–6
    classification and categorization, 82–4,
        265–7
    clinical interviews, 88–9, 268, 270
    comorbidity, 221–2, 309–11
    fire raising, 229–30, 241–2
    harmful sexual behaviour, 238,
        240–1, 244, 331–2, 334–6, 343–4,
        416–17
    legal issues, 97–8
    people with intellectual disability,
        227–45
    personality disorders, 265–72,
        281–7
    practitioner bias, 92–3
    psychometric assessment tools, 89–90,
        91–2
    risk assessment, 97–108, 128, 242–4,
        281–7, 343–4, 348, 349–50,
        415–22
    'scientist practitioner' approach,
        81–4
    self-report questionnaires, 268–70

substance use disorders, 301–2,
    303
validity and reliability, 90–3, 100–7,
    275–6, 292–5, 303, 343–4
Association of Chief Police Officers,
    40, 372
attention deficit hyperactivity disorder,
    127–8, 164–5, 233
Attica prison riot, 203
Attorney General, 24, 27

'Barnum' effects, 38–9
base rates, 91, 101, 107n
Beck Anxiety Inventory, 238
Beck Depression Inventory,
    237–8
Behavioral Science Unit (FBI), 34
behaviourism, 84
benzodiazepine, 304
biodeterminism, 218–19
biopsychosocial model, 219–20
'black swan' events, 106–7
Blair, Tony, 151
Blom-Cooper Report (1992),
    428–9, 434n
Boynton Report (1980), 427–8
brain, 116–21
brain imaging data, admissibility as
    evidence, 126
Brief Symptom Inventory (BSI),
    238–9
British Association for Counselling and
    Psychotherapy (BACP), 407–8,
    409–10
British Cohort Study, 168–9
British Crime Survey, 342
British Psychological Society (BPS), 220,
    227–9, 406, 410–11, 417, 420, 422,
    434n, 437
Bromley Briefing Factfile, 25
brothel-keeping, 348

Forensic Psychology, Second Edition. Edited by David A. Crighton and Graham J. Towl.
© 2015 John Wiley & Sons, Ltd. Published 2015 by British Psychological Society and John Wiley & Sons, Ltd.

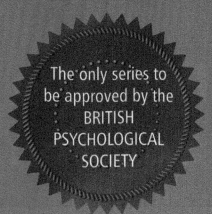

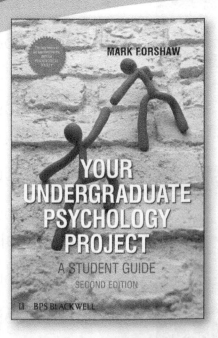

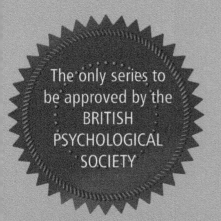
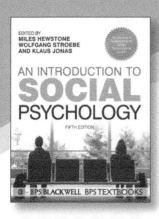

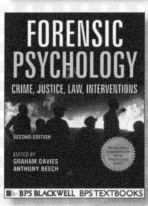

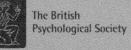

Printed and bound by CPI Group (UK) Ltd, Croydon, CR0 4YY